The Law of Gambling
and Regulated Gaming

The Law of Gambling and Regulated Gaming

Cases and Materials

Anthony N. Cabot

PARTNER AND PRACTICE GROUP LEADER OF THE
GAMING LAW PRACTICE GROUP,
LEWIS AND ROCA LLP

Keith C. Miller

ELLIS AND NELLE LEVITT DISTINGUISHED PROFESSOR OF LAW,
DRAKE UNIVERSITY LAW SCHOOL

CAROLINA ACADEMIC PRESS
Durham, North Carolina

ISBN: 978-1-59460-758-5
LCCN: 2010941997

Carolina Academic Press
700 Kent Street
Durham, North Carolina 27701
Telephone (919) 489-7486
Fax (919) 493-5668
www.cap-press.com

Printed in the United States of America

Anthony Cabot dedicates this book to his wife, Linda,
and his children, Trace and Dani, for just being special.
He thanks his law firm, Lewis and Roca, for fostering an environment
that encourages academic and social contributions to our community
and the legal profession.

Keith Miller dedicates the book to Liz and Dori.
The smiles, love, and support of Liz help to keep things in perspective.
So does the affection of my faithful Golden Retriever, Dori.

Contents

Part II: Casino Gambling

Table of Cases

Principal cases are set in **bold**, while cases cited in the text and in the authors' notes are set in roman type.

Preface and Acknowledgments

A class in gaming law provides a unique opportunity to study how legal doctrine, politics, economics, social policy, religion, and even mathematics coalesce to regulate an activity that humans have engaged in for thousands of years. Lawyers serve in a variety of advocacy, regulatory, and policy-making roles in the gaming field, and an awareness of the basics of gaming law and its elaborate regulatory framework is critical to informed consideration of these issues. While for much of our nation's history, legal issues surrounding gambling were confined to criminal law, the regulated gaming industry has undergone tremendous expansion in the past twenty years. Indeed, areas like tribal gaming and Internet gaming have grown so rapidly that they warrant, and have received, discrete academic treatment. In this book, we strive to provide an introduction to the regulation of gaming law in the varied contexts in which it arises.

We welcome comments from you about the materials and are happy to talk to you about your use of the materials. Our contact information is Professor Keith C. Miller, Drake University Law School, (515) 271-2071, keith.miller@drake.edu, and Anthony Cabot, Lewis and Roca, (702) 949-8280, ACabot@LRLaw.com.

Many people have provided valuable assistance to us as we prepared these materials. Author Cabot would like to acknowledge the leadership, assistance and counsel of his fellow lawyers in the International Masters of Gaming Law, whose dedication to gaming law education through publication and seminars has raised the standards of gaming law throughout the world. He also would like to note the contributions of Robert Faiss and the late Grant Sawyer who mentored him in gaming law in the early 1980s when no legal resources on gaming law were available.

Author Miller offers his deepest thanks to his research assistants at Drake, Jordan Smith and Ben Arato. They worked long and hard on matters large and small and were a source of support and mature professional judgment. They will be a credit to the legal profession.

Part I
Fundamentals of Gambling

Chapter 1

The History and Basics of Gambling

1. The History and Basics of Gambling

Modern commercial gambling law concerns privileges as opposed to rights. The privilege comes from exceptions to general criminal prohibitions against gambling. In particular, a governmental license is a privilege granted by the government and those licensed are considered to be engaged in commercial gambling. In contrast, those who conduct gambling activities without a license are typically subject to criminal sanctions. Hence, two distinct sets of gambling laws arise. The first set is criminal gambling laws that define the general prohibitions and penalties against gambling activities. The second set is regulatory laws that define the exceptions to the prohibition and govern the conduct of commercial gambling.

Before progressing to why most gambling is prohibited and why exceptions for privileged licenses exist, a good place to begin any study of gambling law is an understanding of the history of gambling. Gambling predates the founding of America. Records of gambling are almost as old as recorded human history. The earliest known form of gambling was a kind of dice game played with what was known as an astragalus, or knuckle-bone. This early ancestor of today's dice was a squarish, solid and virtually indestructible bone taken from the ankles of sheep or deer. Egyptian tomb paintings portray games played with astragali dating from 3500 BC, and Greek vases show young men tossing the bones into a circle. The ancient history of gaming is chronicled in PETER L. BERNSTEIN, AGAINST THE GODS: THE REMARKABLE STORY OF RISK (Wiley & Sons, Inc., 1998). For a comprehensive account of the role of gambling throughout history, see DAVID G. SCHWARTZ, ROLL THE BONES: THE HISTORY OF GAMBLING (Gotham Books 2006).

While many ancient cultures were known to play games of skill and chance for amusement, in the United States, traditional lotteries are early examples of a sanctioned gambling activity that supported social, educational and political causes. Ancient India, China, Greece, and Japan had lotteries as well. Government-organized lotteries appeared in Europe in the early sixteenth century in the Italian city-state of Florence and its popularity spread across Europe and then to the New World.

Each of the thirteen colonies established lotteries to raise revenue. Ben Franklin, John Hancock, and George Washington all prominently sponsored the use of lotteries for public works projects. "[L]otteries were used to ... finance county and municipal buildings, repair streets, ensure the water supplies of the cities, and build roads, canals and bridges." REUVEN BRENNER & GABRIELLE A. BRENNER, GAMBLING AND SPECULATION: A THEORY, A HISTORY, AND A FUTURE OF SOME HUMAN DECISIONS 14 (Cambridge Univ. Press 1990). To carry on the war against England, $10 million was severely needed, and because the national legislative body lacked the power to tax, a national lottery was created. The lottery had to be abandoned, however, because it was too large, badly managed, and too few tickets were sold. Moreover, several institutions of higher learning, including Yale and Harvard, were financed in part by lotteries. A lottery is a simple gambling activity. Persons buy tickets. One part of the ticket would be retained by the player and another retained by the lottery operator. A ticket, or "lot" would be drawn at random from the operator's tickets and the holder of that particular number would receive the particular prize upon surrender of the player's ticket. Between 1790 and 1860, twenty-four of the thirty-three states used lotteries for revenue building purposes. Lotteries were considered so respectable that in 1794 the General Assembly of Rhode Island approved a lottery to complete the building of a church, sanctioning the lottery as a promotion of "Public Worship, and the advancement of Religion." This era peaked in 1831, when eight states ran 420 lottery games that sold more than $66 million in tickets, a sum five times that of the federal budget.

As lottery activities expanded, their character changed. The small local lotteries of the 1700s gave way to the large and profit oriented lotteries of the 1800s. Private lottery contractors assumed control of the games. Wholesaling and retailing of tickets became a major line of business. This system not only provided more opportunities to gamble but also provided more opportunities for fraud. Lotteries were soon afflicted with scandals and swindles and lost public support.

State after state began to abolish lotteries and prohibited private parties from selling tickets. In 1833, Pennsylvania and Massachusetts abolished legal lotteries. Many states added a prohibition against lotteries within their state constitutions. By the Civil War, only three states still permitted lotteries. Soon thereafter, by state constitutional provisions or statutes, all states specifically prohibited lotteries. For more discussion of early American gambling history see HENRY CHAFETZ, PLAY THE DEVIL: A HISTORY OF GAMBLING IN THE UNITED STATES FROM 1492 TO 1950 (1960); JOHN M. FINDLAY, PEOPLE OF CHANCE: GAMBLING IN AMERICAN SOCIETY FROM JAMESTOWN TO LAS VEGAS (Oxford Univ. Press 1986); WILLIAM N. THOMPSON, LEGALIZED GAMBLING (1994); Duane V. Burke, *The Legalization of Gambling in the United States: An Analysis and Forecast, in* GAMBLING AND SOCIETY: INTERDISCIPLINARY STUDIES ON THE SUBJECT OF GAMBLING (William R. Eadington, ed., 1976).

Besides lotteries, other gambling games existed. The two other predominate forms of gambling were horse racing and poker. Betting on horseracing survived the initial gambling purge. Poker had a more difficult run.

Poker originated about 1830 in the French-dominated area of New Orleans. Many researchers credit the derivation of old 20-card poker to the Persian game of As-Nas, a game whose origin and age are in dispute, and its various descendants. Comedian Joe Cowell, in a book published in 1844, described how he first encountered the game, whose origin he attributed to Henry Clay, aboard a steamboat from Louisville to New Orleans in December 1829:

> The aces are the highest denomination: then the kings, queens, jacks and tens: the smaller cards are not used; those I have named are all dealt out, and carefully concealed from one another; old players pack them in their hands, and peep at them as if they were afraid to trust even themselves to look.

JOE COWELL, THIRTY YEARS PASSED AMONG THE PLAYERS IN ENGLAND AND AMERICA (1844).

Following the Gold Rush and silver strikes in the West, gambling dives began to permeate the mining boom towns of the West and a saloon with a Poker table could be found in just about every settlement. By the mid 1800s lavish casinos were established that featured table games, such as craps, roulette, poker, faro, and monte. Before long, many of the frontier camps such as Deadwood and Tombstone became as well known for their gunfights over card games as they did for their wealth of gold and silver ore. Since that time, there have been three prevailing versions of Poker, namely: 5 Card Draw, 7 Card Stud, and Texas Hold'em.

Older decisions, most of which were decided around the turn of the twentieth century, found poker to be an illegal game of chance. *See e.g.,* Collet v. Beutler, 76 P. 707 (1904); State ex re. Sonner v. Dean, 126 S.E. 411 (W. Va. 1925). The game, however, was legal in several states, mostly in the western United States. For example, while the Nevada Constitution adopted in 1864 prohibited lotteries, the Nevada legislature legalized poker and other casino-style games in 1869. Poker and other card games remained legal to this day with the exception of a short time from 1910 to 1915. For a discussion of the origins of the game of poker see A. ALVAREZ, POKER: BETS, BLUFFS, AND BAD BEATS (Chronicle Books 2001); HERBERT ASBURY, SUCKER'S PROGRESS: AN INFORMAL HISTORY OF GAMBLING IN AMERICA (Basic Books 1938); MICHAEL DUMMETT, THE GAME OF TARO, (U.S. Games Systems 1980); DAVID PARLETT, THE HISTORY OF CARD GAMES 115 (Oxford Univ. Press 1991); DAVID SPANIER, TOTAL POKER (High Stakes 2002).

Bookmaking, principally on horse racing, was also common in the nineteenth century. The sport was brought to America by British settlers in the seventeenth century and by the mid-eighteenth century patrons of the turf in New York City, tidewater Virginia and low-country South Carolina had erected circular race tracks, purchased purebred horses, and adopted formal racing seasons. Such developments followed English precedent and lent to the dignity, ceremony and orderliness of the "Sport of Kings." Indeed, wagering on horse racing was, at first, an activity that took place among "gentlemen," and was considered more of a sporting matter than true gambling. Betting was done among the patrons or with bookies at the track.

As adventurers continued to migrate westward and cultivate new forms of gambling, a style of horse racing developed in western settlements to suit the rugged early frontier. Pioneers lacked the means to build tracks and institute racing seasons. They resorted to quarter-mile sprints that took place on a straight stretch of road, typically next to a local tavern that served as a kind of community center. This new style of racing, known as "Quarter-racing," prevailed in the westernmost communities and continued to move westward as migrants to each new frontier eventually reproduced eastern culture.

By 1897 there were 314 tracks operating across the United States. This mushrooming of race tracks around the country led to the formation of the American Jockey Club in 1894. So far as it could, the Jockey Club began to regulate the sport and its betting, and in the key state of New York, it quickly acquired exclusive control for licensure, trainers and owners. For a discussion of the history of horse racing and bookmaking, *see* RICHARD SASULY, BOOKIES AND BETTORS: TWO HUNDRED YEARS OF GAMBLING 78 (Holt, Henry & Co., 1982); WILLIAM N. THOMPSON, GAMBLING IN AMERICA: AN ENCYCLOPEDIA OF HISTORY, ISSUES, AND SOCIETY 225 (ABC-CLIO 2001); JOHN M. FINDLAY, PEOPLE OF CHANCE: GAMBLING IN AMERICAN SOCIETY FROM JAMESTOWN TO LAS VEGAS 31 (Oxford Univ. Press 1986).

Of the three forms of gambling, the courts and the governments historically have shown the most hostility towards lotteries. The first campaign against lotteries arose in the early to mid nineteenth century, because Americans grew more disposed to reform society by removing temptations such as gambling that were seen to impede the pursuit of individual perfectibility. Although many groups generally opposed gambling on moral grounds, the flames of opposition were fanned by the prevalence of scandals and a belief that lotteries targeted the poor. As one court noted: "Of all the forms of gambling, lotteries have been the most condemned by the courts." Mobil Oil Corp. v. Danforth, 455 S.W.2d 505, 509 (Mo. 1970) (citing Lucky Calendar Co. v. Cohen, 117 A.2d. 487, 492–93 (N.J. 1955). Historical references to the social evils of lotteries date over 150 years. In 1850, the United States Supreme Court noted:

> Experience has shown that the common forms of gambling are comparatively innocuous when placed in contrast with the widespread pestilence of lotteries. The former are confined to a few persons and places, but the latter infests the whole community: it enters every dwelling; it reaches every class; it preys upon the hard earnings of the poor; it plunders the ignorant and simple.

Phalen v. Commonwealth of Virginia, 49 U.S. (8 How.) 163, 168 (1850).

A reference from the Librarian of Congress in 1893 shared these sentiments: "a general public conviction that lotteries are to be regarded, in direct proportion to their extension, as among the most dangerous and prolific sources of human misery." Ronald J. Rychlak, *Lotteries, Revenues, and Social Costs: A Historical Examination of State-Sponsored Gambling*, 34 B.C. L. Rev. 11, 12–13 (1992) (quoting A.R. Spoffard, *Lotteries in American History*, S. Misc. Doc. No. 57, 52d Cong., 2d Sess. 194-95 (1893) (Annual Report of the American Historical Society)).

At the turn of the twentieth century, horse racing also was almost wiped out by antigambling sentiment. In 1911 the New York tracks were shut down. Other racing states, including California and Louisiana, followed New York's lead. Of the three major forms of gambling, horseracing was the first to reapply as a legal activity. The Depression triggered resurgence in the sport as state governments charted a trend of expanding track wagering and taxing pari-mutuel betting in a quest for new revenues.

Casinos and lotteries lagged in comparison. Nevada stood alone for many years after it legalized casino gambling in 1931. The real resurgence of lawful casinos did not occur until 1979 when New Jersey authorized casinos along the famous boardwalk in Atlantic City.

Legal lotteries ceased to exist in the United States until New Hampshire authorized a state-run sweepstakes in 1963. The New Hampshire sweepstakes was not an overwhelming success, but it did revive interest in the lottery idea. In 1967, New York started a lottery, followed by the very successful New Jersey State Lottery in 1971. New Jersey's success interested several other states. By 1994, thirty-eight states had legalized lotteries. John Lyman Mason & Michael Nelson, Governing Gambling 9 (Cen. Foundation Press 2001).

Despite the seeming ambiguity of gambling opportunities in America, legal gambling remains the exception as opposed to the rule. The general prohibition against lotteries and other games of chance found in state constitutions and statutes often have remained unchanged from the Civil War Era, as have later enacted statutory prohibitions against card games and sports wagering. Permitted forms of gambling, therefore, remain the exception to the general prohibitions and, hence, licenses to conduct these activities are privileges bestowed by the state governments.

2. What Is Gambling?

Laws governing skill games developed separate from gambling laws. They were initially designed to govern carnival and midway games and coin-operated prize redemption games in arcades. In some states, separate laws regulated a variety of sporting contests like fishing and bowling tournaments.

Generally, wagering on the outcome of skill games was treated differently from chance games because they were deemed to have social merit often by teaching valuable skills. As early as medieval times, wagering on horse racing was seen as a method to motivate the training of horse soldiers and improve horse breeding. Simply, skill contests provide motivation to excel at particular activities deemed to have societal benefits. Spelling bees and science competitions furthered academics. Athletics promoted physical prowess.

To accommodate the variety of traditional skill games, a common law definition of gambling in the United States arose that prohibited only those activities where a person pays consideration, usually cash, for the opportunity to win a prize in a game of chance. In time, other definitions of gambling arose to deal with activities that were not strictly games of chance such as sports wagering and certain card games.

Generally, if any of the three elements of games of chance are absent, then the activity is not prohibited. If an activity does not require consideration to play, then it is generally a lawful sweepstakes. A sweepstakes always contains the elements of chance and prize, so the element of consideration must be eliminated to avoid violating the gambling prohibitions. All three elements of gambling, consideration, chance, and prize, cause problems for courts.

A. What Is Consideration?

97 Tenn. Atty. Gen. Op. 025

(1997)

QUESTION

Does the conduct of "rubber duck races," games of chance at which valuable prizes are given away in connection with fund-raising activities, violate Tennessee's gambling statutes or lottery prohibitions?

OPINION

Yes. The conduct of the type of game of chance described herein would be sufficient to support a finding by a trier of fact of a violation of <sic> Tenn. Code Ann. § 39-17-503 (gambling promotion). An objective analysis of this game also would be sufficient to support a determination by a trier fact that it constitutes an illegal lottery, in violation of Tenn. Code Ann. § 39-17-506 and Article XI, § 5 of the Constitution of Tennessee.

ANALYSIS

This Office has received several opinion requests relating to the legality of "rubber duck races," games of chance in which the contestants "adopt" numbered rubber ducks. All of the ducks, up to 60,000 in number, are released into a river at one time and float along a predetermined course toward the established finish line. According to the rules, the race course will close twenty minutes after the first duck has crossed the finish line and/or is gathered in a duck trap. Persons whose names appear on the entry tickets corresponding to the numbers listed on the first ducks in order of finish are awarded prizes. The proceeds from the contest benefit specific charitable organizations and persons "adopting" ducks are urged to pay a "recommended donation" of $5.00 per duck.

The front of an entry brochure promoting one "rubber duck race" emphasizes: "Over $30,000 in Prizes." On the inside cover, prizes such as a new truck, a dream vacation, a home entertainment center, a yard tractor, multiple gift certificates, and other prizes valued at over $500 or more are identified. The promotional material for another race highlights "Win $5,000 Cash" in its largest print. On the entry portion of the promotional brochure, a person may state how many ducks he or she wishes to adopt along with how much he or she is enclosing for these adoptions. It contains the following language: "Please consider a gift of $5.00 or more per adoption because the purpose of this event is to benefit the [specified entity]. Make check or money order payable to the [specified entity] or use your MasterCard or Visa." At the perforation to remove the entry portion, the promoters instruct, "To adopt rubber duck: Tear envelope off at perforation above, fill out adoption papers, and enclose your donation. Seal envelope...." This entry portion, which apparently must be returned in order to adopt a duck, and the side of the brochure describing the various prizes do not disclose that no donation is required. In describing "[w]hat" is the "Great Rubber Duck Race," that side of the promotional brochure explains "[e]ach duck will be numbered and each purchaser will receive a corresponding Adoption Number."

Additionally, the promotional brochure provides the rules and regulations for the contest in small print relative to the promotional language. Not until midway through the numerous rules, which appear in the smallest print on the brochure, is it stated that: "No purchase is necessary in order to enter or win. Presenter does encourage a donation of at least $5.00 per duck adoption to benefit the [specified entity], a charitable organization under Section 501(c)(3) of the Internal Revenue Code." The promotional material does not specify the manner in which "free" ducks may be obtained. It is not clear from the promotional brochure whether persons "donating" for ducks may enter in a different manner from persons who seek "free" ducks.

By design, the definitions in the current gambling provisions of the criminal code are broader than those found in earlier law.[1] Following an amendment in 1989, "Gambling" is presently defined in Tenn. Code Ann. § 39-17-501(1) as "*risking anything of value for a profit* whose return is to any degree contingent on chance but does not include a lawful business transaction" (emphasis added). The Sentencing Commission's comments to this section state:

> This section contains the definitions for gambling offenses. *The definitions are intentionally broader than those found in prior law. The commission intends to include any scheme by which value is risked upon a chance for greater value as a 'gambling' offense.* The definition of 'gambling' includes lotteries, chain or pyramid clubs, numbers, pinball, poker or any as yet unnamed scheme where value is risked for profit. The definition of "lawful business transaction," however, makes it clear that futures and commodities trading is not included in gambling. This is a change from prior code § 39-6-627, which prohibited such trading under certain circumstances as gambling.

(emphasis added)

Thus, the scope of the definition of gambling in the 1989 code includes not only games that qualify as a "lottery," but also "any ... scheme where value is risked for profit."

---

1. In 1949, the Tennessee Supreme Court defined gaming as "any agreement between two or more persons to risk money or property on a contest or chance of any kind, when one must be gainer, and the other loser.... It matters not what the unlawful device is upon which the money is received as a hazard, it is gaming." Cleek v. State, 225 S.W.2d 70, 71 (Tenn. 1949) (citing Mitchell v. Orr, 64 S.W. 476 (Tenn. 1901)).

The current criminal code applies this definition of "gambling" in Tenn. Code Ann. §§ 39-17-502 and 39-17-503, which respectively prohibit "gambling" and "gambling promotion." Tenn. Code Ann § 39-17-502 provides:

(a) A person commits an offense who knowingly engages in gambling.

(b) The offense of gambling is a Class C misdemeanor.

Tenn. Code Ann. § 39-17-503 defines the offense of gambling promotion as follows:

(a) A person commits an offense who *knowingly induces or aids another to engage in gambling,* and:

(1) Intends to derive or derives an economic benefit other than personal winnings from the gambling; or

(2) Participates in the gambling and has, other than by virtue of skill or luck, a lesser risk of losing or greater chance of winning than one (1) or more of the other participants.

(b) The offense of gambling promotion is a Class B misdemeanor.

(emphasis added)

We believe that the facts outlined above would provide an objective trier of fact with sufficient evidence to conclude that the "rubber duck races" violate these gambling prohibitions. It is evident that the "rubber duck races" in question contain the elements of a possible profit whose return is entirely contingent upon chance. Thus, if any person pays to "adopt" a duck with intent to obtain the chance to gain a profit, i.e., a valuable prize, then that person has risked something of value (the "suggested donation") on a chance to win and has committed the offense of "gambling" in violation of Tenn. Code Ann. § 39-17-502. Common sense suggests that, in the game promoted as outlined above, most people are not paying a "suggested donation" per adopted duck merely for the benefits to be derived from making a charitable contribution. Rather, they are paying in order to acquire the chance to win one of the advertised prizes.

Since the scheme outlined above provides a basis sufficient to permit a trier of fact to find that game participants have engaged in "gambling," it follows that the promoters of the games could also be found to have committed the offense of "gambling promotion" in violation of Tenn. Code Ann. § 39-17-502. Plainly, the promoters know that the prizes to be awarded are an inducement to the participants to make "recommended donations," and the promoters intend to derive an economic benefit from the game in the form of "recommended donations." Indeed, we are not aware of any instance when a rubber duck race awarding valuable prizes has been marketed without a concurrent request for "recommended donations." In these circumstances, a trier of fact could reasonably find all of the elements of the offense of "gambling promotion."

A trier of fact could also conclude that a "rubber duck race" prize contest conducted in the manner described above constitutes an illegal "lottery," in violation of Tenn. Code Ann. § 39-17-506 and Article XI, § 5 of the Constitution of Tennessee. Lotteries for any purpose, charitable or otherwise, are unlawful in Tennessee. Secretary of State v. St. Augustine Church/St. Augustine School, 766 S.W.2d 499, 500 (Tenn. 1989). Article XI, Section 5 of the Tennessee Constitution expressly provides: "The Legislature shall have no power to authorize lotteries for any purpose, and shall pass laws to prohibit the sale of lottery tickets in this State." Early Tennessee decisions defined a lottery as "a game of hazard in which small sums are ventured for the chance of obtaining a larger value either in money or articles." France v. State, 65 Tenn. 478, 484 (1873). Under the traditional test, three elements must be present in order for a transaction to be considered a lottery: (1) chance, (2) prize, and (3) consideration. State ex rel. District Attorney General v. Crescent Amusement Co., 95 S.W.2d 310, 312 (Tenn. 1936).

While the exact factual situation at issue has not been previously addressed, this Office has opined in an analysis of prize giveaways in general that if a prize giveaway lacks the element of "consideration" being ventured or risked, the scheme will not be deemed a "lottery." In Op. Atty. Gen. No. 89-72, May 3, 1989, this Office opined that:

> Tennessee case law indicates that an organization, charitable or otherwise, may lawfully conduct a cash or prize giveaway if all persons wishing to participate are given an opportunity to do so without being required to pay any money, make any donation, or purchase any product or service.

We explained, however, in footnote 4 of that Opinion that:

> [I]f, in reality, all participants in a type of prize giveaway are not paying or giving anything of value to participate, then there is no consideration. "Consideration" is negated *when no participants pay to play.*

(emphasis added)

This Office has further noted and clarified that merely labeling the payments of prize giveaway participants as "suggested" or "voluntary" donations (or as otherwise not being required) does not in and of itself alter the fact that "consideration" is present, if in reality participants are paying or giving anything of value in order to participate. September 15, 1989 Memorandum, "Legality of Proposed Types of Prize Giveaways."[2] ... We believe it clear that "for a prize giveaway to fall outside the proscription provided by the constitutional ban, participation in the prize giveaway must be objectively independent from any charge made or received, directly or indirectly, by donation or otherwise, for a product, service, membership, or event." Id. (emphasis added). The contests here at issue provide a sufficient basis for a trier of fact to conclude that, for many of the participants, their decision to pay the recommended donation for adopting ducks is not objectively independent from the desire to win the contest.[3]

...

In summary, it is the opinion of this Office that the facts outlined above would provide a trier of fact with sufficient evidence to find a violation of Tenn. Code Ann. § 39-17-503 (gambling promotion), as well as a violation of the lottery prohibitions contained in Tenn. Code Ann. § 39-17-506 and Article XI, § 5 of the Constitution of Tennessee.

---

2. In St. Augustine, the Court noted that for a transaction to be a lottery, three elements must be present: consideration, prize, and chance.

In the statutes which were under consideration [in St. Augustine], the General Assembly undertook to remove the game of bingo from the definition of a lottery by terming the consideration paid by a customer as a charitable contribution rather than a wager. This, in our opinion, is an ineffective means to circumvent the Constitutional prohibition, so long as the other elements of prize and chance are present. *Id.* at 501 (emphasis added).

3. These "duck race" promotions are distinguishable from the scenario presented in the Lincoln County Fair prize giveaway addressed in Attorney General Op. 96-109 (August 30, 1996). In that case, which is similar to Crescent Amusement, it was assumed that the promoter clearly and conspicuously disclosed to all patrons who did not pay admission to the fair that it was necessary to participate in the giveaway and that no admission could be charged for persons wishing to enter the grandstand where the drawing would occur. As previously stated herein, the promotional literature for the duck races clearly emphasizes the recommended donation and prizes, but makes mention only once, in its smallest type, that no purchase is necessary. The entry portion of the brochure does not make this disclosure in any fashion and emphasizes making a recommended donation.

Notes

1. This Tennessee Attorney General opinion addresses the situation where the promoter has attempted to eliminate the element of consideration by making the payment optional. Yet promotional sweepstakes attempt to avoid the prohibition against gambling also by offering an alternative method of entering (often referred to as AMOE) the game for free. This is permitted in the majority of states even though most people receive their entries into the game through the purchase of the product being promoted. Examples of popular AMOE's are mail-in entries or entry via an 800 telephone number.

The AMOE also typically must have "equal dignity" with the purchase method of entry: any material disparity (actual or perceived) between paying and non-paying entrants may invalidate the AMOE. This means that nonpaying participants must have equal opportunity to both enter and win the sweepstakes. Equal opportunity to enter requires that the entry mechanism for nonpaying participants be comparable to those of paying participants. Likewise, a person who enters by paying cannot get a disproportionate number of entries compared to nonpaying entries. Equal opportunity to win also means that a nonpaying customer has equal chances to win all prizes offered. For example, separate prize pools may invalidate the AMOE because the non-paying participants do not have the opportunity to win any prize. Likewise, nonpaying participants should not face greater odds or obstacles to winning the prizes. The Deceptive Mail Prevention and Enforcement Act, 39 U.S.C § 3001, specifically requires disclosure of the AMOE to be "clear and conspicuous," so that consumers are adequately informed of the existence of a non-purchase method of entry.

2. Promotional activities where the participants directly or indirectly pay fees to play a game tend to come under greater legal scrutiny. This higher scrutiny results from situations where the promoters attempt to make money not from the sale of a product unrelated to the sweepstakes, but from paying customers who desire to win prizes in the sweepstakes. This is a very real distinction in some court cases. As one court noted:

> A distinction exists between promotion of a primary business of selling a meal or a drink for valuable consideration together with a chance to win a business related prize, in kind or, albeit, as a sweepstakes prize which attracts sales, and promotion of a non-primary business related and incidental activity for valuable consideration together with a chance to win a prize unrelated to either the primary business activity or attraction of sales. The difference in the distinction is in the essence of the product: [t]he former promotes sales of the primary business product, e.g., food, while the latter promotes the prize and the product (coupon) is unrelated to either the primary business purpose of the promoter, of the distributor ...

F.A.C.E Trading, Inc. v Carter, 821 N.E.2d 38, 42 (Ind. Ct. App. 2005).

3. Over the years, various promoters have attempted to use the AMOE exception to devise schemes that prosecutors often describe as "*a thinly veiled lottery.*" Perhaps the most well known of these schemes was the "Lucky Shamrock." In the late 1990s and through the first part of the early 2000s, several court opinions and attorney general opinions addressed the "Lucky Shamrock" phone card sweepstakes and mechanical dispensers. The Lucky Shamrock emergency phone card was a one or two minute long distance phone card, usually sold at market value, that also had a sweepstakes entry attached to the card. The Lucky Shamrock emergency phone card dispensers came in two varieties: one which dispensed the cards with a pull tab sweepstakes entry, and one that displayed the sweepstakes results in a display as the card was dispensed. Regardless of delivery and sales method, the Lucky Shamrock sweepstakes offered an alternative free method of entry.

Many courts determined that the Lucky Shamrock promotion and dispenser violated criminal gambling laws in their states. Only the Kansas Attorney General provided an opinion that the sweepstakes was likely to be legal because the contest would lack consideration if the AMOE was free, not overly burdensome and offered an equal chance of winning to non-paying contestants. In every other instance, the AMOE was held to be ineffective or likely to be ineffective. *See* Sun Light Prepaid Phonecard Co. v. State, 600 S.E.2d 61 (S.C. 2004). A good example is this quote from the Illinois Attorney General: "although the scheme has been carefully designed to appear to meet the criteria generally prescribed by the courts in approving giveaway schemes, a review of the underlying purpose of the scheme leads inexorably to the conclusion that the Lucky Shamrock sweepstakes is but a thinly veiled lottery." 98 Op Att'y Gen IL 010 (1992).

4. Can fast food restaurants conduct prize giveaways that involve buying hamburgers to reveal prizes?

5. Laws in most states are easily able to recognize the difference between risking money on a roulette table as opposed to competing for a scholarship in a science competition. But what about competitions that mix both skill and chance? What should be the standards for when an activity blurs the line between legal and illegal?

B. Skill? Chance? Both?

Morrow v. Alaska

511 P.2d 127 (Ala. 1973)

Appellant, Joseph Robert Morrow, was charged with selling a ticket in a lottery.

The ticket involved is commonly called a "football card." Such a card lists numerous football games to be played on certain days, from which the purchaser selects from three to ten winning teams. The adds are listed at the bottom of the card. The selection of any winning team is useless unless it beats the opposing team by more than the "point spread" listed to the right of the teams.

The district court concluded that the football predictions were based on skill and, therefore, the scheme was not a lottery. For this reason it dismissed the complaint. The state sought review of that decision. The superior court reversed the dismissal, holding as a matter of law that the card was a ticket in a lottery. Morrow appeals from that decision.

I.

Lotteries constitute a distinct form of gambling, prohibited by Alaska statute. Where the term "lottery" is not defined by statute, courts generally adopt a definition including three essential elements: consideration, chance, and prize.[4] All three elements must be present for the scheme to constitute a lottery. If one of them is absent, the scheme is not a lottery, regardless of its purpose. If all of the elements are present, the scheme is a lottery, regardless of the purpose of its sponsor.

---

4. A fourth element is occasionally required for a lottery in some jurisdictions: the scheme must also be a public nuisance or a widespread pestilence in order to constitute a lottery. However, courts generally hold that a scheme constitutes a lottery even though it is not a widespread pestilence. State v. Coats, 158 Ore. 122, 74 P.2d 1102, 1105 (1938); Note, Lotteries-Nature and Elements-Regulations, 16 Ore.L.Rev. 164, 168 (1937).

In the case at bar, consideration and prize are present; the controversy concerns the element of chance.

In determining whether chance is present, courts generally employ one of two guides: (1) the pure chance doctrine, under which a scheme is considered a lottery when a person's judgment plays no part in the selection and award of the prize, and (2) the dominant factor doctrine, under which a scheme constitutes a lottery where chance dominates the distribution of prizes, even though such a distribution is affected to some degree by the exercise of skill or judgment. Most jurisdictions favor the dominant factor doctrine.

We agree that the sounder approach is to determine the character of the scheme under the dominant factor rule. We think that a game should be classified as one of skill or chance depending on the dominating element, not on the presence or absence of a small element of skill, which would validate the game under the pure chance doctrine. The pure chance doctrine would legalize many guessing contests and other schemes, where only a small element of skill would remove such games from classification as lotteries. This could lead to large-scale evasion of the statutory purpose. In many instances the gambling aspect of a lottery could be cleverly concealed so that ignorant and unwary persons would be enticed into participation before they became aware of the true nature of the scheme.

The following aspects are requisite to a scheme where skill predominates over chance. (1) Participants must have a distinct possibility of exercising skill and must have sufficient data upon which to calculate an informed judgment. The test is that without skill it would be absolutely impossible to win the game. (2) Participants must have the opportunity to exercise the skill, and the general class of participants must possess the skill. Where the contest is aimed at the capacity of the general public, the average person must have the skill, but not every person need have the skill. It is irrelevant that participants may exercise varying degrees of skill. Johnson v. Phinney, 218 F.2d 303, 306 (5th Cir. 1955). The scheme cannot be limited or aimed at a specific skill which only a few possess. '(W)hether chance or skill was the determining factor in the contest must depend upon the capacity of the general public—not experts—to solve the problems presented.' State ex inf. McKittrick v. Globe-Democrat Publishing Co., 110 S.W.2d 705, 717 (Mo. 1937). (3) Skill or the competitors' efforts must sufficiently govern the result. Skill must control the final result, not just one part of the larger scheme. Commonwealth v. Plissner, 4 N.E.2d 241 (Mass. 1936). Where 'chance enters into the solution of another lesser part of the problems and thereby proximately influences the final result,' the scheme is a lottery. State ex inf. McKittrick v. Globe-Democrat Publishing Co., supra. Where skill does not destroy the dominant effect of chance, the scheme is a lottery. Horner v. United States, 147 U.S. 449, 459, (1893). (4) The standard of skill must be known to the participants, and this standard must govern the result. The language used in promoting the scheme must sufficiently inform the participants of the criteria to be used in determining the results of the winners. The winners must be determined objectively. Note, *Contest and the Lottery Law*, 45 Harv. L. Rev. 1196, 1216 (1932).

II.

Turning to the case at bar, we feel that the question of which element predominates—skill or chance—is for the trier of fact to determine. We cannot, as a matter of law, conclude that the football pool in this case is not a lottery, because we do not have evidence before us as to the relevant importance of chance and skill. Appellant is entitled to a trial on the factual issue of the predominance of chance or skill, and the state has the burden of showing that chance predominates.

Therefore, we reverse and remand to the superior court for further remand to the district court for proceedings consistent with the views expressed in this opinion.

Reversed and remanded.

Boardwalk Regency Corp. v. Attorney General of New Jersey
457 A.2d 847 (N.J. 1982)

Gruccio, A.J.S.C.

In this action, plaintiffs Boardwalk Regency Corporation and American Backgammon Championships, Inc. seek a declaratory judgment that a proposed backgammon tournament scheduled to be held on March 16–20, 1983 at the Boardwalk Regency casino hotel would not violate any state laws and therefore would not subject plaintiffs to criminal prosecution by defendant in the event the tournament is held.

. . .

In the statutory scheme, "gambling" is defined as:

> Staking or risking something of value upon the outcome of a contest of chance or a future contingent event not under the actor's control or influence, upon an agreement or understanding that he will receive something of value in the event of a certain outcome. N.J.S.A. 2C:37-1(b)

"Contest of chance" is defined as:

> Any contest, game, pool, gaming scheme or gaming device in which the outcome depends in a material degree upon an element of chance, notwithstanding that skill of the contestants or some other persons may also be a factor therein. N.J.S.A. 2C:37-1(a)

Plaintiffs place great reliance on this latter definition in support of their argument that skill predominates over chance to such a great extent in tournament backgammon that the element of chance, represented by the results of the dice roll on each turn, is reduced to an immaterial factor in the determination of the outcome of the competition.

After reviewing the exhibits admitted into evidence and the testimony elicited from plaintiffs' expert witness, Paul Magriel, the court acknowledges that backgammon, played on its highest level, can and does involve complex strategies and maneuvers incorporating sophisticated theories of mathematics and statistics which at least some highly intelligent players are able to utilize. Furthermore, credible evidence indicates that such strategies on the part of these players, coming into effect after the rolls of the dice, amount to skill which in certain instances can play a significant role in the outcome of tournament play. (It is apparent that the average backgammon player is not as highly competent in these sophisticated systems as plaintiffs' expert, and accordingly that such strategies which Magriel may utilize are not uniformly applied in the game.)

But this recognition of the skill factor is not determinative on the issue of whether chance plays a material or immaterial role in the outcome of the activity. Indeed, the statute acknowledges that a game may be a "contest of chance" "notwithstanding that skill of the contestants … may also be a factor therein." N.J.S.A. 2C:37-1(a). Thus, the proper focus of the inquiry here is not on the level of skill which may affect the outcome of the contested activity but rather on whether the element of chance is a factor that is material to the final result.

The court, reviewing all of the evidence, finds that the element of chance, represented by the rolling of two dice to begin the game and at the beginning of each player's turn, is a decidedly material element in the game of backgammon. The rolling of the dice constitutes a "future contingent event not under the actor's control or influence" (see N.J.S.A. 2C:37-1(b)) upon which the players risk something of value.

Plaintiffs' expert testified that, in his opinion, the rolls of the dice are a "given" element; that the numbers displayed are a mere background upon which the game's complex strategies are played, and that it is the skill in developing these strategies which are more important than the numbers rolled. However, the credible evidence indicates that this characterization is an unmistakable understatement as to the role of the dice. The game itself could not be played without the independent chance element provided by the dice. Each turn of the players is begun by the throw of the dice, and each throw determines the moves, and accompanying strategies, that are possible under the rules. The dice are also rolled at the start of each game to decide who plays first, bringing at least some advantage to that player, according to plaintiffs' expert.

Another point deserves mention. Plaintiffs' expert testified on cross-examination that in a backgammon tournament, as more games or points are required to win a match, the role of chance in the final outcome will correspondingly be reduced. Yet in the hardbound, 404-page book entitled *Backgammon*, introduced into evidence as Exhibit P-7, the author, plaintiffs' expert, writes (at 269):

> Doubling is one of the most important aspects of backgammon; correct doubling decisions alone will give a player an enormous advantage over his opponent. The doubling cube holds the key to being a winner or loser.

In the stipulation of facts submitted to the court, the doubling cube is described. The stipulation explains that the doubling element, when utilized at the option of either player, results in increasing in the number of points attributable to each game, thereby also decreasing the length of a match or round. These factors, when considered in their entirety, indicate to the court that the doubling technique, so vital to the outcome of tournament backgammon play, substantially increases not only the importance of a single game but also the importance attached to the independent, uncontrollable element of chance.

Finally, an article in the June 4, 1979 issue of *Sports Illustrated* magazine, introduced in evidence as exhibit P-1, provides eyewitness coverage of the final round of a tournament in which plaintiffs' expert was a participant. The article's introduction, reads (at 69), "Paul Magriel is a mathematician and backgammon champion of the world. His enemy is the dice, which obscure the intricate and beautiful patterns of his game." The same account concludes (at 82) as follows:

> With one man left to bring into his homeboard in order to start bearing off, Magriel rolled a horrible 1-1. Samuels bore off two more men. He had only two men left on his No. 1 point and would with the game on his next roll. However, Magriel was still in the match so long as he didn't roll 1-1, 2-1, 3-1 or 3-2. Any other roll—29 of 36 possibilities in all—would allow Magriel to bring his last man into his home board and bear one man off. He was slightly better than a 4-to-1 favorite note to get gammoned.

> Magriel shook his cup and let the dice fall. They bounced crazily around the board and came to a stop. Magriel stared. Samuels stared.

> Double aces!

A pause. Then a roar from the crowd. Samuels leaped up and shook Magriel's hand. He had beaten the world champion. The crowd swirled around him. They carried him off to the bar to celebrate.

Magriel sat in his chair in the now empty room, staring in dismay at the double aces. He could not believe what had happened. Resting on the felt surface of the backgammon board, the dice seemed to be mocking him. Magriel shook his head.

There they still were. Double aces. Snake eyes. On this night, the enemy, the agent of disorder and chaos, had triumphed.

This report, offered by plaintiffs and admitted by the participant, Magriel, to be an accurate account upon examination by the court, removes all doubt from this court that the element of chance plays at least a material role in determining the outcome of this activity on which money is risked, no matter how much it is claimed that the role of skill predominated or allowed the finalist to reach that stage in the tournament.

Therefore, the court concludes that (a) under the New Jersey Constitution the proposed backgammon tournament is a form of "gambling" which has not been authorized by the people and (b) the game of backgammon in the stated context is a "contest of chance" and "gambling" within the express provisions of N.J.S.A. 2C:37-1 et seq. Accordingly, this action must be resolved in favor of defendant.

Notes

1. A key difference between the *Morrow* and *Boardwalk* cases is the standard that the court adopted for determining whether a game should be classified as a lawful contest of skill or an unlawful game of chance. In *Morrow*, the Alaskan court adopted the predominance test, while the New Jersey legislature adopted the material element test by statute. The material element test recognizes that although skill may primarily influence the outcome of a game, a state may prohibit wagering on the game if chance has more than an incidental effect on the game. Unlike the predominance test, the material element test is more subjective. The court determines the level of chance in a particular game and makes a judgment as to when that chance becomes material to the outcome. Some other states analyze the role chance plays in a game by determining whether a particular game contains "any" chance that affects the outcome of the game. As virtually every game has some element of chance, most skill games may not survive scrutiny in these states. Do games exist that do not contain any chance whatsoever?

2. Simply knowing the test used in each state is insufficient. An understanding of the concept of chance is needed to properly apply the tests. The idea of random events as an indicator of chance is easy to understand. In many games, the chance element is obvious. In Scrabble, it is the random selection of tiles. In poker, it is the shuffle and deal of the cards. This is systemic chance, or in other words, a randomizer that is an integrated part of game play.

Yet, other forms of chance can impact outcome. Take, for example, the game of rock, paper and scissors. The game does not have systemic chance. Likewise, in duplicate bridge, players do not know what cards are in their opponents' hands. This phenomenon is called imperfect information, where skill is not the sole determinant but is influenced by not having complete information of all factors that can impact game results. In contrast, perfect information is a state of complete knowledge about the rules of the game, factors that can impact outcome and information about the actions of other contestants that is instantaneously updated to allow a skilled response. What are some perfect information games? Can a perfect information game also be a game of chance?

Other forms of chance may exist. Specifically, this may occur where a game is designed to negate skill by either making the skill levels beyond the capabilities of the participants or so easy that every participant can always display perfect skill. For example, imagine administering a multiple choice test on quantum physics to ordinary eight year olds. Would the test results be based on skill or chance? Likely, most fifth graders would simply be guessing at the correct answer. For additional discussion, *see* Anthony N. Cabot, Glenn J. Light & Karl F. Rutledge, *Alex Rodriguez, a Monkey, and the Game of Scrabble: The Hazard of Using Illogic to Define Legality of Games of Mixed Skill and Chance*, 57 Drake L. Rev. 383 (2009).

3. Knowing the test for whether a game is skill-based and the types of chance only provide the courts with the rules to decide cases involving prize games. Courts also need to apply these rules to the particularities of each game offered by an Internet site. The actual court determination of whether a particular game is a game of chance or a game of skill is a question of fact, not of law. Effectively, this means that each side—the prosecutor and the defendant—must introduce evidence of the chance and skill elements of the game and try to convince the jury or judge that the game has the requisite legal standards of one or the other.

Proof that a game is skill-based can come from many sources, such as expert witnesses and books or articles discussing and analyzing skill. Perhaps the most compelling is mathematical evidence. One such solution is to do statistical trials showing that over time, skilled contestants prevail over non-skilled contestants. But does this really prove that a game is a game of skill? The "law of large numbers" is one of several theorems expressing the idea that as the number of trials of a process increases, the percentage difference between the expected and actual values goes to zero. Suppose a game is 99% luck and 1% skill. If one contestant possesses that skill and the other does not, then in a small number of games, the skilled contestant does not have a decided advantage. Nevertheless, after thousands of games, the skilled contestant is undoubtedly going to prevail. These results only prove that skill is an element. Evidence is still required to prove that in any given game that the skill levels meet the test for the type of game being presented.

C. What Is a Prize?

Wisconsin v. Hahn
553 N.W.2d 292 (Wis. Ct. App. 1996)

Sundby, Judge.

In this appeal, the State candidly acknowledges that it seeks to establish that video poker machines are "gambling machine[s]" per se. In its prosecution of defendant Lester Hahn for collecting the proceeds of "any gambling machine," contrary to § 945.03(5), Stats.,[1] it claims that it need prove only that Hahn knew that the proceeds he collected resulted from the operation of video poker machines. The trial court disagreed and in a

---

1. Section 945.03(5), Stats., provides in part:
    Whoever intentionally does any of the following is engaged in commercial gambling and is guilty of a Class E felony: ...
        (5) Sets up for use for the purpose of gambling or collects the proceeds of any gambling machine ...
(emphasis added)

pre-trial order proposed to instruct the jury that before they could find Hahn guilty, they had to be satisfied beyond a reasonable doubt that he knowingly and intentionally collected gambling proceeds from the video poker machines. We granted the State's motion for leave to appeal the order and now affirm in part and reverse in part with directions.

For purposes of this appeal, it is undisputed that Hahn, through his employee, collected the proceeds from video poker machines he placed in three taverns in Jefferson County, Wisconsin. The State contends that this proof establishes the offense of collecting the proceeds of a gambling machine. It proposes that the trial court instruct the jury that a violation of § 945.03(5), Stats., requires a showing of two elements: "First, that the machine [from which defendant collected the proceeds] ... was a gambling machine. Second, that the defendant collected the proceeds of the gambling machine."

The instruction proposed by the State defines "gambling machine" in terms of § 945.01(3), Stats., but does not assist the jury in determining whether the video poker machines involved in this prosecution meet that definition. The State assumes that video poker machines are gambling machines per se and no further instruction is necessary. We disagree. We conclude that because a video poker machine may be used for either amusement or gambling, the trial court must instruct the jury as to what the evidence must show to establish that the machine from which defendant collected proceeds was a "gambling machine."

Section 945.01(3), Stats., defines "gambling machine" as follows:

> (a) A gambling machine is a contrivance which for a consideration affords the player an opportunity to obtain something of value, the award of which is determined by chance, even though accompanied by some skill and whether or not the prize is automatically paid by the machine.

> (b) "Gambling machine" does not include any of the following:

> 2. Any amusement device if it rewards the player exclusively with one or more nonredeemable free replays for achieving certain scores and *does not* change the ratio or *record the number of the free replays so awarded.*

(emphasis added)

Under this definition, we conclude that the jury may find that Hahn violated § 945.03(5), Stats., if they are satisfied that he collected the proceeds from video poker machines knowing they were being used for gambling and that the proceeds he collected were derived from such gambling.

If the evidence at trial is consistent with the testimony of the tavern operators at Hahn's preliminary examination, Hahn cannot claim that the video poker machines were "amusement device[s]." At Hahn's preliminary hearing, the operators of taverns in which he placed video poker machines testified that the machines awarded successful players free replays which were recorded by the machines. The tavern keepers paid the successful player cash for the accumulated free replays and by operation of a remote control device behind the bar expunged the replays.

A video poker machine operated in this way is not an "amusement device" under § 945.01(3)(b)2, Stats., for two reasons. First, it rewards the player with redeemable free replays. Second, it records the number of free replays awarded.

The "free replay" language was added to § 945.01(3)(b)2, Stats., by Laws of 1979, ch. 91. The analysis by the Legislative Reference Bureau states that the purpose of the amendment was to change the result of State v. Lake Geneva Lanes, Inc., 125 N.W.2d 622 (Wis.

1963), where the court held that a free replay awarded the operator of a pinball machine was "something of value" and therefore pinball machines were "gambling machine[s]." 1979 Assembly Bill 512, LRB-2456/2. However, the amendment made two important qualifications: (1) the free replays had to be "nonredeemable;" and (2) the amusement device could not record the number of free replays awarded.

The prohibition against redeeming free replays is consistent with the requirement that a contrivance be only an "amusement device" and not a "gambling machine." Not so clear, however, is why an "amusement device" cannot record free replays. We may assume, however, that the drafters of the amendment were aware that free replays are "an incentive that fosters the gambling spirit." People v. Cerniglia, 11 N.Y.S.2d 5 (1939), quoted in Robert J. Urban, *Gambling Today Via The "Free Replay" Pinball Machine*, 42 Marq. L. Rev. 98, 111 (1958). For years, the status of free replays awarded by amusement devices was debated in courts and legislatures across the country. *See* 42 Marq. L. Rev. at 104–14. In 1957, the Wisconsin legislature defeated a bill to permit pinball machines which paid off in free replays because of opposition of law enforcement agencies which believed that this latitude would open the door to syndicate gambling. Id. at 101 & n. 27. Urban noted that the view of the Lake Geneva Lanes court was being challenged by "an ever-stronger minority." Id. at 109–10. He suggested that perhaps the reason the minority view did not prevail was that state legislatures were revising anti-gambling laws to permit free replays awarded by machines of one sort or another. Id. at 110 & n. 88.

In Laws of 1979, Ch. 91, the Wisconsin legislature joined those state legislatures which distinguished between machines whose free replays were not recorded and those machines which metered or recorded extra games. See id. at 113. Urban commented:

> The object of this rather recent test, applied where the free replay is permitted under general, partially definitive, or specific statutes is to diminish the danger of actual pay-offs made on the number of additional plays, by eliminating any accurate registration of such to determine pay-off amounts. This added precaution seems to recognize, of necessity, the inherent tendency and actual practice of using such devices for gambling purposes.

Id. (footnotes omitted).

While a jury could find that the video poker machines which are the subject of this prosecution do not qualify as "amusement device[s]," we reject the State's argument that they are gambling machines, per se. A video poker machine need not record or redeem free replays. We agree with the Attorney General that, "[a]s a general proposition, an article which is capable of innocent uses is usually held not to be a gambling device unless expressly so defined by statute or unless shown to have been used for gambling." 30 Op. Att'y Gen. 300, 301 (1941); see also Dallmann v. Kluchesky, 282 N.W. 9 (Wis. 1938) (basketball machine not gambling machine where there was no pay-off device, and it was not possible to play more than one game with a single coin). A video poker machine may be used for innocent purposes if the machine either does not award free replays or requires that the replays be used as earned. The machines in question do not have these innocent characteristics.

The fact that a video poker machine does not meet the definition of an "amusement device" does not require the conclusion that it is a gambling machine; it simply does not satisfy the exception as an amusement device. However, the video poker machines which are the subject of this action are "gambling machine[s]" because they "afford" the successful player an opportunity to obtain "something of value" even if the player's "prize" is not automatically awarded by the machine but is awarded by the owner or lessee of the machine. Section 945.01(3)(a), Stats., only requires that the machine afford the player the opportunity to obtain a prize; the machine itself need not award the prize. A "contrivance" is a "gambling machine" "whether or not the prize is automatically paid by the machine." Id. The legislature's choice of the word "affords" is significant. If the legislature had intended that the contrivance itself must award a prize before it may be considered a gambling machine, it would have defined "any gambling machine" as "any contrivance which rewards the player with something of value."

The trial court's order correctly states the law as far as it goes. However, its proposed instruction is incomplete in that it does not inform the jury as to what it must find to conclude that the video poker machines in question are gambling machines. Upon completion of the trial, we direct that the trial court instruct the jury according to the principles stated in this opinion.

Order affirmed in part; reversed in part and cause remanded with directions.

Notes

1. An activity where the contestants cannot win prizes is rarely considered gambling. The advent of traditional poker and slot machines with free replays forced state legislatures to reconsider the traditional definitions of games of chance.

2. Besides a general prohibition on games of chance, most states expressly prohibit wagering and bookmaking. These prohibitions are typically stated applying to "staking or risking something of value upon the outcome of a contest of chance or a future contingent event not under the person's control or influence" and to bookmakers who accept these types of wagers. The difference between wagering/bookmaking and most other gambling/lottery laws may be explained as follows: notwithstanding a state's exclusion of skill gaming from its general gambling prohibitions, if a contestant wagers on someone else's skill, not his or her own, a bookmaking violation may have occurred. For example, in those states that have adopted the Dominant Factor Test, a player in a chess tournament can probably wager on his or her own performance by paying an entry fee into a contest in which he or she hopes to finish first, but cannot normally wager on the expected performance of someone else in that chess tournament.

Georgia laws provide a good example of this requirement. A Georgia court drew a sharp distinction between a game of skill, baseball, and the wagering on such game of skill, which is a game of chance, stating:

> … [A] game of chance may be found under certain circumstances to be played between persons who wager or bet … upon the outcome of a game although not actually participating in the game itself, which may or may not have been inaugurated primarily for the purpose of affording an opportunity for wagering or betting, even though the game is a game of skill, between the players who participated therein.

Grant v. State, 44 S.E.2d 513, 515 (Ga. Ct. App. 1947). Thus, case law still suggests that wagering on one's own personal skill in a game of skill is not prohibited gambling. Wagering on the outcome of a game of skill where you are not a participant, however, can be a violation of wagering or bookmaking laws.

Chapter 2

Gambling, Public Policy and Regulatory Models

1. Introduction

Gambling as an activity has long been controversial. For many years after legalizing casino gambling in 1931, Nevada's casinos were considered a pariah industry. All the other states maintained a prohibitory stance toward most forms of gambling. With the exception of horse race wagering, no other form of commercial gambling was legal in the United States. Nevada's casinos had no competition until New Jersey passed legislation in 1978 to authorize casinos in Atlantic City. When it did so, New Jersey's regulatory system was markedly different from Nevada in several respects. For example, while Nevada allowed its casinos to freely grant credit, New Jersey restricted credit by allowing only check cashing with strict deposit requirements. These differences were not isolated to casino credit but reflected a different overriding public policy concerning casino gaming. From these different public policies, three basic gaming system models emerged: the Prohibitory Model, the Government Interest Model, and the Player Protection Model. Each model has distinct characteristics; however, jurisdictions often adopt regulatory systems that use principles invoking more than one model or an amalgam of different models. ANTHONY CABOT, CASINO GAMING: POLICY, ECONOMICS, AND REGULATION (UNLV Int'l Gaming Institute 1996); JOHN DOMBRINK & WILLIAM THOMPSON, THE LAST RESORT: SUCCESS AND FAILURE IN CAMPAIGNS FOR CASINOS (Univ. of Nevada Press, 1990); Jerome Skolnick & John Dombrink, *The Limits of Gaming Control*, 12 CONN. L. REV. 770 (1980).

A. Prohibitory Model

Georgia Constitution, Article I, Section II

Paragraph VIII: Lotteries and nonprofit bingo games.

(a) Except as herein specifically provided in this Paragraph VIII, all lotteries, and the sale of lottery tickets, and all forms of pari-mutuel betting and casino gambling are hereby prohibited; and this prohibition shall be enforced by penal laws.

Idaho Constitution

Article III Section 20: Gambling Prohibited.

(1) Gambling is contrary to public policy and is strictly prohibited except for the following:

a. A state lottery which is authorized by the state if conducted in conformity with enabling legislation; and

b. Pari-mutuel betting if conducted in conformity with enabling legislation; and

c. Bingo and raffle games that are operated by qualified charitable organizations in the pursuit of charitable purposes if conducted in conformity with enabling legislation.

(2) No activities permitted by subsection (1) shall employ any form of casino gambling including, but not limited to, blackjack, craps, roulette, poker, bacarrat, keno and slot machines, or employ any electronic or electromechanical imitation or simulation of any form of casino gambling.

(3) The legislature shall provide by law penalties for violations of this section.

(4) Notwithstanding the foregoing, the following are not gambling and are not prohibited by this section:

a. Merchant promotional contests and drawings conducted incidentally to bona fide nongaming business operations, if prizes are awarded without consideration being charged to participants; and

b. Games that award only additional play.

Notes

1. Jurisdictions that follow the Prohibitory Model maintain an underlying public policy that gambling is an evil or a burden that needs to be banned. These proscriptions can be in the form of a constitutional prohibition that bans the state from adopting laws that permit games of chance or lotteries and institutes criminal penalties on those who operate a gambling game or engage in the game as a player.

While support for opposition to gambling may be founded on philosophic, economic, or social thought, the religious orientation of a society is often paramount. Many of the world's major religions including Judaism, Islam, Hindu, Buddhism, Shintoism and several divisions of Christianity take an absolutist attitude that gambling is an evil or a sin.

Particularly in secular societies, determining whether the prohibition on gambling is based on religious or pragmatic grounds is difficult. Religious and utilitarian views on gambling are often similar in result if not in analysis. Nevertheless, religious orientation of a society is a good predictor of whether that society will allow gambling. Moreover, the secular laws of societies with a dominant religion tend to follow the teachings of the predominant religion.

Arguments for prohibition also can rest on moral as opposed to religious grounds. Moralists maintain positions based on subjective personal feelings dictated either by theology or personal notions of social order. The teaching of Patrick Devlin typifies the moralist position. He states:

> Societies disintegrate from within more frequently than they are broken up by external pressures. There is disintegration when no common morality is observed, and history shows that the loosening of moral bonds is often the first stage of disintegration so that society is justified in taking the same steps to preserve its moral code as it does to preserve its government and other essential institutions.

PATRICK DEVLIN, THE ENFORCEMENT OF MORALS 13 (Oxford Univ. Press 1965).

Moralists claim that gambling influences the general public's values and priorities. In essence, people may interact with others differently in a community with gambling as opposed to a community without it. Gambling's emphasis on hedonism, luck, and wealth may affect the nature of these interactions. Therefore, moralists maintain that undesirable attributes in the community at large may emerge, including that persons are better off being lucky than working hard and that wealth is the most important attribute. Therefore, everyone must have a price.

2. Besides moral and religious grounds, utilitarian arguments for the prohibition of gambling are common. Amoral pragmatic arguments assess whether an activity should be legal based on an objective evaluation that considers many principles and effects. For example, Professor William Eadington suggests that governments considering legalizing gambling should first weigh the benefits, such as taxes, jobs, economic stimulation, and the fulfillment of consumer demands, against costs, such as economic displacement, effects on crime, and dysfunctional gambling. Governments should next consider reasonable cost-effective methods to minimize the costs. Then, according to Eadington, "If, at that point, aggregate benefits do not exceed aggregate costs, or the proposed gambling industry is not economically viable, then creation of a new gambling industry would not be wise." William Eadington, *Problem Gambling and Public Policy: Alternatives in Dealing with Problem Gamblers and Commercial Gambling*, in COMPULSIVE GAMBLING THEORY, RESEARCH, AND PRACTICE 175 (Howard Shaffer et al., eds.) (Lexington Books 1989).

Prohibition can be coupled with either rigid or lax enforcement. Disrespect for the law through non-enforcement also may occur where people adopt an attitude that not all laws need to be taken seriously. An example was the attempt to ban alcohol consumption in the United States in the 1920s. The government ultimately abandoned prohibition because of strong commercial demand. This resulted, however, in the first widespread incidence where the public openly defied the laws. Moreover, non-enforcement may lead the public to believe that the police are corrupt. One national study concluded that "citizens are very likely to view non-enforcement of gambling laws as an indication of police corruption." FLOYD J. FOWLER, GAMBLING LAW ENFORCEMENT IN MAJOR AMERICAN CITIES (National Institute of Law Enforcement & Criminal Justice, 1978).

B. Player Protection Model

R. v. Police Commissioner of the Metropolis
2 Q.B. 118, (1968)

LORD DENNING, M.R.:

The applicant, Mr. Blackburn moves for a mandamus against the Commissioner of Police of the Metropolis. He says that it was the commissioner's duty to enforce the law against gaming houses: and that he has not done it. The applicant seeks an order to compel the commissioner to do it....

1. The law as to gaming houses.

The common law of England has always condemned gaming houses. This is not because gambling is wicked in itself, but because of the evils attendant on it. HAWKINS in his PLEAS OF THE CROWN (Book I, Ch. 75, sect. 6) writes that:

"All common gaming houses are nuisances in the eye of the law; not only because they are great temptations to idleness, but because they are apt to draw together great numbers of disorderly persons, which cannot but be very inconvenient to the neighbourhood."

The statute law of England has likewise condemned gaming houses. As early as 1541 in the time of Henry VIII Parliament enacted that no person should for his gain keep a gaming house. The reason then was because gambling disturbed the military training. It distracted the young men from practising archery which was needed for the defence of the country. Several statutes have been passed since. All of them condemned gaming houses because of the mischiefs attendant on them. When roulette was first introduced over two hundred years ago, Parliament tried to stop it. A statute of 1744 recited that the "pernicious" game called roulette or roy-poly was practised. It prohibited any person from keeping any house for playing it.

All these statutes, however, proved of no avail to prevent the mischief. BLACKSTONE said that the legislature had been careful to pass laws to prevent "this destructive vice," but these laws had failed to achieve their object. The reason for the failure was because the gamblers were too quick-witted for the law to catch them. He said that:

"The invention of sharpers being swifter than the punishment of the law which only hunts them from one device to another ..."

See his COMMENTARIES, BOOK IV, Ch. 13, p. 173. So much so that by the beginning of the nineteenth century gaming houses were a scandal. The Victorian legislation, aided by the Victorian judges in Jenks v. Turpin, 13 Q.B.D. 505 (1884), reduced the evil but did not exterminate it.

History has repeated itself in our own time. Parliament made an attempt in 1960 to put the law on a sound footing. It had before it the Report of the Royal Commission on the subject. The report drew a clear distinction between promoters who organised gaming for their own profit (which was an evil) and those who arranged gaming for the enjoyment of others without making a profit out of it themselves (such as gaming in a members' club which was innocent). The Royal Commission thought that

"the main object of the criminal law should be to prevent persons being induced to play for high stakes for the profit of the promoter."

They recommended legislation to achieve this object. The draftsmen set to work and produced the bill which became the Betting and Gaming Act, 1960, since re-enacted in the Betting, Gaming and Lotteries Act 1963. The old common law was abolished. The old statutes were repealed. New sections were enacted with the intention of ensuring that promoters did not make high profits out of gaming, either in clubs or elsewhere.

These sections have lamentably failed to achieve their object. Just as in BLACKSTONE'S time, so in ours. The casino companies have set up gaming houses and made large profits out of them. They always seem to be one device ahead of the law. The first device they used after the Act of 1960 was to levy a toll on the stakes. They used to promote roulette without a zero and demand sixpence for themselves on every stake. That device was declared unlawful in Quinn v. Mackinnon, 1 Q.B. 874 (1963). Next, they claimed that they could take sixpence from every player on every spin of the wheel. That device too was held to be unlawful by this court in J. M. Allan (Merchandising), Ltd. v. Cloke, 2 Q.B. 340 (1963). Then they claimed that they could charge every player 10s. for every twenty minutes. That too was found to be unlawful in Kelland v. Raymond, 2 Q.B. 108 (1964). One of their devices at this time, however, succeeded. It was in chemin-de-fer. The promoters charged every player £5 for every "shoe" which took about thirty-five minutes. This was held to be lawful in Mills v. Mackinnon, 2 Q.B. 96 (1964). I must say I doubt that decision. I should have thought that £5 for every thirty-five minutes was worse than ten shillings every twenty minutes. At any rate, it is more profitable.

After those cases, the casino companies thought out a new device which proved to be far more profitable. They promoted roulette with a zero. This is a game in which the chances over a long period mightily favour the holder of the bank. Under this new device, the organisers so arranged things that they themselves nearly always held the bank; but they claimed it was lawful because the croupier every half hour "offered the bank" to the players. Very rarely, if ever, was the offer accepted: for the simple reason that it may be ruinous to hold the bank for only a few spins of the wheel. It is only worth holding if you can hold it for a long time, such as a week or a month. Nevertheless the organisers claimed that this "offer of the bank" rendered the gaming lawful.

. . .

2. The steps taken by the applicant:

In 1966 the applicant was concerned about the way in which the big London clubs were being run. He went to see a representative of the Commissioner of Police and told him that illegal gaming was taking place in virtually all London casinos. He was given to understand, he says, that action would be taken; but nothing appeared to be done. On Mar. 15, 1967, the applicant wrote a letter to the commissioner in which he again stated that illegal gaming was taking place. He asked the commissioner to assist him in prosecuting several London clubs. Following that letter he was seen by Mr. Bearman on behalf of the commissioner. Mr. Bearman explained to him that there were difficulties in enforcing the provisions of the Act of 1963. He added that the way in which police manpower was used was a matter for the discretion of the commissioner; and that it was felt that, as the gaming law stood, there were higher priorities for the deployment of police manpower. He also stated that it would be contrary to a policy decision for him to promote or assist in the promotion of a prosecution for breach of s. 32 of the Act of 1963.

The applicant was dissatisfied and made application to the divisional court for a mandamus directed to the commissioner requiring three things: (i) to assist him and others to prosecute gaming clubs; (ii) to assist him in a particular complaint against a named club; and (iii) to reverse the policy decision. The divisional court rejected his application. He appeals in person to this court.

. . .

4. The duty of the Commissioner of Police:

The office of Commissioner of Police within the metropolis dates back to 1829 when SIR ROBERT PEEL introduced his disciplined Force. The commissioner was a justice of the peace specially appointed to administer the police force in the metropolis. His constitutional status has never been defined either by statute or by the courts. It was considered by the Royal Commission on the Police in their report in 1962 (Cmnd. 1728). I have no hesitation, however, in holding that, like every constable in the land, he should be, and is, independent of the executive. . . .

He must take steps so to post his men that crimes may be detected; and that honest citizens may go about their affairs in peace. He must decide whether or no (sic) suspected persons are to be prosecuted; and, if need be, bring the prosecution or see that it is brought; but in all these things he is not the servant of anyone, save of the law itself. No

Minister of the Crown can tell him that he must, or must not, keep observation on this place or that; or that he must, or must not, prosecute this man or that one. Nor can any police authority tell him so. The responsibility for law enforcement lies on him. He is answerable to the law and to the law alone.

...

Although the chief officers of police are answerable to the law, there are many fields in which they have a discretion with which the law will not interfere. For instance, it is for the Commissioner of Police, or the chief constable, as the case may be, to decide in any particular case whether enquiries should be pursued, or whether an arrest should be made, or a prosecution brought. It must be for him to decide on the disposition of his force and the concentration of his resources on any particular crime or area. No court can or should give him direction on such a matter. He can also make policy decisions and give effect to them, as, for instance, was often done when prosecutions were not brought for attempted suicide; but there are some policy decisions with which, I think, the courts in a case can, if necessary, interfere. Suppose a chief constable were to issue a directive to his men that no person should be prosecuted for stealing any goods less than £100 in value. I should have thought that the court could countermand it. He would be failing in his duty to enforce the law.

...

5. Conclusions:

This case has shown a deplorable state of affairs. The law has not been enforced as it should. The lawyers themselves are at least partly responsible. The niceties of drafting and the refinements of interpretation have led to uncertainties in the law itself. This has discouraged the police from keeping observation and taking action; but it does not, I think, exempt them also from their share of the responsibility. The proprietors of gaming houses have taken advantage of the situation. By one device after another they have kept ahead of the law. As soon as one device has been held unlawful, they have started another; but the day of reckoning is at hand. No longer will we tolerate these devices. The law must be sensibly interpreted so as to give effect to the intentions of Parliament; and the police must see that it is enforced. The rule of law must prevail.

...

The chief function of the police is to enforce the law. The divisional court left open the point whether an order of mandamus could issue against a chief police officer should he refuse to carry out that function. Constitutionally it is clearly impermissible for the Home Secretary to issue any order to the police in respect of law enforcement. In this court it has been argued on behalf of the commissioner that the police are under no legal duty to anyone in regard to law enforcement. If this argument were correct, it would mean that insofar as their most important function is concerned, the police are above the law and therefore immune from any control by the court. I reject that argument. In my judgment the police owe the public a clear legal duty to enforce the law — a duty which I have no doubt they recognise and which generally they perform most conscientiously and efficiently. In the extremely unlikely event, however, of the police failing or refusing to carry out their duty, the court would not be powerless to intervene. For example, if, as is quite unthinkable, the chief officer in any district were to issue an instruction that as a matter of policy the police would take no steps to prosecute any house-breaker, I have little doubt but that any householder in that district would be able to obtain an order of mandamus for the instruction to be withdrawn. Of course, the police have a wide discretion whether or not they will prosecute in any particular case. In my judgment, however, the action which I have postulated would be a clear breach of duty. It would be so improper that it could not amount to an exercise of discretion.

The object of s. 32 to s. 40 of the Betting, Gaming and Lotteries Act 1963, and the corresponding provisions of the Betting and Gaming Act, 1960, which the Act of 1963 replaced, was quite simply to protect society against the evils which would necessarily follow were it possible to build up large fortunes by the exploitation of gaming. The Acts of 1960 and 1963 were designed to prevent such exploitation and would have been entirely effective to do so had they been enforced. Regrettably they have not been properly enforced. As a result, and entirely contrary to the intention or contemplation of Parliament, an immense gaming industry, particularly in London, has been allowed to grow up during the past seven years. This has inevitably brought grave social evils in its train — protection rackets, crimes of violence and widespread corruption. There are no doubt a few large establishments which are respectably run and from which these evils are excluded; but for every one of these, there are scores of others. As long as it remains possible for large fortunes to be made by the private exploitation of gaming, the evils to which I have referred will grow and flourish until they threaten the whole fabric of society. Since large fortunes can be made out of the exploitation of gaming, naturally a great deal of ingenuity has been exercised to devise schemes for the purpose of evading the law. With a little more resolution and efficiency, these schemes could and should have been frustrated.

In the present case we are concerned chiefly with the game of roulette played with a zero. For the reasons which appear in the evidence before us, so long as the odds offered against any one number are no more than thirty-five to one the chances favour the bank by three to ten per cent., according to the way the bets are laid. If the house holds the bank, the house in the long run is bound to win. It follows that this contravenes s. 32(1)(a) and (b) of the Act of 1963, for the "chances in the game are [not] equally favourable to all the players, of whom the bank is one' (cf., sub-s. (1)(a)), and the "gaming is so conducted that the chances therein are [not] equally favourable to all the players" (cf., sub-s. (1)(b)). We have all heard of the very old song, "The Man that Broke the Bank at Monte Carlo." The bank could, of course, have a very bad run of luck during one evening and lose heavily. It could perhaps have a very bad run of luck for days and even for weeks, but month in and month out, it is bound to win. This, amoungst other reasons, is why the house which holds that bank month in and month out is bound to be more favourably placed than any player who may hold it sporadically for comparatively short periods of time.

In Kursaal Casino, Ltd. v. Crickitt (No. 1), 2 All E.R. 639 (1966), which was decided in the divisional court on Mar. 23, 1966, the justices had held that for the house to hold the bank contravened the law. The point taken by the prosecution, which to my mind was manifestly a good point, was that whoever held the bank was ex hypothesi a player and accordingly the game could not be equally favourable to all players and was therefore illegal. It would, therefore, make no diffence that the house went through the motions of offering the bank to the players and that very occasionally the offer was accepted for short periods of time. The defense had argued that as the bank was offered at regular intervals to all the players, the chances were equal for all. The justices convicted. Incidentally, they also held that as there must be very many players who could not afford to take the bank, the offer, therefore, was in any event neither genuine nor realistic. The divisional court upheld the conviction and concluded that there was ample evidence to support the finding that the offer of the bank was neither genuine nor realistic.

...

In no circumstances can roulette be legal when played with a zero and when the odds are thirty-five to one or less against any one number turning up. The correct odds are, of course, thirty-six to one, since including zero there are thirty-seven numbers on the roulette wheel.

According to the evidence before this court, however, most of the gaming houses in London, in direct defiance of the law as laid down by the House of Lords, are still playing roulette, unmolested, in exactly the same way (save for one immaterial variation to which I will refer) as they were doing prior to Dec. 19, 1967. The variation is as follows: If the number backed by a player for, say, one chip turns up, he receives thirty-five ordinary chips and one special chip of a different colour. He is not allowed to play with this chip or to exchange it for an ordinary chip. The normal practice is for the players to toss the special chips back to the croupier. Clearly the players are under no illusion. They realise that these special chips are but a hollow sham devised to deceive the exceptionally gullible into thinking that the odds being paid out are thirty-six to one when in reality they are thirty-five to one. If anyone with a special chip chooses (and very few of them do) to take it to the cash desk to be cashed, it is duly cashed but the player concerned has to pay a fee, for example, of £10 in the Golden Nugget Casino Club and £50 in the Victoria Sporting Club. It may be that gamblers are reluctant to cash the chips because they do not like paying the fee or because, rightly or wrongly, they fear that they may be barred—and most gamblers would rather sacrifice a shade of odds than lose the chance of gambling.

However that may be, it is obvious that in reality the odds on the overwhelming number of bets remain at the rate of thirty-five to one against a single number turning up. What otherwise could be the object of having a different coloured chip to make the odds up to thirty-six to one and charging a fee for cashing it? At most it amounts to giving a player an option either to pay a fee or to play in a game in which the chances are not equally favourable to all players. There is certainly nothing here for a test case. This could only serve to give the gaming houses a further breathing space for another long spell, at the end of which no doubt an equally transparent ruse would be devised. What is now urgently needed is that energetic steps should immediately be taken to prosecute a substantial number of major London gaming houses in which the law is being defied. It may be that even when very heavy fines are imposed, they will be ineffective, in which event the Attorney-General would no doubt consider the advisability of bringing relator actions to restrain the present abuses by injunction.

...

Gaming Act 1968, Chapter 65, Part I: Gaming Elsewhere Than on Premises Licensed or Registered under Part II of this Act (Great Britain)

§ 16 Provision of Credit for Gaming

(1) Subject to [subsections [(2) to (2A)] of this section], where gaming to which this Part of this Act applies takes place on premises in respect of which a license under this Act is for the time being in force, neither the holder of the license nor any person acting on his behalf or under any arrangement with him shall make any loan or otherwise provide or allow to any person any credit, or release, or discharge on another person's behalf, the whole or part of any debt,—

(a) for enabling any person to take part in the gaming, or

(b) in respect of any losses incurred by any person in the gaming.

(2) Neither the holder of the license nor any person acting on his behalf or under any arrangement with him shall accept a cheque and give in exchange for it cash or tokens for enabling any person to take part in the gaming unless the following conditions are fulfilled, that is to say—

(a) the cheque is not a post-dated cheque, and

(b) it is exchanged for cash to an amount equal to the amount for which it is drawn, or is exchanged for tokens at the same rate as would apply if cash, to the amount for which the cheque is drawn, were given in exchange for them; but, where those conditions are fulfilled, the giving of cash or tokens in exchange for a cheque shall not be taken to contravene subsection (1) of this section....

...

(3) Where the holder of a license under this Act, or a person acting on behalf of or under any arrangement with the holder of such a license, accepts a cheque in exchange for cash or tokens to be used by a player in gaming to which this Part of this Act applies [or a substitute cheque, he shall not more than two banking days later cause the cheque to be delivered to a bank for payment or collection....

...

(4) In this section "banking day" means a day which is a business day in accordance with section 92 of the Bills of Exchange Act 1882....

...

§ 17 Exclusion of Persons under 18

Except as provided by section 20 or section 21 of this Act, no person under eighteen shall be present in any room while gaming to which this Part of this Act applies takes place in that room.

§ 18 Gaming on Sundays

[(1) ... no gaming shall take place on any Sunday between the hours of four in the morning and two in the afternoon on any premises in respect of which a license under this Act is for the time being in force.]

(2), (3)....

...

§ 42 Restrictions on advertisements relating to gaming

(1) Except as provided by this section, no person shall issue, or cause to be issued, any advertisement—

(a) informing the public that any premises in Great Britain are premises on which gaming takes place or is to take place, or

(b) inviting the public to take part as players in any gaming which takes place, or is to take place, on any such premises, or to apply for information about facilities for taking part as players in any gaming which takes place, or is to take place, in Great Britain, or

(c) inviting the public to subscribe any money or money's worth to be used in gaming whether in Great Britain or elsewhere, or to apply for information about facilities for subscribing any money or money's worth to be so used, [....

. . .

(3D) Subsection (1) of this section does not apply to the publication of an advertisement relating to premises, other than bingo club premises, in respect of which a license under this Act is for the time being in force if—

(a) the advertisement is contained in a publication which is not published wholly or mainly for the purpose of promoting premises on which gaming takes place or is to take place; and

(b) the advertisement contains no more than—

(i) the name, logo, address, telephone and facsimile numbers of the premises; and

(ii) factual written information about the facilities provided on the premises, the ownership of the premises, the persons who may be admitted to the premises and the method by which such persons may become eligible to take part in gaming on the premises.]

(4) Subsection (1) of this section does not apply to the publication of an advertisement in a newspaper which circulates wholly or mainly outside Great Britain. . . .

. . .

(8) In this section — "advertisement" includes every form of advertising, whether in a publication or by the display of notices or by means of circulars or other documents or by an exhibition of photographs or a cinematograph film, or by way of sound broadcasting or television or by inclusion in a programme service (within the meaning of the Broadcasting Act 1990) that is not a sound or television broadcasting service and references to the issue of an advertisement shall be construed accordingly;

. . .

Notes

1. If gambling is not inevitable, then the government can effectively eliminate gambling from its culture by enforcement of laws. If gambling is inevitable, when society criminalizes gambling, it will suffer costs from the illegal gambling. These costs may include providing a source of funds for criminals, police corruption, and loss of respect for enforcement. Legalizing and controlling gambling may alleviate these costs. Additionally, a government that permits gambling may be able to prevent excessive gambling, and assure that the casino provides fair and honest games. Legalizing gambling also may allow the government to best allocate its resources to control the deviant behavior of its citizens. Limited law enforcement resources (police, judges, prosecutors, and even prisons) can be concentrated on serious deviant behavior. In contrast, "victimless" deviant behavior, although not encouraged, is permitted and controlled through regulation. D. Miers, *Eighteenth Century Gaming: Implications for Modern Casino Control, in* HISTORY AND CRIME 169–92 (James A Inciardi & Charles E Faupel, eds., 1980).

2. The predominant theme throughout a regulatory system based on the Player Protection Model is to sanction casino gaming without overtly encouraging consumers to en-

gage in casino gaming. The United Kingdom's gaming regulations were structured in this way. The United Kingdom has had legal casino gaming since 1960. However, as noted in R. v. Police Commissioner Of The Metropolis, the industry initially was not well regulated. This lack of efficient regulation led to a rise in criminal activity and exploitation of the casino gambler. As a result, to effectively control legal casinos and curtail the expansion of casino gaming, the Gaming Act of 1968 was introduced. *See* Antony Seely, *Gaming: Regulation & Taxation of Casinos*, Report to the House of Commons, *available at* http://www.parliament.uk/commons/lib/research/rp2000/rp00-057.pdf. The Act set forth extensive regulations, delegated policy on gambling to the Home Secretary, and created the Gaming Board, a five member board appointed by the Home Secretary, which controls the daily operations of the gaming industry. *Id.* To curtail expansion of the casino gaming industry, which was "flourishing like weeds in many parts of the country" when not heavily regulated, the Gaming Act of 1968 introduced mechanisms to reduce the number of casinos. A large part of that mechanism included stringent licensing and operation procedures for new facilities based on the principle of unstimulated demand. *See* Royal Commission on Gambling (The Rothschild Report), July 1978, Cmnd. 7200 at 286.

3. Licensing Standards. Under the Player Protection Model, licensing authorities considering applications for casino licenses ordinarily require that a substantial demand exists for the kind of facilities proposed and that such demand is not already satisfied by available facilities reasonably accessible to prospective players in the area. Nigel Kent-Lemon, *A New Approach To Casino Licensing Problems In The United Kingdom*, 10 J. Gambling Stud., 295–304 (1994).

4. Advertising Restrictions. Under the Player Protection Model, a jurisdiction may prohibit advertising, which is a general method of demand stimulation that can be directed at any market segment. Governments usually justify a total ban on the basis that all forms of gaming advertising create more burdens than benefits.

The United States Supreme Court in Condado Holiday Inn v. Tourism Company Of Puerto Rico, 478 U.S. 328, 341 (1986), described this interest as follows:

> The interest at stake in this case, as determined by the Superior Court, is the reduction of demand for casino gambling by the residents of Puerto Rico. Appellant acknowledged the existence of this interest in its February 24, 1982, letter to the Tourism Company. See App. to Juris. Statement 2h ("The legislators wanted the tourists to flock to the casinos to gamble, but not our own people"). The Tourism Company's brief before this Court explains the legislature's belief that "[e]xcessive casino gambling among local residents ... would produce serious harmful effects on the health, safety and welfare of the Puerto Rican citizens, such as the disruption of moral and cultural patterns, the increase in local crime, the fostering of prostitution, the development of corruption, and the infiltration of organized crime." Brief for Appellees 37. These are some of the very same concerns, of course, that have motivated the vast majority of the 50 States to prohibit casino gambling. We have no difficulty in concluding that the Puerto Rico Legislature's interest in the health, safety, and welfare of its citizens constitutes a "substantial" governmental interest. *Cf.* Renton v. Playtime Theaters, Inc., 475 U. S. 41, 54 (1986) (city has substantial interest in "preserving the quality of life in the community at large").

5. Two debated areas are gambling on credit and the consumption of alcohol by patrons. Credit play occurs when a patron borrows money from a casino to allow him to make wagers. Three principal policy arguments against casino credit are that credit (1)

will allow casinos to engage in undesirable methods of collection, (2) could allow unscrupulous operators to skim funds, or (3) will result in patrons losing more than they can afford. Credit play in some casinos accounts for most of the resort's revenues from table games. Without the ability to offer credit, however, casinos would lose a substantial amount of business. Where permitted, gamblers can arrange discounts on their losses in advance, as well as complimentaries and reimbursements. Discounts in practice reduce the price that persons pay to gamble. Patrons may view credit play from a business perspective in that casinos, unlike banks, charge no interest on these loans. Therefore, if they lose, they can delay paying their losses, and use the money until the debt becomes due. Issues regarding the offering of credit are covered in greater detail in chapter 5. *See also* ROBERT HANNUM, & ANTHONY CABOT, PRACTICAL CASINO MATH 215–36 (Trace Publication 2005).

6. What other types of activities might the government look to reduce or eliminate to assure that a casino does not stimulate demand?

C. Government Interest Model

Nev. Rev. Stat. § 463.0129: Public Policy of State Concerning Gaming; License or Approval, Revocable Privilege

1. The legislature hereby finds, and declares to be the public policy of this state, that:

(a) The gaming industry is vitally important to the economy of the state and the general welfare of the inhabitants.

(b) The continued growth and success of gaming is dependent upon public confidence and trust that licensed gaming and the manufacture, sale and distribution of gaming devices and associated equipment are conducted honestly and competitively, that establishments which hold restricted and nonrestricted licenses where gaming is conducted and where gambling devices are operated do not unduly impact the quality of life enjoyed by residents of the surrounding neighborhoods, that the rights of the creditors of licensees are protected and that gaming is free from criminal and corruptive elements.

(c) Public confidence and trust can only be maintained by strict regulation of all persons, locations, practices, associations and activities related to the operation of licensed gaming establishments, the manufacture, sale or distribution of gaming devices and associated equipment and the operation of inter-casino linked systems.

(d) All establishments where gaming is conducted and where gaming devices are operated, and manufacturers, sellers and distributors of certain gaming devices and equipment, and operators of inter-casino linked systems must therefore be licensed, controlled and assisted to protect the public health, safety, morals, good order and general welfare of the inhabitants of the state, to foster the stability and success of gaming and to preserve the competitive economy and policies of free competition of the State of Nevada.

(e) To ensure that gaming is conducted honestly, competitively and free of criminal and corruptive elements, all gaming establishments in this state must remain open to the general public and the access of the general public to gaming activities must not be restricted in any manner except as provided by the legislature.

2. No applicant for a license or other affirmative commission approval has any right to a license or the granting of the approval sought. Any license issued or other commission approval granted pursuant to the provisions of this chapter or chapter 464 of NRS is a revocable privilege, and no holder acquires any vested right therein or thereunder.

3. This section does not:

(a) Abrogate or abridge any common law right of a gaming establishment to exclude any person from gaming activities or eject any person from the premises of the establishment for any reason; or

(b) Prohibit a licensee from establishing minimum wagers for any gambling game or slot machine.

Notes

1. In the Government Interest Model, the predominant goal is protecting economic interests. These can be varied, but may include protecting jobs, state taxes, encouraging tourism, investment and construction, urban redevelopment, or simply stopping the flow of residents' money to foreign casinos. The Government Interest Model typically includes a high degree of regulation, specifically for licensing, accounting, auditing, and reporting procedures within the gaming industry. Under this model, although the regulations are intended to protect players, a predominant goal is to portray to the public the image that gaming is tightly controlled and heavily regulated, thereby discouraging many of the perceived criminal or unsavory aspects stereotypically conjured up with the grant of legalized gaming. Under the Government Interest Model, the government's interest in maximizing tax revenues and employment dictates a general policy of allowing casinos to stimulate demand. This general policy, however, is not without limitations. The most obvious limitations arise out of deceptive and fraudulent practices. The government may realize that the general effect on the casino industry is negative if the fraudulent or deceptive practices of one casino are widely publicized. Similarly, the government may decide that certain methods of demand stimulation, while not fraudulent or deceptive, create such a probability of negative repercussion that they should be prohibited.

2. With the exception of demand stimulation, the regulatory models adopted pursuant to the Government Interest Model and the Player Protection Model are similar. Take for example licensing: in the Government Interest Model, licensing is important to keep out persons who would, indirectly or directly, jeopardize the government's economic stake in the casino industry. Persons who can do direct harm are those who skim funds without paying taxes, are likely to cheat patrons, or are so incompetent that the government will lose tax revenues through employee or patron theft or poor management. Assuring the honesty of the games is important because the public must perceive that gambling is honest before it will gamble. If one operator cheats, the public may believe or fear that the entire industry is dishonest. Other persons can do indirect harm to the government's economic interest because their mere presence taints the industry such that legislators may consider making gaming illegal, or existing and prospective patrons may be dissuaded from coming to the casinos. Under the Player Protection Model, the focus shifts from economic considerations to protecting the gambler. Unsuitable persons include those who cheat the patron, evade regulations that discourage the stimulation of demand in casino gaming, or are so incompetent

that they cannot detect and prevent schemes by employees or patrons to cheat other patrons.

2. When Interests Collide

Commonwealth of Puerto Rico Tourism Company Regulations with Respect to The Games of Chance Act, as Amended

Section 3.1 Advertising; General Rule.

(a) Any Franchise Licensee of a casino duly authorized to operate in Puerto Rico may advertise or promote itself within the jurisdiction of Puerto Rico, only and exclusively when its advertisements or promotions:

(1) are directed at foreign tourists, even though said advertisements incidentally may reach the residents of Puerto Rico, and

(2) do not invite residents of Puerto Rico to visit the casinos.

(b) In accordance with the provisions of paragraph (a) above, all casino Franchise Licensees duly authorized to operate in Puerto Rico are authorized to:

(1) Distribute and place advertisements or promotions of its casinos in:

(i) airplanes that have landed in Puerto Rico;

(ii) cruise ships that are in Puerto Rico territorial waters;

(iii) areas restricted to passengers in Puerto

Rico airports; and

(iv) tourist piers in Puerto Rico;

(2) Publish advertisements or promotions of its casinos in magazines or other publications the distribution in Puerto Rico of which is mainly directed or oriented to informing foreign tourists of the tourist attractions and facilities of Puerto Rico, even though such magazines may be also accessible to residents of Puerto Rico;

(3) Publish advertisements or promotions in newspapers and magazines, tape or film advertisements in movies, television or radio of its casinos for the promotion of foreign tourism in Puerto Rico, even though the same may be incidentally circulated or shown in Puerto Rico; and

(4) Place advertisements or promotions of its casinos within the hotel premises.

(c) Under no circumstances shall the above list be deemed to limit any other type of advertisement or promotion, provided that the advertisement or promotion complies with the public policy of promoting foreign tourism. Any advertisement or promotion of a casino shall be submitted in advance to the Company for its approval.

(d) Nothing of the above-mentioned shall be interpreted as preventing that the name of a hotel includes the word "casino" or any other word that implies that such hotel has a casino. Except as otherwise provided in this section and in section 3.1 of these Regulations, when the word "casino" is used as part of the name of the hotel, it shall be of a size similar to the rest of the name of the hotel and may never be used on its own.

Metropolitan Creditors Service of Sacramento v. Soheil Sadri

15 Cal. App. 4th 1821; 19 Cal. Rptr. 2d 646 (1993)

I. INTRODUCTION

In this case we hold that a Nevada cause of action to enforce gambling debts incurred at a casino for the purpose of providing the debtor with funds for gambling violates California's public policy against gambling on credit and thus is unenforceable in this state.

Metropolitan Creditors Service of Sacramento (MCS) challenges a municipal court judgment declining to enforce gambling debts incurred by Soheil Sadri at a Lake Tahoe casino. We affirm.

II. BACKGROUND

Sadri, a California resident, incurred debts totaling $22,000 over a two-day period in 1991 while gambling at Caesar's Tahoe casino in Nevada. On January 13 and 14 he wrote the casino two personal checks for $2,000 and $10,000. On January 14 he executed two memoranda of indebtedness for $5,000 each. In exchange for the checks and memoranda, Sadri received chips, which he lost playing the game of baccarat. Sadri subsequently stopped payment on the checks and memoranda, which were drawn on his account at a Redwood City bank.

A Nevada statute makes credit instruments evidencing gambling debts owed to licensed persons, and the debts represented, valid and enforceable by legal process. NEV. REV. STAT. ANN. §463.368 (Michie 1991). This law took effect in 1983. NEV. REV. STAT. ANN. §463.368, subd. (1) (Michie 1991). Gambling debts were previously unenforceable in the Nevada state courts. *See e.g.*, West Indies v. First Nat. Bank of Nevada, 214 P.2d 144 (1950).

Caesar's Tahoe did not, however, seek a judgment in Nevada on Sadri's debts. Instead, the casino assigned its claims to MCS for collection, and MCS sued Sadri in California, filing a complaint in municipal court in San Mateo County.

The municipal court rendered judgment for Sadri, ruling that under established public policy his gambling debts were unenforceable in California. The Appellate Department of the San Mateo County Superior Court affirmed the judgment, and on its own motion certified the case for transfer to the Court of Appeal (Cal. Rules of Court, rule 63(a)), which we ordered (Cal. Rules of Court, rule 62(a)).

III. DISCUSSION

...

California has always had a strong public policy against judicial enforcement of gambling debts, going back virtually to the inception of statehood. This prohibition is deeply rooted in Anglo-American jurisprudence, originating in England in 1710 in the Statute of Anne, which made gambling debts "utterly void, frustrate, and of none effect, to all intents and purposes whatsoever...." 9 Anne, ch. 14, § 1.

In the earliest California case, Bryant v. Mead, 1 Cal. 441 (1851), the defendant lost $4,000 playing faro at the plaintiff's San Francisco gaming house. The defendant paid the debt with two checks, but then stopped payment on them. The Supreme Court refused to enforce the debt on the ground, among others, that "wagers, which tend to excite a breach of the peace, or are *contra bonos mores*, or which are against the principles of sound policy, are illegal; and no contract arising out of any such illegal transaction, can be enforced." *Id.* at 444. At that time the statutes of California permitted operation of licensed gaming houses, and the plaintiff was apparently unlicensed, but the court commented that even if the plaintiff had held a license "such license should not be construed as conferring a *right to sue* for a gaming debt, but as a *protection* solely against a criminal action." *Ibid.*, original italics.

Two years later, in Carrier v. Brannan 3 Cal. 328 (1853), where the defendant lost $17,000 in a gaming house playing faro, the Supreme Court reaffirmed the rule against judicial enforcement of gambling debts. The court stated, "It needs no authority or arguments to satisfy this court that the practice of gaming is vicious and immoral in its nature, and ruinous to the harmony and well-being of society. Neither do we think that gaming debts have been legalized by the operation of the act of the legislature licensing gaming-houses. The legislature, finding a thirst for play so universally prevalent throughout the State, and despairing of suppressing it entirely, have attempted to control it within certain bounds, by imposing restrictions [*sic*] and burdens upon persons carrying on this kind of business. The license simply operates as a permission, and removes or does away with the misdemeanor which existed at common law without changing the character of the contract." Id. at 329.

After gambling at most games of chance was criminalized (*see* Pen. Code, § 330 et seq.), the rule of *Bryant* and *Carrier* was restated in statutory terms. In Union Collection Co. v. Buckman, 88 P. 708 (Cal. 1907) the defendant gave the plaintiff's assignor three promissory notes for a $1,300 gambling loss. Citing Civil Code sections 1607 and 1667, the Supreme Court said the assignor and hence the plaintiff could not recover on the notes because "under the settled law of this state the consideration for such notes was *contra bonos mores* and unlawful...." Section 1607 states that consideration for a contract must be lawful. Section 1667 states that a contract is unlawful if it is contrary to "an express provision of law," "the policy of express law, though not expressly prohibited," or "good morals."

Following the advent of legalized gambling in the State of Nevada, the rule in California against enforcement of gambling debts was once again put to the test, and it again prevailed. In Hamilton v. Abadjian, 179 P.2d 804 (Cal. 1947), the defendant gave a Las Vegas hotel six checks totaling $11,450, used part of the proceeds to finance his gambling, and then stopped payment on the checks. The Supreme Court reaffirmed *Bryant, Carrier* and *Union Collection Co.,* noting that the courts of California—and also, at that time, Nevada—"refuse to lend their process to recover losses in gambling transactions of the type here involved." *Abadjian, supra,* 30 Cal.2d at p. 51.

The *Hamilton* court also stated the anti-enforcement rule within a context more specific to the facts of that case, as well as to the present case: "The owner of a gambling house who honors a check for the purpose of providing a prospective customer with funds with which to gamble and who then participates in the transaction thus promoted by his act cannot recover on the check." 30 Cal.2d at p. 52; accord, Braverman v. Horn, 198 P.2d 948 (Cal. App. 1948); see also Sasner v. Ornsten, 209 P.2d 44(1949); Rose v. Nelson, 180 P.2d 749 (Cal. App. 1947).

Shortly after *Hamilton,* in a decision reminiscent of the early days of legalized gambling in California and the *Bryant* and *Carrier* cases, the court in Lavick v. Nitzberg 188 P.2d 758 (Cal. App. 1948), refused to compel payment on checks totaling $2,000 given to the owner of a California gaming house to purchase chips lost at draw poker, which is a lawful game in California. The *Lavick* court reasoned that even though draw poker is not made a crime by Penal Code section 330, a contract founded upon a gambling consideration is still against public policy and contrary to good morals under Civil Code section 1667, and thus the contract itself is unlawful and unenforceable. 83 Cal. App.2d at pp. 382–83. Echoing *Hamilton,* the *Lavick* court concluded that "promissory notes given in a gaming-house to the keeper of the house for the purpose of enabling the maker to participate in any game of chance with the keeper or his employees are unenforceable under the provisions of *section 1667 of the Civil Code.*" *Id.* at 383.

The most recent statement of the *Hamilton* rule occurred in Lane & Pyron, Inc. v. Gibbs, 71 Cal. Rptr. 817 (Cal. App. 1968). In that case the defendant cashed five checks totaling $1,900 at a Lake Tahoe casino and subsequently stopped payment on the checks. Noting that a sister state cause of action will not be enforced if it "offends deeply held notions of local public policy," the court invoked the policy in California and Nevada against judicial enforcement of gambling debts and concluded that "California's rejection of such claims is an application of Nevada law as well as domestic public policy." *Id.* at 65.

The *Hamilton* rule is on all fours with the present case. Caesar's Tahoe honored Sadri's checks and memoranda of indebtedness for the purpose of providing him with funds with which to gamble, and then participated in the game. Thus, if *Hamilton* still reflects the public policy of the State of California, it precludes judicial enforcement of Sadri's gambling debts in California state courts; as explained in *Lavick,* the contracts underlying the debts are against public policy and contrary to good morals under Civil Code section 1667, and thus the contracts are unlawful and the debts unenforceable.

Two things have changed in the 46 years since *Hamilton* was decided. First, under Nevada state law, credit instruments evidencing gambling debts owed to licensed persons are now enforceable by legal process in that state, and have been since 1983. NEV. REV. STAT. ANN. § 463.368 (Michie 1991). This point is inconsequential, however, since the rule of *Hamilton,* its predecessors and its progeny rests not on the public policy of Nevada, but on the public policy of California.

Second, the people of California have demonstrated increased tolerance for gambling through the passage, by initiative measure, of the California State Lottery Act of 1984. Gov. Code, § 8880 et seq. Indeed, several forms of institutionalized legal gambling in California predate *Hamilton,* including pari-mutuel horse racing (Bus. & Prof. Code, § 19400 et seq.) and draw poker clubs (by the omission of draw poker from the list of games proscribed by Penal Code section 330), which are now subject to registration with the Attorney General. Bus. & Prof. Code, § 19800 et seq. This state of affairs led one California court to observe, in requiring relief on a contract for the sale of a Nevada casino, that "Californians cannot afford to be too pious about this matter of gambling." Nevcal Enterprises, Inc. v. Cal-Neva Lodge, Inc., 14 Cal. Rptr. 805 (Cal. App. 1961).

This brings us to Crockford's Club Ltd. v. Si-Ahmed, 250 Cal. Rptr. 728 (Cal. App. 1988). In that case, Smail Si-Ahmed passed bad checks to an English casino in exchange for tokens, which he then lost at gambling. The casino obtained a default judgment against Si-Ahmed in England, and then obtained a default judgment in California enforcing the English judgment. On appeal, Si-Ahmed argued that gambling debts are unenforceable in California as against public policy. The court rejected this argument, noting that casino gambling is legal in England and concluding that "in view of the expanded acceptance of gambling in this state as manifested by the introduction of the California lottery and other innovations [citation], it cannot seriously be maintained that enforcement of said judgment 'is so antagonistic to California public policy interests as to preclude the extension of comity in the present case.'" (at p. 1406, quoting Wong v. Tenneco, Inc., *supra,* 39 Cal.3d at p. 136.)

The posture of *Crockford's Club* is similar to that of the present case in that both turn on the question of public policy in California.

...

The court in *Crockford's Club* did not specifically address the question whether enforcement of gambling debts is still against public policy in California. Indeed, the court did not even discuss the *Hamilton* rule or mention any of the other California cases on point. The court simply relied on California's "expanded acceptance" of gambling *itself* as indicating enforcement of the English judgment was not against public policy. (Crockford's Club Ltd. v. Si-Ahmed, *supra,* 203 Cal. App.3d at p. 1406.)

It cannot be denied that California's historical public policy against gambling has been substantially eroded. Pari-mutuel horse racing, draw poker clubs, and charitable bingo games have proliferated throughout the state. These forms of gambling are indulged by a relatively small segment of the population, but the same cannot be said of the California State Lottery, which was passed by initiative measure and has become firmly rooted in California's popular culture. Lottery tickets are now as close as the nearest convenience store, turning many Californians into regular gamblers. The "thirst for play" of Californians, as noted in 1853 in *Carrier v. Brannan, supra, 3 Cal. at page 329,* has not abated. If it was true as observed in 1961 that "Californians cannot afford to be too pious about this matter of gambling" Nevcal Enterprises, Inc. v. Cal-Neva Lodge, Inc., *supra,* 194 Cal. App.2d at p. 180, then all the more so in 1993 would expressions of piety on the subject ring hollow. On this score, the *Crockford's Club* decision has a point.

But the court in *Crockford's Club* failed to draw the critical distinction between public acceptance of gambling itself and California's deep-rooted policy against enforcement of gambling debts—that is, gambling *on credit*. While the public policy against the former has been substantially eroded, the public policy against the latter has not.

This is because California's rule against enforcing gambling debts has never depended upon the criminalization of gambling itself. At the inception of the rule in the early 1850s, in Bryant v. Mead, *supra,* 1 Cal. 441, and Carrier v. Brannan, *supra,* 3 Cal. 328, licensed gaming houses were statutorily sanctioned. As the Supreme Court observed in both cases, the licensing of a gaming house did not make enforceable a gambling debt incurred there. Carrier v. Brannan, *supra,* 3 Cal. at p. 329; Bryant v. Mead, *supra,* 1 Cal. at p. 444. In 1948, the matter of gambling debts incurred at legal gaming houses was revisited, and the prohibition against enforcement reaffirmed, in Lavick v. Nitzberg, *supra,* 83 Cal. App.2d 381.

Indeed, the prohibition against legalized gambling on credit goes all the way back to 1710 in the Statute of Anne, which permitted gambling "at the palaces of St. James, or Whitehall when the sovereign is in residence" but limited such gambling to "ready money only." 9 Anne, ch. 14, § 9.

Thus, it matters little that gambling itself has become more accepted in California. The cornerstone of the *Hamilton* rule against enforcement of gaming house debts is not simply that the game played is unlawful, but that the judiciary should not encourage gambling *on credit* by enforcing gambling debts, whether the game is lawful or not.

This distinction between gambling itself and gambling on credit was elucidated in King International Corp. v. Voloshin, 366 A.2d 1172 (Conn. 1976). Defendant in that case stopped payment on a check given in exchange for chips at a licensed casino in Aruba, and the casino's owner sued in Connecticut to enforce the debt. The court refused enforcement, concluding that despite Connecticut's embrace of various forms of legalized gambling such as pari-mutuel racing, jai alai and a state lottery, "Connecticut has never deviated from its ancient prohibition of gambling on credit." 366 A.2d at p. 1174, fn. omitted. The court explained, "It is not incongruous for a legislature to sanction certain forms of gambling and still to refuse the collection of gambling debts.... [P] While the state's heretofore ancient and deep-rooted policy condemning gambling has been eroded to some degree by its legalization of certain types of gambling, the state has, nevertheless, been intransigent in its policy prohibiting the extension of credit for the promotion of gambling activity—and with good reason. One need not have the gambling sagacity of the famed Las Vegas oddsmaker Jimmy the Greek to recognize the potential dangers in the extension of credit to the gambler or the possibly unfortunate incidents, to employ a euphemism, that could well result from the nonpayment of the gambling bettor to his creditor." 366 A.2d at pp. 1174–1175; *accord*, Casanova Club v. Bisharat, 458 A.2d 1, 4 (Conn 1983).

Courts in other jurisdictions have similarly concluded that a shift in public policy with regard to gambling itself, for example through the advent of legalized forms of gambling such as lotteries, is not inconsistent with a continued public policy against gambling on credit. *E.g.*, Carnival Leisure Industries, Ltd. v. Aubin 938 F.2d 624, 626 (5th Cir. 1991); Resorts International, Inc. v. Zonis, 577 F. Supp. 876, 878–79 (N.D. Ill. 1984). "Even while legal gambling spreads throughout the country, the public policy of virtually every state makes legal gambling debts unenforceable, treating a casino marker the same as a contract for prostitution." Rose, *Gambling and the Law—Update 1993* 15 HASTINGS COMM. & ENT. L.J. 93, 95(1992).

There is a special reason for treating gambling on credit differently from gambling itself. Gambling debts are characteristic of pathological gambling, a mental disorder which is recognized by the American Psychiatric Association and whose prevalence is estimated at 2 to 3 percent of the adult population. Diagnostic & Statistical Manual of Mental Disorders (3d ed. rev. 1987) pp. 324–325. "Characteristic problems include extensive indebtedness and consequent default on debts and other financial responsibilities, ... and financially motivated illegal activities to pay for gambling." (at p. 324.) Having lost his or her cash, the pathological gambler will continue to play on credit, if extended, in an attempt to win back the losses.

Pathological gambling is to be distinguished from "social gambling," where "acceptable losses are predetermined." Diagnostic & Statistical Manual of Mental Disorders, *supra*, p. 324. The social gambler comes prepared to leave the game with an empty wallet or purse, but not with a heavy debt. In contrast, the pathological gambler is out of control, risking extensive debt and possibly financial ruin—perhaps even "unfortunate incidents, to employ a euphemism." King International Corp. v. Voloshin, *supra*, 366 A.2d at p. 1175.

In our view, this is why enforcement of gambling debts has always been against public policy in California and should remain so, regardless of shifting public attitudes about gambling itself. If Californians want to play, so be it. But the law should not invite them to play themselves into debt. The judiciary cannot protect pathological gamblers from themselves, but we can refuse to participate in their financial ruin.

...

We conclude that California's strong public policy against enforcement of gambling debts remains unaffected by increased public tolerance of gambling itself or by the limited legalization of certain forms of gambling in this state. That public policy is so fundamental and deep-rooted as to justify our refusal to enforce a sister state cause of action. *See* Wong v. Tenneco, Inc., supra, 39 Cal.3d at p. 135; Knodel v. Knodel, *supra*, 14 Cal.3d at p. 765, fn. 15; Loucks v. Standard Oil Co., supra, 120 N.E. at p. 202.

We therefore reaffirm the commitment of the California courts to the *Hamilton* rule: "The owner of a gambling house who honors a check for the purpose of providing a prospective customer with funds with which to gamble and who then participates in the transaction thus promoted by his act cannot recover on the check." Hamilton v. Abadjian, supra, 30 Cal.2d at p. 52.

...

IV. DISPOSITION

The judgment of the municipal court is affirmed.

Notes

1. The Puerto Rico regulations and the California case are examples of conflicting interests. In Puerto Rico, the government was attempting to achieve two goals, to reduce demand for gaming by prohibiting advertising in its jurisdiction, but to allow advertising outside the jurisdiction to stimulate tourism. Governments may justify geographic-based restrictions on two bases. First, a government may decide its obligation to protect gamblers does not extend beyond its own citizens. Therefore, preventing casinos from stimulating demand outside its jurisdiction serves no policy goals. Second, governments may decide that problem gambling is more likely to affect those with easy access to the casino. This conflict, however, was the subject of a Supreme Court challenge described in Chapter 13.

2. Demographic-based restrictions attempt to minimize the impact of casino gaming on particular socioeconomic classes. Demographic-based restrictions usually attempt to discourage or prohibit gambling by the poor. For example, a regulation requiring casinos to have high table limits might discourage gambling among the poor. Here, the government is making the decision that the poor should use their funds for necessities or for things, such as training, which can improve their social conditions.

3. The *Metropolitan Creditors* case demonstrates conflicts both between states and within a state based on changing policies. In this case, a conflict existed between Nevada and California regarding the enforceability of gaming debts and within California regarding public policy toward gambling. This conflict as it relates to the enforcement of gambling debts is discussed in greater detail in Chapter 5.

Part II
Casino Gambling

Chapter 3

Fundamentals of Regulatory Oversight

1. Introduction

State gaming laws typically entrust numerous responsibilities to the regulatory bodies they create. Many of these duties involve the agency acting in a quasi-legislative role, whereby it promulgates rules and regulations that govern the operation of the gambling entities in the state. This process helps to further the policies expressed in the gaming laws. A regulatory body may also perform judicial functions such as resolving disputes between patrons and licensees, and even deciding tax questions. To promote the efficient operation of the agency, the agency employs and trains staff members, and develops budgeting plans. Likewise, auxiliary services such as computer information services and equipment supply and maintenance form an important support element to the agency's work.

While regulating bodies may be delegated many responsibilities by state law, this chapter focuses on three key elements of gaming regulation: 1) implementation of accounting and audit rules; 2) enforcement of gambling statutes and regulations; and 3) measures to protect the regulatory process itself. These three components of gaming regulation are essential to the integrity of gaming laws, and gaming itself, within a state. Chapter 4 focuses on another aspect of regulation, licensing.

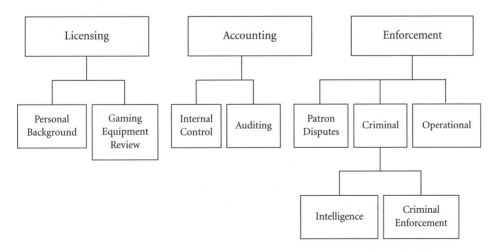

After licensing, the focus of regulation shifts from attempting to predict future behavior to policing the existing licensees. Regulation has no meaning if licensees can violate the rules without the ability of the regulators to enforce them. Enforcement has two critical elements: detection and disciplinary action. Through regulatory functions, such as an audit or observation of the casino operations, the regulators may detect a violation of those rules. Once detected, disciplinary action allows the regulators to bring an action, either administratively or judicially, against the offending licensee. It involves deciding if the licensee violated the rules and, if so, what is appropriate punishment.

2. Audit and Accounting

The casino industry presents unique accounting issues because it differs from businesses where each cash transaction is recorded. Most retail stores, for example, keep written evidence, such as cash register receipts, of each item sold. Reconciliation between inventory and sales can allow the business to detect and, if necessary, control theft. Other cash businesses, such as money exchanges or banks, record each individual transaction. These records provide a method to both account for and audit the financial transactions of the business. In the casino, recording each bet made is impractical particularly on table games. Therefore, governments and the casinos must rely on accounting by aggregate. A good general article on the topic is Michael Santaniello, *Casino Gambling: The Elements of Effective Control*, 6 SETON HALL LEGIS. J. 23 (1982). The accuracy of this type of accounting necessarily relies on accurate and secure handling of all casino transactions: collecting, transferring and paying cash, granting and recording credit, and exchanging, collecting, and disbursing gaming chips and tokens.

Government auditing and internal accounting controls help maintain the integrity of a tax system. Internal controls are procedures that a casino must implement to prevent or detect errors or irregularities. Accounting regulations control and protect the flow of revenues generated by the gaming activities. Government has two principal objectives in setting regulations governing the accounting and auditing of casinos. First, accounting regulations can inhibit non-licensed persons from sharing in the casino revenues. Audits can help regulators detect if an unsuitable person is profiting from the casino. This may help assure that unsuitable persons are not evading the licensing process through "hidden interests." Second, the government has an interest in assuring that all revenues are properly accounted for so that it can receive all taxes. This prevents "skimming," where the owners receive revenues but do not pay taxes on it, and deters employee theft and embezzlement.

Another important function of audits is to assure that the casinos are complying with internal controls and regulations. Because the casino industry is a significant cash business, controls and regulations dealing with cash and cash equivalents predominate over other regulations. Audits can often detect violations of these controls and regulations better than other forms of enforcement.

Accounting controls can take various forms, from actual governmental participation in the accounting process to simply reporting. Governments may impose any of the following requirements: (1) governmental participation; (2) governmental audits; (3) independent audits; (4) minimum internal controls; (5) recordkeeping requirements; and (6) reporting requirements.

A. Minimum Internal Control Procedures

Application of Playboy-Elsinore Associates
497 A.2d 526 (N.J. Super 1985)

The opinion of the court was delivered by COHEN, J.A.D.

Elsinore Shore Associates (ESA) is a New Jersey partnership.[1] It owns and operates a casino hotel in Atlantic City, known as Elsinore Atlantis, which opened in 1981 under the authority of a temporary casino permit issued by the Casino Control Commission. N.J.S.A. 5:12-95.1 *et seq.* (repealed). In April 1982, the Commission issued it an annual casino license, N.J.S.A. 5:12-87, and renewed it in April 1983, N.J.S.A. 5:12-88. In March 1984, the Commission heard ESA's application for renewal and granted it, effective April 14, 1984.

. . .

Another of the conditions, # 142, read as follows:

That to ensure the independence of the Licensee's internal audit and surveillance departments pursuant to N.J.A.C. 19:45-1.11(c), both the Director of Internal Audit and the Director of Surveillance shall report directly to Elsinore Corporation's Board of Director's Audit Committee and that appropriate documentation defining the authority and responsibility of these two departments be provided to the Commission.

On appeal to this court, ESA challenges both of these conditions on the grounds that they are unauthorized by statute or regulation and are arbitrary and unlawful. . . . We disagree with ESA, however, on Condition # 142, and confirm its validity.

Condition # 142 arose out of ESA's unusual business organization. When formed in 1979, ESA was a partnership of Playboy of Atlantic City, also a partnership, and Elsub Corporation, a subsidiary of Elsinore Corporation, which is publicly owned. In 1984, Elsub bought most of the interest of ESA owned by Playboy of Atlantic City, as a result of which Elsub now owns 91.5% of ESA. ESA, as a partnership, has no board of directors, but only a two-person executive committee, consisting of the president and vice president of Elsub and Elsinore.[2]

Part of the Commission's statutory responsibilities is to see to it that a system of internal controls is established by each casino. N.J.S.A. 5:12-99. The Commission adopted N.J.A.C.19:45-1.11 to create standards for those controls. The various operations of a casino are to be divided into at least seven departments: surveillance, internal audit, casino, slot, credit, security and casino accounting. The regulation provides that the surveillance and internal audit departments should

. . . report directly to the Board of Directors, or its audit committee or equivalent regarding matters of policy, purpose, responsibilities and authority. . . . [N.J.A.C.19:45-1.11(C)(1) and 19:45-1.11(C)(3).]

The idea is to establish lines of reporting that will guarantee independence of the various departments from one another, independence for the more sensitive functions from operating management and clear responsibility at the highest level for internal audit and surveillance responsibilities.

---

1. Its name was changed after the relevant events from Playboy-Elsinore Associates.
2. Pursuant to N.J.S.A. 5:12-82(b)(4) and N.J.A.C. 19:41-3.1(a)(3), the Commission did not issue ESA's license until being satisfied of the qualifications of Elsub, Elsinore and a number of individuals involved in the ownership and management of the corporations.

If ESA's surveillance and internal audit departments reported to its two-person executive committee, the result would frustrate the Commission's valid goal of assigning and insulating responsibility, institutionalizing oversight over operating management and creating checks and balances within the casino operation. Therefore, it required the two departments to report directly to the audit committee of the board of directors of the publicly traded parent, Elsinore. ESA complains here, as it did to the Commission, that the regulation does not permit the Commission to impose responsibilities on the directors of unregulated parent corporations and that imposing surveillance and internal audit responsibilities on Elsinore's corporate directors is burdensome, inconvenient and unnecessary. We disagree.

We will not rehearse the sound and frequently repeated reasons for the detailed, intensive and pervasive regulation of casino operations in New Jersey. *See* Knight v. Margate, 86 N.J. 374 (1981); Bally Mfg. Corp. v. N.J. Casino Control Comm'n., 85 N.J. 325, *app. dism.* 454 U.S. 804 (1981). It is a legitimate part of the regulatory fabric to require corporate structures that will create highest level responsibility and independence from operating management for such sensitive casino functions as surveillance and internal audit. A publicly traded company cannot isolate itself from responsibility by operating a casino through a subsidiary corporation and a partnership with only two managers. Faced with such an operation, the Commission has sufficient flexibility under N.J.A.C. 19:45-1.11 to impose the kind of responsibilities on the parent corporation that are involved here. *See* N.J.S.A. 5:12-70; 5:12-80; *In re* Boardwalk Regency Corp. Casino License, 90 N.J. 361, *app. dism.* 459 U.S.1081 (1982). *Cf.* N.J.S.A. 5:12-82(c)(3).

It is of no consequence that the operations of the license applicant may be relatively free of violations. The Commission's reasonable role includes requiring business structures that will keep them that way. It does not matter that the parent's board of directors is not prepared to undertake the responsibilities which the Commission imposed on it. The Commission's response to its legitimate concerns is a reasonable one, and the board of directors will have to accommodate to it. The Commission need not accept the relationship between the casino licensee and its parent, if, as here, alteration is necessary to meet significant regulatory interests. Condition # 142 will stand.

. . .

The imposition of Condition # 142 is confirmed as valid.

Nevada Gaming Commission Regulation § 6.090

Internal control for Group I licensees. As used in this section, "licensee" means a Group I licensee and "chairman" means the chairman or other member of the state gaming control board.

1. Each licensee shall establish administrative and accounting procedures for the purpose of determining the licensee's liability for taxes and fees under chapters 463 and 464 of NRS and for the purpose of exercising effective control over the licensee's internal fiscal affairs. The procedures must be designed to reasonably ensure that:

(a) Assets are safeguarded;

(b) Financial records are accurate and reliable;

(c) Transactions are performed only in accordance with management's general or specific authorization;

(d) Transactions are recorded adequately to permit proper reporting of gaming revenue and of fees and taxes, and to maintain accountability for assets;

(e) Access to assets is permitted only in accordance with management's specific authorization;

(f) Recorded accountability for assets is compared with actual assets at reasonable intervals and appropriate action is taken with respect to any discrepancies; and

(g) Functions, duties, and responsibilities are appropriately segregated and performed in accordance with sound practices by competent, qualified personnel.

2. Each licensee and each applicant for a nonrestricted license shall describe, in such manner as the chairman may approve or require, its administrative and accounting procedures in detail in a written system of internal control. Each licensee and applicant for a license shall submit a copy of its written system to the board. Each written system must include:

(a) An organizational chart depicting segregation of functions and responsibilities;

(b) A description of the duties and responsibilities of each position shown on the organizational chart;

(c) A detailed, narrative description of the administrative and accounting procedures designed to satisfy the requirements of subsection 1;

(d) A written statement signed by the licensee's chief financial officer and either the licensee's chief executive officer or a licensed owner attesting that the system satisfies the requirements of this section;

(e) If the written system is submitted by an applicant, a letter from an independent accountant stating that the applicant's written system has been reviewed by the accountant and complies with the requirements of this section; and

(f) Such other items as the chairman may require....

8. The licensee may not implement a system of internal control procedures that does not satisfy the minimum standards unless the chairman, in his sole discretion, determines that the licensee's proposed system satisfies subsection 1, and approves the system in writing....

9. Each licensee shall require the independent accountant engaged by the licensee to examine the financial statements or to review the licensee's financial statements to submit to the licensee 2 copies of a written report of the compliance of the procedures and written system with the minimum internal control standards. Using the criteria established by the chairman, the independent accountant shall report each event and procedure discovered by or brought to the accountant's attention that the accountant believes does not satisfy the minimum standards or variations from the standards that have been approved by the chairman pursuant to subsection 8. Not later than 150 days after the end of the licensee's business year, the licensee shall submit a copy of the accountant's report or any other correspondence directly relating to the licensee's systems of internal control to the board accompanied by the licensee's statement addressing each item of noncompliance noted by the accountant and describing the corrective measures taken....

13. Each licensee shall comply with its written system of internal control submitted pursuant to subsection 2 as it relates to compliance with the minimum standards, variations from the minimum standards approved pursuant to subsection 8, and Regulation 14 associated equipment approvals.

14. Failure to comply with subsection 13 is an unsuitable method of operation.

15. Using guidelines, checklists, and other criteria established by the chairman, the licensee's internal auditor shall perform observations, document examinations, and inquiries of employees to determine compliance with applicable statutes, regulations, and minimum internal control standards. Two copies of the internal auditor's report summarizing all instances of noncompliance and management responses must be submitted to the board within 120 days after the end of the first six months of the licensee's business year and must include all work required to be performed during that six-month period along with any additional procedures that were performed. Noncompliance noted in the second half of the business year must be submitted to the board within 120 days after the end of the business year unless the noncompliance is to be disclosed in the independent accountant's report submitted pursuant to Regulation 6.090(9).

Notes

1. **Internal Controls** should safeguard the assets of a casino, maintain accountability for transactions, and prevent and detect any errors and irregularities that might occur in a timely manner. E. MALCOLM GREENLEES, CASINO ACCOUNTING FINANCIAL MANAGEMENT (Univ. of Nev. Press, 1988); Barry P. Robbins & Gary P. LeVan, *A Comparison and Analysis of Internal Control Regulations in New Jersey and Nevada Casinos*, The Gambling Papers: Proceedings of the Fifth National Conference on Gambling and Risk Taking (1982), *available at* http://knowledgecenter.unr.edu/specoll/mss/nc1216.html. As the *Elsinore* case indicates, regulators may, in an effort to promote accountability, insist on certain internal standards and a particular departmental structure. The objectives noted above can be achieved by three primary types of internal controls: Access Controls, Documentation Controls, and Personnel Controls.

2. **Access Controls** are physical safeguards, such as surveillance cameras, and lock-and-key devices. Access Controls generally involve security devices. Susan H. Ivancevich, *Casino Surveillance: Internal Control Structure and Beyond, The Bottom Line*, 10 J. INT'L ASS'N OF HOSPITALITY ACCT., 30, 30–33 (1995). This factor makes physical safeguards appealing to operational divisions that involve cash or costly inventory and fixed-asset items. Since most operating departments of a casino handle large amounts of cash, physical safeguards are common. Access to most sensitive areas in a casino (*e.g.*, cashier's cage, slot booths, hard and soft count rooms, etc.) is physically restricted, and is closely monitored by surveillance cameras. Access Controls, however, are not always practical and do not apply to some transactions. For example, physical safeguards could not be used to control the issuance of casino credit. Instead, requiring management authorization for credit issuance and maintaining documentation of credit extensions are the only practical ways to control these types of transactions.

3. **Documentation Controls**, as the name implies, are internal controls that result in physical evidence of a transaction from its origin through recording the financial records of the casino. Most businesses use extensive documentation controls to create an "audit trail" of transactions. Casinos, however, are limited in the level of document controls available to trail cash transactions such as cash wagers that occur on the gaming floor. Documentation Controls, nevertheless, are effective in many areas of a casino operation. For example, accounting department employees can use an audit checklist to document the procedures performed to verify the casino's financial activity. This checklist then forms the means by which the Accounting Department can prove compliance with regulatory auditing standards. Maintaining systems whereby transactions can be documented, reviewed, authorized, and verified (whenever possible) is an important element of any internal control environment.

4. The final internal control category is broadly described as **Personnel Controls**. Personnel Controls create a chain of command for approval of, and accountability for, transactions. Examples of Personnel Controls include staff supervision, secondary review and approval of transactions, and appropriate segregation of job duties so that the recording function, custody, and accountability of company assets are performed independently. According to the American Institute of Certified Public Accountants, "As in any sound system of internal accounting control, segregation of duties is of paramount importance in the overall control considerations." American Institute of Certified Accountants, *Audits of Casinos* (1984). For example, in a casino environment, Personnel Controls are critical. In the casino pit, a floor supervisor, pit boss, shift manager, and casino manager all typically observe table game activities. Similarly, casino cage activity is supervised by a cashier supervisor, shift supervisor, and cage manager. In both the pit and the cage, at least one supervisor reviews and approves all notable transactions.

5. Internal control procedures established in a casino environment incorporate combinations of Access Controls, Documentation Controls, and Personnel Controls. As an example, internal controls are critical in a table game environment since gaming activity is conducted by individuals (as opposed to mechanical devices). These table games also often involve substantial dollar amount wagers that the casinos stores in diverse locations throughout the casino. Table games typically have a "drop box" that is used to store currency received from patrons until it is counted and recorded in the casino's financial records. To avoid theft, the drop box is secured with several locks, each of which requires a different key. These all act as Access Controls. Surveillance cameras and security officers also monitor all table game activity.

During the course of table game play, if a particular table game has paid out more in winnings than it has collected in losing wagers, the inventory of chips at that table may become low. Conversely, if losing wagers exceeds winning payouts, the table inventory may contain an excess of chips. To bring the table's chip inventory back to normal, the pit will either request additional chips from the cage (this is called a *fill*) or send excess chips back to the cage (this is known as a *credit*). Activities such as chip fills and credits are monitored using Document Controls. To prevent a person from creating a fictitious transaction, special forms designed to record the event are prepared, verified, and signed by the individuals who participate in the transaction (*e.g.,* cage cashier, dealer). The forms are subsequently audited by the Accounting Department.

Personnel Controls also are used extensively to monitor table game activity. Dealers put the currency received from players in exchange for chips directly into the locked drop box under the gaming table through a slot on the top. Table supervisory personnel carefully observe these transactions and others such as patron wagers, chip purchases, winning wager payouts to ensure that improper activities do not occur. Table game supervisors, however, cannot handle chips or currency. Moreover, persons who count the cash stored in the drop boxes at each gaming table (called the "Soft Count Team") are independent of the Table Games Department. The Soft Count Team counts the currency in a separate room that has special access controls. The locked drop boxes are typically transported to this room by security. These soft count rooms are locked and monitored by surveillance. Soft Count Team members must wear uniforms that have been designed to prevent concealment of currency. Ultimately, the information recorded by the Soft Count Team is verified by the Accounting Department as an additional Documentation and Personnel Control.

6. Documentation control is of little value unless the records are maintained. Therefore, governments usually mandate that the casinos keep all required records for a spec-

ified time, often as long as six years. This facilitates the audit process by government and independent auditors, and allows for government investigations into the casino's activities.

7. Besides independent audits, governments usually require the casinos to provide many periodic reports. Most common are tax returns. Other reports that governments may require include employee lists, loans, equipment purchases, junket agent and junket lists, bad debts, involvement in foreign gaming, and significant contracts.

B. Governmental Participation and Audits

Governments can ensure that all revenues are properly accounted for by having a physical presence in the accounting process. In a casino environment, this involves government investigators participating in major transactions that involve the transfer of money, credit, or monetary equivalents, such as chips. For example, a government agent may be present whenever casino employees access drop boxes which hold the cash and chips under the gaming devices and gaming tables. They also may observe and verify the transport of the drop boxes to a room where they would be counted. For a discussion of the origin and purpose of these regulations, *see* Arthur Neilson, *Government Regulation of Casino Gaming in Australia: The Political and Bureaucratic Components and Some Myths, in* GAMBLING AND PUBLIC POLICY 363, 384 (1991). A comprehensive physical presence would also require that government review and approve extension and collection of gaming credit. Surveillance would also require government personnel to be present.

As one could imagine, this type of comprehensive system would be financially impractical unless a jurisdiction had only a single large casino—or other conducive characteristics. A common circumstance would be where gaming is restricted to gaming devices. Here, government accountants can monitor play as it occurs through on-line systems. For example, Louisiana uses an on-line system to monitor gaming device activity at private "truck stop" casinos with up to fifty games, and taverns and other locations with up to three games. The advantages and disadvantages of online slot monitoring systems and states where they are implemented can be found in Eugene Christiansen, *Central Systems for Machine Gaming: A Good Policy?* (2003), http://www.cca-i.com/central%20 systems%20for%20machine%20gaming.pdf.

A government audit requires the retention of a trained and competent staff to conduct the audits with sufficient regularity to be a deterrent force to illegal or poor accounting practices. Typical audit objectives are to ensure that a licensed casino (1) is not paying or allowing unlicensed persons to receive gaming revenues; (2) has adequate internal control procedures; (3) is following its internal control procedures; (4) is properly reporting its revenues; and (5) is paying all taxes and fees.

Government audits are often unannounced and/or occur at irregular intervals. This prevents licensees from simply following good accounting principles and complying with the laws only when they expect to be audited. They may involve long detailed reviews or spot compliance with certain regulations or procedures.

Another method of helping to meet governmental accounting objectives is to require casinos to undergo annual audits by independent outside accounting firms. They may require these firms to conduct an audit of the casino's financial statement and a review of the casino's compliance with its internal control submission. *See* Nev. Gaming Comm. Reg. § 6.080.

C. Currency Reporting

i. Generally

Because of the often large and unique cash transactions that occur in casinos, the federal government has adopted special regulations governing reporting of these transactions. The purpose of these regulations is to provide the government with the tools to track cash transactions related to criminal activity involving money laundering. Money laundering is the process by which criminals transform the money that they receive from criminal activities into funds that appear to have been generated by lawful means and cannot be traced by law enforcement to their illicit sources.

ii. Currency Transaction Reports

31 CFR § 103.22 Reports of transactions in currency.

(a) General. This section sets forth the rules for the reporting by financial institutions of transactions in currency. The reporting obligations themselves are stated in paragraph (b) of this section. The reporting rules relating to aggregation are stated in paragraph (c) of this section. Rules permitting banks to exempt certain transactions from the reporting obligations appear in paragraph (d) of this section.

...

(2) Casinos. Each casino shall file a report of each transaction in currency, involving either cash in or cash out, of more than $10,000.

(i) Transactions in currency involving cash in include, but are not limited to:

(A) Purchases of chips, tokens, and other gaming instruments;

(B) Front money deposits;

(C) Safekeeping deposits;

(D) Payments on any form of credit, including markers and counter checks;

(E) Bets of currency including money plays;

(F) Currency received by a casino for transmittal of funds through wire transfer for a customer;

(G) Purchases of a casino's check;

(H) Exchanges of currency for currency, including foreign currency; and

(I) Bills inserted into electronic gaming devices.

(ii) Transactions in currency involving cash out include, but are not limited to:

(A) Redemptions of chips, tokens, and other gaming instruments;

(B) Front money withdrawals;

(C) Safekeeping withdrawals;

(D) Advances on any form of credit, including markers and counter checks;

(E) Payments on bets;

(F) Payments by a casino to a customer based on receipt of funds through wire transfers;

(G) Cashing of checks or other negotiable instruments;

(H) Exchanges of currency for currency, including foreign currency;

(I) Travel and complimentary expenses and gaming incentives; and

(J) Payment for tournament, contests, and other promotions.

(iii) Other provisions of this part notwithstanding, casinos are exempted from the reporting obligations found in §§ 103.22(b)(2) and (c)(3) for the following transactions in currency or currency transactions:

(A) Transactions between a casino and a currency dealer or exchanger, or between a casino and a check casher, as those terms are defined in § 103.11(uu), so long as such transactions are conducted pursuant to a contractual or other arrangement with a casino covering the financial services in §§ 103.22(b)(2)(i)(H), 103.22(b)(2)(ii)(G), and 103.22(b)(2)(ii)(H);

(B) Cash out transactions to the extent the currency is won in a money play and is the same currency the customer wagered in the money play, or cash in transactions to the extent the currency is the same currency the customer previously wagered in a money play on the same table game without leaving the table;

(C) Bills inserted into electronic gaming devices in multiple transactions (unless a casino has knowledge pursuant to § 103.22(c)(3) in which case this exemption would not apply); and

(D) Jackpots from slot machines or video lottery terminals.

...

(3) Multiple transactions — casinos. In the case of a casino, multiple currency transactions shall be treated as a single transaction if the casino has knowledge that they are by or on behalf of any person and result in either cash in or cash out totaling more than $10,000 during any gaming day. For purposes of this paragraph (c)(3), a casino shall be deemed to have the knowledge described in the preceding sentence, if: any sole proprietor, partner, officer, director, or employee of the casino, acting within the scope of his or her employment, has knowledge that such multiple currency transactions have occurred, including knowledge from examining the books, records, logs, information retained on magnetic disk, tape or other machine-readable media, or in any manual system, and similar documents and information, which the casino maintains pursuant to any law or regulation or within the ordinary course of its business, and which contain information that such multiple currency transactions have occurred.

Notes

1. The CTR requirement is not limited to casinos, although the regulation is very detailed in the ways in which the greater than $10,000 threshold may be triggered in a casino setting. Whether in a casino or elsewhere, the CTR is designed to be one mechanism for preventing the laundering of money. Part (3) of the regulation is a reference to what is called "structuring." Efforts to break a single transaction exceeding $10,000 into multiple transactions amounting to less than that amount would be a clear evasion of the CTR requirement. Therefore, they must be treated as a single transaction. As described below, when one attempts to structure a transaction, it may also trigger other casino reporting.

2. For discussion of the application of money laundering laws to casino operations, *see* Mark D. Schopper, *Internet Gambling, Electronic Cash & (and) Money Laundering: The Unintended Consequences of a Monetary Control Scheme*, 5 Chap. L. Rev. 303 (2002); Joseph M. Kelly & Mark Clayton, *Money Laundering and Land Based Casinos*, 14 Gaming L. Rev. & Econ. 275 (2010); John J. Ensminger, *Increasingly Complex Financial Offerings*

Make Casinos a Higher Priority in Anti-Money Laundering Enforcement, 21 J. Tax'n & Reg. Fin. Institutions, 41 (2008); Sara A. Hallmark & Megan L. Wolf, *Financial Institutions Fraud*, 47 Am. Crim. L. Rev. 595 (2010); Michael F. Zeldin & Richard W. Harms, *Anti-Money Laundering Compliance Programs: Principles from Traditional Financial Institutions Applied to Casinos*, 1 Gaming L. Rev. 343 (1997); John Mills & Thomas Doyle, *Money Laundering: New Challenges for Casino and Other Corporate Internal Auditors*, Mgmt. Acct., 73 (Jan. 1992); John R. Mills, *Understanding the Money Laundering Control Act and its Implementation Costs in the United States, in* Gambling & Public Policy: International Perspectives 169 (1991); *Money Laundering: Rapid Growth Of Casinos Makes Them Vulnerable* (U.S. General Accounting Office 1996).

iii. SAR-C (Suspicious Activity Report by Casinos and Card Clubs)

31 CFR § 103.21 Reports by casinos of suspicious transactions.

(a) *General.* (1) Every casino shall file with FinCEN, to the extent and in the manner required by this section, a report of any suspicious transaction relevant to a possible violation of law or regulation. A casino may also file with FinCEN, by using the form specified in paragraph (b)(1) of this section, or otherwise, a report of any suspicious transaction that it believes is relevant to the possible violation of any law or regulation but whose reporting is not required by this section.

(2) A transaction requires reporting under the terms of this section if it is conducted or attempted by, at, or through a casino, and involves or aggregates at least $5,000 in funds or other assets, and the casino knows, suspects, or has reason to suspect that the transaction (or a pattern of transactions of which the transaction is a part):

(i) Involves funds derived from illegal activity or is intended or conducted in order to hide or disguise funds or assets derived from illegal activity (including, without limitation, the ownership, nature, source, location, or control of such funds or assets) as part of a plan to violate or evade any federal law or regulation or to avoid any transaction reporting requirement under federal law or regulation;

(ii) Is designed, whether through structuring or other means, to evade any requirements of this part or of any other regulations promulgated under the Bank Secrecy Act, Public Law 91–508, as amended, codified at 12 U.S.C. 1829b, 12 U.S.C. 1951–1959, and 31 U.S.C. 5311–5332;

(iii) Has no business or apparent lawful purpose or is not the sort in which the particular customer would normally be expected to engage, and the casino knows of no reasonable explanation for the transaction after examining the available facts, including the background and possible purpose of the transaction; or

(iv) Involves use of the casino to facilitate criminal activity.

. . .

(e) *Confidentiality of reports; limitation of liability.* No casino, and no director, officer, employee, or agent of any casino, who reports a suspicious transaction under this part, may notify any person involved in the transaction that the transaction has been reported. Thus, any person subpoenaed or otherwise requested to disclose a SARC or the information contained in a SARC, except where such disclosure is requested by FinCEN or another appropriate law enforcement or regulatory agency, shall decline to produce the SARC or to provide any information that would disclose that a SARC has been prepared or filed, citing this paragraph (e) and 31 U.S.C. 5318(g)(2), and shall notify FinCEN of any such request and its response thereto. A casino, and any director, officer, employee, or agent of such casino, that makes a report pursuant to this section (whether such report is required by this section or made voluntarily) shall be protected from liability for any disclosure contained in, or for failure to disclose the fact of, such report, or both, to the extent provided by 31 U.S.C. 5318(g)(3).

(f) *Compliance.* Compliance with this section shall be audited by the Department of the Treasury, through FinCEN or its delegees, under the terms of the Bank Secrecy Act. Failure to satisfy the requirements of this section may constitute a violation of the reporting rules of the Bank Secrecy Act and of this part.

Financial Crimes Enforcement Network Advisory
FIN-2009-A003

Issued: July 1, 2009

Subject: Structuring by Casino Patrons and Personnel

The Financial Crimes Enforcement Network ("FinCEN") recently received information from law enforcement and regulatory authorities that certain casino personnel may have complied with requests from patrons to evade, or provided instructions to patrons on how to evade, reporting and recordkeeping requirements under the Bank Secrecy Act ("BSA").[1] It appears that casino patrons and personnel may have engaged in "structuring" certain transactions to evade such requirements.[2] The BSA prohibits any person, for the purpose of evading the requirement to report currency transactions or evading recordkeeping requirements under the BSA, from causing or attempting to cause a casino not to file a currency transaction report, to file a currency transaction report with material misstatements or omissions, not to maintain records required under the BSA, or to maintain these records in a form that is incomplete or inaccurate.[3] FinCEN is issuing this advisory to remind casinos and card clubs that structuring is unlawful, and that such activity can give rise to significant civil and criminal penalties under the BSA.[4] FinCEN is authorized to impose civil money penalties against casinos violating the BSA, and the U.S. Department of Justice prosecutes criminal violations of the BSA and related money-laundering statutes.[5]

Casinos subject to the BSA are required to develop and implement a compliance program reasonably designed to manage the risk of illicit activity and ensure compliance with the BSA and its implementing regulations.[6] The BSA requires casinos to file reports, properly identify customers conducting transactions, and maintain appropriate records of transactions. These reports and records are highly useful in criminal, tax, or regulatory investigations or proceedings, or in the conduct of intelligence or counterintelligence activities, including analysis, to protect against international terrorism.[7]

Recent accounts from law enforcement and regulatory authorities allege that certain casino patrons may have conspired with casino personnel to structure transactions to

---

1. *See* 31 U.S.C. §5311 *et seq.* and 31 C.F.R. Part 103.

2. Structuring is a money laundering and terrorist financing "placement" technique. Structuring includes, among other activities, the "breaking up" of transactions for the purpose of evading BSA currency transaction reporting requirements. See 31 U.S.C. §5324 and 31 C.F.R. §§103.11(gg) and 103.63.

3. *See* 31 U.S.C. §5324.

4. *See* 31 U.S.C. §§5321 and 5324.

5. *See* 31 U.S.C. §§5321(a)(4) and 5324 and 31 C.F.R. §§103.57(e) and 103.63; see also 18 U.S.C. §§1956 and 1957 (money laundering violations).

6. *See* 31 C.F.R. §§103.64 and 103.120(d).

7. *See* 31 U.S.C. §5311 and 31 C.F.R. §§103.12 and 103.31.

evade BSA reporting and/or recordkeeping requirements. The following scenarios are il-lustrative of the relevant conduct being alleged:[8]

- A premium player induces casino personnel to allow breaking up of a transaction into multiple transactions so as to fall below the $10,000 BSA currency transaction reporting threshold.

- A patron persuades casino personnel to alter or omit transaction information (e.g., a player rating record) or identification information on casino records.

- A player with chips amounting to more than $10,000 is told by a cage cashier that reducing the amount of the chip redemption to $10,000 or below will avoid currency transaction reporting, and the player redeems less than $10,000.

- A patron obtains assistance from a pit boss to allow the patron to intentionally coordinate buy-ins with the time of day when the casino's business or gaming day is concluded, in order to split cash transactions among different gaming days.

For any of these types of activities, casinos are obligated to file FinCEN Form 102, Suspicious Activity Report by Casinos and Card Clubs ("SARC"). Since structuring or any suspicious activity by casino personnel and patrons, including collusion and/or misuse of position by casino personnel including a casino host, constitutes reportable activity under the SARC provisions, a casino or card club is required to provide full disclosure of the subjects, identifying information and affiliations, business or employee relationships and associations in the applicable reporting items of the SARC, including the narrative part of the form.

Casinos are required also to deter, detect and report structuring by implementing a compliance program reasonably designed to prevent casino personnel and patrons from circumventing BSA requirements. A casino's written anti-money laundering program must be tailored to the risks of its business, and ensure that internal controls, training, independent testing and designated personnel are in place to deter, detect and report structuring.[9] If structured transactions involve or aggregate to at least $5,000 in funds or other assets, a casino must file a suspicious activity report.[10]

FinCEN is authorized to assess civil money penalties against a casino, card club, or any partner, director, officer, or employee thereof, for willful violations of BSA anti-money laundering program, reporting, and recordkeeping requirements, as follows:

- A penalty of $25,000 per day may be assessed for failure to establish and implement an adequate written BSA compliance or anti-money laundering program, including program failures that led to instances of undetected structuring. A separate violation occurs for each day the violation continues.[11]

- A penalty not to exceed the greater of the amount involved in the transaction (but capped at $100,000) or $25,000 may be assessed for each currency transaction or suspicious activity reporting violation.[12]

---

8. These examples are in addition to those set forth in FinCEN's previous guidance on "Recognizing Suspicious Activity—Red Flags for Casinos and Card Clubs" (FIN-2008-G007, August 1, 2008).

9. For additional guidance on BSA compliance programs, see FinCEN's Frequently Asked Questions—Casino Recordkeeping, Reporting and Compliance Program Requirements (FIN-2007-G005, November 14, 2007), questions and answers 21 through 23.

10. *See* 31 U.S.C. § 5318(g) and 31 C.F.R. § 103.21(a)(2)(ii).

11. *See* 31 U.S.C. § 5321(a)(1).

12. *See* 31 U.S.C. § 5321(a)(1) and 31 C.F.R. § 103.57(f).

- A penalty up to the amount of the coins and currency involved in the transaction[s] for structuring, attempting to structure, or assisting in structuring.[13]

FinCEN may also seek injunctive relief against future violations of the BSA.[14]

...

* * *

Notes

1. FinCEN (Financial Crimes Enforcement Network) is a part of the U.S. Department of the Treasury. According to FinCEN's web site, "FinCEN's mission is to enhance U.S. national security, deter and detect criminal activity, and safeguard financial systems from abuse by promoting transparency in the U.S. and international financial systems," http://www.fincen.gov. As with CTRs, this is not limited to casino reporting. However, the web site has extensive informational materials, as well as formal Guidance and Advisory Statements, for casinos, http://www.fincen.gov/financial_institutions/casinos/.

2. Note that the FinCen regulations prohibit casinos from telling patrons that their conduct will lead to the casino filing a SAR-C. The SAR-C report form requires a detailed narrative of the factual basis for the suspicious activity. If the suspicious activity turns out to be innocent, does it seem appropriate to deny recourse to the patron who has been reported to the government by the casino? What if the report lacks any serious merit?

3. For discussion of the role of SARCs in the gaming industry, *see* I Nelson Rose, *Casinos Stuck Under New Anti-Terrorism Law*, 8 GAMING L. REV. 1 (2004); Edward Magaw, *Suspicious Activity Reporting and Casinos: The Life and Death of Nevada's Regulation of Casino Suspicious Activity Reporting*, 7 GAMING L. REV. 427 (2003).

3. Enforcement

A. Generally

Colorado Limited Gaming Act of 1991

12-47.1-204. **Investigator — peace officers.** (1) All investigators of the division of gaming, and their supervisors, including the director and the executive director, shall have all the powers of any peace officer to:

(a) Make arrests, with or without warrant, for any violation of the provisions of this article, article 20 of title 18, C.R.S., or the rules and regulations promulgated pursuant to this article, any other laws or regulations pertaining to the conducting of limited gaming in this state, or any criminal law of this state, if, during an officer's exercise of powers or performance of duties under this section, probable cause is established that a violation of any said law or rule or regulation has occurred;

---

13. *See* 31 U.S.C. §§ 5321(a)(4) and 5324 and 31 C.F.R. §§ 103.57(e) and 103.63.
14. *See* 31 U.S.C. § 5320.

(b) Inspect, examine, investigate, hold, or impound any premises where limited gaming is conducted, any devices or equipment designed for or used in limited gaming, and any books and records in any way connected with any limited gaming activity;

(c) Require any person licensed pursuant to this article, upon demand, to permit an inspection of such person's licensed premises, gaming equipment and devices, or books or records; and to permit the testing and the seizure for testing or examination purposes of all such devices, equipment, and books and records;

(d) Serve all warrants, notices, summonses, or other processes relating to the enforcement of laws regulating limited gaming;

(e) Serve distraint warrants issued by the department of revenue pertaining to limited gaming;

(f) Conduct investigations into the character, record, and reputation of all applicants for limited gaming licenses, all licensees, and such other persons as the commission may determine pertaining to limited gaming;

(g) Investigate violations of all the laws pertaining to limited gaming and limited gaming activities;

(h) Assist or aid any sheriff or other peace officer in the performance of his duties upon such sheriff's or peace officer's request or the request of other local officials having jurisdiction.

(2) Criminal violations of this article discovered during an authorized investigation or discovered by the commission shall be referred to the appropriate district attorney.

(3) The investigators of the division, including the director of the division, shall be considered peace officers, as described in sections 16-2.5-101 and 16-2.5-123, C.R.S. The executive director of the department of revenue shall be considered a peace officer as described in sections 16-2.5-101 and 16-2.5-121, C.R.S.

(4) Nothing in this section shall be construed to prohibit local sheriffs, police departments, and other local law enforcement agencies from enforcing the provisions of this article, and the rules and regulations promulgated pursuant to this article, or from performing their other duties to the full extent permitted by law. All such sheriffs, police officers, district attorneys, and other local law enforcement agencies shall have all the powers set forth in subsection (1) of this section.

Nevada Gaming Commission Regulation § 5.045

Compliance review and reporting system.

1. Whenever the commission is acting upon any application of a licensee or registrant, or pursuant to its powers provided in NRS 463.310, and if the commission determines that special circumstances exist which require additional management review by a licensee or registrant, the commission may impose a condition upon any license or order of registration to require implementation of a compliance review and reporting system by the licensee or registrant....

4. The compliance review and reporting system shall be created for the purpose of monitoring activities relating to the licensee's or registrant's continuing qualifications under the provisions of the Nevada Gaming Control Act and regulations of the commission in accordance with a written plan to be approved by the board administratively or as otherwise ordered by the commission.

5. The written plan must provide for the operation of the compliance review and reporting system and must designate who shall be responsible for said system. The plan must provide for involvement of at least one person knowledgeable of the provisions of the Nevada Gaming Control Act and the regulations of the commission. The plan must require periodic reports to senior management of the licensee or registrant. Such reports shall be advisory and the licensee or registrant shall maintain responsibility for compliance with the Gaming Control Act and regulations of the commission. Copies of the reports must be provided to the board.

6. The activities to be monitored must be set forth in the written plan and must be determined by the circumstances applicable to the licensee or registrant. Without limitation, the activities that may be required to be monitored pursuant to the compliance review and reporting system include the following:

(a) Associations with persons denied licensing or other related approvals by the commission or who may be deemed to be unsuitable to be associated with a licensee or registrant;

(b) Business practices or procedures that may constitute grounds for denial of a gaming license or registration;

(c) Compliance with other special conditions that may be imposed by the commission upon the licensee or registrant;

(d) Review of reports submitted pursuant to the Nevada Gaming Control Act and regulations of the commission;

(e) Compliance with the laws, regulations, or orders of duly constituted governmental agencies or entities having jurisdiction over the gaming affairs, or such other business activities which the board or the commission may deem necessary or proper, of the licensee, registrant, or its affiliates; and

(f) Review of such other activities determined by the board or the commission as being relevant to the licensee's or registrant's continuing qualifications under the provisions of the Nevada Gaming Control Act and the regulations of the commission.

Notes

1. Many methods of detection of a statutory or regulatory violation are available, such as self-reporting or audits. A common method, however, is field observation, which is the equivalent of a casino patrol officer. This may involve both overt investigations in response to reported problems, and covert or undercover observations. Field observation is used to detect cheating scams, underage gambling, and casino floor regulatory violations. The last of these may include whether casino employees properly carry out mandated procedures, such as observing and documenting fills and credits. Undercover operations allow regulatory agents to uncover cheating scams, skimming, credit, and currency violations. The casino equivalent to "beat" police officers is on-site government inspectors. For example, New Jersey requires government inspectors to be on the premises at each casino. Under N.J.S.A. § 5:12-63, the Casino Control Commission must be

> present through its inspectors and agents at all times, except as provided by section 4 of P.L.2008, c.23 (C.5:12-211), during the operation of any casino or simulcasting facility for the purpose of certifying the revenue thereof, receiving complaints from the public relating to the conduct of gaming and simulcast wagering operations, examining records of revenues and procedures, and con-

ducting periodic reviews of operations and facilities for the purpose of evaluating current or suggested provisions of P.L.1977, c.110 (C.5:12-1 et seq.) and the regulations promulgated thereunder.

2. Governments can use compliance committees to assure proper accounting and regulatory compliance. For a good explanation of compliance committees *see* Grant Thornton, *Getting in the Game A Guide to Successful Gaming Company Compliance* (Lewis & Roca 2010); David O. Stewart, *Basics of Criminal Liability for Corporations and their Officials, and Use of Compliance Programs and Internal Investigations*, 22 Pub. Contact L. J. 81 (1993). *See also* Dominic P. Gentile, *Is Your Compliance Program Prepared for Success?*, 1 Gaming L. Rev. 191 (1997); Fredric E. Gushin & William R. Kisby, *The Compliance Department: Key to Protecting Gaming Domestically and Internationally*, 7 Gaming L. Rev. 149 (2003); David D. Waddell & Douglas L. Minke, *The Increasing Federal Regulation of Casinos: What a Casino Compliance Team Needs to Know*, 14 Gaming L. Rev. 609 (2010).

3. Regulatory agencies often dictate the membership criteria of compliance committees, but they usually include one or more outside members. These committees periodically meet to review the casino's compliance with all gaming laws. They also may conduct investigations, and provide advice to the casinos. Corporate compliance committees need to meet objectives to be effective. First, the committee should be able to implement procedures within the company that increase the probability of regulatory compliance. Second, the procedures should apply at all levels of the corporation from the president to dealers. Third, all employees should be trained as to the program, its purposes, its procedures, and their responsibility. Employees should know the proper method of reporting non-compliance. Available methods include ombudsmen, telephone hotlines and boxes. The procedure should require employees to complete periodic reports. Fourth, the company should dedicate itself to the implementing the compliance program. Fifth, the program should provide meaningful discipline for employees that violate its provisions. Sixth, the program should be reviewed and modified periodically.

B. Disciplinary Actions

Regulators have many tools by which to assure regulatory compliance. Regulators may use advice or directives, fines, suspension, conditions to continued licensing, or revocation of the license, to control the behavior of the offending licensee or, to remove the offender from the regulated industry. Isolated and unintentional violations that do not compromise gaming control may be dealt with through working with the licensee to improve training or control.

If a casino licensee has a pattern of unintentional violations that shows a lack of commitment to hiring competent personnel or to training, other sanctions may be appropriate. In a regulatory environment, a fine should not be used as punishment, but a motivational tool intended to deter behavior and ensure future compliance. If regulators believe that the licensee cannot, through lesser sanctions, conform its behavior to meet regulatory goals, then the solution is license revocation. In the regulatory scheme, revocation of a gaming license is tantamount to the death penalty.

Whether an agency can use disciplinary actions to punish the offender, as opposed to regulate the industry, is an unresolved constitutional issue. The United States Supreme Court has held that an agency violates the double jeopardy clause of the United States Constitution if it fines a person more than needed to compensate the government. United States

v. Harper, 450 U.S. 435 (1989). This logic, however, has not been applied to whether agencies can constitutionally assess penalties to punish offenders.

Romano v. Bible
169 F.3d 1182 (9th Cir. 1999)

Before: FLETCHER, FERGUSON, and THOMPSON, Circuit Judges.

FERGUSON, Circuit Judge:

Frank Romano voluntarily relinquished his gaming license and later wanted it back, claiming that the defendants violated his due process and equal protection rights. When the Nevada Gaming Commission refused to revisit the issue, Frank and Maria Romano brought this action for civil damages pursuant to 42 U.S.C. § 1983 against the Nevada Attorney General and current and former members of the Nevada Gaming Commission and the Nevada Gaming Control Board. The Romanos contend that the defendants violated their constitutional rights by depriving Mr. Romano of his gaming license. The district court granted the state defendants' motion to dismiss on seven alternate grounds. We have jurisdiction pursuant to 28 U.S.C. § 1291. We affirm on the grounds that absolute immunity and the Eleventh Amendment shield the defendants from liability.

I. BACKGROUND

We state the facts, as we must in this appeal, as they are set forth in the Romanos' complaint. Since 1981, the Nevada Gaming Commission ("Commission") licensed Mr. Romano to own, manufacture, and distribute gaming devices as a partner in American Coin Companies. In 1989, the Nevada Gaming Control Board ("Board"), which investigates and prosecutes violations of the gaming laws, filed a complaint with the Commission seeking disciplinary action against Mr. Romano and his partners, Rudolph and Rudolph M. LaVecchia. The Board alleged that the LaVecchias altered gaming devices to defraud players, a practice known as "gaffing," and that Mr. Romano was vicariously criminally liable for their conduct. The LaVecchias fled Nevada, leaving Mr. Romano to contend with the authorities.

For a number of reasons, including the government's failure to cooperate with discovery and ineffective assistance of counsel, Mr. Romano entered into a stipulation with the Board in 1990 agreeing to relinquish his gaming license and to pay a fine. As part of the stipulation, Mr. Romano waived his statutory right to a hearing and waived any legal rights that he might have against Board members. While acknowledging that the stipulation was voluntarily signed, Mr. Romano did not admit liability.

As a result of the revocation of Mr. Romano's license and the closure of his businesses, the Romanos suffered financial losses and filed for bankruptcy in 1992. The Romanos also filed an adverse complaint in the bankruptcy proceeding against the LaVecchias. During that proceeding, an investigator employed by the Board testified to Mr. Romano's lack of knowledge concerning the fraud. One of the bankruptcy court's factual findings was that Mr. Romano was not culpable for his partners' conduct.

Consequently, Mr. Romano petitioned the Commission to vacate its order approving the stipulation which had resulted in the voluntary relinquishment of his gaming license. The Commission concluded that it lacked jurisdiction to hear the petition. Nevada law provides that, if no petition for judicial review has been filed, a motion for rehearing must be brought within 10 days of the Commission's order. Seven years had elapsed since Mr. Romano entered into the stipulation. The Commission also declined to consider Mr.

Romano's petition under a regulation permitting it to issue discretionary rulings. The result was that Mr. Romano could not obtain discovery.

The Romanos then filed this action, contending that the failure of the Board to provide them with evidence in its possession tending to exculpate Mr. Romano violated their due process rights. In addition, the plaintiffs alleged that by instituting disciplinary action against Mr. Romano, the Board selectively enforced the Nevada Gaming Act in violation of the plaintiffs' equal protection rights. The complaint sought compensatory and punitive damages. After a hearing, the district court granted the state's motion to dismiss pursuant to Federal Rule of Civil Procedure 12(b)(6). The court concluded that: (1) the Romanos did not have a property right in the gaming license; (2) the Romanos failed to allege an equal protection violation in the pleadings; (3) Mr. Romano waived his right to file a § 1983 action against state officials by signing the stipulation; (4) the statute of limitations prohibits the action; (5) the Eleventh Amendment bars the action against all defendants; and (6) both absolute and qualified immunity shield the defendants from liability.

II. DISCUSSION

. . . .

A. Eleventh Amendment

Whether a state is immune from suit under the Eleventh Amendment is a question of law which we review *de novo*. Micomonaco v. Washington, 45 F.3d 316, 319 (9th Cir. 1995). The Nevada Gaming Control Board and the Nevada Gaming Commission as agency defendants in this action are immune from suit. The Eleventh Amendment bars suits against the State or its agencies for all types of relief, absent unequivocal consent by the state. Pennhurst v. Halderman, 465 U.S. 89, 100 (1984). Nevada has not consented to suit by expressly waiving its Eleventh Amendment immunity. N.R.S. § 41.031(3). Accordingly, we affirm the district court's dismissal as to the state agency defendants.

The Eleventh Amendment also bars the Romano's claims against the remaining defendants in their *official* capacities. The amendment prohibits actions for damages against an "official's office," that is, actions that are in reality suits against the state itself. Stivers v. Pierce, 71 F.3d 732, 749 (9th Cir. 1995).

However, the Romanos have brought suit against individual Board and Commission members in their *personal* capacities as well. They assert that, while acting under color of state law, the defendants deprived Mr. Romano of a protected property interest in violation of due process. They need to allege nothing more to avoid the Eleventh Amendment's shield. The Supreme Court has made it clear that a plaintiff can establish *personal* liability in a § 1983 action simply by showing that the official acted under color of state law in deprivation of a federal right. Hafer v. Melo, 502 U.S. 21, 25 (1991). We also have presumed that officials necessarily are sued in their personal capacities where those officials are named in a complaint, even if the complaint does not explicitly mention the capacity in which they are sued. *See* Shoshone-Bannock Tribes v. Fish & Game Comm'n, 42 F.3d 1278, 1284 (9th Cir. 1994); Cerrato v. San Francisco Community College Dist., 26 F.3d 968, 973 n.16 (9th Cir. 1994). Consequently, the Eleventh Amendment imposes no bar to the Romanos' action against the individual defendants in their personal capacities.

B. Absolute Immunity

The district court concluded that absolute immunity protected the individual defendants named by the Romanos. We review *de novo* the district court's determination regarding immunity. Trevino v. Gates, 23 F.3d 1480, 1482 (9th Cir. 1994).

Absolute immunity extends to agency officials when they preside over hearings, initiate agency adjudication, or otherwise perform functions analogous to judges and prosecutors. Butz v. Economou, 438 U.S. 478, 514–15 (1978). The Supreme Court has adopted a "functional approach" to determine whether an official is entitled to absolute immunity. This approach looks to the nature of the function performed, not the identity of the actor who performed it. Buckley v. Fitzsimmons, 509 U.S. 259, 269, (1993). Judges and those performing quasi-judicial functions are absolutely immune from damages for acts performed *within their judicial capacities.* Stump v. Sparkman, 435 U.S. 349, 360 (1978). Prosecutors are extended absolute immunity from damages when performing activities closely associated with the judicial process. Imbler v. Pachtman, 424 U.S. 409, 430–31 (1976). Quasi-prosecutorial immunity, however, does not attach to administrative or investigatory acts by prosecutors unrelated to their preparation for and initiation of prosecution. *Buckley,* 509 U.S. at 273. In extending absolute immunity to those within administrative agencies who perform prosecutorial and judicial functions, the Court recognized that administrative proceedings are usually adversarial in nature and provide many of the same features and safeguards that are provided in court. *Butz,* 438 U.S. at 513. Thus, we must assess the function that Nevada gaming officials performed when they engaged in the alleged unconstitutional conduct to determine if they are entitled to absolute immunity from damages.

The Romanos contend that the individual defendants acted outside the scope of their duties. We disagree. Under Nevada law, Board and Commission members have access to all gaming premises to inspect or seize any gaming devices or documents relevant to suspected violations of the gaming laws. N.R.S. § 463.140. The Board must investigate the qualifications of each applicant for a gaming license and has discretion to recommend denial or revocation of a license. N.R.S. § 463.1405(1), (2). The Commission then may deny or revoke a license for "any cause deemed reasonable." N.R.S. § 463.1405(3). Both Board and Commission members can issue subpoenas, compel the attendance of witnesses, administer oaths, and require testimony under oath. N.R.S. § 463.140(5).

Within the gaming regulatory scheme, the attorney general provides legal advice to the Board and Commission and represents them in proceedings initiated against them. N.R.S. § 463.0199. Either agency may recommend that the attorney general prosecute any public offense committed in violation of the gaming laws. N.R.S. § 463.141. In Mr. Romano's case, Attorney General Frankie Sue Del Papa is the predecessor of the attorney general who prepared the stipulation on behalf of the Board. The Romanos sued her as the party "responsible for the ... supervision and prosecution" of Mr. Romano's case. She is entitled to absolute immunity because the activity of representing the Board and Commission in the disciplinary action against Mr. Romano is within the scope of her duties in pursuing quasi-judicial proceedings. *See* Hirsh v. Justices of Supreme Court of Cal., 67 F.3d 708, 715 (9th Cir. 1995) (concluding that the California Attorney General was entitled to absolute immunity for his limited role in the Bar disciplinary system).

The Gaming Control Board conducts investigations and decides whether to file complaints with the Commission disciplining a licensee. N.R.S. § 463.310. In so doing, it acts much like a prosecutor. The Board initiated disciplinary proceedings against Mr. Romano and entered into settlement negotiations with him, actions that are prosecutorial in nature. Moreover, prosecutorial functions that require the exercise of discretion are absolutely immune, and the decision whether to disclose exculpatory evidence which has not been requested is such a function. *See Imbler,* 424 U.S. at 431–32 n.34. Thus, the Board is entitled to absolute immunity as well.

Commission members adjudicate disciplinary proceedings against licensees. They conduct hearings with many of the traditional safeguards of courts, and they issue orders. Every party to a hearing before the Commission can call and examine witnesses, introduce exhibits, cross-examine opposing witnesses, impeach witnesses, and offer rebuttal evidence. N.R.S. § 463.313. The Commission may take "judicial notice" of facts and may cite parties for contempt like any Article III court. *Id.*; N.R.S. § 463.314. Members who hear the evidence against a licensee must render a written decision on the merits which includes findings of fact. N.R.S. § 463.3145. Here, as with any judicial plea bargain, the Commission approved the stipulation entered into by Mr. Romano and the Board to resolve his disciplinary proceeding. Like the other defendants, Commission members carried out acts of independent decision-making integral to the functioning of a quasi-judicial process.

In *Butz,* the Court considered several other factors to be characteristic of the judicial process and, thus, relevant to the absolute immunity inquiry. These factors include the adversarial nature of the process, the correctability of errors on appeal, and the presence of safeguards in the regulatory framework to control unconstitutional conduct and to insulate the adjudicators from political influence. 438 U.S. at 512–13. Statutory procedural safeguards in the gaming disciplinary process satisfy these factors. In addition to the safeguards noted above, licensees are entitled to judicial review of the Commission's decision. N.R.S. §§ 463.315, 463.318. The Commission may grant a rehearing upon petition if additional material evidence exists. N.R.S. § 463.3145. Parties may have counsel. Besides the opportunity to present and cross-examine witnesses, parties are provided with adequate notice of the hearing and a copy of the charges against them. N.R.S. § 463.312. Nevada also attempts to shield Commission members from political influence. The governor appoints members of the Commission for staggered terms of four years, and each member can be removed by the governor. N.R.S. § 463.024; 1985 Nev. Stat., ch. 266, § 2 at 804. No elected official or officer of any political party can serve as Commissioner, or any person with a pecuniary interest in the gaming industry. N.R.S. §§ 463.023, 463.025. Not more than three members can be of the same major political party. *Id.*

In addition, other courts have extended *Butz* to state agency officials involved in the adjudication of state regulatory matters, at least where the regulatory scheme provided safeguards against arbitrary and biased decision-making. *See, e.g., Hirsh,* 67 F.3d at 715 (Bar Court judges and prosecutors in attorney disciplinary actions have quasi-judicial or quasi-prosecutorial immunity); Bermudez v. Duenas, 936 F.2d 1064, 1066 (9th Cir. 1991) (parole board officials entitled to absolute immunity for activities which are part of the decision to grant, deny or revoke parole).

III. CONCLUSION

The case at the bar underscores the importance of extending absolute immunity to gaming officials involved in disciplinary proceedings. The highly regulated gaming industry in Nevada generates millions of dollars. Where these dollars go turn on decisions made by Board and Commission members, who determine which people will or will not be "players" in the industry. With so much at stake in their decisions, these officials must be able to pursue disciplinary proceedings "free from intimidation and harassment." *Butz,* 438 U.S. at 516. To deny them immunity would be to disservice the broader public interest in having people perform these functions without fear of having to personally defend their actions in civil damages lawsuits like the Romanos'. *See* Babcock v. Tyler, 884 F.2d 497, 502 (9th Cir. 1989). We conclude that absolute immunity should protect these gaming decisions.

AFFIRMED.

Notes

1. In *Romano*, the court alluded to the presence of procedural protection necessary to meet constitutional due process standards. As will be discussed in Chapter 4, a person who holds a license has a protected property interest in the license. Therefore, the government cannot fine the person or revoke his license without affording that person procedures that include notice and an opportunity to be heard. A regulatory agency may establish procedures for an administrative hearing to decide whether a licensee violates any civil gaming laws and, if so, the appropriate penalty. In some respects, these administrative proceedings may be similar to the role a regulatory agency may play in granting licenses. Both instances involve the regulators serving in a quasi-judicial role. Disciplinary actions, however, differ in several ways. Most importantly, as noted, a licensee in a disciplinary action has greater constitutional protections. In an influential law review article, Judge Henry Friendly identified four procedural safeguards he considered fundamental to fair adjudicatory decision-making: (1) notice of the proposed action and the grounds asserted for it; (2) an opportunity to present reasons why the action should not be taken; (3) an unbiased tribunal; and (4) a statement of reasons. These four minimum procedures are less than what a person is entitled to in a typical judicial proceeding. Judge Friendly identified six other procedural aspects of traditional trials: (1) the right to present evidence, including the right to call witnesses; (2) the right to know opposing evidence;(3) the right to cross examination adverse witnesses; (4) decision based exclusively on the evidence presented; (5) right to counsel and; (6) requirement that the tribunal prepare a record of the evidence presented. Henry J. Friendly, *Some Kind of Hearing*, 123 U. Pa. L. Rev. 1267 (1975).

2. Many jurisdictions that provide for administrative determination of disciplinary actions afford most of these procedures to the accused licensee. The extent to which a jurisdiction must provide all these procedures in a disciplinary proceeding is unresolved. The United States Supreme Court has adopted a flexible analysis in reviewing whether the government has accorded a person due process in a particular case. In Mathews v. Eldridge, the United States Supreme Court established the following test:

> '[D]ue process,' unlike some legal rules, is not a technical conception with a fixed content unrelated to time, place and circumstances. ... [O]ur prior decisions indicate that identification of the specific dictates of due process generally requires consideration of three distinct factors: First, the private interest that win be affected by the official action; second, the risk of an erroneous deprivation of such interest through the procedures used, and the probable value, if any, of additional or substitute procedural safeguards; and finally, the Government's interest, including the function involved and the fiscal and administrative burdens that the additional or substitute procedural requirement would entail.

Mathews v. Eldridge, 424 U.S. 319, 335 (1976).

4. Protecting the Regulatory Process

A. Political Protection

Casino Association of Louisiana v. Foster

820 So.2d 494 (La. 2002), *cert. denied* 537 U.S. 1226 (2003)

Supreme Court of Louisiana.

VICTORY, J.

This case is before us on direct appeal of a finding by the district court that the statutes prohibiting campaign contributions from the riverboat and land-based casino industries are unconstitutional. After reviewing the record and the applicable law, we reverse the judgment of the district court and uphold the constitutionality of these statutes.

FACTS AND PROCEDURAL HISTORY

On September 20, 2000, the Casino Association of Louisiana ("CAL")[1] and its individual members filed a Petition for Declaratory Judgment in the 19th Judicial District Court alleging that the provisions of La. R.S. 18:1505.2(L) prohibiting campaign contributions by the riverboat and land-based casino industries are unconstitutional. Treasure Chest Casino, LLC ("TCC")[2] and two Harrah's entities, Harrah's Operating Company, Inc. and Harrah's Entertainment, Inc. (jointly "Harrah's"),[3] were permitted to intervene in the lawsuit in light of their respective interests in the laws that regulate the casino gaming industry.

Harrah's, TCC, CAL and its individual members are prohibited from making campaign contributions to candidates or to political committees of candidates by operation of La. R.S. 18:1505.2(L), which provides in pertinent part as follows:

> L. (1) The legislature recognizes that it is essential to the operation of effective democratic government in this state that citizens have confidence in the electoral process and that elections be conducted so as to prevent influence and the appearance of influence of candidates for public office and of the election process by special interests, particularly by persons substantially interested in the gaming industry in this state.
>
> (2) No person to whom this Subsection is applicable as provided in Paragraph (3) of this Subsection shall make a contribution, loan, or transfer of funds, including but not limited to any in-kind contribution, as defined in this Chapter, to any candidate, any political committee of any such candidate, or to any other political committee which supports or opposes any candidate.
>
> (3) This Subsection shall be applicable to all of the following:
>
> ...

---

1. CAL is a corporation which represents the interests of the owners and operators of riverboat casinos within this state.

2. TCC is a member of CAL and is licensed by the State to conduct riverboat gaming operations upon its licensed riverboat located in Kenner, Louisiana.

3. Harrah's, through certain subsidiaries, is authorized to conduct riverboat gaming operations upon three licensed riverboats, one of which is located in Shreveport, Louisiana, and two of which are located in Lake Charles, Louisiana, and also owns a 49% interest in JCC Holding Co., the sole member of the land-based casino gaming operator, Jazz Casino Company LLC ("JCC").

(a)(ii) Any person who holds a license to conduct gaming activities on a riverboat, who holds a license or permit as a distributor or supplier of gaming devices or gaming equipment including slot machines, or who holds a license or permit as a manufacturer of gaming devices or gaming equipment including slot machines issued pursuant to the Louisiana Riverboat Economic Development and Gaming Control Act [La. R.S. 27:41 *et seq.*], and any person who owns a riverboat upon which gaming activities are licensed to be conducted.

(iii) Any person who holds a license or entered into a contract for the conduct of casino gaming operations, who holds a license or permit as a distributor of gaming devices or gaming equipment including slot machines, or who holds a license or permit as a manufacturer of gaming devices or gaming equipment including slot machines issued pursuant to the Louisiana Economic Development and Gaming Corporation Act [La. R.S. 27:201 *et seq.*], and any person who owns a casino where such gaming operations are licensed.

. . .

(b)(i) Any person who has an interest, directly or indirectly, in any legal entity included in Subparagraph (a) of this Paragraph. "Interest," as defined in this Subparagraph, means ownership by an individual or spouse, either individually or collectively, of an interest which exceeds ten percent of any legal entity. An indirect interest is ownership through any number of layers of legal entities when twenty-five percent or more or each legal entity is owned by the legal entity ownership beneath it.

(ii) Any holding, intermediary, or subsidiary company of any person included in Subparagraph (a) of this Paragraph and any officer, director, trustee, or partner thereof.

(c) Any officer, director, trustee, partner, or senior management level employee or key employee as defined in R.S. 27:205(19) of any person included in Subparagraph (a) or (b) of this Paragraph.

. . .

(e) The spouse of any person to whom this Subsection is made applicable by this Paragraph.

Following a hearing, the district court, Judge Timothy Kelley presiding, declared La. R.S. 18:1505.2(L)(3)(a)(ii) and La. R.S. 18:1505.2(L)(3)(b)(c)(e), insofar as they are applicable to La. R.S. 18:1505.2(L)(3)(a)(ii) and (iii), unconstitutional. The court also declared unconstitutional a corresponding provision of the Louisiana Administrative Code, 42 LA-ADC Pt. IX, § 2941, insofar as it applies to the owners of any holding company of the casino gaming operator, their affiliated companies, and all of their officers, directors, partners, senior management, and key employees. In support, the district court relied upon the reasoning of the majority of this Court in Penn v. State, 99-2337, 751 So.2d 823 (La. 1999), *cert. denied,* 529 U.S. 1109 (2000), which declared unconstitutional provisions of La. R.S. 18:1505.2(L) barring campaign contributions by the video poker industry. The State has appealed the district court's judgment directly to this Court pursuant to La. Const. Art. V, § 5(D).

DISCUSSION

In *Penn,* in a four-three per curiam decision, this Court declared unconstitutional La. R.S. 18:1505.2(L)(3)(a)(i), La. R.S. 18:1505.2(L)(3)(b)(i) insofar as it is applied to La. R.S. 18:1505.2(L)(3)(a)(i), and Rule 107 of Title 42 of the Louisiana Administrative Code, insofar as Rule 107 precludes candidate and political committee contributions by video draw poker licensees.[4] For the reasons that follow, we decline to follow *Penn* and hold that the legislative bans on campaign contributions by riverboat gaming and land-based casino interests do not violate the First and Fourteenth Amendments to the United States Constitution.[5]

The First Amendment provides that "Congress shall make no law … abridging the freedom of speech." U.S. Const. Amend. I. The Fourteenth Amendment makes this most important guarantee applicable to the states as well as the Congress. Buckley v. Valeo is the seminal United States Supreme Court case on modern campaign finance reform in the context of the First Amendment. 424 U.S. 1. In reviewing the contribution[6] and expenditure[7] limits contained in the 1974 amendments to the Federal Election Campaign Act of 1971 (the "Act"),[8] the *Buckley* Court made clear that restrictions on campaign contributions and expenditures "operate in an area of the most fundamental First Amendment activities," namely, the rights of freedom of association and freedom of expression. 424 U.S. at 14. In discussing the Act's impact on the First Amendment's guarantee of freedom of expression, the Court distinguished between expenditure restrictions and contribution restrictions, characterizing expenditure restrictions as follows:

> A restriction on the amount of money a person or group can spend on political communication during a campaign necessarily reduces the quantity of expression by restricting the number of issues discussed, the depth of their exploration, and the size of the audience reached. This is because virtually every means of communicating ideas in today's mass society requires the expenditure of money.…
>
> The *expenditure limitations* contained in the Act represent *substantial rather than merely theoretical restraints* on the quantity and diversity of political speech.…

424 U.S. at 19 (emphasis added).

In discussing restraints on contributions in the context of freedom of expression rights, the Court held:

---

4. In *Penn,* Chief Justice Calogero, Justices Kimball and Johnson, and former Justice Harry Lemmon, issued concurring opinions and the author of this opinion and Justices Traylor and Knoll issued dissenting opinions.

5. The per curiam opinion in *Penn* noted that while other sections of La. R.S. 18:1505.2(L) also prohibit certain persons from contributing to candidates and political committees of candidates, those sections were not under attack in *Penn* and therefore *Penn* did not consider the validity of those provisions. 751 So.2d at 824, n.2.

6. The Act defines a "contribution" as "any gift, subscription, loan, advance, or deposit of money or anything of value made by any person for the purpose of influencing any election for Federal office;" or "the payment by any person of compensation for the personal services of another person which are rendered to a political committee without charge for any purpose." 2 U.S.C. 431(8).

7. The Act defines an "expenditure" as "any purchase, payment, distribution, loan, advance, deposit, or gift of money or anything of value, made by any person for the purpose of influencing any election for Federal office." 2 U.S.C. 431(9)(A)(i). An "expenditure" is also a "written contract, promise, or agreement to make an expenditure."

8. The statutes at issue, Federal Election Campaign Act of 1971, 86 Stat. 3, as amended by the Federal Election Campaign Act Amendments of 1974, 88 Stat. 1263, contained the following provisions: individual political contributions are limited to $1,000 to any single candidate per election, with an overall annual limitation of $25,000 by any contributor; independent expenditures by individuals and groups "relative to a clearly identified candidate" are limited to $1,000 a year; campaign spending by candidates for various federal offices and spending for national conventions by political parties are subject to prescribed limits; contributions and expenditures above certain threshold levels must be reported and publicly disclosed.

By contrast with a limitation upon expenditures for political expression, a limitation upon the amount that any one person or group may contribute to a candidate or political committee entails *only a marginal restriction upon the contributor's ability to engage in free communication.* A contribution serves as a general expression of support for the candidate and his views, but does not communicate the underlying basis for the support. The quantity of communication by the contributor does not increase perceptibly with the size of his contribution, since the expression rests solely on the undifferentiated, symbolic act of contributing. At most, the size of the contribution provides a very rough index of the intensity of the contributor's support for the candidate. A limitation on the amount of money a person may give to a candidate or campaign organization thus involves little direct restraint on his political communication, for it permits the symbolic expression of support evidenced by a contribution but does not in any way infringe the contributor's freedom to discuss candidates and issues. While contributions may result in political expression if spent by a candidate or an association to present views to the voters, the transformation of contributions into political debate involves speech by someone other than the contributor (emphasis added).

Id., 424 U.S. at 21.

...

The Court in *Buckley* also held that the Act's contribution and expenditure limits "impinge on protected associational freedoms," as follows:

Making a contribution, like joining a political party, serves to affiliate a person with a candidate. In addition, it enables like-minded persons to pool their resources in furtherance of common political goals. The Act's contribution ceilings thus limit one important means of associating with a candidate or committee, but leave the contributor free to become a member of any political association and to assist personally in the association's efforts on behalf of candidates. And the Act's contribution limitations permits associations and candidates to aggregate large sums of money to promote effective advocacy.

Id., 424 U.S. at 22–23.

Thus, in addressing the contribution limitations, the Court held that the "*primary* problem raised by the Act's contribution limitations is their restriction of *one aspect* of the contributor's freedom of political association." *Id.*, 424 U.S. at 24 (emphasis added).

In discussing the appropriate standard of review to be used to determine whether the contribution limitations violated the contributor's freedom of political association rights, the *Buckley* Court held:

In view of the fundamental nature of the right to associate, governmental "action which may have the effect of curtailing the freedom to associate is subject to the closest scrutiny." NAACP v. Alabama, 357 U.S. 449, 460–61 (1958). Yet, it is clear that "[n]either the right to associate nor the right to participate in political activities is absolute." CSC v. Letter Carriers, 413 U.S. 548, 567 (1973). Even a "significant interference with protected rights of political association" may be sustained if the State demonstrates a sufficiently important interest and employs means closely drawn to avoid unnecessary abridgment of associational freedoms.

Id., 424 U.S. at 25. The Supreme Court has recently identified further reasons for the differing standards of review that the Court applies to restrictions on political expenditures and political contributions as follows:

> Spending for political ends and contributing to political candidates both fall within the First Amendment's protection of speech and political association. *Buckley,* 424 U.S. at 14–23. But ever since we first reviewed the 1971 Act, we have understood that limits on political expenditures deserve closer scrutiny than restrictions on political contributions. *Ibid; see also, e.g., Shrink Missouri,* 528 U.S. at 386; *Colorado I, supra,* at 610, 614–615; *Massachusetts Citizens for Life,* 479 U.S. at 259–60. Restrictions on expenditures generally curb more expressive and associational activity than limits on contributions do. *Shrink Missouri, supra,* at 386–88; *Colorado I, supra,* at 615; *Buckley,* 424 U.S. at 19–23. A further reason for the distinction is that limits on contributions are more clearly justified by a link to political corruption than limits on other kinds of unlimited political spending are (corruption being understood not only as quid pro quo agreements, but also as undue influence on an officerholder's judgment, and the appearance of such influence, *Shrink Missouri, supra,* at 388–89). At least this is so where the spending is not coordinated with the candidate or his campaign....
>
> Given these differences, we have routinely struck down limitations on independent expenditures by candidates, other individuals, and groups, *see* Federal Election Comm'n v. National Conservative Political Action Comm., 470 U.S. 480, 490–501 (1985) (political action committees); *Buckley, supra,* at 39–58 (individuals, groups, candidates, and campaigns), while repeatedly upholding contribution limits, *see Shrink Missouri, supra* (contributions by political action committees); California Medical Assn. v. Federal Election Comm'n, 453 U.S. 182, 193–99 (1981) (contributions by individuals and associations); *Buckley, supra,* at 23–36 (contributions by individuals, groups, and political committees).

Colorado II, supra, 533 U.S. at 440.

In applying that standard of review and in upholding the constitutionality of the contribution limitations, the *Buckley* Court found that the Act's primary purpose of limiting the actuality and appearance of corruption resulting from large individual financial contributions was a constitutionally sufficient justification for the limitations. Specifically, the Court held that "[t]o the extent that large contributions are given to secure political quid pro quo's from current and potential office holders, the integrity of our system of representative democracy is undermined," and that "[o]f almost equal concern as the danger of actual quid pro quo arrangements in the impact of the appearance of corruption stemming from public awareness of the opportunities for abuse inherent in a regime of large individual financial contributions." *Id.*, 424 U.S. at 26–7. The Court opined that "Congress could legitimately conclude that the avoidance of the appearance of improper influence 'is also critical ... if confidence in the system of representative Government is not to be eroded to a disastrous extent.'" *Id.* (citing CSC v. Letter Carriers, *supra,* 413 U.S. at 565, n.29).

In *Penn,* wherein a majority of this Court declared unconstitutional provisions of La. R.S. 18:1505.2(L) that barred campaign contributions by the video poker industry, the common thread among the four concurring opinions is the authors' beliefs that *Buckley* identified only a "single narrow exception" to the rule that limits on political activity are contrary to the First Amendment, and that, because the statutes at issue "prohibited" rather that "limited" the contributions, they did not fit into the "exception" and were therefore unconstitutional. These concurrences base their reasoning on language in *Buckley* that emphasized that the contribution limitation was only a "marginal restriction" because it still permitted "the symbolic expression of support evidenced by a contribution" even if the contribution would not be a significant one. Thus, they reasoned, because the statutes at issue in *Penn*, like in this case, prohibit contribution, they did not allow a "symbolic expression of support" and were therefore unconstitutional.

What the majority of the court in *Penn* failed to realize is that under La. R.S. 18:1505.2(L), as pointed out by the Attorney General's office and the Counsel for the Supervisory Committee on Campaign Finance Disclosure in their brief to this Court, the parties prohibited from making campaign contributions to a candidate or political committee of a candidate can still make *unlimited independent expenditures* supporting or opposing a candidate. This allows much more room for political expression and association than the statute involved in *Buckley*, where the statute also limited campaign expenditures. In this case, there is no need to resort to finding a right to "the symbolic expression of support evidenced by a contribution," however small, to save this statute from the doom of unconstitutionality, as these parties still have the full right to political expression and association by making unlimited political expenditures in favor of the candidate of their choice. In addition, they have the same rights the Court recognized as significant in *Buckley, i.e.*, they can still become a member of a political association and personally assist in the association's effort on behalf of candidates; they can still urge their employees to support or oppose particular candidates; they may still openly support individual candidates by displaying yard signs and voluntarily working in political campaigns; and they may sponsor phone banks to encourage persons to vote.

Furthermore, there is no indication in *Buckley* that a contribution limit of zero, as opposed to a contribution limit of $1,000.00, would be unconstitutional. In fact, since *Penn*, the United States Supreme Court has clarified and explained the holding in *Buckley*, and has specifically addressed the issue of what limit would possibly be too low to withstand constitutional scrutiny. In Nixon v. Shrink Mo. Gov't PAC, the Court held that *Buckley* was authority for state limits on contributions to state political candidates but that the state limits did not need to be "pegged to *Buckley's* dollars." 528 U.S. 377, 381 (2000).[9] The *Shrink Missouri* court clearly stated that "[i]n *Buckley*, we specifically rejected the contention that $1,000 *or any other amount*, was a constitutional minimum below which the legislatures could not regulate." *Id.*, 528 U.S. at 397 (emphasis added). The Court set out the proper standard for determining when a minimum might be too low to withstand constitutional scrutiny as follows:

> As indicated above, [in *Buckley*] we referred instead to the outer limits of contribution regulation by asking whether there was any showing that the limits were so low as to impede the ability of candidates to "amass the resources necessary for effective advocacy." 424 U.S. at 21. We asked, in other words, whether the contribution limitation was so radical in effect as to render political association ineffective, drive the sound of a candidate's voice below the level of notice, and render the contributions pointless. Such being the test, the issue in later cases cannot be truncated to a narrow question about the power of the dollar, but must go to mount a campaign with all the dollars likely to be forthcoming. *Id.*

---

9. *Shrink Missouri* involved a Missouri statute which imposed contribution limits ranging from $250 to $1,000, subject to adjustment each even-numbered year based the cumulative consumer price index.

Unlike the across-the-board restrictions involved in *Buckley* and *Shrink Missouri,* the restrictions in this case involve just one licensed land-based casino and 15 licensed riverboat gaming facilities throughout Louisiana. Thus, clearly, in this case, the ban will have a very minimal effect on the candidates' ability "to amass the resources necessary for effective advocacy." *Id.*

We must also point out that seven other states have enacted statutes that *prohibit* campaign contributions by certain gaming interests.[10] Further, three other states' appellate courts that have considered whether a complete prohibition on campaign contributions, rather than a monetary limitation, is constitutional in light of *Buckley* have answered in the affirmative. State v. ACLU, 978 P.2d 597 (Ala. 1999), *cert. denied,* 528 U.S. 1153, (2000) (upholding complete ban on campaign contributions by out-of-district lobbyists); In re Petition of Soto, 236 N.J. Super. 303, 565 A.2d 1088 (1989), *certif. denied,* 121 N.J. 608, 583 A.2d 310 (1990), *cert. denied,* 496 U.S. 937 (1990) (upholding New Jersey's complete ban on campaign contributions by gaming interests; Louisiana's statute is based on this, *see* pp. 506–507, *infra*);[11] Schiller Park Colonial Inn, Inc. v. Berz, 63 Ill.2d 499, 349 N.E.2d 61 (1976) (upholding complete ban on campaign contributions by liquor licensees or their representatives).[12] In addition, two federal courts have upheld complete bans on campaign contributions by lobbyists, both holding that the fact that the contribution restrictions were bans, rather that monetary limits, did not render them unconstitutional under *Buckley.* North Carolina Right to Life, Inc. v. Bartlett, 168 F.3d 705 (4th Cir. 1999), *cert. denied,* 528 U.S. 1153 (2000); Inst. of Governmental Advocates v. Fair Political Practices Comm'n, 164 F. Supp.2d 1183 (E.D. Cal. 2001). Finally, corporate contributions to candidates and candidate committees have long been prohibited completely at the federal level. 2 U.S.C. § 441b(a). Twenty-two states also ban corporate contributions. *See, generally,* Chart 2A, Federal Election Commission, E. Feigenbaum & J. Palmer, Campaign Finance Law 98 (1998).

Thus, contrary to the concurring opinions' viewpoints that carried the day in *Penn,* we find the fact that the campaign contribution ban found in La. 18:1505.2(L)(2) is a

---

10. Indiana, Ind. Stats. 4-33-10-21.1 (prohibits contributions from any officer or person who holds an interest in a gaming entity); Iowa, Iowa Stats. 99F.6(4)(a) (prohibits contributions from riverboat gambling corporations); Kentucky, Rev. Stats. 154(a).160 (prohibits contributions from persons owning lottery contracts); Michigan, Mich. Stats. 7(b)(4)-(5) (prohibits contributions from any licensee or person who has an interest in a gaming entity); Nebraska, Neb. Stats. 49-1469.01 (prohibits contributions from lottery contractors for duration of contract and three years after); New Jersey § 5:12-138 (prohibits contributions from casino officers or key employees); Virginia, § 59.1-375, 376 (prohibits contributions from pari-mutual corporations, executives and their spouses and families).

11. In *Petition of Soto,* a casino employee challenged the constitutionality of a New Jersey statute that prohibited any casino key employee from contributing any money or thing of value to any political candidate or committee of any political party. In holding the statute constitutional, the court found a compelling state interest in preventing the appearance of impropriety given the "acknowledged vulnerability of the casino industry to organized crime and the compelling interest in maintaining the public trust, not only in the casino industry but also the governmental process which so closely regulates it." 565 A.2d at 1098. In addition, the court found that the statute had been narrowly drawn and precisely tailored, commenting that gambling "is an activity rife with evil" and that it was the pronounced policy of the State "to regulate and control the casino industry with the utmost strictness." *Id.*

12. Other courts have also upheld campaign contribution restrictions of certain regulated industries and professions. *See* Blount v. SEC, 61 F.3d 938, 941–48 (D.C. Cir.1995) (upholding regulation restricting ability of municipal securities professionals to contribute to or solicit contributions for political campaigns of elected officials from whom they may obtain business).

prohibition on contributions, rather than a *limitation,* does not render it per se unconstitutional under *Buckley.* Instead, the restriction is to analyzed under the burden of proof enunciated in *Buckley,* as clarified in by later Supreme Court cases, i.e., "that a contribution limit involving 'significant interference' with associational rights, could survive if the Government demonstrated that the contribution regulation was "closely drawn" to match a "sufficiently important interest ..." *Shrink Missouri,* 528 U.S. at 387–88 (citing *Buckley,* 424 U.S. at 25).

In order to conduct this analysis, we must get to the heart of the matter, the history of gambling in Louisiana. This history was ably explained by Justice Knoll in her dissent in *Penn:*

> The Louisiana Constitution of 1879 declared gambling a "vice" and the Legislature was directed to enact laws for its suppression. LA. CONST. art. 172 (1879). Louisiana's Constitutions of 1898, 1913, and 1921 all contained similar provisions regarding gambling. See LA. CONST. art. 19, Sec. 8 (1921); LA. CONST. arts. 178, 188, 189 (1913); LA. CONST. arts. 178, 188, 189 (1898). Although the delegates to the Constitutional Convention which convened on January 5, 1973, eliminated the moral condemnation of gambling and chose to suppress gambling rather than prohibit it, it is clear that the Legislature continued its role of defining gambling. Polk v. Edwards, 626 So.2d 1128, 1141 (La. 1993). Thus, the Louisiana electorate ratified the Constitution of 1974 which followed its predecessor documents with the inclusion of article XII, Sec. 6(B) that "gambling shall be defined by and suppressed by the Legislature." In order to understand the reasons for these constitutional declarations throughout the period of Louisiana's statehood, reference to the history of gambling in this State is essential.

> Historically, gambling has been recognized as a vice activity which poses a threat to public health and public morals. Although the vice of gambling existed throughout the State during the eighteenth and nineteenth centuries, New Orleans was recognized as the gambling capital. See Timothy L. O'Brien, *Bad Bet: The Inside Story of the Glamour, Glitz, and Danger of America's Gambling Industry* (1998). The State outlawed gambling in 1812, but New Orleans received a special exemption that allowed gambling to continue.

> When federal troops occupied New Orleans from 1862 to 1877, the Louisiana Lottery Company, a private corporation, went into business. O'Brien, *supra,* at 105–106. Even though the Constitution had previously declared lotteries illegal, a constitutional amendment was passed in 1866 and the Louisiana Lottery Corporation was given a 25-year charter to operate. *Id.* The Lottery was marketed nationwide via the mail and branch offices and by 1890 was taking in $28 million yearly. *Id.* at 106–107. Lottery proceeds not only paid for the first waterworks in New Orleans, but this lucre supported the New Orleans charity hospital and upgraded the public schools. *Id.* at 107; Stephanie A. Martz, *Note, Legalized Gambling and Public Corruption: Removing the Incentive to Act Corruptly, or, Teaching an Old Dog New Tricks,* 13 J.L. & Pol. 453, 458–59 (1997). In 1893, the federal government intervened in the Louisiana Lottery and passed a law prohibiting any form of lottery sales and promotion. Martz, *supra* at 459.

> Gambling remained available in New Orleans during the first decades of the twentieth century in small establishments around the city, even though the Constitution had outlawed all gambling. *O'Brien, supra,* at 108. In 1934, Huey P.

Long allowed slot machines in New Orleans and several casinos outside the city. *Id.* In the 1950s a reform movement ran the larger casinos away, but the slot machines and back-alley casinos stayed in business until the 1970s. *Id.* at 109.

With the boom of the petrochemical industry during the 1970s and 1980s, the State's economy was revitalized. *Id.* There was no longer a need for gambling proceeds to fund government projects, that is until the bottom fell out of the oil industry. *See Id.* However, when the State's economy went into a tailspin with the decline in the oil industry, the State Legislature, armed with its constitutional authority to "define gambling," turned to legalized gambling as a means out of the fiscal doldrums. *See Id.* In a series of enactments in 1991 and 1992, the Legislature passed four acts providing for the licensing of gaming, to-wit: at a land-based casino in New Orleans, La. R.S. 4:601-686; on cruise ships operating out of New Orleans, La. R.S. 14:90(B); on river boats operating on designated rivers in the state, La. R.S. 4:501-562; and by means of video poker machines located throughout the State, La. R.S. 33:4862.1-19.

In *Polk*, although this Court upheld the power of the Legislature to provide for the licensing of gaming, it further recognized that the Legislature's authority to regulate gambling constitutes a legitimate exercise of police power. *Id.* at 1137; see also Theriot v. Terrebonne Parish Police Jury, 436 So.2d 515, 516 (La. 1983); State v. Mustachia, 152 La. 821, 94 So. 408 (1922); Ruston v. Perkins, 114 La. 851, 38 So. 583 (1905). "Defining and prescribing means of suppression are left to the state Legislature and the legislative determination in this regard constitutes an appropriate exercise of police power for the protection of the public." *Theriot,* 436 So.2d at 521. Moreover, in *Polk* this Court further held that the power to suppress gambling and "to determine how, when, where, and in what respects gambling shall be prohibited or permitted" has been constitutionally delegated to the Legislature. *Polk,* 626 So.2d at 1128.

In 1996, the Legislature, pursuant to its constitutional mandate to define and suppress gambling, enacted the Louisiana Gaming Control Law, La. R.S. 27:1-:392. From the outset, the legislation announced the public policy of this State concerning gaming. In La. R.S. 27:2(A), the Legislature stated:

The legislature hereby finds and declares it to be the public policy of the state that the development of a controlled gaming industry to promote economic development of the state requires thorough and careful exercise of legislative power to protect the general welfare of the state's people by keeping the state free from criminal and corrupt elements. The legislature further finds and declares it to be the public policy of the state that to this all persons, locations, practices, associations, and activities related to the operation of licensed and qualified gaming establishments and the manufacture, supply, or distribution of gaming devices and equipment shall be strictly regulated.

This legislation further declared that any license, casino operating contract, permit, approval, or thing obtained or issued pursuant to the provisions of this Title or any other law relative to the jurisdiction of the board is expressly declared by the legislature to be a pure and absolute revocable privilege and not a right, property or otherwise, under the constitution of the United States or of the state of Louisiana.

La. R.S. 27:2(B); *see also* Catanese v. Louisiana Gaming Control Bd., 712 So.2d 666, 670 (La. App. 1998), *writ denied,* 726 So.2d 30 (La. 1998); Eicher v. Louisiana

State Police, Riverboat Gaming Enforcement Div., 710 So.2d 799, 807 (La. App. 1998), *writ denied*, 719 So.2d 51 (La. 1998).

In the same legislative session, the Legislature enacted La. R.S. 18:1505.2(L) relative to campaign finance.

Penn, supra at 849 (Knoll, J., dissenting).

With this background in mind, the legislative intent behind the enactment of this statute can be easily gleaned from the legislative committee meeting notes. *See* Committee on Senate and Governmental Affairs, Verbatim Transcript Meeting of March 26, 1996, Senate Bill 12 by Senator Dardenne. Senator Dardenne introduced the bill with the following information:

> … we're attempting to track as well in this legislation what was done in New Jersey [an obvious reference to the *Soto* case] which is the only state we know of that has imposed a statutory ban on gambling contributions.
>
> …
>
> … I think unfortunately we can make a strong argument in Louisiana that there is a compelling state interest to prevent the gambling industry from making contributions and there has been unfortunate data that would support that based upon some investigations that have been underway and the problems we've seen.…
>
> …
>
> … I think that this industry stands onto itself and ought to stand onto itself as one that we ought to be singling out for the purpose of trying to limit their involvement in the legislative process and unfortunately I think it is appropriate to look to what has happened over the course of the past couple of years specifically on how individuals within the industry have been accused of attempting to influence the legislative process based upon the industry's entry into the state.… it is directed to specifically at the gambling industry and to say we believe in Louisiana; we ought to limit the gambling industry's influence in the political process.
>
> …
>
> … I will say this about this particular bill. I don't know of any other industry that was singled out in the past campaign as something for the public to look at when you had gubernatorial candidates, you had legislative candidates saying I'm not going to take money from the gambling industry or making a campaign issue over where contributions came from. This is a major, major source of concern in the minds of the public from my viewpoint as to what influence the gambling industry has had over this legislature and this government during its infancy in Louisiana and I think it is an appropriate bill to advance in the legislature to say that we are going to say it is not appropriate for the gambling industry to be making political contributions.

Id.

As stated in *Shrink Missouri*, the Court in *Buckley* found "the prevention of corruption and the appearance of corruption" to be a "constitutionally sufficient justification" for campaign contribution restrictions. 528 U.S. at 388 (citing *Buckley*, 424 U.S. at 25–26). The obvious purpose behind the statute at issue in this case is the prevention of corruption and the appearance of corruption by the gaming industry upon the political process, and under *Buckley* and *Shrink Missouri*, this is a constitutionally sufficient justification for the campaign contribution restrictions.

The gaming interests argue that the statute is unconstitutional because it has an unlawful purpose, as stated in the statute, "to prevent influence and the appearance of influence of candidates for public office and of the election process by special interests." La. R.S. 18:1505.2(L)(2). They argue that preventing "influence" or the "appearance of influence" is not a recognized legitimate governmental interest under *Buckley* and its progeny. However, a clear reading of the statute in light of the history of gambling in this State along with the legislative history of the statute leaves no doubt that the purpose of the statute is to prohibit the corruption and appearance of corruption which the legislature has determined will not be permitted in the highly regulated gaming industry. As the Court explained in *Shrink Missouri:*

> In speaking of "improper influence" and "opportunities for abuse" in addition to "quid pro quo arrangements," we recognized a concern not confined to bribery of public officials, but extending to the broader threat from politicians too compliant with the wishes of large contributors. These were the obvious points behind our recognition that the Congress could constitutionally address the power of money "to influence governmental action" in ways less "blatant and specific" than bribery.

Shrink Missouri, supra at 389, *(citing Buckley,* 424 U.S. at 28).[13]

The gaming interests also argue that the government's burden to show that a speech restriction actually advances the asserted governmental interest is not satisfied by mere speculation or conjecture, and that instead, the government must demonstrate that the harms it recites are real and that its restriction will in fact alleviate them to a material degree. This proposition was also offered by Justice Johnson in support of her concurring opinion in *Penn.* However, *Shrink Missouri* specifically rejected this proposition in the context of campaign contribution restrictions, holding that "as to [what is necessary as a minimum evidentiary showing], respondents are wrong in arguing that in the years since *Buckley* came down we have 'supplemented' its holding with a new requirement that governments enacting contribution limits must 'demonstrate that the recited harms are real, not merely conjectural ...'" *Id.,* 528 U.S. at 391–92. The Court held that "the quantum of empirical evidence needed to satisfy heightened judicial scrutiny of legislative judgments will vary up or down with the novelty and plausibility of the justification raised." *Id.*

Evidence provided to the trial court in this case included affidavits outlining the public perception that gaming is associated with political corruption, information that within the last ten years, nine states (including Louisiana) have prosecuted governmental officials in gaming cases, and statistics showing the staggering sum of money collected by those within the gaming industry. This evidence illustrates why the legislature found it was imperative to prohibit campaign contributions from persons engaged in the gaming industry. Given the history of the gaming industry and its connection to public corruption and the appearance of public corruption, it is completely plausible, and not at all novel, for the Louisiana legislature to have concluded that it was necessary to distance gaming interests from the ability to contribute to candidates and political committees which support candidates. *See also Shrink Missouri,* 528 U.S. at 390 (*"Buckley* demonstrates that the dangers of large, corrupt contributions and the suspicion that large contributions are corrupt are neither novel nor implausible").

---

13. *See also* Federal Election Comm'n v. National Conservative Political Action Comm., 470 U.S. 480, 497 (1985) ("Corruption is a subversion of the political process. Elected officials are influenced to act contrary to their obligations of office by the prospect of financial gain to themselves or infusions of money into their campaigns").

The United States Supreme Court has also repeatedly rejected the gaming interests' argument that the statute is not "closely drawn" to support a sufficiently important government interest because there are less restrictive measures on the books, such as contribution limits,[14] disclosure laws[15] and anti-bribery statutes, that would solve the problem that this more restrictive statute seeks to address. The *Buckley* Court rejected the argument that the contribution limits must be invalidated because bribery laws and narrowly drawn disclosure requirements constitute a less restrictive means of dealing with the problem, finding that bribery laws only criminalize the most blatant attempts to influence governmental action and that Congress was entitled to conclude that the disclosure provisions were only a partial measure. *Buckley, supra,* 424 U.S. at 27–28. The Court concluded that the Act's contribution limitation "focuses precisely on the problem of large campaign contributions—the narrow aspect of political association where the actuality and potential for corruption have been identified—while leaving persons free to engage in independent political expression, to associate actively through volunteering their services, and to assist to a limited but nonetheless substantial extent in supporting candidates and committees with financial resources." *Id.; see also Shrink Missouri, supra,* 528 U.S. at 396; *California Medical Ass'n, supra,* 453 U.S. at 199, n.20 (concluding that a limit on the amount that unincorporated associations could contribute to political committees was not required to be the least restrictive means of accomplishing the intent of the statute and that Congress could have reasonably concluded that the statute was a useful supplement to other anti-fraud provisions).

For the same reasons, we also reject the gaming interests' argument that the statute serves no legitimate purpose because other statutes, such as La. R.S. 27:310(B)-(C) already impose rigorous background checks and strict licensing restrictions on gaming interests, guaranteeing that anyone who obtains a gaming interest is "suitable" and honest.

Further, we note that there are significant differences between the video poker industry, as addressed in *Penn,* and the riverboat and land-based casino gaming industries. For example, there are no limits on the number of persons who may be licensed to operate video poker in this state. In contrast, the Legislature has authorized only a single land-based casino and only 15 riverboats. La. R.S. 27:241 and 27:65. Another notable distinction is that the prohibitions at issue in *Penn* did not apply equally to all persons engaged in the video poker industry. *Penn, supra* at 830 (Johnson, J., concurring). In contrast, the restrictions applicable to those involved in the riverboat and land-based casino gaming industries are uniform.

CONCLUSION

Restrictions on campaign contributions operate in an area protected by the First Amendment, particularly the right of freedom of association. However, a campaign contribution restriction, including a complete ban on campaign contributions, can withstand constitutional scrutiny if the State demonstrates a sufficiently important interest and employs means closely drawn to avoid unnecessary abridgment of associational freedoms. Thus, under *Buckley* and its progeny, we find that the campaign contribution restrictions on the riverboat and land-based casino gaming industries are closely drawn to match a sufficiently important interest in that they focus precisely on the problem of campaign contributions by the gaming industry—the narrow aspect of political association where the actuality and potential for corruption have been identified—while leaving such persons free to engage in independent political expression, to associate actively

---

14. La. R.S. 18:1505.2(H)(1)(a).
15. La. R.S. 18:1482 *et seq.*

through volunteering their services, and to assist to a substantial extent in supporting candidates and committees by making independent expenditures.[16] Therefore, we find that the provisions of La. R.S. 18:1505.2(L) which prohibit riverboat and land-based casino gaming interests from making campaign contributions to candidates or to political committees of candidates do not violate the First Amendment.[17]

DECREE

For the foregoing reasons, we reverse the judgment of the trial court and uphold the constitutionality of La. R.S. 18:1505.2(L)(3)(a)(ii) and La. R.S. 18:1505.2(L)(3)(b)(c)(e), insofar as they are applicable to La. R.S. 18:1505.2(L)(3)(a)(ii) and (iii), as well as 42 LA ADC Pt. IX, § 2941, insofar as it applies to the owners of any holding company of the casino gaming operator, their affiliated companies, and all of their officers, directors, partners, senior management and key employees.

REVERSED.

CALOGERO, C.J., dissents and assigns reasons.

KIMBALL, J., dissents and assigns reasons.

JOHNSON, J., dissents and assigns reasons.

CALOGERO, Chief Justice, dissents and assigns reasons.

Notes

1. Other courts have addressed similar limitations on campaign contributions. In De-Paul v. Commonwealth, 969 A.2d 536 (Pa. 2009), the Supreme Court of Pennsylvania considered a claim by a person who held an interest in a business entity that was planning to build a casino within the state. Under Pennsylvania law, there was an absolute ban on state political contributions by specified individuals in the gaming industry. The court held that this absolute limitation violated provisions of the Pennsylvania Constitution guaranteeing rights of freedom of expression and association. For a discussion of these issues, *see* Bonny Bumiller, *Legalized Gaming and Political Contributions: When the Ice-*

---

16. Having found no First Amendment violation in the provisions of La. R.S. 18:1505.2(L) which prohibit riverboat gaming and land based casino interests from making campaign contributions, we need not address the argument that the statute conflicts with the "doctrine of unconstitutional conditions." *See* 44 Liquormart v. Rhode Island, 517 U.S. 484, 513 (1996).

17. The riverboat and land-based casino gaming interests also argue that the statutes at issue are violative of the equal protection clause of the Fourteenth Amendment. They argue that the statute respects the right of some persons to associate and speak in support of political candidates, but strips that right from others, i.e., those who work in the gaming industry. The trial court did not address this issue, specifically stating "[h]aving found that La. R.S. 18:1505.2(L)(a)(ii) and La. R.S. 18:1505.2(L)(3)(b)(c)(e), insofar as they are applicable to La. R.S. 18:1505.2(L)(3)(a)(ii), are unconstitutional [under the First and Fourteenth Amendments], there is no need for this Court to address the Equal Protection arguments of the parties."

Article V, Section 5(F) of the Louisiana Constitution provides that if the Supreme Court has appellate jurisdiction under Section 5, then that jurisdiction *may* extend over all issues involved in the civil action before it. "However, this Court has repeatedly interpreted Article V, Section 5(F) to mean that our appellate jurisdiction does not extend over *all* issues raised in the plaintiff's petition, but only those on which the trial court has ruled." Cat's Meow, Inc. v. City of New Orleans Through Dept. of Finance, 720 So.2d 1186, 1199 (La. 1998); Church Point Wholesale Beverage Co. v. Tarver, 614 So.2d 697 (La. 1993). Accordingly, because the trial court specifically did not rule on the allegation that the statute at issue violated the equal protection clause of the Fourteenth Amendment, this Court is without jurisdiction under Article V to rule on this issue on direct appeal.

man Cometh, Will Corruption Goeth?, 40 J. Marshall L. Rev. 1089 (2007); Colin A. Black, Brown v. State: *The Louisiana Supreme Court Considers Free Speech, Campaign Finance, and Legalized Gambling*, 71 Tul. L. Rev. 1593 (1997); Stephanie A. Martz, Note, *Legalized Gambling and Public Corruption: Removing the Incentive to Act Corruptly, or, Teaching an Old Dog New Tricks*, 13 J.L. & Pol. 453 (1997).

2. In Citizens United v. Federal Election Commission, 130 S. Ct. 876 (2010), the United States Supreme Court held that political spending is protected under the First Amendment as a form of speech. This means that government may not prohibit corporations or unions from spending money to support or oppose individual candidates in elections. Though corporations or unions may not give money directly to campaigns, they may seek to persuade the voting public through other means, including political ads. Does the *Citizens United* decision call into question limitations on corporations or individuals in the gaming sector from likewise engaging in this form of speech?

B. Other Protections

i. Conflicts of Interest Regulations

Michigan Gaming Control & Revenue Act of 1997 — (PA 69)

Section 4d: Member, employee, or agent of board; conduct generally

432.204d Member, employee, or agent of board; conduct generally.

Sec. 4d. (1) By January 31 of each year, each member of the board shall prepare and file with the office of the board, a board disclosure form in which the member does all of the following:

(a) Affirms that the member or the member's spouse, parent, child, or child's spouse is not a member of the board of directors of, financially interested in, or employed by a licensee or applicant.

(b) Affirms that the member continues to meet any other criteria for board membership under this act or the rules promulgated by the board.

(c) Discloses any legal or beneficial interests in any real property that is or that may be directly or indirectly involved with gaming or gaming operations authorized by this act.

(d) Discloses any other information as may be required to ensure that the integrity of the board and its work is maintained.

(2) By January 31 of each year, each employee of the board shall prepare and file with the office of the board an employee disclosure form in which the employee does all of the following:

(a) Affirms the absence of financial interests prohibited by this act.

(b) Discloses any legal or beneficial interests in any real property that is or that may be directly or indirectly involved with gaming or gaming operations authorized by this act.

(c) Discloses whether the employee or the employee's spouse, parent, child, or child's spouse is financially interested in or employed by a supplier licensee or an applicant for a supplier's license under this act.

(d) Discloses such other matters as may be required to ensure that the integrity of the board and its work is maintained.

(3) A member, employee, or agent of the board who becomes aware that the member, employee, or agent of the board or his or her spouse, parent, or child is a member of the board of directors of, financially interested in, or employed by a licensee or an applicant shall immediately provide detailed written notice thereof to the chairperson.

(4) A member, employee, or agent of the board who has been indicted, charged with, convicted of, pled guilty or nolo contendre to, or forfeited bail concerning a misdemeanor involving gambling, dishonesty, theft, or fraud or a local ordinance in any state involving gambling, dishonesty, theft, or fraud that substantially corresponds to a misdemeanor in that state, or a felony under Michigan law, the laws of any other state, or the laws of the United States, or any other jurisdiction shall immediately provide detailed written notice of the conviction or charge to the chairperson.

(5) Any member, employee, or agent of the board who is negotiating for, or acquires by any means, any interest in any person who is a licensee or an applicant, or any person affiliated with such a person, shall immediately provide written notice of the details of the interest to the chairperson. The member, employee, or agent of the board shall not act on behalf of the board with respect to that person.

(6) A member, employee, or agent of the board may not enter into any negotiations for employment with any person or affiliate of any person who is a licensee or an applicant, and shall immediately provide written notice of the details of any such negotiations or discussions to the chairperson. The member, employee, or agent of the board shall not take any action on behalf of the board with respect to that person.

(7) Any member, employee, or agent of the board who receives an invitation, written or oral, to initiate a discussion concerning employment or the possibility of employment with a person or affiliate of a person who is a licensee or an applicant shall immediately report that he or she received the invitation to the chairperson. The member, employee, or agent of the board shall not take action on behalf of the board with respect to the person.

(8) A licensee or applicant shall not knowingly initiate a negotiation for or discussion of employment with a member, employee, or agent of the board. A licensee or applicant who initiates a negotiation or discussion about employment shall immediately provide written notice of the details of the negotiation or discussion to the chairperson as soon as he or she becomes aware that the negotiation or discussion has been initiated with a member, employee, or agent of the board.

(9) A member, employee, or agent of the board, or former member, employee, or agent of the board, shall not disseminate or otherwise disclose any material or information in the possession of the board that the board considers confidential unless specifically authorized to do so by the chairperson or the board.

(10) A member, employee, or agent of the board or a parent, spouse, sibling, spouse of a sibling, child, or spouse of a child of a member, employee, or agent of the board may not accept any gift, gratuity, compensation, travel, lodging, or anything of value, directly or indirectly, from any licensee or any applicant or affiliate or representative of an applicant or licensee, unless the acceptance conforms to a written policy or directive that is issued by the chairperson or the board. Any member, employee, or agent of the board who is offered or receives any gift, gratuity, compensation, travel, lodging, or anything of value, directly or indirectly, from any licensee or any applicant or affiliate or representative of an applicant or licensee shall immediately provide written notification of the details to the chairperson.

(11) A licensee or applicant, or affiliate or representative of an applicant or licensee, may not, directly or indirectly, give or offer to give any gift, gratuity, compensation, travel,

lodging, or anything of value to any member, employee, or agent of the board which the member, employee, or agent of the board is prohibited from accepting under subsection (10).

(12) A member, employee, or agent of the board shall not engage in any conduct that constitutes a conflict of interest, and shall immediately advise the chairperson in writing of the details of any incident or circumstances that would present the existence of a conflict of interest with respect to the performance of the board-related work or duty of the member, employee, or agent of the board.

(13) A member, employee, or agent of the board who is approached and offered a bribe in violation of section 118 of the Michigan penal code, 1931 PA 328, MCL 750.118, or this act shall immediately provide written account of the details of the incident to the chairperson and to a law enforcement officer of a law enforcement agency having jurisdiction.

(14) A member, employee, or agent of the board shall disclose his or her past involvement with any casino interest in the past 5 years and shall not engage in political activity or politically related activity during the duration of his or her appointment or employment.

(15) A former member, employee, or agent of the board may appear before the board as a fact witness about matters or actions handled by the member, employee, or agent during his or her tenure as a member, employee, or agent of the board. The member, employee, or agent of the board shall not receive compensation for such an appearance other than a standard witness fee and reimbursement for travel expenses as established by statute or court rule.

(16) A licensee or applicant or any affiliate or representative of an applicant or licensee shall not engage in ex parte communications with a member of the board. A member of the board shall not engage in any ex parte communications with a licensee or an applicant or with any affiliate or representative of an applicant or licensee.

(17) Any board member, licensee, or applicant or affiliate or representative of a board member, licensee, or applicant who receives any ex parte communication in violation of subsection (16), or who is aware of an attempted communication in violation of subsection (16), shall immediately report details of the communication or attempted communication in writing to the chairperson.

(18) Any member of the board who receives an ex parte communication which attempts to influence that member's official action shall disclose the source and content of the communication to the chairperson. The chairperson may investigate or initiate an investigation of the matter with the assistance of the attorney general and state police to determine if the communication violates subsection (16) or subsection (17) or other state law. The disclosure under this section and the investigation shall remain confidential. Following an investigation, the chairperson shall advise the governor or the board, or both, of the results of the investigation and may recommend action as the chairperson considers appropriate.

(19) A new or current employee or agent of the board shall obtain written permission from the executive director before continuing outside employment held at the time the employee begins to work for the board. Permission shall be denied, or permission previously granted will be revoked, if the nature of the work is considered to or does create a possible conflict of interest or otherwise interferes with the duties of the employee or agent for the board.

(20) An employee or agent of the board granted permission for outside employment shall not conduct any business or perform any activities, including solicitation, related to out-

side employment on premises used by the board or during the employee's working hours for the board.

(21) Whenever the chairperson, as an employee of the board, is required to file disclosure forms or report in writing the details of any incident or circumstance pursuant to this section, he or she shall make such filings or written reports to the board.

(22) The chairperson shall report any action he or she has taken or contemplates taking under this section with respect to an employee or agent or former employee or former agent to the board at the next meeting of the board. The board may direct the executive director to take additional or different action.

(23) Except as follows, no member, employee, or agent of the board may participate in or wager on any gambling game conducted by any licensee or applicant or any affiliate of an applicant or licensee in Michigan or in any other jurisdiction:

(a) A member, employee, or agent of the board may participate in and wager on a gambling game conducted by a licensee under this act, to the extent authorized by the chairperson or board as part of the person's surveillance, security, or other official duties for the board.

(b) A member, employee, or agent of the board shall advise the chairperson at least 24 hours in advance if he or she plans to be present in a casino in this state or in another jurisdiction operated by a licensee or applicant, or affiliate of a licensee or an applicant, outside the scope of his or her official duties for the board.

(24) Violation of this section by a licensee or applicant, or affiliate or representative of a licensee or applicant, may result in denial of the application of licensure or revocation or suspension of license or other disciplinary action by the board.

(25) Violation of this section by a member of the board may result in disqualification or constitute cause for removal under section 4(7) or other disciplinary action as determined by the board.

(26) A violation of this section by an employee or agent of the board will not result in termination of employment if the board determines that the conduct involved does not violate the purpose of this act, or require other disciplinary action, including termination of employment. However, employment will be terminated as follows:

(a) If, after being offered employment or beginning employment with the board, the employee or agent intentionally acquires a financial interest in a licensee or an applicant, or affiliate or representative of a licensee or applicant, employment with the board shall be terminated.

(b) If a financial interest in a licensee or an applicant, or affiliate or representative of a licensee or applicant, is acquired by an employee or agent that has been offered employment with the board, an employee of the board, or the employee's or agent's spouse, parent, or child, through no intentional action of the employee or agent, the individual shall have up to 30 days to divest or terminate the financial interest. Employment may be terminated if the interest has not been divested after 30 days.

(c) Employment shall be terminated if the employee or agent is a spouse, parent, child, or spouse of a child of a board member.

(27) Violation of this section does not create a civil cause of action.

(28) As used in this section:

(a) "Outside employment" includes, but is not limited to, the following:

(i) Operation of a proprietorship.

(*ii*) Participation in a partnership or group business enterprise.

(*iii*) Performance as a director or corporate officer of any for-profit corporation or banking or credit institution.

(b) "Political activity" or "politically related activity" includes all of the following:

(*i*) Using his or her official authority or influence for the purpose of interfering with or affecting the result of an election.

(*ii*) Knowingly soliciting, accepting, or receiving a political contribution from any person.

(*iii*) Running for the nomination or as a candidate for election to a partisan political office.

(*iv*) Knowingly soliciting or discouraging the participation in any political activity of any person who is either of the following:

(A) Applying for any compensation, grant, contract, ruling, license, permit, or certificate pending before the board.

(B) The subject of or a participant in an ongoing audit, investigation, or enforcement action being carried out by the board.

Notes

1. Prohibiting a regulator from having an interest in a licensed casino operation is a common feature of most regulatory systems. This prohibition usually extends to a financial interest, including ownership or employment. The latter may create a problem where regulators are part-time government employees. Conflict-of-interest rules often extend beyond those that would disqualify a person from being a regulator. For example, suppose the regulator is an accountant, and his firm had done work for a person appearing before the agency. This might be a conflict of interest requiring the regulator to disqualify himself from considering the matter.

2. Simply being employed in the casino industry before appointment should not necessarily be a disqualification. Having regulators who have gained experience and knowledge through their previous employment may provide substantial benefit to the regulatory agency. Appointing only persons with no prior gaming experience to the regulatory agency would be the equivalent of appointing only persons to judgeships who have never practiced law. Moreover, by only appointing persons who were employed as agents to regulatory agencies, government may narrow the perception of the agency.

3. A background check of candidates for regulatory positions may reveal risks involved in appointments to sensitive positions of public trust. Such background checks are common for appointments to judicial office. They are similar to the background investigation conducted on applicants for casino licenses, and may involve the same criteria, such as honesty, criminal history, associations with unsuitable persons, and management abilities. The investigation also may include review of financial and familial information to assure no conflicts of interest exist.

4. A seasoned and concrete policy on complimentaries is more important in gaming than most other industries, because the giving of complimentaries is common practice and authority to give them often extends to low level employees. Preventing casinos from giving certain gifts or complimentaries to regulators and staff is without serious debate. What is questioned is the threshold for prohibiting such gifts.

5. Political influence over regulatory action is more likely if the regulators that sit on a multi-member board are from the same political party. Decisions of the agency may

reflect a political bias toward supporters of that political party and against those of opposing political parties. Requiring the membership of a multi-member regulator agency to reflect at least minority membership from different political parties may further the independence of the agency. Such requirements, however, may result in a less qualified person being appointed to the agency because the more qualified person is prohibited because of his political party affiliation.

6. Usually the legislature decides the jurisdiction's budget and allocates funding to the various government programs based on how it believes the funds can be best spent. Under this system, the legislature is politically accountable to the voting public for the spending of public funds. Because this system results in the legislature deciding the budget of the regulatory agency, it allows the legislature to assert some influence over the agency. To many, this would not appear problematic because the agency is under a directive to attempt to achieve the policy goals established by the legislature. If the legislature, as a whole, uses the funding process to indicate that the agency is not meeting its expectations, then this may serve as a valuable check on the power and direction of the agency. More problematic, however, is when the legislature is fragmented and a particular member of the legislature effectively controls the funding for the regulatory agency. This may occur where the person is a powerful chair of an appropriations committee. Moreover, unlike a chief executive who is elected by and answerable to all the voters, the powerful legislator needs only to answer to his or her constituency. This leaves the possibility that that legislator can influence regulatory actions or policy for her own benefit or the benefit of the region that she represents. This problem, however, is one that is not unique to regulatory agencies and can affect all agencies and legislation. It must be addressed in the method that the jurisdiction uses to establish budgets. To avoid both the political influence from the legislature and specific legislators, New Jersey attempted to protect its Gaming Commission by having its funding come from a casino control fund derived from gaming taxes. Robert P. Culleton, *The Implementation of the Credit Controls of the 1977 New Jersey Casino Control Act, in* GAMBLING & PUB. POL'Y 203 (1991). This funding method poses two problems. First, it may create a built-in inefficiency because the Commission may feel it needs to use all the funds available even if they exceed what is needed to effectively regulate the industry. Second, no political accountability exists for the spending of government funds. No one reviews whether the funds spent to achieve a particular goal were excessive or could have been used more wisely elsewhere.

ii. "Cooling-Off" Period Employment Restrictions
NJ Casino Control Commission Regulations

19:40-2.6 Post-employment restrictions

(a) For purposes of this section, a "policy-making management position" means:

1. For the Commission, the Executive Secretary; the Chief of Staff; a Director of any Division; the General Counsel; the Public Information Officer; the Equal Employment Opportunity and Affirmative Action Officer; and any other person designated to serve on the Commission's management advisory team; and

2. For the Division, the Director; the Deputy Director; the Executive in Charge of Investigations; the Attorney Administrator, Licensing Prosecution Bureau; the Attorney Administrator, Regulatory Prosecution Bureau; the Agent Administrator, Licensing Investigations; and the Agent Administrator, Regulatory Enforcement.

(b) No employee of the Commission or employee or agent of the Division shall solicit or accept employment with, or acquire any direct or indirect interest in, any person who is an applicant, licensee or registrant with the Commission for a period of two years from the date of termination of his or her employment with the Commission or Division. Notwithstanding the foregoing:

1. A secretarial or clerical employee may solicit and accept such employment at any time after termination of employment with the Commission or the Division;

2. Any employee, other than a person subject to (c) below, who is terminated as the result of a reduction in workforce at the Commission or the Division may accept employment otherwise prohibited by this subsection upon application to and the approval of the Commission pursuant to (d) and (e) below;

3. Nothing in this section shall prohibit a former employee of the Commission or a former employee or agent of the Division from soliciting or accepting employment with, or acquiring an interest in, any person who is licensed as a casino service industry enterprise pursuant to subsection 92c of the Act or is an applicant for such licensure.

(c) At the end of two years from termination of employment, and for a period of two years thereafter, any person who held a policy-making management position with the Commission or Division at any time during the five years prior to termination of employment shall not:

1. Solicit employment with an applicant, licensee or registrant unless he or she has provided prior written notice of an intent to solicit such employment to the Commission's General Counsel; or

2. Accept or commence employment with, or acquire an interest in, an applicant, licensee or registrant except upon application to and the approval of the Commission pursuant to (d) below for that particular employment or interest.

(d) A petition for waiver pursuant to (b)2 or (c) above shall be in writing and shall identify the following:

1. The applicant, licensee or registrant that has made an offer of employment, or in which the petitioner will acquire an interest;

2. The position to be held and the specific nature of the duties to be performed for the applicant, licensee or registrant, or the nature of the interest to be acquired; and

3. Any positions held and the specific nature of the duties performed while employed by the Commission or Division.

(e) The Commission may grant a waiver upon a finding that the acceptance of the employment or the acquisition of the interest identified in the petition will not create the appearance of a conflict of interest or evidence a conflict of interest in fact.

(f) The Commission's General Counsel shall review each petition for waiver and supporting documentation and shall make a recommendation to the Commission, with copies to the Division and the petitioner, within 10 days of the receipt of a completed petition.

(g) Any waiver granted pursuant to (e) above shall apply only to the applicant, licensee or registrant and the position or interest identified in the petition for waiver. No person subject to post-employment restriction pursuant to (b)2 or (c) above shall accept or commence employment in any other position or with any other applicant, licensee or registrant, or acquire any other interest that is otherwise prohibited unless a waiver has been granted by the Commission for such employment or interest.

Notes

1. A potential way that the industry may attempt to influence, or "capture," regulators is through the promise of private employment after government service. A method of preventing this is through "cooling off" periods. This prevents regulators from leaving their positions to take gaming-industry jobs. The purpose is to avoid the appearance that the casino industry can influence a regulator by holding out the possibility of post-government service employment. *See* Jeffrey Lowenhar, *et al., Regulatory Requirements and Legalized Casino Gaming in New Jersey: The Case for Change, in* Gambling & Pub. Pol'y 266, 269 (1991) (discussing the history of "cooling off" regulations in New Jersey).

2. Two problems occur with the "cooling off" period. First, knowing that one cannot use skills learned while working for the government in the private sector will make the government job less appealing. Therefore, it will lower the quantity and quality of applicants for regulatory employment. With the proliferation of gaming, this is less of a problem. Former gaming agents from one jurisdiction often can find lucrative jobs with companies elsewhere that do not hold a license in the place that the former agent worked. Moreover, the impact of a "cooling off" period may be significantly diminished if government employment is as attractive as private employment. This would include salaries and benefits for the gaming agents and regulators that are competitive with the industry. A second problem is scope. The "cooling off" period often does not prevent professionals, such as accountants or lawyers, from representing casinos before their agency immediately after leaving government employment. A "cooling off" period may be extended to prevent representation of gaming clients by former regulators, their employees, and attorneys. This would prevent a former regulator who is an attorney from representing applicants shortly after resigning.

Chapter 4

Licensing

1. Generally

Gaming licensing is not unique. Governments often impose licensing requirements on various professions to protect the public. A primary reason for licensing is to shield the public from abuse—particularly where the person being licensed holds a special position of trust, and the public is in a more vulnerable position. Licensing has its best advantage in situations where regulatory violations are difficult to detect and enforcement is of limited utility. For example, regulating legal services has many practical problems because unethical behavior often is difficult to detect unless the client lodges a complaint. Even then, the client may lack the sophistication to know what constitutes an unethical practice. In such cases, the client must rely on the state's licensing of attorneys as an indication of minimum competency and ethical compliance.

Similarly, government has an interest in protecting the public by assuring that certain persons are not involved in its casino industry. For example, the public could easily be victimized by rigged games at gaming establishments. Unsuitable persons also may include those who are so incompetent that they cannot detect and prevent schemes by employees or patrons to cheat other patrons.

The government may have a more selfish reason to prevent the involvement persons who could, indirectly or directly, jeopardize the government's economic stake in the casino industry. Persons who can do direct harm include those who skim funds without paying taxes or are so incompetent that the government will lose tax revenues through employee or patron theft or poor management.

Assuring the honesty of the games also is important because the public must perceive that gambling is honest before it will gamble. If one operator cheats, the public may believe or fear that the entire industry is dishonest. Other persons can do indirect harm to the government's economic interest because their mere presence taints the industry, because legislators may consider making gaming illegal, or existing and prospective patrons may be dissuaded from coming to the casinos. The gaming industry can suffer credibility problems if the media exposes a casino owner or operator having criminal ties, regardless of whether the owner or operator otherwise complies with all regulations and acts ethically.

Licensing is a prophylactic exercise. Regulators are attempting to exclude unfit persons before they get their license. Some debate whether character investigations of applicants for professional and privileged licenses are the best vehicle for assuring ethical conduct and regulatory compliance. While enforcement concentrates on verification of the licensee's activities through oversight, licensing attempts to rely on the regulator's ability to predict the applicant's future behavior. The major attributes of gaming regulatory enforcement were covered in Chapter Three.

Licensing systems have five distinct characteristics: breadth, depth, criteria, level of review, and standards. Breadth means the extent to which a government requires persons or entities associated with the casino industry to obtain a license. Depth of licensing means the extent to which government requires persons within a licensable entity to undergo an individual investigation. Criteria are those matters that the government considers in granting licenses such as having good character or the lack of a felony conviction. Level of review refers to the intensity of the investigative process. A low-level review might include simple checks with law enforcement agencies to learn whether the applicant has an arrest record. A high-level review may entail the regulatory agency training special agents to conduct complete and independent reviews of the applicant, including both background and finances. This investigation may be more intense than that required by a government for the highest security clearances. Standards relate to the burden of proof the applicant must meet, and the nature of the proof that applicants must offer to qualify for licensing. These refer to how rigid the regulators will be in applying the criteria. For example, under the same set of facts, an applicant may obtain a license in one jurisdiction, but not another.

Gaming licenses can be either mandatory or discretionary. Mandatory licenses are licenses that are required for operation of or association with the casino. Discretionary licenses are required to be obtained upon the discretionary review of the regulators.

For good overviews of the licensing process *see* Lester B. Snyder, *Regulation of Legalized Gambling, An Inside View*, 12 Conn. L. Rev. 665, 714 (1980). *See also* Note, *Control of Gaming in Nevada: A Look at Licensing*, 16 Cal. W. L. Rev. 500 (1980); Shannon Bybee, *The Legal Status of Gaming and Its Impact on Licensing*, 2 Gaming Res. & Rev. J. 61 (1995).

2. Breadth

Casinos do not operate in a vacuum. They contract with, and rely on, many other entities and persons to carry on business. These include contractors, and suppliers of many types of goods and services, including gaming equipment. Breadth of licensing concerns how governments attempt to prevent unsuitable persons from associating with or profiting from the gaming industry. For example, suppose a casino operator has a valid license, but an unsuitable associate has a hidden interest in the operation. Licensing attempts to prevent the unsuitable associate from sharing in casino revenues through third party relationships. The associate's challenge is to obtain a share of the revenue without attracting the attention of the gaming regulators. Methods to siphon revenues from the casino include selling goods or services to the casino at prices far beyond market price, and charging exorbitant "finder's" fees for arranging financing for the casino. Licensing also prevents unsuitable persons from attempting to influence operations through control of some goods or services critical to the casino or gaining influence through the ability to control labor unions.

A. Mandatory Licensing

86 Illinois Administrative Code § 3000.200:
Classification of Licenses

The Board may classify an activity to be licensed in addition to, different from, or at a different level than the classifications set forth in this Subpart.

a) Owner's License. An owner of a Riverboat Gaming Operation is required to hold an Owner's license.

b) Supplier's License. The following persons or entities are required to hold a Supplier's License:

1) Supplier of Gaming Equipment/Supplies, including a manufacturer, distributor, wholesaler, or retailer. All manufacturers of Electronic Gaming Devices, Chips, and Tokens must be licensed as a Supplier regardless of whether the manufacturer uses an independent distributor or wholesaler to distribute its Equipment/Supplies.

2) Supplier of Gaming Equipment maintenance or repair services.

3) Supplier of security services.

4) Lessors of Riverboat and/or dock facilities.

5) Junketeers.

6) Any other purveyor of goods or services to a Riverboat Gaming Operation, as deemed necessary by the Board.

c) Occupation License. A person employed at a Riverboat Gaming operation is required to hold an Occupation license. ...

New Jersey Stat. § 5:12-82: Casino License—
Applicant Eligibility

a. No casino shall operate unless all necessary licenses and approvals therefore have been obtained in accordance with law.

b. Only the following persons shall be eligible to hold a casino license; and, unless otherwise determined by the commission with the concurrence of the Attorney General which may not be unreasonably withheld in accordance with subsection c. of this section, each of the following persons shall be required to hold a casino license prior to the operation of a casino in the casino hotel with respect to which the casino license has been applied for:

(1) Any person who either owns an approved casino hotel or owns or has a contract to purchase or construct a casino hotel which in the judgment of the commission can become an approved casino hotel within 30 months or within such additional time period as the commission may, upon a showing of good cause therefore, establish;

(2) Any person who, whether as lessor or lessee, either leases an approved casino hotel or leases or has an agreement to lease a casino hotel which in the judgment of the commission can become an approved casino hotel within 30 months or within such additional time period as the commission may, upon a showing of good cause therefore, establish;

(3) Any person who has a written agreement with a casino licensee or with an eligible applicant for a casino license for the complete management of a casino and, if applicable, any authorized games in a casino simulcasting facility; and

(4) Any other person who has control over either an approved casino hotel or the land thereunder or the operation of a casino.

c. Prior to the operation of a casino and, if applicable, a casino simulcasting facility, every agreement to lease an approved casino hotel or the land thereunder and every agreement for the management of the casino and, if applicable, any authorized games in a casino simulcasting facility, shall be in writing and filed with the commission. No such agreement shall be effective unless expressly approved by the commission. The commission may require that any such agreement include within its terms any provision reasonably necessary to best accomplish the policies of this act. Consistent with the policies of this act:

(1) The commission, with the concurrence of the Attorney General which may not be unreasonably withheld, may determine that any person who does not have the ability to exercise any significant control over either the approved casino hotel or the operation of the casino contained therein shall not be eligible to hold or required to hold a casino license;

(2) The commission, with the concurrence of the Attorney General which may not be unreasonably withheld, may determine that any owner, lessor or lessee of an approved casino hotel or the land thereunder who does not own or lease the entire approved casino hotel shall not be eligible to hold or required to hold a casino license;

(3) The commission shall require that any person or persons eligible to apply for a casino license organize itself or themselves into such form or forms of business association as the commission shall deem necessary or desirable in the circumstances to carry out the policies of this act;

(4) The commission may issue separate casino licenses to any persons eligible to apply therefor;

(5) As to agreements to lease an approved casino hotel or the land thereunder, unless it expressly and by formal vote for good cause determines otherwise, the commission shall require that each party thereto hold either a casino license or casino service industry enterprise license and that such an agreement be for a durational term exceeding 30 years, concern 100% of the entire approved casino hotel or of the land upon which same is located, and include within its terms a buy-out provision conferring upon the casino licensee-lessee who controls the operation of the approved casino hotel the absolute right to purchase for an expressly set forth fixed sum the entire interest of the lessor or any person associated with the lessor in the approved casino hotel or the land thereunder in the event that said lessor or said person associated with the lessor is found by the commission to be unsuitable to be associated with a casino enterprise;

(6) The commission shall not permit an agreement for the leasing of an approved casino hotel or the land thereunder to provide for the payment of an interest, percentage or share of money gambled at the casino or derived from casino gaming activity or of revenues or profits of the casino unless the party receiving payment of such interest, percentage or share is a party to the approved lease agreement; unless each party to the lease agreement holds either a casino license or casino service industry enterprise license and unless the agreement is for a durational term exceeding 30 years, concerns a significant portion of the entire approved casino hotel or of the land upon which same is located, and includes within its terms a buy-out provision conforming to that described in paragraph (5) above;

. . .

New Jersey Stat. § 5:12-93:
Registration of Labor Organizations

a. Each labor organization, union or affiliate seeking to represent employees who are employed in a casino hotel, casino or casino simulcasting facility by a casino licensee shall register with the commission annually, and shall disclose such information to the commission as the commission may require, including the names of all affiliated organizations, pension and welfare systems and all officers and agents of such organizations and systems; provided, however, that no labor organization, union, or affiliate shall be required to furnish such information to the extent such information is included in a report filed by any labor organization, union, or affiliate with the Secretary of Labor pursuant to 29 U.S.C. 431 et seq. or 1001 et seq. if a copy of such report, or of the portion thereof containing such information, is furnished to the commission pursuant to the aforesaid federal provisions. The commission may in its discretion exempt any labor organization, union, or affiliate from the registration requirements of this subsection where the commission finds that such organization, union or affiliate is not the certified bargaining representative of any employee who is employed in a casino hotel, casino or casino simulcasting facility by a casino licensee, is not involved actively, directly or substantially in the control or direction of the representation of any such employee, and is not seeking to do so.

b. No person may act as an officer, agent or principal employee of a labor organization, union or affiliate registered or required to be registered pursuant to this section if the person has been found disqualified by the commission in accordance with the criteria contained in section 86 of that act. The commission may, for purposes of this subsection, waive any disqualification criterion consistent with the public policy of this act and upon a finding that the interests of justice so require.

c. Neither a labor organization, union or affiliate nor its officers and agents not otherwise individually licensed or registered under this act and employed by a casino licensee may hold any financial interest whatsoever in the casino hotel, casino, casino simulcasting facility or casino licensee whose employees they represent.

d. Any person, including any labor organization, union or affiliate, who shall violate, aid and abet the violation, or conspire or attempt to violate this section is guilty of a crime of the fourth degree.

e. The commission or the division may maintain a civil action and proceed in a summary manner, without posting bond, against any person, including any labor organization, union or affiliate, to compel compliance with this section, or to prevent any violations, the aiding and abetting thereof, or any attempt or conspiracy to violate this section.

f. In addition to any other remedies provided in this section, a labor organization, union or affiliate registered or required to be registered pursuant to this section may be prohibited by the commission from receiving any dues from any employee licensed or registered under that act and employed by a casino licensee or its agent, if any officer, agent or principal employee of the labor organization, union or affiliate has been found disqualified and if such disqualification has not been waived by the commission in accordance with subsection b. of this section. The commission or the division may proceed in the manner provided by subsection e. of this section to enforce an order of the commission prohibiting the receipt of dues.

g. Nothing contained in this section shall limit the power of the commission to proceed in accordance with subsection c. of section 107 of P.L.1977, c.110 (C.5:12-107).

Brown et al. v. Hotel & Restaurant Employees & Bartenders Int'l Union Local 54

468 U.S. 491 (1984)

Justice O'CONNOR delivered the opinion of the Court.

In 1976, the citizens of New Jersey amended their State Constitution to permit the legislative authorization of casino gambling within the municipality of Atlantic City.[1] Determined to prevent the infiltration of organized crime into its nascent casino industry and to assure public trust in the industry's integrity, the New Jersey Legislature enacted the Casino Control Act (Act), N.J. Stat. Ann. § 5:12-1 et seq. (West Supp. 1983–84), which provides for the comprehensive regulation of casino gambling, including the regulation of unions representing industry employees. Sections 86 and 93 of the Act specifically impose certain qualification criteria on officials of labor organizations representing casino industry employees. Those labor organizations with officials found not to meet these standards may be prohibited from receiving dues from casino industry employees and prohibited from administering pension and welfare funds. The principal question presented by these cases is whether the National Labor Relations Act (NLRA), as amended, 29 U.S.C. § 141 et seq., precludes New Jersey from imposing these criteria on those whom casino industry employees may select as officials of their bargaining representatives. We hold that it does not.

A subsequent amendment permits revenues to be used as well as to provide health and transportation benefits for eligible senior citizens and disabled residents. Ibid.

I

A

The advent of casino gambling in New Jersey was heralded with great expectations for the economic revitalization of the Atlantic City region, but with equally great fears for the potential for infiltration by organized crime. The state legislature conducted extensive hearings and, in cooperation with the Governor, commissioned numerous studies on how best to prevent infiltration by organized crime into the casino industry.[2] These studies confirmed the fact that the vast amount of money that flows daily through a casino operation and the large number of unrecorded transactions make the industry a particularly attractive and vulnerable target for organized crime. The New Jersey Commission of Investigation (NJCI), for example, found that there was a "well-organized highly functional organized crime network in [New Jersey]" which had become more interested in

---

1. That amendment provides in part:

"It shall be lawful for the Legislature to authorize by law the establishment and operation, under regulation and control by the State, of gambling houses or casinos within the boundaries, as heretofore established, of the city of Atlantic City, ... and to license and tax such operations and equipment used in connection therewith. Any law authorizing the establishment and operation of such gambling establishments shall provide for the State revenues derived therefrom to be applied solely for the purpose of providing reductions in property taxes, rentals, telephone, gas, electric, and municipal utilities charges of, eligible senior citizens and disabled residents of the State ..." N.J. Const., Art. 4, §7, 2D.

2. See generally Cohen, *The New Jersey Casino Control Act: Creation of a Regulatory System*, 6 SETON HALL LEGIS. J. 2–5 (1982); Note, The Casino Act: Gambling's Past and the Casino Act's Future, 10 Rutgers-Camden L.J. 279 (1979).

investing funds in legitimate enterprises.[3] The NJCI feared that such an incursion by organized crime into the Atlantic City casinos might also be accompanied by extortion, loan sharking, commercial bribery, and tax and antitrust violations. It was on the basis of these hearings and empirical studies that New Jersey finally adopted the Act, a comprehensive statutory scheme that authorizes casino gambling and establishes a rigorous system of regulation for the entire casino industry.

In order to promote "public confidence and trust in the credibility and integrity of the regulatory process and of casino operations," the Act "extend[s] strict State regulation to all persons, locations, practices and associations related to the operation of licensed casino enterprises and all related service industries." N.J. Stat. Ann. § 5:12-1(b)(6) (West Supp. 1983–84). The Casino Control Commission (Commission), an independent administrative body, possesses broad regulatory authority over the casinos and other related industries, §§ 5:12-63 to 5:12-75. The Division of Gaming Enforcement (Division), a part of the Attorney General's Office, is charged with the responsibility for investigating license and permit applicants and for prosecuting violators of the Act, §§ 5:12-76 to 5:12-79.

The Act imposes strict licensing requirements on any business seeking to own and operate a casino hotel, §§ 5:12-84(a)–(c); on suppliers of goods and services to casino hotels, §§ 5:12-12, 5:12-92; on all supervisory employees involved in casino operations, §§ 5:12-9, 5:12-89; and on all employees with access to the casino floor, §§ 5:12-7, 5:12-90. The Act requires registration, rather than licensing, for employees of casino hotels. Casino hotel employees include those performing "service or custodial duties not directly related to operations of the casino, including, without limitation, bartenders, waiters, waitresses, maintenance personnel, kitchen staff, but whose employment duties do not require or authorize access to the casino." § 5:12-8. Most relevant to this litigation, § 93(a) of the Act also requires labor organizations that represent or seek to represent persons employed in casinos or casino hotels to register annually with the Commission, § 5:12-93(a).

All those entities and persons required to be licensed or registered are subject to the disqualification criteria set forth in § 86 of the Act. Section 86 specifically lists criteria for the disqualification of casino licensees. The Commission is authorized to revoke, suspend, limit, or otherwise restrict the registration of any casino hotel employee who would be disqualified for a casino license. N.J. Stat. Ann. §§ 5:12-86, 5:12-91(b) (West Supp. 1983–84). All industries offering goods or services to the casinos are also subject to the disqualification criteria of § 86. § 5:12-92.

Section 93(b) directly subjects registered labor organizations to the § 86 disqualification criteria and imposes two express penalties for noncompliance:

> "No labor organization, union or affiliate registered or required to be registered pursuant to this section and representing or seeking to represent employees licensed or registered under this act may receive any dues from any employee

---

3. *See* NJCI, Report and Recommendations on Casino Gambling 1C-2C (1977). Most relevant to these cases, this study specifically noted: "[E]xperience and collected intelligence regarding organized crime strongly suggests [sic] that there are few better vehicles utilized by organized crime to gain a stranglehold on an entire industry than labor racketeering. Organized crime control of certain unions often requires the legitimate businessmen who employ the services of the union members to pay extra homage to the representatives of the underworld. Moreover the ready source of cash which union coffers provide can be employed as financing of all sorts of legitimate or illicit ventures." *Id.*, at 1-H.

licensed or registered under this act and employed by a casino licensee or its agent, or administer any pension or welfare funds, if any officer, agent, or principal employee of the labor organization, union or affiliate is disqualified in accordance with the criteria contained in section 86 of this act. The commission may for the purposes of this subsection waive any disqualification criterion consistent with the public policy of this act and upon a finding that the interests of justice so require."

The disqualification criteria referred to in § 86 include convictions for a list of enumerated offenses or "any other offense which indicates that licensure of the applicant would be inimical to the policy of this act and to casino operations." N.J. Stat. Ann. § 5:12-86(c)(4) (West Supp. 1983–84). Disqualification may also result if an individual is identified "as a career offender or a member of a career offender cartel or an associate of a career offender or career offender cartel in such a manner which creates a reasonable belief that the association is of such a nature as to be inimical to the policy of this act and to gaming operations." § 5:12-86(f).[4]

B

Appellee Hotel and Restaurant Employees and Bartenders International Union Local 54 (Local 54) is an unincorporated labor organization within the meaning of § 2(5) of the NLRA, 29 U.S.C. § 152(5). Local 54 represents in collective bargaining approximately 12,000 employees, 8,000 of whom are employed in casino hotels in Atlantic City. All of Local 54's casino hotel employees work in traditional hotel and restaurant service-related positions; none are employed in direct gambling operations. Appellee Frank Gerace is the president of Local 54.

In 1978, Local 54 began filing with the Commission the annual registration statement required by § 93(a) of the Act. Following a lengthy investigation, the Division in 1981 reported to the Commission that, in its view, Local 54's President Gerace, Secretary-Treasurer Robert Lumio, and Grievance Manager Frank Materio were disqualified under the criteria of § 86. Pursuant to that section, the Commission scheduled a hearing on the Division's allegations. When Local 54 raised objections to the constitutionality of § 86 and § 93, the Commission ruled that it lacked the authority to consider such challenges to its enabling statute. In response, appellees filed a complaint in District Court,[5] seeking declaratory and injunctive relief on the grounds that § 86 and § 93 impermissibly regulate areas which are pre-empted by the NLRA, the Employee Retirement Income Security Act (ERISA), 29 U.S.C. § 1001 et seq., and the Labor-Management Reporting and Disclosure Act of 1959 (LMRDA), 29 U.S.C. § 401 et seq., and that § 86(f) violates the Constitution because it is both overbroad and vague. Appellees also filed a motion for preliminary in-

---

4. A "career offender," in turn, is defined as "any person whose behavior is pursued in an occupational manner or context for the purpose of economic gain, utilizing such methods as are deemed criminal violations of the public policy of this State." N.J. Stat. Ann. § 5:12-86(f) (West Supp. 1983–84).

5. Defendants in that action, now appellants before this Court, included G. Michael Brown, the Director of New Jersey's Department of Law and Public Safety, Division of Gaming Enforcement; the Division itself; and Thomas Kean, Governor of New Jersey. These appellants filed an appeal in No. 83-498, and are referred to collectively as appellant Division. Also defendants below were Martin Danziger, Acting Chairman of the Commission, along with the other members constituting the Commission. These appellants are referred to as appellant Commission, and their appeal, No. 83-573, has been consolidated with No. 83-498.

junctive relief alleging irreparable injury from being forced to participate in further Commission proceedings.

After a hearing, the District Court denied the motion for a preliminary injunction, concluding that appellees were unlikely to succeed on the merits of their claims.[6] 536 F. Supp. 317 (N.J. 1982). Since no preliminary injunction was entered, the Commission went forward with its disqualification hearing. The Commission concluded that Gerace and Materio were disqualified under § 86(f) because they were associated with members of organized crime in a manner inimical to the policy of the Act and to gaming operations. Local 54's Business Agent, Karlos LaSane, was also held disqualified under § 86(c) because he had been convicted in 1973 of extortion from persons doing business with Atlantic City while he was a City Commissioner.[7] On the basis of its findings, the Commission ordered that these individuals be removed as officers, agents, or principal employees of Local 54, failing which Local 54 would be barred from collecting dues from any of its members who were licensed or registered employees under the Act. See App. to Juris. Statements 206a–207a. The Commission later issued a supplemental decision, determining that the prohibition against dues collection would suffice to effectuate the removal of the three union officials and that it was therefore unnecessary to invoke the additional sanction of prohibiting the disqualified officials from administering pension and welfare funds. *Id.*, at 208a–215a.

Subsequent to the Commission's decision, a divided panel of the United States Court of Appeals for the Third Circuit issued a ruling concluding that the District Court had erred in refusing to grant the preliminary injunction. 709 F.2d 815 (1983). Reaching the merits of the underlying complaint, the court decided that § 93 of the Act is pre-empted by § 7 of the NLRA insofar as it empowers the Commission to disqualify elected union officials and is pre-empted by ERISA insofar as it empowers the Commission to prohibit administration of pension and welfare funds.[8]

We noted probable jurisdiction, and consolidated the separate appeals of the Commission and the Division to consider the pre-emption issue, 464 U.S. 990 (1983).[9]

---

6. Appellants had in turn moved to dismiss the complaint on abstention grounds, relying on the various strands of that doctrine as enunciated in Railroad Comm'n of Texas v. Pullman Co., 312 U.S. 496 (1941); Burford v. Sun Oil Co., 319 U.S. 315 (1943); and Younger v. Harris, 401 U.S. 37 (1971). The District Court concluded that none of these abstention doctrines was applicable to this case. 536 F. Supp. 317, 324–325 (N.J. 1982).

7. One of the officials earlier identified in the Division's report, Secretary-Treasurer Lumio, died in June 1981, prior to the Commission's decision.

8. The Court of Appeals also concluded that the District Court was correct in declining to abstain. Because its decision on the NLRA and ERISA pre-emption issues sufficed to dispose of the appeal, the Court of Appeals had no occasion to pass on Local 54's overbreadth and vagueness contentions, nor do we. Local 54 did not challenge on appeal the District Court's decision that LMRDA does not pre-empt the sanctions provided by the Act.

9. As a preliminary matter, we note appellant Commission's contention that, despite the decision below, the case should still be dismissed under the abstention doctrine of Younger v. Harris, *supra*. The New Jersey Attorney General — representing appellants Division, its Director, and the Governor — does not, however, press the Younger abstention claim before this Court, and instead submits to the jurisdiction of this Court in order to obtain a more expeditious and final resolution of the merits of the constitutional issue. Brief for Appellant Division 14, n. 6. Since the State's Attorney General has thereby agreed to our adjudication of the controversy, considerations of comity are not implicated, and we need not address the merits of the Younger abstention claim. *See* Ohio Bureau of Employment Services v. Hodory, 431 U.S. 471, 480 (1977).

II

When federal pre-emption is invoked under the directive of the Supremacy Clause, it falls to this Court to examine the presumed intent of Congress. *See* Fidelity Federal Savings & Loan Assn. v. De la Cuesta, 458 U.S. 141, 152–53 (1982). Our task is quite simple if, in the federal enactment, Congress has explicitly mandated the pre-emption of state law, *see* Shaw v. Delta Air Lines, Inc., 462 U.S. 85, 95–100 (1983), or has adequately indicated an intent to occupy the field of regulation, thereby displacing all state laws on the same subject, Rice v. Santa Fe Elevator Corp., 331 U.S. 218, 230 (1947). Even in the absence of such express language or implied congressional intent to occupy the field, we may nevertheless find state law to be displaced to the extent that it actually conflicts with federal law. Such actual conflict between state and federal law exists when "compliance with both federal and state regulations is a physical impossibility," Florida Lime & Avocado Growers, Inc. v. Paul, 373 U.S. 132, 142–43 (1963), or when state law "stands as an obstacle to the accomplishment and execution of the full purposes and objectives of Congress," Hines v. Davidowitz, 312 U.S. 52, 67 (1941). *See* Michigan Canners & Freezers Assn., Inc. v. Agricultural Marketing and Bargaining Board, 467 U.S. 461, 469 (1984); Fidelity Federal Savings & Loan Assn. v. De la Cuesta, *supra*.

These pre-emption principles are no less applicable in the field of labor law. Section 7 of the NLRA, 49 Stat. 452, as amended, 29 U.S.C. § 157, the provision involved in this case, neither contains explicit pre-emptive language nor otherwise indicates a congressional intent to usurp the entire field of labor-management relations. *See* New York Telephone Co. v. New York State Dept. of Labor, 440 U.S. 519, 540 (1979); Garner v. Teamsters, 346 U.S. 485, 488 (1953) ("The national ... Act ... leaves much to the states, though Congress has refrained from telling us how much"). The Court has, however, frequently applied traditional pre-emption principles to find state law barred on the basis of an actual conflict with § 7. If employee conduct is protected under § 7, then state law which interferes with the exercise of these federally protected rights creates an actual conflict and is pre-empted by direct operation of the Supremacy Clause. *See, e.g.,* Nash v. Florida Industrial Comm'n, 389 U.S. 235, 239–40 (1967) (invalidating state unemployment compensation law); Bus Employees v. Missouri, 374 U.S. 74, 81–82 (1963) (striking down state statute prohibiting peaceful strikes against public utilities); Bus Employees v. Wisconsin Board, 340 U.S. 383, 394 (1951) (same); Automobile Workers v. O'Brien, 339 U.S. 454, 458–59 (1950) (invalidating state "strike-vote" legislation).

Appellants argue that the appropriate framework for pre-emption analysis in these cases is the balancing test applied to those state laws which fall within the so-called "local interests" exception to the pre-emption doctrine first set forth in San Diego Building Trades Council v. Garmon, 359 U.S. 236, 243–44 (1959). They contend that because New Jersey's interest in crime control is "so deeply rooted in local feeling and responsibility," *ibid.*, the Act may yet be sustained as long as the magnitude of the State's interest in the enactment outweighs the resulting substantive interference with federally protected rights. *See* Operating Engineers v. Jones, 460 U.S. 669, 683 (1983). This argument, however, confuses pre-emption which is based on actual federal protection of the conduct at issue from that which is based on the primary jurisdiction of the National Labor Relations Board (NLRB). *See, e.g.,* Railroad Trainmen v. Terminal Co., 394 U.S. 369, 383, n. 19 (1969). In the latter situation, a presumption of federal pre-emption applies even when the state law regulates conduct only arguably protected by federal law. Such a pre-emption rule avoids the potential for jurisdictional conflict between state courts or agencies and the NLRB by ensuring that primary responsibility for interpreting and applying this body of labor law remains with the NLRB. *See* Motor Coach Employees v. Lockridge, 403

U.S. 274, 286–89 (1971); San Diego Building Trades Council v. Garmon, *supra*, 459 U.S. at 244–45. This presumption of federal pre-emption, based on the primary jurisdiction rationale, properly admits to exception when unusually "deeply rooted" local interests are at stake. In such cases, appropriate consideration for the vitality of our federal system and for a rational allocation of functions belies any easy inference that Congress intended to deprive the States of their ability to retain jurisdiction over such matters. We have, therefore, refrained from finding that the NLRA pre-empts state court jurisdiction over state breach of contract actions by strike replacements, Belknap, Inc. v. Hale, 463 U.S. 491 (1983), state trespass actions, Sears, Roebuck & Co. v. Carpenters, 436 U.S. 180 (1978), or state tort remedies for intentional infliction of emotional distress, Farmer v. Carpenters, 430 U.S. 290 (1977).

If the state law regulates conduct that is actually protected by federal law, however, pre-emption follows not as a matter of protecting primary jurisdiction, but as a matter of substantive right. Where, as here, the issue is one of an asserted substantive conflict with a federal enactment, then "[t]he relative importance to the State of its own law is not material ... for the Framers of our Constitution provided that the federal law must prevail." Free v. Bland, 369 U.S. 663, 666 (1962). We turn, therefore, to consider whether New Jersey's Act actually conflicts with the casino industry employees' § 7 rights.

III

Section 7 guarantees to employees various rights, among them the right "to bargain collectively through representatives of their own choosing." 29 U.S.C. § 157. In a straightforward analysis, the Court of Appeals found that this express right of employees to choose their collective-bargaining representatives encompasses an unqualified right to choose the officials of these representatives. Because § 93(b) of the Act precludes casino industry employees from selecting as union officials individuals who do not meet the § 86 disqualification criteria, the Court of Appeals determined that this provision clearly and directly conflicts with § 7 and, under traditional pre-emption analysis, must be held preempted.

The Court of Appeals relied heavily on this Court's decision in Hill v. Florida ex rel. Watson, 325 U.S. 538 (1945), as support for the threshold proposition that § 7 confers an unfettered right on employees to choose the officials of their own bargaining representatives. Hill involved a Florida statute that provided for state licensing of union business agents and prohibited the licensing of individuals who had not been citizens for more than 10 years, who had been convicted of a felony, or who were not of "good moral character." The statute also required the unions to file annual reports. Pursuant to this law, the Florida Attorney General obtained injunctions against a union and its business agent, restraining them from functioning until they had complied with the statute.

On review, the Court found that Florida's statute as applied conflicted with § 7, explaining:

> "The declared purpose of the Wagner Act, as shown in its first section, is to encourage collective bargaining, and to protect the 'full freedom' of workers in the selection of bargaining representatives of their own choice. To this end Congress made it illegal for an employer to interfere with, restrain or coerce employees in selecting their representatives. Congress attached no conditions whatsoever to their freedom of choice in this respect. Their own best judgment, not that of someone else, was to be their guide. 'Full freedom' to choose an agent means freedom to pass upon that agent's qualifications." 325 U.S. at 541.

The decision in Hill does not control the present cases, however, because Congress has, in our view, subsequently disclaimed any intent to pre-empt all state regulation which touches upon the specific right of employees to decide which individuals will serve as officials of their bargaining representatives. As originally enacted, and as interpreted by the Court in Hill, §7 imposed no restrictions whatsoever on employees' freedom to choose the officials of their bargaining representatives. In 1959, however, Congress enacted the Labor-Management Reporting and Disclosure Act (LMRDA), designed in large part to address the growing problems of racketeering, crime, and corruption in the labor movement. *See* S. Rep. No. 187, 86th Cong., 1st Sess., 12–16 (1959); H.R. Rep. No. 741, 86th Cong., 1st Sess., 9–12 (1959), U.S. Code Cong. & Admin. News 1959, p. 2318. Title V of LMRDA imposes various restrictions on labor union officials and defines certain qualifications for them. Specifically, 29 U.S.C. §504(a) provides in pertinent part:

> "No person ... who has been convicted of, or served any part of a prison term resulting from his conviction of [a series of enumerated crimes] shall serve ... as an officer, director, trustee, member of any executive board or similar governing body, business agent, manager, organizer ... of any labor organization ... for five years after such conviction or after the end of such imprisonment ..."

By enacting §504(a), Congress has unmistakably indicated that the right of employees to select the officers of their bargaining representatives is not absolute and necessarily admits of some exception. Of course, a strong counter-argument can be made that Congress intended §504(a) to be the very measure of the exception, thereby cutting back on the pre-emptive effect of §7 only to that extent and no more. Although this is certainly a conceivable reading of congressional intent, we are, however, not persuaded by it.

As the Court has already recognized, another provision of LMRDA, §603(a),[10] is "an express disclaimer of pre-emption of state laws regulating the responsibilities of union officials, except where such pre-emption is expressly provided ..." De Veau v. Braisted, 363 U.S. 144, 157 (1960) (plurality opinion); *see also id.*, at 160–61 (BRENNAN, J., concurring in judgment) (LMRDA "explicitly provides that it shall not displace such legislation of the States").[11] In affirmatively preserving the operation of state laws, §603(a) indicates that Congress necessarily intended to preserve some room for state action concerning the responsibilities and qualifications of union officials. Moreover, §504 itself makes clear that Congress did not seek to impose a uniform federal standard on those who may serve as union officials. An individual is disqualified from holding office for five years under §504 only if he has been convicted of certain state law crimes. His eligibility for union office may be restored earlier depending on the various state laws providing for the restoration of citizen rights to convicted felons. *See* 104 Cong. Rec. 10991–10994 (1958) (remarks of Sen. McNamara). Thus, the federal law's disqualification criteria themselves are premised on state laws which of course

---

10. Section 603(a), as set forth in 29 U.S.C. §523(a), provides:
   "Except as explicitly provided to the contrary, nothing in this chapter shall reduce or limit the responsibilities of any labor organization or any officer ... under any other Federal law or under the laws of any State, and, except as explicitly provided to the contrary, nothing in this chapter shall take away any right or bar any remedy to which members of a labor organization are entitled under such other Federal law or law of any State." *See also* 29 U.S.C. §524 (separate "saving clause" which explicitly preserves state authority to enforce general criminal laws).

11. It was upon the authority of *De Veau* that the District Court in the instant cases rejected appellees' argument that §93 of the Act was directly pre-empted by LMRDA. *See* 536 F. Supp., at 326–328. Appellees no longer press this contention.

vary throughout the Nation. Finally, our conclusion that Congress might not view such state regulation as necessarily interfering with national labor policy is buttressed by consideration of the concerns that led Congress to enact LMRDA in the first place. Congress was prompted to take action in large part because the governmental machinery was not "effective in policing specific abuses at the local level" and in "stamp[ing] out crime and corruption [in unions]." S. Rep. No. 187, *supra*, at 6, U.S. Code Cong. & Admin. News 1959, p. 2322. Consistent with this overreaching legislative purpose, we can more readily presume that Congress would allow a State to adopt different and more stringent qualification requirements for union officials to effectuate this important goal.

In De Veau v. Braisted, *supra*, this Court first squarely confronted the issue of post-Hill congressional intent in the context of a challenge to § 8 of the New York Waterfront Commission Act. The New York statute prohibited any labor organization representing waterfront employees from collecting dues if any of its officers or agents had been convicted of a felony and had not subsequently been pardoned or cleared by the parole board. The statute had been enacted in furtherance of an interstate compact between New York and New Jersey, establishing a bistate commission intended to combat crime and corruption on the States' mutual waterfront. The compact had been expressly approved by Congress pursuant to Art. I, § 10, of the Federal Constitution. The argument urged upon the Court was that the New York statute was pre-empted by § 7 of the NLRA as conflicting with Hill's guarantee of "complete freedom of choice in the selection of [waterfront employees'] representatives." 363 U.S. at 152. In an opinion for a four-Justice plurality, Justice Frankfurter rejected this pre-emption argument and upheld the challenged statute.

The plurality opinion began by noting that the NLRA "does not exclude every state policy that may in fact restrict the complete freedom of a group of employees to designate 'representatives of their own choosing.'" *Ibid.* The plurality reasoned:

> "It would misconceive the constitutional doctrine of pre-emption—of the exclusion because of federal regulation of what otherwise is conceded state power—to decide this case mechanically on an absolute concept of free choice of representatives on the part of employees, heedless of the light that Congress has shed for our guidance. The relevant question is whether we may fairly infer a congressional purpose incompatible with the very narrow and historically explained restrictions upon the choice of a bargaining representative embodied in § 8 of the New York Waterfront Commission Act. Would Congress, with a lively regard for its own federal labor policy, find in this state enactment a true, real frustration, however dialectically plausible, of that policy?" *Id.*, at 153 (emphasis added).

After thus framing the inquiry, the plurality concluded that the Court need not in fact "imaginatively summon" a hypothetical congressional response since, in light of Congress' express approval of the compact, federal pre-emption could not be found. *Ibid.*

De Veau's direct relevance for these cases lies less in its approach to determining § 7's pre-emptive scope than in its focus on the indicia of congressional intent that can be garnered from Congress' approval of the compact. At congressional hearings, labor union officials testified against the compact's ratification on the specific ground that the New York statute conflicted with federal labor policy and that approval of the compact would therefore appear to sanction all such state restrictions. *See* 363 U.S. at 151 (citing to testimony of International Longshoremen's Association). In approving the compact over such objections, Congress apparently concluded that, at least where the States were confronted with the "public evils"[12] of "crime, corruption, and racketeering,"[13] more stringent state regulation of the qualifications of union officials was not incompatible with the national labor policy as embodied in § 7.[14]

In short, given Congress' intent as expressed in its enactment of LMRDA and its approval of the bistate compact at issue in *De Veau*, it can no longer be maintained that § 7 necessarily and obviously conflicts with every state regulation that may restrict the right of employees to select certain individuals to serve as the officials of their bargaining representatives. Nor can we find that New Jersey's imposition of its disqualification criteria in any way "stands as an obstacle to the accomplishment and execution of the full purposes and objectives of Congress." Hines v. Davidowitz, 312 U.S. at 67. In its enactment of LMRDA and its awareness of New York's comparable restrictions when approving the bistate compact, Congress has at least indicated both that employees do not have an unqualified right to choose their union officials and that certain state disqualification requirements are compatible with § 7. This is particularly true in the case of New Jersey's disqualification criteria, the purpose of which is identical to that which motivated those New York restrictions implicitly approved by Congress: Both statutes form part of comprehensive programs designed to "vindicate a legitimate and compelling state interest, namely, the interest in combating local crime infesting a particular industry." De Veau v. Braisted, *supra*, 363 U.S. at 155. In the absence of a more specific congressional intent to the contrary, we therefore conclude that New Jersey's regulation of the qualifications of casino industry union officials does not actually conflict with § 7 and so is not preempted by the NLRA.

We emphasize that this conclusion does not implicate the employees' express § 7 right to select a particular labor union as their collective-bargaining representative, but only their subsidiary right to select the officials of that union organization. While the Court in Hill v. Florida ex rel. Watson, 325 U.S. 538 (1945), apparently assumed that the two rights were undifferentiated and equally protected, our reading of subsequent legislative action indicates that Congress has since distinguished between the two and has accorded less than absolute protection to the employees' right to choose their union officials. In this litigation, the casino industry employees' freedom in the first instance to select Local 54 to represent them in collective bargaining is simply not affected by the qualification criteria of New Jersey's Act....

V

We find that § 93 of New Jersey's Act is not pre-empted by § 7 of the NLRA to the extent that it imposes certain limitations on whom casino industry employees may choose to serve as officials of their bargaining representatives. On remand, the District Court should determine whether imposition of § 93(b)'s sanction of prohibiting the collection of dues from casino industry employees will effectively prevent the union from performing its statutory functions as bargaining representative for its members. The judgment of the Court of Appeals is therefore vacated, and the cases are remanded to the Court of Appeals with instructions to remand to the District Court for further proceedings consistent with this opinion.

It is so ordered.

---

12. H.R. Rep. No. 998, 83d Cong., 1st Sess., 1 (1953).

13. *Ibid.* See also S. Rep. No. 583, 83d Cong., 1st Sess., 1–2 (1953).

14. In recommending approval of the compact, the House Judiciary Committee distinguished between state laws directed specifically at labor-management relations and those state laws directed at entirely separate problems: "The compact to which the committee here recommends that Congress grant its consent is in no sense anti-labor legislation, but rather, antiracketeering legislation." H.R. Rep. No. 998, *supra*, at 6.

Justice BRENNAN and Justice MARSHALL took no part in the decision of these cases.

Justice WHITE, with whom Justice POWELL and Justice STEVENS join, dissenting.

Section 93(b) of the New Jersey Casino Control Act restricts the activities of unions representing workers employed in the casino industry. In particular, it provides that a union may not collect dues from casino workers or administer pension or welfare funds if any of its officials is disqualified under the criteria set forth in §86. The Court purports to save some portion of this statute[15] by holding that a state law restricting the class of individuals who can serve as officers in a union is not pre-empted by federal labor law. If §93(b) did no more than that, I would agree with the Court's resolution of these cases because, as the Court amply demonstrates, Congress' actions in enacting the LMRDA indicate that federal labor law does not pre-empt state laws which prevent certain types of individuals from serving as union officials.[16] However, §93(b) is not directed at the individuals who are disqualified under §86. It imposes sanctions on the union itself and, in so doing, infringes on the employees' federally protected rights.

Section 7 of the NLRA grants covered employees the right "to bargain collectively through representatives of their own choosing." 29 U.S.C. §157.[17] A bargaining representative achieves this status by being "designated or selected for the purposes of collective bargaining by the majority of the employees in a unit appropriate for such purposes." 29 U.S.C. §159(a). The employees' right to exercise this right is protected from employer, 29 U.S.C. §158(a)(1), labor organization, 29 U.S.C. §158(b)(1), and state, Hill v. Florida ex rel. Watson, 325 U.S. 538 (1945), interference. The employees whose rights are involved in these cases have exercised this right by selecting Local 54 as their bargaining representative.[18] The State, acting pursuant to §93(b), has sought to prohibit Local 54

---

15. It is not clear what portion of the statute the Court upholds since it expressly refuses to decide whether the dues prohibition and fund administration provisions are valid. Section 93(b) does nothing more than impose those two restrictions on unions whose officials are disqualified under the criteria set forth in §86. It does not, by its terms, provide a mechanism for disqualifying any union officer. Therefore, while it appears that the Court holds that a State is free to disqualify certain individuals from acting as union officials as long as it does not impose sanctions on the union itself, it is not clear that anything in §93(b) enables the State to do that.

16. If these cases required us to determine whether New Jersey could enforce the limits in §86 by imposing sanctions directly against the disqualified individual, for example by imposing fines or criminal penalties on those who hold union office after being disqualified, I would hold that it could. Section 93(b) does not purport to do that, however, and it is that statute which we are asked to review.

17. The Court correctly recognizes that there is a fundamental difference between the employees' absolute §7 right to choose which labor organization will act as their bargaining representative and their less absolute right to determine who will serve as officers in that organization. One need only examine the actual workings of most unions in order to realize that the two rights are not coextensive. For example, while a nonunion employee in an agency shop retains his §7 right to participate in the selection of the bargaining representative, he often has no say in who will serve as officers of the union that represents him in the bargaining process since such decisions are generally made by union members only. Similarly, while only the members of a particular collective-bargaining unit are empowered to decide which union will act as their bargaining representative, all members of the union, even those not in the particular bargaining unit, are generally free to participate in the process of electing union officials. Thus, in a large union, it is possible that a substantial majority of the members of a particular bargaining unit may vote against the union official who is eventually elected. Even though the members of the bargaining unit are unable to select the union official of their choice in such situations, there would be no legitimate claim that this somehow interfered with their §7 right to bargain through the representative of their choice.

18. Under the NLRA, an individual, as well as a labor organization, can serve as the exclusive bargaining representative. 29 U.S.C. §152(4). See Louisville Sanitary Wiper Co., 65 N.L.R.B. 88 (1945); Robinson-Ransbottom Pottery Co., 27 N.L.R.B. 1093 (1940). The employees whose interests are at stake

from collecting dues from these employees, thereby effectively preventing the union from carrying out the collective-bargaining function and nullifying the employees' exercise of their § 7 right.

In Hill v. Florida ex rel. Watson, the Court held that federal labor policy prohibits a State from enforcing permissible regulations by the use of sanctions that prevent the union "from functioning as a labor union." *Id.*, at 543. Allowing the State to so restrict the union's conduct infringes on the employees' right to bargain collectively through the representative of their own choosing because it prevents that representative from functioning as a collective-bargaining agent. The same effect would occur if New Jersey were to enjoin Local 54 from collecting dues from employees in the casino industry. A union which cannot sustain itself financially obviously cannot effectively engage in collective-bargaining activities on behalf of its members. Unlike the Court, I see no need to remand these cases in order to determine whether, as a factual matter, Local 54 is so dependent on dues that it will be prevented from effectively functioning as a bargaining representative if that source of revenue is cut off. I am willing to hold that, as a matter of law, a statute like § 93(b), which prohibits a union from collecting dues from its members, impairs the union's ability to represent those members to such an extent that it infringes on their § 7 right to bargain through the representative of their choice. Since the Court refuses to strike down the statute on this ground, I respectfully dissent.

B. Discretionary Licensing

Mississippi Code Ann. § 75-76-61:
Operation of Gaming Establishment

(1) Except for persons associated with licensed corporations or limited partnerships and required to be licensed, each employee, agent, guardian, personal representative, lender or holder of indebtedness of a gaming licensee who, in the opinion of the commission, has the power to exercise a significant influence over the licensee's operation of a gaming establishment shall be required to apply for a license.

(2) A person required to be licensed pursuant to subsection (1) of this section shall apply for a license within thirty (30) days after the executive director requests that he do so.

(3) If an employee required to be licensed under subsection (1):

(a) Does not apply for a license within thirty (30) days after being requested to do so by the executive director, and the commission makes a finding of unsuitability for that reason, or

(b) Is denied a license, or

(c) Has a license revoked by the commission, the licensee by whom he is employed shall terminate his employment in any capacity in which he is required to be licensed and shall not permit him to exercise a significant influence over the operation of the gaming establishment upon being notified by registered or certified mail of that action.

. . .

---

in these cases have chosen a union (Local 54), rather than an individual, as their bargaining representative.

Nevada v. Glusman
651 P.2d 639 (Nev. 1982)

STEFFEN J.

These consolidated appeals stem from issues involving the constitutional validity of Nevada gaming statute NRS 463.160(8)(a), hereinafter frequently referred to as "the statute",[1] and the jurisdiction of the district court to grant injunctive relief against the implementation thereof by state gaming authorities. After preventing enforcement of the statute through issuance of a preliminary injunction, the district court determined that the legislation was constitutional and dissolved the injunction. We qualifiedly affirm the decision supporting the statute, but hold that the district court was without jurisdiction to enjoin its enforcement.

Frederick J. Glusman is an officer, director and sole shareholder of International Dress Shop, Inc. (International). International is engaged in the retail clothing business on the premises of the Las Vegas Hilton and Stardust hotels under the name of Fredde's Dress Shops. The International shops at the Hilton and Stardust have operated continuously under leases dated in 1968 and 1977, respectively.

Pursuant to the recommendation of the Nevada Gaming Control Board (Board), the Nevada Gaming Commission (Commission) issued an order directing Glusman to apply to the latter agency for a determination of suitability to be associated with a gaming enterprise. The statutory authority for the order, NRS 463.160(8)(a), reads as follows:

If the premises of a licensed gaming establishment are directly or indirectly owned or under the control of the licensee therein, or of any person controlling, controlled by, or under common control with the licensee, the commission may, upon recommendation of the board, require the application of any business or person for a determination of suitability to be associated with a gaming enterprise if the person or business:

(a) Does business on the premises of the licensed gaming establishment.

Glusman responded to the order by filing a complaint for declaratory and injunctive relief with the district court, asserting constitutional infirmity in the questioned statute. The district court granted Glusman and International a preliminary injunction from which the State of Nevada, State of Nevada Gaming Commission and State of Nevada Gaming Control Board (the State) appealed under Case No. 12946. During the pendency of the latter appeal, the district court heard the complaint for declaratory relief and held against Glusman and International, thus prompting the appeal in Case No. 13217. (Hereafter, for purposes of this opinion, Glusman and International will alternatively be referred to as appellants).

In a major sense, the determination of the issues before us is dictated by the unique setting of the Nevada gaming industry. The peculiar nature of the gaming industry presents numerous concerns and problems of control, the resolution of which must be readily available to cognizant government authorities of this state. It has been clearly recognized by our earlier decisions that gaming longevity and vitality, under continuing state authority, are dependent upon effective control mechanisms which will assure appropriate deference to the health, safety and welfare of the citizenry. It is in that context that the Nevada Legislature has enacted legislation designed to provide effective and timely management of the gaming industry. NRS ch. 463.

---

1. N.R.S. 463.160(8)(a) is the applicable statute designated in effect in 1980. *See* N.R.S. 463.167(2).

...

Appellants assert error by the district court in finding NRS 463.160(8)(a) constitutional on its face and as applied to them. We do not agree. We have long recognized, as a general principle, that statutes should be construed, if reasonably possible, so as to be in harmony with the constitution.... In the face of attack, every favorable presumption and intendment will be brought to bear in support of constitutionality. As previously held, "[a]n act of the legislature is presumed to be constitutional and should be so declared unless it appears to be clearly in contravention of constitutional principles." State ex rel. Tidvall v. Eighth Judicial District Court, 91 Nev. 520, 526, 539 P.2d 456, 460 (1975). In the case before us, the statute attacked must be considered in light of this state's policy regarding the gaming industry as expressed in NRS 463.130(1). NRS 463.130(1) provides in pertinent part:

(c) Public confidence and trust can only be maintained by strict regulation of all persons, locations, practices, associations and activities related to the operation of licensed gaming establishments and the manufacture or distribution of gambling devices and equipment.

(d) All establishments where gaming is conducted and where gambling devices are operated, manufacturers, sellers and distributors of certain gambling devices and equipment in the state shall therefore be licensed, controlled and assisted to protect the public health, safety, morals, good order and general welfare of the inhabitants of the state, to foster the stability and success of the gaming industry and to preserve the competitive economy and policies of free competition of the State of Nevada.

As used in this provision, the word establishment is defined as "any premises wherein or whereon any gaming is done."

Appellants first contend that NRS 463.160(8)(a) is constitutionally infirm by reason of vagueness and overbreadth. The criterion under which we examine the assertion of vagueness is whether the statute "either forbids or requires the doing of any act in terms so vague that men of common intelligence must necessarily guess at its meaning and differ as to its application...." Connally v. General Construction Co., 269 U.S. 385 (1926) cited by this Court in In re Laiolo, 83 Nev. 186, 426 P.2d 726 (1967). Equally important in a facial challenge for vagueness is whether the statute impinges upon First Amendment freedoms. If not, a statute may be stricken as unconstitutionally vague only if it is found to be so "in all of its applications." Hoffman Estates v. Flipside, Hoffman Estates, 455 U.S. 489 (1982). Further, our standard of review is less strict under a challenge for vagueness where the statute is directed at economic regulations.

It is argued that the language of the statute fails to provide clarity of meaning or application, thereby subjecting those affected by the statute to uncertainty as to what constitutes acceptable conduct. It is true, of course, that the statute in question does not attempt to define the type of conduct which would actuate the investigatory machinery of the statute. Such definition is supplied, however, by reference to NRS 463.170(2).[19]

---

19. N.R.S. 463.170(2) provides:

An application to receive a license or be found suitable shall not be granted unless the commission is satisfied that the applicant is:

(a) A person of good character, honesty and integrity;

(b) A person whose prior activities, criminal record, if any, reputation, habits and associations do not pose a threat to the public interest of this state or to the effective regulation and control of gaming, or create or enhance the dangers of unsuitable, unfair or illegal practices, methods and activities in the conduct of gaming or the carrying on of the business and financial arrangements incidental thereto; and

(c) In all other respects qualified to be licensed or found suitable consistently with the declared policy of the state.

The latter statute describes with specificity the standards of conduct applicable to a determination of suitability and, by converse logic, that conduct which is inconsistent with suitability and which, if suspected, may prompt invocation of the investigation and qualifying aspects of NRS 463.160(8)(a).

Under the terms of the statute, any person or entity that does business on the premises occupied by a specified, licensed gaming establishment may be required to apply for a determination of suitability. The statute is precise. Regulation 1.050(12) of the Commission defines "premises" to mean "land together with all buildings, improvements and personal property located thereon." It is clear that the purpose of the statute is to provide a basis for investigating and qualifying or disqualifying as suitable, persons and businesses who choose to conduct non-gaming business operations on the premises of a gaming establishment. This purpose is both legitimate and reasonable. Human experience has shown gaming to be like quicksilver, and unless controls are complete and resourceful, the industry will be fraught with conditions of potential threat to its continued existence.

The United States Supreme Court recently sustained a city ordinance challenged for impermissible vagueness in the case of City of Mesquite v. Aladdin's Castle, Inc., 455 U.S. 283 (1982). There the city ordinance under fire was a licensing ordinance for coin-operated amusement establishments. The ordinance included a provision directing the chief of police to, inter alia, investigate an applicant's "connections with criminal elements." In reversing the court of appeals, the high court held:

> The Federal Constitution does not preclude a city from giving vague or ambiguous directions to officials who are authorized to make investigations and recommendations. There would be no constitutional objection to an ordinance that merely required an administrative official to review 'all relevant information' or 'to make such investigation as he deems appropriate' before formulating a [licensing] recommendation. *Id.* at 161.

In the instant proceeding, the statute is merely an investigative vehicle for confirming or dispelling concerns over the suitability of a person or business to conduct business operations on the same premises as a gaming establishment. The application and implicit investigation in connection therewith represent the total operative scenario attributable to NRS 463.160(8)(a). Obviously, the finding of suitability referred to in the statute is analogous to the ultimate licensing purpose of the city ordinance in *Mesquite*, and in both instances the eventual critical determination must result from the evaluation of facts obtained from the investigation and applied to well-defined criteria requisite to suitability or licensure. Therefore, we hold that the challenged statute is not susceptible to constitutional infirmity for vagueness since it purports to do nothing more than provide a basis for an investigation preliminary to a determination of suitability.

Appellants also contend that the statute is overbroad because it impermissibly regulates all types of businesses irrespective of any nexus with gaming. Generally, an overbreadth argument is only available for the purpose of challenging the validity of statutes which chill First Amendment rights. Anderson v. State, 562 P.2d 351 (Alaska 1977). The Supreme Court in Moose Lodge No. 107, 407 U.S. 163, 168 stated:

> [w]hile the doctrine of 'overbreadth' has been held ... to accord standing by reason of the 'chilling effect' that a particular law might have upon the exercise of the First Amendment rights, that doctrine has not been applied to constitutional litigation in areas other than those relating to the First Amendment.

In the case before us, none of appellants' First Amendment rights is impaired by reason of the questioned statute. Appellants do assert a denial of the First Amendment right to freedom of association, but such contention lacks merit. The type of association protected by the First Amendment is that which is related to the cherished right of freedom of speech, namely, "the freedom to associate for the promotion of political and social ideas." Lewitus v. Colwell, 479 F.Supp. 439 (D.C. Md. 1979), citing Bates v. Little Rock, 361 U.S. 516 (1960); Sweezy v. New Hampshire, 354 U.S. 234 (1957). Accordingly, appellants' argument supporting constitutional infirmity for overbreadth cannot prevail since appellants failed to demonstrate that NRS 463.160(8)(a) has any impermissible impact on First Amendment freedoms. The statute here challenged is constitutional on its face.

Appellants maintain that the statute represents an excessive, pervasive and therefore, unconstitutional exercise of the police power of the state. Appellants concede the vital role of gaming in the economy of the state and further acknowledge the right of the state to regulate and control the gaming industry consonant with the health, safety and welfare of the public. They conclude, however, that since appellants operate dress shops and have no relationship to gaming, it is an unwarranted and unconstitutional intrusion on private rights to include them within the penumbra of the statute. It is unquestionably true that there are limitations on the police power of the state. Not only must the ends and means of the legislative enactment of the power be reasonable, but the objective of its exercise must be so manifestly in the public interest as to strongly justify any intrusion on the basic rights of individuals.... However, appellants erroneously contend that NRS 463.160(8)(a) extends to all non-gaming businesses throughout the state. It does not. It applies only to businesses who elect to locate on certain premises shared by a gaming establishment. We hold that it is a reasonable exercise of the state's police power to subject businesses sharing premises with certain gaming establishments to a determination of suitability to be thus located. Having so held, however, does not dispose of the issue concerning the effect of the legislative scheme as applied to appellants.

Under the Nevada Gaming Control Act, the state is empowered to investigate and impose heavy sanctions, both civil and criminal, for the violation of Nevada's gaming laws. The statute in question facilitates the investigation of such violations or suspected violations by requiring investigatees to submit a detailed application and supportive information to gaming authorities. A finding of suitability by the Commission does not, however, constitute a license to participate in gaming. It merely provides official validation of the applicant's right to continue its non-gaming business on the premises shared by a gaming enterprise. The "finding of suitability" thus constitutes a form of acquittal from whatever suspicions prompted the investigation. It leaves the "suitable" business in no better position than its non-gaming neighbors who remain impliedly "suitable" until such time as they might be called forward under the statute to justify their continued suitability. Indeed, an applicant who has survived the "suitability" process has sustained losses of time, effort and expense necessitated by the preparation and submission of a detailed application[6] required by the gaming authorities. More importantly, however, an applicant is subject to the payment of all investigative costs incurred by the state during the course of its investigation. NRS 463.331.

The combined effect of NRS 463.160(8)(a) and NRS 463.331(1) constitutes an unreasonable and fundamentally unfair burden on those who are required to submit to the

---

6. The magnitude of the application is illustrated by the following requested information: Personal History Record (personal, marital, family, military, residence, employment and arrest information); and Invested Capital Questionnaire (detailed statement of all assets and liabilities).

qualifying procedures of the challenged statute. If the Commission determines that the applicant is "suitable," this simply means that the applicant is free of gaming involvement or impact and entitled to continue its non-gaming business on the same premises as a gaming establishment. The net effect to the non-gaming, "suitable" business could be financial decimation. We are thus faced with a situation where non-gaming applicants may be forced to underwrite their own financial demise even though they are totally free of gaming involvement. It is one thing to charge investigatory costs to those who are seeking licensure in the gaming industry; it is altogether different to subject one who, at least ostensibly, has no relationship to gaming beyond that of sharing space with a gaming enterprise, to potentially prohibitive costs of investigation as a condition precedent to the continuance of a non-gaming business. To impose such costs on non-gaming applicants is unreasonable and beyond the legitimate public purposes of the law. It is an impermissible extension of the police power to predicate a non-gaming applicant's economic survival upon an ability or willingness to underwrite the costs of investigation. There is no essential symbiosis between NRS 463.160(8)(a) and NRS 463.331(1). The right to investigate under the former need not depend on the discriminatory subvention of the latter. It is not within the scope or purpose of gaming control to selectively impose on non-gamers the financial burden of gaming enforcement.

It is unavailing to argue that since the costs of investigation may be waived by the Commission[7] no harm may in fact result from the cost assessment potential under NRS 463.331(1). A selective waiver of costs would serve to intensify the arbitrary and discriminatory effect of the provision. We accordingly hold that the combined effect of the aforementioned statutes is an unreasonable intrusion on the private rights of appellants and others similarly situated.... Consequently, we declare that part of NRS 463.331(1) which assesses costs to applicants for findings of suitability an invalid and excessive use of the police power of the state.

Appellants insist that the district court erred in construing the statutory phrase, "associated with a gaming enterprise," to include them since they are assertedly not rationally tied to gaming. We disagree. The words of a statute should be construed, if reasonably possible, so as to accommodate the statutory purpose.... It is manifestly clear that the statute would be shorn of any meaningful purpose if it were held to apply only to those who were overtly associated in the gaming industry. Such persons or associates would require gaming licenses and would be subjected to investigation incidental thereto, thereby rendering NRS 463.160(8)(a) completely redundant. On the other hand, it poses no threat to reason to view the phrase "associated with" in the context of a spatial relationship or association, i.e., a joining together in the use of the entire space referred to in the statute as "the premises." Such a connotation is consonant with the legislative history of the statute as contained in the record, and promotes the legitimate purposes of the legislation.

Appellants next assert that NRS 463.160(8)(a) violates their constitutional right to privacy. We hold, however, that the legislature had a compelling interest in subjecting persons and businesses engaged in commerce and sharing space with gaming establishments to selective investigation and a finding of suitability. Such an interest is more than sufficient to sustain the statute in the face of a constitutional challenge based upon invasion of privacy assertions.... A person or entity voluntarily situated and doing business within such proximity of gaming establishments cannot override legitimate government control mechanisms by invoking a superior right of privacy. To do so would substantially frus-

---

7. Gaming Commission Regulation 4.070(8) provides that: the board may, in its discretion, waive payment of an investigative fee or cost.

trate the state's capacity to regulate the gaming industry. Furthermore, appellants' claim that disclosure of financial information violates their right to privacy is also unfounded since any financial information obtained from appellants in the investigative process is confidential and immune from public disclosure by law. NRS 463.120(4). Any invasion of appellants' privacy is minimal and therefore constitutionally permissible....

We next turn to the argument that NRS 463.160(8)(a) impairs appellants' contract rights without just compensation. This contention immediately fails as to the Stardust shop because the lease under which appellants maintain their business expressly covers the possibility of a suitability determination and termination of the lease in the event of denial. In any event, it is well established that the police power concerns of public health, safety and welfare may be invoked where reasonably necessary to control even contractually vested rights antecedent to regulating legislation without running afoul of the impairment of contracts clause of the state and federal constitutions.... is equally settled that vested rights in a given profession or calling may be made subject to licensing or qualification enactments post dating such rights without running afoul of the impairments clause.... Here appellants enjoy whatever advantages exist in doing business in juxtaposition with gaming establishments. That spatial relationship will not be impaired if appellants are operating according to the laws of this state. We may not presume that a finding of suitability will be denied appellants if their business is consistent with their representations in this action. We accordingly hold that appellants have suffered no impairment of contracts as a result of the challenged statute.

Appellants' claim that NRS 463.160(8)(a) impairs their right to hold specific employment is also without merit. A finding of unsuitability by the Commission would not prevent appellants from engaging in the retail clothing business. It would only affect appellants' right to maintain their businesses in conjunction with gaming establishments at particular locations. This is not constitutionally prohibited.... Given the apparent extent of appellants' investments in their longstanding retail businesses, we are not suggesting, however, that appellants' interests are not substantial. Still, the public welfare far transcends any interest on the part of appellants to retain their existing locations. We are not unmindful, however, of the obvious differences between one who seeks and is denied a gaming license and one who, after investing substantial time and money in business locations held under lease, is thereafter found unsuitable to continue with such businesses. We trust the state will be equally mindful of such differences.... In any event, under the worst scenario, appellants would not be foreclosed from continued retail operations at non-gaming locations, and their existing shops presumably could be sold.

Lastly, appellants complain of a discriminatory application of NRS 463.160(8)(a) in violation of the equal protection clauses of our state and federal constitutions. Appellants argue that they have been singled out of a large class and, unlike the remainder of the class, subjected to a determination of suitability. This argument is unsound. All members of the class to which the statute is directed are subject to the requirement of a suitability determination. It is of no constitutional moment that appellants have been ordered to apply for a determination of suitability whereas others within the class have not. We have previously upheld the discretionary power of the Commission. State v. Rosenthal, *supra*. Gaming control would be intolerably burdened if selective investigation were disallowed. The statutory scheme provides a basis for requiring suitability determinations when, for whatever reason, gaming authorities have concern over the activities of those who share space with gaming establishments. The power to confirm or allay such concerns through selective investigation and qualification represents an important aspect of control which the legislature has deemed to be vital to the maintenance of our gaming economy. We hold that the class created by NRS 463.160(8)(a) is reasonable and necessary to the fulfillment of a legitimate legislative purpose and that the statute does not discriminate against appellants....

For the reasons above stated, we affirm as qualified, the decision of the district court in holding that NRS 463.160(8)(a) is constitutional, but we reverse as to the district court's jurisdiction to enjoin its enforcement.

Notes

1. Jurisdictions often vary as to the categories of businesses or persons associated with casinos that must obtain a license. In most jurisdictions, casino owners, casino operators and gaming device manufacturers must obtain a license. Regarding other businesses, such as the manufacturer of chips and cards, the need to obtain a license will vary between jurisdictions. In many cases, this distinction can result from the government's perception of the need to maintain a level of regulatory control over a particular occupation or business. For example, if organized crime in a particular jurisdiction had a strong influence over labor unions and the construction trade, this may justify moving labor unions and construction contractors into a higher tier that gives regulators greater ability to scrutinize their involvement with the gaming industry.

2. Breadth of licensing also can be impacted by the jurisdiction's capabilities and budget. Placing all groups into a mandatory licensing tier with full investigations may require a substantial government commitment of trained personnel to conduct the investigations even if only a single casino exists in the jurisdiction. Therefore, a government may need to place groups into a lower tier of licensing or forego licensing altogether on a priority basis. Usually, top priorities include owners and operators, followed by persons sharing in profits, distributors, manufacturers, and key employees. It may then assign lower levels of licensing scrutiny to lower tiers, taking into account the budget and capacity of its investigative division. In some cases, it may only fully investigate owners and operators.

3. Another consideration is the economic impact of requiring licenses of certain groups. Requiring licensure may discourage persons from applying because they are unwilling to devote the time, pay the cost, or suffer the embarrassment of the licensing process. For example, a small jurisdiction with only a few casinos might have difficulty attracting chip suppliers if they had to undergo full licensing.

4. Finally, decisions on whether to require certain groups to undergo licensing are based on other considerations. For example, if a state legislature decides that the gaming industry must begin to realize revenues quickly to help a dire economic crisis, it may require the regulators to prioritize the businesses which will require licensure.

3. Depth

A. Generally

When a government requires a license to engage in a business related to gaming, the entity that must apply and obtain the license typically is not an individual. For example, the owners of most Nevada casinos are owned directly or indirectly by publicly traded corporations. Depth of licensing refers to which persons associated with the applicant-entity must file an application and obtain a license.

B. Individuals

Casino operators must go through full investigation and licensing. When the operator is an individual, called a "sole proprietor," requiring that person to submit the application and undergo an investigation is obvious. If casino licenses were issued only to individuals, the licensing process would be simple. Individual ownership is the least complex business form. To license an individual, the authorities need only to investigate that person and specified employees by job responsibilities and not an entire business entity.

C. Corporations

A corporation is an artificial person or legal entity that the government authorizes to conduct business. The principal benefits of a corporation over other forms of business enterprises are limited liability of equity owners known as shareholders, transferability of interest, and continuity of existence.

Structures for corporations differ between jurisdictions, but usually involve officers, directors, and shareholders. Shareholders are persons or entities that hold equity, as represented by shares, in a company. Shares entitle the holders to control the corporation through voting for the board of directors. In the discretion of the board of directors, shareholders are entitled to earnings through current or accumulated dividends and to pro-rata distribution of assets upon liquidation. Shareholders elect directors who manage the corporation through the corporate officers. The directors have a duty to the corporation to use their best judgment in deciding and executing corporate policy. Among other things, their duties typically include: (1) selecting officers and setting officer salary and compensation; (2) making major policy decisions; and (3) deciding major financial matters, including dividends and financing. Officers are corporate agents, and have management responsibilities that the board of directors delegates to them. Typical officers are the president, who serves as the general manager; the treasurer, who is the chief financial officer; and the secretary, who is the ministerial officer. Corporations also may have one or more vice presidents and assistant officers.

Depth of licensing for corporations concerns which officers, employees, directors, and shareholders must undergo licensing scrutiny. Similar considerations apply to other business formations, such as general and limited partnerships, trusts, joint ventures, limited liability companies, and joint stock associations.

D. Publicly-Traded Corporations

Public company stock is attractive to investors because it usually provides liquidity. If a person buys the stock, he can readily sell it in the public market. The corporation benefits because capital is easier to raise in liquid markets. Allowing publicly traded corporations to own and operate casinos, however, poses regulatory issues. As a practical matter, a publicly traded corporation cannot be licensed if all its shareholders must be licensed. Often a public company will have thousands of shares traded daily. Therefore, if a jurisdiction wants to encourage publicly traded corporations to invest in its casino industry, it must allow licensing without each shareholder having to obtain a license.

Waiving licensing requirements for some shareholders, however, may allow unsuitable persons to buy shares and have an ownership interest in the casino companies. This may not pose substantial problems if the person owns a few shares out of millions, but can create regulatory issues if the person owns a significant percentage of the stock.

i. Shareholders

68 Indiana Admin. Code § 5-1-4:
Publically Traded Corporations

Sec. 4. (a) Each person (other than an institutional investor who complies with subsection (c)) who, individually or in association with others, acquires, directly or indirectly, the beneficial ownership of:

(1) five percent (5%) or more of any class of voting securities of a publicly traded corporation that is required to contain the charter provisions set forth in 68 IAC 4-1-8; or

(2) five percent (5%) or more of the beneficial interest in a riverboat licensee, riverboat license applicant, or supplier licensee, directly or indirectly, through any class of voting securities of any holding or intermediary company of a riverboat licensee, riverboat license applicant, or supplier licensee;

shall apply to the commission for a finding of suitability within forty-five (45) days after acquiring the securities. A riverboat licensee or supplier licensee shall notify each person who is subject to this section of its requirements, provided that the obligations of the person subject to this rule are independent of, and unaffected by, the corporation's failure to give notice.

(b) Each institutional investor who, individually or in association with others, acquires, directly or indirectly, beneficial ownership of:

(1) five percent (5%) or more of any class of voting securities of a publicly traded corporation that is required to contain the charter provisions set forth in 68 IAC 4-1-8;

or

(2) five percent (5%) or more of the beneficial interest in a riverboat licensee, riverboat license applicant, or supplier licensee through any class of voting securities of any holding company or intermediary company of a riverboat licensee, riverboat license applicant, or supplier licensee;

shall notify the commission within ten (10) business days after the person acquires the securities and files Form 13-D or 13-G with the Securities and Exchange Commission and shall provide additional information and may be subject to a finding of suitability as required by the commission. A riverboat licensee or supplier licensee shall notify each person who is subject to this section of its requirements as soon as the corporation becomes aware of the acquisition, provided that the obligations of the persons subject to this rule are independent of, and unaffected by, the corporation's failure to give notice.

(c) An institutional investor who would otherwise be subject to subsection (a) shall, within forty-five (45) days after acquiring the interests set forth in subsection (b), submit the following information to the commission:

(1) A description of the institutional investor's business and a statement as to why the institutional investor is within the definition of institutional investor set forth in 68 IAC 1-1-52.

(2) A certification made under oath and the penalty of perjury that the voting securities were acquired and are held for investment purposes only and were acquired and are held in the ordinary course of business as an institutional investor and not for the purpose of causing, directly or indirectly, the election of a majority of the board of directors, any change in the corporate charter, bylaws, management, policies, or operations of a riverboat licensee, supplier licensee, or affiliate. The signatory shall also explain the basis of his or her authority to sign the certification and to bind the institutional investor to its terms. The certification shall also provide that the institutional investor is bound by and shall comply with the Act (IC 4-33) and this title, is subject to the jurisdiction of the courts of Indiana, and consents to Indiana as the choice of forum in the event any dispute, question, or controversy arises regarding the application of this rule.

(3) The name, address, telephone number, and Social Security number of the officers and directors, or their equivalent, of the institutional investor as well as those persons who have direct control over the institutional investors's holdings of voting securities of the riverboat licensee, riverboat license applicant, supplier licensee, or affiliate.

(4) The name, address, telephone number, and Social Security number or federal tax identification number of each person who has the power to direct or control the institutional investor's exercise of its voting rights as a holder of voting securities of the riverboat licensee, riverboat license applicant, supplier licensee, or affiliate.

(5) The name of each person who beneficially owns five percent (5%) or more of the institutional investor's voting securities or other equivalent.

(6) A list of the institutional investor's affiliates.

(7) A list of all securities of the riverboat licensee, riverboat license applicant, or supplier licensee that are or were, directly or indirectly, beneficially owned by the institutional investor or its affiliates within the preceding one (1) year period, setting forth a description of the securities, the amount of the securities, and the date of the acquisition, sale, or both.

(8) A list of all regulatory agencies with which the institutional investor or any affiliate that beneficially owns voting securities of the riverboat licensee, supplier licensee, or affiliate files periodic reports, and the name, address, and telephone number of the person, if known, to contact at each agency regarding the institutional investor.

(9) A disclosure of all criminal sanctions imposed during the preceding ten (10) years. A disclosure of all regulatory sanctions imposed during the preceding ten (10) years and of any administrative or court proceedings filed by any regulatory agency in the preceding five (5) years against the institutional investor, its affiliates, any current officer or director, or any former officer or director whose tenure ended within the preceding twelve (12) months.

(10) A copy of any filing made under 15 U.S.C. 18a with respect to the acquisition or proposed acquisition of voting securities of the riverboat or supplier licensee or affiliate.

(11) Any additional information the commission may request to ensure compliance with the Act and this title.

(d) Each institutional investor who, individually or in association with others, acquires, directly or indirectly, the beneficial ownership of:

(1) fifteen percent (15%) or more of any class of voting securities of a publicly traded corporation that is required to contain the charter provisions set forth in 68 IAC4-1-8; or

(2) fifteen percent (15%) or more of the beneficial interest in a riverboat licensee, riverboat license applicant, or supplier licensee directly or indirectly, through any class of voting securities of any holding company or intermediary company of a riverboat or supplier licensee;

shall apply to the commission for a finding of suitability within forty-five (45) days after acquiring the securities. A riverboat licensee or supplier licensee shall notify each person who is subject to this section of its requirements, provided that the obligations of the person subject to this rule are independent of, and unaffected by, the corporation's failure to give notice.

(e) The commission may require that any applicant for an ownership interest apply for a finding of suitability in accordance with this rule if the commission deems the finding of suitability necessary to ensure compliance with the Act and this title.

(f) The following activities shall be deemed to be consistent with holding voting securities for investment purposes only under subsection (c)(2):

(1) Voting, directly or indirectly, through the delivery of a proxy furnished by the board of directors, on all matters voted on by the holders of such voting securities.

(2) Serving as a member of any committee of creditors or security holders formed in connection with a debt restructuring.

(3) Nominating any candidate for election or appointment to the board of directors in connection with a debt restructuring.

(4) Accepting appointment or election as a member of the board of directors in connection with a debt restructuring and serving in that capacity until the conclusion of the member's term.

(5) Making financial and other inquiries of management of the type normally made by securities analysts for information purposes and not to cause a change in its management, policies, or operations.

(6) Such other activities the commission determines to be consistent with such investment intent.

(g) A person who acquires beneficial ownership of any voting security in a riverboat licensee, riverboat license applicant, supplier licensee, holding company, or intermediary company of any riverboat licensee, riverboat license applicant, or supplier licensee created under the laws of a foreign country shall file such reports as the commission may prescribe and is subject to a finding of suitability under the Act and 68 IAC 2-1-5(c).

(h) Any person whose application was denied by the commission shall not hold, directly or indirectly, the beneficial ownership of any voting security of a riverboat licensee, riverboat license applicant, supplier licensee, holding company, or intermediary company thereof beyond that period of time prescribed by the commission, and must be removed immediately from any position as a director, officer, or employee of such riverboat licensee, riverboat license applicant, supplier licensee, holding company, or intermediary company thereof.

(i) Subsections (a), (b) and (d) shall not apply to any underwriter during the first ninety (90) days of the underwriting.

Notes

1. Jurisdictions that allow publicly traded corporations to hold gaming licenses must balance regulatory concerns with market realities. They can do this by setting thresholds

at which shareholders in publicly traded corporations must apply for and obtain a gaming license. In the United States, common levels are set at either five-percent or ten-percent. The five-percent level is tied to federal requirements on the reporting of stock ownership. An advantage of tying gaming approvals to SEC reporting is that the SEC rules on who has to report are well-established and supported by legal precedent. Under SEC requirements, a person acquiring more than five-percent of the beneficial ownership of any class of voting securities in a publicly traded corporation must report such to the SEC (usually an SEC Schedule 13D or 13G). The purpose of this filing is to inform the company and the public of the person's ownership and his or her intentions, such as an attempt to acquire control or to merely be a passive investor. Attempting to require persons owning less than five-percent to obtain a license is unworkable because the identity of these shareholders is difficult to discover. For example, the stock can be held in street names that effectively prevent gaming regulators from learning the identities of those owning less than five-percent of the equity securities of a company. Therefore, the only practical way that regulators may acquire knowledge of beneficial ownership of voting securities of registered publicly-traded corporations is through SEC reporting requirements.

2. A jurisdiction may decide that a five-percent threshold is too low because it can exclude publicly traded companies that have passive shareholders that hold more than five-percent. This is particularly common in a market that is dominated by funds or groups that collectively pool assets, such as mutual funds, pension funds, and insurance companies. In other cases, the five-percent shareholders are individual passive investors. A five-percent rule will move many corporations with large institutional investors and passive investors out of the jurisdiction. A ten-percent rule also has a foundation in federal securities law. Under section 16(a) of the Securities and Exchange Act of 1934, beneficial owners of more than ten-percent of a class of equity securities registered under section 12 of the Act must disclose their holdings, and any changes to them, in a filing with the SEC. A purpose of this requirement is that holders of ten-percent or greater are deemed "insiders" whose transactions can be followed by the media and public. Moreover, these individuals may be subject to short-swing profit recovery under section 16(d) of the Act. A ten-percent threshold has the advantage of permitting more corporations the opportunity to enter a jurisdiction. Moreover, a party that owns less than ten-percent is unlikely to control a publicly-traded corporation even if its stock is widely-held.

3. Still, if a concern exists that a shareholder (under either the five or ten percent rule) can influence corporate decisions, a jurisdiction can adopt exceptions to the exemptions from licensing. These exceptions might target activity that is inconsistent with the notion of the shareholder as a passive investor, such as sitting on the board of directors, causing a change in the majority of the board, or causing a change in the charter, bylaws, management, policies or operations of the publicly traded corporation or its casino subsidiary.

4. Many jurisdictions now allow institutional investors to hold over ten-percent. Institutional investors are entities such as banks, insurance companies, registered investment companies, advisors, and employee benefit or pension funds. These jurisdictions often require the institutional investors to apply for and obtain waivers. Besides Indiana, referenced above, examples include Michigan, Mich. Comp. Laws Ann. § 432.206c (allowing up to ten %); Nev. Gaming Comm. Reg. § 16.430 (an institutional investor is allowed to beneficially own up to and including 25% of any class of a PTC's voting securities and still qualify for a waiver); Ohio Rev. Code Ann. § 3772.10 (allowing up to ten %); N. J. Stat. Ann. § 5:12-85(f) (allowing up to ten %).

ii. Officers and Employees

Application of Lisa M. Lavigna for a
Casino Key Employee License

Casino Control Commission, 95 N.S.A.R.2d (CCC) 1, Sept. 30, 1992

Perskie, Chairman

Initial Decision: Introduction

This case involves the application of Lisa M. Lavigna (Applicant) for a casino key employee license. Applicant is an attorney-at-law licensed to practice in New Jersey. It is the first contested employee license case involving the qualifications of an attorney to arise under the Casino Control Act (Act), N.J.S.A. 5:12-1 et seq. Thus, it marks the initial occasion for the Commission to consider, from its regulatory perspective, the role of the casino counsel and the standards to which counsel may be held accountable by this body.

Procedural History

By letter dated November 15, 1990, the Division of Gaming Enforcement (Division) recommended that the application be granted but cited certain negative information uncovered in the course of its investigation. Specifically, the Division cited charges on July 5, 1984, which were disposed of in municipal court by plea and conviction for a traffic offense (failing to have driver's credentials, N.J.S.A. 39:3-29), and a then-pending administrative complaint filed with the Commission against Applicant's former employer, TropWorld Hotel and Casino (TropWorld). The complaint, which did not name Applicant (or any other TropWorld employee) as a party respondent, involved the employment of Applicant as an assistant corporate counsel, a position requiring a casino key employee license, from July 31, 1989 through December 6, 1989. During this period Applicant held only a casino hotel employee registration and was listed on documents supplied to the Commission by TropWorld as a legal secretary.

When the Commission reviewed the license application in December 1990, it deferred any action pending disposition of the casino violation complaint. The complaint was resolved on November 12, 1991, by approval of a stipulation of settlement that called for imposition of a civil penalty totaling $17,500 for two violations: permitting an employee to work without the proper credential and inaccurate reporting to the Commission.

Upon reconsideration of this application for key licensure on November 20, 1991, the Commission referred the matter for a contested case hearing. A prehearing conference was held on April 22, 1992. The hearing was conducted on June 10, 1992, at the conclusion of which the record was closed.

Issues

The Prehearing Conference Memorandum recites that this case involves but one issue: does Applicant possess the good character, honesty and integrity required for a casino key employee license pursuant to N.J.S.A. 5:12-89(b)(2). However, as the hearing progressed, it became evident that this was not merely a matter of balancing the "negative" aspects of Applicant's life the only relevant one being her employment without proper credentials against the positive aspects, of which there were many. Rather, in this instance the significance of the global "character" issue was subsumed by a more particularized inquiry into Applicant's competence to hold a license issued by the Commission for service as counsel to a casino licensee. Recognizing that a question of competence is, in the Act's terminology, more a matter of business ability and experience (section 86(b)(3)) than it is of good character, honesty and integrity, counsel for Applicant acknowledged the pertinence of the question and interposed no objection to its consideration.

However, such an inquiry necessarily raises significant and complex questions regarding the ambit of this Commission's authority to "regulate" attorneys in the practice of law. The preeminent concern is whether the application of our statutory employee licensing criteria encroaches impermissibly upon the province of the Supreme Court of New Jersey to regulate the practice of law in this State. At the hearing, I asked counsel for Applicant if the fact that the Supreme Court issued Applicant a license to practice law was dispositive. He responded: "I wouldn't say it's dispositive. I'd say it's highly probative of her ability to serve as corporate counsel." T52-9 to 10. I agree.

Other questions of delicate intricacy may arise concerning the standards to be applied. Putting aside the difficulty of articulating the standards,[1] what is their relationship to the Rules of Professional Conduct (R.P.C. 1.1 et seq.) which govern the legal profession in this State?

Such questions will be addressed here only insofar as they need be in order to resolve the ultimate issue of Applicant's licensure. The essential resolution of these and other related questions will be left for another day. It is hoped that merely identifying some potential issues will have the salutary effect of initiating a process that will yield answers to more probing and substantive questions. To this end, I invite all interested parties, particularly the Casino Association, the Casino Law Section of the New Jersey Bar Association and the Division to join the Commission in an effort to provide more expansive answers to these decidedly difficult and important questions.

Findings Of Fact

The facts regarding the incident which gave rise to the concern over Applicant's suitability for licensure as a casino key employee are not in dispute.

Applicant was admitted to the New Jersey bar in December 1988. T15-10 to 12. Thereafter she worked for brief periods with two law firms in the Atlantic City area. In late July 1989, Applicant secured an offer of employment from Steven R. Bolson, an attorney-at-law and Vice President of Legal and Corporate Affairs of TropWorld, to work as an Assistant Corporate Counsel. At the direction of Solson or Idelle Goldberg, also an attorney and then Assistant Corporate Counsel, or both, Applicant filed for and obtained a casino hotel employee registration. The position of Assistant Corporate Counsel was, according to TropWorld's Commission-approved Jobs Compendium,[2] a position requiring a casino key employee license. Pursuant to section 106, TropWorld could not employ anyone in that capacity unless he or she possessed a valid casino key employee license.[3]

Applicant applied for a casino key employee license on September 5, 1989; she was issued a temporary key license on December 6 of that year. From July 3l, 1989 through November 1, 1989, Applicant was reported to the Commission in TropWorld's Work Permit reports (sections 48 and 106 of the Act; N.J.A.C. 19:41-1.7) as holding employment in the position of "Senior Secretary IV/Legal." This secretarial position required only a

---

1. For a provocative discourse on problems of this sort see Cox, Regulation of Attorneys Practicing Before Federal Agencies, 34 Case W. Res. 173 (1983–84).

2. N.J.A.C. 19:45-1.11(a) requires casino licensees to submit a detailed list of positions of its employees, including, "proposed registration or license endorsement consistent with the requirements of the Act and the Commission's rules...."

3. Section 117 of the Act subjects both the individual and the employer-casino to criminal penalties for employment without the requisite credential. However, no criminal complaint was ever filed in connection with these particular violations.

casino hotel employee registration. From the time she began her employment at TropWorld to her termination in June 1990 (for reasons unrelated to this case), Applicant worked as Assistant Corporate Counsel. She represented TropWorld in several matters presented to the Commission, at least one of which involved the licensing of casino security employees. At no time did Applicant work as a secretary.

The critical factual inquiry concerns Applicant's awareness of the licensing requirements of her corporate counsel position, and more importantly, her actions when she knew or should have known that she was not appropriately licensed. Within days of her hiring, TropWorld issued an identification badge to Applicant which showed her to be employed in the capacity of legal secretary. Out of "curiosity," she questioned first Goldberg and later the Personnel Department about the badge. Applicant was informed that this was "the way it was done," and that she would be issued a new identification card indicating a corporate counsel position when her temporary key license was granted. Goldberg further informed Applicant that this was consistent with the way her own licensure had been handled when she was first employed. Applicant thereafter dismissed any concern from her mind. She placed the badge in her pocketbook and used it only occasionally to gain access to the cafeteria at TropWorld.

Applicant repeatedly maintained at the hearing that neither she, the supervisors who hired her, nor the Personnel Department at TropWorld acted with any fraudulent intent or design to deceive. Rather it was, as they understood it, the way it was always done: one worked as an attorney on a "registration" until a key credential was issued. Applicant relied in particular on Bolson due to his extensive experience in the casino industry.

At the hearing Applicant readily acknowledged that this practice, and her participation in it, were wrong. She placed principal, but not exclusive, responsibility for the error on Bolson. Nevertheless, she acknowledged initially with reticence, belatedly with fervor that she should have looked into it further and should have exercised better judgment.

Two witnesses testified as character witnesses, one a long-time friend who had occasion to avail herself of Applicant's legal counsel, the other an attorney acquainted with Applicant primarily through his representation of TropWorld in the casino violation case which resulted from the Applicant's employment without the proper credential. Both witnesses alluded favorably to Applicant's character and veracity. The friend added that Applicant had done a "wonderful job" representing her in personal and business matters and was always "extremely ethical." She further described Applicant as a person who has done "a lot of volunteer work" for charity. In addition, two favorable character reference letters from acquaintances of Applicant were received into the record without objection.

As noted, none of the foregoing statements was disputed and I therefore find them as fact. I specifically find that Applicant was, at least in the initial stages of her employment at TropWorld, ignorant, and blissfully so, of the law regarding licensing requirements under the Act and its attendant regulations. Further, I find that within a matter of a few days after her hiring, Applicant was notified that she was listed on TropWorld's records as holding a position she did not, in fact, hold. Her efforts to resolve what in her mind was a mere curious quandary were minimal and inadequate. She asked her supervising attorney, whose judgment on this point appears at least equally dubious, and some unidentified person in the casino's personnel department why this was so. Upon hearing the explanation, "that's the way it's done," Applicant dismissed any further thought of the matter from her mind. I accept Applicant's assertion that her acts and omissions were without guile or devious intent. I am satisfied, rather, that she was personally irresponsible, professionally ignorant and ethically obtuse.

Finally, I find that in the early stages of the hearing, particularly during her direct and cross-examination as well as in her initial responses to my own inquiries, Applicant was not noticeably cognizant of the full measure of her responsibilities as an attorney. However, on the re-direct examination which followed an extended colloquy between her counsel and me, Applicant demonstrated an awareness and comprehension of the fact that the exercise of informed, independent judgment, together with technical expertise concerning the Act and Commission regulations, and a sound sense of right and wrong, were integral elements of the professional responsibility expected of attorneys seeking or holding a license to serve as casino counsel.

Conclusions Of Law

Among the Commission's many duties is the obligation "to hear and decide promptly and in reasonable order all license ... applications ..." N.J.S.A. 5:12-63(a). Applicant submitted her application after her employer had gained approval of its job compendium (see n.2 ante) which indicated that her position required a casino key employee license. Key employee licenses are governed by section 89 of the Act, subsection (b) of which requires each applicant to establish by clear and convincing evidence: (1) financial stability, integrity and responsibility; (2) good character, honesty and integrity; (3) business ability and casino experience sufficient to establish "the reasonable likelihood of success and efficiency in the particular position involved;" and (4) residency in the State of New Jersey (subject to waiver under circumstances not here relevant).

A casino key employee is defined in section 9:

"Casino Key Employee" Any natural person employed in the operation of a licensed casino in a supervisory capacity or empowered to make discretionary decisions which regulate casino operation, including, without limitation, pit bosses; shift bosses; credit executives; casino cashier supervisors; casino managers and assistant managers; and managers or supervisors of casino security employees; or any other natural person empowered to make discretionary decisions which regulate the management of an approved hotel including, without limitation, hotel managers; entertainment directors; and food and beverage directors; or any other employee so designed by the Casino Control Commission for reasons consistent with the policies of this act.

The Commission has not heretofore been requested to make nor has it issued any blanket rule determining that all corporate counsel and assistant corporate counsel employed by casinos require a key employee license or any other specific credential. In point of fact, the credential requirements vary from casino to casino, depending in large measure upon the duties of the particular position. Perhaps some standardization in this area would be desirable, but that is not a matter to be decided here. In this instance, the determination that a key license is required was a product of the jobs compendium process.

...

It is also obvious that the best interests of the casino-client will be furthered by faithful compliance with the regulatory strictures. The regulatory framework in which casinos must operate is described in the complex, sometimes arcane language of the law. The concepts, even where plainly stated, are not always easily understood by one not fortified with legal training and ability. It is therefore essential that casinos receive competent legal advice. Such advice is marked by sound, independent judgment and thorough knowledge of the Act and Commission regulations, as well as awareness and understanding of Commission policies and procedures. Moreover, all casino counsel are specifically and individually accountable in this respect, not only to their employer but, as holders of licenses, to this Commission as well. This applies to neophyte lawyers and seasoned practitioners alike. Just as the obligation to comply with the ethics rules comes with admission to the bar, the obligation to know and comply with the Act and Commission regulations comes with the issuance of an employee license or registration.[4] The Commission expects all casino employees to be familiar with those provisions of the Act and regulations that affect their positions of employment. We also visit upon those with discretionary functions the duty to exercise sound judgment. See State v. Resorts International Hotel, Inc., et al., Docket Nos. 91-291 through 294 (Commission decision January 22, 1992), where in a case involving the acceptance of stolen money orders, the Commission observed that casinos and cashiers must apply "reasoned judgment" before accepting cash equivalents. (Slip opinion at 7). We expect nothing less, indeed, considerably more, from casino counsel. Their knowledge of the Act and Commission regulations must be plenary, and their professional conduct beyond reproach.

Turning, then, to the application of these standards to the conduct and judgment of Applicant at the outset of her employment, it is obvious and certain that she simply did not fulfill our requirements. She violated the statute by working without a proper license. She is charged with the knowledge that her status was affirmatively misrepresented to the Commission and the Division. She failed to take any action to correct or even object to the violation. She abdicated her responsibilities to the blithe assurance that "that is the way it is done." And, of course, she came to a recognition that her conduct was unacceptable only when, as the late, former Commissioner Joel Jacobson so poetically once described it, she was "pounding on the pearly gates of licensure," and even then with ever so much difficulty.

Were I to base my decision solely on an evaluation of her qualifications at that time I would surely find her unqualified. Her actions reflected an alarming absence of the very qualities that are essential to the position she held, i.e., sound, independent judgment, a thorough, detailed knowledge of the law and, not least, a clear understanding of her personal obligation to assure compliance with all applicable provisions of the law. Her failure at the time to assume personal responsibility for her acts and deficiencies is both startling and troublesome.

But that is not the limit of the present inquiry. A license determination is essentially a predictive judgment. It is largely governed by the events, good and bad, of the applicant's past, but it is in the final analysis a present determination of the likelihood of successful future experience in the casino industry. Having considered the entire record before me, and noting that Applicant is a licensed attorney in good standing, I am convinced that she currently meets the criteria for licensure. I believe Applicant now recognizes the deficiencies she previously manifested and understands both her professional responsibilities and the fact that those responsibilities cannot be evaded or delegated. On balance, I view her conduct in 1989 as aberrational and attributable to though certainly not excused by her relative inexperience. I am satisfied that the likelihood of a further default in her professional responsibility is remote, and that she has, by the requisite standard of clear and convincing evidence, established her business ability (and, as noted, her character) and therefore her qualification for licensure.

---

4. Of course, this assumes compliance with the Act's requirements regarding appropriate licensure before commencing casino employment. See discussion of sections 106 and 117, ante. When, as here, the employment preceded licensure in derogation of the licensing scheme I would not and do not hesitate to visit these obligations as of the time Applicant assumed the responsibilities of the position of casino counsel. In this instance, that occurred in July 1989, notwithstanding that a formal (temporary) license was not issued until December 1989.

Before concluding, however, I must comment on the evidence that two attorneys senior to Applicant in the TropWorld legal department were at least as irresponsible as she regarding the circumstances of her improper licensure. Such conduct, if it occurred as described in this record, does not mitigate Applicant's responsibility for her own acts and omissions. Nevertheless, while I do not conclude that the persons identified in this record are culpable without affording them an opportunity to present evidence on the subject it would be unfair to do so.[5] I would remind all supervising casino counsel of their own ethical and professional obligations with respect to lawyers in their organizations. R.P.C. 5.1(a); Matter of Yacavino, 100 N.J. 50, 55–56 (1985), where the Court issued a similar directive and advised that the "attitude of leaving new lawyers to 'sink or swim' will not be tolerated.

Disposition

I recommend that the casino key employee license application of Lisa M. Lavigna be GRANTED. I further recommend that the casino hotel employee registration, issued to Applicant under pretenses which I find to have been false, be administratively revoked.

I hereby FILE my Initial Decision with the CASINO CONTROL COMMISSION for consideration....

Note

Why wouldn't an otherwise suitable person seek the proper license? Should failure to apply for a proper license affect a person's suitability for a license? Why shouldn't holding a license to practice law *automatically* mean a person was entitled to a gaming license? What are the similarities and differences in the licensing of lawyers and the issuance of gaming licenses?

4. Criteria

A. Generally

Criteria are what the regulatory agency considers when granting a license. They may include moral character, honesty, financial ability, association with unsavory characters, and business experience. When analyzing an applicant, the regulatory body sets the standard, or minimum, level an applicant must satisfy for licensure within the regulatory provisions.

i. Personal Suitability

Nev. Rev. Stat. § 463.170: Qualifications for License, Finding of Suitability or Approval, Regulations

1. Any person who the commission determines is qualified to receive a license, to be found suitable or to receive any approval required under the provisions of this chapter,

---

5. As to Bolson, presumably these issues will be raised in the context of an application to renew his key employee license, which will expire in a few months. As to Goldberg, whose license was recently renewed, it would appear incumbent upon the Division to consider what action would be appropriate in light of the evidence presented here. *See* N.J.S.A. 5:12-94(d).

or to be found suitable regarding the operation of a charitable lottery under the provisions of chapter 462 of NRS, having due consideration for the proper protection of the health, safety, morals, good order and general welfare of the inhabitants of the State of Nevada and the declared policy of this state, may be issued a state gaming license, be found suitable or receive any approval required by this chapter, as appropriate. The burden of proving his qualification to receive any license, be found suitable or receive any approval required by this chapter is on the applicant.

2. An application to receive a license or be found suitable must not be granted unless the commission is satisfied that the applicant is:

(a) A person of good character, honesty and integrity;

(b) A person whose prior activities, criminal record, if any, reputation, habits and associations do not pose a threat to the public interest of this state or to the effective regulation and control of gaming or charitable lotteries, or create or enhance the dangers of unsuitable, unfair or illegal practices, methods and activities in the conduct of gaming or charitable lotteries or in the carrying on of the business and financial arrangements incidental thereto; and

(c) In all other respects qualified to be licensed or found suitable consistently with the declared policy of the state.

3. A license to operate a gaming establishment or an inter-casino linked system must not be granted unless the applicant has satisfied the commission that:

(a) The applicant has adequate business probity, competence and experience, in gaming or generally; and

(b) The proposed financing of the entire operation is:

(1) Adequate for the nature of the proposed operation; and

(2) From a suitable source.

Any lender or other source of money or credit which the commission finds does not meet the standards set forth in subsection 2 may be deemed unsuitable.

4. An application to receive a license or be found suitable constitutes a request for a determination of the applicant's general character, integrity, and ability to participate or engage in, or be associated with gaming or the operation of a charitable lottery, as appropriate.

...

Michigan Compiled Laws § 432.206: Casino Licenses

...

Sec. 6. (4) An applicant is ineligible to receive a casino license if any of the following circumstances exist:

(a) The applicant has been convicted of a felony under the laws of this state, any other state, or the United States.

(b) The applicant has been convicted of a misdemeanor involving gambling, theft, dishonesty, or fraud in any state or a local ordinance in any state involving gambling, dishonesty, theft, or fraud that substantially corresponds to a misdemeanor in that state.

(c) The applicant has submitted an application for a license under this act that contains false information.

(d) The applicant is a member of the board.

(e) The applicant fails to demonstrate the applicant's ability to maintain adequate liability and casualty insurance for its proposed casino.

(f) The applicant holds an elective office of a governmental unit of this state, another state, or the federal government, or is a member of or employed by a gaming regulatory body of a governmental unit in this state, another state, or the federal government, or is employed by a governmental unit of this state. This section does not apply to an elected officer of or employee of a federally recognized Indian tribe or to an elected precinct delegate.

(g) The applicant or affiliate owns more than a 10% ownership interest in any entity holding a casino license issued under this act.

(h) The board concludes that the applicant lacks the requisite suitability as to integrity, moral character, and reputation; personal and business probity; financial ability and experience; responsibility; or means to develop, construct, operate, or maintain the casino proposed in the certified development agreement.

(i) The applicant fails to meet other criteria considered appropriate by the board. The criteria considered appropriate by the board shall not be arbitrary, capricious, or contradictory to the expressed provisions of this act.

(5) In determining whether to grant a casino license to an applicant, the board shall also consider all of the following:

(a) The integrity, moral character, and reputation; personal and business probity; financial ability and experience; and responsibility of the applicant and of any other person or means to develop, construct, operate, or maintain a casino that either:

(i) Controls, directly or indirectly, the applicant.

(ii) Is controlled, directly or indirectly, by the applicant or by a person who controls, directly or indirectly, the applicant.

(b) The prospective total revenue to be derived by the state from the conduct of casino gambling.

(c) The financial ability of the applicant to purchase and maintain adequate liability and casualty insurance and to provide an adequate surety bond.

(d) The sources and total amount of the applicant's capitalization to develop, construct, maintain, and operate the proposed casino.

(e) Whether the applicant has adequate capitalization to develop, construct, maintain, and operate for the duration of a license the proposed casino in accordance with the requirements of this act and rules promulgated by the board and to responsibly pay off its secured and unsecured debts in accordance with its financing agreement and other contractual obligations.

(f) The extent and adequacy of any compulsive gambling programs that the applicant will adopt and implement if licensed.

(g) The past and present compliance of the applicant and its affiliates or affiliated companies with casino or casino-related licensing requirements, casino-related agreements, or compacts with the state of Michigan or any other jurisdiction.

(h) Whether the applicant has been indicted, charged, arrested, convicted, pleaded guilty or nolo contendere, forfeited bail concerning, or had expunged any criminal offense under the laws of any jurisdiction, either felony or misdemeanor, not including traffic violations, regardless of whether the offense has been expunged, pardoned, or reversed on appeal or otherwise.

(i) Whether the applicant has filed, or had filed against it, a proceeding for bankruptcy or has ever been involved in any formal process to adjust, defer, suspend, or otherwise work out the payment of any debt.

(j) Whether the applicant has been served with a complaint or other notice filed with any public body regarding a payment of any tax required under federal, state, or local law that has been delinquent for 1 or more years.

(k) The applicant has a history of noncompliance with the casino licensing requirements of any jurisdiction.

(l) The applicant has a history of noncompliance with any regulatory requirements in this state or any other jurisdiction.

(m) Whether at the time of application the applicant is a defendant in litigation involving its business practices.

(n) Whether awarding a license to an applicant would undermine the public's confidence in the Michigan gaming industry.

(o) Whether the applicant meets other standards for the issuance of a casino license which the board may promulgate by rule. The rules promulgated under this subdivision shall not be arbitrary, capricious, or contradictory to the expressed provisions of this act.

(6) Each applicant shall submit with its application, on forms provided by the board, a photograph and 2 sets of fingerprints for each person having a greater than 1% direct or indirect pecuniary interest in the casino, and each person who is an officer, director, or managerial employee of the applicant.

(7) The board shall review all applications for casino licenses and shall inform each applicant of the board's decision. Prior to rendering its decision, the board shall provide a public investigative hearing at which the applicant for a license shall have the opportunity to present testimony and evidence to establish its suitability for a casino license. Other testimony and evidence may be presented at the hearing, but the board's decision shall be based on the whole record before the board and is not limited to testimony and evidence submitted at the public investigative hearing.

(8) A license shall be issued for a 1-year period. All licenses are renewable annually upon payment of the license fee and upon the transmittal to the board of an annual report to include information required under rules promulgated by the board.

(9) All applicants and licensees shall consent to inspections, searches, and seizures and the providing of handwriting exemplar, fingerprints, photographs, and information as authorized in this act and in rules promulgated by the board.

(10) Applicants and licensees shall be under a continuing duty to provide information requested by the board and to cooperate in any investigation, inquiry, or hearing conducted by the board.

(11) Failure to provide information requested by the board to assist in any investigation, inquiry, or hearing of the board, or failure to comply with this act or rules promulgated by the board, may result in denial, suspension, or, upon reasonable notice, revocation of a license.

Notes

1. Criteria can be either set or discretionary. An example of set criteria is the prohibition in Michigan that a person who has been convicted of a felony is ineligible for a gaming license. Discretionary criteria are illustrated by the Nevada requirement that a person must be of good character, honesty and integrity to obtain a gaming license.

2. Integrity, truthfulness, and honesty are related concepts but have different meanings. Truthfulness means simply telling the truth. Truthfulness is only one component of honesty. One can be truthful but dishonest. It is dishonest to use some facts but not disclose other facts to create a false impression. For example, a person who was arrested by state police may be able to state truthfully that he was never arrested by city police. If, however, that was in response to a question as to whether the applicant has a criminal record, it would be dishonest. So, it is not enough to simply be truthful. How useful is honesty as a criterion? Shakespeare wrote, in *Hamlet*: "Ay, Sir, to be honest, as this world goes, is to be one man picked out of ten thousand." Thomas Fuller conveyed similar thought in *Gnomologia* when he wrote: "He that resolves to deal with none but honest men must leave off dealing." The sentiments that both men convey is that no matter how committed to honesty a person may be, few people can claim to be completely honest in all their dealings. When applying the honesty criteria, regulators usually apply a "materiality standard." An applicant is unlikely to be denied a license if he told his son that he could not take him fishing because he had to work, when, in fact, he was going to a football game with his buddies. The honesty criterion generally is reviewed in a business as opposed to a personal relationship. This is justified because the purpose of licensing is to predict the behavior of the applicant as a gaming licensee. Thus, his behavior in other business relationships is more germane to the inquiry than his personal relationships. Moreover, honesty in business conduct usually becomes more relevant with the importance of the transaction. For example, it may be of minor materiality that an applicant, in order to cut short a telephone conversation, lied to a salesman when he told him that he recently bought the product being offered. The materiality increases dramatically if the applicant misrepresents the value of inventory to convince a lender to loan money to his business.

3. Honesty is only one component of integrity, which means soundness of moral character, as shown by dealings with others. A person can be honest but lack integrity if, for example, he knowingly takes advantage of people in his business dealings. While, conceptually, integrity appears preferable to honesty, it is difficult to assess and apply. Integrity is a complex concept that involves coherent commitment to a personal order of moral principles. Commitments can include honesty, family, friendship, religion, honor, country or fairness. Persons order these commitments in such a way that it is acceptable to violate some commitments in order to honor others. For many people it is acceptable to lie, if necessary, to protect another from harm or injustice. For example, integrity is not compromised if a person shelters a victim of spousal abuse and lies to the spouse when questioned as to the individual's whereabouts. Integrity means upholding these commitments in the face of temptation or challenge for the right reasons. Attempting to test a person's integrity consistently tests the skills of the regulators. They must understand the person's personal order of commitment, then decide whether the person consistently is true to these commitments.

4. Take two different scenarios that the gaming regulators might face in deciding whether to license an applicant for a casino license:

    1) The applicant is forty-four years old with a college education. He has worked in the gaming industry for seventeen years and is now a casino

manager at a major casino. Both his record in the industry and his reputation are very good. He has only a minor criminal record for larceny as a teenager. He befriended a person in the fifth grade. His friend started in the gaming industry as a dealer but had his work permit revoked for stealing from a player and the casino. His friend has since been involved in many crimes and has been linked to a local member of a Chicago crime family. Unlike the prior applicant, this applicant has no criminal record and has no involvement with the criminal matters but remains fiercely loyal to his childhood friend, even to the point of posting bail money.

2) The applicant is the same as the above except that instead of having a notorious friend, his father is the local member of a Chicago crime family. While he maintains a normal father-son relationship, he is not involved in any criminal activities and does not associate with any of his father's friends.

Integrity might be inconsistent with regulatory policy based on the ordering of the applicant's commitments. Take the first scenario. Here, the applicant values personal friendship highly. Unfortunately, he chose poorly in his childhood. The regulators demand licensees not to associate with such persons, but the applicant's personal integrity places his personal commitment to friendship above the dictates of regulation. If the applicant were a person of little integrity, he might lie to the regulators and tell them he will not socialize with his friend in the future. If the applicant was a person of integrity, his personal order of commitment might dictate that he maintain his friendship and tell the regulators. Here, the regulators must assess whether the relationship and the applicant's refusal to sever it pose such a threat to the industry as to justify denying the license. In this situation, an applicant may be denied a license, not because he lacks integrity, but because his high commitment to friendship is inconsistent with good regulation. How would you access this scenario if you were a regulator considering this application?

The second scenario is even more difficult because most people consider commitments to one's family more important than to friends. As the saying goes, "You can pick your friends, but you can't pick your family." Here the regulators must decide whether to license the person despite his relationship with his father, require the applicant to dissociate himself from his father, or deny the application because the mere involvement of the father taints the industry.

5. A major criticism of pre-licensing inquiry is that it is flawed when its purpose is to predict the future behavior of an individual. Commentators have expressed doubt as to the accuracy of such predictions. *See* Banks McDowell, *The Usefulness of "Good Moral Character,"* 33 Washburn L.J. 323, 327 (1992). Attempting to predict future behavior assumes that people have fundamental character traits that govern their conduct. The validity of this assumption is questioned. According to critics, character assessments have little predictive value because conduct is contextual in nature, and "the situational nature of moral conduct makes predictions of behavior uncertain under any circumstances." Noted one commentator, "a half century of behavioral research underscores the variability and contextual nature of moral behavior: A single incident or small number of acts committed in dissimilar social settings affords no basis for reliable generalizations." Deborah L. Rhode, *Moral Character as a Professional Credential*, 94 Yale L.J. 491, 560 (1985). Nevertheless, social scientists can predict behavior in groups. For example, they can use statistics to predict that some recovering alcoholics will relapse, but that prediction cannot be extended to an individual alcoholic with any reliability. Regulators may decide that persons who by past actions put themselves into high risk categories should not be licensed even if the regulators cannot predict if a particular applicant is likely to cre-

ate problems. Therefore, despite the criticism, all established governments that allow gambling impose some form of pre-licensing inquiry.

ii. Business and Financial Suitability

Nevada Gaming Commission & State Gaming Control Board Regulation § 3.050: Financial Requirements

1. No license will be issued for use in any establishment until satisfactory evidence is presented that there is adequate financing available to pay all current obligations and, in addition, to provide adequate working capital to finance opening of the establishment.

2. The commission may require a licensee to provide security for the payment of future wages, salaries or other obligations, either as a condition precedent to issuance or renewal of any license or at any other time the commission determines that such requirement would be in the public interest. The security required shall be in such form and amount as the commission may from time to time determine.

Nevada Gaming Commission and State Gaming Control Board Regulation § 3.090: Standards for Commission Action

1. No license, registration, finding of suitability, or approval shall be granted unless and until the applicant has satisfied the commission that the applicant:

(a) Is a person of good character, honesty, and integrity;

(b) Is a person whose background, reputation and associations will not result in adverse publicity for the State of Nevada and its gaming industry; and

(c) Has adequate business competence and experience for the role or position for which application is made.

2. No license, registration, finding of suitability, or approval shall be granted unless and until the applicant has satisfied the commission that the proposed funding of the entire operation shall be (a) adequate for the nature of the proposed operation, and (b) from a suitable source. The suitability of the source of funds shall be determined by the standards enumerated in paragraph 1(a), (b) and (c) above.

New Jersey Stat. § 5:12-84: Casino License— Applicant Requirements

Any applicant for a casino license must produce information, documentation and assurances concerning the following qualification criteria:

a. Each applicant shall produce such information, documentation and assurances concerning financial background and resources as may be required to establish by clear and convincing evidence the financial stability, integrity and responsibility of the applicant, including but not limited to bank references, business and personal income and disbursement schedules, tax returns and other reports filed with governmental agencies, and business and personal accounting and check records and ledgers. In addition, each applicant shall, in writing, authorize the examination of all bank accounts and records as may be deemed necessary by the commission or the division.

...

d. Each applicant shall produce such information, documentation and assurances as may be required to establish by clear and convincing evidence that the applicant has sufficient business ability and casino experience as to establish the likelihood of creation and maintenance of a successful, efficient casino operation. The applicant shall produce the names of all proposed casino key employees as they become known and a description of their respective or proposed responsibilities, and a full description of security systems and management controls proposed for the casino and related facilities.

e. Each applicant shall produce such information, documentation and assurances to establish to the satisfaction of the commission the suitability of the casino and related facilities subject to subsection i. of section 83 of P.L.1977, c.110 (C.5:12-83) and its proposed location will not adversely affect casino operations. Each applicant shall submit an impact statement which shall include, without limitation, architectural and site plans which establish that the proposed facilities comply in all respects with the requirements of this act and the requirements of the master plan and zoning and planning ordinances of Atlantic City, without any use variance from the provisions thereof; a market impact study which analyzes the adequacy of the patron market and the effect of the proposal on such market and on the existing casino facilities licensed under this act; and an analysis of the effect of the proposal on the overall economic and competitive conditions of Atlantic City and the State of New Jersey.

New Jersey Admin. Code § 19:43-4.2: Financial Stability

(a) Each casino licensee or applicant shall establish its financial stability by clear and convincing evidence in accordance with section 84(a) of the Act and this subchapter.

(b) The Commission may consider any relevant evidence of financial stability; provided, however, that a casino licensee or applicant shall be considered to be financially stable if it establishes by clear and convincing evidence that it meets each of the following standards:

1. The ability to assure the financial integrity of casino operations by the maintenance of a casino bankroll or equivalent provisions adequate to pay winning wagers to casino patrons when due. A casino licensee or applicant shall be found to have established this standard if it maintains, on a daily basis, a casino bankroll, or a casino bankroll and equivalent provisions, in an amount which is at least equal to the average daily minimum casino bankroll or equivalent provisions, calculated on a monthly basis, for the corresponding month in the previous year. For any casino licensee or applicant which has been in operation for less than a year, such amount shall be determined by the Commission based upon levels maintained by a comparable casino licensee;

2. The ability to meet ongoing operating expenses which are essential to the maintenance of continuous and stable casino operations. A casino licensee or applicant shall be found to have established this standard if it demonstrates the ability to achieve positive gross operating profit, measured on an annual basis;

3. The ability to pay, as and when due, all local, State and Federal taxes, including the tax on gross revenues imposed by subsection 144(a) of the Act, the investment alternative tax obligations imposed by subsection 144(b) and section 144.1 of the Act, and any fees imposed by the Act and Commission rules;

4. The ability to make necessary capital and maintenance expenditures in a timely manner which are adequate to ensure maintenance of a superior first class facility of

exceptional quality pursuant to subsection 83(i) of the Act. A casino licensee or applicant shall be found to have established this standard if it demonstrates that its capital and maintenance expenditures, over the five-year period which includes the three most recent calendar years and the upcoming two calendar years, average at least five percent of net revenue per annum, except that any casino licensee or applicant which has been in operation for less than three years shall be required to otherwise establish compliance with this standard; and

5. The ability to pay, exchange, refinance or extend debts, including long-term and short-term principal and interest and capital lease obligations, which will mature or otherwise come due and payable during the license term, or to otherwise manage such debts and any default with respect to such debts. The Commission also may require that a casino licensee or applicant advise the Commission and Division as to its plans to meet this standard with respect to any material debts coming due and payable within 12 months after the end of the license term.

New Jersey Admin. Code § 19:43-3.1: Undue Economic Concentration

(a) In accordance with N.J.S.A. 5:12-82e, no casino license shall be issued to or held by a person if the Commission determines that such issuance or holding will result in undue economic concentration in Atlantic City casino operations by that person. Whether a person is considered the holder of a casino license is defined in N.J.S.A. 5:12-82e.

(b) For purposes of N.J.S.A. 5:12-82e and this section, "undue economic concentration" means that a person would have such actual or potential domination of the casino gaming market in Atlantic City as to substantially impede or suppress competition among casino licensees or adversely impact the economic stability of the casino industry in Atlantic City.

(c) In determining whether the issuance or holding of a casino license by a person will result in undue economic concentration, the Commission shall consider the following criteria:

1. The percentage share of the market presently controlled by the person in each of the following categories:

i. The total number of licensed casinos in this State;

ii. Total casino and casino simulcasting facility square footage;

iii. Number of guest rooms;

iv. Number of slot machines;

v. Number of table games;

vi. Net revenue;

vii. Table game win;

viii. Slot machine win;

ix. Table game drop;

x. Slot machine drop; and

xi. Number of persons employed by the casino hotel;

2. The estimated increase in the market shares in the categories in (c)1 above if the person is issued or permitted to hold the casino license;

3. The relative position of other persons who hold casino licenses, as evidenced by the market shares of each such person in the categories in (c)1 above;

4. The current and projected financial condition of the casino industry;

5. Current market conditions, including level of competition, consumer demand, market concentration, any consolidation trends in the industry and any other relevant characteristics of the market;

6. Whether the licensed casinos held or to be held by the person have separate organizational structures or other independent obligations;

7. The potential impact of licensure on the projected future growth and development of the casino industry and Atlantic City;

8. The barriers to entry into the casino industry, including the licensure requirements of the Act, and whether the issuance or holding of a casino license by the person will operate as a barrier to new companies and individuals desiring to enter the market;

9. Whether the issuance or holding of the license by the person will adversely impact on consumer interests, or whether such issuance or holding is likely to result in enhancing the quality and customer appeal of products and services offered by casino licensees in order to maintain or increase their respective market shares;

10. Whether a restriction on the issuance or holding of an additional license by the person is necessary in order to encourage and preserve competition and to prevent undue economic concentration in casino operations; and

11. Any other evidence deemed relevant by the Commission.

Arch-View Casino Cruises, Inc. v. Illinois Gaming Board
636 N.E.2d 42 (Ill. App. 1994)

GREEN, J.

This case is before us for judicial review pursuant to section 17.1(a) of the Riverboat Gambling Act (Act) (230 ILCS 10/17.1(a) (West 1992)) and Supreme Court Rule 335 (134 Ill.2d R. 335) from a final order of the Illinois Gaming Board (Board) (230 ILCS 10/5(a)(1) (West 1992)) denying petitioner Arch-View Casino Cruises, Inc. (Arch-View), an owner's license to conduct a riverboat gambling operation (230 ILCS 10/6, 7 (West 1992)). The order was entered orally by the Board on May 3, 1993, by adoption of a recommended decision of an administrative law judge. Notice of that decision was mailed by the Board to Arch-View's counsel on May 5, 1993.

Arch-View contends that the Board's decision should be set aside because (1) the decision was contrary to the manifest weight of the evidence; (2) Arch-View was improperly denied its rights under the contested hearing provisions of the Illinois Administrative Procedure Act (Procedure Act) (5 ILCS 100/10-5 et seq. (West 1992)); and (3) Arch-View was denied due process rights. We disagree and affirm.

Section 7(e) of the Act (230 ILCS 10/7(e) (West 1992)) permitted the Board to issue up to five owner's licenses to become effective not earlier than January 1, 1991, and another five licenses to become effective not earlier than March 1, 1992, with one of that five to authorize gambling on the Des Plaines River in Will County. Arch-View sought one of the latter four licenses for a boat to be docked on a pier at the Village of Sauget, Illinois, a community of 197 people situated on the east bank of the Mississippi River in St. Clair County.

Section 7(b) of the Act (230 ILCS 10/7(b) (West 1992)) sets forth the factors for the Board to consider in passing upon an application for an owner's license. They are (1) the character, reputation, experience, and financial integrity of the applicant or persons having direct or indirect ability to control the applicant; (2) the facilities available for the gambling; (3) the revenue the State is likely to receive from the gambling; (4) the good faith of the applicant in providing an affirmative action plan to recruit, train, and upgrade minorities in all employment classifications; (5) the ability of the applicant to provide liability and casualty insurance; (6) the adequacy of the applicant's capitalization; and (7) the extent to which the applicant meets other requirements the Board may adopt by rule. The Board adopted rules which also require an applicant to have (1) a background, reputation, and associations which will not result in adverse publicity for the State and its gaming industry; (2) adequate business competence and experience; and (3) adequate funding for the entire operation from a suitable source. 86 Ill. Adm. Code § 3000.230(c)(2) (1992).

The recommended order adopted by the Board emphasized that section 2 of the Act described a legislative intent to benefit the people of the State by assisting economic development and promoting tourism, which can be done only if public confidence and trust in the credibility and integrity of the gambling operation and regulating process are maintained. (230 ILCS 10/2(a), (b) (West 1992)). The order then (1) found a lack of showing that the operation would be adequately financed; (2) deemed the existing type of entertainment at the establishments near the docks as being too low-grade to attract tourists; (3) noted the lack of hotels in the area; (4) questioned the accuracy of calculations of the number of likely customers for the gambling boat; (5) questioned the reputation of at least one of the prospective employees; (6) noted that a person who would profit greatly if the boat was a success was a relative of the mayor of Sauget and a local official; and (7) pointed out that two Super Fund hazardous waste sites were close to the dock area.

The evidence presented before the Board was that Arch-View had only a minimum of cash and substantial debts, but almost all of its shares were owned by George E. Middleton. He did not testify, and he had not signed a purported financial statement of his which had been furnished with the application. Middleton's chief financial advisor, Gary Gill, testified that Middleton had accumulated a fortune of approximately $44 million through his ownership of Pizza Hut restaurants and could put $21 million into the instant project. Gill described Middleton as a very able person who had worked on the "Gemini" project for the Federal government at one time. According to Gill, Middleton had put approximately $453,000 into the project to get the riverboat but had never been involved before in gaming operations. As Arch-View's financing was almost entirely dependent upon Middleton, and he had neither testified nor signed the financial statement which accompanied the application, the Board was justified in finding that Arch-View's ability to finance the project was not proved.

The evidence was undisputed that several of the few places of entertainment in Sauget were places where women entertainers remove their clothes. Reasonable minds may differ as to whether that atmosphere is likely to attract or turn away prospective gamblers. Some evidence was presented of plans to erect hotels in the area but no assurance existed that this would take place. The Board's decision that this environment would deter gamblers from coming to Sauget was not contrary to the manifest weight of the evidence.

Evidence was presented that originally, a well-established gaming company had been sought to manage the boat's gaming operation, but that plan had been abandoned because that company's fee request was too high. Instead, Jack Speelman was hired as gaming manager. He had been involved in the gambling industry since 1954 mostly in Las Vegas, Nevada, but he had never operated a gaming boat or an operation under Illinois law. He had been fired by the Tropicana Casino in that city. There, a dispute had arisen concerning an "irregularity" affecting a game that Speelman's daughter was supervising. He had hired her but did not fire her or other employees involved in that situation. Speelman testified that his firing was for other reasons. Speelman testified he had hired his daughter to be an assistant pit boss supervising certain game tables on the proposed boat.

Originally Middleton had a 60% interest in Arch-View and Vincent and Richard Sauget had most of the rest of the interest in equal shares. Vincent died and Richard succeeded to his interest. Others dropped out. Richard then entered into an agreement with Arch-View whereby Arch-View purchased and redeemed Richard's shares for a purchase price which was dependent upon the issuance of an owner's license and the successful operation of the gaming boat but which could result in a payment to Richard of between $600,000 and $1 million. Richard is a trustee of the Village of Sauget and a member of the St. Clair County Building Commission. His uncle is mayor of Sauget, and his cousin is on the township board. Richard is also the owner of or a substantial creditor of many of the businesses in the area. Richard clearly had an interest in the success of Arch-View and also obligations to the governmental units with which Arch-View would be dealing. While all concerned would benefit by the success of Arch-View, the interrelationships involved were matters of concern for the Board as they could affect the reputation of the operation or its integrity.

The proposed dock site was approximately 1,000 feet north of a proposed Super Fund hazardous waste site and approximately 12,000 feet west of another such site. Testimony of an Illinois Environmental Protection Agency (Agency) project manager indicated that the sites "released or threatened releases of contamination impacting human health or the environment" with high levels of hazardous chemicals, including a carcinogen. He described the north site as one of the worst in the State. He noted that the Village had placed a playground near it despite his warning. While the existence of these nearby sites is not directly listed as one for consideration in deciding whether to grant an owner's license, we hold that their existence bears upon the quality of the facilities available for gambling.

Gary Gill praised Middleton as an able, successful, and trustworthy business person. Several witnesses projected that the proposed boat would have sufficient customers to make the project profitable for its promoters, increase the revenue of the State, and promote, through tourism, the Sauget area. With projected highways being completed, the site could be reached from St. Louis in a very short time. Other testimony indicated that the dock site was excellent for keeping the boat. Other testimony indicated the project would create a substantial number of jobs, and the Village of Sauget had agreed to a plan for sharing the revenue with other hard-pressed areas.

However, the factual determination of the administrative agency must be upheld unless it is contrary to the manifest weight of the evidence. Abrahamson v. Illinois Department of Professional Regulation, 153 Ill.2d 76, 88, 180 Ill. Dec. 34, 40, 606 N.E.2d 1111, 1117 (1992). Considering (1) the uncertain nature of the financing of Arch-View; (2) the question of whether the area surrounding the dock would attract customers and tourists; (3) the present lack of hotels; and (4) the evidence of proximity of a highly hazardous site near the boat dock, we cannot find that the decision of the Board to deny the owner's license was contrary to the manifest weight of the evidence. We have not discussed the contention that the survey of the number of probable customers testimony was invalid, because that is complicated and need not be shown to support the Board's decision.

Arch-View correctly points out that the supreme court made clear in Balmoral Racing Club, Inc. v. Illinois Racing Board, 151 Ill.2d 367, 403, 177 Ill. Dec. 419, 434–35,

603 N.E.2d 489, 504–05 (1992), that in licensing proceedings before administrative agencies where notice and a right to be heard was involved, 1010-65(a) of the then Procedure Act (Ill. Rev. Stat.1991, ch. 127, par. 10-65(a)) required that the contested case provision of the Procedure Act apply and that the parties involved are entitled to due process. Arch-View further notes that section 17 of the Act (230 ILCS 10/17 (West 1992)) also grants them the right to the contested case provision. It maintains it was granted neither those statutory rights nor due process.

Arch-View maintains that the Board considered factors not designated by section 7(b) of the Act. As we have indicated, we deem the matters considered do bear upon the section 7(b) factors. It asserts that it was denied an opportunity to make an offer of proof as to certain testimony Gill would make. The record indicates that a voluminous written offer was made, considered, and denied. The offer is replete with matter otherwise shown of record, hearsay, and argument. No error resulted from the refusal of the admission of the information set forth therein. Moreover, the purport of the matters set forth there is that Arch-View was unfairly treated because the Board did not act more rapidly. The information presented tends to indicate that the Board was slowed by change in membership and uncertainty arising from litigation concerning the validity of language in section 7(e) of the Act (230 ILCS 10/7(e) (West 1992)) which purported to require that one of the first five owner's licenses be from a dock at East St. Louis. The delay was unfortunate, but nothing alleged indicates it deprived Arch-View of any statutory or constitutional right.

Citing McCabe v. Department of Registration & Education, 90 Ill.App.3d 1123, 1131, 46 Ill. Dec. 240, 246, 413 N.E.2d 1353, 1359 (1980); Wegmann v. Department of Registration & Education, 61 Ill.App.3d 352, 356, 18 Ill. Dec. 661, 665, 377 N.E.2d 1297, 1301(1978), Arch-View asserts it was prejudiced by the failure of the Board to turn over to it information which was favorable to Arch-View. Those cases concerned the right of a person, respondent to a petition to revoke his or her license, to have such helpful information. Regardless of whether the holding of those cases is applicable here, no error resulted in this case. Arch-View indicates it did not know of a letter authored by the Agency representative who testified about the hazardous waste sites which impeached his testimony. However, Arch-View had the letter in time to use it to cross-examine that witness.

Arch-View argues that it cannot argue about the use it would put to information advantageous to it which the Board possessed but did not reveal to it, because it has no way of knowing what that information is. At the heart of Arch-View's concern is its contention that the Board did not treat it evenly with other applicants for license. It seems to believe it is entitled to discovery as to every bit of information that bore upon the issuance of other licenses. It is entitled to obtain all public records it wishes in regard to the Board's activities but to require the Board to furnish all of the information it seeks and to allow it to use that information in support of its request would create interminable dispute. We know of no rule that requires that.

Arch-View places substantial significance to section 5(c)(1) of the Act, which empowers the Board:

"To investigate applicants and determine the eligibility of applicants for licenses and to select among competing applicants the applicants which best serve the interests of the citizens of Illinois" (emphasis added) (230 ILCS 10/5(c)(1) (West 1992)).

Arch-View maintains that no other application for an owner's license was before the Board at the time the Board denied Arch-View a license. As the interests of Illinois citizens is not mentioned in section 7(b) of the Act, Arch-View maintains the Board showed it considered an improper factor when it mentioned the "interests of citizens of Illinois" in denying Arch-View a license. While the Board should be careful in following only stated factors in passing upon license applications, we will not hold it to that much care with its language. Moreover, the words used by the Board referred to the stated purposes of the Act, which are inherently a matter to be considered as long as the evidence of specific factors supports the Board's order.

The evidence supported the Board's determination in denying the license application. We find no reversible error in the conduct of the hearing or the decision process. Accordingly, we affirm the order denying the owner's license.

Affirmed.

KNECHT and COOK, JJ., concur.

Notes

1. A government may have varying degrees of concern with the financial ability of an applicant for a casino license to succeed. In a monopoly or small oligopoly situation, the government may have a strong interest in assuring that the prospective casino operator is properly financed, particularly where the government is committing its own resources to the project through infrastructure, committing community development funds, hiring additional city personnel, or buying new city equipment. A government may have legitimate concerns that, after committing its financial resources, the casino may never open or will close shortly after opening because its owners did not have sufficient financial resources. This may become even more acute where the government borrows the money to make the infrastructure improvements and is relying on gaming taxes to pay it back. Here, the financial failure of the casino may bankrupt or severely strain the government.

2. Governments also may have a concern as to the financial stability of the casino where it is meant to serve as an icon for tourism. In this environment, where one or two casinos in a resort area are meant to provide a spectacular amenity to promote tourism, a casino closing can harm tourism. Not only would the closing eliminate the amenity, but if the casino is well known, it may signal to the tourist market that the location is declining as a tourist destination.

3. In a competitive economy, the government may not share these reasons to refuse a license to a new casino operation because it questions its economic viability. Market forces in a competitive economy often are the best judge of what is viable. If this is done by the government, the market may lose a potential competitor that could succeed by introducing innovations or creating new markets. If the regulators question the viability of an operation, there may be some legitimate concerns. For example, will the operator go to some unsuitable source to get money if times turn tough or will it try to create profits by cheating patrons? *See* Guy S. Michael, *Whose License Is It, Anyway? The Evaluation of the Suitability of a Corporation for a Casino License*, 6 Seton Hall Legis. J. 41 (1983)

iii. Location Suitability

Nevada Gaming Commission & State Gaming Control Board Regulation § 3.010: Unsuitable Locations

The board may recommend that an application for a state gaming license be denied, if the board deems that the place or location for which the license is sought is unsuitable for the conduct of gaming operations. The commission may deny an application for a state gaming license if the commission deems that the place or location for which the license is sought is unsuitable for the conduct of gaming operations.

Without limiting the generality of the foregoing, the following places or locations may be deemed unsuitable:

1. Premises located within the immediate vicinity of churches, schools and children's public playgrounds. The board may recommend and the commission may determine that premises located in the vicinity of churches, schools, and playgrounds are nevertheless suitable upon a sufficient showing of suitability by the applicant. In making their determinations, the board and commission may consider all relevant factors including but not limited to whether the premises have been used previously for licensed gaming or are located in a commercial area.

2. Premises located in a place where gaming is contrary to a valid zoning ordinance of any county or city. The board may recommend and the commission may determine that premises located where gaming is contrary to a valid zoning ordinance are nevertheless suitable upon a sufficient showing by the applicant that the premises have been used for licensed gaming prior to the effective date of the zoning ordinance and that there is good cause why the use should be allowed to continue.

3. Premises having a substantial minor clientele. The board may recommend and the commission may determine that premises having a substantial minor clientele are nevertheless suitable if the applicant demonstrates that it has taken sufficient precautions to separate areas frequented by minors from the gaming operation.

4. Premises lacking adequate supervision or surveillance.

5. Premises difficult to police.

6. Brothels.

7. Any other premises where the conduct of gaming would be inconsistent with the public policy of the State of Nevada.

Mississippi Gaming Commission
Regulation & Licensing: Qualifications

Section 2. Location

(a) The legislature has declared gaming operations legal if licensed by the Commission and conducted upon establishments, vessels and cruise vessels located in certain statutorily described areas where voters have not voted to prohibit gaming. The Commission, as authorized by law and in conformity with the power and responsibility vested in it by the legislature, finds that gaming licensees may operate at the following locations. Nothing in this section shall act to prevent the Commission from denying a gaming license or preliminary site approval based on the unsuitability of a particular site.

(1) Cruise Vessels. Waters within the State of Mississippi which lie adjacent to the three (3) most southern counties of the State. In addition to the Mississippi Sound, this would include St. Louis Bay, Biloxi Bay and Pascagoula Bay. However, the rivers, bayous, lakes and back bays leading into these bays, including but not limited to the Jourdan River, Wolf River, Bernard Bayou, Tchoutacabouffa River, Pascagoula River and Escatawpa River, Biloxi River, Big Lake and Back Bay of Biloxi are not within the authorized area. In determining where the river ends and the bay begins, an imaginary line shall be drawn from the foremost land mass at the intersection of the river and bay, straight across the river to the foremost land mass of the intersection on the other side. In determining where

Back Bay of Biloxi ends and Biloxi Bay begins, an imaginary line shall be drawn beginning at a point 1200 feet west of the center line of Interstate 110 on the northern shore to a point on the center line of Interstate 110 on the southern shore.

(2) Vessels. Vessels must be on the Mississippi River or navigable waters within any county bordering on the Mississippi River when such navigable waters run into the Mississippi River. Navigable waters mean any rivers, creeks, bayous or other bodies of water that are used or susceptible of being used as an artery of commerce and which either in their natural or improved condition are used or suitable for use as an artery of commerce or are used for the docking or mooring of a vessel, notwithstanding interruptions between the navigable parts of such rivers, creeks, bayous or other bodies of water by falls, shallows, or rapids compelling land carriage.

Vessels may be located (1) on the Mississippi River, including oxbow lakes immediately adjacent to the Mississippi River, that communicate with the Mississippi River and are characterized by currents which reverse seasonally, running one direction when the Mississippi River rises, and the opposite direction when it falls, and (2) on navigable waters.

"Navigable Waters" are defined as rivers, creeks, bayous or other naturally occurring bodies of water that, at the time of application and prior to improvements to accommodate a vessel.

- empty into the Mississippi River in the county where the applicant casino is located;
- are located within a county where gaming is legal, in other words, do not border a county where gaming is illegal;
- are used or susceptible of being used as an artery of commerce for substantial commercial traffic;
- either in their natural or improved condition are used or suitable for use as an artery of commerce for substantial commercial traffic or are used for docking or mooring of a vessel; and
- are of a sufficient depth and width at least thirty (30) days of the calendar year to accommodate a vessel of at least 150' in length and the proposed width of the applicant vessel.

Naturally occurring interruptions between the navigable parts of such rivers, creeks, bayous or other bodies of water by falls, shallows, or rapids compelling land carriage do not deprive it of its classification of navigable. Artificial impediments to navigation for substantial commercial traffic do not deprive rivers, creeks, bayous or other bodies of water of their status as navigable.

In accordance with the above, vessels must be west of the main line levee that runs from the border between the states of Mississippi and Tennessee to the end of the main line levee in Warren County and west of the naturally occurring levee system or bluffs from Warren County to the border between Wilkinson County, Mississippi and West Feliciana Parish, Louisiana, except vessels may be located on the Yazoo River within Warren County and the Big Black River where it forms the border between Warren and Claiborne Counties.

(3) Establishments. The part of the structure in which licensed gaming activities are conducted is located entirely in an area which is located no more than eight hundred (800) feet from the mean high-water line (as defined in Section 29-15-1) of the waters within the State of Mississippi, which lie adjacent to the State of Mississippi south of the three (3) most southern counties in the State of Mississippi, including the Mississippi Sound, St. Louis Bay, Biloxi Bay and Pascagoula Bay, or, with regard

to Harrison County only, no farther north than the southern boundary of the right-of-way for U.S. Highway 90, whichever is greater; and

In the case of a structure that is located in whole or part on shore, the part of the structure in which licensed gaming activities are conducted shall lie adjacent to state waters south of the three (3) most southern counties in the State of Mississippi, including the Mississippi Sound, St. Louis Bay, Biloxi Bay and Pascagoula Bay. When the site upon which the structure is located consists of a parcel of real property, easements and rights-of-way for public streets and highways shall not be construed to interrupt the contiguous nature of the parcel, nor shall the footage contained within the easements and rights-of-way be counted in the calculation of the distances specified in the above paragraph.

(b) The Executive Director may make a recommendation to the Commission regarding the qualification of a location for gaming operations upon the request of an applicant for an operator's license or upon a finding by the Executive Director that such determination is necessary and in accord with public policy.

(c) These amendments shall apply to all existing, pending, renewal and new applicants for a license or preliminary site approval.

Indiana Code § 4-33-6-7: Consideration in License Determination—Assurance of Economic Development

Sec. 7. (a) In granting a license under this chapter, the commission may give favorable consideration to the following:

(1) Economically depressed areas of Indiana.

(2) Applicants presenting plans that provide for significant economic development over a large geographic area.

(b) This subsection applies to any owner's license issued for a city described in section 1(a)(1) of this chapter. The commission must require the applicant to provide assurances that economic development will occur in the city and that adequate infrastructure and site preparation will be provided to support the riverboat operation. In order to prove the assurance that economic development will occur, the applicant must:

(1) construct or provide for the construction of an approved hotel; or

(2) cause economic development that will have an economic impact on the city that exceeds the economic impact that the construction of an approved hotel would have.

Sec. 18. (a) This subsection applies to cities described in section 1(a)(1) through 1(a)(4) or section (1)(b) of this chapter. The commission may not issue a license authorizing a riverboat to dock in a city unless the legislative body of the city has approved an ordinance permitting the docking of riverboats in the city.

(b) This subsection applies to a county described in section 1(a)(5) of this chapter if the largest city in the county is contiguous to the Ohio River. The commission may not issue a license authorizing a riverboat to dock in the county unless an ordinance permitting the docking of riverboats in the county has been approved by the legislative body of the largest city in the county. The license must specify that the home dock of the riverboat is to be located in the largest city in the county.

(c) This subsection applies to a county described in section 1(a)(5) of this chapter if the largest city in the county is not contiguous to the Ohio River. The commission may not issue a license authorizing a riverboat to dock in the county unless an ordinance permitting the docking of riverboats in the county has been approved by the county fiscal body.

(d) This subsection applies to a county described in section 1(a)(6) of this chapter. The commission may not issue a license authorizing a riverboat to dock in the county unless an ordinance permitting the docking of riverboats in the county has been approved by the county fiscal body.

Notes

1. Why are the criteria for location suitability so different between Nevada and Mississippi? What are the purposes for the respective policies? What is the potential economic impact of such decisions?

2. Site suitability in some states has been controversial. For additional discussion of this topic, *see* Ben H. Stone, J. Adrian Smith, Scott E. Andress & Thomas L. Carpenter, Jr., *Site Approval of Casinos in Mississippi: A Matter of Statutory Construction, or a Roll of the Dice?*, 64 Miss. L.J. 363 (1995); Klaus J. Meyer-Arendt, *What Is a Legal Casino Site in Mississippi?*, 1 Gaming L. Rev. 55 (1997); Allan B. Solomon & Gregory D. Guida, *Riverboat Gaming: Legislation, Licensing, Site Selection, and Case Law*, 29 J. Mar. L. & Com. 215 (1998).

5. Level of Review[1]

A. Full Investigation and Licensing

Gaming attorneys are often called upon to assist their clients through the gaming licensing process. This is often a much different role than an attorney normally serves in representing a client. While individual states often follow different investigative procedures, the similarities far outweigh the differences. A description of the investigative process and the attorney's role in it is critical to understanding the lawyering process for the gaming attorney.

A full licensing investigation is a comprehensive independent review of the applicant's financial history and personal background. In some respects, a gaming investigation is easier than criminal investigations because the gaming applicant must cooperate by providing information and files. Because of this, requiring the applicant to complete extensive forms can provide the investigators with a wealth of useful information that can build a framework on which to conduct the investigation. Typically, these forms include:

A **personal history form** that elicits personal, familial, educational, marital, civil litigation, criminal, and residential information. This form also may request employment history, licensing background, and character references.

A **personal financial form** that asks for financial information including the amount and source of investment in the gaming establishment, tax information, bankruptcy disclosures, salary information, and a detailed statement of assets and liabilities.

---

1. This section is generally adopted from Anthony Cabot, *Obtaining a Non-Restricted Gaming License in Nevada* (Lewis & Roca 2008).

Besides these basic forms, regulators can request many releases, waivers, and other relinquishments of rights or privileges. The most important waiver is that the applicant must agree not to sue the gaming regulators or their investigators for anything related to the gaming application or the investigation process. A separate release form often contains this provision. This form serves to protect the government and the regulators from civil liability. Suppose, for example, a gaming investigator shares negative or false information with the applicant's banker. If the banker subsequently cancels a loan with the applicant, the applicant could not successfully sue the investigator or the regulators if he signed a release.

Typical application forms also include releases that allow third persons to share information with the investigators and shield those third parties from a lawsuit by the applicant for libel, slander or any other reason. Moreover, these releases may allow third parties to provide information that they could not otherwise legally provide. For example, courts may be able to reopen sealed criminal records. Any person given this form can provide all information that the investigators request, despite a legal privilege not to have to provide the information. For example, accountants may otherwise refuse to give a client's accounting information to investigators by citing an accountant-client privilege.

Some jurisdictions require the applicant to provide sworn statements attesting to the accuracy of both the information contained in personal history and financial forms. This form may also request the applicant to keep the regulators consistently informed of any changes in the information provided in the application. Fingerprint cards are used to verify the applicant's identity, and to obtain criminal records. These cards may be sent to central processing agencies, such as the Federal Bureau of Investigation, to learn if the applicant has a criminal history.

Investigations are usually preplanned and logical. Where an regulatory agency has the capabilities, it often uses a team approach to complex investigations. An investigative team can have as few as one investigator or as many as a dozen. The size of the team depends on the regulators' capabilities, the complexity of the investigation, and time requirements, and other considerations. Some regulatory agencies have a small staff and limited resources. These agencies can only place one or two investigators on an investigation despite the complexity. The highest-ranking member of the team is usually an experienced investigator. This person has direct responsibility for the daily activities of the investigators involved in the investigation. The ranking member provides guidance to the investigators in his charge, and formulates the investigative strategy. The team may have financial investigators that hold degrees in accounting. Financial investigators are responsible for investigating the applicant's current financial status, past financial activities, general business probity, and the financial status of the proposed gaming operation. Background investigators would have responsibility for investigating the applicant's background, general reputation, and personal and business associates.

The initiation of the investigation often involves the investigators reviewing the application, and accessing easily available information, such as that contained in the agency's files. The agents also may reconcile the information in the application. For example, investigators review whether the past addresses provided by the applicant reconcile with where the applicant listed as previous places of employment. Another area is to uncover any unexplained gaps in the records. The investigators attempt to assure that all the information that they are working with is accurate and complete.

An investigation may commence with an opening interview with the applicant to review and verify information on an application, and to discuss inconsistencies, omissions or potential issues. Two primary purposes of the background investigation are to verify the information provided by the applicant and to uncover information that the applicant may not have revealed. Because of the nature of fieldwork, an applicant may not have much contact with the background agents. They often work with other law enforcement agencies and conduct extensive interviews to learn the character of the applicant.

Background agents have very broad powers. They can request the applicant to supply documents such as:

- birth certificate;

- current and previous passports;

- a copy of the applicant's last will and testament;

- copies of any trust agreements, trust tax returns, and a list and valuation of assets held by the trusts, of which the applicant is a party;

- a copy of any current employment and/or stock option agreement(s);

- copies of any federal, state, county or city licenses held by the applicant individually or as a representative of a business;

- detailed narrative of any questioning by any governmental agencies including dates, circumstances, and dispositions; and

- copies of any pleading and orders in litigation and arbitration for the applicant as an individual, member of a partnership, member/manager of a limited liability company, or shareholder, director, or officer of a corporation. Involvement can be as either a plaintiff/defendant or defendant/respondent.

Background agents can inspect premises and demand access to inspect, examine, and photocopy records and interview witnesses. This can extend to requesting company and individual computer hard drives to review files and email correspondence. Anything written down or memorialized in electronic or any other form may be the subject of a request from a background agent regardless of whether it is personal or business related.

Schools and universities can be contacted to verify education. Military information is verified with the respective branch with attention on any disciplinary or other derogatory information. Marital information is reviewed with attention to divorces. This is important because divorces often are acrimonious and the files (or the ex-spouse) can be valuable sources for allegations of wrongdoing.

Background agents can verify criminal information on the applicant. Most important are the circumstances of all arrests or detentions and whether the applicant revealed all of them. Agents may discover that the applicant failed to reveal a criminal record by checking court records. The major sources of information, however, are police records and law enforcement information systems. These include local sheriffs, local police, the Federal Bureau of Investigation, the Drug Enforcement Administration, customs and immigration, organized crime task forces, other gaming regulatory agencies, and liquor and other privileged license agencies. Among the types of law enforcement information available are arrest reports, incident reports, field interrogation reports, and intelligence reports. Police records often have information that was not presented to the court because the witness could not be found or the police failed to follow constitutional guidelines in obtaining it. Unlike criminal actions, gaming regulatory agencies are not burdened by the same rules about what can be considered.

Records of civil court proceedings also often provide information that proves relevant to a background or financial investigation. These lawsuits may contain allegations of unscrupulous business practices and the identity of persons who have had unsatisfactory business experiences with the applicant. Evidence of disposition of the civil cases is also important. Beyond the nature or omission of civil lawsuits, a review of litigation may reveal that an applicant abuses the civil court system to gain economic advantages. The existence of many lawsuits may show a pattern of using the judicial system to avoid or compromise legitimate debts, to harass or damage competitors, or to create unlawful competitive advantages.

Besides criminal and civil court records, governments maintain substantial information on people much of which may be relevant to the person's suitability as a gaming licensee. For example, a state's consumer affairs division may have complaints filed by customers of the applicant's business that contain allegations of fraud or deceptive trade practices. Similarly, the equal opportunity employment offices may have complaints alleging sexual or racial discrimination in the workplace.

Governments usually have a considerable amount of public information on corporations and partnerships. Individual applicants for casino licenses often have extensive business backgrounds, which may involve prior and contemporaneous businesses. The review of corporate information about these businesses may further reveal the applicant's associations. Often whether a person acted as an incorporator, director, or officer is public information that can be found through government offices, such as a corporate register or secretary of state. These searches also may reveal corporations not listed on an application.

Corporate books also contain a wealth of information. Incorporation papers show the date of incorporation and number of authorized shares. Subsequent filings usually show the list of initial officers and directors and any changes to them, along with dates of each change. The corporate minutes contain information on significant events, such as major acquisitions or loans, and the hiring or firing of key personnel.

Verification of employment history is done for many reasons including establishing the person's experience in a particular area and exploring the applicant's honesty. Here the agents often go beyond the stated reasons for changing employment and decide if other reasons exist. An agent may take advantage of the applicant's release of all liability to convince the employer to detail the facts leading to the applicant's firing or resignation.

Financial agents are the beneficiaries of most documentation supplied by an applicant and may use the documentation for many reasons. Requested documentation can include copies of:

- Federal, State and Local individual income tax returns for past five years (minimum), including all supporting schedules (W-2's, 1099's and K-1's);
- bank and brokerage account records for a five year period;
- original note receivable agreements;
- escrow documents such as mortgage loan statements or notes, trust deeds, and settlement statements for the purchase of all real estate currently owned;
- statements pertaining to any pension or retirement funds, IRAs, and annuities;
- life insurance policies and statements confirming current cash surrender values; and
- notes payable and credit line agreements incurred.

Later supplemental requests may include other financial records such as certificates of deposit; cashier's checks purchased; notes and loans receivable or payable, financial statements; accountant's work papers; brokerage accounts; contingent liabilities (i.e., guarantees); and business investments.

If the applicant provides part or all of the financing for the gaming establishment, these records reveal the adequacy of the applicant's resources and the suitability of his sources. Financial records often reveal identities and financial arrangements with the applicant's associates. Financial agents also scrutinize sources of income and records of payments through these documents.

Tasks that financial agents can perform during their investigation include:

- source of funds analysis;
- tracing primary holdings to their original sources;
- verifying personal income information to confirm that current holdings are consistent with income reported to the tax authorities;
- preparing a cash-flow analysis; and
- verifying the applicant's net worth.

A source of funds analysis traces where the applicant receives income and the source of funds from which assets are purchased. A common regulatory goal is to assure that the applicant is not a front for unsuitable individuals who are financing the acquisition of a casino. It also provides insight into the applicant's business and associations. Bank records are the most common vehicles for establishing source of funds, provided all accounts are revealed. Bank statements, in particular, are the beginning points because they contain both deposits and withdrawals. Deposits often reveal sources of income. As such, all deposits are reviewed to learn if they are ordinary, such as salary deposits, or extraordinary, such as the one-time sale of an automobile. Large extraordinary deposits will be verified by reviewing source documents.

Standard bank records that agents may review include (1) signature cards showing who is authorized to use the bank account; (2) monthly statements showing all activity on the account, including deposits, withdrawals, and checks paid; (3) canceled checks; and (4) deposit tickets showing a breakdown of checks, cash deposited, and identification of the checks. The applicant may have other documentation that will greatly help in the investigation, such as check registers, copies of all checks deposited, and the canceled checks.

Bank accounts are the usual, but not exclusive place into which funds can be deposited. Other possible depositories include brokerage accounts and savings and loans associations. An agent will often review all accounts before conducting a cash-flow analysis or reconciling income to expenses.

A principal concern of many regulators is the protection of tax revenues. Applicants who intentionally fail to pay taxes, such as federal income tax, may be unqualified to hold a gaming license. A primary method of investigating whether a person fully pays federal income tax is to compare cash flow with reported income. If a substantial difference exists, the agent may confront the applicant for explanation of the difference. Beyond this, tax returns provide information on sources of income, verify businesses, and provide information on associations.

Financial and background agents work closely together. For example, financial agents can learn of the applicant's business associates by reviewing financial documents such as bank deposits or partnership agreements. The financial agents may pass this information to the background agent to do police checks on these associates.

At the conclusion of their investigation, the agents typically prepare a report for consideration by the person or agency responsible for determining the applicant's suitability. This forms the basis for the agency's consideration. Determination of suitability, however, is typically done in a public hearing. Because the applicant typically has the burden of proving his suitability, he can introduce evidence of such suitability or to counter any evidence contained in the investigative report.

Legal counsel plays three important roles during the investigation. First, counsel serves as the "point man" for coordinating the agents' requests for documents or information. Requests are usually made by letter to the applicant with copies to his counsel or by telephone call to counsel. The speed and accuracy of the assembly and transmission of requested information has a direct impact upon the length and cost of the investigation. By coordinating the production of documents and information, counsel can review the materials for responsiveness, clarity, accuracy and completeness. The applicant's level of preparation and cooperation largely determines the length of the investigation.

Counsel's second role is that of an "observer." If requests are made without notice to the applicant's counsel, the applicant should inform counsel of the request. By analyzing the nature of the information requested and observing the direction of the investigation, counsel can make educated guesses about the agents' concerns or areas of interest. With this knowledge, the applicant has the ability to dispel any misconceptions and to prepare ahead of time any necessary rebuttal for the Board and Commission hearings.

Counsel's third role is "presenter." An applicant's counsel, being familiar with the Board and Commission hearings, will be presenting and introducing the applicant in front of the Board and Commission.

B. Limited Investigation

Limited investigations involve reviewing only specific areas on each application. A limited investigation is usually only a check for negative criminal history, reviewing responses from the applicant's references, and sometimes a personal interview. Limited investigations have disadvantages because of the minimal personal contact with the applicant and time involved in the investigative process. Nevertheless, a partial investigation provides some benefits. Most notably, it may inhibit persons with extensive criminal histories from obtaining employment in a casino. Moreover, regulators may obtain useful derogatory information on applicants from third parties that may lead to denial of the applicant despite the absence of a negative criminal record.

Limited investigations are common with casino employees. In this case, the extent of the limited investigation can be tiered, with key employees being subjected to higher review than lower-level employees. Similarly, the licenses issued can restrict the person's activities very specifically, such as a dealer only, or by category, such as in New Jersey, which issues different licenses to key casino employees, regular casino employees, and non-casino employees. To differentiate types of licenses, some jurisdictions will use different terminology, such as a work "permit" or "card" for the licensing of casino and non-casino employees.

C. Transactional and Temporary Approvals

Transactional and temporary approvals address the problems created when the cost of licensing poses an absolute or significant barrier to potential suppliers. A jurisdiction that has only one or a few casinos may have problems in attracting casino suppliers if they must undergo a full licensing investigation to sell a small amount of goods. This may prevent the goods from being available or available at a price that not only includes the cost of licensing, but also the reduction in competition created.

For example, gaming device manufacturers may attempt to be the first manufacturer to obtain a license in a small market. If a manufacturer succeeds, it can grab a significant market share of the total potential market. The considerations for other manufacturers to seek a license now differ because the total potential sales in that jurisdiction are less. If other manufacturers decide not to enter the market, the sole licensed manufacturer has monopoly power and may charge corresponding prices.

A transactional approval allows the applicant to enter a specific transaction, such as supplying a fixed number of gaming devices to a casino. A temporary approval allows the supplier to make unlimited sales in a jurisdiction for a limited time.

Temporary approvals can create a competitive market before the regulatory agency can process the applications of competing suppliers. By granting several temporary licenses, the regulators can assure a competitive market at its inception. Even in established markets, regulators can use temporary approvals to rectify market imperfections quickly. This would allow introduction of competing products pending the completion of a full investigation.

In contrast, transactional approvals usually apply to types of transactions that are sensitive, but where requiring licensing would result in the market not being served or significantly under-served. Before granting a transactional approval, the regulators may require some background information on the applicant and full disclosure of the transaction that is the subject of the approval. Because the purpose of transactional approvals is to avoid either the costs or time associated with full licensing, the time and expense relevant to the transactional approval should reflect the purpose of the approval and market conditions. For example, if the sale of gaming chips requires transactional approval, the regulators may need to expedite this approval if the casino has a critical shortage of chips.

D. Preliminary Approvals

A preliminary approval differs from a temporary approval in that the former does not allow the applicant to engage in the licensed activity, but suggests that he likely will be approved in the future, absent changed circumstances. For example, suppose an applicant wishes to invest $80 million in a new casino, but has never been licensed. A preliminary approval gives him some assurances that he and the proposed location and design of the new casino are suitable before committing his capital. Because incidents may occur between the preliminary and final approvals, regulators may reserve discretion to change the preliminary approval if new facts show that the applicant is unsuitable.

E. Final Approvals

A final approval can have different levels of permanency. One common application is to limit the license to a fixed period, such as three years. At the end of this period, the license expires. Therefore, before the end of the period, the licensee must reapply for a new gaming license if it wishes to continue operations. This method has various advantages. First, it provides regulators an opportunity to periodically investigate and review their licensees to ensure that they are meeting the minimum standards expected under the law and regulations. Second, it may deter licensees from committing acts that fall below these minimum standards because the periodic investigation is likely to expose these transgressions. Third, regulators may not have to accord full due-process rights to a licensee seeking a new license, but would have to afford such rights if it attempted to revoke a license.

Requiring periodic relicensing has various disadvantages. First, it is expensive. Investigations of applicants, particularly large corporations, can be costly for both regulators and applicants. Licensees attempt to pass these extra costs on to the patrons as higher costs. Second, investigations consume both agency and licensee time and effort and divert their efforts from other business matters and pursuits. Where the licensee is conscientious, it may be a poor use of agency and licensee time. Third, it introduces more risk to the business opportunity. All other things being equal, a company looking to invest in a casino may choose a jurisdiction where a license can be revoked only by a disciplinary action as opposed to expiring on specified dates. Fourth, financial markets may be less willing to lend funds to companies whose license expires before the loan is due because without a license, the company may not pay the loan.

A jurisdiction can use both temporary and permanent approvals. One method mandates that all first-time licenses are temporary and expire after a time (probationary), but that the second license is a permanent license. Another method is to allow the regulators to decide whether a license will be temporary or permanent.

6. Standards of the Licensing Process

In the Matter of the Application of Boardwalk Regency Corporation for a Casino License

434 A.2d 1111 (N.J. Super. 1981)

The opinion of the court was delivered by FRITZ, P.J.A.D.

Following extensive investigation and formal hearings on the application of Boardwalk Regency Corporation (BRC) for a plenary casino license, the Casino Control Commission (Commission) determined that BRC qualified except for the presence of Stuart Z. and Clifford S. Perlman, brothers with extensive interests in the operation. As a consequence, the grant of a plenary license was conditioned in effect on divestiture of any Perlman interest which had any capacity for exerting control over BRC or any related entity. These consolidated appeals by BRC, Caesars World, Inc. (CWI), Caesars New Jersey, Inc. (CNJ) and Stuart and Clifford Perlman challenge that ruling and the constitutionality of N.J.S.A. 5:12-89.

Direct and indirect Perlman interest in and influence upon the affairs of BRC and ample cause for the insistence of the Commission that it be persuaded of the qualification of each of the brothers as a "casino key employee" (N.J.S.A. 5:12-85 c and d) appear indisputably from the genesis of the corporation and are in fact not disputed.[1] BRC is a wholly-owned subsidiary of CNJ, 86% of the stock of which is in turn owned by CWI.

---

1. One of the expressed concerns of all the appellants is that the Perlmans are such a prime force in the corporate structure and interstructure that their departure would seriously impair the capacity of the corporations to borrow money and otherwise intrude upon the financial operations of the corporations to their detriment.

A creature of humble beginnings, CWI was launched in 1956 when Stuart and Clifford Perlman purchased a "Lum's" restaurant, a small fast-food eating establishment that specialized in hot dogs steamed in beer. The purchase price was $25,000, "half down and the balance over three years." About 1965 the Perlmans started franchising the Lum's stores. Ultimately there were almost 400 of these restaurants in 30 or more states. Lum's was listed on the New York stock exchange in 1969.

1969 was also the year the Perlmans negotiated the purchase of Caesars Palace for 60 million dollars. In 1971 the recession in the restaurant business and the need of the growing Caesars Palace for money produced the sale of the restaurants and the change of the corporate name to Caesars World.

Today CWI is listed on the New York and Pacific Coast stock exchanges. Its 26,100,000 shares of outstanding stock are owned by 70,000 shareholders. Consolidated revenues approximate a half billion dollars annually. Clifford Perlman, chairman of the board and chief executive officer of CWI, owns approximately 10% of the outstanding stock. His brother Stuart owns about 8% of the stock of CWI and holds the position of vice-chairman of the board of directors.

At the conclusion of the hearings the Commission noted, with respect to one of the individuals in the corporate structure who was found to be qualified: "As in all areas of human endeavor, there is in the regulatory process never a situation absent some scintilla, some particle of doubt." Nevertheless, it found qualified for a license the corporation and all the persons required to qualify by N.J.S.A. 5:12-85 c and d, except Clifford and Stuart Perlman. Upon clearly articulated findings and for reasons expressed at length, it announced that it was unable "to find by clear and convincing evidence that Clifford Perlman possesses the good character, honesty and integrity demanded by the Casino Control Act," and that "BRC has failed to meet the affirmative responsibility of establishing the good character, honesty and integrity of Stuart Perlman." The substance of the consequent order was that the application of BRC for a license would be granted but only upon the conditions that

> ... both Clifford and Stuart Perlman ... dispose of any interest whatsoever which either of them may hold in Caesars World, Inc., Caesars New Jersey, Inc. or in any and all subsidiary companies of Caesars World, Inc. in this or any other jurisdiction; ... both Clifford and Stuart Perlman be removed from any position as an officer, director or employee of Caesars World, Inc., Caesars New Jersey, Inc., Boardwalk Regency Corporation and any and all subsidiary companies of Caesars World, Inc. in this or any other jurisdiction; ... [and that] neither Clifford or Stuart Perlman shall receive any remuneration in any form, whether for services rendered or otherwise, from Caesars World, Inc., Caesars New Jersey, Inc., Boardwalk Regency Corporation, or from any other subsidiary company of Caesars World, Inc., in this or any other jurisdiction.

The order further provided for the submission of "a detailed plan and timetable for accomplishing the divestiture of all such securities and removal from all such positions."

...

As noted above, the conclusionary finding of the Commission respecting both Perlmans was that it had not been persuaded by clear and convincing evidence that either of them possessed the good character, honesty and integrity required by the Casino Control Act to qualify for a license. The basic or evidentiary facts upon which this conclusion was founded included among others: Clifford Perlman's "repeated and enduring" relationship with one Alvin I. Malnik, "a person of unsuitable character and unsuitable reputation ... [who] associated with persons engaged in organized criminal activities, and ... [who had] himself participated in transactions that were clearly illegitimate and illegal," at times subsequent to the media identification of an alleged business connection between Malnik and Meyer Lansky, a reputed organized crime figure. It was stipulated that the CWI directors were told as early as July 1971 that although Malnik, once indicted for tax fraud, had never been convicted of a crime, the "Federal law enforcement agencies apparently believed Malnik was involved in organized crime." The Commission found that the Malnik-Perlman association persisted long after Clifford Perlman's attention was called to the allegations of unsavoriness respecting Malnik's other friends. Indeed, it found that it persisted even after Philip Hannifan, chairman of the Nevada Gaming Control Board, had "voiced his concerns over Mr. Perlman's association with an individual of Mr. Malnik's reputation," and had received a commitment from Perlman "to extricate himself from the Cricket Club [one of the Perlman-Malnik associations] if Mr. Malnik would not institute a libel suit against Hank Messick, the author of *Lansky*."

Appellants' response is impassioned and zealous. They point to evidence that "[i]n 1972, when Clifford Perlman entered into the Cricket Club transaction, he had no reason to believe that there was any obstacle to his doing so.... [M]any other reputable individuals and financial institutions saw no problem at this time in associating with Malnik." They explain the continuance of the Cricket Club relationship by saying that "Perlman tried repeatedly to sever his connections with the venture, and subsequently did terminate his ties with the Cricket Club, after great difficulty and heavy personal financial sacrifice." They direct our attention to the fact that "In its eagerness to make its point, the Commission suppresses the testimony of Hannafin that he never took Perlman's expression of intent to get out of the deal as a commitment." Both briefs emphasize that Hannafin, no longer a Nevada official, testified he was satisfied with Perlman's efforts.

The foregoing is only one area of several which troubled the Commission. It is typical of the others. As is most certainly to be anticipated, a large portion of the testimony was susceptible not only of varying inferences but of varying conclusions. In like fashion, appellants point to substantial areas of testimony which are highly complimentary and praiseful of the Perlman brothers, most of it from business and banking.

Appellants claim the Commission distorted the evidence. Whether by unintentional hyperbole or as a result of faithful (but we believe misplaced) conviction, they assert that the findings are "completely unsupported by the record." These things are just not so. The Commission chose between conflicts in evidence, conflicts in available reasonable inferences and conflicts in conclusions which might be drawn. This was not only their right, it was their duty. A careful review of the record convinces us that regardless of evidence to the contrary, the findings they reached were reasonably available on the whole record and we will not disturb those findings [citation omitted].

With respect to the contention of Stuart Perlman that his disqualification, at least, resulted from "administrative afterthought" on a record where there is "virtually no evidence ... directed specifically against him," we say only that we are in hearty agreement with the conclusion of the Commission: "Stuart and Clifford Perlman are more than just brothers." We are persuaded, as was the Commission, that the affairs of the brothers are inextricably entwined. Parenthetically, we observe that judicious administrative afterthought may well be a salutary purpose of the administrative hearing. What one perceives to be "afterthought," another might regard as "careful consideration."

Appellants Perlman also complain of that which they characterize as a "procedural inadequacy" respecting the findings of fact. They claim that in marshalling its findings the

Commission ignored (or at least was unconcerned with) "overwhelming evidence" of distinguished business careers and model corporate existence of praiseworthy propriety. Citing the concurring opinion of Justice Handler in *In re* Kessler Mem. Hosp. Reimbursement, 78 N.J. 564, 573, 578–79 (1979), they charge that the agency has failed to identify the evidence it found insufficient.

The Commission did not ignore the favorable testimony. Quantitating the supportive factual presentation in terms of "a great deal of evidence," it said:

> In an effort to meet its statutorily imposed burden, BRC produced a great deal of evidence in support of both the good reputation of Clifford Perlman and the good character, honesty and integrity of Clifford Perlman. Several witnesses testified as to Clifford Perlman's good reputation in the financial community, in the casino hotel industry and in the communities where he lives and works. Most of these witnesses also testified as to his good character, honesty and integrity. Suffice it to say that the Commission has very carefully examined, considered and weighed all of this evidence.

It also spoke of the evidence produced "in support of the qualification of Stuart Perlman all of which has been carefully examined, considered and weighed." The distinction between findings of proof and findings of nonproof or inadequate proof or proofs which are not creditable, and the consequent obligations of a reviewing court, are discussed in Kaplowitz v. K & R Appliances, Inc., 108 N.J. Super. 54, 61–62 (App. Div. 1969), *certif. den.* 55 N.J. 452 (1970).

We have no doubt at all respecting "the grounds upon which the administrative agency has acted, its reasoning, and the manner in which the evidence of record has been transmuted into ultimate conclusions." *In re* Kessler Mem. Hosp. Reimbursement, *supra*, Handler, J., concurring, 78 N.J. at 578–79. We are satisfied that these have been "clearly disclosed and carefully explained." *Ibid.* Indeed, it is the clarity of that explanation that convinces us the Commission assuredly heard what was being said by the financial community, the personal community and the industry favorable to the Perlmans. Despite this, the Commissioners believed the shortcomings to be in fatally critical areas. This is exemplified by a question posed in their opinion:

> Once again, in the absence of any credible explanation presented in this record, we are left with a serious question. Why did Clifford Perlman, in late 1974, lead his company into its second (and his third) business entanglement with Alvin Malnik, especially in light of his November 1972 discussion with the Chairman of the Nevada Gaming Control Board?

In the conclusion implicit in this inquiry, and after an extraordinarily careful review of the record in view of the importance and novelty of the questions before us, we will not substitute our judgment for that of the agency. New Jersey Guild of Hearing Aid Dispensers v. Long, *supra*.

Although the statute is discussed in greater detail below, we pause to note that the appellants Perlman at one point in their brief contend simply that the "Commission's findings do not support a bad character conclusion." Such a conclusion is unnecessary. The statutory burden to demonstrate affirmatively the qualifying attributes, whatever they might be, has been expressly and clearly placed on the applicant by the Legislature and is subject to the canon of clear and convincing evidence. N.J.S.A. 5:12-84, 5:12-89. It is not necessary to disqualification that the applicant or any personnel required to be qualified be of demonstrably bad character. Disqualification is justified by their failure to prove themselves qualified by clear and convincing evidence. Such evidence is that which "produce[s] in the mind of the trier of fact a firm belief or conviction as to the truth of the allegations sought to be established," evidence "so clear, direct and weighty and convincing as to enable [the factfinder] to come to a clear conviction, without hesitancy, of the truth of the precise facts in issue." Aiello v. Knoll Golf Club, 64 N.J. Super. 156, 162 (App. Div. 1960). Particularly in this sensitive field, N.J.S.A. 5:12-1 b(9); Bally Mfg. Corp. v. N.J. Casino Control Comm'n, 85 N.J. 325, 331 (1981), to doubt is most certainly to deny.

. . .

Except respecting the requirement of divestiture as it applies to non-New Jersey nongaming subsidiaries of CWI, we affirm the administrative determination. We remand to the Casino Control Commission for recasting of the order consistent with the foregoing and for reasonable revision of the timetable. The stay imposed by the Supreme Court shall remain in effect pending the recasting of the order of the Commission and thereafter until further order of this court or the Supreme Court on motion. Other than with respect to the stay as noted, we do not retain jurisdiction.

Notes

1. In licensing matters, the burden of proof is usually on the applicant. For example, Mississippi gaming regulations provide: "An application for a state gaming license or any other affirmative Commission action is seeking the granting of a privilege, and the burden of proving his qualification to receive any license, registration, finding of suitability or approval, is at all times on the applicant." Miss. Gaming Reg. (II)(A)(1)(b). This is logical because the applicant has the most direct access to that information on which the regulators may decide his suitability. If the applicant cannot produce this evidence, then it probably does not exist. Similarly, the burden of persuading the regulators of the applicant's suitability should be on the applicant.

2. A party that has the burden of proof must, at a minimum, present evidence to support the requested decision. For example, if an applicant has the burden of proving his suitability, then the applicant must provide at least enough evidence to allow the regulators to decide whether the applicant is suitable. In matters such as licensing, the burden of proof may also implicate the burden to persuade the regulators of the applicant's suitability.

3. A regulatory agency decides factual matters by weighing the evidence and making a decision. But not all decisions are made by stacking evidence on different sides of the scale and choosing the side with the most substantial evidence. Decision-makers have different ways to "weigh" evidence. Perhaps the most commonly known are "beyond a reasonable doubt," "clear and convincing evidence" and "a preponderance of evidence." The former emanates from the standard used in criminal trials. Here, the amount of evidence supporting a particular decision should be substantial so as to eliminate any reasonable doubt that a contrary conclusion could be reached. Here is how one court described the difference between the three standards:

> We have generally applied three different standards of proof: preponderance, clear and convincing, and beyond a reasonable doubt. Evid. R. 1(4). Our courts have stated that the differences between these classifications are not semantic.

> Clear and convincing evidence should produce in the mind of the trier of fact "a firm belief or conviction as to the truth of the allegations sought to be established." Aiello v. Knoll Golf Club, 64 N.J. Super. 156, 162 (App. Div. 1960); *see also In re* Boardwalk Regency Casino License Application, 180 N.J. Super. 324,

339 (App. Div. 1981), *aff'd except as modified*, 90 N.J. 361 (1982). In *Aiello* the court, in defining the phrase, "clear and convincing," quoted the following language from Tapler v. Frey, 184 Pa. Super. 239, 132 A.2d 890, 893 (1957): "[The evidence must be] so clear, direct and weighty and convincing as to enable either a judge or jury to come to a clear conviction, without hesitancy, of the truth of the precise facts in issue." "Clear and convincing" is said to establish a standard of proof falling somewhere between the other two categories. It has also been said to be more closely akin to proof beyond a reasonable doubt. *See* State v. Cale, 19 N.J. Super. 397, 400 (App. Div. 1952).

Preponderance of evidence on the other hand is evidence sufficient to generate a belief that the conclusion advanced is likely. It has been stated in terms of reasonable probability. *See* Kahalili v. Rosecliff Realty, Inc., 26 N.J. 595, 607 (1958); *see also In re* Polk License Revocation, 90 N.J. 550 (1982) (noting difference between the preponderance and the clear and convincing standards.)

State v. Williams, 459 A.2d 651, 661–62 (1983) (Schreiber, J., dissenting).

4. Does the nature of the burden of proof and the standard applied in a licensing hearing affect how a gaming attorney approaches the proceeding? Is the attorney more inclined to approach the licensing hearing along the lines of defending a criminal case, or being a party to a civil matter?

7. The Legal Nature of a Gaming License

Nevada v. Rosenthal
559 P.2d 830 (Nev. 1977)

OPINION

THOMPSON, Justice:

This matter comes to us on direct appeal from a judgment of the Eighth Judicial District Court. That judgment declared certain licensing provisions of the Nevada Gaming Control Act unconstitutional for want of standards. It also found that the hearings before the Gaming Control Board and the Gaming Commission on Frank Rosenthal's application for a gaming license were conducted in such fashion as to violate federal constitutional proscriptions. Finally, the district court nullified the decision of the Gaming Commission that Frank Rosenthal is a person whose licensing would reflect or tend to reflect discredit upon the State of Nevada. For reasons hereafter stated we reverse that judgment in all respects and reinstate the decision of the Gaming Commission.

On January 23 and 24, 1975, the Gaming Commission held an investigative hearing to determine whether Frank Rosenthal was a key employee exercising significant influence over decisions of Argent Corporation, a holding company, which then owned three major hotel-casinos in Clark County. Rosenthal was executive consultant to the Chairman of the Board of Argent Corporation. It is clear that he significantly influenced policy decisions concerning the conduct of gaming in the three hotel-casinos. Consequently, the Commission directed him to submit an application for a gaming license as a key employee. The application submitted by him described his duties "to consult with and to recommend to the Chairman; to advise, to administrate, delegate and supervise Corporate standards, procedures and policies."

The application first was considered by the Gaming Control Board at a hearing on January 14, 1976. The members of that Board voted unanimously to recommend to the Nevada Gaming Commission denial of the application.

On January 22, 1976, the Gaming Commission heard the matter and voted unanimously to deny the application for license. The Commission found: "The applicant is a person whose licensing by the State would reflect or tend to reflect discredit upon the State of Nevada by reason of: A) A North Carolina court finding of guilt for conspiracy to bribe an amateur athlete; B) Testimony of Mickey Bruce in Senate subcommittee hearings that applicant attempted to bribe him to throw outcome of 1960 Oregon-Michigan football game; (C) Statements by police officers Dardis and Clode to Senate subcommittee and to Florida Racing Commission that applicant admitted he was corrupting public officials in return for protection; D) The applicant's being barred from race tracks and parimutuel operations in the State of Florida."

On February 17, 1976, Rosenthal filed a petition for judicial review of the decision of the Commission. He premised his petition upon NRS 463.315, alleging that the decision of the Commission violated constitutional provisions, was in excess of its jurisdiction, made upon unlawful procedures, was unsupported by any evidence, and was arbitrary and capricious and otherwise not in accordance with law. The petition did not assert that the licensing provisions of the Gaming Control Act were unconstitutional for want of standards. The district court, sua sponte, declared NRS 463.140 and 463.220 unconstitutional, and nullified the decision of the Gaming Commission.

1. It is established beyond question that gaming is a matter of privilege conferred by the State rather than a matter of right. The legislature has so declared. "Any license issued pursuant to this chapter shall be deemed to be a revocable privilege and no holder thereof shall be deemed to have acquired any vested rights therein or thereunder." NRS 463.130(2). In 1931 this court wrote: "We think the distinction drawn between a business of the latter character (liquor) and useful trades, occupations, or businesses is substantial and necessary for the proper exercise of the police power of the state. Gaming as a calling or business is in the same class as the selling of intoxicating liquors in respect to deleterious tendency. The state may regulate or suppress it without interfering with any of those inherent rights of citizenship which it is the object of government to protect and secure." State ex rel. Grimes v. Board, 53 Nev. 364, 372, 373, 1 P.2d 570, 572 (1931). *Accord:* Dunn v. Tax Commission, 67 Nev. 173, 187, 216 P.2d 985 (1950).

The licensing and control of gaming requires special knowledge and experience. Nev. Tax Com. v. Hicks, 73 Nev. 115, 119, 310 P.2d 852 (1957); Dunn v. Tax Commission, *supra*. In *Hicks*, this court observed "the risks to which the public is subjected by the legalizing of this otherwise unlawful activity are met solely by the manner in which licensing and control are carried out. The administrative responsibility is great." *Id.* at 120, 310 P.2d at 854.

The legislature has been sensitive to these basic concepts. Members of the Gaming Control Board and Gaming Commission must have special qualifications suited to the important duties with which they are charged. NRS 463.023; 463.040. Their powers are comprehensive. NRS 463.130-144. Court intrusion is limited. As we noted in Gaming Control Bd. v. Dist. Ct., 82 Nev. 38, 409 P.2d 974 (1966): "Any effort to obstruct the orderly administrative process provided by the Gaming Control Act casts serious doubt upon the ability of Nevada to control the privileged enterprise of gaming. Control does not exist if regulatory procedures are not allowed to operate. Courts owe fidelity to the legislative purpose...." *Id.* at 40, 409 P.2d at 975. Indeed, judicial review is confined to a final decision or order of the Commission and then only in specified instances.

With these basic principles in mind we turn to consider the issues of this appeal.

2. In the district court the State and the Gaming Commission moved to dismiss the petition for review for want of jurisdiction. We particularly note that the petition did not challenge the constitutionality of the licensing statutes. Had such challenge been made, a court would have to resolve it. Jurisdiction to decide that issue would exist since the courts are charged with the duty to decide such a question.

The petition for review was presented pursuant to NRS 463.315. That statute provides that "Any person aggrieved by a final decision or order of the commission made after hearing or rehearing by the commission pursuant to NRS 463.312 ... may obtain a judicial review thereof in the district court...." An examination of NRS 463.312 reveals its application only to disciplinary or other action against a licensee. It does not contemplate court review of the denial of a gaming license application. The sole responsibility for licensing is vested exclusively in the commission. NRS 463.220(6) so provides. "The commission shall have full and absolute power and authority to deny any application (for a license) for any cause deemed reasonable by such commission...." In Nev. Tax Com. v. Hicks, 73 Nev. 115, 121, 310 P.2d 852, 855 (1957), the court wrote: "It is not the province of the courts to decide what shall constitute suitability to engage in gambling in this state." In this regard the law has not changed since *Hicks*.

The legislature carefully has distinguished between persons who have been licensed and those who never have been licensed. In the former case judicial review of disciplinary action is provided; in the latter instance, it is not. This is a reasonable distinction since licensees possess property interests which those who have never been licensed do not have. The district court should have granted the motion to dismiss filed by the State and the Commission. Instead, that court declared the licensing provisions of the Gaming Control Act unconstitutional for want of standards, notwithstanding the absence of an allegation in the petition placing that question in issue. We proceed, therefore, to resolve that question.

3. The sections declared unconstitutional are NRS 463.140 and 463.220. In discussing this issue we do not decide whether licensing standards for the privileged enterprise of gaming must be expressed legislatively. State ex rel. Grimes v. Board, 53 Nev. 364, 1 P.2d 570 (1931), may be read to mean that uniform rules and standards are not essential to state control of gaming since it is a privileged enterprise subject to total state regulation and suppression. The legislature, however, has expressed standards which have been implemented administratively. When one considers the interrelationship of the statutory standards, United States v. Polizzi, 500 F.2d 856 (9th Cir. 1974), and the regulations adopted administratively, any contention that there is an absence of appropriate standards must fail.

The basic standard is stated in NRS 463.130. Gaming shall be licensed and controlled "so as to protect the public health, safety, morals, good order and general welfare of the inhabitants of the State of Nevada, and to preserve the competitive economy and the policies of free competition of the State of Nevada." The statutes which were ruled unconstitutional by the court below simply state that gaming licenses shall be administered "for the protection of the public and in the public interest in accordance with the policy of this state," NRS 463.140, and that the Gaming Commission has full power to deny any application "for any cause deemed reasonable," NRS 463.220.

Administrative regulations have been adopted by the Commission pursuant to legislative authorization. NRS 463.150(1). Relevant to this case is Regulation 3.090. There, it is stated: "1. No license, registration, finding of suitability, or approval shall be granted unless and until the applicant has satisfied the Commission that the applicant: a) Is a person of good character, honesty, and integrity; b) Is a person whose background, reputation and associations will not result in adverse publicity for the State of Nevada and its gaming industry; and c) Has adequate business competence and experience for the role or position for which application is made." If we were to assume that the standards announced in NRS 463.140 and 463.220 are inadequate legislative expressions for the control of licensing in a privileged industry, the implementing regulation would serve to cure the defect since the "gaps" may be filled in administratively. Dunn v. Tax Commission, 67 Nev. 173, 216 P.2d 985 (1950).

Persons of ordinary intelligence surely can understand the intent and purpose of the standards expressed in the quoted regulation.

We wish, however, explicitly to state that the statutory standards alone are sufficient since "reasonable" action by the Commission is required in the light of the public interest involved. It is entirely appropriate to lodge such wide discretion in the controlling administrative agency when a privileged enterprise is the subject of the legislative scheme. State ex rel. Grimes v. Board, 53 Nev. 364, 1 P.2d 570 (1931); Gragson v. Toco, 90 Nev. 131, 520 P.2d 616 (1974). We, therefore, find no basis for the ruling below that NRS 463.140 and NRS 463.220 are unconstitutional.

4. The district court also found that the applicant was denied procedural due process at the hearings before the Board and Commission. For reasons already stated, the court lacked jurisdiction to so rule. Notwithstanding this fact, the record refutes the court finding. The applicant and his two attorneys were present at each hearing. The applicant testified at each hearing and was given the opportunity to explain certain past alleged criminal activities and argue his position. Seventeen witnesses testified on his behalf, and seven letters attesting his good character and reputation were read into the record.

The district court, by ruling Rosenthal's due process had been violated because he had not been notified of the charges against him, misconceived the purpose of the hearings. They were not criminal proceedings in which Rosenthal had charges against him, but merely administrative proceedings wherein Rosenthal had the burden of proving his qualifications to receive a license. NRS 463.170. Further, the court mistakenly held that Rosenthal was denied his right to cross-examine apparently because the Board and Commission considered certain "hearsay" evidence consisting of the McClellan subcommittee transcript which was taken under oath, judicial papers from North Carolina, and investigative reports by the North Carolina State Bureau of Investigation. However, these hearings need not technically comport with strict rules of evidence, and hearsay can be accepted and considered by the agencies. NRS 463.312(13)(f); Citizens Bk. of Nev. v. Robison, 74 Nev. 91, 323 P.2d 705 (1958).

The district court ruling was premised upon the federal constitution. Although due process was not denied the applicant, it is worthwhile briefly to consider whether federal constitutional proscriptions are involved at all.

As before noted, gaming is a privilege conferred by the state and does not carry with it the rights inherent in useful trades and occupations. State ex rel. Grimes v. Board, 53 Nev. 364, 1 P.2d 570 (1931); Dunn v. Tax Com., 67 Nev. 173, 216 P.2d 985 (1950); NRS 463.130(2).

We view gaming as a matter reserved to the states within the meaning of the Tenth Amendment to the United States Constitution.[1] Within this context we find no room for

---

1. U.S. Const. amend. X: "The powers not delegated to the United States by the Constitution, nor prohibited by it to the States, are reserved to the States respectively, or to the people."

federally protected constitutional rights. This distinctively state problem is to be governed, controlled and regulated by the state legislature and, to the extent the legislature decrees, by the Nevada Constitution. It is apparent that if we were to recognize federal protections of this wholly privileged state enterprise, necessary state control would be substantially diminished and federal intrusion invited.

In this opinion we heretofore have noted the distinction drawn by the legislature between persons who have been licensed and those who never have been licensed. Judicial review is provided for disciplinary action against licensees. It is not provided for one who has not been licensed.

With regard to licensees the legislature, in vague fashion, has recognized that a decision of the gaming commission may violate "constitutional provisions." NRS 463.315(11)(a). We use the term "vague" advisedly. The "constitutional provisions" which the legislature had in mind are not designated. This, along with the mandate of NRS 463.130(2) that any license is a revocable privilege without vested rights, makes it difficult to fathom legislative intent.

Our obligation is to construe the mentioned statutory provisions in such manner as to render them compatible with each other. Bodine v. Stinson, 85 Nev. 657, 461 P.2d 868 (1969). With this principle in mind we interpret NRS 463.315(11)(a) to refer only to the concept of procedural due process which is embraced within Nev. Const. art 1, §8, no person shall "be deprived of life, liberty, or property, without due process of law." Thus construed, the two statutes are compatible. The license which is declared to be a revocable privilege, may not be revoked without procedural due process first being afforded the licensee.

5. As a gaming employee, Frank Rosenthal was required to hold a valid work permit. NRS 463.335(3). The denial of his application for a gaming license as a key employee may have caused an automatic revocation of his work permit if NRS 463.595 and Regulation 5.011(6) are to be literally applied,[2] thus precluding his right to work in a gaming establishment in any capacity. Revocation of a work permit is subject to judicial review, NRS 463.337(4), although the denial of his application to be licensed is not for reasons already stated.

---

2. NRS 463.595. "1. Each officer, employee, director, partner, principal, trustee or direct or beneficial owner of any interest in any holding company or intermediary company, who the commission determines is, or is to become, engaged in the administration or supervision of, or any other involvement with, the gaming activities of a corporate licensee, must be found suitable therefor and may be required to be licensed by the commission, prior to such engagement.

"If any officer, employee, director, partner, principal, trustee or direct or beneficial owner required to be found suitable pursuant to subsection 1 fails to apply for a gaming license within 30 days after being requested so to do by the commission, or is not found suitable by the commission, or his suitability or license is rescinded after such finding by the commission, the holding company or intermediary company, or both, shall immediately remove such officer, employee, director, partner, principal, trustee or owner from any position wherein he is engaged in the administration or supervision of, or any other involvement with, the gaming activities of a corporate licensee. If the commission suspends the suitability or license of any such officer, employee, director, partner, principal, trustee or owner, the holding company or intermediary company, or both, shall, immediately and for the duration of such suspension, suspend such person from performing any duties wherein he is engaged in administration or supervision of the gaming activities of the corporate licensee and from any other involvement therewith."

Regulation 5.011(6): "Employing in any capacity in or about any licensed establishment (including hotel, restaurant or bar facilities, as well as the gaming casino) any person who has been denied a state gaming license on the grounds of unsuitability or who has refused to submit an application for licensing as a key employee when so requested by the commission, or whose past activities and reputation would tend to bring discredit on the industry or the State of Nevada."

The hearings before the Board and Commission were focused entirely upon the suitability of Rosenthal to be licensed as a key employee since he did significantly influence policy. His right to work in a capacity other than that of a key employee was not in issue at all. His suitability to work as a gaming employee has never been questioned by the gaming authorities of this state. To this extent, O'Callaghan v. District Court, 89 Nev. 33, 505 P.2d 1215 (1973), is in point. There, an employee's right to work as a gaming employee was revoked without prior notice and an opportunity to be heard. We ruled such action improper.[3] It follows that an automatic revocation of an employee's work permit also must fail for want of fairness.

We, therefore, find Regulation 5.011(6) to be inconsistent with the statutes providing for administrative and judicial review of the revocation of a work permit. The regulation cannot stand. Cashman v. Nevada Gaming Comm'n, 91 Nev. 424, 538 P.2d 158 (1975).

A portion of NRS 463.595 likewise may be read to require automatic revocation of a work permit held by one found unsuitable to be licensed by reason of the oft repeated phrase in the statute "or any other involvement with, the gaming activities of a corporate licensee." An employee with a work permit is involved with the gaming activities of a corporate licensee. This portion of the statute does not square with the statutes providing for administrative and judicial review of the revocation of a work permit and cannot stand.

A reasonable distinction exists between the status of one who seeks to acquire a license, and the status of one who possesses a work permit as a gaming employee. The former does not have existing privileges, but is attempting to acquire them. The latter does have an existing privilege, and is entitled to receive notice and a hearing before his privilege to work as a gaming employee can be nullified.

Therefore, we conclude that Frank Rosenthal may continue to enjoy a work permit as a gaming employee. Our conclusion, however, shall not be construed to preclude further action by the gaming authorities to revoke his work permit should they deem such action advisable.

The judgment of the district court is reversed, and the decision of the Nevada Gaming Commission is reinstated. We particularly point to the fact that this opinion rests solely upon the State Gaming Control Act and Nevada case precedent. As we view this case, a federal question is not present.

BATJER, C.J., and ZENOFF, MOWBRAY and GUNDERSON, JJ., concur.

Jacobson v. Hannifin

627 F.2d 177 (9th Cir. 1980)

Before HUG and SKOPIL, Circuit Judges, and MUECKE, Chief District Judge.

HUG, Circuit Judge:

Nathan S. Jacobson and certain business interests (collectively, "Jacobson") brought this action against the State of Nevada and against members of the Nevada Gaming Control Board and the Nevada Gaming Commission (collectively, "the State"). The complaint demands $7,000,000 in damages allegedly caused by the State's conspiratorial deprivation of Jacobson's constitutional rights in violation of 42 U.S.C. §§ 1983 and 1985. Specifically, Jacobson alleges that the Board and the Commission denied his request for licensing

---

3. Since the O'Callaghan decision NRS 463.335 was amended to provide for judicial review. See: 1975 Stats., p. 686.

as the landlord of a hotel-casino in a manner which violates due process and equal protection. Jacobson appeals from summary judgment for the State. We affirm.

I

The parties do not dispute the essential historical facts that shape this controversy. At one time, Jacobson was licensed to operate the Kings Castle Hotel and Casino as a gaming establishment. In 1972, however, financial difficulties forced Kings Castle into bankruptcy. Operations ceased, and Jacobson's license expired for nonpayment of the quarterly licensing tax. A reorganization plan that was developed during bankruptcy proceedings provided that Jacobson would not be engaged in the active conduct of the hotel-casino, but would remain only as landlord of the property.

Jacobson notified the State of the reorganization plan and formally applied for licensing as landlord. After a hearing, the Gaming Control Board recommended that Jacobson be found suitable as landlord, subject to several conditions to be imposed upon the license. In a hearing before the Gaming Commission, Jacobson objected to the conditions recommended by the Board. Jacobson proposed to the Commission four alternatives, ranging in descending order of preferability from a finding of suitability without conditions to an outright sale of property. The Commission did not expressly rule on the first three of these alternatives. Instead, it adopted Jacobson's fourth proposal, and Kings Castle was sold.

Jacobson filed this action in the district court, claiming that the actions of the Board and the Commission denied him due process and equal protection. The district court granted summary judgment for the State on alternative grounds: (1) the defendants acted in good faith and were thus protected by qualified immunity, and (2) Jacobson failed to state a claim for denial of due process or equal protection.

II

Our standard of review on appeal from summary judgment is set forth in Yazzie v. Olney, Levy, Kaplan & Tenner, 593 F.2d 100 (9th Cir. 1979):

> Under Fed. R. Civ. P. 56(c), summary judgment is proper only where there is no genuine issue of any material fact or where, viewing the evidence and the inferences which may be drawn therefrom in the light most favorable to the adverse party, the movant is clearly entitled to prevail as a matter of law. Our role in reviewing the grant of summary judgment is to determine whether there is any genuine issue of material fact underlying the adjudication and, if not, whether the substantive law was correctly applied.

Id. at 102 (citations omitted).

Jacobson's principal claim is that the State denied him due process in the manner in which it rejected his request for an unqualified license to act as landlord. Because we find that Jacobson has no protectible property interest in a new gaming license, we uphold the district court's conclusion that Jacobson failed to state a claim for denial of due process.

There is no dispute that Jacobson's gaming licenses in the Kings Castle Hotel and Casino had expired before he applied to the State for license to act as landlord. We agree with the district court that Jacobson thus "stood in a position no different from that of any other first-time applicant."

We must first determine whether Jacobson, in the position of a first-time applicant for a license, had a property interest protected by the due process clause.

A property interest in a benefit protected by the due process clause results from a legitimate claim of entitlement created and defined by an independent source, such as state or federal law. Board of Regents v. Roth, 408 U.S. 564, 577 (1972); Perry v. Sindermann, 408 U.S. 593 (1972); Russell v. Landrieu, 621 F.2d 1037, 1040 (9th Cir. 1980).

The specific question before us is whether the Nevada Gaming Control Act, Nev. Rev. Stat., ch. 463, provides in Jacobson an expectation of entitlement to a license sufficient to create a property interest. *See* Griffeth v. Detrich, 603 F.2d 118, 120–21 (9th Cir. 1979), *cert. denied*, 445 U.S. 970 (1980). That will depend largely upon the extent to which the statute contains mandatory language that restricts the discretion of the Commission to deny licenses to applicants who claim to meet minimum eligibility requirements. *See id.*; *cf.* Bowles v. Tennant, 613 F.2d 776 (9th Cir. 1980) (liberty interest in parole).

The Nevada gaming statute grants to the Gaming Commission "full and absolute power and authority to deny any application for any cause deemed reasonable by such commission." Nev. Rev. Stat. § 463.220(6); *see also* Nev. Rev. Stat. §§ 463.130(2), 463.140(2). The only substantive restriction imposed upon the Commission's exercise of authority is the requirement that the basis for its decisions be reasonable. *See* State v. Rosenthal, 559 P.2d 830, 835 (Nev. 1977). This wide discretion resting with the Gaming Commission negates Jacobson's claim to a protectible property interest created by the State. *See* United States v. Goldfarb, 464 F. Supp. 565, 572–74 (E.D. Mich. 1979). *Cf.* Medina v. Rudman, 545 F.2d 244, 250–51 (1st Cir. 1976), *cert. denied*, 434 U.S. 891 (1977) (racing license under New Hampshire law). Moreover, Jacobson's interest in a gaming license is not so fundamental as to warrant constitutional protection apart from its status under state law. *See id.* at 251–52.

Jacobson suggests that a protectible interest is created by certain procedural requirements within the Gaming Control Act. He contends that the Commission violated those requirements by failing to rule expressly upon his first three alternative proposals and by failing to issue a written decision supporting its action.[1] Assuming, without deciding, that Jacobson's factual assertions and his interpretation of the procedural requirements of the Act are correct, we find that these requirements do not create a property interest entitled to constitutional protection.

Procedural guarantees ordinarily do not transform a unilateral expectation into a constitutionally protected interest. *E. g.,* Hayward v. Henderson, 623 F.2d 596 (9th Cir. 1980); Wells Fargo Armored Service Corp. v. Georgia Public Service Commission, 547 F.2d 938, 942 (5th Cir. 1977); Lake Michigan College Federation of Teachers v. Lake Michigan Community College, 518 F.2d 1091, 1095 (6th Cir. 1975), *cert. denied*, 427 U.S. 904 (1976); *see also* United States v. Caceres, 440 U.S. 741, 755–57 (1979). A property interest may be created if "procedural" requirements are intended to operate as a significant substantive restriction on the basis for an agency's actions. *See* Davis v. Oregon State University, 591 F.2d 493, 497 (9th Cir. 1978); Young v. United States, 498 F.2d 1211, 1220 (5th Cir. 1974). However, that is clearly not the case here. The Gaming Control Act unmistakably commits the substance of decisions regarding licensing applications to the discretion of the Commission. The procedural guarantees claimed by Jacobson do not enhance his expectation of obtaining a license to a degree sufficient to create a protectible interest.

---

1. Jacobson cites specifically to Nev. Rev. Stat. § 463.220(6), which provides:

    The commission shall have full and absolute power and authority to deny any application for any cause deemed reasonable by such commission. In the event an application is denied, the commission shall prepare and file its written decision upon which its order denying such application is based.

Jacobson has also raised claims of conspiracy, facial invalidity of provisions of the Gaming Control Act, and deprivation of his right to equal protection. Those claims are clearly without merit and were correctly dismissed by the district court on summary judgment. Because we affirm the district court's finding that Jacobson failed to state a claim for deprivation of constitutional rights, we need not review the district court's alternative holding based on immunity. *See* Klopfenstein v. Pargeter, 597 F.2d 150, 151, n.1 (9th Cir. 1979).

The judgment of the district court is AFFIRMED.

Kraft v. Jacka

872 F.2d 862 (9th Cir. 1989)

Before CHOY, CANBY and TROTT, Circuit Judges.

CHOY, Circuit Judge:

Sydell R. Kraft ("Kraft"), Levin International Corporation ("LIC"), Trans Atlantic Games, Inc. ("TAG"), and Trans Atlantic Games of Nevada ("TAG-Nevada") (collectively referred to as "plaintiffs") appeal from the district court's grant of summary judgment in their action under 42 U.S.C. § 1983 against members of the Nevada Gaming Board ("Board" or "Board members"). This action arose from the Board's refusal to extend further licensing to the plaintiffs after expiration of their one-year limited gaming licenses.

The district court concluded that the Board members were protected by absolute immunity. Alternatively, the district court ruled that the Board members were entitled to qualified immunity because plaintiffs had not shown that the Board violated clearly established constitutional rights of which a reasonable person would have known. Harlow v. Fitzgerald, 457 U.S. 800, 818 (1982). In part, this ruling was based on the court's determination that plaintiffs had no protected property or liberty interest and thus could not make out a claim for violation of due process rights.

Without reaching the issue of immunity, we affirm and hold that the plaintiffs have failed to establish a violation of procedural due process. Plaintiffs had no protected property interest in further licensing and could show no other property or liberty interest that would trigger due process protection. In addition, we hold that plaintiff Kraft has failed to establish a violation of her fourteenth amendment right to freedom of intimate association.

BACKGROUND

In 1984, plaintiffs applied to the Board for licenses to manufacture, distribute, and operate gaming devices in Nevada. The Board considered the applications at a public meeting on February 13, 1985. At that meeting, Board members raised several concerns regarding matters uncovered during the investigation of plaintiffs. Specifically, the Board was concerned that plaintiffs had engaged in the sale and distribution of slot machines within Nevada without a license, had shipped a machine into the state which had been approved in a particular form but had been modified without approval, and apparently had difficulty maintaining control of their machines in Nevada. The Board also was concerned that Howard Levin ("Levin"), who was then president of all the plaintiff corporations, had been associating with a convicted felon.

The Board ultimately voted to recommend approval of one-year limited licenses. The Board advised plaintiffs that its action was merely a recommendation to the Nevada Gaming Commission ("Commission"), which would make the final decision.

The Commission considered the recommendation at a public meeting on February 21, 1984. After raising several of the same concerns expressed by the Board, the Commission voted three to two to issue licenses in accordance with the Board's recommendation. Each license stated that it was a "[l]imited license to expire on date of Nevada Gaming Commission meeting of February, 1986." The Commission's orders of registration of LIC and TAG also stated that the sale of any equity in LIC or TAG:

> shall be void unless approved in advance by the ... Board. Such approval is deemed granted if an application ... has been filed with the Board for 30 days and the Board has not ... ordered acceleration or extension of time, or issued a stop order during such period.

In October, 1985, LIC filed a preliminary prospectus with the SEC in connection with a proposed public offering. On November 20, 1985, the Board issued an order stopping the offering. Two days later, the Board rescinded the order.

Plaintiffs and Levin subsequently applied for licenses to become effective at the end of the one-year period. The Board considered these applications at a meeting on February 6, 1986. Kraft and Levin attended the meeting. The Board members again raised numerous concerns, including Levin's substantial gambling debts and the possibility that he had used subterfuge to avoid repayment of those debts. Prior to any decision of the Board, plaintiffs requested withdrawal of the LIC and TAG applications and a continuance of the Board's consideration of the TAG-Nevada application. This continuance allowed LIC, TAG, and Levin time to transfer their interests to Kraft so that only Kraft and TAG-Nevada would be under consideration.

One week later, the Board considered the revised applications at a public meeting. The Board expressed concerns about the financial strength of TAG-Nevada, the continued involvement of Levin, and the genuineness of the separation of Levin from Kraft and TAG-Nevada. The Board ultimately voted unanimously to recommend denial of the applications "without prejudice," meaning that the applicants could attempt to cure the deficiencies in their applications and reapply.

On February 20, 1986 (one week later), the Commission considered the Board recommendation at a public meeting. Kraft attended the meeting with her attorney. The Commission echoed the concerns of the Board, and voted four to one against approval of either permanent licenses or six-month limited licenses.

The one-year licenses expired on February 21, 1986. On March 7, 1986, Board Chairman Jacka wrote to all Nevada licensees and their affiliates to notify them of the denial of new licenses to plaintiffs, quoting provisions of Nevada law requiring Commission approval prior to engaging in business transactions with denied applicants.

On July 18, 1986, plaintiffs filed their complaint in district court against S. Barton Jacka, Michael D. Rumbolz, and Guy T. Hillyer, members of the Board, and Larry G. Hickman, an employee of the Board. The complaint included two claims for relief under RICO, a claim based on common law fraud, and a request for injunctive relief. The complaint also included two claims under 42 U.S.C. §§ 1983, 1985, and 1986. The plaintiffs alleged their civil rights had been violated because they had been deprived of protected property and liberty interests without due process of law.

The Board moved for summary judgment on October 3, 1986. On August 31, 1987, the district court held a hearing on the motion. On September 4, 1987, the court issued its opinion granting the motion for summary judgment. Kraft v. Jacka, 669 F. Supp. 333 (D. Nev. 1987). The district court concluded that the Board members were entitled to absolute immunity. Alternatively, the court held that the Board members were entitled to qualified immunity on the civil rights claims. The court determined that there was no procedural due process violation because plaintiffs could not show a protected property interest in further licensing after the limited licenses expired automatically in February, 1986. *Id.* at 337–39. The court further determined that the Board was not the actual or proximate cause of the injuries stemming from the refusal to license, since the Board only made recommendations and the Commission was responsible for the ultimate decision to license.[1] *Id.* at 339.

On appeal, plaintiffs attack a variety of the findings and conclusions of the district court with respect to their action under 42 U.S.C. § 1983.[2] The plaintiffs contend that the district court erred by failing to view factual disputes in a manner most favorable to them as opponents of a summary judgment motion. Further, they contend that they were denied their procedural due process rights in the licensing proceedings and that the district court erred by failing to find protected property or liberty interests that would entitle them to due process of law. Plaintiff Kraft contends that the Board violated her right to free association by denying her application for a license because she would not terminate her personal relationship with Levin. Finally, the plaintiffs contend that the district court erred in determining that the Board was immune from suit.

STANDARD OF REVIEW

We review *de novo* a grant of summary judgment, using the same standard that is used by the trial court. Bonner v. Lewis, 857 F.2d 559, 561 (9th Cir. 1988). Summary judgment is appropriate if, viewing the evidence in the light most favorable to the party opposing the motion, the court finds that there is no genuine issue of material fact and the moving party is entitled to judgment as a matter of law. Fed. R. Civ. P. 56(c); Lundy v. Union Carbide Corp., 695 F.2d 394, 396 (9th Cir. 1982), *cert. denied,* 474 U.S. 848 (1985).

DISCUSSION

I. Protected Property or Liberty Interests

As a threshold requirement to any due process claim, the plaintiffs must show that they have a protected property or liberty interest. Board of Regents v. Roth, 408 U.S. 564, 569–71 (1972). The plaintiffs contend they were deprived of two separate property interests: (1) the property interest of TAG-Nevada in its limited licenses, and (2) the property interest of LIC in its common stock. In addition, plaintiffs assert that a protected liberty interest in reputation was violated. Plaintiffs TAG and LIC assert that their interest in reputation was violated by a finding of unsuitability issued by the Board without notice to them. Plaintiffs TAG-Nevada and Kraft contend that their reputations were damaged by the letter the Board sent to all Nevada gaming licensees, informing the licensees that Kraft and TAG-Nevada had been denied further licensing.

---

1. The district court noted that the plaintiffs had voluntarily withdrawn their claims under RICO. 669 F. Supp. at 337. The court dismissed the plaintiffs' 42 U.S.C. § 1985 claim because plaintiffs failed to allege class-based animus. The court denied the request for injunctive relief. Finally, having granted summary judgment on the federal claims, the court noted that its pendent jurisdiction over the state fraud claim was lost. *Id.* at 340–41. Plaintiffs do not raise the § 1985 claim or the state fraud claim on appeal, nor do they discuss injunctive relief.

2. To proceed under 42 U.S.C. § 1983, plaintiffs must allege deprivation of a constitutionally protected right under color of state law. Learned v. City of Bellevue, 860 F.2d 928, 933 (9th Cir. 1988).

A. Protected Property Interests

1. TAG-Nevada's Property Interest in its Limited Licenses

Plaintiffs contend that TAG-Nevada had a property interest in its limited licenses which was protected by due process. Property rights protected by procedural due process "are not created by the Constitution. Rather, they are created and their dimensions are defined by existing rules or understandings that stem from an independent source such as state law—rules or understandings that secure certain benefits and that support claims of entitlement to those benefits." *Roth*, 408 U.S. at 577. Thus, the issue before us is whether state law or any other source confers upon a limited licensee an expectation of entitlement to continued licensing that would give rise to a property interest protected by the federal Constitution. "A reasonable expectation of entitlement is determined largely by the language of the statute and the extent to which the entitlement is couched in mandatory terms." Association of Orange County Deputy Sheriffs v. Gates, 716 F.2d 733, 734 (9th Cir. 1983), *cert. denied sub nom.* Singer v. Gates, 466 U.S. 937 (1984).

The district court determined that plaintiffs stood in the shoes of first time applicants as of the date their limited licenses expired.[3] Relying on Jacobson v. Hannifin, 627 F.2d 177, 179 (9th Cir. 1980), in which we held that a first time applicant has no protected property interest in a new gaming license, the district court concluded that plaintiffs had no constitutional or statutory right to further licensing.

Plaintiffs make two arguments that the district court erred in holding they had no expectation of entitlement to continued licensing. First, plaintiffs assert that they were licensed and in active business at the time their limited licenses were reviewed and thus the refusal to extend any further licensing to them was more a revocation of existing licenses than a denial of new licensing. As holders of existing gaming licenses, they contend that they had a sufficient property interest to warrant procedural due process protection upon revocation of the licenses.[4]

We need not decide whether there is a state-created property interest in an existing gaming license that would be protected by the federal Constitution. A close look at the statutory scheme governing licensing and the specific purposes behind issuance of a limited license instead of a permanent license reveals that the decision to deny further licensing did not operate as a revocation or suspension of an existing license. Rather, it is clear as a matter of statutory interpretation that plaintiffs stood in the shoes of first time

---

3. Plaintiffs contend that the district court was required to characterize TAG-Nevada's property interest in the limited licenses in the light most favorable to them, as required by Fed. R. Civ. P. 56(c). This contention is meritless. Fed. R. Civ. P. 56(c) requires only that the *evidence* be construed most favorably to the opponent of a summary judgment motion. The characterization of TAG-Nevada's property interest depends primarily on statutory construction and is thus a question of law which does not need to be construed most favorably to either party. This court reviews questions of law *de novo*. Brock v. Plumbers Int'l Union of America Local 375, 860 F.2d 346, 349 (9th Cir.1988).

4. Plaintiffs cite Barry v. Barchi, 443 U.S. 55 (1979), and Kerley Industries, Inc. v. Pima County, 785 F.2d 1444 (9th Cir. 1986), to support their argument that the holder of an existing gaming license would have a property interest in revocation or suspension of that license. In *Barry*, the Supreme Court determined that a harness racing trainer had a property interest in his racing license that was protected by the Due Process Clause against suspension or revocation without proof of culpable conduct. In *Kerley*, the owner of a chemical plant was granted a conditional permit allowing the plant to operate for a limited period of time. The County subsequently revoked the conditional permit without prior notice and a hearing. State law set forth detailed provisions for suspension and revocation of conditional use permits. We concluded that "[t]his body of law endowed appellant with a sufficient claim of entitlement to its conditional use permit … to establish a property right and to trigger the constitutional requirement of due process." *Id.* at 1446.

applicants when they appeared before the Board in 1986. As first time applicants, plaintiffs had no protected property interest in further licensing. *Jacobson*, 627 F.2d at 180.

Under the Nevada Gaming Control Act (the "Act"), Nev. Rev. Stat. §§ 463.010 *et seq.*, gaming is regulated primarily through licensing and control by the Commission and the Board. The Board has "full and absolute power and authority to recommend [to the Commission] the denial of any application, the limitation, conditioning, or restriction of any license … [or] the suspension or revocation of any license … for any cause deemed reasonable by the board."[5] Nev. Rev. Stat. § 463.1405(2). The Commission has the same broad authority in making final rulings on licensing applications. *Id.* § 463.1405(3).

In making a licensing decision, the Board and Commission are required to consider numerous factors which indicate whether the applicant is suitable to participate in Nevada gaming.[6] *See* Nev. Rev. Stat. §§ 463.1405, 463.170. The Board has discretion to recommend issuance of a limited license, rather than a permanent license, when there are serious concerns regarding an applicant's suitability. A limited license is issued to allow a licensee to engage in business temporarily, as a testing period. If the concerns regarding suitability are resolved during the term of the limited license, the Board recommends further licensing. If the concerns are not resolved, the Board has discretion to recommend denial of an application for further licensing.

We conclude that the Nevada legislature could not have intended to confer any entitlement to further licensing on licensees who initially had not been considered suitable enough for the Board to recommend issuance of a permanent license. This conclusion is consistent with the sections of the Act that govern renewal and revocation or suspension of permanent licenses. A permanent license must be renewed each year on January 1, but renewal is virtually automatic upon payment of the proper fees and taxes.[7] Nev. Rev. Stat. § 463.270. Presumably, the holder of a permanent license could allow the license to ex-

---

5. A gaming license can be restricted or nonrestricted. A restricted license is a license to operate no more than 15 slot machines. All other licenses are nonrestricted. Nev. Gaming Comm'n Reg. 4.030(1); Nev. Rev. Stat. §§ 463.0177, 463.0189. A nonrestricted license can be limited to a set period of time or conditioned on the performance of certain acts. The licenses possessed by the plaintiffs were nonrestricted, subject to certain conditions, and limited to a period of one year.

6. Nev. Rev. Stat. § 463.170 provides in part:

2. An application to receive a license or be found suitable shall not be granted unless the commission is satisfied that the applicant is:

(a) A person of good character, honesty and integrity;

(b) A person whose prior activities, criminal record, if any, reputation, habits and associations do not pose a threat to the public interest of this state or to the effective regulation and control of gaming … ; and

(c) In all other respects qualified to be licensed or found suitable consistently with the declared policy of the state.

3. A license to operate a gaming establishment shall not be granted unless the applicant has satisfied the commission that:

(a) He has adequate business probity, competence and experience, in gaming or generally; and

(b) The proposed financing of the entire operation is:

(1) Adequate for the nature of the proposed operation; and

(2) From a suitable source.

7. Nev. Rev. Stat. § 463.270 provides, in part:

1. Subject to the power of the commission to deny, revoke, suspend, condition or limit licenses, any state license in force may be renewed by the commission for the next succeeding license period upon proper application for renewal and payment of state license fees and taxes as required by law and the regulations of the commission.

2. All state gaming licenses are subject to renewal on the 1st day of each January.

pire by failing to pay the renewal fees. As long as fees are paid, however, the holder has a continuing license unless the Board, upon proper investigation, decides to initiate a hearing before the Commission to limit, condition, suspend, or revoke the license. *See* Nev. Rev. Stat. § 463.310(2).

TAG-Nevada's limited licenses differed from a permanent license in that they were set to expire automatically in February, 1986. During the term of the licenses, the Board presumably would have been required to initiate a hearing before it could revoke or suspend the licenses. However, in the 1986 licensing proceedings, the Board had the option to allow the limited licenses to expire without further action by the Board or to grant TAG-Nevada's request for further licensing. The Board was not required to revoke the limited licenses and TAG-Nevada was not automatically entitled to renewal upon payment of fees. TAG-Nevada's position was indistinguishable from that of any other first time applicant.

Our conclusion that plaintiffs had no entitlement to further licensing also is consistent with our reasoning in *Jacobson*. In *Jacobson*, we determined that the Commission's broad discretion to grant or deny gaming license applications negated a claim to a state-created property interest in a new gaming license. 627 F.2d at 180. We stated:

> [t]he specific question before us is whether the Nevada Gaming Control Act provides in Jacobson an expectation of an entitlement to a license sufficient to create a property interest. That will depend largely upon the extent to which the statute contains mandatory language that restricts the discretion of the Commission to deny licenses to applicants who claim to meet minimum eligibility requirements.

627 F.2d at 179–80 (citations omitted). As was the case in *Jacobson* which dealt with a new applicant, the Nevada legislature has done nothing to restrict the Board's discretion to deny further licensing to a licensee when suitability concerns have not been resolved during the term of a limited license. The limited licenses possessed by plaintiffs were set to expire automatically on the date of the Nevada Gaming Commission meeting of February, 1986. The Board's total discretion to deny further licensing beyond that date once again "negates [plaintiffs'] claim to a protectible property interest created by the State." *Id.* at 180.

The plaintiffs' second argument is that they were assured by the Board that they would be granted continued licensing if they met with certain conditions attached to the limited licenses. They contend that they have invested hundreds of thousands of dollars in their business in reliance on this assurance and that they strictly adhered to the conditions attached to their licenses. Because of their compliance with the conditions, they contend that they had a reasonable expectation of entitlement to further licensing.

This contention is without merit. Assuming that such an assurance by the Board could give rise to an entitlement sufficient to trigger procedural due process protections,[8] there is absolutely no support for the plaintiffs' contention that the promise was made. The sole basis for plaintiffs' assertion is a statement by one Board member at the first licensing proceeding in 1985 that if, during the term of the one-year license, the Board found no "material problems," the Board "may very well entertain going to the full license." This is hardly an assurance that further licensing would be automatic. There is no other place in the record before the district court where any Board member makes

---

8. A property interest *may* be established through an implied contract or "by some other 'mutually explicit understandings.'" Parks v. Watson, 716 F.2d 646, 656 (9th Cir. 1983) (quoting Perry v. Sindermann, 408 U.S. 593, 601 (1971)).

any assurance to the plaintiffs that satisfaction of the conditions would result in automatic permanent licenses. In addition, as the Board and the Commission pointed out in the 1986 proceedings, such an assurance would be contrary to their duty to consider all of the statutory criteria that would indicate the plaintiffs were suitable to operate a gaming establishment.

The transcripts of the Board and Commission hearings, which were part of the record before the district court, contain no assurance of continued licensing. No other evidence of an assurance, other than that dealt with above, was presented. Thus, there was no issue of material fact on this point and the plaintiffs cannot establish an entitlement to further licensing on the basis of the Board's alleged promise. Since plaintiffs stood in the shoes of first time applicants in the 1986 licensing proceedings and have not established an entitlement to permanent licensing on any other ground, plaintiffs had no protected property interest in further licensing.

2. LIC's Property Interest in its Common Stock

Plaintiffs next argue that the Board violated their constitutional right by issuing a stop order as to an out-of-state sale of corporate securities by LIC. They contend that the Board's action deprived them of corporate property in violation of the Commerce Clause, and thus in violation of 42 U.S.C. § 1983.

The Commerce Clause places restraints upon the power of the states. Philadelphia v. New Jersey, 437 U.S. 617, 623 (1978). It divides power between the states and the federal government. We have previously stated that "§ 1983 was not intended to encompass those constitutional provisions which allocate power between the state and federal government." White Mountain Apache Tribe v. Williams, 810 F.2d 844, 848 (9th Cir. 1984) (Supremacy Clause, which establishes federal-state priorities, does not secure individual rights under § 1983), *cert. denied*, 479 U.S. 1060 (1987); *see also* Consolidated Freightways Corp. v. Kassel, 730 F.2d 1139, 1144 (8th Cir. 1984) (The Commerce Clause is "an allocating provision, not one that secures rights cognizable under § 1983."), *cert. denied*, 469 U.S. 834 (1984). Thus, assuming that the Board's actions in any way implicated the Commerce Clause, the plaintiffs cannot state a cause of action under § 1983 for violation of the Clause.

B. *Liberty Interests in Reputation*

The plaintiffs make two arguments that they were deprived of a protected liberty interest in reputation without due process of law. Plaintiffs TAG and LIC contend that they were deprived of their liberty interest when the Board, without first giving notice to the two companies, issued an order finding them unsuitable to engage in Nevada gaming. In addition, plaintiffs TAG-Nevada and Kraft contend that they were deprived of their liberty interest when the Board sent out a letter to all Nevada licensees informing the licensees that the application of TAG-Nevada and Kraft had been denied.

An interest in reputation "is, without more, 'neither "liberty" nor "property" guaranteed against state deprivation without due process of law.'" Fleming v. Department of Public Safety, 837 F.2d 401, 409 (9th Cir. 1988) (quoting Paul v. Davis, 424 U.S. 693, 713 (1976)), *cert. denied*, 109 S. Ct. 222 (1988). To implicate constitutional liberty interests, state action must be "sufficiently serious to 'stigmatize' or otherwise burden the individual so that he is not able to take advantage of other … opportunities." Bollow v. Federal Reserve Bank of San Francisco, 650 F.2d 1093, 1101 (9th Cir. 1981) (citing Board of Regents v. Roth, 408 U.S. at 573–74), *cert. denied*, 455 U.S. 948 (1982). The statements at issue must involve charges which rise to the level of "moral turpitude"; "charges that do not reach this level of severity do not infringe constitutional liberty interests." *Id.*

1. *Liberty Interests of TAG and LIC*

At the February 13, 1986, meeting, the Board voiced concerns regarding Kraft's and TAG-Nevada's continued involvement with LIC, TAG, and Levin. The Board issued an order recommending to the Commission that TAG-Nevada's application be denied. That order stated that one reason for recommending denial was that Kraft had proposed to continue her business association with TAG, LIC, and Levin, "all of whom are found to be unsuitable by the Board." Neither TAG nor LIC was represented at the February 13 meeting because both companies had withdrawn their license applications. Plaintiffs contend that the Board's statement regarding unsuitability "banished" both TAG and LIC from association with gaming in Nevada, and thus stigmatized them sufficiently to impair liberty interests. Since they were not present at the meeting, they contend that this finding of unsuitability violated due process.

Neither TAG nor LIC was directly affected by the Board's statement that they were unsuitable. Because neither company was before the board as an applicant, the statement did not have the effect of a "finding" of unsuitability which would result in denial of a licensing application. The Board was required to consider Kraft's associations, both business and personal, in ruling on TAG-Nevada's licensing application. Nev. Rev. Stat. §§ 463.170(2)(b), (3)(b)(2). The Board's statement constituted only a determination that TAG-Nevada should not be allowed to participate in gaming because the company's president, Kraft, had unsuitable associations. TAG and LIC were not "banished" from Nevada gaming by virtue of the Board's statement. Since the plaintiffs have not shown that the statement had a stigmatizing effect on the companies' ability to pursue future licensing applications, the asserted interest in reputation does not rise to the level of a constitutional liberty interest.

2. *Liberty Interests of TAG-Nevada and Kraft*

After the Commission issued its order denying TAG-Nevada's application for further licensing, the Board sent a letter to all Nevada gaming licensees informing them that TAG-Nevada and Kraft were no longer able to conduct business in the gaming industry. The Board's action did not invade a constitutional liberty interest in reputation. "Unpublicized accusations do not infringe constitutional liberty interests because, by definition, they cannot harm 'good name, reputation, honor or integrity.'... When reasons are not given, inferences drawn from [the state action at issue] are simply insufficient to implicate liberty interests." *Bollow*, 650 F.2d at 1101 (quoting Bishop v. Wood, 426 U.S. 341, 348 (1976)). The Board's letter did not state any reasons for the denial and did not even say that TAG-Nevada or Kraft had been declared unsuitable. An inference of unsuitability could have been drawn from the denial alone. However, as we stated in *Bollow,* a mere inference is not sufficient to implicate a liberty interest in reputation.

Plaintiffs had no protected property interest in further licensing and could not make out a claim under § 1983 for an alleged violation of the Commerce Clause. In addition, plaintiffs have failed to establish a protected liberty interest in reputation. Since plaintiffs had no protected property or liberty interests, they cannot show that their due process rights were violated. *Roth,* 408 U.S. at 569–71.

II. *Kraft's Free Association Claim*

Kraft contends that the Board violated her free association rights by basing the denial of TAG-Nevada's application on her personal association with Levin. Kraft and Levin live together as single adults.

There are two possible sources of constitutional protection for personal relationships. The first amendment protects expressive associations that involve the other activities protected by the amendment such as speaking, religious exercise, and petitioning the government. IDK, Inc. v. Clark County, 836 F.2d 1185, 1192 (9th Cir. 1988). The fourteenth amendment protects "'certain intimate human relationships ... against undue intrusion by the State because of the role of such relationships in safeguarding the individual freedom that is central to our constitutional scheme.'" Id. at 1191 (quoting Roberts v. United States Jaycees, 468 U.S. 609, 617–18 (1984)). Kraft contends that the Board's denial of her licensing application violated her fourteenth amendment right to free association, because the Board's denial was based on its disapproval of her personal relationship with Levin.

During the Board's meeting on February 6, 1986, it became obvious that the Board was concerned with Levin's suitability and was prepared to deny his application for licensing. The Board granted plaintiffs a continuance of their applications so that LIC, TAG, and Levin could transfer their interests in TAG-Nevada to Kraft. Kraft purchased TAG-Nevada, in exchange for a promissory note, so that only Kraft and TAG-Nevada would be under consideration.

At the February 13 Board meeting, the Board expressed serious concerns about the financial stability of TAG-Nevada and the possibility that Levin would continue to participate in the management of the company.[9] In the Board's order recommending denial of TAG-Nevada's application, the Board stated as one reason for the recommendation that "the applicant, SYDELL R. KRAFT, has proposed to continue her *business association* with TAG, [LIC], and Howard S. Levin, all of whom are found to be unsuitable by the Board, and this association will create or enhance the danger of unsuitable practices, methods and activities in the carrying on of business and financial arrangements incidental to the conduct of gaming by the applicants...." (emphasis added). Business relationships do not fall within the fourteenth amendment's protection of intimate associations. *IDK, Inc.,* 836 F.2d at 1193. If the Board had denied the application solely on the basis of Kraft's business ties with Levin, there clearly would be no constitutional violation.

However, the transcript of the Board meeting shows that the Board also was concerned that Kraft would continue to have a personal relationship with Levin.[10] In fact, one Board member stated that Kraft "could not have structured this deal to [his] satisfaction ... because the only way [he] would be willing to look at this favorably would be with conditions that Sydell Kraft *not work for nor be associated with* LIC, TAG, Inc., or Howard Levin" (emphasis added). Another Board member stated that "[i]f [he] were to move forward as one Board member today with a recommendation to approve this transaction, it would be with a condition that [Kraft] sever herself totally from Mr. Levin." Thus, we

---

9. There was some doubt that the company would be able to make enough money to support itself and it seemed more likely that the company would operate at a loss. The Board was concerned that Levin, through TAG and LIC, held the promissory note on TAG-Nevada and would be able to exert some control over the company because of that. Also, there was some discussion about whether Kraft intended to hire Levin as a consultant for mathematical or statistical services and whether he would have any management role in the company. Finally, Kraft stated that she intended to continue working for TAG and LIC in the same position that she had previously held.

10. The transcript contains the following testimony:

Member Hillyer: Mrs. Kraft, how about your personal relationship with Mr. Levin? ... Are you still going to be sharing a household?

Ms. Kraft: That is what we are doing today.... We have a very close personal relationship. I hope that it continues, but there are no guarantees....

Member Hillyer: So the personal relationship with Mr. Levin as it stands right now is planned to continue status quo; is that correct?

Ms. Kraft: As far as personal relationship, as far as I know from today, yes.

must decide whether the Board violated Kraft's free association rights when it denied her licensing application.

We have previously stated that the freedom of intimate association is coextensive with the right of privacy. Fleisher v. City of Signal Hill, 829 F.2d 1491, 1500 (9th Cir. 1987), *cert. denied,* 108 S. Ct. 1225 (1988). As we noted in *Fleisher,* the Supreme Court has extended the right of privacy to unmarried individuals only in cases involving contraception and abortion. *Id.* at 1497. The relationship between Kraft and Levin as cohabiting, single adults may fit within our description of an intimate protected association in IDK, Inc. v. Clark County, 836 F.2d at 1193. However, we need not decide whether the relationship between Kraft and Levin is a protected one, because we conclude that the Board's actions did not intrude on Kraft's free association right.

Neither the right to privacy nor the right to free association is absolute. In some cases, these rights must give way to compelling governmental interests. *See Fleisher,* 829 F.2d at 1500 (no violation of free association rights when police officer was terminated for having sexual relationship with a minor); Fugate v. Phoenix Civil Serv. Bd., 791 F.2d 736, 741 (9th Cir. 1986) (no violation of right to privacy when police officers were terminated for having sexual relationships with prostitutes); *see also* Karst, *The Freedom of Intimate Association,* 89 Yale L.J. 624, 627 (1980) (freedom of intimate association is presumptive rather than absolute and may give way to overriding governmental interests in particular cases). "The more fundamental the rights on which the state's activities encroach, the more weighty must be the state's interest in pursuing that course of conduct." Thorne v. City of El Segundo, 726 F.2d 459, 471 (9th Cir. 1983) (citing Moore v. City of East Cleveland, 431 U.S. 494, 499 (1977), and Kelley v. Johnson, 425 U.S. 238, 245 (1976)).

On the surface, the Board might appear to be violating Kraft's fourteenth amendment right by conditioning receipt of a gaming license on the termination of a possibly protected relationship. However, the Board did not deny licensing because it disapproved of the fact that Levin and Kraft were unmarried. The personal relationship between Kraft and Levin was not even the principal reason for the denial. The Board members clearly indicated that the personal relationship would not have been a deciding factor in the decision to deny further licensing if the transfer of control over TAG-Nevada from Levin to Kraft had not looked so much like a mere subterfuge.[11]

In this case, there was a significant governmental interest that justified the intrusion on any free association right Kraft might have. The Nevada Gaming Control Act sets forth the declared public policy of the state that "[t]he continued growth and success of gam-

---

11. The transcript of the February 13 Board meeting contains the following testimony:

Member Rumbolz: [T]he question of Mr. Levin's relationship with her, frankly, I was prepared to consider under the totality of the circumstances.

....

Mr. Silver: Well, I think if in fact you had indicated that Miss Kraft could not be associated with Mr. Levin, knowing that she had this relationship, that it would be an unfair burden on us coming forward, and if we had been told of that fact, probably we would have made other arrangements.

Member Rumbolz: Mr. Silver, I am talking about right now. As I mentioned to you earlier, I was prepared to look at that relationship after having seen all of the other severances of relationships and her good faith intent to be out here running a company.

....

Chairman Jacka: If I were to move forward as one Board member today with a recommendation to approve this transaction, it would be with a condition that she sever herself totally from Mr. Levin. Financially she cannot do that by her own admission today. And then that puts the company in a very tenuous position from a financial perspective.

ing is dependent upon public confidence and trust that licensed gaming is conducted honestly and competitively, that the rights of the creditors of licensees are protected and that gaming is free from criminal and corruptive elements." Nev. Rev. Stat. § 463.0129. This public confidence and trust is to be maintained by "strict regulation of all persons, locations, practices, associations and activities related to the operation of licensed gaming establishments and the manufacture or distribution of gambling devices and equipment." *Id.* In considering the qualifications of a licensee, the Board is required to consider whether the licensee's associations will adversely affect the operation of a gaming establishment. Nev. Rev. Stat. § 463.170(2)(b).[12]

The Board determined that Levin was unsuitable to be associated with Kraft because he lacked the business probity, competence, and experience to be in control of a gaming operation. The Board was concerned that Levin's personal relationship with Kraft would allow him to continue to exercise substantial control over TAG-Nevada.[13] In addition, the Board was concerned that the transfer of TAG-Nevada stock from Levin to Kraft was a mere subterfuge, because the entire transfer was financed through promissory notes, Kraft's personal relationship with Levin remained unchanged, and Kraft intended to continue working for TAG and LIC in the same position she had previously held.[14]

The state of Nevada has a significant interest in ensuring that only suitable individuals will have control of gaming operations. Here, the Board was concerned that Kraft's personal relationship with Levin would allow Levin to exert indirect control over TAG-Nevada even though he was not considered suitable to hold a gaming license. This concern is directly related to the state's interest in maintaining public trust and confidence in the gaming industry. The denial of Kraft's application was based in part on her refusal to sever her personal ties with Levin. However, the Board's action was not directed at the per-

---

12. Nev. Rev. Stat. § 463.170(2)(b) provides that "[a]n application to receive a license or be found suitable shall not be granted unless the commission is satisfied that the applicant is: ... (b) A person whose ... reputation, habits and associations do not pose a threat to the public interest of this state or to the effective regulation and control of gaming, or create or enhance the dangers of unsuitable, unfair or illegal practices methods and activities in the conduct of gaming or the carrying on of the business and financial arrangements incidental thereto...."

13. As Board member Rumbolz stated during the licensing proceedings,

Mr. Levin was not in my mind unsuitable because of associations with organized crime members or some nefarious criminal past he may himself have had. However, I am very concerned since he is the gentleman that's been teaching this lady her management in gaming companies, since he is the gentleman that will undoubtedly be the person she looks to for advice for management of a gaming company, that she will be receiving advice and has received training from somebody who does not understand this industry and is unsuitable for licensing.

....

LIC and TAG, Inc., are unsuitable companies.... I also feel Mr. Levin is unsuitable. I think that should have been abundantly clear from our meeting last week.

I have a real concern that you are going to continue to work for two unsuitable companies while you are purportedly the head of a company that would hold a Nevada gaming license. In addition, I am concerned that you would continue to have a personal relationship with someone I consider to be unsuitable while you were the purported head of a company with a Nevada gaming license.

14. Board member Rumbolz stated:

[W]hat we have is your client continuing her employment as an employee of Mr. Levin, continuing to live with him, continuing to live in the East Coast, putting nothing at risk in purchasing this company, and as far as I can see, having no different involvement with this company than she had before, other than the name change of title.

I view this as nothing more than a subterfuge. I think this is Howard Levin using Sydell Kraft to maintain the same relationship he had before....

sonal aspects of the relationship. Instead, the Board's decision was based on the appearance of subterfuge and the possibilities Levin would have to exert control over TAG-Nevada through his personal relationship with Kraft. Because the Board's denial of licensing was directly related to a significant state interest, the Board's action did not violate any free association right Kraft may have.

CONCLUSION

Plaintiffs have failed to establish protected liberty or property interests that would trigger procedural due process protections. In addition, plaintiff Kraft has failed to establish a violation of any free association right that may arise from her relationship with Levin. Because we conclude that plaintiffs cannot succeed on the merits of their claims, we find it unnecessary to address the issues of immunity and causation. The district court's order of summary judgment in favor of the Board is AFFIRMED.

CANBY, Circuit Judge, concurring:

I concur in Judge Choy's thorough opinion. I write separately only because I wish to add a few words regarding Kraft's freedom of association claim. Kraft contends that the Board violated her free association rights by basing its denial of TAG-Nevada's license on her personal relationship with Levin.

That claim, however, misperceives the record. Kraft's intimate association was far from the focus of the Board's action. The uncontroverted evidence makes clear that the Board's central concern was that Levin, whom it had found unsuitable to hold a Nevada gaming license, remained in effective control of TAG-Nevada. The totality of circumstances known to the Board lent substance to its fears. Levin had conveyed the ownership interest in TAG-Nevada to Kraft only after it became clear that the Board would deny a license if Levin remained as owner. Kraft gave only a note in return for the ownership interest; she made no other investment in TAG-Nevada and remained financially dependent upon Levin. And she continued to live with Levin. None of these facts is controverted. For the Board to have determined from all of the circumstances that Levin remained in control, or was likely to resume control, of TAG-Nevada was certainly permissible. To characterize the Board's action as a penalty or condition imposed on Kraft's intimate association with Levin is to ignore most of the evidence.

It is true that Kraft's living with Levin was one of the many circumstances that the Board considered relevant to the question of Levin's control of TAG-Nevada. To the extent that such consideration may be viewed as an incidental burden on Kraft's associational interests, it was justified in the circumstances of this case by Nevada's governmental interest in maintaining the integrity of public licensed gaming. *See* Nev. Rev. Stat. § 463.0129. Whether the Board would or could prevail if it were faced *only* with the fact of Kraft's personal relationship with Levin need not be decided; the Board acted on the totality of circumstances. In so acting, it did not infringe Kraft's rights.

Notes

1. The government's action in deciding whether to approve a gaming application is based on principles different from the criminal law that requires the process be fair, even if guilty persons occasionally go free. Instead, the basic belief behind stringent gaming licensing is that persons meet strict standards even if qualified persons do not obtain a license. Unlike the presumption of innocence in criminal proceedings, the applicant for a gaming license is not presumed suitable. Instead, an applicant must prove his suitability to hold a license.

2. Under the above trio of cases, is a gaming license considered a "privilege" or a "right"? What is the meaning and consequences of this distinction? Does this change once a license has been granted? If so, how and why?

3. Not all businesses are "useful trades and occupations." A person engaging in an excluded trade is not afforded due process protection. Typical of this genre are trades "inherently harmful and dangerous to society or the public welfare." These trades may have "license requirements and exactions ... to discourage and to even amount to a prohibition of them." Earlier Nevada court decisions have held that gaming is one of those inherently harmful businesses. In a 1931 case, the court said that "[g]aming as a calling or business is in the same class as the selling of intoxicating liquors in respect to deleterious tendency." Grimes v. Board of Commissioners, 1 P.2d 570, 572 (Nev. 1931). The court reasoned, "The State may regulate or suppress it without interfering with any of those inherent rights of citizenship which it is the object of government to protect and secure." *Id.* In 1957, Nevada's Supreme Court wrote that "if Nevada gambling is to succeed as a lawful enterprise, [it] must be free from the criminal and corruptive taint acquired by gambling beyond its borders. If this is to be accomplished, not only must the operation of gambling be carefully controlled, but the character and background of those who would engage in gambling in this State must be carefully scrutinized.... The risks to which the public is subjected by the legalizing of this otherwise unlawful activity are met solely by the manner in which licensing and control are carried out. The administrative responsibility is great." Nevada Tax Commission v. Hicks, 310 P.2d 852, 854 (Nev. 1957).

Chapter 5

Gaming Contracts: Player Disputes and Casino Debt Collections

1. Introduction

A contract is a promise or a set of promises that the law will enforce. Casino-style wagering breaks down into a series of contracts. The wager itself is an adhesion contract, or a "take-it-or-leave-it" contract, between the casino and its players. An adhesion contract is non-negotiable. The casino defines the terms of the contract (the rules of the wager) and allows players to play the game as-is, with no possibility of changing the rules. The nature of gaming necessitates such adhesion contracts. Casinos are in the business of making money. Therefore, the casino typically only enters into contracts that have a statistical advantage favoring the casino. Altering the terms of this contract could change the statistical advantage by changing the probability of winning or losing the wager. *See generally*, RESTATEMENT (SECOND) OF CONTRACTS § 1 (1978); E. ALLAN FARNSWORTH, CONTRACTS 312 (2d ed. 1990).

Once the wager is made by the player and accepted by the casino, then a contract is formed. Ultimately, Lady Luck and perhaps some skill from the player determine whether the casino keeps or returns the player's wager or must pay a larger prize. Disputes may arise when the casino and player disagree either about the terms of the contract or about the result of the event that determines the outcome.

The wager itself is not the only potential contract between the casino and a player. Sometimes, the casino will provide credit to the player to allow the player to gamble. Credit play occurs when a player borrows money from a casino to allow him to make wagers. Credit play in some casinos accounts for over 60% of the resort's total table game drop. Credit is extended to players who fill out an application form. The form includes detailed personal information, including the player's bank and bank account information. This allows the casino to determine the creditworthiness of the player. When credit is extended, the player can draw on the line of credit to the extent approved by requesting that the casino issue a "marker." A marker is a negotiable instrument that bears the instruction PAY TO THE ORDER OF. It authorizes the casino to fill in details regarding the transaction and to present the instrument for payment to the bank which the player provided on his credit application. Typically, this presentation is only done after the casino has failed in informal attempts to have the player repay the amount extended as credit.

In some instances, the casino may allow a player to make a bet at a table through the use of "rim" credit, which is credit given without signing a formal document, like a verbal IOU. In addition, checks are a form of credit because the casino relies on the player's financial standing to assure that the bank will pay the check when presented for payment. For example, New Jersey requires that the casino present the check within a certain number of days depending on the amount of the check. Small checks must be presented within a shorter time than larger checks. New Jersey's system is based on the belief that players will not spend more than the available cash in their checking accounts if they know the casino will present the check for payment within a short period. In all cases of credit extension, the casino is relying on the player's creditworthiness to assure that the checks will be paid when presented to the bank. Alvin J. Hicks, *No Longer the Only Game in Town: A Comparison of the Nevada and New Jersey Regulatory Systems of Gaming Control*, 12 Sw. U. L. Rev. 620 (1981). Missouri and several other states prohibit the use of credit altogether. Robert D. Faiss, *Nevada Gaming Industry Credit Practices and Procedures*, 3 Gaming L. Rev. 145 (1999).

Both the wager and credit extended pose legal considerations that distinguish them from ordinary contracts.

2. Are Gaming Debts Enforceable?

West Indies, Inc. v. First National Bank of Nevada
214 P.2d 144(Nev. 1950)

PRIEST, District Judge.

This is an appeal from a final judgment of dismissal of an action commenced in the Second Judicial District Court of Washoe County, after issue joined on the pleadings. Appellant was plaintiff and respondent was defendant in the trial court.

The complaint alleges that on October 23, 1948, decedent Leonard H. Wolff, drew three checks upon respondent in the respective amounts of $7,000.00; $29,000.00; and $50,000.00, ... and alleges that same were presented to respondent for payment on October 24, 1948, and dishonored; that Leonard H. Wolff died testate on October 23, 1948; that on November 22, 1948, the respondent was appointed by the Second Judicial District Court, administrator, ... and on said date qualified, and is now qualified and acting as such administrator of the estate of the said Leonard H. Wolff; that on February 15, 1949, the appellant duly presented its claim to said administrator for the sums set out in said checks totaling $86,000.00, which claim was rejected and refused of February 16, 1949, by an instrument in writing. Plaintiff prayed for judgment against the defendant as administrator of the estate of Leonard H. Wolff, in the sum of $86,000.00 and for costs of suit, payable out of said estate in due course of administration.

Respondent answered and set up as an affirmative defense that the said checks had been given by decedent to plaintiff in payment of money theretofore won by plaintiff from defendant at the gambling game of 'twenty one' and for no other purpose and that the sole consideration for the execution and delivery thereof was money theretofore won by plaintiff from decedent at said gambling game.

Plaintiff's reply admitted the allegations of the affirmative defense heretofore set out. Subsequent to the filing of its reply the plaintiff moved the court for an order permitting an amendment to the reply in such a manner as to show that at all times material to the action, appellant was regularly licensed by state authorities as by law provided and required, to operate the said game referred to. Without objection this proposed amendment was allowed.

Defendant then moved the court for the entry of judgment on the pleadings dismissing the action, upon the ground that if said checks were so executed and delivered, they were executed upon the sole consideration of money won at gambling.... Upon presentation and argument the court entered an order granting the motion for judgment on the pleadings and accordingly entered judgment for defendant. From the judgment of dismissal plaintiff appeals.

. . . .

There is ... one question presented here to this court, viz: May a gambling house or the proprietor thereof maintain an action at law for the collection of money won at a duly licensed game? We have thus limited the inquiry and have omitted from this determination the question of collectibility of money by a patron of winnings from a duly licensed game. Such question is not presented here.

Appellant contends: That the earlier decisions of this court are not controlling being decided under other statutes declaratory of a different public policy; that the English common law, if adopted by Nevada, has been altered by statute; that since 1909 the public policy of this state has been substantially altered with reference to gambling; that licensed gambling is no longer a public nuisance or contrary to public policy, and that our gambling enactments are repugnant to the English statutes.

Respondent contends: That a portion of the common law known as the Statute of Anne, 9 Anne, c. 14, 4 Bac. Abr. 456, relevant to gambling has been effectually adopted by this state; that if not effectually adopted heretofore it is nevertheless an integral part of the law of this state; that the statute is severable and the adoption of a pertinent part is not dependent upon the adoption of the whole; that the law does distinguish in its regulatory power between useful callings and those that do not contribute to the economic good; that the statute is prohibitive rather than permissive; that an express clause in the act making such accounts collectible would have been ineffectual in the absence of a change of title; and that the social consequences of a change in the recognized law are great and that an intent to repeal by implication should not be imputed to the legislature in the absence of a clear showing.

The first pronouncement of this court upon this question was in Scott v. Courtney, 1872, 7 Nev. 419, in which case the court construed the statute of 1869.... [This statute prohibited gambling from being offered without a license and prescribed how licenses could be obtained.]

. . . .

In Scott v. Courtney, *supra*, suit was brought by the proprietor of a duly licensed game to collect money lost at such game. Without a declaration that Nevada had adopted any portion of the common law of England known as the Statute of Anne, ... the court nevertheless concluded, in reliance principally upon decisions of the state courts under similar statutes, that the so-called indebtedness was not collectible and that the action could not be maintained.... The court said:

> In the United States, wagering and gaming contracts seem to have met with no countenance from the courts, and consequently in nearly every state they are held illegal, as being inconsistent with the interests of the community and at variance with the laws of morality. 2 Smith's Leading Cases, 343.

Section 9021 N.C.L. of 1929, provides as follows: 'The common law of England, so far as it is not repugnant to, or in conflict with the constitution and laws of the United States, or the constitution and laws of this state, shall be the rule of decision in all the courts in this state.' This has been held to include the English statutes in force at the time of the American Declaration of Independence. Ex parte Blanchard, 9 Nev. 101....

In Evans v. Cook, 11 Nev. 69, decided in 1876, [the court]proceeded to determine whether the proprietor of an establishment could maintain an action for money won by it at one of its duly licensed games. The court then held that there had been an adoption of the applicable portions of the Statute of Anne.

. . . .

In Burke & Co. v. Buck, 1909, 31 Nev. 74, decided under the statute of 1879, the uncontroverted evidence showed that Buck while playing roulette at a Goldfield saloon, endorsed and delivered a negotiable certificate of deposit of $500.00 back to the house. Buck then notified John S. Cook and Co., the issuing corporation, that he had lost possession of same, without consideration and requested said company to refuse payment of said certificate. Judgment was for plaintiff, the gambling house proprietor, in the trial court and upon appeal reversed. The opinion refers approvingly to Evans v. Cook, *supra*, and approves the adoption of all parts not inconsistent, of the English Statute of Anne. Again there is a declaration as in Scott v. Courtney, *supra*, that the licensing of gambling is merely permissive, and serves to give immunity from criminal prosecution and nothing more.

In Menardi v. Wacker, 105 P. 287, 288, it was held that 'A check given for a gambling debt is void under the law of this state, and, there being no valid obligation, there could be no lawful consideration for the security as a pledge.'...

Looking at the matter historically and by way of throwing light upon the question of legislative intent, it is deemed fitting to show that in or about the year 1909, the pendulum of public opinion had reached the extreme right, and from 1909 through 1915 a series of anti gambling statutes were enacted. Sufficient to conclude without going into great detail that this was a period of extreme conservatism in the public policy of the state with reference to gambling. This attitude was first manifested by a statute of 1909, p. 307, entitled; 'An Act prohibiting gambling, providing for the destruction of gambling property and other matters relating thereto.'....

Public opinion having changed again toward liberality the legislature enacted the so-called open gambling law in 1931. The statute is entitled: 'An Act concerning slot machines, gambling games, and gambling devices; providing for the operation thereof under license; providing for certain license fees and the use of the money obtained therefrom; prohibiting minors from playing and loitering about such games; designating the penalties for violations of the provisions thereof; and other matters properly relating thereto.' Statutes of 1931, 165–169, Secs. 3302-3302.16, N.C.L. Supplement 1931–1941.

Appellant as a result of tireless and exhaustive research shows to the court that a great deal of the gambling law of England in force at the time of the American Declaration of Independence, is peculiarly applicable to that country because of the structure of their government. From this he argues that under our form of government and particularly in view of the liberality of our statutory enactments pertaining to this subject, from the year 1931, no part of the said Statute of Anne can now have any controlling force. In support of this position appellant shows:

. . . .

That the Statute of Anne does not, as do the Nevada statutes, license gambling;

. . . .

We understand that certain of the statutes of England, not here under investigation, but which cast light upon the gambling status and public policy of England at that particular time, are discussed only for these purposes.

Certain portions of the Statute of Anne that are at hopeless variance with the structure of government in America, were equally at hopeless variance at the time of the admission of Nevada to statehood. Admittedly, without attempting to define just which portions, certain portions of the Statute of Anne are not in harmony with the structure of government here, either national or state. But from this fact we cannot conclude that no part of the statute has been adopted unless the statute itself is totally inseparable, or non-severable. Apparently this question of severability has not been raised or urged in any of the gambling cases heretofore decided by this court. Such contention therefore merits careful consideration....

The determination of Evans v. Cook, *supra*, and Burke v. Buck, *supra*, elicited the declaration that the first section of the Statute of Anne had been adopted. The wording of the first section alone was required to sustain the conclusion reached. The first section of said statute reads as follows:

> That all notes, bills, bonds, judgments, mortgages, or other securities or conveyances whatsoever given, granted, drawn, or entered into, or executed by any person or persons whatsoever, where the whole, or any part of the consideration of such conveyances or securities shall be for any money, or other valuable thing whatsoever, won by gaming or playing at cards, dice, tables, tennis, bowls, or other game or games whatsoever, or by betting on the sides or hands of such as to game at any of the games aforesaid, or for the reimbursing or repaying any money knowingly lent or advanced at the time and place of such play, to any person or persons so gaming or betting as aforesaid, or that shall, during such play, so play or bet, shall be utterly void, frustrate, and of none effect, to all intents and purposes whatsoever.

The first section heretofore quoted, provides that gambling debts may not be collected at law; the second section that money lost at gambling and paid over may be recovered by the loser....

The first and second sections of the statute are entirely independent and severable. The first provides a shield for one who has lost at gambling but has not paid his losses, while the second provides a sword by which he may recover back what he has paid over. The first provides a defense and the second a remedy. It is difficult or impossible to conceive of a single transaction in which both sections could be invoked. The first section cannot be invoked if the gambling debt has been paid. The second section cannot be invoked if the gambling debt has not been paid....

Only such portions of the common law as are applicable to our conditions, have been adopted as the law of this state.... We are satisfied that there has been an effectual declaration of adoption of the first section of the Statute of Anne. We are not required to decide if more was adopted and without limiting such possibility we pass the matter for future determination in a proper case.

We are now confronted with the question of whether any of the gambling statutes enacted from the date 1931, have in legal effect repealed by implication the first section of the Statute of Anne. Such repeal would necessarily be by implication for there is nothing in any of the statutes repealing it directly, i. e. there is no provision in any of the statutes to the effect that money won by the establishment at a licensed game may be collected by suit at law.

.....

Appellant's contention for a repeal by implication is based particularly upon three points, viz;

> 1. That the use of the word 'checks' in the statute of 1931 impliedly authorizes suit to collect same.

2. That the statute of 1931 in omitting the immunity clause contained in the earlier statute did so with the intent of giving authority to the licensee to maintain an action for winnings of licensed games.

3. That if the repeal of the first section of the Statute of Anne was not effected by the act of 1931 it nevertheless was effected by the act of 1945, p. 492, under the terms and provisions of which it is urged 'the state became a partner'.

In all of the statutes under scrutiny, 1869, 1879, 1931, in which gambling under license is authorized, the word 'checks' appears. It is not new to the statute of 1931, which statute is clearly modeled from the other statutes. The first section deals with the unlawful and is prohibitive rather than permissive. In effect it declares that it is unlawful for all persons, natural or artificial, to carry on certain games of chance, enumerating them, for property of all kinds unless properly licensed. It cannot be legally inferred from this wording of the statute that the statute is a grant of authority to take checks in properly licensed games, and that there is a corollary power granted to maintain an action at law for the collection of such checks.

. . . .

But to resolve this question of repeal by implication, we are not required to indulge in speculation, we can reach it very directly. We quote from 15 C.J.S., Commerce, § 12, p. 620, as follows:

> Although the common law may be impliedly repealed by a statute which is inconsistent therewith, or which undertakes to revise and cover the whole subject matter, repeal by implication is not favored, and this result will be reached only where there is a fair repugnance between the common law and the statute, and both cannot be carried into effect.

The statute of 1931 did not attempt to 'revise and cover the whole subject matter', as evidenced by the fact that section 10201 N.C.L. of 1929, which was a law with reference to gambling effective January 1, 1912, was amended in 1941 p. 64: Sec. 10201, 1931–1941 N.C.L. Supplement.

In Cunningham v. Washoe County, 203 P.2d 611, 613, in which appellant contended for repeal of the common law by implication, Mr. Justice Badt stated the law applicable to this action at bar in these words:

> Nevada has by statute adopted the principles of the common law and has in a number of instances modified the common law by statutory enactment. That this may be done by way of constructive repeal of the common law (as in cases where a statute has revised the whole subject) or that it may be the result of 'the clear and unquestionable implication from legislative acts,' as maintained by appellant, we may concede to be true where such situations sufficiently appear. However to sustain a justification of the particular acts under this theory, where such acts are not authorized by the express terms of the statute under which the justification is made, we should have to find the plainest and most necessary implication in the statute itself. This rule appears to be frankly admitted even in the authorities submitted by appellant.

We now approach the question of liberal and strict construction.

. . . .

Statutes in derogation of the common law are to be strictly construed. Sutherland Statutory Constitution, Third Edition, Vol. 3, Art. 6202. '* * * statutes granting special privileges to a group of persons who are in no particular need may be strictly construed against such beneficiaries.' Sutherland Statutory Construction, Third Edition, Vol. 3, Art. 5503, Note 9. 'One of the best illustrations of such legislation is laws granting special franchises and privileges.' Charles River Bridge v. Warren Bridge, 11 Pet. 420, 36 U.S. 420.

Considering the limitations placed by law upon the license, the special class of industry licensed and its deleterious effect, the fact that it is in contravention of the common law, the fact that it is a statute granting special privileges, we entertain no doubt but that the statute is one meriting strict construction against the licensee, and must therefore conclude from the application of the rule of strict construction, that the omission of the immunity clause in the statute of 1931, does not in legal effect grant the right to maintain an action for winnings at a duly licensed game. There is no such 'clear and unquestionable implication from legislative acts'....

Finally does the fact that the state now accepts two per cent of the gross income from duly licensed games, confer the right upon the licensee of such games to maintain an action for his winnings at such games?

It has been urged that such license fee in which the state has this direct interest, confers such right by operation of law. Under the statutes of 1869 and 1879 the state and county both had a financial interest in the proceeds of the license. Under the present law the state receives far more money, of that there can be no doubt, but the financial interest of the state and county has been present under all of the gambling statutes. It might be said that under the earlier laws the interest of the state was in licensing and nothing more, and that the state was not concerned with the success of the licensed games. In a restricted and limited sense that is true, and yet on the other hand an unsuccessful game could not or would not under the earlier statutes, continue from quarter to quarter to be licensed. It is therefore true that under all license laws the state has been financially interested in the success of the games, machines or devices so licensed. The distinction between the application of the old laws and the present law is therefore a distinction of quantity and not quality. We must therefore conclude that the enactment of the laws of 1945, p. 492, and of 1947, p. 734, by which a license fee of one (1%) per cent and later two (2%) per cent of gross income, was and is charged, does not alter the conclusions formerly reached.

. . . .

For the reasons heretofore given it is ordered that the judgment of the District Court be, and the same is hereby affirmed, with costs.

HORSEY, C. J., and BADT, J., concur.

Resorts International Hotel, Inc. v. Agresta

569 F. Supp. 24 (E.D. Va. 1983)

OPINION AND ORDER

WARRINER, District Judge.

Plaintiff's amended complaint ... alleges that during May and June, 1982, defendant came to plaintiff's place of business in Atlantic City ... and engaged in and lost a substantial sum of money in games of chance. To pay the loss defendant drew a series of three drafts payable to plaintiff on the account of one Edward Hamway in a Philadelphia, Pennsylvania, bank. The drafts were dishonored by the bank and returned to the plaintiff. Defendant thereupon executed a note in payment of the loss providing that defendant would pay plaintiff the principal sum of $10,000 together with eight percent (8%) interest. The note authorized defendant's attorney-in-fact, Benjamin B. Wooldridge, to confess judgment against defendant in the amount of $10,000 (face value of the note), plus interest, costs, and collection charges. Plaintiffs allege that the note plus interest and collection charges is now due and owing from defendant to plaintiff. Plaintiff claims that demand has been made upon defendant to honor the obligation under the note, but that defendant has failed and refused to pay plaintiff the sum due.... For the reasons set forth herein the action will be dismissed.

Plaintiff, Resorts International Hotel, Inc., is a New Jersey corporation with its principal place of business in the State of New Jersey. Plaintiff does not transact business in the Commonwealth of Virginia and has no principal place of business here. Defendant is a citizen of the Commonwealth.... The Court looks to the substantive law of the Commonwealth of Virginia for the basis of its decision.

The general rule is that contracts and liabilities recognized as valid by the laws of the State or the country where made or established may be enforced in the courts of another State or country where the action is brought unless such contract or liability is contrary to morals, public policy, or the positive law of the latter.... In New Jersey, gambling has been legalized and a contract such as that in the present case would presumably be enforceable in its courts. Thus under ordinary principles of law the debt would be enforceable in the courts of the Commonwealth. The fact that the debt is, in fact, a gambling debt removes it from the ordinary and requires the Court to determine whether it is collectible in this Court. The question is whether enforcing the debt would be contrary to the morals, public policy, or the positive law of Virginia.

In Virginia any person who illegally gambles is guilty of a Class 3 misdemeanor. Va. Code § 18.2-326 (1982). Persons who operate an illegal gambling enterprise are guilty of a Class 6 felony. Va. Code § 18.2-328 (1982). Possession of a gambling device constitutes a Class 1 misdemeanor. Va. Code § 18.2-331 (1982). The public policy of the Commonwealth expressed through statutory provisions has been since 1740 that all promises, agreements, mortgages, and securities, and the like, where the consideration was based on wagers are void. *See* Commonwealth v. Shelton, 49 Va. (8 Gratt.) 592 (1851). The applicable Virginia statute, Va. Code § 11-14 (1982) provides that:

> All wagers, conveyances, assurances, and all contracts and securities whereof the whole or any part of the consideration be money or other valuable thing, won, laid, or bet, at any game, horse race, sport or pastime, and all such contracts to repay any money knowingly lent at the time and place of such game, race, sport, or pastime, to any person for the purpose of so gaming, betting, or wagering, or to repay any money so lent to any person who shall, at such time and place, so pay, bet, or wager, shall be utterly void.

Id. The Supreme Court of Virginia has recently interpreted Va. Code § 11-14 (1982). In Kennedy v. Annandale Boys Club, Inc., ... plaintiff sought to recover a judgment against defendant Boys Club for $6,000. She alleged that she won the money in a bingo game conducted in Virginia at defendant club. The Supreme Court affirmed the lower court in sustaining defendant's demurrer to plaintiff's motion for judgment. The Court found that the contract was not merely voidable but utterly void, and therefore, unenforceable. The Court reasoned that even though the General Assembly had removed the "taint of illegality" from the operation of bingo games in the Commonwealth, it had not repealed or amended Va. Code § 11-14 (1982).

The Virginia Supreme Court held that the plain and unambiguous language of the statute should be construed strictly. The language makes plain that the General Assembly has not made the State court system available to unpaid gambling winners. There can be no claim made on any contract founded upon gaming. The Virginia Court concluded that the General Assembly's failure to amend Va. Code § 11-14 (1982) could not be inadvertent in light of the change in law to allow bingo in the Commonwealth. The Court also found that the legislature's refusal to permit enforcement in its courts of a gambling contract presented no constitutional question, State or federal....

In light of the General Assembly's express and unmistakable policy and the Virginia Supreme Court's interpretation thereof in a case much more persuasive than this one, there can be no other conclusion than that the enforcement of such a contract would be against the express public policy and positive law of the Commonwealth.

This Court is mindful of a recent opinion by another judge of this Court directly on point holding to the contrary. I am not aware of the authorities cited in that case and none are specified in the bench opinion. But the controlling law in this diversity case is that of Virginia, under the principles above mentioned, and I am not persuaded that I can ignore the plain language of Virginia's statute and the equally plain language of its Supreme Court.

Accordingly, this Court cannot, despite defendant's failure to plead or otherwise defend this case, contravene the positive law of the Commonwealth of Virginia in a diversity case and enforce a contract that offends two centuries of State policy....

Accordingly, for the above reasons, the amended complaint shall be DISMISSED.

And it is so ORDERED.

Notes

1. Just because a jurisdiction allows gambling, it does not necessarily follow that it will allow credit to be extended to the player. The *West Indies* case illustrates that permitting casinos to offer credit is a fairly recent phenomenon. Even now, not all states permit their licensed casinos to grant credit. Three principal arguments against casino credit are (1) credit allows casinos to engage in undesirable collection methods; (2) credit allows unscrupulous operators to skim funds; and (3) credit results in players losing more than they can afford. Given the numerous problems related to the granting of credit and collecting on debt, why would a casino want to bother with granting credit to players?

2. Several jurisdictions prohibit all forms of gambling credit for player protection reasons. For example, in Germany, players may only gamble with cash or cash equivalents, such as traveler's checks. Prohibiting or restricting casinos from granting credit is behavior-based. The government seeks to limit or prohibit a particular type of behavior in the casino, specifically gambling on credit. Therefore, to be effective, the government needs to impose parallel restrictions or prohibitions on third parties providing the funds to gamble on credit. Otherwise, loan sharks or others may attempt to operate on or near the casino grounds. This may present a more substantial problem than if the casinos grant credit because these individuals may not seek to establish long-term players, or may grant credit more liberally or employ unacceptable collection methods.

3. A jurisdiction may employ regulatory strategies short of prohibition. One such strategy is a regulation capping the percentage of credit that can be written off as uncollectible. In New Jersey, as an example, a casino cannot include in deductible operating expenses "losses on bad debt instruments from gaming operations in excess of the lesser of such instruments actually uncollected or 4% of gross revenues" as it relates to certain taxes and fees. N.J. Stat. 5:12–147. This requires the casinos to be more selective and conser-

vative in the granting of credit. A second strategy is to allow the casinos only to accept checks from a player.

4. The related issue of course is the ability of a casino to enforce a gambling debt. As the *Resorts International* case illustrates, some states will refuse to entertain a cause of action to enforce a gambling debt incurred in a state where gambling is legal. *See also* Gulf Collateral, Inc. v. Morgan, 415 F. Supp. 319 (D. Ga. 1976); Condado Aruba Caribbean Hotel, N.V. v. Tickel, 561 P.2d 23 (Colo. App. 1977); Hilton of San Juan, Inc. v. Lateano, 305 A.2d 538 (Conn. Cir. 1972).

At least one court has held that laws prohibiting the enforcement of gaming debts are not based on whether gaming is legal. Rather, they are concerned with the problems associated with credit play. In this case, a California resident incurred debts of $22,000 at Caesars Tahoe. Metropolitan Creditors Service v. Soheil Sadri, 15 Cal. App. 4th 1821, 1828, 1830 (1993). The California player stopped payment on the checks. Caesars Tahoe assigned the debt to a collection agency, which, in turn, sued the player. In 1993, the California Appellate Court held that it would not require the player to repay the debt. California courts have historically refused to enforce gaming debts. The court was not persuaded by plaintiff's argument that the recent proliferation of legal gaming in California should cause the court to come to a different conclusion now than it had in the past. The court reasoned: "California's rule against enforcing gambling debts has never depended upon the criminalization of gambling itself." Instead, the court viewed gambling on credit as the real culprit. The court took the position that granting debts are characteristic of pathological gambling, stating "Because of this, gaming on credit will not be enforced regardless of shifting public attitudes about gambling itself." The court noted, "If Californians want to play, so be it. But, the law should not invite them to play themselves into debt. The judiciary cannot protect pathological gamblers from themselves, but we can refuse to participate in their financial ruin."

5. When states do permit casinos to offer credit, a detailed statutory and regulatory regime will exist that sets out the way in which this is executed. The following provisions are from the Nevada code:

463.01467. "Credit instrument" defined.

"Credit instrument" means a writing which evidences a gaming debt owed to a person who holds a nonrestricted license at the time the debt is created, and includes any writing taken in consolidation, redemption or payment of a previous credit instrument.

463.361. Enforceability and resolution of gaming debts.

1. Except as otherwise provided in NRS 463.361 to 463.366, inclusive, and 463.780, gaming debts that are not evidenced by a credit instrument are void and unenforceable and do not give rise to any administrative or civil cause of action.

2. A claim by a patron of a licensee for payment of a gaming debt that is not evidenced by a credit instrument may be resolved in accordance with NRS 463.362 to 463.366, inclusive:

(a) By the Board; or

(b) If the claim is for less than $500, by a hearing examiner designated by the Board.

463.368. Credit instruments: Validity; enforcement; redemption; penalties; regulations.

1. A credit instrument accepted on or after June 1, 1983, and the debt that the credit instrument represents are valid and may be enforced by legal process.

2. A licensee or a person acting on behalf of a licensee may accept an incomplete credit instrument which:

(a) Is signed by a patron; and

(b) States the amount of the debt in figures,

and may complete the instrument as is necessary for the instrument to be presented for payment.

3. A licensee or person acting on behalf of a licensee:

(a) May accept a credit instrument that is payable to an affiliated company or may complete a credit instrument in the name of an affiliated company as payee if the credit instrument otherwise complies with this subsection and the records of the affiliated company pertaining to the credit instrument are made available to agents of the Board upon request.

(b) May accept a credit instrument either before, at the time or after the patron incurs the debt. The credit instrument and the debt that the credit instrument represents are enforceable without regard to whether the credit instrument was accepted before, at the time or after the debt is incurred.

4. This section does not prohibit the establishment of an account by a deposit of cash, recognized traveler's check, or any other instrument which is equivalent to cash.

5. If a credit instrument is lost or destroyed, the debt represented by the credit instrument may be enforced if the licensee or person if acting on behalf of the licensee can prove the existence of the credit instrument.

6. A patron's claim of having a mental or behavioral disorder involving gambling:

(a) Is not a defense in any action by a licensee or a person acting on behalf of a licensee to enforce a credit instrument or the debt that the credit instrument represents.

(b) Is not a valid counterclaim to such an action.

7. Any person who violates the provisions of this section is subject only to the penalties provided in NRS 463.310 to 463.318, inclusive. The failure of a person to comply with the provisions of this section or the regulations of the Commission does not invalidate a credit instrument or affect the ability to enforce the credit instrument or the debt that the credit instrument represents.

8. The Commission may adopt regulations prescribing the conditions under which a credit instrument may be redeemed or presented to a bank or credit union for collection or payment.

MGM Desert Inn, Inc. v. Holz
411 S.E.2d 399 (N.C. App.1991)

PARKER, Judge.

In this civil action under the Uniform Enforcement of Foreign Judgments Act, N.C.G.S. §§ 1C-1701 to 1708 (1991), ("uniform act") defendant appeals from summary judgment entered in favor of plaintiff. We affirm the judgment of the trial court.

The pleadings, answers to interrogatories and affidavits before the trial court show that in June 1989 defendant traveled to Las Vegas, Nevada, where he visited plaintiff's casino. According to defendant's affidavit, on 7 June he "commenced to gamble with dice, the dice, or crap table, provided by the Plaintiff." Defendant lost all his cash, $2,700.00, but was advised by plaintiff's agent that credit was available to him if he would make application. Defendant went to an office on plaintiff's premises, completed some forms and was told to return the next day to determine if credit would be available to him. On 8 June defendant returned to the casino and was told credit was available; all he had to do was sign a marker signifying the amount of credit he desired. On that same day, over the course of several hours during which he lost $20,000.00 at the dice table, defendant signed ten markers, each in the amount of $2,000.00.

Although defendant paid some of this debt, plaintiff sued for the unpaid balance; and in April 1990 judgment by default was entered against defendant in the district court of Clark County, Nevada. The default judgment was in the amount of $14,000.00, with prejudgment interest from 8 June 1989 to the date of entry of judgment at the statutory rate, costs of $104.00, and reasonable attorney's fees of $3,500.00; the total of all these sums was to bear interest at the statutory rate from 16 March 1990 until the judgment was satisfied.

Plaintiff subsequently sued in North Carolina on the Nevada default judgment. Pursuant to the uniform act, plaintiff filed a copy of the judgment in the office of the Clerk of Carteret Superior Court, *see* N.C.G.S. § 1C-1703 (1991), and on 12 July 1990, pursuant to N.C.G.S. § 1C-1704, served notice of this filing on defendant. On 19 July 1990 defendant filed a motion for relief from judgment and notice of defense pursuant to N.C.G.S. § 1C-1705. In this pleading defendant alleged (i) the default judgment was void as being contrary to the public policy of North Carolina and (ii) the uniform act prohibits enforcement of foreign judgments based on claims contrary to the public policies of North Carolina. Defendant also moved for dismissal of the proceeding pursuant to Rule 12(b)(1) of the North Carolina Rules of Civil Procedure. Plaintiff's reply alleged that the federal and state constitutions require the enforcement in North Carolina of foreign judgments. Both parties moved for summary judgment; plaintiff's motion was granted and defendant's was denied.

On appeal defendant contends that (i) plaintiff's claim, being predicated on a gaming debt, is contrary to the public policies of North Carolina, (ii) plaintiff was unable to raise this defense in Nevada, whose laws permit enforcement of such debts, (iii) plaintiff's action is barred by the uniform act, and (iv) the superior court lacked jurisdiction to enforce a foreign judgment predicated on a gaming debt. While we agree that gaming debts incurred in North Carolina are not enforceable in the courts of this state, we find defendant's remaining arguments unpersuasive.

General Statutes, Chapter 16, provides as follows:

> All wagers, bets or stakes made to depend ... upon any gaming by lot or chance ... shall be unlawful; and all contracts, judgments ... and assurances for and on account of any money ... so wagered, bet or staked, or to repay, or to secure any money ... lent or advanced for [such] purpose ... shall be void. N.C.G.S. § 16-1 (1983).

Similarly, futures contracts

> shall be utterly null and void; and no action shall be maintained ... to enforce any such contract, whether ... made in or out of the State ... nor shall any party to any such contract ... have or maintain any action or cause of action on account of any money ... paid or advanced ... on account of such contract ... nor shall the courts of this State have any jurisdiction to entertain any suit or action brought upon a judgment based upon any such contract. N.C.G.S. § 16-3 (1983).

The Uniform Enforcement of Foreign Judgments Act provides, "The provisions of this Article shall not apply to foreign judgments based on claims which are contrary to the public policies of North Carolina." N.C.G.S. § 1C-1708 (1991).

The federal constitution provides, "Full Faith and Credit shall be given in each State to the public Acts, Records, and judicial Proceedings of every other State; And the Congress may by general Laws prescribe the Manner in which such Acts, Records and Proceedings shall be proved, and the Effect thereof." U.S. Const. art. IV, §1. Congress subsequently prescribed the manner and effect of such judicial proceedings thus:

> The records and judicial proceedings of any court of any such State ... or copies thereof, shall be proved or admitted in other courts within the United States ... by the attestation of the clerk and seal of the court annexed, if a seal exists, together with a certificate of a judge of the court that the said attestation is in proper form.

> Such ... judicial proceedings or copies thereof, so authenticated, shall have the same full faith and credit in every court within the United States ... as they have by law or usage in the courts of such State ... from which they are taken.

28 U.S.C.A. § 1738 (West 1966) (formerly 28 U.S.C. § 687).

In Fauntleroy v. Lum, 210 U.S. 230 (1908), the United States Supreme Court considered whether the State of Mississippi had to enforce a Missouri judgment based on a gambling transaction in cotton futures. The original cause of action arose in Mississippi, where such transactions were illegal and void. Nevertheless the matter was submitted to arbitration in Mississippi, the question of illegality not being included in the submission, and the result was an award against defendant. Finding defendant in Missouri, plaintiff sued on the Mississippi award. The jury found for plaintiff and judgment was entered against defendant. Plaintiff then sued in Mississippi to enforce the Missouri judgment. *Id.* at 234.

On appeal defendant argued that since the law of Mississippi made dealing in futures a misdemeanor and provided that futures contracts would not be enforced by that state's courts, the Mississippi court was deprived of jurisdiction. *Id.* The Court, however, found this argument unpersuasive. Instead the Court framed the issue as "whether the illegality of the original cause of action in Mississippi can be relied upon there as a ground for denying a recovery upon a judgment of another State." *Id.* at 236. Citing the predecessor of 28 U.S.C. § 1783, the Court said

> Whether the award would or would not have been conclusive, and whether the ruling of the Missouri court upon that matter was right or wrong, there can be no question that the judgment was conclusive in Missouri on the validity of the cause of action. A judgment is conclusive as to all the *media concludendi;* and ... it cannot be impeached either in or out of the state by showing that it was based upon a mistake of law. Of course, a want of jurisdiction over either the person or the subject-matter might be shown. But, as the jurisdiction of the Missouri court is not open to dispute, the judgment cannot be impeached in Mississippi even if it went upon a misapprehension of the Mississippi law.

Id. at 237 (citations omitted).

In Mottu v. Davis, 65 S.E. 969 (N.C. 1909), plaintiff instituted an action in North Carolina on a Virginia judgment predicated on a gaming debt. Defendant filed two answers to plaintiff's complaint; the second ("further") answer raised the defense that the Virginia judgment was rendered on a demand arising from a gambling transaction. The Court stated

> As we have said, this further answer alleges that the original demand was on a gambling contract; that a recovery thereon is forbidden, both by our public pol-

icy and our statute law, and contends that this defense is now open to the defendant, notwithstanding the rendition of the Virginia judgment, but the question presented has been recently decided against the defendant's position by the Supreme Court of the United States, the final arbiter in such matters, in Fauntleroy v. Lum, 210 U.S., 230.

Mottu v. Davis, 65 S.E. at 970–71.

After Fauntleroy the United States Supreme Court considered whether a federal district court in Illinois should entertain jurisdiction of an action on a valid Wisconsin judgment predicated on income tax due from defendant to the State of Wisconsin. Milwaukee County v. White Co., 296 U.S. 268 (1935). The Court considered the narrow question of whether the courts of one state, even though not required to entertain a suit to recover taxes levied under the statutes of another state, "must nevertheless give full faith and credit to judgments for such taxes." *Id.* at 275. The Court stated

> A cause of action on a judgment is different from that upon which the judgment was entered. In a suit upon a money judgment for a civil cause of action the validity of the claim upon which it was founded is not open to inquiry, whatever its genesis. Regardless of the nature of the right which gave rise to it, the judgment is an obligation to pay money in the nature of a debt upon a specialty. Recovery upon it can be resisted only on the grounds that the court which rendered it was without jurisdiction; or that it has ceased to be obligatory because of payment or other discharge; or that it is a cause of action for which the state of the forum has not provided a court, unless it is compelled to do so by the privileges and immunities clause; or possibly because procured by fraud.

Id. at 275–76 (citations omitted). In the case under review defendant argues that the statutory denial of jurisdiction to North Carolina courts to hear suits on judgments based on gaming debts or futures contracts has been upheld as an exception to the application of the full faith and credit clause described by the Court in *Milwaukee County* as "a cause of action for which the state of the forum has not provided a court." *See* Lockman v. Lockman, 16 S.E.2d 670 (N.C. 1941); Cody v. Hovey, 14 S.E.2d 30 (N.C. 1941). We disagree.

Admittedly, language in Lockman and Cody suggests such an exception exists; but after these cases were decided, the United States Supreme Court citing Fauntleroy, reiterated that virtually no exceptions exist to the granting of full faith and credit to the judgments of sister states:

> From the beginning this Court has held that these provisions have made that which has been adjudicated in one state res judicata to the same extent in every other. Even though we assume for present purposes that the command of the Constitution and the statute is not all-embracing, and that there may be exceptional cases in which the judgment of one state may not override the laws and policy of another, this Court is the final arbiter of the extent of the exceptions. And we pointed out in *Williams v. North Carolina* that "the actual exceptions have been few and far between...."

We are aware of no such exception in the case of a money judgment rendered in a civil suit. Nor are we aware of any considerations of local policy or law which could rightly be deemed to impair the force and effect which the full faith and credit clause and the Act of Congress require to be given to such a judgment outside the state of its rendition.

The constitutional command requires a state to enforce a judgment of a sister state for its taxes or for a gambling debt.... Magnolia Petroleum Co. v. Hunt, 320 U.S. 430, 438–39 (1943) (citations and footnote omitted), *reh'g denied,*321 U.S. 801 (1944).

Similarly, this Court has stated

> The "Fauntleroy Doctrine" was followed by our own Supreme Court in Mottu
> v. Davis, 65 S.E. 969 (N.C. 1909)....

Defendant points to numerous decisions in which we have stated that a judgment of
a court in another state may be attacked on grounds of lack of jurisdiction, fraud in the
procurement, *or as being against public policy.* Although we have so asserted, it is rare that
we will disregard a sister state judgment on public policy grounds. The *Fauntleroy* decision, as noted by a recent commentator, "narrows almost to the vanishing point the area
of state public policy relief from the mandate of the Full Faith and Credit Clause — at
least so far as the judgments of sister states are concerned." One exception to the full faith
and credit rule is a penal judgment; a state need not enforce the penal judgment of another state. Another exception is when the judgment sought to be enforced is against the
public policy of the state where it was initially rendered. The exceptions, however, are
few and far between. In general, we are bound by the Full Faith and Credit Clause to recognize and enforce a valid judgment for the payment of money rendered in a sister state.
FMS Management Systems v. Thomas, 309 S.E.2d 697, 699 (N.C. App. 1983) (emphasis
in original, citations omitted) (quoting S.W. Wurfel, *Recognition of Foreign Judgments,*
50 N.C.L. Rev. 21, 43 (1971)), *aff'd per curiam,*314 S.E.2d 545 (N.C. 1984).

In light of the foregoing principles we hold that notwithstanding language in the anti-
gambling statutes and uniform act suggesting otherwise, no exception to the full faith and
credit clause exists to prohibit enforcement in North Carolina of the Nevada judgment
against defendant. Defendant has raised no question as to the jurisdiction of the Nevada district court over either his person or the original claim against him. "[S]ummary judgment
will be granted 'if the pleadings, depositions, answers to interrogatories, and admissions
on file, together with the affidavits, if any, show that ... any party is entitled to a judgment
as a matter of law.' N.C.R.Civ.P. 56(c)."Collingwood v. G.E. Real Estate Equities, 376 S.E.2d
425, 427 (N.C. 1989). As a matter of law, upon plaintiff's action properly instituted under
the Uniform Enforcement of Foreign Judgments Act, this state cannot refuse to enforce the
Nevada judgment against defendant, even though predicated on a gaming debt. Therefore,
we hold the trial court did not err in granting summary judgment in favor of plaintiff.

Affirmed.

WELLS and WYNN JJ., concur.

Notes

1. The *MGM* case illustrates a different approach to enforcing a gambling debt. In
Agresta, supra, the casino brought the action in a state which did not allow gambling or
allow for the offering of credit. Even though the gambling debt was valid in the state in
which it was incurred, the court held that such a cause of action violated the state's public policy and the claim would not be entertained. In *MGM,* rather than bringing the
original action in the state where the player/debtor lives, the casino initially brings the
claim in the state where the debt was incurred and recovers a judgment against the player.
It then goes to a sister state and registers the judgment to have it enforced in the state
where the debtor lives and/or has financial assets which can be seized in payment of the
gambling debt. The Full Faith and Credit Clause of the United States Constitution does
not have a public policy exception and the sister state is obliged to honor the judgment.
How does the casino/creditor gain personal jurisdiction over the player/creditor sufficient to obtain an in personam judgment against them if they are not a resident of that

state? For other cases applying this rule see Coghill v. Boardwalk Regency Corp., 396 A.2d 838 (Va. 1990); Marina Assocs., v. Barton, 563 N.E.2d 1110 (Ill. App. 1990); M & R Investments, Co., v. Hacker, 511 So.2d 1099 (Fla. App. 1987); GNLV Corp. v. Jackson, 736 S.W.2d 893 (Tex. App. 1987).

2. When dealing with foreign players, the considerations regarding legal enforcement change dramatically. American casinos do not have the benefit of constitutional full faith and credit tools when attempting to enforce a judgment against a player in a foreign jurisdiction. While many foreign courts will give deference to an American judgment under a legal principle called "comity", the foreign court is under no obligation to do so. Where the enforcement of the American judgment would violate the laws or public policy of the foreign jurisdiction, the foreign courts will frequently not recognize the judgment and will apply the law of the forum to the transaction. Joseph Kelly, *Caught In The Intersection Between Public Policy And Practicality: A Survey Of The Legal Treatment Of Gambling-Related Obligations In The United States,* 5 Chap. L. Rev. 87 (2002) (containing an appendix detailing international treatment of gaming debts); Maria Angela Jardim de Santa Cruz Oliveira, *Recognition and Enforcement of United States Money Judgments in Brazil,* 19 N.Y. Int'l. L. Rev. 1 (2006).

3. The enforceability, or unenforceability, of gambling debts in many states is extensively covered in Joseph Kelly, *Caught In The Intersection Between Public Policy And Practicality: A Survey Of The Legal Treatment Of Gambling-Related Obligations In The United States,*5 Chap. L. Rev. 87 (2002). *See also* Anthony N. Cabot, *Casino Collection Lawsuits: The Basics,* 4 Gaming L. Rev. 319 (2000); Note, *A Continuing Debate: Public Policy And Welfare Versus Economic Interests Regarding Enforcement Of Gambling Debts In State v. Dean,* 46 Loy. L. Rev. 299 (2000); Jeffrey R. Soukup, *Rolling the Dice on Precedent and Wagering on Legislation: The Law of Gambling Debt Enforceability in Kentucky After* Kentucky Off-Track Betting, Inc. v. McBurney *and KRS § 372.005,* 95 Ky. L.J. 529 (2007)

4. Because the dishonored "marker" is tantamount to a normal check being returned by a bank, state law provisions making the passing of "bad" checks a criminal offense may be invoked. Of course, a casino can only refer such matters to the local prosecuting authorities for action. What are the factors a casino would consider in deciding whether to direct a collection matter to the criminal justice system? *See, e.g.,* Nev. Rev. Stat. § 205.130 (providing for prosecution of an unpaid check); Fleeger v. Bell, No. CV-99-0155, 2001 WL 1491252 (9th Cir. Nov. 26, 2001) (holding that under Nevada law, a marker is treated the same as a check); I. Nelson Rose, *In Nevada, It's Pay Your Markers or Go to Jail,* 5 Gaming L. Rev. 425 (2001).

5. Enforcing gambling debts incurred at sea present unique issues is detailed in Robert Jarvis, *Gambling Debts at Sea,* 39 Mar. L. & Com. 505 (2008).

3. Defenses Available to the Debtor

Hakimoglu v. Trump Taj Mahal Associates
70 F.3d 291 (3rd Cir. 1995)

OPINION OF THE COURT

ALITO, Circuit Judge:

This case presents the question whether under New Jersey law a casino player may recover from a casino for gambling losses caused by the casino's conduct in serving alcoholic beverages to the player and allowing the player to continue to gamble after it becomes obvious that the player is intoxicated.

The plaintiff in this case, Ayhan Hakimoglu, filed two separate actions in the United States District Court for the District of New Jersey against defendants associated with two Atlantic City casinos. Invoking the district court's diversity jurisdiction, his complaints alleged that the defendants had "intentionally and maliciously enticed him" to gamble at the casinos on numerous occasions by providing him with free alcoholic beverages and other amenities; that while he gambled he was served free alcoholic beverages until he became intoxicated; that after he became "visibly and obviously intoxicated" the defendants "invited and permitted him to continue to gamble in that condition" for lengthy periods; and that he consequently incurred "substantial gambling losses." Asserting claims for negligence, intentional and malicious conduct, and unjust enrichment, he sought to recover compensatory and punitive damages, as well as other relief.

In both cases, the district court dismissed the plaintiff's claims for failure to state a claim on which relief could be granted.... The plaintiff appealed in both cases, and the appeals were consolidated.

. . .

Our task in this appeal is to predict whether the Supreme Court of New Jersey would recognize claims such as those asserted by the plaintiff. Unfortunately, we must make this prediction without specific guidance from the New Jersey appellate courts, for neither the Supreme Court of New Jersey nor the Appellate Division has addressed the question that is now before us or any closely related question. If New Jersey law, like that of some other states,[1] permitted us to certify the question at issue to the Supreme Court of New Jersey, we would seek to do so here, because the question is both difficult and important. New Jersey law, however, does not allow such certification, and therefore we are relegated to predicting what the Supreme Court of New Jersey would do if it were confronted with this question [footnote omitted].

While we are required to venture this prediction and while we recognize the need to issue a published opinion for the guidance of the district courts in the circuit, we understand that our decision here is unlikely to have—and should not have—lasting precedential significance. We expect that claims such as those advanced by the plaintiff in this case will work their way up through the New Jersey court system and that the New Jersey appellate courts will provide a definitive answer to the question before us. For this reason and because most of the chief arguments on both sides of this question have already been set out in excellent published district court opinions, we do not find it necessary to engage in a lengthy discussion here. The opinion in GNOC Corp. v. Aboud, ...

---

1. *See, e.g.,* Del. Const., art. IV, sec. 9; Del. Sup. Ct. R. 41(a)(ii).

argues forcefully that the New Jersey Supreme Court would recognize claims like those in this case. By contrast, the published opinion of the district court in one of the cases now before us and the opinion in Tose v. Greate Bay Hotel and Casino Inc., ... persuasively set out the opposite case.[2]

Although it is not clear which way the New Jersey Supreme Court would rule on this question—as the conflicting district court opinions illustrate—it seems to us more likely that the New Jersey Supreme Court would not recognize claims such as those that the plaintiff asserted. In reaching this conclusion, we find it significant that, except in cases involving minors, the New Jersey courts have not extended "the liability of servers of alcoholic beverages beyond injuries related to drunken driving, barroom accidents and barroom brawls." ... The intense state regulation of casinos is also important because, as the district court observed in this case:

> [e]xtending common law dram-shop liability into an area so fully regulated, without a glimmer of legislative intent, is not a predictable extension of common law tort principles, and has not been foreshadowed by the New Jersey courts.

... And as the district court noted in Tose:

> [c]onsidering the breadth of areas covered by statute and regulation, it would seem that if it were indeed the public policy of New Jersey to impose liability on casinos for allowing intoxicated players to gamble, that policy would have been enacted. The State has regulated the minutiae of gaming rules and alcohol service and expressly permitted the serving of free drinks to players at the gambling tables. Surely it could not have been unaware that the cognitive functioning of many gamblers would be impaired by drinking or of the consequences of permitting persons so impaired to gamble.

> ...

We are also influenced by the difficult problems of proof and causation that would result from the recognition of claims such as those involved here. As the district court judge in this case aptly put it:

> enlargement of [the doctrine of dram-shop liability] to casino gambling losses could present almost metaphysical problems of proximate causation, since sober gamblers can play well yet lose big, intoxicated gamblers can still win big, and under the prevailing rules and house odds, "the house will win and the gamblers will lose" anyway in the typical transaction....

---

2. On appeal in *Greate Bay*, we did not decide the question that is now before us.... In that case, the casino sued Tose for gambling debts, and Tose responded with a counterclaim similar to the claims of the plaintiff here.... The counterclaim was tried to a jury, and Tose lost. Tose appealed the district court's denial of his motion for a new trial, and the casino argued, among other things, that the district court should not have exercised jurisdiction over the counterclaim because it lay within the exclusive primary jurisdiction of the state Casino Control Commission. We rejected this argument, as well as Tose's contentions regarding the denial of the new trial motion. We expressly declined to predict whether the state supreme court would hold that Tose's counterclaim stated a claim on which relief could be granted.... We did observe: "[W]hile we do not make a ruling on the point, a reasonable argument can be made that a casino owes a common law duty to a player to prevent him from gambling when it knows he is intoxicated." ... This comment did not decide the question presented in this case; nor do we interpret it as inconsistent with our holding in this appeal. We completely agree that "a reasonable argument can be made" in support of a result contrary to the one we reach. However, forced to predict whether the New Jersey Supreme Court would accept that argument, we predict that it would not.

Moreover,

> such a cause of action could be fabricated with greater ease than a dram-shop action involving personal injury, since in the accident case the occurrence of the accident is a specific notable event and reliable evidence of blood alcohol content is usually obtained; in the gambling loss case, on the other hand, a dram-shop negligence claim might be brought up to two years after the gambling events concerning plays of which no casino dealer or server could have reason to recollect. Although sometimes highstakes table games are videotaped using surveillance cameras, such tapes from multiple cameras would amount to hundreds of hours of films per day that are routinely recycled rather than retained if no incident is reported within thirty days. The New Jersey Supreme Court has expressed concern for the reliability of evidence of intoxication and its effects, ... and such reliability is largely absent after-the-fact in the casino gaming environment.

> ...

For these reasons and many of the others mentioned in the district court opinions in this case and Tose, we predict that the New Jersey Supreme Court would not permit recovery on claims such as those asserted by the plaintiff here. Accordingly, we affirm the district court's dismissal of the plaintiff's claims in both cases, and we remand to the district court for further proceedings on the defendants' counterclaims.

BECKER, Circuit Judge, Dissenting.

Ayhan Hakimoglu played his hand, and lost. Now we are being asked to make our own bet.... As the majority points out, we must [predict how the New Jersey Supreme Court would rule] with little guidance from New Jersey law. But that is an incident — and a flaw — of the regime of diversity jurisdiction. I believe that the New Jersey Supreme Court would recognize a cause of action, in tort, allowing players to recover gambling debts from casinos that serve them alcohol after they are visibly intoxicated.[3] This prediction is founded on long standing trends in New Jersey law recognizing new causes of action, even in areas pervaded by legislation.

---

3. In addition to the tort theory Hakimoglu has pursued, a gambler in his position may have a claim in contract. The gambler's obvious intoxication, one might argue, voided the gambling contract. *See, e.g.,* Feighner v. Sauter, 614 A.2d 1071, 1075 (App. Div. 1992) (listing grounds for contract rescission, including intoxication); Onderdonk v. Presbyterian Homes of New Jersey, 425 A.2d 1057, 1062 (1981) (every contract has "implied covenant of good faith and fair dealing"). The district court seemed to doubt the existence of this "so-called gambling 'contract'" because "there is no mutuality." Hakimoglu v. Trump Taj Mahal Associates, 876 F. Supp. 625, 633 n.7 (D.N.J. 1994)."The player does not negotiate the terms of his relationship with the casino," the court explained, "nor can the player or the casino vary the rules of the game, the odds, or the payoffs." Id.; see also Tose v. Greate Bay Hotel and Casino, Inc., 819 F. Supp. 1312, 1317 n.8 (D.N.J.1993) ("[B]ecause every aspect of the relationship between the gambler and the casino is minutely regulated by the state[,] there is little freedom of contract in the usual sense."). But the player retains the choice whether to play, and how much to bet. Thus, this situation is little different from most sales contracts. Purchasing a hair dryer, for example, forms a contract even though the price is set and the characteristics of the good are heavily regulated. On what other basis is the casino legally able to keep the gambler's money after he loses? Moreover, the pervasive regulation of the gambling relationship does not nullify its contractual nature. New Jersey courts have held that gambling on credit markers forms a contract between the casino and the player, *see* Lomonaco v. Sands Hotel, 614 A.2d 634 (N.J. Law Div. 1992), and that the Casino Control Act did not abrogate traditional common law contract defenses such as intoxication. *See id.* However, Hakimoglu has declined to press a contract claim and hence we do not decide the question.

In my view, the New Jersey Supreme Court is especially likely to create a cause of action where a defendant profits from conduct causing the foreseeable injury, and has the ability, in the exercise of due care, to prevent such injury at small cost to itself. Because this case presents these factors, and because I am unpersuaded by the majority's arguments, I would reverse the judgment of the district court and remand for trial on the merits. I also write to underscore a crucial point mentioned by the majority: as New Jersey has no certification procedure, we are forced to make important state policy with little guidance. I therefore suggest that New Jersey, to serve its own interests and ours, enact a certification provision.

I.

...

II.

Analysis of this case under the principles of New Jersey tort law supports the conclusions of *Aboud* and *Tose* that New Jersey's highest court would recognize Hakimoglu's cause of action. In Hopkins v. Fox & Lazo Realtors, the New Jersey Supreme Court set out its standard for determining when a tort duty, and thus a cause of action in negligence, exists. The inquiry, "ultimately a question of fairness," requires the court to weigh (1) the relationship of the parties; (2) the nature of the risk; (3) the opportunity and ability to exercise care; and (4) the public interest in the proposed solution. *Id.* These factors support a cause of action in this case.

First, the relationship of the parties argues strongly for casino liability. Casinos, perhaps the ultimate for-profit institution, make their money from players' losses. Gambling losses are the casino's business. The casino and the gambler, therefore, are linked in an immediate business relationship much like that from which dram shop liability sprang — the tavern and the player.... Like the tavern owner, the casino's control over the environment into which the player places himself, and its ability to open or close the alcohol spigot, imposes on the casino some concomitant responsibility toward that player. Just as the tavern owner must make sure that drinking does not cause her player to hurt himself or others, the casino should ensure that its alcohol service does lead its player to hurt himself through excessive gambling.

Second, the nature of the risk — essentially a test of foreseeability — also points to casino liability. Gamblers come to the casino to gamble; the casino supplies free alcohol; the odds favor the casino. Losses are the natural result, if not the intent, of this situation. Unacceptable losses due to alcohol consumption are certainly foreseeable.

This foreseeability factor explains the inapplicability of contrary authority. The New Jersey Supreme Court's recent limitations of dram shop liability, fairly read, all turn on a lack of foreseeability....

Lack of foreseeability also explains why the New Jersey courts and legislature have never extended liability for tavern owners and social hosts (as opposed to casinos) beyond physical injuries and property damage.... Casinos, on the other hand, can plainly foresee large and unacceptable losses from players they help get drunk. And the New Jersey Supreme Court has made clear that tort is an appropriate basis for liability (possibly in addition to a contract theory, ... even if no physical damage occurs, when the losses are foreseeable....

Finally, the presence of foreseeability rebuts the casinos complaint that recognizing liability in this case would lead to unfair and extreme results. A restaurant located near a casino would be held liable, the casinos argue, if it served alcohol to a player who became intoxicated, entered the casino, and lost money. This, they imply, would be unfair. That may be so. But because foreseeability is lacking in the casinos' hypothetical, the analogy to the present case does not withstand scrutiny. The restaurant and its customer, in the casinos' hypothetical, do not stand in a similar posture to a casino and its gambling player. The restaurant is not in the gambling business and does not necessarily know whether the dining player would later be gambling. The loss involved, therefore, is too remote to fairly and rationally hold the restaurant accountable. By contrast, in a casino setting with gambling as the primary activity, there is no difficulty in foreseeing that the player will engage in that activity and the high chance that he will suffer financial losses under a state of intoxication.

The third factor—the opportunity and ability to exercise care—further suggests liability here. To a much greater degree than tavern owners, casino operators can readily protect themselves against the type of liability sought to be imposed here. Unlike most tavern owners, restauranteurs or social hosts, casinos generally have huge staffs and sophisticated surveillance cameras. Gamblers, particularly high rollers, are constantly monitored by a dealer, floor persons, a pit boss, hidden cameras, and sometimes even officials of the New Jersey Casino Control Commission.... When the line is crossed, the casino need only refuse to serve more alcohol.[4]

Of course, the player is also in a position to exercise care by not getting drunk. But this does not undermine my argument. New Jersey has made it clear that if the intoxicated person sues for injuries to himself, he may be charged with contributory negligence.... Imposing contributory negligence is not a retreat from the policy underlying dram shop liability; rather, it is best explained as an effort to fairly apportion the loss among all who bear some responsibility.... This holding also ensures, from the standpoint of deterrence, that both parties in a position to avert the harm take steps to prevent it.

Finally, the public interest in the proposed solution also leads to the conclusion that New Jersey would recognize this cause of action. Throughout its history, New Jersey has exercised strict control over various types of gambling.... Indeed, only by a constitutional provision or amendment can any type of gambling be lawfully conducted in this state, subject to approved "restrictions and control."... In an environment where gambling has been regarded as "an activity rife with evil," the state's general ban on casino gambling should be no surprise....

...

When it passed the [1977 Casino Control] Act, the New Jersey legislature recognized that casinos—with their concentration of wealth—have disproportionate power over the political process.... As expressed in the Act, it is New Jersey's pronounced policy to regulate casinos "with the utmost strictness to the end that public confidence and trust in the honesty and integrity of the State's regulatory machinery can be sustained."... The historical background reveals that New Jersey recognizes an important public interest in protecting gamblers. From New Jersey's perspective, requiring casinos to protect gamblers from losses flowing from their excessive service of alcohol would probably also be in the public interest.

---

4. Again, on the theory that Hakimoglu pursues (based on dram shop liability), the casino presumably would need only to stop serving the player alcohol after he became obviously and visibly intoxicated. It would not need to bar him from further gambling, though hopefully the refusal to serve might serve as a "wake-up call." On the broader theory articulated in *Aboud*, however, the casino might have to keep a player from gambling, even if he had become drunk elsewhere.

The most plausible objection to my position is that torts of negligence generally seek to deter and compensate for the destruction of wealth, while the tort in this case is arguably merely allocative. In other words, a typical economic tort would redress negligence that shut down a factory, causing a loss in production, while in this case the alleged tortfeasor casino coaxes the money from the gambler and then retains it. Society is no worse off; different parties just possess the wealth....

...

VI. CONCLUSION

The majority fairly observes that this case is a difficult one and that reasonable arguments support either side. Nevertheless, I believe that the better arguments should lead us to predict that New Jersey would find a cause of action here, subject to the defense of contributory fault. The New Jersey Supreme Court has been highly hospitable to recognizing causes of action, even in areas where the legislature has acted, for foreseeable injuries. The four factors the court uses for evaluating whether a duty exists—(1) the relationship of the parties; (2) the nature of the risk; (3) the opportunity and ability to exercise care; and (4) the public interest—all point toward finding a cause of action here. And the policy objections of the majority and the litigants either miss the point or are overstated. For all of the foregoing reasons, I believe the New Jersey Supreme Court would recognize a cause of action, in tort, allowing players to recover gambling debts from casinos that serve them alcohol after they are visibly intoxicated. I therefore respectfully dissent.

Notes

1. Intoxication as a defense to the enforcement of a debt is not new. While policy issues concerning alcohol use transcend casino gambling, the casino industry is unusual in the prevalence of complimentary alcoholic beverages as a part of the contract process. To be bound by a contract, the player must have the capacity to incur the debt. The general rule is that a person has the capacity to incur contractual obligations unless special circumstances exist. Players have argued incapacity based on severe intoxication. The impact of intoxication on gambling contracts is explored in Jeffrey C. Hallam, *Rolling The Dice: Should Intoxicated Gamblers Recover Their Losses*, 85 Northwestern L. Rev. 240 (1990); *see also* Jessica Krentzman, *Dram Shop Law—Gambling While Intoxicated: The Winner Takes It All? The Third Circuit Examines A Casino's Liability for Allowing a Patron to Gamble While Intoxicated*, 41 Vill. L. Rev. 1255 (1996). Doubt exists whether, in many states, incapacity due to voluntary intoxication is a recognized defense. This is the result of the influence of the common law of England that voluntary intoxication is not a defense to a contract action. "As for a drunkard who is voluntarious daemon," stated the Lord Coke, the leading 17th Century commentator on the English common law, "he hath ... no privilege thereby." Even under the more liberal rule adopted in some American states, intoxication is no defense unless the level is so severe as to render the person unable to understand the nature and consequences of the transaction. E. Allan Farnsworth, Contracts 240 (2d ed. 1990).

Moreover, most courts that recognize the defense also require the other party to the contract to have reason to know that the intoxicated person lacks the capacity to understand or control his acts.

2. The lack of mental capacity also is a viable defense in certain circumstances. The general rule is that mental illness or a defect is a viable defense if the person is "unable to understand in a reasonable manner the nature and consequences of the transaction or

unable to act in a reasonable manner in relation to the transaction and the other person has reason to know of his condition." E. ALLAN FARNSWORTH, CONTRACTS 240 (2d ed. 1990).

3. Defendants in gaming debt cases have sought to avoid obligations by establishing mental incapacity through various means. The most common are players who argue that compulsive gambling is a mental defect, which robbed them of the capacity to act in a reasonable manner. The Nevada Legislature addressed this issue by codification of Nev. Rev. Stat § 463.368(6). That section provides that a player cannot claim a mental or behavioral disorder as a defense or a counterclaim to a licensee's efforts to enforce a credit instrument.

4. New Jersey decisions do not recognize compulsive gambling alone to be a viable defense to set aside a gambling obligation, but might permit it if compulsive gambling is coupled with some other common law defense, such as duress or unconscionability. Lomonaco v. Sands Hotel Casino and Country Club, 614 A.2d 634, 639 (N.J. Super 1992) "This court in so holding finds no support in legislation or case law that the disorder of compulsive gambling should, in and of itself, be recognized as a defense to capacity to contract which will render a contract void." In that case, a gambler who incurred $285,000 in casino markers sought a declaratory judgment that the casino's action in allowing him credit — notwithstanding his abusive conduct, his admission he was a compulsive gambler, and his marathon sessions — violated New Jersey law and that the markers should be unenforceable because of duress and unconscionability. The casino moved for summary judgment arguing that New Jersey casino law prohibited implied causes of action, and that to allow such a defense "would improperly cause the judiciary to usurp the Commission's oversight responsibility and violate the separation of powers doctrine." The court concluded that because the Casino Control Act did not "do away with" common law defenses of duress and unconscionability "which plaintiff alleges would be present here if plaintiff suffered from the illness of compulsive gambling." The court rejected a finding that "it was the legislature's intent to abolish all defenses to such contracts for casino credit even under circumstances in which the casino issued credit to a player whom the casino clearly knows cannot form freely the intent to enter such a contract, or if the casino knows or should know the player does not have the financial means to perform on such a contract." The court concluded that issues of material fact existed and "specifically and narrowly h[eld] that, under the facts as alleged in this case, the circumstances of plaintiff's bizarre behavior causing his compulsive gambling and signing of casino markers may be such that the contracts may be void due to a lack of free will on the part of the plaintiff to have entered into such contracts due to duress or unconscionability."

5. The Puerto Rico Civil Code of 1931 provides a "good father" defense: "Civil liability in a game or bet not prohibited. A person who loses in a game or a bet which is not prohibited is civilly liable. Nevertheless, the judicial authority may either not admit the claim when the sum which was wagered in the game or bet is excessive, or may reduce the obligation to the amount it may exceed the customs of a good father of a family."

6. Because a gaming contract is merely a type of contract arising out of a gaming transaction, all of the defenses available to a contract debtor are available to the gaming debtor. Like any other contract case, certain jurisdictional defenses are available to defendants such as improper service and lack of jurisdiction. Certain defenses, however, are unique to gaming debt collection including violation of public policy, failure to follow statutory guidelines for collecting the debt and "good father" statutes.

7. Most states that allow credit have created statutory schemes regulating the collection of gaming debts. In New Jersey, non-compliance with the statutory scheme can be a defense to the enforcement of a credit instrument. According to the New Jersey courts, only literal and absolute compliance will allow a casino to collect on an outstanding credit instrument. *See* Nemtin v. Zarin, 577 F. Supp. 1135, 1146 (D.N.J. 1983), *see also* Resorts Int'l Hotel, Inc. v. Salomone, 178 N.J. Super. 598 (App. Div. 1981). In Nevada, however, the Nevada Legislature wanted to ensure that statutory noncompliance, although giving rise to potential disciplinary action against the casino, would not impair legal enforceability of the markers. Accordingly, pursuant to Nev. Rev. Stat. § 463.368(7), statutory noncompliance is not a defense to a marker collection claim. Rather, statutory noncompliance results only in a disciplinary action against the licensee pursuant to Nev. Rev. Stat § 463.310 to 463.318.

8. The incapacity of minors to contract can be established by statute. Under the common law, the age of majority was reached when a person is of 21 years of age. The age of majority brought with it the capacity to contract. Most states, however, have passed statutes lowering the majority age to 18. In most states, however, the legal age for gaming remains at 21. A casino granting credit to an underage gambler likely has no legal right to recover the debt. In addition, the casino might face criminal or regulatory disciplinary action for allowing the minor to gamble.

4. Resolution of Patron Disputes

Erickson v. Desert Palace, Inc., et al.
942 F.2d 694 (9th Cir. 1991)

BRUNETTI, Circuit Judge:

Appellants Russell, Beth, and Kirk Erickson appeal the district court's order dismissing their complaint for lack of subject matter jurisdiction and for failure to state a claim. The Ericksons brought this action against corporate defendants operating Caesar's Palace Casino in Las Vegas, Nevada, seeking to recover a $1,061,812.00 slot machine jackpot won by Kirk, a minor. The Erickson's alleged breach of contract, quasi-contract, fraud and cheating, and interference with contract, and sought declaratory judgment regarding the unconstitutional implementation and enforcement of a Nevada statute. The Ericksons appeal only the dismissal of their third cause of action alleging fraud and cheating. We have jurisdiction pursuant to 28 U.S.C. § 1291 and affirm.

We review de novo the dismissal of a complaint for lack of subject matter jurisdiction under Fed. R. Civ. P. 12(b)(1) or for failure to state a claim pursuant to Fed. R. Civ. P. 12(b)(6). Kruso v. Int'l Tel. & Tel. Corp., 872 F.2d 1416, 1421 (9th Cir. 1989) *cert. denied*, 496 U.S. 937 (1990). Dismissal is proper when it appears the plaintiff can prove no set of facts in support of his claim which would entitle him to relief. Love v. United States, 871 F.2d 1488, 1491 (9th Cir. 1989).

The Ericksons assert diversity jurisdiction. Therefore state law applies to this action and we are bound by Nevada's Supreme Court case law.

I.

On August 5, 1987, the Ericksons visited Caesar's Palace Casino in Las Vegas, Nevada. Kirk, then 19, purchased tokens and won a jackpot of $1,061,812.00. Because Kirk was under 21, the legal gambling age in Nevada, the casino refused to pay him the jackpot. See NRS 463.350.

Under Nevada law, an unpaid slot machine jackpot is a gaming debt not evidenced by a credit instrument. Harrah's Club v. State Gaming Control Bd., 766 P.2d 900 (Nev. 1988) (casino player's claim to an unpaid slot machine jackpot considered "disputed gaming debt"); State Gaming Control Bd. v. Breen, 661 P.2d 1309, 1311 (Nev. 1983) (player seeking recovery of unpaid keno winnings found to have "no claim other than a gambling debt").

NRS 463.361, enacted in 1983, states: "Except as provided in NRS 463.361 to 463.366, inclusive, gaming debts not evidenced by a credit instrument are void and unenforceable and do not give rise to any administrative or civil cause of action." NRS 463.362 to 463.366 provide for review of a casino's refusal to pay alleged winnings to a player by the State Gaming Control Board (the "Board"). NRS 463.3662 to 463.3668 provide for review of the Board's decision by a Nevada District Court and by the State Supreme Court. NRS 463.3668(2) provides that judicial review by the state courts is the exclusive method for review of the Board's actions.

The Ericksons filed a formal complaint under NRS 463.363 with the Board on August 7, 1987. When the Board's Enforcement Division denied the Erickson's claims on November 9, 1988, they filed a petition seeking reconsideration which was also denied. Specifically, the Board found that NRS 463.350 prohibited Kirk Erickson from collecting the slot machine jackpot and that any contract that may have existed between the defendant casino and Erickson was inoperative because it violated NRS 463.350. The Board also held that Erickson had not properly stated a claim for restitution, quasi contract or unjust enrichment, because he sought payment of the jackpot rather than return of the three $1 tokens he had used, and those theories permit only damages to the extent of the benefit to the defendant. Finally, the Board held because the Casino had properly warned Erickson that the legal gambling age is twenty-one and had made no misrepresentations of gambling rules, defendant was not guilty of fraud.

Pursuant to NRS 463.3662, the Ericksons petitioned the Eighth Judicial District Court of Nevada for Clark County to review the Board's ruling. The district court affirmed the denial of the claim, whereupon the Ericksons petitioned the Nevada Supreme Court for judicial review. The Nevada Supreme Court dismissed the appeal on May 21, 1990. The Court agreed with the Board that NRS 463.350 prohibited Erickson from collecting the jackpot, and that there was no evidence the casino "knowingly allowed Kirk Erickson to gamble while underage," which might support a claim of fraud.

II.

The Erickson's filed a complaint in federal district court on August 11, 1988, before the decision of the Board. Defendants State of Nevada, Nevada Gaming Control Board, and Caesars filed motions to dismiss the action. The district court granted the motions dismissing the complaint for lack of subject matter jurisdiction due to the Erickson's failure to exhaust the administrative remedies provided by Nevada law. Because the Nevada Supreme Court has issued its decision, the Ericksons now have exhausted their administrative remedies.

We decline to remand this case to the district court, however, because that court provided an alternative ground for dismissing the complaint. The court found that NRS 463.361 limits a plaintiff to an administrative proceeding followed by judicial review in state court. The court therefore determined the Ericksons could not state a claim upon which relief could be granted. Fed. R. Civ. P. 12(b)(6). The district court held because "plaintiffs claim can most accurately be characterized as an attempt to recover a gaming debt not evidenced by a credit instrument ... plaintiffs cannot maintain a civil action to recover a jackpot, but instead are limited to an administrative proceeding followed by judicial review."

III.

A. Appellants assert the Nevada statute should not bar this action because it does not involve a "gaming debt." We agree with the district court that "Nevada characteristically categorizes suits to collect unpaid gambling winnings as gaming debts." Harrah's Club v. State Gaming Control Bd., 766 P.2d 900 (Nev. 1988); State Gaming Control Bd. v. Breen, 661 P.2d 1309, 1311 (Nev. 1983); Corbin v. O'Keefe, 484 P.2d 565 (Nev. 1971). The district court correctly held that NRS 463.361 to 463.3688 limits a plaintiff's recovery of a gaming debt to the exclusive administrative/judicial review procedure contained therein.

B. Plaintiffs also assert the limitation imposed by NRS 463.361 does not apply in this case because the casino's refusal to pay the slot machine jackpot amounts to fraud. They cite Berman v. Riverside Casino Corp., 323 F.2d 977 (9th Cir. 1963) and Zaika v. Del E. Webb Corp., 508 F. Supp. 1005 (D. Nev. 1981).

In *Berman*, appellant sued a casino to recover money he lost allegedly as a result of the casino's use of "loaded" dice. Although at the time of the action, Nevada made no statutory provision for suit to recover gambling losses, we held the appellant had properly asserted a cause of action for fraud: "The common law of England, in effect when Nevada became a state is, except as modified by statute or decision of Nevada's courts, the law of Nevada. And the common law rule, as of the time of Nevada's admission to the Union, appears to have been that one who lost money in a crooked gambling game could recover in a civil action." *Id.* at 979 (citations omitted) (emphasis added). Berman thus provides for a cause of action for fraud to recover losses sustained in a gambling transaction.

Berman does not, however, remove this action from the purview of NRS 463.361. The Ericksons did not sue to recover losses sustained as the result of a "crooked gambling game." Rather appellants sought damages for fraud in the amount they would have won had Russell been a legal gambler. Whether or not appellees refusal to turn over the casino jackpot amounted to fraud, the remedy sought here is recovery of an alleged gaming debt. Since the passage of NRS 463.361, any action to recover such a debt is confined to the administrative process.

Zaika is likewise inapposite. In that case plaintiff claimed he was defrauded by a casino that used an extra card in its blackjack decks. He sought to recover losses resulting from the alleged fraud. Appellant filed a claim against the casino, which was rejected by the Board, and then a federal court action for misrepresentation and fraud. Defendant moved for dismissal of the claim, arguing that under the doctrine of res judicata, a decision by an administrative agency (i.e., the Board) that the casino had acted properly should preclude a federal court action.

The district court disagreed. It held that a player who claims she has been cheated by a casino has two distinct remedies: she may pursue a hearing before the Gaming Control Board, *id.* at 1007–08, or she may bring a civil suit under Berman. Zaika pursued the administrative relief and was rebuffed. The district court decided, however, that res judicata would not bar a subsequent civil action: "The opportunity to seek judicial review from an administrative determination is implicit in the doctrine[] of res judicata...." *Id.* at 1009. Under NRS 463.315 a casino has a right to judicial review of a Board decision ordering it to pay a claim. The court found, however, that "neither the Nevada statutes nor gaming regulations provide a similar procedure for review to a complainant, such as plaintiff here, who receives an adverse decision from the Gaming Control Board." *Id.* at 1010. Because of this inequality of judicial review the court held res judicata was inapplicable.

Zaika simply reaffirms the rule in Berman that a party may assert an action outside the administrative process to recover gambling losses sustained due to casino fraud. We reiterate, however, the suit in this case does not involve an attempt to recover such losses. We do not believe the Nevada legislature intended to allow parties to avoid the administrative process simply by alleging fraud in a patent attempt to force a casino to turn over alleged winnings. Under NRS 463.361, parties who assert they are owed a gaming debt, fraud or no fraud, are confined to the administrative process followed by state judicial review.

Because NRS 463.361 precludes Appellants' fraud action, they have failed to state a claim upon which relief can be granted. Fed.R.Civ.P. 12(b)(6). We therefore affirm the decision of the district court.

AFFIRMED.

Eash v. Imperial Palace of Mississippi, LLC
4 So. 3d 1042 (Miss. 2009)

GRAVES, PRESIDING JUSTICE, FOR THE COURT:

This is a patron dispute between Florida Eash and the Imperial Palace Casino (Imperial Palace). Eash was playing a slot machine at Imperial Palace and hit a winning combination. She subsequently initiated a patron dispute over the award for her winning play. The Mississippi Gaming Commission (the Commission) made a final decision in favor of Eash. Imperial Palace sought judicial review, and the circuit court reversed the final decision of the Commission. Aggrieved by this decision, Eash appeals to this Court.

FACTS

On February 19, 2006, Florida Eash was playing a $5 Double Top Dollar slot machine at the Imperial Palace Casino in Biloxi, Mississippi. It was the first time that Eash had played this particular machine, and she testified that she did not read the instructions or the description of the possible awards listed on the front of the machine before playing. A patron could play this machine with one or two five-dollar credits wagered. After several plays, and with two five-dollar credits wagered, Eash hit a winning combination — three double diamond symbols lined up on the single pay line. After Eash hit the winning combination, the following words scrolled across the electronic display on the machine (also referred to as the "door VFD"[1]): "Hand Pay Jackpot 200,000 credits." The keypad LCD[2] (also referred to as the "NexGen display") showed that the winnings totaled $1,000,000. Eash and the other patrons around her thought that she had won $1,000,000. However, the front of the Double Top Dollar machine (also referred to as the "belly glass" or the "awards glass") displayed the permanent rules and instructions of the game, and it stated that the maximum award on that particular machine was $8,000.[3] Nothing on the machine indicated that a patron could win more than $8,000.[4]

When Eash hit the winning combination, staff members of the Imperial Palace were notified of the win and approached Eash and the machine. In order to disperse the crowd that had gathered, a staff member cleared the keypad LCD showing the $1,000,000 win.

---

1. Vacuum fluorescence display.
2. Liquid crystal display.
3. A patron could win a larger sum of money on the bonus round of the game, but the bonus round is not at issue in this case.
4. Again, the bonus round is not at issue here.

Agent Daniel Pearson of the Commission's Enforcement Division was called in to investigate. Imperial Palace staff members informed Eash that she would be paid only $8,000 for her win and, as a result, she initiated a patron dispute claim with the casino.

Soon after the incident and on the next day, Agent Pearson ran a battery of tests on the machine and reviewed the videotape of the incident. He concluded that the International Game Technology (IGT) programmer who set up the machine mistakenly entered $1,000,000 as the jackpot, rather than $8,000. The machine was also mistakenly programmed as a "Stand Alone Progressive" machine, although nothing on the exterior of the machine indicated that it was a progressive machine.

On March 22, 2006, the executive director of the Commission issued a written decision stating that Eash was entitled to $1,000,000. On April 13, 2006, Imperial Palace timely filed a Petition to Reconsider the executive director's decision, requesting a hearing before a hearing examiner appointed by the Commission. At the hearing, Imperial Palace presented testimony from Agent Pearson, Eash, an IGT employee, and two Imperial Palace employees. Eash appeared *pro se* and, after being questioned by Imperial Palace, she presented her son and daughter as witnesses and recalled Agent Pearson. The hearing officer subsequently issued a written decision reversing the executive director's decision. The hearing examiner reasoned that, because the Double Top Dollar machine clearly indicated that the maximum award on that machine was $8,000 and because there was no signage on or around the machine indicating that a patron could win more than $8,000, Eash was entitled to only $8,000 for her winning combination.

Eash appealed the hearing examiner's decision to the Commission. On March 15, 2007, after reviewing the record, the Commission entered a final decision reinstating the executive director's decision that Eash was entitled to $1,000,000.

Imperial Palace then appealed to the Circuit Court of Harrison County. Both parties presented arguments to the circuit court at a hearing on the matter. At the conclusion of the hearing, the circuit court ruled in favor of Imperial Palace and found that Eash was entitled to only $8,000. The circuit court subsequently issued a written decision reversing the Commission's decision on the ground that it prejudiced the substantial rights of Imperial Palace in that it "was not made in accordance with the law, arbitrary and maybe arbitrary and capricious, and was made upon unlawful procedure." Eash timely appealed to this Court.

On appeal, Eash argues that this Court should reverse the circuit court's decision because the substantial rights of Imperial Palace were not prejudiced by the Commission decision, and because the Commission's decision was supported by the evidence, was not made upon unlawful procedure, was not arbitrary or capricious, and was made in accordance with the law. Imperial Palace claims that the substantial rights of Imperial Palace were prejudiced by the Commission's decision, which was also arbitrary or capricious, was not in accordance with the law, was violative of state and federal law, was unsupported by any evidence, and was made in excess of the Commission's statutory authority. Eash contests Imperial Palace's assertions in rebuttal.

ANALYSIS

This Court applies the same standard of review that the lower courts are bound to follow when reviewing the decisions of a chancery or circuit court concerning an agency action.... According to Mississippi Code Section 75-76-171(2), when reviewing the final decision or order of the Commission, the circuit court's review is conducted "without a jury and must not be a trial de novo but is confined to the record on review. "Miss. Code Ann. 75-76-171(2) (Rev. 2000). Section 75-76-171(3) sets out the deferential standard of review:

(3) The reviewing court may affirm the decision and order of the commission, or it may remand the case for further proceedings or reverse the decision if the substantial rights of the petitioner have been prejudiced because the decision is:

(a) In violation of constitutional provisions;

(b) In excess of the statutory authority or jurisdiction of the commission;

(c) Made upon unlawful procedure;

(d) Unsupported by any evidence; or

(e) Arbitrary or capricious or otherwise not in accordance with law.

Miss. Code Ann. 75-76-171; *see also* Miss. Gaming Comm'n v. Freeman, 747 So.2d 231 238 (Miss. 1999). If this Court agrees that the circuit court properly found that the substantial rights of Imperial Palace had been prejudiced because of anyone of the five reasons stated in Section 75-76-171, then this Court will affirm the circuit court's decision. Miss. Code Ann. §75-76-171 (3). If this Court finds otherwise, then this Court must reverse the circuit court's decision. Id.

Accordingly, we must first determine whether or not the Commission's final decision prejudiced the substantial rights of Imperial Palace. The Commission's final decision requires that Imperial Palace pay Eash $1,000,000 on a machine that was intended to pay a maximum award of $8,000. Eash argues that the substantial rights of Imperial Palace were not prejudiced because Imperial Palace has an indemnity agreement with IGT. The only reference to an indemnification agreement in the record is in the Flat Fee/Stand Alone/Rental and Servicing Agreement between IGT and Imperial Palace. The agreement states, in relevant part:

9. Lessee (i.e., Imperial Palace) shall maintain adequate liability insurance, naming IGT as an additional insured, and to the extent not covered by insurance shall hold IGT harmless and indemnify IGT from all claims which may arise as a result of the existence, use or operation of the Equipment on the Lessee's premises....

15. Lessee agrees to indemnify IGT and hold IGT harmless from and against liability or damage from injury or loss arising out of the possession or use of the Equipment on the premises of Lessee, over which IGT has no control. Within the warranty limitations set forth above, IGT shall be responsible for the acts and omissions of its employees and agents.

The warranty portion of the agreement states

4. IGT warrants that during the term of this Agreement the IGT Equipment installed hereunder will be in good working order. Lessee sole and exclusive remedy is expressly limited to the restoration of the Equipment to good working condition by adjustment, repair or replacement of defective parts, at IGT's election. Except as specifically provided in this Agreement, there are no other warranties, express or implied, including, but not limited to warranties of merchantability or fitness for a particular purpose. No affirmation of fact, including but not limited to statements regarding suitability for use, performance or percentage hold or par value of the Equipment shall be or be deemed to be a warranty of IGT for any purpose ...

This agreement covers thirty IGT machines that Imperial Palace leased, including the Double Top Dollar machine in question.

From the language in the agreement, it is clear that Imperial Palace agreed to indemnify IGT against any claims, and it is equally clear that IGT had not agreed to indemnify Imperial Palace. Any payment required by the Commission's final decision would be paid by Imperial Palace. Therefore, we find Eash's argument that the substantial rights of Imperial Palace were not prejudiced to be without merit. The rights of Imperial Palace have clearly been prejudiced by the Commission's final decision.

Next, we must determine whether or not the substantial rights of Imperial Palace were prejudiced for one of the five reasons set out in Section 75-76-171 (3). Miss. Code Ann. § 75-76-171(3) (Rev. 2000). Subsection (e) of Section 75-76-171(3) states, in part, that the Commission's decision may be reversed if it is "not in accordance with the law." Consistent with Section 75-76-171(3), this Court has recognized that agencies are constrained to follow the law. For example, this Court has stated that "an agency's findings may not be disturbed by appellate courts where ... the relevant law was properly applied to the facts. Mickle v. Miss. Employment Sec. Comm'n., 765 So.2d 1259, 1261 (Miss. 2000). It follows, therefore that if the agency did not properly apply the relevant law to the facts, then an appellate court may reverse an agency's decision.

In this case, the hearing examiner's decision that Eash was entitled to only $8,000 was based largely on contract law. The hearing examiner's decision states that "(w)hen a patron plays a casino slot machine, the patron is entering into a contract with the casino.... The express terms of the contract are those that are stated in writing. Imperial Palace of Miss., LLC v. Eash, Mississippi Gaming Commission Hearing Examiner Decision No. 06-00076(SD), at 7 (Oct. 16 2006) (citations omitted). Because the Double Top Dollar machine clearly displayed its terms in writing on the belly glass of the machine, the hearing examiner decided that Eash was bound by those terms, which limited her winnings to $8,000. The circuit court's decision to reverse the Commission's decision was also based largely on the contract law analysis applied by the hearing examiner in her decision.

Although this Court has not explicitly stated that a patron enters into a contract with a casino when playing a particular machine in that casino, this Court did apply contract principles when reviewing the patron dispute in IGT v. Kelly. *Kelly*, 778 So.2d 773 (Miss. 2001). In *Kelly*, the question was whether Kelly's play on a progressive poker machine — a descending sequential royal heart flush — entitled her to the primary progressive jackpot, which was the advertised award for a sequential royal flush in hearts. *Id.* at 774. IGT, the maker of the machine, argued that the primary progressive jackpot was intended only for an *ascending* sequential royal heart flush and that Kelly was, therefore, only entitled to the secondary progressive jackpot. *Id.* at 775–76. The hearing examiner found that Kelly was entitled to the primary progressive jackpot. *Id.* at 774. The Commission adopted the hearing examiner's decision, and the circuit court affirmed the Commission's decision. *Id.*

This Court stated that the signage on the poker machine in Kelly was ambiguous because it did not specify that a patron could win the primary progressive jackpot only with an ascending sequential royal heart flush. *Id.* at 775–76. Therefore, this Court concluded that Kelly was entitled to the primary progressive jackpot for her descending sequential royal heart flush. *Id.* In reaching this conclusion, this Court relied on a longstanding principle of contract construction. *See, e.g.,* Miss. State Highway Comm n v. Dixie Contractors, Inc., 375 So.2d 1202, 1205 (Miss.1979) ("[A]mbiguities in a written contract [must] be resolved unfavorably to the party who drafted the contract."). In *Kelly*, this Court stated that "if the posted rules in a casino are ambiguous, then the agency will interpret the rule in favor of the patron if the rule can be reasonably read in that fashion." *Id.* at 777. The Commission had also announced this rule in its prior decisions. *Id.*

Although the patron won the jackpot in *Kelly*, that case cannot be cited in support of awarding Eash $1,000,000 for her winning combination, because the facts of Kelly are distinguishable from the facts in this case. While there was ambiguity in the permanent signage on the progressive poker machine in *Kelly*, there was no ambiguity in the permanent signage on the Double Top Dollar machine here. The signage on the machine in this case clearly stated that a winning combination entitled the patron to $8,000. When Eash or any other patron played that Double Top Dollar slot machine, she was playing for a chance to win $8,000 and nothing more. The fact that the electronic displays erroneously stated that Eash won $1,000,000 after she hit the winning combination does not create an ambiguity analogous to the one in *Kelly*. Though it unfortunately caused some confusion, there was no indication from anything on the machine *before* Eash began playing that indicated that a patron could win anything more than $8,000 with three double diamonds lined up on the pay line. In other words, there was no question *ex ante* as to what a winning combination was or what the corresponding award would be on the machine in this case. In contrast, in *Kelly*, the permanent signage on the machine was unclear (at all times) as to what constituted a winning combination. *Kelly*, 778 So.2d 773.

In Allen v. Isle of Capri, Vicksburg, the hearing examiner stated that a "contract between the patron making the bet and the casino" is formed when the patron places "a wager ... of the amount allowable in the particular game." Allen v. Isle of Capri, Vicksburg, Mississippi Gaming Commission Hearing Examiner Decision No. 97-00285, at 5 (June 24, 1997). The formation of a contract between a patron and a casino has also been recognized in the gaming industry. *See* Anthony Cabot & Robert Hannum, Advantage Play and Commercial Casinos, 74 Miss. L.J. 681, 682–83 (2005) ("Casino-style gambling involves a contract, which is simply a promise, or set of promises, between the casino and the player.... [T]he casino promises to pay the patron a predetermined sum if certain conditions are met. In turn, the patron agrees to place the sum of the wager at risk if those certain conditions are not met.").

In this case, the Commission decided that Eash was entitled to $1,000,000 because of the Commission's "broader responsibility in some cases, without ignoring the law or regulations, to ensure that reasonable fairness and the perception of fairness prevails. However, in deciding that Eash was entitled to $1,000,000 for hitting a winning combination on a machine that advertised a maximum award of $8,000, the Commission did ignore the law. Contract law dictates that when Eash put her money into the Double Top Dollar machine, she and Imperial Palace entered into a contract whereby Imperial Palace would pay her $8,000 if her ten-dollar wager resulted in three double diamond symbols lined up on the single pay line. Since her play resulted in that winning combination, Eash is entitled to $8,000. The Double Top Dollar machine clearly stated that the maximum award on that machine was $8,000, and no information was displayed on the machine that indicated otherwise. Therefore, despite the regrettable programming error that led Eash to believe that she had won $1,000,000, she is entitled only to an $8,000 award.

It should be noted that this Court's decision in Pickle v. IGT also supports the result reached by this Court today. Pickle v. IGT, 830 So.2d 1214 (Miss.2002). The patron dispute in *Pickle* concerned whether or not Pickle had hit the progressive jackpot on a Wheel of Fortune game when her play resulted in a non-winning combination. *Id.* at 1215. The bells, whistles, and other indicators showed that she had hit the jackpot. *Id.* at 1215. However, the Commission's Gaming Laboratory found that Pickle's combination was not a winning combination, and that the bells, whistles, and other secondary indicators were activated because of a "technical problem." *Id.* at 1218. The hearing examiner made a similar finding, which the Commission adopted. *Id.* at 1219. The circuit court subsequently affirmed the Commission's decision, and this Court affirmed the circuit court. *Id.* at 1219, 1221–22.

Thus, this Court found in *Pickle* that a patron's award (or lack thereof) is determined by the combination resulting from the patron's play, and not the secondary indicators activated by the play. *Id.* at 1221. In the same way, the proper award here is determined by the rules and instructions on the permanent signage on the Double Top Dollar machine, and not the information displayed electronically on the machine after the winning combination was hit.

Because this Court finds that the Commission's final decision is not in accordance with the law, the arguments made regarding the other grounds for reversal of the Commission's decision need not be addressed. See Miss. Code Ann. § 75-76-171(3) (Rev. 2000).

CONCLUSION

This Court finds that the Commission's final decision in favor of Eash is not in accordance with the law. Therefore, the circuit court's decision to reverse the Commission final decision is affirmed.

Notes

1. Player disputes can involve either questions of fact or interpretation of laws or rules. In the former, the issue is what happened. For example, did the player place a bet at the roulette table on the winning number or on a losing number? More common, however, are player disputes that involve application and interpretation of law and rules to particular facts. This requires understanding and interpretation of the contract between the player and the casino governing the play of a game. An interesting question is identifying the offer and the acceptance. If a casino displays a table game or a gaming device that lists the terms and conditions of the wager, is this an offer? Courts do not consider this an offer but merely a solicitation of an offer. Instead, the offer is the player's action in placing a wager and the acceptance is when the casino acknowledges the wager typically by beginning the game. For example, a casino's display of a blackjack table is not the offer. When the player places a wager on the table, an offer is made. The casino does not need to accept that wager, but can refuse the wager for any of a myriad of reasons. Once accepted, however, a contract is formed.

2. To be entitled to a prize or jackpot, the player must comply with the terms and conditions of the contest or game. Two types of terms or conditions govern a gaming contract, express and implied. Express terms or conditions are those in writing or expressly agreed to by the parties. An example of an express term is the statement on a gaming device that three cherries on the pay line pay ten coins for each coin played. Also, the felt on a blackjack table might read that a blackjack pays two to one. Implied terms govern the gaming contract but are not expressed on the felt or the face of the gaming device or elsewhere. For example, if a blackjack player receives two aces, these cards may be split but the player can only receive one additional card for each split hand. This basic rule is rarely written on the felt or on signs, but is, through custom, as much a part of the contract as express terms and conditions. *See generally*, E. ALLAN FARNSWORTH, CONTRACTS 565 (2d ed. 1990).

3. Interpretation of express conditions is rarely the subject of player disputes. However, there are exceptions. Suppose the player claimed a jackpot for lining up the required symbols on the third line of the gaming device. The gaming device could accept up to three coins, and each coin lit up a different pay line. The gaming device had signs that stated all payouts were made on lighted lines only, and that the player was responsible for making certain the deposit of the coin registered and lighted the line. The player deposited three coins

in the machine, but only two registered. The third coin momentarily caught in the coin acceptor, and did not register until the next play. Who should have won this dispute? Why?

4. If the express conditions do not resolve the dispute, the decision-maker must supply the omitted term or condition. The first basis for implication is the actual expectations of the parties. If both parties shared a common expectation, the law will give effect to that expectation, though the parties did not reduce it to words. Absent shared expectations, the court will substitute an objective test for the subjective test of shared expectation. The aspects of the objective test most relevant to gaming devices are course of dealing and trade custom. Course of dealing looks at previous conduct between the parties to see if it forms a common understanding. U.C.C. § 1-205 (2004). For example, suppose a casino knowingly allowed a player to play a machine with a defect. If that defect results in a jackpot that the player would not, under normal circumstances, be allowed, then the player may argue that the failure to correct the defect, and permitting play to continue, form a basis for course of dealing. Trade custom or usage is a method of dealing that has enough regularity in the casino industry to justify an expectation that it will be observed in all wagers.

5. Contractual rights and obligations of parties can be superseded by statutory laws. In the gaming industry, these statutory laws are often implemented by governments to assure the honesty and fairness of the games and to protect the player. These statutes and regulations can impact the terms and conditions of the contract between the casino and the player in many ways. For example, the law can and often does hold that gambling contracts are void and unenforceable. In less dramatic ways, the law can dictate mandatory terms of a contract between a casino and a player, such as requiring that the casino must pay out a minimum average return on wagers (such as 75% in slot machines) or actually dictating the exact terms of the contract by statutorily setting the rules on how the games must be played.

6. Disputes typically fall into one of three categories. The first is where no malfunction occurs with the device (or human error occurs) but a disagreement arises as to the terms of the offer. For example, in Semaan v. IGT, 126 Fed. Appx. 794 (9th Cir. 2005), a jackpot winner claimed immediate payment of the full amount of the jackpot rather than in 25 installments because the larger sign on the slot machine did not contain such qualification. Instead, it was contained on a smaller placard on the face of the machine. The court disagreed, noting that the terms of the contract were clear on the placard and nothing on the larger sign contradicted these terms.

7. A second category of disputes is where no malfunction occurs but the parties disagree as to whether the patron meet the terms of the agreement to be paid. In Marcangelo v. Boardwalk Regency, 847 F. Supp. 1222 (D. N.J. 1994) Marcangelo was playing on a Pokermania machine. The machine had signage on it indicating it had two progressive payoffs: "a sequential royal flush," defined on the face of the machine as the left to right sequence of 10, Jack, Queen, King, and Ace of a specified suit, would win the primary Pokermania progressive jackpot, known as the "Pokermania jackpot", and in addition, a "royal flush" defined as a combination of 10, Jack, Queen, King, and Ace, all of the same suit, in any order, would win a secondary jackpot known as "Mini-Mania." Marcangelo's play resulted in a suited Ace, King, Queen, Jack, Ten (a reverse sequential royal flush). The casino was only willing to pay the secondary jackpot. The player who was denied the primary jackpot commenced the action. The court ultimately determined that no cause of action existed because the requirement that the Casino Control Commission approve all signage preempted a private right of action against the casino. The court noted, however, that *even if* the court were to recognize this cause of action, Marcangelo would not prevail. As a unilateral mistake, Marcangelo could merely collect his

initial $1.25, not the difference between the primary and secondary progressive jackpots. This should be contrasted with the *Kelly* case, described in depth in the *Eash* case, above.

8. A third broad category is where a machine malfunctions or a human error occurs by a casino employee. Pickle v. IGT, 830 So. 2d 1214 (Miss. 2002) also described in the *Eash* case is illustrative. Other cases involving malfunctions include Dockery v. Sam's Town, 2007 WL 3023928 (W.D. La. 2007), Sengel v. IGT, 2 P.3d 258 (Nev. 2000); Sister Nira Ledoux v. Grand Casino-Coushatta, 954 So. 2d 902 (La. App. 2007) (holding in favor of the patron because the casino could not prove a malfunction); Griggs v. Harrah's Casino, 929 So. 2d 204 (La. App. 2006); Grand Casino Biloxi v. Hallman, 823 So. 2d 1185 (Miss. 2002) (holding for the player because the casino failed to preserve evidence of the malfunction).

9. How would you decide the following cases and why?:

Case 1: A player claims to have put three coins in a slot machine and lined up the symbols to win a progressive jackpot. Yet, when casino personnel check, the machine showed that the player deposited only two coins. The third coin jammed in the coin acceptor. The sign on the machine made it the player's responsibility to make certain all coins registered before pulling the handle.

Case 2: The player put in the proper number of coins. The slot machine appeared to function properly. After the reels had stopped spinning, the symbols on three of the four reels had lined up perfectly to reveal a winning combination. Yet, the position of the symbol on the fourth reel necessary for the winning combination was such that the patron claimed it appeared on the payout line. The casino disagreed. According to its internal record, the slot machine did not align a jackpot. Instead, the outer reel that contained the symbol in question had slipped slightly to appear roughly halfway between the payout line and the line above.

Case 3: The dealer at a blackjack game inadvertently skips a player that is holding a soft 14 and wants a hit. The dealer gives his card to the player to next player. The card is a seven. When the player objects, the dealer realized his mistake. He then deals a new card to the player rather than back up the seven. The new card is a ten. The player takes another card and busts.

10. As the cases illustrate, the process for a player contesting a decision by a casino not to pay money the player believes he is owed is governed by statute or regulation. These procedures typically relegate the player to an administrative process which must be exhausted before any resort to the courts is possible. As an example, the procedure for Indiana is outlined below.

Indiana Administrative Code § 18-1-2 Player dispute process:

Sec. 2. (a) The riverboat licensee shall attempt to resolve all player disputes with the player.

(b) If the riverboat licensee and the player cannot resolve the dispute, the riverboat licensee must advise the player of the player's right to file a complaint with the commission. The complaint may be:

(1) received by the commission agent; or

(2) sent to the commission office in Indianapolis, Indiana.

The riverboat licensee shall provide a player with a complaint form upon request.

(c) The complaint shall contain, at a minimum, the following information:

(1) The name, address, and telephone number of the player.

(2) A summary of the nature of the player complaint, including the date and time on which the incident leading to the dispute occurred.

(3) A list of the names, if known, of any occupational licensees that were involved in or a witness to the incident that led to the player dispute.

(4) The name, address, and telephone number, if known, of any witnesses to the incident that led to the player dispute.

(5) A summary of the riverboat licensee's attempt to resolve the player dispute.

(6) Any other information deemed necessary by the executive director or the commission.

The player shall submit the complaint within five (5) business days of the incident that led to the player dispute. The player shall provide a copy of the complaint to the riverboat licensee at the same time the player submits the complaint to the commission.

(d) The riverboat licensee shall respond to a player complaint within two (2) business days of receiving a copy of the complaint.

68 Indiana Administrative Code § 18-1-3 Investigation; possible disciplinary action

Sec. 3. The executive director or the executive director's designee shall determine and conduct any investigation deemed necessary. If it is determined that the riverboat licensee or an occupational licensee violated the Act or this title, the commission may initiate a disciplinary action under 68 IAC 13-1.

Chapter 6

Exclusions and Problem Gambling

1. Generally

The "exclusion" that this chapter refers to is the situation where a patron is denied the opportunity to gamble at a licensed facility. There are a number of applications of this idea.

First, a licensed facility such as a pari-mutuel facility or a casino clearly has the authority to exclude a person from their premises when they believe the person is cheating or attempting to cheat. Cheating can take many forms, from a gambler altering the value of a chip to a gambler trying to change the "elements of chance, method of selection or criteria" of a game. Nev. Rev. Stat. § 465.015. Chapter 7 considers the issue of "advantage play," where a bettor uses lawful means to maximize the opportunity of winning. The most common, and controversial, form of advantage play is "card counting," a tactic employed by blackjack players. As the material in Chapter 7 makes clear, this is *not* cheating.

Second, there are some people who want to gamble who are *required* to be excluded by the licensed facility. Known cheaters, crime figures, and other unsavory persons fall into this category. Laws and regulations in the gaming-heavy states of Nevada and New Jersey provide for "exclusion lists." In Nevada, the list can include those "whose presence in the establishment is determined by the [Gaming Control] Board and the Commission to pose a threat to the interests of this state or to licensed gaming." Nev. Rev. Stat. § 463.151.2. Similarly, in New Jersey those "whose presence in a licensed casino establishment would be inimical to the interest of the State of New Jersey or licensed gambling therein," as demonstrated by a list of offenses, can likewise be placed on the exclusion list. N.J. Stat. Ann. § 19:48-1.3(a)(1). Both states have a detailed statutory and regulatory mechanism implementing this authority. *See* Nev. Rev. Stat. §§ 463.151-463.155; Nevada Gaming Commission and State Gaming Control Board Regulations 28.010–28.090. The Nevada "rogue's gallery," otherwise known as the "Excluded Person List" can be viewed at http://gaming.nv.gov/loep_main.htm. For New Jersey, *see* N.J. Stat. Ann § 19:48-1.3 (Criteria for Exclusion).

Third, and most controversial, is the exclusion of a patron for a reason that is sometimes difficult to ascertain. There may be a claim that the person's presence is "inimical" to the interests of the facility. But it may also just be that the facility says they simply do not want the gambler's "action." Why would this be? Is the person winning too much? Is it sporting to exclude a person who is a winning bettor rather than a losing one? When facilities exclude a patron in this situation the question often arises of whether there is a statutory or common law right to exclude a person from a gambling operation. As will be discussed below, there are two venues where this issue has been prominent: the pari-mutuel facility and the casino. Once again, the blackjack "card counter" is at the center of this controversy for casinos. While the issues raised in the pari-mutuel setting are similar, the differences between the two warrants separate treatment.

A fourth area involving exclusions is the "self-exclusion." Sometimes gamblers recognize they have a problem controlling their gambling. In an attempt to remedy their problem, they sign a document telling the casino they should not be permitted to return and that they may be removed if they do. Many states provide for this, in an effort to combat gambling addiction. Admirable as this policy may be, it is not without controversy.

Related to self-exclusion is the issue of problem gambling. Even if one thinks of gambling as a form of entertainment, there is no question that a person who cannot control his gambling can bring ruinous consequences upon himself and others. There are certainly ways of treating this addiction, but are there ways to reduce the chance it will occur? What is the responsibility of a gambling establishment to recognize a "problem" gambler and to take steps to protect him, or at least not exploit his weakness?

2. At the Track: Power to Exclude Licensees and Patrons

Bresnik v. Beulah Park LTD Partnership, Inc.
617 N.E.2d 1096 (1993)

Syllabus by the Court

R.C. Chapter 3769 and its accompanying regulations do not abolish the common-law right of proprietors to exclude individuals from their property.

This case arises from a dispute over the right of an owner of a private racetrack to exclude a state licensee from its premises. The facts stated below are as alleged in the complaint. Appellee, Edward Bresnik, held a valid license as a jockey agent from the Ohio State Racing Commission. This license allowed appellee to represent jockeys in their racing arrangements at state-licensed horse racing tracks. Appellee had oral contracts to represent two jockeys, Luis Gonzalez and Robert McWhorter.

Appellants, Beulah Park Limited Partnership, Inc., Buckeye Turf Club, Inc. and Capital Racing Club, Inc. ("Beulah Park") operate a thoroughbred racetrack pursuant to a permit issued by the Ohio State Racing Commission.

On February 3, 1991, appellee was informed by a security officer that he was no longer permitted on the grounds of Beulah Park.

Due to this exclusion, the appellee, on February 25, 1991, filed a complaint in the Court of Common Pleas of Franklin County, alleging tortious interference with a business relationship. The appellee also requested a temporary restraining order and a preliminary injunction to prevent Beulah Park from barring his entry into the race park. Beulah Park filed a motion to dismiss the complaint for failure to state a claim, which the trial court granted.

Appellee then appealed to the Court of Appeals for Franklin County. The court of appeals reversed the trial court's judgment, and remanded the case for further proceedings. Beulah Park then filed a notice of appeal with the Ohio Supreme Court. The cause is now before this court pursuant to the allowance of a motion to certify the record....

PFEIFER, J. Beulah Park has a common-law right to exclude persons from its business premises absent specific legislative language to the contrary. The Revised Code contains no such language.

Appellee contends that R.C. Chapter 3769, which empowers the Ohio State Racing Commission with the right to exclude jockey agents from racetracks, abrogates any common-law rights of racetrack owners to exclude jockey agents from their premises. Appellee also argues that Ohio Adm. Code 3769-2-05 and 3769-4-22(B) authorize racing stewards to exclude jockey agents from a racetrack, and, thus, abolish Beulah Park's common-law right. We disagree.

As the late Justice Thurgood Marshall noted, the common-law right to exclude has long been a fundamental tenet of real property law:

"The power to exclude has traditionally been considered one of the most treasured strands in an owner's bundle of property rights." Loretto v. Teleprompter Manhattan CATV Corp., 458 U.S. 419, 435 (1982). Proprietors of private enterprises, such as Beulah Park, possess this right. Fletcher v. Coney Island, Inc., 134 N.E.2d 371 (Ohio 1956). In *Fletcher,* this court held at paragraph one of the syllabus that:

"At common law, proprietors of private enterprises such as places of amusement and entertainment can admit or exclude whomsoever they please, and their common-law right continues until changed by legislative enactment."

Because horse racing tracks certainly qualify as "places of amusement and entertainment," Beulah Park possesses the common-law right to exclude whomsoever it pleases, provided the General Assembly has not abolished that right.

Contrary to appellee's assertion, R.C. Chapter 3769 and its accompanying regulations do not abolish the common-law right of proprietors to exclude individuals from their property. Not every statute is to be read as an abrogation of the common law. "Statutes are to be read and construed in the light of and with reference to the rules and principles of the common law in force at the time of their enactment, and in giving construction to a statute the legislature will not be presumed or held, to have intended a repeal of the settled rules of the common law *unless the language employed by it clearly expresses or imports such intention*" (emphasis added). State v. Sullivan, 90 N.E. 146 (Ohio 1909), paragraph three of the syllabus.

The rules and statute cited by the appellee provide a right to exclude to the racing commission and racing stewards, who are not addressed by the common law. This does not mean that racetrack owners who possessed this right at common law have lost that right due to rules and statutes providing the same right to others. R.C. Chapter 3769 and its accompanying regulations supplement the common law by providing the racing commission and stewards with a right to exclude jockey agents from a racetrack in addition to the right to exclude held by the proprietors of the track. Thus, the decision of the court of appeals is reversed.

Judgment reversed.

MOYER, C.J., and DOUGLAS, RESNICK and FRANCIS E. SWEENEY, Sr., JJ., concur.

A. WILLIAM SWEENEY, J., dissenting. While at first blush the underlying theme of the majority's position appears unassailable, *i.e.,* that racetrack operators should be permitted to control whoever is on their premises so long as such control is not motivated by discrimination on grounds of race, color, religion, etc., I believe a closer examination of the Revised Code and related Administrative Code provisions compels a different result. Since I believe the court of appeals below correctly analyzed the statutory language and manifest intent of the General Assembly in this realm, I must respectfully dissent from the majority opinion.

The majority asserts that appellant Beulah Park has a "common-law right to exclude whomsoever it pleases," since racetracks qualify as "places of amusement and entertainment." First of all, however, the case upon which the majority relies for this proposition, Fletcher v. Coney Island, Inc., 134 N.E.2d 371 (1956), paragraph one of the syllabus, is readily distinguishable from the cause *sub judice. Fletcher* dealt with the exclusion of mere patrons of amusement facilities, whereas the appellee herein was on the racetrack grounds engaged in his employment by virtue of his license, which is authorized and regulated by the Ohio State Racing Commission. Second, assuming, *arguendo,* that racetracks qualify as the type of place characterized by the majority, a review of the pertinent statutes and regulations reveals that racetracks are a highly regulated industry in this state, unlike ordinary places of amusement or entertainment.

R.C. 3769.03 provides as follows:

"The state racing commission shall prescribe the rules and conditions under which horse racing may be conducted * * *."

"The state racing commission may issue, deny, suspend, or revoke licenses to such persons engaged in racing and to such employees of permit holders as is in the public interest for the purpose of maintaining a proper control over horse-racing meetings. The *commission* may also, as is in the public interest for the purpose of maintaining proper control over horse-racing meetings, rule any person off a permit holder's premises * * *" (emphasis added).

"With respect to the issuance, denial, suspension, or revocation of a license to a participant in horse racing, the action of the commission shall be subject to Chapter 119 of the Revised Code. * * *"

As I see it, the foregoing statutory language gives the State Racing Commission plenary power over the regulation of horse racing, including the power to determine who may be ruled off a permit holder's premises.

In the exercise of the regulatory power granted by the legislature, the State Racing Commission promulgated Ohio Adm. Code 3769-2-05, which provides:

"All thoroughbred racing in Ohio over which the commission has jurisdiction and supervision shall be conducted under the rules and regulations which the commission has set forth for such racing. If any case occurs which is not provided for in the rules of the Ohio state racing commission, the matter shall be determined by the stewards or by the commission as the case may be."

Additionally, Ohio Adm. Code 3769-4-22(B) appears to grant all power to the race stewards with regard to matters concerning licensees of the commission:

"The stewards * * * shall determine all questions with regard to racing arising during the meeting * * * and in such questions their orders shall supersede the orders of the other officials of the permit holder."

Furthermore, stewards "have general supervision over all other persons licensed by the Ohio state racing commission while such persons are on the premises of a permit holder." Ohio Adm. Code 3769-4-26(B). Among the licensed persons subject to supervision by the steward are the track's general manager and head of security. Ohio Adm. Code 3769-2-24.

In my view, R.C. Chapter 3769 and the supporting Administrative Code rules clearly restrict a racetrack operator's power to control persons on its property, because persons involved in racing cannot enter the racetrack grounds unless they are licensed by the commission. Ohio Adm. Code 3769-2-27(A). Assuming, *arguendo,* that racetrack operators had a common-law right to exclude whomever they please from their premises, I believe that such prior right was clearly and substantially altered by R.C. Chapter 3769 in its scheme of licensing and regulation by the State Racing Commission.

Given the extensive regulatory scheme with respect to horse racing, I believe that a licensee, such as plaintiff, excluded by a track operator deserves the type of due process that the statutes and rules allow when a steward or an agent of the State Racing Commission excludes a licensee from a permit holder's premises. However, by adopting the position of appellants, the majority holds that a licensee must prove illegal discrimination in order to obtain any relief for a wrongful exclusion. In essence, the majority decision herein grants permit holders the power to exclude anyone for any other reason. However, such a position, and the reasoning behind it, should not be countenanced by this court, especially in light of several illuminating examples provided by *amicus curiae,* Horseman's Benevolent and Protective Association, in support of appellee:

"For example, the Permit Holder could arbitrarily exclude a licensed trainer from the racetrack premises because the trainer has objected to the safety of the racetrack surface. The Permit Holder could also arbitrarily exclude a licensed owner from the racetrack premises because the owner brought suit against the Permit Holder due to injuries sustained as a result of such unsafe conditions. The unfettered ability of the Permit Holder to act arbitrarily in excluding these licensed individuals from the racetrack premises would have the [e]ffect of not only barring such individuals from earning a livelihood in the horse racing industry, but could also be used as an unfair business practice which imposed unsafe or hazardous working conditions upon both licensed horsemen and their horses."

"Clearly, the Ohio legislature envisioned that this heavily regulated industry would be governed by the State in a fair and impartial manner rather than by private individuals whose actions would be without recourse for those affected."

However, under the sweeping language of the majority opinion herein, a racetrack operator is judge, jury and executioner to anyone who enters its grounds, regardless of whether such person is licensed to be there by the State Racing Commission. Clearly, this is not what the General Assembly intended when it enacted R.C. Chapter 3769. Nevertheless, under today's majority opinion, the power of the State Racing Commission is subject to the whim and caprice of the individual racetrack operators.

The better view, in my opinion, was cogently expressed by the court of appeals in its unanimous decision below:

"The state has issued a license authorizing plaintiff to act as a jockey agent at the racetrack in question, which necessarily requires him to enter the permit holder's premises in order to make mandatory reports. Under such circumstances, the apparent arbitrary exclusion of plaintiff by defendants from the permit premises is in conflict with the regulations and statutes. As to access to the premises by persons licensed by the commission to engage in racing upon the premises, the common law power of the permit holder over his premises has been altered. By applying for and accepting a permit to conduct horse racing, defendants have surrendered a substantial portion of the power and control they otherwise would have over the permit premises and expressly agree to abide by the rules and regulations of the commission and the regulations and orders of the stewards."

"Although there is no express provision in the regulations requiring a permit holder to admit the holder of a license issued by the commission to engage in some aspect of racing on the permit premises, it is a necessary corollary to the issuance of the license, which necessarily requires the person for the proper utilization of that license to enter upon the permit premises."

Based on all of the foregoing, I would affirm the judgment of the court of appeals below.

WRIGHT, J., concurs in the foregoing dissenting opinion.

Ziskis v. Kowalski

726 F. Supp. 902 (D. Conn. 1989)

RULING ON CROSS-MOTIONS FOR SUMMARY JUDGMENT

NEVAS, District Judge.

On August 30, 1977, Harvey Ziskis was summarily ejected from the jai-alai fronton in Hartford, Connecticut. He brought suit in 1980, pursuant to 42 U.S.C. Section 1983 and Connecticut common law, against various officials of the State of Connecticut and the Connecticut Commission on Special Revenue (now the Division of Special Revenue) (collectively, the "public defendants"), and Hartford Jai-Alai, Inc., World Jai-Alai, Inc., WJA Realty, and EHP Corporation (collectively, the "private defendants"). Nine years and a multitude of pleadings, motions, and rulings later, the court has before it cross-motions for summary judgment, brought by the plaintiff, the public defendants, and the private defendants. For the reasons that follow, the plaintiff's motion for summary judgment is denied and the defendants' motions for summary judgment are granted.

Background

The undisputed facts in this case support the following narrative. The plaintiff Harvey Ziskis ("Ziskis"), at times prior to this action, was a frequent bettor at jai-alai games. Defendant Hartford Jai-Alai, Inc. ("HJA") was a private corporation licensed by the State of Connecticut Commission on Special Revenue ("Commission") to operate the Hartford Jai-Alai fronton and was subject to the Commission's rules and regulations. Defendants World Jai-Alai, Inc., WJA Realty and EHP Corporation are or were private organizations with ownership or associated interests in HJA.

On August 30, 1977, Ziskis was ejected and permanently barred from the Hartford Jai-Alai fronton after he had cashed, but retained possession of, a winning jai-alai ticket.[2] The ejection was effected by Gerald Coakley, then assistant general manager and director of security of HJA, in accordance with Commission Regulation 12-574-D25(c)(2),[3]

---

2. The Notice form, with the name of the plaintiff filled in, stated that:
   The Management of Hartford Jai-Alai, Inc. has determined that the presence of Harvey L. Ziskis ... on the property of Hartford Jai-Alai is not desirable. The Management of Hartford Jai-Alai has further determined that Harvey L. Ziskis is an undesirable individual who is hereby barred from the premises of Hartford Jai-Alai permanently. The reason for the ejection was handwritten at the bottom of the form as follows: "Subject presented trifecta ticket for 9th game and took it back after he was paid for it. Window # 167."

3. Conn. Agencies Regs. Section 12-574-D25(c)(2) provides that:
   [A]n Association conducting Jai Alai games under license from the Commission shall eject from its grounds all unauthorized persons, known undesirables, touts, persons believed to be bookmakers or connected with bookmakers, persons under suspension or ruled off, persons of lewd or immoral character, and persons guilty of other conduct detrimental to Jai Alai or the public welfare.

then in effect. Subsequent to his ejection, the plaintiff unsuccessfully appealed to fronton management for reinstatement and to the Commission on Special Revenue for a hearing. In the absence of a statutory and/or regulatory requirement to comply, the Commission did not respond.

In September of 1977, after being denied reinstatement by fronton management, the plaintiff brought allegations before the Commission of various wrongdoings taking place at the Hartford Jai-Alai and other frontons in the state. The Commission initiated an investigation into plaintiff's allegations on systems betting and commenced a formal inquiry through a series of hearings which extended from November 1977 until January 1978.[5] The plaintiff testified at those hearings regarding his claimed knowledge of violations of Commission rules and regulations by HJA management. In the course of the Commission's investigation, Commission representatives received reports from employees of HJA alleging that the plaintiff was involved in "game fixing" at the state jai-alai frontons, and that HJA had failed to report these allegations to the Commission. As a result, the Commission held disciplinary hearings in March and April, 1978 concerning HJA's noncompliance with Commission rules. At the hearings, Ziskis was subpoenaed but refused to testify, relying on his fifth amendment privilege to remain silent.

In March 1978, the Commission invited Ziskis to submit a written specific request for a hearing. On May 15, 1980, Ziskis requested "a patron reinstatement hearing." The Commission agreed to hold a patron reinstatement hearing, even though not required by statute or regulation to do so, with the reservation that Ziskis be prepared to answer questions about the allegations made against him concerning player fixing. A hearing was scheduled and held on September 8, 1980. However, Ziskis did not attend.

Discussion of the Law

. . . .

B. Existence of a Protectable Liberty or Property Interest in Gambling. The heart of this dispute involves whether or not there are protected property or liberty interests of which the plaintiff was deprived. The court finds that such interests are not present and that there is no reason, therefore, to address other issues.

---

5. Because of Ziskis's allegations regarding player fixing at HJA, the Commission conducted hearings from November 1977 to January 1978 on the operation of "systems betting" at Hartford Jai-Alai and in March–April 1978 on HJA's non-compliance with Commission Regulations. In its final decision, In the Matter of the Commission on Special Revenue v. Hartford Jai-Alai (Sept. 20, 1978), the Commission found that John Dewees, an employee of HJA who worked for Rodney Woods, a large systems bettor, had informed HJA's Director and Chief of Security Gerald Coakley that

> [I]n April 1977 ... Mr. Ziskis allegedly stated to Dewees that he had some players under his control, that he was paying certain players to throw points thereby insuring that they would finish out of the money in a particular game, and that he wanted Dewees to leave out certain numbers when Dewees punched tickets for certain systems bettors, and that they would then split the money that was left out between he (sic) and Ziskis.

> *Id.* at 3. This conversation was reported to the management of HJA who failed to report these violations to the Commission. Instead, HJA conducted its own investigation and, having formed an opinion that Ziskis was an undesirable person at the fronton, made no effort to eject him. As a result, the Commission and state police were not able to investigate the player fixing allegations. The Commission thus fined Hartford Jai-Alai and closed it down for a week from September 27 to October 7, 1978.

In this case the plaintiff claims that his ejection from Hartford Jai-Alai deprived him, under color of state law, of substantive and procedural due process-loss of liberty, suspension from his employment as a bettor, loss of livelihood, and deprivation of property without due process of law-in contravention of the first, fifth and fourteenth amendments and in violation of his civil rights under 42 U.S.C. Section 1983. The threshold issue before this court, therefore, is whether there exists a protected liberty or property interest in the profession of gambling, the deprivation of which constitutes a denial of due process and thus a violation of section 1983.

In order to maintain an action under section 1983, a plaintiff must show that he has been deprived of a constitutional right by a person acting under color of state law.... The initial inquiry, however, is whether the plaintiff has been deprived of any *protected* liberty or property interest. If there has been no deprivation of liberty or property, then no process is due and the court need not address the issue of whether the deprivation occurred under color of state law....

To establish a property interest in this case, there must be a federal or state statute or rule of law or understanding that entitles the plaintiff to participate as a gambler in state parimutuel activities. Thus, in order for Ziskis successfully to argue that he was deprived of a hearing, he must first point to a specific state or federal law source for his claimed property or liberty interest in pursuing his profession of gambling. Unless Ziskis can clear this initial hurdle, the court need not even reach the state action question....

1. No Federal Property Interest in Gambling

There is no federal rule of law creating a general right to be a patron of a jai-alai fronton or other gambling establishment. Title II of the Civil Rights Act of 1964, 42 U.S.C. Section 2000a(c), which deals with public accommodations, including places of amusement, creates only a right not to be discriminated against on the basis of race, color, religion, or national origin. Indeed, the plaintiff does not argue that there exists a right to gamble secured by the Constitution, claiming instead that "[i]t was purely and simply the existence of State laws which gave rise to the plaintiff's protectable liberty and property interests." ...

2. No Property Interest in Connecticut For a Patron To Gamble

The plaintiff contends that he had a legitimate claim of entitlement, a property interest in pursuing his career in gambling, secured by existing state law. The plaintiff cites Conn. Gen. Stat. Section 53-35 as a state law source for his entitlement to attend jai-alai exhibitions.... This statute, which deals with public accommodations, including places of amusement, like the federal statute, creates only a right not to be discriminated against on the basis of race, color, religion, or national origin. It does not provide a patron with a constitutional right to attend jai-alai exhibitions....

The plaintiff also cites Conn. Gen. Stat. Section 12-573a, authorizing the operation of frontons, and Conn. Gen. Stat. Section 12-574, requiring the licensing of gambling related activities, which the plaintiff refers to as "special revenue activities," as state law sources for his entitlement to pursue his career in gambling.... Yet the list of gambling-related activities enumerated in the statute regulating licensing, such as operating gambling associations, and working as a concessionaire, vendor, or totalizator at a state-licensed gambling facility does *not* include gambling per se. Indeed, the State of Connecticut does not grant patrons licenses to gamble. Thus, plaintiff's reliance on this statute licensing gambling-related activities for his state-created entitlement to gamble is misplaced, since gambling is not a licensed activity, and it is the licensing of an activity which has been held to create a property interest. In Staino v. Pennsylvania State Horse Racing Comm'n, 98

Pa. Commw. 461, 470, 512 A.2d 75, 78 (1986), the court distinguished a licensee from a patron:

> The difference in procedural due process accorded patrons and licensees can be explained [by the fact that] [l]icensees, unlike patrons, have more than an abstract desire for or a unilateral expectation of admission to the racetrack by virtue of the license given them to exercise their occupation at the race track. Denial of admission to or ejection of a licensee thus constitutes denial of the liberty to exercise his occupation which triggers the procedural protections of the Fourteenth Amendment.

See also Cox v. National Jockey Club, 323 N.E.2d 104, 109 (Ill. App. 1974) (distinguishing a racetrack owner's common law right to exclude patrons from the exclusion of a licensed jockey "who was being arbitrarily deprived of his fundamental right to engage in his chosen occupation"); Jacobson v. New York Racing Ass'n, 33 N.Y.2d 144, 150, 350 N.Y.S.2d 639, 642–43, 305 N.E.2d 765, 768 (1973) (contrasting a racetrack proprietor's "common-law right to exclude undesirable patrons" with "an absolute immunity from having to justify the exclusion of an owner and trainer whom the State has deemed fit to license"). In contrast, the plaintiff's characterization of gambling, although unlicensed, as a special revenue activity thereby entitling him to a protected property interest in gambling is not supported by the caselaw. Although the plaintiff claims to have been licensed as a food concessionaire who could not get his license renewed because of the ejection and subsequent ruling off, that claim is not in the complaint; nor is there supporting evidence in the materials submitted with the plaintiff's motion for summary judgment. Nor can the plaintiff claim a property right to a license in other gambling-related activities from which he may have been banned as a result of the ejection, i.e., the ability to race dogs in other states. Rather, a property right arises, if it arises at all, only after a license has been granted.... In Lasky v. Van Lindt, 115 Misc.2d 259, 263, 453 N.Y.S.2d 983, 986 (1982), the court upheld the denial of a thoroughbred racehorse owner's license to a professional tout since there is no absolute right to a racehorse owner's license and thus no claim of entitlement requiring a hearing, since licensing touts was not in the best interests of racing. As the first circuit stated in Medina v. Rudman, 545 F.2d 244, 245, 250 (1976), the state had created no vested right or status in favor of potential greyhound license applicants, although once a license is granted "a right or status recognized under state law would come into being, and the revocation of the license would require notice and a hearing."

The licensing statute is an inapposite source of a state law entitlement to gambling. It concerns the licensing of activities for the purpose of regulating gambling (because it is a suspect activity) rather than the rights of patrons to participate in gambling. The weight of the case law upholds the common law rule that owners of places of amusement, like theaters and racetracks, are permitted to exclude patrons without cause. At common law a person engaged in a public calling, such as an innkeeper or common carrier, was held to have a duty to the general public to serve without discrimination all who sought service. In contrast, owners of private enterprises, such as places of amusement and resort, were under no such obligation, enjoying an absolute power to serve whom they pleased. Madden v. Queens County Jockey Club, 296 N.Y. 249, 253, 72 N.E.2d 697, 698, *cert. denied*, 332 U.S. 761, 68 S. Ct. 63, 92 L. Ed. 346 (1947). *See also* Marrone v. Washington Jockey Club, 227 U.S. 633, 636 (1913) (Holmes, J.) (upholding the common law rule that a ticket of admission to a racetrack does not create a right in rem precluding patron's ejection); Brooks v. Chicago Downs Ass'n, 791 F.2d 512, 519 (7th Cir. 1986) ("the common law rule, relic though it may be, still controls," conferring an absolute right to owners of racetracks to eject undesirable patrons); People v. Licata, 28 N.Y.2d 113, 115, 320 N.Y.S.2d 53, 55, 268 N.E.2d 787, 788 (1971) (reaffirming *Madden* based on a regulation similar to the Connecticut rule under which Ziskis was ejected); Contra Uston v. Resorts Int'l Hotel, 89 N.J. 163, 175, 445 A.2d 370 (1982) (casino precluded from excluding patron based on his "card counting" method of playing blackjack, where there was no indication that patron violated any Commission rule on the playing of blackjack.) *But see* Marzocca v. Ferone, 93 N.J. 509, 516, 461 A.2d 1133, 1137 (1983) (reaffirming the common law right of racetrack owner in New Jersey to exclude "notwithstanding the dicta in *Uston.*")

The plaintiff argues that since he was ejected pursuant to a Commission regulation, the common law right to exclude patrons had been abrogated. However, the case law supports the defendants' contention that the Connecticut regulation under which Ziskis was ejected did no more than codify the existing common law.... The courts of other jurisdictions have held that despite heavy regulation, the common law of exclusion was not changed....

Furthermore, the regulation under which Ziskis was ejected did not require a hearing. In the only case involving a patron ejection from a jai-alai fronton in Connecticut, Herman v. Division of Special Revenue, 193 Conn. 379, 477 A.2d 119 (1984), the Connecticut Supreme Court held that the reinstatement hearing held by the Division of Special Revenue upon the request of a patron ejected from the Milford Jai-Alai Fronton in 1979, pursuant to the same regulation under which Ziskis was ejected, did not qualify as a hearing because the plaintiff lacked the "right to be heard" under the statute. 193 Conn. at 387, 477 A.2d at 124.

Thus, Connecticut law creates no right of admission to jai-alai, no right not to be ejected, no property right of which Ziskis was deprived, and, therefore, no entitlement to a hearing. On similar facts, the Court of Appeals for the Sixth Circuit in *Rodic,* 615 F.2d at 736, addressed the question whether a patron at an Ohio racetrack had been deprived of a constitutional right when he was barred permanently from the racetrack without receiving a hearing. The sixth circuit stated that *Rodic* had no property interest in attending races at Thistledown since there was no federal law creating a general right to be admitted to racetracks and since Ohio law permitted racetracks to admit and exclude whom they pleased, so long as the exclusion was not based on race, creed, color, or national origin. The court held that Rodic "had no liberty or property interest in attending races at Thistledown on which to base a due process claim under Section 1983." *Rodic,* 615 F.2d at 738. In *Staino,* as in the instant case, the plaintiff was ejected pursuant to a regulation that did not specifically require a hearing in the event of a patron ejection, whereas a hearing was required, if requested, for an ejected licensee. 98 Pa. Commw. at 470, 512 A.2d at 79. The *Staino* court held that an ejected patron of a racetrack "has no constitutional right to a seat at the racetrack denial of which by state action would entitle him to the procedural protections of the Fourteenth Amendment" because "the statutory law of Pennsylvania accords no property right to a seat at a race track to a patron." 98 Pa. Commw. at 468, 512 A.2d at 78. Similarly, in Medina v. Rudman, 545 F.2d 244 (1st Cir. 1976), *cert. denied,* 434 U.S. 891 (1977), the court found the due process clause "inapplicable" and, consequently, a section 1983 claim groundless where a plaintiff's "interest in participating in the ownership of a parimutuel greyhound racetrack is neither a right recognized under New Hampshire law nor is it a 'fundamental' or 'natural' right." *Id.* at 250.

Like the ejected patrons in *Rodic* and *Staino,* Ziskis can point to no state statute, rule of law or understanding that entitles him to participate as a gambler in state parimutuel activities. He can thus make no claim that he was deprived of any protected property interest which would have entitled him to a due process hearing. The State of Connecticut accords no property right to gamble to a patron at jai-alai. Therefore, Ziskis had no property interest in gambling on which to base a due process claim under section 1983.

3. *No Liberty Interest in Gambling*

A. Gambling is not a Common Occupation

The plaintiff argues that by legalizing gambling in 1972, the State of Connecticut created a common occupation out of gambling related activities, including gambling per se, which plaintiff refers to as "special revenue activities." ... Thus, the plaintiff claims that his ejection as a patron from Hartford Jai-Alai violated his "liberty interest in pursuing a common occupation in special revenue activities." To support this proposition, the plaintiff cites cases holding that there is a fundamental right to pursue a common occupation. In Meyer v. Nebraska, 262 U.S. 390 (1923), the Supreme Court stated that the liberty guaranteed by the fourteenth amendment:

> denotes not merely freedom from bodily restraint but also the right of the individual to contract, *to engage in any of the common occupations of life,* to acquire useful knowledge, to marry, establish a home and bring up children, to worship God according to the dictates of his own conscience, and generally to enjoy those privileges long recognized at common law as essential to the orderly pursuit of happiness by free men.

Id. at 399 (emphasis added).... Yet the plaintiff cites no cases which hold that gambling is a common occupation. However, in Medina v. Rudman, 545 F.2d 244, 251 (1976), the first circuit held, to the contrary, that racetrack ownership is not "one of life's 'common occupations.' Gambling is traditionally suspect in our society, and investment in such an enterprise, when permitted at all, is plainly open to the strictest kind of supervision." The *Medina* court affirmed the district court's rejection of "any notion that Mrs. Medina's application [for a license to own a racetrack] involved a 'fundamental' or 'natural' right — such as the right to earn a living and engage in one's chosen occupation — which might, apart from state law, be a protected 'liberty' interest." *Id.* at 249. Similarly in Lasky v. Van Lindt, 115 Misc.2d 259, 263, 453 N.Y.S.2d 983, 986 (1982) the court held that " ... owning, training and racing horses is not one of life's common occupations." *See also* Note, *Legal Aspects of Public Gaming,* 12 CONN. L. REV., 870, 874 (1980) (distinguishing gambling-related jobs and businesses from the common occupations).

These courts' characterization of only certain occupations as "common occupations" and therefore a protected liberty interest can be analogized to the Supreme Court's definition of a family by its living arrangements in Moore v. East Cleveland, 431 U.S. 494, 504–05, 97 (1977) (children living with a grandparent constitute a family) and in Village of Belle-Terre v. Boraas, 416 U.S. 1 (1974) (unrelated people living together do not constitute a family). Similarly, certain professions have been held to constitute common occupations, while others, like gambling, traditionally a suspect activity, have not. Indeed, gambling remains a suspect activity in Connecticut, even though it has been legalized. *See* King Int'l Corp. v. Voloshin, 33 Conn. Supp. 166, 171, 366 A.2d 1172, 1175 (1976):

> While the state's heretofore ancient and deep-rooted policy of condemning gambling has been eroded to some degree by its legalization of certain types of gambling, the state has, nevertheless, been intransigent in its policy of prohibiting the extension of credit for the promotion of gambling activity — and with good reason. One need not have the gambling sagacity of the famed Las Vegas oddsmaker Jimmy the Greek to recognize the potential dangers in the extension of credit to the gambler or the possibly unfortunate incidents, to employ a euphemism, that could well result from the nonpayment of the gambling bettor to his creditor.

B. No First Amendment Right to Gamble

Nor has gambling been held to be a first amendment right. The plaintiff argues that he had a first amendment right to associate with the other members of his profession of gambling. Yet, the plaintiff cites no cases to support this claim. In contrast, the court in Allendale Leasing, Inc., v. Stone, 614 F. Supp. 1440, 1454 (D.R.I.1985) held that "there is no First Amendment right to conduct or play Bingo, ... a game of chance; in less euphemistic terms, ... commonly known as gambling ... regardless of whether the game is completely prohibited or statutorily permitted subject to regulation."

Conclusion

Since the plaintiff has failed to show the existence of a liberty or property interest in pursuing gambling as a livelihood, this court holds that, as a matter of law, the plaintiff cannot claim entitlement to a due process hearing and, as a consequence, has no claim under 42 U.S.C. Section 1983. The plaintiff's motion for summary judgment is therefore denied. The defendants' motions for summary judgment are granted.

SO ORDERED.

Notes

1. When racing authorities seek to exclude persons they invoke the broad discretionary powers they have to protect the integrity of pari-mutuel activities. Courts tend to validate this action when it involves those who have been licensed as participants in the racing activity, such as jockeys and trainers, and those who participate in handling the wagers such as pari-mutuel clerks. *See e.g.,* Lee v. Walters, 433 F.3d 672 (9th Cir. 2005) (horse owners could be excluded from race track by Oregon Racing Commission for improper use of funds); Phillips v. Graham, 427 N.E.2d 550 (Ill. 1981) (harness racing drivers, owners, and trainers could be excluded pursuant to statute by formal order of Racing Board for indictment based on bribery charges); Morrison v. Cal. Horse Racing Bd., 252. Cal. Rptr. 293 (Cal. Ct. App. 1988) (licensee can be excluded for any reason horse racing authority considers appropriate including off track offenses); Boyce v. State Horse Racing Comm'n, 651 A.2d 656 (Pa. Commw. Ct. 1994) (ejection of state licensee from a horseracing track does not prevent the licensee from working at another track. However, license revocation does.).

2. Exclusion of non-licensed individuals such as patrons may be based on a statutory provision or a claimed common law right of exclusion. There is disagreement in the courts regarding the common law right of exclusion in the pari-mutuel setting as well as in the casino patron exclusion case. For statutory exclusion authority, *see* 810 Ky. Admin. Regs. 1:026 § 23 (ejection or exclusion from Association grounds); N.D. Admin. Code 69.5-01-02-06 (2009) (exclusion of patrons); Md. Code Regs. 09.10.01.45. §§ (V), (Y) (power of stewards to exclude those licensed and unlicensed). *See also* Narragansett Racing Ass'n v. Mazzaro, 357 A.2d 442 (R.I. 1976) (statute abrogated track's common law right to exclude, as statute required racetrack to show cause that such person is undesirable and that presence would interfere with the proper conduct of races).

On the issue of common law exclusion, *see* Marrone v. Washington Jockey Club, 227 U.S. 633 (1913) (seminal decision written by Justice Holmes applying the English common law rule established in Wood v. Leadbitter, 153 Eng. Rep. 351 (Ex. 1845), holding that horserace tracks had the common law right to exclude patrons); Tropical Park, Inc. v. Jock, 374 So. 2d 639 (Fla. Dist. Ct. App. 1979) (statutes did not preempt racetrack operator's common law right to absolutely exclude patrons); James v. Churchill Downs,

Inc., 620 S.W.2d 323 (Ky. Ct. App. 1981). *See also* John J. Kropp et al., *Exclusion of Patrons and Horsemen From Racetracks: A Legal, Practical and Constitutional Dilemma*, 74 Ky. L.J. 739 (1986) (comprehensive look at the historical development of the common law and statutory rights of exclusion and the challenges thereto).

3. Exclusions at the Casino:
"We Don't Want Your Action."

Uston v. Resorts International Hotel, Inc.
445 A.2d 370 (1982)

PASHMAN, J.

Since January 30, 1979, appellant Resorts International Hotel, Inc. (Resorts) has excluded respondent, Kenneth Uston, from the blackjack tables in its casino because Uston's strategy increases his chances of winning money. Uston concedes that his strategy of card counting can tilt the odds in his favor under the current blackjack rules promulgated by the Casino Control Commission (Commission). However, Uston contends that Resorts has no common law or statutory right to exclude him because of his strategy for playing blackjack.

We hold that the Casino Control Act, N.J.S.A. 5:12-1 to -152 gives the Commission exclusive authority to set the rules of licensed casino games, which includes the methods for playing those games. The Casino Control Act therefore precludes Resorts from excluding Uston for card counting. Because the Commission has not exercised its exclusive authority to determine whether card counters should be excluded, we do not decide whether such an exclusion would be lawful.

I

Kenneth Uston is a renowned teacher and practitioner of a complex strategy for playing blackjack known as card counting. Card counters keep track of the playing cards as they are dealt and adjust their betting patterns when the odds are in their favor. When used over a period of time, this method allegedly ensures a profitable encounter with the casino.

Uston first played blackjack at Resorts' casino in November 1978. Resorts took no steps to bar Uston at that time, apparently because the Commission's blackjack rules then in operation minimized the advantages of card counting.

On January 5, 1979, however, a new Commission rule took effect that dramatically improved the card counter's odds. N.J.A.C. 19:47-2.5. The new rule, which remains in effect, restricted the reshuffling of the deck in ways that benefitted card counters. Resorts concedes that the Commission could promulgate blackjack rules that virtually eliminate the advantage of card counting. However, such rules would slow the game, diminishing the casino's "take" and consequently its profits from blackjack gaming.

By letter dated January 30, 1979, attorneys for Resorts wrote to Commission Chairman Lordi, asking the Commission's position on the legality of summarily removing card counters from its blackjack tables. That same day, Commissioner Lordi responded in writing that no statute or regulation barred Resorts from excluding professional card counters from its casino. Before the day had ended, Resorts terminated Uston's career at its blackjack tables, on the basis that in its opinion he was a professional card counter. Resorts subsequently formulated standards for identification of card counters and adopted a general policy to exclude such players.[2]

The Commission upheld Resorts' decision to exclude Uston. Relying on Garifine v. Monmouth Park Jockey Club, 29 N.J. 47, 148 A.2d 1 (1959), the Commission held that Resorts enjoys a common law right to exclude anyone it chooses, as long as the exclusion does not violate state and federal civil rights laws. The Appellate Division reversed. Although we interpret the Casino Control Act, N.J.S.A. 5:12-1 to -152 somewhat differently than did the Appellate Division, we affirm that court's holding that the Casino Control Act precludes Resorts from excluding Uston. The Commission alone has the authority to exclude patrons based upon their strategies for playing licensed casino games. Any common law right Resorts may have had to exclude Uston for these reasons is abrogated by the act. We therefore need not decide the precise extent of Resorts' common law right to exclude patrons for reasons not covered by the act. Nonetheless, we feel constrained to refute any implication arising from the Commission's opinion that absent supervening statutes, the owners of places open to the public enjoy an absolute right to exclude patrons without good cause. We hold that the common law right to exclude is substantially limited by a competing common law right of reasonable access to public places.

II

This Court has recognized that "[t]he statutory and administrative controls over casino operations established by the [Casino Control] Act are extraordinarily pervasive and intensive." The almost 200 separate statutory provisions "cover virtually every facet of casino gambling and its potential impact upon the public." These provisions include a preemption clause, stating that the act prevails over "any other provision of law" in conflict or inconsistent with its provisions. N.J.S.A. 5:12-133(b). Moreover, the act declares as public policy of this State "that the institution of licensed casino establishments in New Jersey be strictly regulated and controlled." N.J.S.A. 5:12-1(13).

At the heart of the Casino Control Act are its provisions for the regulation of licensed casino games. N.J.S.A. 5:12-100 provides:

> ... e. All gaming shall be conducted according to rules promulgated by the commission. All wagers and pay-offs of winning wagers at table games shall be made according to rules promulgated by the commission, which shall establish such minimum wagers and other limitations as may be necessary to assure the vitality of casino operations and fair odds to and maximum participation by casino patrons;....

This provision on games and gaming equipment reinforces the general statutory provisions codified at N.J.S.A. 5:12-70. Those provisions provide in part:

> The Commission shall, without limitation on the powers conferred in the preceding section, include within its regulations the following specific provisions in accordance with the provisions of the act;
>
> ....
>
> f. Defining and limiting the areas of operation, the rules of authorized games, odds, and devices permitted, and the method of operation of such games and devices;....

Pursuant to these statutes, the Commission has promulgated exhaustive rules on the playing of blackjack.... These rules cover every conceivable aspect of the game, from de-

---

2. Since then an industry-wide policy has developed to ban card counters. Each casino maintains its own list of persons to be barred as card counters.

termining how the cards are to be shuffled and cut, ... to providing that certain cards shall not be dealt "until the dealer has first announced 'Dealer's Card' which shall be stated by the dealer in a tone of voice calculated to be heard by each person at the table." ... It is no exaggeration to state that the Commission's regulation of blackjack is more extensive than the entire administrative regulation of many industries.

These exhaustive statutes and regulations make clear that the Commission's control over the rules and conduct of licensed casino games is intended to be comprehensive. The ability of casino operators to determine how the games will be played would undermine this control and subvert the important policy of ensuring the "credibility and integrity of the regulatory process and of casino operations." N.J.S.A. 5:12-1(b).[3] The Commission has promulgated the blackjack rules that give Uston a comparative advantage, and it has sole authority to change those rules. There is no indication that Uston has violated any Commission rule on the playing of blackjack.... Put simply, Uston's gaming is "conducted according to rules promulgated by the Commission." ... Resorts has no right to exclude Uston on grounds that he successfully plays the game under existing rules.

The Attorney General interpreted §71 to be a tightly circumscribed intrusion on common law rights. We need not determine whether §71, standing alone, would give the Commission the authority to exclude card counters....

III

Resorts claimed that it could exclude Uston because it had a common law right to exclude anyone at all for any reason. While we hold that the Casino Control Act precludes Resorts from excluding Uston for the reasons stated, it is important for us to address the asserted common law right for two reasons. First, Resorts' contentions and the Commission's position concerning the common law right are incorrect. Second, the act has not completely divested Resorts of its common law right to exclude.

The right of an amusement place owner to exclude unwanted patrons and the patron's competing right of reasonable access both have deep roots in the common law.... In this century, however, courts have disregarded the right of reasonable access in the common law of some jurisdictions at the time the Civil War Amendments and Civil Rights Act of 1866 were passed....

The current majority American rule has for many years disregarded the right of reasonable access,[4] granting to proprietors of amusement places an absolute right arbitrarily to eject or exclude any person consistent with state and federal civil rights laws....

At one time, an absolute right of exclusion prevailed in this state, though more for reasons of deference to the noted English precedent of Wood v. Leadbitter, 13 M&W 838, 153 Eng. Rep. 351, (Ex.1845), than for reasons of policy....

In view of the substantially uniform approval of, and reliance on, the decision in Wood v. Leadbitter in our state adjudications, it must fairly be considered to be adopted as part

---

3. The Appellate Division relied on N.J.S.A. 5:12-71 (§71) to establish the Commission's right to exclude Uston. That provision directs the Commission to compile a list of persons to be excluded from gaming casinos whose presence in the casino would be inimical to the interests of casino gambling in New Jersey. N.J.S.A. 5:12-71(a)(3). The section applies to persons whose backgrounds or occupations indicate either criminal activity or actions hostile to the integrity of licensed casino gambling. We do not rely on this portion of the statute.

4. The denial of freedom of reasonable access in some States following passage of the Fourteenth Amendment, and the creation of a common law freedom to arbitrarily exclude following invalidation of segregation statutes, suggest that the current majority rule may have had less than dignified origins.

of our jurisprudence, and whatever views may be entertained as to the natural justice or injustice of ejecting a theater patron without reason after he has paid for his ticket and taken his seat, we feel constrained to follow that decision as the settled law.

It hardly bears mention that our common law has evolved in the intervening 70 years. In fact, *Leadbitter* itself was disapproved three years after the *Shubert* decision by Hurst v. Picture Theatres Limited, (1915) 1 K.B. 1 (1914). Of far greater importance, the decisions of this Court have recognized that "the more private property is devoted to public use, the more it must accommodate the rights which inhere in individual members of the general public who use that property." State v. Schmid, 84 N.J. 535, 562, 423 A.2d 615 (1980).

Schmid involved the constitutional right to distribute literature on a private university campus. The Court's approach in that case balanced individual rights against property rights. It is therefore analogous to a description of the common law right of exclusion. Balancing the university's interest in controlling its property against plaintiff's interest in access to that property to express his views, the Court clearly refused to protect unreasonable exclusions. Justice Handler noted that:

> Regulations ... devoid of reasonable standards designed to protect both the legitimate interests of the University as an institution of higher education and the individual exercise of expressional freedom cannot constitutionally be invoked to prohibit the otherwise noninjurious and reasonable exercise of [First Amendment] freedoms." *Id.* at 567, 423 A.2d 615.

Schmid recognizes implicitly that when property owners open their premises to the general public in the pursuit of their own property interests, they have no right to exclude people unreasonably. On the contrary, they have a duty not to act in an arbitrary or discriminatory manner toward persons who come on their premises. That duty applies not only to common carriers, innkeepers, owners of gasoline service stations, or to private hospitals, but to all property owners who open their premises to the public. Property owners have no legitimate interest in unreasonably excluding particular members of the public when they open their premises for public use.

No party in this appeal questions the right of property owners to exclude from their premises those whose actions "disrupt the regular and essential operations of the [premises]," State v. Schmid, 84 N.J. at 566, 423 A.2d 615 (quoting Princeton University Regulations on solicitation), or threaten the security of the premises and its occupants.... In some circumstances, proprietors have a duty to remove disorderly or otherwise dangerous persons from the premises.... These common law principles enable the casino to bar from its entire facility, for instance, the disorderly, the intoxicated, and the repetitive petty offender.

Whether a decision to exclude is reasonable must be determined from the facts of each case.[5] Respondent Uston does not threaten the security of any casino occupant. Nor has he disrupted the functioning of any casino operations. Absent a valid contrary rule by the Commission, Uston possesses the usual right of reasonable access to Resorts International's blackjack tables.

IV

Although the Commission alone has authority to exclude persons based upon their methods of playing licensed casino games, that authority has constitutional and statu-

---

5. We need not decide whether the common law allows exclusion of those merely suspected of criminal activity, *see Garifine, supra*, 29 N.J. at 57, 148 A.2d 1, because the Casino Control Act clearly vests such decisions in the Commission alone. N.J.S.A. 5:12-71.

tory limits. We expressly decline to decide whether the Casino Control Act empowers the Commission to exclude card counters.

If the Commission decides to consider promulgating a rule banning card counters, it should review the statutory mandates regarding both the public policy of this State and the rules of licensed games. The Casino Control Act commands the Commission to regulate gambling with such "limitations as may be necessary *to assure the vitality of casino operations and fair odds to and maximum participation by casino patrons,*" N.J.S.A. 5:12-100(e) (emphasis added). The Court recognizes that the goals of casino vitality, fair odds to all players and maximum player participation may be in conflict. It is the Commission which must strike the appropriate balance.

The Commission should also consider that the Legislature has declared as public policy of this state that "[c]onfidence in casino gaming operations is eroded to the extent the State of New Jersey does not provide a regulatory framework for casino gaming that permits and promotes stability and continuity in casino gaming operations." N.J.S.A. 5:12-1(14). Moreover, "[a]n integral and essential element of the regulation and control of such casino facilities by the State rests in the public confidence and trust in the credibility and integrity of the regulatory process and of casino operations." N.J.S.A. 5:12-1(6). The exclusion of persons who can play the licensed games to their advantage may diminish public confidence in the fairness of casino gaming. To the extent persons not counting cards would be mistakenly excluded, public confidence might be further diminished. However, the right of the casinos to have the rules drawn so as to allow some reasonable profit must also be recognized in any realistic assessment. The Commission should consider the potentially broad ramifications of excluding card counters before it seeks to promulgate such a rule. Fairness and the integrity of casino gaming are the touchstones.

V

In sum, absent a valid Commission regulation excluding card counters, respondent Uston will be free to employ his card-counting strategy at Resorts' blackjack tables. There is currently no Commission rule banning Uston, and Resorts has no authority to exclude him for card counting. However, it is not clear whether the Commission would have adopted regulations involving card counters had it known that Resorts could not exclude Uston. The Court therefore continues the temporary order banning Uston from Resorts' blackjack tables for 90 days from the date of this opinion. After that time, respondent is free to play blackjack at Resorts' casino absent a valid Commission rule excluding him.

Uston v. Hilton Hotels Corp.

448 F. Supp. 116 (D. Nev. 1978)

MEMORANDUM OPINION

ROGER D. FOLEY, Chief Judge.

This action is one of several cases filed by Kenneth Uston in this court and others over the last two years. In all, Uston has sought damages as well as injunctive relief to enjoin the respective casinos from refusing to allow him to play the game of "21". The present action arises from an event which occurred at the Flamingo Hilton Hotel casino on June 29, 1975. At approximately 6:00 P.M., Uston was approached by two security guards at a "21" table and was requested to leave the premises. The two guards escorted Uston to the hotel's entrance where Uston was read the Nevada trespass statute. Uston thereafter departed. Uston alleges that he was asked to leave because he is a "better than average black jack ("21") player."[1]

This case is presently before this Court on the defendants' motion for summary judgment. For the reasons set forth below, it is the conclusion of this Court that summary judgment be granted in favor of the defendants.

Uston's complaint contains various causes of action which may be divided into the state law claims and the federal law claims. The claims based on federal law will be discussed first.

This action is brought under various provisions of Title 28, United States Code, most notably §§ 1332 and 1343(3), and under the provisions of Title 42, United States Code, §§ 1983, 1985 and 1986. Uston asserts that certain rights secured by the due process and equal protection clauses of the Fourteenth Amendment of the United States Constitution have been denied him. After having considered the pleadings, affidavits and written arguments of counsel, it is the finding of this Court that there are no pertinent genuine issues of fact. Further, it is the finding of this Court that Uston has failed to state any federally recognized cause of action.

In order to predicate an action under 42 U.S.C. § 1983, it must be demonstrated, inter alia, that the deprivation of constitutional rights, the injury complained of, was brought about by state action, that is, took place under color of state law. It is well established that private conduct without some significant state involvement is not actionable under 42 U.S.C. § 1983. In opposing the defendants' motion for summary judgment, Uston asserts that the actions of the defendants in preventing him from playing the game of "21" were tantamount to state action (1) because of the extent to which the State of Nevada regulates the gaming industry, and (2) because the State of Nevada, charged with the enforcement of the gaming laws, has refused to prohibit the discrimination against card counters. Both contentions are without merit.

Mere state regulation of a private industry in and of itself does not constitute state action. Something more, more in the nature of a substantial and direct state involvement in promoting the challenged activity, must be demonstrated in order to establish state action. In Jackson v. Metropolitan Edison Co., 419 U.S. 345 (1974), a private electric utility was subject to pervasive and detailed state regulation and licensing, similar to the extent that the gaming industry is controlled by Nevada. The Court, in holding that such licensing and regulation did not constitute state action, stated, at page 358:

"Metropolitan is a privately owned corporation, and it does not lease its facilities from the State of Pennsylvania. It alone is responsible for the provision of power to its customers. In common with all corporations of the State it pays taxes to the State, and it is subject to a form of extensive regulation by the State in a way that most other business enterprises are not. But this was likewise true of the appellant club in Moose Lodge No. 107 v. Irvis, *supra*, where we said:

'However detailed this type of regulation may be in some particulars, it cannot be said to in any way foster or encourage racial discrimination. Nor can it be said to make the State in any realistic sense a partner or even a joint venturer in the club's enterprise.' 407 U.S. at 176–77.

"All of petitioner's arguments taken together show no more than that Metropolitan was a heavily regulated, privately owned utility, enjoying at least a partial monopoly in

---

1. Uston, apparently, is a "card counter." With respect to the game of "21", a card counter is a person that attempts to know every card both in and out of the deck, thereby enhancing his chances of placing a favorable wager. This practice is not considered cheating, nor is it illegal.

the providing of electrical service within its territory, and that it elected to terminate a service to petitioner in a manner which the Pennsylvania Public Utility Commission found permissible under state law. Under our decision this is not sufficient to connect the State of Pennsylvania with the respondent's action so as to make the latter's conduct attributable to the State for purposes of the Fourteenth Amendment."

In the case at hand, there has been no demonstration that the State of Nevada, either through its regulation and/or licensing of the gaming industry, has to any significant degree promoted or participated in the exclusion of persons suspected by gaming establishments to be card counters or in Uston's words, "better than average black jack players."

Similarly, the State of Nevada is under no obligation, statutory or otherwise, which, by its refusal to compel gaming establishments to allow card counters to play "21", would attribute the defendants' actions to state action. Uston has asserted that the omission by the State of Nevada to take any affirmative action to alleviate the discrimination against card counters, in light of Nevada Revised Statutes 463.151, is akin to approval of same, and therefore state action. NRS 463.151 requires the exclusion from gaming establishments of certain persons named on a list compiled by the Nevada Gaming Commission for various reasons, one of which is not card counting. In essence, Uston argues that since the State of Nevada has enacted measures that require the exclusion of a limited class of undesirable persons, of which Uston is not a member, it thereby undertook the affirmative duty to compel the admittance of all persons, such as Uston, who were not named on the list compiled by the Nevada Gaming Commission. Such an argument strains logic. It is the judgment of this Court that NRS 463.151 gives rise to no affirmative obligation by the State of Nevada to compel gaming establishments to admit persons thought to be card counters. Since no duty exists, the failure to prohibit private action is not state action. As was stated in Cohen v. Illinois Institute of Technology, 524 F.2d 818 (7th Cir. 1975), at 826:

"Finally, we are not persuaded that the omission of any affirmative prohibition against sex discrimination, even against the background of detailed State regulation of the Institute, is tantamount to express State approval of the objectionable policy. The holding of the Supreme Court in Moose Lodge No. 107 v. Irvis, *supra*, requires us to reject such an argument. For it is abundantly clear that the State of Pennsylvania had ample power to revoke the liquor license of the Lodge No. 107, and further that the State could not constitutionally endorse the Lodge's discriminatory practices. If a State's mere failure to prohibit could be equated with express approval, the *Moose Lodge* case would have been decided differently."

As such, since Uston has been unable to persuade this Court that any of the activities involved in his removal from the casino of the Flamingo Hilton amounted to state action, this Court concludes that Uston has failed to state a claim under 42 U.S.C. § 1983.

Next, Uston asserts that the defendants have conspired to deprive him of the opportunity to play "21" which is actionable under 42 U.S.C. s 1985. In order to state a claim under 42 U.S.C. s 1985(3), it must be asserted that the defendants conspired to deprive Uston of equal protection of the laws, hence causing injury to him or his property. However, in Griffin v. Breckenridge, 403 U.S. 88 (1971), at 101 and 102, the Court stated that 42 U.S.C. s 1985 was not "intended to apply to all tortious, conspiratorial interferences with the rights of others," but only to those which were founded upon "some racial, or perhaps otherwise class-based, invidiously discriminatory animus." ...

In the case at hand, Uston has failed to allege that the "conspiracy" between the defendants to eliminate the class of "better than average black jack players" was brought about by racial or any other invidiously discriminatory animus. Therefore, Uston has failed to state a claim under 42 U.S.C. § 1985....

Turning now to Uston's state law claims, it is the finding of this Court that it is without jurisdiction to entertain same. Based on the same series of events upon which Uston predicated his federal law claims, he alleges state law claims of assault, false imprisonment, intentional infliction of emotional harm, and violation of the state public accommodation law. Since all the federal law claims have been dismissed, the only jurisdictional base upon which this Court could entertain the state law claims is Uston's assertion that this Court has diversity jurisdiction under 28 U.S.C. § 1332.

Diversity jurisdiction exists only if there is complete diversity. Uston alleges that he is a citizen of California, and for complete diversity to exist none of the defendants can be citizens of California. One of the named defendants, Hilton Hotels Corporation, has as its principal place of business the State of California. 28 U.S.C. § 1332(c) provides:

"For the purposes of this section and section 1441 of this title, a corporation shall be deemed a citizen of any State by which it has been incorporated and of the State where it has its principal place of business: ..."

For purposes of 28 U.S.C. § 1332, Hilton Hotels Corporation is a citizen of the State of California. As such, there is no diversity jurisdiction. Therefore, Uston's state law claims shall be dismissed.

Notes

1. In a later case, the Supreme Court of New Jersey reiterated the principle that the power of the state Casino Control Commission (CCC) over the conduct of casino games was comprehensive. The decision noted that after the *Uston* case, the CCC did not pass a regulation that allowed casinos to bar card counters. However, the CCC did authorize the use of "countermeasures" which the plaintiff alleged were being applied against him in a discriminatory manner. The court ruled that while the CCC had primary jurisdiction over issues involving the interpretation of the state gambling laws and regulations, this did not convert the CCC into a "court of claims" for claims of discriminatory treatment by patrons, and these claims could be heard in the courts. While the court found no private cause of action for money damages against a casino generally, there was a common law basis for a claim of discriminatory treatment, for, "[e]ven without statutory or regulatory support, a casino has a common-law duty to treat patrons fairly." Ultimately, the plaintiff's damage award was overturned and the case was remanded to the lower court. Campione v. Adamar of New Jersey, 714 A.2d 299, 309 (1998). Thus, New Jersey recognizes, at least in theory, that casinos may not have the authority to exclude a person merely for being a card counter, though they can make life very difficult through the use of countermeasures. The topic of countermeasures and advantage play is addressed in chapter 7.

2. The Nevada Supreme Court has not definitively ruled on the legality of exclusions in Nevada. In one case, a card counter, Mark Estes, was evicted from a casino and arrested for trespassing. He sued the casino, arguing it had no legal basis for excluding him. According to one source:

> What followed next can only be considered an embarrassment to the legal system of Nevada. In a short, two-page Order, the Nevada Supreme Court dismissed Estes' appeal. Nevada's public accommodation law prohibits discrimination 'on the ground of race, color, religion, national origin or physical or visual hand-

icap,' NRS 651.070, and the Court refused to follow other modern courts in protecting anyone else but these special classes from discrimination.... Estes v. State, Sup. Ct. Nev. No. 10420 (Mar. 13, 1980).

It is significant to note that this Nevada Supreme Court Order was not published. When a court opinion ... is not published there are two important consequences: first, it is very difficult for anyone to find out exactly what the court has done; and, second, the opinion has no legal precedential value.

Apparently, the Nevada Supreme Court did not want to go on public record as siding with the casinos on the dubious claim that a casino can discriminate against whomever they wish.

I. NELSON ROSE & ROBERT A. LOEB, BLACKJACK AND THE LAW 18–19 (RGE Publishing 1998).

Nevada law does not provide that card counters can be excluded, nor does it provide for their protection as any type of "protected class." Nev. Rev. Stat. §463.151. But card counting is not listed as cheating under the Nevada code, nor does it satisfy the statutory definition of cheating, "to alter the elements of chance, method of selection or criteria which determine: (a) The result of a game." Nev. Rev. Stat. §465.015. Does the statutory and judicial silence suggest that the state would just like the issue to go away? Are the authors quoted above correct in their belief that policy makers do not want to be seen as favoring casinos over a player?

3. Is there a contractual component to the exclusion issue? By offering the games to a player, does the casino enter into an agreement that it will allow a player to use his skills, including card counting to try to win? Presumably, a player who sees that countermeasures are being used by the casino will know that the terms of the contract, or the casino's "offer" to play, have changed. What if a casino used "smart" tables that could keep track of the cards played and calculate when the deck favored the player. Would a player have a valid complaint if the casino used this technology to determine when, for example, a mid-deck shuffle would take place?

4. There is little precedent in other states on the casino's right to exclude. *See* Donovan v. Grand Victoria Casino & Resort, L.P., 915 N.E.2d 1001 (Ind. App. 2009) (because Indiana Gaming Regulations set forth exhaustive set of blackjack regulations, and such regulations did not prohibit card counting, casino's common law right of exclusion had been abrogated by statute), *opinion vacated* 929 N.E.2d 786 (Ind. 2010); Termini v. Missouri Gaming Comm'n, 921 S.W.2d 159 (Mo. App. 1996) (commission's exclusion of a patron based on its asserted authority set forth in the commissions regulations did not exceed the authority of the commission); *see also* Silbert v. Ramsey, 482 A.2d 147 (Md. 1984) (racetrack operator had common law right to exclude patron without sufficient reason or excuse, provided that the exclusion was not based on race, creed, color, sex or national origin, and such common law right was not abrogated by State law); Winfield v. Noe, 426 S.E.2d 1148 (Fla. App. 1983) (state's attempt to regulate pari-mutuel wagering did not abrogate the common law right of exclusion).

5. Is the exclusion issue that important as a practical matter? If a state says a casino cannot exclude patrons, but can employ various countermeasures against them, is the gambler really any better off? Might there be some casinos that would advertise they *welcomed* card counters, believing that the action they would receive from bad counters would more than offset what is paid out to the successful counter? Is there a market solution to this issue? For discussion of the exclusion issue see Anthony Cabot & Robert Hannum, *Advantage Play and Commercial Casinos*, 75 MISS. L.J. 681 (2005); Tom Julian, *Exclusions and Countermeasures: Do Card Counters Have a Right to Play?*, 9 GAMING L. REV. 165 (2005).

4. Problem Gambling and Self-Exclusions

A. Problem Gambling Generally

There is no question that gambling gets the better of some people. This goes beyond a person losing some money from gambling and lamenting his bad luck. The "compulsive" or "problem" gambler is not a myth. Various studies of the issue estimate that one to two percent of the adult population fit the definition of a pathological or problem gambler. In Nevada, a 2002 study estimated that 3.5% of the adult population in that state were pathological gamblers and 2.9% could be classified as problem gamblers. The costs to society of such activity are staggering. Job loss, personal debt, bankruptcy, damage to health, divorce, and suicide are all remarkably higher for the compulsive gambler. These costs are borne not just by the gambler. Dependents can suffer as well, and society bears many of the costs for those who have hit bottom and have no means of caring for themselves. Society benefits by implementing preventive and therapeutic mechanisms for treating this problem, and few would argue with the idea that it is the "right thing" to do. It may seem that the gambling industry benefits financially when people gamble away all their money. After all, the house expects to win. But stories of problem gamblers cast a pall over the industry. If policy-makers thought the industry had an uncaring attitude about pathological gamblers, or worse, exploited them, unwelcome regulation of the gaming industry might result. This raises the question: how should society, including policy-makers and courts, address the problem of the gambler who cannot set limits for himself? What obligations do casinos have to these people?

Taveras v. Resorts Intern. Hotel, Inc.
2008 WL 4372791 (D.N.J. 2008)

I. Introduction

This matter comes before the Court upon the defendants' motions to dismiss plaintiff's Amended Complaint for failure to state a claim upon which relief may be granted, for insufficient service of process, and for failure to plead a short and plain statement of the claims showing entitlement to relief. The Defendants are Bally's Park Place, Atlantic City Showboat, Harrah's Entertainment, Inc., Colony Capital, LLC, Sun International Hotels Limited, Trump Plaza Associates, LLC, Trump Taj Mahal Associates, LLC, Resorts International Hotel, Inc., Bob Benz, and Elizabeth D'Andrea, (the "Defendants"), all casinos, casino owners, and/or casino employees. Plaintiff Arelia Margarita Taveras ("Plaintiff") patronized Defendant-casinos during a 14-month period in 2004 and 2005.

Plaintiff alleges the Defendants facilitated Plaintiff's gambling addiction and induced her to gamble away money belonging to her and others, causing her loss of money, emotional injury, and damage to reputation. Plaintiff, who is a former attorney, also alleges the Defendants' conduct caused her disbarment. Specifically, Plaintiff alleges, Defendants breached their common-law duty of care to her, breached contractual obligations owed to her, conspired against her in violation of federal racketeering laws, and failed to report her casino transactions as required by federal law.

Defendants now move ... to dismiss the Amended Complaint for failure to state a legally cognizable claim; ... For the reasons set forth below, the Court grants Defendants' motions to dismiss for failure to state a claim....

II. Facts

Plaintiff Arelia Margarita Taveras, formerly an attorney in New York, gambled recreationally at various casinos between 2000 and 2004. She contends that her "gambling went from recreational to compulsive during the latter part of 2004 and the year of 2005." In that time, she gambled at a number of different casinos. Plaintiff's compulsive gambling, manifest over a 14-month period, resulted in substantial financial losses. As a result of Plaintiff's gambling addiction, she neglected her professional duties and gambled away client funds. She was subsequently disbarred.[2]

On numerous occasions, Plaintiff's behavior during that period consisted of "consecutive days of gambling, without eating or sleeping...." Plaintiff alleges that certain casino employees "refused to permit [her] family members from taking her home," and continued to allow her to gamble in spite of clear indications that she was a compulsive gambler, confirmed by information about her condition provided to casino employees by her brother. At the height of her addiction, Plaintiff was gambling five days per week and losing an average of $5,000 per hour. In a weekend of continuous gambling, Plaintiff lost $150,000.

During this period, Plaintiff alleges, she received numerous "enticements" from Defendant-casinos, including casino event promotions, gambling tournament invitations, promotions for free televisions, as well as free limousine rides, hotel rooms, food, entertainment, and gift coupons.

Plaintiff was hospitalized twice for "serious mental and physical ailments," and ultimately underwent in-patient treatment for her gambling addiction at a facility in Minnesota for nine months. She filed this action against Defendant casinos, casino owners, and casino employees, on September 20, 2007 for relief in the amount of $20,000,000....

All Defendants have filed motions to dismiss the Amended Complaint for failure to state a claim upon which relief may be granted pursuant to Federal Rule of Civil Procedure 12(b)(6).

....

IV. Discussion

Plaintiff's Amended Complaint purports to plead twelve causes of action, however it raises essentially only three categories of claims: claims sounding in tort (Negligence (Count II), Intentional and Reckless Disregard for Plaintiff's Safety (Count III), Breach of Common Law Duty of Care (Count IV); Strict Liability (Count V), Respondeat Superior (Count VI), Negligent and Intentional Infliction of Emotional Distress (Counts XI and XII)); claims deriving from contract (Breach of the Implied Covenant of Good Faith and Fair Dealing (Count VII) and Unjust Enrichment (Count VIII)); and allegations of statutory and regulatory violations (The Federal Racketeer Influenced and Corrupt Organizations Act (RICO), 18 U.S.C. §§ 1961–1968 (Count I); the Bank Secrecy Act, 31 U.S.C. §§ 5311–32 (Count IX); and, IRS regulations regarding the obligation to report cash transactions in excess of $10,000 (Count X)).

---

2. Plaintiff's disbarment is a matter of public record. *See* In re Taveras, 42 A.D.3d 258 (N.Y. App. Div. 2007). On June 12, 2007, Plaintiff was disbarred without opposition for "engaging in a pattern and practice of converting escrow funds entrusted to her as a fiduciary, knowingly providing altered and falsified records of her attorney escrow account to the Grievance Committee, improperly commingling personal and fiduciary funds, improperly drawing an escrow check to cash, and failing to maintain required records for her IOLA account...." *Id.*

A. Tort Claims

1. Negligence

Most of the allegations in the Amended Complaint amount to variations of a simple negligence claim. Counts II, III, IV, V, VI, and XII all rely on Plaintiff's assertion that Defendants owed a common-law duty to her, which, she alleges, they breached.

For a complaint alleging negligence to survive a motion to dismiss, the Court must find as a matter of law that Defendants owed Plaintiff a duty. GNOC Corp. v. Aboud, 715 F. Supp. 644, 652 (D.N.J. 1989). To determine whether a duty was owed, the Court must apply the substantive law of the State of New Jersey. *Id.* Where, as here, the New Jersey Supreme Court has not squarely addressed the critical issue at bar, the federal court "must be governed by a prediction of how the state's highest court would decide were it confronted with the problem." McKenna v. Ortho Pharmaceutical Corp., 622 F.2d 657, 661 (3d Cir. 1980).

Plaintiff offers a number of different accounts for why Defendants have a duty to identify and exclude compulsive gamblers from their casinos. She first asserts that Defendants owed her "a general duty to exercise reasonable care in the operation of its (sic) casino and gaming activities." She also claims that "Defendants were under a duty to use reasonable care under all attendant circumstances to make the premises safe for invitees...."[3] Plaintiff is correct inasmuch as land-occupiers in Defendants' position "must refrain from conduct that is foreseeably and unreasonably dangerous to [their] invitee[s]." 5 *Harper, James, & Gray on Torts*, § 27.1, at 145 (2008). However, Plaintiff's argument assumes that her continued gambling was an unreasonable danger foreseeable to Defendants.

Plaintiff does not point to any authority in support of this strained understanding of casinos' common-law duties. In fact, the great weight of authority supports Defendants' position that common-law tort principles do not require casinos to rescue compulsive gamblers from themselves. *See, e.g.,* Hakimoglu v. Trump Taj Mahal Assoc., 70 F.3d 291, 293–94 (3d Cir. 1995); Rahmani v. Resorts Int'l Hotel, Inc., 20 F. Supp. 2d 932, 937 (E.D. Va. 1998); Merrill v. Trump Indiana, Inc., slip op., 2002 WL 1307304, *5 (N.D. Ind. May 9, 2002).[4]

The strongest argument against the existence of a casino's duty to restrain compulsive gamblers is the State's deliberate decision not to impose such a duty. "[S]tatutory and administrative controls over casino operations ... are extraordinary[,] pervasive and intensive.... [State law regulates] virtually every facet of casino gambling and its potential impact upon the public. The regulatory scheme is both comprehensive and minutely elaborate." *Knight v. City of Margate*, 86 N.J. 374, 381, 431 A.2d 833 (1981). Yet, in spite of the "extraordinary[,] pervasive and intensive" regulations over "virtually every facet of casino gambling," *id.*, the State's policymakers have notably declined to impose the duty upon which Plaintiff relies here.

In Tose v. Greate Bay Hotel & Casino Inc., 819 F. Supp. 1312, 1319 (D.N.J. 1993) and Hakimoglu v. Trump Taj Mahal Assoc., 876 F. Supp. 625 (D.N.J. 1994) *aff'd* 70 F.3d 291

---

3. Plaintiff's papers correctly note that land-occupiers have a heightened duty of care to their invitees. However, this heightened duty applies only to dangerous *conditions* on the premises, not the potentially hazardous *conduct* of the land-occupier. As to their conduct, businesses have the same duty to act with reasonable prudence toward their invitees as everyone else. *See* 5 *Harper, James, & Gray on Torts*, § 27.1, at 145 (2008). However, even if Plaintiff were entitled to the heightened duty imposed for conditions on the premises, as she suggests, Defendants would satisfy their duty merely by warning casino-patrons of the hazards associated with gambling....

4. One notable and well-reasoned opinion issued by this Court could be read to provide support for Plaintiff's argument. *See* GNOC Corp. v. Aboud, 715 F. Supp. 644, 651–56 (D.N.J. 1989). This view was expressly abrogated by the Third Circuit in *Hakimoglu*, however. 70 F.3d at 293.

(3d Cir. 1995), this Court similarly noted the conspicuous refusal of state law to impose such duties in light of the State's vast regulatory scheme. Again today, the Court declines Plaintiff's invitation to impose a public policy on the State that the State itself has disclaimed.[5]

Plaintiff asks this Court to adopt an extreme position, which departs radically from the New Jersey courts' formulation of the common-law duty of care. Plaintiff requests that the Court innovate a new doctrine akin to dram-shop liability in which casinos would have a duty to identify and exclude gamblers exhibiting compulsive tendencies. In *Hakimoglu*, the Third Circuit declined to expand dram-shop liability to make casinos responsible for the gambling losses of intoxicated patrons. 70 F.3d at 293–94. Here, Plaintiff asks the Court to go even further, imposing upon casinos a duty to stop sober casino patrons who are gambling too much. The Court is unwilling to do so. Plaintiff's theory would, in effect, have no limit. For example, if adopted by this Court, her theory would impose a duty on shopping malls and credit-card companies to identify and exclude compulsive shoppers.[6] This Court will not sacrifice common sense and stretch the common-law duty of care as Plaintiff urges.

In addition to her simple negligence claims, Plaintiff asserts that Defendants are strictly liable for her injuries on a theory that gambling is an "abnormally dangerous activity." ... This argument has no merit. The New Jersey Supreme Court has applied the analysis set out in Restatement (Second) of Torts § 520 in determining whether an activity is so "abnormally dangerous" that it is worthy of strict liability. N.J. Dept. of Environm'l Prot'n v. Ventron Corp., 94 N.J. 473, 491–92, 468 A.2d 150 (1983). Factors to be considered in this analysis include whether the activity's risk can be eliminated with the exercise of reasonable care, whether the activity is a matter of common usage, and whether the activity is inappropriate for its location. *Id.* Needless to say, gambling can indeed be a safe activity, gambling is common, and state-regulated casinos are not inappropriate locations for gambling. Playing blackjack, roulette, or the slots bears no likeness to dumping toxic waste into environmentally sensitive areas, *id.* at 492–93, demolition of buildings in populated areas, Majestic Realty Assoc., Inc. v. Toti Contracting *Co.*, 30 N.J. 425, 153 A.2d 321 (1959), and transportation of highly flammable substances, Biniek v. Exxon Mobil Corp., 358 N.J. Super. 587, 818 A.2d 330 (2002). Strict liability is simply inappropriate.

2. Intentional Infliction of Emotional Distress

Plaintiff's only cause of action sounding in tort that does not require a common-law duty of care is her claim of intentional infliction of emotional distress.... She asserts that it was foreseeable to Defendants that she would become addicted to gambling and that Defendants "intentionally caused [her] severe emotional distress by continuing to entice her into gaming activities." ... This claim, too, is without merit.

"[T]o establish a claim for intentional infliction of emotional distress, the plaintiff must establish intentional and outrageous conduct by the defendant, proximate cause, and distress that is severe." Buckley v. Trenton Saving Fund Soc., 111 N.J. 355, 366, 544 A.2d 857 (1988). The conduct must be either intentional, meaning the defendant must intend to produce emotional distress, or reckless, meaning the defendant must act in deliberate disregard of a high degree of probability that emotional distress will follow. *Id.*

---

5. Notably, while patrons may voluntarily place their names on lists of persons to be excluded from casinos, state law expressly absolves casinos from liability for failure to exclude these self-identified persons from gambling. N.J.S.A. 5:12-71.2(c).

6. "Uncontrolled buying, defined by the presence of repetitive impulsive and excessive buying that leads to personal and familial distress, is a psychiatric disorder...." M. Lejoyeux, et al., *Phenomenology and Psychopathology of Uncontrolled Buying*, 153 Am. J. Psychiatry 1524 (1996).

In a conclusory fashion, the Amended Complaint asserts that Defendant "knew that its acts would cause severe emotional and mental distress if they continued to solicit the plaintiff...." ... Even if this brute assertion were sufficient, Plaintiff cannot establish "extreme and outrageous conduct" by the Defendants.

To establish "extreme and outrageous conduct," Plaintiff must show that the conduct was "so outrageous in character, and so extreme in degree, as to go beyond all possible bounds of decency, and to be regarded as atrocious, and utterly intolerable in a civilized community." *Buckley,* 11 N.J. at 366 (citing Restatement (Second) of Torts, §46 cmt. d (1965)). Since "[t]he severity of the emotional distress raises questions of both law and fact [,] ... the court decides whether as a matter of law such emotional distress can be found, and the jury decides whether it has in fact been proved." *Id.* at 367.

The Court holds that such "outrageous," "extreme," "atrocious," and "utterly intolerable" conduct cannot be found in this case. New Jersey law sets a high bar for establishing extreme and outrageous conduct.... In allowing, even encouraging, Plaintiff to continue gambling, Defendants acted well within the bounds of the community norms reflected in state law. As a matter of law, therefore, Plaintiff's Amended Complaint falls far short of the high bar for claims of intentional infliction of emotional distress.

Each of Plaintiff's claims sounding in tort—Counts II, III, IV, V, VI, XI, and XII of the Amended Complaint—therefore fail to state a claim upon which relief may be granted.

B. Contract Claims

Plaintiff asserts two causes of action based in contract: breach of the implied covenant of good faith and fair dealing (Count VII) and unjust enrichment (Count VIII). Plaintiff asserts in her brief that she had a contract with Defendant-casinos, because she "sign[ed] a form for their various card programs which offers players 'comps' and player incentives based on gaming activity...." ... However, this Court has previously rejected the concept of a gambling contract. *See Hakimoglu,* 876 F. Supp. at 633 n.7.[8] Moreover, signing a form does not necessarily create a contract; and even if it did, Plaintiff does not specify what terms of this alleged contract Defendants breached.

In short, Plaintiff's causes of action for breach of the implied covenant of good faith and fair dealing and for unjust enrichment fail to state a cognizable claim. There is no "generalized duty to act in good faith toward others in social intercourse," Joseph M. Perillo, *Calamari and Perillo on Contracts* 474 (2003), nor has Plaintiff pled an equitable contract substitute, like promissory estoppel or quasi-contract. Similarly, "unjust enrichment" is not a stand-alone claim; it is a doctrine measuring restitution recovery in quasi-contract. Perillo, *supra,* at 622. Even if she had pled a quasi-contract claim, it would not state a legally cognizable claim. Plaintiff clearly received the benefit of her relationship with Defendant casinos: she spent money on the bona fide chance that she might win more money. In short, she gambled. The mere fact that Defendants profited from her misfortune, while lamentable, does not establish a cognizable claim in the law. "[S]it-

---

8. This Court has opined that the gambling relationship may not be contractual, since "[t]he patron does not negotiate the terms of his relationship with the casino, nor can the patron or casino vary the rules of the game, the odds, or the payoffs, as those are established in New Jersey by the Casino Control Commission. In short, in the so-called gambling 'contract' there is no mutuality." *Hakimoglu,* 876 F. Supp. at 633 n. 7. *See also Tose,* 819 F. Supp. at 1316 n.8 ("[B]ecause every aspect of the relationship between the gambler and the casino is minutely regulated by the state and there is little freedom of contract in the usual sense, there seems to be at least significant doubt that the New Jersey Supreme Court would recognize obligations not specifically called for by the statute or regulations.").

uations exist where one's sense of justice would urge that unjust enrichment has occurred, yet no relief is available." *Id.* Although Plaintiff may feel wronged by Defendant-casinos, unjust enrichment and a lack of good-faith are not available to her as avenues for relief.

C. Statutory/Regulatory Claims

1. RICO Act

Plaintiff alleges that Defendants "engaged in a pattern of racketeering activity" in violation of the Racketeer Influenced and Corrupt Organizations Act ("RICO"), 18 U.S.C. §§ 1961–68. . . . She claims that Defendants used advertisements and solicitations, sent by mail to her home and business, to mislead her into thinking that gambling "would result in high returns and rewards.". . . .

To establish a RICO claim, one must plead predicate criminal acts that constitute a threat of continuing racketeering activity. "Where the alleged predicate acts involve mail and wire fraud, the allegations must meet the rigorous pleading requirements of Rule 9(b) of the Federal Rules of Civil Procedure." Bologna v. Allstate Ins. Co., 138 F. Supp. 2d 310, 321 (E.D.N.Y. 2001) (internal citations omitted). "To specify acts of alleged wire and mail fraud with the necessary particularity, the complaint should contain evidence of the content, time, place, and speaker of each alleged mailing or wire transmission. In addition, mail and wire fraud claims must set forth (1) the existence of a scheme to defraud; (2) the defendant's knowledge or intentional participation in the scheme; and (3) the use of interstate mails or wires to further the fraudulent scheme." *Id.*

Plaintiff's Amended Complaint falls far short of this minimum standard. In fact, in the Amended Complaint's 37 paragraphs setting out its RICO claim, Plaintiff fails to identify with particularity (by quoting, for example) even a single falsehood or misleading statement sent through the mail by a particular Defendant. Plaintiff nonetheless argues that her RICO claim should be subject to the fact-finding inquiry of a trial. The requirement that plaintiffs plead the predicate fraudulent acts with particularity, however, exists to protect defendants from defending against spurious charges. Seville Indus. Mach. Corp. v. Southmost Mach. Corp., 742 F.2d 786, 791 (3d Cir. 1984).

Failure to plead fraud with particularity in a RICO claim is a proper basis for dismissal of the claim. Lum v. Bank of America, 361 F.3d 217, 227 (3d Cir. 2004). The Court therefore need not reach the question of whether Plaintiff has adequately pled a racketeering "enterprise" under the statute. The Court dismisses Plaintiff's RICO claim for failure to plead the predicate criminal act of mail fraud with particularity.

2. Other Federal Regulatory Claims

Finally, causes of action IX and X in Plaintiff's Amended Complaint allege that Defendants failed to report certain gaming activities as required by 26 U.S.C. § 60501, 31 C.F.R. § 103 and the Bank Secrecy Act (31 U.S.C. §§ 5311–32). Plaintiff alleges that Defendants' failure to report her high-stakes gambling activity precluded state and federal authorities from interceding to curb her behavior. . . . Setting aside this Court's doubts as to whether Plaintiff has standing to bring such a claim, she has no private right of action under these statutes. *See* James v. Heritage Valley Fed. Credit Union, 197 Fed. Appx. 102, 106 (3d Cir. 2006) (declining to recognize a private right of action in the Bank Secrecy Act); Deleu v. Scaife, 775 F. Supp. 712, 716–17 (S.D.N.Y. 1991) (declining to recognize a private right of action for tax code violations). Plaintiff therefore cannot state a claim upon which relief may be granted under these statutes and regulations.

. . . .

V. Conclusion

For the aforementioned reasons, Defendants' motion to dismiss the Amended Complaint is granted. An appropriate Order will issue this date.

Tose v. Greate Bay Hotel and Casino Inc.
819 F. Supp. 1312 (D.N.J. 1993)

IRENAS, District Judge:

On January 9, 1991, the Sands casino sued Leonard H. Tose to recover alleged gambling debts. Mr. Tose filed a counterclaim seeking to recover gambling losses incurred at the Sands while he was alleged to be obviously and visibly intoxicated.

Presently before the court in this tort action are questions presented by the parties regarding proper instructions for the jury. Specifically, defendants wish to have the jury instructed on the defense of comparative negligence against plaintiff, and on the issue of proximate cause. For the reasons stated below, the court will not charge the jury on either of these issues.

A jury trial on Tose's counterclaim was conducted from February 16, 1993 through March 5, 1993. Before the conclusion of the trial, defendant requested that the jury be charged on the issue of plaintiff's comparative negligence. Defendant argued that plaintiff's becoming voluntarily intoxicated was contributory negligence, and that defendant's liability should thus be reduced to the extent that this negligence contributed to his losses. In addition, defendant requested that the jury receive a proximate cause charge, which would instruct that plaintiff could recover only for those losses which were causally related to the casino's permitting plaintiff to gamble while drunk....

Plaintiff's claim is based on the decision in GNOC v. Aboud, 715 F. Supp. 644 (D.N.J. 1989), where Judge Mitchell H. Cohen predicted that the New Jersey courts would hold that "a casino has a duty to refrain from knowingly permitting an invitee to gamble where that patron is obviously and visibly intoxicated and/or under the influence of a narcotic substance." *Id.* at 655. Although there was no New Jersey state court authority imposing such potential liability on the casinos, Judge Cohen analogized the claim to a dram-shop action and found that imposition of this liability furthers New Jersey's public policy of "protect[ing] ... gambling patrons from the deleterious effects of alcohol imbibement." *Id.* 715 F. Supp. at 654....

In Lee v. Kiku Restaurant, 127 N.J. 170, 182, 603 A.2d 503 (1992), the court stated that once a person is visibly intoxicated he is presumed to have lost the capacity to evaluate the risk of driving while intoxicated, or the risk of being a passenger with an intoxicated driver. 127 N.J. at 184, 187. The server is liable for continuing to serve a patron only after he has reached this incapacitated state. Likewise, *Aboud* imposes liability on casinos for failing to protect clearly intoxicated patrons who have lost the ability to "comprehend[ ] the consequences of continued, protracted gambling." 715 F. Supp. at 655.

However, while the actions of the casino defendants may be analogous to the actions of other dram-shop defendants, the significance of the plaintiffs' actions, particularly before becoming visibly and obviously intoxicated, is quite different. In dram-shop cases, New Jersey has held that an individual plaintiff has a duty not to increase her risk of physical injury, either by becoming voluntarily intoxicated, being unduly careless, or otherwise.

The crucial question in the instant case is whether the State of New Jersey imposes on a gambling casino patron a duty to protect herself from the financial injury which might occur if she gambles while her mental facilities are impaired by alcohol. Certainly the public policy of this state imposes such a duty on a negligent driver or foolhardy pedestrian through the doctrine of comparative negligence. Does the *Aboud* analogy to dramshop liability dictate the same result for a gambler who carelessly becomes intoxicated?

Gambling, like other human activities, can create a risk of harm to one who engages in it. However, the state has a long history of seeking to protect the gambler from her own weakness or foolishness-prior to 1976 by a broad-based ban on gambling activity and thereafter by comprehensive regulation of casino activities.

New Jersey's restrictions on gambling date back to at least 1844, when the State adopted a constitution that made lotteries unlawful. N.J. Const. art. IV, § 7, par. 2 (1844), reprinted in N.J. Stat. Ann. (West 1971). That section of the constitution was amended in 1897 and again in 1939 to encompass additional forms of gambling, including "roulette ... game[s] of chance of any form ... pool-selling, book-making, or gambling of any kind...." *Id.*; ...

In its Constitution of 1947, New Jersey again incorporated a general prohibition on "gambling of any kind," N.J. Const. art. IV, § 7, ¶ 2. Gambling may only be authorized if it is of a type permitted in the constitution, or if it is submitted to and authorized by a majority of the people voting at a general election. Id. The current statutes of New Jersey also provide that "[a]ll wagers, bets or stakes made to depend upon ... any gaming by lot or chance ... shall be unlawful." N.J.S.A. § 2A:40-1.

Courts have viewed the temptation to gamble as extremely powerful. In Lucky Calendar Co., Inc. v. Cohen, 19 N.J. 399, 117 A.2d 487 (1955), the New Jersey Supreme Court referred to "the lure of the chance for 'easy money,'" which "has not changed in the [past] century." *Id.* 19 N.J. at 410. The court also quoted other judicial opinions describing lotteries specifically as "prey[ing] upon the hard earnings of the poor," "plunder[ing] the ignorant and simple," and "arous[ing] the desire to gain something for nothing." *Id.* 19 N.J. at 410, 413 (citations omitted).

New Jersey's restrictions on gambling are thus intended to protect both the individual gambler, and society, from the harms of gambling. *See Lucky Calendar*, 19 N.J. at 410–11 (restrictions prevent "catering to the weakness of those whom the statute seeks to protect, primarily for the benefit of society in general"). New Jersey's policy of protecting those who fall prey to gambling is also evident from N.J.S.A. § 2A:40-5, which provides that a person who loses money or property in an unlawful gambling operation may sue to recover the value of what was lost. *See also* N.J.S.A. § 2C:37-2(c) (providing defense to criminal prosecution for gambling if person was only a "player," i.e. bettor); *but cf. Rucker*, 46 N.J. Super. at 171, 134 A.2d at 413–14 (although in many instances New Jersey legislature has chosen not to punish bettors, some statutes can be construed to encompass player as violator).

In 1976 the citizens of New Jersey voted to create an exception to the general ban on casino gambling. At that time a majority of voters approved an amendment to the state constitution that made lawful the establishment of gambling houses or casinos within Atlantic City. See N.J. Const. art. IV, § 7, ¶ 2(D); ... In response to this constitutional amendment, the legislature passed the Casino Control Act in 1977. *See* N.J.S.A. 5:12-1 to 5:12-190.

As described by New Jersey's Supreme Court, the Casino Control Act's "statutory and administrative controls over casino operations ... are extraordinary pervasive and intensive.... Over 11 statutory articles and almost 200 separate provisions cover virtually every facet of casino gambling and its potential impact upon the public. The regulatory scheme is both comprehensive and minutely elaborate." *Knight*, 86 N.J. at 381. The Legislature recognized that the public had authorized this exception to the general policy against gambling in order to promote the economic welfare of Atlantic City, "and therefore determined casino gambling to be a revocable, highly regulated and conditioned privilege." *Id.*

Given this historical background, it cannot be said that New Jersey has generally placed upon potential gamblers the burden of protecting themselves from gambling losses. Whether through outright prohibitions or minute regulation, New Jersey has throughout its history exercised a high degree of control over gambling by regulating gambling operators, and not by penalizing bettors.

Furthermore, it would make no sense for New Jersey to authorize casino gambling while at the same time imposing a "duty" on a gambler to protect himself from loss. It is clear that gamblers are at a high risk of losing money in a casino — otherwise, the casino could not stay in business. Rules governing the play of casino gambling games are fixed by the Casino Control Commission, and these rules determine the odds which a gambler has of winning, odds which always favor the casino. *Cf., e.g.,* N.J. Admin. Code tit. 19, § 19:47-1.4 (1993) (payout odds for craps); § 19:47-2.7 (payout odds for blackjack); § 19:47-3.3 (payout odds for baccarat-punto banco). Only by choosing not to gamble at all can an individual insure freedom from gambling losses.

Yet even if a sober gambler has no duty to protect herself from loss, does it necessarily follow that one has no duty to avoid increasing the risk of greater losses by becoming intoxicated? Although a gambler can't change the advantage the house has in every game, an individual can minimize the amount of her loss by betting in a manner which gives her the best odds of winning, by placing smaller or fewer bets and, maybe most importantly, by leaving the gaming tables before the losses grow to unacceptable levels. Since drinking will often impair cognitive functioning, an individual who drinks while gambling may be unable to take those actions which are necessary to minimize loss. *Cf. Aboud*, 715 F. Supp. at 655 (noting the risk of "continued, protracted gambling").

The New Jersey legislature has not clearly indicated an intention to impose on a gambler the duty to avoid becoming intoxicated while gambling. Specifically, the legislature has explicitly permitted casinos to serve alcoholic beverages at gaming tables upon request of the patron, see N.J.S.A. 5:12-103(g)(1), and these beverages may be served without cost to a patron and her guests, see N.J.S.A. § 5:12-102(m)(1). Although there is a regulation which forbids a casino to serve alcohol to a visibly and obviously intoxicated patron, there is no regulation which either forbids the casino or the patron from gambling while in this condition. Nor does there appear to be any legislative or regulatory recognition of the self-evident proposition that many people's mental abilities and judgment will be impaired by alcohol consumption before they become visibly and obviously intoxicated.

A gambler, particularly a high roller like the plaintiff[11] is under constant surveillance by a dealer, a floor person, a pit boss, hidden overhead cameras, and sometimes even by officials of the New Jersey Casino Control Commission. Since the regulation that prohibits serving a visibly intoxicated patron is based on the premise that casino employees

---

11. The term "high roller" is used by the casinos to describe patrons who bet large sums. Plaintiff would often bet $10,000 on a single hand of blackjack and would sometimes play five or more hands at the same time. Casinos, for obvious reasons, find high rollers to be desirable customers and make special efforts to attract their patronage. The Casino Control Act permits casinos to offer free food, lodging, transportation and other inducements to potential customers. *See* N.J.S.A. § 5:12-29 (defining "junket" as providing complimentary transportation, food, lodging, and entertainment based on person's propensity to gamble); § 5:12-102 (regulating junkets).

can determine when a patron is visibly and obviously intoxicated, since it is a simple matter for the casino to prevent a patron from gambling while in this condition, and considering the extraordinary degree of regulation and control that the State exercises over casinos, the absence of a regulation barring gambling by a drunk patron cannot be considered an oversight or mistake. At the very least the State condones casino patrons drinking while they place bets, and the policy of providing free drinks on request could arguably be said to actively encourage this conduct.

Aboud was decided at the summary judgment stage and did not specifically consider the issues of comparative negligence and proximate cause which are the subjects of this opinion. Because that court relied on the theory of dram-shop liability in predicting that New Jersey would recognize the theory of liability espoused in this case, it is tempting merely to apply the analogy in all its particulars, including the applicability of comparative negligence as determined in *Lee v. Kiku*. However, a closer analysis suggests at least seven major differences between the two situations:

... (i) While there is clearly an overwhelming state policy against an intoxicated individual driving or engaging in any other activity which risks bodily injury or property damage, New Jersey at the very least condones drinking while gambling.

(ii) With dram-shop liability, and the related doctrine of social-host liability, the defendant's negligent act is serving alcohol. In this case, defendant's negligent "act" seems more like an omission-defendant has failed to prevent plaintiff from engaging in a risky activity, gambling while intoxicated. Framed this way, the issue becomes whether defendant has an affirmative duty to protect a drunken patron, beyond its duty not to continue serving alcohol to the person. *Cf.* Prosser & Keeton § 56 (discussing some exceptions to general common-law rule that person has no legal duty to aid another).

(iii) In the context of a dram-shop case the ability of a server of alcohol to anticipate or prevent harm is somewhat limited. A bartender will often not know whether a patron who leaves the bar is going to drive, and even if she does, she will have very little if any ability to prevent the driving or any subsequent calamity. A casino patron's gambling activity is always totally controlled by casino employees who are in a position to immediately stop the gambling of any patron they know to be drunk.

(iv) In a typical dram-shop case the harm being redressed is physical injury or property damage, and there can be little doubt that New Jersey public policy actively discourages conduct which leads to this kind of harm. In an *Aboud*-type case the harm is loss at the gambling tables, something the state as a general matter anticipates and on which it has based a large and substantial industry. Nobody is encouraged in New Jersey to go out and cause a "reasonable" amount of property damage and personal injury. The same cannot be said about gambling losses.

(v) Although dram-shop liability attaches even where the only harm caused by an inebriate is to himself, there is a substantial risk that bodily injury or other harm will result to innocent third parties, and the respective legal obligations of the server of alcohol and the drinker must be considered in this light. For the most part a drunken gambler is a menace only to herself.

(vi) As noted ... supra, New Jersey's public policy over the years has been to protect gamblers from consequences of their own weakness and folly, either by banning gambling or by minutely regulating those who operate games of chance. Public policy towards those who create the risk of personal injury has been to make them legally responsible for their conduct, a liability generally developed by common law courts rather than by legislation.

(vii) When allocating the respective obligations of the patron and the server in a dram-shop case, we must consider that the profit to the seller of alcohol earned by serving a few drinks too many is relatively small. As the allegations in this case demonstrate, letting a visibly and obviously intoxicated high roller gamble for even a short period of time can yield enormous profits to a casino.

Assuming, as this opinion does, that New Jersey would recognize the *Aboud* cause of action, the court cannot find that New Jersey would apply comparative negligence to a person who drinks, gambles, and loses. The public policies of New Jersey condone, and in certain ways even encourage, drinking, gambling and losing in a licensed casino. Accordingly, the court will not instruct the jury on comparative negligence.

B. Proximate Cause Instruction

At trial, defendants also raised the issue of what, if any, instruction the jury would be given on proximate cause. Such a charge would instruct the jury to make a finding as to whether the casino's act of permitting plaintiff to gamble while visibly and obviously intoxicated was the proximate cause of plaintiff's financial losses.

As described by the courts of New Jersey, a tortfeasor "is generally answerable for an injury that results from his wrongful act in the ordinary course of events.... [U]nless so highly extraordinary that they cannot be considered natural, consequences which follow in unbroken sequence from the original negligent act, without an intervening efficient cause, are natural and proximate...." Lutz v. Westwood Transp. Co., 31 N.J. Super. 285, 289–90, 106 A.2d 329, 331 (App. Div. 1954), *certif. denied*, 16 N.J. 205, 108 A.2d 120 (1954).

An initial consideration in the "proximate cause" determination is whether defendant's conduct was a "cause in fact" of plaintiffs' loss. Plaintiff must show that the particular harmful event at issue would not have occurred but for the defendant's negligence. *Id.* As to the necessary degree of causation, "it is generally sufficient if [defendant's] negligent conduct was a substantial factor in bringing about the injuries." *Rappaport*, 31 N.J. at 203;....

In the instant case, the court finds as a matter of law that, if proven, the defendant casino's negligent conduct was a cause-in-fact of plaintiff's injury. If defendant had not breached its duty—i.e., if plaintiff had been stopped from further gambling once intoxicated—plaintiff would not have incurred any gambling losses at all. As discussed above, the activity of gambling contemplates that the gambler will lose at least some of the time. By permitting someone to gamble, a casino almost invariably will thereby "cause" that person to lose money. It thus follows that defendant's conduct is also a "substantial factor" that caused plaintiff's injuries.

Furthermore, as a matter of policy the court finds that it is impossible to allocate how much of any losses incurred would be specifically attributable to defendant's actions. One cannot make any reasonable calculation of what losses a sober gambler would have incurred compared to a drunken gambler, and it would be senseless to instruct the jury to do so. Maybe the sober gambler would not in fact have gambled for as long a time; maybe she would have placed smaller bets; maybe she would have played the cards differently. There is simply no prototype "normal" or "reasonable" gambler, and the jury should not be permitted to speculate on what losses a sober gambler would have incurred. *Aboud* says a patron who is visibly and obviously intoxicated should not be permitted to gamble at all.

Accordingly, the court holds that any and all losses incurred while the plaintiff was allowed to gamble while drunk will be considered proximately caused by defendant's negligence, as a matter of law. The jury will therefore not be instructed to make a specific finding concerning proximate cause.[17]

Notes

1. The consequences that can result from compulsive gambling are made clear in *Taveras*, i.e., the destruction of a person's professional career. The question raised by the case is whether a duty is owed by a casino to a patron it has reason to know is a problem gambler. One way of dealing with the issue is to hold the casino financially responsible for damages caused by allowing the person to continue to gamble. The court in *Taveras* rejects this as a matter of common law. Would recognizing such a claim provide incentives for people not to take responsibility for their own actions? Does this create a type of "moral hazard" that improperly shifts liability to the casino?

2. The court in *Taveras* stated that if it were to impose a duty on a casino to stop problem gamblers, there would likewise have to be a duty on the part of shopping malls and credit card companies to discover and stop compulsive shoppers. Does this seem like a suitable analogy? Likewise, are analogies to premises liability cases helpful here? Given the interest in reducing activity that has such serious negative consequences throughout society, does it really make sense to view a case where the casino is at least arguably complicit in enabling a compulsive gambler in the same way the court would a slip and fall case in the casino? Are the causes, effects, and implications of the two cases fundamentally different?

3. Are the "enticements" referred to in *Taveras*, things like promotions, free limousine rides, free hotel rooms, food and drinks simply a matter of a casino rewarding its best customers? Or do these tactics have a predatory quality as they relate to the problem gambler? Should there be marketing limitations on casinos? What other measures could be taken to make it more difficult for the compulsive gambler to lose vast sums of money?

4. Among the many claims advanced by Taveras, and rejected by the court, was a claim that she and the casino had a contractual relationship. For a discussion of the problems with such a contract claim, *see* Anthony Cabot & Robert Hannum, *Advantage Play and Commercial Casinos*, 74 Miss. L.J. 681, 720–25 (2005).

5. If gaming regulators are serious about reducing the incidence of problem gambling, wouldn't a fairly obvious measure be to forbid the serving of alcohol in casinos? Since the de-inhibiting qualities of alcohol are well-known, why would regulators permit this? If this seems too extreme, can the lesson of the *Tose* case be that casinos should not be permitted to ply patrons with free alcohol when it is clear they are already intoxicated? Why wouldn't such a common sense measure be instituted?

6. Several other cases have considered claims similar to that in the *Tose* case. While some of the decisions have favorable language for the patron trying to recoup his gambling losses, ultimately they have not been successful. *See, e.g.,* GNOC Corp. v. Aboud, 715 F. Supp. 644 (D.N.J. 1989) (patron did not meet burden of proof that casino knowingly permitted him to continue to gamble when he was visibly intoxicated); Hakimoglu

---

17. [O]ne can view an *Aboud* action as sounding in contract rather than tort. In this light, plaintiff's suit can be considered a rescission action to restore the parties to their respective positions before they began entering gambling contracts while the plaintiff was visibly and obviously intoxicated. This approach yields the same result as the court's holding, which has been analyzed in a tort context....

v. Trump Taj Mahal Associates, 876 F. Supp. 625 (D.N.J. 1994), *aff'd* 70 F.3d 291 (3d Cir. 1995) (patron could not assert dram shop claim as way of recovering his gambling losses). For additional discussion of the possibility of a losing gambler trying to offer such defenses, see Chapter 5 on casino debt collections.

B. Self-Exclusion Programs

Merrill v. Trump Indiana, Inc.

320 F.3d 729 (7th Cir. 2003)

TERENCE T. EVANS, Circuit Judge.

Mark Merrill robbed banks in December 1998 and January 1999 and for that activity he was convicted and is now serving time at a federal prison in Florida. But this is not a criminal case dealing with the robberies: it's a civil suit, under our diversity jurisdiction, alleging that a riverboat casino didn't do what it was supposed to do to prevent Merrill from gambling. His substantial gambling losses fueled a need for money, and although his complaint doesn't come right out and say it, Merrill's present predicament can be traced to his need for cash to cover his gambling tab.

Trump Indiana operates a riverboat casino on the shore of Lake Michigan in Gary, Indiana. We recently noted some of the political machinations that led to the licensing of the casino in the mid-1990s. *See* Mays v. Trump Indiana, Inc., 255 F.3d 351 (7th Cir. 2001). Mr. Merrill, by his own admission, is a compulsive gambler. Like East and West, this is a twain that should never meet. But it did.

According to the third version of Merrill's complaint, which seeks over $6 million in damages, he entered a clinic for compulsive gamblers in Peoria, Illinois, in 1996. The clinic soon became his "guardian/custodian/trustee in all matters pertaining to the recognition and treatment of the symptoms and underlying causes of [his] addictive and compulsive behaviors...." Acting in that capacity, Merrill alleged that his rehab counselor at the clinic contacted the casino in 1996 and formed with it an oral contract to keep Merrill off its premises. The consideration for this contract, it is alleged, was that the clinic would "publicize to the community" the casino's support of programs to help compulsive gamblers get over their addictions. Discovery in the case, particularly a deposition given by the rehab counselor, however, disclosed that no oral contract was created. But it is undisputed that Merrill himself, in 1996, wrote to the casino asking that he be evicted from it if he ever showed up to gamble. And Merrill's name does appear on the casino's "eviction list."

In 1998, Merrill relapsed and returned to gambling at the casino. And now, as we said, he's serving federal time for bank robbery.

Merrill's complaint alleged causes of action for fraud, constructive fraud, strict liability, breach of contract, intentional and reckless disregard for others' safety (willful and wanton misconduct), negligence, and breach of the implied covenant of good faith and fair dealing. The district court dismissed the constructive fraud and strict liability claims on a Rule 12(b)(6) motion and, a year later, granted summary judgment for Trump on all other counts. The court concluded that Trump never promised to honor Merrill's self-exclusion request and so no contract existed between Trump and Merrill. The court further found that, because Trump owed no statutory or contractual duty to Merrill, it did not act negligently or engage in willful and wanton misconduct.

On appeal, Merrill does not contest the district court's finding that he and Trump did not have a contract. He challenges only the grant of summary judgment on his tort claims. Merrill argues that the court erred in holding that Trump had neither violated a duty of care nor engaged in willful and wanton misconduct when it allowed Merrill to gamble in its casino....

In Indiana, the existence of a tort duty is a question of law. Thus, we review *de novo* whether Trump owed a duty to Merrill. We resolve the issues in this case as we believe Indiana courts would resolve them.

A defendant is not liable for negligence unless it owes a duty of care to an injured plaintiff. Merrill argues that Indiana statutory provisions and administrative regulations impose a duty on Trump to exclude gamblers who ask to be placed on the casino's eviction list. The Indiana Gaming Commission is empowered by statute to eject or exclude individuals who "call into question the honesty and integrity of the gambling operations." Ind. Code § 4-33-4-7 (2002). But it is not clear that Merrill's conduct while in the casino put the "honesty and integrity" of Trump's operations in question. Moreover, the statute addresses exclusion by the gaming commission, not the casinos.

Indiana regulations do require casinos to maintain an eviction list, including individuals who request to be excluded, and to prohibit entry to those on the list: "Each riverboat licensee shall maintain a list of evicted persons.... At minimum, the eviction criteria shall include ... [a] person [who] requests that his or her own name be placed on the riverboat licensee's eviction list." Ind. Admin. Code tit. 68, r. 6-2-1 § 1(c)(5) (2002). But this is a recent amendment, implemented in 2000. In 1998, when Merrill's relapse occurred, no statute or regulation explicitly obligated Indiana casinos to honor self-eviction requests.

Even if the amended regulation applied, however, it is by no means certain that the regulation would sustain a cause of action against Trump. Trump is required by regulation to maintain an exclusion log and to add to that list individuals who request to be put on it. But Trump's obligation to follow regulations promulgated by the Indiana Gaming Commission does not automatically translate into a duty of care owed to compulsive gamblers. At most, the rules impose upon Trump a duty to the state through the gaming commission, not to a self-requesting evictee.

If Trump violates regulations, it must answer to the gaming commission — the current rules provide for administrative and disciplinary hearings, as well as sanctions against casinos, including fines and rescindment of licenses. Ind. Admin. Code tit. 68, r. 13-1-1 *et seq.* But neither the regulations nor the statute expressly creates a private cause of action against nonconforming casinos. When a statute is silent regarding the imposition of civil liability, the Indiana Supreme Court looks to legislative intent to determine whether a private cause of action exists. As the district court noted, the statutory provisions and administrative rules surrounding gambling are voluminous, and although the legislature was silent regarding civil liability, it specifically created administrative penalties to be enforced through the gaming commission. Given the extent of gambling regulation in Indiana, we conclude that the Indiana Supreme Court would not conclude that the legislature intended to create a private cause of action....

But Merrill also argues that, even in the absence of a statutory duty, Trump owed him a duty of care under common law. We can find no Indiana case addressing the extent of the duty owed by casinos to their patrons. Indeed, it appears that no court has addressed the specific issue whether casinos can be sued in tort when they fail to evict a gambler who requests his own exclusion.

Courts elsewhere that have addressed the liability of casinos to injured plaintiffs have imposed on casinos no higher duty to their patrons than any on other business. Lundy v. Adamar of N.J., Inc., 34 F.3d 1173, 1180–81 (3d Cir. 1994) (casino had duty to summon aid and take reasonable first aid measures); Marmer v. Queen of New Orleans at the Hilton, J.V., 787 So.2d 1115, 1120 (La. Ct. App. 2001) (casino has duty to protect patrons from foreseeable criminal acts); Saucier v. Players Lake Charles, 751 So.2d 312, 319 (La. Ct. App. 1999) (casino has duty to take reasonable care of patrons' safety); Joynt v. Cal. Hotel & Casino, 108 Nev. 539, 835 P.2d 799, 801 (1992) (casino has duty to maintain reasonably safe premises). Under Indiana law, a business owes its invitees a duty to take reasonable care for their safety. Ellis v. Luxbury Hotels, Inc., 716 N.E.2d 359, 360 (Ind. 1999). Merrill never alleged in district court that Trump had not taken reasonable care for his safety or that he ever felt unsafe on the premises.

The closest analogy to Merrill's situation is that of a tavern's liability to exercise reasonable care to protect its patrons. In Indiana, a tavern proprietor serving alcohol can be held liable, under certain conditions, if an intoxicated patron injures another patron or a third party. But a patron who drives while intoxicated, causing his own injuries, cannot recover from the tavern that served him alcohol. Essentially, Merrill thinks that the casino should be held responsible for the destructive effects of his 1998 relapse into gambling. But Indiana law does not protect a drunk driver from the effects of his own conduct, and we assume that the Indiana Supreme Court would take a similar approach with compulsive gamblers.

Merrill's last argument is that the court erred in granting Trump summary judgment on his willful and wanton misconduct claim. In Indiana, a defendant engages in willful and wanton misconduct when it consciously acts or refuses to act knowing, or with reckless disregard to the probability, that injury will result to the plaintiff from its conduct or from its failure to take steps to avoid an impending danger. The defendant must know that injury is probable or likely, as opposed to possible. Under this standard, we cannot conclude that the district court erred in concluding that Merrill raised no issue of material fact that could lead a jury to find that Trump engaged in willful and wanton misconduct. For these reasons, the judgment of the district court is AFFIRMED.

Notes

1. All states that offer casino style gaming have some form of self-exclusion program. In many states, this is administered by the state. The gambler would follow the process prescribed by state law for providing identification and petitioning for exclusion. There is considerable variation in the terms of self-exclusion programs, involving such matters as the length of time the exclusion is effective, to measures that protect the privacy of the gambler. One example is from New Jersey's administrative code:

19:48-2.2 Request for self-exclusion

(a) Any person may have his or her name placed on the self-exclusion list by submitting a request for self-exclusion in the form and manner required by this section.

(b) Any person requesting placement on the self-exclusion list shall submit, in person, a completed request for self-exclusion as required in (c) below. The request shall be delivered to either the Employee License Information Unit of the Commission located at the Arcade Building, Tennessee Avenue and the Boardwalk, in Atlantic City, or to the Trenton office of the Division of Gaming Enforcement located at 140 East Front Street. The Commission may designate other locations for submission of completed requests for self-exclusion in accordance with these rules, which locations may be designated on a temporary basis. Any person submitting a self-exclusion request shall be required to present valid identification credentials containing his or her signature and either a photograph or a general physical description. Any person requesting self-exclusion pursuant to this subchapter shall be required to have his or her photograph taken by the Commission or Division upon submission of the request.

(c) A request for self-exclusion shall be in a form prescribed by the Commission, which form shall include:

1. The following identifying information concerning the person submitting the request for self-exclusion:

i. Name, including any aliases or nicknames;

ii. Date of birth;

iii. Address of current residence;

iv. Telephone number of current residence;

v. Social security number, which information is voluntarily provided in accordance with section 7 of the Privacy Act, 5 U.S.C. § 552a; and

vi. A physical description of the person, including height, weight, gender, hair color, eye color and any other physical characteristic that may assist in the identification of the person;

2. The length of minimum self-exclusion requested by the person:

i. One year;

ii. Five years; or

iii. Lifetime;

3. A waiver and release which shall release and forever discharge the State of New Jersey, the Commission and its employees, the Division and its employees and agents, and all casino licensees and their employees and agents from any liability to the person requesting self-exclusion and his or her heirs, administrators, executors and assigns for any harm, monetary or otherwise, which may arise out of or by reason of any act or omission relating to the request for self-exclusion or request for removal from the self-exclusion list, including:

i. Its processing or enforcement;

ii. The failure of a casino licensee to withhold gaming privileges from, or restore gaming privileges to, a self-excluded person;

iii. Permitting a self-excluded person to engage in gaming activity in a licensed casino or simulcasting facility while on the list of self-excluded persons; and

iv. Disclosure of the information contained in the self-exclusion request or list, except for a willfully unlawful disclosure of such information;

4. The signature of the person submitting the request for self-exclusion indicating acknowledgment of the following statement:

"I am voluntarily requesting exclusion from all gaming activities at all New Jersey licensed casinos and simulcasting facilities because I am a problem gambler. I certify that the information that I have provided above is true and accurate, and that I have read and understand and agree to the waiver and release included with this request for self-exclusion. I am aware that my signature below authorizes the Casino Control Commission to direct all New Jersey casino licensees to restrict my gaming activities in accordance with this request and, unless I have requested to be excluded for life, until such time as the Commission removes my name from the self-exclusion list in response to my written request to terminate my voluntary self-exclusion. I am aware and agree that during any period of self-exclusion, I shall not collect any winnings or recover any losses resulting from any gaming activity at all licensed casinos and simulcasting facilities, and that any money or thing of value obtained by me from, or owed to me by, a casino licensee as a result of wagers made by me while on the self-exclusion list shall be subject to forfeiture.";

5. The type of identification credentials examined containing the signature of the person requesting self-exclusion, and whether said credentials included a photograph or general physical description of the person; and

6. The signature of a Commission or Division employee authorized to accept such request, indicating that the signature of the person on the request for self-exclusion appears to agree with that contained on his or her identification credentials and that any photograph or physical description of the person appears to agree with his or her actual appearance.

2. In a few states, most notably Nevada, the self-exclusion program is administered by the casino. One justification for this is that slot machines are ubiquitous in Nevada— they are found in gas stations, supermarkets, and convenience stores. It is argued that an across-the-board exclusion program would not be practicable. Nevada gaming regulations do not require casinos to operate self-exclusion measures. The regulations do require procedures that "[e]ach licensee that engages in the issuance of credit, check cashing, or the direct mail marketing of gaming opportunities, shall implement a program ... that allows patrons to self-limit their access to the issuance of credit, check cashing, or direct mail marketing by that licensee."

Nevada Gaming Commission Reg. § 5.170 (2010).

Casinos can offer programs that allow for self-exclusion. One large casino company, Harrah's, markets its "Commitment to Responsible Gaming," which includes self-exclusion. *See* http://www.harrahs.com/harrahs-corporate/about-us-responsible-gaming.html for the details of this program.

3. What happens if a patron who has put himself, one way or another, on the self-exclusion list, disregards the self-banishment and gambles at a casino? Depending on the state, the person can be removed from the premises, charged with trespass, and forfeit winnings. If winnings have to be forfeited, should losses be replenished?

4. As part of a state-administered program, regulations will provide for the internal controls casinos must establish for implementation. In addition to refraining from sending marketing materials to those on the list, the casino typically has to train its personnel to identify these people. One question raised in *Merrill* is whether, apart from administrative sanctions that might be imposed, a gambler has a cause of action against a casino which allegedly does not follow these state regulatory procedures. *Merrill* represents the approach courts have taken so far, namely, that no such cause of action exists. *See, e.g.,* Nelson v. MGM Grand Hotel, LLC, 287 Fed. Appx. 587 (9th Cir. 2008); Fleeger v. Bell, 23 Fed. Appx. 741 (9th Cir. 2001); Williams v. Aztar Ind. Gaming Corp., 2003 WL 1903369 (S.D. Ind. Apr. 5, 2003). In New Jersey, the casino's freedom from liability in this setting is now statutory:

c. A licensed casino or simulcasting facility or employee thereof shall not be liable to any self-excluded person or to any other party in any judicial proceeding for any harm, monetary or otherwise, which may arise as a result of:

(1) the failure of a licensed casino or simulcasting facility to withhold gaming privileges from, or restore gaming privileges to, a self-excluded person; or

(2) otherwise permitting a self-excluded person to engage in gaming activity in such licensed casino or simulcasting facility while on the list of self-excluded persons.

N.J. Stat. Ann. § 5: 12-71.2 (West 1996 & Supp. 2010). Is it good public policy to immunize casinos from civil liability when they violate the spirit and letter of a self-exclusion process? In light of this immunity, what incentive does a casino have to be scrupulous in its enforcement of a patron's self-exclusion?

5. For a discussion of the issues of self-exclusion, *see* William N. Thompson, Robert Stocker, II, & Peter J. Kulick, *Remedying the Lose-Lose Game of Compulsive Gambling: Voluntary Exclusions, Mandatory Exclusions, or an Alternative Method?*, 40 J. Marshall L. Rev. 1221 (2007) (in addition to surveying the treatment given to these issues in the United States, the article examines how foreign countries deal with compulsive gambling); Andy Rhea, *Voluntary Self Exclusion Lists: How They Work and Potential Problems*, 9 Gaming L. Rev. 462 (2005) (describes duties taken on by gambler and casino when gambler is on self-exclusion list); Irina Slavina, *Don't Bet on It: Casinos' Contractual Duty to Stop Compulsive Gamblers from Gambling*, 85 Chi.-Kent L. Rev. 369 (2010) (analyzes cases where gamblers seek damages from casinos when self-exclusion list is not enforced).

Chapter 7

Casino Crimes and Advantage Play

1. Casino Crimes Generally

Casino crimes generally fall into one of three broad categories. The first category is skimming and cheating by owners. Skimming is the taking of money from the casino's proceeds before it is counted for tax purposes. It is called tax evasion in other industries. Governments often tax casinos based on gross revenues, i.e., the difference between all amounts received as winnings less all amounts paid out as losses. Dishonest owners can avoid paying "gross revenue" taxes (and income tax), if they can remove winnings before they are counted. Skimming also can be used as a method to hide an unlicensed person's involvement in a casino operation. Owners have also been known to cheat their customers. Owners may steal from patrons by rigging the games to ensure that the patron loses.

The second category of gaming crimes is employee theft. Unscrupulous employees may steal from both their employers and casino patrons. In most thefts the casino is the victim, but the government also suffers. Cheating takes profits from the bottom line and deprives the government of taxes. Ways that employees can steal from a casino are nearly endless. A simple theft may involve a count room employee taking some money from a drop box. Other thefts are elaborate. One race and sports book kept unclaimed winning tickets in a locked box. An employee, who had access to the box, reviewed the tickets and found those with large payouts. He then had a friend pose as a tourist claiming to have "lost" his portion of the winning ticket. The book verified the ticket in the unclaimed ticket box, and paid the "tourist." There are literally hundreds of other schemes by which employees can steal from a casino. Employees also can steal from casino patrons. For example, an employee can palm a chip from the patron's stack and hide it on his person until the end of his shift.

The third category of casino crimes is theft by third parties against a casino or its patrons. Again, these thefts can range from simple to extremely complex. Many cheating crimes involve the player attempting to gain an advantage over the casino—such as switching out a poorer card in the player's blackjack hand for a better card. All advantage play, however, is not cheating.

For excellent references on cheating and advantage play, *see* DUSTIN MARKS, CHEATING AT BLACKJACK AND ADVANTAGE PLAY 101 (1994); BILL ZENDER, HOW TO DETECT CASINO CHEATING AT BLACKJACK (1999).

2. Crimes by Owners

A. Skimming

United States v. DeLuna
763 F.2d 897 (8th Cir. 1985)

McMILLIAN, Circuit Judge.

Carl Wesley Thomas, Carl Angelo DeLuna, Carl James Civella, Charles David Moretina, and Anthony Chiavola, Sr., appeal from a final judgment entered in the District Court for the Western District of Missouri upon a jury verdict finding them guilty of knowingly transporting stolen money in interstate commerce, travelling in and utilizing the facilities of interstate commerce with the intention of establishing and managing an unlawful interest in a Nevada gaming establishment, and conspiring with others to accomplish these ends in violation of 18 U.S.C. §§ 2, 371, 1952, 2314 (1982). For reversal appellants argue that the district court erred in (1) refusing to grant their motions for judgment of acquittal (Travel Act violations),

...

For the reasons discussed below, we affirm the judgments of the district court.

On November 5, 1981, eleven defendants were charged in a seventeen-count indictment with conspiracy and substantive offenses in violation of 18 U.S.C. §§ 2, 371, 1952, 2314. Charges against six of the eleven defendants were dismissed or disposed of in proceedings separate from the trial where the five appellants in this case were convicted. Defendant Nick Civella died before trial. Defendants Donald Joe Shepard, Billy Clinton Caldwell and Joseph Vincent Agosto entered guilty pleas before trial. (Agosto, now deceased, was the government's principal witness against the other defendants.)

...

During the period covered by the indictment (January 1, 1975, to April 1, 1979), the state of Nevada required that persons conducting gaming operations be licensed in accordance with state law and regulations. Any person who owned, managed, or operated a gambling casino, or received directly or indirectly a share of the moneys played therein, had to make his identity known to Nevada gaming authorities and had to be licensed. Key employees, that is, persons who had significant influence over casino management, were required to be licensed. Certain employees, including managers, were required to obtain work permits. Persons who had been convicted of felonies, had poor reputations, or were excluded by law from casinos, and others known to associate with such persons were not likely to be licensed. Donald Shepard and Billy Caldwell were licensed with respect to the Tropicana casino in Las Vegas. Carl Thomas was licensed with respect to his own casinos, Bingo Palace and Slots-of-Fun. None of the other defendants charged in the indictment was licensed or had been issued a work permit.

The government charged and sought to prove that the defendants conspired to gain control over the casino operations at the Tropicana Hotel and Country Club in Las Vegas, Nevada, in order to "skim" money from the casino by removing cash before it was counted or reported and to transport this skimmed money in interstate commerce. The evidence consisted primarily of the testimony of co-conspirator Joseph Agosto, tape recordings, notes made by DeLuna and other defendants, surveillance testimony by FBI agents, testimony of Tropicana officials, and stipulations. The events described below are based primarily on Agosto's testimony.

Agosto met with Carl DeLuna and Nick and Carl Civella in January 1975 to discuss means by which Agosto could infiltrate and obtain control of the Tropicana so that Agosto could eventually skim money from the casino. DeLuna and the Civellas told Agosto that they would see to it that a Teamsters loan to Tropicana's part-owner Deil Gustafson would be disapproved in order to facilitate Agosto's takeover. The Tropicana at the time was in serious financial trouble. Agosto purchased the Folies Bergere, the successful floor show at the Tropicana, and used this as a base to acquire influence over casino operations.

Agosto, a convicted felon, knew he could never be licensed by the Nevada gaming authorities. The Civellas were in the "Black Book" of persons excluded from Nevada casinos and therefore knew that they could not be licensed. Because Agosto and the Civellas could not be licensed, they agreed to use code names to "camouflage" their true identities and connections with the Tropicana.

Nick Civella instructed Agosto to keep DeLuna informed of his progress in infiltrating the casino. Agosto began to acquire great influence over the daily operations of the hotel and casino. Agosto reported this to DeLuna, who in turn informed the Civellas. Agosto frequently travelled from Las Vegas to Kansas City to meet with DeLuna, Moretina and the Civellas, who occasionally travelled to Las Vegas to discuss Agosto's progress.

At Agosto's request in 1975, Nick Civella was able to rid the Tropicana of competing "hidden" interests. Agosto, DeLuna, and the Civellas then decided to use Carl Thomas to take charge of the skimming at the Tropicana.

Later in 1975, Mitzi Briggs became part-owner of the Tropicana and Agosto's infiltration and exercise of authority ceased temporarily because of Briggs' distrust of Agosto. By 1977, however, Agosto was able to gain Briggs' confidence and by 1978, Agosto was effectively running the hotel and casino. Briggs never knew that any skimming was taking place.

Upon Carl Thomas' recommendation, Agosto hired Shepard as casino manager. Later Agosto hired Caldwell as assistant casino manager. Shepard and Caldwell were to do the actual skimming under Thomas' supervision.

In March 1978, Agosto and Thomas met or spoke with Nick Civella in Los Angeles and Civella ordered them to start skimming. In April 1978, $11,500 was skimmed by Shepard and transported to Kansas City by DeLuna.

In May 1978, Shepard hired Jay Gould as cashier to skim cash from the cashier's cage of the casino and to falsify fill slips to document the "loss" of cash. Signatures and initials of other casino employees were forged by Caldwell. Caldwell supervised Gould, who passed the skimmed money to Shepard. This money was skimmed before the casino owner or the Nevada gaming authorities knew of its existence.

From June through October 1978, Shepard, Caldwell and Gould skimmed over $40,000 a month and gave it to Agosto. Agosto then gave it to Carl Caruso, who transported the money to Kansas City and delivered it to Moretina. Caruso made at least eighteen trips between Las Vegas and Kansas City. Moretina gave Caruso $1,000 after each delivery. The remaining money was distributed to Joseph Aiuppa and Jack Cerone in Chicago. Anthony Chiavola, Sr., the nephew of the Civellas and a Chicago police officer, aided DeLuna and Nick Civella in the distribution of Aiuppa's and Cerone's shares. Moretina acted as DeLuna assistant in dealing with Agosto and in receiving the skimmed money from Caruso.

By late September 1978, Agosto and the Civellas were concerned that Shepard or his subordinates might be doing "unauthorized" skimming on their own, thereby reducing their profits. At Agosto's suggestion, a "moratorium" on skimming was ordered by Nick Civella in the months of November and December 1978, so that Carl Thomas could do a study of the Tropicana to determine if unauthorized skimming was occurring. In these same months, Agosto sent $50,000 and $60,000 of his own money to the Civellas because they still demanded money. Agosto was later reimbursed for $30,000 of this amount by Shepard with skimmed Tropicana money.

On November 26, 1978, Agosto and Thomas flew to Kansas City to meet with the Civellas and DeLuna to discuss lifting the moratorium and more efficient ways of skimming. Skimming resumed in January 1979 and $80,000 in skimmed money was transported to Kansas City on February 14, 1979. Several defendants' homes were searched on that date by FBI agents pursuant to search warrants. The FBI seized $80,000 from Caruso. Notes (referred to during the trial as a "dairy") and other items were seized from DeLuna and Tamburello.

From approximately June 1978 until March 1979, many telephones and meeting places of the defendants were subject to court-authorized electronic surveillance. Immediately following the searches, Agosto, the other defendants, Aiuppa, and Cerone engaged in a series of meetings and telephone conversations to assess the damage done by the searches. Evidence about these meetings and telephone conversations obtained by electronic and visual surveillance and from government witness Agosto was introduced at the trial.

Travel Act Violations

Appellants argue that the district court erred in refusing to grant their motions for judgment of acquittal on the ground that the government failed to prove an essential element of the conspiracy charged in count one of the indictment and of the substantive Travel Act violations, 18 U.S.C. § 1952. Appellants argue that the government failed to prove any criminal violations of Nevada gaming law. We disagree.

Count one of the indictment charged appellants and others with conspiring in violation of 18 U.S.C. § 371 from about January 1, 1975, to about April 1, 1979, to travel in interstate commerce and to use facilities in interstate commerce with the intent to promote, manage, establish, carry on and facilitate the promotion, management, establishment and carrying on of an unlawful activity, namely: the management, operation, conducting, maintaining and carrying on of gaming operations of a licensed gaming establishment in Las Vegas, Nevada, that is, the Tropicana Hotel and Country Club, and the indirect receipt of moneys played therein, by persons who were not licensed or found suitable for licensing by, and whose interests in said gaming establishment had been concealed from, agencies of the State of Nevada, in violation of the Nevada Gaming Control Act, including Sections 463.130, 463.160, 463.165, 463.170, 463.200, 463.335, 463.339, 463.360 and 463.530 of the Nevada Revised Statutes, and regulations of the Nevada Gaming Commission promulgated thereunder, including Regulations 3.080, 3.100, 3.110, 8.010 and 15.1594-6, and to thereafter perform and attempt to perform acts to promote, manage, establish, carry on and facilitate the promotion, management, establishment, and carrying on of said unlawful activity in violation of Title 18, United States Code, Section 1952.

The indictment also alleged appellants and others conspired to "transport in interstate commerce moneys having a value in excess of $5,000, knowing the same to have been stolen, converted, and taken by fraud, in violation of Title 18, United States Code, Section 2314."

Appellants argue that the government proved only that an unlicensed show producer had assumed de facto control of some operations of the Tropicana Hotel through which he ultimately brought employees into the hotel to steal casino revenues. Appellants argue that theft is a crime in Nevada but not under the Nevada gaming laws. Appellants also argue that the operation or control of a gambling game without a license is not a criminal offense under Nevada law and that such conduct in violation of Nevada gaming regulations only cannot support a Travel Act violation.

Similar arguments involving the Nevada gaming laws and federal prosecution for violations of the Travel Act were rejected by the Sixth Circuit in a comprehensive opinion in United States v. Goldfarb, 643 F.2d 422, 426–32 (6th Cir.), *cert. denied*, 454 U.S. 827 (1981). The Travel Act, 18 U.S.C. § 1952, prohibits travel in interstate commerce or the use of facilities of interstate commerce to "promote, manage, establish, carry on, or facilitate the promotion, management, establishment, or carrying on, of any unlawful activity," which is further defined as "any business enterprise involving gambling ... in violation of the laws of the State in which they are committed." "[I]t is the violation of federal law which is the gravamen of a Travel Act offense." United States v. Goldfarb, 643 F.2d at 426 (citations omitted). As noted in [that case] which involved conduct similar to that alleged in the present case, "[i]t is abundantly clear that as a predicate to a Travel Act conviction, absent a distinct violation of a law of the United States, the defendants must have engaged in some form of unlawful activity prohibited by the law of the State of Nevada."

We agree with the Sixth Circuit that "a violation of a Nevada Gaming Commission regulation could [not in and of itself] form the predicate state law violation required for a federal prosecution under the Travel Act." *Id.* at 429; *cf.* United States v. Gordon, 464 F.2d 357 (9th Cir. 1972) (violation of nonpenal regulations of state gaming commission insufficient for engaging in "illegal gambling business" in violation of 18 U.S.C. § 1855). However, according to the government's indictment and the district court's instructions, the unlawful activity under the Travel Act in the present case was not based upon violation of state regulations alone but also upon violation of the related Nevada *statutes*. *See* United States v. Goldfarb, 643 F.2d at 430.

Appellants also argue that the unlawful activity with which they are accused is not a crime under Nevada state law. The government argues that appellants violated Nevada state law by conducting gambling operations without the necessary licenses, Nev. Rev. Stat. § 463.160(1)(a), and by indirectly receiving gambling moneys without the necessary licenses, *id.* § 463.160(1)(c). Although there is no specific penalty for violation of these provisions, the "catch-all" section, *id.* § 463.360, which makes such a violation a gross misdemeanor, and thus a crime, would apply....

Notes

1. Skimming can occur in many ways. The most obvious is the taking of cash from the drop boxes of the table or gaming devices, or from the hopper of gaming devices, before it is counted. Some governments have on-line monitoring systems for gaming devices that count the money as the patrons play, and base the taxes on the number of coins played, less the number of coins paid out and the hand-paid jackpots. This avoids basing gross revenue on the owner's count of the coins. Other jurisdictions do not trust the owner to conduct the hard count or even open a gaming device without a government inspector present to observe. For other cases discussing the issue of skimming, *see* United States v. Manarite, 44 F.3d 1407 (9th Cir. 1995); State v. Erickson, 534 N.W.2d 804 (N.D. 1995).

2. Policing the count of cash from tables is more difficult. Unlike gaming devices, tables do not have meters that count the number of dollars placed in the drop box. Unscrupulous operators may not put all money collected into the drop box. The use of credit also makes it more difficult to properly track gross revenues. A common "skim" method of the 1950s was to allow patrons to play on "rim" credit. Here, the patron would ask for credit and receive chips. The credit would be registered only by a button or marker placed by the dealer on the edge of the table without any written documentation. After the patron accumulated a large debt, the owner could ask the patron to come to his office, where the debt would be settled in cash for less than the face value of the rim credit. The owner would return to the table and remove the marker. The skim was completed with no paper trail whatsoever. Most regulatory authorities either prohibit rim credit or attempt to control it by imposing internal controls that the casino must follow when granting rim credit.

3. Another method of skimming is to exaggerate losses. This is simpler in jurisdictions that allow credit. Suppose an owner grants credit to a co-conspirator in the amount of $100,000, which the co-conspirator takes in chips. Rather than gambling, the co-conspirator exchanges the chips for cash, and gives the cash to the owner. At the end of the day, the casino has paid out $100,000 in cash, and holds a check for $100,000. If the casino never collects the check, it never receives cash in the win column, but has recorded a $100,000 loss.

B. Cheating by Owners

NRS 465.083 Cheating. It is unlawful for any person, whether the person is an owner or employee of or a player in an establishment, to cheat at any gambling game.

NRS 465.015 Definitions. As used in this chapter:

1. "Cheat" means to alter the elements of chance, method of selection or criteria which determine:

(a) The result of a game;

(b) The amount or frequency of payment in a game;

(c) The value of a wagering instrument; or

(d) The value of a wagering credit.

2. The words and terms defined in chapter 463 of NRS have the meanings ascribed to them in that chapter.

Nevada Tax Commission v. Mackie
333 P.2d 985 (Nev. 1959)

MERRILL, Chief Justice.

This matter is before this court on review of action taken by the Nevada tax commission. The commission revoked the gambling licenses theretofore issued by the state to respondents as partners in the operation of a gambling enterprise. Judgment of the court below, on review, modified that order and the commission has appealed from that judgment.

The principal question involved is whether the district court on review has authority to modify the commission's order by substituting a limited suspension of license for the outright revocation ordered by the commission.

On May 22, 1958 the respondents were cited to appear before the Nevada gambling control board and show cause why their license should not be revoked upon the grounds that they were operating a cheating game and conducting their business in an unsuitable manner. Hearing was had before the control board on June 10, 12, 16 and 17, 1958. On July 23, 1958 the board formally recommended to the commission the revocation of respondents' licenses. Hearing before the commission on this recommendation was had that day and on July 26, 1958 the commission entered its order of revocation supported by its findings of fact and conclusions of law.

On July 28, 1958 respondents filed a petition for review with the court below. Hearing before the district court was had on this petition on August 8 and 9, 1958, and on the latter date judgment was rendered modifying the revocation order in three respects: substituting a 60-day suspension for revocation of the license as to twenty-one games, substituting a 30-day suspension for revocation of the license as to crap games, reversing the revocation as to slot machines.

The appeal of the commission is taken from this judgment. The commission contends that the reviewing court is without authority to modify the commission's order in this manner. We have concluded that the position of the commission has merit and that the judgment below must be reversed.

NRS 463.140, dealing with the powers and duties of the tax commission, provides in part, "The Nevada tax commission shall have full and absolute power and authority * * * to limit, restrict, revoke or suspend any license for any cause deemed reasonable by the commission." The same language is to be found in NRS 463.310(4) dealing with suspension or revocation of licenses.

In Nevada Tax Commission v. Hicks, 310 P 2d.852, this court carefully delineated the area within which the courts may act in judicial review of commission action. From that opinion it follows that it is not the province of the courts to decide what shall be reasonable cause for revocation of license; that such determination is an administrative one to be made by the commission in the exercise of its judgment based upon its specialized experience and knowledge. Whether reasonable cause for revocation, as the commission may have defined it, exists in the particular case, is the question which the courts may review.

The commission has determined that the operation of a cheating game is a reasonable cause for revocation of license. That determination is not subject to judicial review in the absence of a showing that the determination was arbitrary or capricious or for some other reason was beyond the administrative authority of the commission. Nevada Tax Commission v. Hicks, *supra*.

The court below made no express determination upon the question whether the record supported the finding of the commission that a cheating game had been operated by the respondents. However, since its judgment provided for suspension of license as to two games, such a determination appears by necessary implication.

Such being the case, the modification of the commission's order in this case amounted to administrative rather than judicial action and was beyond the authority of a reviewing court.

Respondents contend that court authority to modify a commission order is expressly granted by statute. NRS 463.310(6) provides, "Any such limitation, revocation or suspension so made shall be and remain effective until reversed or modified by a court of competent jurisdiction upon review."

Reading this language in the context of the remainder of the section, the provision for reversal or modification by a court of competent jurisdiction must be held to apply to such reversal or modification as may be exercised by the court in a judicial capacity. It cannot reasonably be held to confer administrative powers upon the court.

Upon the appeal of the tax commission, the judgment must be reversed.

Respondents have taken a cross-appeal from the judgment of the court below, contending that there is no substantial evidence to support a determination that they had operated a cheating game.

There was direct and positive testimony by eye witnesses that they had observed cheating in the twenty-one games operated by respondents. The witnesses qualified themselves as persons of knowledge and experience in matters of gambling and in methods of cheating at cards. This testimony, if credible, constituted substantial evidence in support of the commission's findings. The problem, then, is not one of substance but one of credibility.

Respondents contend that this testimony was rendered incredible by cross examination. They point to many instances of inconsistencies and improbabilities. There is no need to detail these matters. Upon the precise points involved they may well have affected the weight of the testimony. They cannot, however, be said to have destroyed the probative value of the evidence of cheating or to have rendered it incredible as a matter of law. These matters, then, posed questions of weight and credibility which it was the function of the control board and the tax commission to resolve in their capacities as finders of the facts. It can hardly be questioned that their specialized knowledge and experience are of peculiar value in the performance of these functions upon factual issues such as are here involved.

Their decision to believe the testimony that cheating was observed is a determination with which we shall not interfere upon review.

[The court considered the cross-appeal of the Respondents and concluded they were without merit.]

Reversed and remanded with instructions that the order of revocation of license issued by the Nevada tax commission be reinstated and affirmed.

Notes

1. Without proper regulation, casino operators can cheat patrons. Some casinos were known as "bust out" houses or "clip joints" because their sole purpose was to dishonestly separate the player from his money. Gaming devices are the easiest for the casino operator to modify (or gaff). In more modern machines, this is as simple as altering the software to decrease the chances of winning. In older machines, the casino operator could weigh or alter the gears in the machine to guarantee that certain winning combinations never appeared. A fascinating description of how unregulated casinos in the 1940s rigged the games to cheat customers is found in WARREN NELSON, ALWAYS BET ON THE BUTCHER 168–69 (University of Nevada Oral History Project 1994).

2. Sixty years ago, the most common buyers of loaded dice were the illegal casinos operating from Steubenville, Ohio, to Galveston, Texas. The 1.414% house advantage provided by the game of craps did not provide enough money to bribe the sheriff, the judge, and the politicians and still make a reasonably high profit and some illegal casinos resorted to using loaded dice. But, these casinos faced a dilemma. They wanted to use loaded dice, but they did not want players to do the same. So they demanded the exacting standards of the dice maker to protect them from the cheats. These included distinct logos, serial numbers, and sealed containers. The illegal operators convinced unscrupu-

lous dice makers to make almost identical sets of dice with the same serial numbers. The major difference, however, was that the second set was loaded to cheat the gamblers. The loaded dice would see the felts at the appropriate times and "cool" a table. Besides "loaded" dice, casinos can use other types of altered dice to cheat the patron. *See generally,* An-thony Cabot, Casino Gaming: Policy, Economics and Regulation 480 (1996).

3. A casino operator also can cheat at blackjack. A simple method is to remove some high cards from a multi-deck shoe. This improves the casino's theoretical advantage over the patrons. Another method is for the dealer to peek at the top card of the deck or to use a marked or blistered deck to learn if that card would cause him or a patron to "bust." If it would, the dealer would deal "seconds," a technique where it appears that the dealer is dealing the top card, but actually is dealing another card of his choice. By this method, the dealer can decide when he wants to avoid "busting" or when to cause the patron to "bust." Many other ways exist for operators to increase the house advantage to their own favor. Dealers can stack the deck in favor of the house by picking up discards in a particular order and engaging in a non-random shuffle. Dealers also can switch their hole card by slight-of-hand to achieve a better hand. All these maneuvers significantly increase the house advantage.

4. Roulette tables can be gaffed with magnets that cause a steel-core ball to fall in one of four segments of the wheel. By looking at the various bets on the table, the operator can choose that segment of the wheel that has the lowest potential for the player to win.

5. Dealers or gaming devices also can short players on winning hands or plays. For example, instead of paying 100 coins on a slot jackpot, a machine could be set to pay 98 coins. Similarly, a dealer at a table can rearrange the player's bet on a table by removing a chip during the process of paying him, causing the original bet and the payoff to be decreased.

6. Few reported cases involve the casino or casino employees cheating the player. A notable exception was Kelly v. First Astri Corporation, 72 Cal. App. 4th 462, 84 Cal. Rptr.2d 810 (1999), where a player was denied the right to sue casino employees that rigged a blackjack games with marked cards to the detriment of some players. The court relied on California public policy that prohibits the judicial resolution of claims arising out of gambling contracts regardless of cheating or fraud.

3. Crimes by Employees

Dumas v. Mississippi
806 So. 2d 1009 (Miss. 2000)

PRATHER, Chief Justice, for the Court:

STATEMENT OF THE FACTS AND CASE

1. On June 9, 1997, Johnny Dumas ("Dumas") was indicted on thirteen separate counts of "unlawfully, wilfully, and feloniously taking an amount greater than the amount won at the game of blackjack" at the Lady Luck Casino in Coahoma County, in violation of Miss. Code Ann. §75-76-301 (Supp.1999). Dumas was also indicted under the same statute for "altering or misrepresenting the outcome of the game of blackjack" and for unlawfully canceling a bet after acquiring knowledge of the outcome of the game. On November 12, 1998, Dumas was tried before a duly empaneled jury in the Circuit Court of Coahoma County.

2. At trial, the State built its case upon the testimony of three witnesses as well as upon videotape allegedly showing Dumas committing illegal acts at the blackjack table at the Lady Luck Casino. Michael Bush ("Bush"), a surveillance supervisor at Lady Luck, testified that, on April 20, 1997, he had supervised the videotaping of the gambling which had occurred at the blackjack table of Tyrone Wells ("Wells"), a dealer at the casino. In conjunction with Bush's testimony, the State played for the jury videotape taken of Wells' blackjack table on the day in question.

3. The defense successfully objected when Bush attempted to testify that one frame showed a dealer overpaying a customer, and the trial judge ruled that it was for the jury to decide whether the videotape depicted such overpaying. The judge did allow Bush to testify as to the general violations which, in his view, were depicted on the videotape. Bush testified that, in his opinion, the following violations occurred:

> Oh, overpayments, getting paid for hands that did not win, the dealer making his self [sic.] bust out, taking to many cards for his self [sic.] and paying — and the dealer paying losing hands.

4. Clay Barnett, an employee of the Mississippi Gaming Commission, testified that he was called to the Lady Luck Casino on April 20, 1997 in order to investigate allegations that a dealer had been "dumping the game on blackjack." Barnett testified that he was led to the security department of the casino, where he encountered dealer Wells and two patrons, including Dumas. Barnett testified that he asked Dumas whether he knew Wells or if he had any knowledge of cheating at the table, and Barnett testified that Dumas responded "no."

5. Barnett conceded on cross-examination that he had also interviewed Wells and that Wells had "fully admitted to wrongdoing" but had asserted that Dumas was not involved in the crime. Specifically, Barnett testified that:

> Q: And he told you that Mr. Dumas had nothing to do with it; isn't that correct?
>
> A: Correct. He said he didn't know any of the players at the table.

Thus, according to Barnett's testimony, both Dumas and Wells claimed that they did not know each other. However, the State produced Nita Dumas-Wells, the sister of Dumas, who acknowledged that she was married to Tyrone Wells. Upon eliciting this testimony, the State rested, and the defense rested without calling any witnesses.

6. The jury returned a verdict finding Dumas not guilty of six counts of the indictment and finding him guilty of seven counts. Dumas was sentenced to serve a term of two years in the custody of the Mississippi Department of Corrections, and he was ordered to pay a fine of five hundred dollars. Dumas' post-trial motions for JNOV and/or new trial were denied, and he timely appealed to this Court.

   I. The trial court committed reversible error in not sustaining Appellant's motion for a directed verdict of not guilty at the close of the State's case in chief and at the close of all of the evidence, and in failing to sustain Appellant's motion for judgment of acquittal, or in the alternative, new trial.

   ...

8. The jury returned a verdict finding Dumas not guilty of six counts of the indictment and finding him guilty of seven counts. Six of the seven counts on which Dumas was convicted were identical, except for the video footage to which they refer. These identical counts read as follows:

> That Tyrone C. Wells, Johnny Dumas, and James Darryl Luckadue, individually or while aiding or abetting and/or acting in concert with each other, late of Coa-

homa County, Mississippi, on or about April 20, 1997, in the County and State aforesaid, and within the jurisdiction of this Court, did unlawfully, wilfully, and feloniously, at the Lady Luck Rhythm and Blues Casino, as shown at the time of ____ on surveillance video, take an amount greater than the amount won at the game of blackjack, contrary to the form of the statute in such cases made and provided and against the peace and dignity of the State of Mississippi.

These counts are based on the language of Miss. Code Ann. § 75-76-301(c) (Supp. 1999), which provides that:

> It is unlawful for any person (c) To claim, collect or take, or attempt to claim, collect or take, money or anything of value in or from a gambling game, with intent to defraud, without having made a wager contingent thereon, or to claim, collect, or take an amount greater than the amount won. Dumas argues that the State failed to prove an intent to defraud on his part and that the jury's verdict should accordingly be reversed.

9. Although the evidence of an intent to defraud on the part of Dumas is not overwhelming, this Court concludes that a reasonable juror could have found that such intent to defraud was established by the State beyond a reasonable doubt. All parties concede that fraud did take place at Tyrone Wells' blackjack table, and Wells himself admitted that he did, in fact, knowingly commit fraud against the casino. Thus, there is clear evidence that a crime took place at Wells' blackjack table on April 20, 1997, and the only issue in question is whether Dumas knowingly participated in this crime.

10. The State presented testimony that Wells and Dumas were brothers-in-law, but testimony established that both Wells and Dumas had falsely represented that they were not even acquainted. In the view of this Court, the fact that the parties were related makes the State's case a stronger one as it relates to the possibility of a common scheme or purpose to defraud the casino. Moreover, the fact that the parties both lied about this relationship makes the State's case much stronger in this regard.

11. Also supportive of the jury's verdict is the fact that the crime was recorded on videotape. The jurors clearly examined the videotapes carefully, as evidenced by the fact that they requested and were granted a magnifying glass to view the video footage more carefully. The jurors' close attention to the videotape is also evidenced by the fact that they returned "not guilty" and "guilty" verdicts with regard to different counts of the indictment which were worded exactly the same, except with regard to the time at which the videos were taken.

12. The fact that the jury returned differing verdicts with regard to otherwise identical counts, depending upon which video frames were referenced, clearly indicates that the jurors based their verdict upon their evaluation of the conduct which they observed on the videotape. Such being the case, the present appeal does not present a compelling case for reversal, given that this Court should properly show deference to the trier of fact in its evaluation of duly admitted evidence such as the videotape. It is entirely plausible that a juror might have been able to gain insights into Dumas' state of mind by observing his "body language" on the videotape. While it can not be said with any certainty that this is the case, this Court must give all reasonable inferences which can be drawn from the evidence to the State in the present appeal.

13. Also, the fact that the jurors found that Dumas had, as stated in the indictment, "take(n) an amount greater than the amount won" on six separate occasions could lead to an inference of fraud by Dumas, more so than if the jury had found that Dumas had done so on only one or two occasions. This Court concludes that the evidence presented

in the present case could lead a reasonable juror to conclude that Dumas did knowingly take part in the crime, and this point of error is without merit.

14. This Court's final basis for affirming the jury's verdict comes from a review of the videotape itself. While it is not for this Court on appeal to conduct a de novo review of the evidence, we conclude that the videotape does depict activities which a reasonable juror could consider to be in violation of Miss. Code Ann. § 75-76-301 (Supp.1999).

15. The only other count on which Dumas was convicted was Count III, which reads as follows:

> That Tyrone C. Wells, Johnny Dumas, and James Darryl Luckadue, individually or while aiding or abetting and/or acting in concert with each other, late of Coahoma County, Mississippi, on or about April 20, 1997, in the County and State aforesaid, and within the jurisdiction of this Court, did unlawfully, wilfully, and feloniously, at the Lady Luck Rhythm and Blues Casino, as shown at the time of ____ on surveillance video, alter or misrepresent the outcome of the game of blackjack on which wagers had been made after the outcome was made sure but before it was revealed to the players by withholding a hit card, contrary to the form of the statute in such cases made and provided and against the peace and dignity of the State of Mississippi.

In convicting Dumas on this count, the jury concluded that Dumas had "aided or abetted" Wells in "misrepresenting the outcome of the game of blackjack on which wagers had been made after the outcome was sure but before it was revealed to the players by withholding a hit card."

16. In this regard, this Court's analysis of Dumas' convictions on the previous counts is equally applicable in the present context. Dumas argues that the decision of whether or not to withhold a hit card is the dealer's alone, and he notes once again that Wells asserted that he had acted alone. This Court concludes, however, that a reasonable juror could have refused to believe this assertion by Wells, given his close relationship to Dumas, given the fact that both parties had lied about that relationship, and given that the incriminating conduct was captured on videotape. This Court also concludes that a reasonable juror could have found Dumas to have aided and abetted Wells in withholding a hit card. As with the previous counts, the jurors were able to personally view the alleged crime, and they concluded that the State met its burden of proving that Dumas had in fact aided and abetted Wells in this regard.

17. Moreover, this Court may take judicial notice of the fact that a blackjack player, rather than dealer, decides whether to request his own hit card, and a player's knowing silence or inaction when the dealer withholds a hit card could clearly be considered aiding or abetting in this regard. This is particularly true when the evidence establishes, to the jury's satisfaction, that the parties were actively engaged in a criminal act at the time the hit card was withheld. Dumas' arguments in the present context would likely carry more weight if the jury had not found that he was guilty of defrauding the casino on several other counts as well. This Court concludes that the jury's convictions were based on legally sufficient evidence and should be affirmed.

    . . .

Notes

1. Cheaters can most easily cheat a casino game where the dealer is working with a person posing as a patron. This is known as "dumping off" the game. Four common meth-

ods are the "push and pay," "flashing," "peeking," and "stacking." In the "push and pay," the dealer simply pays or pushes on losing hands in black jack. The dealer also can overpay on winning hands. Success of this technique depends on the level of surveillance and skill of the employees that watch the game. "Flashing" is when the dealer intentionally exposes either his "hole card" or the top card of the deck to the player-accomplice. The player then can use this information to guide his play. In some schemes, he can use the information to guide his own play and, in others, to attempt to cause the dealer to bust more often than usual. The latter can allow other accomplices at the table, who are betting higher amounts, a greater opportunity to win. "Peeking" is similar to "flashing," except that the dealer is the person that sees the top card. The dealer can then signal his accomplice, who plays accordingly. "Stacking" is a method where the dealer appears to shuffle the deck, but does not randomly mix the cards. Instead, cards picked up from the previous hand are segregated and left in the same position after the final "shuffle." The dealer then deals the arranged cards to allow his accomplice-player to win the hand. *See generally*, BILL ZENDER, HOW TO DETECT CASINO CHEATING AT BLACKJACK (RGE Publishing 1999).

2. Casino employees also may have opportunities to steal from casino patrons without the knowledge of their employer. A common method is to steal chips off the table and conceal them somewhere on the employee's person. After his or her shift ends, the employee may pass the chips to a conspirator who cashes them at the cage. The simplest way for a dealer to steal from the patrons is to palm chips from the patron's stack and drop them into hidden pockets in his clothing. Mario Puzo, in his novel, *Fools Die*, describes the origin of dealers clapping their hands and turning their palms to the sky as: "Far off, down the rows of blackjack tables, those dealers going off duty washed their hands high in the air to show they were not palming chips." Bill Zender describes the use of hidden pockets by dealers mainly to steal chips from the tray as opposed to the patrons. BILL ZENDER, HOW TO DETECT CASINO CHEATING AT BLACKJACK (RGE Publishing 1999).

3. Cases involving employees cheating in casinos include Washington v. Heffner, 110 P.3d 219 (Wash. App. 2005) (casino dealer's conviction for theft was upheld based on his manipulation of cards to the favor of the casino patrons to generate higher tips); United States v. Hung Quoc, 1998 WL 141334 (9th Cir. Mar. 25, 1998) (conviction upheld for a dealer and players where the dealer conspired with the players to execute a "false shuffle" at a mini-baccarat "game that allowed the players to determine the outcome of upcoming hands and bet accordingly"); United States v. Vaccaro, 115 F.3d 1211 (5th Cir. 1997) (upholding a conviction for a conspiracy where a group of casino employees schemed with others in placing decks of previously marked cards on blackjack tables).

4. Cheating by Patrons

NRS 465.070 Fraudulent acts. It is unlawful for any person:

1. To alter or misrepresent the outcome of a game or other event on which wagers have been made after the outcome is made sure but before it is revealed to the players.

2. To place, increase or decrease a bet or to determine the course of play after acquiring knowledge, not available to all players, of the outcome of the game or any event that affects the outcome of the game or which is the subject of the bet or to aid anyone in acquiring such knowledge for the purpose of placing, increasing or decreasing a bet or determining the course of play contingent upon that event or outcome.

3. To claim, collect or take, or attempt to claim, collect or take, money or anything of value in or from a gambling game, with intent to defraud, without having made a wager contingent thereon, or to claim, collect or take an amount greater than the amount won.

4. Knowingly to entice or induce another to go to any place where a gambling game is being conducted or operated in violation of the provisions of this chapter, with the intent that the other person play or participate in that gambling game.

5. To place or increase a bet after acquiring knowledge of the outcome of the game or other event which is the subject of the bet, including past-posting and pressing bets.

6. To reduce the amount wagered or cancel the bet after acquiring knowledge of the outcome of the game or other event which is the subject of the bet, including pinching bets.

7. To manipulate, with the intent to cheat, any component of a gaming device in a manner contrary to the designed and normal operational purpose for the component, including, but not limited to, varying the pull of the handle of a slot machine, with knowledge that the manipulation affects the outcome of the game or with knowledge of any event that affects the outcome of the game.

8. To offer, promise or give anything of value to anyone for the purpose of influencing the outcome of a race, sporting event, contest or game upon which a wager may be made, or to place, increase or decrease a wager after acquiring knowledge, not available to the general public, that anyone has been offered, promised or given anything of value for the purpose of influencing the outcome of the race, sporting event, contest or game upon which the wager is placed, increased or decreased.

9. To change or alter the normal outcome of any game played on an interactive gaming system or a mobile gaming system or the way in which the outcome is reported to any participant in the game.

Sheriff of Washoe County v. Martin

662 P.2d. 634 (Nev. 1983)

MOWBRAY, Justice:

Respondent was arrested and charged with two counts each of card cheating in violation of NRS 465.083 and conspiracy to commit card cheating in violation of NRS 199.480 and NRS 465.083. After being bound over to the district court for trial, respondent petitioned the district court for a writ of habeas corpus. Among other contentions, he argued that the definition of cheating in NRS 465.015, on which the charges against him rested, was unconstitutionally vague. The district court agreed, and dismissed the charges. We hold that the statutory definition of cheating is not unconstitutionally vague, and therefore reverse and remand for trial.

THE FACTS

The following facts were adduced at respondent Martin's preliminary hearing. On April 10, 1982, Martin was playing "21" at Boomtown, in Verdi, Nevada. He was seated to the left of a known card crimper, Dennis Wayne Petersen. Card crimping is the act of deforming a card, often by bending the corners, to make the point value of the card readable to the crimper from the back as well as the face of the card.

Casino employees and Gaming Control Board agents placed the table under observation. The deck in play was exchanged for a new deck, and the used deck was found to contain many crimped cards. Petersen was observed crimping several cards in the new deck.

Martin consistently asked Petersen how he should play his cards. Before the deck was changed, Petersen watched the deck closely as the cards were being dealt, frequently standing up to do so. He was playing a single hand and betting $5–$10 per hand, while Martin was betting about $100 per hand. Petersen also hit his hand in an unusual pattern. Immediately after the deck was changed, Petersen ceased watching the deck and began to play two hands, while Martin's bets dropped to about $25 per hand. After a period of ten to fifteen minutes, during which Petersen was observed crimping cards in the new deck, Petersen went back to playing a single hand, and Martin's bets went back up to about $100 per hand. A Gaming Control agent also noted a correlation between Petersen's touching of a particular stack of chips and Martin's taking a hit. A card expert employed by the casino testified that Martin's and Petersen's behavior indicated that they were working together. Martin was ahead several hundred dollars at the time he and Petersen were removed from the table and detained by casino security personnel.

Martin and Petersen were arrested and charged with two counts each of card cheating in violation of NRS 465.083 and conspiracy to commit card cheating in violation of NRS 199.480 and NRS 465.083 (one count for each deck of cards). Petersen jumped bail, and the State proceeded against Martin alone. After his preliminary hearing Martin was bound over to the district court for trial. Martin subsequently petitioned the district court for a writ of habeas corpus, challenging the legality of his restraint on several grounds. After a hearing on the petition, the district court entered an "Order of Discharge" under NRS 34.500(8), dismissing the charges against Martin on the ground that the definition of cheating in NRS 465.015, on which NRS 465.083 rests, is unconstitutionally vague. This appeal followed.

NRS 465.015 IS NOT UNCONSTITUTIONALLY VAGUE

NRS 465.083, as amended in 1981, provides that "[i]t is unlawful for any person, whether he is an owner or employee of or a player in an establishment, to cheat at any gambling game." NRS 465.015, added in 1981, provides that "'[c]heat' means to alter the selection of criteria which determine: (a) The result of a game; or (b) The amount or frequency of payment in a game." The district court held that the phrase "to alter the selection of criteria" made the penal statute unconstitutionally vague.

It is well settled that the Due Process Clause of the Fourteenth Amendment prohibits the states from holding an individual "criminally responsible for conduct which he could not reasonably understand to be proscribed." United States v. Harriss, 347 U.S. 612, 617–18 (1954). See Rose v. Locke, 423 U.S. 48, 49 (1975). Laws must give a person of ordinary intelligence a reasonable opportunity to know what is prohibited, so that he may act accordingly, and must also provide explicit standards for those who apply the laws, to avoid arbitrary and discriminatory enforcement.

A statute therefore violates the due process requirement of specificity if it "either forbids or requires the doing of any act in terms so vague that men of common intelligence must necessarily guess at its meaning and differ as to its application...." Nev. Gaming Comm'n v. Glusman, 651 P.2d 639, 644 (Nev. 1982), quoting Connally v. General Construction Co., 269 U.S. 385, 391 (1926). However, "[t]he Constitution does not require impossible standards of specificity in penal statutes. The test of granting sufficient warning as to proscribed conduct will be met if there are well settled and ordinarily understood meanings for the words employed when viewed in the context of the entire statutory provision." Woofter v. O'Donnell, 542 P.2d 1396, 1400 (Nev. 1975). As the High Court noted in Rose v. Locke, supra, the prohibition against excessive vagueness:

> does not invalidate every statute which a reviewing court believes could have been drafted with greater precision.

Even trained lawyers may find it necessary to consult legal dictionaries, treatises, and judicial opinions before they may say with any certainty what some statutes may compel or forbid.... All the Due Process Clause requires is that the law give sufficient warning that men may conduct themselves so as to avoid that which is forbidden.

Id. 423 U.S. at 49–50. Moreover, if an enactment does not implicate constitutionally protected conduct, the court may strike it down as vague on its face only if it is impermissibly vague in all of its applications. A challenger who has engaged in conduct that is clearly proscribed cannot complain of the vagueness of the law as applied to the conduct of others.

Acts of the Legislature are presumed to be constitutional, and the party challenging an enactment bears the burden of making a "clear showing" of invalidity. Where the intention of the Legislature is clear, it is the duty of the court to give effect to such intention and to construe the language of the statute to effectuate rather than nullify its manifest purpose.

Applying these rules, we find that the definition of cheating in NRS 465.015 is not unconstitutionally vague on its face or as applied to respondent. The Legislature sought by this generic definition to prohibit all forms of cheating, and thus to avoid the many gaps and loopholes left by the prior cheating statutes. *See* NRS 465.070–465.083 (1979). While we have never before construed the phrase "to alter the selection of criteria which determine [the outcome of the game]," the words bear an easily ascertainable meaning. Webster's Third New International Dictionary (1976) defines "criterion" as either a characterizing mark or trait, or a standard on which a decision or judgment may be based. The same dictionary defines "selection" as either the act or process of selecting, or that which is selected (choice). In light of the statutory purpose, we interpret the current cheating statutes to proscribe the alteration of the group of characteristics which identify and define the game in question. The attributes of the game—its established physical characteristics and basic rules—determine the probabilities of the game's various possible outcomes. Changing those attributes to affect those probabilities is a criminal act.

In addition, the statutes and the legislative history do not suggest that the Legislature intended to remove from the crime of cheating the requirement of fraudulent intent. *See* NRS 199.480(2)(d). We have consistently drawn parallels between cheating and fraudulent conduct.... Thus, if a player or dealer deceitfully alters the identifying characteristics or attributes of a game with the intent to deprive another of money or property by affecting the otherwise established probabilities of the game's various outcomes, he or she is guilty of cheating within the meaning of NRS 465.015 and NRS 465.083.

By crimping cards, respondent's alleged coconspirator in effect made the cards readable on both sides. While this did not alter the location of the cards in the deck, which was established randomly by the dealer's shuffling, it did alter a crucial characteristic of the game. The card crimper by his actions eliminated the element of chance as to himself and respondent concerning the point value of the top cards in the deck at the time of deciding whether or not to take a hit. The other players' knowledge of those cards was based solely on their observation of the cards already played and the laws of probability. "What a man does not know and cannot find out is chance as to him, and is recognized as chance by the law." Dillingham v. McLaughlin, 264 U.S. 370, 373 (1924).

By way of contrast, a card counter—one who uses a point system to keep track of the cards that have been played—does not alter any of the basic features of the game. He merely uses his mental skills to take advantage of the same information that is available to all players.

The evidence adduced at Martin's preliminary hearing was sufficient on the elements of conduct and intent to warrant binding him over for trial, and indicates that he was or should have been on notice that his conduct was proscribed by NRS 465.083 and NRS 199.480. We therefore reverse the order of the district court dismissing the charges against Martin, and remand the matter to the district court for trial.

Notes

1. While cheating in the context of non-gaming activities is theoretically no different than cheating at casino games, most casino states have adopted special statutes to cover casino crimes. While many reasons may exist for creating special statutes, the myriad of different methods of cheating can explain the need for specific legislation to address each methodically. *See* Casino Control Act, N.J. Stat. Ann. § 5:12-113; Cal. Penal. Code § 337 et. seq.

2. One form of cheating by patrons is an effort to eliminate the random outcome of the event that determines the outcome of the contract. More colorful methods may include the use of loaded dice in a craps game or marking cards in blackjack. Switching a prearranged deck of cards with a deck used in the game is another form of cheating. This type of cheat, known as a cooler, usually requires the aid of at least one casino employee. A person also may attempt to alter or misrepresent the outcome of a game or event after the outcome is made sure, but before the casino reveals it to the players wagering on the game.

For example, during a card game it is unlawful to switch cards with another person. The Nevada Supreme Court held that blackjack players who—in any manner—switch or change dealt cards and attempt to play different cards than those dealt to him, or who offer cards back to the dealer for payoff either as a winning hand or because the dealer "broke," violate the law. Moore v. State, 692 P.2d 1278, 1279 (Nev. 1984).

Lyons v. Nevada
775 P.2d 219 (Nev. 1989)

OPINION

STEFFEN, Justice:

This appeal raises the issue of whether the State may induce an accused to plead guilty to a non-committed crime by unwittingly convincing the accused that the noncriminal conduct for which he was arrested constituted a criminal offense. The issue, thus stated, represents an accurate but somewhat convoluted distillate of appellant's complaint. It also explains why appellant's conviction must be reversed.

Lyons, who is no stranger to the criminal justice system in general and to gaming crimes in particular, was charged with cheating at gambling, conspiracy to cheat at gambling, and being an habitual criminal. The underlying conduct leading to Lyons' arrest involved what has come to be known as "handle popping" a slot machine. The term refers to a process of handle manipulation that enables a player to exploit mechanically vulnerable slot machines.

Lyons was apprehended as a result of his handle popping activities at Harrah's Tahoe Casino. Subsequent to his preliminary hearing, Lyons assented to a plea bargain that allowed him to enter an *Alford* plea to the non-committed crime of attempting to obtain money by false pretenses. The original charges were dropped in exchange for entry of the plea.

Lyons raises four issues on appeal, only one of which requires discussion because it is dispositive of the entire matter.

...

Turning to the paramount substantive issue, Lyons contends that NRS 465.015, which defines cheating at gambling, is unconstitutionally vague as applied to slot machine handle manipulation. We are convinced that he is correct. In United States v. Harriss, 347 U.S. 612 (1954), the United States Supreme Court declared:

> The Constitutional requirement of definiteness is violated by a criminal statute that fails to give a person of ordinary intelligence fair notice that his contemplated conduct is forbidden by the statute. The underlying principle is that no man shall be held criminally responsible for conduct which he could not reasonably understand to be proscribed (footnote omitted).

In analyzing the clarity of definition and notice supplied by NRS 465.015 as applied to "handle popping," we also recognize that statutes providing criminal sanctions must reflect a higher standard of certainty than civil statutes.

This court has previously declared NRS 465.015 constitutionally acceptable on its face and as applied to the practice of "card crimping." However, we have never had the occasion to consider the constitutional validity of NRS 465.015 *as applied* to the practice of "handle popping" or handle manipulation of a slot machine. We are constrained to do so now, as the State has seen fit to use handle manipulation as a basis for charging Lyons with the commission of a felony, thereby inducing him to plead to a crime not committed, but otherwise free of controversy.

As previously noted in *Harriss,* persons are deemed to have been given fair notice of a criminal offense if the statutorily proscribed conduct has been described with sufficient clarity to be understood by individuals of ordinary intelligence. 347 U.S. at 617. And statutes challenged for vagueness are evaluated on an as-applied basis where, as here, first amendment interests are not implicated.

Turning now to an analysis of NRS 465.015 as applied to "handle popping," it will be seen that the statute fails to address such conduct in terms that would alert persons of ordinary intelligence that they were committing a crime.

The obvious purpose of NRS 465.015 is to prevent persons from taking unlawful advantage of Nevada's gaming industry by cheating. In specific terms, the statute declares:

1. "Cheat" means to alter the selection of criteria which determine:

(a) The result of a game; or

(b) The amount or frequency of payment in a game....

The statute thus addresses knowing, purposeful, unlawful conduct designed to alter the criteria that determines the outcome of any lawful gambling activity. Thus, in *Martin,* we held that the statute had clear application to one who attempted to enhance his chances of winning by crimping cards. Having thus made it possible to identify certain cards, Martin was able to supplant elements of chance with actual knowledge that substantially altered both the nature of the game and the criteria for winning. The statute clearly proscribed such conduct. Similarly, those who, by resorting to mirrors, confederates, electronic equipment, magnets, tools or other devices, alter the play of a game or machine to increase their prospects of winning, would have no difficulty understanding that they are cheating within the definition of the statute.

In contrast, consider the gaming patrons who are specially gifted and can increase the odds in their favor by "card counting." Or perhaps the patron who notices and takes advantage of a dealer's habit of play that will occasionally provide an unintended view of the dealer's cards. Unquestionably, neither category of patron would be subject to prosecution under the statute, although casino management may take measures to deny them the right to play. In both cases, the players simply exploit what their skills and the play of the games will afford them. And yet, they are altering the *usual* criteria, i.e., the characteristic complex or standard of play that determines the frequency of payment.

Because handle popping neither damages nor mechanically alters a slot machine, the innocent novice may "stumble across" the technique and use it as effectively as the professional who adroitly identifies and depletes the mechanically deficient machines. Players engaging in handle manipulation do nothing more than take advantage of what the slot machines will give them, just as card players may exploit a dealer's unintended revelation of his cards. In a sense, slot machine handle manipulators are analogous to all slot machine patrons who shuffle from machine to machine and casino to casino in the hope of favorably changing their luck. In the one case, such hope is manifested by varying the motion by which the handle is pulled; in the other, by a move to another machine or environment. In either case, the desire is to somehow change the odds in favor of the player.

In Sheriff v. Martin, 662 P 2d.at 638, we recognized the requirement of fraudulent intent as an element of cheating. Moreover, we also observed that "the attributes of the game — its established physical characteristics and basic rules — determine the probabilities of the game's various possible outcomes. Changing those attributes to affect those probabilities is a criminal act." *Id.*; 662 P 2d.at 638. Games in the form of slot machines have established physical characteristics that are not altered by handle popping. Furthermore, we are unaware of any rules, written or otherwise, directing slot machine patrons to pull the handles in a specific manner. Certain gaming sophisticates — such as Lyons — would undoubtedly manipulate handles with a form of scienter because of their awareness that the procedure forms a basis for criminal prosecution in Nevada. Others, like Coolidge Brown (*see* El Dorado v. Brown), who stumble across a more favorable method of play, will handle pop without an intent to cheat or defraud. It is clear, however, that crime categories do not materialize or disappear on an ad hoc basis because of the presence or absence of scienter. Public offenses are defined by statute, ordinance or the common law. *in See* NRS 193.050.

Because varying the pull of a slot machine handle has never been expressly proscribed by Nevada statute or ordinance or the common law of England, the status of handle popping as a public offense is entirely dependent upon its fair inclusion in the language of NRS 465.015. Fairly read, we do not perceive a description of handle popping within the statutory language. The physical characteristics and potential pay offs of slot machines are not altered by handle manipulators. They are, therefore, similar to card counters who, without altering the physical characteristics or payment potential of card games do, by their skillful play, increase the frequency of payments. Such activities do not constitute criminal conduct under existing law in Nevada.

. . .

If the State and the gaming industry desire to make handle popping or handle manipulation of slot machines a crime in Nevada, it will be necessary to do so in clearly expressed, specific statutory terms. Moreover, given the fact that innocent, well-intentioned patrons may so easily adopt various methods of handle manipulation in an attempt to change their fortune, it will be necessary to provide conspicuous notices on or about the machines to inform patrons which methods of handle pulling are lawful and which methods are felonious. In lieu of criminal sanctions, it should be apparent that gaming establishments will be able to curtail handle popping losses by promptly retiring and repairing or replacing machines vulnerable to such manipulation.

For the reasons stated above, we hold that NRS 465.015 is unconstitutional as applied to handle popping or handle manipulation of slot machines that does not damage the machines. Accordingly, the judgment of conviction entered pursuant to Lyons' *Alford* plea is vacated, and if Lyons remains in custody pursuant to the instant conviction, he is to be released immediately.

MOWBRAY, Judge, with whom YOUNG, Chief Judge, agrees, dissenting:

Respectfully, I dissent.

The bottom line issue in this appeal is whether Nevada's anti-cheating statute, NRS 465.015, is unconstitutionally vague as applied to slot machine manipulation commonly called "cheating by handle popping." My learned brethren of the majority have held the statute constitutionally infirm because it fails to give a person of ordinary intelligence fair notice that his contemplated conduct is forbidden by statute; or that a reasonable man of ordinary intelligence would not understand that slot machine handle popping was proscribed. I disagree.

It is difficult to draft a definition to cover all cases of cheating in the gaming industry. The legislature in its wisdom has come forward with the best possible definition that covers the problem, a definition that can be understood by those who wish to understand it.

NRS 465.015 is not a trap for the unwary, uninitiated novice who seeks to play the slots. I do not believe it is necessary at this juncture to post in blueprint detail in and about and around the slot machines warnings to the uninformed neophytes how to pull the handle of a slot machine. However, the professional "popper," as in the instant case, comes to the casino well trained in how to jerk, wrench, wrack and otherwise abuse the slot machines in order to alter the "selection of the criteria" proscribed in NRS 465.015.[1]

I conclude that people of ordinary intelligence would understand that a method of play which permits only one reel of a slot machine to spin as the "popper" does alters the selection of criteria which determines the result of the game. Therefore, I would hold NRS 465.015 constitutional in the instant case.

. . .

Notes

1. While no longer a relevant concern to the casino industry because of advanced technologies, slot handle manipulation was the basis for significant litigation. The "cherry

---

1. Mr. Lyons, the appellant, has incurred at least seven arrests in Nevada and one arrest in New Jersey for slot machine cheating. He was indicted by a grand jury in Clark County, Nevada for (1) racketeering, (2) conspiracy to manufacture methamphetamines, (3) possession of ephedrine for sale, (4) attempt to manufacture methamphetamine, (5) trafficking in methamphetamine, and (6) possession of cocaine.

The Nevada Gaming Commission has entered Mr. Lyons' name in their "Black Book" excluding him from licensed gaming establishments in the State of Nevada. The Commission noted therein that "[o]ver the past 35 years there have been few time periods when Lyons was not either a fugitive from justice, facing criminal prosecution, or incarcerated in a correctional facility. He has been arrested in excess of thirty (30) times, and has numerous felony and misdemeanor convictions."

squeeze," or "handle popping" involved the handle manipulation of mechanical or electro-mechanical slot machines to control the reel alignment.

2. The Nevada Supreme Court did not follow the same reasoning used for slot manipulation in a case involving dice sliding. In craps, players are given the opportunity to "toss" two dice that will result in numbers between two and twelve, although these numbers come up with different frequencies. This "toss" is the random event upon which the gaming contracts between the casino and the players at that table will be decided. Dice sliding refers to the skilled player who is able to slide one or both dice across the table rather than tossing them and allowing them to roll. Thus, a predetermined "roll" may be chosen and the outcome of the game manipulated by the slider. In Skipper v. State, 879 P.2d 732, 734 (Nev. 1994), a dice slider challenged his cheating conviction on the same ground as that raised by the handle popping slot player in *Lyons*. Claiming that the criminal statutes were unconstitutionally vague, Skipper argued that the statutes failed to alert the average dice player that dice sliding constituted criminal conduct. The Nevada Supreme Court rejected the argument, finding that the rules of craps clearly require a roll of the dice (the random event that is the basis of the contract). As the dice do not roll when they are slid, dice sliding violated the rules of the game and, as such, provide adequate notice to the average player that sliding violates the anti-cheating statutes.

Dice sliding should be contrasted with dice setting. The latter is a process by the shooter or thrower in a dice game to exert some control over the numbers that the dice will show after they have been tossed. The concept is that the thrower arranges the dice in their hand before throwing them. By controlling (and standardizing) the motion of the throw, dice setters claim to be able alter the random selection of results to favor certain dice combinations that will give them an advantage over the casino. Dice setting is different than dice sliding because the dice setter is working within the prescribed rules of play to attempt to influence the roll. The casino may prescribe the rule with the belief that regardless of what proper method that the advantage player employs, it will not impact the random-aspect of the throw. In other words, the casino considers dice setting to be more based on superstition than science.

3. Besides card crimping discussed in *Martin*, above, a player may attempt to cheat the casino through the a process known as card marking. A card marker can alter the backs of cards, and figure out the value of the dealer's hole card in blackjack. Knowledge of the dealer's hole card assures the player of an advantage over the casino.

4. Another major method of cheating is for the person to steal from casinos or other players by playing gaming devices or a table game without making a wager. For example, in one reported case, an individual played a quarter gaming device at the Thunderbird Hotel. The coin he used had a mono-filament string attached that made it possible to play the same machine several times while using only one coin. This type of cheat is known as a "stringer." See Smith v. Nevada, 482 P.2d 302 (Nev. 1971). "Sluggers" also were a persistent problem. Slugs are counterfeit tokens used to play gaming devices. In Wallace v. Nevada, No. 51904, slip op., 2010 WL 3295117 (Nev. July 12, 2010), a person was convicted for using a light optic device to manipulate slot machines to release tokens not won by playing the device. For other cases involving cheating, *see* State v. Barr, 651 P.2d 649 (Nev. 1982); Isbell v. State, 626 P.2d 1274 (Nev. 1981); Graham v. State, 467 P.2d 1016 (Nev. 1970).

NRS 465.080 Possession, use, sale or manufacture of counterfeit, unapproved or unlawful instruments or items; possession of certain unlawful devices or paraphernalia for manufacturing slugs.

1. It is unlawful for any licensee, employee or other person, not a duly authorized employee of a licensee acting in furtherance of his or her employment within an establishment, to possess, use, sell or manufacture counterfeit chips, counterfeit debit instruments or other counterfeit wagering instruments in a gambling game, associated equipment or a cashless wagering system.

2. It is unlawful for any licensee, employee or other person, not a duly authorized employee of a licensee acting in furtherance of his or her employment within an establishment, to possess, use, sell or manufacture any counterfeit instruments, counterfeit tickets or other counterfeit items that are used to determine the outcome of any contest or promotional activity conducted by or on behalf of any licensee.

3. It is unlawful for any person, in playing or using any gambling game, associated equipment or cashless wagering system designed to be played with, receive or be operated by chips, tokens, wagering credits or other wagering instruments approved by the State Gaming Control Board or by lawful coin of the United States of America:

(a) Knowingly to use other than chips, tokens, wagering credits or other wagering instruments approved by the State Gaming Control Board or lawful coin, legal tender of the United States of America, or to use coin or tokens not of the same denomination as the coin or tokens intended to be used in that gambling game, associated equipment or cashless wagering system; or

(b) To use any device or means to violate the provisions of this chapter.

4. It is unlawful for any person, not a duly authorized employee of a licensee acting in furtherance of such employment within an establishment, to have on his or her person or in his or her possession on or off the premises of any licensed gaming establishment any device intended to be used to violate the provisions of this chapter.

5. It is unlawful for any person, not a duly authorized employee of a licensee acting in furtherance of such employment within an establishment, to have on his or her person or in his or her possession on or off the premises of any licensed gaming establishment any key or device known to have been designed for the purpose of and suitable for opening, entering or affecting the operation of any gambling game, cashless wagering system or drop box, or any electronic or mechanical device connected thereto, or for removing money or other contents therefrom.

6. It is unlawful for any person, not a duly authorized employee of a licensee acting in furtherance of such employment within an establishment, to have on his or her person or in his or her possession any paraphernalia for manufacturing slugs. As used in this subsection, "paraphernalia for manufacturing slugs" means the equipment, products and materials that are intended for use or designed for use in manufacturing, producing, fabricating, preparing, testing, analyzing, packaging, storing or concealing a counterfeit facsimile of the chips, tokens, debit instruments or other wagering instruments approved by the State Gaming Control Board or a lawful coin of the United States, the use of which is unlawful pursuant to subsection 3. The term includes, but is not limited to:

(a) Lead or lead alloys;

(b) Molds, forms or similar equipment capable of producing a likeness of a gaming token or United States coin;

(c) Melting pots or other receptacles;

(d) Torches;

(e) Tongs, trimming tools or other similar equipment; and

(f) Equipment which can be reasonably demonstrated to manufacture facsimiles of debit instruments or wagering instruments approved by the State Gaming Control Board.

7. Possession of more than one of the devices, equipment, products or materials described in this section permits a rebuttable inference that the possessor intended to use them for cheating.

State v. Smith

2009 WL 3337632 (Iowa Ct. App. Oct. 9, 2009)

MANSFIELD, J.

This case requires us to decide whether Iowa Code section 99F.15(4)(i) (2005) applies to a form of cheating at blackjack, where the player increases or "caps" his or her bet after seeing that he or she has a favorable hand. The issue presented is whether a casino patron who engages in this practice "claims, collects, or takes an amount of money or thing of value of greater value than the amount won." *See* Iowa Code § 99F.15(4)(i). Because we conclude that capping does not violate this specific subsection, we reverse the defendant's conviction and remand for dismissal of the trial information.

I. Facts.

On the evening of December 23, 2006, the defendant, Mitchell Terrell Smith, was playing blackjack at the Riverside Casino and Golf Resort. Smith had played blackjack at the same casino about a month before.

In the version of blackjack played at Riverside Casino, all players place their bets before the cards are dealt. Two cards are then dealt face up to each player. The dealer receives one card face up and one card face down. At this point, players are not allowed to add chips to their bet unless they are doubling down or splitting pairs.

Capping, a form of cheating, involves slipping one or more additional chips into one's bet after the cards have been dealt. Capping, in effect, allows the player to adjust his or her bet retroactively after learning that he or she will likely have a better hand than the dealer. Since a winning hand normally returns the amount that the player bet, a player who can increase his or her bet after observing the deal gains an unfair advantage.

Smith was seated next to the "third base" position at the table. This area is to the dealer's right, and is favored by individuals who want to engage in capping because they can do so more easily while the dealer is first addressing other players to his or her left.

A nearby "relief" dealer noticed that Smith appeared to be capping. He alerted his supervisor, and the surveillance video of Smith's table was reviewed. The video showed Smith on several occasions adding a chip to his wager stack after the cards had been dealt. On the video, Smith appeared to be acting deliberately, with a quick motion intended to escape the dealer's notice.

Smith was taken away from the gaming table and questioned by an Iowa Division of Criminal Investigation (DCI) agent. In his statement to the DCI, Smith admitted that he had been adding to his bets after the cards had been dealt, but denied he knew it was against the rules. He also wrote, falsely, in a statement, "I never played blackjack at a casino in my life." In fact, Smith later conceded, as shown by the Riverside Casino's electronic records, that he had played over two hours of blackjack at the same casino about a month before.

Smith was charged with prohibited gaming activities in violation of Iowa Code section 99F.15(4)(i). That provision makes it an offense if a person:

Claims, collects, or takes, or attempts to claim, collect, or take, money or anything of value in or from the gambling games, with intent to defraud, without having made a wager contingent on winning a gambling game, or claims, collects, or takes an amount of money or thing of value of greater value than the amount won.

Smith went to trial before the court on May 22, 2008. On June 4, 2008, the district court issued a written ruling finding Smith guilty as charged. From his conviction, Smith appeals, arguing that his motion for judgment of acquittal should have been granted because there was insufficient evidence that he committed the crime charged.

II. Analysis.

. . .

The State apparently concedes that Smith did not violate the first part of section 99F.15(4)(i) because he did not claim, collect, or take anything of value "without having made a wager contingent on winning a gambling game." In each of the nine instances where he capped his bet, Smith *did* make a wager. Rather, the State claims that Smith violated the second part of section 99F.15(4)(i) by claiming, collecting, or taking a thing of value "of greater value than the amount won." The State argues that by capping, Smith was able to collect "more than he legitimately won."

Smith, on the other hand, contends that he did not collect more than he won. While Smith may have won more chips than he was entitled to win if he had been following the rules of the game, he maintains that his chips reflected his actual winnings.

Upon our review, we agree with Smith's reading of the statute for several reasons. To begin with, when the text of a statute is plain and its meaning clear, we do not search for a meaning beyond the express terms of the statute. By its literal terms, section 99F.15(4)(i) applies to situations where the defendant claimed or collected more than his or her actual winnings. The relevant language reads: "of greater value than the amount won." The State is seeking to rewrite the statute as if it read: "of greater value than the amount *legitimately* won." That is a broader concept. We are not at liberty to expand the legislature's definition of a crime.

Furthermore, section 99F.15(4) contains a separate prohibition on cheating. Thus, the statute reads as follows:

A person commits a class "D" felony and, in addition, shall be barred for life from excursion gambling boats under the jurisdiction of the commission, if the person does any of the following:

. . . .

(d) Cheats at a gambling game.

. . . .

(i) Claims, collects, or takes, or attempts to claim, collect, or take, money or anything of value in or from the gambling games, with intent to defraud, without having made a wager contingent on winning a gambling game, or claims, collects, or takes an amount of money or thing of value of greater value than the amount won.

According to Smith, "An argument could be made that defendant violated Iowa Code section 99F.15(4)(d) which prohibits cheating at a gambling game, but he did not violate section 99F.15(4)(i) as alleged in the trial information." We agree.

As a general rule, we interpret statutes to give effect to the entire statute and to avoid sur-plusage. *See* Iowa Code §4.4(2). If section 99F.15(4)(i) covered any situation where the defendant claimed more than he or she "legitimately won," what would be the need for a separate prohibition on cheating in section 99F.15(4)(d)? Any cheating would already violate section 99F.15(4)(i). An interpretation that renders part of a statute superfluous is disfavored.

Furthermore, although the case law on provisions similar to section 99F.15(4)(i) is fairly sparse, this language does appear to be designed to cover situations where the defendant used some kind of fraud to collect more than he or she actually won at the game, rather than cheated at the game itself. Thus, in People v. Kolaj, No. 262205 (Mich. Ct. App. Oct. 26, 2006), the court upheld the defendant's conviction for violating Michigan Compiled Laws section 432.218(2)(j) where the defendant fraudulently altered non-winning tickets to make them appear to be winning tickets before having them cashed. Michigan Compiled Laws section 432.218(2)(j) is identically worded to Iowa Code section 99F.15(4)(i) and makes it a crime if the defendant:

> [c]laims, collects, takes, or attempts to claim, collect, or take money or anything of value in or from gambling games, with intent to defraud, without having made a wager contingent on winning a gambling game, or claims, collects, or takes an amount of money or thing of value of greater value than the amount won.

Iowa Code §99F.15(4)(i), Mich. Comp. Laws §432.218(2)(j).

Finally, we are mindful that criminal statutes are to be strictly construed with doubts resolved in favor of the accused.

For all these reasons, we hold that Iowa Code section 99F.15(4)(i) does not cover Smith's conduct in this case, and accordingly reverse the judgment and remand for dismissal of the charge.

REVERSED AND REMANDED.

Notes

1. This case illustrates yet another major form of cheating against a casino. This involves increasing or decreasing the amount of one's wager after learning the result of the random event. A cheat with a losing hand in blackjack, for example, can "pinch the bet" by palming one chip in the stack wagered. If the cheat adds a chip after learning that he has a winning hand, he pressed or past-posted the bet. Unlike the holding in the *Smith* case, past posting is explicitly prohibited in Nevada by statute,

2. Similar cheating can occur against other patrons. Observing a craps game is a bewildering experience for the uninitiated. One quickly wonders how it is possible to keep track of the bets. Sometimes even the patrons forget a bet they have on the table. Cheaters however also can claim another person's winnings. This may happen in a craps game where players may lose track of all their wagers. This allows a cheat to claim the winnings of other players that lose track of their bets. Besides claiming another person's winnings, a thief can simply steal the other players' wagers or chips. In some cases, the thief may use a "clip cup" to take the chips. A common ploy is for an "intoxicated" or "interested" bystander to drop a pack of cigarettes over a player's chips. The back of the pack has an adhesive that sticks to a chip. When the player retrieves his cigarettes, he also retrieves the chip.

3. Cheating and theft are tremendous problems for casino operators. Like other businesses, casinos may face a dilemma in apprehending persons suspected of cheating. As noted in the leading legal text on torts, a business proprietor:

who has good reason to believe that he has caught a customer in the act of stealing, of defrauding him of goods, or of sneaking out without paying for goods or services, is placed in a difficult position. He must permit the suspected wrongdoer to walk out, and probably say good-bye to both goods and payment, or run the risk that he will be liable for heavy damages in any detention.

PROSSER & KEETON ON TORTS 141 (5th Edition 1984).

For cases involving casinos detaining players, *see* Grosjean v. Imperial Palace, Inc., 212 P.3d. 1068 (Nev. 2009); Romanski v. Detroit Entertainment, LLC, 428 F. 3d 629 (6th Cir. 2005); Moore v. Detroit Entertainment, L.L.C., No. 275157, 2008 Mich. App. LEXIS 1105 (Ct. App. May 27, 2008); El Dorado Hotel, Inc., v. Coolidge Brown, 691 P.2d 436 (Nev. 1984). *See also* Ted Connell, *Mississippi Casinos and the Detention of a Patron: What Are the Limits to a Casino's Powers in Detaining a Patron and the Subsequent Liability?*, 1 GAMING L. REV. 361 (1997), Christopher Pastore & Crystal Tatco, *Under Color of State Law*, CASINO ENTERPRISE MGNT., at 8–11 (2009).

4. Some states have given business owners a limited privilege to detain persons suspected of theft for a short time to investigate whether the person actually stole property or services. But, at best, this privilege is limited to brief "on the spot" inquiries. To provide protection from civil lawsuits, some jurisdictions provide more extensive statutory protection. While a jurisdiction could give absolute immunity, or in other words, bar all lawsuits against the casino, most statutes that exist give only limited protection. For example, under Nevada Revised Statute 465.101, a gaming licensee or his agents have the right to take any individual suspected of cheating into custody, detain him in the establishment, and question him. If the limitations of the common law are honored, the casino and its employees may be immune from criminal and civil liability for false arrest, false imprisonment, slander, or unlawful detention. In such cases, courts have imposed liability only where the casino did not follow the statute. *See* Jacobson v. State, 510 P.2d 856 (Nev. 1973).

Hazelwood v. Harrah's, 862 P.2d 1189 (Nev. 1993) is illustrative. In that case, the player, Hazelwood, was playing keno. Upon learning that a winning keno ticket was not redeemed, and with the permission of a casino employee, he searched through the trash and found and redeemed the winning ticket. Nevertheless, the casino decided to contact the gaming control board. In the interim, casino employees asked Hazelwood to accompany them to the manager's office. After arrival, the gaming control board agents later informed the player that Nevada law prohibited someone from claiming winnings from a gambling game with the intent to defraud without having a wager contingent on the game. No casino employee was present at that time. The player then sued Harrah's for false imprisonment based on its actions in holding him while awaiting the gaming control board agents to arrive. The Nevada Supreme Court upheld the claim and refused to recognize the immunity from civil liability. The court noted:

> Harrah's argues that it is immune from civil liability for false imprisonment under NRS 465.101(1) which provides that any licensee or his officers may question any person in his establishment suspected of violating any of the gaming statutes without incurring civil liability. In addition, this statute also allows the licensee to detain the suspect provided the detention is for a reasonable time and the licensee has probable cause to believe a violation has occurred, again without incurring civil liability for false imprisonment.

> The district court correctly points out that the Harrah's employees involved failed to obtain more information concerning Hazelwood's possible violation of any statute. This failure to act caused the detention to be unreasonable and without proba-

ble cause. Therefore, we hold that the district court was correct in finding that Harrah's was not immune from civil liability under NRS 465.101(1).

862 P.2d at 1193.

5. Many jurisdictions have struggled with whether the use of a computer to predict outcomes of games should be a crime. Patrons who use computers to analyze play strategy can greatly increase their probability of success. In some cases, the patron can achieve a statistical advantage over the casino. Jurisdictions vary on the legality of using of computers to analyze strategy in casino games. For example, under Nevada law, "It is unlawful for any person at a licensed gaming establishment to use, or possess with the intent to use, any device to assist: 1) In projecting the outcome of the game; 2) In keeping track of the cards played; 3) In analyzing the probability of the occurrence of an event relating to the game; or 4) In analyzing the strategy for playing or betting to be used in the game, except as permitted by the Commission." Nev. Rev. Stat. 465.075. The policy underlying their prohibition is premised on two arguments. First, computers can be used to analyze strategy in games such as blackjack. Here their purpose is not to remove the randomness from the game, but to allow the patron the opportunity to play in such a manner as to maximize the potential to win. In other circumstances, however, persons may use computers to assist in cheating. Because the casino and regulatory agents cannot learn the intended use of the computer, the only effective method of preventing cheating is to prohibit the use of computers. Second, the nature of gaming is such that the parties to the gaming transaction should not have an unfair advantage over each other. Just like it would seem unfair for the casino to use computers in blackjack to decide when to shuffle the deck, it would be unfair for the patron to use computers to obtain an advantage over the casino. This is particularly appropriate when the casino is not a participant in the gaming transaction, such as in poker. In this situation the player using a computer can acquire an advantage over the other players.

If a jurisdiction decides to prohibit the use of computers, it must adopt laws that define the offense. In a Nevada case applying such a law, the person was playing blackjack. Sheriff v. Anderson, 746 P.2d 643 (Nev. 1987), *abrogated by* City of Las Vegas v. Clark County, 59 P.2d 477 (Nev. 2002) (holding that statutory vagueness creates a valid facial challenge to the statute, even when there is no implication of First amendment concerns). While playing, a surveillance camera operator noticed that he moved his toes often during the game. His toe movements corresponded to the appearance of certain cards. After casino security officials confronted him, the patron, a computer expert, admitted that he had hidden a microcomputer in his shoe. To pull off his "computer shoe" scam, the patron cut his socks to allow his bare toes to input data into the computer. Velcro held the switches in his shoes. Wires extended up his legs to a battery pack located in his left rear pocket. He strapped the main portion of his computer to his left calf, and the computer sent vibratory signals to a special receiver located inside his athletic supporter. The signal told him whether to hit, stand, double down, or split. The computer calculated his advantage or disadvantage with the casino, and advised him of the remaining cards in the deck. The police arrested the patron, and charged him with having and using a device at a casino to keep track of cards played. He was charged under Nevada Statute section 465.075, noted above. The patron argued that the statute was vague on what type of conduct it prohibits. The court restated the standard for evaluating vagueness. The test is whether a person of ordinary intelligence has a reasonable opportunity to know what conduct is prohibited. The court found that the law was not vague as applied to the patron because the use of a hidden computer is precisely the type of conduct envisioned by the law. In finding that no person of ordinary intelligence could believe otherwise, the court stated that whatever else the term "device" meant, it included computers. For other examples of state statutes prohibiting the use of devices to aid a patron during a game, *see* Colo. Rev. Stat. § 12-47.1-824; Miss. Code Ann. § 75-76-303; N.J. Stat. Ann. § 5: 12-113.1.

5. Advantage Play

Bartolo v. Boardwalk Regency Hotel Casino
449 A.2d 1339 (1982)

SKILLMAN, J.S.C.

Is it permissible for a casino to detain a patron suspected of being a "card counter" for the purpose of questioning? This issue is presented in the context of a tort action brought by four patrons of a casino who allege that they were falsely imprisoned by its security personnel. Defendants are the Boardwalk Regency Hotel Casino and several of its employees.

The matter is before the court on a motion for summary judgment filed by defendants. Therefore, the court must accept as true for the purpose of the motion the descriptions of the incident provided by plaintiffs in their depositions.

Plaintiffs are two brothers and two of their friends. All four are occasional social gamblers. They arrived at the Boardwalk Regency on December 26, 1979, played various casino games, including blackjack, and lost money. They returned to the gambling area around 11 a.m. the next morning and began playing blackjack. After playing for about an hour they were approached by two casino security guards dressed in uniforms. Plaintiffs were notified that they had been identified as card counters and were directed to accompany the guards. One plaintiff was grabbed by the back of the collar and pulled away from the blackjack table. The others were grabbed by the arms and led away. This physical removal happened so quickly and so forcefully that some plaintiffs were unable even to remove their chips from the table. All four were led to a nearby area where they were joined by a games manager, who ordered them to produce identification so that they could be registered and prevented from playing blackjack. At first plaintiffs refused to produce identification, protesting that they were not card counters. However, they were threatened with arrest if they refused to cooperate, and they then acceded to the demand. When identifications were produced, the games manager wrote plaintiffs' names on a pad, told them they would not be permitted to play blackjack again at the Boardwalk Regency or any other casino and directed them to leave. During this entire confrontation the two uniformed casino security guards remained on either side of plaintiffs. The three plaintiffs who were deposed all testified that they did not feel free to leave the casino between the time they were pulled away from the blackjack table and when they produced identification.

After unsuccessfully seeking to lodge a complaint concerning the incident with an official of the New Jersey Casino Control Commission, plaintiffs arranged a meeting with the assistant manager of the casino. The assistant manager acknowledged that the casino personnel had been at fault and said that he would like to make amends by buying plaintiffs a meal and allowing them back into the blackjack game. However, plaintiffs declined the offer and departed from the casino. This lawsuit followed.

The complaint sets forth three separate theories of liability arising out of this incident: assault and battery, slander and false imprisonment. However, defendants concede that a contested material issue of fact is presented by the assault and battery claim, and plaintiffs concede that their slander claim must be dismissed due to an inability to show any damage to their business, professional or personal reputations resulting from the incident. Therefore, the sole question at this juncture is whether there is a contested material issue of fact on the false imprisonment claim.

The tort of false imprisonment is established upon showing any "unlawful restraint upon a man's freedom of locomotion." Earl v. Winne, 14 N.J. 119, 128 (1953). The unlawful restraint need not be imposed by physical force. As observed in Earl v. Winne:

> This constraint may be caused by threats as well as by actionable force, and the threats may be by conduct or by words. If the words or conduct are such as to include a reasonable apprehension of force and the means of coercion is at hand, a person may be as effectually restrained and deprived of liberty as by prison bars. [at 127]

Furthermore, the assertion of legal authority to take a person into custody, even where such authority does not in fact exist, may be sufficient to create a reasonable apprehension that a person is under restraint.

There can be no serious doubt that the elements of false imprisonment would be established if plaintiffs' version of this incident were believed by a jury. According to plaintiffs, they were accosted by uniformed security guards who physically removed them from the blackjack table. They were then subjected, while surrounded by security guards, to an interrogation by a games manager, who said that they would be arrested unless identification was produced. Under these circumstances, plaintiffs reasonably could have concluded that they would be forcibly restrained if they attempted to leave the site of this interrogation without producing identification and that they were thus under confinement.

Defendants do not seriously dispute that the incident, as described by plaintiffs, contains the essential elements of a false imprisonment. However, they assert that a casino has the legal right to detain temporarily a patron suspected of being a card counter. Hence, they argue that any restraint imposed upon plaintiffs was not "unlawful." Defendants assert that they have the same right to detain a suspected card counter as a retail store owner has to detain a suspected shoplifter. See N.J.S.A. 2C:20-11e. In the words of defendants, it is their position that "a casino, in order to protect its interests, may reasonably detain a suspected card counter, and may not be held liable for false imprisonment in so doing."

To assess this contention, it is appropriate to consider the nature of card counting and the asserted justification for casinos to exclude the persons who engage in this activity from blackjack tables. Former Casino Control Commissioner Prospero De Bona issued an addendum to a report on the exclusion of card counters from casinos which described the card counting process as containing three basic elements:

> The first is the method for keeping track of, or "counting," the cards that have been dealt. This is usually accomplished by assigning a certain plus or minus value to each card in the deck and keeping a "running total or count" of these values as the cards are being dealt. The "running count" is then converted into a "true count" which depends upon the number of cards left to be dealt. The second element of these systems is the strategy to be followed for hitting, standing, doubling down, splitting pairs or surrendering. This strategy is a variable one which depends on the specific cards held by the player, the exposed card of the dealer, and the plus or minus value of the count at that particular time. The third component of these systems is the ability to vary the amount of each wager so that minimal amounts are bet when the "count" is unfavorable and larger amounts when the "count" is favorable.

Thus, card counting does not involve dishonesty or cheating. On the contrary, a card counter is simply a highly skilled player who analyzes the statistical probabilities associated with blackjack and, based upon those probabilities, develops playing strategies which may afford him an advantage over the casino. It was solely this loss of the normal "house advantage" which caused the casinos to exclude card counters from the blackjack tables.

The Casino Control Commissioner upheld this exclusion policy on the grounds that the common law right of the proprietor of a business to exclude a person from its establishment for any reason it chooses (*see* Garifine v. Monmouth Park Jockey Club, 29 N.J. 47 (1959)) encompasses the right of a casino to exclude a patron who has devised a technique for winning at blackjack. That determination of the Casino Control Commission was reversed by the Appellate Division (Uston v. Resorts Int'l Hotel, Inc., 179 N.J. Super. 223 (1981)), and the issue is now before the Supreme Court of New Jersey, certification having been granted. 87 N.J. 419–20 (1982). Whichever way the issue ultimately may be resolved, the only point which needs to be made here is that the decision of the Casino Control Commission upholding the exclusion of card counters from blackjack tables was not predicated on the view that such conduct is dishonest or that it is prohibited by statute or administrative regulation, but solely upon the asserted common law rights of casinos as private entrepreneurs.

This circumstance sharply distinguishes the detention of suspected card counters from the detention of alleged shoplifters. Shoplifting is a crime. N.J.S.A. 2C:20-11(e). To aid in the apprehension of shoplifters as well as to enable retail stores to protect themselves from this form of criminal activity, the Legislature has provided that "a merchant, who has probable cause for believing that a person has willfully concealed unpurchased merchandise and that he can recover the merchandise by taking the person into custody, may, for the purpose of attempting to effect the recovery thereof, take the person into custody and detain him in a reasonable manner for not more than a reasonable time." *Ibid.* Furthermore, to ensure that merchants will be able to exercise this power without inhibition, the Legislature has specifically provided that a merchant who takes a suspected shoplifter into custody as provided by this statute shall not be "civilly liable in any manner or to any extent whatever." *Ibid.* The decision in Cooke v. J.J. Newberry & Co., 96 N.J. Super. 9 (App. Div. 1967), upon which defendants place primary reliance in support of their motion for summary judgment, simply interprets the predecessor to this statutory provision authorizing the detention of suspected shoplifters. Therefore, it obviously has no pertinency to a case where no legislation has been enacted providing immunity for conduct which otherwise would constitute false imprisonment.

However, defendants contend that N.J.S.A. 5:12-121(b) confers an immunity upon casinos comparable to that which N.J.S.A. 2C:20-11(e) confers upon retail merchants. This section provides in pertinent part:

> Any licensee or its officers, employees or agents who shall have probable cause for believing there has been a violation of sections 113 through 116 of this act in the casino by any person may take such person into custody and detain him in the establishment in a reasonable manner for a reasonable length of time, for the purpose of notifying law enforcement or commission authorities. Such taking into custody and detention shall not render such licensee or its officers, employees or agents criminally or civilly liable for false arrest, false imprisonment, slander or unlawful detention unless such taking into custody or detention is unreasonable under all of the circumstances.

To be sure, this section authorizes casino officials to detain patrons under certain circumstances and provides an accompanying qualified immunity from civil liability. However, the operation of this section can be triggered only by the existence of probable cause to believe that "there has been a violation of sections 113 through 116 of this act." These sections (N.J.S.A. 5:12-112 through 5:12-116) make it a crime of the fourth degree or a misdemeanor to use bogus chips, marked cards, loaded dice, sleight of hand tricks and a variety of other devices to cheat or swindle a casino. However, there is no basis upon which card counting can be viewed as cheating or swindling a casino and hence a violation of one of these criminal provisions. Rather, it is simply a skillful technique for playing blackjack which negates the normal advantage of the casino over the player. Therefore, N.J.S.A. 5:12-121(b) affords no authorization to a casino to detain a suspected card counter.

Absent any affirmative statutory authorization to detain suspected card counters, the plaintiffs' version of the incident at the Boardwalk Regency would constitute false imprisonment. Therefore, the defendants' motion for summary judgment, except that part directed at the claim for slander, will be denied.

Notes

1. Card counting is *not* illegal under New Jersey or Nevada law. Capmione v. Adamar of New Jersey, Inc, 714 A.2.d. 299 (N.J. 1998); Chen v. Nevada State Gaming Control Bd., 994 P.2d. 1551 (Nev. 2000) (implied in the majority opinion and noted in the dissent). This has also been recognized by Federal courts in Mississippi. *See* Cashio v. Alpha Gulf Coast, Inc., 77 F.3d 477 (5th Cir. 1995). No state has either statutes or regulations prohibiting card counting.

2. Advantage play is a broad term to describe a situation in which a player through some method of play can acquire an advantage over the casino. In other words, advantage play is where the player can overcome the mathematical advantage that is built into every house-banked casino game. Advantage play is more than a hypothetical question. Some experts believe that advantage players take as much as three percent of all moneys wagered in commercial casinos. Some advantage play is clearly cheating, such as card crimping or marking. Some forms of advantage play are legal, such as card counting. Other types of advantage play meet the same criteria as card counting, i.e. where the player uses superior skill to analyze factors within the game rules that are available to all players. Another example is slot teams. Progressive slots are slot machines in which one or more of the payouts increase by a set amount for each coin or credit played that does not result in the player winning that payout. *See generally,* DAVID SKLANSKY, GETTING THE BEST OF IT 199 (1997). While slot machines are games of pure chance, on accession the slot machines, typically with progressive jackpots, may provide the player with a positive expectation or advantage. Knowing when a machine with a progressive jackpot provides a positive expectation involves skill. For example, suppose a progressive slot machine has a top payout of $100 and 5 cents of every dollar bet increases the progressive jackpot. If the player plays the machine for $1 and does not win, the progressive jackpot will increase to $100.05. The progressive jackpot will increase in this way until it is won and it will then be reset to its original starting point. If the progressive jackpot increases to a certain point without being won, then the theoretical payout results in a positive player advantage. This slight statistical advantage is what attracts the professional slot teams. These are organized and financed teams of professional slot players that attempt to exploit those progressive slots that have a positive player expectation. Only certain progressive slot machines will meet the slot team's criteria. First, the number of slot machines

that are linked to the progressive jackpot must be manageable. The team needs to monopolize all the slot machines to avoid the risk that a non-member will win the jackpot. Second, the slot team must know certain fundamental aspects of the machine including its house advantage and frequency of payout for all reel combinations. Third, the statistical frequency of hitting the progressive jackpot must be consistent with the slot team's bankroll. No slot team has an unlimited bankroll. Based on probabilities, the team needs to have enough cash on hand to play all the linked machines with the progressive jackpot until one team member hits the progressive jackpot.

3. Some advantage players create the advantage by intentionally exploiting mistakes by the casino, its employees or by malfunctioning gaming devices. A good example is the advantage player or team of players that are present on opening nights of any new casino. They understand that errors are most likely to occur when a casino is in the midst of training employees and deploying several hundred or thousand new gaming devices. In an unreported case, a newspaper described the exploits of one such player that began on the opening night of a casino as follows:

> He noticed a bank of slot machines where the payouts for the $100 machines and the $1 machines had been mistakenly reversed. Over the course of several hours, he won $27,000 in cash and comps by collecting $100 machine payouts from $1 machines.

> Rod Smith, *Civil Liberties: Disadvantaged: Casinos, Police Officials Often Intimidate Legal Patrons, Lawyers Say,* Las Vegas Rev. J. (July 6, 2003).

4. Other advantage players attempt to find slot machines that are overpaying or, in other words, have defective software or hardware resulting in the player receiving a greater number of coins than they would otherwise be entitled to.

5. Another type of advantage play is hole-carding, which is a technique used primarily in blackjack to learn the value of the dealer's hole card before the player needs to make a decision on how to play his or her hand. The advantage derived from hole-carding can be more substantial than card counting. Most hole-carding is done intentionally. One surveillance expert described a typical team that took advantage of a weak dealer. In that case, the team consisted of two people. One person was in the "third base side," meaning the seat nearest to the dealer's right hand, and the other in the first spot, nearest the dealer's left hand. "Not only was the third base player slouching in his seat, his signals to the other player were simple. The hole-carder on the third-base side of the game had a stock of green ($25 chips) and red ($5 chips). To signal stand, he touched the red (stand/stop), to signal hit, he touched the green (hit/go) and for insurance he tapped the green stack with a chip pinched between his fingers to represent an 'I' (insurance). The dealer later was proven to be a weak dealer and not in the group...." In the case of the player sitting on the third base side, slouching, he was right "74 percent of the time at reading the hole card." Douglas Florence, Advantage Play: Blackjack, Global Gaming Bus., at 18 (July 2004). If a person knows the dealer's hole card, the player has an advantage over the casino through having additional information to figure out whether to double his bet, surrender a hand (thus, only losing half a bet), or determining whether to hit or stand. The impact that "hole-carding" has on the house advantage will vary depending on the advantage player's proclivity to correctly identify the hole card and to what advantage he uses the information. If the player knows the dealer's hole card every time and played every hand to maximum advantage, it would result in a ten percent advantage over the house. The typical advantage player, however, would not play to maximum advantage because, for example, hitting a nineteen against the dealer's twenty would be too suspicious and draw inquiry. Stafford Wong, Basic Blackjack (1992).

Chapter 8

Ethical Issues and Duties Arising in the Gaming World[*]

1. Introduction

In many contexts, the ethical standards most common to the practice of gaming law are obvious. For example, an attorney can be disbarred for soliciting millions of dollars from gaming applicants to corrupt and manipulate the application process in connection with the lawyer's father—the Governor—and disguising them as attorney's fees. In re Stephen R. Edwards, 879 So. 2d 718 (La. 2004). Nor is it surprising that an attorney who knowingly files an application containing false information is subject to discipline. This chapter, however, addresses situations of greater nuance that, while not necessarily unique to gaming attorneys, may occur more frequently in a gaming law practice. Several hypothetical questions are included that examine common ethical problems faced by the gaming attorney.

2. Who Is the Client?

Corporations and organizations are fictitious legal entities that can only speak and act through authorized agents, shareholders, officers, directors or other employees. In representing organizations, lawyers must necessarily interact with people acting for the organizations. Lawyers must be mindful, however, that these individuals merely serve as proxies or representatives of the organization. A lawyer's frequent interaction with the organization's representatives may result in mistaken assumptions by the representatives that they are the client rather than the organization itself.

Obviously, no problem arises in cases when the interests of the organization and the organization's representative are compatible. However, the interests of the organization and the organization's representative may eventually conflict. These conflicts frequently are not readily discernable at the outset of the representation. As a result, by the time the friction is realized, the lawyer is deeply entrenched in the representation. The emerging conflicts give rise to a disconcerting dilemma for the lawyer. That is, who does the lawyer represent: the organization, or the individual(s) acting on behalf of the organization [hereinafter "individual constituent"]?

These very real issues are common in the context of gaming representation, particularly licensing. Gaming attorneys often represent a corporation applying for a gaming li-

---

[*] Coauthored by Martha Denning Moore, Assistant Dean and Professor, Thomas M. Cooley Law School.

cense. In most cases, this involves filing an application for the corporation and certain of its officers, directors, and shareholders.

Hypothetical

A group of four individuals schedule an appointment to meet you for consultation regarding obtaining a gaming license. The group, which includes two investors, a casino executive, and a builder, is constructing a new casino. The investors are providing the capital, the builder is providing construction services, and the casino executive is providing development and casino operational experience. Each group member will own 25% of the casino, but the two investors want to control the decisions of the group. After consulting with corporate counsel, the decision is made to create a Limited Liability Corporation allowed under state law that will give control over the entity to the two investors, who will serve as managing members, but also give an equity interest in the entity to the casino executive and the builder. You commence the application process by gathering information from the four individuals, all of whom must be licensed independently.

For the most part, the information is not unusual. One applicant, the builder, has a twenty-year-old arrest for underage drinking. The investor has a few lawsuits related to a failed business. You complete the individual applications and the company application and submit them to the gaming authorities. As the investigation progresses, negative information regarding the casino executive begins to surface. He apparently left an earlier employment at one casino amidst an internal investigation that he had abused his executive privileges by extending complimentary services to persons who were not patrons of the casino but actually customers of his wife's design firm. The casino executive defended his decisions because he asserted that these individuals were excellent potential casino customers. The gaming executive discloses to you that while he may not have extended the complimentaries without the relationships to his wife's business, he believed he was within company policy.

You defended the applicant before the gaming authorities on the basis that he was within company policy and the persons were wealthy and thus potential customers. Later, however, another issue arose regarding a different employer. In this case, the casino executive resigned under another internal investigation centering on the executive purchasing four custom wheels for his personal automobile on a company account. After discussing this with the casino executive, you decide that it is basically indefensible. His only explanation is that he got "stiffed" on the year-end bonus and he deserved the wheels. Based on the accumulated evidence, you become concerned that the casino executive is not suitable for a license. You conclude it is in the best interests of the LLC and its managing members to terminate both his employment and his equity interest.

Query: Before learning of the custom wheels issue, could you, as gaming counsel, represent both the corporation and the corporate officers in a licensing investigation? Why or why not? Who is the client—the LLC, its managing partners, or the casino executive? Do you have an obligation to inform the managing partners of the LLC upon discovery of issue regarding potential abuse of complimentary privileges? At what point, if at all, did the interests of the casino executive and the LLC diverge such that you could no longer represent both the LLC and the casino executive?

In this case, the best interests of the casino executive may be to try to convince the regulators that the purchase of the custom wheels was legitimate because the automobile was used primarily for business. If you represent the LLC, what are your obligations to the LLC? To the casino executive? To the gaming regulators?

Assume for argument that the best interests of the corporation are to have the casino executive resign his position and sell his interest in the LLC. What are the ethical considerations?

Under what circumstances should the corporate officer obtain new counsel?

Rules

Nevada Professional Conduct Rule 1.13: Organization as Client

Rule 1.13. Organization as Client.

(a) A lawyer employed or retained by an organization represents the organization acting through its duly authorized constituents.

(b) If a lawyer for an organization knows that an officer, employee or other person associated with the organization is engaged in action, intends to act or refuses to act in a matter related to the representation that is a violation of a legal obligation to the organization, or a violation of law that reasonably might be imputed to the organization, and that is likely to result in substantial injury to the organization, then the lawyer shall proceed as is reasonably necessary in the best interest of the organization. Unless the lawyer reasonably believes that it is not necessary in the best interest of the organization to do so, the lawyer shall refer the matter to higher authority in the organization, including, if warranted by the circumstances, to the highest authority that can act on behalf of the organization as determined by applicable law.

(c) Except as provided in paragraph (d), if

(1) despite the lawyer's efforts in accordance with paragraph (b), the highest authority that can act on behalf of the organization insists upon or fails to address in a timely and appropriate manner an action, or a refusal to act, that is clearly a violation of law, and

(2) the lawyer reasonably believes that the violation is reasonably certain to result in substantial injury to the organization, then the lawyer may reveal information relating to the representation whether or not Rule 1.6 permits such disclosure, but only if and to the extent the lawyer reasonably believes necessary to prevent substantial injury to the organization.

(d) Paragraph (c) shall not apply with respect to information related to a lawyer's retention by an organization to investigate an alleged violation of law, or to defend the organization or an officer, employee or other constituent associated with the organization against a claim arising out of an alleged violation of law.

(e) A lawyer who reasonably believes that he or she has been discharged because of the lawyer's actions taken pursuant to paragraphs (b) or (c) or who withdraws under circumstances that require or permit the lawyer to take action under either of those paragraphs, shall proceed as the lawyer reasonably believes necessary to assure that the organization's highest authority is informed of the lawyer's discharge or withdrawal.

(f) In dealing with an organization's directors, officers, employees, members, shareholders or other constituents, a lawyer shall explain the identity of the client to the constituent and reasonably attempt to ensure that the constituent realizes that the lawyer's client is the organization rather than the constituent. In cases of multiple representation such as discussed in paragraph (g), the lawyer shall take reasonable steps to ensure that the constituent understands the fact of multiple representation.

(g) A lawyer representing an organization may also represent any of its directors, officers, employees, members, shareholders or other constituents, subject to the provisions of Rule 1.7. If the organization's consent to the dual representation is required by Rule 1.7, the consent shall be given by an appropriate official of the organization other than the individual who is to be represented, or by the shareholders.

Notes

1. In light of the Rule set out above, whose interests should the lawyer advocate? How should the lawyer resolve this predicament?

2. Under limited circumstances, a lawyer may represent the organization and its employees, officers, directors, or shareholders. However, this dual/multiple representation is a potential minefield. In carrying out the dual/multiple representation, the lawyer must be cognizant of and comport with the constraints of the applicable conflict rules. Nevada Professional Conduct Rule 1.7 (2006); RESTATEMENT (THIRD) OF THE LAW GOVERNING LAWYERS § 131 cmt. e (2000). The lawyer must obtain the written, informed consent of all clients to the representation. Under a rule found in most states:

> A lawyer who represents two or more clients shall not participate in making an aggregate settlement of the claims of or against the clients, or in a criminal case an aggregated agreement as to guilty or nolo contendere pleas, unless each client gives informed consent, in a writing signed by the client. The lawyer's disclosure shall include the existence and nature of all the claims or pleas involved and of the participation of each person in the settlement.

NEVADA RULES OF PROF'L CONDUCT R. 1.8(g). The lawyer must also advise each client that any information received in the course of the dual/multiple representation will be shared with the other client(s) and that such information is not protected by the ethical duty of confidentiality between them. Further, the lawyer must keep each client adequately informed, enabling each client to make informed decisions about the representation.

> Unless all affected clients consent to the representation under the limitations and conditions provided..., a lawyer may not represent both an organization and a director, officer, employee, shareholder, owner, partner, member, or other individual or organization associated with the organization if there is a substantial risk that the lawyer's representation of either would be materially [limited] and adversely affected by the lawyer's duties to the other.

RESTATEMENT (THIRD) OF THE LAW GOVERNING LAWYERS § 131 (2000). As with any minefield, such dual/multiple representation is a treacherous venture, which must be maneuvered with rigorous scrutiny and vigilance. Indeed, the prudent course of action would be to avoid the minefield altogether. Therefore, lawyers must be painstakingly cognizant of the identity of the actual client and attendant obligations.

Longstanding law recognizes that the organization's lawyer represents the organization, not the organization's individual constituent. *See* Upjohn Co. v. United States, 449 U.S. 383 (1981). The organization's lawyer is obligated to advocate in the best interest of the organization. In this regard, the lawyer owes the organization the duty of confidentiality, diligence, and loyalty even to the detriment of the organization's individual constituents.

3. The lawyer's special duties in representing organizations are enumerated in Nevada Professional Conduct Rule 1.13. Organizations include, but are not limited to, profit and non-profit corporations, limited liability companies, labor unions, trade associations,

unincorporated associations, general and limited partnerships, "joint venture[s], trust[s], estate[s], or similar entit[ies] with a recognizable form, internal organization, and relative permanence." RESTATEMENT (THIRD) OF THE LAW GOVERNING LAWYERS § 131 cmt. a (2000).

4. Notwithstanding the plain language of Rule 1.13 defining the lawyer's role, frequent challenges exist in the practical application of this rule. Learning or uncovering negative information about the individual constituent is not unusual for a lawyer in the routine course of dealing with an individual constituent on behalf of an organization. The individual constituent may have unwittingly supplied negative information to the lawyer under the mistaken belief that the information would be protected from disclosure to the organization by virtue of the ethical duty of confidentiality. Thus, in representing organizations, lawyers must be ever vigilant of adverse consequences to the lawyer if the lawyer fails to clarify the lawyer's role at the outset of the representation.

5. A constituent may mistakenly assume that the lawyer will act to further the personal interests of the constituent, perhaps even against the interest of the organization. Such a mistake on the part of the constituent can occur after an extended period of working with the lawyer on matters of common interest to the organization and the constituent, particularly if the lawyer has formerly provided personal counsel to the constituent, and may be more likely to occur with inside legal counsel due to greater personal acquaintanceship. Such an assumption, although erroneous, may be harmless so long as the interests of the constituent and the organization do not materially conflict. When those interests do materially conflict, however, the lawyer's failure to warn the constituent of the nature of the lawyer's role could prejudicially mislead the constituent, impair the interests of the organization, or both.

6. An adequate clarification is required to protect the interest of the organization in unencumbered representation. Failing to clarify the lawyer's role and the client's interests may redound to the disadvantage of the organization if the lawyer, even if unwittingly, thereby undertakes concurrent representation of both the organization and the constituent. RESTATEMENT (THIRD) OF THE LAW GOVERNING LAWYERS § 103 cmt. e (2000).

7. If a conflict develops between an organization and the individual constituent, and the lawyer failed to clarify the lawyer's role at the outset of the representation, causing the individual to reveal what the individual believed was confidential information to the lawyer, the lawyer may be required to withdraw from the representation of the organization and the individual.

8. Lawyers should also identify and clarify the lawyer's role, emphasizing to the organization's agents, officers, directors, or employees that the lawyer represents the organization rather than the individual. This initial early clarification of the lawyer's role, along with advice that the individual constituent secure separate counsel obviates the need for the lawyer to forfeit both clients should a conflict later materialize.

9. In situations where the lawyer fully clarified his role at the commencement of the representation and subsequently learns of adverse information about an individual constituent that may cause substantial harm to the organization, the lawyer is absolutely obligated to act in the best interests of the organization, which may require disclosure of the information albeit to the detriment of the individual constituent.

10. Not only does the organization's lawyer have a duty to act in the best interests of the organization, but the lawyer also has an affirmative duty to report wrongdoing by individual constituents. Breaches of fiduciary duty or illegal activity likely to result

in substantial injury to the organization must be reported up the organizational ladder, beginning with the chief legal officer, the chief executive officer, or the equivalent thereof.

3. Candor to the Tribunal

A. Disclosure

Confidentiality is fundamental to the attorney-client relationship. The objective of the ethical duty of confidentiality is to promote frankness and candidness by clients in dealing with their lawyers. Confident that information shared with their lawyers will be kept confidential, clients are free to fully converse with their lawyers, even disclosing embarrassing and/or detrimental information. This open and candid flow of information enables lawyers to consider all information relevant to the cause, whether good, bad or neutral. Lawyers are then equipped to thoroughly and fairly evaluate their clients' matters and to provide optimal advice and counsel. The ethical duty of confidentiality, however, can be inconsistent with strict gaming law regulations that often require applicants to consent to inspections, searches and seizures, and to disclosure of information otherwise protected by the attorney-client privilege. With certain exceptions, lawyers have an ethical duty to keep confidential all information relating to the representation of a client. NEW JERSEY RULES OF PROF'L CONDUCT R. 1.6(2005). This ethical duty is broader than the attorney client privilege, which extends only to communications between the attorney and client and may be waived by the client's disclosure to third parties. *See* Brennan's Inc. v. Brennan's Restaurants, Inc., 590 F.2d 168, 172 (5th Cir. 1979). For example, an applicant for a Nevada gaming license must sign a release of information form that authorizes and requests "all persons to whom this request is presented ... to furnish such information ... whether or not such information would otherwise be protected from disclosure by any constitutional, statutory, or common law privilege." Nevada State Gaming Control Board, Investigations Division, Form 18 (revised May 2004).

Hypothetical

You represent an applicant for a casino license. The licensing authorities have a standard application form that requires the disclosure of certain personal information including criminal history. Specifically, the question asks: "Have you ever been arrested, detained, charged, indicted, or summoned to answer for any criminal offense or violation for any reason whatsoever, regardless of the disposition of the event? (Except minor traffic citations)." In your first meeting with the client, you explain the need to fully, fairly and honestly respond to all questions on the application and stress that failure to disclose past arrests is especially problematic because it invokes suitability issues regarding personal background and candor. At a scheduled meeting, the applicant wants to discuss two "minor" issues. He informs you that when he was sixteen years old, some twenty years ago, he and his friends were "partying" down by the river when a park ranger happened upon them. The park ranger found marijuana and drug paraphernalia. The applicant explains, however, that he was never charged after he and his parents met with the park rangers. It is highly unlikely that regulators will ever uncover the arrest, thus Applicant did not disclose it. How should you respond as gaming counsel? Does a gaming attorney have the responsibility to disclose negative information on a client if such information might materially impact the client's ability to obtain a license? Why or why not?

The second "minor" issue involves Applicant's brother, who unexpectedly appeared at Applicant's home one day, claiming that he was down on his luck and needed cash. Applicant gives his brother money and tells him never to return. The next day, the police question Applicant's parents about the brother's whereabouts because he is wanted on outstanding warrants for possession and sale of drugs. After Applicant's brother was apprehended, Applicant became concerned that the police might conclude that he aided a fugitive. If regulators learn that Applicant provided money to a fugitive, regulators would likely want to explore the matter in greater detail notwithstanding Applicant's reasonable explanation. Do you as the gaming attorney have any ethical obligations to inform regulators of the incident? What if regulators ask you if you are aware of any facts that could impact the suitability of Applicant? What if your client, Applicant, knew his brother was a fugitive before giving him money? What if Applicant refuses to allow you to disclose the information to regulators?

Rules

New Jersey Rules Prof'l Conduct R. 1.6(b): Confidentiality of Information

(a) A lawyer shall not reveal information relating to representation of a client unless the client consents after consultation, except for disclosures that are impliedly authorized in order to carry out the representation, and except as stated in paragraphs (b) and (c).

(b) A lawyer shall reveal such information to the proper authorities, as soon as, and to the extent the lawyer reasonably believes necessary, to prevent the client:

(1) from committing a criminal, illegal or fraudulent act that the lawyer reasonably believes is likely to result in death or substantial bodily harm or substantial injury to the financial interest or property of another;

(2) from committing a criminal, illegal or fraudulent act that the lawyer reasonably believes is likely to perpetrate a fraud upon a tribunal.

(c) A lawyer may reveal such information to the extent the lawyer reasonably believes necessary:

(1) to rectify the consequences of a client's criminal, illegal or fraudulent act in the furtherance of which the lawyer's services had been used;

(2) to establish a claim or defense on behalf of the lawyer in a controversy between the lawyer and the client, or to establish a defense to a criminal charge, civil claim or disciplinary complaint against the lawyer based upon the conduct in which the client was involved; or

(3) to comply with other law.

(d) Reasonable belief for purposes of RPC 1.6 is the belief or conclusion of a reasonable lawyer that is based upon information that has some foundation in fact and constitutes prima facie evidence of the matters referred to in subsections (b) or (c).

Notes

1. One of the fundamental tenets of the attorney-client relationship is the lawyer's ethical duty of confidentiality. Any information obtained in the course of the attorney-client relationship that is not general knowledge is protected by the broad ethical duty of confidentiality. This duty survives the termination of the attorney-client relationship, and even survives the client's death. In fact, the ethical duty of confidential-

ity lasts forever. The lack of full disclosure by clients may cause substantial harm to the clients' matters, oftentimes resulting in prejudicial surprise or the complete disassembling of a case.

2. Given the broad reach of the ethical duty of confidentiality, lawyers may not disclose negative information about a client without the client's informed consent, implied authority, or an exception under New Jersey Rule Professional Conduct 1.6(b). Where a gaming regulation requires a waiver of the attorney-client privilege, a gaming lawyer must communicate to clients the advantages, disadvantages, and the consequences of granting such consent (often in the form of a waiver). The client has the ultimate decision whether to execute such a waiver, notwithstanding the almost certain negative outcome of the gaming matter absent the execution of the waiver. Clients only then can make informed decisions about the waiver.

3. Undoubtedly, the preservation of confidential client information is a high-stakes game and lawyers must be vigilant in safeguarding client confidences and secrets. Nevertheless, lawyers are always free to counsel clients and to advise them of attendant benefits to full disclosure. After fully considering counsel's advice, an increased likelihood exists that clients will authorize disclosure of negative information, thereby alleviating the issue altogether.

4. Lawyers also must be cognizant that while the ethical duty of confidentiality is expansive, it is not absolute. The duty does not extend to a client's intentions to commit a crime or fraud. This holds especially true in the gaming industry, where vigilant regulatory agencies keep watchful eyes to guard against the infiltration of criminal activity. Nor does the duty permit lawyers to conceal or participate in a client or witness' lack of candor before a tribunal, gaming regulatory bodies, or administrative agencies.

5. As stated above, lawyers may not disclose negative information pertaining to a client, whether perceived or real, absent client consent, implied authority, or the application of an exception under the New Jersey Rule Professional Conduct 1.6(b). However, lawyers in the discharge of their duties should advise clients of the benefits of full disclosure at the outset. The forthright disclosure of "not per se" negative information will likely foster trust with gaming regulators. Similarly, up-front disclosures signal openness and trustworthiness to gaming officials, which can only enhance the clients' cause.

6. On the other hand, the likely eventual discovery of the "not per se" negative information may lead gaming regulators to draw negative inferences from the mere fact that the information was not disclosed in the first place, regardless of the "responsible explanation." Further, prompt disclosure of "not per se" negative information provides lawyers with the opportunity to fully explain the information and to dispel its negative flavor, an unequivocal benefit to clients in the course of an investigation.

B. Honesty

Rules

Colorado Rule and Comments

Rule 3.3. Candor Toward The Tribunal

(a) A lawyer shall not knowingly:

(1) make a false statement of material fact or law to a tribunal or fail to correct a false statement of material fact or law previously made to the tribunal by the lawyer;

(2) fail to disclose to the tribunal legal authority in the controlling jurisdiction known to the lawyer to be directly adverse to the position of the client and not disclosed by opposing counsel; or

(3) offer evidence that the lawyer knows to be false. If a lawyer, the lawyer's client, or witness called by the lawyer has offered material evidence and the lawyer comes to know of its falsity, the lawyer shall take reasonable remedial measures, including, if necessary, disclosure to the tribunal. A lawyer may refuse to offer evidence, other than the testimony of a defendant in a criminal matter, that the lawyer reasonably believes is false.

(b) A lawyer who represents a client in an adjudicative proceeding and who knows that a person intends to engage, is engaging or has engaged in criminal or fraudulent conduct related to the proceeding shall take reasonable remedial measures, including, if necessary, disclosure to the tribunal.

(c) The duties stated in paragraphs (a) and (b) continue to the conclusion of the proceeding, and apply even if compliance requires disclosure of information otherwise protected by Rule 1.6.

(d) In an ex parte proceeding, a lawyer shall inform the tribunal of all material facts known to the lawyer that will enable the tribunal to make an informed decision, whether or not the facts are adverse.

People v. Lopez
796 P.2d 957 (Colo. 1990)

The respondent, Andrew M. Lopez, was charged with professional misconduct in his representation of Halina Topa (Topa) and for his participation in the acquisition and later sale of a bar, when he knew or should have known of a conflict of interest that he had with his client. Topa is the complaining witness in this case. The hearing panel of the Grievance Committee approved the findings of fact, conclusions, and recommendations of the hearing board and the recommendation that the respondent be suspended for thirty days and be assessed the costs of these proceedings. We approve the findings and conclusions, but impose a six-month suspension upon the respondent for his professional misconduct and order that he pay the costs incurred in these proceedings.

Respondent Andrew M. Lopez was admitted to the bar of this court on May 19, 1975, and is subject to the jurisdiction of this court and its Grievance Committee. C.R.C.P. 241.6. The respondent is engaged in the general practice of law, but limits his practice to business matters and liquor license proceedings. The respondent met Halina Topa in May 1982. They developed a close personal and social relationship that later became business oriented. The disciplinary complaint asserts fraud, conflicts of interest, and that the respondent had taken advantage of Topa by engaging in conduct prejudicial to her interests and had failed to account to her for proceeds he received for her benefit while he was her lawyer. Topa was from Poland, was fluent in five languages, had a degree in business, and was licensed by the New York Stock Exchange. She also owned an interest in real property, which was valued at $50,000 and provided her with rental income.

Topa desired to acquire a business and sought to use her rental property as a down payment to purchase an interest in a business. The respondent assisted her in her efforts to purchase several bars, but, in each instance, her offers were refused because the bar owners were not willing to accept Topa's income property as a down payment. Thereafter, the respondent introduced her to Jackson St. James who bought, sold, and operated bars. St. James agreed to help Topa purchase a bar and entered into a management agreement with Topa. In the agreement St. James covenanted to train Topa to operate and manage a bar. The respondent also recommended Russell Berget, a real estate broker, to assist her in the sale of her income property and the income property was listed with Berget. Topa also entered into a business agreement with the respondent for legal services in the acquisition of a bar. Eventually, the respondent, St. James, and Berget formed JAR Associates, a partnership, to buy and sell bars and taverns, and purchased a bar known as Savanna's using funds or property provided by Topa. The transactions leading to the purchase, sale, repossession, and resale of the bar provide the basis for this disciplinary proceeding.

Both the hearing board and the hearing panel concluded that an attorney-client relationship existed that required that the respondent protect his client against any injury that might arise out of a conflict of interest. Although the respondent denies that he had an attorney-client relationship with Topa, the finding that an attorney-client relationship existed is supported by an abundance of evidence in the record.[1]

COUNT I

JAR Associates located a bar called Savanna's, which was closed and needed extensive repairs, and spent $9,000 to purchase the equipment in the restaurant, which was valued at $45,000. JAR Associates also paid $7,000 on the lease and outstanding taxes and fees to maintain the liquor license. To facilitate the sale and transfer of Savanna's to Topa, a new corporation called the South Holly Corporation was formed and Topa was issued all of the stock of that corporation. The respondent prepared the documents and obtained a transfer of the liquor license to the South Holly Corporation.

On March 5, 1984, Topa signed a lease to operate Savanna's. For a short period of time Topa and St. James operated Savanna's. Pursuant to St. James' agreement with Topa, Topa was paid for working at the bar. Not long after the purchase, an offer was made by Floyd Steven Laneer, who worked at Savanna's, to buy the bar and the offer was accepted by both Topa and JAR Associates. Laneer agreed to buy the stock of the South Holly Corporation, which owned Savanna's for $90,000. The purchase agreement included an earnest money payment of $2,000 and a payment of $8,000 at the time of closing. The $10,000 was paid to JAR Associates by Laneer and the funds were used to pay outstanding debts of Savanna's and certain claims by Topa. No formal accounting was made to Topa at the Laneer closing but a promissory note was executed by Laneer to Topa on July 18, 1984. The note required the payment of $1,093.15 per month. Some payments were collected by Topa but Laneer defaulted and the bar reverted to the South Holly Corporation.

In February 1985, a new buyer for Savanna's was located and a new contract was prepared by the respondent. Herman Sidkey and Rita Tulper agreed to purchase the bar for $105,000. The contract specified that $2,500 was to be paid as earnest money and $22,500 upon the assumption of the operation of the bar. Rita Tulper executed an $80,000 promis-

---

1. On at least one occasion the respondent brought suit to collect a debt for Topa. He also sued on behalf of Topa and a number of others to obtain specific performance on a contract to purchase Ryan's Off Market bar when Ryan refused to go through with Topa's contract to purchase Ryan's Off Market bar. The respondent prepared the contracts and documents for the acquisition of a number of bars by Topa. Topa, in connection with a number of the prospective bar or tavern transactions, obtained independent counsel who testified that the respondent and Topa had a business but not an attorney-client relationship.

sory note payable to Topa with interest at 11% for the balance of the purchase price. The down payment was made to JAR Associates who permitted the purchasers to reduce their cash payment to $15,000 to provide funds for the operation of the bar with JAR Associates carrying back a $5,000 loan to Sidkey. The $15,000 paid to JAR Associates was used to pay back taxes, debts, and expenses incurred at the bar prior to the sale but no formal accounting was provided to Topa. $1,500 was used to pay for repairs on Topa's rental property and to repay security deposits that Topa owed her tenants.

While the complaining witness was working at Savanna's, she met a customer who was in the oil exploration business in Cyprus and whom she subsequently married. Thereafter the relationship between the respondent and Topa deteriorated and she filed a lawsuit against JAR Associates, the respondent, St. James, and Berget. Berget settled the claim for $6,000. St. James moved to Florida, and a judgment was obtained against the respondent who filed for bankruptcy. The complaining witness, alleging fraud, sought to prevent the respondent's discharge in bankruptcy. After a full hearing in the bankruptcy court, the respondent's debt to Topa was discharged. A complaint was then filed with the Grievance Committee.

No evidence was presented that would establish that there was any attempt to defraud or take advantage of the complaining witness who the hearing board described as sophisticated, intelligent, and knowledgeable about all of the transactions that took place. The monetary loss that was suffered resulted from the default on Tulper's note, which was part of the consideration for the purchase of Savanna's. In addition, Topa was paid more than $16,000 for her services at Savanna's pursuant to her contract with St. James and she is now endeavoring to collect on the note. She acknowledges that Tulper has offered to pay $50,000 for the note, but is not willing to pay both the outstanding principal and interest. The evidence does not establish fraud, deceit, defalcation, overreaching, or misapplication of funds by JAR Associates, or the respondent, St. James, or Berget who were the partners in JAR Associates.

The complex business transactions to acquire different bars and taverns brought about a complaint that produced massive amounts of conflicting testimony. In all of the transactions both the respondent and Topa had a mutual interest in bringing about a successful conclusion to the transaction. The social relationship between the complaining witness and the respondent turned into a business relationship that did not turn out to the satisfaction of any of the parties.

COUNT II

Count II of the complaint relates to false statements included in applications filed by the respondent before the Colorado Liquor Licensing Authority. Findings also were made to support the claims relating to the false statements and failure to disclose interest in other bars when applications were made for a liquor license. The evidence presented established that the respondent is presently engaged in the general practice of law, and limits his practice to business matters and liquor licensing proceedings. The respondent served as attorney, corporate officer, and co-business participant in the purchase and sale of liquor establishments. The Hearing board found by clear and convincing evidence in Count II of the Complaint that in preparing liquor license applications the respondent failed on at least two occasions to disclose his interests in other liquor establishments, as required by subsection 12-47-129(4)(a), 5 C.R.S. (1985). The respondent also did not report the execution of a power of attorney in one of his liquor operations, in violation of subsection 12-47-106(9), 5 C.R.S. (1985). This clear and convincing evidence sustains the Disciplinary Counsel's exception to the determination by the Hearing board and Hearing panel that respondent's preparation and filing of the liquor license applications did not involve dishonesty, fraud, deceit, or misrepresentation, in violation of DR 1-102(A)(4).[2]

The respondent admits that as an attorney he is experienced in handling matters relating to the purchase, sale, and ownership of liquor establishments. The respondent's knowing failure to disclose his interests in other liquor establishments was an act involving dishonesty and misrepresentation, even though there may not have been fraudulent motive or intent to deceive. People v. McDowell, 718 P.2d 541, 546 (Colo.1986). The evidence supporting the false statements in the applications for liquor licenses was not in dispute and supports the allegations in the complaint.

DISCIPLINARY SANCTION

The hearing panel recommended a thirty-day suspension as the proper sanction. We conclude that a six-month suspension should be imposed for the respondent's violation of C.R.C.P. 241.6 and the Code of Professional of Responsibility. In addressing Count I, the hearing board concluded that the respondent failed to fully disclose his conflict of interest between JAR Associates and Topa regarding the purchase of Savanna's and concluded that the respondent violated DR5-101(A)[3] in representing Topa. Respondent failed to fully disclose his involvement with St. James and Berget, and of his conflicts of interest, and those of JAR Associates, with the complaining witness. The hearing board found that the respondent failed to advise Topa that the respondent had a mixed allegiance and that Topa could not rely on his advice.

The respondent also violated DR5-104(A).[4] The respondent and the complaining witness were in business together. The respondent had different business interests than Topa and should have limited his business relations with her. The respondent failed to insure that Topa was aware that he may not be using his professional judgment on her behalf and might be acting where there was a conflict of interest. See People ex rel. Kent v. Denious, 196 P.2d 257, 266–67 (Colo. 1948). The board also found that the respondent violated DR5-105(A).[5] The finding was based upon the fact that the respondent had both a personal and professional business relationship with Topa and his representation of JAR Associates involved serious conflicts of interest between Topa and JAR Associates. The multiple violations of the disciplinary rules by the respondent in and of themselves constitute grounds for disciplinary sanctions. DR1-102(A) (1) (a lawyer shall not violate a disciplinary rule).

In addition, the charges in Count II were proven by clear and convincing evidence and constitute a violation of C.R.C.P. 241.6. The hearing board found by clear and convincing evidence that the respondent violated DR1-102(A)(4)[6] by failing to list his involve-

---

2. DR 1-102(A)(4) provides that "[a] lawyer shall not: … engage in conduct involving dishonesty, fraud, deceit, or misrepresentation."

3. DR5-101(A) provides: "Except with the consent of his client after full disclosure, a lawyer shall not accept employment if the exercise of his professional judgment on behalf of his client will be or reasonably may be affected by his own financial, business, property, or personal interests."

4. DR5-104(A) provides: "A lawyer shall not enter into a business transaction with a client if they have differing interests therein and if the client expects the lawyer to exercise his professional judgment therein for the protection of the client, unless the client has consented after full disclosure."

5. DR5-105(A) provides: "A lawyer shall decline proffered employment if the exercise of his independent professional judgment in behalf of a client will be or is likely to be adversely affected by the acceptance of the proffered employment, or if it would be likely to involve him in representing differing interests, except to the extent permitted under DR 5-105(C)."

6. DR 1-102(A)(4) provides: "A lawyer shall not … [e]ngage in conduct involving dishonesty, fraud, deceit, or misrepresentation."

ment in other liquor establishments when he made application for a liquor license for a bar he was attempting to acquire for Topa. His failure to list his involvement in other liquor establishments adversely reflects on his fitness to practice law since buying and selling bars is his field of expertise. DR1-102(A) (6).

Relying on section 4.32 of the American Bar Association Standards for Imposing Lawyer Sanctions, the hearing board recommended suspension because the respondent knew or should have known of the conflict of interest and failed to disclose the possible effect of that conflict to his client resulting in her detriment. In reviewing aggravation and mitigation pursuant to section 9.2 of the standards, the hearing board found multiple offenses and a pattern of misconduct as aggravating factors. The respondent's lack of a disciplinary record and his absence of a dishonest or selfish motive were mitigating factors. Accordingly, a recommendation of suspension for thirty days was made to this court. Compare People v. Underhill, 683 P.2d 349 (Colo.1984) (representation of multiple parties with different interests in the sale of bars without insuring that full disclosure occurred, coupled with neglect and delay, warranted a one-year suspension) with People v. McDowell, 718 P.2d 541 (Colo.1986) (suspension for six months for withholding knowledge and fraud in representing both the seller and purchaser when obvious conflicts of interest existed). The hearing board, in recommending a thirty-day suspension, considered our decisions in both the *Underhill* and *McDowell* cases. Both cases had significant factual differences. In our view, the respondent's professional misconduct, which not only included his representation of Topa when there was an obvious conflict of interest but also the making of false representations in applications for liquor licenses, requires a six-month suspension.

Accordingly, we order that the respondent, Andrew M. Lopez, be suspended from the practice of the law for a period of six months effective thirty days after the date of this opinion. The respondent is ordered to comply with the provisions of C.R.C.P. 241.21 relating to the termination of all legal matters, the giving of notice to all clients and opposing counsel, and maintenance of appropriate records as proof of compliance. The respondent is also ordered to pay the cost of these proceedings in the amount of $1,499.45 and deliver that amount to the Grievance Committee at 600-17th Street, Suite 500S, Denver, Colorado 80202, within thirty days of this date.

Notes

1. Lawyers may not present false evidence to a tribunal. Nor may lawyers assist clients in a crime or fraud. Significantly, while lawyers may be unable to unilaterally disclose negative information about clients, lawyers may not assist clients in presenting false evidence to a tribunal or gaming administrative agencies. Colorado Rule of Professional Conduct 1.2(d) provides that:

> A lawyer shall not counsel a client to engage, or assist a client, in conduct that the lawyer knows is criminal or fraudulent, but a lawyer may discuss the legal consequences of any proposed course of conduct with a client and may counsel or assist a client to make a good faith effort to determine the validity, scope, meaning or application of the law.

In other words, while lawyers may be required to remain hushed about negative information pertaining to clients, lawyers may not actively participate in presenting this same negative information to a tribunal or administrative body on behalf of clients. Notably, the rules governing conduct of lawyers delineate minimum standards by which lawyers must conduct themselves. However, exceptional lawyers conduct themselves in a manner exceeding the prescribed minimum standards. While lawyers must generally place client interests above their own, lawyers must purposefully and deliberately guard and protect their reputations for honesty and integrity.

2. A lawyer's good reputation is expedient in establishing and maintaining a successful gaming practice. This holds exceptionally true in the gaming arena, often perceived in a suspicious and negative light, whether rightly or wrongly. Correspondingly, if clients ultimately reject their lawyers' advice to disclose negative information, lawyers should seek to withdraw from the representation.

C. Zealous Advocacy

Lawyers must provide zealous advocacy on behalf of clients. Zealous advocacy, however, is not unrestricted combat; there are necessary rules to the game. The representation, although zealous, must occur within the bounds of legal and ethical constraints. Lawyers also are required to preserve confidential client information as set forth in Colorado Rule of Professional Conduct 1.6. However, the ethical duty of confidentiality is not absolute. The duty to preserve confidential client information is sometimes at odds with the superior duty of honesty and truthfulness toward the tribunal. Peculiarly, "lawyer[s] [have] a duty to know everything, to keep it in confidence, and to reveal it to the court." Gavin Mackenzie, Lawyers and Ethics Professional Responsibility and Discipline 7-1 (2001) (citations omitted).

Colorado Rule of Professional Conduct 3.3 resolves this dilemma. This rule provides that a lawyer shall not make a false statement of fact or law to a tribunal. Administrative regulatory agencies, such as gaming boards, are considered tribunals subject to Colorado Rule 3.3. Pursuant to Colorado Rule 3.9:

> A lawyer representing a client before a legislative body or administrative agency in a nonadjudicative proceeding shall disclose that the appearance is in a representative capacity and shall conform to the provisions of the Rules 3.3(a) through (c) [Candor Towards the Tribunal], 3.4(a) and (b) [Fairness To Opposing Counsel], and 3.5 [Impartiality and Decorum of the Tribunal].

Colorado Rules of Prof'l Conduct R. 3.9 (2008).

Notes

1. In Nix v. Whiteside, 475 U.S. 157 (1986), a criminal defendant insisted that he be allowed to provide false testimony at trial. The lawyer refused, and the defendant was convicted. The defendant filed an appeal raising ineffective assistance of counsel based on his attorney's refusal to permit the false testimony at trial. The United States Supreme Court rejected the ineffective assistance claim, holding that a lawyer's compliance with the rules governing candor towards the tribunal does not violate a client's constitutional rights.

2. Because of the overarching goal of preserving the integrity of the judicial system in its truth-seeking mission, the rules governing candor towards the tribunal trumps all other rules, including the rules pertaining to the ethical duty of confidentiality.

3. Truth seeking is fundamental to the hearing process. This holds especially true in the gaming law area, which is already clouded with suspicion and mistrust. Preserving the

integrity of the gaming regulatory process simply takes precedence over the duty of preserving client confidential information and zealous advocacy. While clients are entitled to zealous advocacy, they are not entitled to the zealous advancement of perjury to the tribunal. The lawyer's duty to take remedial action continues to the conclusion of the case, which includes the exhaustion of the appellate process. It must be emphasized that the lawyer is required to take remedial action only if the lawyer knows that the client or witness will lie, is lying, or has lied.

4. Gaming lawyers must not wheel and deal with presenting false evidence to the tribunal. Rather, gaming lawyers must maintain integrity when dealing with the tribunal, even if it requires disclosure of confidential information.

5. In a civil matter, if a lawyer knows that a client or a witness will give false testimony, the lawyer is absolutely precluded from calling the witness at the hearing or trial and soliciting false testimony. This requirement is not discretionary for the lawyer—it is mandatory. Whoever flouts or disobeys this requirement is loosely gambling with his or her license to practice law, not to mention his or her reputation, and perhaps even his or her freedom, as this conduct may constitute criminal conduct.

6. If the lawyer reasonably believes that the civil client or witness will lie, then the lawyer has the option of determining whether to call the client or witness. This holds true even if the client insists that the client or witness be called. However, mere suspicion that a civil client or witness will lie is insufficient. In this case, the lawyer should err on the side of the client and call the client or witness.

7. In a criminal case, if the lawyer knows that the defendant will lie, the lawyer may not constitutionally prevent the defendant from testifying. Unlike a civil client, a lawyer's reasonable belief that a criminal defendant will lie is insufficient for the lawyer to refuse to call the criminal defendant to testify.

8. Criminal defendants have a constitutional right to testify. The criminal defendant's "right to testify is one of the rights that are essential to due process of law in a fair adversary process" and is protected by the Fifth, Sixth, and Fourteenth Amendments of the United States Constitution. People v. Johnson, 62 Cal. App. 4th 608, 617, 72 Cal. Rptr. 2d 805, 809 (1998) (quoting Rock v. Ark, 483 U.S. 44, 51).

9. However, the lawyer may not elicit false testimony from criminal defendants. While the criminal defendant has the right to testify, the criminal defendant does not have the right to commit perjury. Instead, the usual question-and-answer format is discarded and the defendant is allowed to testify in a narrative fashion. People v. Johnson, 72 Cal Rptr. 2d at 813.

10. The gaming lawyer must refrain from referring to any of the perjured testimony in the closing argument, and is also prohibited from sitting idly by with knowledge of false statements.

11. Colorado Rule 3.3(b) requires lawyers to take remedial action upon learning that a client "intends to engage, is engaging or has engaged in" a fraud or crime upon the tribunal. The remedial action commences with the lawyer's frank attempt to dissuade the client from continuing with the wrongful conduct. The lawyer should try to convince the client to abandon the plan to lie or to recant or correct the erroneous statements to the court. The wise client will heed the lawyer's advice. However, if the client rejects the lawyer's advice, the lawyer is required to take further remedial action, including disclosure to the tribunal, even if such information would otherwise be protected by the ethical duty of confidentiality.

12. When a lawyer's state of knowledge is relevant, in the absence of circumstances indicating otherwise, a lawyer may assume that a client will use the lawyer's counsel for proper purposes. Mere suspicion on the part of the lawyer that the client might intend to commit a crime or fraud does not constitute knowledge.

13. Under the actual knowledge standard a lawyer is not required to make a particular kind of investigation to ascertain more certainly what the facts are. Only information known to the lawyer at the time the lawyer provides the assistance is relevant, not information learned afterwards. Restatement (Third) of the Law: The Law Governing Lawyers § 94 cmt. g (2000).

D. Competency

Rules

Nevada Rule of Professional Conduct Rule 1.1: Competence

A lawyer shall provide competent representation to a client. Competent representation requires the legal knowledge, skill, thoroughness and preparation reasonably necessary for the representation.

Nevada Rule of Professional Conduct Rule 1.16 (a): Declining or Terminating Representation

(a) Except as stated in paragraph (c), a lawyer shall not represent a client or, where representation has commenced, shall withdraw from the representation of a client if:

(1) The representation will result in violation of the Rules of Professional Conduct or other law;

(2) The lawyer's physical or mental condition materially impairs the lawyer's ability to represent the client; or

(3) The lawyer is discharged.

Notes

1. Competence is the first rule of ethics. Nevada Rule of Prof'l Conduct 1.1 (2006). A lawyer shall provide competent representation to a client. Competent representation requires the legal knowledge, skill, thoroughness and preparation reasonably necessary for the representation. Competence is not a game of chance. Rather, competence requires that a lawyer possess "legal knowledge, skill, thoroughness and preparation" when representing a client. *Id.*

2. Given the highly regulatory nature of gambling, it is essential that lawyers who practice gaming law be conversant of the countless statutes and fully equipped to provide competent representation. Notwithstanding the desire to secure a lucrative client, if the lawyer is not competent in gaming law or cannot become competent with reasonable preparation and research, or associate with a competent gaming attorney, the lawyer must decline the representation. Nevada Rules of Prof'l Conduct R. 1.16 (2006). A lawyer's ignorance of strict gaming law requirements, including the myriad of statutes and regulations, may result in grave consequences to gaming clients. Incompetence may also result in grave consequences to the lawyer: a malpractice action, a bar grievance, or the diminution of the lawyer's reputation.

E. Communication

Rules

Nevada Rule of Professional Conduct 1.4(a): Communication

(a) A lawyer shall:

(1) Promptly inform the client of any decision or circumstance with respect to which the client's informed consent is required by these Rules;

(2) Reasonably consult with the client about the means by which the client's objectives are to be accomplished;

(3) Keep the client reasonably informed about the status of the matter;

(4) Promptly comply with reasonable requests for information; and

(5) Consult with the client about any relevant limitation on the lawyer's conduct when the lawyer knows that the client expects assistance not permitted by the Rules of Professional Conduct or other law.

Michigan Rule 1.4 (a): Communication

(a) A lawyer shall keep a client reasonably informed about the status of a matter and promptly comply with reasonable requests for information. A lawyer shall notify the client promptly of all settlement offers, mediation evaluations, and proposed plea bargains.

Notes

1. Not only does inadequate communication result in uninformed clients and the diminution of the lawyer-client relationship, but poor communication also often results in ethics charges, bar grievances and even legal malpractice suits. Inescapably, communication is an important arsenal in the practice of law. Good lawyers must be proficient in the art of communication. Alarmingly, however, many lawyers lack basic communication skills.

2. There are ten fundamental rules that all lawyers should use in their practice. These rules, if practiced, will enable lawyers to achieve unwavering lawyer-client relationships and avoid bar grievances.

1) **Discuss and settle upon the preferred method of communication with clients.**

The technology explosion has resulted in augmented means of communication. Traditional methods of communication, such as letter writing and the use of home telephones have been eclipsed by numerous contemporary methods of communication, such as fax, e-mail, text messaging and personal cell phones. Given the several communication options, lawyers must know how to communicate with clients so as to preserve attorney confidences and secrets. Lawyers can ill afford to assume a client's favored mode of communication. With increased technology comes increased responsibility and vigilance. For example, lawyers cannot simply dial a client's home telephone number and leave a message or send an e-mail to a common family e-mail address. Doing so may result in the divulgence of client confidences, a violation of the rules governing the ethical duty of confidentiality.

2) **Confirm the content of conversations in writing.**

Attorneys are not immune from the litigious environment in which we live. Accordingly, it is imperative that lawyers protect themselves by memorializing client conversations in writing. Writings protect lawyers against spurious allegations made by disgruntled clients. Writings also thwart client confusion, misapprehensions and mistakes.

3) **Offer candid advice to clients, considering not only law, but moral, economic, social and political considerations as well.**

Nevada Rule 2.1 provides that in "representing a client, a lawyer shall exercise independent professional judgment and render candid advice. In rendering advice, a lawyer may refer not only to law, but also to other considerations such as moral, economic, social and political factors that may be relevant to the client's situation."

4) **Provide clients with sufficient information to make informed decisions about the representation.**

Nevada Rule 1.0(e) defines informed consent as "the agreement by a person to a proposed course of conduct after the lawyer has communicated adequate information and explanation about the material risks of, and reasonably available alternatives to, the proposed course of conduct." In short, lawyers must advise clients of all relevant facts, including "the good, the bad and the ugly," to enable the client to make informed decisions about the representation.

5) **Keep the client reasonably informed of the status of the matter.**

Lawyers can easily fulfill this ethical obligation by providing clients with copies of correspondence, applications or other documents generated in the matter. Whatever the method of communication, lawyers must ensure that clients are aware of the status of their applications and other legal matters.

6) **Respond promptly to inquiries.**

Clients are entitled to reasonably prompt responses to their inquiries. While lawyers are not required to respond to every client inquiry, lawyers must act in a reasonable, responsible and professional manner. Game playing (so as to avoid communicating with clients) must be avoided. For example, don't play telephone tag with clients — purposefully calling a client at 5:30 p.m. knowing that the client routinely leaves the office at 5:00 p.m. This requirement holds especially true when dealing with pesky or difficult clients, as it is these clients who are likely to malign a lawyer's reputation and file bar grievances.

7) **Demonstrate great care in communicating with clients.**

Lawyers must not only scrutinize the means of communication, but they must also examine the tone and substance of the communication. Lawyers must refrain from demeaning or belittling clients. Rather, they must treat clients with courtesy, dignity and respect — even the most obnoxious and unpleasant client. Seemingly trivial details matter. Be sure to properly spell the client's name, for example.

8) **Be honest.**

9) **Advise the client of the limits of the representation if the client expects legal services that would constitute a violation of the rules of professional conduct.**

Lawyers must be forthright, frank and firm in conveying the lawyer's ethical restraints so as to escape unfair expectations and other disappointments.

10) **Listen.**

Listening is a crucial communication tool that is often disregarded. Yet, listening is crucial to the development of a vital lawyer-client relationship. Admittedly, lawyers are trained communicators. However, lawyers must occasionally stop and listen. In listening, lawyers gain an understanding and appreciation for client objectives and concerns, which in turn leads to optimal legal representation.

Part III
Native American Gambling

Chapter 9

History and Pre-Statutory Development

One of the most complex and richly textured areas of American law deals with the Indian tribes of North America. The interaction between the tribes and the federal and state governments in the gaming context exposes the contradictory policies that have informed all of Indian regulation. While no division of a topic as vast as Indian gaming can be precise, there is no question that the Indian Gaming Regulatory Act (IGRA), enacted in 1988, was the transformative event in the regulation of Indian gaming. The world of Indian gaming that existed before the passage of this law was forever altered. Yet, it is important to have an understanding of the pre-IGRA world in which Indian gaming operated. The current issues that challenge the gaming lawyer are a product of the historical and political dynamics that have marked the relationship between the tribes and the federal and state governments. Chapter 9 develops the issues up to the passage of IGRA. Chapter 10 examines the legal issues created by that statute.

1. Introduction to Tribal Sovereignty and Tribal Gaming

Two of the leading scholars on Indian gaming concisely summarize the history of relations between Indian tribes and pre- and post-Constitutional America:

> Indian gaming is fundamentally different than most forms of gambling, from church bingo nights to the slots at Las Vegas's Bellagio Hotel and Casino, because it is conducted by tribal governments as an exercise of their sovereign rights. Tribal sovereignty—a historically rooted doctrine recognizing tribes' inherent rights as independent nations, preexisting the United States and its Constitution—is the primary legal and political foundation of federal Indian law and policy and thus, Indian gaming. Yet the legal doctrine of tribal sovereignty is perhaps the most misunderstood aspect of tribal gaming. This in large part is due to the convoluted body of federal Indian law and resultant public policy that has shaped the doctrine over the course of more than 200 years. [14]

---

14. In this section, we draw upon Kathryn R.L. Rand & Steven A. Light, *Virtue or Vice? How IGRA Shapes the Politics of Native American Gaming, Sovereignty, and Identity*, 4 Va. J. Soc. Pol. & L., 385–96. For a highly readable summary of the relationship between the United States Constitution and Native American nations and tribes, *see* DAVID E. WILKINS, AMERICAN INDIAN POLITICS AND THE AMERICAN POLITICAL SYSTEM, Chapter 2 (Rowman &Littlefield 2002). For a thorough treatment of the legal doctrine of tribal sovereignty, *see* DAVID E. WILKINS, AMERICAN INDIAN SOVEREIGNTY AND THE

Prior to the arrival of Western colonizers, Native American tribes were sovereign nations in the territory that became the United States. Although recognizing the sovereign status of the tribes, the colonizers believed that tribal sovereignty rightly was limited both by settlers' "manifest destiny" and the perceived primitiveness of indigenous societies. The foundations of the modern legal doctrine of tribal sovereignty, which governs the relationship among the tribes, the federal government, and the states, reflects these early colonial conceptions. The doctrine was established by Chief Justice John Marshall in the U.S. Supreme Court's infamous "Marshall trilogy," handed down in the early 1800s. In the trilogy, the Court held that all tribes were incorporated into the United States through a "doctrine of discovery," through which "civilized" Western colonizers had rights that trumped those of the "savage" tribes of America. Tribes thus were "domestic dependent nations," possessing only limited sovereignty subject to Congress's asserted plenary power over tribes under the U.S. Constitution's Indian Commerce Clause.[15]

The Marshall trilogy occurred during the first post-Constitution stage of federal Indian policy, the hallmarks of which were forced relocation and land cessions. After halting treaty making with the tribes in 1871, the United States adopted a policy of forced assimilation designed to eradicate Native traditions and culture. During the 1920s and 1930s and throughout the middle of the twentieth century, federal Indian policy reflected the termination and allotment era. Tribal lands were sold to non-Natives and Native Americans were provided incentives to move off-reservation. After the Civil Rights Movement, the federal government promulgated a new policy of tribal self-determination. By the 1970s and 1980s, this policy drove cuts in federal assistance to tribes while encouraging tribal economic self-sufficiency. Leveraging limited reservation resources to promote economic growth and development proved extremely difficult, however, and many tribes faced the continuing realities of crushing poverty and other economic and social ills.

...

Native American tribes now have a special status outside as well as within the American federal system that is, under federal law, defined and circumscribed by the historical development of the legal and political doctrine of tribal sovereignty. In essence, the modern legal doctrine means that the United States recognizes tribes as independent sovereign nations, and their location within the boundaries of a state does not subject them to the application of state law, yet they are subject to Congress's asserted plenary power and bound by the trust relationship between the federal government and tribes. [16] Tribes therefore have a

---

U.S. Supreme Court: The Masking of Justice (Univ. of Tex. Press 1997). For an argument that tribes' inherent right of self-determination, rather than the federal legal doctrine of tribal sovereignty, should guide Indian gaming policy, see Light and Rand, *Indian Gaming and Tribal Sovereignty: The Casino Compromise.*

15. *See generally* Worcester v. Georgia, 31 U.S. (6 Pet.) 515 (1832); Cherokee Nation v. Georgia, 20 U.S. (5 Pet.) 1 (1831); Johnson v. M'Intosh, 21 U.S. (8 Wheat.) 543 (1823); *see also* U.S. Const., art. I, §8, cl. 3 ("The Congress shall have Power ... to regulate commerce ... with the Indian tribes...."). For a critical analysis of the Marshall Trilogy and the so-called plenary power, *see* David E. Wilkins & K. Tsianina Lomawaima, Uneven Ground: American Indian Sovereignty and Federal Law (Univ. of Okla. Press 2001).

16. Rand & Light, *Virtue or Vice?*, 382; *see also* Wilkins, *American Indian Politics*, Chapter 2.

unique semi-sovereign status under federal law, and accordingly may be regulated by Congress.[17]

...

To a large extent, state and local gambling laws simply do not apply to Indian gaming. Tribal sovereignty and Congress's constitutional authority place regulatory power over Indian gaming primarily with the tribes and federal government. But state interests are not absent from Indian gaming—far from it.

KATHRYN R.L. RAND & STEPHEN ANDREW LIGHT, INDIAN GAMING LAW AND POLICY, 10–13 (Carolina Academic Press 2006). So much attention is focused on the gambling by non-Indians on tribal lands that gambling by tribe members themselves often is overlooked. As Professors Rand and Light describe, however, gambling plays an important role in many tribal cultures.

The tribes of North America share a rich history of traditional tribal gaming. Many tribal games have their roots in cultural creation stories and myths. Often, the rules of the game were determined by the elements of the story and the characters portrayed. They mythical foundation also provided the sacred circumstances of the game and frequently taught a moral lesson.[18] Traditional tribal games reflect a profound relationship between the game, the community, and spirituality. Contestants prepared mentally, physically, and spiritually for the game with the participation and help of the community. This spiritual aspect highlighted the importance of the contestants' personal conduct during the game, including responsibility to team members and fairness to the opposition. In that respect, tribal games resembled ceremonies more than sporting events.[19]

Although each tribe is unique—and often a game is unique to a particular tribe—universal tribal games or categories of games exist in Native American history and culture.[20] Two broad categories of traditional games are games of dexterity and games of chance, both of which often involved gambling or wagering.[21]

Games of dexterity were defined by physical skill, such as speed and agility in foot races and lacrosse, and strength and coordination in hoop and pole and archery games. Besides the athletes themselves, community members participated in dexterity contests by placing bets on the games. Wagering was part of the social activity surrounding the games; the more significant the game was to

---

17. Although beyond the scope of this book, it is important to understand that the federal legal doctrine is not the only, and certainly not the best, definition of tribal sovereignty. A broader and more accurate definition, rooted in tribal rather than U.S. legal and political conceptions, is that tribal sovereignty is tribes' inherent right of self-determination, with legal, political, cultural, and spiritual dimensions. For a thorough treatment of Indian gaming centered on indigenous perspectives on tribal sovereignty, *see* KATHRYN R.L. RAND & STEPHEN ANDREW LIGHT, INDIAN GAMING AND TRIBAL SOVEREIGNTY: THE CASINO COMPROMISE (Univ. Press of Kan. 2005).

18. Stewart Culin, *Games of the North American Indians* (Dover Publications, Inc., 1975 (republication of Accompanying Paper, "Games of the North American Indians," in W.H. Holmes, *Twenty-Fourth Annual Report of the Bureau of American Ethnology to the Smithsonian Institution*, 1902–1903 (Government Printing Office, 1907))), 31–32; Kathryn Gabriel, *Gambler Way: Indian Gaming in Mythology, History and Archaeology in North America* 19 (Johnson Books 1996).

19. JOSEPH B. OXENDINE, AMERICAN INDIAN SPORTS HERITAGE 3–5, 15–17. (Human Kinetics Publishers 1988).

20. *Id.* at xix.

21. *Id.* at 141; Culin, *Games of the North American Indians*, 31.

the community, the higher the stakes.[22] Betting on games of dexterity was common, especially in foot racing; however, there also were specific games in which wagering played an integral part for the players and the community.[23]

Games of chance included dice games and various forms of guessing games, such as stick games and the moccasin game, and traditionally involved wagering as part of the play.[24] Dice games were universally popular among Native American tribes.[25] The game consisted of players throwing dice, sometimes made of stones, buttons, seeds, or similar objects, against a blanket or a hide. Each player's score was determined by how the dice landed on the ground.[26] Stick games, a type of guessing game, involved an uneven number of sticks grouped together. One player divided the group of sticks into two groups, and the opposing player guessed which group contained an even or uneven number of sticks, or which group of sticks contained a special stick.[27] The moccasin game was another guessing game, widely known today as the shell game. An object was placed under one of a number of moccasins and the player guessed which moccasin hid the object.[28]

Although one common western view, at least at different times throughout history, is that gambling is evil or immoral, tribal communities generally did not share that perspective.[29] For many tribes, wagering was viewed as an act of generosity that helped to regularly redistribute wealth within the community.[30] Traditional Native gambling myths place a "sacred significance" on wagering and express a "divine origin, power, and symbolism of the games." They often depict "good" gamblers, who play according to the rules and in appropriate context and moderation, and "bad" gamblers, who cheat or wager excessively. In Native mythology, the good gambler prevails over the bad gambler and restores the balance in nature.[31]

The stakes, and thus the rewards for winning, were as varied as the types of games. Depending on the prestige of the game, players would wager money, clothing, jewelry, guns, horses, saddles, and lodges. Besides the cautionary tales of gambling myths, tribal communities commonly addressed potential negative effects of gambling through various social norms and practices. Bets could only be placed in the amount of goods or cash the gambler had available at the time, creating wagering limits. Community members looked unfavorably on those who gambled excessively, and gamblers were not allowed to incur debt. Because gambling was a means of redistributing wealth, the community took steps to ensure gambling did not impoverish individuals.[32]

---

22. Oxendine, *American Indian Sports Heritage*, 81–82.
23. *Id.* at 81–82, 142.
24. *Id.* at 142.
25. Culin, *Games of the North American Indians*, 44–45.
26. Oxendine, *American Indian Sports Heritage*, 144–149.
27. *Id.* at 149–150.
28. *Id.* at 151.
29. Gabriel, *Gambler Way*, 22–23.
30. Oxendine, *American Indian Sports Heritage*, 143.
31. Gabriel, *Gambler Way*, 17.
32. Oxendine, *American Indian Sports Heritage*, 144, 156.

As an integral component of traditional tribal games, tribal communities viewed gambling as part of their social and cultural heritage.[33] Traditional tribal games, like other Native customs and practices, were impacted by increasing contact with Europeans and the pressures of colonization and westward expansion. The influence of colonial religious teachings, and the laws and policies of the United States, actively discouraged gambling by tribal members. At the same time, white settlement had negative effects on the wealth of tribal communities, resulting in less leisure time to play and fewer goods to wager.[34] Nevertheless, many tribes have retained traditions of games of chance and wagering, and continue to play these games in modern times, often in conjunction with social or religious ceremonies and events.

KATHRYN R.L. RAND & STEPHEN ANDREW LIGHT, INDIAN GAMING LAW AND POLICY, 17–19 (Carolina Academic Press 2006).

2. Early (Pre-IGRA) Regulation

Seminole Tribe of Florida v. Butterworth
658 F.2d 310 (5th Cir. 1981)

LEWIS R. MORGAN, Circuit Judge:

This appeal involves a question arising under Public Law 280, the federal law permitting states to exercise civil and criminal jurisdiction over the Indian tribes. All parties agree that the case turns on the determination of whether Florida Statute Section 849.093 which permits bingo games to be played by certain qualified organizations subject to restrictions by the state is civil/regulatory or criminal/prohibitory in nature. If the statute is civil/regulatory within the meaning of Bryan v. Itasca County, 426 U.S. 373 (1976), the statute cannot be enforced against the Seminole Tribe of Florida.

This lawsuit commenced when the Seminole Indian tribe brought an action under 28 U.S.C. §§ 2201 and 2202, seeking a declaratory judgment and injunctive relief against Robert Butterworth, the sheriff of Broward County, Florida. The Seminole tribe had contracted with a private limited partnership that agreed to build and operate a bingo hall on the Indian reservation in exchange for a percentage of the profits as management fees. Anticipating violation of the Florida bingo statute, Sheriff Butterworth informed the tribe that he would make arrests for any violations of Fla. Stat. § 849.093. [Lengthy footnote setting out bingo laws of state omitted]. The attorney general of the state of Florida filed a petition on behalf of the state seeking leave to participate in the case as amicus curiae, and leave was granted. Relying on stipulated facts, the parties filed cross motions for summary judgment, presenting the question to the district court, 491 F. Supp. 1015, whether the statute could be enforced against the Indian nation. After finding that the case satisfied the "case or controversy" requirement of the Constitution, the district judge granted the plaintiff's motion for summary judgment on the ground that the statute in question was regulatory in nature and therefore could not be enforced against the Indian tribe.

---

33. *Id.* at 142, 156.
34. *Id.* at 141–44.

The lower court enjoined the sheriff from enforcing the statute against the plaintiff. The sheriff of Broward County and the State of Florida appealed the lower court's decision to this court, but agreeing with the lower court, we affirm its decision.

I. Can Indians Operate Bingo Halls?

The states lack jurisdiction over Indian reservation activity until granted that authority by the federal government; however, Sections 2 and 4 of Public Law 280[2] granted certain states the right to exercise criminal jurisdiction and limited civil jurisdiction over the Indian tribes. Section 7 of the Act[3] granted to other states the right to assume criminal and civil jurisdiction by legislative enactment, and although this section was repealed in 1968 by Section 403(b) of Public Law 90-284, any cessions of jurisdiction made pursuant to the Act prior to its repeal were not affected. Pursuant to the former Public Law 280 the state of Florida assumed criminal jurisdiction over reservation Indians in Fla. Stat. §285.16. By this enactment, Florida assumed jurisdiction over the Indians to the full extent allowed by the law.

The repeal changed the law to require the consent of the Indians to any further assumption of jurisdiction.

In Bryan v. Itasca County, *supra*, 426 U.S. at 383, the Supreme Court of the United States interpreted Public Law 280 as granting civil jurisdiction to the states only to the extent necessary to resolve private disputes between Indians and Indians and private citizens. In Bryan the petitioner Indian sought relief from a personal property tax that the state had levied against his mobile home. The Court interpreted the language of Section 4(a) of Public Law 280[4] providing for civil jurisdiction as follows:

(S)ubsection (a) seems to have been primarily intended to redress the lack of Indian forums for resolving private legal disputes between reservation Indians, and between Indians and other private citizens, by permitting the courts of the States to decide such disputes.... (The statute) authorizes application by the state courts of their rules of decision to decide such disputes. *Id.* at 383–84.

After further discussion the Court concluded that "if Congress in enacting Pub. L. 280 had intended to confer upon the States general civil regulatory powers, including taxation over reservation Indians, it would have expressly said so." *Id.* at 390. Although the Supreme Court was interpreting the language of Public Law 280 as directed at the six mandatory states, it is clear that these same limitations on civil jurisdiction would apply to a state that assumed jurisdiction pursuant to Section 7 of the former Public Law 280.

---

2. The two sections were codified at 18 U.S.C.A. §1162 and 28 U.S.C.A. §1360, respectively. The first section concerned state assumption of criminal jurisdiction and the second involved assumption of civil jurisdiction. These sections were directed at the willing states of California, Minnesota, Nebraska, Oregon and Wisconsin (later adding Alaska), which are sometimes referred to as the mandatory states because the assumption of jurisdiction was dictated by the statute.

3. 67 Stat. 590 (1953) (repealed by Pub. L. 90-284, Title IV, §403, 82 Stat. 79 (1968). The former section provided: The consent of the United States is hereby given to any other state not having jurisdiction with respect to criminal offenses or civil causes of action, or with respect to both, as provided for in this act, to assume jurisdiction at such time and in such manner as the people of the state shall by affirmative legislative action obligate and bind the state to assumption thereof.

4. See note 2 supra. Section 4(a) provides:(a) Each of the States or Territories listed ... shall have jurisdiction over civil causes of action between Indians or to which Indians are parties which arise in the areas of Indian country ... to the same extent that such State or Territory has jurisdiction over other civil causes of action, and those civil laws of such State or Territory that are of general application to private persons or private property shall have the same force and effect within such Indian country as they have elsewhere within the State or Territory....

Thus, the mandate from the Supreme Court is that states do not have general regulatory power over the Indian tribes.

The difficult question remaining in a case such as the present one is whether the statute in question represents an exercise of the state's regulatory or prohibitory authority. The parties have presented the question for decision to this court in that form, and several cases out of the Ninth Circuit have addressed similar Indian problems with the same or a similar analysis.... Thus, under a civil/regulatory versus criminal/prohibitory analysis, we consider the Florida statute in question to determine whether the operation of bingo games is prohibited as against the public policy of the state or merely regulated by the state.

Fla. Stat. Section 849.093 provides that the general prohibition against lotteries does not apply to prevent "nonprofit or veterans' organizations engaged in charitable, civic, community, benevolent, religious or scholastic works or other similar activities ... from conducting bingo games or guest games, provided that the entire proceeds derived from the conduct of such games shall be donated by such organizations to the endeavors mentioned above." Id. Section 2 of the statute sets out conditions of operation for organizations not engaged in the charitable activities listed above. The remaining sections of the statute state restrictions for the operation of bingo games and penal sanctions for violation of those provisions. Although the inclusion of penal sanctions makes it tempting at first glance to classify the statute as prohibitory, the statute cannot be automatically classified as such. A simplistic rule depending on whether the statute includes penal sanctions could result in the conversion of every regulatory statute into a prohibitory one.... The classification of the statute is more complex, and requires a consideration of the public policy of the state on the issue of bingo and the intent of the legislature in enacting the bingo statute.

The Florida Constitution provides: "lotteries, other than the types of pari-mutuel pools authorized by law..., are hereby prohibited in this state." Art. X, s 7, Fla. Const. The legislature has the power to prohibit or regulate all other forms of gambling, and in Greater Loretta Improvement Ass'n. v. State ex rel. Boone, 234 So.2d 665 (Fla. 1970), the Florida Supreme Court recognized that bingo was one of the forms of gambling, along with horse racing, dog racing, and jai alai, excepted from the lottery prohibition and permitted to be regulated by the state. Based on the definition of "pari-mutuel" and the fact that the bingo statute was enacted the same year that the Constitution was revised, the court held that the bingo statute did not violate the Constitution of Florida. In a later constitutional challenge, Carroll v. State, 361 So.2d 144 (Fla. 1978), the Supreme Court of Florida stated that

> while the legislature cannot legalize any gambling device that would in effect amount to a lottery, it has an inherit power to regulate or to prohibit any and all other forms of gambling. In exercising this power to regulate, the legislature, in its wisdom, has seen fit to permit bingo as a form of recreation, and at the same time, has allowed worthy organizations to receive the benefits (citations omitted) (emphasis added) *Id.* at 146–47.

Although this language suggesting that the legislature has chosen to regulate bingo is not binding on this court as to whether the statute is regulatory or prohibitory, the language indicates that the game of bingo is not against the public policy of the state of Florida.... Bingo appears to fall in a category of gambling that the state has chosen to regulate by imposing certain limitations to avoid abuses. Where the state regulates the operation of bingo halls to prevent the game of bingo from becoming a money-making business,[7] the Seminole Indian tribe is not subject to that regulation and cannot be prosecuted for violating the limitations imposed.

In holding that the bingo statute in question is regulatory, we must address two Ninth Circuit cases in which similar issues were raised. In United States v. Marcyes, *supra,* 557 F.2d at 1364, the Ninth Circuit held that a fireworks statute of the state of Washington was a prohibitory statute of the state, and therefore was necessarily included within the ambits of the Assimilative Crimes Act, 18 U.S.C. § 13. The fireworks statute, like the bingo statute in question, permitted the activity to take place under certain circumstances. Despite these exceptions, to the statute, however, the Ninth Circuit found that the statute's "intent was to prohibit the general possession and/or sale of dangerous fireworks" and that it was "not primarily a licensing law." *Id.* The lower court in the present case relied on *Marcyes* for its discussion of the regulatory/prohibitory distinction, but distinguished the case based on the fact that fireworks are dangerous items that, if bought on an Indian reservation, can be carried off of it. The operation of bingo halls, on the other hand, must necessarily remain on the reservation. Although the distinction is a legitimate one, the determination underlying it is a legislative decision which we are not at liberty to make. Instead we find that the real distinction between the cases lies in the reference to each state's law as to whether the statutes in question were prohibitory or regulatory. Legislative intent determines whether the statute is regulatory or prohibitory, and although the state of Florida prohibits lotteries in general, exceptions are made for certain forms of gambling including bingo. All parties agree that forms of gambling such as horse racing are regulated in Florida, and indeed the petitioner admits that the Indians could engage in the operation of horse racing activities without interference by the state. Petitioner suggests that the distinction between bingo and horse racing lies within the licensing requirements; however, we find that argument without merit. Regulation may appear in forms other than licensing, and the fact that a form of gambling is self-regulated as opposed to state-regulated through licensing does not require a ruling that the activity is prohibited.

In a more recent and in some respects more similar case, United States v. Farris, *supra,* 624 F.2d 890, the Ninth Circuit found that members of the Puyallup Indian tribe could not be prohibited from operating a gambling casino on the reservation because the state of Washington had not assumed jurisdiction over gambling offenses. However, in considering whether the provisions of 18 U.S.C. § 1955 of the Organized Crime Control Act of 1970 could apply to non-Indians gambling on the reservation, the Ninth Circuit analyzed the public policy of the state of Washington and determined that the state prohibited professional gambling. The court found that the "violation of a law of a state" requirement of section 1955 was intended to exempt from federal prosecution the operators of gambling business in states where gambling was not contrary to the public policy of the state, and the legislative declaration in Washington's gambling statute indicated

---

7. Arguably, the Florida bingo statute could be viewed as a narrow exception to the general prohibition against lotteries, permitting bingo operations only when the activity was recreational or charitable, and not for profit. Under this view urged by petitioner, professional, money-making bingo operations continue to be prohibited. Even if we were to accept this view of the statute as prohibiting professional bingo, the Seminole Indian tribe could arguably qualify as a nonprofit organization "engaged in charitable, civic, community, benevolent, religious or scholastic works or other similar activities" as prescribed in the statute. The Seminole's complaint alleges that the profits received by the tribe from the bingo activities are to be invested for the betterment of the Indian community. Although the Indian nation may not qualify as a charitable organization within the letter of the statute, the Seminole tribe could be said to fall within the spirit of its permissive intent.

a clear legislative intent to prohibit professional gambling.[8] Specifically noting the exception of Florida fronton operators to the gambling provisions, the court reiterated that the federal statute could apply only in states where gambling was illegal. Washington, unlike Florida, was such a state, and thus the statute could be enforced against non-Indians gambling on the reservation. *Cf.* Rincon Band of Mission Indians v. County of San Diego, 324 F. Supp. 371 (S.D. Cal. 1971), *rev'd on other grounds*, 495 F.2d 1 (9th Cir. 1974) (court held local ordinance prohibiting gambling was within ambit of phrase "laws of such state" of Public Law 280 so that gambling provisions could apply to Indians on the reservation).

II. Can Non-Indians Play?

Although the Ninth Circuit found that the casino operation of the Puyallup Indians was a "violation of the law of a state" for which non-Indians could be prosecuted under the federal gambling law, the case supports the proposition that the state's public policy determines whether the activity is prohibited or regulated. Although the Florida Constitution, the Florida Supreme Court, and the Florida legislature have in various forms denounced the "evils of gambling," it is clear from the provisions of the bingo statute in question and the statutory scheme of the Florida gambling provisions considered as a whole that the playing of bingo and operation of bingo halls is not contrary to the public policy of the state. Other courts prohibiting other forms of gambling have found those forms of gambling contrary to the public policy of the state. As the district court noted, this case presents a close and difficult question. The Supreme Court in interpreting Public Law 280 has stated that "statutes passed for the benefit of dependent Indian tribes ... are to be liberally construed, doubtful expressions being resolved in favor of the Indians." Bryan v. Itasca County, *supra*, 426 U.S. at 392. Although the regulatory bingo statute may arguably be interpreted as prohibitory, the resolution must be in favor of the Indian tribe.

Although we have concluded that the Florida bingo statute cannot be enforced against the Seminole tribe, Sheriff Butterworth and the State of Florida petition this court for a ruling requiring the Seminole Indians to distinguish between Indians and non-Indians and abide by the restrictions of the statute as to non-Indians. It is not altogether clear how petitioner proposes that such distinctions practically could be made without prohibiting non-Indians from play or imposing the restrictions on all players, Indian and non-Indian alike. Furthermore, the relief sought continues to request the right to enforce regulation of the Indians operation of bingo games. We reject petitioner's argument for these and the following reasons.

... [W]e note that the statute in question, Fla. Stat. §849.093, makes no reference to violations of its restrictions by the players of bingo. Sheriff Butterworth suggests that several general lottery prohibition statutes, such as Fla. Stat. §§849.08, 849.09(1)(b), and 849.09(2), permit the arrest of bingo players as players of illegal lotteries; however, we refuse to recognize in one breath that bingo is excluded from the general lottery prohibition and in the next permit the arrest of bingo players as players of illegal lotteries. The statutes cited must be considered in pari materia with the bingo statute permitting the operation of bingo games. The bingo statute does not prohibit the playing of bingo games in violation of its restrictions, and if the legislature of the state of Florida desires to prohibit such, then it must act accordingly. The courts that have prohibited Indians or non-Indians from gambling on reservations have done so in light of a statute that specifically

---

8. The Wash. Rev. Code §9.46.010 provides: It is hereby declared to be the policy of the legislature, recognizing the close relationship between professional gambling and organized crime, to restrain all persons from seeking profit from professional gambling activities in this state; (and) to restrain all persons from patronizing such professional gambling activities. ...

prohibits the act of gambling. In Florida, unlike in Washington, no distinction exists between Indians and non-Indians for the legality (or illegality) of certain gambling activities. Thus, petitioner's attempts to require the Seminoles to distinguish between Indian and non-Indian players are to no avail.... The decision of the lower court is

AFFIRMED.

Barona Group of the Capitan Grande Band of Mission Indians v. Duffy
694 F.2d 1185 (9th Cir. 1982)

BOOCHEVER, Circuit Judge:

Barona Group of the Capitan Grande Band of Mission Indians ("Barona") filed suit requesting declaratory and injunctive relief from the enforcement against them of certain county and state laws pertaining to the operation of bingo games by John Duffy, the Sheriff of San Diego County, California (the County). Summary judgment was entered for the County on March 26, 1982, and Barona has appealed. We reverse.

FACTS

Barona is an independent Indian Nation recognized by federal statute with its reservation in the County of San Diego.... On April 20, 1981, the Tribal Council of the Barona Tribe, the Tribe's governing body, enacted a Tribal Ordinance authorizing, with certain restrictions, the playing of bingo within the reservation. The Tribe subsequently entered into a management agreement with American Amusement Management, Inc., to commence a bingo operation within the reservation.

On June 25, 1981 the undersheriff of the County informed representatives of Barona that the bingo ordinance of the County of San Diego prohibited the Tribe's bingo operation. The undersheriff also said that the ordinance would be enforced to the extent of entry on Indian territory to cite or arrest the participants in the bingo operation. The Tribe then sought injunctive and declaratory relief against the Sheriff on the ground that the Sheriff is without lawful authority to enforce the state or county laws regarding bingo on the Barona Reservation.

STANDARD OF REVIEW

In reviewing a grant of summary judgment, our task is identical to that of the trial court. State ex rel. Edwards v. Heimann, 633 F.2d 886, 888 n.1 (9th Cir. 1980). Viewing the evidence *de novo,* in the light most favorable to the party against whom summary judgment is granted, we must determine whether the trial court correctly found that there was no genuine issue of material fact and that the moving party was entitled to judgment as a matter of law.... The present case is suitable for summary judgment because there is no genuine issue of material fact. We reverse, however, on the basis of the legal issues involved.

DISCUSSION

I.

Statutes Involved

The California legislature, in accordance with state constitutional limitations,[2] adopted Cal. Penal Code § 326.5 (West Supp.1982) which controls the conduct of bingo games. This

---

2. Article 4, § 19 of the California State Constitution states:(a) The Legislature has no power to authorize lotteries and shall prohibit the sale of lottery tickets in the State.... (c) Notwithstanding sub-

statute removes from the general prohibition of various forms of gambling the conduct of bingo games pursuant to city or county ordinance as provided in the California Constitution. The County passed such an ordinance allowing bingo games conducted by certain charitable organizations. Barona contends that these provisions do not apply to them because the state and county lacked a grant of power from the federal government to impose or enforce these laws within the confines of the reservation. The County contends that such power is granted under the Act of August 15, 1953, Pub. L. No. 83-280, 67 Stat. 588 (commonly known as "Public Law 280").

Public Law 280 does provide some applicability of state law over on-reservation activities. Section 4, codified at 28 U.S.C. § 1360, grants states civil jurisdiction over Indian reservations in words that on the surface seem to make all state laws of general application effective. The Supreme Court, however, has construed this section to mean that states have jurisdiction only over private civil litigation involving reservation Indians in state court. Bryan v. Itasca County, 426 U.S. 373, 385 (1976). Thus, a state may not impose general civil/regulatory laws on the reservation. Section 2 of Public Law 280, codified at 18 U.S.C. § 1162, however, confers on certain states, including California, full criminal jurisdiction over offenses committed by Indians on the reservation. Thus, whether the state and county laws apply to the Tribe's bingo enterprise depends on whether the laws are classified as civil/regulatory or criminal/prohibitory.

II.
The Caselaw

We addressed this issue in United States v. Marcyes, 557 F.2d 1361 (9th Cir. 1977). In that case, members of the Puyallup Indian Tribe were convicted for possessing certain unmarked and unclassified fireworks in violation of Washington State Law. The court was construing the Assimilative Crimes Act, 18 U.S.C. §§ 13, 1152 (1976). That Act was held to have incorporated the general criminal laws of a state, but not the civil/regulatory laws. Marcyes, 557 F.2d at 1364. In determining that the Washington law was prohibitory rather than regulatory, the court said:

> Even though the Washington scheme allows for limited exceptions (i.e., public displays, ... movies, ...), its intent is to prohibit the general possession and/or sale of dangerous fireworks and is not primarily a licensing law.

> The possession of fireworks is not the same situation encountered in other regulatory schemes such as hunting or fishing, where a person who wants to hunt or fish merely has to pay a fee and obtain a license. The purpose of such statutes is to regulate the described conduct and to generate revenues. In contrast, the purpose of the fireworks laws is not to generate income, but rather to prohibit their general use and possession in a legitimate effort to promote the safety and health of all citizens. Moreover, by allowing appellants to operate their stands on the reservation or in any federal enclave would entirely circumvent Washington's determination that the possession of fireworks is dangerous to the general welfare of its citizens.

Marcyes, 557 F.2d at 1365. We are confronted with the question of whether the County's bingo laws are similarly prohibitory.

The Fifth Circuit has recently distinguished Marcyes in determining the scope of Public Law 280 jurisdiction to facts almost identical to the present case. We find Seminole

---

division (a), the Legislature by statute may authorize cities and counties to provide for bingo games, but only for charitable purposes.

Tribe of Florida v. Butterworth, 658 F.2d 310 (5th Cir.1981), persuasive. In *Butterworth*, like the present case, pursuant to a state constitutional grant of power, the state statute excepted bingo operations by certain charitable organizations and under certain conditions from a general prohibition of gambling.[5] The Fifth Circuit determined that whether a statute may be classified as regulatory or prohibitory depended on whether the legislature deemed the activity to be against the public policy of the state. Evaluating the statute, the court determined that the legislature meant only to regulate bingo. The court based this determination on the fact that bingo is allowed in Florida as a form of recreation, that certain worthy organizations are allowed to benefit from bingo and that the state regulates bingo halls only to prevent the game of bingo from becoming a money-making venture. 658 F.2d at 314–15. *Marcyes* was distinguished on the basis that the *Marcyes* court had found that possession of dangerous fireworks was "generally" prohibited and not merely licensed. This evidenced Washington's public policy against dangerous fireworks.

Another Ninth Circuit case, United States v. Farris, 624 F.2d 890 (9th Cir. 1980) (1981), gives additional support for the "public policy" test. In *Farris*, the court was considering whether the provisions of the Organized Crime Control Act of 1970, 18 U.S.C. § 1955 (1976), could apply to gambling on the Puyallup Indian reservation. The court found that the "violation of the law of state" requirement of § 1955 was intended to include in the federal prohibition those gambling operations contrary to state public policy, as was the Puyallup gambling. Based on this analysis, the *Butterworth* court concluded that the state's public policy determines whether the activity is prohibited or regulated.

The scope of Public Law 280 as applied to bingo games is also addressed in Oneida Tribe of Indians v. Wisconsin, 518 F. Supp. 712 (W.D. Wis. 1981). In *Oneida* the district court was confronted with a factual situation and state statutory scheme virtually identical to those found in *Butterworth*. Using what it called a *Marcyes/Butterworth* analysis, the *Oneida* court also determined that the bingo laws were regulatory and not prohibitory. The court rested its decision primarily on the fact that the Wisconsin statute only provided penalties for operation of bingo games not in accordance with the statute. The general populace was allowed to *play* at will. Thus, the court reasoned that bingo was not contrary to public policy.

Although the test for determining when a state statutory scheme such as the present one should apply to tribal members on their reservation is not susceptible of easy application, we conclude for a number of reasons that the County's bingo laws are regulatory and of a civil nature.

First, the state statute authorizes bingo operations by tax exempt organizations including, for example, fraternal societies, recreational clubs, senior citizen organizations, real estate boards and labor and agricultural groups. Cal. Penal Code § 326.5(a) (West Supp. 1982). There is no general prohibition against playing bingo as there was against

---

5. When the Florida statute was first enacted, it contained no sanctions for its violation. The court recognized in a footnote that this arguably indicates a legislative intent that the statute be construed as regulatory. *Butterworth*, 658 F.2d at 314 n.6. The district court in the present case placed heavy emphasis on this factor in distinguishing the *Butterworth* case. It is clear from the text of the *Butterworth* opinion, however, that the Fifth Circuit did not rely heavily on the presence of penal sanctions in classifying the statute. *Butterworth*, 658 F.2d at 314; *see also Marcyes*, 557 F.2d at 1364 (state not allowed to enforce regulatory system on Indian reservation by making criminal failure to comply with regulations). Rather, that court relied on a consideration of a "public policy" test developed from Ninth Circuit cases. Moreover, criminal sanctions had been enacted before the *Butterworth* case was filed, so that the provisions considered by the Fifth Circuit were essentially the same as those of the County's ordinance.

fireworks in *Marcyes*. As in *Butterworth*, the California statute regulates bingo as a money making venture by limiting size of prizes, requiring that all proceeds be applied to charitable purposes, and requiring that the game be operated by volunteers from the authorized organization. The fact that so many diverse organizations are allowed to conduct bingo operations, albeit under strict regulation, is contrary to a finding that such operations violate California public policy.

Second, as was pointed out in the *Oneida* case, the general public is allowed to play bingo at will in an authorized game. This cuts against a public policy prohibition.

Third, the Supreme Court has laid down several rules of construction applicable to statutes affecting Indian affairs which undercut application of the bingo laws in this case. Ambiguities in statutes concerning dependent tribes are to be resolved in favor of the Indians. Oliphant v. Suquamish Indian Tribe, 435 U.S. 191, 208 n.17 (1978); Bryan v. Itasca County, 426 U.S. 373, 392 (1976). State jurisdiction over reservations, historically, is strongly disfavored. *Bryan*, 426 U.S. at 376 n.2; McClanahan v. Arizona State Tax Commission, 411 U.S. 164, 168 (1973). Moreover, enforcement of the bingo laws is contrary to the present federal policy of encouraging tribal self-government. *See* United States v. Wheeler, 435 U.S. 313, 322–26 (1978); *Bryan*, 426 U.S. at 388–89 n.14; *see also* the Indian Self-Determination and Education Assistance Act, 25 U.S.C. §450 et seq. (1976); Civil Rights Act of 1968, Title IV, 25 U.S.C. §§1321–1326 (1976) (requiring tribal consent to further state assumption of jurisdiction under Public Law 280). The decisions addressing similar bingo statutes have acknowledged the closeness of the question, but have found in favor of the reservation Indians on the basis of these strong policies.

Finally, the stated purpose of the tribal bingo ordinance is to collect money "for the support of programs to promote the health, education and general welfare" of the Barona Tribe. This intent to better the Indian community is as worthy as the other charitable purposes to which bingo proceeds are lawfully authorized under the California statute. Although the Barona bingo operation does not fully comply with the letter of the statutory scheme, it does at least fall within the general tenor of its permissive intent.[6]

III.
The Federal Organized Crime Control Act

Appellee argues that it can prohibit the tribal bingo operation under federal law, regardless of whether the state laws are civil or criminal, by reliance on the Organized Crime Control Act of 1970, 18 U.S.C. §1955 (1976). This federal law incorporates by reference certain state gambling laws and makes the violation of the state provisions a federal offense.

In United States v. Farris, 624 F.2d 890 (9th Cir. 1980), we held that whether a tribal activity is "a violation of the law of a state" within the meaning of §1955 depends on whether it is contrary to the "public policy" of the state. *Id.* at 895–96. Thus, *Farris* makes co-extensive the tests for application of state law to Indian reservations under §1955 and for direct application of state law under Public Law 280. Because we have concluded that bingo games are not contrary to the public policy of California, the activity is not violative of §1955.

---

6. The trial court emphasized that the statutory scheme is not for the purpose of licensing or raising revenue. But as the *Butterworth* court recognized, "[r]egulation may appear in forms other than licensing, and the fact that a form of gambling is self-regulated as opposed to state-regulated through licensing does not require a ruling that the activity is prohibited." 658 F.2d at 315. Further, zoning laws do not license and do not raise revenue, but have been held regulatory and inapplicable to Indian reservations. United States v. County of Humboldt, 615 F.2d 1260 (9th Cir. 1980).

The summary judgment is reversed and the case is remanded for the purpose of entering judgment for Barona.

REVERSED and REMANDED.

Notes

1. *Butterworth* and *Barona* are illustrations of how courts interpreted Public Law 280. This law, in its amended codified form, 18 U.S.C. § 1162, 28 U.S.C. §§ 1360, 1362, as well as other parts of the United States Code, gave Alaska, California, Minnesota, Nebraska, Oregon, and Wisconsin jurisdiction over specified tribes within those states. Other states also had some basis for exercising authority over tribes within the state borders. The grant of jurisdiction to the state over criminal offenses committed on tribal lands was broad. However, Public Law 280 gave more limited authority to states on matters of civil jurisdiction. This division of jurisdiction was the basis for the "prohibitory/regulatory" distinction often used by courts in these pre-IGRA cases. That is, if a state did not allow gambling of any kind, tribes within the state which did were violating a criminal, i.e., prohibitory, provision. On the other hand, when states allowed some form of gambling, the attempt to prevent similar gaming on tribal lands was view as a civil, i.e., regulatory matter. For a discussion and analysis of the history of Public Law 280, *see* Carole Goldberg & Duane Champagne, *Is Public Law 280 fit for the Twenty-First Century? Some Data at Last*, 38 Conn. L. Rev. 697 (2006); Arthur F. Foerster, *Divisiveness and Delusion: Public Law 280 and the Evasive Criminal/Regulatory Distinction*, 46 UCLA L. Rev. 1333 (1999); Vanessa J. Jimenez, *Concurrent Tribal and State Jurisdiction Under Public Law 280*, Am. U. L. Rev. 1627 (1998); Carole Goldberg-Ambrose, Planting Tail Feathers: Tribal Survival and Public Law 280 (UCLA Am. Indian Stud. Center 1997).

2. Many other cases analyzed the relationship between the tribes and the federal and state governments in the pre-IGRA era. *See, e.g.,* United States v. Dakota, 796 F.2d 186 (6th Cir. 1986) (tribes issuance of commercial gambling licenses violated Michigan law and therefore was also in violation of Organized Crime Control Act of 1970); Langley v. Ryder, 602 F. Supp. 335 (D. La. 1985) (state jurisdiction over gambling offenses committed on Indian lands preempted by doctrine of tribal sovereignty); Oneida Tribe of Indians of Wisconsin v. Wisconsin, 518 F. Supp. 712 (D. Wis. 1981) (state gaming law does not apply to tribal bingo operations under Public Law 280 as it is a civil regulation); Val/Del, Inc. v. Pima County Superior Court, 703 P.2d 502 (Ariz. Ct. App. 1985) (tribe waived sovereign immunity when it entered into contract with management company containing arbitration clause and therefore civil jurisdiction properly lay with the state).

3. The *Barona* decision noted that: ambiguities in statutes concerning dependent tribes are to be resolved in favor of the Indians; state jurisdiction over reservations, historically, is strongly disfavored; and enforcement of bingo laws is contrary to the federal policy of encouraging tribal self-government. Thus while the *Cabazon* case, set out below, may have come as a surprise to the states, there were indications that the United States Supreme Court was taking a narrower view of the state's authority to regulate gaming on tribal lands.

4. As Professors Rand and Light state, the role of gaming on tribal lands as a form of economic self-sufficiency was growing:

> The colonization of the New World and the subsequent history of federal-tribal relations in the United States more widely resulted in what has been termed the

"Indian problem."[35] Through the early twentieth century, the so-called problem involved western settlement of tribal lands, "solved" through armed conflict, treaties, and forced relocation of tribal members onto reservations.[36] In more recent years, the Indian problem has referred to the wide-spread extraordinary poverty and accompanying social ills on reservations. By the late twentieth century, over a third of reservation Indians lived in poverty and unemployment rates topped 50 percent in many tribal communities.[37] Native Americans living on reservations had lower life expectancy and higher infant mortality rates than the general U.S. population, along with higher incidences of violent crime, suicide, substance abuse, mental health problems, and mortality from illnesses such as diabetes, tuberculosis, and alcoholism.[38]

At the same time, the federal government adopted a policy of "self-determination" towards tribes, including encouragement of tribal economic development. But contributing to extreme levels of poverty and unemployment on reservations were high barriers to tribal enterprise. Typically, reservations afforded few opportunities for successful commercial business ventures or efforts to market on-reservation goods and services to non-Native populations.[39] Nevertheless, and against the odds, many tribes pursued some form of economic development, perhaps purely as a means of survival for tribal communities in the face of depressed reservation economies and the Reagan Administration's policy of encouraging tribal self-sufficiency and economic development while cutting funding to Indian programs.[40]

In the late 1970s and early 1980s, a few tribes, notably in California and Florida, opened high-stakes bingo palaces as a means of raising revenue. As one of the few viable strategies for reservation economic development, bingo presented an attractive option to tribal governments: start-up costs were relatively low, the facilities had a minimal impact on the environment, and the game had potential for high returns on the tribes' investment.[41]

Bingo was legal in both California and Florida, as it was in many states at the time, but state law stringently regulated bingo enterprises through both civil and

---

35. *See, e.g.,* Murray L. Wax & Robert W. Buchanan, eds., *Solving "The Indian Problem": The White Man's Burdensome Business,* N.Y. TIMES, 1975.

36. *See generally,* STEPHEN CORNELL, RETURN OF THE NATIVE: AMERICAN INDIAN POLITICAL RESURGENCE 33–50 (Oxford Univ. Press, 1988); ANGIE DEBO, A HISTORY OF THE INDIANS OF THE UNITED STATES (Univ. of Okla. Press, 1970).

37. *See* FRANK POMMERSHEIM, BRAID OF FEATHERS: AMERICAN INDIAN LAW AND CONTEMPORARY TRIBAL LIFE 7 (Univ. of Cal. Press 1995). In 1990, the U.S. Census found that 31 percent of Native Americans, living both on and off the reservation, earned incomes below the poverty line, the largest percentage of the five identified racial groups in the United States. U.S. Census Bureau, *Social and Economic Characteristics, American Indian and Native Alaska Areas* (Washington, DC 1990) (hereinafter cited as 1990 U.S. Census, *American Indians*).

38. *See, e.g.,* U.S. Commission on Civil Rights, *A Quiet Crisis: Federal Funding and Unmet Needs in Indian Country* 34–35 (July 2003).

39. *See, e.g.,* Kathryn R.L. Rand and Steven A. Light, *Raising the Stakes: Tribal Sovereignty and Indian Gaming in North Dakota,* 5 GAMING L. REV. 334 (2001).

40. For an overview of federal Indian policy during the Reagan era, see Samuel R. Cook, *Ronald Reagan's Indian Policy in Retrospect: Economic Crisis and Political Irony,* 24 POL'Y STUD. J., 11–27 (1996).

41. *See generally* Eduardo E. Cordeiro, *The Economics of Bingo: Factors Influencing the Success of Bingo Operations on American Indian Reservations, reprinted in* WHAT CAN TRIBES DO? STRATEGIES AND INSTITUTIONS IN AMERICAN INDIAN ECONOMIC DEVELOPMENT, UCLA Am. Indian Stud. Center (Steven Cornell & Joseph P. Kalt, eds. 1992).

criminal penalties. Based on federal Indian law's general prohibition against state regulation of tribes, the tribes offered games in their bingo halls that did not comply with state regulations. The states, however, argued that state regulation had been authorized by Congress and attempted to fine or shut down the tribal bingo and card games for violations of state law.[42]

KATHRYN R.L. RAND & STEPHEN ANDREW LIGHT, INDIAN GAMING LAW AND POLICY 20–21 (Carolina Academic Press 2006). As the cases discussed above demonstrate, states had limited success in putting limits on this form of tribal activity. Perhaps the states would have continued these efforts, hoping for a victory every so often, had it not been for the *Cabazon* case. It is what can safely be called a game-changer.

California v. Cabazon Band of Mission Indians
480 U.S. 202 (1987)

Justice WHITE delivered the opinion of the Court.

The Cabazon and Morongo Bands of Mission Indians, federally recognized Indian Tribes, occupy reservations in Riverside County, California. Each Band, pursuant to an ordinance approved by the Secretary of the Interior, conducts bingo games on its reservation. The Cabazon Band has also opened a card club at which draw poker and other card games are played. The games are open to the public and are played predominantly by non-Indians coming onto the reservations. The games are a major source of employment for tribal members, and the profits are the Tribes' sole source of income. The State of California seeks to apply to the two Tribes Cal. Penal Code Ann. § 326.5 (West Supp.1987). That statute does not entirely prohibit the playing of bingo but permits it when the games are operated and staffed by members of designated charitable organizations who may not be paid for their services. Profits must be kept in special accounts and used only for charitable purposes; prizes may not exceed $250 per game. Asserting that the bingo games on the two reservations violated each of these restrictions, California insisted that the Tribes comply with state law. Riverside County also sought to apply its local Ordinance No. 558, regulating bingo, as well as its Ordinance No. 331, prohibiting the playing of draw poker and the other card games.

The Tribes sued the county in Federal District Court seeking a declaratory judgment that the county had no authority to apply its ordinances inside the reservations and an injunction against their enforcement. The State intervened, the facts were stipulated, and the District Court granted the Tribes' motion for summary judgment, holding that neither the State nor the county had any authority to enforce its gambling laws within the reservations. The Court of Appeals for the Ninth Circuit affirmed, ...

The Court has consistently recognized that Indian tribes retain "attributes of sovereignty over both their members and their territory," ... and that "tribal sovereignty is dependent on, and subordinate to, only the Federal Government, not the States". It is clear, however, that state laws may be applied to tribal Indians on their reservations if Congress has expressly so provided. Here, the State insists that Congress has twice given its express consent: first in Pub. L. 280 in 1953, 67 Stat. 588, as amended, 18 U.S.C. § 1162, 28 U.S.C. § 1360 (1982 ed. and Supp. III), and second in the Organized Crime Control Act in 1970, 84 Stat. 937, 18 U.S.C. § 1955. We disagree in both respects.

---

42. Florida's and California's position on the issue had some support from the limited federal grant of authority in Public Law 280, which is discussed in more detail below.

In Pub. L. 280, Congress expressly granted six States, including California, jurisdiction over specified areas of Indian country within the States and provided for the assumption of jurisdiction by other States. In § 2, California was granted broad criminal jurisdiction over offenses committed by or against Indians within all Indian country within the State.[6] Section 4's grant of civil jurisdiction was more limited.[7] In Bryan v. Itasca County, 426 U.S. 373, ... we interpreted § 4 to grant States jurisdiction over private civil litigation involving reservation Indians in state court, but not to grant general civil regulatory authority. Id., at 385, 388–390. We held, therefore, that Minnesota could not apply its personal property tax within the reservation. Congress' primary concern in enacting Pub. L. 280 was combating lawlessness on reservations. Id., at 379–80. The Act plainly was not intended to effect total assimilation of Indian tribes into mainstream American society. Id., at 387. We recognized that a grant to States of general civil regulatory power over Indian reservations would result in the destruction of tribal institutions and values. Accordingly, when a State seeks to enforce a law within an Indian reservation under the authority of Pub. L. 280, it must be determined whether the law is criminal in nature, and thus fully applicable to the reservation under § 2, or civil in nature, and applicable only as it may be relevant to private civil litigation in state court.

The Minnesota personal property tax at issue in Bryan was unquestionably civil in nature. The California bingo statute is not so easily categorized. California law permits bingo games to be conducted only by charitable and other specified organizations, and then only by their members who may not receive any wage or profit for doing so; prizes are limited and receipts are to be segregated and used only for charitable purposes. Violation of any of these provisions is a misdemeanor. California insists that these are criminal laws which Pub. L. 280 permits it to enforce on the reservations.

Following its earlier decision in Barona Group of Capitan Grande Band of Mission Indians, San Diego County, Cal. v. Duffy, 694 F.2d 1185 (9th Cir. 1982) ... which also involved the applicability of § 326.5 of the California Penal Code to Indian reservations, the Court of Appeals rejected this submission.... In Barona, applying what it thought to be the civil/criminal dichotomy drawn in Bryan v. Itasca County, the Court of Appeals drew a distinction between state "criminal/prohibitory" laws and state "civil/regulatory" laws: if the intent of a state law is generally to prohibit certain conduct, it falls within Pub. L. 280's grant of criminal jurisdiction, but if the state law generally permits the conduct at issue, subject to regulation, it must be classified as civil/regulatory and Pub. L. 280 does not authorize its enforcement on an Indian reservation. The shorthand test is whether the conduct at issue violates the State's public policy. Inquiring into the nature

---

6. Section 2(a), codified at 18 U.S.C. § 1162(a), provides: "Each of the States ... listed in the following table shall have jurisdiction over offenses committed by or against Indians in the areas of Indian country listed ... to the same extent that such State ... has jurisdiction over offenses committed elsewhere within the State..., and the criminal laws of such State ... shall have the same force and effect within such Indian country as they have elsewhere within the State ...:
    * * *
    "California.... All Indian country within the State."
7. Section 4(a), codified at 28 U.S.C. § 1360(a) (1982 ed. and Supp. III) provides: "Each of the States listed in the following table shall have jurisdiction over civil causes of action between Indians or to which Indians are parties which arise in the areas of Indian country listed ... to the same extent that such State has jurisdiction over other civil causes of action, and those civil laws of such State that are of general application to private persons or private property shall have the same force and effect within such Indian country as they have elsewhere within the State:
    * * *
    "California.... All Indian country within the State."

of § 326.5, the Court of Appeals held that it was regulatory rather than prohibitory.[8] This was the analysis employed, with similar results, by the Court of Appeals for the Fifth Circuit in Seminole Tribe of Florida v. Butterworth, 658 F.2d 310 (5th Cir. 1981), which the Ninth Circuit found persuasive.

We are persuaded that the prohibitory/regulatory distinction is consistent with *Bryan's* construction of Pub. L. 280. It is not a bright-line rule, however; and as the Ninth Circuit itself observed, an argument of some weight may be made that the bingo statute is prohibitory rather than regulatory. But in the present case, the court reexamined the state law and reaffirmed its holding in *Barona*, and we are reluctant to disagree with that court's view of the nature and intent of the state law at issue here.

There is surely a fair basis for its conclusion. California does not prohibit all forms of gambling. California itself operates a state lottery, Cal. Govt. Code Ann. § 8880 et seq. (West Supp.1987), and daily encourages its citizens to participate in this state-run gambling. California also permits parimutuel horse-race betting. Cal. Bus. & Prof. Code Ann. §§ 19400–19667 (West 1964 and Supp.1987). Although certain enumerated gambling games are prohibited under Cal. Penal Code Ann. § 330 (West Supp.1987), games not enumerated, including the card games played in the Cabazon card club, are permissible. The Tribes assert that more than 400 card rooms similar to the Cabazon card club flourish in California, and the State does not dispute this fact.... Also, as the Court of Appeals noted, bingo is legally sponsored by many different organizations and is widely played in California. There is no effort to forbid the playing of bingo by any member of the public over the age of 18. Indeed, the permitted bingo games must be open to the general public. Nor is there any limit on the number of games which eligible organizations may operate, the receipts which they may obtain from the games, the number of games which a participant may play, or the amount of money which a participant may spend, either per game or in total. In light of the fact that California permits a substantial amount of gambling activity, including bingo, and actually promotes gambling through its state lottery, we must conclude that California regulates rather than prohibits gambling in general and bingo in particular.[10]

---

8. The Court of Appeals questioned whether we indicated disapproval of the prohibitory/regulatory distinction in Rice v. Rehner, 463 U.S. 713 (1983). We did not. We rejected in that case an asserted distinction between state "substantive" law and state "regulatory" law in the context of 18 U.S.C. § 1161, which provides that certain federal statutory provisions prohibiting the sale and possession of liquor within Indian country do not apply "provided such act or transaction is in conformity both with the laws of the State in which such act or transaction occurs and with an ordinance duly adopted by the tribe having jurisdiction over such area of Indian country...." We noted that nothing in the text or legislative history of § 1161 supported the asserted distinction, and then contrasted that statute with Pub. L. 280. "In the absence of a context that might possibly require it, we are reluctant to make such a distinction. Cf. Bryan v. Itasca County, 426 U.S. 373, 390 (1976) (grant of civil jurisdiction in 28 U.S.C. § 1360 does not include regulatory jurisdiction to tax in light of tradition of immunity from taxation)." 463 U.S. at 734, n.18.

10. Nothing in this opinion suggests that cock-fighting, tattoo parlors, nude dancing, and prostitution are permissible on Indian reservations within California. See post, at 1095. The applicable state laws governing an activity must be examined in detail before they can be characterized as regulatory or prohibitory. The lower courts have not demonstrated an inability to identify prohibitory laws. For example, in United States v. Marcyes, 557 F.2d 1361, 1363–65 (9th Cir. 1977), the Court of Appeals adopted and applied the prohibitory/regulatory distinction in determining whether a state law governing the possession of fireworks was made applicable to Indian reservations by the Assimilative Crimes Statute, 62 Stat. 686, 18 U.S.C. § 13. The court concluded that, despite limited exceptions to the statute's prohibition, the fireworks law was prohibitory in nature. See also United States v. Farris, 624 F.2d 890 (9th Cir. 1980), discussed in n.13, infra.

California argues, however, that high stakes, unregulated bingo, the conduct which attracts organized crime, is a misdemeanor in California and may be prohibited on Indian reservations. But that an otherwise regulatory law is enforceable by criminal as well as civil means does not necessarily convert it into a criminal law within the meaning of Pub. L. 280. Otherwise, the distinction between §2 and §4 of that law could easily be avoided and total assimilation permitted. This view, adopted here and by the Fifth Circuit in the *Butterworth* case, we find persuasive. Accordingly, we conclude that Pub. L. 280 does not authorize California to enforce Cal. Penal Code Ann. §326.5 (West Supp.1987) within the Cabazon and Morongo Reservations.[11]

California and Riverside County also argue that the Organized Crime Control Act (OCCA) authorizes the application of their gambling laws to the tribal bingo enterprises. The OCCA makes certain violations of state and local gambling laws violations of federal law. The Court of Appeals rejected appellants' argument, relying on its earlier decisions in United States v. Farris, 624 F.2d 890 (9th Cir. 1980), and Barona Group of Capitan Grande Band of Mission Indians, San Diego County, Cal. v. Duffy, 694 F.2d 1185 (9th Cir. 1982). 783 F.2d, at 903. The court explained that whether a tribal activity is "a violation of the law of a state" within the meaning of OCCA depends on whether it violates the "public policy" of the State, the same test for application of state law under Pub. L. 280, and similarly concluded that bingo is not contrary to the public policy of California.

The Court of Appeals for the Sixth Circuit has rejected this view. United States v. Dakota, 796 F.2d 186 (6th Cir. 1986). Since the OCCA standard is simply whether the gambling business is being operated in "violation of the law of a State," there is no basis for the regulatory/prohibitory distinction that it agreed is suitable in construing and applying Pub. L. 280. 796 F.2d, at 188. And because enforcement of OCCA is an exercise of federal rather than state authority, there is no danger of state encroachment on Indian tribal sovereignty. *Ibid.* This latter observation exposes the flaw in appellants' reliance on OCCA. That enactment is indeed a federal law that, among other things, defines certain federal crimes over which the district courts have exclusive jurisdiction. There is nothing in OCCA indicating that the States are to have any part in enforcing federal criminal laws or are authorized to make arrests on Indian reservations that in the absence of OCCA they could not effect. We are not informed of any federal efforts to employ OCCA to prosecute the playing of bingo on Indian reservations, although there are more than 100 such enterprises currently in operation, many of which have been in existence for several years, for the most part with the encouragement of the Federal Government. Whether or not, then, the Sixth Circuit is right and the Ninth Circuit wrong about the coverage of OCCA, a matter that we do not decide, there is no warrant for California to make arrests on reservations and thus, through OCCA, enforce its gambling laws against Indian tribes.

---

11. Nor does Pub. L. 280 authorize the county to apply its gambling ordinances to the reservations. We note initially that it is doubtful that Pub. L. 280 authorizes the application of any local laws to Indian reservations. Section 2 of Pub. L. 280 provides that the criminal laws of the "State" shall have the same force and effect within Indian country as they have elsewhere. This language seems clearly to exclude local laws. We need not decide this issue, however, because even if Pub. L. 280 does make local criminal/prohibitory laws applicable on Indian reservations, the ordinances in question here do not apply. Consistent with our analysis of Cal. Penal Code Ann. §326.5 (West Supp.1987) above, we conclude that Ordinance No. 558, the bingo ordinance, is regulatory in nature. Although Ordinance No. 331 prohibits gambling on all card games, including the games played in the Cabazon card club, the county does not prohibit municipalities within the county from enacting municipal ordinances permitting these card games, and two municipalities have in fact done so. It is clear, therefore, that Ordinance No. 331 does not prohibit these card games for purposes of Pub. L. 280.

II

Because the state and county laws at issue here are imposed directly on the Tribes that operate the games, and are not expressly permitted by Congress, the Tribes argue that the judgment below should be affirmed without more. They rely on the statement in Mc-Clanahan v. Arizona State Tax Comm'n, 411 U.S. 164 (1973), that "'[s]tate laws generally are not applicable to tribal Indians on an Indian reservation except where Congress has expressly provided that State laws shall apply'.... Our cases, however, have not established an inflexible per se rule precluding state jurisdiction over tribes and tribal members in the absence of express congressional consent.[17] "[U]nder certain circumstances a State may validly assert authority over the activities of nonmembers on a reservation, and ... in exceptional circumstances a State may assert jurisdiction over the on-reservation activities of tribal members." New Mexico v. Mescalero Apache Tribe, 462 U.S. 324, 331–332 (1983) (footnotes omitted). Both Moe v. Confederated Salish and Kootenai Tribes, 425 U.S. 463 (1976), and Washington v. Confederated Tribes of Colville Indian Reservation, 447 U.S. 134 (1980), are illustrative. In those decisions we held that, in the absence of express congressional permission, a State could require tribal smokeshops on Indian reservations to collect state sales tax from their non-Indian customers. Both cases involved nonmembers entering and purchasing tobacco products on the reservations involved. The State's interest in assuring the collection of sales taxes from non-Indians enjoying the off-reservation services of the State was sufficient to warrant the minimal burden imposed on the tribal smokeshop operators.

This case also involves a state burden on tribal Indians in the context of their dealings with non-Indians since the question is whether the State may prevent the Tribes from making available high stakes bingo games to non-Indians coming from outside the reservations. Decision in this case turns on whether state authority is pre-empted by the operation of federal law; and "[s]tate jurisdiction is pre-empted ... if it interferes or is incompatible with federal and tribal interests reflected in federal law, unless the state interests at stake are sufficient to justify the assertion of state authority." *Mescalero*, 462 U.S. at 333, 334. The inquiry is to proceed in light of traditional notions of Indian sovereignty and the congressional goal of Indian self-government, including its "overriding goal" of encouraging tribal self-sufficiency and economic development. *Id.* at 334–35....

These are important federal interests. They were reaffirmed by the President's 1983 Statement on Indian Policy.[20] More specifically, the Department of the Interior, which has the primary responsibility for carrying out the Federal Government's trust obligations to Indian tribes, has sought to implement these policies by promoting tribal bingo enterprises. Under the Indian Financing Act of 1974, 25 U.S.C. § 1451 et seq..., the Secretary of the Interior has made grants and has guaranteed loans for the purpose of constructing bingo facilities. See S. Rep. No. 99-493, p. 5 (1986); Mashantucket Pequot Tribe v. McGuigan, 626 F. Supp. 245, 246 (Conn. 1986). The Department of Housing and Urban Development and the Department of Health and Human Services have also provided financial assistance to develop tribal gaming enterprises. See S. Rep. No. 99-493, supra, at 5. Here, the Secretary of the Interior has approved tribal ordinances establishing and regulating the gaming activities involved. *See* H.R. Rep. No. 99-488, p. 10 (1986). The Sec-

---

17. In the special area of state taxation of Indian tribes and tribal members, we have adopted a per se rule....

20. "It is important to the concept of self-government that tribes reduce their dependence on Federal funds by providing a greater percentage of the cost of their self-government." 19 Weekly Comp. of Pres. Doc. 99 (1983).

retary has also exercised his authority to review tribal bingo management contracts under 25 U.S.C. § 81, and has issued detailed guidelines governing that review.

These policies and actions, which demonstrate the Government's approval and active promotion of tribal bingo enterprises, are of particular relevance in this case. The Cabazon and Morongo Reservations contain no natural resources which can be exploited. The tribal games at present provide the sole source of revenues for the operation of the tribal governments and the provision of tribal services. They are also the major sources of employment on the reservations. Self-determination and economic development are not within reach if the Tribes cannot raise revenues and provide employment for their members. The Tribes' interests obviously parallel the federal interests.

California seeks to diminish the weight of these seemingly important tribal interests by asserting that the Tribes are merely marketing an exemption from state gambling laws. In Washington v. Confederated Tribes of Colville Indian Reservation, 447 U.S. at 155, we held that the State could tax cigarettes sold by tribal smokeshops to non-Indians, even though it would eliminate their competitive advantage and substantially reduce revenues used to provide tribal services, because the Tribes had no right "to market an exemption from state taxation to persons who would normally do their business elsewhere." We stated that "[i]t is painfully apparent that the value marketed by the smokeshops to persons coming from outside is not generated on the reservations by activities in which the Tribes have a significant interest." *Ibid*. Here, however, the Tribes are not merely importing a product onto the reservations for immediate resale to non-Indians. They have built modern facilities which provide recreational opportunities and ancillary services to their patrons, who do not simply drive onto the reservations, make purchases and depart, but spend extended periods of time there enjoying the services the Tribes provide. The Tribes have a strong incentive to provide comfortable, clean, and attractive facilities and well-run games in order to increase attendance at the games.[23] The tribal bingo enterprises are similar to the resort complex, featuring hunting and fishing, that the Mescalero Apache Tribe operates on its reservation through the "concerted and sustained" management of reservation land and wildlife resources. New Mexico v. Mescalero Apache Tribe, 462 U.S. at 341. The Mescalero project generates funds for essential tribal services and provides employment for tribal members. We there rejected the notion that the Tribe is merely marketing an exemption from state hunting and fishing regulations and concluded that New Mexico could not regulate on-reservation fishing and hunting by non-Indians. *Ibid*. Similarly, the Cabazon and Morongo Bands are generating value on the reservations through activities in which they have a substantial interest.

The State also relies on Rice v. Rehner, 463 U.S. 713 (1983), in which we held that California could require a tribal member and a federally licensed Indian trader operating a general store on a reservation to obtain a state license in order to sell liquor for off-premises consumption. But our decision there rested on the grounds that Congress had never recognized any sovereign tribal interest in regulating liquor traffic and that Con-

---

23. An agent of the California Bureau of Investigation visited the Cabazon bingo parlor as part of an investigation of tribal bingo enterprises. The agent described the clientele as follows:
   "In attendance for the Monday evening bingo session were about 300 players.... On row 5, on the front left side were a middle-aged latin couple, who were later joined by two young latin males. These men had to have the game explained to them. The middle table was shared with a senior citizen couple. The aisle table had 2 elderly women, 1 in a wheelchair, and a middle-aged woman.... A goodly portion of the crowd were retired age to senior citizens." App. 176. We are unwilling to assume that these patrons would be indifferent to the services offered by the Tribes.

gress, historically, had plainly anticipated that the States would exercise concurrent authority to regulate the use and distribution of liquor on Indian reservations. There is no such traditional federal view governing the outcome of this case, since, as we have explained, the current federal policy is to promote precisely what California seeks to prevent.

The sole interest asserted by the State to justify the imposition of its bingo laws on the Tribes is in preventing the infiltration of the tribal games by organized crime. To the extent that the State seeks to prevent any and all bingo games from being played on tribal lands while permitting regulated, off-reservation games, this asserted interest is irrelevant and the state and county laws are pre-empted.... Even to the extent that the State and county seek to regulate short of prohibition, the laws are pre-empted. The State insists that the high stakes offered at tribal games are attractive to organized crime, whereas the controlled games authorized under California law are not. This is surely a legitimate concern, but we are unconvinced that it is sufficient to escape the pre-emptive force of federal and tribal interests apparent in this case. California does not allege any present criminal involvement in the Cabazon and Morongo enterprises, and the Ninth Circuit discerned none. 783 F.2d, at 904. An official of the Department of Justice has expressed some concern about tribal bingo operations,[24] but far from any action being taken evidencing this concern — and surely the Federal Government has the authority to forbid Indian gambling enterprises — the prevailing federal policy continues to support these tribal enterprises, including those of the Tribes involved in this case.[25]

We conclude that the State's interest in preventing the infiltration of the tribal bingo enterprises by organized crime does not justify state regulation of the tribal bingo enterprises in light of the compelling federal and tribal interests supporting them. State regulation would impermissibly infringe on tribal government, and this conclusion applies equally to the county's attempted regulation of the Cabazon card club. We therefore affirm the judgment of the Court of Appeals and remand the case for further proceedings consistent with this opinion.

It is so ordered.

Notes

1. The majority opinion refers to Justice Stevens' dissenting opinion. It was joined by Justices O'Connor and Scalia. The opinion pointed out that while California permitted some forms of bingo, it was according to specific regulations and stakes limits that the Indian casinos would not be subject to. This was a clear violation of the state's public policy and

---

24. Hearings on H.R. 4566 before the House Committee on Interior and Insular Affairs, 98th Cong., 2d Sess., 15–39, 66–75 (1984); App. 197–205.

25. Justice STEVENS' assertion, post, at 1097, that the State's interest in restricting the proceeds of gambling to itself, and the charities it favors, justifies the prohibition or regulation of tribal bingo games is indeed strange. The State asserted no such discriminatory economic interest; and it is pure speculation that, in the absence of tribal bingo games, would-be patrons would purchase lottery tickets or would attend state-approved bingo games instead. In any event, certainly California has no legitimate interest in allowing potential lottery dollars to be diverted to non-Indian owners of card clubs and horse tracks while denying Indian tribes the opportunity to profit from gambling activities. Nor is California necessarily entitled to prefer the funding needs of state-approved charities over the funding needs of the Tribes, who dedicate bingo revenues to promoting the health, education, and general welfare of tribal members.

seemingly required other exemptions for such "illegal but profitable enterprises" such as "cockfighting, tattoo parlors, nude dancing, [and] houses of prostitution." 480 U.S. at 224.

2. Congressional legislative initiatives relating to Indian gaming had been percolating for several years before the *Cabazon* decision. These efforts focused primarily on authorizing states to regulate gaming on tribal lands. The *Cabazon* ruling certainly added urgency to this activity. If it was thought that gaming on Indian lands would be limited to bingo, even of the high-stakes variety, perhaps the reaction would not have been as intense. But many interests feared that *Cabazon* presaged an explosion of full-blown casino gambling on tribal lands. This raised concerns that gambling generally would increase substantially, and that the risk of organized crime infiltrating the tribal gaming would likewise be greater. Of greatest concern perhaps was the prospect that a robust gambling environment for tribal casinos would come at the expense of private gaming facilities. This would cause a corresponding decline in state tax revenues. At this time, the latest nationwide expansion of gambling was still in its nascent stages. This meant that much of the opposition to tribal gaming came from interests in Nevada and New Jersey.

Thus, Congress had many policies to balance in creating a regulatory template for Indian gaming:

- promoting the tribal economic self-sufficiency that gaming could provide;
- respecting the historical sovereignty accorded the tribes in the United States;
- creating conditions that put some limits on the overall growth of gambling in the United States;
- protecting the expanding tribal gaming industry from organized crime elements;
- preserving the tax revenues states derived from gambling; and
- respecting the primacy of the federal government's constitutional role in regulating Indian tribes.

Chapter 10 will examine the Indian Gaming Regulatory Act and the student can decide how well the law balanced these various interests.

3. For detailed examinations of *Cabazon* and the lead-up to IGRA, see KATHRYN R.L. RAND & STEPHEN ANDREW LIGHT, INDIAN GAMING LAW AND POLICY 29–33 (Carolina Academic Press 2006); KATHRYN R.L. RAND & STEPHEN ANDREW LIGHT, INDIAN GAMING AND TRIBAL SOVEREIGNTY: THE CASINO COMPROMISE 40–44 (Univ. Press of Kan. 2005); Joseph M. Kelly, *Indian Gaming Law*, 43 DRAKE L. REV. 501, 502–507 (1995); Roland J. Santoni, *The Indian Gaming Regulatory Act: How Did We Get Here? Where Are We Going?*, 26 CREIGHTON L. REV. 395 (1992); Virginia W. Boylan, *Reflections on IGRA Twenty Years After Enactment*, 42 ARIZ. ST. L.J. 1 (2010); Linda King Kading, Note, *State Authority to Regulate Gaming Within Indian Lands: The Effect of the Indian Gaming Regulatory Act*, 41 DRAKE L. REV. 317 (1992); Kevin J. Worthen, *Who Will Control the Future of Indian Gaming? "A Few Pages of History are Worth a Volume of Logic,"* 1996 BYU L. REV. 407; Alexander Tallchief Skibine, *Cabazon and its Implications for Indian Gaming*, in INDIAN GAMING: WHO WINS? (Mullis & Kamper, eds.); Harry Reid, *The Indian Gaming Act and the Political Process*, in INDIAN GAMING AND THE LAW (Eadington, ed.).

4. The troubled relationship between North American Indian tribes and the state and federal governments predated gaming issues. Of course, volumes have been written about this history. Some awareness of these historical dynamics assists in the understanding of how the gaming debate developed and evolved. Some sources to consider are: JOHN H. VINZANT, THE SUPREME COURT'S ROLE IN AMERICAN INDIAN POLICY (LFB Scholarly Pub-

l'g 2009) (providing an overview of the numerous approaches taken by the Supreme Court when dealing with tribal/state relationships); DAVID E. WILKINS, AMERICAN INDIAN SOVEREIGNTY AND THE U.S. SUPREME COURT: THE MASKING OF JUSTICE (Univ. of Tex. Press, 1997) (an examination of fifteen landmark cases that significantly limited Indian rights); BURKE A. HENDRIX, OWNERSHIP, AUTHORITY, AND SELF-DETERMINATION (Penn. State Univ. Press 2008) (discussing the concept, origins, and justifications for governmental authority over American Indian tribes and the problems presented when that authority is challenged).

Chapter 10

Gaming on Indian Lands under the Indian Gaming Regulatory Act (IGRA)

1. Background of IGRA

The *Cabazon* decision certainly affected the future course of Indian gaming regulation. It is important, however, to note that Indian gaming had drawn congressional attention several years before *Cabazon* and initiatives to legislate in this area had been numerous and varied. Unquestionably, *Cabazon* gave urgency to these efforts. Without federal legislation regulating gambling on Indian lands, the decision in *Cabazon* was seen as opening the door for widespread and unregulated gambling there. Such growth was threatening to casino gambling on non-tribal lands, which could diminish a source of state tax revenue. The political history of what culminated in the Indian Gaming Regulatory Act of 1988 (IGRA) is a fascinating study in the operation of the American political process. For discussion of this *see* Franklin Ducheneaux, *The Indian Gaming Regulatory Act: Background and Legislative History*, 42 ARIZ. ST. L.J. 99 (2010) (providing a broad overview of Indian law from Chief Justice John Marshall's Cherokee Cases to pre-IGRA decisions interpreting Public Law 280, and discussing the Reagan Administration's policy of decreasing federal subsidies for Indian tribes, while at the same time calling for a way to promote the economic self-sufficiency of the tribes); Roland J. Santoni, *The Indian Gaming Regulatory Act: How Did We Get Here? Where Are We Going?* 26 CREIGHTON L. REV. 387 (1993) (discussing the political discord and the accompanying amendment process that preceded the passage of IGRA); STEPHEN ANDREW LIGHT & KATHRYN R. L. RAND, INDIAN GAMING & TRIBAL SOVEREIGNTY: THE CASINO COMPROMISE 42–44 (Univ. Press of Kan. 2005) (focusing on the competing political concerns of the states and the tribes, and discussing the efforts of Senator Harry Reid (D-Nev.), Senator Daniel Inouye (D-Haw.), and Representative Morris Udall (D-Ariz.) to create a viable compromise); Harry Reid, *in* INDIAN GAMING & THE LAW 17 (William R. Eadington, ed., 1998) (discussing his general opposition to the proliferation of gambling outside the state of Nevada, as well as how the competing interests of the Indian tribes—who desired little or no federal control over Indian gaming—and the state and local officials—who demanded that states have the right to regulate gambling inside their borders—led to the Class III tribal-state compact compromise that helped end the stalemate and lead to the passage of IGRA); John R. Mills, *in* INDIAN GAMING & THE LAW 119 (William R. Eadington, ed., 1998) (predicting massive growth in Indian gaming as well as a vast new confusing array of state-specific regulations, restrictions, and procedures as each state creates and implements their own tribal compacts).

2. Basic Structure of IGRA

The makeup of IGRA is informed by the Legislative Findings and Declaration of Policy in the Act. 25 U.S.C. §2701 provides:

> The Congress finds that:
>
> (1) Numerous Indian tribes have become engaged in or have licensed gaming activities on Indian lands as a means of generating tribal governmental revenue;
>
> (2) Federal courts have held that section 81 of this title requires Secretarial review of management contracts dealing with Indian gaming, but does not provide standards for approval of such contracts;
>
> (3) Existing Federal law does not provide clear standards or regulations for the conduct of gaming on Indian lands;
>
> (4) A principal goal of Federal Indian policy is to promote tribal economic development, tribal self-sufficiency, and strong tribal government; and
>
> (5) Indian tribes have the exclusive right to regulate gaming activity on Indian lands if the gaming activity is not specifically prohibited by Federal law and is conducted within a State which does not, as a matter of criminal law and public policy, prohibit such gaming activity.

Note the reference in subsection four to the importance of tribal self-sufficiency. This reinforces the Supreme Court's decision in *Cabazon* that Indian tribes need opportunities to provide for themselves and that gambling may provide such an opportunity. The other prominent component of the Findings is the need for developing "clear standards [and] regulations" for Indian gaming, found in subsection three. These interests coalesce in section 2702:

> The purpose of this chapter is:
>
> (1) To provide a statutory basis for the operation of gaming by Indian tribes as a means of promoting tribal economic development, self-sufficiency, and strong tribal governments;
>
> (2) to provide a statutory basis for the regulation of gaming by an Indian tribe adequate to shield it from organized crime and other corrupting influences, to ensure that the Indian tribe is the primary beneficiary of the gaming operation, and to assure that gaming is conducted fairly and honestly by both the operator and players; and
>
> (3) to declare that the establishment of independent Federal regulatory authority for gaming on Indian lands, the establishment of Federal standards for gaming on Indian lands, and the establishment of a National Indian Gaming Commission are necessary to meet congressional concerns regarding gaming and to protect such gaming as a means of generating tribal revenue.

The statutory scheme established by IGRA has many components and these will be addressed in the following materials. For example, IGRA creates the National Indian Gaming Commission (NIGC) which has power over certain aspects of Indian gaming. The law also sets out the requirements for conducting gaming on tribal lands acquired after the passage of IGRA. Perhaps the most fundamental element of IGRA is its division of Indian gaming into Class I, II, or III. Although one may see references to "Class III gaming" outside of the Indian context, it is only in IGRA where the classification is made part of federal law.

Class I "means social games solely for prizes of minimal value or traditional forms of Indian gaming engaged in … as a part of, or in connection with, tribal ceremonies or celebrations." 25 U.S.C. § 2703(4), (6). IGRA expressly excludes this type of gaming from the coverage of the Act. 25 U.S.C. § 2710(a) (1).

Class II gaming means bingo, pull-tabs, lotto, punch boards, tip jars, instant bingo, "and other games similar to bingo." 25 U.S.C. § 2703(7) (a). It also includes card games played in conformity with state law. But this does not include "banked" card games such as blackjack. The distinction is between card games such as poker where the house is not the opponent, and blackjack where it is. The NIGC has monitoring and oversight authority of Class II gaming.

Class III gaming is defined somewhat cryptically by IGRA as "all forms of gaming that are not Class I or Class II gaming." 25 U.S.C. § 2703(8). These are the "casino-style" games such as slot machines, roulette, and banked card games like blackjack. To offer Class III gaming, the tribe has to enter into a compact with the state where the tribal lands are located, and it must be a state that "permits such gaming." 25 U.S.C. § 2710(d).

The descriptions above are over-simplified. Indeed, the bulk of this Chapter is devoted to a study of the many complex legal issues that have arisen over the meaning and implementation of this language.

3. Classification and Regulation: The Vagaries of Class II Gaming

United States v. 162 Megamania Gambling Devices
231 F.3d 713 (10th Cir. 2000)

BRORBY, Circuit Judge.

The United States filed a civil complaint in the Northern District of Oklahoma seeking the forfeiture of "MegaMania" machines operated in Indian country. The government asserted the machines operating the game "MegaMania" are unlawful gambling devices operated in violation of the Johnson Act. A district judge subsequently issued a warrant to seize the MegaMania machines. The machines are owned by the Cherokee Nation of Oklahoma and the Seneca-Cayuga Tribe of Oklahoma (the Tribes). The Tribes and Multimedia Gambling Devices, Inc. (Multimedia), the manufacturer of the machines, filed claims and answers seeking a declaratory judgment determining the machines are lawful under the Indian Gaming Regulatory Act, and not illegal gambling devices under the Johnson Act. The district court granted summary judgment in favor of Multimedia and the Tribes, ruling the MegaMania machines are utilized for a "Class II" game permitted by the Indian Gaming Regulatory Act and are not illegal gambling devices under the Johnson Act. The district court subsequently denied the government's motion to alter or amend the judgment. The government appeals the decision of the district court.

I. BACKGROUND

A. The Game

At the heart of this dispute is the nature of the game MegaMania. Thus, we begin our discussion with a description of this game, which the Tribes and Multimedia liken to bingo or a game similar to bingo. MegaMania is played on a machine called an electronic player station. These player stations are located on Indian lands in Oklahoma, California, and elsewhere. A person playing MegaMania begins the game by electronically selecting up to four cards with randomly generated numbers. The player must pay twenty-five cents per card to begin the game. A game will commence once at least twelve players nationwide purchase at least forty-eight cards. A bingo "blower" located in Indian country in Oklahoma selects three numbered balls, and a human operator transmits the numbers on the balls by computer to Multimedia's headquarters where they are sent through a computer network to each player station. The player then touches the corresponding space or spaces on the player's card appearing on the MegaMania station screen. To continue playing the game, a player must pay an additional twenty-five cents per card in exchange for the numbers on the next three balls. These numbers are transmitted in roughly ten second intervals. Consequently, the player must continue to pay twenty-five cents to one dollar every ten seconds to stay in the game.

With the purchase of these numbers, a MegaMania player simultaneously engages in two aspects of the game, namely "straight-line" bingo and "CornerMania." Straight-line bingo is won by the first player or simultaneous players to cover or "daub" five spaces in a straight line on the player's bingo card image displayed on the screen. Once one or more players cover five spaces in a row on a card, either horizontally, vertically or diagonally, the game terminates unless no player has won at CornerMania. The amount the straight-line winners take depends on a variety of factors: the number of cards played; the number of balls drawn; the amount of money carried over from prior games; and the number of simultaneous straight-line winners.

The object of the CornerMania portion of the game is to cover two, three or four corners of a card and win an interim monetary prize. CornerMania is played until the straight-line bingo is won. If the straight-line bingo ends with no CornerMania winner, additional balls, at three-ball increments, are drawn until at least one CornerMania winner is announced. The amount a player wins at CornerMania is based on a fixed formula that depends solely on the number of corners covered and the number of balls drawn at the time the corners are covered.

On average, Multimedia and the Tribes retain fifteen percent of the amount taken in by the machines and the winning players receive eighty-five percent. In every game of MegaMania, there is at least one straight-line bingo winner and one CornerMania winner.

B. The Statutes

Two pieces of legislation are relevant to this case—the Johnson Act and the Indian Gaming Regulatory Act. Both pertain to gaming activities in Indian country. The Johnson Act makes it unlawful within Indian country to possess or use any "gambling device."

The [Indian] Gaming [Regulatory] Act defines Class II games to include "the game of chance commonly known as bingo (whether or not electronic, computer or other technologic aids are used in connection therewith) ... including (if played in the same location) pull-tabs, lotto, punch boards, tip jars, instant bingo, *and other games similar to bingo....*" 25 U.S.C. § 2703(7) (A) (emphasis added). Class II games are regulated by the National Indian Gaming Commission (Commission) and can be operated on Indian lands without a tribal-state compact. *Id.* at §§ 2703(7), 2710(b). All other gaming activity is Class III gaming and is allowed only where a tribal-state compact is entered. *Id.* at §§ 2703(8), 2710(d). The central issues of this case are whether the MegaMania game is properly classified as a Class II or III game, and whether the MegaMania machines are illegal gambling devices under the Johnson Act....

A. The Designation of MegaMania as a Class II Game Under the Indian Gaming Regulatory Act

The Gaming Act defines Class II gaming as:

(A) (i) the game of chance *commonly known as bingo* (whether or not electronic, computer, or *other technologic aids* are used in connection therewith)—

(I) which is played for prizes, including monetary prizes, with cards bearing numbers or other designations,

(II) in which the holder of the card covers such numbers or designations when objects, similarly numbered or designated, are drawn or electronically determined, and

(III) in which the game is won by the first person covering a previously designated arrangement of numbers or designations on such cards, including (if played in the same location) pull-tabs, lotto, punch boards, tip jars, instant bingo, *and other games similar to bingo,*

. . . .

(B) The term "class II gaming" does not include—

(i) *any banking card games,* including baccarat, chemin de fer, or blackjack (21), or

(ii) *electronic or electromechanical facsimiles of any game of chance or slot machines of any kind.*

25 U.S.C. § 2703(7) (emphasis added). Thus, subsections A(i) (I), (II) and (III) set forth three explicit criteria for classification as a Class II game.

In this case, MegaMania meets these three criteria. Specifically, it is played with an electronic card that looks like a regular paper bingo card containing a grid of numbers, and the first persons to cover a previously designated arrangement of numbers—in this case five straight-line spaces and the necessary corner spaces—wins a monetary prize. The Ninth Circuit, in addressing the same issues connected with MegaMania, reached the same conclusion in United States v. 103 Electronic Gambling Devices, 223 F.3d 1091, 1095 (9th Cir. 2000).

As it did before the Ninth Circuit, the government points to certain variations in the game MegaMania which it asserts make it a Class III game. Specifically, the government argues MegaMania fails to meet the statutory definition of a Class II "bingo" game because: 1) CornerMania is a house banking game, and thus is properly categorized as Class III gaming; 2) the CornerMania game is played concurrently with the straight-line bingo game and includes multiple winners per game; 3) the "ante up" feature fundamentally alters the game to the extent it is no longer a Class II game; 4) the MegaMania machines more closely resemble slot machines than the game commonly known as bingo; and 5) the MegaMania machines are prohibited electromechanical facsimiles of the game of bingo. We are not persuaded by these arguments for the following reasons.

In order to determine whether the game MegaMania is a Class II or III game, we turn for guidance to the definitions relating to Class II games set forth by the Commission as published in the Code of Federal Regulations. In § 502.3(a), the Commission defined Class II gaming as "bingo or lotto (whether or not electronic, computer, or other technological aids are used)" and followed the definition of bingo described in 25 U.S.C. § 2703(7). The Commission defined "[g]ame[s] similar to bingo" as "any game that meets the requirements for bingo under § 502.3(a) of this part and that is not a house banking game under § 502.11 of this part." 25 C.F.R. § 502.9. The phrase "house banking game" does not appear in the definition of bingo set forth in the Gaming Act. However, Congress specified Class II gaming does not include "(i) any *banking card games*, including baccarat, chemin de fer, or blackjack (21), or (ii) electronic or electromechanical facsimiles of any game of chance or slot machines of any kind." 25 U.S.C. § 2703(7) (B) (emphasis added). The Commission defined a "house banking game" as "any game of chance that is played with the house as a participant in the game, where the house takes on all players, collects from all losers, and pays all winners, and the house can win." 25 C.F.R. § 502.11. In determining whether MegaMania is a Class II game, we note the Gaming Commission expressed its opinion the variations of the game "commonly known as bingo" featured in the MegaMania game are minor, do not alter the fundamental characteristics of the game of bingo, and meet the criteria of the Class II game of bingo or a game "similar to bingo."

1. House Banking Game

The government asserts the availability of jackpot prizes and the "continuous win" feature of the CornerMania game render MegaMania a Class III house banking game because the house takes fifteen percent of the money paid in and "the house may have to pay out more in winnings than it receives in bets" in a "particular game or series of games." It also contends CornerMania is played against the house and not other players, and violates § 2703(7) (A) (i) (III), which it reads as requiring only one winner. We disagree.

In order to win at either straight-line bingo or CornerMania, the winners must defeat other players, not a machine. The house, in this case the Tribes and Multimedia, is not a "participant" because it does not play a bingo card which players must beat, nor is it ever a "winner" in the game. *See also 103 Electronic Gambling Devices*, 223 F.3d at 1099. As discussed in the next section, CornerMania is clearly an interim part of the game, similar to recognized variations of traditional bingo where more than one prize is allowed for filling in corners. Furthermore, even if the jackpot and CornerMania features make it possible for players to win more than the total amount wagered by all the players, the Commission recognized jackpots are permissible in Class II gaming provided the jackpot, as it does here, remains in place for players to win in future games. *See* Definitions Under the Indian Gaming Regulatory Act, 57 Fed. Reg. at 12,382, 12,382 (1992). Finally, nothing in the Gaming Act or in the regulation's definition of a "house banking game" prohibits a game where the house may on occasion pay out more than it takes in, or forbids the house from earning a profit. *See* 25 C.F.R. § 502.11; *see also 103 Electronic Gambling Devices*, 223 F.3d at 1099 (explaining "[i]n any church-hall bingo game, the 'house' regularly nets some portion of the money it takes in, or there would be no point in sponsoring the game."). We find the Commission's reasoning persuasive and thus conclude MegaMania is not a "house banking game" as defined by the Code of Federal Regulations. Our holding is reinforced by the following discussion specifically concerning the CornerMania aspect of the game.

2. The Interim Win Feature of CornerMania

As part of its argument MegaMania is a "house banking game," the government contends CornerMania converts the game into a Class III game because a player does not have to be the first player to cover the designated pattern of numbers to win at CornerMania. The government points out a player can win at CornerMania at any time before a winner of the straight-line bingo game is identified, and a player can win multiple prizes in CornerMania during one session of MegaMania. Thus, the government contends MegaMania fails to meet the criteria set forth in § 2703(7) (A) (i) (III) that a Class II game "is won by the first person 'covering' the designated arrangement of numbers."

The Commission Chairman addressed these same issues in an opinion letter written to the President of Multimedia, who requested a determination as to whether MegaMania is a Class II game. Regarding CornerMania, the Chairman noted a number of bingo handbooks, manuals and catalogues describe interim win games where a player in a traditional bingo game may win an interim prize by being the first player to cover a predetermined corner pattern of numbers "while playing toward a regular predetermined pattern on the bingo card." Accordingly, the Chairman concluded CornerMania "conforms to these pregame prizes which are a part of the game commonly known as bingo."

In addressing the government's argument, the district court correctly pointed out nothing in the Gaming Act or regulations prohibits more than one winner or "interim prizes" during a game of bingo. The Ninth Circuit reached the same conclusion, holding "winning" does not necessarily mean "vanquishing" all other opponents, and identifying Congress' intent to permit interim prizes, given that some traditional variants of bingo allow them. *See 103 Electronic Gambling Devices*, 223 F.3d at 1098–99. Moreover, nothing in the Act or regulations outlines what configuration the predetermined numbers or pattern must be in, i.e., in a straight-line, a corner configuration, or both. *Id.* at 1098. Thus, the language in the Act concerning the "first person" to win is not limited to a straight-line game and should not be read in isolation from the traditional variations of bingo that allow interim prizes and simultaneous winners. For these reasons, we agree with the Chairman, the district court, and the Ninth Circuit in concluding CornerMania does not affect the designation of MegaMania as a Class II game.

3. The "Ante Up" Feature

The government further contends MegaMania is not the game commonly known as bingo or a game "similar to bingo" because instead of paying one up-front price for a bingo card, a MegaMania player must continuously feed money into the machine to receive bingo balls and to continue playing the game. The parties refer to this as the "ante up" feature of the game. The district court determined the ante up feature did not fundamentally alter the game, relying on the following comment made by the Commission during the adoption of the regulations governing the Gaming Act:

F. Players Participating on Equal Basis

> One commenter questioned whether the definition of bingo should require that all players participate on an equal basis. The commenter stated that in a traditional bingo game, all cards are purchased for a preset price, notwithstanding limited promotional discounts. The Commission believes that such considerations are marketing decisions and are outside the Act's purview. Therefore, the Commission rejected this suggestion.

The Acting General Counsel of the Commission also concluded MegaMania is properly categorized as a Class II game not subject to state regulation, stating in an opinion letter to the President of Multimedia:

> Finally, a question has been raised about the ante up feature of your game. While I am cognizant of the similarities between such a feature and slot machines, this feature is not essential to the MegaMania game nor does it appear to impact negatively on our analysis of the statutory and regulatory criteria for "bingo" or a game "similar to bingo." The feature is essentially similar to the paper card "speed bingo" or "chip up bingo" games played in halls where the player antes up money for each number called. Therefore, while not traditional bingo, the ante up aspect does not change the game so fundamentally that it prevents me from ultimately determining that this is a game similar to bingo.

We begin our discussion on this issue by noting, as did the Ninth Circuit, that nothing in the Gaming Act or the Commission's regulations explicitly or implicitly prohibits the "ante-up" or "pay as you go" system for Class II games. *See 103 Electronic Gambling Devices,* 223 F.3d at 1097. When the Commission commented that the preset price feature in traditional bingo games concerned a marketing decision and was outside the Gaming Act's purview, it implicitly recognized the Act's silence on this matter. While the Commission may or may not have contemplated the "ante-up" scenario before us, its legal counsel directly addressed the matter in the opinion letter. Although succinct, we find this opinion consistent with the Commission's earlier determination that price-setting features for Class II games are beyond the scope of the Act. The Commission's counsel's reasoning that the "ante-up" feature does not change the statutory criteria for bingo is sound and supported by the explanation that certain other forms of bingo hall games use "ante-up" features. *Id.* (holding more weight may be given to well-reasoned non-binding agency interpretations.) Given the Act's silence on the pricing system for Class II games, and our agreement with the Commission's reasoning, we hold the "ante-up" feature does not change MegaMania's Class II status. Any perceived ambiguity concerning the Act's silence on this matter is resolved by applying the canons of construction which require us to construe ambiguous statutes in favor of the Indians. If Congress wants to add a pricing or payment requirement to the definition of bingo or games "similar to bingo," it will do so.

4. MegaMania's Similarities to a Slot Machine

The government also contends MegaMania more closely resembles a slot machine than the game commonly known as bingo. The government points out the MegaMania machines are designed to resemble slot machines, are faster-paced than traditional or manual bingo, require more investment by the participants than bingo, and cause the individual player to run a greater risk of loss than the average bingo player in a traditional bingo parlor. While the speed, appearance and stakes associated with MegaMania are different from traditional, manual bingo, MegaMania meets all of the statutory criteria of a Class II game, as previously discussed. Moreover, as the Ninth Circuit pointed out, "[u]nlike a slot machine, MegaMania is ... being played outside the terminal; the terminal merely permits a person to connect to a network of players comprising each MegaMania game, and without a network of at least 12 other players playing at other terminals, an individual terminal is useless." *103 Electronic Gambling Devices,* 223 F.3d at 1100. We therefore reject the government's argument that MegaMania stations are similar to slot machines.

For all the reasons set forth above, we conclude the MegaMania game challenged here meets the statutory criteria for a Class II game in the Gaming Act, 25 U.S.C. § 2703(7) (A) (i). We proceed to analyze whether MegaMania falls within the definition of those games specifically excluded from Class II characterization under 25 U.S.C. § 2703(7) (B) and therefore constitutes an illegal gambling device prohibited by the Johnson Act.

B. Whether MegaMania is an Electromechanical Facsimile of the Game of Bingo and a Gambling Device Under the Johnson Act

In addition to the criteria for Class II games set forth in § 2703(7) (A) (i) of the Gaming Act, Congress specifically excluded from Class II characterization as games that are house "banking card games" or "electromechanical facsimiles" of such games. 25 U.S.C. § 2703(7) (B) Electromechanical facsimiles are defined in the Code of Federal Regulations as "any gambling device as defined in 15 U.S.C. §§ 1171(a) (2) or (3) [the Johnson Act]." 25 C.F.R. § 502.8. Thus, the definition of electromechanical facsimile incorporates the Johnson Act's definition of a gambling device. A gambling device is defined in the Johnson Act as:

any other machine or mechanical device (including, but not limited to, roulette wheels and similar devices) designed and manufactured primarily for use in connection with gambling, and (A) which when operated may deliver, as the result of the application of an element of chance, any money or property, or (B) by the operation of which a person may become entitled to receive, as the result of the application of an element of chance, any money or property.

15 U.S.C. § 1171(a) (2).

However, the Gaming Act explicitly permits "electronic, computer, or other technologic aids" for use in bingo. 25 U.S.C. § 2703(7) (A) (i). An electronic, computer or other technologic aid is defined in the Code of Federal Regulations as:

a device such as a computer, telephone, cable, television, satellite or bingo blower and that when used —

(a) Is not a game of chance but merely assists a player or the playing of a game;

(b) Is readily distinguishable from the playing of a game of chance on an electronic or electromechanical facsimile; and

(c) Is operated according to applicable Federal communications law.

25 C.F.R. § 502.7.

The Tribes and Multimedia contend MegaMania is not an electromechanical facsimile of the game of bingo, but rather is merely a technological aid to playing bingo, and as such, is properly classified as a Class II game under § 2703(7) (A) (i) of the Gaming Act. Courts reviewing the legislative history of the Gaming Act have recognized an electronic, computer or technological aid must possess at least two characteristics: (1) the "aid" must operate to broaden the participation levels of participants in a common game, *see* Spokane Indian Tribe v. United States, 972 F.2d 1090, 1093 (9th Cir. 1992); and (2) the "aid" is distinguishable from a "facsimile" where a single participant plays with or against a machine rather than with or against other players. Cabazon Band of Mission Indians v. National Indian Gaming Comm'n, 14 F.3d 633, 636–37 (D.C. Cir.), *cert. denied*, 512 U.S. 1221 (1994) (Cabazon *III*). Courts have adopted a plain-meaning interpretation of the term "facsimile" and recognized a facsimile of a game is one that replicates the characteristics of the underlying game. *See* Sycuan Band of Mission Indians v. Roache, 54 F.3d 535, 542 (9th Cir. 1994) ("the first dictionary definition of 'facsimile' is 'an exact and detailed copy of something.'" (quoting Webster's Third New Int'l Dictionary 813 (1976)), *cert. denied*, 516 U.S. 912 (1995); *Cabazon II*, 827 F. Supp. at 32 (same); *Cabazon III*, 14 F.3d at 636 (stating "[a]s commonly understood, facsimiles are exact copies, or duplicates.").

In the present case, the district court determined the MegaMania machines act as aids to the game of bingo rather than unlawful electromechanical facsimiles. We agree. First, the MegaMania machines link up many different players, thus broadening the participation level of the traditional game of bingo. Second, because each player competes against other players to achieve a "bingo" rather than with or against a machine or the "house," the machines are an aid to bingo, rather than a facsimile. We are not persuaded by the government's argument the CornerMania game renders MegaMania an electronic facsimile of the game of bingo because more than one person may win at CornerMania. As discussed above, this is an interim game that is a traditional part of the game of bingo and specifically approved by the Commission. Finally, although MegaMania satisfies the statutory criteria for a Class II game, it cannot fairly be described as an exact copy or replica of the traditional game of bingo, as required to satisfy the plain-meaning definition of "facsimile." We therefore conclude MegaMania is not an electronic facsimile of, but is an aid to, the game of bingo as defined in the Code of Federal Regulations. Accordingly, Mega-Mania is not excluded from the Gaming Act's definition of a Class II game.

We further conclude Congress did not intend the Johnson Act to apply if the game at issue fits within the definition of a Class II game, and is played with the use of an electronic aid. *See 103 Electronic Gambling Devices,* 223 F.3d at 1101–02 (holding "[t]he text of [the Gaming Act] quite explicitly indicates that Congress did not intend to allow the Johnson Act to reach bingo aids."); *Cabazon II,* 827 F. Supp. at 31–32 (concluding the Johnson Act does not apply to aids to Class II games, and a narrow interpretation of the Johnson Act's definition of a gambling device is appropriate);....[9] We conclude the Johnson and Gaming Acts are not inconsistent and may be construed together in favor of the Tribes.... For these reasons, we join the Ninth Circuit in concluding MegaMania is not a gambling device as contemplated by either Act, but rather an electronic aid to bingo or a game "similar to bingo."[10]

United States v. Santee Sioux Tribe of Nebraska
324 F.3d 607 (8th Cir. 2003)

I. BACKGROUND

This is our third review of this case, which has an extensive factual and procedural history. In early 1993, the Tribe attempted to negotiate a compact with the State of Nebraska that would have permitted class III gaming on tribal lands, pursuant to the Indian Gaming Regulatory Act, 25 U.S.C. § 2701 *et seq.* (IGRA). No agreement was reached, but the Tribe nevertheless opened a class III gambling casino on the reservation in 1996. Thereafter, the Chairman of the National Indian Gaming Commission (NIGC) issued a closure order against the Tribe because the Tribe was illegally participating in class III gaming activities. [After initially complying with the NIGC order, the tribe reopened the casino with Class III gaming devices. Eventually, members of the tribe were held in contempt.]

In May 2001, the Tribe ceased operation of its class III gaming devices. It eventually replaced them with what is commonly known as "Lucky Tab II" machines, in part because the NIGC's Chief of Staff wrote a letter to the Tribe's legal counsel suggesting that the Tribe install and operate the Lucky Tab II dispensers. The NIGC thereafter dissolved its closure order because it took the position that the Lucky Tab II is not a class III gaming device. Accordingly, the Tribe brought this action, seeking relief from the prior order of contempt. The government, however, contends that the Lucky Tab II is a class III device, or, in the alternative, that even if it is a class II device, it is prohibited by the Johnson Act, 15 U.S.C. § 1171 *et seq.*

At trial, the following evidence was adduced regarding the Lucky Tab II machines. First, the instruments look and sound very much like traditional slot machines. Inter-

---

9. The State of Oklahoma, as *amicus curiae,* argues the district court's determination MegaMania is not a gambling device under the Johnson Act creates a dangerous precedent under which "all electronic slot machines and similar devices could be converted into non-gaming devices by simply networking them with a separate computer or device which provided part or all of the element of chance." Our decision rests on our determination the MegaMania game is bingo or a game "similar to bingo" and the MegaMania machines meet the statutory definition of an "aid to bingo." Our holding in this case therefore is limited to the MegaMania form of bingo currently at issue.

10. The Ninth Circuit concluded MegaMania is "bingo." *See 103 Electronic Gambling Devices,* 223 F.3d at 1102. Having determined MegaMania is a Class II game, we see no reason to go any further, and leave the specific question whether MegaMania is bingo or a "game similar to bingo" for future resolution.

nally, the device is essentially a computer. It also has a manual feed for money, a roll of paper pull-tabs, a bar code reader to read the back of each pull-tab, a rubber roller to dispense the pull-tabs, a cutter which cuts the pull-tabs from the roll, and a cash drawer. The bar code reader reads the pull-tab as it passes through the machine to the player, and based on this reading, a video screen displays the contents of the pull-tab—whether it is a winner or loser. The machine also emits different sounds, depending on whether it has read a winning or losing ticket.

A player begins playing by feeding money into the machine, but the machine cannot give change. The player presses a start button and after approximately two and a half seconds an animated display appears, announcing winner or loser status. The machine then dispenses the paper pull-tab to the player. At this point, the player can either pull back the paper tab to verify the contents, or continue playing by feeding more money into the machine and pressing the start button again. If the pull-tab is a winner, the machine cannot pay the player or give credits for accumulated wins; instead, the machine tells the player to go to the cashier and present the pull-tab to redeem winnings.

The pull-tabs themselves are small, preprinted, two-ply paper cards. The player peels off the top layer to reveal symbols and patterns which indicate a winning or losing card. The pull-tabs also indicate the number manufactured, game type, and unique sequence number. The back of the pull-tab shows an encrypted bar code with fifteen characters. The bar code must be scanned with a laser light to determine if the card is a winner or a loser. Because the information is encrypted, the data on the bar code is unknowable without the proprietary software from the manufacturer, World Gaming Technologies. Also, anti-tampering devices ensure that a pull-tab that has already been scanned will be rejected and that the tabs will be dispensed in the correct sequence. Without a roll of paper pull-tabs in place, the machine cannot function—it will not accept money or display any symbols.

The evidence suggested that, as a practical matter, players often take the winning tickets, unopened, to the cashier for redemption. Furthermore, players frequently leave the losing tickets, unopened, in the dispenser drawer of the Lucky Tab II machines.

The district court found that the machines at issue were class II devices because: the machines do not determine the winner or loser, pull-tabs can be played without these machines, the player does not play against the machine, and no winnings are paid or accumulated by the machines. The district court followed the reasoning in Diamond Game Enters., Inc. v. Reno, 230 F.3d 365 (D.C. Cir. 2000), in coming to this conclusion. United States v. Santee Sioux Tribe of Neb., 174 F. Supp. 2d 1001, 1008–09 (D. Neb. 2001).

II. DISCUSSION

. . . .

The first issue in this case necessitates our delving into the relationship between the IGRA and the Johnson Act. The government argues that if Lucky Tab II is construed to be a class II gaming device, it is still a "gambling device" within the parameters of the Johnson Act[2] and therefore prohibited. If that is the case, the Tribe cannot be granted relief

---

2. The Johnson Act defines "gambling device" to include all slot machines with a drum or reel with insignia, 15 U.S.C. § 1171(a) (1), and also:

> any other machine or mechanical device ... designed and manufactured primarily for use in connection with gambling, and (A) which when operated may deliver, as the result of the application of an element of chance, any money or property, or (B) by the operation of which a person may become entitled to receive, as the result of the application of an element of chance, any money or property.

from the contempt order. The Tribe argues that the Johnson Act defines "gambling device" so expansively that it would include any device which is "electric" or "mechanical," including those which are allowable class II gaming devices. Because class II gaming is permitted under one federal law (the IGRA), but the machines which facilitate class II gaming are arguably prohibited under another (the Johnson Act), the Tribe argues that the IGRA has repealed the Johnson Act by implication.

The IGRA, in section 2710(b) (1) (A), states that an Indian tribe may engage in class II gaming where the state in which it is located permits similar games "and such gaming is not otherwise specifically prohibited on Indian lands by Federal law." 25 U.S.C. § 2710(b) (1) (A). This section, the government argues, shows that the two acts can be read together because the IGRA contemplated prohibition of certain class II games if the devices used to carry out the gaming are prohibited Johnson Act gambling devices.

We agree with the government that the two acts can be read together. [The two statutes] are not irreconcilable, and the Tribe must not violate either act if it is to gain relief from the prior order of contempt.

The government argues that if the Johnson Act applies, the Lucky Tab II machines are prohibited "gambling devices" under that act, and the Tribe is still operating gambling equipment in contravention of federal law. We disagree because we do not believe the Lucky Tab II machines are "gambling devices" within the meaning of the Johnson Act. Lucky Tab II machines are not slot machines as apparently contemplated by 15 U.S.C. § 1171(a) (1), because they do not randomly generate patterns displayed on a screen, pay out money or otherwise determine the outcome of a game of chance. Nor do these machines fall within the strictures of sections 1171(a) (2) (A) and (B), which state, as earlier indicated, that a gambling device includes any machine:

> designed and manufactured primarily for use in connection with gambling, and (A) which when operated may deliver, as the result of the application of an element of chance, any money or property, or (B) by the operation of which a person may become entitled to receive, as the result of the application of an element of chance, any money or property.

15 U.S.C. § 1171(a) (2) (A), (B).

Lucky Tab II machines clearly do not fall within subsection A because the machines do not deliver any money or property. Subsection B seems a more likely candidate to ensnare these machines, but upon close examination, we find it does not. This section states that the operation of a machine designed and manufactured primarily for gambling use is a gambling device if, "*as the result of the application of an element of chance*" a person can be entitled to receive money or property. 15 U.S.C. § 1171(a) (2) (B) (emphasis added). The key words are highlighted, and demonstrate why the Lucky Tab II devices do not fit within this definition. As the trial testimony indicates, these machines do not generate random patterns with an element of chance. They simply distribute the pull-tab tickets and display the contents of the tickets on a screen for the user. The user of the machine does not become entitled to receive money or property as a result of the *machine's* application of an element of chance, which is what the statute clearly contemplates. *See id.* ("by the operation of [the gambling device] a person may become entitled to receive, as the result of the application of an element of chance [by the machine], any money or property").

The Johnson Act does not bar this type of machine, because it is merely a high-tech dispenser of pull-tabs. If, however, the Lucky Tab II machines were computer-generated versions of the game of pull-tabs itself, or perhaps, even if it randomly chose which pull-tab from the roll it would dispense, it could fall within this subsection. However, it is clear the machines do neither of these things. Instead, they dispense, in identical order from the roll as physically placed in the machine, pull-tabs from that roll. The machines, as noted, have a cutting device which separate the tabs from the roll, and then feed the pull-tab to the player. This action does not describe the "application of the element of chance." Therefore, although we find that the IGRA does not repeal the Johnson Act, either explicitly or implicitly, we also find that the Tribe does not violate the Johnson Act by operating the Lucky Tab II machines.

However, this does not end the inquiry. Instead, the key question becomes whether Lucky Tab II is an IGRA-prohibited class III gaming device.... According to the statute, ... pull-tabs is a class II game. However, "electronic or electromechanical facsimiles of any game of chance" are not class II games. Such facsimiles constitute class III gaming. *Id.* The government argues that Lucky Tab II machines *are* electromechanical facsimiles of the game of pull-tabs, making their use prohibited class III gaming. The Tribe argues that these machines are technological "aids" within the meaning of section 2703(7) (A), and therefore fall within the parameters of permitted class II gaming. We do not fully agree with either of these positions, and in that regard, we pause to clarify a terminology issue.

Other courts have construed this statute and concluded that the phrase "whether or not electronic, computer, or other technologic aids are used in connection therewith" modifies both the game of bingo and also other games mentioned later in the section, specifically "pull-tabs, lotto, punch boards, tip jars, instant bingo, and other games similar to bingo." These courts thus have found that games other than bingo could be technologically aided. *E.g., Diamond Game*, 230 F.3d at 367 (noting that pull-tabs is a class II game by statute, and that the IGRA specifically allows use of technologic aids "in connection with class II games"). We disagree with this reading of the statute. Instead, we believe that the phrase "whether or not electronic, computer, or other technologic aids are used in connection therewith" applies only to bingo. *See* 25 U.S.C. § 2703(7) (A). However, we also note that nothing in the statute *proscribes* the use of technological aids for any games, so long as the resulting exercise falls short of being a facsimile. Therefore, while we quarrel somewhat with the posture in which the parties, and other cases, have placed the issues, we agree with the ultimate conclusion that if the devices are not facsimiles within the meaning of the statute, they are not prohibited, regardless of whether or not they are labeled technological "aids." With that caveat, we apply the "aids" and "facsimiles" terminology.

The District of Columbia Circuit recently considered whether the same Lucky Tab II machines at issue here were permitted class II gaming devices under the IGRA. The court distinguished the Lucky Tab II machines from the machines at issue in that circuit's earlier decision, *Cabazon Band*, 14 F.3d 633. In *Cabazon Band*, the court examined electronic pull-tab machines which randomly selected a card for the player, electronically "pulled" the tab off the card at the player's direction, and displayed the results onscreen. Because that game "exactly replicate[d]" the game of video pull-tabs in computer form, it was a facsimile and not a class II device. *Id.* at 636.

The *Diamond Game* court observed that the Lucky Tab II machines were "quite different" from the machines in *Cabazon*. 230 F.3d at 369. The court found that the presence of the video monitor did not render Lucky Tab II a computerized version of pull-tabs because the computer did not select the patterns; instead, the machines merely cut tabs from paper rolls, displayed and dispensed them. "In other words, the game is in the paper rolls, not, as in the case of the *Cabazon* machine, in a computer." *Id.* at 370. Furthermore, citing Webster's Dictionary for a definition of aid, the court found that the machines "'help[ed] or support[ed]' or 'assist[ed]' the paper game of pull-tabs." *Id.* (citing Webster's Third New International Dictionary 44 (1993)). Noting that a Lucky Tab II machine was "little more than a high-tech dealer," the *Diamond Game* court held that "Lucky Tab II is not a facsimile of paper pull-tabs, it *is* paper pull-tabs." 230 F.3d at 370 (emphasis in original).

The Lucky Tab II machines, ... display the results of the game in a novel way and do not directly affect the outcome of the game. While the Lucky Tab II machines read the pull-tab card for the player and display the results on screen in a novel way, the paper pull-tab card itself is the player's only path to winning. The machines have nothing to do with the outcome of the game.

The *Diamond Game* court used a similar analysis to reach its conclusion about the Lucky Tab II machines. The government had offered a device called a "Tab Force Validation System" as an example of a class II aid. Under this system, a player buys a pull-tab from a clerk, and instead of peeling off the top layer, inserts the pull-tab into a scanner which reads a bar code and displays the results on a video screen. The *Diamond Game* court could find no discernable difference between the two systems:

Both devices electronically "read" paper pull-tabs and display their contents on a screen, and neither can "change the outcome of the game." Unlike the machine involved in *Cabazon,* neither contains an internal computer that generates the game. Rather, both machines facilitate the playing of paper pull-tabs. They are thus Class II aids.

While this case presents a close call, we think the better view is that operation of the Lucky Tab II machines does not change the fundamental fact that the player receives a traditional paper pull-tab from a machine, and whether he or she decides to pull the tab or not, must present that card to the cashier to redeem winnings. We agree with the reasoning of the *Diamond Game* court that the machines do not replicate pull-tabs; rather, the player using the machines *is playing* pull-tabs.[3]

The most recent amendments to the NIGC-enacted regulations also support this conclusion. Prior to July 2002, the regulations defined facsimile with direct reference to the Johnson Act. The regulation in effect as of July 17, 2002, defines "facsimile" as

a game played in an electronic or electromechanical format that replicates a game of chance by incorporating all of the characteristics of the game, except when, for bingo, lotto, and other games similar to bingo, the electronic or electro-mechanical format broadens participation by allowing multiple players to play with or against each other rather than with or against a machine.

25 C.F.R. § 502.8 (July 17, 2002).

Furthermore, the regulations effective July 17, 2002, define an "aid" as an electronic, computer, or other technologic device that assists the playing of a game. *Id.* § 502.7(a)(1). Significantly, the regulation gives the following examples of gaming aids, "pull *tab dispensers and/or readers,* telephones, cables, televisions, screens, satellites, bingo blowers, electronic player stations, or electronic cards for participants in bingo games." *Id.* § 502.7(c) (emphasis added).

The current regulations seem to expressly contemplate the use of Lucky Tab II pull-tab dispensers/readers, suggesting that the NIGC has now given its imprimatur to these types of machines. *Cf. Diamond Game,* 230 F.3d at 369 (noting at that time that the NIGC took

---

3. We have considered, and rejected, the government's argument that the Lucky Tab II machines are facsimiles of slot machines. These machines may look and sound like slot machines, but they cannot make change, accumulate credits, or pay out winnings. Thus, they are not exact copies (the commonly understood definition of a facsimile, *see Cabazon Band,* 14 F.3d at 636) of a slot machine.

no official position on the Lucky Tab II's class of gaming). Based on our review of the record and of the case law, the NIGC's conclusion that Lucky Tab II is a permissible class II gaming device seems to be a reasonable interpretation of the IGRA. *Cf.* Chevron U.S.A. Inc. v. Natural Res. Def. Council, Inc., 467 U.S. 837, 844 (1984) (holding that agency interpretation which is reasonable is entitled to deference).

III. CONCLUSION

Because we conclude that the Lucky Tab II machines are not prohibited Johnson Act gambling devices and are not prohibited "facsimiles" within the meaning of 25 U.S.C. § 2703(7), the Tribe is not conducting class III gaming in contravention of the federal court's prior order. We therefore affirm the judgment of the district court.

Notes

1. As the court in one case asked, "what is bingo?" United States v. 103 Electronic Gambling Devices, 223 F.3d 1091, 1093 (9th Cir. 2000). Old-style, traditional bingo conjures up images of slow-paced games with numbers being called and daubed on cards by players surrounded by many other participants. At one point a player will call out "Bingo!" and win a prize of relatively modest size. After reading the two principal opinions here, it is evident that what is involved is not your father's bingo. Technology has enhanced the ability to offer bingo, and "other games similar to bingo" in an electronic format. The machine offering the bingo game may resemble a slot machine. Indeed, this is done intentionally because it is thought to attract more players. Some of the same issues are presented here as in the case of video lottery terminals (VLT), discussed in Chapter 16. In both cases, however, there is a fundamental difference between the bingo and VLTs on the one hand, and a slot machine on the other. Because of the electronic nature of VLTs, they are able to be connected to a central computer system, which is programmed in advance to determine the total number—and total amount—of payouts that will occur for the connected VLTs. The outcome of each individual wager is determined by a random number generator in the central computer system. A traditional slot machine, on the other hand, is a self-contained unit, and the outcome of each wager is determined by the random number generator located inside the machine—not by any outside factors. *See* Texas House of Representatives House Research Organization, Betting on Video Lottery Terminals to Raise Revenue (Mar. 5, 2004), *available at* http://www.hro.house. state.tx.us/focus/vlt78-14.pdf; KyCasinos.com, *What is a Video Lottery Terminal?*, http:// kycasinos.us/vlt.php.

The efforts to increase the attractiveness of, and revenue from, bingo games are most pressing in states where tribes cannot offer Class III gaming. Without the more lucrative slot machines and table games, tribes want to maximize revenues from the bingo games, and technological advances have made this possible. Additionally, even in states where tribes may offer Class III gaming, tribes have incentives to have these games considered Class II and not Class III devices. The most important reason is that Class II revenues do not have to be shared with the state pursuant to a tribe-state compact, while Class III gaming revenues typically do.

According to one highly respected report, in calendar year 2007, Class II gaming produced $3.8 billion in gaming revenue, which represents 14% of total gaming revenue from tribal casinos. Alan P. Meister, Casino City's Indian Gaming Industry Report 3 (2008–2009 ed.). Currently three states have only Class II gaming, Alabama, Alaska, and Texas. *See* National Congress of American Indians, *Gaming Compacts*, http://www.ncai.org/GamingCompacts.103.0.html (last visited July 10, 2010).

2. The NIGC has authority under IGRA to promulgate regulations regarding whether a game is a Class II game. § 2706(a)(10). The NIGC website has a page entitled, "Game Classification Opinions," which sets out the Commission's decision on particular games. *See* NIGC webpage, http://www.nigc.gov/Reading_Room/Game_Classification_Opinions.aspx. As noted in the two principal opinions, IGRA and the Johnson Act have somewhat parallel application to the bingo games. Between 2004 and 2006, because of concerns that the line between Class II and Class III machines was being erased, the NIGC sought to clarify the standards for classifying machines as Class II or Class III. While the NIGC was offering clarifications to IGRA, the Department of Justice asserted that the NIGC regulations did not go far enough and proposed amendments to the Johnson Act that would have resulted in the machines being considered Class III games. Tribes obviously were opposed to the DOJ initiative, in part because it would trigger the potential revenue-sharing provisions of tribal-state compacts. The DOJ proposal also would have required significantly slower play and this would have reduced the revenues flowing from those games. The DOJ's proposed amendments did not gain support in Congress. Despite a series of meetings and proceedings involving the NIGC, tribes, and game manufacturers, no clarifying rules have yet been issued. For a discussion of these issues, *see* Alex Tallchief Skibine, *Indian Gaming and Cooperative Federalism*, 42 ARIZ. ST. L.J. 253 (2010); Matthew L.M. Fletcher, *Bringing Balance to Indian Gaming*, 44 HARV. J. LEGIS. 29 (2007); Heidi McNeil Staudenmaier, *Proposed NIGC Class II Game Classification Standards: End of Class II Gaming Debate ... or Just Further Fuel for Fire?*, 10 GAMING L. REV. 527 (2006); Heidi McNeil Staudenmaier & Andrew D. Lynch, *The Class II Gaming Debate: The Johnson Act vs. The Indian Gaming Regulatory Act*, 74 MISS. L.J. 843 (2005).

3. During the 1990s many courts undertook the analysis of the "facsimile" vs. "technological aid" issue for bingo machines. In line with the *MegaMania* case above, there was a strong consensus that the electronic machines were aids and not facsimiles. *See* Seneca-Cayuga Tribe of Okla., 327 F.3d 1019 (10th Cir. 2003); United States v. 103 Elec. Gambling Devices, 223 F.3d 1091 (9th Cir. 2000); Diamond Game Enters., Inc. v. Reno, 230 F.3d 365 (D.C. Cir. 2000). *But see* Cabazon Band of Mission Indians v. Nat'l Indian Gaming Commission, 14 F.3d 633 (D.C. Cir.), *cert denied* 512 U.S. 1221 (1994); Sycuan Band of Mission Indians v. Roache, 54 F.3d 535 (9th Cir. 1994); Spokane Indian Tribe v. United States, 972 F.2d 1090 (9th Cir. 1992). Does there seem to be a clear basis for distinguishing a "facsimile" from an "aid"? Could it be a futile effort to try to articulate such a difference in light of the ability of technology to adapt more quickly than the law can? Is it likewise of limited value to try to determine legislative intent from the history of the enactment of IGRA in 1988, a time that, in technologic terms anyway, is nearly pre-historic?

4. Casino Gaming on Tribal Lands — Class III

There is no question that Class III gaming is the largest revenue producer in the tribal gaming world. Slot machines, card games that are "banked' by the casino, and other casino games accounted for nearly $23 billion of revenue in 2007, approximately 86% of total tribal gaming revenue. In 2008, total tribal gaming revenue grew to almost $27 billion and Class III activities again constituted the overwhelming bulk of that number. *See* Kathryn Rand, *Indian Gaming Industry Report for 2009–2010 Released*, http://indiangamingnow.com/blog/indian-gaming-industry-report-2009-2010-released. The Congressional response to the 1987 *Cabazon* decision by the Supreme Court is most pointed and observable in IGRA's regulation of Class III tribal gaming. In order for a tribe to offer Class III gaming, the tribal land must be "located in a state that permits such gaming." That is, if the tribe is located in a state without casino type gaming, the tribe would be restricted to Class II gaming only. Second, the tribe can offer Class III gaming only when it is "conducted in conformance with a Tribal-state compact." 25 U.S.C. § 2710(d)(1). These provisions invest states with considerable authority over tribal gaming, authority that *Cabazon* had previously denied to the states. Although the compacts have to be approved by the Secretary of the Interior, and the NIGC retains some oversight power, IGRA emphatically puts states in a powerful position when dealing with tribes that want to conduct Class III gaming.

As befitting an enterprise involving many billions of dollars, the legal issues surrounding Class III tribal gaming are diverse, evolving, and complex. They implicate the historical, political, and cultural dynamics that make Indian/governmental relations so fascinating.

A. Is the State Required to Negotiate a Compact with a Tribe?

Mashantucket Pequot Tribe v. State of Connecticut
913 F.2d 1024 (2d Cir. 1990)

The Indian Gaming Regulatory Act ("IGRA") establishes three classes of gaming activity. The Mashantucket Pequot Tribe (the "Tribe") seeks to operate casino-type games of chance on its reservation located in Ledyard, Connecticut (the "Reservation"). The contemplated games are class III gaming activities, which are allowed only in conformance with a tribal-state compact. Accordingly, the Tribe requested that the State of Connecticut enter into negotiations with the Tribe concerning the formation of a compact. The state refused to negotiate, and when no compact had been completed more than 180 days after the request to negotiate, the Tribe filed this action against the State of Connecticut and Governor William A. O'Neill (collectively the "State") in the United States District Court for the District of Connecticut pursuant to 25 U.S.C. § 2710(d) (7) (1988). The Tribe sought (1) an order directing the State to conclude within sixty days a tribal-state compact with the Tribe governing the conduct of gaming activities on the Reservation, pursuant to section 2710(d) (7) (B) (iii), and appointing a mediator to resolve any impasse in accordance with section 2710(d) (7) (B) (iv); and (2) a declaratory judgment that the IGRA obliges the State to negotiate in good faith with the Tribe regarding the conduct of gaming activities on the Reservation.

Both sides moved for summary judgment. Agreeing with the Tribe that the only precondition to the State's obligation to negotiate is a request by the Tribe to negotiate in accordance with section 2710(d) (3) (A), the district court 737 F. Supp. 169 granted summary judgment to the Tribe directing the State to enter into good faith negotiations with the Tribe, and directing that the State and the Tribe conclude a tribal-state compact within sixty days.

We affirm.

The IGRA declares its primary purpose to be the provision of "a statutory basis for the operation of gaming by Indian tribes as a means of promoting tribal economic development, self-sufficiency, and strong tribal governments." § 2702(1). Its enactment followed court decisions upholding the right of tribes to conduct public bingo games on Indian lands. *See* California v. Cabazon Band of Mission Indians, 480 U.S. 202, ...

Under section 2710(d) (1), class III gaming activities are lawful on Indian lands only if such activities are:

(A) authorized by an ordinance or resolution that—

(i) is adopted by the governing body of the Indian tribe having jurisdiction over such lands,

(ii) meets the requirements of subsection (b) of this section, and

(iii) is approved by the Chairman [of the NIGC],

(B) located in a State that permits such gaming for any purpose by any person, organization, or entity, and

(C) conducted in conformance with a Tribal-State compact entered into by the Indian tribe and the State under paragraph (3) [of section 2710(d)] that is in effect.

25 U.S.C. § 2710(d) (1) (1988). A tribal-state compact is "in effect" when "notice of approval by the Secretary [of the Interior] of such compact has been published by the Secretary in the Federal Register." § 2710(d) (3) (B). In sum, class III gaming activities are subject to tribal and state regulation, as provided by a tribal ordinance, a tribal-state compact, and the IGRA.

The Tribe sought to expand its gaming activities to include class III games of chance, such as those activities permitted by Connecticut law for certain nonprofit organizations during "Las Vegas nights." Conn. Gen. Stat. §§ 7-186a to 7-186p (1989).[5] Accordingly, counsel for the Tribe wrote a letter dated March 30, 1989 to the governor of Connecticut, William A. O'Neill, "to request that the State of Connecticut enter into negotiations with the Tribe for the purpose of entering into a Tribal-State compact governing the conduct of expanded gaming activities on the Tribe's reservation in Ledyard, Connecticut." By letter dated May 1, 1989, Governor O'Neill responded that he had requested that the State's Acting Attorney General, Clarine Nardi Riddle, review the IGRA and determine the State's obligations there under.

By letter dated July 19, 1989, Acting Attorney General Riddle advised the Tribe that the State would not negotiate concerning the operation of games of chance or "Las Vegas nights" on the reservation, since the Tribe only had a "right to conduct 'Las Vegas Nights' on the premises of the reservation subject ... to those restrictions contained in the Connecticut General Statutes (§ 7-186a, et seq.) and the regulations of the Division of Special Revenue which are generally applicable to those groups authorized to conduct such a form of entertainment." The letter also stated that the State was willing "to negotiate, in good faith, with the Tribe, concerning other permissible forms of gaming in Connecticut," and that Governor O'Neill would "shortly be appointing a task force or negotiating team specifically for this purpose."

By letter dated August 1, 1989, counsel for the Tribe expressed to Acting Attorney General Riddle their pleasure "to hear of the impending appointment of a negotiating team for the State, and [their] hope to meet with [the] negotiating team as soon as possible," while soliciting an expression of the legal analysis underlying the State's view that it was under no obligation to negotiate concerning class III gambling. Responding by letter dated Au-

---

5. The games of chance that Connecticut permits at the "Las Vegas nights" include blackjack, poker, dice, money-wheels, roulette, baccarat, chuck-a-luck, pan game, over and under, horse race games, acey-deucy, beat the dealer, and bouncing ball. *See* Division of Special Revenue, Administrative Regulations: Operation and Conduct of Games of Chance § 7-186k-15 (1988).

gust 23, 1990, Acting Attorney General Riddle offered additional arguments for the State's position, discussed the State's amenability to litigation to resolve the issue, and raised the question whether the Tribe had enacted a gaming ordinance. Despite the State's asserted "readiness to resolve the issue of casino type gambling" on the Reservation, however, prior to this litigation the State never entered into actual negotiations with the Tribe, nor was the Tribe ever advised of the appointment of any negotiating committee by the State.

Section 2710(d)(7)(B)(i) authorizes an Indian tribe to commence an action in district court against a state for failure to negotiate if a 180-day period has elapsed since the tribe requested that the state enter into negotiations. On November 3, 1989, after more than 200 days had elapsed since the Tribe requested negotiations, the Tribe filed its complaint in this action in the United States District Court for the District of Connecticut, invoking jurisdiction under section 2710(d)(7)(A)(i).

On January 25, 1990, the Tribe moved for summary judgment: (1) declaring that the State is required by the IGRA to negotiate with the Tribe concerning the terms of operation of games of chance on the Reservation, including any rules concerning prizes, wagers and frequency; (2) ordering the State and Tribe to conclude a tribal-state compact governing gaming activities on the Reservation within sixty days pursuant to section 2710(d)(7)(B)(iii); and (3) ordering the appointment of a mediator to resolve any impasse in accordance with section 2710(d)(7)(B)(iv)(vii)....

The Tribe contended that the only precondition to negotiation was a request to negotiate in accordance with section 2710(d)(3)(A), which had been made, and that because the State permitted certain non-profit organizations to conduct "Las Vegas nights," the games of chance the Tribe desired were generally permitted, albeit regulated, within the meaning of section 2710(d)(1)(B).

On May 15, 1990, the district court granted summary judgment in favor of the Tribe and denied the State's cross-motion. The court ordered the State to "enter into good faith negotiations with the Tribe for the purpose of formulating a Tribal-State compact governing the conduct of games of chance defined in Conn. Gen. Stat. § 7-186a, *et seq.*, on its reservation," and ordered further that the State and the Tribe conclude a tribal-state compact within sixty days of the ruling, in accordance with section 2710(d)(7)(B)(iii). The State appealed to this court on May 25, 1990....

A. The State's Obligation to Negotiate.

The State first contends that no obligation to negotiate a compact has yet arisen, because the Tribe has not adopted a tribal ordinance that has been approved by the chairman of the NIGC and authorizes the conduct of Class III gaming on the Reservation, as required by subparagraph (A) of section 2710(d)(1), and the adoption of such an ordinance is a precondition to the State's obligation to negotiate a tribal-state compact regarding class III gaming. We disagree.

Section 2710(d)(1) on its face lists several conditions that must be satisfied before a tribe can lawfully engage in class III gaming. Although the adoption of an appropriate tribal ordinance is the first requirement set forth in section 2710(d)(1), nothing in that provision requires sequential satisfaction of its requirements, nor does its legislative history suggest that a tribal ordinance must be in place before a state's obligation to negotiate arises. Indeed, section 2710(d)(2)(C) provides that effective with the publication of a tribal ordinance in the Federal Register, "class III gaming activity on the Indian lands of the Indian tribe shall be fully subject to the terms and conditions of the Tribal-State compact entered into under paragraph (3) of the Indian tribe *that is in effect*" (emphasis added), thus suggesting that the consummation of the compact will *precede* enactment of the tribal ordinance.

Moreover, the IGRA plainly requires a state to enter into negotiations with a tribe upon request. Section 2710(d)(3)(A) provides:

> Any Indian tribe having jurisdiction over the Indian lands upon which a class III gaming activity is being conducted, or is to be conducted, *shall request* the State in which such lands are located to enter into negotiations for the purpose of entering into a Tribal-State compact governing the conduct of gaming activities. *Upon receiving such a request, the State shall negotiate* with the Indian tribe in good faith to enter into such a compact.

Id. (emphasis added). Further, the IGRA permits a tribe to initiate an action upon the state's failure to negotiate, after a waiting period timed from the date of the request. *See* § 2710(d)(7)(B). Thus, the only condition precedent to negotiation specified by the IGRA is a request by a tribe that a state enter into negotiations.

Finally, the State's argument that the adoption of a tribal ordinance must occur first among the three conditions specified in section 2710(d)(1) because it is listed first (in subparagraph (A)) encounters the obstacle that the condition which is listed second (in subparagraph (B)) will, of necessity, preexist and precede the adoption of a tribal ordinance. Subparagraph (B) requires that the proposed gaming activities be "located in a State that permits such gaming for any purpose by any person, organization, or entity." Obviously, if a state does not permit "such gaming," the matter is at an end, and the adoption of a tribal ordinance will never occur.

For all the foregoing reasons, the district court correctly concluded that the State was required to negotiate with the Tribe upon request.

B. Gaming Activities Subject to Negotiation.

[In this portion of the opinion, the court addressed the issue of which specific casino games would be subject to negotiation. This issue will be considered in the next section of the materials.]

C. The Negotiation Mandate.

Finally, the State contends that under the admittedly mandatory provision of section 2710(d)(7)(B)(iii), the district court is required to order the State and the Tribe to conclude a tribal-state compact within sixty days only if it finds that "the State has failed to negotiate in good faith with the Indian tribe," *id.*, with respect to such a compact. Maintaining that the court below "nowhere found that the State had failed to negotiate in good faith," the State argues that the district court's order directing the conclusion of a compact within sixty days must be reversed.

The district court made no express finding as to the State's lack of good faith, probably because the State did not raise the issue below. As the district court noted in its Ruling on Motion for Stay of Judgment, the State "did not specifically object to the sixty-day requirement or assert that it was not applicable in this instance." Thus, the issue was not preserved for appeal. *See* Radix Org., Inc. v. Mack Trucks, Inc., 602 F.2d 45, 48 (2d Cir. 1979). In any event, the State's contention fails on the merits.

First, despite the absence of an explicit finding as to the State's good faith, the district court substantially addressed that issue. The court (1) noted at the outset of its Ruling on Cross-Motions for Summary Judgment that "[the Tribe] asserts that the State has not appointed [a negotiating] team nor commenced negotiations and that over six months has [sic] elapsed since [the Tribe's] request [to negotiate];" (2) addressed in that opinion the central issue whether the State was obligated to negotiate in good faith; and (3) entered a judgment directing the State to "enter into good faith negotiations with the Tribe."

Furthermore, the jurisdictional provision of the IGRA vests jurisdiction in district courts over "any cause of action … arising from the failure of a State to enter into negotiations … *or* to conduct such negotiations in good faith." § 2710(d)(7)(A)(i) (emphasis added). In addition, section 2710(d)(7)(B)(ii) provides that:

> [U]pon the introduction of evidence by an Indian tribe that—
>
> (I) a Tribal-State compact had not been entered into…, and
>
> (II) the State did not respond to the request of the Indian tribe to negotiate such a compact *or* did not respond to such request in good faith,
>
> the burden of proof shall be upon the State to prove that the State *has negotiated with the Indian tribe in good faith* to conclude a Tribal-State compact governing the conduct of gaming activities.

25 U.S.C. § 2710(d)(7)(B)(ii) (1988) (emphasis added).

When a state wholly fails to negotiate, as did Connecticut in the instant case, it obviously cannot meet its burden of proof to show that it negotiated in good faith. *See* NLRB v. Katz, 369 U.S. 736, 743 (1962) ("there is no occasion to consider the issue of good faith if a party has refused even to negotiate").

The State's protestations that its failure to negotiate resulted from sincerely held views as to the meaning of the IGRA, and that it declared its willingness to resolve these legal issues of first impression by litigation, do not alter the outcome. The statutory terms are clear, and provide no exception for sincere but erroneous legal analyses. Further, the manifest purpose of the statute is to move negotiations toward a resolution where a state either fails to negotiate, or fails to negotiate in good faith, for 180 days after a tribal request to negotiate. The delay is hardly ameliorated because the state's refusal to negotiate is not malicious.

Conclusion

The judgment of the district court is affirmed.

Seminole Tribe of Florida v. Florida
517 U.S. 44 (1996)

Chief Justice REHNQUIST delivered the opinion of the Court.

The Indian Gaming Regulatory Act provides that an Indian tribe may conduct certain gaming activities only in conformance with a valid compact between the tribe and the State in which the gaming activities are located. 102 Stat. 2475, 25 U.S.C. § 2710(d)(1)(C). The Act, passed by Congress under the Indian Commerce Clause, U.S. Const., Art. I, § 8, cl. 3, imposes upon the States a duty to negotiate in good faith with an Indian tribe toward the formation of a compact, § 2710(d)(3)(A), and authorizes a tribe to bring suit in federal court against a State in order to compel performance of that duty, § 2710(d)(7). We hold that notwithstanding Congress' clear intent to abrogate the States' sovereign immunity, the Indian Commerce Clause does not grant Congress that power, and therefore § 2710(d)(7) cannot grant jurisdiction over a State that does not consent to be sued. We further hold that the doctrine of Ex parte Young, 209 U.S. 123, (1908), may not be used to enforce § 2710(d)(3) against a state official.

I

Congress passed the Indian Gaming Regulatory Act in 1988 in order to provide a statutory basis for the operation and regulation of gaming by Indian tribes. *See* 25 U.S.C.

§2702. The Act divides gaming on Indian lands into three classes—I, II, and III—and provides a different regulatory scheme for each class. Class III gaming ... is the most heavily regulated of the three classes. The Act provides that class III gaming is lawful only where it is: (1) authorized by an ordinance or resolution that (a) is adopted by the governing body of the Indian tribe, (b) satisfies certain statutorily prescribed requirements, and (c) is approved by the National Indian Gaming Commission; (2) located in a State that permits such gaming for any purpose by any person, organization, or entity; and (3) "conducted in conformance with a Tribal-State compact entered into by the Indian tribe and the State under paragraph (3) that is in effect." §2710(d)(1)....

§2710(d)(3) describes the process by which a State and an Indian tribe begin negotiations toward a Tribal-State compact:

> "(A) Any Indian tribe having jurisdiction over the Indian lands upon which a class III gaming activity is being conducted, or is to be conducted, shall request the State in which such lands are located to enter into negotiations for the purpose of entering into a Tribal-State compact governing the conduct of gaming activities. Upon receiving such a request, the State shall negotiate with the Indian tribe in good faith to enter into such a compact."

The State's obligation to "negotiate with the Indian tribe in good faith" is made judicially enforceable by §§2710(d)(7)(A)(i) and (B)(i):

> "(A) The United States district courts shall have jurisdiction over—
>
> "(i) any cause of action initiated by an Indian tribe arising from the failure of a State to enter into negotiations with the Indian tribe for the purpose of entering into a Tribal-State compact under paragraph (3) or to conduct such negotiations in good faith....
>
> "(B) (i) An Indian tribe may initiate a cause of action described in subparagraph (A) (i) only after the close of the 180-day period beginning on the date on which the Indian tribe requested the State to enter into negotiations under paragraph (3) (A)."

Sections 2710(d)(7)(B)(ii)–(vii) describe an elaborate remedial scheme designed to ensure the formation of a Tribal-State compact. A tribe that brings an action under §2710(d)(7)(A)(i) must show that no Tribal-State compact has been entered and that the State failed to respond in good faith to the tribe's request to negotiate; at that point, the burden then shifts to the State to prove that it did in fact negotiate in good faith. §2710(d)(7)(B)(ii). If the district court concludes that the State has failed to negotiate in good faith toward the formation of a Tribal-State compact, then it "shall order the State and Indian Tribe to conclude such a compact within a 60-day period." §2710(d)(7)(B)(iii). If no compact has been concluded 60 days after the court's order, then "the Indian tribe and the State shall each submit to a mediator appointed by the court a proposed compact that represents their last best offer for a compact." §2710(d)(7)(B)(iv). The mediator chooses from between the two proposed compacts the one "which best comports with the terms of [the Act] and any other applicable Federal law and with the findings and order of the court," *ibid.*, and submits it to the State and the Indian tribe, §2710(d)(7)(B)(v). If the State consents to the proposed compact within 60 days of its submission by the mediator, then the proposed compact is "treated as a Tribal-State compact entered into under paragraph (3)." §2710(d)(7)(B)(vi). If, however, the State does not consent within that 60-day period, then the Act provides that the mediator "shall notify the Secretary [of the Interior]" and that the Secretary "shall prescribe ... procedures ... under which class III gaming may be conducted on the Indian lands over which the Indian tribe has jurisdiction." §2710(d)(7)(B)(vii).

In September 1991, the Seminole Tribe of Florida, petitioner, sued the State of Florida and its Governor, Lawton Chiles, respondents.... [P]etitioner alleged that respondents had "refused to enter into any negotiation for inclusion of [certain gaming activities] in a tribal-state compact," thereby violating the "requirement of good faith negotiation" contained in § 2710(d)(3).... Respondents moved to dismiss the complaint, arguing that the suit violated the State's sovereign immunity from suit in federal court. The District Court denied respondents' motion, ...

The Court of Appeals for the Eleventh Circuit reversed the decision of the District Court, holding that the Eleventh Amendment barred petitioner's suit against respondents. The court agreed with the District Court that Congress in § 2710(d)(7) intended to abrogate the States' sovereign immunity, and also agreed that the Act had been passed pursuant to Congress' power under the Indian Commerce Clause, U.S. Const., Art. I, § 8, cl. 3. The court disagreed with the District Court, however, that the Indian Commerce Clause grants Congress the power to abrogate a State's Eleventh Amendment immunity from suit, and concluded therefore that it had no jurisdiction over petitioner's suit against Florida. The court further held that Ex parte Young, 209 U.S. 123 (1908), does not permit an Indian tribe to force good-faith negotiations by suing the Governor of a State. Finding that it lacked subject-matter jurisdiction, the Eleventh Circuit remanded to the District Court with directions to dismiss petitioner's suit....

[W]e granted certiorari, in order to consider two questions: (1) Does the Eleventh Amendment prevent Congress from authorizing suits by Indian tribes against States for prospective injunctive relief to enforce legislation enacted pursuant to the Indian Commerce Clause?; and (2) Does the doctrine of Ex parte Young permit suits against a State's Governor for prospective injunctive relief to enforce the good-faith bargaining requirement of the Act? We answer the first question in the affirmative, the second in the negative, and we therefore affirm the Eleventh Circuit's dismissal of petitioner's suit.

The Eleventh Amendment provides:

> "The Judicial power of the United States shall not be construed to extend to any suit in law or equity, commenced or prosecuted against one of the United States by Citizens of another State, or by Citizens or Subjects of any Foreign State."

Although the text of the Amendment would appear to restrict only the Article III diversity jurisdiction of the federal courts, "we have understood the Eleventh Amendment to stand not so much for what it says, but for the presupposition ... which it confirms." Blatchford v. Native Village of Noatak, 501 U.S. 775, 779 (1991). That presupposition, first observed over a century ago in Hans v. Louisiana, 134 U.S. 1 (1890), has two parts: first, that each State is a sovereign entity in our federal system; and second, that "'[i]t is inherent in the nature of sovereignty not to be amenable to the suit of an individual without its consent,' id. at 13.... For over a century we have reaffirmed that federal jurisdiction over suits against unconsenting States "was not contemplated by the Constitution when establishing the judicial power of the United States." Hans, supra, at 15....

Here, petitioner has sued the State of Florida and it is undisputed that Florida has not consented to the suit.... Petitioner nevertheless contends that its suit is not barred by state sovereign immunity. First, it argues that Congress through the Act abrogated the States' sovereign immunity. Alternatively, petitioner maintains that its suit against the Governor may go forward under Ex parte Young, supra. We consider each of those arguments in turn.

II

Petitioner argues that Congress through the Act abrogated the States' immunity from suit. In order to determine whether Congress has abrogated the States' sovereign immunity, we ask two questions: first, whether Congress has "unequivocally expresse[d] its intent to abrogate the immunity," Green v. Mansour, 474 U.S. 64, 68 (1985); and second, whether Congress has acted "pursuant to a valid exercise of power," ibid.

A

Congress' intent to abrogate the States' immunity from suit must be obvious from "a clear legislative statement." Blatchford, *supra*, 501 U.S. at 786....

Here, we agree with the parties, with the Eleventh Circuit in the decision below, and with virtually every other court that has confronted the question that Congress has in §2710(d)(7) provided an "unmistakably clear" statement of its intent to abrogate.... [W]e think that the numerous references to the "State" in the text of §2710(d)(7)(B) make it indubitable that Congress intended through the Act to abrogate the States' sovereign immunity from suit.

B

Having concluded that Congress clearly intended to abrogate the States' sovereign immunity through §2710(d)(7), we turn now to consider whether the Act was passed "pursuant to a valid exercise of power." Green v. Mansour, 474 U.S. at 68. Before we address that question here, however, we think it necessary first to define the scope of our inquiry.

Petitioner suggests that one consideration weighing in favor of finding the power to abrogate here is that the Act authorizes only prospective injunctive relief rather than retroactive monetary relief. But we have often made it clear that the relief sought by a plaintiff suing a State is irrelevant to the question whether the suit is barred by the Eleventh Amendment....

Thus our inquiry into whether Congress has the power to abrogate unilaterally the States' immunity from suit is narrowly focused on one question: Was the Act in question passed pursuant to a constitutional provision granting Congress the power to abrogate? *See, e.g.*, Fitzpatrick v. Bitzer, 427 U.S. 445, 452–56 (1976). Previously, in conducting that inquiry, we have found authority to abrogate under only two provisions of the Constitution. In *Fitzpatrick*, we recognized that the Fourteenth Amendment, by expanding federal power at the expense of state autonomy, had fundamentally altered the balance of state and federal power struck by the Constitution. *Id.* at 455. We noted that §1 of the Fourteenth Amendment contained prohibitions expressly directed at the States and that §5 of the Amendment expressly provided that "The Congress shall have power to enforce, by appropriate legislation, the provisions of this article." *See id.* at 453 (internal quotation marks omitted). We held that through the Fourteenth Amendment, federal power extended to intrude upon the province of the Eleventh Amendment and therefore that §5 of the Fourteenth Amendment allowed Congress to abrogate the immunity from suit guaranteed by that Amendment.

In only one other case has congressional abrogation of the States' Eleventh Amendment immunity been upheld. In Pennsylvania v. Union Gas Co., 491 U.S. 1 (1989), a plurality of the Court found that the Interstate Commerce Clause, Art. I, §8, cl. 3, granted Congress the power to abrogate state sovereign immunity, stating that the power to regulate interstate commerce would be "incomplete without the authority to render States liable in damages." 491 U.S. at 19–20. Justice White added the fifth vote necessary to the result in that case, but wrote separately in order to express that he "[did] not agree with much of [the plurality's] reasoning." *Id.* at 57 (opinion concurring in judgment in part and dissenting in part)....

Following the rationale of the *Union Gas* plurality, our inquiry is limited to determining whether the Indian Commerce Clause, like the Interstate Commerce Clause, is a grant of authority to the Federal Government at the expense of the States. The answer to that question is obvious. If anything, the Indian Commerce Clause accomplishes a greater transfer of power from the States to the Federal Government than does the Interstate Commerce Clause. This is clear enough from the fact that the States still exercise some authority over interstate trade but have been divested of virtually all authority over Indian commerce and Indian tribes. Under the rationale of *Union Gas*, if the States' partial cession of authority over a particular area includes cession of the immunity from suit, then their virtually total cession of authority over a different area must also include cession of the immunity from suit. *See id.* at 42 ... We agree with petitioner that the plurality opinion in *Union Gas* allows no principled distinction in favor of the States to be drawn between the Indian Commerce Clause and the Interstate Commerce Clause.

Respondents argue, however, that we need not conclude that the Indian Commerce Clause grants the power to abrogate the States' sovereign immunity. Instead, they contend that if we find the rationale of the *Union Gas* plurality to extend to the Indian Commerce Clause, then "*Union Gas* should be reconsidered and overruled." Brief for Respondents 25. Generally, the principle of stare decisis, and the interests that it serves, viz., "the even-handed, predictable, and consistent development of legal principles, ... reliance on judicial decisions, and ... the actual and perceived integrity of the judicial process," Payne v. Tennessee, 501 U.S. 808, 827 (1991), counsel strongly against reconsideration of our precedent. Nevertheless, we always have treated stare decisis as a "principle of policy," Helvering v. Hallock, 309 U.S. 106, 119 (1940), and not as an "inexorable command," *Payne*, 501 U.S. at 828. "[W]hen governing decisions are unworkable or are badly reasoned, 'this Court has never felt constrained to follow precedent.'" *Id.* at 827. Our willingness to reconsider our earlier decisions has been "particularly true in constitutional cases, because in such cases 'correction through legislative action is practically impossible.'" *Payne, supra,* at 828.

The Court in *Union Gas* reached a result without an expressed rationale agreed upon by a majority of the Court.... Since it was issued, *Union Gas* has created confusion among the lower courts that have sought to understand and apply the deeply fractured decision....

The plurality's rationale also deviated sharply from our established federalism jurisprudence and essentially eviscerated our decision in *Hans*.... It was well established in 1989 when *Union Gas* was decided that the Eleventh Amendment stood for the constitutional principle that state sovereign immunity limited the federal courts' jurisdiction under Article III. The text of the Amendment itself is clear enough on this point: "The Judicial power of the United States shall not be construed to extend to any suit...." And our decisions since *Hans* had been equally clear that the Eleventh Amendment reflects "the fundamental principle of sovereign immunity [that] limits the grant of judicial authority in Art. III," Pennhurst State School and Hospital v. Halderman, 465 U.S. 89, 97–98 (1984); *see Union Gas, supra,* at 38, ("'[T]he entire judicial power granted by the Constitution does not embrace authority to entertain a suit brought by private parties against a State without consent given ...'") (SCALIA, J., dissenting).... As the dissent in *Union Gas* recognized, the plurality's conclusion—that Congress could under Article I expand the scope of the federal courts' jurisdiction under Article III "contradict[ed] our unvarying approach to Article III as setting forth the exclusive catalog of permissible federal-court jurisdiction." *Union Gas, supra,* 491 U.S., at 39.

Never before the decision in *Union Gas* had we suggested that the bounds of Article III could be expanded by Congress operating pursuant to any constitutional provision other than the Fourteenth Amendment. Indeed, it had seemed fundamental that Congress could not expand the jurisdiction of the federal courts beyond the bounds of Article III....

The plurality's extended reliance upon our decision in Fitzpatrick v. Bitzer, 427 U.S. 445 (1976), that Congress could under the Fourteenth Amendment abrogate the States' sovereign immunity was also, we believe, misplaced. *Fitzpatrick* was based upon a rationale wholly inapplicable to the Interstate Commerce Clause, viz., that the Fourteenth Amendment, adopted well after the adoption of the Eleventh Amendment and the ratification of the Constitution, operated to alter the pre-existing balance between state and federal power achieved by Article III and the Eleventh Amendment. *Id.* at 454....

In the five years since it was decided, *Union Gas* has proved to be a solitary departure from established law.... Reconsidering the decision in *Union Gas*, we conclude that none of the policies underlying stare decisis require our continuing adherence to its holding. The decision has, since its issuance, been of questionable precedential value, largely because a majority of the Court expressly disagreed with the rationale of the plurality.... The case involved the interpretation of the Constitution and therefore may be altered only by constitutional amendment or revision by this Court. Finally, both the result in *Union Gas* and the plurality's rationale depart from our established understanding of the Eleventh Amendment and undermine the accepted function of Article III. We feel bound to conclude that *Union Gas* was wrongly decided and that it should be, and now is, overruled....

In overruling *Union Gas* today, we reconfirm that the background principle of state sovereign immunity embodied in the Eleventh Amendment is not so ephemeral as to dissipate when the subject of the suit is an area, like the regulation of Indian commerce, that is under the exclusive control of the Federal Government. Even when the Constitution vests in Congress complete law-making authority over a particular area, the Eleventh Amendment prevents congressional authorization of suits by private parties against unconsenting States. The Eleventh Amendment restricts the judicial power under Article III, and Article I cannot be used to circumvent the constitutional limitations placed upon federal jurisdiction. Petitioner's suit against the State of Florida must be dismissed for a lack of jurisdiction.

III

Petitioner argues that we may exercise jurisdiction over its suit to enforce § 2710(d)(3) against the Governor notwithstanding the jurisdictional bar of the Eleventh Amendment. Petitioner notes that since our decision in *Ex parte Young*, 209 U.S. 123 (1908), we often have found federal jurisdiction over a suit against a state official when that suit seeks only prospective injunctive relief in order to "end a continuing violation of federal law." Green v. Mansour, 474 U.S. at 68. The situation presented here, however, is sufficiently different from that giving rise to the traditional *Ex parte Young* action so as to preclude the availability of that doctrine.

Here, the "continuing violation of federal law" alleged by petitioner is the Governor's failure to bring the State into compliance with § 2710(d) (3). But the duty to negotiate imposed upon the State by that statutory provision does not stand alone. Rather, as we have seen, ... Congress passed § 2710(d) (3) in conjunction with the carefully crafted and intricate remedial scheme set forth in § 2710(d) (7).

Where Congress has created a remedial scheme for the enforcement of a particular federal right, we have, in suits against federal officers, refused to supplement that scheme with one created by the judiciary.... Here, of course, the question is not whether a remedy should be created, but instead is whether the Eleventh Amendment bar should be lifted, as it was in *Ex parte Young,* in order to allow a suit against a state officer. Nevertheless, we think that the same general principle applies: Therefore, where Congress has prescribed a detailed remedial scheme for the enforcement against a State of a statutorily created right, a court should hesitate before casting aside those limitations and permitting an action against a state officer based upon *Ex parte Young.*

Here, Congress intended § 2710(d)(3) to be enforced against the State in an action brought under § 2710(d)(7); the intricate procedures set forth in that provision show that Congress intended therein not only to define, but also to limit significantly, the duty imposed by § 2710(d)(3). For example, where the court finds that the State has failed to negotiate in good faith, the only remedy prescribed is an order directing the State and the Indian tribe to conclude a compact within 60 days. And if the parties disregard the court's order and fail to conclude a compact within the 60-day period, the only sanction is that each party then must submit a proposed compact to a mediator who selects the one which best embodies the terms of the Act. Finally, if the State fails to accept the compact selected by the mediator, the only sanction against it is that the mediator shall notify the Secretary of the Interior who then must prescribe regulations governing class III gaming on the tribal lands at issue. By contrast with this quite modest set of sanctions, an action brought against a state official under *Ex parte Young* would expose that official to the full remedial powers of a federal court, including, presumably, contempt sanctions. If § 2710(d)(3) could be enforced in a suit under *Ex parte Young,* § 2710(d)(7) would have been superfluous; it is difficult to see why an Indian tribe would suffer through the intricate scheme of § 2710(d)(7) when more complete and more immediate relief would be available under *Ex parte Young.*

Here, of course, we have found that Congress does not have authority under the Constitution to make the State suable in federal court under § 2710(d)(7). Nevertheless, the fact that Congress chose to impose upon the State a liability that is significantly more limited than would be the liability imposed upon the state officer under *Ex parte Young* strongly indicates that Congress had no wish to create the latter under § 2710(d)(3). Nor are we free to rewrite the statutory scheme in order to approximate what we think Congress might have wanted had it known that § 2710(d)(7) was beyond its authority. If that effort is to be made, it should be made by Congress, and not by the federal courts. We hold that *Ex parte Young* is inapplicable to petitioner's suit against the Governor of Florida, and therefore that suit is barred by the Eleventh Amendment and must be dismissed for a lack of jurisdiction.

IV

The Eleventh Amendment prohibits Congress from making the State of Florida capable of being sued in federal court. The narrow exception to the Eleventh Amendment provided by the Ex parte Young doctrine cannot be used to enforce § 2710(d)(3) because Congress enacted a remedial scheme, § 2710(d)(7), specifically designed for the enforcement of that right. The Eleventh Circuit's dismissal of petitioner's suit is hereby affirmed.

It is so ordered.

[Dissenting opinions of Justice Stevens and Justice Souter (joined by Justices Ginsburg and Breyer) omitted.]

Notes

1. *Seminole Tribe* was a 5–4 decision. The dissenting opinions of Justices Stevens and Souter criticized the majority opinion on several bases: first, the dissent argued that Congress had broad constitutional authority to regulate commerce, and this was even more the case when Indian nations were concerned. Second, Indian relations had been interpreted as being the "exclusive province of federal law." *Cabazon* established that this was emphatically the case as it related to gaming on tribal lands. According to Justice Souter then, "since the States have no sovereignty in the regulation of commerce with the tribes … there is no source of sovereign immunity to assert in a suit based on regulation of that commerce." 517 U.S. at 148. Third, the dissents disagreed with the narrow reading of *Ex parte Young* given by the majority, arguing that the *Young* doctrine did not create a new cause of action which would allow a tribe "more complete and immediate relief" than provided for by IGRA, but merely provided a jurisdictional basis for the tribe to proceed against a state officer. In addition, the dissent chastised the Court for not reading IGRA in such a way as to "avoid constitutional infirmity" and choosing a reasonable interpretation of the statute rather than confronting the constitutional issue head on, as the majority chose to do. Such well-established doctrines would require the application of *Young*. *See* Wayne L. Baker, Seminole *Speaks to Sovereign Immunity and* Ex Parte Young, 71 St. John's L. Rev. 739 (1997) (providing an examination of the widely different approaches embraced by the majority and dissent in *Seminole Tribe*).

2. *Seminole Tribe* is a staple of constitutional law casebooks. It is illustrative of the Rehnquist Court's movement in a number of cases to use the Tenth and Eleventh Amendments, and a narrow reading of the Commerce Clause, to protect the interests of states against perceived federal encroachment. *See, e.g.,* United States v. Morrison, 529 U.S. 598 (2000) (holding that neither the Commerce Clause nor the Fourteenth Amendment gave Congress the power to create a civil cause of action in federal court for gender-motivated violence); Printz v. United States, 521 U.S. 898 (1997) (holding that Congress did not have the power to require state law enforcement officials to conduct background checks for handgun purchases in compliance with the Brady Act); United States v. Lopez, 514 U.S. 549 (1995) (limiting Congress' Commerce Clause power to the channels of interstate commerce; persons, things or instrumentalities in interstate commerce; and, activities that are substantially affected or related to interstate commerce); New York v. United States, 505 U.S. 144 (1992) (holding that Congress' Low-Level Radioactive Waste Policy Amendments Act requiring state that did not comply with the Act to "take title" to the waste produced by the State was impermissible use of Commerce Clause power and therefore not enforceable). The legal literature assessing the "New Federalism" approach of the Rehnquist Court is extensive. *See, e.g.,* Mitchell F. Crusto, *The Supreme Court's "New" Federalism: An Anti-Rights Agenda?* 16 Ga. St. U.L. Rev. 517 (2000) (examining the effect of "New" Federalism on the constitutional rights of individuals and minorities, concluding that the approach is inherently flawed and a threat to individual rights); David H. Getches, *Beyond Indian Law: The Rehnquist Court's Pursuit of States' Rights, Color-Blind Justice and Mainstream Values,* 86 Minn. L. Rev. 267 (2001) (arguing that the new federalism approach of the Rehnquist Court has had the effect of drastically reshaping Federal Indian law by ignoring precedent and tradition); Brent E. Simmons, *The Invincibility of Constitutional Error: The Rehnquist Court's States' Rights Assault on Fourteenth Amendment Protections of Individual Rights,* 11 Seton Hall Const. L.J. 259 (2001) (arguing that the new federalism approach of the Rehnquist court signals a direct threat to liberties secured by the Fourteenth Amendment); Robert J. Pushaw, Jr., *Bridging the Enforcement Gap in Constitutional Law: A Critique of the Supreme Court's Theory that Self-Restraint Promotes Fed-*

eralism, 46 Wm. & Mary L. Rev. 1289 (2004) (arguing that, contrary to the assertion of the Supreme Court, the purpose of an independent federal judiciary was to ensure the uniformity and supremacy of federal law, not to protect the autonomy of state courts as equal enforcers of federal law); Hon. Randall T. Shepard, *The Renaissance in State Constitutional Law: There are few Dangers, But What's the Alternative?* 61 Alb. L. Rev. 1529 (1998) (arguing that "the difference between legitimate and illegitimate state constitutional decision-making is not so much a matter of how one perceives the current relationship between state and federal governments, as it is a matter of maintaining an internal sort of interpretative integrity.").

3. In the majority opinion, the Court declined to consider whether this portion of IGRA also violated the Tenth Amendment, which provides in pertinent part, "[t]he powers not delegated to the United States by the Constitution, nor prohibited by it to the States, are reserved to the States respectively...." Some commentators have made the argument that IGRA cannot be squared with the Tenth Amendment. *See, e.g.*, Neil Scott Cohen, Note, *In What Often Appears to be a Crapshoot Legislative Process, Congress Throws Snake Eyes When It Enacts the Indian Gaming Regulatory Act*, 29 Hofstra L. Rev. 277 (2000). For judicial consideration of the issue, *see* Ponca Tribe v. Oklahoma, 37 F.3d 1422 (10th Cir. 1994), *judgment vacated by* 517 U.S. 1129 (1996), *rev'd on other grounds*, 89 F.3d 690 (10th Cir. 1996); Cheyenne River Sioux Tribe v. South Dakota, 3 F.3d 271 (8th Cir. 1993).

4. What part of IGRA was declared unconstitutional in *Seminole Tribe*? Was it just the part of section 2710(d) relating to the tribe suing the state in federal court? Or did the Supreme Court's decision effectively make *all* of section 2710(d)—the part of IGRA describing the compact process for Class III gaming—unconstitutional? IGRA does have a severability clause, which creates a presumption that if one provision of the law is ruled unconstitutional, the remainder of the statute remains valid. *See* § 2721. But one court has ruled that the "presumption is not conclusive; we must still strike down other portions of the statute if we find strong evidence that Congress did not mean for them to remain in effect without the invalid section." United States v. Spokane Tribe of Indians, 139 F.3d 1297, 1299 (9th Cir. 1998). What would be the effect of declaring all of the Class III compact process unconstitutional? Would there then be a reversion to the law as of 1987, the date of the *Cabazon* decision? Would this be a result favorable to states?

5. What recourse does a tribe have after *Seminole Tribe* if a state refuses to negotiate a Class III compact in good faith? The most likely result is the tribe has no recourse if a state invokes its immunity when sued in federal court. Note 4 suggested another possibility, the return of the pre-*Cabazon* days. But a third possibility is what is sometimes referred to as an "administrative compact." After *Seminole Tribe*, the Secretary of the Interior promulgated regulations that gave the Secretary the power to authorize class III gaming in the absence of a tribe-state compact. According to the regulations, which became effective in 1999, this could be done when, "A State and an Indian tribe are unable to voluntarily agree to a compact; and, [t]he State has asserted its immunity from suit [under the Seminole Tribe decision.]" 25 C.F.R. § 291.1 (2010). The procedures themselves are very detailed, but basically track the compact negotiation rules of IGRA.

The asserted statutory authority for taking this action is somewhat tenuous. Two general provisions of federal law giving power to the Bureau of Indian Affairs state that:

> The Commissioner of Indian Affairs shall, under the direction of the Secretary of the Interior, and agreeably to such regulations as the President may prescribe, have the management of all Indian affairs and of all matters arising out of Indian relations. 25 U.S.C. § 2.

> The President may prescribe such regulations as he may think fit for carrying into effect the various provisions of any act relating to Indian affairs, and for the settlement of the accounts of Indian affairs. 25 U.S.C. § 9.

More specifically, IGRA itself provides that the Secretary of the Interior *shall* prescribe procedures for Class III gaming on a tribal land that are "consistent with the proposed compact selected by the mediator" appointed by a court in a case where the tribe has sued the state claiming the state has not bargained in good faith. 25 U.S.C. § 2710(d)(7)(B)(vii)(I)–(II). Of course, *Seminole Tribe* established that this procedure could not be pursued if the State asserted its immunity. But the Court did not consider the constitutionality of the administrative compact, though Justice Stevens' dissent suggested that with the administrative compact possibility the dispute might "begin and end in the Executive Branch." 517 U.S. at 99 (Stevens, J., dissenting).

Does the Secretary have the authority under federal law to apply this procedure, especially in light of *Seminole Tribe*? In Texas v. United States, 497 F.3d 491 (5th Cir. 2007), the Fifth Circuit ruled that it was "legal alchemy" to infer from IGRA or the "general authority" statutes that the Secretary of the Interior had the power "to promulgate a wholesale substitute for the judicial process." 497 F.3d at 503. The tribal-state compact was the "lynchpin" of IGRA's balancing of interests, and "Congress viewed the compact as an indispensable prerequisite to Class III gaming." *Id.* at 507. Consequently, the procedures for an "administrative compact" violated "the unambiguous language of IGRA and congressional intent by bypassing the neutral judicial process that centrally protects the state's role in authorizing tribal Class III gaming." *Id.* at 511.

At least one court of appeals decision suggests that the Secretary's authority to prescribe compact regulations was not negated by the *Seminole Tribe* decision. In United States v. Spokane Tribe, 139 F.3d 1297 (9th Cir. 1998), the court noted that while it had previously scorned the Eleventh Circuit's rationale that the Secretary would retain the authority to prescribe regulations, that was before *Seminole Tribe* had changed the scope of IGRA.

> [W]e considered the Eleventh Circuit's suggestion and said that "such a result would pervert the congressional plan," turning the Secretary of the Interior into "a federal czar." However, that was in the context of our (incorrect) assumption that tribes could sue states. We were pointing out that the Eleventh Circuit's suggestion would not be as close to Congress's intent as the scheme Congress in fact passed. True. But the Supreme Court has now told us that Congress's scheme is unconstitutional; the Eleventh Circuit's suggestion is a lot closer to Congress's intent than mechanically enforcing IGRA against tribes even when states refuse to negotiate. Whether or not such rulemaking would bring IGRA's operation close enough to Congress's intent to save the statute depends on the as yet undisclosed details of the proposed regulations.

139 F.3d at 1301–02. *See also* Santee Sioux Nation v. Norton, No. 8:05CV147, 2006 WL 2792734 at *6 (D. Neb. Sept. 26, 2006) ("Congress intended that the Secretary review and approve Class III gaming by tribes. This court agrees with the Eleventh and Ninth Circuits which have found that a tribe could request the Secretary determine gaming procedures pursuant to [IGRA]."). *But see* United States v. Confederated Tribes of Colville Reservation, No. 99-35153, 1999 WL 1269335 (9th Cir. Dec 28, 1999) (declining to rule on tribe's request for a stay on the proceeding pending completion of regulations promulgated by the Department of the Interior which would operate in place of a tribal-state compact; issue could be resolved with a determination of whether the gaming devices

seized were legal in the state of Washington and statutory and constitutional issues need not be reached); Robinson Band of Pomo Indians of Robinson Rancheria v. Babbitt, No. C 98-0294, 1998 WL 355580 (N.D. Cal. June 26, 1998) (granting Secretary of Interior's Motion to Dismiss; tribe's claim that Secretary must adopt class III gaming procedures because negotiations with State of California had broken down was premature, as California had not yet raised a defense of sovereign immunity defense to the bad faith claims of the tribe).

Which of these views seems correct? Is the "administrative compact" an attempted "end run" around *Seminole Tribe*? When critics of *Seminole Tribe* say that it disrupted a "carefully constructed balance" between tribal and state interests by depriving tribes of a judicial remedy, does that necessarily mean that Congress would have viewed the "administrative compact" as a fallback for the tribe? Could this be determined by the legislative history of IGRA? Would post-*Seminole Tribe* decision statements by the Congressional sponsors of IGRA to the effect that they intended the administrative compact process to operate as a fallback be relevant? Could the administrative compact process make the *tribe* less likely to negotiate in good faith? How?

There have been few occasions where the Secretary of the Interior has resorted to the administrative compact process. Usually, the political process will sort out these issues. Florida's experience is instructive here. After losing the right to sue the state to resolve their compact dispute, the Seminole tribe requested that the Secretary create new gaming regulations for the tribe, which he did. The regulations were to go into effect in 2007 if the tribe and the state could not reach an agreement. Governor Crist reached an agreement with the tribe in 2007 and the compact was signed. The compact was challenged by the Florida legislature and quickly invalidated by the Florida Supreme Court. The court stated that because the compact had not been approved by the legislature, and Governor Crist did not have the authority to bind the state to such a compact, the agreement was therefore invalid. *See* Florida House of Representatives v. Crist, 999 So. 2d 601 (Fla. 2008). However, the legislature was merely unhappy with the terms of the agreement, and was not opposed to signing a compact with the tribe. In an extended 2008 session, the legislature submitted a proposal to the tribe for a new compact. Changes made to the proposal by Governor Crist and the tribe were not approved by the legislature, and this second proposal fell apart. Finally, in April, 2010, an agreement was reached between the parties and Governor Crist signed the compact. *See* Mary Ellen Klas, *Crist Signs $1Billion Seminole Gambling Deal*, Miami Herald, April 29, 2010, http://www.miamiherald.com/ 2010/04/29/1603451/crist-signs-1-billion-seminole.html. The Department of the Interior approved the compact and the last pin is finally in place after nearly two decades of negotiations and legal battles. *See* Josh Hafenbrack, *Florida's Gambling Deal with Seminoles is OK'd*, Miami Herald, July 7, 2010, http://www.miamiherald.com/2010/07/07/1718508/floridas-gambling-deal-with-seminoles.html.

The situation in Texas that led to the Fifth Circuit's decision in *Texas v. United States* is slightly different. The Kickapoo tribe had requested that the Secretary of the Interior promulgate regulations to allow them to operate Class III gaming in the state, after eight years of little progress at the negotiation table. Unlike Florida, which treated the request as an incentive to negotiate more earnestly with the Seminole tribe, Texas was not so enticed, and sued the Secretary of the Interior seeking an injunction, which was granted. *See* John H. Douglas, Texas v. United States: *Will IGRA Allow the States to have Their Cake and Eat it too?*, http://www.indiangaming.com/regulatory/view/?id=86 (last visited August 1, 2010).

For a discussion of many of these issues, *see* Rebecca S. Lindner-Cornelius, *The Secretary of the Interior as Referee: The States, the Indian Nations, and how Gambling led to the Illegality of the Secretary of the Interior's Regulations in 25 C.F.R. §29*, 84 Marq. L. Rev. 685 (2001); Sean Cunniff, Texas v. United States: *Mind the Gap*, 39 N.M. L. Rev. 527 (2009); Kevin K. Washburn, *Recurring Problems in Indian Gaming*, 1 Wyo. L. Rev. 427 (2001).

B. What Games Are Subject to Compact Negotiation?

Northern Arapaho Tribe v. Wyoming
389 F.3d 1308 (10th Cir. 2004)

SEYMOUR, Circuit Judge.

The Northern Arapaho Tribe brought an action seeking a declaration that the state of Wyoming failed to negotiate in good faith with the Tribe in violation of the Indian Gaming Regulatory Act (IGRA), 25 U.S.C. §§2701 *et seq.* Partially granting the Tribe's motion for judgment on the pleadings, the district court held that Wyoming failed to negotiate in good faith with regard to calcutta and parimutuel wagering and ordered the parties to complete a compact within sixty days. The court further held that casino-style gaming and slot machine wagering were against Wyoming public policy and thus not subject to negotiation. Both parties appeal. We affirm in part and reverse in part.

I

The Northern Arapaho Tribe is a federally recognized Indian tribe with a reservation in the State of Wyoming. Under the IGRA, a tribe must negotiate with the state and enter into a "tribal-state" compact in order to engage in gaming on Indian lands. 25 U.S.C. §2710(d)(1)(C). Seeking to engage in a casino-style gaming operation on the Wind River Indian Reservation, the Tribe submitted a written request to the state for tribal-state compact negotiations.

The Tribe submitted a proposal to the state under which it would be entitled to operate gaming and gaming machines including poker, video poker, roulette, dice games, sportsbook, parimutuel, wheel of fortune, keno, video keno, raffle/lottery, multi-line slot, regular slot, blackjack, video blackjack, video pull-tab, and video horse racing. In response, the state took the position that because Wyoming has a broad criminal prohibition against gambling and exceptions to that prohibition are narrowly drawn, the IGRA requires it to negotiate only regarding the games that Wyoming law specifically permits for commercial purposes. According to the state, the compact negotiations with the Tribe were thus limited to raffles, bingo, pull tabs, calcuttas, and parimutuel wagering.

The Tribe disagreed, claiming that Wyoming was required to negotiate regarding all games listed in the Tribe's proposed compact because state law permitted a nearly unlimited variety of gaming, including "any game, wager or transaction," albeit only for social or non-profit purposes. Wyo. Stat. §6-7-101(a)(iii)(E). Over one hundred eighty days passed without a gaming compact, prompting the Tribe to file suit seeking a declaration that Wyoming had failed to negotiate in good faith in violation of the IGRA. *See* 25 U.S.C. §2710(d)(7)(B)(i). In addition, the Tribe requested the court to order the state to enter into a tribal-state compact within sixty days. *Id.* §2710(d)(7)(B)(iii). In the alternative, the Tribe sought an injunction to prevent the state from interfering with the Tribe's alleged right to conduct or regulate class III gaming on Indian lands within Wyoming.

The district court partially granted a motion for judgment on the pleadings in favor of the Tribe, holding that the state's refusal to bargain on calcutta or parimutuel wagering, other than in strict conformity with state law restrictions that do not apply to tribes under the IGRA, constituted a failure to negotiate in good faith. The court further held, however, that the state was not required to negotiate regarding "casino-style" games or "gaming machines," notwithstanding Wyoming's permissiveness in allowing casino-style gambling for social purposes. The court ordered the parties to enter into a compact within sixty days with regard to calcutta and parimutuel betting.

II

....

The IGRA was enacted in 1988 in order to "promot[e] tribal economic development, self-sufficiency, and strong tribal governments." 25 U.S.C. § 2702(1). The statute provides a comprehensive system to regulate gambling activities on Indian lands. The IGRA explicitly states that "Indian tribes have the exclusive right to regulate gaming activity on Indian lands if the gaming activity is not specifically prohibited by Federal law and is conducted within a state which does not, as a matter of criminal law and public policy, prohibit such gaming activity." *Id.* § 2701(5). This declaration is consistent with Supreme Court's seminal pre-IGRA decision:

> if the intent of a state law is generally to prohibit certain conduct, it falls within [the state's] criminal jurisdiction, but if the state law generally permits the conduct at issue, subject to regulation, it must be classified as civil/regulatory.... The shorthand test is whether the conduct at issue violates the State's public policy.

California v. Cabazon Band of Mission Indians, 480 U.S. 202, 209 (1987). Accordingly, the primary issue in this case is whether "such gaming activity" in which the Northern Arapaho Tribe wishes to engage is "prohibited" or merely regulated by the state of Wyoming.

The IGRA divides Indian gaming into three classes:.... Class III gaming activities are "lawful on Indian lands only if such activities are ... (A) authorized [by an approved Tribal] ordinance or resolution..., (B) located in a State that permits such gaming *for any purpose by any person, organization, or entity,* and (C) conducted in conformance with a Tribal-State compact...." *Id.* § 2710(d) (emphasis added). In order to engage in Class III gaming activities, the Tribe must "request the State in which such lands are located to enter into negotiations for the purpose of entering into a Tribal-State compact governing the conduct of gaming activities." *Id.* § 2710(d)(3)(a). The state must negotiate in good faith with the tribe upon receipt of such a request. *Id.*

The controversy between the Tribe and the state of Wyoming centers on the phrase "located in a State that permits such gaming for any purpose by any person, organization, or entity." *Id.* § 2710(d)(1)(B). As the district court detailed in its opinion, this statutory language has spawned at least two different approaches regarding the scope of negotiations required between tribes and states under the IGRA.

The "Wisconsin" analysis or "categorical" approach requires courts to first review the general scope of gaming permitted by the state. *See, e. g., Lac du Flambeau Band of Lake Superior Chippewa Indians v. Wisconsin,* 770 F. Supp. 480 (W.D. Wis. 1991). If the state permits any form of Class III gaming, the tribe must negotiate to offer all forms of Class III gaming because the state is merely "regulating," rather than "prohibiting," this type of gambling. *Id.* at 484–88. This categorical approach has been adopted by at least one circuit. *See Mashantucket Pequot Tribe v. Connecticut,* 913 F.2d 1024, 1031–32 (2d Cir. 1990).

The "Florida" analysis or "game-specific" approach requires courts to review whether state law permits the specific game at issue. *See, e.g.,* Coeur d'Alene Tribe v. Idaho, 842 F. Supp. 1268, 1278 (D. Idaho 1994) (citing Seminole Tribe of Florida v. Florida, 1993 WL 475999 (S.D. Fla. Sept.22, 1993)). If the state allows a particular game for any purpose, it must negotiate with the tribe over that specific game. *Id.* at 1279–80. Similarly, if the state entirely prohibits a particular game, the state is not required to negotiate with the Tribe as to that game, even if the state permits other games in the same category. *Id.* Under this approach, the state's permissive treatment as to one type of Class III game does not mean that the state must negotiate with tribes as to all Class III games. At least two circuits follow the "game-specific" approach. *See* Rumsey Indian Rancheria of Wintun Indians v. Wilson, 64 F.3d 1250, 1257–58 (9th Cir. 1994); Cheyenne River Sioux Tribe v. South Dakota, 3 F.3d 273, 278–79 (8th Cir. 1993).

The district court specifically adopted the "Florida" or "game-specific" approach. We need not decide whether to follow the Wisconsin or Florida analysis regarding the scope of gaming under the IGRA because we conclude that Wyoming must negotiate with the Tribe under either approach regarding the full gamut of "any game, wager or transaction," Wyo. Stat. §6-7-101(a)(iii)(E).

In order to determine the appropriate scope of negotiations between the Tribe and the state under either analysis, it is critical to determine the scope of gaming permitted by state law. Under Wyoming law, Class III calcutta wagering is permitted on "amateur contests, cutter horse racing, dog sled racing, professional rodeo events or professional golf tournament[s]" if "conducted by a bona fide nationally chartered veterans', religious, charitable, educational or fraternal organization or non-profit local civic or service club...." Wyo. Stat. §6-7-101. For-profit parimutuel wagering is permitted on specified events so long as the profits are limited to 25.90% of the total wagers per event. *Id.* §11-25-102.

The district court held that because Wyoming law specifically authorizes calcutta and parimutuel wagering, the state is required to negotiate with the Tribe regarding the full gamut of those types of games. The fact that calcutta wagering, under state law, may only be conducted by incorporated non-profit groups for non-profit purposes is inapposite: the tribe is not limited to "just wagering subject to the conditions of Wyo. Stat. §6-7-101(a)(iii)(F) and 11-25-105." Aplt. App. at 139. In other words, the district court held that state law "person" or "purpose" restrictions on calcutta or parimutuel wagering do not apply to tribes under the IGRA.

The state argues that the district court erred in concluding the IGRA requires the state to negotiate with the Tribe as to calcutta and parimutuel wagering without regard to the limitations of Wyoming law. If the state's approach were correct, however, "[t]he compact process that Congress established as the centerpiece of the IGRA's regulation of Class III gaming would thus become a dead letter; there would be nothing to negotiate, and no meaningful compact would be possible." *Mashantucket Pequot Tribe,* 913 F.2d at 1031. Furthermore, "the legislative history [of the IGRA] reveals that Congress intended to permit a particular gaming activity, *even if conducted in a manner inconsistent with state law,* if the state law merely regulated, as opposed to completely barred, that particular gaming activity." United States v. Sisseton-Wahpeton Sioux Tribe, 897 F.2d 358, 365 (8th Cir. 1990) (emphasis added).

It is clear under Wyoming law that the state regulates, rather than prohibits, calcutta and parimutuel wagering. Thus, the IGRA's requirement that Class III gaming be "located in a State that permits such gaming for any purpose by any person, organization, or entity" is fulfilled. 25 U.S.C. §2710(d)(1)(B). The state is therefore clearly required to conduct negotiations with the Tribe concerning the full gamut of calcutta and parimutuel wagering.

With regard to the broader issue of other casino-style Class III gambling, the district court recognized that Wyoming allows such activities because it permits "any game, wager or transaction" for social and non-profit purposes. Wyo. Stat. §6-7-101(a)(iii)(E). The court stated that "[u]nder a straightforward Florida analysis, Wyoming would have to negotiate over casino-style gambling with the Arapaho because it allows such gaming for any purpose; namely, a social one." Nonetheless, the court held the state was not required to negotiate regarding casino-style gambling. Forcing the state to do so simply because Wyoming permits social gambling, the court concluded, would lead to an "absurd result." *Id.* at 140–42. We disagree.

As the district court acknowledged with respect to calcutta and parimutuel wagering, if gaming is permitted by a state "for any purpose by any person," such gaming is lawful on Indian land without the restrictions otherwise imposed on off-reservation gaming as a matter of state law. 25 U.S.C. §2710(d)(1). The Tribe contends that because the state broadly permits any casino-style gaming for social and non-profit purposes, it is required to negotiate with the Tribe concerning the full gamut of "any game, wager or transaction." Wyo. Stat. §6-7-101(a)(iii)(E).

The state argues that its limited authorization of casino-style gambling for social purposes does not amount to a general allowance of "such gaming" within the contemplation of the IGRA. 25 U.S.C. §2710(d)(1)(B) (Class III gambling is lawful if "located in a State that permits such gaming for any purpose by any person, organization, or entity"). The state apparently claims that the appropriate baseline category to which the term "such gaming" refers is neither all Class III gambling games nor all casino-style gambling games, but rather the subset of specific Class III games at issue — in this instance, casino-style gambling games for non-commercial purposes. The state's argument fails under either the Wisconsin or Florida analysis.

Under the Wisconsin or "categorical" approach, the state must negotiate concerning all forms of Class III gaming because Wyoming permits and regulates "such gaming," albeit only for social and non-profit purposes. Under the Florida or "game-specific" approach, the state must negotiate regarding the broad category of "any game, wager or transaction" because the state specifically permits and regulates all types of "such gaming" for certain purposes by certain people and organizations. We are aware of no court that has approved a state law restriction against gaming "for-profit," "professionally," or anything similar when the state permits the same type of gaming for social and non-profit purposes. Instead, courts have rejected states' attempts to limit negotiations with Tribes due to state law restrictions against commercial gaming. *See, e.g., Mashantucket Pequot Tribe,* 913 F.2d at 1032 (holding that limited permission by state for occasional, charitable gaming does not preclude commercial gambling by Tribe under the IGRA); Ysleta Del Sur Pueblo v. Texas, 852 F. Supp. 587, 595–96 (W.D. Tex. 1993) (holding that limited permission for only social gaming under state law does not preclude commercial gambling the Tribe seeks under the IGRA), *rev'd on other grounds,* 36 F.3d 1325 (5th Cir. 1994). In sum, if a state permits Class III gaming under the "Wisconsin" approach, or if a state permits any specific games (here, all games) in any fashion under the "Florida" approach, that state must negotiate a compact for those games even if state law restricts the sponsors or purposes of such gaming. The district court erred in concluding to the contrary.

Finally, the state contends the Tribe produced no evidence that the state failed to respond in good faith to the request of the Tribe to negotiate a compact. The district court held that because (1) Wyoming had a duty to negotiate for terms beyond those Wyoming law expressly permits and (2) the state conceded that it only negotiated to the extent that Wyoming law permitted parimutuel and calcutta gaming, the state had not negotiated in good faith. We agree.

The IGRA provides that:

> upon the introduction of evidence by an Indian tribe that ... (I) a Tribal-State compact has not been entered into ... and (II) the State did not respond to the request of the Indian tribe to negotiate such a compact or did not respond to such request in good faith, the burden of proof shall be upon the State to prove that the State has negotiated with the Indian tribe in good faith to conclude a Tribal-State compact governing the conduct of gaming activities.

25 U.S.C. § 2710(d)(7)(B)(ii). The Tribe alleged and the state conceded that Wyoming only negotiated regarding "raffles, bingo, pull tabs, calcuttas, and parimutuel wagering" and only to the extent state law permits such activities. When a state refuses to negotiate beyond state law limitations concerning a game that it permits, the state cannot be said to have negotiated in good faith under the IGRA given the plain language of the statute. Moreover, "when a state wholly fails to negotiate," as Wyoming did here concerning casino-style gambling, "it obviously cannot meet its burden of proof to show that it negotiated in good faith." *Mashantucket Pequot Tribe*, 913 F.2d at 1032.

The judgment of the district court is **AFFIRMED** in part, **REVERSED** in part, and **REMANDED** for further proceedings in accordance with this opinion. Appellee's motion to file a supplemental appendix is granted.

Notes

1. For a tribe to conduct Class III gaming, IGRA provides that it must be pursuant to a tribal-state compact and be "located in a State that permits such gaming." The question that has been presented in several cases is the meaning of the words "permits such gaming." As the Tenth Circuit's opinion sets out, there are two basic approaches courts have taken to this. Some cases apply what is called a "categorical" analysis. If a state permits Class III gaming of *any* type, then any other form of Class III gaming is subject to negotiation. For example, a state allowing pari-mutuel betting would have no basis for refusing to negotiate with a tribe wanting to offer a casino game like blackjack. Both are categorized as Class III gaming and satisfy the "permits such gaming" requirement. This would be the case even if no venue in the state offered blackjack. Cases following this analysis include Lac du Flambeau Band of Lake Superior Chippewa Indians v. Wisconsin, 770 F. Supp. 480, 487–88 (W.D. Wis. 1991), *appeal dismissed*, 957 F.2d 515 (7th Cir.), *cert denied*, 506 U.S. 829 (1992) ("It was not Congress's intent that the states would be able to impose their gaming regulatory schemes on the tribes.... [T]he state is required to negotiate with plaintiffs over the inclusion ... of any activity that includes the elements of prize, chance and consideration and that is not prohibited expressly by the Wisconsin Constitution or state law."); Mashantucket Pequot Tribe v. Connecticut, 913 F.2d 1024 (2d Cir. 1990) (this is a principal case discussed above on issue of state's requirement to negotiate in good faith. The court ruled that because the state allowed "Las Vegas nights" to be offered by nonprofit groups, it regulated rather than prohibited games of chance. Moreover, the state also permitted other forms of gambling such as jai alai, bingo, and a state-operated lottery. In light of these two considerations, the state had duty to negotiate with the tribe on casino-style games.); United States v. Sisseton-Wahpeton Sioux Tribe, 897 F.2d 358, 365 (8th Cir. 1990) ("legislative history [of IGRA] reveals that Congress intended to permit a particular gaming activity, even if conducted in a manner inconsistent with state law, if the state law merely regulated, as opposed to completely barred, that particular gaming activity."). Note that these cases emphasize the "regulatory-prohibitory" distinction that pre-dated IGRA and was part of the Public Law 280 analysis discussed in Chapter 9.

2. The other approach noted in the principal case is the "game-specific" approach. Just because a state offers one type of Class III gaming does not mean it is required to negotiate with a tribe on other forms of Class III gaming that are not offered in the state. If a tribe wants to offer the game of blackjack, the state must "permit" blackjack in the state. Otherwise, it cannot be said that the state "permits such gaming." Cases following the "game-specific" approach include Rumsey Indian Rancheria of Wintun Indians v. Wilson, 64 F.3d 1250 (9th Cir. 1994), *cert. denied*, 521 U.S. 1118 (1997) ("IGRA does not require a state to negotiate over one form of Class III gaming activity simply because it has legalized another, albeit similar form of gaming.... In other words, a state need only allow Indian tribes to operate games that others can operate, but need not give tribes what others cannot have."); Cheyenne River Sioux Tribe v. South Dakota, 3 F.3d 273, 279 (8th Cir. 1993) (tribe wanted to offer game of keno; state permitted video keno games; "the 'such gaming' language of [IGRA] does not require the state to negotiate ... [on] forms of gaming it does not presently permit. Because video keno and traditional keno are not the same and video keno is the only form of keno allowed under state law, it would be illegal, [and] unfair to the other tribes, for the tribe to offer traditional keno ..."); and Coeur d'Alene Tribe v. Idaho, 842 F. Supp. 1268 (D. Idaho 1994) (after tribe requested Class III negotiations, Idaho Constitution was amended to make gambling illegal except for the state lottery, certain pari-mutuel racing, and charitable bingo and raffle games. According to IGRA and Supreme Court's *Cabazon* decision, state only had duty to negotiate with tribe on issues of lottery and horse, mule, and dog races.).

3. Note that in the cases adopting the broader categorical approach, the courts focus on whether the state has forbidden certain games, while in the game-specific analysis, courts ask whether the state has authorized the game the tribe wants to negotiate on. Are these really just two sides of the same coin?

4. What are the interests that support the two identified approaches? Did Congress intend to give the tribes broad authority to offer Class III gaming, so long as the state did not have a blanket policy against any type of Class III gaming? Does the game-specific approach give states an incentive to make subtle distinctions between games that are offered in the state? As one court stated, a state should not be permitted "to regulate and prohibit, alternately, game by game and device by device, turning its public policy off and on by minute degrees." Sycuan Band of Mission Indians v. Roache, 54 F.3d 535, 539 (9th Cir. 1994). Is a court's decision distinguishing keno and video keno as two different games consistent with IGRA?

On the other hand, is it a stretch to require a state that allows *only* a state-operated lottery to negotiate with a tribe on the full panoply of casino games, which would include everything from slot machines, to blackjack, to craps, to roulette? Does such a result seem consistent with Congress's intent for IGRA? Is the problem the ambiguity of IGRA itself, that is, the "permits such gaming" language? If Congress were to revisit and try to clarify this issue, how would you advise the drafters on the language they should use?

5. In the principal case, the state of Wyoming had waived its Eleventh Amendment immunity and was fully participating in the compact process prescribed by IGRA. Why would a state decline to assert its *Seminole Tribe*/Eleventh Amendment immunity and subject itself to the full scope of IGRA?

6. The state of California has a robust tribal gaming industry. As of 2007, California generated $7.8 billion of gaming revenue from tribes, over 29% of total tribal gaming revenue. The evolution of tribal gaming in California is an interesting study in politics. Soon after the enactment of IGRA, tribes asked the state of California to negotiate a com-

pact for various types of Class III gaming. After the state refused, the tribes and the state agreed to seek a judicial determination whether the state was obligated to negotiate with the tribes on these matters. The tribe argued that because the state permitted some forms of Class III gaming, such as pari-mutuel betting, the state regulated rather than prohibited all Class III gaming. This meant that "such gaming" was permitted in California. The court disagreed, and, as indicated in note 2 above, the court took the "game-specific" approach, ruling that the state did not have to negotiate with the tribes over these Class III games. Rumsey Indian Rancheria of Wintun Indians v. Wilson, 64 F.3d 1250 (9th Cir. 1994), *cert. denied*, 521 U.S. 1118 (1997). The tribe then gathered over 800,000 signatures and, under the referendum provisions of California law, a proposal for tribal casino-style gaming was put to a popular vote. "Proposition 5" passed with 63% of the vote, despite the determined opposition of an array of interests, including Nevada casinos, anti-gambling groups, and non-tribal gambling interests. According to some accounts, over $100 million was spent by all parties before Proposition 5 was voted on.

Soon after the passage of Proposition 5, however, the California Supreme Court ruled that it was unconstitutional. A 1984 amendment to the California Constitution declared that, "The Legislature has no power to authorize, and shall prohibit casinos of the type currently operating in Nevada and New Jersey." Proposition 5, according to the court, did just that by allowing for Class III banked card games on tribal lands. Hotel Employees & Restaurant Employees Int'l Union v. Davis, 981 P.2d 990 (Cal. 1999). This did not discourage the tribes, however. They then gathered enough signatures for Proposition 1A to be put on the ballot, an effort also supported by the state government. This was a proposed amendment to the California Constitution that permitted tribes to offer casino-style games upon negotiation of a compact with the Governor. Proposition 1A passed with a wider margin than Proposition 5. Since that time, more than fifty tribes have negotiated compacts in California. As the discussion that follows indicates, however, the terms of some of these compacts have been challenged in the courts. In any event, the confluence of political and financial considerations is quite profound.

7. For commentary on the game negotiation issue, *see e.g.*, Melissa S. Taylor, *Categorical vs. Game Specific: Adopting the Categorical Approach to Interpreting "Permits Such Gaming,"* 43 Tulsa L. Rev. 89 (2007); Steve J. Coleman, Note, *Lottery Logistics: The Potential Impact of a State Lottery on Indian Gaming in Oklahoma*, 27 Am. Indian L. Rev. 515 (2003); Alex Tallchief Skibine, *Scope of Gaming, Good Faith Negotiations and the Secretary of Interior's Class III Gaming Procedures: Is IGRA Still a Workable Framework After Seminole?* 5 Gaming L. Rev. 401 (2001); Kevin K. Washburn, *Recurring Problems in Indian Gaming*, 1 Wyo. L. Rev. 427 (2001).

C. Compact Terms under IGRA

Rincon Band of Luiseno Mission Indians of the Rincon Reservation v. Schwarzenegger

602 F.3d 1019 (9th Cir. 2010)

MILAN D. SMITH, JR., Circuit Judge:

The Indian Gaming Regulatory Act (IGRA), 25 U.S.C. §2701 et seq., provides that a state must negotiate in good faith with its resident Native American tribes to reach compacts concerning casino-style gaming on Native American lands. Defendants-Appellants/Cross-Appellees the State of California (the State) and Governor Arnold

Schwarzenegger (Governor Schwarzenegger) (collectively as parties to this litigation, the State) appeal the district court's finding that, in violation of IGRA, 25 U.S.C. §2710(d) (3) (A), the State negotiated in bad faith with Plaintiff-Appellee/Cross-Appellant the Rincon Band of Luiseno Mission Indians (Rincon) concerning amendments to the parties' existing tribal-state gaming compact.

The district court based its bad faith finding on the State's repeated insistence that Rincon pay a portion of its net revenues into the State's general fund, which the district court determined to be an attempt by the State to impose a tax on the tribe in violation of 25 U.S.C. §2710(d) (4).

The State challenges the district court's characterization of its requests as an attempt to impose a tax, and argues that even if it was attempting to impose a tax, that alone is insufficient to support the finding of bad faith. We affirm.

FACTUAL AND PROCEDURAL BACKGROUND

The 1999 Compacts

In the fall of 1999, the State (through then-governor Gray Davis) and Rincon negotiated a compact granting Rincon the right to operate casino-style gaming on its lands located near San Diego, California, subject to certain limitations. Simultaneously, the State's negotiations also resulted in similar compacts with dozens of other tribes across California. Although some of the 1999 compacts have since been renegotiated, the 1999 compact between Rincon and the State remains operative.

While negotiations over the 1999 compacts were pending, the California Supreme Court handed down its decision in Hotel Employees & Restaurant Employees International Union v. Davis, 21 Cal. 4th 585, 88 Cal. Rptr.2d 56, 981 P.2d 990 (1999). In that case, the California Supreme Court determined that the California constitution prohibited everyone in the state, including Indian tribes, from operating Las Vegas-style casinos. As a major consideration, and in order to make the proposed 1999 compacts legally enforceable, the State sponsored a constitutional amendment—Proposition 1A—that would authorize tribal gaming in California.

In March 2000, California voters approved Proposition 1A, thereby vivifying the 1999 compacts. Not only did Proposition 1A permit tribes to conduct class III gaming lawfully, it effectively gave tribes a state constitutional monopoly over casino gaming in California. In re Indian Gaming Related Cases (*Coyote Valley II*, 331 F.3d 1094, 1103 (9th Cir. 2003)).

Revenue Sharing Under the 1999 Compacts

In consideration for the State's efforts in securing the passage of Proposition 1A (without which the tribes would have been barred from conducting class III gaming in the State of California), the tribes agreed to share a portion of their expected revenues.... The State originally took the position that the revenue should be for general use, but abandoned that position during the negotiations in favor of tribal proposals.... The tribes agreed to pay a portion of their revenues into two funds: the Revenue Sharing Trust Fund (RSTF) and the Special Distribution Fund (SDF).... Monies paid into the RSTF are redistributed to tribes who choose not to, or are unable to, conduct their own gaming activities.... Monies paid into the SDF, on the other hand, are used to fund:

> (a) grants for programs designed to address gambling addiction; (b) grants for the support of state and local government agencies impacted by tribal gaming; (c) compensation for regulatory costs incurred by the State Gaming Agency and the state Department of Justice in connection with the implementation and ad-

ministration of the compact; (d) payment of shortfalls that may occur in the RSTF; and (e) "any other purposes specified by the legislature."[5]

In *Coyote Valley II*, appellants questioned whether the RSTF and SDF provisions of the 1999 compacts were lawful since IGRA, 25 U.S.C. § 2710(d)(4), precludes states from imposing taxes on Indian gaming. 331 F.3d 1094. We held that the RSTF and SDF were permissible notwithstanding § 2710(d)(4) because, as more fully explained infra, the nature of the revenue sharing and the constitutional exclusivity obtained in consideration for it were primarily motivated by a desire to promote tribal interests. 351 F.3d at 1110–15. We further concluded that by virtue of the 1999 compacts and Proposition 1A, the State gave all tribes in California significant opportunities to benefit from gaming without taking anything significant for itself, beyond what was required to protect its citizens from the adverse consequences of gaming, and to fulfill other regulatory and police functions contemplated by IGRA. *Id.*

The 2003–2006 Compact Renegotiations

Operating under its 1999 compact, Rincon began to generate significant revenue that enabled it to improve tribal governmental functions and become economically self-sufficient. By 2003, Rincon desired to expand its operations beyond what the 1999 compact permitted. Accordingly, in March of that year, Rincon notified the State of its interest in renegotiating certain provisions of the 1999 compact.

Negotiations began in 2003 in response to Rincon's request, but in October of that year, California voters recalled Governor Davis and elected Governor Schwarzenegger in his stead. Although negotiations eventually reconvened, they quickly assumed a decidedly different tone. Instead of requesting funds to help defray the costs of gaming, or to benefit Indian tribes, the State demanded that Rincon pay a significant portion of its gaming revenues into the State's general fund.

The State made its first offer to Rincon on November 10, 2005. The State offered Rincon the opportunity to operate 900 additional devices plus the 1600 devices Rincon already operated, but only if Rincon would agree to pay the State 15% of the net win on the new devices, along with an additional 15% annual fee based on Rincon's total 2004 net revenue. In exchange for the 15% revenue share demanded, the State offered Rincon an "exclusivity provision."

Rincon countered that, in order to obtain additional devices, it would agree to some per device fees. Rincon emphasized, however, that the use of any fees it paid had to be limited to paying for the costs of regulating gaming, building infrastructure needed to support gaming operations, and mitigating adverse impacts caused by gaming operations. Rincon further stated that "with all due respect, we are not asking for exclusivity and the State's analysis does not hold water as it relates to Rincon in its current circumstance."

Rincon also noted that Proposition 1A already provided for tribal gaming exclusivity, so it was not seeking whatever further exclusivity might provide. Rincon's lands are located in the middle of a saturated tribal gaming market. Accordingly, no form of tribal exclusivity could shelter Rincon from substantial competition. As long as the proposed exclusivity provision related only to freedom from non-tribal competition, "exclusivity"

---

5. In this opinion, we focus only on subsections (a), (b) and (e) of the SDF. Subsection (c) is expressly authorized by § 2710(d) (3) (C) (iii), and the State does not rely upon it in its quest because it seeks to deposit funds into its general fund, not one with earmarked uses. Subsection (d) is effectively part of the RSTF so it need not be analyzed separately. We have previously construed subsection (e) to cover only those purposes directly related to gaming. *Coyote Valley II*, 331 F.3d at 1113–14.

would not provide Rincon with any meaningful economic advantages that would warrant the tribe making the requested payments.

The State interpreted Rincon's counterproposal for limited-use, per device fees and its rejection of exclusivity to be a request that the State agree to allow Rincon to operate additional devices beyond the 1999 compact limits "without offering the State anything meaningful in return." The State held firm in its demand that a portion of tribal gaming revenues be paid into the State's general fund, rather than into an earmarked fund.

Rincon re-countered with an offer substantially mirroring its previous offer, but offering slightly increased per device fees. Rincon also presented several expert reports on the financial impact the State's offer would have on Rincon. By Rincon's calculations,

> "the State's offer ... would require Rincon to pay an additional $23 million in fees for the machines currently in play at Rincon's gaming operation pursuant to the 1999 Compact.... By imposing the 15% fee on the Tribe's net win as of Fiscal year 2004, the Tribe would be required to pay 15 to 20 times what it is paying now without adding a single machine onto the gaming floor! The State's proposal is a poorly disguised tax, which is impermissible under IGRA."

The State made its next counteroffer on October 23, 2006. That offer included substantially the same terms as its November 10, 2005 offer, but offered that the compact term would be extended for five years, and that Rincon would pay an annual fee equal to 10% (instead of 15%) of its net win based on fiscal year 2005 (instead of 2004). The State noted that the terms it was offering Rincon were similar to those already accepted by a handful of other tribes and approved by the Department of the Interior. At Rincon's request, on October 31, 2006, the State made an alternative offer to allow Rincon to operate 400 additional devices with no other changes to the existing compact. In exchange for the 400 additional devices, Rincon would have to pay $2 million annually to the RSTF, plus 25% of Rincon's net win on those additional 400 devices to the State's general fund.

The State accompanied this last counteroffer with its own expert analysis comparing the value to Rincon of continuing to operate its current 1600 devices under the 1999 compact to the value to Rincon of accepting the State's counteroffer of 2500 devices with a 10% annual fee. The State's expert concluded that if Rincon accepted the State's offer, it would pay California $38 million and retain $61 million in net revenue. If Rincon maintained its operations under the 1999 compact, it would pay the State nothing and retain $59 million in net revenue. Hence, according to the State's expert, Rincon stood to gain $2 million in additional revenues if it accepted the amendment. In contrast, the State stood to gain $38 million. Rincon rejected the State's counteroffer, and the record of negotiations then closed.

Having reached an impasse, the parties filed cross-motions for summary judgment in the district court. The district court granted summary judgment in favor of Rincon, and this timely appeal followed.

JURISDICTION AND STANDARD OF REVIEW

IGRA grants district courts original federal jurisdiction over tribal claims that a state has failed to negotiate in good faith concerning class III gaming rights. 25 U.S.C. §2710(d)(7)(A)(i). California has waived its Eleventh Amendment immunity from such suits.[8] ...

---

8. Many states have not waived their Eleventh Amendment immunity under IGRA as California has. The dissent's reliance on the prevalence of compacts containing revenue sharing provisions is therefore suspect because that reliance ignores the fact that many of the states involved in those compacts would not permit tribes to challenge state demands as made in bad faith. *See, e.g.,* Seminole Tribe of Florida v. Florida, 517 U.S. 44 (1996) (holding that IGRA did not abrogate state Eleventh

DISCUSSION

From the advent of colonists in North America, the new arrivals promptly began encroaching on Indian lands, and frequently treating Indians unfairly....

Mindful of this ignominious legacy, Congress enacted IGRA to provide a legal framework within which tribes could engage in gaming—an enterprise that holds out the hope of providing tribes with the economic prosperity that has so long eluded their grasp—while setting boundaries to restrain aggression by powerful states.... In passing IGRA, Congress assured tribes that the statute would always be construed in their best interests....

Under IGRA, a tribe may conduct class III gaming only once a compact with its home state is in effect. Because the compact requirement skews the balance of power over gaming rights in favor of states by making tribes dependent on state cooperation, IGRA imposes on states the concomitant obligation to participate in the negotiations in good faith.... If a court finds that a state has failed to negotiate in good faith, IGRA empowers the court to order additional negotiations and, if necessary, to order the parties into mediation in which a compact will be imposed....

In evaluating a State's good faith, the district court:

(I) may take into account the public interest, public safety, criminality, financial integrity, and adverse economic impacts on existing gaming activities, and

(II) shall consider any demand by the State for direct taxation of the Indian tribe or of any Indian lands as evidence that the State has not negotiated in good faith.

§ 2710(d) (7) (B) (iii) (emphasis added)....

In addition to specifying criteria for evaluating a state's good faith, IGRA outlines permissible tribe-state negotiation topics.

(C) Any Tribal-State compact ... may include provisions relating to—

(i) the application of the criminal and civil laws and regulations of the Indian tribe or the State that are directly related to, and necessary for, the licensing and regulation of such activity;

(ii) the allocation of criminal and civil jurisdiction between the State and the Indian tribe necessary for the enforcement of such laws and regulations;

Amendment immunity, so Florida state actors could not be sued by tribe to force good faith negotiations); Mescalero Apache Tribe v. New Mexico, 131 F.3d 1379, 1384–85 (10th Cir. 1997) (holding that New Mexico has not waived its Eleventh Amendment immunity to IGRA suits); Ponca Tribe of Okla. v. Oklahoma, 89 F.3d 690 (10th Cir. 1996) (same for Oklahoma); Santee Sioux Tribe of Neb. v. Nebraska, 121 F.3d 427, 431 (8th Cir. 1997) (same for Nebraska); Sault Ste. Marie Tribe of Chippewa Indians v. Michigan, 800 F. Supp. 1484 (W.D. Mich. 1992) (same for Michigan). Tribes in states that have not waived their Eleventh Amendment immunity for IGRA suits have no recourse to challenge the validity of revenue sharing, and some therefore choose to accept revenue sharing rather than go without a compact. See Pueblo of Sandia v. Babbitt, 47 F. Supp. 2d 49, 51, 56–57 & n. 7 (D.D.C.1999) (explaining that the Department of the Interior believed the revenue sharing provision was illegal, but also believed that it had no choice but to allow the compact to go into effect because the tribe would have no recourse against the state to obtain a legal compact). Moreover, this reality—for better or worse—will prevent the proliferation of lawsuits feared by our dissenting colleague. The dissent suggests that 25 C.F.R. §§ 291.1 et seq. is a potential vehicle for tribes to challenge state demands, ..., but the only circuit court to consider the question has held the regulations invalid. Texas v. United States, 497 F.3d 491 (5th Cir. 2007), cert. denied sub nom. Kickapoo Traditional Tribe of Tex. v. Texas, ___ U.S. ___, 129 S. Ct. 32, 172 L. Ed.2d 18 (2008). The validity of the regulations is not before us, and we therefore do not find it appropriate to rely on them, or express any opinion as to their validity.

(iii) the assessment by the State of such activities in such amounts as are necessary to defray the costs of regulating such activity;

(iv) taxation by the Indian tribe of such activity in amounts comparable to amounts assessed by the State for comparable activities;

(v) remedies for breach of contract;

(vi) standards for the operation of such activity and maintenance of the gaming facility, including licensing; and

(vii) any other subjects that are directly related to the operation of gaming activities.

§ 2710(d) (3) (C). However, the list of permissible negotiation topics is circumscribed by one key limitation on state negotiating authority:

Except for any assessments that may be agreed to under [§ 2710(d) (3) (C) (iii)], nothing in this section shall be interpreted as conferring upon a State ... authority to impose any tax, fee, charge, or other assessment upon an Indian tribe.... No State may refuse to enter into the negotiations ... based upon the lack of authority in such State ... to impose such a tax, fee, charge, or other assessment.

25 U.S.C. § 2710(d)(4). IGRA limits permissible subjects of negotiation in order to ensure that tribal-state compacts cover only those topics that are related to gaming and are consistent with IGRA's stated purposes, *see Coyote Valley II*, 331 F.3d at 1111, which are:

(1) to provide a statutory basis for the operation of gaming by Indian tribes as a means of promoting tribal economic development, self-sufficiency, and strong tribal governments;

(2) to provide a statutory basis for the regulation of gaming by an Indian tribe adequate to shield it from organized crime and other corrupting influences, to ensure that the Indian tribe is the primary beneficiary of the gaming operation, and to assure that gaming is conducted fairly and honestly by both the operator and players; and

(3) to declare that the establishment of independent Federal regulatory authority for gaming on Indian lands, the establishment of Federal standards for gaming on Indian lands, and the establishment of a National Indian Gaming Commission are necessary to meet congressional concerns regarding gaming and to protect such gaming as a means of generating tribal revenue.

§ 2702 (emphasis added).

Here, the State repeatedly demanded that Rincon agree to pay into the State's general fund 10–15% of Rincon's annual net win, and up to 25% of Rincon's revenue from any new devices Rincon would operate under an amended compact. Once Rincon proffered evidence suggesting that the State had acted in bad faith by attempting to impose taxation, "the burden of proof [shifted to] the State to prove that the State has negotiated with the Indian tribe in good faith to conclude a Tribal-State compact governing the conduct of gaming activities." § 2710(d)(7)(B)(ii). We conclude that the State failed to meet its burden.

I. Taxation Demands "Shall" Be Considered Evidence of Bad Faith

Under § 2710(d)(7)(B)(iii)(II), a court must consider a "demand" for a tax to be made in bad faith. A tax is "a charge, usu[ally] monetary, imposed by the government on persons, entities, transactions, or property to yield public revenue." Black's Law Dictionary 1594 (9th ed. 2009) (emphasis added). The State insisted that Rincon pay at least 10% of its net profits into the State's general fund. According to California Government Code

§ 16300, "[t]he General Fund consists of money received into the treasury and not required by law to be credited to any other fund." No amount of semantic sophistry can undermine the obvious: a non-negotiable, mandatory payment of 10% of net profits into the State treasury for unrestricted use yields public revenue, and is a "tax." Moreover, unlike what occurred in the 1999 negotiations, none of the State's communications during the renegotiations that occurred after the change in administration in 2003 reflected a willingness to take its general fund revenue sharing demand off the table. The State repeatedly emphasized its position that it would not give Rincon more devices or time without a reciprocal benefit to the State, and the record reveals that no other "benefit" was demanded besides monetary payments into the general fund.... Under the plain language of § 2710(d)(7)(B)(ii)(II), the State's demand for the payment of a tax is evidence of the State's bad faith.

Our dissenting colleague faults us for our characterization of the 10–15% revenue share as a "tax," primarily because he contends we fail to appreciate the import of the word "imposed" in the definition of a "tax.".... He argues that IGRA merely creates a context for "voluntary" negotiations, and that no matter how "hard line" the State's position is, it still has not attempted to exercise authority to "impose" a tax.

The flaw in this argument—related to a faulty assumption made throughout the dissent—is that it ignores the plain fact that neither tribes nor states enter IGRA negotiations "voluntarily" in the way parties do in all the examples cited by the dissent. IGRA negotiations are therefore distinguishable from regular contract negotiations. When private parties, or independent sovereign entities, commence contract negotiations, they generally do so because each has something of value the other wants, and each side has the right to accept or reject an offer made, based on the desirability of the terms. If negotiations fail, neither party has a right to complain. Not so in IGRA negotiations. In IGRA, Congress took from the tribes collectively whatever sovereign rights they might have had to engage in unregulated gaming activities, but imposed on the states the obligation to work with tribes to reach an agreement under the terms of IGRA permitting the tribes to engage in lawful class III gaming activities. If IGRA negotiations break down between a state and a tribe because the state does not come to the bargaining table in good faith, IGRA specifically provides that courts, and the Secretary of the Interior, can intervene to impose a gaming arrangement without the affected state's approval. See § 2710(d)(7)(B)(iii-vii). Thus, while IGRA was designed to give states a voice in Indian gaming, it was not designed to give states complete power over tribal gaming such that each state can put the opportunity to operate casinos up for sale to the tribe willing to pay the highest price....

The dissent acknowledges that in this case "California has insisted that the Band share its gaming revenues as a condition to receiving authorization for additional gaming devices," but then concludes that this is simply "hard-line" negotiating for revenue sharing, not imposing a tax.... If there is a distinction between insisting on obtaining a share of Rincon's income as a non-negotiable condition of granting it a compact, and demanding a tax or "refus[ing] to enter into the negotiations ... based upon the lack of authority ... to impose such a tax, fee, charge, or other assessment," § 2170(d)(4), it is a distinction without a difference. In either case, the state is using its power over negotiations to force Rincon to pay the State a portion of its income into the State's general fund (and not for any use for the benefit of Rincon or other tribes) in order to engage in class III gaming. If § 2710(d)(4) means anything, it means that California cannot do that—whatever one calls it.

In *Coyote Valley II*, we explained that IGRA requires courts to consider a state's demand for taxation as evidence of bad faith, not conclusive proof.... However, "[d]epending on the nature of both the fees demanded and the concessions offered in return, such demands might, of course, amount to an attempt to impose a fee, and therefore amount to bad faith on the part of a State."…. For the reasons described in greater detail infra, when the "nature of the fees" is general fund revenue sharing—a bald demand for payment of a tax—the State faces a very difficult task to rebut the evidence of bad faith necessarily arising from that demand. *See* § 2710(d)(3)(B)(iii)(II.)

Under IGRA, the State may attempt to rebut bad faith by demonstrating that the revenue demanded was to be used for "the public interest, public safety, criminality, financial integrity, and adverse economic impacts on existing gaming activities." § 2710(d)(3)(B)(ii)…. The State's need for general tax revenues is not in the list. Even if "the public interest" or "financial integrity" could conceivably be construed to implicate the State's need for general funds, IGRA's purposes do not permit such a construction. Instead, those terms clearly apply to protecting the State against the adverse consequences of gaming activities…. Moreover, construing those terms broadly in favor of the State's interests would be inconsistent with our obligation to construe IGRA most favorably towards tribal interests….

Critically, the State does not even seek to justify its general fund revenue sharing demands directly under any of the factors in § 2710(d)(7)(B)(ii)(I). Rather, the State relies on its interpretation of our decision in *Coyote Valley II*. The State's reliance is misplaced. *Coyote Valley II* is an exceptional case whose facts are readily distinguishable from those in this case.

II. Coyote Valley II

Coyote Valley II considered objections to, among other things, the RSTF and SDF provisions of the 1999 compacts. We held those funds to be authorized subjects of negotiation under 25 U.S.C. § 2710(d)(3)(C)(vii) (subjects "directly related to the operation of gaming"). The SDF was clearly "directly related" to gaming because all uses of SDF funds were earmarked for gaming-related purposes…. The RSTF funds similarly were related to gaming because, by redistributing gaming funds from gaming to non-gaming tribes, they are entirely consistent with the IGRA goal of using gaming to foster tribal economic development…. Notably, we expressly declined to decide if the RSTF or SDF were "taxes," because they were decidedly not "imposed" in bad faith. Rather, the tribes themselves suggested them, and were willing to pay into them in exchange for the "meaningful concession" of constitutional exclusivity.

Coyote Valley II thus stands for the proposition that a state may, without acting in bad faith, request revenue sharing if the revenue sharing provision is (a) for uses "directly related to the operation of gaming activities" in § 2710(d)(3)(C)(vii), (b) consistent with the purposes of IGRA, and (c) not "imposed" because it is bargained for in exchange for a "meaningful concession." The State's offers in this case fail on all three prongs of that proposition.

A. "Directly Related to the Operation of Gaming Activities"

The State asserts that, like the RSTF and SDF, its revenue sharing demands were authorized under § 2710(d)(3)(C)(vii) because they involve a subject directly related to gaming. The State misunderstands….

Whether revenue sharing is an authorized negotiation topic under § 2710(d)(3)(C)(vii) … depends on the use to which the revenue will be put, not on the mere fact that the revenue derives from gaming activities. General fund revenue sharing, unlike funds paid into the RSTF and SDF, has undefined potential uses…. Therefore, payments into the general fund cannot be said to be directly related to gaming. Indeed, in *Coyote Valley II* we expressly recognized the distinction between general fund revenue sharing and the RSTF and SDF.... Consequently, we hold that general fund revenue sharing is not "directly related to the operation of gaming activities" and is thus not an authorized subject of negotiation under §2710(d)(3)(C)(vii)....

B. Consistent with the Purposes of IGRA

According to §2702, IGRA is intended to promote tribal development, prevent criminal activity related to gaming, and ensure that gaming activities are conducted fairly. In *Coyote Valley II* we construed the meaning of subjects "directly related to the operation of gaming" in §2710(d)(3)(C)(vii) broadly to include revenue sharing because the RSTF is consistent with the plain language of §2702 (listing tribal economic self-sufficiency as one of IGRA's purposes). *See Coyote Valley II*, 331 F.3d at 1111. By contrast, we cannot read §2710(d)(3)(C)(vii) broadly here to include general fund revenue sharing because none of the purposes outlined in §2702 includes the State's general economic interests. The only *state* interests mentioned in §2702 are protecting against organized crime and ensuring that gaming is conducted fairly and honestly. §2702(2)....

The State ... directs us to a ... statement from *Coyote Valley II* that "Congress ... did not intend to require that States ignore their economic interests when engaged in compact negotiations." ... The State's reliance on this statement is ... misplaced. When we said that Congress did not intend for states to ignore their economic interests, we were not deciding whether states were allowed to pursue their own economic objectives affirmatively through compact negotiations. Rather, we decided only whether the State could require the tribes to pay into the SDF to cover the government's costs of dealing with the fallout of gaming. It is one thing to ask the tribes to contribute funds so the State is not left bearing the costs for gaming-related expenses; it is quite another to ask the tribes to help fix the State's budget crisis. The State is therefore incorrect that pursuit of state general economic interests is consistent with IGRA's purposes.

As already explained, IGRA's stated purposes include ensuring that tribes are the primary beneficiaries of gaming and ensuring that gaming is protected as a means of generating tribal revenue. §2702. We therefore find particularly persuasive the fact that the revenue sharing demanded in this case would result in $38 million in additional net revenue to the State compared to $2 million for the tribe. In such case, it is the State, not the tribe, that would be the "primary beneficiary" of the gaming rights under negotiation....

C. "Meaningful Concessions"

Because we hold above that general fund revenue sharing is neither authorized by IGRA nor reconcilable with its purposes, it is difficult to imagine what concessions the State could offer to rebut the strong suggestion of bad faith arising from such demands. But even if it were possible to conjure up an exceptional circumstance where such would be the case, where, as here, the State demands significant taxes and fails to offer any "meaningful concessions" in return, a finding of bad faith is the only reasonable conclusion.

The relevance of "meaningful concessions" arises from §2710(d)(4). We have interpreted §2710(d)(4) as precluding state authority to impose taxes, fees, or assessments, but not prohibiting states from negotiating for such payments where "meaningful concessions" are offered in return....

In 1999, the California constitution prohibited casino-style gaming, and the State was therefore under no obligation to allow tribes to conduct it, or even negotiate concerning it.... The State nonetheless negotiated the 1999 compacts with dozens of tribes, and to make the 1999 compacts fully operable, the State promoted a constitutional amendment exempting tribes, and tribes alone, from the constitutional prohibition....

The value of a monopoly is obvious, and the value of a monopoly that cannot be altered except by the extraordinary act of further constitutional amendment is even greater. Such a benefit was well beyond anything IGRA required the State to offer.... Specifically, IGRA provides that tribes can engage in class III gaming to the same extent as others in the state. § 2710(d)(1). Thus, IGRA only requires that states treat tribes equally. However, with the strong encouragement of the then governor, California voters gave the tribes an economic opportunity denied to everyone else. The State's agreement (with the consent of the voters) to confer such a substantial benefit on the tribes proved that its request that more successful tribes financially assist the less fortunate ones (and that the tribes agree to cover the costs of adverse impacts) was freely negotiated. Indeed, in a rare example of generosity to tribes, the State conferred a valuable economic right on the tribes in exchange for a program under which all of the significant benefits of the compact were to be enjoyed by the tribes themselves.

In short, we approved exclusivity as a "meaningful concession" in *Coyote Valley II* because it was exceptionally valuable and bargained for. By contrast, in the current legal landscape, "exclusivity" is not a new consideration the State can offer in negotiations because the tribe already fully enjoys that right as a matter of state constitutional law. Moreover, the benefits conferred by Proposition 1A have already been used as consideration for the establishment of the RSTF and SDF in the 1999 compact.... The State asserts that it would be unfair to permit Rincon to keep the benefit of exclusivity conferred by Proposition 1A without holding the tribe to an ongoing obligation to periodically acquiesce in some new revenue sharing demand. While we do not hold that no future revenue sharing is permissible, it is clear that the State cannot use exclusivity as new consideration for new types of revenue sharing since it and the collective tribes already struck a bargain in 1999, wherein the tribes were exempted from the prohibition on gaming in exchange for their contributions to the RSTF and SDF....

The State offers various alternative arguments to support its claim that it offered more than illusory consideration. We find all of the State's arguments unpersuasive.

1. Revised and Expanded Exclusivity

The State first claims that it offered Rincon revised and expanded exclusivity, which had even greater economic value than the exclusivity originally granted by Proposition 1A....

[But] Rincon did not request or desire a revised local tribal gaming exclusivity provision because such a provision—which would not apply to other tribes—would not protect Rincon against the high degree of tribal competition it experiences in its core geographic market. Freedom from nontribal competition in its core geographic market therefore provides Rincon with no significant additional economic advantages over whatever value Rincon receives from the statewide exclusivity it already enjoys.

More importantly, even if there were some enhanced value in the proposed revised and expanded exclusivity provision, the calculations presented by the State's own expert reveal that the financial benefit to Rincon from the amendments proposed would be negligible: Rincon stood to gain only about $2 million in additional revenues compared to the State's expected $38 million....

Our conclusion is buttressed by the fact that the State never wavered from its general fund revenue sharing demands. We do not mean to suggest that the State is guilty of bad faith whenever it takes a "hard line" negotiating position.... As already suggested supra, a "hard line" stance is not inappropriate so long as the conditions insisted upon are related to legitimate state interests regarding gaming and the purposes of IGRA. *See* § 2710(d)(3)(B)(iii)(I). We hold only that a state may not take a "hard line" position in IGRA negotiations when it results in a "take it or leave it offer" to the tribe to either accept nonbeneficial provisions outside the permissible scope of §§ 2710(d)(3)(C) and 2710(d)(4), or go without a compact....

2. More Devices and Time

The State's next argument is that, at the very least, it is entitled to some new consideration in exchange for giving Rincon expanded gaming rights, and the increased revenue share it requested was the only possible new consideration it could seek.

The State is correct that general contract principles dictate that new or additional consideration for a compact amendment is required. However, as already explained, IGRA does not permit the State and the tribe to negotiate over any subjects they desire; rather, IGRA anticipates a very specific exchange of rights and obligations, defined in §§ 2710(d)(3)(C) and (d)(4)....

As held above, general fund revenue sharing is not a state public policy interest directly related to gaming and is not an authorized negotiation topic under § 2710(d)(3)(C). Therefore, gaming rights that tribes are entitled to negotiate for under IGRA, like device licensing and time, ... cannot serve as consideration for general fund revenue sharing; the consideration must be for something "separate" than basic gaming rights.... In order to obtain additional time and gaming devices, Rincon may have to submit, for instance, to greater State regulation of its facilities or greater payments to defray the costs the State will incur in regulating a larger facility. *See* 25 U.S.C. § 2710(d)(3)(C)(i, iii). Rincon need not, however, submit to demands that it assist the State in addressing its budget crisis....

To hold otherwise would effectively mean that states could put gaming rights "up for sale." That would be inconsistent with IGRA's spirit, and its express refusal to allow states to use their right to engage in compact negotiations as a means to extract fees. § 2710(d)(4).

3. "Exclusive Gaming Rights"

Next, the State argues that the value of its offers during compact negotiations should be analyzed as a whole, not piecemeal. Specifically, the State contends that we should evaluate its offer not simply by considering the value of the exclusivity provision itself, but rather the value of the entire bundle of "exclusive gaming rights" that Rincon would obtain under an amended compact. Viewing its offer in this way, the State contends it negotiated in good faith.

If there is a meaningful distinction between "exclusivity" and "gaming rights" as stand alone terms and "exclusive gaming rights," it is too minuscule to see. Because exclusivity exists independent of the current compact negotiations, the negotiations concern only the extent of gaming rights, which are, by nature as a result of California constitutional law, exclusive. Were we to accept the State's view that whenever it negotiates with a tribe, it offers "meaningful concessions" because the gaming rights offered will, as a matter of law, be exclusive, we would effectively be holding that, as a matter of law, the State is entitled to insist on significant general fund revenue sharing whenever a tribe wants to renegotiate basic terms. We reject the State's view....

Further, we disagree that the State makes "meaningful concessions" whenever it offers a bundle of rights more valuable than the status quo. As previously explained,

IGRA endows states with limited negotiating authority over specific items. Accepting the State's "holistic" view of negotiations would permit states to lump together proposals for taxation, land use restrictions, and other subjects along with IGRA class III gaming rights. Such a construction of IGRA would violate the purposes and spirit of that law.

III. Other Evidence of Good Faith

The State raises one final argument in support of its position. Specifically, the State contends that it genuinely believed its revenue sharing demands were authorized by *Coyote Valley II*, approved by the Department of the Interior, and fair because other tribes had accepted them. The State therefore urges us to find that its demands, even though herein held improper under IGRA, were nonetheless made in good faith.

IGRA does not provide express guidance about whether good faith is to be evaluated objectively or subjectively. However, we are influenced by the factors outlined in § 2710(d)(7)(B)(iii), which lend themselves to objective analysis and make no mention of unreasonable beliefs. Further, the structure and content of § 2710(d) make clear that the function of the good faith requirement and judicial remedy is to permit the tribe to process gaming arrangements on an expedited basis, not to embroil the parties in litigation over their subjective motivations. We therefore hold that good faith should be evaluated objectively based on the record of negotiations, and that a state's subjective belief in the legality of its requests is not sufficient to rebut the inference of bad faith created by objectively improper demands....

Here, the State's belief that IGRA permitted the revenue sharing it sought was objectively unreasonable. IGRA expressly condemns state attempts to compel fees for purposes other than those specified in § 2710(d)(3)(C)(iii). The State does not even attempt to fit its general fund revenue sharing demand within § 2710(d)(3)(C)(iii).... As explained supra, the rationale for permitting revenue sharing under 2710(d)(3)(C)(vii) in *Coyote Valley II* is not present in this case, and the State was unreasonable to rely on *Coyote Valley II* for propositions not decided, or expressly reserved.... Further, the Department of the Interior has frequently noted its concerns about the legitimacy of general fund revenue sharing.... The Department of the Interior has approved compacts with general fund revenue sharing provisions agreed to by other California tribes, but has done so reluctantly, and only after the tribes themselves confirmed the desirability of the amendments.... The State therefore could not reasonably have relied on the Department of the Interior's approval of certain other compacts as proof that its demands to Rincon were lawful. This is especially true since IGRA anticipates that, even if some tribes agree to a waiver of their rights not to be taxed by a state, such a waiver cannot be a basis for the State expecting the same from Rincon....

The State's demand for 10–15% of Rincon's net win, to be paid into the State's general fund, is simply an impermissible demand for the payment of a tax by the tribe.... None of the State's arguments suffices to rebut the inference of bad faith such an improper demand creates.

In so holding, we are mindful that many states, and especially California, are currently writhing in the financial maw created by the clash of certain mandatory state expenditures at a time when state revenues have plummeted from historic levels. However, we are also keenly aware of our nation's too-frequent breach of its trust obligations to Native Americans when some of its politically and economically powerful citizens and states have lusted after what little the Native Americans have possessed. In developing IGRA, Congress anticipated that states might abuse their authority over compact negotiations to force tribes to accept burdens on their sovereignty in order to obtain gaming opportunities.... That is why the good faith requirement exists, and why IGRA condemns state taxation demands.

CONCLUSION

We AFFIRM the district court's finding that the State of California negotiated with Rincon in bad faith by conditioning its agreement to expand Rincon's class III gaming rights on Rincon's agreement to pay a percentage of its revenues to the State's general fund. The district court's order compelling the parties to reach a compact or submit their best offers to a mediator pursuant to § 2710(d)(7) is effective forthwith.

AFFIRMED.

Notes

1. Compact terms negotiated by tribes and states can vary widely. As the court in *Rincon* notes, IGRA provides for several items that are permissible topics of negotiation. This includes measures relating to the state and tribal laws applicable to gaming activities, standards for the operation of the tribal casino, and other matters that "are directly related to the operation of gaming activities." § 2710(d)(3)(C)(vii). In addition, IGRA provides that states can recover the costs they incur in regulating the tribal gaming. Costs for such things as improved roads leading to the tribal casino or enhanced sewer facilities that are necessary because of the greater number of people visiting tribal lands may be the subject of negotiation. Even local governments may be affected by the tribal casino and a compact might provide for payment of the costs of those operations. Typically, none of these issues present problems under IGRA and are left to the negotiation process.

2. *Rincon*, however, deals with costs that exceed assessments for costs the state incurs in regulating tribal gaming. Apart from these expenses, IGRA denies to a state the "authority to impose any tax, fee, charge, or other assessment upon an Indian tribe," or the authority to refuse to negotiate with a tribe because of the absence of such taxes or fees. § 2710(d)(4). In other words, states cannot force a tribe to give the state a portion of the gaming revenue the tribe collects. Because the Secretary of the Interior has to approve a compact before it becomes effective, a proposed compact that included such taxes would be fatally flawed and subject to disapproval.

3. Despite the clear language of IGRA, many tribal/state compacts have included "revenue sharing provisions," where the tribe pays the state a percentage of its gaming revenue. Such agreements are commonplace, found in compacts for tribal casinos located in states like Connecticut, California, Wisconsin, New York, Arizona, New Mexico, as well as others. If a tribe can point to the clear language of IGRA that seems to proscribe such an arrangement, why would a tribe ever agree to this "revenue sharing?" Part of the answer goes back to the *Seminole Tribe* decision. Recall that even if a state refuses to bargain in good faith, such as by insisting on revenue sharing, it may invoke its immunity under the Eleventh Amendment when the tribe sues in federal court. If the compact deal was "sweetened" by the tribe offering to share a portion of its gaming revenue with the state, that might be enough for the state to agree to waive its immunity. As in *Rincon*, a number of states have waived their immunity and have subjected themselves to IGRA's provisions. In footnote 8, the court states, "Tribes in states that have not waived their Eleventh Amendment immunity for IGRA suits have no recourse to challenge the validity of revenue sharing, and some therefore choose to accept revenue sharing rather than go with-

out a compact." Is the state's insistence on revenue sharing a form of political coercion the states are exercising against the tribes?

4. Note 3 ought to cause a student to ask, "I thought IGRA expressly forbade this very type of revenue sharing or refusal to negotiate because of the absence of revenue sharing? How can it be this practice is so widespread?" Part of the answer lies in the interpretation of IGRA given by the Secretary of the Interior, and is a significant part of the *Rincon* decision. If the state offers the tribe a "valuable economic benefit," the Secretary will not find a revenue sharing agreement to be necessarily in contravention of IGRA. *See Oversight Hearing on Indian Gaming Regulatory Act; Role and Funding of the National Indian Gaming Commission, Part 2, Before the S. Comm. On Indian Affairs*, 108th Cong. 2 (2003) (Statement of Aurene M. Martin, acting assistant secretary, Indian Affairs, Department of the Interior). In *Rincon*, the "valuable economic benefit" the state alleged it offered was "exclusivity" in the gaming marketplace. Although the court rejected this, "exclusivity" is an important economic benefit that can justify a revenue sharing provision. For example, a state may agree to prohibit or severely limit the commercial (non-tribal) gaming within the state or within a particular region of the state. Should this be sufficient to allow for the evasion of the clear prohibition in IGRA of such agreements? Does the fact that the tribe agrees to this ameliorate the problem, or should that be irrelevant? Other than exclusivity, what other "valuable economic benefits" could a state offer a tribe? Does the Secretary of the Interior's position on this issue simply reflect the post-*Seminole Tribe* reality that the state can refuse to negotiate a compact unless there is the revenue sharing incentive available? Is the effect of *Seminole Tribe* to create more opportunities for compact negotiation leading to beneficial and cooperative results for both the state and the tribe? Or is it, as suggested above, another way that tribes are treated unfairly. For a discussion of these issues, *see* Ezekiel J.N. Fletcher, *Negotiating Meaningful Concessions from States in Gaming Compacts to Further Tribal Economic Development: Satisfying the "Economic Benefits" Test*, 54 S.D. L. Rev. 419 (2009) (arguing that tribes should negotiate "non-traditional" subjects in compacts such as those relating to taxation or acquisition of tribal lands to satisfy the "substantial economic benefits" requirement); Katie Eidson, Note, *Will States Continue to Provide Exclusivity in Tribal Gaming Compacts or Will Tribes Bust on the Hand of the State in Order to Expand Indian Gaming*, 29 Am. Indian L. Rev. 319 (2004) (examining the trend towards substantial exclusivity as a bargaining chip in compact negotiations in various states); Eric S. Lent, Note, *Are States Beating the House?: The Validity of Tribal-State Revenue Sharing Under the Indian Gaming Regulatory Act*, 91 Geo. L.J. 451 (2003) (arguing that revenue-sharing agreements violate IGRA and suggesting remedies that would protect Indian gaming rights).

5. *Rincon* gives some of the background to the ongoing California experience with tribal/state compacts. As the court noted, the RSTF and SDF funds that were created as part of the 1999 compacts were held to be permissible in the "Coyote Valley II" case. In re Indian Gaming Related Cases, 331 F.3d 1094, 1103 (9th Cir. 2003). Look at the description of the purpose of these funds in the *Rincon* case. Is the fact the money does not go into the state's general fund that significant? Do these funds seem to be nothing more than thinly veiled revenue sharing plans?

When Arnold Schwarzenegger was elected to succeed the recalled Governor Gray Davis in 2004, he continued the effort begun by Davis to renegotiate the compacts that were the result of the passage of Proposition 1A amending the California Constitution to allow for tribal gaming. Schwarzenegger campaigned with a pledge to have the tribes pay their "fair share" of gaming revenue to the state; he referred to the tribes in California as "special interests." New compacts were negotiated with many tribes which increased payments to the state in exchange for the state allowing the tribes to offer more slot machines on their property. The Rincon tribe objected to this, claiming the state was simply trying to impose a tax in violation of IGRA. This led to the Ninth Circuit decision set out above. If, as the Ninth Circuit ruled, the state had no legal basis for making the tribes pay this money, would the tribes who had acceded to the government's compact demands have a basis for recovering the "illegal" payments they made to the state? For further discussion of the California issues, *see* Rubin Ranat, Note, *Tribal State Compacts: Legitimate or Illegal Taxation of Indian Gaming in California?*, 26 WHITTIER L. REV. 953 (2005); Alan P. Meister, *Tribal-State Gaming Compacts and Revenue Sharing: A California Case Study*, 7 GAMING L. REV. 347 (2003); Peter Hecht, *Judges Rules That Schwarzenegger Strongarmed Gaming Tribe*, SACRAMENTO BEE, Apr. 21, 2010, at 1A, *available at* http://www.sacbee.com/2010/04/21/2693660/judges-rule-that-schwarzenegger.html; Dan Morain, Op-Ed, *Ruling May Backfire on Tribal Casinos*, SACRAMENTO BEE, Apr. 29, 2010, at 17A, *available at* http://www.sacbee.com/2010/04/29/2713620/ruling-may-backfire-on-tribal.html; John Wildermuth, *Expensive Ballot Fight Looms on February Vote Over Indian Casinos*, S.F. CHRON., Dec. 7, 2007, http://links.sfgate.com/cgi-bin/article.cgi?f=/c/a/2007/12/07/BAM9TM776.DTL.

6. Another state with a large tribal gaming market is Florida. After years of negotiations, court battles, and political intrigue, the state in 2010 entered a compact with the Seminole Tribe of Florida. Among other things, the state authorized the tribe to offer card games like blackjack at several of its casinos. These card games are not legal anywhere else in Florida. It also gave the tribe the exclusive operation of slot machines at casinos outside Miami-Dade and Broward counties. In return, the tribe guaranteed the state $1 billion over five years and up to 10% of its net revenue on its banked card games for 15 years after that.

7. The gaming moneys states derive from tribes is substantial and has become an important part of state revenues. One respected analyst of the tribal gaming industry has written,

> On the whole, Indian gaming continues to make significant contributions to the U.S. economy.... The fiscal benefits of Indian gaming go beyond just tax revenue from secondary economic activity. Many tribes also made direct payments to federal, state, and local governments, including payments to defray regulatory costs, revenue sharing with local governments, and revenue sharing with states. In calendar year 2007, the total of all identifiable direct payments to federal, state, and local governments was approximately $1.3 billion. This included: $58.2 million in payments to defray federal and state regulatory costs ($15.0 million federal and $43.2 million state*); $155.6 million in local revenue sharing; and $1.1 billion in state revenue sharing.*

ALAN P. MEISTER, CASINO CITY'S INDIAN GAMING INDUSTRY REPORT 3 (Casino City Press 2009) (emphasis added). For a discussion of these issues, *see* Alan P. Meister, Kathryn R.L. Rand, & Steven Andrew Light, *Indian Gaming and Beyond: Tribal Economic Development and Diversification*, 54 S.D. L. REV. 375 (2009); William N. Thompson & Christopher Stream, *Casino Taxation and Revenue Sharing: A Budget Game, or a Game for Economic Development?*, 22 T.M. COOLEY L. REV. 515 (2005); Steven Andrew Light, Kathryn R.L. Rand, & Alan P. Meister, *Spreading the Wealth: Indian Gaming and Revenue-Sharing Agreements*, 80 N.D. L. REV. 657 (2004).

8. Do Indian tribes have to pay federal or state income tax on gaming revenue they generate? The answer is yes to the former and no to the latter. *See* Chickasaw Nation v.

United States, 534 U.S. 84 (2001). *See also* Kevin K. Washburn, *The Legacy of* Bryan v. Itasca County: *How an Erroneous $147 County Tax Notice Helped Bring Tribes $200 Billion in Indian Gaming Revenue*, 92 Minn. L. Rev. 919 (2008) (arguing that the Supreme Court's decision in *Bryan*, holding that Public Law 280 did not confer to the states civil regulatory power over Indian tribes and therefore did not subject them to state taxes, paved the way for the success of Indian gaming).

9. The Ninth Circuit's *Rincon* decision is the only federal case dealing with the revenue sharing issue under IGRA. Does this surprise you? Why haven't there been more cases where tribes contest this questionable arrangement?

D. Who Has the Authority to Negotiate the Compact?

Florida House of Representatives v. Crist

999 So. 2d 601 (Fla. 2008)

CANTERO, J.

After almost sixteen years of sporadic negotiations with four governors, in November 2007 the Seminole Indian Tribe of Florida signed a gambling "compact" (a contract between two sovereigns) with Florida Governor Charles Crist. The compact significantly expands casino gambling, also known as "gaming," on tribal lands. For example, it permits card games such as blackjack and baccarat that are otherwise prohibited by law. In return, the compact promises substantial remuneration to the State.

The Florida Legislature did not authorize the Governor to negotiate the compact before it was signed and has not ratified it since. To the contrary, shortly after the compact was signed, the Florida House of Representatives and its Speaker, Marco Rubio, filed in this Court a petition for a writ of quo warranto disputing the Governor's authority to bind the State to the compact. We have exercised our discretion to consider such petitions, *see* art. V, §3(b) (8), Fla. Const., and now grant it on narrow grounds. We hold that the Governor does not have the constitutional authority to bind the State to a gaming compact that clearly departs from the State's public policy by legalizing types of gaming that are illegal everywhere else in the state.

In the remainder of this opinion, we describe the history of Indian gaming compacts in general and the negotiations leading up to the compact at issue. We then explain our jurisdiction to consider the petition. Finally, we discuss the applicable constitutional provisions, statutes, and cases governing our decision....

B. The Negotiations Between the Tribe and the State

[The court described the basic provisions of IGRA, especially as they relate to the negotiation of a compact to allow Class III gaming on Indian lands, and the authority of the Secretary of the Interior to issue regulations allowing tribes to conduct gaming in the absence of a compact.] With this statutory framework in mind, we briefly describe the protracted history of the Seminole Tribe's efforts to negotiate a compact for conducting Class III gaming in Florida. These negotiations spanned sixteen years and four different governors.

The Seminole Indian Tribe is a federally recognized Indian tribe whose reservations and trust lands are located in the State. The Tribe currently operates Class II gaming facilities, offering low stakes poker games and electronically aided bingo games. The Tribe first sought a compact allowing it to offer Class III gaming in 1991. That January, the Tribe and Governor Lawton Chiles began negotiations, but they ultimately proved fruitless. That same year, the Tribe filed suit in federal court alleging that the State had failed to negotiate in good faith.... [T]he Supreme Court ultimately ruled that the State could assert immunity, and it did. *See Seminole Tribe,* 517 U.S. at 47, *aff'g* Seminole Tribe of Fla. v. Fla., 11 F.3d 1016 (11th Cir. 1994).

Over the next several years, the Tribe repeatedly petitioned the Department to establish Class III gaming procedures. In 1999, the Department did so. It found the Tribe eligible for the procedures and called an informal conference, which was held in Tallahassee that December. At the State's suggestion, however, the Tribe agreed to suspend the conference, though only temporarily. In January 2001, the Secretary issued a twenty-page decision allowing the Tribe to offer a wide range of Class III games. When the State requested clarification, however, the Secretary withdrew the decision. The delay continued. Finally, five years later—in May 2006—the Department reconvened the conference in Hollywood, Florida, and in September of that year warned that if the Tribe and the State did not execute a compact within 60 days, the Department would issue Class III gaming procedures. Despite the parties' failure to negotiate a compact, however, the Department never issued procedures.

Apparently exasperated with the slow progress of the procedures, in March 2007 the Tribe sued the Department in federal court.... The Department then urged Governor Crist to negotiate a compact, warning that if a compact was not signed by November 15, 2007, the Department would finally issue procedures. Under the proposed procedures, the State would not receive any revenue and would have no control over the Tribe's gaming operations. The Tribe would be authorized to operate slot machines and "card games," defined as "a game or series of games of poker (other than Class II games) which are played in a nonbanking manner" (emphasis added). Notably, the alternative procedures would not have permitted the Tribe to operate banked card games such as blackjack.

On November 14—the day before the deadline—the Governor agreed to a compact with the Tribe (Compact). Five days later, the House and its Speaker, Marco Rubio, filed this petition disputing the Governor's authority to bind the State to the Compact without legislative authorization or ratification. We allowed the Tribe to join the action as a respondent.

On January 7, 2008, upon publication of the Secretary's approval, the Compact went into effect.... The parties agree, however, that the Secretary's approval does not render the petition moot.

C. The Compact

The Compact recites that the Governor "has the authority to act for the State with respect to the negotiation and execution of this Compact." It covers a period of twenty-five years and allows the Tribe to offer specified Class III gaming at seven casinos in the State. It establishes the terms, rights, and responsibilities of the parties regarding such gaming. We discuss only its more relevant provisions.

The Compact authorizes the Tribe to conduct "covered gaming," which includes several types of Class III gaming: slot machines; any banking or banked card game, including baccarat, blackjack (twenty-one), and chemin de fer; high stakes poker games; games and devices authorized for the state lottery; and any new game authorized by Florida law. The Compact expressly does not authorize roulette- or craps-style games. The gaming is limited to seven casinos on tribal lands in six areas of the state: Okeechobee, Coconut Creek, Hollywood (two), Clewiston, Immokalee, and Tampa....

The Compact grants the Tribe the exclusive right to conduct certain types of gaming. That is, the Tribe may conduct some Class III gaming, such as banked card games, that is prohibited under state law. Based on that "partial but substantial exclusivity," the Tribe must pay the State a share of the gaming revenue. That share is based in part on amounts that increase at specified thresholds: when the Compact becomes effective, the State receives $50 million. Over the first twenty-four months of operation, it will receive another $175 million. Thereafter, for the third twelve months of operation the State will receive $150 million, and for each twelve-month cycle after that, a minimum of $100 million. If the State breaches the exclusivity provision, however—by legalizing any Class III gaming currently prohibited under state law—the Tribe may cease its payments. The Compact (attached as an appendix to this opinion) is thirty-seven pages long and contains several other provisions we need not detail here.

II. JURISDICTION

[The court concluded that it had authority to issue a writ of quo warranto, a writ used to determine whether a state official is improperly exercising a power derived from the state. Quo warranto, rather than an action seeking a declaratory judgment, was appropriate because the compact was about to become effective. If the Governor lacked authority to enter into the compact, the declaratory judgment action would not be heard before the gaming on tribal lands had begun.]

III. DISCUSSION OF LAW

We now discuss the law that applies to this inter-branch dispute. In deciding whether the Governor or the Legislature has the authority to execute a compact, we first define a "compact" and its historical use in Florida. We then discuss how other jurisdictions have resolved this issue. Next, we review the relevant provisions of our own constitution. Finally, we explain our conclusion that the Governor lacked authority under our state's constitution to execute the Compact because it changes the state's public policy as expressed in the criminal law and therefore infringes on the Legislature's powers.

A. Compacts and their Use in Florida

A compact is essentially a contract between two sovereigns.... The United States Supreme Court has described compacts as "a supple device for dealing with interests confined within a region." State ex rel. Dyer v. Sims, 341 U.S. 22 (1951). The United States Constitution provides that "[n]o State shall, without the Consent of Congress ... enter into any Agreement or Compact with another State, or with a foreign Power." U.S. Const, art. I, § 10. IGRA establishes the consent of Congress to execute gaming compacts, but requires federal approval before they become effective. See 25 U.S.C. § 2710(d)(8).

Like many states, Florida has executed compacts on a range of subjects, including environmental control, water rights, energy, and education—more than thirty in all. The vast majority were executed with other states. In most cases, the Legislature enacted a law.... In others, the Legislature authorized the Governor to execute a compact in the form provided in a statute.... In a few—including a compact among the State, the Tribe, and the South Florida Water Management District regulating water use on Tribal lands—the Legislature by statute approved and ratified the compact. § 285.165, Fla. Stat. (2007). Thus, by tradition at least, it is the Legislature that has consistently either exercised itself or expressly authorized the exercise of the power to bind the State to compacts. We have found no instance in which the governor has signed a compact without legislative involvement.

Although tradition bears some relevance, it does not resolve the question of which branch actually has the constitutional authority to execute compacts in general and gaming compacts in particular. As explained above, the Compact here governs Class III gaming on certain tribal lands in Florida. The issue is whether, regardless of whether the Governor bucked tradition, he had constitutional authority to execute the Compact without the Legislature's prior authorization or, at least, subsequent ratification.

B. How Other Courts Have Answered the Question

Although Florida has not addressed a governor's authority to bind a state to an IGRA compact, other states have. We examine but a few. In State ex rel. Stephan v. Finney, 251 Kan. 559, 836 P.2d 1169, 1182 (1992), the governor executed the compact. In deciding his authority to do so, the Kansas Supreme Court examined the "the nature of the obligations undertaken" by the executed IGRA compact. The court noted that many of the compact's provisions were "clearly legislative in nature," such as creating a state agency and assigning new duties to extant state agencies, and concluded that many provisions "would operate as the enactment of new laws and the amendment of existing laws." *Id.* at 1185. The court therefore held that, although the governor had authority to negotiate the compact, "the Governor ha[d] no power to bind the State to the terms thereof." *Id.*

The New York Court of Appeals has arrived at the same conclusion. After examining IGRA's list of several permissible areas of negotiation for a tribal-state compact, *see* 25 U.S.C. §1071(d) (3) (C), the court concluded that "these issues necessarily make fundamental policy choices that epitomize 'legislative power.'" Saratoga County Chamber of Commerce, Inc. v. Pataki, 100 N.Y.2d 801, 766 N.Y.S.2d 654, 798 N.E.2d 1047, 1060 (2003). Further, like the Kansas Supreme Court, the court found that the compact's designation of an agency to oversee the gaming and the authority of the agency to promulgate rules "usurped the Legislature's power." 766 N.Y.S.2d at 668, 798 N.E.2d at 1061. The court held that the governor "lack[ed] the power unilaterally to negotiate and execute tribal gaming compacts under IGRA." *Id.*

Applying the test of "whether the Governor's action disrupts the proper balance between the executive and legislative branches," the New Mexico Supreme Court similarly found a gaming compact unduly disruptive of the legislature's powers. State ex rel. Clark v. Johnson, 120 N.M. 562, 904 P.2d 11, 23 (1995). The court found that the compact granted extended gaming rights, authorized gaming in contravention of legislative policy, and assigned the roles of the state and the tribe with respect to gaming regulation and civil and criminal jurisdiction. *Id.* at 23–24. Stating that "[r]esidual governmental authority should rest with the legislative branch rather than the executive branch," *id.* at 24, the court held that the "Governor lacked authority under the state Constitution to bind the State by unilaterally entering into the compacts and revenue-sharing agreements in question." *Id.* at 25; *see also* Panzer v. Doyle, 271 Wis.2d 295, 680 N.W.2d 666, 698, 700 (2004) (where a state statute authorized the governor to execute a gaming compact, holding that the governor exceeded his power by permitting the tribes to engage in certain games prohibited by state law and to waive state sovereign immunity).

Federal courts, too, have concluded that a state's governor did not have the authority to bind the state to a gaming compact. In Pueblo of Santa Ana v. Kelly, 104 F.3d 1546, 1548 (10th Cir. 1997), the circuit court held that the Secretary's approval of a compact could not cure an ultra vires act by the state's governor, and the question of "whether a state has validly bound itself to a compact" must be decided under state law. *Id.* at 1557. Noting the New Mexico Supreme Court's "thorough and careful analysis of state law" in Clark, the Tenth Circuit accepted it as determinative on the question of whether its governor had authority to bind the state to the compacts. *Id.* at 1559.

In all these cases, to determine which branch had the authority to bind the state to the compact, courts analyzed the nature and effect of the IGRA compact at issue and compared it to the powers the state constitution delegated to the respective branches. The courts found the compacts within the legislative power because they created or assigned new duties to agencies, conflicted with state law, changed state law, or restricted the legislature's power. Finally, recognizing that state legislative power is limited only by the state and federal constitutions, several courts have ascribed to the legislature, rather than the executive, any residual power on which the state constitutions were silent.... We now review our own state constitution in the context of IGRA's provisions and the Compact signed in this case.

C. Florida Constitutional Provisions

The House contends that several of the Compact's provisions encroach on the Legislature's law- and policy-making powers. To answer the question, we first review the separation-of-powers provisions of the Florida Constitution and our interpretations of it. We then discuss one specific provision on which the Governor relies: the "necessary business" clause.

1. The Florida Constitution's Delegation and Separation of Powers

The Florida Constitution generally specifies the relative powers of the three branches of government. Article II, section 3 provides innocuously that "[t]he powers of the state government shall be divided into legislative, executive and judicial branches. No person belonging to one branch shall exercise any powers appertaining to either of the other branches unless expressly provided herein." In construing our constitution, we have "traditionally applied a strict separation of powers doctrine." Bush v. Schiavo, 885 So.2d 321, 329 (Fla. 2004) (quoting State v. Cotton, 769 So.2d 345, 353 (Fla. 2000)).

These provisions are not specific, however.... Both the Governor and the House concede that the state constitution does not expressly grant either branch the authority to execute compacts.

We must therefore expand our analysis beyond the plain language of the constitution. We have held that the powers of the respective branches "are those so defined ... or such as are inherent or so recognized by immemorial governmental usage, and which involve the exercise of primary and independent will, discretion, and judgment, subject not to the control of another department, but only to the limitations imposed by the state and federal Constitutions." *Id.* at 974. A branch has "the inherent right to accomplish all objects naturally within the orbit of that department, not expressly limited by the fact of the existence of a similar power elsewhere or the express limitations in the constitution." ... As we noted over seventy-five years ago, what determines whether a particular function is legislative, executive, or judicial "so that it may be exercised by appropriate officers of the proper department" is not "the name given to the function or to the officer who performs it" but the "essential nature and effect of the governmental function to be performed." Florida Motor Lines v. Railroad Comm'rs, 100 Fla. 538, 129 So. 876, 881 (1930).

The House argues that, precisely because the state constitution does not expressly grant the governor authority to execute compacts, such authority belongs to the Legislature. In other words, the "residual" power—that is, powers not specifically assigned to the governor—belongs to the Legislature. Albeit many years ago and under different circumstances, we have implied as much. *See* State ex rel. Green v. Pearson, 153 Fla. 314, 14 So.2d 565, 567 (1943) ("The legislative branch looks to the Constitution not for sources of power but for limitations upon power. But if such limitations are not found to exist, its discretion reasonably exercised may not be disturbed by the judicial branch of the government.") ... And, as we noted above, other state courts have ascribed to their legislatures any residual power on which the state constitutions were silent. *See Clark*, 904 P.2d at 25....

We need not decide, however, whether the authority to bind the state to compacts always resides in the legislature. Although the line of demarcation is not always clear, we have noted that "the legislature's exclusive power encompasses questions of fundamental policy and the articulation of reasonably definite standards to be used in implementing those policies." B.H. v. State, 645 So.2d 987, 993 (Fla. 1994).... Therefore, even if the Governor has authority to execute compacts, its terms cannot contradict the state's public policy, as expressed in its laws.

2. IGRA and the "Necessary Business" Clause

The Governor argues that his authority to execute the Compact derives from article IV, section 1 of the Florida Constitution. That provision states in part that "[t]he governor shall take care that the laws be faithfully executed ... and transact all necessary business with the officers of government." Art. IV, § 1(a), Fla. Const. The Governor submits that the phrase "transact all necessary business with the officers of government" includes negotiating with the Tribe and that he cannot ignore the federal directive to "negotiate"; therefore, negotiating the Compact was "necessary business" under IGRA.

IGRA provides that a tribe seeking to offer Class III gaming must "request [that] the State ... enter into negotiations" for a compact and that the "State shall negotiate with the Indian tribe in good faith." 25 U.S.C. § 2710(d)(3)(A). The Governor is therefore correct that IGRA requires states to negotiate. As other courts have recognized, however, nowhere does IGRA equate "the state" with "the governor." *See Seminole Tribe*, 517 U.S. at 75 n.17.... In addition, when a state fails to negotiate, a tribe must sue the state, not the governor. *Seminole Tribe*, 517 U.S. at 74–75 (holding that Congress intended § 2710(d)(3) to be enforced against the state, not the governor)....

More importantly, a State's "duty to negotiate" under IGRA cannot be enforced. A state may avoid its duty, as Florida has effectively done, by asserting its immunity. *Seminole Tribe*, 517 U.S. at 47. Therefore, although IGRA requires a state to negotiate, it does not impose any duty on a state's governor. Moreover, IGRA does not prescribe the terms of a compact, *see* 25 U.S.C. § 2710(d), and it does not confer on the governor the authority to bind the state to a compact or act in contravention to state law. In other words, IGRA does not grant a governor, or any state actor, any powers beyond those provided by the state's constitution and laws....

We express no opinion on whether the "necessary business" clause may ever grant the governor authority to bind the State to an IGRA compact. We do conclude, however, that the clause does not authorize the governor to execute compacts contrary to the expressed public policy of the state or to create exceptions to the law. Nor does it change our conclusion that "the legislature's exclusive power encompasses questions of fundamental policy and the articulation of reasonably definite standards to be used in implementing those policies." *B.H.*, 645 So.2d at 993.

We now discuss why, in authorizing conduct prohibited by state law, the Governor exceeded his authority.

D. The Compact Violates the Separation of Powers

The House claims that the Compact violates the separation of powers on a number of grounds.[8] We find one of them dispositive. The Compact permits the Tribe to conduct certain Class III gaming that is prohibited under Florida law. Therefore, the Compact violates the state's public policy about the types of gambling that should be allowed. We hold that, whatever the Governor's authority to execute compacts, it does not extend so far. The Governor does not have authority to agree to legalize in some parts of the state, or for some persons, conduct that is otherwise illegal throughout the state.

We first discuss whether state laws in general, and gaming laws in particular, apply to Indian tribes. We next discuss Florida law on gaming. We then address the House's argument that IGRA prohibits compacts from expanding the gaming allowed under state law. Finally, we explain why the Governor lacked authority to bind the State to a compact, such as this one, that contradicts state law.

1. State Gaming Laws Apply to the Tribe

Generally, state laws do not apply to tribal Indians on Indian reservations unless Congress so provides.... Therefore, the extent to which a state may enforce its criminal laws on tribal land depends on federal authorization.... Congress has, however, conferred on the states the authority to assume jurisdiction over crimes committed on tribal land, *see* Act of Aug. 15, 1953, Pub. L. No. 280 § 6, 67 Stat. 588, 590 (1953), and Florida has assumed such jurisdiction.... The state's law is therefore enforceable on tribal lands to the extent it does not conflict with federal law.... In regard to gambling in particular, federal law provides that, except as provided in a tribal-state compact, state gambling laws apply on tribal lands. *See* 18 U.S.C. § 1166(a) (2000).

Based on these state and federal provisions, what is legal in Florida is legal on tribal lands, and what is illegal in Florida is illegal there. Absent a compact, any gambling prohibited in the state is prohibited on tribal land.

2. Florida's Gaming Laws

It is undisputed that Florida permits limited forms of Class III gaming. The state's constitution authorizes the state lottery, which offers various Class III games, and now permits slot machines in Miami-Dade and Broward Counties. *See* art. X, §§ 7, 15, Fla. Const. For a long time, the State also has regulated pari-mutuel wagering—for example, on dog and horse racing. *See* ch. 550, Fla. Stat. (2007) (governing pari-mutuel wagering).

It is also undisputed, however, that the State prohibits all other types of Class III gaming, including lotteries not sponsored by the State and slot machines outside Miami-Dade and Broward Counties. Florida law distinguishes between nonbanked (Class II) card games and banked (Class III) card games. A "banking game" is one "in which the house is a par-

---

8. The House argues that the Compact significantly changes Florida law and policy in a number of ways: it authorizes Class III slot machines outside of Broward County; it allows blackjack and other banked card games that are currently illegal throughout Florida; it provides for collection of funds from tribal casinos for State purposes under a revenue-sharing agreement and penalizes the State for any expansion of non-tribal gaming; it allows an exception to Florida's substantive right of access to public records for information dealing with Indian gaming; it changes the venue of litigation dealing with individual disputes with the tribal casinos; it sets procedures for tort remedies occurring in certain circumstances; it waives sovereign immunity to the extent that it creates enforceable contract rights between the State and the Tribe; and it establishes a regulatory mechanism to be undertaken by the Governor or his designee. Because of our resolution of this case, we need not consider whether these other provisions encroach on the legislature's policy-making authority.

ticipant in the game, taking on players, paying winners, and collecting from losers or in which the cardroom establishes a bank against which participants play." § 849.086(2)(b); *see* § 849.086(1), Fla. Stat. (deeming banked games to be "casino gaming"). Florida law authorizes cardrooms at pari-mutuel facilities for games of "poker or dominoes," but only if they are played "in a nonbanking manner." § 849.086(2), Fla. Stat.; *see* § 849.086(1)-(3). Florida law prohibits banked card games, however. *See* § 849.086(12) (a), (15)(a). Blackjack, baccarat, and chemin de fer are banked card games. They are therefore illegal in Florida.

3. Does IGRA Permit Compacts to Expand Gaming?

Contrary to Florida law, the Compact allows banked card games such as blackjack, baccarat, and chemin de fer. The House argues that the Compact therefore violates IGRA itself, which permits Class III gaming only if the state "permits such gaming for any purpose by any person, organization, or entity." 25 U.S.C. § 2710(d)(1). The Governor, on the other hand, contends that, once state law permits any Class III gaming, a compact may allow all Class III gaming.

The meaning of the phrase "permits such gaming" has been heavily litigated. The question is whether, when state law permits some Class III games to be played, a tribe must be permitted to conduct only those particular games or all Class III games. *See* Kathryn R.L. Rand, Caught in the Middle: How State Politics, State Law, and State Courts Constrain Tribal Influence Over Indian Gaming, 90 Marq. L. Rev. 971, 983 (2007) (citing cases). The Secretary's interpretation of this provision supports the House's argument. *See* Class III Gaming Procedures, 63 Fed. Reg. 3289, 3293 (Jan. 22, 1998) (Proposed Rules) ("IGRA thus makes it unlawful for Tribes to operate particular Class III games that State law completely and affirmatively prohibits."). So do a majority of federal courts.... Our Attorney General has agreed with the majority interpretation. *See* Op. Att'y Gen. Fla. 2007–36 at 3 (2007) ("[I]n light of the greater weight of federal case law and the Department of the Interior's interpretation of IGRA, Class III gaming activities subject to mandatory negotiations between a state and an Indian tribe do not include those specifically prohibited by state law.").

Whether the Compact violates IGRA, however, is a question we need not and do not resolve. Given our narrow scope of review on a writ of quo warranto, the issue here is only whether the Florida Constitution grants the Governor the authority to unilaterally bind the State to a compact that violates public policy. We conclude that even if the Governor is correct that IGRA permits the expansion of gaming on tribal lands beyond what state law permits, such an agreement represents a significant change in Florida's public policy. It is therefore precisely the type of action particularly within the Legislature's power. We now discuss that issue.

4. The Compact Violates Florida's Public Policy on Gaming

Article II, section 3 of the Florida Constitution prohibits the executive branch from usurping the powers of another branch. Enacting laws—and especially criminal laws—is quintessentially a legislative function.... By authorizing the Tribe to conduct "banked card games" that are illegal throughout Florida—and thus illegal for the Tribe—the Compact violates Florida law.... The Governor's action therefore encroaches on the legislative function and was beyond his authority. Nor does it matter that the Compact is a contract between the State and the Tribe. Neither the Governor nor anyone else in the executive branch has the authority to execute a contract that violates state criminal law....

IV. CONCLUSION

We conclude that the Governor's execution of a compact authorizing types of gaming that are prohibited under Florida law violates the separation of powers. The Governor has no authority to change or amend state law. Such power falls exclusively to the Legislature. Therefore, we hold that the Governor lacked authority to bind the State to a compact that violates Florida law as this compact does. We need not resolve the broader issue of whether the Governor ever has the authority to execute compacts without either the Legislature's prior authorization or, at least, its subsequent ratification. Because we believe the parties will fully comply with the dictates of this opinion, we grant the petition but withhold issuance of the writ.

It is so ordered.

Notes

1. In line with the *Crist* case, a commanding majority of the cases considering this issue place limits on a governor's authority to negotiate or execute a compact. *See, e.g.,* State ex rel. Stephan v. Finney, 836 P.2d 1169 (Kan. 1992) (governor had authority to enter into compact negotiations with tribe, but had no power to bind state to terms thereof absent appropriate delegation of power by state legislature or legislative approval of compact); Pueblo of Santa Ana v. Kelly, 104 F.3d 1546 (10th Cir. 1997), *cert. denied,* 522 U.S. 807 (1997) (holding that compacts were invalid because the Governor of New Mexico lacked authority under New Mexico law to execute the compacts on behalf of the state); Saratoga County Chamber of Commerce, Inc. v. Pataki, 798 N.E.2d 1047 (N.Y. 2003) (gaming compacts address issues involving licensing, taxation and criminal and civil jurisdiction and necessarily involve fundamental policy choices that epitomize legislative power; these are tasks the multimember, representative Legislature is entrusted to perform under state's constitutional structure); Narragansett Indian Tribe of Rhode Island v. State, 667 A.2d 280, 282 (R.I. 1995) ("[T]he Governor as Chief Executive lacked both constitutional as well as legislative authority to bind the State of Rhode Island by executing the Tribal-State Compact dated August 29, 1994, between the State of Rhode Island and the Narragansett Indian Tribe.").

2. Two cases support wider authority for a Governor to negotiate compacts. *See* Willis v. Fordice, 850 F. Supp. 523 (S.D. Miss. 1994) (Mississippi law provided that, "governor shall transact all the business of the state," and this gave governor authority to enter into compact with tribe); Dewberry v. Kulongoski, 406 F. Supp. 1136 (D. Or. 2005) (Oregon Constitution provides that Governor "shall transact all necessary business," and negotiation of compact with tribe was necessary business).

3. The *Crist* decision is subtle in its holding and its effects. The court ruled that the type of gaming authorized in the compact was not legal in Florida, and that the question of whether gaming on tribal lands "beyond what state law permits" was an important public policy issue that was within the Legislature's authority to address, not the Governor's. Therefore, the court stated that it "need not resolve the broader issue of whether the Governor ever has the authority to execute compacts without either the Legislature's prior authorization or, at least, its subsequent ratification." 999 So. 2d at 616. The court also did not invalidate the compact or rule that the compact violated IGRA. Was the effect of the ruling the closure of the tribal casinos that were beginning to operate pursuant to the compact? That was clearly not the case. The Secretary of the Interior had approved the compacts, so the tribe maintained that it had the authority to operate the games and it did so. Would the state have had the authority under IGRA to close down those games?

4. While IGRA requires a tribal-state compact for the tribe to offer Class III gaming, it does not, as the preceding materials illustrate, specify who on behalf of the state (or the tribe) has the authority to negotiate the compact terms. For the state, the governor or

the legislature, or both, may have this authority. This is a matter that has been left to state statutes and state constitutional law. Would it be better if IGRA were amended, or the Secretary of the Interior promulgated a regulation, to provide specifically who should negotiate the contract on behalf of the state? Or should federal law be left out of this issue? Does the holding in *Crist* suggest that IGRA could eliminate the uncertainty of who is the proper negotiator and make the process more efficient? For that matter, wasn't one of the central purposes of IGRA to make the regulation of tribal gaming a matter of federal law, with states having specifically stated and limited authority? If so, is there an argument that IGRA constitutionally pre-empts the operation of state law on this issue?

5. IGRA also does not specify who on behalf of the tribe is authorized to negotiate a tribal-state compact. This is a matter of tribal law. *See* David E. Wilkins, American Indian Politics and the American Political System (Rowman & Littlefield) (2007); Tracy Burris, *How Tribal Gaming Commissions are Evolving*, 8 Gaming L. Rev. 243 (2004).

6. For additional consideration of the authority to negotiate issues, *see* Chris Rausch, *The Problem with Good Faith: The Indian Gaming Regulatory Act a Decade After* Seminole, 11 Gaming L. Rev. 423 (2007); Kathryn R.L. Rand & Steven Andrew Light, *How Congress Can and Should "Fix" the Indian Gaming Regulatory Act: Recommendations for Law and Policy Reform*, 13 Va. J. Soc. Pol'y & L. 396 (2006); Steven D. Hamilton, Note, Panzer v. Doyle: *The Wisconsin Supreme Court Fires a Near Fatal Shot at the "New Buffalo"*, 55 DePaul L. Rev. 1341 (2006); Rebecca Tsosie, *Negotiating Economic Survival: The Consent Principle and Tribal-State Compacts Under the Indian Gaming Regulatory Act*, 29 Ariz. St. L.J. 25 (1997).

E. Where Can Tribe-Operated Gaming Take Place?

The title of this section asks a question that many people would say has an obvious answer—tribal gaming occurs on tribal lands. This part of IGRA contains two elements that are critical to tribal gaming: the land must be territorially confined to the Indian reservation, and the United States government must hold the property in trust. As defined by IGRA:

(4) The term "Indian lands" means:

(A) all lands within the limits of any Indian reservation; and

(B) any lands title to which is either held in trust by the United States for the benefit of any Indian tribe or individual or held by any Indian tribe or individual subject to restriction by the United States against alienation and over which an Indian tribe exercises governmental power.

25 U.S.C. §2703. Predictably, however, IGRA adds political layers to these simple legal concepts, and thereby expands the possibilities for where tribal gaming can operate.

Lac Courte Oreilles Band of Lake Superior Chippewa Indians of Wisconsin v. United States
367 F.3d 650 (7th Cir. 2004)

FLAUM, Chief Judge.

The Plaintiff Tribes appeal the district court's opinion and order declaring the gubernatorial concurrence provision of the Indian Gaming Regulatory Act ("IGRA") constitutional and not in violation of the federal government's trust obligation to Indians. For the reasons set forth in the following opinion, we affirm the judgment of the district court.

I. Background

Plaintiffs are three federally-recognized Indian Tribes with reservations in sparsely populated areas of northern Wisconsin ("the Tribes"). While each of the Tribes operates a casino on reservation land, these casinos do not generate income comparable to casinos operated by tribes who have reservations near Wisconsin's urban centers or destination resorts. Seeking to advance their tribal and economic development, the Tribes joined together for the purpose of establishing a jointly owned and operated off-reservation gaming facility in a lucrative location.

The Tribes found a struggling pari-mutuel greyhound racing facility in Hudson, Wisconsin that they wished to acquire and convert into a casino gaming facility. Hudson was attractive to the Tribes because they believed its proximity to the metropolitan areas of Minneapolis and St. Paul and easy accessibility to Interstate Highway 94 would ensure a broad customer base. In October 1992 the Tribes formally submitted their application under the Indian Gaming Regulatory Act ("IGRA") 25 U.S.C. §§ 2701 et seq. to the Department of the Interior seeking to have the Hudson property taken into trust for their benefit for the purpose of operating a casino gaming facility.

The Secretary of the Interior has broad discretion to acquire lands in trust for the benefit of Indian tribes pursuant to Indian Reorganization Act of 1934, 25 U.S.C. § 465. However, this authority is limited by IGRA, which prohibits certain types of gaming on lands acquired in trust by the Secretary of the Interior after October 17, 1988 ("after-acquired lands"). 25 U.S.C. § 2719(a). The Tribes hoped that their application would be favorably received pursuant to 25 U.S.C. § 2719(b)(1)(A), an exception to IGRA's general ban on gaming on after-acquired lands. That exception provides that the general prohibition on gaming shall not apply where:

> the Secretary, after consultation with the Indian tribe and appropriate State and local officials, including officials of other nearby Indian tribes, determines that a gaming establishment on newly acquired lands would be in the best interest of the Indian tribe and its members, and would not be detrimental to the surrounding community, but only if the Governor of the State in which the gaming activity is to be conducted concurs in the Secretary's determination.

25 U.S.C. § 2719(b)(1)(A).

The Department of the Interior initially denied the Tribes' application, but later vacated the rejection following a lawsuit and settlement. In February 2001, the Department of the Interior issued findings that the proposal was in the best interests of the Tribes and would not be detrimental to the surrounding community. The Department of the Interior sent the matter to then Governor of Wisconsin Scott McCallum for his concurrence. In May 2001, Governor McCallum issued a letter declining to concur in the Secretary's findings, citing Wisconsin's general disapproval of off-reservation gaming and public policy of permitting only "limited exceptions to the general prohibition against gambling." Governor McCallum opined that the public interest would not be served by the addition of another major casino gaming facility to the seventeen casino gaming facilities already operating in Wisconsin. In June 2001, the Department of the Interior issued a final decision denying the Tribes' application on the grounds that, absent the Governor's concurrence, the exception provided in 25 U.S.C. § 2719(b)(1)(A) did not apply and 25 U.S.C. § 2719(a) precluded the acquisition of the land for the purposes of gaming.

The Tribes initiated this litigation in the United States District Court for the District of Columbia in May 2001 seeking a declaration that the gubernatorial concurrence provision of § 2719(b)(1)(A) was unconstitutional. [The] Tribes [also asked that they] be permitted to add a claim that Governor McCallum had relied on improper factors in refusing to concur, in the event that the court upheld the constitutionality of the gubernatorial concurrence provision of § 2719(b)(1)(A).

In April 2003, the district court granted the defendants' motions for judgment on the pleadings, finding that the gubernatorial concurrence provision is not an unconstitutional delegation of power, nor does it violate the separation of powers doctrine, the Appointments Clause, Art. II, § 2, or the Tenth Amendment. Further, the district court found that the Tribes' claim that the gubernatorial concurrence requirement represented a breach of trust was barred by sovereign immunity and was without support in law.... We uphold the judgment of the district court because we conclude that § 2719(b)(1)(A) does not violate separation of powers principles, the nondelegation doctrine, the Appointments Clause, principles of federalism, or the federal government's trust obligations to Indians.

II. Analysis

The Tribes challenge the constitutionality of the gubernatorial concurrence provision of the Indian Gaming Regulations Act ("IGRA"), 25 U.S.C. § 2719(b)(1)(A) on multiple grounds....

At issue in this litigation is § 2719(b)(1)(A), which allows the Secretary of the Interior to deviate from IGRA's general prohibition of gaming on after-acquired lands if certain prerequisites are met. Under § 2719(b)(1)(A), the Secretary of the Interior may take land not contiguous to the reservation of the applicant Indian tribe into trust for the purpose of operating a gaming establishment if the Secretary finds that two factual predicates exist, namely, whether (1) "a gaming establishment on newly acquired lands would be in the best interest of the Indian tribe and its members," and (2) "would not be detrimental to the surrounding community," and if the "Governor of the State in which the gaming activity would be conducted" concurs in the Secretary's favorable determination. 25 U.S.C. § 2719(b)(1)(A).

A.

The Tribes assert that the gubernatorial concurrence provision of § 2719(b)(1)(a) violates the separation of powers doctrine because it prevents the Executive Branch from executing the laws. In their view, § 2719(b)(1)(A) unconstitutionally diverts to the Governors of the 50 States the final decisional authority delegated by IGRA to the Secretary of the Interior. The Tribes submit that § 2719(b)(1)(A) requires a governor to review the Secretary of the Interior's analysis of the two factual predicates and empowers the governor to "veto" the Secretary of the Interior's conclusion by withholding concurrence. The Tribes cite INS v. Chadha, 462 U.S. 919 (1983) for the proposition that Congress cannot confer upon itself or an actor external to the federal Executive Branch the power to veto the President's execution of federal law.

At issue in Chadha was Section 244(c) (2) of the Immigration and Nationality Act, 8 U.S.C. § 1254(c)(2), which authorized either House of Congress, by resolution, to veto the Attorney General's decision to suspend the deportation of a particular alien. The Supreme Court noted that the one-house veto served an "essentially legislative ... purpose and effect," id. at 952, ... and was therefore subject to the procedural requirements for enacting legislation set forth in the Constitution: bicameral passage, ... and presentment to the President, Chadha, 462 U.S. at 954–55. [T]herefore [the Court] concluded that the House of Representatives lacked authority under the Constitution to veto the Attorney General's decision to suspend the petitioner's deportation. *Id.* at 956–57. Finally, the *Chadha* Court noted that to maintain the separation of powers, "the carefully defined limits on the power of each Branch must not be eroded." 464 U.S. at 962.

Unlike the one-House veto provision at issue in *Chadha*, the gubernatorial concurrence provision does not prevent the Executive Branch from accomplishing its delegated function under IGRA. Section 2719(b)(1)(A) assigns the Secretary of the Interior two responsibilities: (1) to evaluate whether gaming on the proposed trust land would be in the best interest of the applicant tribe and not detrimental to the surrounding community; if so, then (2) to ascertain whether the Governor of the State where the proposed trust land is located concurs with his or her favorable determination. A governor's concurrence is no less a precondition to the Executive Branch's authority to waive IGRA's general prohibition of gaming on after-acquired lands than are the factual circumstances that give rise to Secretary of the Interior's conclusion that gaming on the proposed trust land would be in the Indian tribe's best interests and would not be detrimental to the surrounding community. Unless and until the appropriate governor issues a concurrence, the Secretary of the Interior has no authority under § 2719(b)(1)(A) to take land into trust for the benefit of an Indian tribe for the purpose of the operation of a gaming establishment.

.... [In *Chadha*], the one-House veto wrested final decision-making power away from the Executive Branch over an issue that had been legislatively entrusted to the Attorney General and thereby directly impeded the Attorney General from accomplishing the function delegated: to determine whether to suspend, and to suspend, the deportation of a particular alien. In contrast, after the two preconditions to the Secretary of the Interior's authority are met—i.e., the two factual predicates exist and the governor issues a concurrence—the Secretary of the Interior's decision to execute § 2719(b)(1)(A) by taking the proposed land into trust is not subject to review.

We agree with the Ninth Circuit that § 2719(b)(1)(A) is an example of contingent legislation, wherein Congress restricted the authority to execute federal legislation contingent upon the approval of an actor external to the federal Executive Branch. Confederated Tribes of Siletz Indians of Oregon v. United States, 110 F.3d 688, 694–95 (9th Cir. 1997). As the Supreme Court established in Currin v. Wallace, 306 U.S. 1, 15 (1939), Congress may place "a restriction upon its own regulation by withholding its operation" unless a specified percentage of those affected by the regulation agree to submit to it. In *Currin*, the Supreme Court upheld a federal statute that authorized the Secretary of Agriculture to designate markets for the sale of tobacco, but only if two-thirds of affected tobacco growers favored the designation.... As in *Currin*, where the Secretary of Agriculture's authority was conditioned on a favorable vote of the affected farmers, the Secretary of the Interior's authority to act is conditioned on the concurrence of the relevant governor. This condition does not impermissibly interfere with the Executive Branch's execution of federal law, so much as its occurrence is a prerequisite to the Executive Branch's authority to act pursuant to § 2719(b)(1)(A)....

We find that the remaining separation of powers issues illustrated by the one-House veto in *Chadha* are not present here. The gubernatorial concurrence provision does not aggrandize the power of the Legislative Branch at the expense of the Executive Branch. The Secretary of the Interior would have no authority to permit gaming on after-acquired trust lands absent the power delegated by Congress in IGRA. Congress may, consistent with the doctrine of separation of powers, condition that delegation on the approval of an actor external to the Executive Branch.... Congress has not wrongfully enhanced its power by the use of the contingent legislation mechanism; whether the governor concurs and thereby triggers the Secretary of the Interior's power under § 2719(b)(1)(A) is a circumstance outside of Congress's influence or control....

Finally, the Tribes argue that § 2719(b)(1)(A) violates the separation of powers doctrine because it transfers control over the execution of federal law from the Executive Branch to the Governors of the 50 States, citing Printz v. United States, 521 U.S. 898 (1997). In *Printz*, at issue were certain interim provisions of the Brady Handgun Violence Prevention Act ("Brady Act"), 18 U.S.C. § 922, which obliged state law enforcement officers to conduct background checks of prospective handgun purchasers until a national system became operative. *Id.* at 903. The Supreme Court held that the interim provisions unconstitutionally transferred the responsibility of the President to "take Care that the Laws be faithfully executed," U.S. Const. Art. II, § 3, to the law enforcement officers of the 50 States, "who are left to implement the program without meaningful Presidential control." *Id.* at 922. The *Printz* Court noted that, by accomplishing the execution of the law through state officers, Congress had denigrated the President's power by circumventing the Executive Branch and had weakened the accountability and vigor of that Branch. *Id.*

Unlike the Brady Act's requirement that state officers temporarily execute federal law by performing background checks, the gubernatorial concurrence provision does not require or even permit any governor to execute federal law. The execution of § 2719(b) (1) (A) occurs when the Secretary of the Interior takes land into trust for the benefit of Indians for the purpose of operating a gaming establishment. IGRA does not empower any governor to perform that function. For example, even if a governor believed that taking land into trust for an Indian tribe for the purpose of gaming "would be in the best interest of the Indian tribe" and "would not be detrimental to the surrounding community," if the Secretary of the Interior disagreed, the governor would be unable to execute § 2719(b)(1)(A) by taking the land into federal trust.

As only the Secretary of the Interior may execute the § 2719(b)(1)(A) exception to IGRA's general prohibition of gaming on after-acquired land, the Executive Branch retains control over IGRA's execution, and therefore there is no *Printz* separation of powers problem. In conclusion, we hold that the contested provision of IGRA does not violate the separation of powers doctrine by interfering with the Executive Branch's execution of federal law.

B.

We now turn to the Tribes' argument that Congress violated a related branch of the separation of powers jurisprudence: the nondelegation doctrine. In the Tribes' view, if § 2719(b)(1)(A) does not require a governor to decide whether to concur based on his or her analysis of the two factual predicates that bind the Secretary of the Interior's determination, but instead directs each governor to select any standard on which to base the decision, then Congress has abdicated its duty to guide the execution of the law.... According to the Tribes, Congress failed to adequately constrain the discretion of the Governors, and § 2719(b)(1)(A) therefore requires the Governors to establish Congressional policy, in violation of U.S. Const. Art. 1, § 1.

The Supreme Court has explained that the nondelegation doctrine generally prohibits Congress from delegating its legislative power to another Branch of the federal government.... We conclude that the nondelegation doctrine is not implicated by the provision at issue because § 2719(b)(1)(A) does not delegate any legislative power to the Governors of the 50 States. When Congress enacts contingent legislation, it does not "abdicate, or ... transfer to others, the essential legislative functions with which it is vested by the Constitution, U.S.C.A. Art. 1, sec. 1." ... There is no "delegation of legislative authority" to the actor whose assent is a precondition to the execution of the law. *Id.* ...

Congress exercised its legislative authority by enacting IGRA's general prohibition of gaming on after-acquired land, creating an exception to that rule in § 2719(b)(1)(A), and dictating the prerequisites for the application of that exception. A governor does not enact federal policy by issuing a concurrence, but instead merely waives one legislatively enacted restriction on gaming. Nor does a governor impact federal policy by declining to concur; in that event, IGRA's policy of prohibiting gaming on after-acquired lands remains in force....

During oral argument, it became evident that the Tribes' concern is not so much the unconstrained discretion that Congress permitted the Governors of the 50 States to exercise under §2719(b)(1)(A), but that Congress had delegated any power to the Governors at all. The Tribes conceded that they would not have objected on nondelegation grounds had Congress conditioned the Secretary's power to take land into trust not upon the concurrence of a governor, but rather upon the majority vote of the Indian tribes with reservations encompassed by the state where the proposed trust land is located. In the Tribes' view, the Governor of Wisconsin is an improper delegatee because his administration oversees the Wisconsin State Lottery, which they maintain is in competition with the casinos subject to regulation under IGRA. The Tribes rely on Carter v. Carter Coal Co., 298 U.S. 238, 311 (1936) for the proposition that Congress may not delegate to a private party the power to regulate an industry when the delegatee has "interests [that] may be and often are adverse to the interests of others in the same business."...

We conclude that the gubernatorial concurrence provision does not raise the concerns presented in *Carter*. The Governors of the 50 States are politically accountable to their constituencies and will therefore be motivated to maximize the public good, contrary to the chief coal producers in *Carter*, whose relationship with minor coal producers was "conflicting and even antagonistic," and whose motivations were self-serving.... Even if a particular governor might enjoy ultimate authority over a state lottery or gaming system, that role will surely be eclipsed by the governor's responsibility to regulate the broader state economy.

In conclusion, we find that §2719(b)(1)(A) does not violate the nondelegation doctrine because it does not entrust to the Governors of the 50 States any legislative power, nor does it violate the principles of *Carter* by wrongfully authorizing a self-interested leader of private industry to regulate its competitors.

[The court also ruled against the tribe's arguments that the gubernatorial concurrence provision violates the Appointments Clause, that basic principles of federalism were compromised, and that the federal government's trust responsibility to Indians was violated by the gubernatorial concurrence provision.]

Notes

1. It is likely that when IGRA was drafted Congress contemplated that most tribal gambling would be on tribal lands, sometimes referred to as "Indian Country." Certainly, there was no thought that tribes would be setting up casinos in major cities. Generally speaking then, IGRA prohibited gaming on lands acquired after the passage of IGRA in 1988, so-called "newly acquired" lands. But along with the general prohibition, IGRA sets forth several exceptions, such as lands located within or contiguous to the tribe's existing reservation, lands placed in trust as a settlement of a land claim, the initial reservation of a federally recognized tribe, and the restoration of lands for a tribe whose federal recognition is restored. *See* 25 U.S.C. §2719(a) (2009).

2. The exception that was at the heart of the principal case is the "best interests" exception. Indian gaming can take place "off-reservation"—that is, on newly acquired

land—if a two part process is satisfied. First, the Secretary of the Interior must determine that a "gaming establishment on newly acquired lands would be in the best interest of the Indian tribe and its members, and would not be detrimental to the surrounding community." But even if the Secretary, "after consultation with the Indian tribe and appropriate State and local officials," decides that these criteria are satisfied, the tribe cannot offer this gaming unless "the Governor of the State in which the gaming activity is to be conducted concurs in the Secretary's determination." 25 U.S.C. § 2719(b)(1)(A). This provision gives a governor a veto over the expansion of Indian gaming to newly-acquired lands.

3. Some may wonder why a tribe would want to expand gaming operations to an area not near its traditional lands. Many tribal lands are in rural areas, far from population centers that might support a casino. The opportunity to develop a casino in another area of the state serves one of IGRA's objectives of tribal economic development and self-sufficiency. Also, the off-reservation facility would be subject to the compacting requirements for Class III gaming, thus providing an opportunity for a state to benefit through revenue sharing. Accordingly, states would seem to have incentives to approve such initiatives.

Nevertheless, this is one of the most controversial aspects of Indian gaming. Efforts to take Indian land into trust for the purpose of off-reservation gaming has often drawn intense opposition from local communities, state governments, and even other tribes. Sometimes this process is termed "reservation shopping." The phrase reflects the concern that "investors" wanting to develop casinos will contact Indian tribes and propose the acquisition of non-tribal land for the tribe to develop into a casino, with the non-Indian entity profiting from this arrangement. In one instance, a member of Congress stated:

> Attempts at off-reservation gaming and the practice of reservation shopping have increased dramatically in California over the past 5 years … [it] is now estimated that there may be over 20 proposals to game outside of tribal lands in California.
>
> I have watched as out-of-state gaming developers have sought out tribes offering to assist them in developing casinos near lucrative sites in urban areas, and along central transit routes far from any nexus to their historic land.

A Bill to Modify the Date as of which Certain Tribal Land of the Lytton Rancheria of California is Deemed to be Held in Trust: Hearing Before the S. Comm. on Indian Affairs, 109th Cong. 5 (2005) (statement of Sen. Dianne Feinstein).

In fact, the number of tribes that have gotten the dual approval needed to offer gaming on these off-reservation lands has been few. *See* City of Rossville v. Norton, 219 F. Supp. 2d 130 (D.D.C. 2002) (holding that acceptance of fifty acres of land in trust by United States constituted a "restoration of lands," thereby satisfying IGRA requirements, and was not an unconstitutional delegation of congressional authority); Confederated Tribes of Siletz Indians of Oregon v. United States, 110 F.3d 688 (9th Cir. 1997) (holding Congress has the power to make the execution of federal legislation contingent on the approval of an authority outside of the federal government). For discussion of these issues, *see* Eric M. Jensen, *Indian Gaming on Newly Acquired Lands*, 47 Washburn L.J. 675 (2008); Matthew L.M. Fletcher, *Bringing Balance to Indian Gaming*, 44 Harv. J. on Legis. 39 (2007); Kathryn R.L. Rand & Steven Andrew Light, *How Congress Can and Should "Fix" the Indian Gaming Regulatory Act: Recommendations for Law and Policy Reform*, 13 Va. J. Soc. Pol'y & L. 396 (2006); Heidi MacNeil Staudenmaier, *Off-Reservation Native American Gaming: An Examination of the Legal and Political Hurdles*, 4 Nev. L.J. 301 (2004).

4. The Interior Secretary's authority to take land into trust for the benefit of a tribe is a detailed process that traces its legal provenance to the Indian Reorganization Act of 1934 (IRA). *See* 25 U.S.C. § 476. Until 2008, the process of taking the property into trust for gaming purposes under IGRA was less elaborate than that prescribed by the 1934 law for tribal land generally. It focused on the determination of the "best interests" and "not detrimental" parts of IGRA, rather than the more extensive requirements of the IRA's land-in-trust process.

In January 2008, however, the Interior Department released guidance on the taking of off-reservation land into trust for non-gaming purposes. According to the guidance, applications for off-reservation gaming would be analyzed according to the IRA criteria *before* any consideration of the IGRA exceptions. Notably, the guidance stated that when the proposed gaming facility is not "within a commutable distance of the reservation," the "negative impacts on reservation life could be considerable." The negative impacts noted were the inability of tribal members to take advantage of job opportunities if they did not want to travel, and the possibility they would move off the reservation if they did want jobs at the facility. A commutable distance was defined as "the distance a reservation resident could reasonably commute on a regular basis to work at a tribal gaming facility located off-reservation." When the commutable distance standard was not met, the guidance stated, an application would not be granted "unless it carefully and comprehensively analyzes the potential negative impacts on reservation life and clearly demonstrates why these are outweighed by the financial benefits of tribal ownership in a distance gaming facility."

In addition to the "commutable distance" factor's effect on tribal life, the guidance also noted that the farther from reservation lands the gaming facility was, the "more the transfer of Indian jurisdiction to that parcel of land is likely to disrupt established governmental patterns." Similarly, the farther away the facility, the more difficulty the tribal governments would have "efficiently project[ing] and exercis[ing] [their] governmental and regulatory power." Land use concerns of local officials and the removal of the property from the tax roles also had to be given "greater weight."

The guidance was ill-received by many. Neither IRA nor IGRA constrained the Secretary's authority according to the land's distance from the reservation, bringing into question whether the guidance was flawed in its implementation of those statutes. Further, the guidance made a number of questionable assumptions, including that "employment off the reservation may have greater negative consequences than unemployment *on* the reservation." Kathryn R.L. Rand, Alan P. Meister & Steven Andrew Light, *Questionable Federal "Guidance" on Off-Reservation Indian Gaming: Legal and Economic Issues*, 12 Gaming L. Rev. & Econ. 194, 202 (2008) (emphasis in original). *See also* Alex Tallchief Skibine, *Indian Gaming and Cooperative Federalism*, 42 Ariz. St. L.J. 253 (2010).

With the election of President Obama in November 2008, the make-up of the Bureau of Indian Affairs changed, and this has led some to predict a less restrictive attitude toward the off-reservation gaming issue. *See* I. Nelson Rose, *Indian Gaming Law Update 2009*, 13 Gaming L. Rev. & Econ. 298 (2009) (calling the Obama administration "change tribes can believe in."); Dennis J. Whittlesey, *The NEW Obama Department of the Interior: the Good, the Bad and the Ugly*, Gaming Legal News (Dickinson Wright PLLC), Jan. 29, 2009, http://www.dickinsonwright.com/upload_files/intBE.PDF; Gale Courey Toensing, *Support Grows for 'Guidance Memo' Withdrawal*, Indian Country Today, May 27, 2009, http://www.indiancountrytoday.com/national/45845032.html (discussing letter sent by New York Governor David Paterson to the Department of the Interior urging a reversal of the "misguided policy"). Recently, Secretary Ken Salazar issued a memorandum urging the Department of Indian Affairs to "review current guidance and regulatory standards" when deciding the pending "off-reservation" applications. *See* Memorandum from Department of the Interior Secretary Ken Salazar, to Larry Echo-Hawk, Assistant Secretary of Indian Affairs (June 18, 2010), *available at* http://www.doi.gov/tribes/loader.cfm?csModule=security/getfile&PageID=36783. *See also* Press Release, Department of the Interior, Interior Details Path Forward on Indian Gaming Policy (June 28, 2010), *available at* http://www.doi.gov/news/pressreleases/Interior-Details-Path-Forward-on-Indian-Gaming-Policy.cfm (quoting Larry Echo Hawk as saying "we intend to continue to move forward not only on pending applications and requests for gaming on Indian lands, but also on meaningful consultation on federal Indian gaming policy in accordance with President Obama's commitment to the government-to-government relationship with tribal nations.").

Despite this criticism, are there valid questions about the spread of tribal gaming to locations within a state far-distant from tribal lands? Is it appropriate to require the Secretary to give considerable weight to concerns of local communities which would be impacted by a casino owned by a tribe that has its reservation lands many miles away? Is "reservation shopping" by non-Indian gaming developers a threat to states and local communities? Did IGRA contemplate the expansion of Indian gaming in this way? Or does this controversy just reflect an underlying animus held by many toward Indian gaming, a hostility that may be motivated by anti-competitive interests?

5. The issue of tribal lands and the taking property into trust has longstanding legal, historical, and political significance. While much of this has no direct relation to tribal gaming, a 2009 United States Supreme Court decision, Carcieri v. Salazar, 129 S. Ct. 1058 (2009), is an illustration of how tribal gaming can be affected by land trust issues. The IRA authorizes the Secretary of the Interior to acquire land and hold it in trust "for the purpose of providing land to Indians" and defines "Indian" to include all persons of Indian descent who are members "of any Indian tribe *now* under Federal jurisdiction." 25 U.S.C. § 479 (emphasis added). Through various dealings with the state of Rhode Island, the Narragansett Tribe had ceded their tribal lands and agreed to a "detribalization" law in the nineteenth century. After years of efforts by tribe members, the tribe was again formally recognized in 1983 by the Bureau of Indian Affairs. The tribe then purchased property which upon their request the Secretary of the Interior in 1998 took into trust for their benefit. This action was challenged by the Governor of Rhode Island. The tribe expressed no intention of using the land for a casino. The land, which was adjacent to the tribe's settlement lands, was going to be used for housing and the dispute related to whether the tribe would have to comply with local construction regulations.

The Supreme Court's opinion focused simply on the statutory phrase "now under Federal jurisdiction." Only if the tribe was "now" under the authority of the federal government could the Secretary take land into trust. Did "now" mean as of 1934, the date of the passage of the IRA? Or did "now" mean 1998, the date the Secretary took the property into trust? If the former, it was conceded that in 1934, the Narragansett Tribe was neither federally recognized nor under the jurisdiction of the federal government, and the Secretary therefore would not have the authority to take the tribe's land into trust. In a 6–3 decision, the Court held that the word "now" was in effect frozen in time and that only tribes recognized in 1934, the date of the IRA's enactment, could have property taken into trust for their benefit.

Though not set in a gaming law context, the decision has broad implications for tribes wanting to operate gaming venues. A tribe whose federal status had not been established by 1934 or is not part of a special congressional act will be unable to have the property taken into trust for any use. Since this is simply a matter of statutory interpretation, Congress could amend the IRA to make it clear that "now" meant as of the time the Secretary was taking the property into trust. For discussion of this *see* G. William Rice, *The Indian Reorganization Act, The Declaration on the Rights of Indigenous Peoples, and a Proposed* Carcieri *"Fix": Updating the Trust Land Acquisition Process*, 45 IDAHO L. REV. 575 (2009). Recently, the House Interior Appropriations Subcommittee submitted proposed changes to the IRA that would "fix" the *Carcieri* decision. Approval from Congress is far from certain. *See* Dave Palermo, Carcieri *"Fix" Faces Uncertain Future in Senate*, GAMBLING COMPLIANCE, July 26, 2010, http://www.gamblingcompliance.com/node/43768.

F. The Powers of the National Indian Gaming Commission (NIGC)

i. Generally

Section 5 of IGRA establishes the NIGC within the Department of the Interior. IGRA devotes considerable detail to the creation, staffing, and powers of the NIGC. The chair of the NIGC is appointed by the President for a three year term, while the Secretary of the Interior appoints the two associate members. IGRA specifies political party balance in the membership, and requires that at least two of the members of the NIGC be enrolled members of any Indian tribe. *See* 25 U.S.C. § 2704(b) (3). The "Welcome" page of the NIGC web site describes the purpose of the NIGC:

> The Commission's primary mission is to regulate gaming activities on Indian lands for the purpose of shielding Indian tribes from organized crime and other corrupting influences; to ensure that Indian tribes are the primary beneficiaries of gaming revenue; and to assure that gaming is conducted fairly and honestly by both operators and players.

National Indian Gaming Commission Home Page, www.nigc.gov (last visited August 9, 2010). IGRA sets out the powers of the NIGC primarily in sections 2705 and 2706. The Commission's web site gives some indication of the scope of those powers:

> To achieve these goals, the Commission is authorized to conduct investigations; undertake enforcement actions, including the issuance of violation, assessment of civil fines, and/or issuance of closure orders; conduct background investigations; conduct audits; and review and approve Tribal gaming ordinances.

Id. There are several issues involving the NIGC that create controversy. As discussed previously, NIGC plays a significant role in classifying games as Class II or Class III. If the game is classified as Class II, it may be operated without a tribal-state compact, and such games fall within the monitoring responsibilities of NIGC. Over the years, NIGC has offered advisory opinions on particular games and promulgated regulations on the aid vs. facsimile issue. These "Game Classification Opinions" are compiled on the NIGC website for review. A related power given to NIGC by IGRA is the overall responsibility for monitoring Class II gaming, including inspections, background investigations, and auditing authority. As the subsequent materials demonstrate, while the approval of the Chair of the Commission is required for a tribe to offer Class III gaming, the NIGC's authority over Class III gaming is otherwise significantly circumscribed by IGRA. The following sections focus on two of the most problematic areas of NIGC regulation.

ii. Management Contracts

The Chairman of the NIGC also has the responsibility for approving management contracts that tribes enter into for both Class II and Class III gaming, although the requirements for approval differ according to classification. *See* 25 U.S.C. §2711 (Class II), 25 U.S.C. §2710 (Class III). This power, formerly held by the Secretary of the Interior, was transferred to the Chair of the NIGC in section 2705 of IGRA. As the material below illustrates, failure to obtain approval of a management contract can have grave consequences.

United States ex rel. Bernard v. Casino Magic Corp.

293 F.3d 419 (8th Cir. 2002)

HEANEY, Circuit Judge.

The United States and its realtor, Maynard Bernard, appeal an adverse grant of summary judgment in this qui tam action.[1] We hold the district court erred as a matter of law in concluding there was no management agreement, and reverse and remand for further action consistent with this opinion.

I. Background

A. Management and Consulting Agreements

We adopt the factual findings of the district court, which we summarize here. In 1993, the Sisseton-Wahpeton Sioux Tribe (the Tribe) became interested in building and operating a casino on Indian trust land within the Tribe's Lake Traverse Reservation in North Dakota. The Tribe entered into a management agreement with Casino Magic on July 22, 1994. The agreement, created in accordance with the Indian Gaming Regulatory Act, 25 U.S.C. §2701 et seq. (IGRA), provided that Casino Magic would become the manager of the Sisseton-Wahpeton Dakota Nation Casino Gaming Enterprise, to be known as Dakota Magic Casino. For a management agreement involving Indian land to become a binding legal document, it must be approved by the National Indian Gaming Commission (NIGC). *See* 25 U.S.C. §§2710(d) (9), 2711.[2] The Tribe and Casino Magic agreed that

---

1. United States ex rel. Steele v. Turn Key Gaming, Inc., 260 F.3d 971, 973–74 (8th Cir. 2001) (rehearing en banc denied Oct. 16, 2001) (quoting 25 U.S.C. §81), states:

> 25 U.S.C. §81 governs all contracts with an Indian tribe whereby the tribe trades consideration for "services for said Indians relative to their lands." All such agreements must "bear the approval of the Secretary of the Interior and the Commissioner of Indian Affairs indorsed upon [them]." Any agreement subject to Section 81, but not so indorsed, "shall be null and void, and all money or other thing of value paid to any person by any Indian or tribe ... may be recovered by suit in the name of the United States."

2. "IGRA recognizes a tribe's authority to enter into contracts for the management and operation of an Indian gaming facility by an entity other than the tribe or its employees, so long as certain requirements are satisfied and subject to approval by the Chairman of the National Indian Gaming Commission." Casino Resource Corp. v. Harrah's Entertainment, 243 F.3d 435, 438 n.3 (8th Cir. 2001) (citing 25 U.S.C. §§2710(d)(9), 2711). Although the IGRA was passed in 1988, the regulatory scheme created by the Act did not take effect until the NIGC came into existence, some five years later. The preexisting regulatory scheme, administered by the Bureau of Indian Affairs, remained in effect until 1993. *See* U.S. ex rel. Mosay v. Buffalo Bros. Mgt., Inc., 20 F.3d 739, 744 (7th Cir. 1994). Today, the BIA reviews certain consulting agreements with Tribes related to Indian gaming that do not constitute management agreements subject to NIGC review.

such approval was a condition precedent to the contract becoming a binding legal document. The agreement was submitted to the NIGC but was never approved for reasons not clarified by the record.

On September 15, 1994, after finalizing the terms of the management contract, and perhaps anticipating that the Management Agreement would be approved, the Tribe and Casino Magic entered into a Secured Loan Agreement. Under the terms of this agreement, Casino Magic agreed to loan up to $5 million to the Tribe so that it could begin to build the casino. It was contemplated by both parties that once the management contract was approved, the proceeds of the loan would be repaid. In September 1994, Casino Magic advanced $4,102,718.45 to the Tribe, which the Tribe later repaid once it received a $17.5 million loan from the BNC National Bank of Bismark, North Dakota, (BNC).

Because the Management Agreement was never approved, the parties entered into a Consulting Agreement on March 13, 1996, under which Casino Magic was to become a consultant to assist the Tribe in developing and operating the gaming enterprise. The Consulting Agreement specifically stated that Casino Magic had no management authority over the casino. It agreed to "conduct market feasibility studies, develop and identify market plans, and to provide an accounting system, written system of internal controls, security plan, and a job classification system with training." United States Ex. Rel. Maynard Bernard v. Casino Magic Corp., Civ. 98-1033, slip op. at 4 n. 2 (D. S.D. April 23, 2001).... Casino Magic also agreed to develop a long-term master plan for the casino.

The parties submitted the Consulting Agreement to the NIGC for approval to avoid any future dispute regarding the legitimacy of the agreement. The NIGC determined that the Consulting Agreement was not a management contract and therefore did not require the approval of the NIGC. In its February 7, 1996 letter to the Tribe, the NIGC wrote:

> While Casino Magic will be advising and consulting on many aspects of the gaming enterprise, pursuant to the Consulting Agreement, the Tribe will retain ultimate control and direction of the casino operation. Because the Consulting Agreement does not provide for the management of all or part of the Tribe's gaming operation by any person or entity other than the Tribe or its employees, it is not a management contract. Therefore this Agreement does not require the approval of the Chairman.

The BIA also approved the Consulting Agreement. It sent a Section 81 Accommodation Approval and Disclaimer to the parties in February, 1996. The disclaimer stated in part:

> The Department has reviewed this Agreement, determined that it does not constitute an agreement relative to the Tribe's trust land or other trust assets and, therefore, this Agreement is not subject to the provisions of 25 U.S.C. §81. As a result, this statute does not limit or impair the Tribe's capacity to make or enter into this agreement without obtaining the approval of the Secretary of the Interior and the Commissioner of Indian Affairs.

B. The Construction and Term Loan Agreement and the Participation Agreement

On June 7, 1996, BNC and the Tribe entered into a Construction and Term Loan Agreement. Under the terms of the agreement, BNC agreed to make advances to the Tribe in the aggregate amount of $17.5 million, conditioned upon Casino Magic's commitment to contribute to the loan up to $5 million, or 28.6 percent of the loan. Article V, Section 5.1(p) of the Agreement obliged the Tribe to "accept and comply with all of the recommendations made by the Consultant under the Consulting Agreement, except to the extent that any such recommendations are not consistent with current Indian Gaming Practices or industry standards." ... Casino Magic was not a party to the Construction and Term Loan Agreement. The district court determined that Casino Magic's status as "consultant" continued after the Construction and Term Loan Agreement became effective.

On June 28, 1996, BNC and Casino Magic entered into a Participation Agreement to formalize Casino Magic's consent to contribute a percentage of the Tribe's financing for the casino. The Participation Agreement stated in relevant part: "this loan participation [agreement] constitutes a sale of a percentage ownership interest in the referenced indebtedness, and, collateral security and in the 'loan documents'... and shall not be construed as an extension of credit by [Casino Magic] to [BNC]."

The parties submitted the Construction and Term Loan Agreement to the BIA for § 81 approval, but it was not submitted to the NIGC. On July 10, 1996, the BIA issued a Section 81 Accommodation Approval and Disclaimer letter stating, "The Department has reviewed the documents, determined that they do not constitute an agreement relative to the Tribe's trust land or other trust assets and, therefore, the Documents are not subject to the provisions of 25 U.S.C. § 81."

The Tribe received its first advance from the approved loan after receipt of this letter. As part of this first disbursement, Casino Magic received a cashier's check from BNC in the amount of $4,102,718.45 to satisfy the Tribe's pre-existing loan obligation under the 1994 Secured Loan Agreement.

On January 15, 1998, Casino Magic requested a consulting fee payment from the Tribe under the terms of the Consulting Agreement. On January 28, 1998, before paying the consulting fee, the Tribe terminated the Consulting Agreement. Following termination, the Tribe submitted the Consulting Agreement and the Construction and Term Loan Agreement to the NIGC for joint review. After inspecting both documents, the NIGC stated in relevant part:

> Certain provisions of the submitted documents are of particular concern to the construction of the management contract. More specifically, Section 5.1(p) of the Construction and Term Loan Agreement requires that the Tribe "accept and comply with all of the recommendations made by the Consultant under the Consulting Agreement ..." pg. 17. The Agreement further provides that ... "[T]he Tribe will maintain the Consulting Agreement ... in full force and effect ...", and limits the Tribe's ability to terminate the Agreement while there is any outstanding balance due to the BNC National Bank. Section 5.1(g) pgs. 17–18. As mentioned in your request letter dated February 12, 1998, these provisions call into question the actual relationship between the Sisseton-Wahpeton Sioux Tribe and CMA.
> After careful review, we have determined that the Consulting Agreement and related documents, when considered as a whole, are management contracts. As such, the submitted documents require the approval of the Chairman of the NIGC.

The Tribe replaced Casino Magic with another consulting company, and on October 9, 1997, Bernard filed a qui tam action on behalf of the United States government claiming that 25 U.S.C. § 81, 18 U.S.C. § 438, and 25 U.S.C. § 2711 had been violated. He alleged that the Consulting Agreement and the Construction and Term Loan Agreement, when considered together, comprised a management contract that required NIGC approval. He argued that the parties' failure to seek such approval voided the contracts under § 81, requiring Casino's Magic's return of an amount in excess of $7 million dollars "extracted from the Tribe" under the unapproved agreement.

Casino Magic sought summary judgment as a matter of law, contending that there was no § 81 violation because the Consulting Agreement was approved by the BIA on behalf of the Secretary of the Interior and the Commissioner of Indian Affairs, and was reviewed by the NIGC, which concluded it did not have to approve the contract because it was not a management agreement. Casino Magic also asserted that it had not been paid any fees by the Tribe; it had only been reimbursed the $4,102,718.45 that it had advanced to the Tribe for construction, plus an additional $350,000 it had advanced to the Tribe for other expenses. The district court granted Casino Magic's motion, holding that, contrary to Bernard's contention, the Construction and Term Loan Agreement between the Tribe and BNC did not convert the Consulting Agreement into a management contract requiring the approval of the NIGC. It stated:

> [t]he record is clear that Casino Magic performed its consulting duties in a manner that resulted in the development of a well planned and maintained casino. When the casino became profitable and Casino Magic demanded payment pursuant to the Consulting Agreement, the tribe terminated their relationship and later submitted the Consulting Agreement and the Construction Loan Agreement [sic] to the NIGC with the suggestion that, when read jointly, they comprised a "management contract" requiring approval under 25 U.S.C. § 81 and § 2711. Because Congress never intended the qui tam provision of § 81 to be used in the manner proposed by plaintiff, and based upon the reasons stated above, it is hereby ordered that Casino Magic's motion for [summary judgment] is granted.

United States Ex. Rel. Maynard Bernard v. Casino Magic Corp., Civ. 98-1033, slip op. at 14–15 (D. S.D. April 23, 2001) (order granting motion for summary judgment) (footnote omitted).

On appeal, Bernard asks us to consider whether the district court: erred in granting summary judgment in favor of Casino Magic; ... We reverse the grant of summary judgment, hold that the agreements, when considered together, constituted a management agreement, and remand for action consistent with this opinion.

II. Discussion

....

The primary issue between the parties is whether the Consulting Agreement, the Construction and Term Loan Agreement, and the Participation Agreement together, as a matter of law, comprised a management agreement (or a series of management agreements) not properly approved by the NIGC in accordance with 25 U.S.C. § 2711, and therefore unenforceable. If the agreements were in fact invalid, the Tribe expects Casino Magic to return *any fees* paid to it under the terms of the invalid agreements, excluding the Tribe's secured loan repayment to Casino Magic and any other out-of-pocket expense.

A. The Effect of the Three Agreements

After reviewing the Consulting Agreement and the Construction and Term Loan Agreement entered into by the Tribe and BNC, the district court held that the Tribe's agreement to "accept and comply with all recommendations made by the Consultant" in section 5.1(p) of the Construction and Term Loan Agreement was "insufficient to change Casino Magic's obligations to the tribe from that of a consultant to that of a manager." United States Ex. Rel. Maynard Bernard v. Casino Magic Corp., Civ. 98-1033, slip op. at 14 (D. S.D. April 23, 2001). The court determined that the record was "devoid of any facts from which a reasonable jury could find that Casino Magic began to act as a manager after the Construction and Term Loan Agreement was finalized." *Id.*

We disagree. When the NIGC had the opportunity to review the Consulting Agreement and the Construction and Term Loan Agreement together, it determined that the documents created a management agreement, requiring NIGC approval under 25 U.S.C. § 2711. Without such approval, the agreements were invalid. Moreover, the Participation Agreement gave Casino Magic a percentage ownership interest in the Tribe's indebtedness. That interest, combined with the other documents' impact, transferred more authority to Casino Magic than what the Consulting Agreement, reviewed by the NIGC and the BIA, actually provided. The Consulting Agreement stipulated that the "Consultant has no management authority or control with regard to the Enterprise or the Existing Facilities, but shall act only as a consultant offering consulting services.... [A]ll decision-making authority shall rest solely with the Tribe." ... The Tribe's ultimate authority, however, was effectively revoked by the terms of section 5.1(p) of the Construction and Term Loan Agreement, which mandated the Tribe's compliance with Casino Magic's recommendations.

The district court advanced four reasons for its decision to grant summary judgment in favor of Casino Magic. We do not find these reasons persuasive. First, the court explained that "the post-cancellation of the [Consulting Agreement] does not provide Bernard with a cause of action under § 81." United States Ex. Rel. Maynard Bernard v. Casino Magic Corp., Civ. 98-1033, slip op. at 13 (D. S.D. April 23, 2001).... At first opportunity, the Chairman of the NIGC held that the Consulting Agreement and the Construction and Term Loan Agreement, considered together, were management contracts.... Casino Magic was aware of the combined effect of all agreements, and it assumed the risk of proceeding without having submitted all documents to the Chairman. We therefore find that Bernard did, in fact, have a valid cause of action under § 81.

Second, the district court explained that Casino Magic was not a party to the Construction and Term Loan Agreement, and neither that agreement nor the Participation Agreement mandated the condition that Casino Magic assume managerial responsibilities of the casino. Although this finding is correct, it does not change the fact that Casino Magic was aware of the terms of the Construction and Term Loan Agreement, which limited the Tribe's powers and enhanced those of Casino Magic. A management contract includes the principal contract and "all collateral agreements to such contract that relate to the gaming activity." 25 U.S.C. § 2711(a)(3). The three agreements discussed above served as a management contract implicitly if not explicitly.

Third, the court below stated, "the record is devoid of any facts from which a jury could find that Casino Magic began to act as a manager after the Construction and Term Loan Agreement was finalized." United States Ex. Rel. Maynard Bernard v. Casino Magic Corp., Civ. 98-1033, slip op. at 14 (D. S.D. April 23, 2001) ... In our view, this lack of evidence is irrelevant. The issue is whether Casino Magic, in fact, had managerial control. The NIGC found that it had, given the combined effect of the series of agreements. We defer to that finding. *See* Bruce H. Lien Co. v. Three Affiliated Tribes, 93 F.3d 1412, 1418 n.10 (8th Cir. 1996) ("a permissible agency interpretation on this issue [of whether the management contract requires NIGC review] would merit considerable deference") (citing Arkansas AFL-CIO v. FCC, 11 F.3d 1430, 1441 (8th Cir. 1993)).

Finally, the court explained that Congress did not intend § 81 to be used "as a sword to regain monies paid under a series of agreements" serving only to benefit the Tribe. *Id.* The district court cites no authority for this proposition, and we find none. The law is clear that management agreements must be approved by the Chairman of the NIGC. Without that approval, invalid management fees must be recovered on behalf of the Tribe. We cannot ignore the plain words of § 2711 nor the Chairman's findings that taken as a whole, the series of agreements constituted a management agreement. Thus, appellant is entitled to recover any fees paid by the Tribe to Casino Magic.

....

III. Conclusion

The district court erred in holding as a matter of law that the Consulting Agreement, the Construction and Term Loan Agreement, and the Participation Agreement constituted a consulting agreement rather than a management agreement. We reverse the district court's grant of summary judgment and remand for proceedings consistent with this opinion.

Notes

1. On remand in *Casino Magic*, the district court awarded damages of $350,000. This was affirmed on appeal. 384 F.3d 510 (8th Cir. 2004). Tribes enter management contracts to take advantage of the expertise of entities that have business acumen when it comes to operating a casino and maximizing revenues. NIGC approval of these agreements is apparently an effort at least in part to protect tribes from unscrupulous operators. Is this sort of paternalism really necessary or appropriate? Should tribes be expected to engage in "due diligence" on their own to determine the trustworthiness of a business seeking to enter a management contract with the tribe, and to negotiate a contract that is in its favor?

2. In addition to the management agreement, "collateral" agreements, those that are "related, directly or indirectly, to a management contract, or to any rights duties or obligations created between a tribe ... and a management contractor," must also be submitted to the NIGC for approval. 25 C.F.R. § 502.5 (2007).

Given the consequences of a determination that an agreement with a tribe constitutes a management contract, why wouldn't a party always submit any agreement with a tribe to the NIGC for approval? Consider the following: (1) the approval process can be lengthy and costly. In many business transactions, time is of the essence and waiting for bureaucratic approval may chill the ardor of the parties. This concern creates an incentive to draft an agreement so that is a consulting agreement and not a management agreement; (2) in *Casino Magic*, the court referred to "participation agreements," "loan agreements," "consulting agreements," as well as management agreements. While no one document was titled a management contract, the court agreed with NIGC's conclusion that the other agreements, taken as a whole, constituted a management contract. In other words, it may not be clear that an agreement is a management contract that needs to be submitted for NIGC approval; (3) a party can submit even questionable agreements, that is, ones the party is relatively certain does not constitute a management agreement, with the hope of receiving a "declination" letter from the NIGC. This is a letter indicating the agreement does not need NIGC approval. Even these letters may take some time to obtain, with the concomitant problems of delay. In addition, as the *Casino Magic* case makes clear, subsequent agreements can have an effect on whether an overall set of transactions has produced a management agreement. A party may have to return to the NIGC for another declination letter or confirmation that subsequent agreements have not converted the arrangement into a management contract. Would these requirements frustrate the IGRA objective of giving tribes the opportunity to offer gambling so as to promote tribal self-sufficiency? Is

NIGC's approval role unnecessary given the experience tribes have gained since IGRA was enacted in 1988?

3. The NIGC offers assistance on the management contract issue. There are "Helpful Hints for Submitting a Management Contract and Obtaining the Chairman's Approval;" there is a "Checklist for New Management Contracts;" and examples of "Approved Management Contracts." *See* National Indian Gaming Commission, http://www.nigc.gov/Reading_Room/Management_Contracts.aspx. However, some commentators have questioned the helpfulness of the NIGC regulations on management contracts, and urge counsel to err on the side of submitting agreements to the NIGC. *See, e.g.*, Heidi McNeil Staudenmaier & Ruth K. Khalsa, *Theseus, The Labyrinth, and the Ball of String: Navigating the Regulatory Maze to Ensure Enforceability of Tribal Gaming Contracts*, 40 J. MARSHALL L. REV. 1123 (2007) (noting that NIGC has considered "the method for calculating the contractor's compensation (flat fee or percentage of gaming revenue); the length of the agreement's term; and whether the consultant will also perform activities that the NIGC considers to be management-related" to be important criteria in determining whether an agreement is a management contract). *See also* Heidi McNeil Staudenmaier, *Negotiating Enforceable Tribal Gaming Management Agreements*, 7 GAMING L. REV. 31, 36 (2003) (arguing that *Casino Magic* and other cases "harshly underscore the need of parties pursuing any type of a business relationship with a tribal gaming operation to seek NIGC and BIA review of the transaction documents and, where appropriate, the issuance of a declination letter. Failure to obtain such assurances can lead to void and unenforceable agreements, without remedy or recourse."); Kevin K. Washburn, *The Mechanics of Indian Gaming Management Contract Approval*, 8 GAMING L. REV. 333 (2004) (comprehensive article supplying valuable guidance as to how management agreement process operates).

4. A 2010 federal district court decision, Wells Fargo Bank, N.A. v. Lake of The Torches Economic Development Corp., 677 F. Supp. 2d 1056 (W.D. Wis. 2010), is perhaps the most dramatic example of what can happen when there is a mistaken belief that agreements need not be vetted with the NIGC for entities dealing with tribes. The court ruled that the language of a trust indenture gave a receiver substantial control over key financial and personnel decisions and amounted to a management contract that, because it had not been submitted to NIGC for approval, was invalid. This had the effect of invalidating the $50 million bond agreement. *See* Alexandra Berzon, *Tribal-Casino Loans are Tested by Ruling*, WALL ST. J., May 12, 2010, *available at* http://online.wsj.com/article/NA_WSJ_PUB: SB10001424052748703565804575238621598513454.html (noting that purchasers of bonds had relied on assurances from tribe's attorneys that bond documents did not constitute a management agreement and did not need to be submitted to the NIGC).

5. For other cases dealing with the dynamics of management contracts, *see* Jena Band of Choctaw Indians v. Tri-Millennium Corp. Inc., 387 F. Supp. 2d 671 (W.D. La. 2005) (holding that agreement granting two developers the rights to conduct first gaming operations in casino under construction was management contract requiring approval under IGRA); First Am. Kickapoo Operations, L.L.C. v. Multimedia Games, Inc., 412 F.3d 1166 (10th Cir. 2005) (under Oklahoma law, unauthorized management provisions of agreement were not severable; therefore entire agreement was invalid under IGRA); United States ex rel Saints Regis Mohawk Tribe v. St. Regis Mgmt. Co., 451 F.3d 44 (2d Cir. 2006) (notwithstanding invalidity of management contract, tribe did not have standing to bring declaratory judgment action prior to exhaustion of administrative remedies).

iii. *NIGC Authority over Class III Gaming*

Colorado River Indian Tribes v.
National Indian Gaming Commission

466 F.3d 134 (D.C. Cir. 2006)

RANDOLPH, Circuit Judge.

This is an appeal from an order of the district court, Bates, J., granting summary judgment in favor of the Colorado River Indian Tribes and against the National Indian Gaming Commission, the Commission's Chairman, and two of its members. Colo. River Indian Tribes v. Nat'l Indian Gaming Comm'n, 383 F. Supp. 2d 123 (D.D.C. 2005). The issue is whether the Indian Gaming Regulatory Act, 25 U.S.C. §§ 2701–2721, gives the Commission authority to promulgate regulations establishing mandatory operating procedures for certain kinds of gambling in tribal casinos....

The Tribe operates the BlueWater Resort and Casino on Indian lands in Parker, Arizona. The casino offers what the Act defines as "class II" and "class III" gaming. Class II gaming includes bingo; "non-banking" card games; and pull-tabs, lotto, and other games similar to bingo, if played in the same location. 25 U.S.C. § 2703(7)(A), (B). Class III gaming includes most conventional forms of casino gaming such as slot machines, roulette, and blackjack. *Id.* § 2703(8); 25 C.F.R. § 502.4. Class I gaming consists of social gaming for minimal prizes and traditional forms of Indian gaming in connection with tribal ceremonies. 25 U.S.C. § 2703(6).

The Act treats each gaming class differently.... As to class II gaming, the Commission and the tribes share regulatory authority: the tribes must enact a gaming ordinance applying the Act's minimum regulatory requirements; and the Commission's Chairman must approve the tribal ordinance before gaming may occur. *Id.* § 2710(a)(2), (b). The Act regulates how tribes engaging in class II gaming may make payments to tribal members, *id.* § 2710(b)(3), and it requires an annual outside audit of the gaming and various contracts, *id.* § 2710(b)(2)(C), (D).

Like class II gaming, class III gaming is lawful only if it takes place on Indian land "in a State that permits such gaming for any purpose by any person, organization, or entity...." *Id.* § 2710(d)(1)(B). But unlike class II gaming, a tribe conducts class III gaming pursuant to a compact with the state. *Id.* § 2710(d)(1)(C). The Secretary of the Interior must approve any such compact before it may become effective. *Id.* § 2710(d)(3)(B). Thereafter, the "Tribal-State compact govern[s] the conduct of gaming activities," *id.* § 2710(d)(3)(A), and the tribe's class III gaming operations must be "conducted in conformance" with the compact, *id.* § 2710(d)(1)(C). Tribal-state compacts may contain provisions related to "standards for the operation of such activity" and "any other subjects that are directly related to the operation of gaming activities." *Id.* § 2710(d)(3)(C)(vi), (vii). The Commission must approve any tribal ordinances for regulating and conducting class III gaming and any contracts the tribe enters into for the management of its class III gaming. *Id.* § 2710(d)(1)(A)(iii), (d)(9).

The Colorado River Indian Tribes regulates gaming at its BlueWater casino pursuant to a tribal ordinance and rules contained in a tribal-state class III gaming compact with the State of Arizona ... Both the ordinance and the compact contain their own internal control standards. The most recent version of the compact requires the Tribe's gaming agency to create standards governing operating procedures that are at least as stringent as those contained in the rules the Commission promulgated in 1999. *Gaming Compact* § 3(b)(3)(B). The State of Arizona monitors the Tribe's compliance with the standards, for which the Tribe reimburses the state about $250,000 per year. The Tribe's gaming agency employs twenty-nine employees and has an annual budget of $1.2 million.

In 1999 the Commission promulgated regulations, which it termed "Minimum Internal Control Standards," governing class II and class III gaming. *See* 64 Fed. Reg. 590 (Jan. 5, 1999) (codified as amended at 25 C.F.R. pt. 542). The regulations take up more than eighty pages in the Code of Federal Regulations. No operational detail is overlooked. The rules establish standards for individual games, *see, e.g.,* 25 C.F.R. § 542.7, .8, .10, customer credit, *id.* § 542.15, information technology, *id.* § 542.16, complimentary services, *id.* § 542.17, and many other aspects of gaming. To illustrate, tribes must establish "a reasonable time period" not to exceed seven days for removing playing cards from play, but "if a gaming operation uses plastic cards (not plastic-coated cards), the cards may be used for up to three (3) months if the plastic cards are routinely inspected, and washed or cleaned in a manner and time frame approved by the Tribal gaming regulatory authority." *Id.* § 542.9(d), (e). To take another example the district court mentioned, coin drops are regulated differently according to the size of the gaming facility. *See id.* § 542.21, .31, .41. There are rules prescribing the number and type of employees who must be involved in the removal of the coin drop, *id.* § 542.21(g)(1), the timing of the removal of the coin drop, *id.* § 542.21(g)(2), the tagging and transportation of the coin drop, *id.* § 542.21(g)(4), the manner in which the coin drop must be housed while in the machine, *id.* § 542.21(g)(5), and the purposes for which a coin drop may be used, *id.* § 542.21(g)(6).

In January 2001, the Commission sought to audit the Tribe's class III gaming at the Blue-Water casino in order to determine whether the Tribe was complying with the regulations. The Tribe protested on the ground that the rules exceeded the Commission's authority under the Act. The auditors departed and the Commission issued a notice of violation. After administrative hearings, the Commission fined the Tribe $2,000 for terminating the audit. *Colo. River,* 383 F. Supp. 2d at 130. The Commission denied the Tribe's objection, citing its authority to "promulgate such regulations and guidelines as it deems appropriate to implement the provisions" of the Act, 25 U.S.C. § 2706(b)(10), among which is the provision stating that one of the Act's purposes is to protect the integrity of gaming revenue, *id.* § 2702. In re Colo. River Indian Tribes, NOV/CFA 01-01, 5–6 (Nat'l Indian Gaming Comm'n May 30, 2002) (*NIGC Final Order*). The Commission located its power to audit the casino in § 2706(b)(4), which authorizes the Commission to "audit all papers, books, and records respecting gross revenues of class II gaming conducted on Indian lands and any other matters necessary to carry out the duties of the Commission under this chapter...." *See NIGC Final Order* at 7. The Tribe brought an action in federal district court challenging the decision and the Commission's statutory authority to regulate class III gaming. The district court reached the "inescapable conclusion" that Congress did not intend to give such broad authority to the Commission, and therefore vacated the Commission's decision and declared the regulations unlawful as applied to class III gaming. *Colo. River,* 383 F. Supp. 2d at 132.

There was a time when the Commission agreed with the district court's view of the Act. The first Chairman of the Commission notified the Inspector General of the Department of the Interior in 1993 that "the regulation of class III gaming was not assigned to the Commission but was left to the tribes and the states...." Memorandum from Anthony J. Hope, Chairman, Nat'l Indian Gaming Comm'n to the Assistant Inspector General for Audits, Dep't of the Interior 2 (Oct. 18, 1993). He explained that this was why the Commission had not imposed "gaming control standards" on class III gaming: "the Act assigns those responsibilities to the tribes and/or the states." *Id.* The Commission's Chairman took the same position when he testified before Congress the following year. *See Manner in which Gaming Activities Are Regulated by the Several States and the Role of the Federal Government in the Regulation of Indian Gaming Activities: Hearing Before the S. Comm. on Indian Affairs,* 103d Cong. 7–8 (1994) (testimony of Chairman Hope, Nat'l Indian

Gaming Comm'n). Despite many legislative efforts since then, all of which are cited in Judge Bates's careful opinion, 383 F. Supp. 2d at 142 n.13, Congress has never amended the Act to confer any such express power on the Commission.

Even now the Commission concedes that no provision of the Act explicitly grants it the power to impose operational standards on class III gaming. Section 2706 grants the Commission authority over several aspects of class II regulation. Thus, the Commission "shall monitor class II gaming," and "inspect and examine all premises located on Indian lands on which class II gaming is conducted...." 25 U.S.C. §2706(b)(1), (2). It "may demand access to and inspect, examine, photocopy, and audit all papers, books, and records respecting gross revenues of class II gaming conducted on Indian lands and any other matters necessary to carry out the duties of the Commission under this chapter...." Id. §2706(b)(4). While the statute grants the Commission audit authority over "any other matters necessary to carry out [its] duties," the statute does not indicate that these duties extend to class III regulation. Instead, the main provision dealing with the regulation of class III gaming—§2710(d)—contemplates joint tribal-state regulation. The Act describes tribal-state compacts as agreements "governing the conduct of [class III] gaming activities." Id. §2710(d)(3)(A). A compact may contain provisions relating to "the application of the criminal and civil laws and regulations of the Indian tribe or the State that are directly related to, and necessary for, the licensing and regulation of" class III gaming, id. §2710(d)(3)(C)(i), "standards for the operation of such activity," id. §2710(d)(3)(C)(vi), and "any other subjects that are directly related to the operation of [class III] gaming activities," id. §2710(d)(3)(C)(vii). That the Act sets up concurrent tribal-state regulation of class III gaming, not tribal-state-Commission regulation, is evident from §2710(d)(5): "Nothing in this subsection shall impair the right of an Indian tribe to regulate class III gaming on its Indian lands concurrently with the State, except to the extent that such regulation is inconsistent with, or less stringent than"—not Commission regulations, but—"the State laws and regulations made applicable by any Tribal-State compact entered into by the Indian tribe under paragraph (3) that is in effect." Contrast this provision with §542.4(c) of the regulations, which states that if a standard in the Commission's regulations is more stringent than a standard in a tribal-state compact, the Commission's regulation "shall prevail." 25 C.F.R. §542.4(c). There are other indications that Congress intended to leave the regulation of class III gaming to the tribes and the states, including the fact that the Secretary of the Interior—rather than the Commission—approves (or disapproves) tribal-state compacts regulating class III gaming. 25 U.S.C. §2710(d)(3)(B). The significance of this provision and others is thoroughly discussed in Judge Bates's opinion in the district court, 383 F. Supp. 2d at 135–38, and need not be repeated here.

As against this, the Commission offers three main arguments. One is that the Commission has "oversight" authority over class III gaming, that the dictionary defines "oversight" to mean "supervision," and that the Commission's regulation of class III gaming falls within that definition. The trouble is that the Act does not use the word "oversight." The Commission relies not on statutory language, but on a sentence from the Senate committee report on the Act: "The Commission will have a regulatory role for class II gaming and an oversight role with respect to class III gaming." S. REP. No. 100-446, at 1 (1988), reprinted in 1988 U.S.C.C.A.N. 3071, 3071. But just two sentences before the "oversight" passage, the report states that the Senate bill "provides for a system for joint regulation by tribes and the Federal Government of class II gaming on Indian lands and a system for compacts between tribes and States for regulation of class III gaming." Id. One might wonder why the Committee would rely on tribal-state compacts to regulate class III gaming. The report gives this explanation: "the Committee notes that there is no adequate Federal regulatory system in place for class III gaming, nor do tribes have such systems for the regulation of class III gaming currently in place. Thus a logical choice is to make use of existing State regulatory systems, although the adoption of State law is not tantamount to an accession to State jurisdiction. The use of State regulatory systems can be accomplished through negotiated compacts but this is not to say that tribal governments can have no role to play in regulation of class III gaming—many can and will." *Id.* at 13, 1988 U.S.C.C.A.N. at 3083–84. In addition to the point that a committee report is not law, it is perfectly clear that whatever the Senate committee thought "oversight" might entail, the committee did not foresee the Commission regulating class III gaming.

The Commission's other arguments proceed from the text of the Act. The Commission is funded by a percentage of each tribe's gross gaming revenues from class II and class III gaming. 25 U.S.C. §2717(a). To this end, tribes must submit annual "outside audits" to the Commission of their class II and class III gaming operations. *Id.* §2710(b)(2)(C), (d)(1)(A)(ii). From this the Commission infers that it has the authority to regulate the handling and accounting of gaming receipts in order to ensure the integrity of audits. We cannot see how the right to receive an outside audit, presumably conducted in accordance with Generally Accepted Auditing Standards, translates into a power to control gaming operations. Under the Securities Exchange Act of 1934, public companies must file reports necessary to the protection of investors. *See* 15 U.S.C. §78m(a). If the public company happened to be in the casino business, such as Harrah's Entertainment, Inc., the Commission's logic here would entitle the SEC to dictate the details of how Harrah's conducts its casino operations because the SEC receives reports from the company. The SEC obviously has no such authority, and neither does the Commission.

This brings us to the Commission's third argument—namely, that its regulations are valid in light of its authority to "promulgate such regulations and guidelines as it deems proper to implement the provisions of [the Act]." 25 U.S.C. §2706(b) (10). Mourning v. Family Publications Service, Inc., 411 U.S. 356 (1973), the Commission tells us, states a canon of statutory interpretation for general rulemaking provisions such as this—regulations promulgated pursuant to such statutes are valid so long as they are "reasonably related to the purposes of the enabling legislation." *Id.* at 369 ... Judge Bates rejected this argument and so do we. An agency's general rulemaking authority does not mean that the specific rule the agency promulgates is a valid exercise of that authority.... So here....

In arguing that the regulations implement the provisions of the Act, the Commission points to §2702, the Act's general declaration of policy, which it says embodies the congressional purpose to promote integrity in Indian gaming, a purpose the Commission's regulations further. But this cannot carry the Commission as far as it needs to go. We have observed before that "[a]ll questions of government are ultimately questions of ends and means." ... Agencies are therefore "bound, not only by the ultimate purposes Congress has selected, but by the means it has deemed appropriate, and prescribed, for the pursuit of those purposes." ... The Commission is correct that Congress wanted to ensure the integrity of Indian gaming, but it is equally clear that Congress wanted to do this in a particular way. The declared policy is therefore not simply to shield Indian tribes "from organized crime and other corrupting influences" and "to assure that gaming is conducted fairly and honestly by both the operator and players," 25 U.S.C. §2702(2), but to accomplish this through the "statutory basis for the regulation of gaming" provided in the Act, *id.* This leads us back to the opening question—what is the statutory basis empowering the Commission to regulate class III gaming operations? Finding none, we affirm.

So ordered.

Notes

1. As the *Colorado River* court notes, the "Minimum Internal Control Standards," (MICS) developed by the NIGC for Class III gaming were quite detailed. But the court is emphatic in its conclusion that IGRA grants the authority to regulate Class III gaming to the tribal-state compact process and not NIGC. There is no case to the contrary. Yet, in regulations promulgated by NIGC there still are MICS for Class III gaming, including this provision:

§ 542.4 How do these regulations affect minimum internal control standards established in a Tribal-State compact?

> (a) If there is a direct conflict between an internal control standard established in a Tribal-State compact and a standard or requirement set forth in this part, then the internal control standard established in a Tribal-State compact shall prevail.

> (b) If an internal control standard in a Tribal-State compact provides a level of control that equals or exceeds the level of control under an internal control standard or requirement set forth in this part, then the Tribal-State compact standard shall prevail.

> (c) If an internal control standard or a requirement set forth in this part provides a level of control that exceeds the level of control under an internal control standard established in a Tribal-State compact, then the internal control standard or requirement set forth in this part shall prevail.

Are the regulations promulgated by the NIGC still valid in light of the *Colorado River* case? What exactly was the holding in that case? Was the decision limited to the MICS for Class III gaming, or did it extend more generally to NIGC's lack of authority over Class III gaming apart from what IGRA expressly provided?

2. The interaction between the NIGC and the Department of the Interior regarding the regulation of tribal gaming has not always been friendly. *See* Dennis J. Whittlesey, *Washington's Newest Battle: Indian Gaming v. Indian Gaming*, 12 GAMING L. REV. & ECON. 408 (2008) (describing dispute where Department told the NIGC to "back away" from its decision that an Alabama Indian tribe had the right to conduct casino operations on land that was taken into trust status pursuant to IGRA's special exception for certain categories of newly-acquired land); Kevin K. Washburn, *Agency Conflict and Culture: Federal Implementation of the Indian Gaming Regulatory Act by the National Indian Gaming Commission, The Bureau of Indian Affairs, and the Department of Justice*, 42 ARIZ. ST. L.J. 303 (2010) (describes the inter-agency conflicts over governing Indian gaming and land, stating, "Aside from the Constitution, it is hard to imagine a federal law that disperses power more widely and among more institutions across more levels of government than IGRA.").

Given the uncertainties that can develop over which agency/department has what power, should IGRA be amended to clarify these issues?

3. The *Colorado River Tribe* holding essentially created a loophole in Indian Gaming Regulation. If the NIGC, the federal agency responsible for the oversight of Indian gaming, did not have the authority to monitor the tribe's class III operations, who did? This has led some in Congress to call for a revision of IGRA to "fix" this loophole and re-establish NIGC authority over Class III monitoring. *See* Gale Courey Toensing, *McCain Launches "Broad Based Attack" on Indian Gaming Regulation*, INDIAN COUNTRY TODAY, July 30, 2010, *available at* http://www.indiancountrytoday.com/politics/McCain-launches-broad-based-attack-on-Indian-gaming-regulation-99640774.html?m=y.

iv. NIGC Enforcement Powers

United States v. Seminole Nation of Oklahoma

321 F.3d 939 (10th Cir. 2002)

I. INTRODUCTION

Plaintiff, the United States of America, filed this action in federal district court to enforce temporary closure orders issued to Defendant, Seminole Nation of Oklahoma (the "Nation"), by the Chairman of the National Indian Gaming Commission ("NIGC"). Although the government moved for preliminary injunction, the district court notified the parties by order that the hearing on the government's motion would be combined with a trial on the merits of the government's suit. The district court dismissed the government's suit reasoning that the NIGC Chairman exceeded his authority in ordering the closure of the Nation's gaming facilities rather than just the particular games at issue. The government appeals the district court's dismissal of the suit. This court has jurisdiction under 28 U.S.C. § 1291 and vacates the district court order for the reasons stated below. Further, the Nation's motion to dismiss this appeal for mootness is denied.

II. BACKGROUND

In 1988, Congress enacted the Indian Gaming Regulatory Act ("IGRA") which provided a comprehensive system to regulate gambling activities on Indian lands. *See* 25 U.S.C. §§ 2701–2721....

The NIGC is charged with the development of regulations and administrative enforcement of IGRA. *Id.* §§ 2705, 2706. In accordance with the discharge of this duty, the NIGC Chairman is authorized to order the temporary closure of gaming activities and impose civil fines if he determines that any person or tribe is conducting gaming in substantial violation of IGRA. *Id.* §§ 2705(a), 2713(b)(1). Under the NIGC's regulations, a temporary closure order may extend to "all or part of an Indian gaming operation" and is "effective upon service." 25 C.F.R. §§ 573.6(a), 573.6(b).

The Nation operates gaming activities at four gaming facilities in Seminole County, Oklahoma. In an effort to increase revenues from these facilities, the Nation added "coin-operated amusement games," which it characterizes as games of skill. The Nation offered for play one particular coin-operated amusement game known as "Red Hot Re-Spin."

On May 30, 2000, the NIGC Chairman concluded that the Red Hot Re-Spin machines were impermissible Class III gaming devices and issued a temporary closure order ("May Order") directing the Nation to cease operating these machines. The Nation filed an appeal of the May Order with the NIGC.

After receiving the May Order, the Nation offered for play several new coin-operated amusement machines, in addition to Red Hot Re-Spin, under the following names: "Buffalo Nickels," "Rainbow Reels," "Fantasy Fives," "Pot O Gold," and "Lucky Cherries." On September 12, 2000, the NIGC Chairman determined that these new games were also Class III games. Accordingly, the NIGC Chairman issued a second temporary closure order ("September Order") ordering the Nation to cease all gaming activities in all of its gaming facilities.

On January 19, 2001, the government filed a complaint in federal district court for enforcement of the May and September closure orders. The government moved for a preliminary injunction. The district court notified the parties by order that the hearing on the government's motion would be combined with a trial on the merits of the government's suit. On February 27, 2001, the district court denied the motion and dismissed the suit reasoning that the NIGC Chairman exceeded his authority in ordering the closure of all the Nation's gaming facilities. The government appeals the district court's dismissal of the suit.

On February 4–6, 2002, a hearing was held before a Presiding Official ("PO") appointed by the United States Department of the Interior's Office of Hearings and Appeals on the Nation's appeals from the May and September Orders. On April 8, 2002, the PO issued a Recommended Decision in which he concluded that the NIGC met its burden of proof with regard to the May Order but failed to meet its burden of proof with regard to the September Order. The PO recommended that the May Order be sustained and the September Order be vacated.

The NIGC reviewed the PO's recommendations. In a written Notice of Decision and Order entered on May 7, 2002, the NIGC adopted the PO's recommendation as to the May Order but rejected the PO's recommendation as to the September Order. The NIGC directed that both the May and September Orders become permanent.

On August 16, 2002, the Nation filed suit in federal district court seeking review of the NIGC's permanent closure order. This case is still pending before the district court.

III. DISCUSSION

A. Mootness

The Nation has moved for dismissal, arguing that the government's appeal is moot because the NIGC Chairman's temporary closure orders were superseded by the NIGC's permanent closure order....

The NIGC Chairman's temporary closure orders have been superseded by the issuance of a permanent closure order by the NIGC. Thus, the temporary closure orders are no longer in effect. This case, however, fits the narrow exception to the mootness doctrine for conduct capable of repetition, yet evading review. The NIGC Chairman's temporary closure orders are too short in duration to be fully litigated in court prior to their administrative expiration or replacement by permanent orders. Temporary closure orders, by their very nature, are short in duration. IGRA requires the NIGC to quickly review temporary closure orders and either dissolve them or issue permanent closure orders. 25 U.S.C. § 2713(b)(2) (providing an Indian tribe with the right to a hearing before the Commission to review a temporary closure order within thirty days of its issuance and requiring the Commission to decide whether to dissolve the order or issue a permanent closure order within sixty days of the hearing). The Nation argues, however, the NIGC Chairman's temporary orders are not so short in duration as to require this court to exercise jurisdiction over this appeal. Rather, the Nation argues, the government's failure to seek an expedited appeal and its multiple requests for additional time to file appellate briefs delayed appellate review until after the issuance of the permanent order. The course of proceedings in *this* appeal, however, are irrelevant. The NIGC's statutory obligation to quickly conduct a hearing within thirty days of the issuance of a temporary order and decide whether to dissolve or make permanent the order within sixty days of the hearing, creates a paradigm in which a temporary order will not remain in effect throughout the appellate process. Accordingly, the NIGC Chairman's temporary closure orders are of a sufficiently limited duration to ordinarily escape appellate review.

The Nation also argues that the *issues* in this appeal are not of a limited duration because they will be litigated in the case involving the permanent closure order. The issue in this appeal is whether the NIGC Chairman's statutory authority to issue temporary closure orders extends to the closure of a tribe's entire gaming operation. The NIGC Chairman's statutory authority, however, is not at issue in an appeal from permanent closure orders because the NIGC, and not the NIGC Chairman, issues permanent closure orders under IGRA. 25 U.S.C. § 2713(b)(2). Accordingly, a district court hearing an appeal from a permanent closure order will consider the NIGC's authority to issue the order and the NIGC's conclusion that the gaming operation was in substantial violation of IGRA. *See generally id.* at § 2713(c).

To constitute an exception to the mootness doctrine, it is not enough that an issue will escape review because of limited duration. It is also necessary that there be "a reasonable expectation that the same complaining party ... [will] be subjected to the same action again." *Gannett,* 443 U.S. at 377. Because the district court's denial of injunctive relief was based on the specific facts of this case, the Nation argues, the government has no reasonable expectation that it will bring a substantially similar action for enforcement of a temporary closure order in the future. The Nation also argues that the court should not presume that it will not comply with future temporary closure orders. At oral argument, however, the Nation conceded it would again challenge the scope of the Chairman's authority under IGRA. Accordingly, there is a reasonable expectation that the Nation will again challenge the NIGC Chairman's authority to issue temporary closure orders that apply to all the Nation's gaming facilities.

Therefore, while the NIGC Chairman's temporary orders were superseded by the NIGC's permanent closure order, this court's "jurisdiction is not defeated" because this appeal fits the exception to mootness for conduct capable of repetition, yet evading review. *See id.*

B. IGRA

The district court determined the NIGC Chairman's authority to issue temporary closure orders is limited under 25 U.S.C. § 2713(b)(1) to the closure of individual games. Accordingly, the district court concluded the NIGC Chairman exceeded his statutory authority by issuing the September Order which required closure of all the Nation's gaming facilities. The government argues that the NIGC Chairman is authorized under IGRA to issue a temporary closure order applicable to an entire gaming facility and that the district court, therefore, erred in refusing to enforce the September Order. This court reviews the interpretation of a federal statute *de novo.*

In interpreting a statute, this court gives effect to the statute's unambiguous terms ... "In ascertaining the plain meaning of the statute, the court must look to the particular statutory language at issue, as well as the language and design of the statute as a whole." K Mart Corp. v. Cartier, Inc., 486 U.S. 281, 291 (1988). "[I]f the statute is silent or ambiguous with respect to the specific issue," however, this court defers to the agency's reasonable interpretation of the statute. *Chevron,* 467 U.S. at 843.

The Nation argues that the NIGC Chairman's authority to issue temporary closure orders is limited to the closure of an individual game. To support its argument, the Nation relies on 25 U.S.C. § 2713(b)(1) which states:

The Chairman shall have power to order temporary closure of an Indian game for substantial violation of the provisions of [IGRA, NIGC regulations, and tribal regulations approved under IGRA].

While the narrow term "an Indian game" is used in § 2713(b)(1), when read as a whole IGRA unambiguously authorizes the NIGC Chairman to order the temporary closure of entire gaming operations. In § 2705(a)(1), the NIGC Chairman is authorized to "issue orders of temporary closure of *gaming activities* as provided in section 2713(b)." 25 U.S.C. § 2705(a)(1) (emphasis added). Accordingly, the phrases "gaming activities" and "an Indian game" are used interchangeably in reference to the NIGC Chairman's authority to issue temporary closure orders.

Moreover, the NIGC is required by § 2713(b)(2) to review the NIGC Chairman's temporary closure order and either dissolve it or order "a permanent closure of the gaming operation." *Id.* § 2713(b)(2). Because the NIGC can act to either dissolve or make permanent the Chairman's temporary order, the NIGC's permanent closure order is of the same scope as the NIGC Chairman's temporary closure order. The reference in § 2713(b)(2) to a "gaming operation," therefore, is substantially equivalent to the phrase "an Indian game" in § 2713(b)(1).

Finally, the NIGC Chairman is obligated to approve tribal ordinances which, *inter alia,* provide for the protection of public health and safety at gaming facilities. *Id.* § 2710(b)(2)(E) (authorizing the Chairman to approve tribal ordinances which provide that "construction and maintenance of the gaming facility, and the operation of that gaming is conducted in a manner which adequately protects the environment and the public health and safety"). The NIGC Chairman is authorized to enforce such tribal ordinances through the issuance of temporary closure orders. *Id.* § 2713(b)(1). The Nation conceded at oral argument that the NIGC Chairman's authority to enforce such tribal ordinances is derived from § 2713(b) (1). If the NIGC Chairman's authority to issue temporary closure orders was limited to the closure of individual games, he would be unable to carry out this obligation. Accordingly, when § 2710(b) (2)(E) and § 2713(b)(1) are read together, the NIGC Chairman's authority to issue temporary closure orders clearly includes the power to close entire gaming facilities.

Even assuming, *arguendo,* that the statute authorizing the NIGC Chairman to issue temporary closure orders under IGRA is ambiguous, the NIGC's interpretation of the statute as embodied in their regulations is entitled to deference. *Chevron,* 467 U.S. at 843. Under 25 C.F.R. § 573.6, the NIGC Chairman is authorized to issue "an order of temporary closure of all or part of an Indian gaming operation" if the tribe violates certain provisions of IGRA. 25 C.F.R. § 573.6(a). "The operator of an Indian gaming operation [must] close the operation upon service" of the order. *Id.* § 573.6(b). This regulation is a reasonable interpretation of § 2713(b)(1) and, therefore, is entitled to deference under *Chevron. See* 467 U.S. at 843.

Accordingly, because the NIGC Chairman is authorized under IGRA to issue a temporary closure order of an entire gaming facility, the district court erred in dismissing the government's action seeking enforcement of the September Order.

IV. CONCLUSION

For the reasons stated above,[5] the district court's order is vacated. Further, the Nation's motion to dismiss this appeal for mootness is denied.

---

5. In addition to concluding that the NIGC Chairman exceeded his statutory authority by issuing a temporary closure order relating to all the Nation's gaming facilities, the district court raised, *sua sponte,* the issue of whether the Nation's due process rights were violated. As an additional reason for dismissing the government's suit, the district court determined that the Nation's due process rights were violated. Because resolution of this constitutional issue was unnecessary to the adjudication of the case, the district court abused its discretion in deciding the issue.... Moreover, the Nation has abandoned this issue on appeal. Accordingly, this court does not have the benefit of appellate briefing on this issue. In light of these circumstances and the conclusion that the district court's opinion be vacated, this court will abstain from adjudicating the merits of this issue. Because this action was an enforcement action, the only issue properly addressed by the district court was whether the NIGC Chairman had the authority to order the temporary closure of all the Nation's gaming facilities. Accordingly, the district court lacked jurisdiction over other issues raised by the parties, including the classification of the games at issue and the validity of IGRA provisions requiring that tribal-state compacts be obtained prior to engaging in Class III gaming activities. These issues must be raised in an appeal of the NIGC's permanent order. *See* 25 U.S.C. § 2713(c) (conferring jurisdiction over final, permanent orders of the NIGC on the federal district court). Therefore, this court, like the district court, lacks jurisdiction to resolve these issues.

Notes

1. The NIGC has ordered closures of tribal casinos in many instances. *See, e.g.,* United States v. Seminole Nation of Oklahoma, 321 F.3d 939 (2002) (holding that NIGC has the power to issue temporary closure order for all gaming operations; authority was not limited to single game at issue); Sac and Fox Tribe of the Mississippi in Iowa, No. NIGC 2003-1 (Sept. 10, 2003), *available at* http://www.nigc.gov/Reading_Room/Enforcement_Actions?NOV_03-02_Commission_Decision.aspx (tribal leaders recognized by Interior Department were ousted and new faction continued to operate casino; NIGC ruled that because recognized tribal leadership was not in control of gaming, closure was only effective option); Notice of Violation and Closure Order from Montie R. Deer, Chairman, National Indian Gaming Commission, to Bennett Arkeketa, Chairman, Ponca Tribe of Oklahoma, May 1, 2002, *available at* http://www.nigc.gov/LinkClick.aspx?link=NIGC+Uploads%2freadingroom%2fenforcementactions%2fponcatribeofok%2fCO-02-03.pdf&tabid=124&mid=774 (ordering closure of casino for tribes failure to provide proper employee documentation).

2. NIGC has promulgated a number of regulations setting forth specific violations of IGRA that may lead to a closure order. *See* 25 C.F.R. § 573.6(1)-(13).

5. Issues Created by Tribal Sovereignty

A. Generally

Indian tribes are sometimes referred to as the "third sovereign," along with the federal and state governments. This tribal sovereign immunity allows tribes to invoke immunity in a variety of settings when tribes are sued in state or federal court. The United States Supreme Court has ruled that immunity applies not just to tribal governmental actions, but the commercial activities of a tribe as well. *See* Kiowa Tribe of Oklahoma v. Mfg. Tech., Inc. 523 U.S. 751, 754–55 (1998). In addition, the immunity can extend to the activities of business entities that are functionally a part of the tribe. All this significantly complicates tribal dealings with third parties. Congress can, and has, restricted tribal immunity in various situations, some involving gaming and some not. But it is clear that unless Congress restricts tribal immunity, the only way the immunity can be lost is if it is expressly waived by the tribe.

The overall topic of tribal sovereignty is vast, certainly extends beyond gaming, and is beyond the scope of these materials. What is presented here will impart a sense of the numerous settings in which tribal immunity problems arise.

i. Doing Business and Contracting with Tribes

World Touch Gaming, Inc. v. Massena Management, LLC

117 F. Supp.2d 271 (N.D.N.Y. 2000)

MEMORANDUM-DECISION and ORDER

HURD, District Judge.

Plaintiff World Touch Gaming, Inc. ("World Touch") filed the instant action on December 22, 1999, alleging breach of contract by defendants. World Touch filed an amended complaint on May 4, 2000. Defendants Massena Management, LLC; Massena Management Corp. d/b/a President R.C.-St. Regis Management Company ("Management Company"); Akwesasne Mohawk Casino ("the Casino"); and St. Regis Mohawk Tribe ("the Tribe") move to dismiss the amended complaint for lack of subject matter jurisdiction pursuant to Fed. R. Civ. P. 12(b)(1). Plaintiff opposes the motion. Oral argument was heard on June 9, 2000, in Utica, New York. Decision was reserved.

I. FACTS

The Tribe is a federally-recognized American Indian Tribe whose lands, known as Akwesasne, were reserved to the Tribe by treaty with the United States. The Tribe is governed by its Constitution. In part the Constitution provides that "the Tribe is immune from suit except to the extent that the Tribal Council expressly waives sovereign immunity...." Moreover, the Tribe's Civil Judicial Code provides, inter alia, the following:

> Tribal sovereign immunity is hereby found and stated to be an essential element of self-determination and self-government, and as such will be waived by the Mohawk Tribal Council only under such circumstances as the Mohawk Tribal Council finds to be in the interests of the Tribe in promoting economic or commercial development or for other tribal purposes. Any such specific waivers of sovereign immunity as may from time to time be executed must be clear, explicit and in writing; any such waivers shall be interpreted narrowly and limited to the explicit terms of the waivers; and any such waivers shall not by implication or interpretation be extended in any manner or fashion beyond their narrow, explicit terms.

The Tribe operates a gaming enterprise, the Casino, which is a wholly owned unincorporated subsidiary of the Tribe. The Tribe operates the Casino pursuant to a gaming compact with New York State, as required by the Indian Gaming Regulation Act ("IGRA"). The Tribe entered into an agreement with the Management Company, pursuant to which the Management Company would be the managing agent for the Tribe and operate the Casino under the supervision of the Tribe. According to the sworn testimony of Angus N. McDonald, Executive Director of the Tribe, "The Tribe has never authorized anyone form [sic] the Casino Management to waive the Saint Regis Mohawk Tribe's sovereign immunity. Such an authorization could only be made by resolution of the Tribal Council. No such resolution exists to my knowledge." (McDonald Aff. ¶ 8.)

On May 20, 1999, after some months of selection and negotiation, World Touch and the Casino entered into agreements for the lease and purchase of gallery-style pull tab gaming machines for use in the Tribe's gaming enterprise ("the Lease Agreement" and the "Sales Agreement"). Walter Horn, Senior Vice President of the Management Company, signed the Lease and Sales Agreements as the managing agent of the Casino.

The Lease Agreement provides, inter alia, that the "Lessee [Casino] agrees to waive its Sovereign Immunity from suit to enforce the provisions of this Agreement and acknowledges that this waiver allows Lessor [World Touch] the right to pursue both legal and equitable remedies as Lessor deems necessary." The Sales Agreement provides as follows:

> The parties recognize that the Tribe, being a federally recognized Indian tribe, is a sovereign entity dedicated to promoting the general welfare of its members and their descendants the blessings of liberty and freedom. Nothing in this agreement shall be construed to limit or diminish that sovereignty nor to abridge or waive any sovereign rights, privileges or immunities of the Tribe, its agencies, divisions, corporations or their respective officers and representatives. Notwith-

standing the aforementioned Tribal Sovereignty the Tribe agrees to submit to the jurisdiction of the state and federal courts for the sole and limited purpose of enforcement of the obligations under this contract....

The Casino was to purchase 181 machines from World Touch for a total of $1,176,500.00, to be paid in four equal installments. World Touch alleges that the second and third installment payments were made late and only after considerable collection efforts. Further, World Touch alleges that the final payment due under the Sales Agreement has not been paid.

The Casino was to lease 120 machines, and pay a twenty percent revenue sharing amount for the ninety-day term of the lease. World Touch alleges that the Casino failed to pay the June 1999 and July 1999 revenue sharing amounts when due under the Lease Agreement. While these payments were eventually made, the Casino allegedly failed to make payment of the August 1999 and September 1999 revenue sharing amounts. Additionally, World Touch alleges that the Casino is in default by its failure to purchase the leased machines after ninety days, as was required by the Lease Agreement. World Touch eventually repossessed the leased equipment. World Touch also claims that it is owed $112,236.89 by the Casino for parts and supply orders, transportation, and installation expenses, pursuant to the Lease and Sales Agreements.

For relief World Touch seeks money damages of at least $2,000,000, an accounting to determine the owed revenue sharing amounts, an injunction prohibiting operation of the machines while payment is due, and costs and attorneys fees.

II. DISCUSSION

A. Fed. R. Civ. P. 12(b) (1) Motion to Dismiss Standard

An action must be dismissed when the court lacks jurisdiction over the subject matter. The party asserting subject matter jurisdiction has the burden of proving that such jurisdiction exists. When faced with a motion to dismiss for lack of jurisdiction, the party cannot "rest on [the] mere assertion that factual issues exist." Rather, the party asserting jurisdiction should be permitted discovery of facts relevant to the jurisdictional issue, particularly "where the facts are peculiarly within the knowledge of the opposing party." The parties may submit affidavits in support of and in opposition to a jurisdictional motion, for the court's consideration. The proof of jurisdictional facts must be competent, and guidance regarding the proof can be taken from Fed. R. Civ. P. 56. Finally, a motion brought pursuant to Fed R. Civ. P. 12(b)(1) must be considered before any other motions, as a finding of lack of jurisdiction would render other objections and defenses moot.

B. Sovereign Immunity & Waiver

Defendants contend that subject matter jurisdiction is lacking due to the sovereign immunity of the Tribe, and likewise of the Casino because it is a wholly owned unincorporated enterprise of the Tribe. Plaintiff argues that the Tribe waived its sovereign immunity under the terms of both the Lease Agreement and the Sales Agreement which were signed by Walter Horn, Senior Vice President of the Management Company. In response, the defendants argue that Walter Horn had no authority to waive the Tribe's sovereign immunity and that, as subject matter jurisdiction is lacking over the Tribe and the Casino, and they are indispensable parties, any claims against the Management Company should be dismissed pursuant to Fed. R. Civ. P. 19(b).

The parties agree that the Tribe enjoys sovereign immunity. That being so, the Tribe is immune from suit, absent authorization by Congress, unless it has waived its sovereign immunity. Kiowa Tribe of Oklahoma v. Manufacturing Tech., Inc., 523 U.S. 751,

754 (1998). This immunity extends to tribal enterprises. *Kiowa Tribe of Oklahoma*, 523 U.S. at 757–58. Thus, the Tribe and the Casino are immune from this lawsuit unless the Tribe has waived its sovereign immunity.

World Touch points to the explicit waiver language of the Sales and Lease Agreements, signed by Walter Horn, Senior Vice President of the Management Company, in support of its position that the Tribe and the Casino waived sovereign immunity. However, according to the unequivocal language of the Tribe's Constitution and Civil Judicial Code, only the Tribal Council can waive the Tribe's sovereign immunity, and such waiver must be express. The Tribal Council did not authorize Walter Horn to waive sovereign immunity, nor did the Tribal Council expressly waive the Tribe's sovereign immunity. (*See* McDonald Aff. ¶ 8.) Thus, the Tribe's sovereign immunity was not waived, and it is immune from suit.

World Touch argues first that Walter Horn had express authority to waive the Tribe's sovereign immunity, pursuant to the Management Agreement provision giving exclusive control over the day to day operations of the Casino to the Management Company. *See supra* n.2 for the language referenced by World Touch in support of this proposition. However, giving authority to operate the Casino is not equivalent to authorizing the Management Company to waive the Tribe's sovereign immunity. The Management Agreement, which expressly authorizes the Management Company to operate the gaming enterprise, cannot be read to authorize waiver of sovereign immunity. *See supra* n.2. Simply put, "construct, manage, administer, operate, maintain and improve the gaming facilities ... [and] such other activities as are reasonably related thereto" cannot mean "you have the authority to waive the Tribe's sovereign immunity."

Moreover, as a sophisticated distributor of gaming equipment that frequently deals with Indian gaming enterprises, World Touch should have been careful to assure that either the Management Company had the express authority of the Tribe to waive sovereign immunity, or that the Tribe itself expressly waived sovereign immunity with respect to the Sales and Lease Agreements.[3] World Touch is not a novice in matters relating to In-

---

3. A perfect example of an express waiver of sovereign immunity is found in the agreement between the Tribe and the Management Company, which was signed by the President of the Management Company, and most importantly, by the Tribe. The waiver provision of the management agreement states: 10.8 RESOLUTION OF DISPUTES; LIMITED WAIVER OF SOVEREIGN IMMUNITY. TRIBE and MANAGER hereby covenant and agree that they each may sue or be sued to enforce or interpret the terms, covenants and conditions of this Agreement or to enforce the obligations or rights of the parties hereto in accordance with the terms and conditions set forth in this Section.(A) *Forum.* Any action with regard to a controversy, disagreement or dispute between the TRIBE and MANAGER arising under this Agreement shall be brought before the appropriate United States District Court. In the event such federal court should determine that it lacks subject matter jurisdiction over any such action, such action shall be brought before the appropriate state court.(B) *Waiver of Tribal Remedies.* TRIBE hereby expressly waives any right to proceed before any tribal court or authority of TRIBE and further expressly waives any right which it may possess to require MANAGER to exhaust tribal remedies prior to bringing an action in federal court or state court as provided above.(C) *Limited Waiver of Sovereign Immunity.* TRIBE hereby specifically and expressly waives its sovereign immunity from suit to the extent necessary to allow MANAGER to bring any action at law or in equity to enforce or interpret the terms and conditions of this Agreement, including without limitation the right to obtain injunctive relief and/or monetary damages as determined by a court of competent jurisdiction and to the extent necessary to allow MANAGER to bring any action at law or in equity to challenge, contest or interpret any laws, ordinances, regulations, licensing procedures or enactments of any sort by TRIBE which relate to or affect in any way the ability of MANAGER to engage in gaming under this Agreement, including without limitation the right to obtain injunctive relief and/or monetary damages as determined by a court of competent jurisdiction. Nothing contained in this Agreement shall be construed as waiving sovereign immunity in any suit for payment of damages from lands or funds held in trust for TRIBE by the United States.(D) *Survival.* The waivers con-

dian gaming enterprises and Indian sovereign immunity, and cannot now rely upon naiveté to expand the reading of the Management Agreement to encompass authority to waive sovereign immunity.

World Touch argues alternatively that the Management Company had apparent authority to bind the Casino and the Tribe to all the terms of the contract, including the waiver of sovereign immunity (or a question of fact exists regarding such authority). World Touch cites authority from the law of agency in support of this argument. However, regardless of any apparent or implicit, or even express, authority of the Management Company to bind the Casino and the Tribe to contract terms and other commercial undertakings, such authority is insufficient to waive the Tribe's sovereign immunity. *See* Merrion v. Jicarilla Apache Tribe, 455 U.S. 130 (1982) (sovereign power "remain[s] intact unless surrendered in unmistakable terms"); Santa Clara Pueblo v. Martinez, 436 U.S. 49, 58–59 (1978) ("a waiver of sovereign immunity cannot be implied but must be unequivocally expressed") (internal quotation omitted). Similarly, any argument that subsequent acts, or acquiescence in carrying out the contract entered into with apparent authority, estop the Tribe from claiming sovereign immunity must fail. *See Merrion,* 455 U.S. at 148; *Santa Clara Pueblo,* 436 U.S. at 58–59.

In sum, the Tribe and the Casino enjoy sovereign immunity. The Tribe has not waived its sovereign immunity. Accordingly, the action must be dismissed as against the Tribe and the Casino.

C. Indispensable Parties under Fed. R. Civ. P. 19

Defendants argue that the Tribe and the Casino are indispensable parties under Fed. R. Civ. P. 19(b). Therefore, they argue, the suit should also be dismissed as against the Management Company. Plaintiff makes no argument in opposition.

Rule 19(b) provides that in the absence of an indispensable party the court must determine "whether in equity and good conscience the action should proceed among the parties before it." Fed. R. Civ. P. 19(b). The court should consider "to what extent a judgment rendered in the person's absence might be prejudicial to the person or those already parties; second, the extent to which, by protective provision in the judgment, by the shaping of relief, or other measures, the prejudice can be lessened or avoided; third, whether a judgment rendered in the person's absence will be adequate; [and] fourth, whether the plaintiff will have an adequate remedy if the action is dismissed" under this rule. *Id.*

The basis for this action is the Lease and Sales Agreements between World Touch and the Casino. The Management Company was not a party to the agreements, as Walter Horn signed merely as the agent of the Casino. Moreover, it was the Casino, not the Management Company, that allegedly breached the agreements and defaulted on the required payments and purchases. Accordingly, based upon a review of the record in this matter, a consideration of the requirements set forth in Fed. R. Civ. P. 19(b), and plaintiff's failure to oppose dismissal under Rule 19(b), it is determined that the Tribe and the Casino are indispensable parties and in equity and good conscience the action should not proceed with the Management Company as the sole remaining defendant. Thus, the action is dismissed as against the Management Company.

---

tained in this Section shall survive any termination of this Agreement.
(Def.'s Mem. Reply Ex. D.)

III. CONCLUSION

The Tribe and the Casino are entitled to sovereign immunity, which they have not waived. The action must be dismissed as against these defendants pursuant to Fed. R. Civ. P. 12(b)(1). As the Tribe and the Casino are indispensable parties, the action must be dismissed as against the remaining defendant, the Management Company, pursuant to Fed. R. Civ. P. 19(b)....

Accordingly, it is

ORDERED that defendants' motion to dismiss pursuant to Fed. R. Civ. P. 12(b)(1) and 19(b) is GRANTED and the complaint is DISMISSED in its entirety.

Notes

1. The principal case underscores a vital point in business dealings with tribes: any waiver of tribal immunity must be express and authorized. "Because of the unique sovereign and jurisdictional characteristics attendant to business transactions with tribes and tribal enterprises, certain due diligence should be conducted with respect to the pertinent tribal organizational documents and governing laws, which may collectively dictate and control the business relationship. The most critical contract provision is an express and unequivocal waiver of sovereign immunity." Heidi McNeil Staudenmaier & Metchi Palaniappan, *The Intersection of Corporate America and Indian Country: Negotiating Successful Business Alliances*, 22 T.M. Cooley L. Rev. 569, 602–03 (2005). As seen, it may not be enough just to have a waiver in the contracting documents; there must be authority on the part of the contracting party to waive the immunity. *See also* S. Chloe Thompson, *Exercising and Protecting Tribal Sovereignty in Day-to-Day Business Operations: What the Key Players Need to Know*, 49 Washburn L.J. 661 (2010); Padraic I McCoy, *Sovereign Immunity and Tribal Commercial Activity: A Legal Summary and Policy Check*, 57 Fed. Law. 41 (2010); R. Lance Boldrey & Jason Hanselman, *Proceed with Prudence: Advising Clients Doing Business in Indian Country*, 89 Mich. B.J. 34 (2010). For additional examples of cases dealing with the issue of tribal sovereign immunity, *see* Memphis Biofuels, LLC v. Chickasaw Nation Indus., Inc., 585 F.3d 917 (6th Cir. 2009) (holding that incorporation of a tribal entity under the IRA was not an automatic waiver of immunity; tribal corporation's charter did not contain express waiver of immunity); Rush Creek Solutions, Inc. v. Ute Mountain Ute Tribe, 107 P.3d 402 (Colo. App. 2004) (holding that tribe's CFO held himself out as tribe's agent with requisite authority and therefore contract signed by him which included a waiver of sovereign immunity was enforceable).

2. The *World Touch* court stated that "as a sophisticated distributor of gaming equipment that frequently deals with Indian gaming enterprises," the plaintiff should have taken greater care in its dealings with the tribe. Is this a one-sided arrangement? Should a tribe be allowed to exploit fairly subtle flaws in business documents to escape the duties it has quite clearly undertaken? Does this broad immunity give tribes an incentive to draft documents ambiguously so that they may have an escape hatch? Or are tribal business partners charged with the knowledge that the burden is on them to make sure the immunity is expressly waived? Are there instances where immunity can work against the tribes' interests?

3. In addition to product suppliers, lenders also have to be especially careful in their drafting of documents as to the remedies available in case of default. In the preceding section on management contracts, the case Wells Fargo Bank, N.A. v. Lake of The Torches Economic Development Corp., 677 F. Supp.2d 1056 (W.D. Wis. 2010), was discussed. In that case, the Trust Indenture had a provision where the tribal business entity expressly waived its sovereign immunity. Because the court held the trust indenture itself was void, no enforceable obligation existed, so the waiver was meaningless.

Although the case focused primarily on the court's conclusion that the financial documents amounted to a management contract needing NIGC approval, it is another illustration of how treacherous the business relationship with tribal gaming entities can be. Can this work to the disadvantage of the tribe? If you were a bank or other lender, would you be wary of doing business with the tribe? Would you expect a higher return in exchange for the risk involved?

4. In difficult economic times, casinos can experience downturns like other businesses. When a casino cannot pay its indebtedness, a lender has a number of options available to protect its financial interest. This can include foreclosing on the casino's assets or forcing them into some form of bankruptcy. When tribes operate the defaulting casinos, however, the creditor's options are limited. IGRA prohibits creditors from retaining all tribal revenues, or from operating the casino itself. *See* 25 U.S.C. § 2710. Where a tribe is involved, the creditor cannot simply seize the assets of the casino, even if the provisions of the Uniform Commercial Code would otherwise allow for it. Nor can it contract with another entity to operate the casino during the reorganization period. Similarly, there is substantial doubt that federal bankruptcy laws have application to Indian tribes. This all leads to greater uncertainty for lenders as casino defaults, including tribal casino defaults increase. For more discussion of these issues, *see* STEVEN T. WATERMAN, TRIBAL TROUBLES: WITHOUT BANKRUPTCY RELIEF, AM. BANKR. INST. J. (January 2010), *available at* http://www.dorsey.com/files/upload/TribalTroubles_Waterman10.pdf; Michael M. Eidelman, Terence M. Dunleavy, & Stephanie K. Hor-Chen, *Dealing with Troubled Tribal Casinos*, 6 J. BANKR. L. 302 (2010).

5. Perhaps the greatest success story in Indian gaming is the Foxwoods Resort Casino in Ledyard, Connecticut, operated by the Mashantucket Pequot Tribal Nation. After opening in 1992, Foxwoods grew impressively and total revenue in 2006 was $1.58 billion. This success was too much for investors to ignore. Lenders like banks purchased bonds to fund expansion of the resort. But Foxwoods was not insulated from the economic downturn that hit casinos. Foxwoods saw its revenues, which were used to fund tribal government operations and services, decline sharply. In July 2010, the tribe had over $2 billion in debt that it could no longer repay. After the tribe asked for a restructuring of its debt that would reduce it by nearly half, bondholders scrambled to protect their interests. Matters were complicated by the fact that tribal members received dividends from casino revenues of as much as $120,000. The former chairman of the tribal council had suggested that payments to tribal members would take precedence over payments to debtors. For a description and analysis of this matter, *see* Mike Spector, *Foxwoods Debt Talks Test Tribal Bets*, WALL ST. J., July 2, 2010, *available at* http://online.wsj.comarticle/SB10001424052748704525704575341310022442270.html.

ii. Labor and Employment Issues

San Manuel Indian Bingo and Casino v. N.L.R.B.
475 F.3d 1306 (D.C. Cir. 2007)

BROWN, Circuit Judge.

In this case, we consider whether the National Labor Relations Board (the "Board") may apply the National Labor Relations Act, 29 U.S.C. §§ 151 *et seq.* (the "NLRA"), to employment at a casino the San Manuel Band of Serrano Mission Indians ("San Manuel" or the "Tribe") operates on its reservation. The casino employs many non-Indians and caters primarily to non-Indians. We hold the Board may apply the NLRA to employment at this casino, and therefore we deny the petition for review.

I

San Manuel owns and operates the San Manuel Indian Bingo and Casino (the "Casino") on its reservation in San Bernardino County, California. This proceeding arose out of a competition between the Communication Workers of America ("CWA") and the Hotel Employees & Restaurant Employees International Union ("HERE"), each seeking to organize the Casino's employees. According to HERE's evidence, the Casino is about an hour's drive from Los Angeles. It includes a 2300-seat bingo hall and over a thousand slot machines. It also offers live entertainment. HERE's evidence further suggests the Tribe actively directs its marketing efforts to non-Indians, and the Board found that "many, and perhaps the great majority, of the casino's patrons are nonmembers who come from outside the reservation." San Manuel Indian Bingo & Casino, 341 N.L.R.B. 1055, 1056. The Tribe does not contract with an independent management company to operate the Casino, and therefore many Tribe members hold key positions at the Casino. Nevertheless, given the Casino's size, the Tribe must employ a significant number of non-members to ensure effective operation. *Id.* at 1056, 1061.

The Casino was established by the San Manuel tribal government as a "tribal governmental economic development project," *id.* at 1055, and it operates pursuant to the Indian Gaming Regulatory Act of 1988 ("IGRA"), which authorized gaming on tribal lands expressly "as a means of promoting tribal economic development, self-sufficiency, and strong tribal governments," 25 U.S.C. § 2702(1). According to San Manuel's evidence, its tribal government consists of a "General Council," which elects from among its members a "Business Committee." ... The record also does not indicate the Casino's gross annual revenues, but HERE submitted a declaration indicating that, as of February 8, 2000, the Casino's website was advertising in regard to its bingo operation *"Over 1 BILLION Dollars in Cash and Prizes awarded since July 24th, 1986."* Revenues from the Casino are used to fund various tribal government programs and to provide for the general welfare of Tribe members.

In the Tribe's case, IGRA appears to have fulfilled its purpose, as the Casino has markedly improved the Tribe's economic condition. The Tribe's evidence indicates its one-square-mile reservation consists primarily of steep, mountainous, arid land, most of it unsuitable to economic development. For many years, the Tribe had no resources, and many of its members depended on public assistance. As a result of the Casino, however, the Tribe can now boast full employment, complete medical coverage for all members, government funding for scholarships, improved housing, and significant infrastructure improvements to the reservation. In addition, according to the Tribe's evidence, the tribal government is authorized to make direct per capita payments of Casino revenues to Tribe members, suggesting that improved government services are not the only way Tribe members might benefit from the Casino.

II

On January 18, 1999, HERE filed an unfair labor practice charge with the Board. The charge asserted the Casino "has interfered with, coerced and restrained employees in the exercise of their [collective bargaining] rights, and has dominated and discriminatorily supported the [CWA] by allowing CWA representatives access to Casino property..., while denying the same—or any—right of access to representatives of the Charging Party...." On September 30, 1999, the Board's Regional Director for Region 31 issued an order consolidating the two cases, as well as a consolidated complaint. The complaint alleged the Casino had permitted CWA: (1) to place a trailer on Casino property for the purpose of organizing Casino employees; (2) to distribute leaflets from the trailer; and (3) to communicate with Casino employees on Casino property during working hours. The complaint further alleged the Casino's security guards denied HERE equal access to Casino employees.

The Tribe appeared specially, seeking dismissal for lack of jurisdiction. The Tribe asserted the NLRA does not apply to the actions of tribal governments on their reservations. *See Fort Apache Timber Co.,* 226 N.L.R.B. 503 (1976). On January 27, 2000, the matter was transferred to the Board in Washington, D.C., and on May 28, 2004, the Board issued a decision and order finding the NLRA applicable.

The Board began by reviewing its past decisions regarding application of the NLRA to tribal governments. 341 N.L.R.B. at 1056–57. In *Fort Apache,* the Board had ruled the NLRA did not apply to a tribal government operating a timber mill on Indian land, finding the mill to be akin to a "political subdivision" of a state government and therefore exempt. *Fort Apache,* 226 N.L.R.B. at 506 n. 22. This ruling would arguably apply wherever the tribal government's enterprise was located, but in *Sac & Fox Industries, Ltd.,* 307 N.L.R.B. 241 (1992), the Board found the NLRA applicable to *off-reservation* tribal enterprises. *Id.* at 242–43, 245; … Analyzing these precedents, the Board acknowledged reliance on two basic premises — that location is determinative and that the text of the NLRA supported this location-based rule — and found both flawed. 341 N.L.R.B. at 1057. First, the Board concluded that the NLRA applies to tribal governments by its terms and that the legislative history of the NLRA does not suggest a tribal exemption. *Id.* at 1057–59. Next, the Board held federal Indian policy does not preclude application of the NLRA to the commercial activities of tribal governments. *Id.* at 1059–62.

In regard to the latter point, the Board cited the Supreme Court's statement in Federal Power Commission v. Tuscarora Indian Nation, 362 U.S. 99, 116 (1960), that "a general statute in terms applying to all persons includes Indians and their property interests." The Board noted several contexts in which courts had followed *Tuscarora* and applied federal laws to Indian tribes. 341 N.L.R.B. at 1059. In Donovan v. Coeur d'Alene Tribal Farm, 751 F.2d 1113 (9th Cir. 1985), for example, the Ninth Circuit found the Occupational Safety and Health Act applicable to a farm operated by a tribe and located on the tribe's reservation. The *Coeur d'Alene* court identified only three exceptions to *Tuscarora's* statement that federal statutes apply to tribes. According to the Ninth Circuit, an exception to this general rule is appropriate when: "(1) the law touches 'exclusive rights of self-governance in purely intramural matters'; (2) the application of the law to the tribe would 'abrogate rights guaranteed by Indian treaties'; or (3) there is proof 'by legislative history or some other means that Congress intended [the law] not to apply to Indians on their reservations.…'" *Id.* at 1116 (alterations in original).… The Board adopted the *Tuscarora-Coeur d'Alene* framework in this case, thus overruling the *Fort Apache* decision, 341 N.L.R.B. at 1060, and it concluded that none of the three *Coeur d'Alene* exceptions applied and that therefore what it characterized as *Tuscarora's* general rule was controlling, *id.* at 1063.

But the Board did not stop there. Having found the NLRA applicable according to its terms, and having concluded federal Indian law did not preclude application of the NLRA, the Board considered as a matter of discretion whether to exercise its jurisdiction in light of the need to "accommodate the unique status of Indians in our society and legal culture." *Id.* at 1062. Here, the Board went beyond the *Coeur d'Alene* exceptions, asking if the assertion of jurisdiction would "effectuate the purposes of the [NLRA]," *id.*, and noting that when a tribe "is fulfilling traditionally tribal or governmental functions" that do not "involve non-Indians [or] substantially affect interstate commerce," "the Board's interest in effectuating the policies of the [NLRA] is likely to be lower," *id.* at 1063. The

Board considered the location of the tribal government's activity (that is, whether on or off the Tribe's reservation) relevant but not determinative. *Id.* Because here "the casino is a typical commercial enterprise [that] employs non-Indians[ ] and ... caters to non-Indian customers," *id.*, the Board found the exercise of jurisdiction appropriate, *id.* at 1063–64.

.... The Board issued a cease-and-desist order requiring the Tribe to give HERE access to the Casino and also to post notices in the Casino describing the rights of employees under the NLRA. The Tribe petitioned for review, and the Board filed a cross-application for enforcement of its order.

III

Several factors make resolution of this case particularly difficult. We have before us conflicting Supreme Court canons of interpretation that are articulated at a fairly high level of generality. In addition, the NLRA was enacted by a Congress that in all likelihood never contemplated the statute's potential application to tribal employers, and probably no member of that Congress imagined a small Indian tribe might operate like a closely held corporation, employing hundreds, or even thousands, of non-Indians to produce a product it profitably marketed to non-Indians. Further, the casino at issue here, though certainly exhibiting characteristics that are strongly commercial (non-Indian employees and non-Indian patrons), is also in some sense governmental (the casino is the primary source of revenue for the tribal government). Finally, out-of-circuit precedent is inconsistent as to the applicability of general federal laws to Indian tribes.

The gravitational center of San Manuel's case is tribal sovereignty, but even if we accept the paramount significance of this factor, our resolution of the case depends on how the Supreme Court and Congress have defined the contours and limits of tribal sovereignty. Our central inquiry is whether the relation between the Tribe's sovereign interests and the NLRA is such that the ambiguity in the NLRA should be resolved against the Board's exercise of jurisdiction. By focusing on the sovereignty question and addressing it first, we find the statutory interpretation question resolves itself fairly simply. Thus, we analyze this case in two parts: (1) Would application of the NLRA to San Manuel's casino violate federal Indian law by impinging upon protected tribal sovereignty? and (2) Assuming the preceding question is answered in the negative, does the term "employer" in the NLRA reasonably encompass Indian tribal governments operating commercial enterprises?

A

When we begin to examine tribal sovereignty, we find the relevant principles to be, superficially at least, in conflict. First, we have the Supreme Court's statement in *Tuscarora* that "a general statute in terms applying to all persons includes Indians and their property interests." 362 U.S. at 116. In *Tuscarora*, the Court applied this principle to permit condemnation of private property owned by a tribal government, finding a general grant of eminent domain powers applicable to the tribe.... This *Tuscarora* statement is, however, in tension with the longstanding principles that (1) ambiguities in a federal statute must be resolved in favor of Indians, ... and (2) a clear expression of Congressional intent is necessary before a court may construe a federal statute so as to impair tribal sovereignty, ...

As discussed above, the Board steered its way between these various rules by following the Ninth Circuit's lead in *Coeur d'Alene*, 751 F.2d at 1116, which identified three exceptions to *Tuscarora's* general statement. The Board concluded none of the exceptions applied, and therefore *Tuscarora's* general statement controlled.... Because the Board's expertise and delegated authority does not relate to federal Indian law, we need not defer to the Board's conclusion.... Therefore, we decide de novo the implications of tribal sovereignty on the statutory construction question before us.

Each of the cases petitioners cite in support of the principle that statutory ambiguities must be construed in favor of Indians (as well as the cases we have found supporting the principle) involved construction of a statute or a provision of a statute Congress enacted specifically for the benefit of Indians or for the regulation of Indian affairs. We have found no case in which the Supreme Court applied this principle of pro-Indian construction when resolving an ambiguity in a statute of general application.

With regard to the alternative principle relied on by petitioners, that a clear statement of Congressional intent is necessary before a court can construe a statute to limit tribal sovereignty, we can reconcile this principle with *Tuscarora* by recognizing that, in some cases at least, a statute of general application can constrain the actions of a tribal government without at the same time impairing tribal sovereignty.

Tribal sovereignty is far from absolute, as the Supreme Court has explained:

Indian tribes are distinct, independent political communities, retaining their original natural rights in matters of local self-government. Although no longer possessed of the full attributes of sovereignty, they remain a separate people, with the power of regulating their internal and social relations....

....

As the Court ... [has] recognized, however, Congress has plenary authority to limit, modify or eliminate the powers of local self-government which the tribes otherwise possess.

Santa Clara Pueblo, 436 U.S. at 55–56. An examination of Supreme Court cases shows tribal sovereignty to be at its strongest when explicitly established by a treaty, ... or when a tribal government acts within the borders of its reservation, in a matter of concern only to members of the tribe.... Examples of such intramural matters include regulating the status of tribe members in relation to one another, ... and determining tribe membership, ... Conversely, when a tribal government goes beyond matters of internal self-governance and enters into off-reservation business transaction with non-Indians, its claim of sovereignty is at its weakest.... In the latter situation, courts recognize the capacity of a duly established tribal government to act as an unincorporated legal person, engaging in privately negotiated contractual affairs with non-Indians, but the tribal government does so subject to generally applicable laws.... The primary qualification to this rule is that the tribal government may be immune from suit. *See* Kiowa Tribe v. Mfg. Techs., Inc., 523 U.S. 751, 754 (1998)

Many activities of a tribal government fall somewhere between a purely intramural act of reservation governance and an off-reservation commercial enterprise. In such a case, the "inquiry [as to whether a general law inappropriately impairs tribal sovereignty] is not dependent on mechanical or absolute conceptions of ... tribal sovereignty, but has called for a particularized inquiry into the nature of the state, federal, and tribal interests at stake." *White Mountain Apache Tribe,* 448 U.S. at 145. The determinative consideration appears to be the extent to which application of the general law will constrain the tribe with respect to its governmental functions. If such constraint will occur, then tribal sovereignty is at risk and a clear expression of Congressional intent is necessary. Conversely, if the general law relates only to the extra-governmental activities of the tribe, and in particular activities involving non-Indians ... then application of the law might not impinge on tribal sovereignty. Of course, it can be argued any activity of a tribal government is by definition "governmental," and even more so an activity aimed at raising revenue that will fund governmental functions. Here, though, we use the term "governmental" in a restrictive sense to distinguish between the traditional acts governments perform and collateral activities that, though perhaps in some way related to the foregoing, lie outside their scope.

.... In sum, the Supreme Court's decisions reflect an earnest concern for maintaining tribal sovereignty, but they also recognize that tribal governments engage in a varied range of activities many of which are not activities we normally associate with governance. These activities include off-reservation fishing, investments in non-residential private property, and commercial enterprises that tend to blur any distinction between the tribal government and a private corporation. The Supreme Court's concern for tribal sovereignty distinguishes among the different activities tribal governments pursue, focusing on acts of governance as the measure of tribal sovereignty. The principle of tribal sovereignty in American law exists as a matter of respect for Indian communities. It recognizes the independence of these communities as regards internal affairs, thereby giving them latitude to maintain traditional customs and practices. But tribal sovereignty is not absolute autonomy, permitting a tribe to operate in a commercial capacity without legal constraint.

Of course, in establishing and operating the Casino, San Manuel has not acted solely in a commercial capacity. Certainly its enactment of a tribal labor ordinance to govern relations with its employees was a governmental act, as was its act of negotiating and executing a gaming compact with the State of California, as required by IGRA. *See* 25 U.S.C. § 2710(d) (3). Moreover, application of the NLRA to employment at the Casino will impinge, to some extent, on these governmental activities. Nevertheless, impairment of tribal sovereignty is negligible in this context, as the Tribe's activity was primarily commercial and its enactment of labor legislation and its execution of a gaming compact were ancillary to that commercial activity. The total impact on tribal sovereignty at issue here amounts to some unpredictable, but probably modest, effect on tribal revenue and the displacement of legislative and executive authority that is secondary to a commercial undertaking. We do not think this limited impact is sufficient to demand a restrictive construction of the NLRA.

Therefore, we need not choose between *Tuscarora's* statement that laws of general applicability apply also to Indian tribes and *Santa Clara Pueblo's* statement that courts may not construe laws in a way that impinges upon tribal sovereignty absent a clear indication of Congressional intent. Even applying the more restrictive rule of *Santa Clara Pueblo,* the NLRA does not impinge on the Tribe's sovereignty enough to indicate a need to construe the statute narrowly against application to employment at the Casino. First, operation of a casino is not a traditional attribute of self-government. Rather, the casino at issue here is virtually identical to scores of purely commercial casinos across the country. Second, the vast majority of the Casino's employees and customers are not members of the Tribe, and they live off the reservation. For these reasons, the Tribe is not simply engaged in internal governance of its territory and members, and its sovereignty over such matters is not called into question. Because applying the NLRA to San Manuel's Casino would not impair tribal sovereignty, federal Indian law does not prevent the Board from exercising jurisdiction. This conclusion is consistent with the conclusion of several other circuits in regard to the application of federal employment law to certain commercial activities of certain tribes, although those cases resulted from the application of a framework (*Coeur d'Alene*) different from the one we employ here, and we do not decide how the framework we employ would apply to the facts of those cases. *See, e.g.,* Fla. Paraplegic, Ass'n, Inc. v. Miccosukee Tribe of Indians, 166 F.3d 1126 (11th Cir. 1999) (holding ADA applied to restaurant and gaming facility operated by an Indian tribe); Reich v. Mashantucket Sand & Gravel, 95 F.3d 174 (2d Cir. 1996) (applying OSHA to a tribe-operated construction business); Dep't of Labor v. Occupational Safety & Health Review Comm'n, 935 F.2d 182, 184 (9th Cir. 1991) (applying OSHA to a timber mill that a tribe operated on its reservation and noting "[t]he mill employs a significant number of non-Native Americans and sells virtually all of its finished product to non-Native Americans through channels of interstate commerce"); Smart v. State Farm Ins. Co., 868 F.2d 929 (7th Cir. 1989) (concluding ERISA applied to a health center operated by an Indian tribe on its reservation). *But see* EEOC v. Fond du Lac Heavy Equip. & Constr. Co., 986 F.2d 246 (8th Cir. 1993) (holding ADEA did not apply to an on-reservation employment discrimination dispute between a tribal employer and a tribe-member employee).

B

The second question before us, whether the term "employer" in the NLRA encompasses Indian tribal governments operating commercial enterprises, requires a much briefer analysis. The Board concluded the NLRA's definition of employer extended to San Manuel's commercial activities. Neither the text of the NLRA, nor any other reliable indicator of Congressional intent, indicates whether or not Congress specifically intended to include the commercial enterprises of Indian tribes when it used the term "employer." ...

San Manuel argues, ... that nothing in the legislative history or text of the NLRA indicates a Congressional intent to apply the NLRA to tribal governments.... This point is irrelevant in light of our conclusion above that the NLRA does not impinge on the Tribe's sovereignty enough to warrant construing the statute as inapplicable. In the absence of a presumption against application of the NLRA, the legislative history need not expressly anticipate every category of employer that might fall within the NLRA's broad definition.

San Manuel also argues Congress intended, by enacting IGRA, to give tribes and states a primary role in regulating tribal gaming activities, including labor relations, and that Congress therefore, by implication, foreclosed application of the NLRA to tribal gaming. Among other things, IGRA requires tribes that engage or intend to engage in "class III gaming" (the broad category of gaming at issue here) to negotiate, enter into, and comply with a compact between the tribe and the state in which the gaming will occur. *See* 25 U.S.C. § 2710(d)(1)(C), (3)(A)....

The compact San Manuel entered into with the State of California specifically addresses labor relations, requiring San Manuel to adopt "an agreement or other procedure acceptable to the State for addressing organizational and representational rights of Class III Gaming Employees." San Manuel satisfied this requirement by enacting a detailed labor relations ordinance, which differs substantively from the NLRA.

In addition, IGRA makes class III gaming activities lawful on Indian lands only if authorized by a tribal ordinance or resolution approved by the Chairman of the National Indian Gaming Commission. *Id.* § 2710(d)(1)(A)....

San Manuel argues that IGRA, by authorizing tribes and states to enter into compacts addressing labor-relations issues and by mandating a tribal ordinance or resolution regulating gaming activities, contemplates tribal and state control over gaming and therefore implicitly restricts the scope of the NLRA....

We think San Manuel reads too much into IGRA. IGRA certainly permits tribes and states to regulate gaming activities, but it is a considerable leap from that bare fact to the conclusion that Congress intended federal agencies to have no role in regulating employment issues that arise in the context of tribal gaming. This is not a case in which Congress enacted a comprehensive scheme governing labor relations at Indian casinos, and then the Board sought to expand its jurisdiction into that field.... We find no indication that Congress intended to limit the scope of the NLRA when it enacted IGRA, and certainly nothing strong enough to render the Board's interpretation of the NLRA impermissible....

In sum, the Board has given the NLRA a natural interpretation that falls within the range of interpretations the NLRA permits, and regardless of whether we think the Board's decision wise, we are without authority to reject it. *Id.*

IV

Given that application of the NLRA to the San Manuel Casino would not significantly impair tribal sovereignty, and therefore federal Indian law does not preclude the Board from applying the NLRA, and given that the Board's decision as to the scope of the term "employer" in the NLRA constitutes "a permissible construction of the statute," *id.*, we uphold the Board's conclusion finding the NLRA applicable. In some regards our analysis has differed slightly from that of the Board. These differences do not, however, constitute an improper usurpation of the Board's decisionmaking prerogative, ... because the Board, in reaching its ultimate conclusion, relied on the same factors we rely upon; specifically, that the Casino is a purely "commercial enterprise," 341 N.L.R.B. at 1055, that employs "significant numbers of non-Indians and ... caters to a non-Indian clientele" who live off the reservation, *id.* at 1061....

V

The petition for review is denied, and the cross-application for enforcement is granted. *So ordered.*

Hartman v. Golden Eagle Casino, Inc.
243 F. Supp. 2d 1200 (D. Kan. 2003)
MEMORANDUM AND ORDER

ROGERS, District Judge.

These are employment discrimination cases arising from the Golden Eagle Casino....

I.

In its motion, the defendant contends that the court lacks subject matter jurisdiction over these actions. The defendant argues that the Tribe, not the Casino, is the real party in interest. Based upon that argument, the defendant contends it is entitled to sovereign immunity. Alternatively, the defendant asserts that each plaintiff must exhaust her remedies either administratively or judicially at the tribal court level before proceeding to federal court....

II.

Plaintiffs, who are not Indians, were employed at the Golden Eagle Casino. Tammy Hartman worked as a security guard at the casino until May 15, 2001. Randy Rodvelt was employed as a security supervisor until on or about May 29, 2001. Hartman contends that she was discriminated against by the defendant based upon her sex, race and national origin. She also claims that she was subjected to a hostile work environment and was constructively discharged after being physically assaulted twice by a co-worker. Rodvelt also contends that he was discriminated against because of his sex, race and national origin. He further alleges that he was also the victim of a hostile work environment and constructively discharged from his employment. Plaintiffs seek damages based upon Title VII of the Civil Rights Act of 1964, 42 U.S.C. § 2000e et seq.

The Golden Eagle Casino is owned and operated by the Kickapoo Tribe of Kansas ("Tribe"). The Tribe is a federally recognized Indian tribe with its reservation located in northeast Kansas. In 1995, the Tribe entered into a Gaming Compact (Compact) with the State of Kansas, which allowed the Tribe to conduct gaming on its reservation. The Tribe operates the Casino, a Class II gaming facility, pursuant to the Indian Gaming Regulatory Act (IGRA), 25 U.S.C. § 2701 et seq.

Hartman has previously filed other actions arising from her employment with the Golden Eagle. In 1998, she filed an action in Kickapoo Tribal Court in which she alleged wrongful suspension and deprivation of her due process rights. Following an adverse ruling, she appealed. In 1999, she filed a civil action in this court asserting essentially the same claims that she raised in tribal court. In 2001, Judge Dale Saffels dismissed her case. *See* Hartman v. Kickapoo Tribe Gaming Comm., 176 F. Supp.2d 1168 (D. Kan. 2001). She has appealed that ruling and the appeal remains pending.

III.

Arguments of sovereign immunity and subject matter jurisdiction are inextricably intertwined. Sovereign immunity is a matter of subject matter jurisdiction. E.F.W. v. St. Stephen's Indian High School, 264 F.3d 1297, 1302 (10th Cir. 2001). "Indian tribes are domestic dependent nations that exercise inherent sovereign authority over their members and territories. As an aspect of this sovereign immunity, suits against tribes are barred in the absence of an unequivocally expressed waiver by the tribe or abrogation by Congress." *Id.* at 1304....

IV.

Plaintiffs raise a variety of arguments in response to the defendant's motion to dismiss. These arguments can be characterized as creative and passionate. Nevertheless, they are all lacking in merit.

Plaintiffs initially suggest that Title VII allows the assertion of a claim by them under the circumstances of these cases. Although this contention is urged by the plaintiffs, it is not pressed with great sincerity because most of the plaintiffs' argument is based upon the notion that no remedy presently exists that allows them to proceed against the Tribe for employment discrimination.

Plaintiffs begin initially with a contention that they have properly stated a claim under Title VII. As noted above, these actions involve claims against an Indian tribe. Title VII does not allow private employment discrimination claims against Indian tribes because it specifically exempts Indian tribes from the definition of employer. 42 U.S.C. § 2000e(b); ... Plaintiffs contend that Title VII does provide coverage for them because the Casino is an economic enterprise or commercial activity of the Tribe. Plaintiffs, relying upon EEOC v. Karuk Tribe Housing Authority, 260 F.3d 1071 (9th Cir. 2001), assert that the Title VII exemption for Indian Tribes concerns only those employees involved in "purely internal matters" related to the tribe's self-governance. The court has found no support for this distinction in the legislative history of Title VII or the case law interpreting it. The exclusion of Indian Tribes from the definition of employer has been applied to economic entities of Indian Tribes. *See, e.g.,* Duke v. Absentee Shawnee Tribe of Oklahoma Housing Authority, 199 F.3d 1123, 1125 (10th Cir. 1999) (housing authority designed to further Tribe's economic interest was deemed Tribe under Title VII even though created as state agency under Oklahoma law rather than by tribal ordinance); *see also* Thomas v. Choctaw Management/Services Enterprise, 313 F.3d 910, 2002 WL 31680819 (5th Cir. 2002) (unincorporated business venture owned 100% by Tribe is an "Indian Tribe" expressly exempted from being employer under Title VII).

Plaintiffs next assert they are entitled to bring this action based upon the Compact entered into between the Tribe and the State of Kansas. Plaintiffs contend that they are entitled to bring claims because they are third-party beneficiaries of the Compact. This argument has several facets, all somewhat confusing and many contradictory.

Plaintiffs begin by arguing that the State of Kansas has illegally abrogated their rights to bring employment discrimination claims because the Compact failed to provide employees of the Casino with such rights. This argument is purportedly based upon the Supreme Court's decision in Alexander v. Gardner-Denver Co., 415 U.S. 36 (1974).

In *Alexander*, the Supreme Court held that a plaintiff does not waive the right to a trial de novo on a Title VII claim by first pursuing a grievance and arbitration under a collective bargaining agreement's nondiscrimination clause. 415 U.S. at 51–52. The Court determined that an employee's rights under Title VII cannot be prospectively waived through a union contract. *Id.*

Alexander has no application here for several reasons. *Alexander* did not deal with an employee of an Indian tribe. As noted previously, employees of Indian tribes are specifically exempted under Title VII. Moreover, Indian tribes, as sovereigns, have the power to establish the rights of their employees. In order for their employees to have any rights, the Tribe must either waive their sovereign immunity or Congress must abrogate it. The State of Kansas has no power to do either. Accordingly, we do not find that *Alexander* provides any basis for the plaintiffs' contention. In addition, we find no support for it in any other case law.

Plaintiffs next suggest that the Compact did in fact provide for a remedy for employees of the Casino because of the language used in Section 26(D). The nature of this argument is so unusual that we must pause to decide whether to even mention it. Nevertheless, we plunge on to examine each and every argument asserted by the plaintiffs.

Section 26(D) of the Compact provides as follows:

All key employees, standard gaming employees and on-gaming employees shall be covered by Unemployment Compensation and Workers Compensation benefits equivalent to that provided by state law.

Plaintiffs' position is that this section must be read as follows: "all ... employees ... shall be covered by ... benefits equivalent to that provided by state law." Of course, there are a number of problems with this contention. First, and foremost, the language must be read in a tortured way to reach the result sought by plaintiffs. Certain language must be omitted and the rest must be read out of context. Second, and a more fundamental problem, the language fails to mention how this section constitutes a waiver of immunity concerning Title VII, a federal law. At best, and again this is almost laughable, this section, even under the twisted reading put forth by the plaintiffs, only purports to allow employees coverage based upon state law. Here, plaintiffs have not asserted any claims under state law. Regardless of this flaw, the court finds no merit to this contention. The court is not persuaded that Section 26(D) provides any coverage to employees for claims arising under Title VII. Section 26(D) simply entitles gaming employees to the same unemployment and workers' compensation benefits received by other employees in Kansas.

... In order to avoid sovereign immunity, plaintiffs must show that the Tribe either waived it or Congress abrogated it. The court cannot find that either has occurred here. The Compact does not expressly waive immunity, and the laws allowing for gaming contracts between the States and the Tribes do not abrogate it.

Finally, plaintiffs repeatedly assert that no remedy exists here and, therefore, in the interests of justice, the court should impose one. Plaintiffs have provided the court with a variety of alternatives to make this suggestion happen. The court is confident that the law, as it presently exists, allows for none of these alternatives. In reaching this conclusion, the court must note that plaintiffs have failed to adequately demonstrate that "no remedy" exists for their claims. There has been no showing that a tribal remedy does not exist. In any event, the simple lack of a remedy does not require the imposition of one by the court. In the area of Indian law, the court must tread lightly. We certainly are not persuaded that these cases require the use of the court's equity powers. Accordingly, the court declines the opportunity to make new and creative law.

V.

In sum, the court finds that the defendant's motion to dismiss must be granted. The Tribe enjoys sovereign immunity from the claims asserted by the plaintiffs. Accordingly, the court lacks subject matter jurisdiction here....

Notes

1. In Kiowa Tribe of Oklahoma v. Manufacturing Technologies, Inc., 523 U.S. 751, 759 (1998), the United States Supreme Court stated:

> Like foreign sovereign immunity, tribal immunity is a matter of federal law. Although the Court has taken the lead in drawing the bounds of tribal immunity, Congress, subject to constitutional limitations, can alter its limits through explicit legislation.

> In both fields, Congress is in a position to weigh and accommodate the competing policy concerns and reliance interests. The capacity of the Legislative Branch to address the issue by comprehensive legislation counsels some caution by us in this area. Congress has occasionally authorized limited classes of suits against Indian tribes and has always been at liberty to dispense with such tribal immunity or to limit it. It has not yet done so (quotation marks omitted).

The Court makes clear that tribal immunity is subject to Congress's plenary authority to regulate tribes under the Indian Commerce Clause. Congress has in some instances made federal laws applicable to tribes in express terms. *See, e.g.,* Safe Drinking Water Act, 42 U.S.C. §§ 300(f)–300(j) (2006); Resource Conservation and Recovery Act of 1976, 42 U.S.C. §§ 6901–6992(k) (2006). In other instances, Congress has made federal laws expressly not applicable to tribes. As *Hartman* discussed, this is the case with Title VII, and is also true for the Americans With Disabilities Act, 42 U.S.C. §§ 12,111–12,117 (2006 & Supp. 2008) and the Comprehensive Environmental Response, Compensation and Liability Act, 42 U.S.C. § 9601 et seq. (2006), among others.

2. In the absence of a specific expression of Congressional intent, how should it be determined whether the tribe's immunity has been removed by Congress? One approach, illustrated by the *San Manuel* case above, is to apply the statement from a 1960 United States Supreme Court decision that "general Acts of Congress apply to [individual] Indians as well as to all others in the absence of a clear expression to the contrary." Federal Power

Commission v. Tuscarora Indian Nation, 362 U.S. 99, 120 (1960). This analysis was refined by the Ninth Circuit in 1985 to apply the general presumption of application to tribes unless (1) the law touches "exclusive rights of self-governance in purely intramural matters"; (2) the application of the law would "abrogate rights guaranteed by Indian treaties"; or (3) there is proof "by legislative history or some other means that Congress intended [the law] not to apply to Indians on their reservations." Donovan v. Coeur d'Alene Tribal Farm, 751 F.2d 1113, 1116 (9th Cir. 1985). For cases applying this approach, see Solis v. Matheson, 563 F.3d 425 (9th Cir. 2009); E.E.O.C. v. Fond du Lac Heavy Equip. & Constr. Co., 986 F.2d 246 (8th Cir. 1993); Smart v. State Farm Ins. Co., 868 F.2d 929 (7th Cir. 1989).

A contrasting analysis maintains that because of the importance of tribal sovereignty, it is not to be impaired by federal legislation unless Congress expressly provides so. This analysis builds on the idea expressed by the United States Supreme Court that "statutes are to be construed liberally in favor of the Indians, with ambiguous provisions interpreted to their benefit." Montana v. Blackfeet Tribe of Indians, 471 U.S. 759, 766 (1985). For other case law applying the same approach as *Montana, see* Artichoke Joe's California Grand Casino v. Norton, 353 F.3d 712 (9th Cir. 2003); Fort Independence Indian Community v. California, 679 F. Supp. 2d 1159 (E.D. Cal. 2009); Southern Ute Indian Tribe v. Board of County Comm'rs of the County of La Plata, 855 F. Supp. 1194 (D. Colo. 1994). *See also* S. Chloe Thompson, *Exercising and Protecting Tribal Sovereignty in Day-to-Day Business Operations: What the Key Players Need to Know*, 49 WASHBURN L.J. 661, 667–68 (2010) (analyzing the "two schools of thought" on the issue of whether statutes of general applicability apply to Indian tribes).

3. Which approach seems correct? What are the competing values that have to be resolved to decide this? Is it proper to view tribal gaming the same as gaming by non-tribal entities—as a purely commercial activity? Does treating tribal gaming differently than commercial gaming by giving broad scope to immunity claims by tribes give tribal gaming an unfair edge in the gaming marketplace? In criticizing decisions like the *San Manuel* case above, one commentator has written:

> Care must be taken to remember that Indian gaming is tribal governmental gaming. Its foundation rests upon the inherent and treaty powers of Indian tribes to make and enforce their own laws in their own forums and to govern their own territory. The IGRA was conceived, in part, as a Congressional affirmation of that authority. If Indian gaming is allowed to become nothing but a business venture, if it is treated as only a business venture instead of as a method of raising revenues for the provision of governmental programs and services to tribal peoples and other residents of tribal jurisdictions, there will be criticism and unfortunate results directly related to such a view. But, if gaming is used as a tool to consolidate the tribal land base, to build stronger, more effective tribal governments, and to bring economic opportunities to our family, our bands, clans, and other political subdivisions, and to remember our traditions of reaching a helping hand to our neighboring tribes and other jurisdictions in need, the future of Indian gaming, and the future of Indian people throughout this land will be bright.

G. William Rice, *Some Thoughts on the Future of Indian Gaming*, 42 ARIZ. ST. L.J. 219, 252 (2010).

4. State labor and employment laws also are subject to tribal immunity claims. *See, e.g.*, Oklahoma Tax Comm'n v. Citizen Band Potawatomi Indian Tribe of Oklahoma, 498 U.S. 505 (1991) (while state was free to impose taxes on non-Indian customers purchasing cigarettes from the tribe, tribes sovereign immunity precluded the state

from taxing sales to Indian customers); Williams v. Lee, 358 U.S. 217 (1959) (setting forth general principle that state courts do not have jurisdiction over civil claim by non-Indian against Indian where the cause of action took place on Indian lands absent Congressional approval).

iii. State Tort Claims

Kizis v. Morse Diesel Intern., Inc.
794 A.2d 498 (Conn. 2002)

SULLIVAN, C.J.

The issue presented in this appeal is whether the trial court has subject matter jurisdiction over an action brought to recover for a personal injury that allegedly occurred on land belonging to the Mohegan Tribe of Indians of Connecticut (tribe) when the action was brought by a patron who is not Indian against employees of the tribe and the Mohegan Tribal Gaming Authority (authority) who are not Indian.[1] The plaintiff, Louise E. Kizis, brought this negligence action against eight defendants for injuries resulting from a fall at the Mohegan Sun Casino. Of the eight defendants, two individual defendants moved to dismiss the action, asserting tribal sovereign immunity. The trial court denied the motion.... The trial court did not address whether it had subject matter jurisdiction over this tort action. Hence, we ordered, sua sponte, that the parties file supplemental briefs addressing that issue. We reverse the trial court's decision and order that the action be dismissed for lack of subject matter jurisdiction.

The plaintiff alleged that on August 13, 1998, she fell while entering the Mohegan Sun Casino, and she claimed that the fall was caused by a negligently placed fieldstone in an entrance walkway. Seeking to recover for injuries resulting from the fall, the plaintiff brought this action against the defendants in their capacity as employees of the tribe and the authority. She alleged negligence on their part in allowing a fieldstone to be placed in an entrance to the Mohegan Sun Casino. The defendants, the director of facilities operation employed by the authority and a building official employed by the tribe, moved to dismiss the action on the ground that they were protected from suit by the sovereign immunity of the tribe. The defendants claimed that they were being sued for actions undertaken in their official capacities as representatives of the authority and the tribe, both of which are sovereign entities entitled to immunity from suit. They further claimed that unless the tribe expressly had waived its sovereign immunity with regard to a legal action by the plaintiff, the plaintiff could not recover against the tribe or its officials and employees for actions taken by those individuals in their official capacities.

The plaintiff, in opposition to the motion to dismiss, argued that tribal immunity could be asserted only by the tribe itself and, therefore, was unavailable to the defendants in their capacity as employees. The trial court agreed with the plaintiff and denied the mo-

---

1. The tribe created the authority to facilitate and act as the governmental entity responsible for managing all aspects of the tribe's gaming enterprises. This was accomplished under the authority of article XIII, § 1, of the Constitution of the Mohegan Tribe of Indians of Connecticut, which provides in relevant part: "Creation of Gaming Authority. All governmental and proprietary powers of The Mohegan Tribe over the development, construction, operation, promotion, financing, regulation and licensing of gaming, and any associated hotel, associated resort or associated entertainment facilities, on tribal lands (collectively, 'Gaming') shall be exercised by the Tribal Gaming Authority, provided that such powers shall be within the scope of authority delegated by the Tribal Council to the Tribal Gaming Authority under the ordinance establishing the Tribal Gaming Authority...."

tion to dismiss, concluding that tribal immunity arises out of the tribe's status as a dependent domestic nation and, thus, belongs to the tribe itself and not to employees who are not tribe members and who are sued as individuals.[7] Furthermore, the trial court held that the mere employment relationship of the defendants with the tribe or its entities did not grant them the right to assert the tribe's sovereign immunity.

We reverse the trial court's decision and order that the defendants' motion to dismiss be granted, albeit on different grounds. We conclude that the trial court did not have subject matter jurisdiction over the present action because the proper forum for relief is the Mohegan Gaming Disputes Court....

"Subject matter jurisdiction involves the authority of the court to adjudicate the type of controversy presented by the action before it.... [A] court lacks discretion to consider the merits of a case over which it is without jurisdiction.... The objection of want of jurisdiction may be made at any time ... [a]nd the court or tribunal may act on its own motion, and should do so when the lack of jurisdiction is called to its attention.... The requirement of subject matter jurisdiction cannot be waived by any party and can be raised at any stage in the proceedings.... If at any point, it becomes apparent to the court that such jurisdiction is lacking, the appeal must be dismissed" (citations omitted; internal quotation marks omitted). Lewis v. Gaming Policy Board, 224 Conn. 693, 698–99, 620 A.2d 780 (1993).

"Indian tribes have long been recognized as possessing the common-law immunity from suit traditionally enjoyed by sovereign powers." ... We begin with the premise that "Indian tribes are 'domestic dependent nations' which exercise inherent sovereign authority over their members and territories." ... Because Indian tribes possess this inherent sovereignty they are allowed to form "their own laws and be ruled by them" (internal quotation marks omitted). White Mountain Apache Tribe v. Bracker, 448 U.S. 136, 142 (1980). "Tribal powers of self-government ... are observed and protected ... to insure continued viability of Indian self-government insofar as governing powers have not been limited or extinguished.... The exercise of tribal governing power may ... preempt state law in areas where, absent tribal legislation, state law might otherwise apply" (internal quotation marks omitted). Schaghticoke Indians of Kent, Connecticut, Inc. v. Potter, 217 Conn. 612, 628, 587 A.2d 139 (1991).

"Thus, in order for a state enactment to impinge on tribal sovereignty ... the tribe must have a form of demonstrable sovereignty or functioning self-government. [And], the state act in question must actually infringe [upon the] exercise of tribal government or existing tribal legislation." Schaghticoke Indians of Kent, Connecticut, Inc. v. Potter, *supra,* 217 Conn. at 629, 587 A.2d 139.

Consequently, "[a]s a matter of federal law, an Indian tribe is subject to suit only where Congress has authorized the suit or the tribe has waived its immunity"; Kiowa

---

7. Several cases have established that tribal sovereign immunity does not extend to individual members of a tribe and that the tribe itself must assert immunity. A state court does have the authority to adjudicate actions against tribal members when it properly obtains personal jurisdiction. *See, e.g.,* Puyallup Tribe, Inc. v. Washington Game Dept., 433 U.S. 165 (1977); United States v. James, 980 F.2d 1314, 1319 (9th Cir. 1992), *cert. denied,* 510 U.S. 838 (1993); State v. Sebastian, 243 Conn. 115, 160, 701 A.2d 13 (1997), *cert. denied,* 522 U.S. 1077 (1998). "The doctrine of tribal immunity [however] extends to individual tribal officials acting in their representative capacity and within the scope of their authority" (internal quotation marks omitted). Romanella v. Hayward, 933 F. Supp. 163, 167 (D. Conn. 1996). The doctrine does not extend to tribal officials when acting outside their authority in violation of state law. *See* Puyallup Tribe, Inc. v. Washington Game Dept., *supra,* at 171–72.

Tribe of Oklahoma v. Manufacturing Technologies, Inc., 523 U.S. 751, 754 (1998); and the tribe itself has consented to suit in a specific forum. *See* Santa Clara Pueblo v. Martinez, *supra*, at 436 U.S. at 58. "Absent a clear and unequivocal waiver by the tribe or congressional abrogation, the doctrine of sovereign immunity bars suits for damages against a tribe." Romanella v. Hayward, 933 F. Supp. 163, 167 (D. Conn. 1996). "However, such waiver may not be implied, but must be expressed unequivocally." McClendon v. United States, 885 F.2d 627, 629 (9th Cir. 1989). Further, "[t]he doctrine of tribal immunity extends to individual tribal officials acting in their representative capacity and within the scope of their authority" (internal quotation marks omitted). Romanella v. Hayward, *supra*, at 167.

We now examine the pertinent federal, state and tribal laws to determine whether the tribe has waived its sovereign immunity and, if so, in which forum. The Indian Gaming Regulatory Act (gaming act); 25 U.S.C. §2701 et seq. (1994); regulates gaming operations on tribal land. The gaming act permits a recognized tribe to conduct "Class III" gaming only when the gaming operation is conducted in accordance with a gaming compact with a state and approved by the United States Secretary of the Interior. *See* 25 U.S.C. §2710(d)(1)(C).... The tribe has been recognized by an act of Congress and by the state of Connecticut. In accordance with the gaming act, the tribe and the state of Connecticut entered into the Mohegan Tribe-State of Connecticut Gaming Compact (gaming compact), which governs gaming operations on the tribe's reservation. The gaming compact was approved by the Secretary of the Interior and was incorporated by reference into federal law....

Section 3(g) of the gaming compact provides: "The Tribe shall establish, prior to the commencement of class III gaming, reasonable procedures for the disposition of tort claims arising from alleged injuries to patrons of its gaming facilities. The Tribe shall not be deemed to have waived its sovereign immunity from suit with respect to such claims by virtue of any provision of this Compact, but may adopt a remedial system analogous to that available for similar claims arising against the State or such other remedial system as may be appropriate following consultation with the State gaming agency."

Pursuant to its obligation under the gaming compact, the Mohegan Tribal Council established, in the Constitution of the Mohegan Tribe of Indians of Connecticut, a Gaming Disputes Court and a Gaming Disputes Court of Appeals. Mohegan Const., art. XIII, §2. These courts have jurisdiction over disputes "arising out of or in connection with" tribal gaming operations or the actions of the authority. Mohegan Const., art. XIII, §2. The Mohegan constitution provides that "[t]he Tribal Council shall establish by ordinance, the Gaming Disputes Court, which shall be composed of a Trial Branch and an Appellate Branch. Exclusive jurisdiction for the Tribe over disputes arising out of or in connection with the Gaming, the actions of the Tribal Gaming Authority, or contracts entered into by The Mohegan Tribe or the Tribal Gaming Authority in connection with Gaming, including without limitation, disputes arising between any person or entity and the Tribal Gaming Authority, including customers, employees, or any gaming manager operating under a gaming management agreement with the Tribal Gaming Authority, or any person or entity which may be in privity with such persons or entities as to Gaming matters shall be vested in the Gaming Disputes Court...." Mohegan Const., art. XIII, §2. In addition, the tribe ordinance establishing the Gaming Disputes Court confers "exclusive original jurisdiction over all cases with respect to which the Tribe has conferred subject matter jurisdiction pursuant to Article XIII of the Mohegan Constitution." Ordinance No. 95-4 of the Mohegan Tribe of Indians of Conn., art. V, §501.

The tribe enacted an ordinance[13] establishing the Mohegan Torts Code, which contains a limited waiver of the tribe's sovereign immunity so that the Gaming Disputes Court may adjudicate liability for "(1) [i]njuries proximately caused by the negligent acts or omissions of the Mohegan Tribal Gaming Authority; (2) [i]njuries proximately caused by the condition of any property of the Mohegan Tribal Gaming Authority provided the claimant establishes that the property was in a dangerous condition; [and] (3) [i]njuries caused by the negligent acts or omissions of tribal security officers arising out of the performance of their duties during the course and within the scope of their employment." Ordinance No. 98-1, An Ordinance Amending Ordinance 96-2 Establishing The Mohegan Torts Code, §3(c). The Mohegan Torts Code further provides that the ordinance does not immunize employees of the authority from individual liability, but that all disputes regarding employees that occur on the Mohegan "Gaming Enterprise Site shall be heard only in the Gaming Disputes Court."[14] Ordinance No. 98-1, *supra*, §6.

We recognize that federal law may limit a tribal court's assertion of its own jurisdiction.... Congress, however, only extended Connecticut criminal jurisdiction over the Mohegan Reservation. *See* Mohegan Nation of Connecticut Land Claims Settlement Act of 1994, 25 U.S.C. §1775 et seq. (1994). Furthermore, the legislative history of the Mohegan Nation of Connecticut Land Claims Settlement Act discloses a Congressional intent that "[t]he Mohegan Indian Nation will retain exclusive civil jurisdiction within the boundaries of its reservation...." H. Rep. 103-676, 103d Cong., 2d Sess. 9 (1994). Accordingly, in order for Connecticut to assume civil jurisdiction, the state must first obtain the consent of the affected tribe. *See* 25 U.S.C. §§1322, 1326 (1994). The tribe has not consented to state jurisdiction over private actions involving matters that occurred on tribal land. Indeed, in this instance, the statutes and compacts cited previously, which have been recognized by both the federal government and the state of Connecticut through compliance with the procedures set forth in the gaming act and the Indian Civil Rights Act,[16] explicitly place the present type of tort action in the jurisdiction of the tribe's Gaming Disputes Court. The tribe, as discussed previously, is a sovereign entity with the authority to create and enforce its own laws. The exercise of jurisdiction by state courts in this type of action would be in direct contradiction to the procedures established and consented to by the tribe after negotiation with the state of Connecticut and the federal government. Although Connecticut has a genuine interest in providing a judicial forum to victims of torts, the gaming act provided the state with a mechanism to negotiate with the tribe, to establish the manner in which to redress torts occurring in connection with casino operations on the tribe's land. As a result of these negotiations, the tribe maintained jurisdiction over tort actions of this type.

The two individual defendants being sued are employed by the tribe and the authority, and the alleged incident took place on the Gaming Enterprise Site. The Mohegan Torts Code together with the gaming compact and the Mohegan constitution provide a forum and mechanism to redress the plaintiff's injuries. Therefore, the Connecticut courts do not have subject matter jurisdiction over this claim. Accordingly, the Mohegan Gaming Disputes

---

13. Before conducting a gaming operation, a tribe must also adopt a gaming ordinance and obtain approval for the ordinance from the National Indian Gaming Commission. *See* 25 U.S.C. §2710(d) (1) (A) (1994) and 25 C.F.R. §522.1 et seq. (approval requirements).

14. Section 6 of the Mohegan Torts Code provides: "This ordinance does not immunize employees of the Mohegan Tribal Gaming Authority from individual liability for the full measure of the recovery applicable to a claimant if it is established that their conduct exceeded the scope of their employment or authority. Claims for individual liability arising out of conduct which is found to exceed the scope of employment and which arise on the Gaming Enterprise Site shall be heard only in the Gaming Disputes Court."

16. *See* 25 U.S.C. §§1322, 1326 (1994).

Court is the exclusive forum for the adjudication and settlement of tort claims against the tribe and its employees because it is the forum in which the sovereign has consented to being sued, as set forth in Ordinance No. 98-1 amending the Mohegan Torts Code.

The decision of the trial court is reversed and the case is remanded with direction to grant the motion to dismiss and render judgment thereon.

Notes

1. In Cossey v. Cherokee Nation Enterprises, LLC, 212 P.3d 447 (Okla. 2009), a non-Indian patron brought a premises liability action in Oklahoma state court for injuries he suffered at the tribal casino. The tribal business entity operating the casino claimed immunity, arguing that the case should be heard in the tribal court. The compact the tribe has with the state specified that tort claims could be heard in a "court of competent jurisdiction," and that the compact did "not alter tribal, state civil adjudicatory or criminal jurisdiction." The court held that the tribal court and Oklahoma state court had concurrent jurisdiction and that both were a "court of competent jurisdiction." Because the patron was not a party to the compact, and he had entered no consensual relationship with the tribe, he was guaranteed the right to pursue his claim in state court. Does this result seem to square with the idea that waivers of immunity are to be read narrowly?

2. For other cases dealing with state tort claims against tribes, *see* Terry v. Mohegan Tribal Gaming Authority, 2008 WL 2313677 (Conn. Super. May 16, 2008); Ellis v. Allied Snow Plowing, Removal and Sanding Services Corp., 838 A.2d 237 (Conn. App. 2004); Diepenbrock v. Merkel, 97 P.3d 1063 (Kan. App. 2004).

3. Section 2 of this chapter considered immunity issues in relation to business transactions, presumably with businesses that are aware of tribal immunity implications. Sections 3 and 4 address situations where the person challenging the immunity is more likely an individual who may not be aware, or be properly chargeable with knowledge of, the existence and effects of tribal immunity. Should that fact change the immunity analysis?

4. Does a tribe waive its sovereign immunity by purchasing liability insurance to protect against tort claims brought by patrons? Normally the purchase of such insurance indicates an expectation of, if not a willingness to, being sued by an injured patron. *See* Seminole Tribe of Florida v. McCor, 903 So. 2d 353, 359 (Fla. App. 2005) (purchase of insurance is not clear indication of waiver of immunity, rather "it may simply be a measure to provide protection for the Tribe's assets against the possibility that the Tribe's immunity will be abrogated or ignored."); Campo Band of Mission Indians v. Superior Court, 137 Cal. App. 4th 175, 39 Cal. Rptr. 3d 875 (2006) (in compact with state, tribe unambiguously waived its immunity for patron tort claims to the extent of the insurance coverage). *See also* Venus McGhee Prince, *Making the Gaming Business a 'Safe Bet' for Tribes*, 9 GAMING L. REV. 314 (2005) (notes that tribes are often required in compact to carry liability insurance, and even when they are not it is advisable to obtain such insurance in case their sovereign immunity is circumvented).

5. In Agua Caliente Band of Cahuilla Indians v. Superior Court, 148 P.3d 1126 (Cal. 2006), the California Supreme Court ruled that the Tenth Amendment and the "republican form of government" guaranteed under Article IV, section 4 of the United States Constitution allowed the state to sue to enforce reporting requirements for campaign contributions under the state Political Reform Act. For additional discussion on these constitutional issues, *see* Gary Goldsmith, *Big Spenders in State Elections: Has Financial Participation by Indian Tribes Defined the Limits of Tribal Sovereign Immunity From Suit?* 34 WM. MITCHELL L. REV. 659 (2008); Matthew L.M. Fletcher, *The Supreme Court's Indian Problem*, 59 HASTINGS L.J. 579 (2008).

Part IV
Federal and State Laws Affecting Gambling

Chapter 11

Federal Gaming Law

1. The History of Federal Gaming Regulation

From its earliest legislation, Congress' primary intent in adopting gambling legislation was to assist the states that restrict gambling by regulating interstate activities that are beyond the powers of the individual states to regulate. The United States Supreme Court recognized in United States v. Edge Broadcasting Company, 509 U.S. 418 (1993) that: "Congress has, since the early 19th century, sought to assist the States in controlling lotteries. *See, e.g.*, Act of Mar. 2, 1827, § 6, 4 Stat. 238; Act of July 27, 1868, § 13, 15 Stat. 194, 196; Act of June 8, 1872, § 149, 17 Stat. 283, 302." The purpose of this legislation was not to prohibit certain behavior at the federal level, but rather to provide a mechanism whereby the federal government could enforce violations of state gaming laws. Its first foray into gambling legislation occurred in the late nineteenth century. In 1895, the federal government prohibited interstate transportation of lottery tickets and prize lists. They adopted postal regulations to prohibit the distribution of lottery materials and advertisements. As part of the Communications Act of 1934, the federal government expanded the prohibition of lottery materials and advertisements from the mail to radio broadcasting.

Federal gambling legislation strayed from merely regulating interstate lotteries to a weapon against organized crime primarily through the efforts of Senator Estes Kefauver in the 1950s and Attorney General Robert Kennedy in the early 1960s. In 1950, Senator Estes Kefauver of Tennessee chaired a U.S. Senate Committee, commonly known as the Kefauver Committee, to investigate organized crime's influence in America. The work of this commission determined that a major source of revenue for organized crime was the gambling industry, through both illegal games and the legal casinos. Therefore, for the first time, federal legislation expanded beyond lotteries with the passage of the Gambling Ship Act in 1949 and the Johnson Act in 1951. The Gambling Ship Act attempted to eliminate the presence of stationary gambling ships anchored in international water off the coasts of California and Florida. The Johnson Act was directed at the growing slot machine market. It generally prohibited the transportation of gaming devices into any state or possession of the United States from any place outside such state or possession. The Johnson Act also prohibited the possession and use of such devices in a United States possession or within the United States' maritime jurisdiction. A consequence of this legislation was its impact on the presence of casinos on cruise ships.

The federal government significantly augmented gambling laws in the early 1960s. Then U.S. Attorney General Robert Kennedy sponsored a group of gambling laws as part of the Program to Curb Organized Crime and Racketeering. These laws were designed to involve the federal government in the effort to suppress local criminal activities from which organized crime drew much of their sustenance. United States v. Colacurcio, 499

F.2d 1401 (9th Cir. 1974). The cornerstones of the program were the Travel Act, the Federal Wire Act, and the Wagering Paraphernalia Act. While, according to Kennedy, "the target clearly is organized crime," *Hearing on S. 1653–58, S. 1665, Senate Comm. on Judiciary 87th Congress,* 16 (1961), the laws elevated a wide variety of state crimes, including gambling offenses, to federal offenses if the criminal activity involved crossing state lines and met other minimal requirements.

The Illegal Gambling Business Act, adopted in 1970, continued to target illegal gambling businesses. Much like the impetus for the 1961 federal gambling laws, the purpose of the 1970 Act was to strike at those "illegal endeavors [such] as syndicated gambling, loan sharking, theft and fencing of property, the importation and distribution of narcotics and other dangerous drugs, and other forms of social exploitation, [that allowed organized crime to obtain funds] to infiltrate and corrupt legitimate businesses and labor unions and to subvert and corrupt our democratic processes." *See* United States v. Aquino, 336 F. Supp. 737, 739 (D.C. Mich. 1972).

Excellent sources for the history of Federal gambling legislation include James H. Frey, *Federal Involvement in U.S. Gaming Regulation,* AM. ACAD. POL. SCI., Vol. 556, at 138–53 (1998); Robert Blakey & Philip Kurland, *The Development of the Federal Law of Gambling,* 63 CORNELL L. REV. 923, 958 (1978). For a discussion on the Communications Act of 1934, *see* I. NELSON ROSE, LEGAL GAMBLING: THE RIGHT TO ADVERTISE, THE GAMBLING STUDIES: PROCEEDINGS OF THE SIXTH NATIONAL CONFERENCE ON GAMBLING AND RISK TAKING (1985). Robert Kennedy details how the Wire Act, the Wagering Paraphernalia, the Travel Act and amendments to the Johnson Act were intended to work together in the fight against organized crime in Robert Kennedy, *Proposals for Meeting the Challenge of Interstate Organized Crime, The Program of the Department of Justice,* 38 NOTRE DAME L. REV. 637 (1962). FBI director J. Edgar Hoover provided a similar review of the purpose of the 1961 Federal Gambling Statutes in John Edgar Hoover, *The War on Organized Crime,* 13 DEPAUL L. REV. 195 (1964).

This chapter explores the diverse and unsystematic intervention into gambling regulation and prohibition undertaken by the Federal government. A complete review of Federal legislation also involves consideration of other chapters in this book that address specific government intervention into Indian gaming, sports gambling, and the Internet, all of which deserve special consideration.

2. Gambling on International Waters

In contrast to most land based gaming, the gaming industry on the high seas is not operated under direct government control. No regulations govern these floating casinos, and any person can operate the casino regardless of suitability. A player generally has no governmental assurance that the casino is conducting the games honestly. The casino owner has no requirement to implement accounting controls and pays no gaming taxes.

The concept of a floating gaming establishment is not unique to the cruise ship industry. American history shows a rich tradition of gaming aboard ships. The riverboats of the nineteenth century were infamous havens for the American gambler. In 1840, about 2,000 gamblers plied their trade on the Mississippi River between Louisville and New Orleans. UNITED STATES DEPT. OF COMMERCE, COMMISSION ON THE REVIEW OF THE NATIONAL POLICY TOWARD GAMBLING, GAMBLING IN PERSPECTIVE: A REVIEW OF THE

WRITTEN HISTORY OF GAMBLING AND AN ASSESSMENT OF ITS EFFECT ON MODERN AMER-
ICAN SOCIETY, App. I, 23 (1976). Unlike cruise ships, the riverboats operated within the
jurisdiction of the United States.

In contrast to the riverboat, the voyages on the first cruise ships were conspicuous for
the absence of gambling.

Perhaps the first documented cruise was chronicled by Mark Twain in a book written
in 1868 concerning the 1867 pleasure excursion of the "Quaker City" to Europe, the Holy
Land, and Egypt. In his characteristic wit, Twain wrote:

> The pilgrims played dominoes when too much Josephus or Robinson's Holy Land
> Researches, or book-writing, made recreation necessary—for dominoes is about
> as mild and sinless a game as any in the world, perhaps, excepting always the in-
> effably insipid diversion they call croquet, which is a game where you don't pocket
> any balls and don't carom on anything of any consequence, and when you are
> done nobody has to pay, and there are no refreshments to saw off, and, consequently,
> there isn't any satisfaction whatever about it—they played dominoes till they
> were rested, and then they blackguarded each other privately till prayer-time.

MARK TWAIN, THE INNOCENTS ABROAD 645 (1869). Today, almost all major cruise
ships have casinos. A separate market exists for the "cruise-to-nowhere" voyages. These
are voyages on ships that depart and return to the same port. Typically, these ships cruise
to international waters and then open their casinos. After a short voyage, they close the
casino before entering territorial waters and returning to port. Gambling on cruise ships
and "cruise-to-nowhere" voyages are regulated through a complicated interplay of the
Johnson Act, the Gambling Ship Act, and the Internal Revenue Code.

A. The Johnson Act — 15 U.S.C. § 1171 et seq.

Sec. 1171.—Definitions.

As used in this chapter—

(a) The term "gambling device" means—

(1) any so-called "slot machine" or any other machine or mechanical device an
essential part of which is a drum or reel with insignia thereon, and

(A) which when operated may deliver, as the result of the application of an
element of chance, any money or property, or

(B) by the operation of which a person may become entitled to receive, as the
result of the application of an element of chance, any money or property; or

(2) any other machine or mechanical device (including, but not limited to,
roulette wheels and similar devices) designed and manufactured primarily for
use in connection with gambling, and

(A) which when operated may deliver, as the result of the application of an
element of chance, any money or property, or

(B) by the operation of which a person may become entitled to receive, as the
result of the application of an element of chance, any money or property; or

(3) any subassembly or essential part intended to be used in connection with
any such machine or mechanical device, but which is not attached to any such
machine or mechanical device as a constituent part.

(b) The term "State" includes the District of Columbia, Puerto Rico, the Virgin Islands, and Guam.

(c) The term "possession of the United States" means any possession of the United States which is not named in subsection (b) of this section.

(d) The term "interstate or foreign commerce" means commerce

(1) between any State or possession of the United States and any place outside of such State or possession, or

(2) between points in the same State or possession of the United States but through any place outside thereof.

(e) The term "intrastate commerce" means commerce wholly within one State or possession of the United States.

(f) The term "boundaries" has the same meaning given that term in section 1301 of title 43

Section 1172. Transportation of gambling devices as unlawful; exceptions; authority of Federal Trade Commission.

(a) General rule

It shall be unlawful knowingly to transport any gambling device to any place in a State or a possession of the United States from any place outside of such State or possession: Provided, That this section shall not apply to transportation of any gambling device to a place in any State which has enacted a law providing for the exemption of such State from the provisions of this section, or to a place in any subdivision of a State if the State in which such subdivision is located has enacted a law providing for the exemption of such subdivision from the provisions of this section, nor shall this section apply to any gambling device used or designed for use at and transported to licensed gambling establishments where betting is legal under applicable State laws: Provided, further, That it shall not be unlawful to transport in interstate or foreign commerce any gambling device into any State in which the transported gambling device is specifically enumerated as lawful in a statute of that State.

(b) Authority of Federal Trade Commission

Nothing in this chapter shall be construed to interfere with or reduce the authority, or the existing interpretation of the authority, of the Federal Trade Commission under the Federal Trade Commission Act (15 U.S.C. 41 et. seq.).

(c) Exception

This section does not prohibit the transport of a gambling device to a place in a State or a possession of the United States on a vessel on a voyage, if—

(1) use of the gambling device on a portion of that voyage is, by reason of subsection (b) of section 1175 of this title, not a violation of that section; and

(2) the gambling device remains on board that vessel while in that State.

Notes

1. State and federal jurisdiction within state territorial waters is concurrent. Under the Johnson Act, the states retain the right to control gaming and gambling ships *within* their territorial waters. Thus, states can allow cruise ships to conduct gaming activities within their territorial waters, and can prohibit them from doing so. For example, Louisiana

provides an exception to its general prohibition against gaming for commercial cruise ships. LA. REV. STAT. ANN. § 14:90(b).

2. The broad application to "the special maritime and territorial jurisdiction of the United States" created special consideration for the Great Lakes region of the United States. Another statute specifically includes the Great Lakes within this jurisdiction. Therefore, on its face, the Johnson Act appears to prohibit gambling on the Great Lakes, even those areas that are within state jurisdiction. This interpretation, however, is inconsistent with federal policy to support, not interfere with, the gambling policies of the various states. This ambiguity, however, was sufficient for the State of Indiana to request and receive a special exemption for the casino gambling ship on Lake Michigan. 15 U.S.C. § 1175.

B. The Cruise Ship Competitiveness Act Amends the Johnson Act

A major issue with the Johnson Act was resolved by the passage of legislation in 1992 called the "Cruise Ship Competitiveness Act." 26 U.S.C. § 4472. Before 1992, the federal government treated U.S.-flag and foreign-flag vessels differently for purposes of gambling enforcement. The Department of Justice did not interpret the Johnson Act as applying to foreign-flag vessels. As a result, the American cruise industry had operated under a competitive disadvantage. Foreign-flag vessels could dock at a U.S. port with a casino (including gaming devices) on board, pick up American passengers, and operate the casino once the vessel reached international waters. U.S. flag vessels, however, were prohibited from doing so. The Justice Department's interpretation produced predictable results. As of 1991, there were only two cruise ships registered in the United States, and neither offered gaming. In contrast, about eighty foreign-flag cruise ships served United States ports.

On March 9, 1992, Congress amended the Johnson Act by adding a new section designed to place vessels registered in the United States on equal footing with foreign-flag vessels.

Section 1175. Specific jurisdictions within which manufacturing, repairing, selling, possessing, etc., prohibited; exceptions

(a) General rule

It shall be unlawful to manufacture, recondition, repair, sell, transport, possess, or use any gambling device in the District of Columbia, in any possession of the United States, within Indian country as defined in section 1151 of title 18 or within the special maritime and territorial jurisdiction of the United States as defined in section 7 of title 18, including on a vessel documented under chapter 121 of title 46 or documented under the laws of a foreign country.

(b) Exception

(1) In general

Except for a voyage or a segment of a voyage that begins and ends in the State of Hawaii, or as provided in paragraph (2), this section does not prohibit—

(A) the repair, transport, possession, or use of a gambling device on a vessel that is not within the boundaries of any State or possession of the United States;

(B) the transport or possession, on a voyage, of a gambling device on a vessel that is within the boundaries of any State or possession of the United States, if—

(i) use of the gambling device on a portion of that voyage is, by reason of subparagraph (A), not a violation of this section; and

(ii) the gambling device remains on board that vessel while the vessel is within the boundaries of that State or possession; or

(C) the repair, transport, possession, or use of a gambling device on a vessel on a voyage that begins in the State of Indiana and that does not leave the territorial jurisdiction of that State, including such a voyage on Lake Michigan.

(2) Application to certain voyages

(A) General rule

Paragraph (1)(A) does not apply to the repair or use of a gambling device on a vessel that is on a voyage or segment of a voyage described in subparagraph (B) of this paragraph if the State or possession of the United States in which the voyage or segment begins and ends has enacted a statute the terms of which prohibit that repair or use on that voyage or segment.

(B) Voyage and segment described

A voyage or segment of a voyage referred to in subparagraph (A) is a voyage or segment, respectively—

(i) that begins and ends in the same State or possession of the United States, and

(ii) during which the vessel does not make an intervening stop within the boundaries of another State or possession of the United States or a foreign country.

(C) Exclusion of certain voyages and segments

Except for a voyage or segment of a voyage that occurs within the boundaries of the State of Hawaii, a voyage or segment of a voyage is not described in subparagraph (B) if it includes or consists of a segment—

(i) that begins and ends in the same State;

(ii) that is part of a voyage to another State or to a foreign country; and

(iii) in which the vessel reaches the other State or foreign country within 3 days after leaving the State in which it begins.

(c) Exception for Alaska

(1) With respect to a vessel operating in Alaska, this section does not prohibit, nor may the State of Alaska make it a violation of law for there to occur, the repair, transport, possession, or use of any gambling device on board a vessel which provides sleeping accommodations for all of its passengers and that is on a voyage or segment of a voyage described in paragraph (2), except that such State may, within its boundaries—

(A) prohibit the use of a gambling device on a vessel while it is docked or anchored or while it is operating within 3 nautical miles of a port at which it is scheduled to call; and

(B) require the gambling devices to remain on board the vessel.

(2) A voyage referred to in paragraph (1) is a voyage that—

(A) includes a stop in Canada or in a State other than the State of Alaska;

(B) includes stops in at least 2 different ports situated in the State of Alaska; and

(C) is of at least 60 hours duration

Notes

1. This law was further clarified by amendments in 1996 that limited the states' rights to exclude gambling on segments of voyages that "1) begin and end in the same state; 2) that is part of a voyage to another state or to a Foreign country; and 3) in which the vessel reaches the foreign country or other State within three days after leaving the State in which such segment begins." This limitation, however, does not apply to voyages or segments of voyages in Hawaii. 15 U.S.C. § 1175(b)(2)(C).

2. In contrast, states can limit or prohibit cruises to nowhere. In Casino Venture v. Steward, 183 F.3d 307 (4th Cir. 1999), a company wanting to offer gambling cruises from a port in South Carolina sought a declaration that the Johnson Act preempted state gambling laws. The company wanted to operate day cruises offering gambling when in international waters. The cruises were intended to depart from and return to a port in South Carolina without any intervening stops. South Carolina has general criminal gambling laws that include prohibiting the possession of gambling devices within state territory. Unless preempted, these state statutes would prohibit the possession of the gambling devices when in state waters. The Fourth Circuit held in favor of the states and found that the Johnson Act did not preempt its gambling laws. The court held that without an expressed intention to preempt state law, the court would not imply preemption where no conflicts existed between state and federal law. Moreover, after conducting an historical review of federal laws involved gambling or maritime laws, the court concluded that they "leave room for state regulation." 183 F.3d 307, 311. In contrast, a county — as opposed to a state — cannot opt out of the Johnson Act. Palmetto Princess, LLC v. Georgetown County, 631 S.E.2d 68 (S.C. 2006).

3. The 1996 amendments also provided other exceptions to the Johnson Act. First, it exempted voyages departing from Indiana on Lake Michigan from the prohibitions of the Johnson Act, provided that the ship does not leave the territorial jurisdiction of that state. It also exempted certain voyages to and from Alaska. 15 U.S.C. § 1175.

4. The Johnson Act amendments attempted to provide a major incentive to invest in the American cruise ship industry. Gaming serves as a major source of entertainment on cruises, and gaming revenues can enhance the financial viability of a commercial venture. The amendments do not, however, permit unlimited shipboard gaming. Two significant limitations remain: The Gambling Ship Act of 1949 (prohibiting vessels used principally for the operation of a gaming establishments) and state law.

C. Gambling Ship Act of 1949

In 1949, Congress passed the Gambling Ship Act, 18 U.S.C. § 1081, which prohibited the operation of gambling ships that were either in territorial waters, owned by American citizens or residents, of American registry, or otherwise within the jurisdiction of the United States.

This statute was not aimed toward the operation of cruise ships, but rather the operation of stationary barges located off both the eastern and western seaboards. The advent of these floating casinos occurred in 1926 when the barges appeared and were anchored off the coast near San Francisco for the ostensible purposes of fishing, recreation, and pleasure. Passengers were carried to and from these ships in small speedboats. Shortly after these ships appeared in Northern California, other ships appeared off the coast in Florida and Los Angeles. The ships were anchored about three miles off shore, and were brilliantly lit so as to be clearly visible to those on shore. These ships could provide gaming accommodations to about 600 persons. Ship owners extensively advertised and provided free entertainment and food on board.

The operation of these ships was a continuing problem for state law enforcement officials who lacked jurisdiction over the ships. The end to the stationary gambling ships occurred in 1948 after gambling ship legislation introduced by U.S. Senator William Knowland of California passed Congress. When Congress adopted the Gambling Ship Act, it contained a broad prohibition against gambling aboard American-flag vessels. *See* 18 U.S.C. §§ 1081–1082 (1984). The current version of the Gambling Ship Act is set forth below.

The history of these ships was chronicled in H.R. Rep. No. 1058, 3 (1932) (letter from Arthur J. Tyler, Commissioner of Navigation); H.R. Rep. No. 1700, 2 (1948); E. Cray, *High Rollers on the High Sea*, California Law., Vol. 2, 1982, at 51.

Gambling Ship Act: Sec. 1081.—Definitions

As used in this chapter:

The term "gambling ship" means a vessel used principally for the operation of one or more gambling establishments. Such term does not include a vessel with respect to gambling aboard such vessel beyond the territorial waters of the United States during a covered voyage (as defined in section 4472 of the Internal Revenue Code of 1986 as in effect on January 1, 1994).

The term "gambling establishment" means any common gaming or gambling establishment operated for the purpose of gaming or gambling, including accepting, recording, or registering bets, or carrying on a policy game or any other lottery, or playing any game of chance, for money or other thing of value.

The term "vessel" includes every kind of water and air craft or other contrivance used or capable of being used as a means of transportation on water, or on water and in the air, as well as any ship, boat, barge, or other water craft or any structure capable of floating on the water.

The term "American vessel" means any vessel documented or numbered under the laws of the United States; and includes any vessel which is neither documented or numbered under the laws of the United States nor documented under the laws of any foreign country, if such vessel is owned by, chartered to, or otherwise controlled by one or more citizens or residents of the United States or corporations organized under the laws of the United States or of any State.

The term "wire communication facility" means any and all instrumentalities, personnel, and services (among other things, the receipt, forwarding, or delivery of communications) used or useful in the transmission of writings, signs, pictures, and sounds of all kinds by aid of wire, cable, or other like connection between the points of origin and reception of such transmission

Sec. 1082.—Gambling ships

(a) It shall be unlawful for any citizen or resident of the United States, or any other person who is on an American vessel or is otherwise under or within the jurisdiction of the United States, directly or indirectly—

(1) to set up, operate, or own or hold any interest in any gambling ship or any gambling establishment on any gambling ship; or

(2) in pursuance of the operation of any gambling establishment on any gambling ship, to conduct or deal any gambling game, or to conduct or operate any gambling device, or to induce, entice, solicit, or permit any person to bet or play at any such establishment,

if such gambling ship is on the high seas, or is an American vessel or otherwise under or within the jurisdiction of the United States, and is not within the jurisdiction of any State.

(b) Whoever violates the provisions of subsection (a) of this section shall be fined under this title or imprisoned not more than two years, or both.

(c) Whoever, being

(1) the owner of an American vessel, or

(2) the owner of any vessel under or within the jurisdiction of the United States, or

(3) the owner of any vessel and being an American citizen, shall use, or knowingly permit the use of, such vessel in violation of any provision of this section shall, in addition to any other penalties provided by this chapter, forfeit such vessel, together with her tackle, apparel, and furniture, to the United States

Sec. 1083. — Transportation between shore and ship; penalties

(a) It shall be unlawful to operate or use, or to permit the operation or use of, a vessel for the carriage or transportation, or for any part of the carriage or transportation, either directly or indirectly, of any passengers, for hire or otherwise, between a point or place within the United States and a gambling ship which is not within the jurisdiction of any State. This section does not apply to any carriage or transportation to or from a vessel in case of emergency involving the safety or protection of life or property.

...

Notes

1. Because gambling on ships usually occurs on the high seas, jurisdictional issues play an important part in the implementation of the Gambling Ships Act. In the first instance, the Gambling Ships Act applies to American citizens or residents for violations that occur on the high seas. The United States can proscribe conduct of its citizens beyond the territorial boundaries of the United States. This authority extends to regulating the conduct of American citizens on the high seas. *See, e.g.*, Blackmer v. United States, 284 U.S. 421 (1932). This issue was settled in the only reported case involving a prosecution for operation of a gaming ship. In United States v. Black, 291 F. Supp. 262 (S.D.N.Y. 1968), the defendants, American citizens, operated a non-American vessel on a cruise from New York harbor into international waters and back to New York. Once in international waters, a group, known as "The Sons of Italy," conducted gaming activities in an area set aside by the ship's master. The court held that the indictment was sufficient on the settled principle that citizenship alone is sufficient to confer jurisdiction upon the United States over extraterritorial acts.

2. A second jurisdictional issue is the ability of the federal government to assert jurisdiction over a ship with an American registry. Under settled law, the country of registry has the right to assert jurisdiction upon the fiction that a ship on the high seas is assimilated into the territory of the flag under which it flies.

3. A third jurisdictional issue relates to the federal government's right to assert jurisdiction over ships of foreign registry and ownership. As early as 1887, the Supreme Court recognized the right of a country to exercise jurisdiction over a foreign vessel upon its entering an American port. Mali v. Keeper of the Common Jail of Hudson County, 120 U.S. 1 (1887). The territory, subject to the jurisdiction of the United States, includes "a marginal belt of the sea extending from the coast line outward a marine league, or three geographic miles." Cunard SS. Co. v. Mellon, 262 U.S. 100, 122 (1923). The three nautical mile rule resulted from an executive order issued by President Washington to members of the executive branch. See, e.g., Heinzen, The Three Mile Limit: Preserving the Freedom of the Seas, 11 STAN. L. REV. 597 (1959). One land mile equals .87 nautical miles. Thus, the three nautical mile limit is approximately 3.45 miles. The area between three and twelve miles is considered the contiguous zone. International law recognizes a twelve-mile limit for revenue, customs, sanitation, immigration, and fishing rights. Cf. Law of the Sea: Convention on the Territorial Sea and Contiguous Zone, opened for signature April 29, 1958, 15 U.S.T. 1606, 516 U.N.T.S. 205, art. 24 (establishes a twelve mile limit for contiguous zone and recognizes the competence of coastal States to "exercise the control necessary to ... [p]revent infringement of its customs, fiscal, immigration or sanitary regulations within its territory or territorial sea."). A third zone, called an "exclusive economic zone," extends 200 miles from the coastline. This zone was created to both protect fishing rights and to enforce pollution laws. Adding further confusion was the passage of the Antiterrorism and Effective Death Penalty Act of 1996. Public Law No. 104-132. This Act was intended to extend the jurisdiction of the federal government to fight international terrorism. One of its provisions, however, defines United States territorial jurisdiction for purposes of the Act to "12 nautical miles from the baselines of the United States, determined in accordance with international law." When cruise ship gambling was proposed out of New York City in 1997, a federal prosecutor from New York issued an advisory letter that this Act required proposed cruise ship operators to travel twelve miles from shore before commencing any gambling activities. As a practical matter, this interpretation would have doomed the industry because the travel time would have made the voyages impractical for gambling purposes. The cruise industry, however, was able to convince the Federal District Court in Brooklyn that the three-mile, as opposed to the twelve-mile, territorial limit should apply. This decision was upheld in United States v. One Big Six Wheel, 166 F.3d 498 (2d Cir. 1999). In that case, the court noted:

> Further, as the district court opinion notes, the government's argument leads to an inherent conflict between the terms "territorial waters" and "covered voyage," such that a gambling cruise could travel three nautical miles to constitute a covered voyage under the Internal Revenue Code, but would have to travel twelve nautical miles to avoid criminal liability under the Gambling Ship Act. See id. at 178. But there is nothing in the plain language of AEDPA that indicates an intention to abolish the covered voyage exception in 18 U.S.C. §1081 or to amend 26 U.S.C. §4472 or 26 C.F.R. §43.4472-1(e).

166 F.3d at 502.

D. United States Department of Justice Interpretation

Whether the Gambling Ship Act prohibits luxury ships with a significant casino presents another issue. Under the Act, a gambling vessel is a ship or other vessel capable of floating which is "used principally for the operation of one or more gambling establishments." Certainty, the legislation was intended for "large scale commercial gambling." Unfortunately, the term "principally" is a vague and uncertain term. At best, the term is synonymous with "mainly" or "chiefly." If "principally" can be described in economic terms as representing fifty percent or more of revenues, most cruise ships, even if they cater to gaming clientele, would probably not be considered principally gaming ships. The Criminal Resource Manual of the Department of Justice, which incorporated an April 1991 U.S. Attorney General Opinion from Texas, attempts to explain and define these concepts.

Criminal Resource Manual

2089 The Gambling Ship Act — 18 U.S.C. §§ 1081, et seq.

Section 1081 defines "gambling ship" to mean a vessel used principally for the operation of one or more gambling establishments.

In making a prosecutorial determination whether a particular ship is a gambling ship within the meaning of this definition, it will be presumed that a ship which operates one or more gambling establishments on board is a "gambling ship," unless it cruises for a minimum of 24 hours with meals and lodging provided for all passengers, or unless it docks at a foreign port. The fact that the presumption applies or does not apply in a given situation, however, is not ultimately determinative of compliance with Section 1081, *et seq.*, but merely provides guidance to United States Attorneys in exercising their prosecutorial discretion under the pertinent statutes.

In 1994, Congress amended this definition to further state that "[s]uch term does not include a vessel with respect to gambling aboard such vessel beyond the territorial waters of the United States during a covered voyage (as defined in section 4472 of the Internal Revenue Code of 1986 as in effect on January 1, 1994.)"

Section 4472 of Title 26 defines a "covered voyage" as the voyage of

(i) a commercial passenger vessel which extends over [one] or more nights, or (ii) a commercial vessel transporting passengers engaged in gambling aboard the vessel beyond the territorial waters of the United States, during which passengers embark or disembark the vessel in the United States. Such term does not include any voyage on any vessel owned or operated by the United States, a State, or any agency or subdivision thereof.

The term "covered voyage" also does not include "a voyage by a passenger vessel [vessel having berth or stateroom accommodations for more than sixteen passengers] of less than [twelve] hours between [two] ports in the United States." This definition of a gambling ship severely limits the application of the Gambling Ship Act as many vessels will fall within the "covered voyage" exception.

Section 1082 prohibits operating a gambling ship, holding an interest in a gambling ship or a gambling establishment on a gambling ship, conducting a gambling game or gambling device at a gambling establishment on a gambling ship, or enticing or soliciting a person to bet or play at a gambling establishment on a gambling ship when the vessel is on the high seas or "otherwise under or within the jurisdiction of the United States, and is not within the jurisdiction of any State."

Section 1083 prohibits the operation of shuttle crafts, that is, vessels used to transport passengers between "a point or place within the United States and a gambling ship which is not within the jurisdiction of any State."

An explanation of this Act and related statutes applicable to cruise ship gambling is available from the Organized Crime and Racketeering Section in the Criminal Division.

Notes

1. From what source or authority did the Department of Justice derive the conclusion that "it will be presumed that a ship which operates one or more gambling establishments on board is a 'gambling ship,' unless it cruises for a minimum of 24 hours with meals and lodging provided for all passengers, or unless it docks at a foreign port?"

2. In the mid-1990s, Northwest Airlines attempted to convince Congress to pass legislation similar in impact to the Cruise Ship Competitiveness Act. Then-Washington-Senator Slade Gorton looked to apply the law equally to domestic and foreign airlines but not in the method that Northwest was hoping. His solution was to suggest a ban on all gaming on flights, by both foreign and domestic carriers, departing and landing in the United States. His amendment to the Travel Act adopted by the Congress in July 1994 did this. The amendment provided:

> An air carrier or foreign air carrier may not install, transport, or operate, or permit the use of, any gambling device on board an aircraft in foreign air transportation.

49 U.S.C. § 41311(a)

A history and discussion of Gorton Amendment can be found in Jesse Witt, Comment, *Aces & Boats: As the Popularity of Cruise Ship Gambling Soars, Why Do the Airlines Remain Grounded*, 28 Transp. L.J. 353 (2001); Darren A. Plum, *Flight Check: Are Air Carriers Any Closer To Providing Gambling On International Flights That Land or Depart From the United States?*, 74 Air L. & Com. 71 (2009); Steven Grover, *Blackjack at Thirty Thousand Feet: America's Attempt To Enforce Its Ban on In-Flight Gambling Extraterritorially*, 4 Tex. Wesleyan L. Rev. 231 (1997). *See also* Matthew Sinowetski, *Is It Time Congress Revisits the Laws Restricting Gambling at 35,000 Feet?*, 37 Transp. L. J. 143 (2010) (discussing the wisdom of continuing this policy).

3. Federal Wire Act

Many federal laws regulating gambling were developed in response to advances in communications. Prohibitions against use of the mail to conduct or advertise lotteries came shortly after the establishment of the federal postal system and its use by those promoting a national lottery. Likewise, prohibitions against advertising lotteries over the radio came shortly after the commercial availability of radios and their use by lottery operators. Its prohibitions were then extended to television shortly after its introduction. The Unlawful Internet Gambling Enforcement Act was adopted in response to the growing use of the Internet to conduct gambling transactions.

Federal laws addressing the use of telephones to conduct wagering, however, did not appear until sometime after the discovery and widespread use of Alexander Graham Bell's invention. The Federal Wire Act, along with the Travel Act, was adopted in 1961 as part of a group of laws sponsored by then U.S. Attorney General Robert Kennedy under the banner of the Attorney General's Program To Curb Organized Crime And Racketeering.

These laws were designed to involve the federal government in the effort to help suppress those local criminal activities from which organized crime drew much of their sustenance.

18 U.S.C. § 1084. Transmission of wagering information; penalties

(a) Whoever being engaged in the business of betting or wagering knowingly uses a wire communication facility for the transmission in interstate or foreign commerce of bets or wagers or information assisting in the placing of bets or wagers on any sporting event or contest, or for the transmission of a wire communication which entitles the recipient to receive money or credit as a result of bets or wagers, or for information assisting in the placing of bets or wagers, shall be fined under this title or imprisoned not more than two years, or both.

(b) Nothing in this section shall be construed to prevent the transmission in interstate or foreign commerce of information for use in news reporting of sporting events or contests, or for the transmission of information assisting in the placing of bets or wagers on a sporting event or contest from a State or foreign country where betting on that sporting event or contest is legal into a State or foreign country in which such betting is legal.

(c) Nothing contained in this section shall create immunity from criminal prosecution under any laws of any State.

(d) When any common carrier, subject to the jurisdiction of the Federal Communications Commission, is notified in writing by a Federal, State, or local law enforcement agency, acting within its jurisdiction, that any facility furnished by it is being used or will be used for the purpose of transmitting or receiving gambling information in interstate or foreign commerce in violation of Federal, State or local law, it shall discontinue or refuse, the leasing, furnishing, or maintaining of such facility, after reasonable notice to the subscriber, but no damages, penalty or forfeiture, civil or criminal, shall be found against any common carrier for any act done in compliance with any notice received from a law enforcement agency. Nothing in this section shall be deemed to prejudice the right of any person affected thereby to secure an appropriate determination, as otherwise provided by law, in a Federal court or in a State or local tribunal or agency, that such facility should not be discontinued or removed, or should be restored.

(e) As used in this section, the term "State" means a State of the United States, the District of Columbia, the Commonwealth of Puerto Rico, or a commonwealth, territory or possession of the United States.

Notes

1. The Federal Wire Act mandates that the person be engaged "in the business of betting or wagering." The courts require that the party be engaged in a "continuing course of conduct." United States v. Scavo, 593 F.2d 837, 842 (8th Cir. 1979). Consequently, where a gambling operator charges the customers for its service either through accepting or brokering wagers, the continuing activities of the operators will likely constitute being "engaged in business of betting or wagering," and leave them open to liability under the statute.

2. The language in the statute—"wire communications facility"—refers to the technology that existed at the time of enactment. Under the Act, a wire communication facility is a system that is used to transmit writings, pictures, and sounds "by aid of a wire, cable or

other like connection between the points of origin and reception of such transmission." This statute was initially intended to apply to telephone communications, but also has broader implications. In 1961, the goal may have been to capture transmissions between ticker machines that printed information on paper tape. Such transmissions were common for financial information and adaptable for transmission of horse race information.

3. The Federal Wire Act plays a prominent role in the debate over the legality of Internet gambling and is covered in greater depth in Chapter 12.

4. The Travel Act

18 U.S.C. § 1952. Interstate and foreign travel or transportation in aid of racketeering enterprises

(a) Whoever travels in interstate or foreign commerce or uses the mail or any facility in interstate or foreign commerce, with intent to—

(1) distribute the proceeds of any unlawful activity; or

(2) commit any crime of violence to further any unlawful activity; or

(3) otherwise promote, manage, establish, carry on, or facilitate the promotion, management, establishment, or carrying on, of any unlawful activity,

and thereafter performs or attempts to perform—

(A) an act described in paragraph (1) or (3) shall be fined under this title, imprisoned not more than 5 years, or both; or

(B) an act described in paragraph (2) shall be fined under this title, imprisoned for not more than 20 years, or both, and if death results shall be imprisoned for any term of years or for life.

(b) As used in this section (i) "unlawful activity" means

(1) any business enterprise involving gambling, liquor on which the Federal excise tax has not been paid, narcotics or controlled substances (as defined in section 102(6) of the Controlled Substances Act), or prostitution offenses in violation of the laws of the State in which they are committed or of the United States,

(2) extortion, bribery, or arson in violation of the laws of the State in which committed or of the United States, or

(3) any act which is indictable under subchapter II of chapter 53 of title 31, United States Code, or under section 1956 or 1957 of this title and

(ii) the term "State" includes a State of the United States, the District of Columbia, and any commonwealth, territory, or possession of the United States.

(c) Investigations of violations under this section involving liquor shall be conducted under the supervision of the Attorney General.

Notes

1. Despite the declaration of then U.S. Attorney General Robert Kennedy that the Travel Act was directed at organized crime, it is not limited to "organized crime" enterprises. Therefore, any person that engages in that type of activity violates the Act re-

gardless of affiliation with organized crime. For example, a person who cheats at Gin Rummy can violate the Act despite the absence of any connection to organized crime. *See, e.g.,* United States v. Garramone, 380 F. Supp. 590, 592 (E.D. Pa. 1974); United States v. Roselli, 432 F.2d 879, 886 (9th Cir. 1970); United States v. Herrera, 584 F.2d 1137 (2d Cir. 1978).

2. Under the Travel Act, aiding an illegal gambling enterprise means to "promote, manage, establish, carry on or facilitate" any aspect of the unlawful activity. The word "facilitate" means "to make easy or less difficult." Therefore, in its lowest denominator, if the interstate or foreign acts make any aspect of the gambling enterprise easier, then the element is met. *See, e.g.,* United States v. Judkins, 428 F.2d 333 (6th Cir. 1970).

3. The key elements that differentiate a Travel Act violation from the predicate state crime are interstate or foreign travel or the use of interstate or foreign facilities. The Travel Act covers circumstances where a person intending to aid an illegal gambling enterprise: (1) travels in interstate or foreign commerce; or (2) uses a facility in interstate or foreign commerce.

4. Travel in the context of the Act has its ordinary meaning, which is to physically cross state lines or national borders. A person can be convicted of a violation of the Travel Act where another person involved with the gambling enterprise uses an interstate facility to further the criminal enterprise. This includes both operators and employees of the illegal gambling operation who live in another state and travel to the establishment. United States v. Carpenter, 392 F.2d 205 (6th Cir. 1968) (conviction of employee); United States v. Zizzo, 338 F.2d 577 (7th Cir. 1964) (conviction of operator based on employee's travel); Bass v. United States, 324 F.2d 168 (8th Cir. 1963); United States v. Alsobrook, 620 F.2d 139 (6th Cir. 1980) (conviction of operator based on operator's travel). Travel by co-conspirators can be attributed to a conspirator that did not travel in interstate or foreign commerce. United States v. Bowers, 739 F.2d 1050 (6th Cir. 1984). The third party, for whom the defendant bears responsibility, may even be a government agent traveling at the request of the defendant. *See* United States v. Levy, 969 F.2d 136 (5th Cir. 1992).

5. Courts generally will not attribute travel by customers to the defendant for purposes of meeting the requirements of the Act. In Rewis v. United States, 401 U.S. 808 (1971), the United States Supreme Court held that travel by customers to an illegal gambling facility was insufficient to meet the interstate travel requirement of the Travel Act, where the facts failed to establish that the defendant caused the customers to travel or use an interstate facility. In that case, the customers happened to be residents of nearby states who traveled on their own volition to gamble at the defendant's establishment. Where the defendant requires the customers to use an interstate facility, however, travel by customers can be imputed to the defendant. For example, a national or international bookmaking operation that requires its customers to phone in bets, use the Internet, or send payment by wire, uses an interstate facility. *See, e.g.,* United States v. Kelley, 395 F.2d 727 (2d Cir. 1968).

6. While the Travel Act is aimed at criminal activity that involves interstate or foreign travel, the nature of that travel does not have to be extensive, essential or integral to the criminal activity. United States v. O'Dell, 671 F.2d 191 (6th Cir. 1982). Because of questions related to federalism, the United States Supreme Court has struggled with the concept of whether the Travel Act requires a clear nexus between the interstate travel or use of interstate facilities and the illegal activity. Initially, the court indicated that the balance between federal and state relationships required that the federal government show a clear nexus between the illegal activity and interstate commerce to justify federal intervention.

In the *Rewis* case, supra, the Supreme Court stated: "[A]n expansive Travel Act would alter sensitive federal-state relationships, could overextend limited federal police resources, and might well produce situations in which a geographical origin of customers, a matter of happenstance, would transform relatively minor state offenses into federal felonies." 401 U.S. 808, 812 (1971).

Eight years after *Rewis*, the Supreme Court retreated from its holding and rejected the notion that the nexus need be significant. In Perrin v. United States, 444 U.S. 37, 50 (1979), the Court stated: "[S]o long as the requisite interstate nexus is present, the statute reflects a clear and deliberate intent on the part of Congress to alter the federal-state balance to reinforce state law enforcement."

These conflicting decisions caused a split in various circuits as to the extent of the nexus required between the interstate or foreign travel and the illegal activity. All circuits agree that the interstate travel or the use of interstate facilities need not in itself be illegal. *See, e.g.*, United States v. Bally Mfg. Corp., 345 F. Supp. 410, 420 (E.D. La. 1972). The split revolves around whether the travel or use of the interstate facilities need only have "some" relationship to the illegal enterprise or must have more than a "minimal" or incidental relationship. Circuits adopting the liberal interpretation that the Act requires only "some" relationship include the First, Fourth, Fifth, Sixth, Tenth, and Eleventh Circuits. *See* United States v. Houlihan, 92 F.3d 1271 (1st Cir. 1996); United States v. Lozano, 839 F.2d 1020, 1022 (4th Cir. 1988); United States v. Garrett, 716 F.2d 257 (5th Cir. 1983); United States v. Eisner, 533 F.2d 987 (6th Cir. 1976); United States v. Peveto, 881 F.2d 844 (10th Cir. 1989); United States v. Gonzalez, 921 F.2d 1530 (11th Cir. 1991); United States v. Pepe, 747 F.2d 632 (11th Cir. 1984). A Fifth Circuit case illustrates this interpretation. In United States v. Wilkinson, 601 F.2d 791 (5th Cir. 1979), the court upheld a conviction under the Travel Act where the only nexus between a bookmaking operation and an interstate facility was that the operator knowingly provided "line" information and accepted bets from a customer who telephoned from an adjoining state. There need not be a "substantial and integral involvement of interstate facilities in an illegal activity." United States v. Le Faivre, 507 F.2d 1288, 1293 (4th Cir. 1974). Courts adopting the conservative approach, which requires more than a minimal nexus, include the Second and Seventh Circuits. *See, e.g.* United States v. Herrera, 584 F.2d 1137, 1150 (2d Cir. 1978); United States v. Isaacs, 493 F.2d 1124 (7th Cir. 1974). For example, the mere act by a gambling operator of accepting and depositing customer's checks drawn on out-of-state banks alone is not a sufficient nexus under the conservative approach. In contrast, the Fourth Circuit, which has adopted the liberal approach, held that merely depositing out-of-state checks from bettors was sufficient. *Le Faivre*, 507 F.2d 1288. Under either approach, an illegal gambling operation's advertisement of its operations can establish the necessary nexus. For example, a gambling operator that intended to promote his illegal business by causing a newspaper with gambling ads to be carried by a facility of interstate commerce violated the Travel Act. Erlenbaugh v. United States, 409 U.S. 239 (1972). However, placing advertisements in a local paper with almost exclusively local circulation is not sufficient to violate or implicate the Travel Act simply because some copies may be sent to an adjoining state. United States v. O'Dell, 671 F.2d 191 (6th Cir. 1982).

7. Beyond travel, a violation of the Travel Act can be based on the use of interstate or foreign facilities. Unlike the Federal Wire Act, the Travel Act is not specifically directed at wire communications. Like the Wire Act, several cases have interpreted "facility in interstate commerce" to include the telephone. *See, e.g.*, United States v. Villano, 529 F.2d 1046, 1052 n.6 (10th Cir. 1976); United States v. Archer, 486 F.2d 670, 679 n.10 (2d Cir.

1973). Therefore, use of telegraph, telephone, or, presumably, the Internet, to facilitate an illegal gambling enterprise by placing or accepting wagers, receiving or transmitting wagering information, establishing accounts, facilitating payments or advertising would violate the Travel Act. As important, however, is that other types of interstate "facilities" would include credit cards, bank teller machines, and Federal Express. *See e.g.*, United States v. Walton, 633 F. Supp. 1353 (D. Minn. 1986); United States v. Baker, 82 F.3d 273 (8th Cir. 1996); United States v. Goldman, 750 F.2d 1221, 1223 (4th Cir. 1984). Whether the facility used must involve an interstate transaction is disputed. For example, in the Fourth Circuit, the telephone call must be between states or money withdrawn or transferred must be from an out-of-state account. *See, e.g.*, United States v. Le Faivre, 507 F.2d 1288, 1291 n.5 (4th Cir. 1974). In the Eleventh Circuit, purely intrastate calls were sufficient under a similar statute prohibiting Interstate murder for hire schemes on the theory that the telephone itself is a facility of interstate commerce. United States v. Drury, 396 F.3d 1303, 1311 (11th Cir. 2005). An exception in some circuits is the use of the mails. This is the only facility specifically referenced in the statute. Moreover, some courts have held that intrastate mailings involve the Travel Act because the United States Postal Service is an interstate facility. *See, e.g.*, United States v. Heacock, 31 F.3d 249 (5th Cir. 1994); United States v. Goldberg, 928 F. Supp. 89 (D. Mass. 1996).

8. The Travel Act is different from earlier federal laws that prohibited mailing of lottery material. While those crimes intended to preserve the integrity of the mail system, the purpose of the Travel Act was unrelated to the facilities used. Instead, it gave federal authorities jurisdiction over those illegal activities in which organized crime typically engaged across state lines. Andrew St. Lauren, *Reconstituting* United States v. Lopez: *Another Look at Federal Criminal Law*, 31 Colum. J. L. & Soc. Probs. 61, 73–4 (1972). In this regard, the Travel Act creates a separate offense from the state statute that creates criminal liability for conducting gambling activities. United States v. Barrow, 212 F. Supp. 837 (E.D. Pa. 1962). This is because the Travel Act punishes the use of interstate or foreign facilities in furtherance of enterprises that violate state law, as opposed to simply supplementing the punishment for the underlying state crime. United States v. Campagnuolo, 556 F.2d 1209 (5th Cir. 1977).

9. Unlike the Illegal Gambling Business Act, the government must show evidence of use of interstate facilities. In most circuits, to prove a violation of the Travel Act, the government need not prove that the defendant intended to use interstate or foreign facilities, only that a defendant intended to engage in a specified type of unlawful activity, such as operating an illegal gambling business. Knowing participation in the unlawful activity is sufficient. For example, a person may be convicted for knowingly participating in a bookmaking operation as an accountant even if he was unaware that the operation was accepting interstate wagers using the telephones. *See, e.g.*, United States. v. Vaccaro, 816 F.2d 443, 453 (9th Cir. 1987) (overruled on other grounds). *But see* United States v. Prince, 529 F.2d 1108 (6th Cir. 1976). Under the majority rule, proof of knowledge of the use of interstate or foreign facilities is also not required. *See, e.g.* United States v. Perrin, 580 F.2d 730 (5th Cir. 1978); *but see* United States v. Gallo, 763 F.2d 1504, 1521 (6th Cir. 1985).

10. To be a crime under the Travel Act, the travel or use of the interstate facilities must be with the intent to aid in "an illegal gambling enterprise." An illegal gambling enterprise is a business enterprise involving gambling. The Travel Act does not define a "business enterprise." The courts, however, have drawn on testimony before Congress when the law was adopted in 1961. Then U.S. Attorney General Robert Kennedy testified that a business enterprise involved a "continuous course of conduct," as opposed to "sporadic"

or "casual involvement" in an activity. *The Attorney General's Program to Curb Organized Crime and Racketeering: Hearings on S. 1653–58, S. 1665 before the Senate Comm. on Judiciary,* 87th Cong. 16 (1961) (hereinafter "Travel Act Hearing"). The courts have followed this line of reasoning. *See, e.g.,* United States v. Gallo, 782 F.2d 1191 (4th Cir. 1986); United States v. Vaccaro, 816 F.2d 443, 454 (9th Cir. 1987) (overruled on other grounds). Thus, for example, a person does not violate the Travel Act by placing a single bet. This, however, does not require the defendants to be involved with organized crime, be organized in any sense, or even be successful. For example, a small, unorganized gambling operation is a business enterprise if its activities are frequent or have occurred over time. *See, e.g.,* United States v. Garramone, 380 F. Supp. 590, 592 (E.D. Pa. 1974). Moreover, the defendant need not have been involved personally in a continuous course of conduct. For example, a new participant in an established illegal gambling operation can be convicted under the Travel Act by using an interstate facility to aid the gambling operation. *See, e.g.,* United States v. Anderson, 987 F.2d 251 (5th Cir. 1993) (drug case). All that the Travel Act requires is some evidence that the defendants intended the enterprise to be continuous. This can be shown by repeated activity, even if the gambling enterprise has been in operation only a few weeks. *See* United States v. Brennan, 394 F.2d 151, 153 (2d Cir. 1968).

11. The Travel Act probably applies only to gambling operations conducted for profit because a "business" enterprise connotes an activity done with the intent to profit. *See* United States v. Roselli, 432 F.2d 879, 886 (9th Cir. 1970). In testimony before the Congress, Attorney General Robert Kennedy emphasized that the Act was not intended to apply to social gambling. *Travel Act Hearing,* at 5. Being unprofitable, however, is not a defense. As one court noted, the Act "does not require the accused be successful at gambling." *See* United States v. Lisner, 524 F.2d 1263 (5th Cir. 1975). If an enterprise has two components, one legal and one illegal, the government must show that the illegal component is a continuous course of conduct. For example, suppose an established restaurant had a backroom and one Saturday the owner hosted a poker game. This isolated instance would be insufficient to invoke the Travel Act despite the continuous operation of the restaurant. The result would be different, however, if the poker game was held every Saturday night and the restaurant owner received a fee from the participants.

12. Once a business enterprise is established, a single act involving interstate or foreign travel or use of an interstate or foreign facility is sufficient. *See, e.g.,* United States v. Douglass, 780 F.2d 1472, 1478 (9th Cir. 1986); Marshall v. United States, 355 F.2d 999, 1004 (9th Cir. 1966); United States v. Corbin, 662 F.2d 1066, 1071 (4th Cir. 1981).

13. The Travel Act does not define the term "gambling." The second requirement is that the gambling activity must be "in violation of the laws of the state in which [they are] committed or of the United States." In this context, the underlying state crime need not be a felony. A violation of a state gaming law that is a misdemeanor is sufficient to sustain a conviction under the Travel Act. *See, e.g.,* United States v. Garramone, 380 F. Supp. 590, 593 (E.D. Pa. 1974). Moreover, the state statute need not proscribe the activity in its entirety. For example, conducting an unlicensed gambling operation in a state that has authorized gaming can be a predicate state crime. In United States v. Goldfarb, 643 F.2d 422, 428–30 (6th Cir. 1981), the defendants were convicted for holding a hidden interest in a legal Nevada casino in violation of state law that required licensure. Even a violation of a state gaming regulation can be a predicate crime if it is punishable as a misdemeanor under state law. An illegal gambling business can include a scheme to cheat a gambling establishment, whether legal or not, or to cheat patrons. *See, e.g.,* United States v. Bergland, 318 F.2d 159 (7th Cir. 1963) (upholding convictions for "past-posting");

United States v. Polizzi, 500 F.2d 856 (9th Cir. 1974) (conviction for attempting to rig slot machines in Nevada casinos).

14. Because the federal statute is predicated on a violation of state law, defenses that would prove a substantive defense to the charges are generally available to the defendant. Procedural state defenses, however, are generally not available. *See, e.g.*, United States v. Steele, 685 F.2d 793, 807 (3d Cir.), *cert. denied*, 459 U.S. 908 (1982). Therefore, a defendant cannot avoid liability under the Travel Act because a statute of limitations bars prosecution for the underlying state law violation or even if the defendant has been acquitted of the state charge. *See e.g.*, United States v. Campagnuolo, 556 F.2d 1209 (5th Cir. 1977); United States v. Gonzalez, 907 F. Supp. 785 (D. Del. 1995).

5. Wagering Paraphernalia Act — 18 U.S.C. § 1953

The last of the triad of laws adopted in 1961 was the Wagering Paraphernalia Act. According to former Congressman Emanuel Celler of New York, then Chairman of the House Judiciary Committee, the primary purpose of the Act "is to prevent the transportation in interstate commerce of wagering materials. The purpose actually is to cut off and shut off gambling supplies, in reality to prevent these lotteries and kindred illegal diversions." 107 CONG. REC., 15450–51 (Aug. 21 1961). As the Supreme Court noted, the Act "erects a substantial barrier to the distribution of certain materials used in the conduct of various forms of illegal gambling." Erlenbaugh v. United States, 409 U.S. 239, 246 (1972). The key provision of the act that creates the liability states:

> Whoever, except a common carrier in the usual course of its business, knowingly carries or sends in interstate or foreign commerce any record, paraphernalia, ticket, certificate, bills, slip, token, paper, writing, or other device used, or to be used, or adapted, devised, or designed for use in (a) bookmaking; or (b) wagering pools with respect to a sporting event; or (c) in a numbers, policy, bolita, or similar game shall be fined not more than $10,000 or imprisoned for not more than five years or both. 18 U.S.C. § 1953

Notes

1. The Wagering Paraphernalia Act is directed mainly at persons who send physical materials and supplies needed to conduct bookmaking or lotteries over state lines. The Act addresses only tangible items. Because the Wagering Paraphernalia Act and the Wire Act were both enacted on the very same day, and one addressed transporting tangible items while the other specifically addressed wire communications, it is unlikely that the Wagering Paraphernalia Act was intended to address other electronic transmissions such as those sent over the Internet, or that courts would interpret it that way. The Act does not define the word "send." One federal circuit court refused to believe that Congress intended the terms of Section 1953 to be stretched to address wire communications. *See* Pic-A-State Pa., Inc. v. Commonwealth of Pennsylvania, 42 F.3d 175 (3d Cir. 1994).

2. Rather than defining wagering paraphernalia, Congress chose to insert a "laundry" list of items that could not be carried or sent in interstate or foreign commerce. As a practical matter, these items, which include "any record, paraphernalia, ticket, certificate, bills, slip, token, paper, writing or other device," reach all tangible materials that are in-

tended to be used in specified gambling activities regardless of whether they have uses outside these activities. The best example of this is blank "flash" paper. This is paper that will instantly ignite if exposed to a flame. Traditional bookmakers used flash paper because it was easier to destroy evidence if the police raided a location. Magicians also can use flash paper as part of their act. United States v. Scaglione, 446 F.2d 182 (5th Cir. 1971). A person carrying flash paper to be used for a gambling operation commits a crime. A magician, however, can legally carry it. Whether a computer program can be used for legal or illegal purposes as wagering paraphernalia depends on two factors: first, whether the features of the software are designed for use in illegal bookmaking, such as having a feature that could quickly erase wagering data in the event of a police raid; second, whether the program is targeted toward illegal uses as opposed to legal uses. *See* United States v. Mendelsohn, 896 F.2d 1183 (9th Cir. 1989).

3. The courts have not required that the paraphernalia be necessary to the gambling activity if it has some use. For example, the Supreme Court upheld a conviction for sending an "acknowledgment of purchases" for a sweepstakes race, even though such acknowledgment was not needed to collect a prize, but was sent for psychological purposes only. United States v. Fabrizio, 385 U.S. 263, 270–71 (1966).

4. Like the Travel Act, the Wagering Paraphernalia Act does not apply only to persons involved in organized crime or who participate in illegal gambling activities.

5. Some question exists as to whether a person must have "knowledge and intent to transmit gambling paraphernalia" to be convicted under the Act. According to the Fourth Circuit, this is a requirement. United States v. Chase, 372 F.2d 453, 460 (4th Cir. 1967). In other words, the defendant must know the material that he is carrying or sending is wagering paraphernalia as opposed to merely knowing that he is carrying or sending materials. The Supreme Court, however, called this holding into question when it reasoned that the newspaper exception to the Act was made necessary because without the exception the "knowing" requirement only requires that the actor know that he is carrying a newspaper, not that the newspaper contains wagering information. Erlenbaugh v. United States, 409 U.S. 239, 247–48 (1972). The court reasoned that the exceptions, discussed later, were necessary to protect innocent carriers.

6. The Wagering Paraphernalia Act is unusual in that it defines specific games as opposed to relying on the broader definition of "lottery" used in other federal statutes. It applies to materials used in three types of operations: (1) bookmaking; (2) pari-mutuel sports wagering; and (3) numbers, policy, Bolita, or similar games. This has resulted in the unusual circumstances where the courts need to understand and define the playing of specific games as opposed to merely applying the more generic "prize, consideration, and chance" analysis. Bookmaking is the business of setting lines or odds on sporting events or horse races and accepting wagers on such events with the intent to profit by charging a commission on every wager accepted. Pari-mutuel wagering involves the operator accepting bets on a particular event and taking a "commission" on each wager. The remaining funds are then placed in a pool and divided among those persons placing winning wagers. One court provided this standard definition of the Numbers game:

> "[N]umbers" or the numbers game is that game wherein the "player" wagers or plays that on a certain day a certain series of digits will appear or "come out" in the series, such as the United States Treasury balance or pari-mutuel payoff totals or particular races at a certain racetrack for the day, used as a reference. Though the number of digits is fixed, usually at three, any player is free to select any number or quantity of numbers within the range of those digits, and des-

ignate the amount of his wager upon each. Thus, it is possible for a number of people to play the same number while other numbers go unplayed. The probability odds, for example, of predicting that a certain three digit number will come out is a thousand to one. However, the person known as the backer or "banker", who guarantees the payoffs to the successful player or players, predetermines the rate of the payoffs, which in most instances is pitifully less than the true odds. In such a game neither the number or winning players nor the total amount of the payoffs can be predicted in any one day. Thus, in a single day it is possible for the payoffs to be larger than the total sum wagered. On the other hand at the other extreme it is possible to have no payoffs because no one played the number that came out.

United States v. Baker, 364 F.2d 107, 111–12 (3d Cir. 1966).

7. Policy differs from numbers based on the method of deciding the winning numbers, as the *Baker* court noted "in policy, it is ascertained by the drawing at random from a wheel in which tags, each bearing one of the possible combinations of numbers that can be played, have been played." *Baker*, 364 F.2d at 111–12. Bolita is a Spanish game where only two digit numbers are chosen and drawn. Traditionally, Bolita is played by drawing two balls at random from ten balls numbered one to ten. The game, however, can be played by using digits from other random sources. *See, e.g.* Pinder v. United States, 330 F.2d 119, 121 (5th Cir. 1969).

8. The phrase "or similar games" in the statute has raised the question of whether the Act was meant to apply to lotteries. Clearly, under the broad definition of lottery, adopted by the federal courts, numbers, policy, and Bolita are lotteries. The courts, however, had no problem deciding that because of common characteristics, traditional lotteries were "similar games" to numbers, policy, and Bolita. As one court reasoned, these traditional lottery games involve "the distribution of a prize or prizes by lot or chance, the number and value of which is determined by the operator of the lottery." *See, e.g.*, *Baker*, 364 F.2d at 111.

9. Without an exception, the transportation of any wagering paraphernalia over state lines would be illegal regardless of the legality of gambling or possession of such paraphernalia in either the sending or receiving states. United States v. Fabrizio, 385 U.S. 263, 268–69 (1966). Therefore, the Wagering Paraphernalia Act contains several exceptions. These include:

- Materials carried by a common carrier in the usual course of its business;
- Pari-mutuel betting equipment or tickets where legally acquired;
- Pari-mutuel materials used at racetracks or other sporting events where State law allows such betting;
- Betting materials to be used to place bets or wagers on a sporting event into a State whose laws allow such betting;
- Any newspaper or similar publication;
- Equipment, tickets, or materials to be used in a State-run lottery; and
- Equipment, tickets, or materials designed to be used and transported to a foreign country for a legal lottery. 18 U.S.C. §1953(b).

The "state-run" exemption was created in 1975 to "relieve states operating lotteries from the restrictions federal law then imposed." It was part of a package of amendments to various federal laws that was designed to allow state lotteries to advertise by television, radio or mail in states that had legal lotteries. H.R. REP. No. 1517 (1974). This exception, however, does not allow the transportation of materials to be used in an illegal lottery or bookmaking operation in a state that has a legal lottery. United States v. Stuebben, 799 F.2d 225 (5th Cir. 1986). Moreover, the exception is limited to lotteries that involve the pooling of proceeds derived from the sale of tickets or chances and allotting those proceeds or parts thereof by chance to one or more chance takers or ticket purchasers. "Lottery" does not include the placing or accepting of bets or wagers on sporting events or contests.

10. The newspaper exception has generated controversy. This exception was "primarily designed to exclude ... a newspaper or other publication containing racing results or predictions." H. REP. No. 968 (1961). The Senate Judiciary Committee, in considering Section 1953, reported:

> The committee also felt that the bill, as introduced, might be so interpreted as to bring within its criminal penalties a person who carried a newspaper or other publication containing racing results or predictions. In order to clearly prevent such an interpretation, the committee has excluded the carrying or transporting into interstate or foreign commerce of any newspaper or similar publication from the provisions of the bill.

SEN. REP. No. 589, at 2 (1961).

The issue quickly arose as to whether newspapers containing racing or sports information were exempted. The courts uniformly have held that newspapers and magazines devoted primarily or solely to information on horse racing such as entries, jockeys, track conditions and picks fall under the exception. United States v. Kelly, 328 F.2d 227 (6th Cir. 1964). Likewise, a newspaper devoted to sports information is a newspaper of similar publication under the Wagering Paraphernalia Act. United States v. Arnold, 380 F.2d 366 (4th Cir. 1967). Use of a newspaper to promote an illegal gambling establishment, however, can form the basis for a Travel Act violation even if the newspaper itself is exempted from the prohibition against transporting wagering paraphernalia under the Wagering Paraphernalia Act. United States v. Kish, 303 F. Supp. 1212 (N.D. Ind. 1969).

6. Illegal Gambling Business Prohibition — 18 U.S.C. § 1955

Congress adopted the Illegal Gambling Business Prohibition as part of the Organized Crime Control Act of 1970. Pub. L. No. 91-452, 84 Stat. 922. Much like the impetus for the 1961 federal gambling laws, the purpose of the 1970 Act was to strike at those "illegal endeavors as syndicated gambling, loan sharking, the theft and fencing of property, the importation and distribution of narcotics and other dangerous drugs, and other forms of social exploitation, [that allowed organized crime to obtain funds] to infiltrate and corrupt legitimate businesses and labor unions and to subvert and corrupt our democratic processes." See United States v. Aquino, 336 F. Supp. 737, 739 (D. Mich. 1972).

Illegal gambling was a major concern because Congress felt that it had replaced liquor as the monetary foundation for organized crime. Senator John McClellan of Arkansas noted "gambling is the principal source of income for the elements of organized crime and it is the purpose of this bill to seek to shutoff this flow of revenue by making it a crime to engage in a substantial business enterprise of gambling." Senator McClellan's comments were in relation to a predecessor bill to the Organized Crime Control Act. S. 3564, 114 Cong. Rec. 15,603 (1968).

To accomplish these goals, Congress intentionally altered the historic relationship between the states and the federal government as it related to criminal enforcement. Congress felt that the states were ill-equipped and often lacked motivation to successfully enforce the gambling laws against large organized crime-controlled gambling operations. It attributed some problems to the corruption of police and other officials entrusted to enforcing the laws.

In this regard, the purpose of the Act was not to usurp state and local power to prosecute gambling crimes, but to give federal authorities concurrent authority to investigate and prosecute large-scale gambling operations. To accomplish this goal, various elements of the Act were devoted to giving a definition to what constitutes a "large-scale" gambling operation. The result, however, was legislation that empowers the federal government to investigate and prosecute all but the smallest of illegal gambling operations.

18 U.S.C. § 1955—Prohibition of illegal gambling businesses

(a) Whoever conducts, finances, manages, supervises, directs, or owns all or part of an illegal gambling business shall be fined under this title or imprisoned not more than five years, or both.

(b) As used in this section—

(1) "illegal gambling business" means a gambling business which—

(i) is a violation of the law of a State or political subdivision in which it is conducted;

(ii) involves five or more persons who conduct, finance, manage, supervise, direct, or own all or part of such business; and

(iii) has been or remains in substantially continuous operation for a period in excess of thirty days or has a gross revenue of $2,000 in any single day.

(2) "gambling" includes but is not limited to pool-selling, bookmaking, maintaining slot machines, roulette wheels or dice tables, and conducting lotteries, policy, bolita or numbers games, or selling chances therein.

(3) "State" means any State of the United States, the District of Columbia, the Commonwealth of Puerto Rico, and any territory or possession of the United States.

(c) If five or more persons conduct, finance, manage, supervise, direct, or own all or part of a gambling business and such business operates for two or more successive days, then, for the purpose of obtaining warrants for arrests, interceptions, and other searches and seizures, probable cause that the business receives gross revenue in excess of $2,000 in any single day shall be deemed to have been established.

(d) Any property, including money, used in violation of the provisions of this section may be seized and forfeited to the United States. All provisions of law relating to the seizures, summary, and judicial forfeiture procedures, and condemnation of vessels, vehicles, merchandise, and baggage for violation of the customs laws; the disposition of such vessels, vehicles, merchandise, and baggage or the proceeds from such sale; the remission or mitigation of such forfeitures; and the compromise of claims and the award of compensation to informers in respect of such forfeitures shall apply to seizures and forfeitures incurred or alleged to have been incurred under the provisions of this section, insofar as applicable and not inconsistent with such provisions. Such duties as are imposed upon the collector of customs or any other person in respect to the seizure and forfeiture of vessels, vehicles, merchandise, and baggage under the customs laws shall be performed with respect to seizures and forfeitures of property used or intended for use in violation of this section by such officers, agents, or other persons as may be designated for that purpose by the Attorney General.

(e) This section shall not apply to any bingo game, lottery, or similar game of chance conducted by an organization exempt from tax under paragraph (3) of subsection (c) of section 501 of the Internal Revenue Code of 1986, as amended, if no part of the gross receipts derived from such activity inures to the benefits of any private shareholder, member, or employee of such organization except as compensation for actual expenses incurred by him in the conduct of such activity.

United States v. Mick
263 F.3d 553 (6th Cir. 2001)

OPINION

RONALD LEE GILMAN, Circuit Judge.

Robert Mick was convicted on one count of conducting an illegal gambling business, in violation of 18 U.S.C. § 1955, one count of using a facility of interstate commerce for illegal purposes, in violation of 18 U.S.C. § 1952(a)(3), fifty-nine counts of money laundering, in violation of 18 U.S.C. § 1956(a)(1)(A)(i), and eleven counts of knowingly engaging in monetary transactions using criminally derived property worth more than $10,000, in violation of 18 U.S.C. § 1957. He was subsequently sentenced to spend 57 months in prison, serve 36 months of supervised release, and pay $7,100 as a special assessment.

...

Mick next challenges the sufficiency of the evidence supporting the jury's conclusion that his activities constituted an "illegal gambling business" pursuant to 18 U.S.C. § 1955. In our review of his claim, we must determine "whether, after viewing the evidence in the light most favorable to the prosecution, *any* rational trier of fact could have found the essential elements of the crime beyond a reasonable doubt." Jackson v. Virginia, 443 U.S. 307, 319 (1979) (emphasis in original). We may not, however, "weigh the evidence, consider the credibility of witnesses or substitute our judgment for that of the jury." United States v. Hilliard, 11 F.3d 618, 620 (6th Cir. 1993).

An illegal gambling business is defined as an enterprise that

(i) is a violation of the law of a State or political subdivision in which it is conducted;

(ii) involves five or more persons who conduct, finance, manage, supervise, direct, or own all or part of such business; and

(iii) has been or remains in substantially continuous operation for a period in excess of thirty days or has a gross revenue of $2,000 in any single day.

18 U.S.C. § 1955(b)(1). Mick conceded at trial that his bookmaking activities violated Ohio law, and he does not dispute that his business fell within both prongs of subsection (iii) above. Instead, Mick claims that there was insufficient proof to show, beyond a reasonable doubt, that his business "involves five or more persons who conduct, finance, manage, supervise, direct, or own all or part of such business."

Mick misstates this circuit's interpretation of the five-person jurisdictional requirement. He cites United States v. Murray, 928 F.2d 1242 (1st Cir. 1991), for the proposition that the government must prove that "at all times during some thirty day period at least five persons were involved in conducting the gambling operation." Mick fails to note, however, that our court has interpreted § 1955(b)(1) differently. In 1974, fifteen years before *Murray*, this court held that "[t]he statute, 18 U.S.C. § 1955(b)(1)(iii) clearly makes the thirty day requirement a part of the definition of illegal gambling business *and not* a specific requirement as to the duration of individual participation by persons involved in such business." United States v. Mattucci, 502 F.2d 883, 889 (6th Cir. 1974) (emphasis added). The five-person requirement can therefore be satisfied at any point during the thirty days, regardless of the duration of a person's involvement in the business, so long as his or her participation is either regularly helpful or "necessary to the operation of the gambling enterprise." United States v. King, 834 F.2d 109, 113 (6th Cir. 1987).

In considering whether a person's involvement constitutes sufficient "conduct" to be counted as one of the five people required to satisfy § 1955, this court has held that "Congress intended the word conduct to refer to both high level bosses and street level employees." Mattucci, 502 F.2d at 888 (counting the doorman in a gambling club as one of the jurisdictional five) (internal quotation marks omitted). The Fifth Circuit has even gone so far as counting a line service, similar to the one provided by Don Best Sports, as one of the jurisdictional five. *See* United States v. Heacock, 31 F.3d 249, 252 (5th Cir. 1994). Most importantly, this court has held that layoff bettors may be considered as part of the requisite five members, so long as their dealings with the gambling business are "regular" and not just based on "one contact." *See King*, 834 F.2d at 113–14.

Based on this court's interpretation of the degree of "conduct" necessary to be counted in the jurisdictional requirement of five participants, there is overwhelming evidence to support the jury's conclusion that § 1955 was satisfied. Mick does not dispute that he, Brodzinski, and at least one of his sons can be counted towards the jurisdictional five. There was also abundant evidence supporting the jury's conclusion that bookmakers such as Frank Birch, Richard Gothot, Andrew Schneider, and Eugene Smith placed regular layoff bets with Mick. Furthermore, Mick's agreements with Campbell (who distributed parlay sheets for Mick) and Stoiber (who allowed Mick to utilize a telephone line out of her house) were sufficiently regular and helpful to his gambling business to permit the jury to count them as well. Indeed, the summary above is actually an incomplete listing of all the people who regularly aided Mick's gambling enterprise. We therefore find no merit in Mick's challenge to the jury's conclusion that his activities constituted an "illegal gambling business" pursuant to 18 U.S.C. § 1955.

Notes

1. For any participant to be convicted under Section 1955, the gambling business must "involve five or more persons who conduct, finance, manage, supervise, direct or own all or part of such business." This seemingly simple phrase has involved substantial litigation. The questions include:

- Who can be included to meet the minimum requirement of five persons?
- Must the defendant know of the identity or existence of the other persons?
- Must the same five persons participate for a 30-day period?

- Must at least five persons participate for an entire 30-day period?

- Who is included to meet the minimum requirement?

2. Liability under Section 1955 is conditioned on a person having any one of six roles in an illegal gambling operation. The Act declares that, "[w]hoever conducts, finances, manages, supervises, directs, or owns all or part of an illegal gambling business" is subject to fines, imprisonment or both. Mere bettors are not subject to criminal liability under Section 1955. *See* United States v. Box, 530 F.2d 1258, 1267 (5th Cir. 1976). The six roles that qualify a person as a participant are meant to have their ordinary meanings. Little controversy has arisen over what constitutes "financing," "managing," "supervising," "directing," or "owning" a gambling business. "Supervise" means that the person had the ability to control or direct the actions of another participant. This ability can be found in several types of relationships, such as when the participant is an employee, subordinate, or independent contractor. For a person to have supervised five or more persons, the same type of "superior-subordinate relationship need not exist between the supervisor and each of the five other persons involved." United States v. Phillips, 664 F.2d 971, 1013 (5th Cir. 1981) (overruled on other grounds).

3. The major issue has been whether certain employees or other participants in the gambling operation are liable or count toward the minimum person requirement because they "conduct" gambling operations. The Supreme Court has concluded that "conduct" can be "any degree of participation in an illegal gambling business except participation as a customer." Sanabria v. United States, 437 U.S. 54 (1978). Most circuits have adopted a simple test: a person "conducts" a gambling business if he or she performs any function that is "necessary or helpful in" the business. *See, e.g.,* United States v. Merrell, 701 F.2d 53, 55 (6th Cir. 1983); United States v. Reeder, 614 F.2d 1179 (8th Cir. 1980). Under this analysis, virtually all, if not all, employees count toward the minimum requirement and are subject to liability. Perhaps the extreme limit of this test is illustrated by the Sixth Circuit case where the court held that a janitor who cleaned and straightened up a gambling room "conducted" the gambling operation. United States v. Merrell, 701 F.2d 53, 55 (6th Cir. 1983). Besides employees, the "necessary and helpful" standard can snare most other participants if their activities go beyond that of a mere bettor. *See* United States v. Follin, 979 F.2d 369, 371–72 (5th Cir. 1992). This can include professional line services, runners, agents and independent street sellers. *See, e.g.,* United States v. Heacock, 31 F.3d 249 (5th Cir. 1994); United States v. McHale, 495 F.2d 15, 18 (7th Cir. 1974); United States v. Mackey, 551 F.2d 967 (5th Cir. 1977). In some instances, independent bookmakers who cooperate in their operations can also count toward the minimum requirement. United States v. Bobo, 477 F.2d 974 (6th Cir. 1974); United States v. Avarello, 592 F.2d 1339 (5th Cir. 1979); *but see* United States v. Jenkins, 649 F.2d 273 (4th Cir. 1981). This requires more than merely a casual conversation or single transaction; the regular exchange of line information or a pattern of lay-off wagering is sufficient. *See, e.g.,* United States v. Bouy, 598 F.2d 445 (5th Cir. 1979); United States v. King, 834 F.2d 109 (6th Cir. 1987); United States v. Jones, 712 F.2d 115 (5th Cir. 1983); United States v. Baker, 589 F.2d 1008, 1014 (9th Cir. 1979). The regular lay-offs, however, need not be "a two-way street in order to bring two bookmakers together in an illegal gambling business." United States v. Morris, 612 F.2d 483, 493 (10th Cir. 1979). Likewise, interdependent operations that share common backing or divide profits can be combined to meet the minimum requirements. *See, e.g.,* United States v. Grey, 56 F.3d 1219 (10th Cir. 1995). In these scenarios, the gambling operation can have fewer than five employees or partners, but still subject its participants to liability. For example, the Fifth Circuit held that a bookmaker who employed two clerks and used two different line services met the minimum re-

quirements. *United States v. Heacock*, 31 F.3d 249 (5th Cir. 1994). The Tenth Circuit takes a minority position. It requires that each participant fulfill a function necessary to the gambling operation. *United States v. Boss*, 671 F.2d 396 (10th Cir. 1982). Thus, a cocktail waitress in an illegal casino would be deemed a participant in most circuits, except the Tenth Circuit. *See, e.g., United States v. Bennett*, 563 F.2d 879, 883–84 (8th Cir. 1977); *United States v. Boss*, 671 F.2d 396, 401–2 (10th Cir. 1982). In the First Circuit, a cocktail waitress is included if she serves drinks to those in the process of gambling, but not if she serves drinks in the general tavern area to all customers even though some may be gamblers. *United States v. Murray*, 928 F.2d 1242 (1st Cir. 1991).

United States v. Useni
516 F.3d 634 (7th Cir. 2008)

Before BAUER, MANION, and WOOD, Circuit Judges.

MANION, Circuit Judge.

Under Illinois law, only charitable organizations are allowed to run certain gambling games such as bingo games, pull-tab games, and raffles as fundraisers for their organizations. In this case, the operators of the Grand Palace Bingo Hall (the "Grand Palace") in Northlake, Illinois, used the Italian American War Veterans (the "IAWV"), a charitable organization, as a front to pocket nearly three million dollars in gambling proceeds. Both Fuat "Frank" Useni and Phillip Cozzo worked at the Grand Palace from its inception until it was sold to a group of IAWV members. A jury convicted Useni and Cozzo of conspiring to commit racketeering offenses and operating an illegal gambling business, as well as several counts of mail fraud and tax fraud. Following their convictions, Useni and Cozzo appealed, challenging various aspects of their respective convictions and sentences. On appeal, the principal question in their challenges to their convictions and sentences is the extent of their involvement in the illegal gambling that occurred at the Grand Palace. We affirm.

...

A. Illinois Gambling Laws

Illinois has a network of laws and regulations designed to allow charitable organizations to raise money through limited forms of gambling while, at the same time, strictly limiting the use of the money and facilities involved in the gambling in order to prevent fraud and abuse. At trial, Illinois Department of Revenue employees Polly Kirby, Lisa Roberts, and Randi Kaplan testified about Illinois's regulatory scheme for charitable gambling. According to those witnesses, only certain charitable organizations, such as the IAWV, are permitted to run bingo halls. A charitable organization must have a license issued by the state, to conduct bingo or pull-tab games.[1] *See* 230 ILCS 20/2; 230 ILCS 25/1. A license, which must be renewed annually, allows the charitable organization to hold bingo or pull-tab games once a week. Illinois law also requires that a charitable organization have a license to conduct raffles, but the licensing of raffles is left to each individual municipality rather than the state. In addition, Illinois law prohibits conducting raffles and bingo games on the same premises. 230 ILCS 25/2(11).

A company or person that is not affiliated with a charitable organization may obtain a supplier's license, which allows that company to sell gambling supplies to the charita-

---

1. A pull-tab is a card with a pattern of symbols on the front and perforated tabs on the back. The tabs, when pulled back, reveal colored play symbols. If the symbols on the back match the pattern of symbols on the front of the card, then the player wins the prize indicated on the card.

ble group running the games; or a provider's license, which allows the company to rent a facility to a charitable group conducting games. *See* 230 ILCS 20/3.1; 230 ILCS 25/1.4-.5. The provider's license, like the bingo and pull-tab licenses, has to be renewed yearly by the state of Illinois. Neither the supplier nor the provider may receive any revenue from the games other than a reasonable sum in exchange for providing their services; the net proceeds of the gambling must go to the charitable organization running the games. *See* 230 ILCS 20/4; 230 ILCS 25/2. Furthermore, only the members of the charitable organization are allowed to participate in operating the games, including selling bingo cards or pull-tabs, calling numbers, confirming and paying winners, and handling or counting the proceeds from the sale of cards and pull-tabs. Most importantly, only members of the charitable organization are allowed to handle the money earned from the games. Significantly, the members of the charitable organization involved in operating the games must be volunteers and are themselves prohibited from being compensated for their work in running the games. *See* 230 ILCS 20/4(3); 230 ILCS 25/2(3).

Supplier, pull-tab, and bingo licensees have reporting obligations to the state. Suppliers must file quarterly reports listing such information as the manufacturer's serial number for each pull-tab box sold, the date of the sale, the type of tickets sold, serial numbers for the tickets, and what the ideal gross proceeds would be for each box of pull-tabs. Pull-tab and bingo licensees are required to report quarterly to pay their taxes.[2] On a bingo report, a licensee must list the date, the amount of prizes awarded, and the number of players participating for each bingo session held, as well as the gross proceeds from the games that quarter and the amount of tax owed to the state. In contrast, a pull-tab return must report, among other things, each pull-tab game played, the date the particular pull-tab game was played, the manufacturer's serial number for that game, the gross proceeds from the game, the gross proceeds for the sale of pull-tabs that quarter, and the amount of tax owed.

B. Birth of the Grand Palace

While the network of laws, rules, and regulations were designed to prevent fraud, a gambling operation nevertheless presented a lucrative attraction to someone willing to skirt the law. The Grand Palace was the brainchild of William Shlifka,[3] a man who had no affiliation with the IAWV. Shlifka planned to have several IAWV posts each apply for separate bingo and pull-tab licenses, which would allow Shlifka to run several sessions of gaming a week. In turn, Shlifka would have the Grand Palace apply for provider's and supplier's licenses so that it could supply the gambling equipment and host the sessions. Shlifka would pay each veteran who worked a nightly gaming session $50 per session and would pay each IAWV post $100 for every gaming session they hosted.

From the beginning, Shlifka involved Cozzo, who was also not a member of the IAWV, in the planning of the Grand Palace. Prior to the opening of the Grand Palace, Shlifka, together with Cozzo, met with several people who would be key to the Grand Palace's success: Steven Mariani, a high-ranking IAWV member who would recruit IAWV posts and members; Patrick Marotta, the president of bingo-supply distributor Gore & Kay who would be the main supplier of gambling equipment to the Grand Palace; and Aaron Levitansky, who would do the accounting work for the Grand Palace. According to Mariani's testimony, Shlifka and Cozzo approached Mariani and asked him to recruit IAWV posts to sponsor the games and offered Mariani $100 for each gaming session hosted by

---

2. Bingo and pull-tab licensees are required to pay 5% of the gross proceeds of the games to the Illinois Department of Revenue. 230 ILCS 20/5; 230 ILCS 25/3.

3. Shlifka died after the indictment in this case was handed down but before trial began.

an IAWV post recruited by Mariani. Shlifka also introduced Mariani to "Frank" Useni, another non-IAWV member, as someone who would help run the kitchen and do the janitorial work for the bingo hall. Shlifka and Cozzo next met with Marotta about providing gaming supplies. Marotta testified that Shlifka and Cozzo sought Marotta's advice as to the type of games to run and pull-tabs to use. At that meeting with Marotta, Shlifka referred to Cozzo as his "partner." Shlifka and Cozzo then met with Levitansky about the hall. Levitanksy testified that Shlifka told him that the Grand Palace would make money by renting the hall and selling bingo cards to the IAWV posts, as well as by selling concessions to hall patrons. At that meeting no mention was made of the Grand Palace ever profiting off of the revenue from the games.

After securing the aid of Mariani, Marotta, and Levitansky, Shlifka applied for a provider's license in February 1994, using the names of his wife and daughter as purported officers of the Grand Palace. Several applications for bingo and pull-tab licenses for IAWV posts were also submitted. Donna Dombrowski, Fred Bingham's live-in girlfriend, testified that Bingham, the Grand Palace's bookkeeper and a non-IAWV member, completed the applications for the posts. Each application listed the address of the Grand Palace as the address of the IAWV post submitting the application, though no IAWV post had its place of business at the Grand Palace. Mariani testified that Shlifka, gave the money for the license application fees to him, who in turn had money orders made out to be submitted with the applications.

According to the testimony of Lorraine Mazzei, Cozzo's former girlfriend, Cozzo had one of the bingo license applications signed by Mazzei and his sisters. The bingo application required Mazzei and Cozzo's sisters to make several certifications, including that they were bona fide members of the charitable organization and that they had a copy of the rulebook for conducting charitable games and would "be responsible for the conduct of the games in accordance with the provisions of the laws of the State and the rules and regulations of the department governing the conduct of such games." When the bingo and pull-tab license applications were rejected because they were not signed by members of the IAWV, Mariani testified that Shlifka had him obtain the signatures of veterans on amended license' applications. After they were submitted, the amended applications were accepted and bingo and pull-tab licenses issued. No license to conduct raffles was ever obtained.

While the licenses were being pursued, Shlifka held two planning meetings. Both meetings occurred before the operation of the games commenced, the first being held in January 1994 and the second in May 1994. Mariani and Carmen Trombetta—an IAWV member who, like Mariani, became deeply involved in the Grand Palace—testified that Useni and Cozzo attended both meetings. At the May meeting, Shlifka instructed the IAWV veterans working the games to deny that they were getting paid, if asked.

. . .

Lastly, Cozzo argues that the district court erred in denying his motion to dismiss count two of the indictment. Count two charged the defendants with operating an illegal gambling business in violation of 18 U.S.C. § 1955. Cozzo argues that § 1955 was meant to combat large-scale illegal gambling used to fund organized crime, not the type of "technical" violations of Illinois gambling law involved in this case. Cozzo cites United States v. Zizzo, 120 F.3d 1338 (7th Cir. 1997), as an example of the factual scenario to which § 1955 was meant to apply. *Zizzo* involved an illegal sports-betting organization, the proceeds from which were used to fund the Chicago Outfit, a notorious crime syndicate. 120 F.3d at 1343–44. In contrast to the gambling operation in *Zizzo*, Cozzo argues that, by applying § 1955 to this case, the government is allowed to bring racketeering charges against people whom Congress never intended the racketeering laws to prosecute.

Cozzo's argument is without merit. Nothing in the text of § 1955 prevents its application to misdemeanor violations of state gambling law. Section 1955 makes it a crime to "conduct[ ], finance[ ], manage[ ], supervise[ ], direct or own all or part of an illegal gambling business." 18 U.S.C. § 1955(a). To prove the existence of an illegal gambling business, the government must demonstrate that the business violated "the law of [the] State or political subdivision in which it is conducted." 18 U.S.C. § 1955(b)(1)(i). The text of § 1955 does not distinguish between state misdemeanor and felony law. Rather, all it requires is that the gambling violate state law, regardless of whether the violation amounted to a felony or simply a misdemeanor.

Cozzo fails to point to any case law that undermines our reading of § 1955. Indeed, case law appears contrary to his position. The Eighth Circuit rejected a similar challenge to § 1955 in United States v. Matya, 541 F.2d 741 (1976). The defendants in *Matya* argued that Congress did not intend for § 1955 to be used to elevate a state law misdemeanor into a federal felony. In rejecting that argument, the Eighth Circuit noted that violation of state law is not the sole element of a § 1955 offense, which also requires the involvement of five or more persons in a gambling business either in substantial continuous operation for a period of thirty or more days, or involving gross revenues of $2,000 in any single day. *Id.* at 748. Thus, it was inaccurate to characterize § 1955 as simply "elevating" a state misdemeanor into a federal felony.[4] *Id.* Furthermore, the Eighth Circuit found it significant that the House Report which accompanied the Organized Crime Control Act of 1970, of which § 1955 is a part, made no mention of any distinction between state felonies and state misdemeanors in the application of § 1955. *Id.* Finally, because "[m]ajor gambling activities were a principal focus of congressional concern," the Eighth Circuit found that it could not conclude that Congress had ruled out the use of state misdemeanors as a predicate to a § 1955 violation. *Id.* (quoting Iannelli v. United States, 420 U.S. 770, 787 (1975) (alteration in original)).

We agree with the Eighth Circuit. This case, in fact, offers a perfect example of why Congress did not distinguish between misdemeanor and felony violations of state gambling laws for purposes of § 1955. To operate the Grand Palace in the manner that Cozzo and his cohorts did, the Illinois gambling laws had to be systematically flouted. Though each violation of the Illinois gambling laws in this case, considered individually, may have been a mere "technical" or "minor" violation, in the aggregate they allowed the operators of the Grand Palace to divert from the games almost $3 million in illegal proceeds, a figure which represented the government's conservative estimate of the illegal proceeds.

Cozzo has presented nothing to persuade us, in contravention of the case law and clear text of § 1955, that § 1955 was meant to apply only to felony violations of state gambling law with an organized crime nexus. We therefore do not find any error in the district court's failure to dismiss the § 1955 count because it was predicated on misdemeanor violations of the Illinois gambling laws.

---

4. The Eighth Circuit agreed with the Ninth Circuit's conclusion that it was constitutionally permissible for Congress to define a federal felony partially in terms of a state misdemeanor. *See id. at 749 n. 16* ("Congress's power to proscribe conduct carries with it the power to impose appropriate penalties without attempting to match them to varying state punishments for similar conduct." (quoting United States v. Kerrigan, 514 F.2d 35, 37 n. 1 (9th Cir.1975))).

Notes

1. Section 1955 requires that the gambling business be in "violation of the law of a state or political subdivision in which it is conducted." A split of authority exists as to what types of state law violations can serve as a predicate violation. Clearly, a violation of a state criminal law, whether a misdemeanor or a felony, will suffice. United States v. Matya, 541 F.2d 741 (8th Cir. 1976). Moreover, the activity can be legal under state law, but a violation of a city or county ordinance may still serve as the predicate crime. *See, e.g.,* United States v. Zannino, 895 F.2d 1 (1st Cir. 1990). The Ninth Circuit has held that only acts or omissions that breach a penal statute or ordinance are a "violation of the law of the State," and Section 1955 is inapplicable where state law prescribes only civil sanctions. *See* United States v. Gordon, 464 F.2d 357, 358 (9th Cir. 1972). Conversely, the Sixth Circuit has held that the policy underlying the criminal/prohibitory-civil/regulatory test is not applicable to Section 1955. *See* United States v. Dakota, 796 F.2d 186, 187–88 (6th Cir. 1986). The Second Circuit probably would share this view. *See* United States v. Cook, 922 F.2d 1026, 1034–35 (2d Cir. 1991). The United States Supreme Court has declined to resolve this disagreement. *See* California v. Cabazon Band of Mission Indians, 480 U.S. 202, 214 (1987). However, based on dicta in *Cabazon*, it appears that the interpretation given Section 1955 by the Sixth Circuit is more persuasive. Accordingly, a person who engages in conduct that violates any penal law, and possibly any civil law, of the *situs* state governing gambling might incur Section 1955 criminal liability. In United States v. Bala, 489 F. 3d 334 (8th Cir. 2007), the court held that to be an illegal gambling business, the activity itself must be illegal and not simply the failure of a authorized business to properly pay taxes or otherwise violate some aspect of state law.

2. Section 1955 requires, as one alternative, that the gambling business "has been or remains in substantially continuous operation for a period in excess of thirty days." The other alternative is for the government to show that the operation had gross revenues of $2,000 in a single day.

3. "Substantially continuous operation" does not require that the government prove that the defendants operated gambling on a daily basis. Instead, one court noted that the business only had to be conducted upon a "schedule of regulating sufficient to take it out of [the] casual non-business category." United States v. Trupiano, 11 F.3d 769 (8th Cir. 1993). Therefore, a regularly scheduled weekend casino meets this requirement. United States v. Nerone, 563 F.2d 836, 843–44 (7th Cir. 1977). *See also* United States v. Allen, 588 F.2d 1100, 1102–04 (5th Cir. 1979) (concurring that evidence from eleven days of police surveillance over five months was sufficient to infer that the gambling business was in substantially continuous operation for more than 30 days). Perhaps in the extreme, the Third Circuit upheld a conviction of a person who conducted five poker games over a six month period. United States v. Rieger, 942 F.2d 230, 233 (3d Cir. 1991). Likewise, the operation of five "cock fights" over a two month period was held sufficient. United States v. Real Property Title in the Names of Godfrey Soon Bong Kang and Darrell Lee, 120 F.3d 947 (9th Cir. 1997).

4. A split of authority exists as to whether the five-person requirement and the thirty-day or $2,000 per day requirements are "two separate and independent jurisdictional requirements." United States v. Smaldone, 485 F.2d 1333, 1351 (10th Cir. 1973). The majority rule is that they are dependent or, in other words, requiring the involvement of five or more persons over the thirty day period. United States v. Murray, 928 F.2d 1242 (1st Cir. 1991); United States v. Gilley, 836 F.2d 1206, 1212 (9th Cir. 1988). The Tenth Circuit, however, has held these are independent. United States v. Boss, 671 F.2d 396, 401 n.7 (10th Cir. 1982).

Under the majority rule, however, the same five persons need not participate for the full 30-day period. The Fourth Circuit articulated the rule well in United States v. Gresko, when it stated:

> Since the magnitude of the business does not depend on the identities of its operator, we hold that the statute does not require a showing that the same five persons were involved for the entire thirty-day period. However, there must be evidence that the business involved at least five people at all times for the thirty days.

632 F.2d 1128, 1132–33 (4th Cir. 1980).

Moreover, the five persons that are counted for purposes of the minimum requirement need not all be working on any given day. *See, e.g.*, United States v. Marrifield, 515 F.2d 877 (5th Cir. 1975) (holding that a relief person qualified as the fifth participant).

5. As an alternative to proving the existence of a gambling business for a thirty-day period, a conviction can be sustained by showing the gambling business had gross revenues of $2,000 in a single day. This revenue threshold has remained unchanged since the Act was adopted in 1970. This is a fairly easy threshold to meet given its low amount and the method by which the courts calculate it. The threshold is not determined by net profit or gross gaming win, but by the total amount of wagers placed during a day. *See, e.g.*, United States v. Schaefer, 510 F.2d 1307, 1313 n.9 (8th Cir. 1975); United States v. Ceraso, 467 F.2d 653, 656–57 (3d Cir. 1972). Some circuits even allow side bets among players or wagers placed in common pools to be included for threshold purposes. *See* United States v. Zemek, 634 F.2d 1159 (9th Cir. 1980); *but see* United States v. Tille, 729 F.2d 615 (9th Cir. 1984); United States v. Killip, 819 F.2d 1542 (10th Cir. 1987).

Chapter 12

Internet Gambling

1. Background

The Internet is a fixture of modern life. Traditional newsprint is coming under increased financial pressure as more people use the Internet as a primary source of news. Texting, tweeting, instant messaging, and social networks are becoming primary methods of social interaction for many Americans. Online shopping is now a major retail force in the marketplace. In short, the promise of the information superhighway is at the advent of realization. Among the many uses of the Internet, gambling on poker, sports, and casinos has found a home.

Technical aspects of how the Internet works are less important for public policy and political considerations than the impact of what the Internet allows users to do. Simply put, if parties located in different parts of the planet can transact or communicate without having to be present, the Internet can facilitate it with audio, video, test, displays, and ancillary services. Most activities present few public policy issues. If an American company wants to hire a French marketing consultant, the Internet simply becomes a communication tool. The more difficult policy issues arise when the activity contemplated is legal or permitted in one jurisdiction and prohibited in the other. Perhaps no activity better defines this conflict than Internet gambling. Singling out Internet gambling may seem odd. After all, the Internet is only the latest in the string of communication tools used by gambling operators. For example, a person could place a wager over the telephone by international direct dialing since the 1970s. What distinguishes the Internet is the level of functionality. It can serve as the advertising and marketing medium for the gaming sites, offer fully interactive experiences in casino and multiple player games like poker, and provide fund transfers necessary to collect bets and make payouts. The Internet is a one-stop shop for all gambling activity with the divergent parts of the process potentially operating from different parts of the world. For example, the game servers could be in Malta and the payment servers in Canada.

Internet gambling alone is a threat to traditional government. Max Weber in *Politics as a Vocation* claimed that a governmental state exists in a particular territory only "if and insofar as its administrative staff successfully upholds a claim on the *monopoly* of the *legitimate* use of violence in the enforcement of its order." MAX WEBER, THE THEORY OF SOCIAL AND ECONOMIC ORGANIZATION 154 (1964). Governments dictate order by passing laws that govern the conduct of its citizens and use police force to enforce those laws. If, however, the activity that the government wants to control—such as Internet gaming—occurs on the Internet outside of its territory, the government's ability to punish those who contravene its laws is hindered by both practicalities (e.g. finding the persons who violate the law) and cross border consideration (even if you can find them, how do you prosecute them?).

One federal commission took an early stance against Internet gambling. The National Gambling Impact Study Commission issued its final report in May 1999. The Internet portion of the report reflected disdain for Internet gambling. Among other things, the Commission supported legislation that would:

1. Prohibit Internet gambling "not already authorized within the United States or among parties in the United States and any foreign jurisdiction."

2. Prohibit wire transfers to Internet gambling sites and banks servicing those sites.

3. Prohibit the enforcement of credit card debts incurred for Internet gambling purposes.

The Gambling Impact Study Commission also recommended that the state governments not allow expansion of gambling into homes. What was unusual about the National Gambling Impact Study Commission was that it consisted almost equally of political appointments representing either the casino industry or the religious right of the Republican Party who generally opposed legalized gambling.

Specific legislation addressing Internet gambling, however, was not passed until 2006.

2. The Legality of Internet Gambling under Laws Existing before 2006

United States v. Cohen

260 F.3d 68 (2d Cir. 2001)

Before: LEVAL and PARKER, Circuit Judges, and KEENAN, District Judge.[1]

KEENAN, District Judge:

BACKGROUND

In 1996, the Defendant, Jay Cohen ("Cohen") was young, bright, and enjoyed a lucrative position at Group One, a San Francisco firm that traded in options and derivatives. That was not all to last, for by 1996 the Internet revolution was in the speed lane. Inspired by the new technology and its potential, Cohen decided to pursue the dream of owning his own e-business. By year's end he had left his job at Group One, moved to the Caribbean island of Antigua, and had become a bookmaker.

Cohen, as President, and his partners, all American citizens, dubbed their new venture the World Sports Exchange ("WSE"). WSE's sole business involved bookmaking on American sports events, and was purportedly patterned after New York's Off-Track Betting Corporation.[2] WSE targeted customers in the United States, advertising its business throughout America by radio, newspaper, and television. Its advertisements invited customers to bet with WSE either by toll-free telephone or by internet.

WSE operated an "account-wagering" system. It required that its new customers first open an account with WSE and wire at least $300 into that account in Antigua. A customer seeking to bet would then contact WSE either by telephone or internet to request a particular bet. WSE would issue an immediate, automatic acceptance and confirmation of that bet, and would maintain the bet from that customer's account.

---

1. The Honorable John F. Keenan, United States District Judge for the Southern District of New York, sitting by designation.

2. We note, however, that the Off-Track Betting Corporation's business is limited to taking bets on horseracing, not other sporting events.

In one fifteen-month period, WSE collected approximately $5.3 million in funds wired from customers in the United States. In addition, WSE would typically retain a "vig" or commission of 10% on each bet. Cohen boasted that in its first year of operation, WSE had already attracted nearly 1,600 customers. By November 1998, WSE had received 60,000 phone calls from customers in the United 71 States, including over 6,100 from New York.

In the course of an FBI investigation of offshore bookmakers, FBI agents in New York contacted WSE by telephone and internet numerous times between October 1997 and March 1998 to open accounts and place bets. Cohen was arrested in March 1998 under an eight-count indictment charging him with conspiracy and substantive offenses in violation of 18 U.S.C. § 1084 ("§ 1084"). That statute reads as follows:

> (a) Whoever being engaged in the business of betting or wagering knowingly uses a wire communication facility for the transmission in interstate or foreign commerce of bets or wagers or information assisting in the placing of bets or wagers on any sporting event or contest, or for the transmission of a wire communication which entitles the recipient to receive money or credit as a result of bets or wagers, or for information assisting in the placing of bets or wagers, shall be fined under this title or imprisoned not more than two years, or both.

> (b) Nothing in this section shall be construed to prevent the transmission in interstate or foreign commerce of information for use in news reporting of sporting events or contests, or for the transmission of information assisting in the placing of bets or wagers on a sporting event or contest from a State or foreign country where betting on that sporting event or contest is legal into a State or foreign country in which such betting is legal.

See § 1084(a)-(b). In the conspiracy count (Count One) and in five of the seven substantive counts (Counts Three through Six, and Eight), Cohen was charged with violating all three prohibitive clauses of § 1084(a) ((1) transmission in interstate or foreign commerce of bets or wagers, (2) transmission of a wire communication which entitles the recipient to receive money or credit as a result of bets or wagers, (3) information assisting in the placement of bets or wagers). In two counts, Counts Two and Seven, he was charged only with transmitting "information assisting in the placing of bets or wagers."

Cohen was convicted on all eight counts on February 28, 2000 after a ten-day jury trial before Judge Thomas P. Griesa. The jury found in special interrogatories that Cohen had violated all three prohibitive clauses of § 1084(a) with respect to the five counts in which those violations were charged. Judge Griesa sentenced Cohen on August 10, 2000 to a term of twenty-one months' imprisonment. He has remained on bail pending the outcome of this appeal.

DISCUSSION

On appeal, Cohen asks this Court to consider the following six issues: (1) whether the Government was required to prove a "corrupt motive" in connection with the conspiracy in this case; (2) whether the district court properly instructed the jury to disregard the safe-harbor provision contained in § 1084(b); (3) whether Cohen "knowingly" violated § 1084; (4) whether the rule of lenity requires a reversal of Cohen's convictions; (5) whether the district court constructively amended Cohen's indictment in giving its jury instructions; and (6) whether the district court abused its discretion by denying Cohen's request to depose a foreign witness. We will address those issues in that order.

...

II The Safe Harbor Provision

Cohen appeals the district court for instructing the jury to disregard the safe-harbor provision contained in § 1084(b). That subsection provides a safe harbor for transmissions that occur under both of the following two conditions: (1) betting is legal in both the place of origin and the destination of the transmission; and (2) the transmission is limited to mere information that assists in the placing of bets, as opposed to including the bets themselves. *See* § 1084(b).

The district court ruled as a matter of law that the safe-harbor provision did not apply because neither of the two conditions existed in the case of WSE's transmissions. Cohen disputes that ruling and argues that both conditions did, in fact, exist. He argues that betting is not only legal in Antigua, it is also "legal" in New York for the purposes of § 1084. He also argues that all of WSE's transmissions were limited to mere information assisting in the placing of bets. We agree with the district court's rulings on both issues.

A. "Legal" Betting

There can be no dispute that betting is illegal in New York. New York has expressly prohibited betting in both its Constitution, *see* N.Y. Const. art. I, § 9 ("no ... bookmaking, or any other kind of gambling [with certain exceptions pertaining to lotteries and horseracing] shall hereafter be authorized or allowed within this state"), and its General Obligations Law, *see* N.Y. Gen. Oblig. L. § 5-401 ("[a]ll wagers, bets or stakes, made to depend on any race, or upon any gaming by lot or chance, or upon any lot, chance, casualty, or unknown or contingent event whatever, shall be unlawful"); *see also* Cohen v. Iuzzini, 25 A.D.2d 878, 270 N.Y.S.2d 278, 279 (1966) (ruling that the predecessor statute to N.Y. Gen. Oblig. L. § 5-401 (N.Y. Penal L. § 991) did not apply to bets executed at recognized pari-mutuel tracks). Nevertheless, Cohen argues that Congress intended for the safe-harbor provision in § 1084(b) to exclude only those transmissions sent to or from jurisdictions in which betting was a crime. Cohen concludes that because the placing of bets is not a crime in New York, it is "legal" for the purposes of § 1084(b).

By its plain terms, the safe-harbor provision requires that betting be "legal," *i.e.*, permitted by law, in both jurisdictions. *See* § 1084(b); *see also* Black's Law Dictionary 902 (7th ed. 1999); Webster's 3d New Int'l Dictionary 1290 (1993). The plain meaning of a statute "should be conclusive, except in the rare cases in which the literal application of a statute will produce a result demonstrably at odds with the intentions of its drafters." United States v. Ron Pair Enters., Inc., 489 U.S. 235, 242 (1989) (alteration and internal quotation marks omitted). This is not the rare case.

Although, as Cohen notes, the First Circuit has stated that Congress "did not intend [for § 1084] to criminalize acts that neither the affected states nor Congress itself deemed criminal in nature," it did not do so in the context of a § 1084 prosecution. *See* Sterling Suffolk Racecourse Ltd. P'ship v. Burrillville Racing Ass'n, 989 F.2d 1266, 1273 (1st Cir.1993). Instead, that case involved a private bid for an injunction under RICO (18 U.S.C. § 1961 *et seq.*) and the Interstate Horseracing Act (15 U.S.C. §§ 3001–07) ("IHA"). *Id.* at 1272–73. It does not stand for the proposition that § 1084 permits betting that is illegal as long as it is not criminal.

In *Sterling*, the defendant was an OTB office in Rhode Island that accepted bets on horse races from distant tracks and broadcasted the races. *Id.* at 1267. The office typically obtained the various consents required under the IHA, *i.e.*, from the host track, the host racing commission, and its own racing commission. *Id.* However, it would often neglect to secure the consent of the plaintiff, a live horse-racing track located within the statutory sixty-mile radius from the OTB office. *Id.* at 1268. The plaintiff sought an injunction against the OTB office under RICO, alleging that it was engaged in a pattern of racketeering activity by violating § 1084 through its noncompliance with the IHA. *Id.*

The *Sterling* court affirmed the district court's denial of the RICO injunction. *Id.* at 1273. It noted first that because the OTB office's business was legitimate under all applicable state laws, it fell under the safe-harbor provision in § 1084(b). *Id.* Furthermore, the court held that in enacting the IHA, Congress had only created a private right of action for damages on the part of certain parties; it did not intend for any Government enforcement of the IHA. *Id.* Consequently, the plaintiff could not use the IHA together with § 1084 to transform an otherwise legal OTB business into a criminal racketeering enterprise. *Id.*

Neither *Sterling* nor the legislative history behind § 1084 demonstrates that Congress intended for § 1084(b) to mean anything other than what it says.[3] Betting is illegal in New York, and thus the safe-harbor provision in § 1084(b) cannot not apply in Cohen's case as a matter of law. As a result, the district court was not in error when it instructed the jury to disregard that provision.

B. Transmission of a Bet, Per Se

Cohen appeals the district court's instructions to the jury regarding what constitutes a bet *per se.* Cohen argues that under WSE's account-wagering system, the transmissions between WSE and its customers contained only information that enabled WSE itself to place bets entirely from customer accounts located in Antigua. He argues that this fact was precluded by the district court's instructions. We find no error in those instructions.

Judge Griesa repeatedly charged the jury as follows:

> If there was a telephone call or an internet transmission between New York and [WSE] in Antigua, and if a person in New York said or signaled that he or she wanted to place a specified bet, and if a person on an internet device or a telephone said or signaled that the bet was accepted, this was the transmission of a bet within the meaning of Section 1084. Congress clearly did not intend to have this statute be made inapplicable because the party in a foreign gambling business deemed or construed the transmission as only starting with an employee or an internet mechanism located on the premises in the foreign country.

Jury instructions are not improper simply because they resemble the conduct alleged to have occurred in a given case; nor were they improper in this case. It was the Government's burden in this case to prove that someone in New York signaled an offer to place a particular bet and that someone at WSE signaled an acceptance of that offer. The jury concluded that the Government had carried that burden.

Most of the cases that Cohen cites in support of the proposition that WSE did not transmit any bets involved problems pertaining either to proof of the acceptance of transmitted bets, *see* United States v. Truesdale, 152 F.3d 443 (5th Cir. 1998), McQuesten v. Stein-

---

3. In support of his Congressional intent argument, Cohen offers two passages from the Congressional Reports, neither of which is persuasive. Together, the two passages evidence an intent to assist the states in enforcing gambling "offenses" and in suppressing "organized gambling activities" without preempting the states' own prosecutions of those offenses. *Compare* H.R. Rep. No. 87-967 (1961), *reprinted in* 1961 U.S.C.C.A.N 2631, 2631, *with id.* at 2633. Those passages do not demonstrate an intent to exclude illegal yet non-criminal gambling activity from the statute's purview.

metz, 73 N.H. 9, 58 A. 876 (1904), Lescallett v. Commonwealth, 89 Va. 878, 17 S.E. 546 (1893), or to proof of the locus of a betting business for taxation purposes, *see* Saratoga Harness Racing, Inc. v. City of Saratoga Springs, 55 A.2d 295, 390 N.Y.S.2d 240 (1976).

No such problems existed in this case. This case was never about taxation, and there can be no dispute regarding WSE's acceptance of customers' bet requests. For example, a March 18, 1998 conversation between Spencer Hanson, a WSE employee, and a New York-based undercover FBI agent occurred as follows:

Agent: Can I place a bet right now?

Hanson: You can place a bet right now.

Agent: Alright, can you give me the line on the um Penn State/Georgia Tech game, it's the NIT [T]hird Round game tonight.

Hanson: Its [sic] Georgia Tech minus 7?, total is 147.

Agent: Georgia [T]ech minus 7?, umm I wanna take Georgia Tech. Can I take 'em for 50?

Hanson: Sure.

WSE could only book the bets that its customers requested and authorized it to book. By making those requests and having them accepted, WSE's customers were placing bets. So long as the customers' accounts were in good standing, WSE accepted those bets as a matter of course.

Moreover, the issue is immaterial in light of the fact that betting is illegal in New York. Section 1084(a) prohibits the transmission of information assisting in the placing of bets as well as the transmission of bets themselves. This issue, therefore, pertains only to the applicability of § 1084(b)'s safe-harbor provision. As we have noted, that safe harbor excludes not only the transmission of bets, but also the transmission of betting information to or from a jurisdiction in which betting is illegal. As a result, that provision is inapplicable here even if WSE had only ever transmitted betting information.

III. Cohen's Mens Rea

Cohen appeals the district court's instruction to the jury regarding the requisite *mens rea* under § 1084. Section 1084 prohibits the "knowing" transmission of bets or information assisting in the placing of bets. *See* § 1084(a). The district court instructed the jurors that to convict, they needed only to find that Cohen "knew that the deeds described in the statute as being prohibited were being done," and that a misinterpretation of the law, like ignorance of the law, was no excuse.

Cohen argues that he lacked the requisite *mens rea* because (1) he did not "knowingly" transmit bets, and (2) he did not transmit information assisting in the placing of bets or wagers to or from a jurisdiction in which he "knew" betting was illegal. He contends that in giving its jury charge, the district court improperly instructed the jury to disregard that argument.

The district court was correct; it mattered only that Cohen knowingly committed the deeds forbidden by § 1084, not that he intended to violate the statute. *See Bryan v. United States,* 524 U.S. 184, 193 (1998). Cohen's own interpretation regarding what constituted a bet was irrelevant to the issue of his *mens rea* under § 1084.

In any event, Cohen is culpable under § 1084(a) by admitting that he knowingly transmitted information assisting in the placing of bets. His beliefs regarding the legality of betting in New York are immaterial. The legality of betting in a relevant jurisdiction pertains only to § 1084(b)'s safe-harbor provision. As we have already discussed, that safe-harbor provision, as a matter of law, does not apply in this case.

...

V. Aiding-and-Abetting Liability

Cohen contends that the district court constructively amended his indictment by instructing the jury on criminal aiding-and-abetting liability under 18 U.S.C. § 2(b) rather than under § 2(a) of that title. Cohen argues that as a result, the district court failed to instruct the jury that before convicting Cohen for aiding and abetting his subordinates' conduct, it must find that those subordinates were themselves guilty of crimes. Cohen also argues that he could not have been liable under § 2 for acts committed after his arrest. We find no error in either instance.

A constructive amendment can occur when jury instructions change an essential element of the charges in the indictment so as to "deprive a defendant of an opportunity to meet the prosecutor's case." See United States v. Helmsley, 941 F.2d 71, 90 (2d Cir. 1991) (concluding that "the indictment and the jury charge ... comported with one another in all essential respects, and [the defendant] had adequate notice of the conduct she was called upon to defend").

The district court indicated to the parties at the charging conference that it would only charge aiding-and-abetting liability under § 2(a). Section 2(a) requires proof that someone other than the defendant committed the underlying crime. See United States v. Smith, 198 F.3d 377, 383 (2d Cir. 1999).

Instead, the district court charged the jury under § 2(b), which requires only that the defendant willfully cause another person to commit an act which would have been a crime had the defendant committed it himself. See 18 U.S.C. § 2(b); United States v. Concepcion, 983 F.2d 369, 383–84 (2d Cir. 1992). Section 2(b), unlike § 2(a), does not require proof that someone else committed a crime.

Despite having charged § 2(b) rather than § 2(a), the district court did not amend Cohen's indictment. Cohen was charged in his indictment with violations of 18 U.S.C. § 2, see A15, and the district court gave the jury a proper instruction under that statute. Although there may have been some confusing colloquy between the district court and counsel prior to the jury charge, the charge was consistent with the indictment. There was no amendment.

Furthermore, Cohen could still have been liable for aiding and abetting the acts charged in Counts Seven and Eight of his indictment, even though those counts pertained to transmissions that occurred after his arrest. Cohen was a moving force behind WSE's entire operation, which continued to function after his arrest. Cohen retained his position as President of WSE while on bail after his arrest.

Although Cohen purportedly did not "deal with daily operations" at WSE after his arrest, he also made no effort to curtail those operations. In fact, he benefitted from them by receiving a salary, his travel expenses, and his legal fees from WSE. He clearly was still in a position to cause others, willfully, to commit acts that would have been crimes had he himself committed them. He could, therefore, have been found liable for aiding and abetting WSE's ongoing violation of § 1084.

...

CONCLUSION

For the reasons set forth above, the judgment of the district court is AFFIRMED.

In Re Mastercard International, Inc.

313 F.3d 257 (5th Cir. 2002)

DENNIS, Circuit Judge:

In this lawsuit, Larry Thompson and Lawrence Bradley ("Thompson," "Bradley," or collectively "Plaintiffs") attempt to use the Racketeer Influenced and Corrupt Organizations Act ("RICO"), 18 U.S.C. §§ 1961–1968, to avoid debts they incurred when they used their credit cards to purchase "chips" with which they gambled at on-line casinos and to recover for injuries they allegedly sustained by reason of the RICO violations of MasterCard International, Visa International, and banks that issue MasterCard and Visa credit cards (collectively "Defendants").[1] The district court granted the Defendants' motions to dismiss pursuant to Rule 12(b)(6) of the Federal Rules of Civil Procedure. We AFFIRM.

I.

Thompson and Bradley allege that the Defendants, along with unnamed Internet casinos, created and operate a "worldwide gambling enterprise" that facilitates illegal gambling on the Internet through the use of credit cards. Internet gambling works as follows. A gambler directs his browser to a casino website. There he is informed that he will receive a gambling "credit" for each dollar he deposits and is instructed to enter his billing information. He can use a credit card to purchase the credits.[2] His credit card is subsequently charged for his purchase of the credits. Once he has purchased the credits, he may place wagers. Losses are debited from, and winnings credited to, his account. Any net winnings a gambler might accrue are not credited to his card but are paid by alternate mechanisms, such as wire transfers.

Under this arrangement, Thompson and Bradley contend, "[t]he availability of credit and the ability to gamble are inseparable."[3] The credit card companies facilitate the enterprise, they say, by authorizing the casinos to accept credit cards, by making credit available to gamblers, by encouraging the use of that credit through the placement of their logos on the websites, and by processing the "gambling debts" resulting from the extension of credit. The banks that issued the gamblers' credit cards participate in the enterprise, they say, by collecting those "gambling debts."

Thompson holds a MasterCard credit card issued by Fleet Bank (Rhode Island) NA. He used his credit card to purchase $1510 in gambling credits at two Internet gambling sites. Bradley holds a Visa credit card issued by Travelers Bank USA Corporation. He used his credit card to purchase $16,445 in gambling credits at seven Internet gambling sites. Thompson and Bradley each used his credits to place wagers. Thompson lost everything, and his subsequent credit card billing statements reflected purchases of $1,510 at the casinos. Bradley's winning percentage was higher, but he fared worse in the end. He states his monthly credit card billing statements included $7048 in purchases at the casinos.

---

1. Thirty-three virtually identical cases were transferred to the Eastern District of Louisiana through multidistrict litigation. Of these, the two on appeal were selected as test cases and consolidated for pretrial purposes. *See* In re MasterCard Int'l Inc., Internet Gambling Litigation and Visa Int'l Serv. Ass'n Internet Gambling Litigation, 132 F. Supp.2d 468, 471 n. 1 (E.D.La.2001).

2. Gamblers can purchase the credits through online transactions or by authorizing a purchase via a telephone call. Gamblers also can purchase the credits via personal check or money order using the mails.

3. The Plaintiffs state that 95% of Internet gambling business involves the use of credit cards.

Thompson and Bradley filed class action complaints against the Defendants on behalf of themselves and others similarly situated. They state that the Defendants participated in and aided and abetted conduct that violated various federal and state criminal laws applicable to Internet gambling. Through their association with the Internet casinos, the Defendants allegedly "directed, guided, conducted, or participated, directly or indirectly, in the conduct of an enterprise through a pattern of racketeering and/or the unlawful collection of unlawful debt," in violation of 18 U.S.C. § 1962(c).[4] They seek damages under RICO's civil remedies provision,[5] claiming that they were injured by the Defendants' RICO violations. They also seek declaratory judgment that their gambling debts are unenforceable because they are illegal.

Upon motions by the Defendants, the district court dismissed the Plaintiffs' complaints. In a thorough and careful opinion, the court determined that the Plaintiffs not only could not satisfy the necessary prerequisites to a RICO claim but also could not establish their standing to bring such a claim. The Plaintiffs now appeal.

II.

We review a district court's grant of a Rule 12(b)(6) motion *de novo*, applying the same standard used below.[6] "In so doing, we accept the facts alleged in the complaint as true and construe the allegations in the light most favorable to the plaintiffs."[7] But "conclusory allegations or legal conclusions masquerading as factual conclusions will not suffice to prevent a motion to dismiss."[8]

III.

All RICO violations under 18 U.S.C. § 1962 entail "(1) a *person* who engages in (2) a *pattern of racketeering activity*, (3) connected to the acquisition, establishment, conduct, or control of an *enterprise*."[9] As to the second element, a RICO plaintiff may show that the defendant engaged in the collection of unlawful debt as an alternative to showing the defendant engaged in a pattern or racketeering activity.[10] A RICO claim alleging a violation of § 1962(c), as here, also requires that the defendant "participate[d] in the operation or management of the enterprise itself."[11] Of these required elements, the district court concluded that Thompson and Bradley failed to plead facts showing a pattern of racketeering activity or the collection of unlawful debt; a RICO enterprise; or participation in the operation of management of the enterprise. We agree that the Plaintiffs' allegations do not show a pattern of racketeering activity or the collection of unlawful debt. Because this conclusion, alone, is dispositive, we need not consider whether the Plaintiffs sufficiently alleged the other elements.

---

4. "It shall be unlawful for any person employed by or associated with any enterprise engaged in, or the activities of which affect, interstate or foreign commerce, to conduct or participate, directly or indirectly, in the conduct of such enterprise's affairs through a pattern of racketeering activity or collection of unlawful debt." 18 U.S.C. § 1962(c).

5. 18 U.S.C. § 1964.

6. Nolen v. Nucentrix Broadband Networks, Inc., 293 F.3d 926, 928 (5th Cir. 2002); *see also* Rubinstein v. Collins, 20 F.3d 160, 166 (5th Cir.1994) ("Such dismissals may be upheld only if it appears that no relief could be granted under any set of facts that could be proven consistent with the allegations" (internal quotation and citation omitted)).

7. *Nolen*, 293 F.3d at 928 (citing *Rubinstein*, 20 F.3d at 166).

8. *Id.* (citing Fernandez-Montes v. Allied Pilots Ass'n, 987 F.2d 278, 284 (5th Cir. 1993)).

9. Crowe v. Henry, 43 F.3d 198, 204 (5th Cir. 1995) (citing Delta Truck & Tractor, Inc. v. J.I. Case Co., 855 F.2d 241, 242 (5th Cir. 1988)).

10. 18 U.S.C. § 1962(a)-(c); *see also Nolen*, 293 F.3d at 928–29.

11. Reves v. Ernst & Young, 507 U.S. 170, 185 (1993).

"A pattern of racketeering activity requires two or more predicate acts and a demonstration that the racketeering predicates are related and amount to or pose a threat of continued criminal activity."[12] The predicate acts can be either state or federal crimes.[13] Thompson and Bradley allege both types of predicate acts.

On appeal, Thompson alleges that the Defendants' conduct violated a Kansas statute that criminalizes five types of commercial gambling activity.[14] Only two sections of the statute—sections (c) and (e)—are even remotely relevant here. Neither implicates the Defendants' conduct. Because the Defendants completed their transaction with the Plaintiffs *before* any gambling occurred, that transaction cannot have involved taking custody of something bet or collecting the proceeds of a gambling device. Both of those activities, which constitute commercial gambling under Kansas law, necessarily "can only take place after some form of gambling [has been] completed."[15] Accordingly, we find that Thompson fails to identify a RICO predicate act under Kansas law.[16]

Bradley alleges on appeal that the Defendants' conduct violated a New Hampshire gambling statute aimed at persons who operate or control places where gambling occurs.[17] Bradley did not, however, allege a violation of the statute in his complaint. In any event, this statute is patently inapplicable to the Defendants under the facts alleged. Indeed, Bradley makes no effort in his briefs to explain its applicability. Accordingly, we find that Bradley, too, fails to identify a RICO predicate act under a state criminal law.[18]

Thompson and Bradley both identify three substantive federal crimes as predicates— violation of the Wire Act, mail fraud, and wire fraud.[19] The district court concluded that the Wire Act concerns gambling on sporting events or contests and that the Plaintiffs had failed to allege that they had engaged in internet sports gambling.[20] We agree with the district court's statutory interpretation, its reading of the relevant case law, its summary of the relevant legislative history, and its conclusion. The Plaintiffs may not rely on the Wire Act as a predicate offense here.[21]

---

12. St. Paul Mercury Ins. Co. v. Williamson, 224 F.3d 425, 441 (5th Cir. 2000) (citing Word of Faith World Outreach Ctr. Church, Inc. v. Sawyer, 90 F.3d 118, 122 (5th Cir. 1996)).

13. 18 U.S.C. § 1961(1).

14. Kan. Stat. Ann. § 21-4304. This statute, which states that commercial gambling is a "level 8, nonperson felony," defines commercial gambling as: "(a) Operating or receiving all or part of the earnings of a gambling place; (b) Receiving, recording, or forwarding bets or offers to bet or, with intent to receive, record, or forward bets or offers to bet, possessing facilities to do so; (c) For gain, becoming a custodian of anything of value bet or offered to be bet; (d) Conducting a lottery, or with intent to conduct a lottery possessing facilities to do so; or (e) Setting up for use or collecting the proceeds of any gambling device."

15. *See In re MasterCard,* 132 F. Supp.2d at 479.

16. Thompson has abandoned his reliance on three other violations of Kansas law he alleged below. Violations of those statutes cannot serve as predicates because they identify only misdemeanor offenses. *See* 18 U.S.C. § 1961(1)(A).

17. N.H.Rev.Stat. Ann. § 647:2(I-a)(b). This statute provides that "[a] person is guilty of a class B felony if such person conducts, finances, manages, supervises, directs, or owns all or part of a business and such person knowingly and unlawfully conducts, finances, manages, supervises, or directs any gambling activity on the business premises...."

18. Bradley has abandoned his previous reliance on various New Hampshire civil statutes, each of which was obviously inadequate to identify a predicate crime under 18 U.S.C. § 1961(1)(A).

19. 18 U.S.C. §§ 1084, 1341, 1343.

20. *In re MasterCard,* 132 F.Supp.2d at 480 ("[A] plain reading of the statutory language [of the Wire Act] clearly requires that the object of the gambling be a sporting event or contest.").

21. Bradley criticizes the district court for ignoring his identification of an Internet site named "Sportsbook" in his complaint. The name of the site is irrelevant, for Bradley nowhere alleges that he gambled on sporting events or contests at that or any other site.

The district court next articulated several reasons why the Plaintiffs may not rely on federal mail or wire fraud as predicates.[22] Of these reasons, two are particularly compelling. First, Thompson and Bradley cannot show that the Defendants made a false or fraudulent misrepresentation.[23] Because the Wire Act does not prohibit non-sports internet gambling, any debts incurred in connection with such gambling are not illegal. Hence, the Defendants could not have fraudulently represented the Plaintiffs' related debt as legal because it was, in fact, legal. We agree that "the allegations that the issuing banks represented the credit charges as legal debts is not a scheme to defraud."[24] Second, Thompson and Bradley fail to allege that they relied upon the Defendants' representations in deciding to gamble.[25] The district court correctly stated that although reliance is not an element of statutory mail or wire fraud, we have required its showing when mail or wire fraud is alleged as a RICO predicate.[26] Accordingly, we conclude that Thompson and Bradley cannot rely on the federal mail or wire fraud statutes to show RICO predicate acts.[27]

In the alternative, Thompson and Bradley allege that the Defendants engaged in the collection of unlawful debt. Under § 1961, a RICO plaintiff may attempt to show that the debt is unlawful because it was incurred or contracted in an illegal gambling activity or in connection with the illegal business of gambling or because it is unenforceable under usury laws or was incurred in connection with the business of lending at usurious rates.[28] Neither Thompson nor Bradley raises the specter of usury. And, as we have already found, the Defendants' conduct did not involve any violation of a state or federal gambling law. Thus, we agree with the district court's conclusion that the Plaintiffs have not sufficiently alleged "the collection of unlawful debt."[29]

Because Thompson and Bradley cannot prove a necessary element of a civil RICO claim, namely that the Defendants engaged in a pattern of racketeering activity or the collection of unlawful debt, we hold that dismissal is proper under Rule 12(b)(6).[30]

Finally, we reiterate the district court's statement that "RICO, no matter how liberally construed, is not intended to provide a remedy to this class of plaintiff."[31] Thompson and

---

22. *Id.* at 481–83.

23. *See* In re Burzynski, 989 F.2d 733, 742 (5th Cir. 1993) (stating that an element of a RICO mail fraud claim is "a scheme to defraud by means of false or fraudulent representation").

24. *In re MasterCard*, 132 F. Supp.2d at 482.

25. Based in part on this same failure, the district court correctly determined that the Plaintiffs could not establish standing to sue under 18 U.S.C. § 1964(c). *See id.* at 495–96 (explaining that standing requires a showing of both factual and proximate causation).

26. Summit Props., Inc. v. Hoechst Celanese Corp., 214 F.3d 556, 562 (5th Cir. 2000) (stating that the element of reliance is required to recover damages in a RICO fraud claim); *see also* In re MasterCard, 132 F. Supp.2d at 482, 496 (explaining that the element of reliance is also key to the issue of standing).

27. Because we find neither the Wire Act nor the mail and wire fraud statutes may serve as predicates here, we need not consider the other federal statutes identified by the Plaintiffs: § 1952 (Travel Act); § 1955 (illegal gambling businesses); and § 1957 (money laundering). As the district court correctly explained, these sections may not serve as predicates here because the Defendants did not violate any applicable federal or state law. *See In re MasterCard,* 132 F. Supp.2d at 482–83 & n.6. The Plaintiffs' reliance on § 1960 fails because it is not an authorized RICO predicate under § 1961(1)(B).

28. 18 U.S.C. § 1961(6).

29. *In re MasterCard,* 132 F. Supp.2d at 483.

30. We need not analyze the validity or merit of Plaintiffs' claim based on aiding and abetting liability because (assuming it is valid) it necessarily falls along with the underlying RICO claim. Likewise, we need not consider the merits of the Defendants' motions to join the Internet casinos pursuant to Rule 19 of the Federal Rules of Civil Procedure. We agree with the district court that those motions are moot.

31. *Id.* at 497.

Bradley simply are not victims under the facts of these cases. Rather, as the district court wrote, "they are independent actors who made a knowing and voluntary choice to engage in a course of conduct."[32] In engaging in this conduct, they got exactly what they bargained for—gambling "chips" with which they could place wagers. They cannot use RICO to avoid meeting obligations they voluntarily took on.

IV.

For the foregoing reasons, we AFFIRM the judgment of the district court.

Notes

1. The legality of Internet gambling cannot be adequately explored without distinguishing between types of gambling. These include sports wagering, games of chance such as casino and lottery games, poker, and horseracing. What are the distinguishing features of these four types of gambling that resulted in their deserving separate consideration? What distinguishes *Cohen* and *In Re MasterCard*?

2. In United States v. Lombardo, a federal district court in another circuit concluded the second and third prohibited uses of a wire communication facility under section 1084(a) do not require that the bets or wagers to which those uses relate be limited to bets or wagers placed on sporting events or contests alone. 639 F. Supp.2d 1271, 1282 (D. Utah 2007). The court noted: "The phrase 'sporting event or contest' modifies only the first of these three uses of a wire communication facility. *Id.* Giving effect to the presumably intentional exclusion of the 'sporting event or contest' qualifier from the second and third prohibited uses indicates that at least part of § 1084(a) applies to forms of gambling that are unrelated to sporting events." *Id.* Different commentators have different opinions on these issues. *See e.g.,* Bruce P. Keller, *The Game's the Same: Why Gambling in Cyberspace Violates Federal Law*, 108 YALE L.J. 1569 (1999) (arguing that traditional gambling laws should be applied to Internet Gambling; holding otherwise would strip court of over one-hundred years of case law precedent; send the wrong "hands-off" message to courts already wrestling with the problem, and cause a delay in addressing the immediate problem of off-shore Internet gambling sites); Ryan S. Landes, *Layovers and Cargo Ships: The Prohibition of Internet Gambling and a Proposed System of Regulation,* 82 N.Y.U. L. REV. 913 (2007) (examining the various tactics employed by Congress in the past decade when attempting to combat Internet gambling, and arguing that each method employed fails to solve the problem it addresses). *See also* DAVID G. SCHWARTZ, CUTTING THE WIRE: GAMING PROHIBITION AND THE INTERNET (University of Nevada Press 2005).

3. Assuming that the Federal Wire Act only applies to sports, other federal laws may apply to Internet wagers accepted on non-sporting events. These could include the Federal Wire Act Illegal Gambling Business Act (18 U.S.C. § 1955) and the Travel Act (18 U.S.C. § 1952), discussed in Chapter 11. Both acts, however, require a violation of state law as a predicate to a federal violation. These acts are designed to assist states in enforcement of their state gambling laws. Poker has a more controversial history under state law because it is a game of mixed skill and chance. State courts are almost evenly divided as to whether poker is a legal game of skill or an illegal game of chance. This distinction brings even greater uncertainty as to the application of federal gambling laws to Internet poker offered in certain states.

---

32. *Id.*

4. State laws are inconsistent and application to Internet wagering is often difficult because in many cases state law was adopted over 100 years ago. Often, place-based restrictions in these state laws do not apply to the Internet. The difficulty in applying existing gambling law to the Internet was illustrated in the district court's decision in In Re MasterCard, 132 F. Supp.2d at 478.

> ... the Kansas Criminal Code does establish a felony offense for commercial gambling under Kan. Stat. Ann. § 21-4304. The law establishes four activities as felony offenses, namely (1) operating or receiving all or part of the earnings of a gambling place, (2) receiving, recording or forwarding bets, (3) becoming a custodian of anything of value bet or offered to be bet, (4) conducting a lottery, or (5) setting up for use or collecting the proceeds of any gambling device. Kan. Stat. Ann. 21-4304. Although there are no cases applying the statute to internet gambling, plaintiff cites an opinion issued by the Kansas Attorney General, purporting to deal with the factual scenario before this Court, to support his claims.

> Keeping in mind that the Kansas Supreme Court has stated that "[a]n attorney general's opinion is neither conclusive nor binding on us", Unified School Dist. No. 501 v. Baker, 269 Kan. 239, 6 P.3d 848, 849 (2000)and that such an opinion is merely "persuasive authority", Id., the Court addresses plaintiff's argument. The Kansas Attorney General addressed the issue of "legality of gambling over the internet." Kan. Atty. Gen. Op. No. 96-31,1996 WL 156795 (3/25/96). The attorney general opined that "placing, receiving or forwarding a bet, or conducting a lottery, over the telephone or the internet is illegal." Id. at *2. It also stated that "if a bet is placed or a lottery entered into via a computer located in the state of Kansas ... [then] the crime may be prosecuted in this state." Id. The Court must consider this opinion and the statutory language upon which it is based, remembering that "Kansas courts are required to strictly construe penal statutes in favor of the accused." State v. Hall, 14 P.3d 404, 405 (Kan.2000). The relevant statute, Kan. Stat. Ann. 21-4304, makes five commercial gambling activities felony offenses. The only activity remotely applicable to the instant case is section (e), which makes it a felony to "set[] up for use or collect[] the proceeds of any gambling device." Kan. Stat. Ann. 21-4304(e). As applied to the complaint, plaintiff makes no allegation that either the credit card company or issuing bank collected the proceeds of a gambling device. What plaintiff does state is that he purchased credits using his credit card before he gambled. *See* Thompson Complaint at 23–29. It is a temporal impossibility for the defendants to have completed their transaction with the plaintiff before he gambled and to then be prosecuted for collecting the proceeds of a gambling device, which can only take place after some form of gambling is completed. This analysis is in accord with the Attorney General's opinion, which clearly does not address the conduct alleged against the credit card companies or banks in this case. Indeed, the activities encompassed by the opinion are those of the bettors, the plaintiff here, and the internet casinos, who have not been made a party to this suit. Thus, Thompson has failed to allege that the defendants violated Kansas law.

5. Because of federal requirements that a state law violation is needed to prove a federal violation under the Travel Act or the Illegal Gambling Business Act, several states have specifically banned Internet gambling. An example of a Internet-specific statute from Louisiana states: "Gambling by computer is the intentional conducting, or directly assisting in the conducting as a business of any game, contest, lottery, or contrivance whereby a person risks the loss of anything of value in order to realize a profit when ac-

cessing the Internet, World Wide Web, or any part thereof by way of any computer, computer system, computer network, computer software, or any server." La. Rev.Stat. § 14:90.3 (1998). Other states may have sufficiently broad state gaming prohibitions that could apply to Internet wagering. The Oregon Internet gambling statute, entitled "Internet gambling," states the following:

(1) A person engaged in an Internet gambling business may not knowingly accept, in connection with the participation of another person in unlawful gambling using the Internet:

(a) Credit, or the proceeds of credit, extended to or on behalf of such other person, including credit extended through the use of a credit card;

(b) An electronic funds transfer or funds transmitted by or through a money transmission business, or the proceeds of an electronic funds transfer or money transmission service, from or on behalf of the other person;

(c) Any check, draft or similar instrument that is drawn by or on behalf of the other person and is drawn on or payable at or through any financial institution; or

(d) The proceeds of any other form of financial transaction that involves a financial institution as a payor or financial intermediary on behalf of or for the benefit of the other person.

(2) Violation of subsection (1) of this section is a Class C felony.

Or. Rev. Stat. § 167.109.

Oregon law defines "Internet" as an "interactive computer service or system or an information service, system, or access software provider that provides or enables computer access by multiple users to a computer server and includes, but is not limited to, an information service, system, or access software provider that provides access to a network system commonly known as the Internet, or any comparable system or service and also includes, but is not limited to a World Wide Web page, newsgroup, message board, mailing list or chat area on any interactive computer service or system or other on-line service." Or. Rev. Stat. § 167.117(11). Internet gambling does not apply to an activity licensed by the Oregon racing commission. Or. Rev. Stat. § 167.114.

6. A major location for horserace account wagering is in Oregon, where it is licensed by the Oregon racing commission. Whether Internet wagering on horse racing is legal under federal law is a matter of debate. This type of wagering is often called account wagering because players will place money in an account with the operator and wager using the money in the account. The horse racing interests argued that the Interstate Horse Racing Act, along with section 1084(b) of the Wire Act, implies that interstate off-track wagering is legal under federal law. This would include interstate pari-mutuel poolings and account wagering by telephone or other means. Notwithstanding the foregoing, the United States Department of Justice took the position that interstate pari-mutuel off-track wagering violates the Wire Act. *See Letter from* acting Assistant Attorney General Jon P. Jennings, to Senator Patrick Leahy, *available at* http://www.justice.gov/criminal/cyber crime/s692ltr.htm. *See also Internet Prohibition Act of 1999: Hearings on H.R. 3125 Before the Subcomm. on Telecomm., Trade, and Consumer Protection,* 106th Cong. 34 (2000) (testimony of Kevin V. DiGregory, Deputy Assistant Attorney General).

This dispute came to a head at a Congressional committee hearing in 1999 when the Congress was debating the Internet Gambling Prohibition Act. At that hearing, the DOJ representative stated that he thought that account wagering was unlawful. Understandably, this position generated various concerned responses from horsemen's groups, especially since the DOJ had never previously "used the Wire Act to prosecute any state licensed and regulated entities for conducting interstate simulcasting, commingling of pools or account wagering." Internet Gambling Prohibition Act of 1999: Hearing on H.R. 3125 Before the Subcomm. on Crime of the House Comm. on the Judiciary, 106th Cong. 59 (2000) (statement by Stephen Walters, Chairman, Oregon Racing Commission; *see also* Internet Prohibition Act of 1999: Hearings on H.R. 3125 Before the Subcomm. on Telecomm., Trade and Consumer Protection of the House Commerce Comm. 106th Cong. 43 (2000) (testimony of Anne Poulson, President of the Virginia Thoroughbred Association).

As a direct result of that controversy, the horse racing interests solicited the help of Kentucky Senator McConnell to "fix" the law. The solution was to avoid the controversy with the Federal Wire Act that was attendant with the Internet Gambling Prohibition Act and to seek clarification through an amendment to the Interstate Horse Racing Act of 1978. The amendment was passed in 2000 to clarify that pari-mutuel wagering may be placed, via telephone or other electronic media (including the Internet), and accepted by an off-track betting system where such wagers are lawful in each state involved. The new definition of "inter-state off-track wager" is as follows:

> [I]nterstate off-track wager means a legal wager placed or accepted in one State with respect to the outcome of a horserace taking place in another State and includes pari-mutuel wagers, where lawful in each State involved, placed or transmitted by an individual in one State via telephone or other electronic media and accepted by an off-track betting system in the same or another State, as well as the combination of any pari-mutuel wagering pools.

15 U.S.C. § 3002 (2000).

During Congressional debate, Representative Harold Rogers (R-KY), then Chairman of the Appropriation Subcommittee on Commerce, Justice, and State, assured the amendment was specifically intended to "clarif[y] that the Interstate Horse Racing Act permits the continued merging of any wagering pools and wagering activities conducted between individuals and state-licensed and regulated off-track betting systems, whether such wagers are conducted in person, via telephone, or other electronic media." Yet in spite of the 2000 amendment, the DOJ continues to take the position that the existing prohibitions under the Wire Act were not affected.

7. The DOJ has demonstrated that it may pursue charges against media outlets that accept advertisements of gambling websites under a theory of aiding and abetting, regardless of whether the ads involve print, radio, television or the Internet. In June 2003, the DOJ sent a warning letter to the National Association of Broadcasters ("NAB") and others, warning that the practice of accepting gambling advertising may constitute aiding and abetting illegal conduct under federal anti-gambling laws. Acting on this, in the fall of 2003, the Assistant U.S. Attorney General for the Eastern District of Missouri launched an investigation into advertising for offshore online gaming sites by issuing numerous subpoenas to media outlets. Additionally, in July 2006, the Eastern District of Missouri issued fifteen to twenty "Subject to Settlement Negotiations" letters informing companies that, as previously notified, they had repeatedly violated Title 18, United States Code, Sections 2, 1084, 1952, and 1960, by aiding, abetting, inducing, or procuring violations of federal law involving enterprises conducting such activities and that the DOJ was prepared to take all appropriate steps to collect the proceeds received for promoting the illegal activities. Likewise, in 2004, as reported by the New York Times, the DOJ seized

funds of American media companies earned from offshore sites. *See* Matt Richtel, *U.S. Steps Up Push Against Online Casinos by Seizing Cash*, N.Y. TIMES, May 31, 2004. The DOJ confirmed that it has seized money from media outlets, including about $3.2 million from Discovery Communications, operators of the Discovery Channel. As one commentator noted, the DOJ is showing a "crusader's zeal" against anyone who is in or associated with the chain of commerce of offshore gaming sites. The apparent position of the DOJ is that anyone in or associated with the chain of commerce of offshore gaming sites is aiding and abetting the illegal activity.

On January 20, 2006, *The Sporting News*, a print magazine, agreed to pay a $7.2 million settlement with the U.S. government to resolve claims that it promoted illegal Internet and telephone gambling in print, on its Web site and on its radio stations. The advertising ran from the spring of 2000 through December 2003 in the magazine. *The Sporting News* continued to run the ads for more than six months after the Justice Department sent the June 2003 letter described above. The Sporting News paid a $4.2 million fine and agreed that the remaining $3 million of the settlement will be in the form of public service ads aimed at dissuading people from gambling over the Internet or by telephone. The DOJ also obtained a $31.5 million settlement by Microsoft Corp., Google Inc. and Yahoo Inc. to resolve accusations that the companies promoted illegal Internet gambling by carrying banner ads for illegal gambling on their respective services.

In a unreported federal district court case, Casino City sued the DOJ, seeking declaratory relief to confirm its constitutional right to engage in lawful commercial free speech. Casino City, Inc. vs. United States Department of Justice, CV No. 04-557-B-3 (M.D. La., Feb. 15, 2005). Casino City operated sites that carried advertisements for Internet gambling enterprises and argued that the DOJ's application of the Wire Act, Travel Act, Illegal Gambling Business Act, and "aiding and abetting" statute, as applied to Casino City and other similarly situated entities, violated the First Amendment. Casino City placed advertisements for offshore books and online casinos in its network of a collection of portal sites. Once in cyberspace they were not located in a particular geographical location and therefore arguably became available to anyone in the world who had access to the Internet, including places where the advertised activities might be illegal. The DOJ moved to dismiss, and the court dismissed the suit with prejudice in February 2005. In doing so, the court, in dicta, noted that Casino City never claimed its advertisers did not accept bets from those in the United States, but if it did, the advertising would be illegal and thus not protected by the First Amendment guarantee of free speech. The court stated that Casino City's advertisements for Internet gaming sites was not entitled to First Amendment protections for two reasons. The first was that Internet gambling was an illegal activity and the second was that advertisements for Internet gaming are misleading because they "falsely portray the image that Internet gambling is legal." The court, however, appeared to assume that Internet gambling was illegal solely on the basis that the Department of Justice alleged that it was illegal. Casino City appealed to the Fifth Circuit Court of Appeals. On January 26, 2006, the Fifth Circuit granted the DOJ's unopposed motion to dismiss.

8. Many advertising outlets take these ads for sister sites (generally .net) that have the same brand but do not accept real money bets. Does the make a difference in the legal analysis?

9. Even the World Trade Organization ("WTO") has played a role in shaping Internet gambling policy. An opinion involving Antigua resulted in a demand for remedial action imposed on the United States to place U.S. and non-U.S. suppliers of horse race wagering on equal footing. Antigua brought the action based on commitments made by the

United States under the General Agreement on Trade in Services ("GATS"). The United States agreed that with regard to "recreational services," it would follow two principles: market access and national treatment. Market access means that it will open its markets to recreational services offered from another member country and will not impose trade restraints such as numerical limits. National treatment means that the United States agreed that it would not treat another member country less favorably than it treats its own suppliers of a like service. The United States unsuccessfully claimed that recreational services do not include gambling services. The WTO court also decided that certain United States laws including the Wire Act, the Travel Act and the Illegal Gambling Business Act violated GATS because they have the effect of placing numerical limits on number of services, suppliers, operators and quantity of services output. WTO Appellate Body recognized, however, a Public Morals and Public Order Exemption — in other words, the United States can maintain laws that violate GATS if the exemption is necessary to maintain public morals. Antigua failed to submit evidence that the United States had any regulatory alternatives to prohibition. The Appellate Body found, however, that the Interstate Horse Racing Act ("IHRA") discriminates between foreign and domestic suppliers. The IHRA of 1978 was amended in 2000 to clarify that pari-mutuel wagering may be placed, via telephone or other electronic media (including the Internet), and accepted by an off-track betting system where such wagers are lawful in *each state* involved. The United States failed to "fix" this discrimination by either making all Interstate horserace wagering illegal or opening the U.S. market to foreign operators. The United States did neither and the WTO ultimately ruled that Antigua was entitled to levy $21 million annually in trade sanctions against the United States as compensation. Did the United States win the battle, but set itself up for losing the war? For a further explanation of the WTO case, *see* Marwell, Jeremy C., *Trade and Morality: The WTO Public Morals Exception after Gambling*; 81 N.Y.U. L. Rev. 802 (2006); Michael Grunfeld, *Don't Bet on the United States' Internet Gambling Laws: The Tension between Internet Gambling Legislation and World Trade Organization Commitments*, 2007 Colum. Bus. L. Rev. 200, 439 (2007).

3. The Legality of Internet Gambling under Laws Existing after 2006

Anthony Cabot, *Betting on the Budget: Can State Legislatures Go All In or Will the Federal Government Force Them to Fold?: The Absence of a Comprehensive Federal Policy toward Internet and Sports Wagering and a Proposal for Change*
17 Vill. Sports & Ent. L.J. 271, 298–304 (2010)

The fourth major law that impacts Internet gambling is the Unlawful Internet Gambling Enforcement Act ("UIGEA"). Its passage on September 29, 2006, may have changed the legal landscape for Internet sports wagering — or maybe not. The heart of UIGEA is Sections 5363 and 5364, which respectively contain the criminal prohibitions and the financial regulation provisions that make up the heart of the bill.

Understanding UIGEA and its passage requires understanding of the politics and players beyond the bill. Some efforts were evident, while others were clandestine. UIGEA was a culmination of eight years' efforts of Senator Jon Kyl (R-Arizona). Senator Kyl is generally associated with the evangelical movement in the Republican Party. The evangelical movement is very powerful and led by James Dobson and Pat Robertson. To give an indication of the power of this lobby, when Congress commissioned the National Gambling Impact Study Commission, four of nine commissioners were evangelicals including the President of Regent College and James Dobson himself. The evangelical movement espouses a theocracy based on their vision of a Christian nation. The basic political philosophy of the movement is categorized under an umbrella: family values. Gambling, which is a historical vice, fails under the wrath of family values. Therefore, no surprise exists that efforts to ban Internet gambling emanates from Senator Kyl and the evangelical movement.

Historically, however, Senator Kyl ran into problems with passage. Principal opposition came from the horseracing industry, state-run lotteries, and traditional casinos. Each has strong lobbies in DC and wanted exemptions to any prohibition.

The 2006 Congressional session had two competing bills introduced both by conservative Republican Congressman: James Leach (R-Iowa) (who worked with Kyl) introduced a criminal prohibition while Bob Goodlatte (R-Virginia) offered what was primarily a financial services bill. Both made it through the House, but a protracted fight bogged both pieces of legislation in the Senate.

Coming into the last few months of Congress, a new player, Senator Bill Frist then Senate majority leader, came onto the scene. Frist took up the cause with the fervor of an evangelical minister. Frist's motivation was simple; he wanted to be President. The issue had two benefits. Point #7 of the evangelical movement's top ten "family values" issues, as espoused by its House Leadership, targeted Internet gambling along with the usual suspects: Anti-gay Marriage Amendment, Unborn Child Pain Awareness Act, Human Cloning Prohibition Act, and the Pledge Protection Act. The second benefit to Frist was that supporting Leach, who was from Iowa, could help a presidential campaign where Iowa was so important.

The less likely ally of the evangelical movement was the National Football League. Professional sports had a strong interest in joining the battle — to protect the legality of fantasy sports. Two motivations are evident. The first was preserving increasing revenues that the sports leagues were charging to Internet sites that were operating fantasy sports wagering.[1] The future of fantasy sports would have been placed in jeopardy if Congress

---

1. At the time that the NFL was acting to preserve its licensing revenues, a case was being decided that jeopardizes the leagues' ability to charge fees to fantasy leagues to use player statistics. In a decision from August of 2006, a federal district court held that fantasy operators do not need to pay licensing fees to the sports leagues to use the statistics of players in that league. This was a significant decision because the licensing fees gave the sports leagues a direct interest in the success of the major fantasy leagues.

Two major issues in the case involved a legal doctrine called "right of publicity" and whether the players' names and statistics are copyrightable. The right of publicity is described in Section 46 of the Restatement (Third) of Unfair Competition (2005), Appropriation of the Commercial Value of a Person's Identity: The Right of Publicity. This Restatement provision states that "[o]ne who appropriates the commercial value of a person's identity by using without consent the person's name, likeness, or other indicia of identity for purposes of trade is subject to liability...."

The court reasoned, in part, that "Unlike cases where the commercial advantage element of the right of publicity has been found, there is nothing about CBC's fantasy games which suggests that any Major League baseball player is associated with CBC's games or that any player endorses or sponsors the games in any way. The use of names and playing records of Major League baseball players in CBC's games, moreover, is not intended to attract customers away from any other fantasy game provider because all fantasy game providers necessarily use names and playing records. Indeed, there is no evidence to create a triable issue as to whether CBC intended to create an impression that Major League baseball players are associated with its fantasy baseball games or as to whether a reasonable person would

passed Internet gaming legislation that could have been read to prohibit fantasy sports. The second was to maintain the increased viewership by those that played fantasy sports.

Not surprisingly, the NFL played a major role in the passage of UIGEA. According to a New York Post article: "the National Football League used a big bucks lobbyist to ram through Internet gambling-curbing legislation in the final minutes of the legislative session, sources revealed. But opponents of the bill charge that the NFL broke the rules when it fast-tracked legislation that never even got a vote in the Senate—a trick play that provided a big exemption for fantasy football. The NFL runs its own fantasy football site, and gets royalties from others."[2]

The same New York Post article went on to say "Last month, right before lawmakers left town to campaign, the league was struggling for a way to overcome opposition to clearing the gambling bill. The league decided to try to tack the gambling bill onto final defense legislation that couldn't be amended.... NFL Chairman Roger Goodell and past chairman Paul Tagliabue wrote Senate Armed Services Committee Chairman John Warner (R-Va.) that the bill was an "achievement" he could be proud of, but that couldn't get through the Senate by regular means."

The letter was referring to an attempt by Senator Bill Frist to have the legislation attached to the Defense Appropriations bill then being considered by a joint committee of the Senate and House in the closing days before the 2006 fall adjournment. Senator John Warner (R-Virginia) rejected this attempt in a September 25th letter to Senator Frist that read, in part: "My strong objection is based on the following precedents: Section 102 of S.2349, The Legislative Transparency and Accountability Act of 2006 which passed the Senate on May 23, 2006 clearly expresses the views of the Senate that out-of-scope provisions are not to be included in conference reports."[3]

Undeterred by this rejection, Senator Frist turned to another joint committee, this one considering the Port Safety Act. Unlike Senator Warner, none of the members of the committee objected to the inclusion of the amendment. Once attached, the full legislation went before Congress without the ability of its members to vote against the amendment without voting against the entire bill. The trick worked and the bill passed. Though Frist's presidential campaign failed, this bill is an important part of his legacy.

The bill has two distinct provisions largely because it consisted of a last minute merger of two different bills. The first provision of section 5363 is criminal and is both relatively straightforward and unnecessary. This provision provides that no person or corporation engaged in the business of betting or wagering may knowingly accept, in connection with the participation of another person in unlawful Internet gambling, virtually any type of payment including credit, the proceeds of credit, credit card payments, electronic fund transfers or the proceeds there from, checks, drafts or similar instruments, or the proceeds from any other financial transaction as specified by the Treasury Secretary and the Fed-

---

be under the impression that the baseball players are associated with CBC's fantasy games any more than the players are associated with a newspaper boxscore."

The court concluded "that the undisputed facts establish that the players do not have a right of publicity in their names and playing records as used in CBC's fantasy games and that CBC has not violated the players' claimed right of publicity. The court further finds, alternatively, that even if the players have a claimed right of publicity, the First Amendment takes precedence over such a right. The court further finds that the undisputed facts establish that the names and playing records of Major League baseball players as used in CBC's fantasy games are not copyrightable and, therefore, federal copyright law does not preempt the players' claimed right of publicity." C.B.C. Distribution and Marketing, Inc. v. Major League Baseball Advanced Media, L.P., 505 F.3d 818 (8th Cir. 2007), cert denied, 128 S. Ct. 2872 (2008).

2. Geoff Earle, NFL Makes Fantasy Pass, New York Post, October 10, 2006.

3. Memorandum for Senator Bill First, from Senator John Warner, September 25, 2006.

eral Reserve by regulation. Penalties can include fines and imprisonment for up to five years. The reason that this is unnecessary and has not been controversial is that a person engaged in the business of accepting illegal bets is already violating federal law. The person is merely violating another statute.

Like the previously described Travel Act and Illegal Gambling Business Act, UIGEA only applies to unlawful gambling, which is defined as a bet or wager that is unlawful under any applicable state law in the state in which the bet or wager is initiated, received, or otherwise made.

The standards appear identical to the existing law under the Travel Act and the Illegal Gambling Business Act where federal prosecutors need to show a violation of state law to be a violation of federal law. The words of UIGEA, however, could be read more favorable to the prosecution, which need only prove that the bet or wager is unlawful under state law. For example, some states make it unlawful for persons to play poker for money. These statutes would not directly assess liability on a poker site because they are not players. The bets, however, are unlawful under state law. Therefore, an Internet gambling site may be charged under UIGEA for accepting the financial transfer, even if it does not directly violate the state law.

Section 5364 has been more controversial. First, serious question exists as to whether 5364 was even needed. The Department of Justice was doing just fine under the Patriot Act. Second, serious doubt still exists as to whether the intended regulatory scheme is even workable. Under UIGEA, two agencies, the Federal Reserve Board and the Department of the Treasury, had a nine-month period (until July 2007) in which to enact regulations that would require any financial transaction provider, i.e. credit card companies, banks, or stored value providers (like PayPal) to identify, code and block restricted transactions. Restricted transactions are those transactions where a gambling business accepts funds directly or indirectly from a player in connection with unlawful Internet gambling, i.e. unlawful under state law.

The agencies had four tasks in crafting the regulations. The first was to identify types of policies and procedures that would be reasonable to identify and block restricted transaction. The second was to allow financial transaction providers ("FTPs") to chose alternative methods of blocking restricted transactions. The third was to exempt certain restricted transactions of FTPs from a regulation if the agencies found it is not reasonably practical to identify and block such transactions. Finally, the agencies were tasked to ensure that lawful Internet gambling, such as intrastate casino and lottery wagers and interstate horse race wagers, was not blocked.

When the regulation finally came out in January 2009, the agencies did not seek to directly implement the Congressional mandates. They determined that attempting to identify and block most restricted transactions was not feasible. The agencies justified not following the UIGEA mandates that individual transactions be identified, coded and blocked because the Automated Clearing House (ACH), check cashing and other systems do not enable the exempt participants to reasonably identify and block restricted transactions. In its place, the agencies substituted a different scheme that focuses on participants not transactions. This scheme focuses on the FTP that has the relationship with the gambling business, or is the United States FTP that deals directly or indirectly with the foreign FTP that has the customer relationship with the gambling business. These are the only FTPs not exempted from the regulations. For example, in the check collection system, the non-exempt participant is the depository bank—more specifically the first United States institution to which a check is transferred whether from the gambling business itself or a foreign bank or correspondent. This scheme puts the burden on the first United States entity in the money chain coming from outside the United States.

The regulation requires the non-exempt entities to conduct due diligence and know their customer to assure that it is not involved in restricted transactions. The regulations effectively require that the non-exempt entities "do your due diligence" by "knowing your own customer." The result is that banks that work with foreign banks must pressure the foreign banks to police their own customers, and that non-exempt entities that deal directly with gambling sites must know their own customer. An unknown factor is how the non-exempt FTP will distinguish legal and illegal transactions for the purpose of determining what is a restricted transaction. This is often a nuanced determination that imposes a great burden on the non-exempt entity.

To help elevate this burden, the regulations provided two different methods to determine if the customer was lawfully engaged in gambling transactions. For a non-exempt financial institution to provide financial services to a commercial customer engaging in such Internet business, the commercial customer must provide the financial institution with either a copy of a government-issued or tribe-issued license authorizing such activity or, if the customer does not have such a license, a "reasoned legal opinion" that demonstrates the commercial customer's Internet gambling business does not involve restricted gambling transactions. Under the regulation, a "reasoned legal opinion" means "a written expression of professional judgment by a State-licensed attorney that addresses the facts of a particular client's business and the legality of the client's provision of its services to relevant customers in the relevant jurisdictions under applicable federal and state law, and, in the case of intra-tribal transactions, applicable tribal ordinances, tribal resolutions, and Tribal-State compacts." Issuing a reasoned legal opinion requires an attorney to fulfill these requirements of the regulation while complying with the legal profession's guidelines and standards for ethics and legal opinions.

The notion of identifying, coding and blocking specific transactions envisioned to apply to all financial transactions was imposed only on the credit card industry, which already has a system of identifying, coding and blocking merchant transactions for gambling transactions. Likewise, the agencies did not address the mandate of establishing procedures to assure that legal gambling transactions are not blocked. These regulations, that were suppose to go into effect on December 1, 2009, have been postponed and mandatory compliance with the regulations of UIGEA was delayed until June 1, 2010.

Notes

1. The full text of the Unlawful Internet Gambling Enforcement Act is included in the appendix to this chapter.

2. The controversy surrounding the Unlawful Internet Gambling Enforcement Act has resulted in substantial legal commentary. *See e.g.*, Gerd Alexander, *The U.S. On Tilt: Why The Unlawful Internet Gambling Enforcement Act Is A Bad Bet*, 2008 DUKE L. & TECH. REV. 6 (2008); James N. Brenner, *Betting on Success: Can the Unlawful Internet Gambling Enforcement Act Help the United States Achieve Its Internet Gambling Policy Goals?*, 30 HASTINGS COMM. & ENT. L.J. 109 (2008); Mattia V. Corsiglia Murawski, *The Online Gambling Wager: Domestic and International Implications of the Unlawful Internet Gambling Enforcement Act of 2006*, 48 SANTA CLARA L. REV. 441 (2008); Michael Blankenship, *The Unlawful Internet Gambling Enforcement Act: A Bad Gambling Act? You Betcha!*, 60 RUT-

GERS L. REV. 485 (2008); Brant M. Leonard, *Highlighting the Drawbacks of the UIGEA: Proposed Rules Reveal Heavy Burdens*, 57 DRAKE L. REV. 515 (2009).

3. Since 2006, a federal prosecutorial focus has been on both the seizure of cash associated with Internet gambling and persons involved in expediting the transfer of cash. *See e.g.* United States v. $6,976,934.65, 554 F.3d 123 (2009), United States v. Lombardo, 639 F. Supp.2d 1271 (Utah 2007); V. Smith, *Feds in Maryland Seize Bank Accounts Tied to On-Line Gambling*, BALTIMORE CITY PAPER, September 11, 2009; T. Audi, *U.S. Deals Blow to Online-Poker Players*, WALL ST. J., June 10, 2009.

4. State Laws and Internet Gambling after 2006

Rousso v. Washington
239 P.3d 1084 (Wash. 2010)

OPINION

En Banc

SANDERS, J.—

The question before this court is not whether Internet gambling, including playing poker on-line, should be illegal. That determination is reserved to the legislature, and the legislature addressed the issue by enacting and amending RCW 9.46.240, which criminalizes the knowing transmission and reception of gambling information by various means, including use of the Internet. Since sending and receiving gambling information is illegal, Internet gambling in the state of Washington is effectively banned.[1]

It is not the role of the judiciary to second-guess the wisdom of the legislature, which enacted this ban. The court has no authority to conduct its own balancing of the pros and cons stemming from banning, regulating, or openly permitting Internet gambling. *See* Minnesota v. Clover Leaf Creamery Co., 449 U.S. 456, 470 (1981) ("[I]t is not the function of the courts to substitute their evaluation of legislative facts for that of the legislature."); Ferguson v. Skrupa, 372 U.S. 726, 730 (1963) ("[C]ourts do not substitute their social and economic beliefs for the judgment of legislative bodies, who are elected to pass laws.").

The only issue before this court is whether Washington's ban on Internet gambling is an unconstitutional infringement of the dormant commerce clause. *See* U.S. CONST. art. I, § 8, cl. 3. The commerce clause grants Congress the authority "[t]o regulate commerce with foreign nations, and among the several states, and with the Indian tribes." *Id.* The Supreme Court interpreted a dormant commerce clause from this text, reasoning since Congress has the power to regulate interstate commerce, states are precluded from doing so by enacting laws or regulations that excessively burden interstate commerce. *E.g.*, Maine v. Taylor, 477 U.S. 131, 137 (1986).

Determining whether Washington's ban on Internet gambling violates the dormant commerce clause is a multistep analysis. Outlined briefly, we must first determine whether

---

1. The Internet gambling ban does not include wagering on horse races, which is not considered "gambling" under chapter 9.46 RCW, *see* RCW 9.46.0237, and is treated uniquely among other forms of wagering under federal law, *see* 15 U.S.C. §§ 3001–3007.

Congress has granted the states authority to regulate Internet gambling. If it has, the dormant commerce clause does not apply and RCW 9.46.240 is upheld. *See* Ne. Bancorp, Inc. v. Bd. of Governors, 472 U.S. 159, 174 (1985).

If Congress has not, the dormant commerce clause applies, and we must determine (a) whether the language of the statute openly discriminates against out-of-state entities in favor of in-state ones or (b) whether the direct effect of the statute evenhandedly applies to in-state and out-of-state entities. Bostain v. Food Express, Inc., 159 Wn.2d 700, 718, 153 P.3d 846 (2007).

If the statute does not openly discriminate and applies evenhandedly, it does not violate the dormant commerce clause if (1) there is a legitimate state purpose and (2) the burden imposed on interstate commerce is not "'clearly excessive'" in relation to the local benefit. State v. Heckel, 143 Wn.2d 824, 832, 24 P.3d 404 (2001) (quoting Franks & Son, Inc. v. State, 136 Wn.2d 737, 754, 966 P.2d 1232 (1998)); *accord* Pike v. Bruce Church, Inc., 397 U.S. 137, 142 (1970).

If the statute openly discriminates or does not apply to in-state and out-of-state entities evenhandedly, it is upheld only if it is necessary to achieve an important state interest unrelated to economic protectionism. Mt. Hood Beverage Co. v. Constellation Brands, Inc., 149 Wn.2d 98, 110, 63 P.3d 779 (2003) (quoting New Energy Co. of Ind. v. Limbach, 486 U.S. 269, 274, 276 (1988)).

FACTS AND PROCEDURAL HISTORY

Lee Rousso, a Washington resident, gambled by playing poker on-line and wishes to do so again, but Washington law prohibits it. Rousso sought a declaratory judgment that RCW 9.46.240 is unconstitutional, arguing the statute violates the dormant commerce clause as a state regulation impermissibly burdening interstate and international commerce. The trial court granted summary judgment in favor of the State, holding the statute is constitutional. The Court of Appeals affirmed. Rousso v. State, 149 Wn. App. 344, 347, 204 P.3d 243, *review granted*, 166 Wn.2d 1032, 217 P.3d 337 (2009).

ANALYSIS

I. Has Congress expressly authorized the state regulation of Internet gambling?

Congress has the authority to regulate matters affecting interstate commerce and also the authority to delegate such regulation to the states. *See* Ne. Bancorp, Inc., 472 U.S. at 174. If Congress grants the states authority to regulate a certain matter, a state's regulation is consistent with the commerce clause. *Id.* "[B]ecause of the important role the Commerce Clause plays in protecting the free flow of interstate trade," Congress' delegation of that authority must be "'unmistakably clear.'" *Taylor,* 477 U.S. at 138–39 (quoting S.-Cent. Timber Dev., Inc. v. Wunnicke, 467 U.S. 82, 91 (1984)).

Here, the State argues two Congressional acts manifest "unmistakably clear" intent to delegate to the states the authority to regulate on-line gambling. Neither of these acts manifests such intent. The acts cited recognize and expressly preserve a state's authority to criminalize some or all gambling activities *within the state's borders*, but nothing more.

The Unlawful Internet Gambling Enforcement Act of 2006 (UIGEA), codified as 31 U.S.C. §§ 5363–5367, prohibits any person engaged in the business of gambling from accepting money in any form for participation in *unlawful* Internet gambling. *Id.* § 5363. The UIGEA recognizes that some *types* of bets are rendered unlawful under state law, *id.* § 5362(10)(A), and clarifies that it does not alter any state gambling laws, *id.* § 5361(b). Nowhere does the UIGEA permit the states to regulate gambling activities outside their borders or without regard to the commerce clause.

The federal wire act of 1961 (Wire Act) criminalizes the use of wire communication facilities[2] to place bets through interstate or foreign commerce. 18 U.S.C. § 1084(a). The Wire Act then clarifies it does not prevent transmission of information assisting the placement of bets from a state where the bet is legal to another state where it is legal. 18 U.S.C. § 1084(b). Again, the Wire Act recognizes the states' authority to regulate the type of gambling permitted within its borders but does not delegate any authority to regulate interstate commerce with impunity.

Congress has not delegated to the states its authority to regulate interstate Internet gambling. The dormant commerce clause is applicable here, as the Court of Appeals correctly held. *See Rousso*, 149 Wn. App. at 351–57.

II. Does RCW 9.46.240,[3] by its language or effect, discriminate against interstate commerce in favor of in-state economic interests?

Because a statute that discriminates against interstate commerce is subject to heavier scrutiny under the dormant commerce clause, we must first determine whether RCW 9.46.240 discriminates in its language or direct effect.[4] *See, e.g.*, Brown-Forman Distillers Corp. v. N.Y. State Liquor Auth., 476 U.S. 573, 579 (1986); Bostain, 159 Wn.2d at 718. Here, the language of RCW 9.46.240 is not discriminatory; it equally prohibits Internet gambling regardless of whether the person or entity hosting the game is located in Washington, another state, or another country.

Neither does RCW 9.46.240 have a direct discriminatory effect on interstate commerce. The statute prohibits Internet gambling evenhandedly, regardless of whether the company running the web site is located in or outside the state of Washington. *See* Brown-Forman Distillers Corp., 476 U.S. at 579. The effects imposed on in-state and out-of-state entities engaging or that would engage in Internet gambling are the same. *See* CTS Corp. v. Dynamics Corp. of Am., 481 U.S. 69, 87–88 (1987); Clover Leaf Creamery Co., 449 U.S. at 471–72. RCW 9.46.240 is not discriminatory under the dormant commerce clause.

Rousso argues RCW 9.46.240 is discriminatory because the Internet gambling ban excludes Internet gambling web sites, all of which are out-of-state businesses,[5] from the

---

2. A "'wire communication facility'" is any instrumentality used to transfer information by wire, cable, or a like vehicle. 18 U.S.C. § 1081.

3. "Whoever knowingly transmits or receives gambling information by telephone, telegraph, radio, semaphore, the internet, a telecommunications transmission system, or similar means, or knowingly installs or maintains equipment for the transmission or receipt of gambling information shall be guilty of a class C felony subject to the penalty set forth in RCW 9A.20.021. However, this section shall not apply to such information transmitted or received or equipment installed or maintained relating to activities authorized by this chapter or to any act or acts in furtherance thereof when conducted in compliance with the provisions of this chapter and in accordance with the rules adopted under this chapter." RCW 9.46.240.

4. The question here is not whether the State discriminates between Internet poker and Internet wagering on horse racing, for example. First, the relevant discrimination here is against interstate commerce for the benefit of in-state economic interests, not discrimination among various forms of wagering. Second, the legislature is permitted to ban activities piecemeal when not for the purpose of simple protectionism—for instance, to limit the prevalence of wagering or to limit on-line wagering only to already highly regulated areas. *See* RCWA 9.46.240 Notes; *Clover Leaf Creamery Co.*, 449 U.S. at 467, 471–72.

5. This is an unsurprising statement since running such a web site in Washington would constitute a felony under RCW 9.46.240, preventing Washington businesses from entering the Internet gambling market.

Washington market while leaving untouched an alternative service — *in-state*, "brick and mortar" (i.e., where individuals are physically present) gambling businesses. This argument misconstrues and misapplies the test under the dormant commerce clause in several ways.

First, Rousso misapprehends what constitutes a direct discriminatory effect on interstate commerce. The question is *how* the effects of the ban are imposed on in-state and out-of-state entities, not *what* the effect is on those entities' revenue. The ban on Internet gambling has the same effect on all entities, regardless of origin: a ban on the transfer of gambling information via the Internet.

The Supreme Court addressed this distinction in *CTS Corp.*, 481 U.S. 69. There, state regulations hindering hostile takeovers of Indiana companies were deemed nondiscriminatory because they imposed the same effects on in-state and out-of-state entities. 481 U.S. at 87–88. It was immaterial to the Court's consideration that the majority of entities seeking to effectuate a hostile takeover of an Indiana corporation were out-of-state, and thus the law, as applied, would affect out-of-state entities more often. *Id.* at 88.

Second, Rousso alleges direct discrimination because banning Internet gambling will have a secondary effect of promoting in-state, Internet gambling substitutes — such as brick and mortar gambling. But this misses the mark on two counts. Internet gambling and brick and mortar gambling are two different activities, presenting risks and concerns of a different nature, and creating different regulatory challenges; a state can regulate different *activities* differently. The dormant commerce clause only prevents a state (under most circumstances)[6] from discriminating based on whether the business is in-state or out-of-state. Again, RCW 9.46.240 treats all entities engaging in *Internet* gambling equally, regardless of origin.

Furthermore, the discriminatory effect under this analysis must be *direct*. *Brown-Forman Distillers*, 476 U.S. at 579; *Bostain*, 159 Wn.2d at 718. Here, the ban on Internet gambling has a direct effect on Internet gambling operations, preventing them from doing business in Washington. Rousso argues this ban has an effect on a substitute service — brick and mortar gambling — because individuals will gamble at casinos if they are unable to gamble on-line. But an increase of business for another industry is not a *direct* effect of the ban; the ban makes no mention nor imposes any regulation on brick and mortar gambling. This alleged secondary effect on brick and mortar gambling will also occur for *any* goods or services a person might purchase or use instead of banned Internet gambling — whether a person instead engages in on-line stock trading, buys more snacks for an in-person poker game among friends, or signs up for cello lessons. Increased revenues for in-state banks, snack producers and grocery stores, and music teachers would also constitute "discriminatory effects" under Rousso's argument, but again, these are *secondary* effects. Purchasing substitute goods and services does not constitute *direct* discriminatory effects.

The Supreme Court rejected a secondary effects argument in *Clover Leaf Creamery Co.*, 449 U.S. 456. There, the Minnesota legislature banned the retail sale of milk in *plastic* nonreturnable, nonrefillable containers, yet permitted sale in *paperboard* ones. *Id.* at 458. The state has a large pulpwood industry but no plastic industry, so the plastic ban would shift some business from the wholly out-of-state plastic market to in-state pulpwood businesses. *Id.* at 460. Nevertheless the statute was not discriminatory under the dor-

---

6. A discriminatory state law can still be upheld where it is necessary to achieve an important state interest unrelated to economic protectionism. *See, e.g., Mt. Hood Beverage Co.*, 149 Wn.2d at 110.

mant commerce clause because it precluded the use of plastic milk containers *regardless* of origin. *See id.* at 471–72. The favorable in-state, secondary effect on the pulpwood industry did not render the ban discriminatory under the dormant commerce clause.

The discriminatory language or direct effect step of the dormant commerce clause weeds out laws that regulate by virtue of whether a business is in-state or out-of-state. It ferrets out "'simple protectionism.'" *Id.* at 471. RCW 9.46.240 applies based upon whether an individual—regardless of origin—is engaged in Internet gambling operations. The statute does not directly discriminate against out-of-state businesses in favor of in-state ones.

III. Is the burden on interstate commerce "clearly excessive" in relation to a legitimate state interest?

Because neither the language nor direct effect of RCW 9.46.240 is discriminatory, the statute does not violate the dormant commerce clause *if* (a) there is a legitimate state purpose and (b) the burden imposed on interstate commerce is not "'clearly excessive'" in relation to the local benefit, considering also whether the local interest could be promoted in a way that would impose a lesser impact on interstate commerce. *Heckel,* 143 Wn.2d at 832 (quoting *Franks & Son,* 136 Wn.2d at 747); *accord Pike,* 397 U.S. at 142.

a. State interest and burden on interstate commerce

The State wields police power to protect its citizens' health, welfare, safety, and morals. On account of ties to organized crime, money laundering, gambling addiction, underage gambling, and other societal ills, "[t]he regulation of gambling enterprises lies at the heart of the state's police power." Johnson v. Collins Entm't Co., 199 F.3d 710, 720 (4th Cir. 1999); *see also* Edmonds Shopping Ctr. Assocs. v. City of Edmonds, 117 Wn. App. 344, 352, 71 P.3d 233 (2003).

Internet gambling introduces new ways to exacerbate these same threats to health, welfare, safety, and morals. Gambling addicts and underage gamblers have greater accessibility to on-line gambling—able to gamble from their homes immediately and on demand, at any time, on any day, unhindered by in-person regulatory measures. Concerns over ties to organized crime and money laundering are exacerbated where on-line gambling operations are not physically present in-state to be inspected for regulatory compliance. Washington has a legitimate and substantial state interest in addressing the effects of Internet gambling.

RCW 9.46.240 imposes a burden on interstate commerce by walling off the Washington market for Internet gambling from interstate commerce. The extent of this burden is mitigated somewhat. First, the ban does not prevent or hinder Internet gambling businesses from operating throughout the rest of the world. Second, those businesses can easily exclude Washingtonians. If an individual during registration marks his or her location as the state of Washington, the gambling web site can end the registration there. Nevertheless, preventing Internet gambling businesses from having access to Washington consumers who would otherwise patronize those businesses still has a considerable impact on interstate commerce. This burden on interstate commerce is comparable to the substantial state interest stemming from the State's police power to protect the health, welfare, safety, and morals of its citizens.[7]

---

7. This conclusion may appear abrupt or only loosely anchored to the more rigid distinctions that normally appear as hallmarks of legal reasoning. It is a by-product of the ethereal nature of the dormant commerce clause analysis, a specter that has haunted courts since it materialized from article I, section 8, clause 3 of the United States Constitution. Put simply, how does a court take a vaguely quantified and unitless measure of the burden on interstate commerce and then compare it to an equally vague and unitless measure of a benefit to a state interest? Justice Scalia likened this comparison to determining "whether a particular line is longer than a particular rock is heavy." Bendix Au-

b. Is the burden on interstate commerce "clearly excessive" in relation to a legitimate state interest?

Since the burden on interstate commerce is comparable to the state benefit, the final question is whether that burden is "clearly excessive" in relation to the state interest. *Pike*, 397 U.S. at 142; *Heckel*, 143 Wn.2d at 832. The phrase "clearly excessive" carries with it a sense of "too much"—that is, whether the burden is clearly unnecessary to achieve the state interest, or whether that same interest could be protected in another way while imposing a lesser burden on interstate commerce. We thus consider whether the State *clearly* could avoid threats to health, welfare, safety, and morals posed by Internet gambling equally as well in a manner that imposed less of a burden on interstate commerce.

Rousso argues regulating Internet gambling is a less restrictive alternative. This falls short of the mark because (1) it is not clear regulation that could avoid concerns over Internet gambling as well as a complete ban and (2) it is not clear, even if regulation providing comparable protection is possible, that the burden on interstate commerce would be decreased through that regulation. *See Clover Leaf Creamery Co.,* 449 U.S. at 473–74 (alternatives were rejected because they were "either more burdensome on commerce ... or less likely to be effective ...").

Internet gambling has its own unique dangers and pitfalls. A regulatory system to monitor and address concerns unique to Internet gambling would take significant time and resources to develop and maintain. Even so, no regulatory system is perfect. Some concerns will not be fully addressed, while loopholes may permit others to slip through the cracks. The legislature decided to avoid the shortcomings and ongoing process of regulation by banning Internet gambling altogether. The legislature could have decided to step out in the rain with an umbrella, but instead it decided to stay home, dry, and without the possibility that its umbrella would break a mile from home. The judiciary has no authority to second-guess that decision, rebalancing public policy concerns to determine whether it would have arrived at a different result. Under the dormant commerce clause, we observe only that it is not clear that regulation of Internet gambling could protect state interests as fully as, or at least in a comparable way to,[8] a complete ban.

Moving on to the interstate commerce burden, Washington regulation of Internet gambling would be an interstate-commerce burdening nightmare. Washington heavily regulates brick and mortar gambling operations for the protection of its citizens and to assure financial regularity. As one example, the State can inspect the premises and audit the books of a brick and mortar gambling operation without notice, RCW 9.46.130, for compliance with all regulations, including assuring the State has criminal background checks for all em-

---

tolite Corp. v. Midwesco Enters., Inc., 486 U.S. 888, 897 (1988) (Scalia, J., concurring). Justice Thomas simply viewed comparisons such as this as having "no principled way to decide" them. United Haulers Ass'n v. Oneida-Herkimer Solid Waste Mgmt. Auth., 550 U.S. 330, 353 (2007) (Thomas, J., concurring). Thankfully, here, whether the burden on interstate commerce is indeed sufficient to be comparable to the state benefit does not affect the outcome. If the burden is not, RCW 9.46.240 does not violate the dormant commerce clause, with a small burden on interstate commerce not "clearly excessive" in light of a substantial state interest. And even if the burden is comparable, as we conclude here, the road is longer, as set forth below, but the result is the same.

8. One might argue, if some individuals ignore the ban and gamble on-line, regulation would decrease the ills of Internet gambling because those individuals would be exposed to less harm gambling on-line under Washington regulation than under no Washington regulation, as occurs under the ban. But again, such arguments seek to rebalance public policy concerns. The judiciary in not in a position to agree or disagree with the legislature's balancing of public policy interests or its determination of which citizens it will "save."

ployees working at that time, RCW 9.46.070(7), and the gambling operation has implemented measures to counter pathological gambling, RCW 9.46.071, .072.

Even assuming there is an equally effective, Internet equivalent to Washington's brick and mortar regulations, Washington would need to impose its regulatory requirements and intrusive vigilance on foreign[9] on-line operations to regulate foreign Internet gambling. The very structure and practice of those foreign operations would need to be reorganized in conformity to Washington regulations. When a foreign operation failed to conform, all Washington commerce on that web site would be precluded.

And when the conflict is not with only one web site, but also the regulations of the country of origin of that web site, that country would be blacklisted from Washington on-line gambling. Where Washington blocks commerce with specific countries based upon state determinations of the adequacy of the country's regulations or conduct, it is likely to run afoul of the federal government's power to make treaties under article II, section 2, clause 2 of the United States Constitution. *See, e.g.,* Crosby v. Nat'l Foreign Trade Council, 530 U.S. 363, 380–81 (2000) (striking down a Massachusetts law that restricted state purchase of goods from companies in Burma (Myanmar) due to the state-sanctioned, mass genocide that continues to occur there). Washington regulation of foreign service providers is also likely to run afoul of various international treaties.[10]

Regulation of Internet gambling comparable to that currently imposed on brick and mortar gambling would require Washington to export its considerable regulations to the world—a major burden on interstate commerce. *See* S. Pac. Co. v. Arizona ex rel. Sullivan, 325 U.S. 761, 775 (1945) (a state limiting the length of trains would have the effect of exporting that regulation to other states, where train cars would be split up and reassembled to decrease or increase the length of the train prior to and upon leaving that state, causing a "serious impediment to the free flow of commerce …"); *accord* Am. Library Ass'n v. Pataki, 969 F. Supp. 160, 177 (S.D.N.Y. 1997) (a state projecting its laws into other states via regulation of Internet activity is a per se violation of the commerce clause). Comparable regulations on Internet gambling are not *clearly* less restrictive on interstate commerce.[11]

Rather than impose its pervasive regulation on Internet gambling, Washington could permit Internet gambling without regulating it at all or, as Rousso suggested at oral argument, Washington could trust in the regulatory systems of the native countries of the Internet gambling web sites to protect Washington citizens. But whether either of these options would address the concerns of Internet gambling as effectively as a complete ban is not clearly established here, nor could it be.

---

9. Rousso cites *Wunnicke* for the proposition that state regulation burdening foreign commerce is more heavily scrutinized, *see* 467 U.S. at 100, but this burden on foreign commerce is present whether Washington bans or regulates Internet gambling.

10. For example, the United States defended various *federal* gambling restrictions (including the illegal gambling business act of 1970, 18 U.S.C. § 1955, and the Wire Act) after Antigua and Barbuda alleged the United States violated the World Trade Organization's General Agreement on Trade in Services. *See* REPORT OF THE APPELLATE BODY, WORLD TRADE ORGANIZATION, UNITED STATES—MEASURES AFFECTING THE CROSS-BORDER SUPPLY OF GAMBLING AND BETTING SERVICES ¶ 377, WT/DS285/AB/R (Apr. 7, 2005), *available at* http://www.wto.org/english/tratop_e/dispu_e/285abr_e.pdf. Antigua and Barbuda also challenged various state laws, but those issues were dismissed for failure to establish a prima facie case. *Id.*

11. Considering Internet gambling organizations would have to revamp their entire systems to accommodate the Washington regulations, losing Washington players might actually impose less of a burden. A restaurant might be less affected by having fewer customers than by having to change the way it prepares its food, to limit its ingredients, to scrutinize its customers in a certain way, and to be subject to unannounced raids.

Rousso's suggestion—that the court force the legislature to trust in the regulatory systems of other countries—not only bulldozes any notion of a separation of powers between the judiciary and the legislature, but also prevents the legislature from affording any real protection to Washington citizens. If a country's gambling regulations were inadequate, Washington would either have to endure the social ills it caused—permitting its citizens to be exploited, scammed, or made unwilling participants of money laundering schemes—or attempt to run the gambit of selectively banning certain countries from interacting with Washington citizens, running afoul of article II, section 2, clause 2 and various international treaties, as discussed above.

Amicus Curiae The Poker Players Alliance champions the position that Washington *can* regulate Internet gambling itself, encouraging remand to the trial court for further proceedings to show that since other jurisdictions have had "success" with regulating Internet poker, Washington can too. But what constitutes "success" is a fundamental public policy determination, reserved to the legislature. Even if on remand Rousso were able to produce reports or studies stating some jurisdictions regulate Internet gambling in a manner that addresses gambling addiction, underage gambling, money laundering, and organized crime issues with success comparable to Washington brick and mortar regulation, the trial court would then need to determine (a) whether the findings from those reports and studies were reliable and outweighed contrary findings; (b) whether and to what extent such regulation could be budgeted for and implemented by Washington; and (c) whether gambling would increase due to the ready availability of gambling on a home computer, whether that increase would exacerbate current concerns—e.g., causing individuals to go into debt, and increasing gambling addictions, underage gambling, and the prevalence of gambling in society, and whether such increases were "acceptable." These purely public policy determinations demonstrate why the legislature, and not the judiciary, must make that call. *See Clover Leaf Creamery Co.*, 449 U.S. at 470; *Ferguson*, 372 U.S. at 729 ("Under the system of government created by our Constitution, it is up to legislatures, not courts, to decide on the wisdom and utility of legislation.").

Indeed, the judiciary's making such public policy decisions would not only ignore the separation of powers, but would stretch the practical limits of the judiciary. *See* Brown v. Owen, 165 Wn.2d 706, 718–19, 206 P.3d 310 (2009) (recognizing the separation of powers implicit in the Washington Constitution and the relevance of justiciability concerns like those addressed by the federal political question doctrine (citing Baker v. Carr, 369 U.S. 186, 217 (1962))). This court is not equipped to legislate what constitutes a "successful" regulatory scheme by balancing public policy concerns, nor can we determine which risks are acceptable and which are not. These are not questions of law; we lack the tools. Rousso, "in order to succeed in this action, ask[s] the Court to enter upon policy determinations for which judicially manageable standards are lacking." *Baker*, 369 U.S. at 226. Such is beyond the authority and ability of the judiciary.

This is not to imply the dormant commerce clause can be satisfied any time the State invokes the magic words: "public policy determination." But here there is a legitimate public interest. The ban on Internet gambling is a public policy balance that effectively promotes that interest. A reasonable person may argue the legislature can balance concerns for personal freedom and choice, state finance, and the protection of Washington citizens in a "better" way—but he or she must do so to the legislature.

In contrast the fatal flaw of nondiscriminatory state laws struck down under the dormant commerce clause is often the state law's failure to actually protect the targeted state interest. In Bibb v. Navajo Freight Lines, 359 U.S. 520, 525–29 (1959), the Supreme Court held a state law requiring trucks to use curved mudflaps—when flat ones were permitted in all other states—failed because (1) out-of-state trucks having to pull over at the border and change their mudflaps was a substantial burden to interstate commerce and (2) curved mudflaps provided *no* safety benefits over straight ones and caused increased risks by increasing the heat around the truck's tires.

In *Pataki*, a New York law banned anyone from transmitting sexually explicit content to minors. 969 F. Supp. at 163. Since a person who posts something on a web site has no way of excluding visitors by geographic region, he or she could not prevent a New York minor from accessing his or her web site. Thus, a web site operator would need to remove the content for *all* users—regardless of geographic region—to comply with the New York law, causing a substantial burden on interstate commerce. And yet, although web site operators from other states within the United States might remove sexually explicit content from their web sites for fear of New York prosecution, foreign web site operators—far outside the practical reach of New York prosecution—would not be so deterred. *Id.* at 178. The court reasoned that the law failed to protect minors from sexually explicit content because those minors could just as easily view foreign pornographic web sites after domestic web sites were sanitized. *Id.*

Unlike in *Bibb* and *Pataki*, Rousso fails to show a ban on Internet gambling is useless to address legitimate state interests, including reducing underage gambling, compulsive gambling, and Washingtonians' unintentional support of organized crime and money-laundering operations.

The facts and holding in *Clover Leaf Creamery Co.* bear some constructive similarities to the case at hand. *See* 449 U.S. 456. There the Minnesota legislature banned the retail sale of milk in plastic nonreturnable, nonrefillable containers because they presented a solid waste management problem, caused energy waste, and depleted natural resources. *Id.* at 458. Other nonreturnable, nonrefillable containers, such as ones made from paperboard, raised similar concerns but were not banned. *Id.* Here, both brick and mortar gambling and Internet gambling pose many of the same threats to citizens' health, welfare, safety, and morals, yet only the latter is banned.

Even though plastic and paperboard nonreturnable, nonrefillable containers caused the same ultimate ills, the Supreme Court in *Clover Leaf Creamery Co.* held the ban on plastic containers, which still permitted paperboard containers, was consistent with the dormant commerce clause. *Id.* at 473. Two aspects of this holding, discussed in the context of an equal protection claim and then adopted into the dormant commerce clause analysis, *see id.*, are directly applicable here.

First, the Minnesota legislature was permitted to ban plastic without banning paperboard—even if this ban granted an in-state benefit. *Id.* at 473–74. Although both caused solid waste, energy, and conservation issues (particularly in comparison to recyclable containers), plastic nonreturnable, nonrefillable containers were fairly new to the market, had already become popular, and many Minnesota dairies were preparing to switch to their use. *Id.* at 465–67. Furthermore, the *nature and extent* of the solid waste, energy, and conservation issues differed between plastic and paperboard containers. *Id.* at 466–67. The plastic container ban stemmed the proliferation of a growingly popular substitute for recyclable containers, *id.* at 465–67, thus limiting the solid waste, energy, and conservation issues, *id.* at 467.

Just as plastic and paperboard containers produce different wastes to different extents, both brick and mortar and Internet gambling threaten health, safety, welfare, and morals in different ways and to different extents. Internet gambling provides a means of gambling that is growing in popularity and immediately accessible at home. The

Washington legislature can ban it to limit the threat to health, safety, welfare, and morals caused by gambling, even if it doesn't ban all gambling, as the Minnesota legislature was not compelled to ban *all* types of nonrecyclable containers. *See id.* at 465–67, 473. The Washington legislature is permitted to find that Internet gambling's growing popularity, home-accessibility, and regulatory challenges would undermine Washington's policy to "'prohibit all forms and means of gambling, except where carefully and specifically authorized and regulated.'" RCWA 9.46.240 Notes (quoting Laws of 2006, ch. 290, § 1).

Second, the Supreme Court in *Clover Leaf Creamery Co.* held the Minnesota legislature's ban on plastic nonreturnable, nonrefillable containers was consistent with the dormant commerce clause—including that it was not "clearly excessive" and alternatives could not address the issues more effectively and with less of an interstate commerce burden—even though evidence existed that contradicted the legislature's findings that plastic containers caused more of a waste and energy problem than paperboard ones. *Id.* at 469–70. In fact the Minnesota Supreme Court found that plastic containers required less energy to make and took up less space in landfills. *Id.* Nevertheless, the United States Supreme Court held, regardless of whether the legislature's findings were based upon weak or inconclusive evidence, that these findings did not open the door for the judiciary to substitute its judgment for the legislature's. *Id.* at 469–70.

Here, the legislature balanced public policy concerns and determined the interests of Washington are best served by banning Internet gambling. The legislature chose the advantages and disadvantages of a ban over the advantages and disadvantages of regulation. The evidence is not conclusive. Many may disagree with the outcome. But the court has no authority to replace the legislature's choice with its own. Under the dormant commerce clause, the burden on interstate commerce is not "clearly excessive" in light of the state interests. RCW 9.46.240 does not violate the dormant commerce clause.

CONCLUSION

It is the role of the legislature, not the judiciary, to balance public policy interests and enact law. This court's limited function here is to determine whether RCW 9.46.240, which criminalizes the transmission of gambling information via the Internet, violates the dormant commerce clause. It does not.

Madsen, C.J., and C. Johnson, Alexander, Chambers, Owens, Fairhurst, J.M. Johnson, and Stephens, JJ., concur.

Notes

1. After reviewing the UIGEA, the notes on state regulation of the Internet in the previous section, and the *Rousso* case, is it clear what the proper role of the state is in regulating Internet gaming? For a discussion of this issue, *see* Martin D. Owens, Jr., *If You Can't Beat 'Em, Will They Let You Join? What American States Can Offer to Attract Internet Gambling Operators*, 10 Gaming L. Rev. 26 (2006); Linda J. Shorey, Dennis M. P. Ehling, Ashley J. Camron & Amy L. Groff, *Do State Bans on Internet Gambling Violate the Dormant Commerce Clause?*, 10 Gaming L. Rev. 240 (2006).

2. A number of state legislatures have looked to the possibility of Internet gaming as a way of addressing huge budget deficits. Does it seem more likely that Internet gambling will gain legal traction on a state-by-state basis before there is definitive federal legislation? *See* Robert W. Stocker II, *State Legislatures Consider Legalizing Intrastate Internet Gaming*, 2010 European Gaming Law 16 (Spring Issue).

Appendix
Title VIII—Unlawful Internet
Gambling Enforcement

SEC. 801. SHORT TITLE.

This title may be cited as the "Unlawful Internet Gambling Enforcement Act of 2006".

SEC. 802. PROHIBITION ON ACCEPTANCE OF ANY PAYMENT INSTRUMENT FOR UNLAWFUL INTERNET GAMBLING.

(a) In General. Chapter 53 of title 31, United States Code, is amended by adding at the end the following:

SUBCHAPTER IV—PROHIBITION ON FUNDING OF UNLAWFUL INTERNET GAMBLING.

§ 5361. Congressional findings and purpose.

(a) Findings. Congress finds the following:

(1) Internet gambling is primarily funded through personal use of payment system instruments, credit cards, and wire transfers.

(2) The National Gambling Impact Study Commission in 1999 recommended the passage of legislation to prohibit wire transfers to Internet gambling sites or the banks which represent such sites.

(3) Internet gambling is a growing cause of debt collection problems for insured depository institutions and the consumer credit industry.

(4) New mechanisms for enforcing gambling laws on the Internet are necessary because traditional law enforcement mechanisms are often inadequate for enforcing gambling prohibitions or regulations on the Internet, especially where such gambling crosses State or national borders.

(b) Rule of Construction. No provision of this subchapter shall be construed as altering, limiting, or extending any Federal or State law or Tribal-State compact prohibiting, permitting, or regulating gambling within the United States.

§ 5362. Definitions.

In this subchapter:

(1) Bet or wager. The term 'bet or wager':

(A) means the staking or risking by any person of something of value upon the outcome of a contest of others, a sporting event, or a game subject to chance, upon an agreement or understanding that the person or another person will receive something of value in the event of a certain outcome;

(B) includes the purchase of a chance or opportunity to win a lottery or other prize (which opportunity to win is predominantly subject to chance);

(C) includes any scheme of a type described in section 3702 of title 28;

(D) includes any instructions or information pertaining to the establishment or movement of funds by the bettor or customer in, to, or from an account with the business of betting or wagering; and

(E) does not include:

(i) any activity governed by the securities laws (as that term is defined in section 3(a)(47) of the Securities Exchange Act of 1934 for the purchase or sale of securities (as that term is defined in section 3(a)(10) of that Act);

(ii) any transaction conducted on or subject to the rules of a registered entity or exempt board of trade under the Commodity Exchange Act;

(iii) any over-the-counter derivative instrument;

(iv) any other transaction that:

(I) is excluded or exempt from regulation under the Commodity Exchange Act; or

(II) is exempt from State gaming or bucket shop laws under section 12(e) of the Commodity Exchange Act or section 28(a) of the Securities Exchange Act of 1934;

(v) any contract of indemnity or guarantee;

(vi) any contract for insurance;

(vii) any deposit or other transaction with an insured depository institution;

(viii) participation in any game or contest in which participants do not stake or risk anything of value other than:

(I) personal efforts of the participants in playing the game or contest or obtaining access to the Internet; or

(II) points or credits that the sponsor of the game or contest provides to participants free of charge and that can be used or redeemed only for participation in games or contests offered by the sponsor; or

(ix) participation in any fantasy or simulation sports game or educational game or contest in which (if the game or contest involves a team or teams) no fantasy or simulation sports team is based on the current membership of an actual team that is a member of an amateur or professional sports organization (as those terms are defined in section 3701 of title 28) and that meets the following conditions:

(I) All prizes and awards offered to winning participants are established and made known to the participants in advance of the game or contest and their value is not determined by the number of participants or the amount of any fees paid by those participants.

(II) All winning outcomes reflect the relative knowledge and skill of the participants and are determined predominantly by accumulated statistical results of the performance of individuals (athletes in the case of sports events) in multiple real-world sporting or other events.

(III) No winning outcome is based:

(aa) on the score, point-spread, or any performance or performances of any single real-world team or any combination of such teams; or

(bb) solely on any single performance of an individual athlete in any single real-world sporting or other event.

(2) Business of betting or wagering. The term 'business of betting or wagering' does not include the activities of a financial transaction provider, or any interactive computer service or telecommunications service.

(3) Designated payment system. The term 'designated payment system' means any system utilized by a financial transaction provider that the Secretary and the Board of Governors of the Federal Reserve System, in consultation with the Attorney General, jointly determine, by regulation or order, could be utilized in connection with, or to facilitate, any restricted transaction.

(4) Financial transaction provider. The term 'financial transaction provider' means a creditor, credit card issuer, financial institution, operator of a terminal at which an electronic fund transfer may be initiated, money transmitting business, or international, national, regional, or local payment network utilized to effect a credit transaction, electronic fund transfer, stored value product transaction, or money transmitting service, or a participant in such network, or other participant in a designated payment system.

(5) Internet. The term 'Internet' means the international computer network of interoperable packet switched data networks.

(6) Interactive computer service. The term 'interactive computer service' has the meaning given the term in section 230(f) of the Communications Act of 1934 (47 U.S.C. 230(f)).

(7) Restricted transaction. The term 'restricted transaction' means any transaction or transmittal involving any credit, funds, instrument, or proceeds described in any paragraph of section 5363 which the recipient is prohibited from accepting under section 5363.

(8) Secretary. The term 'Secretary' means the Secretary of the Treasury.

(9) State. The term 'State' means any State of the United States, the District of Columbia, or any commonwealth, territory, or other possession of the United States.

(10) Unlawful internet gambling.

(A) In general. The term 'unlawful Internet gambling' means to place, receive, or otherwise knowingly transmit a bet or wager by any means which involves the use, at least in part, of the Internet where such bet or wager is unlawful under any applicable Federal or State law in the State or Tribal lands in which the bet or wager is initiated, received, or otherwise made.

(B) Intrastate transactions. The term 'unlawful Internet gambling' does not include placing, receiving, or otherwise transmitting a bet or wager where:

(i) the bet or wager is initiated and received or otherwise made exclusively within a single State;

(ii) the bet or wager and the method by which the bet or wager is initiated and received or otherwise made is expressly authorized by and placed in accordance with the laws of such State, and the State law or regulations include:

(I) age and location verification requirements reasonably designed to block access to minors and persons located out of such State; and

(II) appropriate data security standards to prevent unauthorized access by any person whose age and current location has not been verified in accordance with such State's law or regulations; and

(iii) the bet or wager does not violate any provision of:

(I) the Interstate Horseracing Act of 1978 (15 U.S.C. 3001 et seq.);

(II) chapter 178 of title 28 (commonly known as the 'Professional and Amateur Sports Protection Act');

(III) the Gambling Devices Transportation Act (15 U.S.C. 1171 et seq.); or

(IV) the Indian Gaming Regulatory Act (25 U.S.C. 2701 et seq.).

(C) Intratribal transactions. The term 'unlawful Internet gambling' does not include placing, receiving, or otherwise transmitting a bet or wager where:

(i) the bet or wager is initiated and received or otherwise made exclusively:

(I) within the Indian lands of a single Indian tribe (as such terms are defined under the Indian Gaming Regulatory Act); or

(II) between the Indian lands of 2 or more Indian tribes to the extent that intertribal gaming is authorized by the Indian Gaming Regulatory Act;

(ii) the bet or wager and the method by which the bet or wager is initiated and received or otherwise made is expressly authorized by and complies with the requirements of:

(I) the applicable tribal ordinance or resolution approved by the Chairman of the National Indian Gaming Commission; and

(II) with respect to class III gaming, the applicable Tribal-State Compact;

(iii) the applicable tribal ordinance or resolution or Tribal-State Compact includes:

(I) age and location verification requirements reasonably designed to block access to minors and persons located out of the applicable Tribal lands; and

(II) appropriate data security standards to prevent unauthorized access by any person whose age and current location has not been verified in accordance with the applicable tribal ordinance or resolution or Tribal-State Compact; and

(iv) the bet or wager does not violate any provision of:

(I) the Interstate Horseracing Act of 1978 (15 U.S.C. 3001 et seq.);

(II) chapter 178 of title 28 (commonly known as the 'Professional and Amateur Sports Protection Act');

(III) the Gambling Devices Transportation Act (15 U.S.C. 1171 et seq.); or

(IV) the Indian Gaming Regulatory Act (25 U.S.C. 2701 et seq.).

(D) Interstate horseracing.

(i) In general. The term 'unlawful Internet gambling' shall not include any activity that is allowed under the Interstate Horseracing Act of 1978 (15 U.S.C. 3001 et seq.).

(ii) Rule of construction regarding preemption. Nothing in this subchapter may be construed to preempt any State law prohibiting gambling.

(iii) Sense of congress. It is the sense of Congress that this subchapter shall not change which activities related to horse racing may or may not be allowed under Federal law. This subparagraph is intended to address concerns that this subchapter could have the effect of changing the existing relationship between the Interstate Horseracing Act and other Federal statutes in effect on the date of the enactment of this subchapter. This subchapter is not intended to change that relationship. This subchapter is not intended to resolve any existing disagreements over how to interpret the relationship between the Interstate Horseracing Act and other Federal statutes.

(E) Intermediate routing. The intermediate routing of electronic data shall not determine the location or locations in which a bet or wager is initiated, received, or otherwise made.

(11) Other terms.

(A) Credit; creditor; credit card; and card issuer. The terms 'credit', 'creditor', 'credit card', and 'card issuer' have the meanings given the terms in section 103 of the Truth in Lending Act (15 U.S.C. 1602).

(B) Electronic fund transfer. The term 'electronic fund transfer':

(i) has the meaning given the term in section 903 of the Electronic Fund Transfer Act (15 U.S.C. 1693a), except that the term includes transfers that would otherwise be excluded under section 903(6)(E) of that Act; and

(ii) includes any fund transfer covered by Article 4A of the Uniform Commercial Code, as in effect in any State.

(C) Financial institution. The term 'financial institution' has the meaning given the term in section 903 of the Electronic Fund Transfer Act, except that such term does not include a casino, sports book, or other business at or through which bets or wagers may be placed or received.

(D) Insured depository institution. The term 'insured depository institution':

(i) has the meaning given the term in section 3(c) of the Federal Deposit Insurance Act (12 U.S.C. 1813(c)); and

(ii) includes an insured credit union (as defined in section 101 of the Federal Credit Union Act).

(E) Money transmitting business and money transmitting service. The terms 'money transmitting business' and 'money transmitting service' have the meanings given the terms in section 5330(d) (determined without regard to any regulations prescribed by the Secretary thereunder).

§ 5363. Prohibition on acceptance of any financial instrument for unlawful Internet gambling.

No person engaged in the business of betting or wagering may knowingly accept, in connection with the participation of another person in unlawful Internet gambling:

(1) credit, or the proceeds of credit, extended to or on behalf of such other person (including credit extended through the use of a credit card);

(2) an electronic fund transfer, or funds transmitted by or through a money transmitting business, or the proceeds of an electronic fund transfer or money transmitting service, from or on behalf of such other person;

(3) any check, draft, or similar instrument which is drawn by or on behalf of such other person and is drawn on or payable at or through any financial institution; or

(4) the proceeds of any other form of financial transaction, as the Secretary and the Board of Governors of the Federal Reserve System may jointly prescribe by regulation, which involves a financial institution as a payor or financial intermediary on behalf of or for the benefit of such other person.

§ 5364. Policies and procedures to identify and prevent restricted transactions.

(a) Regulations. Before the end of the 270-day period beginning on the date of the enactment of this subchapter, the Secretary and the Board of Governors of the Federal Reserve System, in consultation with the Attorney General, shall prescribe regulations (which the Secretary and the Board jointly determine to be appropriate) requiring each designated payment system, and all participants therein, to identify and block or otherwise prevent or prohibit restricted transactions through the establishment of policies and procedures reasonably designed to identify and block or otherwise prevent or prohibit the acceptance of restricted transactions in any of the following ways:

(1) The establishment of policies and procedures that:

(A) allow the payment system and any person involved in the payment system to identify restricted transactions by means of codes in authorization messages or by other means; and

(B) block restricted transactions identified as a result of the policies and procedures developed pursuant to subparagraph (A).

(2) The establishment of policies and procedures that prevent or prohibit the acceptance of the products or services of the payment system in connection with a restricted transaction.

(b) Requirements for Policies and Procedures. In prescribing regulations under subsection (a), the Secretary and the Board of Governors of the Federal Reserve System shall:

(1) identify types of policies and procedures, including nonexclusive examples, which would be deemed, as applicable, to be reasonably designed to identify and block or otherwise prevent or prohibit the acceptance of the products or services with respect to each type of restricted transaction;

(2) to the extent practical, permit any participant in a payment system to choose among alternative means of identifying and blocking, or otherwise preventing or prohibiting the acceptance of the products or services of the payment system or participant in connection with, restricted transactions;

(3) exempt certain restricted transactions or designated payment systems from any requirement imposed under such regulations, if the Secretary and the Board jointly find that it is not reasonably practical to identify and block, or otherwise prevent or prohibit the acceptance of, such transactions; and

(4) ensure that transactions in connection with any activity excluded from the definition of unlawful internet gambling in subparagraph (B), (C), or (D)(i) of section 5362(10) are not blocked or otherwise prevented or prohibited by the prescribed regulations.

(c) Compliance With Payment System Policies and Procedures. A financial transaction provider shall be considered to be in compliance with the regulations prescribed under subsection (a) if:

(1) such person relies on and complies with the policies and procedures of a designated payment system of which it is a member or participant to:

    (A) identify and block restricted transactions; or

    (B) otherwise prevent or prohibit the acceptance of the products or services of the payment system, member, or participant in connection with restricted transactions; and

(2) such policies and procedures of the designated payment system comply with the requirements of regulations prescribed under subsection (a).

(d) No Liability for Blocking or Refusing To Honor Restricted Transactions. A person that identifies and blocks a transaction, prevents or prohibits the acceptance of its products or services in connection with a transaction, or otherwise refuses to honor a transaction:

    (1) that is a restricted transaction;

    (2) that such person reasonably believes to be a restricted transaction; or

    (3) as a designated payment system or a member of a designated payment system in reliance on the policies and procedures of the payment system, in an effort to comply with regulations prescribed under subsection (a),

shall not be liable to any party for such action.

(e) Regulatory Enforcement. The requirements under this section shall be enforced exclusively by:

    (1) the Federal functional regulators, with respect to the designated payment systems and financial transaction providers subject to the respective jurisdiction of such regulators under section 505(a) of the Gramm-Leach-Bliley Act and section 5g of the Commodities Exchange Act; and

    (2) the Federal Trade Commission, with respect to designated payment systems and financial transaction providers not otherwise subject to the jurisdiction of any Federal functional regulators (including the Commission) as described in paragraph (1).

§ Sec. 5365. Civil remedies.

(a) Jurisdiction. In addition to any other remedy under current law, the district courts of the United States shall have original and exclusive jurisdiction to prevent and restrain restricted transactions by issuing appropriate orders in accordance with this section, regardless of whether a prosecution has been initiated under this subchapter.

(b) Proceedings.

    (1) Institution by federal government.

        (A) In general. The United States, acting through the Attorney General, may institute proceedings under this section to prevent or restrain a restricted transaction.

        (B) Relief. Upon application of the United States under this paragraph, the district court may enter a temporary restraining order, a preliminary injunction, or an injunction against any person to prevent or restrain a restricted transaction, in accordance with rule 65 of the Federal Rules of Civil Procedure.

    (2) Institution by state attorney general.

        (A) In general. The attorney general (or other appropriate State official) of a State in which a restricted transaction allegedly has been or will be initiated, received, or otherwise made may institute proceedings under this section to prevent or restrain the violation or threatened violation.

(B) Relief. Upon application of the attorney general (or other appropriate State official) of an affected State under this paragraph, the district court may enter a temporary restraining order, a preliminary injunction, or an injunction against any person to prevent or restrain a restricted transaction, in accordance with rule 65 of the Federal Rules of Civil Procedure.

(3) Indian lands.

(A) In general. Notwithstanding paragraphs (1) and (2), for a restricted transaction that allegedly has been or will be initiated, received, or otherwise made on Indian lands (as that term is defined in section 4 of the Indian Gaming Regulatory Act):

(i) the United States shall have the enforcement authority provided under paragraph (1); and

(ii) the enforcement authorities specified in an applicable Tribal-State Compact negotiated under section 11 of the Indian Gaming Regulatory Act (25 U.S.C. 2710) shall be carried out in accordance with that compact.

(B) Rule of construction. No provision of this section shall be construed as altering, superseding, or otherwise affecting the application of the Indian Gaming Regulatory Act.

(c) Limitation Relating to Interactive Computer Services.

(1) In general. Relief granted under this section against an interactive computer service shall:

(A) be limited to the removal of, or disabling of access to, an online site violating section 5363, or a hypertext link to an online site violating such section, that resides on a computer server that such service controls or operates, except that the limitation in this subparagraph shall not apply if the service is subject to liability under this section under section 5367;

(B) be available only after notice to the interactive computer service and an opportunity for the service to appear are provided;

(C) not impose any obligation on an interactive computer service to monitor its service or to affirmatively seek facts indicating activity violating this subchapter;

(D) specify the interactive computer service to which it applies; and

(E) specifically identify the location of the online site or hypertext link to be removed or access to which is to be disabled.

(2) Coordination with other law. An interactive computer service that does not violate this subchapter shall not be liable under section 1084(d) of title 18, except that the limitation in this paragraph shall not apply if an interactive computer service has actual knowledge and control of bets and wagers and:

(A) operates, manages, supervises, or directs an Internet website at which unlawful bets or wagers may be placed, received, or otherwise made or at which unlawful bets or wagers are offered to be placed, received, or otherwise made; or

(B) owns or controls, or is owned or controlled by, any person who operates, manages, supervises, or directs an Internet website at which unlawful bets or wagers may be placed, received, or otherwise made, or at which unlawful bets or wagers are offered to be placed, received, or otherwise made.

(d) Limitation on Injunctions Against Regulated Persons. Notwithstanding any other provision of this section, and subject to section 5367, no provision of this subchapter shall be construed as authorizing the Attorney General of the United States, or the attorney general (or other appropriate State official) of any State to institute proceedings to prevent or restrain a restricted transaction against any financial transaction provider, to the extent that the person is acting as a financial transaction provider.

§ Sec. 5366. Criminal penalties.

(a) In General. Any person who violates section 5363 shall be fined under title 18, imprisoned for not more than 5 years, or both.

(b) Permanent Injunction. Upon conviction of a person under this section, the court may enter a permanent injunction enjoining such person from placing, receiving, or otherwise making bets or wagers or sending, receiving, or inviting information assisting in the placing of bets or wagers.

§ Sec. 5367. Circumventions prohibited.

Notwithstanding section 5362(2), a financial transaction provider, or any interactive computer service or telecommunications service, may be liable under this subchapter if such person has actual knowledge and control of bets and wagers, and:

(1) operates, manages, supervises, or directs an Internet website at which unlawful bets or wagers may be placed, received, or otherwise made, or at which unlawful bets or wagers are offered to be placed, received, or otherwise made; or

(2) owns or controls, or is owned or controlled by, any person who operates, manages, supervises, or directs an Internet website at which unlawful bets or wagers may be placed, received, or otherwise made, or at which unlawful bets or wagers are offered to be placed, received, or otherwise made.

(b) Technical and Conforming Amendment. The table of sections for chapter 53 of title 31, United States Code, is amended by adding at the end the following:

Subchapter IV—Prohibition on funding of unlawful Internet gambling.

5361   Congressional findings and purpose.

5362   Definitions.

5363   Prohibition on acceptance of any financial instrument for unlawful Internet gambling.

5364   Policies and procedures to identify and prevent restricted transactions.

5365   Civil remedies.

5366   Criminal penalties.

5367   Circumventions prohibited."

§ Sec. 803. Internet gambling in or through foreign jurisdictions.

(a) In General. In deliberations between the United States Government and any foreign country on money laundering, corruption, and crime issues, the United States Government should:

(1) encourage cooperation by foreign governments and relevant international fora in identifying whether Internet gambling operations are being used for money laundering, corruption, or other crimes;

(2) advance policies that promote the cooperation of foreign governments, through information sharing or other measures, in the enforcement of this Act; and

(3) encourage the Financial Action Task Force on Money Laundering, in its annual report on money laundering typologies, to study the extent to which Internet gambling operations are being used for money laundering purposes.

(b) Report Required. The Secretary of the Treasury shall submit an annual report to the Congress on any deliberations between the United States and other countries on issues relating to Internet gambling.

Approved October 13, 2006.

Chapter 13

Legal Restrictions on Gaming Advertising

1. Introduction

The history of gaming advertising, and the restrictions placed on it, extends back into the mid-nineteenth century. Not surprisingly, these early laws were directed at lotteries, one of the most prevalent types of gambling. The Communications Act of 1934, codified as 18 U.S.C. §§ 1304, 1307, proscribed advertisement of information relating to lotteries. However, this law was read by regulatory bodies and courts to extend to all forms of gambling. Of course, in 1934, the modern wave of widespread gambling in the United States was yet to occur, and lotteries were still viewed as socially undesirable. As will be discussed below, over the years exceptions to the Communication Act's prohibition were created by Congress. These exceptions undermined government enforcement efforts. By the 1960s, states began to legislate in the area as well, passing restrictive limits on gambling advertising.

Challenges to these laws lacked constitutional grounding, for the activity involved (advertising) was not speech or expression, rather it was a promotion of business activity. This paradigm began to change in 1976, however, when the United States Supreme Court for the first time held that "commercial speech" enjoyed some amount of protection under the First Amendment. In Virginia State Board of Pharmacy v. Virginia Citizens Consumer Council, 425 U.S. 478 (1976), the Court declared unconstitutional a ban on the advertising of the price of prescription drugs in Virginia. Although the case did not deal with gaming, the extension of the First Amendment to speech that had no political or social message, and involved only commercial transactions, was a significant one for the future of gaming regulation.

The Court elaborated upon its holding that commercial speech was covered by the First Amendment in 1980, in another non-gaming case. In Central Hudson Gas & Electrical Corp. v. Public Service Commission of New York, 447 U.S. 557 (1980), the Court articulated a four-factor analysis to determine whether commercial speech limitations were constitutional:

> At the outset, we must determine whether the expression is protected by the First Amendment. For commercial speech to come within that provision, it at least must concern a lawful activity and not be misleading. Next, we ask whether the asserted governmental interest is substantial. If both inquiries yield positive answers, we must determine whether the regulation directly advances the governmental interest asserted, and whether it is not more extensive than is necessary to serve that interest. 447 U.S. 557, 566.

While the *Central Hudson* analysis was not set in a gaming context, in 1986 and 1993 the Supreme Court applied the criteria to gaming cases.

2. The Evolution of Gaming Advertising in the Supreme Court

Posadas de Puerto Rico Associates v. Tourism Company of Puerto Rico

478 U.S. 328 (1986)

Justice REHNQUIST delivered the opinion of the Court.

In this case we address the facial constitutionality of a Puerto Rico statute and regulations restricting advertising of casino gambling aimed at the residents of Puerto Rico. Appellant Posadas de Puerto Rico Associates, doing business in Puerto Rico as Condado Holiday Inn Hotel and Sands Casino, filed suit against appellee Tourism Company of Puerto Rico in the Superior Court of Puerto Rico, San Juan Section. Appellant sought a declaratory judgment that the statute and regulations, both facially and as applied by the Tourism Company, impermissibly suppressed commercial speech in violation of the First Amendment and the equal protection and due process guarantees of the United States Constitution.[1] The Superior Court held that the advertising restrictions had been unconstitutionally applied to appellant's past conduct. But the court adopted a narrowing construction of the statute and regulations and held that, based on such a construction, both were facially constitutional. The Supreme Court of Puerto Rico dismissed an appeal on the ground that it "d[id] not present a substantial constitutional question." We postponed consideration of the question of jurisdiction until the hearing on the merits. 474 U.S. 917. We now hold that we have jurisdiction to hear the appeal, and we affirm the decision of the Supreme Court of Puerto Rico with respect to the facial constitutionality of the advertising restrictions.

In 1948, the Puerto Rico Legislature legalized certain forms of casino gambling. The Games of Chance Act of 1948, Act No. 221 of May 15, 1948 (Act), authorized the playing of roulette, dice, and card games in licensed "gambling rooms." § 2, codified, as amended, at P.R. Laws Ann., Tit. 15, § 71 (1972). Bingo and slot machines were later added to the list of authorized games of chance under the Act. See Act of June 7, 1948, No. 21, § 1 (bingo); Act of July 30, 1974, No. 2, pt. 2, § 2 (slot machines). The legislature's intent was set forth in the Act's Statement of Motives:

"The purpose of this Act is to contribute to the development of tourism by means of the authorization of certain games of chance which are customary in the recreation places of the great tourist centers of the world, and by the establishment of regulations for and the strict surveillance of said games by the government, in order to ensure for tourists the best possible safeguards, while at the same time opening for the Treasurer of Puerto Rico an additional source of income." Games of Chance Act of 1948, Act No. 221 of May 15, 1948, § 1.

The Act also provided that "[n]o gambling room shall be permitted to advertise or otherwise offer their facilities to the public of Puerto Rico." § 8, codified, as amended, at P.R. Laws Ann., Tit. 15, § 77 (1972).

---

1. We have held that Puerto Rico is subject to the First Amendment Speech Clause, Balzac v. Porto Rico, 258 U.S. 298, 314 (1922), the Due Process Clause of either the Fifth or the Fourteenth Amendment, Calero-Toledo v. Pearson Yacht Leasing Co., 416 U.S. 663, 668–669, n. 5 (1974), and the equal protection guarantee of either the Fifth or the Fourteenth Amendment, Examining Board v. Flores de Otero, 426 U.S. 572, 599–601 (1976). See generally Torres v. Puerto Rico, 442 U.S. 465, 468–471 (1979).

The Act authorized the Economic Development Administration of Puerto Rico to issue and enforce regulations implementing the various provisions of the Act. See § 7(a), codified, as amended, at P.R. Laws Ann., Tit. 15, § 76a (1972). Appellee Tourism Company of Puerto Rico, a public corporation, assumed the regulatory powers of the Economic Development Administration under the Act in 1970. See Act of June 18, 1970, No. 10, § 17, codified at P.R. Laws Ann., Tit. 23, § 671p (Supp.1983). The two regulations at issue in this case were originally issued in 1957 for the purpose of implementing the advertising restrictions contained in § 8 of the Act. Regulation 76-218 basically reiterates the language of § 8. See 15 R. & R.P.R. § 76-218 (1972). Regulation 76a-1(7), as amended in 1971, provides in pertinent part:

"No concessionaire, nor his agent or employee is authorized to advertise the gambling parlors to the public in Puerto Rico. The advertising of our games of chance is hereby authorized through newspapers, magazines, radio, television and other publicity media outside Puerto Rico subject to the prior editing and approval by the Tourism Development Company of the advertisement to be submitted in draft to the Company." 15 R. & R.P.R. § 76a-1(7) (1972).

In 1975, appellant Posadas de Puerto Rico Associates, a partnership organized under the laws of Texas, obtained a franchise to operate a gambling casino and began doing business under the name Condado Holiday Inn Hotel and Sands Casino (footnote omitted). In 1978, appellant was twice fined by the Tourism Company for violating the advertising restrictions in the Act and implementing regulations. Appellant protested the fines in a series of letters to the Tourism Company. On February 16, 1979, the Tourism Company issued to all casino franchise holders a memorandum setting forth the following interpretation of the advertising restrictions:

"This prohibition includes the use of the word 'casino' in matchbooks, lighters, envelopes, inter-office and/or external correspondence, invoices, napkins, brochures, menus, elevators, glasses, plates, lobbies, banners, flyers, paper holders, pencils, telephone books, directories, bulletin boards or in any hotel dependency or object which may be accessible to the public in Puerto Rico." App. 7a.

Pursuant to this administrative interpretation, the Tourism Company assessed additional fines against appellant. The Tourism Company ordered appellant to pay the outstanding total of $1,500 in fines by March 18, 1979, or its gambling franchise would not be renewed. Appellant continued to protest the fines, but ultimately paid them without seeking judicial review of the decision of the Tourism Company. In July 1981, appellant was again fined for violating the advertising restrictions. Faced with another threatened nonrenewal of its gambling franchise, appellant paid the $500 fine under protest (footnote omitted).

Appellant then filed a declaratory judgment action against the Tourism Company in the Superior Court of Puerto Rico, San Juan Section, seeking a declaration that the Act and implementing regulations, both facially and as applied by the Tourism Company, violated appellant's commercial speech rights under the United States Constitution. The Puerto Rico Secretary of Justice appeared for the purpose of defending the constitutionality of the statute and regulations. After a trial, the Superior Court held that "[t]he administrative interpretation and application has [sic] been capricious, arbitrary, erroneous and unreasonable, and has [sic] produced absurd results which are contrary to law." App. to Juris. Statement 29b. The court therefore determined that it must "override the regulatory deficiency to save the constitutionality of the statute." The court reviewed the history of casino gambling in Puerto Rico and concluded:

"... We assume that the legislator was worried about the participation of the residents of Puerto Rico on what on that date constituted an experiment.... Therefore, he prohibited the gaming rooms from announcing themselves or offering themselves to the public—which we reasonably infer are the *bona fide* residents of Puerto Rico.... [W]hat the legislator foresaw and prohibited was the invitation to play at the casinos through publicity campaigns or advertising in Puerto Rico addressed to the resident of Puerto Rico. He wanted to protect him." *Id.,* at 32b.

Based on this view of the legislature's intent, the court issued a narrowing construction of the statute, declaring that "the only advertisement prohibited by the law originally is that which is contracted with an advertising agency, for consideration, to attract the resident to bet at the dice, card, roulette and bingo tables." *Id.* at 33b–34b. The court also issued the following narrowing construction of Regulation 76a-1(7):

"... Advertisements of the casinos in Puerto Rico are prohibited in the local publicity media addressed to inviting the residents of Puerto Rico to visit the casinos."

* * *

"We hereby allow, within the jurisdiction of Puerto Rico, advertising by the casinos addressed to tourists, provided they do not invite the residents of Puerto Rico to visit the casino, even though said announcements may incidentally reach the hands of a resident. Within the ads of casinos allowed by this regulation figure, for illustrative purposes only, advertising distributed or placed in landed airplanes or cruise ships in jurisdictional waters and in restricted areas to travelers only in the international airport and the docks where tourist cruise ships arrive since the principal objective of said announcements is to make the tourist in transit through Puerto Rico aware of the availability of the games of chance as a tourist amenity; the ads of casinos in magazines for distribution primarily in Puerto Rico to the tourist, including the official guide of the Tourism Company 'Que Pasa in Puerto Rico' and any other tourist facility guide in Puerto Rico, even though said magazines may be available to the residents and in movies, television, radio, newspapers and trade magazines which may be published, taped, or filmed in the exterior for tourism promotion in the exterior even though they may be exposed or incidentally circulated in Puerto Rico. For example: an advertisement in the New York Times, an advertisement in CBS which reaches us through Cable TV, whose main objective is to reach the potential tourist.

"We hereby authorize advertising in the mass communication media of the country, where the trade name of the hotel is used even though it may contain a reference to the casino provided that the word casino is never used alone nor specified. Among the announcements allowed, by way of illustration, are the use of the trade name with which the hotel is identified for the promotion of special vacation packages and activities at the hotel, in invitations, 'billboards,' bulletins and programs or activities sponsored by the hotel. The use of the trade name, including the reference to the casino is also allowed in the hotel's facade, provided the word 'casino' does not exceed in proportion the size of the rest of the name, and the utilization of lights and colors will be allowed if the rest of the laws regarding this application are complied with; and in the menus, napkins, glasses, tableware, glassware and other items used within the hotel, as well as in calling cards, envelopes and letterheads of the hotel and any other use which constitutes a means of identification.

"The direct promotion of the casinos within the premises of the hotels is allowed. In-house guests and clients may receive any type of information and promotion regarding the location of the casino, its schedule and the procedure of the games as well as magazines, souvenirs, stirrers, matchboxes, cards, dice, chips, T-shirts, hats, photographs, postcards and similar items used by the tourism centers of the world.

"Since a *clausus* enumeration of this regulation is unforeseeable, any other situation or incident relating to the legal restriction must be measured in light of the public policy of promoting tourism. If the object of the advertisement is the tourist, it passes legal scrutiny." *Id.* at 38b–40b.

The court entered judgment declaring that appellant's constitutional rights had been violated by the Tourism Company's past application of the advertising restrictions, but that the restrictions were not facially unconstitutional and could be sustained, as "modified by the guidelines issued by this Court on this date" (footnote omitted). *Id.* at 42b.

The Supreme Court of Puerto Rico dismissed appellant's appeal of the Superior Court's decision on the ground that it "d[id] not present a substantial constitutional question." *Id.* at 1a. See P.R. Laws Ann., Tit. 4, §37(a) (1978). Treating appellant's submission as a petition for a writ of review, see §§37(b), (g), the Supreme Court denied the petition. One judge dissented.

We hold that we have jurisdiction to review the decision of the Supreme Court of Puerto Rico....

Because this case involves the restriction of pure commercial speech which does "no more than propose a commercial transaction," Virginia Pharmacy Board v. Virginia Citizens Consumer Council, Inc., 425 U.S. 748, 762 (1976),[7] our First Amendment analysis is guided by the general principles identified in Central Hudson Gas & Electric Corp. v. Public Service Comm'n of New York, 447 U.S. 557 (1980). *See* Zauderer v. Office of Disciplinary Counsel, 471 U.S. 626, 637–638 (1985). Under *Central Hudson,* commercial speech receives a limited form of First Amendment protection so long as it concerns a lawful activity and is not misleading or fraudulent. Once it is determined that the First Amendment applies to the particular kind of commercial speech at issue, then the speech may be restricted only if the government's interest in doing so is substantial, the restrictions directly advance the government's asserted interest, and the restrictions are no more extensive than necessary to serve that interest. 447 U.S. at 566.

The particular kind of commercial speech at issue here, namely, advertising of casino gambling aimed at the residents of Puerto Rico, concerns a lawful activity and is not misleading or fraudulent, at least in the abstract. We must therefore proceed to the three remaining steps of the *Central Hudson* analysis in order to determine whether Puerto Rico's advertising restrictions run afoul of the First Amendment. The first of these three steps involves an assessment of the strength of the government's interest in restricting the speech. The interest at stake in this case, as determined by the Superior Court, is the re-

---

7. The narrowing construction of the statute and regulations announced by the Superior Court effectively ensures that the advertising restrictions cannot be used to inhibit either the freedom of the press in Puerto Rico to report on any aspect of casino gambling, or the freedom of anyone, including casino owners, to comment publicly on such matters as legislation relating to casino gambling. *See* Zauderer v. Office of Disciplinary Counsel, 471 U.S. 626, 637–638, n. 7 (1985) (noting that Ohio's ban on advertising of legal services in Dalkon Shield cases "has placed no general restrictions on appellant's right to publish facts or express opinions regarding Dalkon Shield litigation"); Pittsburgh Press Co. v. Pittsburgh Comm'n on Human Relations, 413 U.S. 376, 391 (1973) (emphasizing that "nothing in our holding allows government at any level to forbid Pittsburgh Press to publish and distribute advertisements commenting on the Ordinance, the enforcement practices of the Commission, or the propriety of sex preferences in employment"); Jackson & Jeffries, *Commercial Speech: Economic Due Process and the First Amendment,* 65 VA. L. REV. 1, 35 n. 125 (1979) (such "'political' dialogue is at the core of ... the first amendment").

duction of demand for casino gambling by the residents of Puerto Rico. Appellant acknowledged the existence of this interest in its February 24, 1982, letter to the Tourism Company. *See* App. to Juris. Statement 2h ("The legislators wanted the tourists to flock to the casinos to gamble, but not our own people"). The Tourism Company's brief before this Court explains the legislature's belief that "[e]xcessive casino gambling among local residents ... would produce serious harmful effects on the health, safety and welfare of the Puerto Rican citizens, such as the disruption of moral and cultural patterns, the increase in local crime, the fostering of prostitution, the development of corruption, and the infiltration of organized crime." Brief for Appellees 37. These are some of the very same concerns, of course, that have motivated the vast majority of the 50 States to prohibit casino gambling. We have no difficulty in concluding that the Puerto Rico Legislature's interest in the health, safety, and welfare of its citizens constitutes a "substantial" governmental interest. Cf. Renton v. Playtime Theatres, Inc., 475 U.S. 41, 54 (1986) (city has substantial interest in "preserving the quality of life in the community at large").

The last two steps of the *Central Hudson* analysis basically involve a consideration of the "fit" between the legislature's ends and the means chosen to accomplish those ends. Step three asks the question whether the challenged restrictions on commercial speech "directly advance" the government's asserted interest. In the instant case, the answer to this question is clearly "yes." The Puerto Rico Legislature obviously believed, when it enacted the advertising restrictions at issue here, that advertising of casino gambling aimed at the residents of Puerto Rico would serve to increase the demand for the product advertised. We think the legislature's belief is a reasonable one, and the fact that appellant has chosen to litigate this case all the way to this Court indicates that appellant shares the legislature's view. *See Central Hudson, supra,* 447 U.S. at 569. ("There is an immediate connection between advertising and demand for electricity. Central Hudson would not contest the advertising ban unless it believed that promotion would increase its sales"); cf. Metromedia, Inc. v. San Diego, 453 U.S. 490, 509 (1981) (plurality opinion of WHITE, J.) (finding third prong of *Central Hudson* test satisfied where legislative judgment "not manifestly unreasonable").

Appellant argues, however, that the challenged advertising restrictions are underinclusive because other kinds of gambling such as horse racing, cockfighting, and the lottery may be advertised to the residents of Puerto Rico. Appellant's argument is misplaced for two reasons. First, whether other kinds of gambling are advertised in Puerto Rico or not, the restrictions on advertising of casino gambling "directly advance" the legislature's interest in reducing demand for games of chance. See *id.* at 511 (plurality opinion of WHITE, J.) ("[W]hether onsite advertising is permitted or not, the prohibition of offsite advertising is directly related to the stated objectives of traffic safety and esthetics. This is not altered by the fact that the ordinance is underinclusive because it permits onsite advertising"). Second, the legislature's interest, as previously identified, is not necessarily to reduce demand for all games of chance, but to reduce demand for casino gambling. According to the Superior Court, horse racing, cockfighting, "picas," or small games of chance at fiestas, and the lottery "have been traditionally part of the Puerto Rican's roots," so that "the legislator could have been more flexible than in authorizing more sophisticated games which are not so widely sponsored by the people." App. to Juris. Statement 35b. In other words, the legislature felt that for Puerto Ricans the risks associated with casino gambling were significantly greater than those associated with the more traditional kinds of gambling in Puerto Rico.[8] In our view, the legislature's separate classification of casino

---

8. The history of legalized gambling in Puerto Rico supports the Superior Court's view of the legislature's intent. Casino gambling was prohibited in Puerto Rico for most of the first half of this cen-

gambling, for purposes of the advertising ban, satisfies the third step of the *Central Hudson* analysis.

We also think it clear beyond peradventure that the challenged statute and regulations satisfy the fourth and last step of the *Central Hudson* analysis, namely, whether the restrictions on commercial speech are no more extensive than necessary to serve the government's interest. The narrowing constructions of the advertising restrictions announced by the Superior Court ensure that the restrictions will not affect advertising of casino gambling aimed at tourists, but will apply only to such advertising when aimed at the residents of Puerto Rico. See also n. 7, *infra;* cf. Oklahoma Telecasters Assn. v. Crisp, 699 F.2d 490, 501 (10th Cir. 1983), *rev'd on other grounds sub nom.* Capital Cities Cable, Inc. v. Crisp, 467 U.S. 691 (1984). Appellant contends, however, that the First Amendment requires the Puerto Rico Legislature to reduce demand for casino gambling among the residents of Puerto Rico not by suppressing commercial speech that might *encourage* such gambling, but by promulgating additional speech designed to *discourage* it. We reject this contention. We think it is up to the legislature to decide whether or not such a "counterspeech" policy would be as effective in reducing the demand for casino gambling as a restriction on advertising. The legislature could conclude, as it apparently did here, that residents of Puerto Rico are already aware of the risks of casino gambling, yet would nevertheless be induced by widespread advertising to engage in such potentially harmful conduct. *Cf.* Capital Broadcasting Co. v. Mitchell, 333 F. Supp. 582, 585 (D.D.C. 1971) (three-judge court) ("Congress had convincing evidence that the Labeling Act of 1965 had not materially reduced the incidence of smoking"), summarily aff'd *sub nom.* Capital Broadcasting Co. v. Acting Attorney General, 405 U.S. 1000 (1972); Dunagin v. City of Oxford, Miss., 718 F.2d 738, 751 (5th Cir. 1983) (en banc) ("We do not believe that a less restrictive time, place and manner restriction, such as a disclaimer warning of the dangers of alcohol, would be effective. The state's concern is not that the public is unaware of the dangers of alcohol.... The concern instead is that advertising will unduly promote alcohol consumption despite known dangers"), *cert. denied,* 467 U.S. 1259 (1984).

In short, we conclude that the statute and regulations at issue in this case, as construed by the Superior Court, pass muster under each prong of the *Central Hudson* test. We therefore hold that the Supreme Court of Puerto Rico properly rejected appellant's First Amendment claim.[9]

---

tury. *See* Puerto Rico Penal Code, § 299, Rev. Stats. and Codes of Porto Rico (1902). The Puerto Rico Penal Code of 1937 made it a misdemeanor to deal, play, carry on, open, or conduct "any game of faro, monte, roulette, fantan, poker, seven and a half, twenty one, hoky-poky, or any game of chance played with cards, dice or any device for money, checks, credit, or other representative of value." See P.R. Laws Ann., Tit. 33, § 1241 (1983). This longstanding prohibition of casino gambling stood in stark contrast to the Puerto Rico Legislature's early legalization of horse racing, see Act of Mar. 10, 1910, No. 23, repealed, Act of Apr. 13, 1916, No. 28, see P.R. Laws Ann., Tit. 15, §§ 181–197 (1972 and Supp.1985); "picas," see Act of Apr. 23, 1927, No. 25, § 1, codified, as amended, at P.R. Laws Ann., Tit. 15, § 80 (1972); dog racing, see Act of Apr. 20, 1936, No. 35, repealed, Act of June 4, 1957, No. 10, § 1, see P.R. Laws Ann., Tit. 15, § 231 (1972) (prohibiting dog racing); cockfighting, see Act of Aug. 12, 1933, No. 1, repealed, Act of May 12, 1942, No. 236, see P.R. Laws Ann., Tit. 15, §§ 292–299 (1972); and the Puerto Rico lottery, see J.R. No. 37, May 14, 1934, repealed, Act of May 15, 1938, No. 212, see P.R. Laws Ann., Tit. 15, §§ 111–128 (1972 and Supp.1985).

9. It should be apparent from our discussion of the First Amendment issue, and particularly the third and fourth prongs of the *Central Hudson* test, that appellant can fare no better under the equal protection guarantee of the Constitution. *Cf.* Renton v. Playtime Theatres, Inc., 475 U.S. 41, 55, n. 4 (1986). If there is a sufficient "fit" between the legislature's means and ends to satisfy the concerns of the First Amendment, the same "fit" is surely adequate under the applicable "rational basis" equal

Justice STEVENS, in dissent, asserts the additional equal protection claim, not raised by appellant either below or in this Court, that the Puerto Rico statute and regulations impermissibly discriminate between different kinds of publications. *Post,* at 2986. Justice STEVENS misunderstands the nature of the Superior Court's limiting construction of the statute and regulations. According to the Superior Court, "[i]f the object of [an] advertisement is the tourist, it passes legal scrutiny." *See* App. to Juris. Statement 40b. It is clear from the court's opinion that this basic test applies *regardless of whether the advertisement appears in a local or nonlocal publication.* Of course, the likelihood that a casino advertisement appearing in the New York Times will be primarily addressed to tourists, and not Puerto Rico residents, is far greater than would be the case for a similar advertisement appearing in the San Juan Star. But it is simply the demographics of the two newspapers' readerships, and not any form of "discrimination" on the part of the Puerto Rico Legislature or the Superior Court, which produces this result.

Appellant argues, however, that the challenged advertising restrictions are constitutionally defective under our decisions in *Carey v. Population Services International,* 431 U.S. 678 (1977), and *Bigelow v. Virginia,* 421 U.S. 809 (1975). In *Carey,* this Court struck down a ban on any "advertisement or display" of contraceptives, 431 U.S. at 700–702, and in *Bigelow,* we reversed a criminal conviction based on the advertisement of an abortion clinic. We think appellant's argument ignores a crucial distinction between the *Carey* and *Bigelow* decisions and the instant case. In *Carey* and *Bigelow,* the underlying conduct that was the subject of the advertising restrictions was constitutionally protected and could not have been prohibited by the State. Here, on the other hand, the Puerto Rico Legislature surely could have prohibited casino gambling by the residents of Puerto Rico altogether. In our view, the greater power to completely ban casino gambling necessarily includes the lesser power to ban advertising of casino gambling, and *Carey* and *Bigelow* are hence inapposite.

Appellant also makes the related argument that, having chosen to legalize casino gambling for residents of Puerto Rico, the legislature is prohibited by the First Amendment from using restrictions on advertising to accomplish its goal of reducing demand for such gambling. We disagree. In our view, appellant has the argument backwards. As we noted in the preceding paragraph, it is precisely *because* the government could have enacted a wholesale prohibition of the underlying conduct that it is permissible for the government to take the less intrusive step of allowing the conduct, but reducing the demand through restrictions on advertising. It would surely be a Pyrrhic victory for casino owners such as appellant to gain recognition of a First Amendment right to advertise their casinos to the residents of Puerto Rico, only to thereby force the legislature into banning casino gambling by residents altogether. It would just as surely be a strange constitutional doctrine which would concede to the legislature the authority to totally ban a product or activity, but deny to the legislature the authority to forbid the stimulation of demand for the product or activity through advertising on behalf of those who would profit from such increased demand. Legislative regulation of products or activities deemed harmful, such as cigarettes, alcoholic beverages, and prostitution, has varied from outright prohibition on the one hand, see, *e.g.,* Cal. Penal Code Ann. § 647(b) (West Supp.1986) (prohibiting soliciting or engaging in act of prostitution), to legalization of the product or activity with restrictions on stimulation of its demand on the other hand, see, *e.g.,* Nev. Rev. Stat. §§ 244.345(1), (8) (1986) (authorizing licensing of houses of prostitution except in coun-

---

protection analysis. *See* Dunagin v. City of Oxford, Miss., 718 F.2d 738, 752–753 (5th Cir. 1983) (en banc), *cert. denied,* 467 U.S. 1259 (1984).

ties with more than 250,000 population), §§ 201.430, 201.440 (prohibiting advertising of houses of prostitution "[i]n any public theater, on the public streets of any city or town, or on any public highway," or "in [a] place of business").[10] To rule out the latter, intermediate kind of response would require more than we find in the First Amendment.

Appellant's final argument in opposition to the advertising restrictions is that they are unconstitutionally vague. In particular, appellant argues that the statutory language, "to advertise or otherwise offer their facilities," and "the public of Puerto Rico," are not sufficiently defined to satisfy the requirements of due process. Appellant also claims that the term "anunciarse," which appears in the controlling Spanish version of the statute, is actually broader than the English term "to advertise," and could be construed to mean simply "to make known." Even assuming that appellant's argument has merit with respect to the bare statutory language, however, we have already noted that we are bound by the Superior Court's narrowing construction of the statute. Viewed in light of that construction, and particularly with the interpretive assistance of the implementing regulations as modified by the Superior Court, we do not find the statute unconstitutionally vague.

For the foregoing reasons, the decision of the Supreme Court of Puerto Rico that, as construed by the Superior Court, § 8 of the Games of Chance Act of 1948 and the implementing regulations do not facially violate the First Amendment or the due process or equal protection guarantees of the Constitution, is affirmed.[11]

It is so ordered.

United States v. Edge Broadcasting Co.
509 U.S. 418 (1993)

Justice WHITE delivered the opinion of the Court, except as to Part III-D.[*]

In this case we must decide whether federal statutes that prohibit the broadcast of lottery advertising by a broadcaster licensed to a State that does not allow lotteries, while

---

10. *See also* 15 U.S.C. § 1335 (prohibiting cigarette advertising "on any medium of electronic communication subject to the jurisdiction of the Federal Communications Commission"), upheld in Capital Broadcasting Co. v. Mitchell, 333 F. Supp. 582 (D.D.C. 1971), summarily aff'd *sub nom.* Capital Broadcasting Co. v. Acting Attorney General, 405 U.S. 1000 (1972); Fla. Stat. § 561.42(10)-(12) (1985) (prohibiting all signs except for one sign per product in liquor store windows); Mass. Gen. Laws § 138:24 (1974) (authorizing Alcoholic Beverages Control Commission to regulate liquor advertising); Miss. Code Ann. § 67-1-85 (Supp.1985) (prohibiting most forms of liquor sign advertising), *upheld in* Dunagin v. City of Oxford, Miss., *supra;* Ohio Rev. Code Ann. §§ 4301.03(E), 4301.211 (1982) (authorizing Liquor Control Commission to regulate liquor advertising and prohibiting off-premises advertising of beer prices), *upheld in* Queensgate Investment Co. v. Liquor Control Comm'n, 433 N.E.2d 138, appeal dismissed for want of a substantial federal question, 459 U.S. 807 (1982); Okla. Const., Art. 27, § 5, and Okla. Stat., Tit. 37, § 516 (1981) (prohibiting all liquor advertising except for one storefront sign), *upheld in* Oklahoma Telecasters Assn. v. Crisp, 699 F.2d 490 (10th Cir. 1983), *rev'd on other grounds sub nom.* Capital Cities Cable, Inc. v. Crisp, 467 U.S. 691 (1984); Utah Code Ann. §§ 32-7-26 to 32-7-28 (1974) (repealed 1985) (prohibiting all liquor advertising except for one storefront sign).

11. Justice STEVENS claims that the Superior Court's narrowing construction creates an impermissible "prior restraint" on protected speech, because that court required the submission of certain casino advertising to appellee for its prior approval. *See Post,* at 2987. This argument was not raised by appellant either below or in this Court, and we therefore express no view on the constitutionality of the particular portion of the Superior Court's narrowing construction cited by Justice STEVENS.

* Justice O'CONNOR joins Parts I, II, III-A, III-B, and IV of this opinion. Justice SCALIA joins all but Part III-C of this opinion. Justice KENNEDY joins Parts I, II, III-C, and IV of this opinion. Justice SOUTER joins all but Parts III-A, III-B, and III-D of this opinion.

allowing such broadcasting by a broadcaster licensed to a State that sponsors a lottery, are, as applied to respondent, consistent with the First Amendment.

I

While lotteries have existed in this country since its founding, States have long viewed them as a hazard to their citizens and to the public interest, and have long engaged in legislative efforts to control this form of gambling. Congress has, since the early 19th century, sought to assist the States in controlling lotteries.... In 1876, Congress made it a crime to deposit in the mails any letters or circulars concerning lotteries, whether illegal or chartered by state legislatures.... This Court rejected a challenge to the 1876 Act on First Amendment grounds in Ex parte Jackson, 96 U.S. 727 (1878). In response to the persistence of lotteries, particularly the Louisiana Lottery, Congress closed a loophole allowing the advertisement of lotteries in newspapers in the Anti-Lottery Act of 1890, ch. 908, § 1, 26 Stat. 465, codified at Supp. to Rev. Stat. § 3894 (2d ed. 1891), and this Court upheld that Act against a First Amendment challenge in In re Rapier, 143 U.S. 110 (1892). When the Louisiana Lottery moved its operations to Honduras, Congress passed the Act of Mar. 2, 1895, 28 Stat. 963, 18 U.S.C. § 1301, which outlawed the transportation of lottery tickets in interstate or foreign commerce. This Court upheld the constitutionality of that Act against a claim that it exceeded Congress' power under the Commerce Clause in *Lottery Case*, 188 U.S. 321 (1903). This federal antilottery legislation remains in effect. See 18 U.S.C. §§ 1301, 1302.

After the advent of broadcasting, Congress extended the federal lottery control scheme by prohibiting, in § 316 of the Communications Act of 1934, 48 Stat. 1064, 1088, the broadcast of "any advertisement of or information concerning any lottery, gift enterprise, or similar scheme." 18 U.S.C. § 1304, as amended by the Charity Games Advertising Clarification Act of 1988, Pub. L. 100-625, § 3(a)(4), 102 Stat. 3206.[1] In 1975, Congress amended the statutory scheme to allow newspapers and broadcasters to advertise state-run lotteries if the newspaper is published in or the broadcast station is licensed to a State which conducts a state-run lottery. See 18 U.S.C. § 1307 (1988 ed., Supp. III).[2] This ex-

---

1. Title 18 U.S.C. § 1304 (1988 ed., Supp. III) provides: "Broadcasting lottery information: "Whoever broadcasts by means of any radio or television station for which a license is required by any law of the United States, or whoever, operating any such station, knowingly permits the broadcasting of, any advertisement of or information concerning any lottery, gift enterprise, or similar scheme, offering prizes dependent in whole or in part upon lot or chance, or any list of the prizes drawn or awarded by means of any such lottery, gift enterprise, or scheme, whether said list contains any part or all of such prizes, shall be fined not more than $1,000 or imprisoned not more than one year, or both."

2. Title 18 U.S.C. § 1307 (1988 ed. and Supp. III) provides in relevant part: "Exceptions relating to certain advertisements and other information and to State-conducted lotteries

"(a) The provisions of sections 1301, 1302, 1303, and 1304 shall not apply to—

"(1) an advertisement, list of prizes, or other information concerning a lottery conducted by a State acting under the authority of State law which is—

"(A) contained in a publication published in that State or in a State which conducts such a lottery; or

"(B) broadcast by a radio or television station licensed to a location in that State or a State which conducts such a lottery; or

"(2) an advertisement, list of prizes, or other information concerning a lottery, gift enterprise, or similar scheme, other than one described in paragraph (1), that is authorized or not otherwise prohibited by the State in which it is conducted and which is—

"(A) conducted by a not-for-profit organization or a governmental organization; or

"(B) conducted as a promotional activity by a commercial organization and is clearly occasional and ancillary to the primary business of that organization."

emption was enacted "to accommodate the operation of legally authorized State-run lotteries consistent with continued Federal protection to the policies of non-lottery States." S. Rep. No. 93-1404, p. 2 (1974). *See also* H.R. Rep. No. 93-1517, p. 5 (1974), U.S. Code Cong. & Admin. News 1974, p. 7007.

North Carolina does not sponsor a lottery, and participating in or advertising nonexempt raffles and lotteries is a crime under its statutes. N.C. Gen. Stat. §§ 14-289 and 14-291 (1986 and Supp.1992). Virginia, on the other hand, has chosen to legalize lotteries under a state monopoly and has entered the marketplace vigorously.

Respondent, Edge Broadcasting Company (Edge), owns and operates a radio station licensed by the Federal Communications Commission (FCC) to Elizabeth City, North Carolina. This station, known as "Power 94," has the call letters WMYK-FM and broadcasts from Moyock, North Carolina, which is approximately three miles from the border between Virginia and North Carolina and considerably closer to Virginia than is Elizabeth City. Power 94 is one of 24 radio stations serving the Hampton Roads, Virginia, metropolitan area; 92.2% of its listening audience are Virginians; the rest, 7.8%, reside in the nine North Carolina counties served by Power 94. Because Edge is licensed to serve a North Carolina community, the federal statute prohibits it from broadcasting advertisements for the Virginia lottery. Edge derives 95% of its advertising revenue from Virginia sources, and claims that it has lost large sums of money from its inability to carry Virginia lottery advertisements.

Edge entered federal court in the Eastern District of Virginia, seeking a declaratory judgment that, as applied to it, §§ 1304 and 1307, together with corresponding FCC regulations, violated the First Amendment to the Constitution and the Equal Protection Clause of the Fourteenth, as well as injunctive protection against the enforcement of those statutes and regulations.

The District Court recognized that Congress has greater latitude to regulate broadcasting than other forms of communication. App. to Pet. for Cert. 14a–15a. The District Court construed the statutes not to cover the broadcast of noncommercial information about lotteries, a construction that the Government did not oppose. With regard to the restriction on advertising, the District Court evaluated the statutes under the established four-factor test for commercial speech set forth in Central Hudson Gas & Elec. Corp. v. Public Serv. Comm'n of N.Y., 447 U.S. 557, 566 (1980)....

Assuming that the advertising Edge wished to air would deal with the Virginia lottery, a legal activity, and would not be misleading, the court went on to hold that the second and fourth *Central Hudson* factors were satisfied: the statutes were supported by a substantial governmental interest, and the restrictions were no more extensive than necessary to serve that interest, which was to discourage participating in lotteries in States that prohibited lotteries. The court held, however, that the statutes, as applied to Edge, did not directly advance the asserted governmental interest, failed the *Central Hudson* test in this respect, and hence could not be constitutionally applied to Edge. A divided Court of Appeals, in an unpublished *per curiam* opinion, affirmed in all respects, ...

Because the court below declared a federal statute unconstitutional and applied reasoning that was questionable under our cases relating to the regulation of commercial speech, we granted certiorari.... We reverse.

II

The Government argues first that gambling implicates no constitutionally protected right, but rather falls within a category of activities normally considered to be "vices," and that the greater power to prohibit gambling necessarily includes the lesser power to ban its advertisement; it argues that we therefore need not proceed with a *Central Hudson* analysis. The Court of Appeals did not address this issue and neither do we, for the statutes are not unconstitutional under the standards of *Central Hudson* applied by the courts below.

III

For most of this Nation's history, purely commercial advertising was not considered to implicate the constitutional protection of the First Amendment.... In 1976, the Court extended First Amendment protection to speech that does no more than propose a commercial transaction. *See* Virginia State Bd. of Pharmacy v. Virginia Citizens Consumer Council, Inc., 425 U.S. 748 (1976). Our decisions, however, have recognized the "'common-sense' distinction between speech proposing a commercial transaction, which occurs in an area traditionally subject to government regulation, and other varieties of speech." Ohralik v. Ohio State Bar Assn., 436 U.S. 447, 455–56 (1978). The Constitution therefore affords a lesser protection to commercial speech than to other constitutionally guaranteed expression....

In *Central Hudson,* we set out the general scheme for assessing government restrictions on commercial speech. *Supra,* 447 U.S. at 566. Like the courts below, we assume that Edge, if allowed to, would air nonmisleading advertisements about the Virginia lottery, a legal activity. As to the second *Central Hudson* factor, we are quite sure that the Government has a substantial interest in supporting the policy of nonlottery States, as well as not interfering with the policy of States that permit lotteries. As in Posadas de Puerto Rico Associates v. Tourism Co. of P.R., 478 U.S. 328 (1986), the activity underlying the relevant advertising-gambling-implicates no constitutionally protected right; rather, it falls into a category of "vice" activity that could be, and frequently has been, banned altogether. As will later be discussed, we also agree that the statutes are no broader than necessary to advance the Government's interest and hence the fourth part of the *Central Hudson* test is satisfied.

The Court of Appeals, however, affirmed the District Court's holding that the statutes were invalid because, as applied to Edge, they failed to advance directly the governmental interest supporting them. According to the Court of Appeals, whose judgment we are reviewing, this was because the 127,000 people who reside in Edge's nine-county listening area in North Carolina receive most of their radio, newspaper, and television communications from Virginia-based media. These North Carolina residents who might listen to Edge "are inundated with Virginia's lottery advertisements" and hence, the court stated, prohibiting Edge from advertising Virginia's lottery "is ineffective in shielding North Carolina residents from lottery information." This "ineffective or remote measure to support North Carolina's desire to discourage gambling cannot justify infringement upon commercial free speech.".... In our judgment, the courts below erred in that respect.

A

The third *Central Hudson* factor asks whether the "regulation directly advances the governmental interest asserted." 447 U.S. at 566. It is readily apparent that this question cannot be answered by limiting the inquiry to whether the governmental interest is directly advanced as applied to a single person or entity. Even if there were no advancement as applied in that manner—in this case, as applied to Edge—there would remain the matter of the regulation's general application to others—in this case, to all other radio and television stations in North Carolina and countrywide. The courts below thus asked the wrong question in ruling on the third *Central Hudson* factor. This is not to say that the validity of the statutes' application to Edge is an irrelevant inquiry, but that issue properly should be dealt with under the fourth factor of the *Central Hudson* test. As we have said, "[t]he last two steps of the *Central Hudson* analysis basically involve a consideration of the 'fit' between the legislature's ends and the means chosen to accomplish those ends." *Posadas, supra,* 478 U.S. at 341.

We have no doubt that the statutes directly advanced the governmental interest at stake in this case. In response to the appearance of state-sponsored lotteries, Congress might have continued to ban all radio or television lottery advertisements, even by stations in States that have legalized lotteries. This it did not do. Neither did it permit stations such as Edge, located in a non-lottery State, to carry lottery ads if their signals reached into a State that sponsors lotteries; similarly, it did not forbid stations in a lottery State such as Virginia from carrying lottery ads if their signals reached into an adjoining State such as North Carolina where lotteries were illegal. Instead of favoring either the lottery or the nonlottery State, Congress opted to support the anti-gambling policy of a State like North Carolina by forbidding stations in such a State from airing lottery advertising. At the same time it sought not to unduly interfere with the policy of a lottery sponsoring State such as Virginia. Virginia could advertise its lottery through radio and television stations licensed to Virginia locations, even if their signals reached deep into North Carolina. Congress surely knew that stations in one State could often be heard in another but expressly prevented each and every North Carolina station, including Edge, from carrying lottery ads. Congress plainly made the commonsense judgment that each North Carolina station would have an audience in that State, even if its signal reached elsewhere and that enforcing the statutory restriction would insulate each station's listeners from lottery ads and hence advance the governmental purpose of supporting North Carolina's laws against gambling. This congressional policy of balancing the interests of lottery and nonlottery States is the substantial governmental interest that satisfies *Central Hudson,* the interest which the courts below did not fully appreciate. It is also the interest that is directly served by applying the statutory restriction to all stations in North Carolina; and this would plainly be the case even if, as applied to Edge, there were only marginal advancement of that interest.

B

Left unresolved, of course, is the validity of applying the statutory restriction to Edge, an issue that we now address under the fourth *Central Hudson* factor, *i.e.,* whether the regulation is more extensive than is necessary to serve the governmental interest. We revisited that aspect of *Central Hudson* in Board of Trustees of State Univ. of N.Y. v. Fox, 492 U.S. 469 (1989), and concluded that the validity of restrictions on commercial speech should not be judged by standards more stringent than those applied to expressive conduct entitled to full First Amendment protection or to relevant time, place, or manner restrictions. *Id.* at 477–78. We made clear in *Fox* that our commercial speech cases require a fit between the restriction and the government interest that is not necessarily perfect, but reasonable. *Id.* at 480. This was also the approach in *Posadas,* 478 U.S. at 344.

We have no doubt that the fit in this case was a reasonable one. Although Edge was licensed to serve the Elizabeth City area, it chose to broadcast from a more northerly position, which allowed its signal to reach into the Hampton Roads, Virginia, metropolitan area. Allowing it to carry lottery ads reaching over 90% of its listeners, all in Virginia, would surely enhance its revenues. But just as surely, because Edge's signals with lottery ads would be heard in the nine counties in North Carolina that its broadcasts reached, this would be in derogation of the substantial federal interest in supporting North Carolina's laws making lotteries illegal. In this posture, to prevent Virginia's lottery policy from dictating what stations in a neighboring State may air, it is reasonable to require Edge to comply with the restriction against carrying lottery advertising. In other words, applying the restriction to a broadcaster such as Edge directly advances the governmental interest in enforcing the restriction in nonlottery States, while not interfering with the policy of lottery States like Virginia. We think this would be the case even if it were true, which it is not, that applying the general statutory restriction to Edge, in isolation, would no more than marginally insulate the North Carolinians in the North Carolina counties served by Edge from hearing lottery ads.

... [W]e have observed that the validity of time, place, or manner restrictions is determined under standards very similar to those applicable in the commercial speech context and that it would be incompatible with the subordinate position of commercial speech in the scale of First Amendment values to apply a more rigid standard to commercial speech than is applied to fully protected speech.... [These cases teach] us that we judge the validity of the restriction in this case by the relation it bears to the general problem of accommodating the policies of both lottery and nonlottery States, not by the extent to which it furthers the Government's interest in an individual case....

C

We also believe that the courts below were wrong in holding that as applied to Edge itself, the restriction at issue was ineffective and gave only remote support to the Government's interest.

As we understand it, both the Court of Appeals and the District Court recognized that Edge's potential North Carolina audience was the 127,000 residents of nine North Carolina counties, that enough of them regularly or from time to time listen to Edge to account for 11% of all radio listening in those counties, and that while listening to Edge they heard no lottery advertisements. It could hardly be denied, and neither court below purported to deny, that these facts, standing alone, would clearly show that applying the statutory restriction to Edge would directly serve the statutory purpose of supporting North Carolina's antigambling policy by excluding invitations to gamble from 11% of the radio listening time in the nine-county area. Without more, this result could hardly be called either "ineffective," "remote," or "conditional," *see Central Hudson,* 447 U.S., at 564, 569, 100 S. Ct., at 2350, 2353. Nor could it be called only "limited incremental support," Bolger v. Youngs Drug Products Corp., 463 U.S. 60, 73 (1983), for the Government interest, or thought to furnish only speculative or marginal support.... Otherwise, any North Carolina radio station with 127,000 or fewer potential listeners would be permitted to carry lottery ads because of its marginal significance in serving the State's interest.

Of course, both courts below pointed out, and rested their judgment on the fact, that the 127,000 people in North Carolina who might listen to Edge also listened to Virginia radio stations and television stations that regularly carried lottery ads. Virginia newspapers carrying such material also were available to them. This exposure, the courts below thought, was sufficiently pervasive to prevent the restriction on Edge from furnishing any more than ineffective or remote support for the statutory purpose. We disagree with this conclusion because in light of the facts relied on, it represents too limited a view of what amounts to direct advancement of the governmental interest that is present in this case.

Even if all of the residents of Edge's North Carolina service area listen to lottery ads from Virginia stations, it would still be true that 11% of radio listening time in that area would remain free of such material. If Edge is allowed to advertise the Virginia lottery, the percentage of listening time carrying such material would increase from 38% to 49%. We do not think that *Central Hudson* compels us to consider this consequence to be without significance.

The Court of Appeals indicated that Edge's potential audience of 127,000 persons were "inundated" by the Virginia media carrying lottery advertisements. But the District Court found that only 38% of all radio listening in the nine-county area was directed at stations that broadcast lottery advertising.[4] With respect to television, the District Court observed that American adults spend 60% of their media consumption time listening to television. The evidence before it also indicated that in four of the nine counties served by Edge, 75% of all television viewing was directed at Virginia stations; in three others, the figure was between 50 and 75%; and in the remaining two counties, between 25 and 50%. Even if it is assumed that all of these stations carry lottery advertising, it is very likely that a great many people in the nine-county area are exposed to very little or no lottery advertising carried on television. Virginia newspapers are also circulated in Edge's area, 10,400 daily and 12,500 on Sundays, hardly enough to constitute a pervasive exposure to lottery advertising, even on the unlikely assumption that the readers of those newspapers always look for and read the lottery ads. Thus the District Court observed only that "a *significant* number of residents of [the nine-county] area listens to" Virginia radio and television stations and read Virginia newspapers. App. to Pet. for Cert. 25a (emphasis added).

Moreover, to the extent that the courts below assumed that §§ 1304 and 1307 would have to effectively shield North Carolina residents from information about lotteries to advance their purpose, they were mistaken. As the Government asserts, the statutes were not "adopt[ed] ... to keep North Carolina residents ignorant of the Virginia Lottery for ignorance's sake," but to accommodate non-lottery States' interest in discouraging public participation in lotteries, even as they accommodate the countervailing interests of lottery States. Reply Brief for Petitioners 11. Within the bounds of the general protection provided by the Constitution to commercial speech, we allow room for legislative judgments. *Fox,* 492 U.S. at 480. Here, as in *Posadas de Puerto Rico,* the Government obviously legislated on the premise that the advertising of gambling serves to increase the demand for the advertised product. See *Posadas,* 478 U.S. at 344. See also *Central Hudson, supra,* 447 U.S. at 569. Congress clearly was entitled to determine that broadcast of promotional advertising of lotteries undermines North Carolina's policy against gambling, even if the North Carolina audience is not wholly unaware of the lottery's existence. Congress has, for example, altogether banned the broadcast advertising of cigarettes, even though it could hardly have believed that this regulation would keep the public wholly ignorant of the availability of cigarettes. *See* 15 U.S.C. § 1335. *See also* Queensgate Investment Co. v. Liquor Control Comm'n, 433 N.E.2d 138, 142 (alcohol advertising), *app. dism'd for want of a substantial federal question,* 459 U.S. 807 (1982). Nor do we require that the Government make progress on every front before it can make progress on any front. If there is an immediate connection between advertising and demand, and the federal regulation decreases advertising, it stands to reason that the policy of decreasing demand for gambling is correspondingly advanced. Accordingly, the Government may be said to advance its purpose by substantially reducing lottery advertising, even where it is not wholly eradicated.

Thus, even if it were proper to conduct a *Central Hudson* analysis of the statutes only as applied to Edge, we would not agree with the courts below that the restriction at issue here, which prevents Edge from broadcasting lottery advertising to its sizable radio audience in North Carolina, is rendered ineffective by the fact that Virginia radio and television programs can be heard in North Carolina. In our view, the restriction, even as

---

4. It would appear, then, that 51% of the radio listening time in the relevant nine counties is attributable to other North Carolina stations or other stations not carrying lottery advertising.

applied only to Edge, directly advances the governmental interest within the meaning of *Central Hudson*.

D

Nor need we be blind to the practical effect of adopting respondent's view of the level of particularity of analysis appropriate to decide its case. Assuming for the sake of argument that Edge had a valid claim that the statutes violated *Central Hudson* only as applied to it, the piecemeal approach it advocates would act to vitiate the Government's ability generally to accommodate States with differing policies. Edge has chosen to transmit from a location near the border between two jurisdictions with different rules, and rests its case on the spillover from the jurisdiction across the border. Were we to adopt Edge's approach, we would treat a station that is close to the line as if it were on the other side of it, effectively extending the legal regime of Virginia inside North Carolina. One result of holding for Edge on this basis might well be that additional North Carolina communities, farther from the Virginia border, would receive broadcast lottery advertising from Edge. Broadcasters licensed to these communities, as well as other broadcasters serving Elizabeth City, would then be able to complain that lottery advertising from Edge and other similar broadcasters renders the federal statute ineffective as applied to them. Because the approach Edge advocates has no logical stopping point once state boundaries are ignored, this process might be repeated until the policy of supporting North Carolina's ban on lotteries would be seriously eroded. We are unwilling to start down that road.

IV

Because the statutes challenged here regulate commercial speech in a manner that does not violate the First Amendment, the judgment of the Court of Appeals is

Reversed.

Notes

1. Note the considerable deference these decisions gave to the proffered governmental interests that supported the advertising restrictions. In *Posadas*, the Court accepted without any proof the government's argument that the regulation—and restriction— on gaming advertising would reduce the undesirable secondary effects of gambling. Likewise in the *Edge Broadcasting* case, the Court was less than exacting in its application of the fourth *Central Hudson* factor.

In *Posadas*, the majority opinion at one point stated that, "the Puerto Rico Legislature surely could have prohibited casino gambling by the residents of Puerto Rico altogether. In our view, the greater power to completely ban casino gambling necessarily includes the lesser power to ban advertising of casino gambling." 478 U.S. 328, 345–46. Does this statement suggest that because a state may outlaw gambling that any regulation of gambling is constitutionally valid? Does the power of government to ban an underlying activity thereby legitimize *any* restriction of speech related to that activity?

2. In the same year *Edge Broadcasting* was decided, the Supreme Court began to give indications that it would scrutinize more carefully the justifications given for restricting commercial speech. This included requiring the government to establish that the challenged regulation advanced the government's interest "in a direct and material way." Edenfield v. Fane, 507 U.S. 761, 767 (1993). *See also* Rubin v. Coors Brewing Co., 514 U.S. 476 (1995) (invalidating a federal law that prohibited putting the alcohol content on beer labels. The government stated that the regulation would inhibit "strength wars" between

brewers, but the Court held that the government provided no evidence that this limitation "directly and materially" advanced that interest, especially because alcohol content could be disclosed through advertising. In a departure from *Posadas* and *Edge Broadcasting*, the Court declared that government restrictions on commercial speech had to be based on more than "anecdotal evidence and educated guesses," in order to pass constitutional muster under the third and fourth criteria of *Central Hudson*. *Id.* at 491).

But it was in the 1996 decision in 44 *Liquormart, Inc. v. Rhode Island*, 517 U.S. 484 (1996) that the Court announced a retreat from the broad deference that had been accorded governments in *Posadas* and *Edge Broadcasting*. That case involved a challenge to Rhode Island law prohibiting advertising the prices of alcohol. The ostensible purpose of the restriction was to prevent price wars among retailers that would lead to increased alcohol consumption. Only the third and fourth *Central Hudson* factors were at issue, as the parties agreed that the advertising regarded a lawful activity, and the Court accepted the state's claim that there was a substantial government interest in moderating alcohol consumption. But the state failed to establish that the governmental interest was advanced by the blanket ban on price advertising, as the Court found insufficient evidence that the ban would significantly reduce alcohol consumption. The state also failed the fourth *Central Hudson* factor because it did not prove a reasonable "fit" between the advertising ban and its objective. That is, it failed to prove a ban was necessary to achieve the state's interest.

The most significant components of the decision in 44 *Liquormart, Inc.* were: (1) The Court repudiated the *Posadas* concept of giving wide deference to governmental justifications for limiting advertising; (2) No special power was conferred on the state to restrict activity because it involved "vice"; (3) Likewise, the Court found unpersuasive the "power to ban the activity necessarily includes the power to prohibit advertising." Taken together, these conclusions demonstrated that the Court would no longer accord the government the deference that *Posadas* had suggested. Although the case was in the context of another vice, alcohol and not gaming, soon the Court would apply this analysis to the limitations on gambling advertising contained in the 1934 Communications Act.

Greater New Orleans Broadcasting Association, Inc. v. United States
527 U.S. 173 (1999)

Justice STEVENS delivered the opinion of the Court.

Federal law prohibits some, but by no means all, broadcast advertising of lotteries and casino gambling. In United States v. Edge Broadcasting Co., 509 U.S. 418 (1993), we upheld the constitutionality of 18 U.S.C. § 1304 as applied to broadcast advertising of Virginia's lottery by a radio station located in North Carolina, where no such lottery was authorized. Today we hold that § 1304 may not be applied to advertisements of private casino gambling that are broadcast by radio or television stations located in Louisiana, where such gambling is legal.

I

Through most of the 19th and the first half of the 20th centuries, Congress adhered to a policy that not only discouraged the operation of lotteries and similar schemes, but forbade the dissemination of information concerning such enterprises by use of the mails, even when the lottery in question was chartered by a state legislature.... Consistent with this Court's earlier view that commercial advertising was unprotected by the First Amendment, ... we found that the notion that "lotteries ... are supposed to have a demoralizing influence upon the people" provided sufficient justification for excluding circulars concerning such enterprises from the federal postal system, Ex parte Jackson, 96 U.S. 727, 736–37 (1878). We likewise deferred to congressional judgment in upholding the similar exclusion for newspapers that contained either lottery advertisements or prize lists.... The current versions of these early antilottery statutes are now codified at 18 U.S.C. §§ 1301–1303.

Congress extended its restrictions on lottery-related information to broadcasting as communications technology made that practice both possible and profitable. It enacted the statute at issue in this case as § 316 of the Communications Act of 1934, 48 Stat. 1088. Now codified at 18 U.S.C. § 1304 ("Broadcasting lottery information"), the statute prohibits radio and television broadcasting, by any station for which a license is required, of

> "any advertisement of or information concerning any lottery, gift enterprise, or similar scheme, offering prizes dependent in whole or in part upon lot or chance, or any list of the prizes drawn or awarded by means of any such lottery, gift enterprise, or scheme, whether said list contains any part or all of such prizes."

The statute provides that each day's prohibited broadcasting constitutes a separate offense punishable by a fine, imprisonment for not more than one year, or both. *Ibid.* Although § 1304 is a criminal statute, the Solicitor General informs us that, in practice, the provision traditionally has been enforced by the Federal Communications Commission (FCC), which imposes administrative sanctions on radio and television licensees for violations of the agency's implementing regulation.... Petitioners now concede that the broadcast ban in § 1304 and the FCC's regulation encompasses advertising for privately owned casinos—a concession supported by the broad language of the statute, our precedent, and the FCC's sound interpretation....

During the second half of this century, Congress dramatically narrowed the scope of the broadcast prohibition in § 1304. The first inroad was minor: In 1950, certain not-for-profit fishing contests were exempted as "innocent pastimes ... far removed from the reprehensible type of gambling activity which it was paramount in the congressional mind to forbid." S. Rep. No. 2243, 81st Cong., 2d Sess., 2 (1950); see Act of Aug. 16, 1950, ch. 722, 64 Stat. 451, 18 U.S.C. § 1305.

Subsequent exemptions were more substantial. Responding to the growing popularity of state-run lotteries, in 1975 Congress enacted the provision that gave rise to our decision in *Edge*, 509 U.S. at 422–23; Act of Jan. 2, 1975, 88 Stat.1916, 18 U.S.C. § 1307; *see also* § 1953(b)(4). With subsequent modifications, that amendment now exempts advertisements of state-conducted lotteries from the nationwide postal restrictions in §§ 1301 and 1302, and from the broadcast restriction in § 1304, when "broadcast by a radio or television station licensed to a location in ... a State which conducts such a lottery." § 1307(a)(1)(B); *see also* §§ 1307(a)(1)(A), (b)(1). The § 1304 broadcast restriction remained in place, however, for stations licensed in States that do not conduct lotteries. In *Edge*, we held that this remaining restriction on broadcasts from nonlottery States, such as North Carolina, supported the "laws against gambling" in those jurisdictions and properly advanced the "congressional policy of balancing the interests of lottery and nonlottery States." 509 U.S. at 428.

In 1988, Congress enacted two additional statutes that significantly curtailed the coverage of § 1304. First, the Indian Gaming Regulatory Act (IGRA), ... authorized Native American tribes to conduct various forms of gambling—including casino gambling—pursuant to tribal-state compacts if the State permits such gambling "for any purpose by any person, organization, or entity." § 2710(d)(1)(B). The IGRA also exempted "any gaming conducted by an Indian tribe pursuant to" the Act from both the postal and transportation restrictions in 18 U.S.C. §§ 1301–1302, and the broadcast restriction in § 1304. 25 U.S.C. § 2720. Second, the Charity Games Advertising Clarification Act of 1988, 18 U.S.C. § 1307(a)(2), extended the exemption from §§ 1301–1304 for state-run lotteries to include any other lottery, gift enterprise, or similar scheme—not prohibited by the law of the State in which it operates—when conducted by: (i) any governmental organization; (ii) any not-for-profit organization; or (iii) a commercial organization as a promotional activity "clearly occasional and ancillary to the primary business of that organization." There is no dispute that the exemption in § 1307(a)(2) applies to casinos conducted by state and local governments. And, unlike the 1975 broadcast exemption for advertisements of and information concerning state-conducted lotteries, the exemptions in both of these 1988 statutes are not geographically limited; they shield messages from § 1304's reach in States that do not authorize such gambling as well as those that do.

A separate statute, the 1992 Professional and Amateur Sports Protection Act, 28 U.S.C. § 3701 et seq., proscribes most sports betting and advertising thereof. Section 3702 makes it unlawful for a State or tribe "to sponsor, operate, advertise, promote, license, or authorize by law or compact"—or for a person "to sponsor, operate, advertise, or promote, pursuant to the law or compact" of a State or tribe—any lottery or gambling scheme based directly or indirectly on competitive games in which amateur or professional athletes participate. However, the Act also includes a variety of exemptions, some with obscured congressional purposes: (i) gambling schemes conducted by States or other governmental entities at any time between January 1, 1976, and August 31, 1990; (ii) gambling schemes authorized by statutes in effect on October 2, 1991; (iii) gambling "conducted exclusively in casinos" located in certain municipalities if the schemes were authorized within 1 year of the effective date of the Act and, for "commercial casino gaming scheme[s]," that had been in operation for the preceding 10 years pursuant to a state constitutional provision and comprehensive state regulation applicable to that municipality; and (iv) gambling on parimutuel animal racing or jai-alai games. § 3704(a); *see also* 18 U.S.C. §§ 1953(b)(1)–(3) (regarding interstate transportation of wagering paraphernalia). These exemptions make the scope of § 3702's advertising prohibition somewhat unclear, but the prohibition is not limited to broadcast media and does not depend on the location of a broadcast station or other disseminator of promotional materials.

Thus, unlike the uniform federal antigambling policy that prevailed in 1934 when 18 U.S.C. § 1304 was enacted, federal statutes now accommodate both progambling and antigambling segments of the national polity.

II

Petitioners are an association of Louisiana broadcasters and its members who operate FCC-licensed radio and television stations in the New Orleans metropolitan area. But for the threat of sanctions pursuant to § 1304 and the FCC's companion regulation, petitioners would broadcast promotional advertisements for gaming available at private, for-profit casinos that are lawful and regulated in both Louisiana and neighboring Mississippi.... According to an FCC official, however, "[u]nder appropriate conditions, some broadcast signals from Louisiana broadcasting stations may be heard in neighboring states including Texas and Arkansas," ... where private casino gambling is unlawful.

Petitioners brought this action against the United States and the FCC in the District Court for the Eastern District of Louisiana, praying for a declaration that § 1304 and the FCC's regulation violate the First Amendment as applied to them, and for an injunction preventing enforcement of the statute and the rule against them. After noting that all parties agreed that the case should be decided on their cross-motions for summary judgment, the District Court ruled in favor of the Government. 866 F. Supp. 975, 976 (1994). The court applied the standard for assessing commercial speech restrictions set out in Central Hudson Gas & Elec. Corp. v. Public Serv. Comm'n of N.Y., 447 U.S. 557, 566 (1980), and concluded that the restrictions at issue adequately advanced the Government's "substantial interest (1) in protecting the interest of nonlottery states and (2) in reducing participation in gambling and thereby minimizing the social costs associated therewith." 866 F. Supp. at 979. The court pointed out that federal law does not prohibit the broadcast of all information about casinos, such as advertising that promotes a casino's amenities rather than its "gaming aspects," and observed that advertising for state-authorized casinos in Louisiana and Mississippi was actually "abundant." Id. at 980.

A divided panel of the Court of Appeals for the Fifth Circuit agreed with the District Court's application of Central Hudson, and affirmed the grant of summary judgment to the Government. 69 F.3d 1296, 1298 (1995). The panel majority's description of the asserted governmental interests, although more specific, was essentially the same as the District Court's:

> "First, section 1304 serves the interest of assisting states that restrict gambling by regulating interstate activities such as broadcasting that are beyond the powers of the individual states to regulate. The second asserted governmental interest lies in discouraging public participation in commercial gambling, thereby minimizing the wide variety of social ills that have historically been associated with such activities." Id. at 1299.

The majority relied heavily on our decision in Posadas de Puerto Rico Associates v. Tourism Co. of P. R., 478 U.S. 328 (1986), ... and endorsed the theory that, because gambling is in a category of "vice activity" that can be banned altogether, "advertising of gambling can lay no greater claim on constitutional protection than the underlying activity," id. at 1302. In dissent, Chief Judge Politz contended that the many exceptions to the original prohibition in § 1304—and that section's conflict with the policies of States that had legalized gambling—precluded justification of the restriction by either an interest in supporting anticasino state policies or "an independent federal interest in discouraging public participation in commercial gambling." Id. at 1303–1304.

While the broadcasters' petition for certiorari was pending in this Court, we decided 44 Liquormart, Inc. v. Rhode Island, 517 U.S. 484 (1996). Because the opinions in that case concluded that our precedent both preceding and following Posadas had applied the Central Hudson test more strictly, 517 U.S., at 509–510 (opinion of STEVENS, J.); id. at 531–32 (O'CONNOR, J., concurring in judgment)—and because we had rejected the argument that the power to restrict speech about certain socially harmful activities was as broad as the power to prohibit such conduct, see id. at 513–14 (opinion of STEVENS, J.); see also Rubin v. Coors Brewing Co., 514 U.S. 476, 482–83, n. 2 (1995)—we granted the broadcasters' petition, vacated the judgment of the Court of Appeals, and remanded the case for further consideration. 519 U.S. 801 (1996).

On remand, the Fifth Circuit majority adhered to its prior conclusion. 149 F.3d 334 (1998). The majority recognized that at least part of the Central Hudson inquiry had "become a tougher standard for the state to satisfy," 149 F.3d at 338, but held that § 1304's restriction on speech sufficiently advanced the asserted governmental interests and was not "broader than necessary to control participation in casino gambling," id. at 340. Because the Court of Appeals for the Ninth Circuit reached a contrary conclusion in Valley Broadcasting Co. v. United States, 107 F.3d 1328, cert. denied, 522 U.S. 1115 (1998), as did a Federal District Court in Players, International, Inc. v. United States, 988 F. Supp.

497 (D.N.J. 1997), we again granted the broadcasters' petition for certiorari. 525 U.S. 1097 (1999). We now reverse.

III

In a number of cases involving restrictions on speech that is "commercial" in nature, we have employed Central Hudson's four-part test to resolve First Amendment challenges....

In this analysis, the Government bears the burden of identifying a substantial interest and justifying the challenged restriction....

The four parts of the *Central Hudson* test are not entirely discrete. All are important and, to a certain extent, interrelated: Each raises a relevant question that may not be dispositive to the First Amendment inquiry, but the answer to which may inform a judgment concerning the other three. Partly because of these intricacies, petitioners as well as certain judges, scholars, and amici curiae have advocated repudiation of the *Central Hudson* standard and implementation of a more straightforward and stringent test for assessing the validity of governmental restrictions on commercial speech.... As the opinions in *44 Liquormart* demonstrate, reasonable judges may disagree about the merits of such proposals. It is, however, an established part of our constitutional jurisprudence that we do not ordinarily reach out to make novel or unnecessarily broad pronouncements on constitutional issues when a case can be fully resolved on a narrower ground.... In this case, there is no need to break new ground. *Central Hudson*, as applied in our more recent commercial speech cases, provides an adequate basis for decision.

IV

All parties to this case agree that the messages petitioners wish to broadcast constitute commercial speech, and that these broadcasts would satisfy the first part of the *Central Hudson* test: Their content is not misleading and concerns lawful activities, i.e., private casino gambling in Louisiana and Mississippi. As well, the proposed commercial messages would convey information—whether taken favorably or unfavorably by the audience—about an activity that is the subject of intense public debate in many communities. In addition, petitioners' broadcasts presumably would disseminate accurate information as to the operation of market competitors, such as pay-out ratios, which can benefit listeners by informing their consumption choices and fostering price competition. Thus, even if the broadcasters' interest in conveying these messages is entirely pecuniary, the interests of, and benefit to, the audience may be broader....

The second part of the *Central Hudson* test asks whether the asserted governmental interest served by the speech restriction is substantial. The Solicitor General identifies two such interests: (1) reducing the social costs associated with "gambling" or "casino gambling," and (2) assisting States that "restrict gambling" or "prohibit casino gambling" within their own borders.... Underlying Congress' statutory scheme, the Solicitor General contends, is the judgment that gambling contributes to corruption and organized crime; underwrites bribery, narcotics trafficking, and other illegal conduct; imposes a regressive tax on the poor; and "offers a false but sometimes irresistible hope of financial advancement." Brief for Respondents 15–16. With respect to casino gambling, the Solicitor General states that many of the associated social costs stem from "pathological" or "compulsive" gambling by approximately 3 million Americans, whose behavior is primarily associated with "continuous play" games, such as slot machines. He also observes that compulsive gambling has grown along with the expansion of legalized gambling nationwide, leading to billions of dollars in economic costs; injury and loss to these gamblers as well as their families, communities, and government; and street, white-collar, and organized crime. *Id.* at 16–20.

We can accept the characterization of these two interests as "substantial," but that conclusion is by no means self-evident. No one seriously doubts that the Federal Government may assert a legitimate and substantial interest in alleviating the societal ills recited above, or in assisting like-minded States to do the same.... But in the judgment of both the Congress and many state legislatures, the social costs that support the suppression of gambling are offset, and sometimes outweighed, by countervailing policy considerations, primarily in the form of economic benefits.[5] Despite its awareness of the potential social costs, Congress has not only sanctioned casino gambling for Indian tribes through tribal-state compacts, but has enacted other statutes that reflect approval of state legislation that authorizes a host of public and private gambling activities.... That Congress has generally exempted state-run lotteries and casinos from federal gambling legislation reflects a decision to defer to, and even promote, differing gambling policies in different States. Indeed, in *Edge* we identified the federal interest furthered by § 1304's partial broadcast ban as the "congressional policy of balancing the interests of lottery and nonlottery States." 509 U.S. at 428.... Whatever its character in 1934 when § 1304 was adopted, the federal policy of discouraging gambling in general, and casino gambling in particular, is now decidedly equivocal.

...

Of course, it is not our function to weigh the policy arguments on either side of the nationwide debate over whether and to what extent casino and other forms of gambling should be legalized. Moreover, enacted congressional policy and "governmental interests" are not necessarily equivalents for purposes of commercial speech analysis.... But we cannot ignore Congress' unwillingness to adopt a single national policy that consistently endorses either interest asserted by the Solicitor General.... Even though the Government has identified substantial interests, when we consider both their quality and the information sought to be suppressed, the crosscurrents in the scope and application of § 1304 become more difficult for the Government to defend.

V

The third part of the *Central Hudson* test asks whether the speech restriction directly and materially advances the asserted governmental interest. "This burden is not satisfied by mere speculation or conjecture; rather, a governmental body seeking to sustain a re-

---

5. Some form of gambling is legal in nearly every State.... Thirty-seven States and the District of Columbia operate lotteries.... National Gambling Impact Study Commission, Staff Report: Lotteries 1 (1999). As of 1997, commercial casino gambling existed in 11 States, see North American Gaming Report 1997, Int'l Gaming & Wagering Bus., July 1997, pp. S4–S31, and at least 5 authorize state-sponsored video gambling, see Del. Code Ann., Tit. 29, §§ 4801, 4803(f)–(g), 4820 (1974 and Supp.1997); Ore. Rev. Stat. § 461.215 (1998); R.I. Gen. Laws § 42-61.2-2(a) (1998); S.D. Const., Art. III, § 25 (1999); S.D. Comp. Laws Ann. §§ 42-7A-4(4), (11A) (1991); W. Va. Code § 29-22A-4 (1999). Also as of 1997, about half the States in the Union hosted Class III Indian gaming (which may encompass casino gambling), including Louisiana, Mississippi, and four other States that had private casinos. United States General Accounting Office, Casino Gaming Regulation: Roles of Five States and the National Indian Gaming Commission 4–6 (May 1998) (including Indian casino gaming in five States without approved compacts); cf. National Gambling Impact Study Commission, Staff Report: Native American Gaming 2 (1999) (hereinafter Native American Gaming) (noting that 14 States have on-reservation Indian casinos, and that those casinos are the only casinos in 8 States). One count by the Bureau of Indian Affairs tallied 60 tribes that advertise their casinos on television and radio. Government Lodging 408, 435–437 (3 App. in Player's Int'l, Inc. v. United States, No. 98-5127 (C.A.3)). By the mid-1990s, tribal casino-style gambling generated over $3 billion in gaming revenue-increasing its share to 18% of all casino gaming revenue, matching the total for the casinos in Atlantic City, New Jersey, and reaching about half the figure for Nevada's casinos.

striction on commercial speech must demonstrate that the harms it recites are real and that its restriction will in fact alleviate them to a material degree." *Edenfield*, 507 U.S. at 770–71. Consequently, "the regulation may not be sustained if it provides only ineffective or remote support for the government's purpose." *Central Hudson*, 447 U.S. at 564. We have observed that "this requirement is critical; otherwise, 'a State could with ease restrict commercial speech in the service of other objectives that could not themselves justify a burden on commercial expression.'" *Rubin*, 514 U.S. at 487, quoting *Edenfield*, 507 U.S. at 771.

The fourth part of the test complements the direct-advancement inquiry of the third, asking whether the speech restriction is not more extensive than necessary to serve the interests that support it. The Government is not required to employ the least restrictive means conceivable, but it must demonstrate narrow tailoring of the challenged regulation to the asserted interest — "a fit that is not necessarily perfect, but reasonable; that represents not necessarily the single best disposition but one whose scope is in proportion to the interest served." *Fox*, 492 U.S. at 480 (internal quotation marks omitted); *see 44 Liquormart*, 517 U.S. at 529, 531 (O'Connor, J., concurring in judgment). On the whole, then, the challenged regulation should indicate that its proponent "'carefully calculated' the costs and benefits associated with the burden on speech imposed by its prohibition." Cincinnati v. Discovery Network, Inc., 507 U.S. 410, 417 (1993) (quoting *Fox*, 492 U.S. at 480).

As applied to petitioners' case, §1304 cannot satisfy these standards. With regard to the first asserted interest — alleviating the social costs of casino gambling by limiting demand — the Government contends that its broadcasting restrictions directly advance that interest because "promotional" broadcast advertising concerning casino gambling increases demand for such gambling, which in turn increases the amount of casino gambling that produces those social costs. Additionally, the Government believes that compulsive gamblers are especially susceptible to the pervasiveness and potency of broadcast advertising.... Assuming the accuracy of this causal chain, it does not necessarily follow that the Government's speech ban has directly and materially furthered the asserted interest. While it is no doubt fair to assume that more advertising would have some impact on overall demand for gambling, it is also reasonable to assume that much of that advertising would merely channel gamblers to one casino rather than another. More important, any measure of the effectiveness of the Government's attempt to minimize the social costs of gambling cannot ignore Congress' simultaneous encouragement of tribal casino gambling, which may well be growing at a rate exceeding any increase in gambling or compulsive gambling that private casino advertising could produce.... And, as the Court of Appeals recognized, the Government fails to "connect casino gambling and compulsive gambling with broadcast advertising for casinos" — let alone broadcast advertising for non-Indian commercial casinos. 149 F.3d at 339....

We need not resolve the question whether any lack of evidence in the record fails to satisfy the standard of proof under Central Hudson, however, because the flaw in the Government's case is more fundamental: The operation of §1304 and its attendant regulatory regime is so pierced by exemptions and inconsistencies that the Government cannot hope to exonerate it.... Under current law, a broadcaster may not carry advertising about privately operated commercial casino gambling, regardless of the location of the station or the casino. 18 U.S.C. §1304; 47 CFR §73.1211(a) (1998). On the other hand, advertisements for tribal casino gambling authorized by state compacts — whether operated by the tribe or by a private party pursuant to a management contract — are subject to no such broadcast ban, even if the broadcaster is located in, or broadcasts to, a jurisdiction with the strictest of antigambling policies. 25 U.S.C. § 2720. Government-operated, nonprofit, and "occasional and ancillary" commercial casinos are likewise exempt. 18 U.S.C. § 1307(a)(2).

The FCC's interpretation and application of §§ 1304 and 1307 underscore the statute's infirmity. Attempting to enforce the underlying purposes and policy of the statute, the FCC has permitted broadcasters to tempt viewers with claims of "Vegas-style excitement" at a commercial "casino," if "casino" is part of the establishment's proper name and the advertisement can be taken to refer to the casino's amenities, rather than directly promote its gaming aspects.[7] While we can hardly fault the FCC in view of the statute's focus on the suppression of certain types of information, the agency's practice is squarely at odds with the governmental interests asserted in this case.

From what we can gather, the Government is committed to prohibiting accurate product information, not commercial enticements of all kinds, and then only when conveyed over certain forms of media and for certain types of gambling—indeed, for only certain brands of casino gambling—and despite the fact that messages about the availability of such gambling are being conveyed over the airwaves by other speakers.

Even putting aside the broadcast exemptions for arguably distinguishable sorts of gambling that might also give rise to social costs about which the Federal Government is concerned—such as state lotteries and parimutuel betting on horse and dog races, § 1307(a)(1)(B); 28 U.S.C. § 3704(a)—the Government presents no convincing reason for pegging its speech ban to the identity of the owners or operators of the advertised casinos. The Government cites revenue needs of States and tribes that conduct casino gambling, and notes that net revenues generated by the tribal casinos are dedicated to the welfare of the tribes and their members. *See* 25 U.S.C. §§ 2710(b)(2)(B), (d)(1)(A)(ii), (2)(A). Yet the Government admits that tribal casinos offer precisely the same types of gambling as private casinos. Further, the Solicitor General does not maintain that government-operated casino gaming is any different, that States cannot derive revenue from taxing private casinos, or that any one class of casino operators is likely to advertise in a meaningfully distinct manner from the others. The Government's suggestion that Indian casinos are too isolated to warrant attention is belied by a quick review of tribal geography and the Government's own evidence regarding the financial success of tribal gaming.... If distance were determinative, Las Vegas might have remained a relatively small community, or simply disappeared like a desert mirage.

Ironically, the most significant difference identified by the Government between tribal and other classes of casino gambling is that the former is "heavily regulated." ... If such direct regulation provides a basis for believing that the social costs of gambling in tribal casinos are sufficiently mitigated to make their advertising tolerable, one would have thought that Congress might have at least experimented with comparable regulation before abridging the speech rights of federally *un*regulated casinos. While Congress' failure to institute such direct regulation of private casino gambling does not necessarily compromise the constitutionality of § 1304, it does undermine the asserted justifications for the restriction before us.... There surely are practical and nonspeech-related forms of regulation—including a prohibition or supervision of gambling on credit; limitations on the use of cash machines on casino premises; controls on admissions; pot or betting

---

7. *See, e.g.,* Letter to DR Partners, 8 FCC Rcd 44 (1992); In re WTMJ, Inc., 8 FCC Rcd 4354 (1993) (disapproving of the phrase "Vegas style games"); *see also* 2 Record 493, 497–498 (Mass Media Bureau letter to Forbes W. Blair, Apr. 10, 1987) (concluding that a proposed television commercial stating that the "odds for fun are high" at the sponsor's establishment would be lawful); *id.* at 492, 500–01.

limits; location restrictions; and licensing requirements—that could more directly and effectively alleviate some of the social costs of casino gambling.

We reached a similar conclusion in *Rubin*. There, we considered the effect of conflicting federal policies on the Government's claim that a speech restriction materially advanced its interest in preventing so-called "strength wars" among competing sellers of certain alcoholic beverages. We concluded that the effect of the challenged restriction on commercial speech had to be evaluated in the context of the entire regulatory scheme, rather than in isolation, and we invalidated the restriction based on the "overall irrationality of the Government's regulatory scheme." *Id.* at 488. As in this case, there was "little chance" that the speech restriction could have directly and materially advanced its aim, "while other provisions of the same Act directly undermine[d] and counteract[ed] its effects." *Id.* at 489. Coupled with the availability of other regulatory options which could advance the asserted interests "in a manner less intrusive to [petitioners'] First Amendment rights," we found that the Government could not satisfy the *Central Hudson* test. *Id.* at 490–91.

Given the special federal interest in protecting the welfare of Native Americans, see California v. Cabazon Band of Mission Indians, 480 U.S. 202, 216–17 (1987), we recognize that there may be valid reasons for imposing commercial regulations on non-Indian businesses that differ from those imposed on tribal enterprises. It does not follow, however, that those differences also justify abridging non-Indians' freedom of speech more severely than the freedom of their tribal competitors. For the power to prohibit or to regulate particular conduct does not necessarily include the power to prohibit or regulate speech about that conduct. *44 Liquormart,* 517 U.S. at 509–11 (opinion of Stevens, J.); . . . . It is well settled that the First Amendment mandates closer scrutiny of government restrictions on speech than of its regulation of commerce alone. . . . And to the extent that the purpose and operation of federal law distinguishes among information about tribal, governmental, and private casinos based on the identity of their owners or operators, the Government presents no sound reason why such lines bear any meaningful relationship to the particular interest asserted: minimizing casino gambling and its social costs by way of a (partial) broadcast ban. . . . Even under the degree of scrutiny that we have applied in commercial speech cases, decisions that select among speakers conveying virtually identical messages are in serious tension with the principles undergirding the First Amendment. . . .

The second interest asserted by the Government—the derivative goal of "assisting" States with policies that disfavor private casinos—adds little to its case. We cannot see how this broadcast restraint, ambivalent as it is, might directly and adequately further any state interest in dampening consumer demand for casino gambling if it cannot achieve the same goal with respect to the similar federal interest.

Furthermore, even assuming that the state policies on which the Federal Government seeks to embellish are more coherent and pressing than their federal counterpart, § 1304 sacrifices an intolerable amount of truthful speech about lawful conduct when compared to all of the policies at stake and the social ills that one could reasonably hope such a ban to eliminate. The Government argues that petitioners' speech about private casino gambling should be prohibited in Louisiana because, "under appropriate conditions," ... citizens in neighboring States like Arkansas and Texas (which hosts tribal, but not private, commercial casino gambling) might hear it and make rash or costly decisions. To be sure, in order to achieve a broader objective such regulations may incidentally, even deliberately, restrict a certain amount of speech not thought to contribute significantly to the dangers with which the Government is concerned. . . . But Congress' choice here was neither a rough approximation of efficacy, nor a reasonable accommodation of competing state and private interests.

Rather, the regulation distinguishes among the indistinct, permitting a variety of speech that poses the same risks the Government purports to fear, while banning messages unlikely to cause any harm at all. Considering the manner in which § 1304 and its exceptions operate and the scope of the speech it proscribes, the Government's second asserted interest provides no more convincing basis for upholding the regulation than the first.

VI

Accordingly, respondents cannot overcome the presumption that the speaker and the audience, not the Government, should be left to assess the value of accurate and nonmisleading information about lawful conduct. *Edenfield*, 507 U.S. at 767. Had the Federal Government adopted a more coherent policy, or accommodated the rights of speakers in States that have legalized the underlying conduct, *see Edge*, 509 U.S. at 428, this might be a different case. But under current federal law, as applied to petitioners and the messages that they wish to convey, the broadcast prohibition in 18 U.S.C. § 1304 and 47 CFR § 73.1211 (1998) violates the First Amendment. The judgment of the Court of Appeals is therefore

Reversed.

Notes

1. The Supreme Court's analysis of commercial speech as it related to gambling advertising made an abrupt turnaround between *Posadas* in 1986 and *Greater New Orleans* in 1999. Commercial "vice" advertising would be treated no differently than any other commercial speech. In fact, the Court drew parallels between gambling advertising and the advertising of drug prices in *Virginia State Board of Pharmacy*. This indicated that as long as the advertising was non-deceptive and related to legal activity, the Court would not make moral judgments about the activity involved. Absent a finding that the gambling advertised was illegal, a point that is directly relevant to advertising for internet gambling discussed in Chapter 12, government would have to identify a "substantial interest" that the restriction "directly and materially advanced" without unduly harming the expression interests involved. After *Greater New Orleans*, the Department of Justice announced that it would not seek to prosecute a casino advertiser under federal law. *See* Letter from Janet Reno, Attorney General of the United States, to the Speaker of the House (Sept. 25, 2000), *available at* http://www.justice.gov/olc/18usc1302.htm.

2. While the federal government may not seek to restrict gambling advertising as noted above, what about states? Do states have the authority to enforce laws restricting this advertising? In 2004, the Nevada Gaming Commission sought to impose disciplinary sanctions on the Hard Rock Casino in Nevada for advertising that was described as "racy."

> A billboard ad which ran during the National Finals Rodeo featured a barely clad woman with her panties around her ankles. The Hard Rock slogan read: "Get ready to buck all night." A radio ad promoting Monday Night Football for the Hard Rock's "young, edgy demographics" declared: "At the Hard Rock we believe in your Monday night rights: large quantities of prescription stimulants, having wives in two states ... Tell your wives you are going; if they are hot, bring them along." Another ad showed a truck driver surrounded by women at the Hard Rock pool. The slogan was: "Rehab" spelled with the "R" shaped like the prescription drug symbol Rx.

> By the beginning of this year, the [Gaming Control Board] had had enough. On January 21, the Board unanimously approved and filed a three-count complaint alleging that the Hard Rock's sexually suggestive ads amounted to a "failure to

conduct advertising and public relations in accordance with decency, dignity, good taste, honesty and inoffensiveness" in violation of a state gaming regulation against unsuitable methods of operation. The ads cited by the GCB were the Hard Rock's "There's always a temptation to cheat," "Get ready to buck all night," and the "Monday night rights: large quantities of prescription stimulants, having wives in two states."

David Thompson, *The Hard Rock Casino: An In-Depth Observation: Constitutional Questions? Or Is There Something Else Involved?* NEV. OBSERVER, Oct. 1, 2004, *available at* http://www.nevadaobserver.com/Archive/041001/Featurestory.htm. The disciplinary action was premised on Nevada gaming regulations which provided:

5.011 Grounds for disciplinary action. The board and the commission deem any activity on the part of any licensee, his agents or employees, that is inimical to the public health, safety, morals, good order and general welfare of the people of the State of Nevada, or that would reflect or tend to reflect discredit upon the State of Nevada or the gaming industry, to be an unsuitable method of operation and shall be grounds for disciplinary action by the board and the commission in accordance with the Nevada Gaming Control Act and the regulations of the board and the commission. Without limiting the generality of the foregoing, the following acts or omissions may be determined to be unsuitable methods of operation:

. . .

Failure to conduct advertising and public relations activities in accordance with decency, dignity, good taste, honesty and inoffensiveness, including, but not limited to, advertising that is false or materially misleading. *See* http://gaming.nv.gov/stats_regs/reg5.pdf.

Ultimately, the enforcement proceedings were dropped after a settlement agreement was reached. Hard Rock Café was required to pay a $100,000 fine, but admitted no wrongdoing. *See* Richard N. Velotta, *Gaming Commission set to Vote on Hard Rock Settlement*, CASINO CITY TIMES, Nov. 16, 2004, *available at* http://www.casinocitytimes.com/article/gaming-commission-set-to-vote-on-hard-rock-settlement-48647. Are there constitutional issues with such enforcement efforts?

3. The issue of the constitutionality of commercial speech regulation has been written about extensively. As it relates to gambling advertising, *see* Michael Hoefges & Milagros Rivera-Sanchez, *Vice Advertising under the Supreme Court's Commercial Speech Doctrine: The Shifting* Central Hudson *Analysis*, 22 HASTINGS COMM. & ENT. L.J. 345 (2000); Kathleen E. Burke, *Greater New Orleans v. United States: Broadcasters Have Lady Luck, or at Least the First Amendment, on Their Side*, 35 NEW. ENG. L. REV. 471 (2001); Megan E. Frese, Note, *Rolling the Dice: Are Online Gambling Advertisers "Aiding and Abetting" Criminal Activity or Exercising First Amendment-Protected Commercial Speech?* 15 FORDHAM INTELL. PROP. MEDIA & ENT. L.J. 547 (2005); Nelson Rose, *The Problem of Advertising Internet and Interactive Gaming*, 13 GAMING L. REV. & ECON. 478 (2009); Kraig P. Grahmann, *Betting on Prohibition: The Federal Government's Approach to Internet Gambling*, 7 Nw. J. TECH. & INTELL. PROP. 161 (2009);

4. As discussed, the *Central Hudson* analysis provides that the activity seeking First Amendment protection "must concern lawful activity." This has become a prominent part of the dispute regarding the advertising of online casinos. If online gaming is illegal, those seeking to advertise their online gambling services would not be protected by the First Amendment. This dispute is one of the core issues involving internet gaming and is addressed in Chapter 12.

Part V
Other Forms of Gambling

Chapter 14

Sports Betting and Poker

1. Introduction

Sports betting is one of America's favorite pastimes. From football to basketball to baseball to hockey to soccer, and so on, America's appetite for placing a "sporting wager" on sports is a substantial one indeed. In 2009, the legal wagers placed in Nevada sports books totaled more than $2.5 billion. The two biggest sports betting events in the United States are the NFL's "Super Bowl" and the NCAA Men's Basketball Championships, often called "March Madness." Recent years have shown nearly $100 million wagered on the Super Bowl in Las Vegas sports books, while March Madness totaled nearly $80 million. Not only are the dollar amounts wagered on sports in Nevada huge, so are the venues created for this activity. For example, at Caesars Palace in Las Vegas, mammoth television screens, 12-by-15 feet, display sporting events for all to see and wager on. One can pick from the multitude of games available for wagering posted on a L.E.D. board, which is even larger than the televisions. A New York Times piece recounted the "cultish" and so-cial nature of this type of gambling. *See* Matt Villano, *Victory Never Smelled Worse,* N.Y. TIMES, Mar. 25, 2007, *available at* 2007 WLNR 5612002, for a detailed description of "March Madness" Las Vegas style.

The large dollar amounts wagered at Nevada sports books on sporting events are dwarfed by the amount bet *illegally*. Of the estimated $8 billion wagered on the Super Bowl, over 97% of that amount is bet illegally. The FBI estimates that $2.5 billion is illegally wagered on March Madness. This does not even take into account amounts put into the ubiquitous "office pool." Enforcing laws prohibiting such gambling is espe-cially challenging given its pervasiveness. The widespread nature of sports betting re-moves, or at least dilutes, the moral stigma attached to it. Along these same lines, issues relating to the incredible explosion of "fantasy sports" have become more promi-nent. Do these activities involve illegal wagering, or are they harmless rites of sport-ing camaraderie?

Sports betting is not confined to the United States. Its vast global presence measures in the hundreds of billions of dollars. Many issues emanating from the emergence of the Internet as a means of gambling relate to sports betting. (*See* Chapter 12 — Internet Gambling).

In the minds of many, poker is a discrete form of gambling that should never be con-sidered in the same context as sports wagering. Nevertheless, money bet on poker legally and illegally is subject to many of the same legal considerations as sports betting.

2. Legal and/or State Regulated Sports Wagering

A. Outside the State of Nevada

For reasons discussed in the next section, few examples of legal sports betting exist outside the state of Nevada. The following case focuses on one sport where betting, illegal and legal, has been prevalent.

National Football League v. Governor of State of Delaware
435 F. Supp. 1372 (D. Del. 1977)

STAPLETON, District Judge:

In August 1976, the Office of the Delaware State Lottery announced a plan to institute a lottery game based on games of the National Football League ("NFL"). Immediately thereafter, the NFL and its twenty-eight member clubs filed suit in this Court against the Governor and the Director of the State Lottery seeking preliminary and permanent injunctive relief barring such a lottery scheme. The State of Delaware intervened, and the complaint was amended to add a request that the Court create a constructive trust on behalf of the NFL clubs of all revenues derived from such a lottery. Finding no threat of immediate irreparable injury to the NFL, the Court denied the prayer for a temporary restraining order.

During the week of September 12, 1976, the football lottery games commenced. Upon defendants' motion, the Court dismissed plaintiffs' claims that the games violated the Equal Protection Clause of the Fourteenth Amendment and the Commerce Clause of the Constitution. With respect to twelve other counts, defendants' motion to dismiss or for summary judgment was denied. The lottery games continued through the season....

FACTUAL BACKGROUND

The Delaware football lottery is known as "Scoreboard" and it involves three different games, "Football Bonus", "Touchdown" and "Touchdown II". All are weekly games based on regularly scheduled NFL games. In Football Bonus, the fourteen games scheduled for a given weekend are divided into two pools of seven games each. A player must mark the lottery ticket with his or her projections of the winners of the seven games in one or both of the two pools and place a bet of $1, $2, $3, $5 or $10. To win Football Bonus, the player must correctly select the winner of each of the games in a pool. If the player correctly selects the winners of all games in both pools, he or she wins an "All Game Bonus". The amounts of the prizes awarded are determined on a pari-mutuel basis, that is, as a function of the total amount of money bet by all players.

In Touchdown, the lottery card lists the fourteen games for a given week along with three ranges of possible point spreads. The player must select both the winning team and the winning margin in each of three, four or five games. The scale of possible bets is the same as in Bonus and prizes are likewise distributed on a pari-mutuel basis to those who make correct selections for each game on which they bet.

Touchdown II, the third Scoreboard game, was introduced in mid-season and replaced Touchdown for the remainder of the season. In Touchdown II, a "line" or predicted point spread on each of twelve games is published on the Wednesday prior to the games. The player considers the published point spread and selects a team to "beat the line", that is, to do better in the game than the stated point spread. To win, the player must choose correctly with respect to each of from four to twelve games. Depending upon the number of games bet on, there is a fixed payoff of from $10 to $1,200. There is also a consolation prize for those who beat the line on nine out ten, ten out of eleven or eleven out of twelve games.

Scoreboard tickets are available from duly authorized agents of the Delaware State Lottery, usually merchants located throughout the State. The tickets list the teams by city names, e. g., Tampa or Cincinnati, rather than by nicknames such as Buccaneers or Bengals. Revenues are said to be distributed pursuant to a fixed apportionment schedule among the players of Scoreboard, the State, the sales agents and the Lottery Office for its administrative expenses.

THE PARTIES' CLAIMS

The core of plaintiffs' objections to Scoreboard is what they term a "forced association with gambling". They complain that the football lottery constitutes an unlawful interference with their property rights and they oppose its operation on a host of federal, state and common law grounds. Briefly stated, their complaint includes counts based on federal and state trademark laws, the common law doctrine of misappropriation, the federal anti-gambling laws, the Civil Rights Act of 1871, (42 U.S.C. § 1983), the Delaware Constitution and the Delaware lottery statute.

The defendants deny that the state-run revenue raising scheme violates any federal, state or common law doctrine. Further, they have filed a counterclaim for treble damages under the Sherman and Clayton Acts for federal antitrust law violations charging, inter alia, that the plaintiffs have brought this litigation for purposes of harassment and that they have conspired to monopolize property which is in the public domain.

For the reasons which follow, I have determined that the plaintiffs are entitled to limited injunctive relief, in the nature of a disclaimer on all Scoreboard materials disseminated to the public. The Touchdown II game will also be invalidated. In all other respects, their claims for relief are denied. The defendants' claim for treble damages is likewise denied.

1. Misappropriation

Plaintiffs have proven that they have invested time, effort, talent and vast sums of money in the organization, development and promotion of the National Football League. They have also convincingly demonstrated the success of that investment. The NFL is now a national institution which enjoys great popularity and a reputation for integrity. It generates substantial revenue from gate receipts, broadcasting rights, film rights, and the licensing of its trademarks.

There also can be no dispute that the NFL popularity and reputation played a major role in defendants' choice of NFL games as the subject matter of its lottery. Defendants concede that in making this election they expected to generate revenue which would not be generated from betting on a less popular pastime.

Based on these facts, plaintiffs assert that defendants are misappropriating the product of plaintiffs' efforts or in the words of the Supreme Court, that the State of Delaware is "endeavoring to reap where it has not sown". International News Service v. Associated Press, 248 U.S. 215, 239 (1918) ("INS "). Thus, plaintiffs maintain the lottery must be halted and the ill-gotten gains disgorged.

This Court has no doubt about the continuing vitality of the INS case and the doctrine of misappropriation which it spawned. I conclude, however, that plaintiffs' argument paints with too broad a brush.

The only tangible product of plaintiffs' labor which defendants utilize in the Delaware Lottery are the schedule of NFL games and the scores. These are obtained from public sources and are utilized only after plaintiffs have disseminated them at large and no longer have any expectation of generating revenue from further dissemination. This fact distinguishes the situation in INS. In that case the Court recognized the right of INS to protection against misappropriation of the news it had collected for so long as that "product" still retained commercial value to AP. The court was careful to note that the injunction issued by the District Court limited the protection granted only until the time when "(the) commercial value as news to ... (AP) and all of its ... (customers had) passed away". 248 U.S. at 245. I do not believe the INS case or any other case suggests use of information that another has voluntarily made available to the public at large is an actionable "misappropriation".

Plaintiffs insist, however, that defendants are using more than the schedules and scores to generate revenue for the State. They define their "product" as being the total "end result" of their labors, including the public interest which has been generated.

It is undoubtedly true that defendants seek to profit from the popularity of NFL football. The question, however, is whether this constitutes wrongful misappropriation. I think not.

We live in an age of economic and social interdependence. The NFL undoubtedly would not be in the position it is today if college football and the fan interest that it generated had not preceded the NFL's organization. To that degree it has benefited from the labor of others. The same, of course, can be said for the mass media networks which the labor of others have developed.

What the Delaware Lottery has done is to offer a service to that portion of plaintiffs' following who wish to bet on NFL games. It is true that Delaware is thus making profits it would not make but for the existence of the NFL, but I find this difficult to distinguish from the multitude of charter bus companies who generate profit from servicing those of plaintiffs' fans who want to go to the stadium or, indeed, the sidewalk popcorn salesman who services the crowd as it surges towards the gate....

The NFL plaintiffs, however, argue that this case is different because the evidence is said to show "misappropriation" of plaintiffs' "good will" and "reputation" as well as its "popularity". To a large extent, plaintiffs' references to "good will" and "reputation" are simply other ways of stating their complaint that defendants are profiting from a demand plaintiffs' games have generated. To the extent they relate to a claim that defendants' activities have damaged, as opposed to appropriated, plaintiff's good will and reputation, I believe one must look to other lines of authority to determine defendants' culpability. In response to plaintiffs' misappropriation argument, I hold only that defendants' use of the NFL schedules, scores and public popularity in the Delaware Lottery does not constitute a misappropriation of plaintiffs' property.

In the event a differing analysis is determined to be appropriate in the course of appellate review, I should add that the plaintiffs have not demonstrated that the existence of gambling on its games, per se, has or will damage its good will or reputation for integrity. By this, I do not suggest that an association of the NFL with a gambling enterprise in the minds of the public would not have a deleterious effect on its business. Such an association presupposes public perception of NFL sponsorship or approval of a gambling enterprise or at least confusion on this score, and I treat this subject hereafter. I do find, however, that the existence of gambling on NFL games, unaccompanied by any confusion with respect to sponsorship, has not injured the NFL and there is no reason to believe it will do so in the future. The record shows that extensive gambling on NFL games has existed for many years and that this fact of common public knowledge has not injured plaintiffs or their reputation.

The most prevalent form of such gambling is the illegal form office polls and head-to-head bets with bookies. Virtually every witness testified that he was familiar with illegal football pools and knew they were available in schools, factories and offices around the country. John J. Danahy, Director of Security for the NFL and a former member of the Federal Bureau of Investigation, estimated that millions of dollars a week are spent for illegal betting on football games and that such gambling provides a major source of income to organized crime.

In addition to the illegal gambling, the evidence shows that there is a substantial volume of legalized sports betting. In Nevada, sports betting, including betting on NFL games, has been legal since 1949. The parties have stipulated that sports betting in Nevada in the fourth quarter of the year, when the betting is primarily on football games, has reached the following levels:

1972	$873,318
1973	$826,767
1974	$3,873,217
1975	$26,170,328

These figures represent both "by event" or "head-to-head" betting and parlay card betting. In addition, pool card gambling on professional football has been legal in Montana since 1974. The NFL has not shown that any of this gambling, legal or illegal, has injured the reputation of professional football or the member teams of the NFL....

2. Trademark and Related Unfair Competition Claims

The Delaware Lottery does not utilize the NFL name or any of plaintiffs' registered service marks for the purpose of identifying, as opposed to describing, the service which it offers. The name utilized for the football related betting games is "Scoreboard" and the individual games are identified as "Football Bonus", "Touchdown" and "Touchdown II". No NFL insignia or the like are utilized in the advertising. The cards on which the customers of the Delaware Lottery mark their betting choices, however, identify the next week's NFL football games by the names of the cities whose NFL teams are scheduled to compete against each other, e. g., Philadelphia v. Los Angeles, Washington v. Baltimore, etc. It is stipulated that, in the context in which they appear, these geographic names are intended to refer to, and are understood to refer to, plaintiffs' football teams. It is in this manner that defendants have made it known that the Delaware Lottery offers the opportunity to bet on NFL football.

Undoubtedly when defendants print "Philadelphia v. Los Angeles", the public reads "Philadelphia Eagles v. Los Angeles Rams", and, in this sense, the words utilized by defendants have a secondary meaning. But I do not understand this fact alone to constitute infringement of plaintiffs' registered marks or unfair competition. Defendants may truthfully tell the public what service they perform, just as a specialist in the repair of Volkswagen cars may tell the public of his specialty by using the word "Volkswagen", and just as the manufacturer of a razor blade may advertise the brand names of the razors they will fit. The same rule prevails in the area of comparative advertising which utilizes the tradenames of competing products.

What one may not do, however, is to advertise one's services in a manner which creates an impression in the mind of the relevant segment of the public that a connection exists between the services offered and the holder of the registered mark when no such connection exists. Moreover, this legal prohibition imposes a duty to take affirmative steps to avoid a mistaken impression which is likely to arise from a truthful description of the service even though it does not literally suggest a connection.

This case presents a novel situation for application of these well established principles. After carefully reading all of the materials disseminated in connection with the Delaware Lottery, I cannot point to any specific statement, symbol, or word usage which tends to suggest NFL sponsorship or approval. At the same time, however, plaintiffs have convinced me that a substantial portion of the present and potential audience for NFL games believes that the Delaware Lottery is sponsored or approved by the NFL....

While defendants are guilty of no affirmative statements suggesting affiliation and may well not have foreseen that a substantial number of people would infer an association with the NFL, the fact remains that the ultimate result of their promotion of the Delaware Lottery is significant public confusion and the loss to the NFL of control of its public image. I conclude that this fact entitles plaintiffs to some relief.

The only monetary relief sought by plaintiffs a judgment directing transfer of the proceeds of the Lottery to NFL Charities Incorporated is inappropriate. These proceeds are not funds that the NFL would have harvested for itself in the absence of the Lottery. Nor is there any reason to believe that the retention by the State of any of these proceeds would result in unjust enrichment. I have previously held that Delaware has a right to profit from a demand for gambling created by NFL games. Relief is appropriate only because of the failure of the defendants to avoid an impression of sponsorship, and this record does not suggest that the proceeds of the Lottery were in any way augmented by any public perception of affiliation. Given the nature of the service provided, I strongly suspect that this limited perception had no effect on revenue.

To eliminate the confusion as to sponsorship, an injunction will be entered requiring the Lottery Director to include on Scoreboard tickets, advertising and any other materials prepared for public distribution a clear and conspicuous statement that Scoreboard is not associated with or authorized by the National Football League....

4. Delaware Lottery Law

The plaintiffs assert that the State Lottery Office is acting ultra vires in conducting the Scoreboard games. The NFL points to Article II, Section 17 of the Delaware Constitution which prohibits all forms of gambling in the State except lotteries under state control, pari-mutuel wagering on State licensed races, and Bingo. The heart of their contention based on Section 17 is that Scoreboard is not a lottery. The NFL further contends that, even if Scoreboard is a lottery within the meaning of the Constitution, the Lottery Office is operating it in a manner inconsistent with the requirements for state lotteries established by the General Assembly. The State's first line of defense is that the NFL lacks standing to raise these ultra vires arguments.... [However, the court finds that] the NFL has standing to make its constitutional claim....

B. Validity Of Scoreboard Under The Delaware Constitution

The 1974 Amendment to Article II, Section 17 of the Delaware Constitution authorizes lotteries under State control. It does not define the term "lottery". The NFL contends that the word lottery has a well established meaning in the law and that the Scoreboard games do not fall within that meaning because they entail an element of skill.

It is unquestioned that there are three elements necessary to a lottery: prize, consideration and chance. However, there is a split of authority as to whether a game that incorporates an element of skill as well can qualify as a lottery. Two approaches to the question have developed:

> Under the English rule, a lottery consists in the distribution of money or other property by chance, and nothing but chance, that is, by doing that which is equivalent to drawing lots. If merit or skill play any part in determining the distribution, there is no lottery.... In the United States, however, by what appears to be the weight of authority at the present day, it is not necessary that this element of chance be pure chance, but it may be accompanied by an element of calculation or even of certainty; it is sufficient if chance is the dominant or controlling factor. However, the rule that chance must be the dominant factor is to be taken in the qualitative or causative sense (footnotes omitted).

3 Wharton's Criminal Law and Procedure s 935 (Anderson ed. 1957).

The Delaware courts have not ruled on whether the "pure chance" or "dominant factor" rule applies in this State.... [However,] support for the dominant factor rule can be found in the legislature's interpretation of the word lottery.... In sum then, I conclude that the legislative interpretation of the term lottery together with the weight of authority in other jurisdictions would persuade the Delaware Supreme Court that "lottery" should be interpreted to encompass not only games of pure chance but also games in which chance is the dominant determining factor. The question that remains is whether chance is the dominant factor in some or all of the Scoreboard games. Both the evidence and the case law suggest that it is.

The operation of Football Bonus, Touchdown and Touchdown II are described above. The winners of each are determined by the outcome of the NFL games. Plaintiffs acknowledge that the results of NFL games are a function of myriad factors such as the weather, the health and mood of the players and the condition of the playing field. Some educated predictions can be made about each of these but each is also subject to last minute changes and to an element of the unknowable, or to put it another way, to an element of chance.

In Scoreboard, the unknowable factors in each game are multiplied by the number of games on which the Scoreboard player bets. None of the games permits head-to-head or single game betting. Thus, the element of chance that enters each game is multiplied by a minimum of three and a maximum of fourteen games. In addition, in Touchdown II, the designated point spread or "line" is designed to equalize the odds on the two teams involved. This injects a further factor of chance.

The evidence tends to show that for the first nine weeks of the 1976 season chance was the dominant factor in the outcome of both the NFL games and the Delaware Football Lottery. "Jimmy the Greek" is a widely recognized oddsmaker, syndicated columnist and television personality who earns his living in part by predicting the outcome of NFL games. The record shows that, although he correctly predicted the winner of 101 out of 126 NFL games from September 12 through November 8, if he had bet on both pools of games in Football Bonus each week, he would have won only three times. He would never have won the All-Game Bonus awarded to those who correctly choose the winners of all fourteen games in a single week. We cannot determine how he would have fared in Touchdown because we do not know which three, four or five games he would have placed wagers on each week. However, he successfully predicted the point spread in only 38 out of 126 games in nine weeks. This strongly suggests that expertise would not have carried the day in this game either.

We do not know anything about football expertise of those who actually played Scoreboard. Nonetheless, over the first nine weeks, the average percentage of winners in each pool of Football Bonus and among the three-game Touchdown bettors hovered around

5%. Among those who bet on five games, the average percentage of winners was .22%. These results lend further support to the contention that chance rather than skill is the dominant factor in the games. . . .

[The court also rejected the claim that the Lottery Director had a statutory duty to enter a "contract of affiliation" with the NFL, thereby obtaining their consent to base a lottery upon its games. It did find, however, that the payoffs from one of the games did not meet the statutorily prescribed figure of 45%.]

[Claims premised on violations of federal anti-gambling laws relating to lotteries were rejected on the grounds that even if such violations occurred, no civil claim could be based on such violation. Finally, the court ruled that no property interest of the plaintiff had been taken without due process.]

Conclusion

For all of the reasons discussed in the foregoing Opinion, the Court will enter an Order (1) enjoining the defendants to include in publicly disseminated Scoreboard materials a clear and conspicuous statement that Scoreboard is not associated with or authorized by the National Football League and (2) declaring Touchdown II in violation of [payoff requirements of the Delaware lottery]. All other requests for relief are denied.

Notes

1. Delaware did not find the football lottery profitable. The state discontinued it in 1977. Other states have had similar small-scale lotteries based on NFL games. For example, from 1989 to 2007, Oregon offered sports lotteries called "Sports Action" and "Monday Night Scoreboard" that were tied to NFL games. In 2006 sales for the two contests totaled $12.7 million, with $2.1 million in profit divided among Oregon's seven state universities. During the 2005 legislative session, however, the legislature voted to prohibit these games, effective at the end of the 2006–2007 season. The reason was that the state wanted to attract NCAA basketball tournament games to the state and the NCAA had said it would not permit a site in Oregon to host tournament games if Oregon offered sports betting on games. The legislation provided that the universities would receive other revenues from the lottery which would apparently exceed what they had received previously. In a statement, the Oregon Lottery said its position on "the matter must remain neutral."

See http://www.oregonlottery.org/sports/pdfs/thank_you_qna.pdf. Does it seem appropriate for an association like the NCAA to withhold an economic benefit from a state unless it changes its laws? Could such demands be viewed as extortionate, or at the least anti-competitive?

Montana is the other state with statutory authority for a sports-based lottery. Since the fall of 2008, it has offered a game called "Montana Sports Action." This game allows contestants to select certain players (or defensive units) from NFL teams to create their own "fantasy" team. Fantasy teams earn points when the selected players score touchdowns, kick field goals, intercept passes, and so on. Points can be garnered in over thirty ways. It is a pari-mutuel game, and according to Montana law 74% of sales must be returned as prizes. Three prizes are awarded weekly to those contestants with the three highest point totals. Proceeds support the horse racing industry in Montana. Not content to limit the action to football, the Lottery began offering Fantasy Auto Racing in February 2009. *See* Montana Sports Action Home Page, http://www.montanasportsaction.com (last visited May 18, 2010).

2. In the *Delaware* case, the court gave some consideration to proof offered by the NFL regarding the effect of legalized gambling on the reputation of the sport. The NFL argued that the surveys indicated that the image of the NFL would suffer if there were legal gambling on the games. However, the court decided not to "credit the data," because "there is overwhelming evidence ... that ... in actual experience, widespread gambling, both illegal and state-authorized, has not hurt the NFL." NFL v. Delaware, 435 F. Supp. 1372, 1379 (D. Del. 1977).

3. Most sports betting in football and basketball is based on the "point spread." With point spread betting, the favored team must defeat the underdog by a set number of points — called the point spread — rather than betting simply on one team to defeat the other. Until the emergence of point spread betting, bookmakers had difficulty generating betting action on a team substantially weaker than its opponent. Few would risk money betting on the much weaker team to defeat the stronger team. With point spread betting, if the stronger team had to defeat the weaker by twenty-five points, one betting on the weaker team could win his bet two ways; first, in the unlikely event the weaker team defeated the stronger; second, by the weaker team losing by *fewer than* twenty-five points. Dispute exists about who was the "father" of the point spread, but soon after World War II the use of point spreads became common in the sports betting world.

Another important aspect of sports betting is the concept of "vigorish" or "juice." If a sports bettor wants to win $10 on an event, he must put up $11, 10% more than the amount he seeks to win. If he wins his bet he gets back his $11 bet, and he wins $10. On the other hand, if he loses his bet, he loses $11. A competent bookmaker does not set the betting point spread, also called the line, according to his expectation of the actual outcome. Rather, he sets a line so as to attract roughly an equal amount of money on each side of the betting line. By doing so, he can "balance his books." That is, if he has the same amount of money bet on each side, he pays off the winners with the losers' money and he keeps the 10% as a commission, or as it has come to be called, the "juice."

This discussion is merely a quick overview of how sports betting operates. The types of sports bets that have been developed show ingenuity and an understanding of mathematics. For a good detailed description of the history of sports betting, richly supplemented by an appendix on the details of the activity, *see* RICHARD O. DAVIES & RICHARD G. ABRAM, BETTING THE LINE: SPORTS WAGERING IN AMERICAN LIFE (Ohio St. Univ. 2001). *See also* JAMES JEFFRIES & CHARLES OLIVER, THE BOOK ON BOOKIES: AN INSIDE LOOK AT A SUCCESSFUL SPORTS GAMBLING OPERATION (Paladin Press 2000); STANFORD WONG, SHARP SPORTS BETTING (2001).

B. The "Las Vegas Loophole": Sports Betting in Nevada and the Closing of the Frontier

Nevada legalized gambling in 1931. For many years, however, sports betting was not a prominent component of the Nevada gaming environment. In 1951, the federal government had imposed a 10% tax on all sports bets, as well as licensing costs that made it unprofitable for casinos to offer sports betting. Although many stand-alone sports books operated in Las Vegas, it was not until 1974, when Congress lowered the tax to two percent, that *casino-based* sports betting in Nevada took off. This popularity no doubt was aided by the increasing numbers of sporting events shown on television and the growth of professional sports, especially football.

The legalization and growth of sports betting did not cause the critics of sports betting to go away quietly. Their opposition was aided by a number of scandals where athletes "shaved points" in return for money from gamblers. There were numerous stories of compulsive gamblers in the sports world who risked corrupting the integrity of the game. Most prominent among this group was Art Schlichter, a quarterback with Ohio State University and the NFL team the Indianapolis Colts, whose chronic gambling addiction was well-documented. The revelation in 1989 that baseball star Pete Rose had bet on baseball games involving the team he managed cast a heavier pall over the activity. Of course, neither Schlichter nor Rose really had anything to do with Nevada sports betting per se, but the impression grew that gambling on sporting events was a threat to the integrity of activities cherished in American society.

The attack on sports betting found its most persuasive voice in Senator Bill Bradley, a former basketball star in both college and the professional ranks. Bradley attacked sports betting as corrupting the integrity of and destroying the public's confidence in American sports. Moreover, legalized sports betting sent the youth of our nation the message that sports were more about money than achievement and sportsmanship. By 1992, the call for action was answered with PASPA, the Professional and Amateur Sports Protection Act, 28 U.S.C. 3701 (1992).

§ 3702. Unlawful sports gambling

It shall be unlawful for—

(1) a governmental entity to sponsor, operate, advertise, promote, license, or authorize by law or compact, or

(2) a person to sponsor, operate, advertise, or promote, pursuant to the law or compact of a governmental entity, a lottery, sweepstakes, or other betting, gambling, or wagering scheme based, directly or indirectly (through the use of geographical references or otherwise), on one or more competitive games in which amateur or professional athletes participate, or are intended to participate, or on one or more performances of such athletes in such games.

The law essentially outlawed sports betting on both amateur and professional sports. But the law had another provision, § 3704, which had several important exceptions:

- it exempted pari-mutuel betting on racing of animals (horses and dogs) and jai-alai, also a sport bet in pari-mutuel fashion;

- it "grandfathered" the states that had been conducting or had authorized sports betting before October 2, 1991. This included Nevada, Delaware, Montana, and Oregon.

- it gave New Jersey, in reality Atlantic City, one year after the effective date of the act to obtain state approval of sports betting.

Proponents of sports betting in New Jersey were not able to convince the state legislature to place a referendum on the ballot that would authorize such betting. Undeterred, supporters of sports betting sought a different path.

In the Matter of the Petition of Casino Licensees for Approval of a New Game, Rulemaking and Authorization of a Test

633 A.2d. 1050 (N.J. Super), *aff'd* 647 A.2d 454 (N.J. 1993)

STEIN, J.A.D.

.... We affirm the determination of the New Jersey Casino Control Commission that it has no constitutional or statutory authority to authorize sports betting in New Jersey's gambling casinos.

Appellants are the operators of all twelve licensed gambling casinos in Atlantic City. Intervenors are the leagues conducting major league professional sports in this country: the National Football League, the National Basketball Association, the National Hockey League and the Commissioner of Baseball. Earlier this year, the Legislature chose not to vote on a joint resolution to place a referendum on the ballot permitting a proposed constitutional amendment authorizing casino betting on sports events. The Leagues were among those who vigorously opposed submission of this proposed constitutional amendment to the voters.

Thereafter, on November 15, 1993, the Casinos filed a petition with the Commission seeking a determination that the 1976 state constitutional provision authorizing casino gambling and the regulatory legislation enacted pursuant to it authorized sports betting operated by casinos as a "gambling game" permissibly conducted in those establishments. N.J. CONST. art. IV, §7, ¶2D. Attached to this petition was a comprehensive set of proposed regulations, modeled after those adopted in the state of Nevada where sports betting is legal. Sports betting, called "sports wagering" in the proposed regulations, is permitted on all sports events, professional and amateur, with the exception of sports contests in which there is participation by an educational institutional or non-professional organization principally located in New Jersey; high school sports events; the outcome of a public election held inside or outside of New Jersey; and any horse race not governed by the Simulcasting Racing Act.

The Casinos required a speedy decision by the Commission. Under the Professional and Amateur Sports Protection Act, governmentally-authorized betting on athletic events generally expired on January 1, 1993. However, the effective date of the prohibition is extended for New Jersey casinos to one year after the effective date of the Act, or January 1, 1994.

The Commission rejected the interpretation advanced by petitioners. So do we.

The constitutional amendment authorizing casino gambling provides:

> It shall be lawful for the Legislature to authorize by law the establishment and operation, under regulation and control by the State, of gambling houses or casinos within the boundaries, as heretofore established, of the city of Atlantic City, county of Atlantic, and to license and tax such operations and equipment used in connection therewith.... The type and number of such casinos or gambling houses and of the *gambling games which may be conducted in such establishment* shall be determined by or pursuant to the terms of the law authorizing the establishment and operation thereof. N.J. CONST. art. IV, §7, ¶2D (emphasis added).

The expression of legislative intent surrounding adoption of this constitutional amendment is so strong that we would be remiss if we were to decide that this constitutional amendment authorizes not only traditional in-house gambling games inside casinos but also permits sports betting therein.

Gambling has been legalized in New Jersey very cautiously, one step at a time. [The court traced the history of amendments to the New Jersey Constitution that over time permitted pari-mutuel betting, charitable bingo games and raffles, and casino gaming in Atlantic City.]

When hearings on the proposed amendment [to allow casinos in Atlantic City] were conducted before the Assembly State Government and Federal and Interstate Relations Committee, Steven P. Perskie, the Assembly sponsor of the proposed amendment, specifically stated that the amendment "would not authorize sports betting of any kind." Perskie is now chairman of the New Jersey Casino Control Commission....

The New Jersey Supreme Court has recognized this state's step-at-a-time approach to the introduction of legalized gambling within our borders. In Atlantic City Racing Ass'n v. Attorney General, 489 A.2d 165 (N.J. 1985), the Court held that a specific constitutional amendment was required to authorize inter-track pari-mutuel betting on simulcast horse racing. Its unanimous opinion authored by Judge Matthews, ..., noted that:

> The evolution of legalized gambling in New Jersey has been grudging. Because of widespread abuses in various gambling activities and the attendant social and economic ills engendered, gambling has historically been viewed as an undesirable activity.

Id. at 165 ...

> New Jersey's comprehensive policy against all forms of gambling (except where specifically authorized by the people) has been clear and long-standing.... This principle remains inviolate to this day. Id. at 165....

The gambling provisions of the state constitution were later amended in 1990 by a provision authorizing the Legislature to permit casinos to accept bets on results of simulcast horse races conducted at tracks within or outside New Jersey....

The constitutional permission to authorize simulcast horse betting did not expand the definition of "gambling games" in subparagraph D [of the New Jersey Constitution]. Instead, a specific provision was added, subparagraph E.

The introduction of various forms of legalized gambling into this state has always been by specific constitutional amendment. Sports betting is not a constitutionally-authorized form of legalized gambling.

Moreover, the Commission lacks legislative as well as constitutional authority to authorize casino-operated sports betting.... Originally, the Legislature authorized only specified games as suitable for casino gambling, a list which was later expanded by statutory amendment so that it included roulette, baccarat, blackjack, craps, big six wheel, slot machines, minibaccarat, red dog, pai gow, and sic bo, and any variations or composites of those games found suitable by the Casino Control Commission for use after an appropriate test or experimental period. Later, the statute was amended to permit any other game which is "determined by the commission to be compatible with the public interest and to be suitable for casino use after such appropriate test or experimental period as the commission may deem appropriate." L. 1992, c. 9, § 1, eff. May 19, 1992.

Before this last amendment was adopted, its sponsors, Senator William L. Gormley and Assemblyman John F. Gaffney, sent a joint letter to the chairman of the Assembly Financial Institutions Committee:

> The question has been raised whether [bills allowing casino games] are intended to grant the Casino Control Commission power to authorize casinos to conduct

wagering on sports events. As sponsors of these companion bills, we advise you that the bills have no such intent. The bills, even if so intended would not have that effect because a constitutional amendment approved by the voters is a prerequisite to the commencement of sports wagering in any form in New Jersey.

[Letter from Gormley and Gaffney to Penn of May 4, 1992.]

The Committee then released the bill with the following statement:

The committee releases this bill after being informed by the sponsors, and with the understanding, that this bill is not intended to and does not grant the Casino Control Commission power to authorize casinos to conduct wagering of any kind on sports events. The committee, by the release of this bill, take no position with respect to sports wagering. The committee agrees with the sponsors that sports wagering can only be authorized by adoption of a constitutional amendment approved by the voters at a general election and by enactment of enabling legislation thereafter.

[Assembly Financial Institutions Committee Statement to Assembly, No. 1233, May 4, 1992.]

Additionally, N.J.S.A. 5:12-194(e) provides that sports betting and casino simulcasting shall be conducted in the same area, and in accordance with regulations of the Casino Control Commission only "if wagering at casinos on sports events is authorized by the voters of this State and by enabling legislation enacted by the Legislature." *Ibid.*

The Commission's conclusion that sports betting is not a permitted form of gambling in Atlantic City's casinos is consistent with the constitutional and statutory scheme which, with one exception, permits only those games which take place completely within the confines of a casino. The conduct of in-house casino games is subject to the strict regulation of the Casino Control Commission, lessening the opportunity of a gambler, casino or third person to fix such games. Pari-mutuel horse betting is specifically permitted by our constitution, as is simulcast betting on horse races, whether the race is conducted inside or outside of this state. Horse racing is also a highly regulated activity stringently supervised by the New Jersey Racing Commission pursuant to N.J.S.A. 5:5-22 to -99. Betting on simulcast horse races is also controlled by the Simulcasting Racing Act, N.J.S.A. 5:5-110 to -126. Regulatory controls exist in every state where pari-mutuel betting is conducted.

Except for constitutionally-authorized simulcast horse race betting, gambling casinos may operate only those games conducted solely in-house. They may not offer betting on events which take place or where the result is determined at a location outside a casino's four walls.

Affirmed.

Notes

1. Although New Jersey missed taking advantage of PASPA's one year grace period to legalize sports betting in Atlantic City, the New Jersey Assembly has since revisited the issue of sports betting in the state. For the past few years the New Jersey Assembly has approved legislation that would put a referendum to voters asking if they wanted to allow sports betting in Atlantic City casinos. In light of PASPA's prohibition, however, even proponents acknowledged that the legislation was an effort to get the public interested in the issue and to draw attention to the federal ban. *See* Tom Hester, *Assembly Backs Sports Betting: But Bill is Merely Symbolic unless Federal Ban is Lifted*, STAR-LEDGER (Newark, N.J.) Feb. 8, 2008, *available at* 2008 WLNR 2475183. One unhappy New Jersey sports bettor challenged

PASPA on the grounds it violated the Tenth Amendment, arguing that that because the Constitution does not refer to gambling, "the decision on whether to allow gambling in general, and gambling on sports specifically, should be reserved to the states." Flagler v. United States, No. 06-3699, 2007 WL 2814657 (D.N.J. Sept. 25, 2007). The court ruled that it lacked subject matter jurisdiction. The court also stated that Flagler lacked standing, because he had not alleged any damage to a legally protected interest.

2. As one of PASPA's "grandfathered states," Delaware was eligible to reinstitute sports betting. Proponents said sports betting would act as a buffer against the advent of slot machines in Maryland, which were approved by voter referendum in 2008. In May 2009, the Governor of Delaware signed into law a bill authorizing sports betting in the state. *See* Chad Millen, *Delaware Allows Sports Betting*, ESPN MAG., May 13, 2009, *available at* http://sports.espn.go.com/espn/news/story?id=4162225 (last visited May 18, 2010). The response from professional sports leagues and the NCAA was swift, and they sought a preliminary injunction against the state on July 28, 2009. A district court ruling denying the injunction was overturned by the Third Circuit Court of Appeals in Commissioner of Baseball v. Markell, 579 F.3d 293 (3d Cir. 2009), *cert. denied*, 2010 WL 342193 (May 3, 2010). The court construed the grandfather exception found in PASPA narrowly. The exception stated that the ban on sports wagering did not apply to a gambling scheme, "to the extent that the scheme was conducted by [Delaware]" after 1976 and before 1990. The court interpreted this to mean that only gambling schemes that were actually conducted by Delaware prior to PASPA's enactment would be exempted, and Delaware could not implement its new sports betting operation.

3. Rather than the momentum moving towards a repeal of PASPA, many people have pressed for its expansion. In 1999, the report of the National Gambling Impact Study Commission (NGISC) recommended that all college and amateur sports betting be made illegal. This would close the so-called "Las Vegas loophole." Beginning in 2000, several Congressional bills proposed to do just that. Proponents assert that if all such sports betting were illegal there would be no reason for newspapers to publish the point spread on college games. This would make it difficult for bookies accepting bets illegally to stay in business. The end result would be a clear message that gambling on amateur sports was a corrupting influence that needed to be eliminated.

Fans of sports betting claim that legal Nevada sports betting helps to maintain the integrity of college sports. On several occasions Nevada officials have alerted law enforcement to unusual betting action on particular college teams and games. One such instance led law enforcement to uncover a point shaving scheme in a highly publicized incident involving Arizona State's basketball team. Nevada sports books have significant incentive to maintain the fairness of college sports, because they stand to lose large amounts of money if bets on corrupted contests are made with them.

The effort to extend PASPA to prohibit sports betting on all amateur sports has been met with strong opposition from Nevada and has not been successful. A considerable literature examining this issue has developed. *See* Ronald J. Rychlak, *Bad Bet: Federal Criminalization of Nevada's Collegiate Sports Book*, 4 NEV. L.J. 320 (2004); Michael P. Fechteau, *All for Integrity or All for Naught: The Battle Over State-Sponsored Sports Betting*, 7 GAMING L. REV. 43 (2003); Aaron J. Slavin, *The 'Las Vegas' Loophole and the Current Push in Congress Towards a Blanket Prohibition on Collegiate Sports Gambling*, 10 U. MIAMI BUS. L. REV. 715 (2002).

4. While the NCAA is adamantly opposed to sports betting, it does not prohibit university athletic departments from taking advertising money from lotteries and casinos.

Although the advertising cannot be used in connection with NCAA championships, athletics departments can otherwise advertise casinos and lotteries at sporting venues. As of early 2009, seven of the ten schools in the Pacific 10 (Pac 10) Conference have a marketing relationship with casinos, lotteries, or both. Regarding this, one NCAA spokesperson, Stacey Osburn, said, "While our rules do not allow sports wagering, decisions regarding institutional funding and advertising are under the purview of each university and college, and not under the control of the NCAA." *See* http://www.signonsandiego.com/union trib/20081205/news1m5arena.html.

Is it a contradiction for the NCAA to take such a strident position against sports betting, while turning a blind eye when it comes to other forms of gambling? Is it a satisfying explanation to say that sports betting is the only form of gambling that needs to be eliminated, and that it can be differentiated from lotteries and casino gaming? Is it appropriate to have advertising of gambling at sporting events where many minors are present?

3. Fantasy Sports — Legal or Illegal?

A. The Birth and Basics of Fantasy Sports

According to legend, fantasy sports traces its roots back to 1980 and to what was first called "Rotisserie Baseball." The name came from a restaurant where the idea for the activity originated. As will be discussed, from that modest beginning fantasy sports participation has come a long way. Fantasy sports are based on the accumulated statistics of the individual performances of real athletes. There are many variations on the fantasy theme, however. Fantasy baseball, for example, typically involves a group of owners having a "draft" or "auction" of players at the beginning of the baseball season. Categories of performance are established for hitters, such as batting average, runs batted in, stolen bases, home runs, and runs scored. For pitchers, relevant performance measures include wins, earned run average, saves, and strikeouts. The fantasy team "owners" keep track of the statistics and standings are thereby created. Trades between owners of players are common, as are payouts and prizes to the winning contestants. The description of a baseball fantasy league should not suggest the activity is limited to baseball. Fantasy football, fantasy basketball, fantasy hockey, fantasy golf, fantasy soccer, even fantasy NASCAR, all have their followers.

The number of participants in fantasy sports ranges from fifteen to thirty million. The internet has been largely responsible for the explosion of fantasy sports. Some estimate that fantasy sports activities generate $500 million in annual global revenues. One competition, the National Fantasy Baseball Championship, requires an entry fee of $1300, with a top prize of $100,000. *See* Vincent M. Mallozzi, *In Fantasy Sports, It Helps Being a Rocket Scientist*, N.Y. TIMES, Apr. 15, 2007, *available at* http://www.nytimes.com/2007/04/15/sports/baseball/15cheer.html. *See also* National Fantasy Baseball Championship Home Page, http://nfbc.fanball.com/my/my_teams.php. As discussed below, the big money of fantasy sports is not just for the participants, but for the organizers.

B. Legal Issues of Fantasy Sports

Several legal issues hover over the fantasy gaming, including its core legality. When one engages in fantasy sports, is one gambling? Does it involve skill, or does luck predominate? Are the same sports leagues which supposedly abhor sports betting complicit in violations of the law by their sponsorship of fantasy sports? What are the property rights of those athletes upon which the activity is based? The legal issues are anything but fantasies.

i. Legality under State Law

The legality of fantasy sports under state laws poses a significant question because no state code specifically provides that fantasy sports competitions are legal. In fact, opinions from the Attorney General of several states maintain that fantasy sports are illegal games of chance. These opinions are not recent, however, and they have not been viewed as authoritative resolutions of the issue. To determine the question under state law, one could look to the general means of classifying activities as gambling, that is the "games of chance" vs. "games of skill" analysis. As discussed in Chapter 1, most states use the common law "dominant factor," or "predominance" test to determine whether an activity falls under state anti-gambling provisions. Clearly fantasy sports involve elements of chance, namely, the uncertain performance of the athletes involved. Many would maintain there is skill involved as well. What skills are there in fantasy sports? Do these skills predominate, or is the chance factor dominant in deciding the success of a fantasy sports participant?

The following decision, applying New Jersey law, illustrates the role of the internet in the expansion of fantasy sports, and the centrality of corporate America in fantasy sports. It also gave a boost to the fantasy sports world.

Humphrey v. Viacom, Inc.

2007 WL 1797648 (D.N.J. 2007)

Dennis M. Cavanaugh, U.S. District Judge

This matter comes before the Court upon motions by Defendants ESPN, Vulcan Sports Media and Sportsline.com ("Defendants") to dismiss Complaint of Charles E. Humphrey, Jr. ("Plaintiff" or "Humphrey") pursuant to Federal Rule of Civil Procedure 12(b)(6).... After carefully considering the submissions of the parties and for the following reasons, Defendants' motions to dismiss Plaintiff's Complaint are granted.

Background

Fantasy Sports

Fantasy sports leagues allow participants to "manage" virtual teams of professional players in a given sport throughout a sport's season and to compete against other fantasy sports participants based upon the actual performance of those players in key statistical categories. Fantasy sports have become extremely popular in recent years. They have earned a place in modern popular culture and are the subject of countless newspaper and magazine articles, books, internet message boards and water-cooler conversations. The enormous popularity of fantasy sports can be attributed in part to the services offered on internet websites, such as those operated by Defendants. The websites provide a platform for real-time statistical updates and tracking, message boards and expert analysis. Compl. ¶¶ 26–31.

Fantasy sports leagues allow fans to use their knowledge of players, statistics and strategy to manage their own virtual team based upon the actual performance of professional athletes through a full season of competition. In the early days of fantasy sports, participants compiled and updated the players' statistics manually. Today, the rapid growth of the internet fostered additional services, such as those offered by Defendants, that provide an internet environment and community for playing and discussing fantasy sports. The technology also allows for automatic statistic updates for players and teams and access to expert fantasy sports analysis. As a result, fantasy sports have become much more accessible and popular throughout the country. *Id.*

Although the rules and services vary somewhat from one fantasy sports provider to another, the websites operate as follows. Participants pay a fee to purchase a fantasy sports team and the related services. The purchase price provides the participant with access to the support services necessary to manage the fantasy team, including access to "real-time" statistical information, expert opinions, analysis and message boards for communicating with other participants. *Id.*

The purchase price also covers the data-management services necessary to run a fantasy sports team. Using these services, the participants "draft" a slate of players and track the performance of those players in key statistical categories throughout the season. Participants are grouped into "leagues" of as many as twelve teams and compete not only against the members of their own leagues, but can also compete against the winners of the other leagues. *Id.* at ¶¶ 45–46.

The success of a fantasy sports team depends on the participants' skill in selecting players for his or her team, trading players over the course of the season, adding and dropping players during the course of the season and deciding who among his or her players will start and which players will be placed on the bench. The team with the best performance-based upon the statistics of the players chosen by the participant—is declared the winner at the season's end. Nominal prizes, such as T-shirts or bobble-head dolls, are awarded to each participant whose team wins its league. Managers of the best teams in each sport across all leagues are awarded larger prizes, such as flat-screen TVs or gift certificates. These prizes are announced before the fantasy sports season begins and do not depend upon the number of participants or the amount of registration fees received by Defendants. *Id.* at ¶¶ 32–48.

Plaintiff's Complaint

Plaintiff filed a Complaint on or around June 20, 2006, against Viacom Inc., the CBS Corporation, the CBS Television Network, Sportsline.com, Inc., The Hearst Corporation, The Walt Disney Company, ESPN, Inc., Vulcan, Inc., Vulcan Sports Media and The Sporting News for alleged violations of the anti-gambling laws of New Jersey and several other states. Only ESPN, Sports line and Vulcan Sports Media remain in the case as Defendants. Plaintiff voluntarily dismissed all other Defendants. The Defendants operate separate pay-for-play online fantasy sport leagues.

The Complaint alleges that Defendants operate three distinct pay-for-play fantasy sports sites in violation of several states' *qui tam* gambling loss-recovery laws. The Complaint indicates that Plaintiff is invoking the *qui tam* laws of [these states] to recover losses incurred by the residents of each state who participated in the Defendants' fantasy sports games. . . .

Through invocation of the various *qui tam* laws, Plaintiff alleges that he is entitled to recover the individual gambling losses of all participants of the Defendants' allegedly unlawful gambling schemes. Plaintiff claims that the registration fees paid by fantasy sports leagues participants constitute wagers or bets, and he seeks to recover these fees pursuant to the *qui tam* gambling loss-recovery statutes. In other words, Humphrey concludes that the Defendants' fantasy sports leagues constitute gambling because the participant "wagers" the entry fee for the chance to win a prize and the winner is determined predominantly by chance due to potential injuries to players and the vicissitudes of sporting events in general.

Qui Tam Statutes

The *Qui Tam* statutes derive from the 1710 Statute of Queen Anne, an English statute that authorized gambling losers and informers to sue to recover [gambling] losses incurred.... The American versions of the Statute of Anne contain similar language and were similarly directed at deterring traditional gambling.... Although the specific elements of the *Qui Tam* statutes vary, they share a common origin and purpose. They were intended to prevent gamblers and their families from becoming destitute due to gambling losses—and thus becoming wards of the State-by providing a method for the gambler's spouse, parent or child to recover the lost money from the winner.

Analysis

Legal Standard on a Motion to Dismiss

In deciding a Rule 12(b)(6) motion to dismiss, the Court is required to accept as true the allegations in the complaint, and to view them in the light most favorable to the plaintiff, but the Court "need not credit a complaint's 'bald assertions' or 'legal conclusions.'"

Stating a Claim under *Qui Tam* Laws

Plaintiff asserts claims under the gambling *qui tam* statutes of the District of Columbia, Georgia, Illinois, Kentucky, Massachusetts, New Jersey, Ohio and South Carolina. Courts have long held that the *qui tam* statutes must be narrowly construed because they are penal in nature.... Courts have also construed the *qui tam* statutes narrowly in light of their history and purpose, in part because they provided a remedy in derogation of the common law.... These principles of strict and narrow construction are particularly appropriate in this case, where Plaintiff seeks to recover unspecified losses to which he has no personal connection. While *qui tam* plaintiffs often have not personally suffered a loss, they are not excused from the obligation to allege specific facts demonstrating that their claims are within the narrow confines of the statutes under which they seek relief.... This Court will not extend the *qui tam* statutes to cover fantasy sports league entry fees unless that coverage is warranted by the explicit language of each statute and is supported by specific allegations of Plaintiff.

Does Plaintiff Allege the Specific Facts Necessary to Pursue a Qui Tam Claim?

Plaintiff must come forth with facts to support his claim that there exists a specific loss that he is entitled to recover under New Jersey's *qui tam* statute.... Plaintiff does not identify any individual who paid an entry fee to play one of the Defendants' fantasy sports games; he does not identify the nature of the "wager" or "bet" made between such an individual and either of the Defendants; he does not allege when the loss occurred; and, as in *Fitzgerald*, he does not allege that such an individual lost such a "wager" or "bet" to either of the Defendants.

Plaintiff fails to identify even one individual who participated in even one of the subject leagues, much less one who allegedly lost money to Defendants in those leagues, and concedes that he has done neither himself. Compl.¶¶ 9, 71. In short, Plaintiff asks this Court to indulge a gambling *qui tam* suit seeking a "recover[y] for his own use, unknown amount of money lost by unnamed and unknowable persons." ... Given the absence of the necessary factual allegations showing a recoverable loss under New Jersey's *qui tam* statute, this Court grants Defendants' motions to dismiss and finds no substantial difference between New Jersey's *qui tam* statute and those of the other jurisdictions under which Plaintiff brought his Complaint.

Is Payment of an Entry Fee to Participate in Fantasy Sports Leagues Gambling?

Defendants argue that Plaintiff fails to state a claim under New Jersey's *qui tam* statute because, as a matter of law, the payment of an entry fee to participate in a fantasy sports league is not wagering, betting or staking money. New Jersey allows recovery only of "wagers, bets or stakes made to depend upon any race or game, or upon any gaming by lot or chance, or upon any lot, chance, casualty or unknown or contingent event." Although Plaintiff uses the words "wager" and "bet" to describe the entry fees for ESPN's fantasy sports games (*e.g.* Complt. ¶¶ 4, 19), those allegations are legal conclusions, and "a court need not credit a complaint's ... legal conclusions when deciding a motion to dismiss."

As Plaintiff alleges, Defendants' fantasy sports league participants pay a set fee for each team they enter in a fantasy sports league. This entry fee is paid at the beginning of a fantasy sports season and allows the participant to receive related support services and to compete against other teams in a league throughout the season. As Plaintiff further alleges, Defendants offer set prizes for each league winner and for the overall winners each season. These prizes are guaranteed to be awarded at the end of the season, and the amount of the prize does not depend on the number of entrants. Moreover, Defendants are neutral parties in the fantasy sports games—they do not compete for the prizes and are indifferent as to who wins the prizes. Defendants simply administer and provide internet-based information and related support services for the games. Plaintiff does not allege otherwise.

New Jersey courts have not addressed the three-factor scenario of (1) an entry fee paid unconditionally, (2) prizes guaranteed to be awarded and (3) prizes for which the game operator is not competing. Courts throughout the country, however, have long recognized that it would be "patently absurd" to hold that "the combination of an entry fee and a prize equals gambling," because if that were the case, countless contests engaged in every day would be unlawful gambling, including "golf tournaments, bridge tournaments, local and state rodeos or fair contests, ... literary or essay competitions, ... livestock, poultry and produce exhibitions, track meets, spelling bees, beauty contests and the like," and contest participants and sponsors could all be subject to criminal liability. State v. Am. Holiday Ass'n, Inc., 727 P.2d 807, 809, 812 (*en banc*).

Courts have distinguished between *bona fide* entry fees and bets or wagers, holding that entry fees do not constitute bets or wagers where they are paid unconditionally for the privilege of participating in a contest, and the prize is for an amount certain that is guaranteed to be won by one of the contestants (but not the entity offering the prize). Courts that have examined this issue have reasoned that when the entry fees and prizes are unconditional and guaranteed, the element of risk necessary to constitute betting or wagering is missing....

Therefore, where the entry fees are unconditional and the prizes are guaranteed, "reasonable entrance fees charged by the sponsor of a contest to participants competing for prizes are not bets or wagers." *Am. Holiday Ass'n*, 727 P.2d at 811.

Plaintiff incorrectly argues that the case law cited by Defendants is inapplicable because it applies only to games of skill. To the contrary, none of the decisions cited by Defendants turn on whether the activity in question is a game of skill or chance. Indeed, courts have made clear that the question whether the money awarded is a *bona fide* prize (as opposed to a bet or wager) can be determined without deciding whether the outcome of the game is determined by skill or chance.... Plaintiff's argument that the distinction between "bets" and "entry fees" is meaningless in the context of a lottery is similarly unavailing. In his brief in opposition to Defendants' motions to dismiss, Plaintiff states that

"Defendants operate[ ] an enterprise that has all of the necessary elements of gambling: 'prize, chance and consideration.' "In the very next line, Plaintiff states that those three elements are essential of a lottery, however a separate statutory scheme governs lotteries.... This case does not concern a lottery.... Because the "prize, chance, consideration" test is irrelevant here, Plaintiff's argument that fantasy sports leagues are games of chance is without effect. Although Defendants deny that fantasy sports leagues are games of chance, this Court need not reach this issue in deciding Defendants' motions.

As a matter of law, the entry fees for Defendants' fantasy sports leagues are not "bets" or "wagers" because (1) the entry fees are paid unconditionally; (2) the prizes offered to fantasy sports contestants are for amounts certain and are guaranteed to be awarded; and (3) Defendants do not compete for the prizes.

Are Defendants "Winners" under the Qui Tam Statutes?

Defendants cannot be considered "winners" as a matter of law. In his opposition brief, Plaintiff asserts that Defendants are winners because they "receive and keep, and thus win, the pay-to-play net consideration that must be paid by the players in order to be allowed to enter theses (sic) fantasy sports games of chance." Plaintiff, however, provides no legal support whatsoever for this assertion....

Defendants plainly are not "winners" as a matter of law, but merely parties to an enforceable contract. Defendants provide substantial consideration, in the form of administration of the leagues and the provision of extensive statistical and analytical services, in exchange for the entry fees paid for participation in the fantasy leagues. At no time do Defendants participate in any bet. Absent such participation, Defendants cannot be "winners" as a matter of law.... To suggest that one can be a winner without risking the possibility of being a loser defies logic and finds no support in the law.

Furthermore, Defendants are not "winners" under the plain terms of the *qui tam* statutes. The statutes make clear that the "winner" must be a participant in the card, dice or other game at issue.... Finally, Plaintiff's allegations in the Complaint confirm that Defendants do not compete against fantasy sports participants in any way, and do not "win" anything from them. Defendants provide extensive services to the participants throughout the course of the relevant sports season. Compl. ¶¶ 45–48, Friedman Decl. Ex. R. at ¶ 2. At the end of the season, Defendants award prizes, in pre-determined amounts fixed by contract, to the team managers who have accrued the most "fantasy points" or victories. At no point do the participant-owners of any team pay anything to Defendants that is in any way dependent on the outcome of any league. Nor do participants ever "risk" losing their entry fee—they irrevocably part with that fee shortly after they enter a league, and receive in exchange substantial services from Defendants over the course of an extended sports season.

Accordingly, because Defendants do not "play" in the fantasy leagues, bet on the side of any of the participants or have any financial interest whatsoever in the outcome of any league, Defendants cannot be "winners" subject to liability under the gambling *qui tam* statutes as a matter of law.

Do Fantasy League Participants Sustain the "Loss" Necessary to Bring a Claim?

A *qui tam* plaintiff like Humphrey has no right to recovery unless a participant in gambling activity wins money from one who loses money in that activity. In addition to the fact that fantasy leagues are not gambling and that defendants do not win anything, participants suffer no "loss" in participating in the fantasy leagues.... No fantasy league participant suffered any such "loss." To the contrary, participants pay Defendants a one-time, non-refundable entry fee to participate in the leagues, and receive in consideration for that fee the benefit of Defendants' extensive administrative, statistical and analytical services throughout the relevant sports season. Only at the end of the sports season are prizes awarded, in amounts fixed by the contracts that govern participation in the leagues. Accordingly, in paying for the right to participate in the leagues and receive Defendants' services, participants simply do not "lose" anything, and certainly suffer no cognizable "gambling" loss. Whether or not a participant is a successful league manager, their entry fee never hangs in the balance in any way in connection with their participation in the league.... Indeed, once participants have selected their team and begin their season, the fee cannot be recovered. There is no "loss" on these facts, and this exchange of consideration is an "ordinary contract," in which "both parties may ultimately gain by entering into the agreement." ...

Because those who participate in Defendants' fantasy sports leagues do not suffer the required "loss" under any of the *qui tam* statutes pursuant to which Plaintiff brings his Complaint, Plaintiff cannot recover as a matter of law.

Notes

1. The court in *Humphrey* refers to the plaintiff's complaint and the description of the many types of fantasy competitions conducted. It is a revealing description of the extent of the activity and the involvement of large corporations in their organization and management. *See* Complaint, Humphrey v. Viacom, 2006 WL 2300429 (D.N.J. 2007) (No. 06CV02768).

2. *Humphrey* is the only full judicial treatment of the legality of fantasy sports under state law. Is it persuasive? Is it as clear as the court suggests that the elements of gambling—consideration, chance, and prize are absent? As will be seen below, the court also drew support for its conclusion from federal law.

ii. Legality under Federal Law

Several possibilities exist for applying federal law to fantasy sports. The Professional and Amateur Sports Protection Act (PASPA) discussed above, makes it unlawful for "a person to sponsor, operate, advertise, or promote, pursuant to the law ... of a governmental entity, a ... betting, gambling, or wagering scheme based, directly or indirectly ... on ... competitive games in which amateur or professional athletes participate, ... or on one or more performances of such athletes in such games." Could PASPA's broad statutory language be applied to fantasy sports? *See* Anthony N. Cabot & Louis V. Csoka, *Fantasy Sports: One Form of Mainstream Wagering in the United States*, 40 J. MARSHALL L. REV. 1195, 1213–1214 (2007) (arguing that PASPA would not seem to apply to fantasy gaming). Other federal laws possibly implicated by fantasy sports include the Wire Act, 18 U.S.C. § 1084 (1994), the Travel Act, 18 U.S.C. § 1952 (1994), and the Illegal Gambling Business Act, 18 U.S.C. § 1955 (1994).

The federal law that is most relevant to fantasy sports is the Unlawful Internet Gaming Enforcement Act (UIGEA), 31 U.S.C. §§ 5361–5367 (Supp. 2007). This statute is discussed in detail in Chapter 12 on internet gaming. Although the law does not specifically ban internet gambling, it prohibits wire transfers, credit card payments, or other funding of internet gambling accounts by banks and credit card companies in the United States. Most significantly, however, the drafters created an exception for fantasy sports. According to the law, an illegal "bet" or "wager" does not include participation in any fantasy or simulation sports game, so long as:

(I) All prizes and awards offered to winning participants are established and made known to the participants in advance of the game or contest and their value is not determined by the number of participants or the amount of any fees paid by those participants.

(II) All winning outcomes reflect the relative knowledge and skill of the participants and are determined predominately by accumulated statistical results of the performance of individuals (athletes in the case of sports events) in multiple real-world sporting or other events.

No winning outcome is based—

(aa) on the score, point-spread, or any performance or performances of any single real-world team or a combination of such teams; or

(bb) solely on any single performance of an individual athlete in any single real-world sporting or other event. 31 U.S.C. §5362(1)(E)(ix)

Although these provisions do not use the term "fantasy sports," all the elements of fantasy betting are present: outcomes are determined by "accumulated statistical results" and not the "score" or "point-spread" of a competition by a "single real-world team," nor the single performance of an individual athlete. The statute contemplates that entry fees will be charged and prizes awarded. In *Humphrey*, the court also cited the provision from UIGEA when confirming that plaintiff's complaint should be dismissed. 2007 WL 1797648, at *11.

In an environment where so much opposition exists to anything resembling sports betting, especially on the internet, why would Congress make a point of reassuring fantasy sports participants and sponsors that they are exempted from the law? According to one person:

In the past, the National Football League has had two very different interests in this legislation-one, to protect the integrity of professional football by prohibiting online betting on NFL games, and, two, to line their pocket with royalties by preserving the legality of wagers involved in the growing fantasy sports industry. The NFL succeeds in protecting both interests in the Goodlatte legislation, which expressly exempts from illegality on-line wagers on fantasy sports teams....
It is disingenuous for the National Football League to present their position as anti-gambling when in fact they support carve outs for Fantasy Sports gambling as well as other forms of gambling.

Remarks of the Rev. Louis P. Sheldon, reported at Joseph M. Kelly, *Living in a Fantasy*, 12 GAMING L. REV. 310, 314 (2008). In fact, the NFL and Major League Baseball, as well as other leagues, make considerable sums of money through licensing arrangements for the purposes of fantasy sports. *See* Anthony N. Cabot & Louis V. Csoka, *Fantasy Sports: One Form of Mainstream Wagering in the United States*, 40 J. MARSHALL L. REV. 1195, 1198–99 (2007). There has been a rapid growth in the legal literature regarding fantasy sports. In addition to the articles cited above, *see* M. Christine Holleman, *Fantasy Football: Illegal Gambling or Legal Game of Skill?*, 8 N.C.J.L. & TECH. 59 (2006); Aaron Levy, Comment, *A Risky Bet: The Future of Pay-to-Play Online Fantasy Sports*, 39 CONN. L. REV. 325 (2006); Jon Boswell, Note, *Fantasy Sports: A Game of Skill that is Implicitly Legal under State Law, and Now Explicitly Legal under Federal Law*, 25 CARDOZO ARTS & ENT. L.J. 1257 (2008); Anthony Vecchione, Comment, *Fantasy Sports: Has Recent Anti-Gambling Legislation 'Dropped the Ball' by Providing a Statutory Carve-Out for the Fantasy Sports Industry?* 61 SMU L. REV. 1689 (2008).

C. Property Rights and Fantasy Sports — Who Owns the Numbers?

The right of publicity is a complicated part of the field of intellectual property. Athletes have a right of publicity which has been acknowledged by courts in several instances. For example, in years past children would trade "baseball cards," cards with a photograph of a player and the player's statistics along with Topps Chewing Gum. A court held, however, that without the player's permission, or the player being compensated, the card infringed on the player's right to publicity. In another case, a court held that the use of players' names and statistics in a board game violated their right of publicity. At the same time, can't it be said that a player's statistics are just that, statistics? As such, can they really be "owned," or are they simply a form of news available to all? The following case and notes impart some idea of the subtleties of the problem.

C.B.C. Distribution and Marketing, Inc. v. Major League Baseball Advanced Media, L.P.

505 F.3d 818 (8th Cir. 2007), *cert denied*, 128 S. Ct. 2872 (2008)

ARNOLD, Circuit Judge.

C.B.C. Distribution and Marketing, Inc., brought this action for a declaratory judgment against Major League Baseball Advanced Media, L.P., to establish its right to use, without license, the names of and information about major league baseball players in connection with its fantasy baseball products. Advanced Media counterclaimed, maintaining that CBC's fantasy baseball products violated rights of publicity belonging to major league baseball players and that the players, through their association, had licensed those rights to Advanced Media, the interactive media and Internet company of major league baseball. The Major League Baseball Players Association intervened in the suit, joining in Advanced Media's claims and further asserting a breach of contract claim against CBC. The district court granted summary judgment to CBC, ... We affirm.

I.

CBC sells fantasy sports products via its Internet website, e-mail, mail, and the telephone. Its fantasy baseball products incorporate the names along with performance and biographical data of actual major league baseball players. Before the commencement of the major league baseball season each spring, participants form their fantasy baseball teams by "drafting" players from various major league baseball teams. Participants compete against other fantasy baseball "owners" who have also drafted their own teams. A participant's success, and his or her team's success, depends on the actual performance of the fantasy team's players on their respective actual teams during the course of the major league baseball season. Participants in CBC's fantasy baseball games pay fees to play and additional fees to trade players during the course of the season.

From 1995 through the end of 2004, CBC licensed its use of the names of and information about major league players from the Players Association pursuant to license agreements that it entered into with the association in 1995 and 2002. The 2002 agreement, which superseded in its entirety the 1995 agreement, licensed to CBC "the names, nicknames, likenesses, signatures, pictures, playing records, and/or biographical data of each player" (the "Rights") to be used in association with CBC's fantasy baseball products.

In 2005, after the 2002 agreement expired, the Players Association licensed to Advanced Media, with some exceptions, the exclusive right to use baseball players' names and performance information "for exploitation via all interactive media." Advanced Media began providing fantasy baseball games on its website, MLB.com, the official website of major league baseball. It offered CBC, in exchange for a commission, a license to promote the MLB.com fantasy baseball games on CBC's website but did not offer CBC a license to continue to offer its own fantasy baseball products. This conduct by Advanced Media prompted CBC to file the present suit, alleging that it had "a reasonable apprehension that it will be sued by Advanced Media if it continues to operate its fantasy baseball games."

The district court granted summary judgment to CBC. It held that CBC was not infringing any state-law rights of publicity that belonged to major league baseball players.... The court reasoned that CBCs fantasy baseball products did not use the names of major league baseball players as symbols of their identities and with an intent to obtain a commercial advantage, as required to establish an infringement of a publicity right under Missouri law (which all parties concede applies here).... The district court further held that even if CBC were infringing the players' rights of publicity, the first amendment preempted those rights.... The court rejected, however, CBC's argument that federal copyright law preempted the rights of publicity claim.... Finally, the district court held that CBC was not in violation of the no-use and no-contest provisions of its 2002 agreement with the Players Association because "the strong federal policy favoring the full and free use of ideas in the public domain as manifested in the laws of intellectual property prevails over [those] contractual provisions" (internal quotations omitted).

Because this appeal is from the district court's grant of summary judgment, our review is *de novo* and ... [w]e also review *de novo* the district court's interpretation of state law, including its interpretation of Missouri law regarding the right of publicity.

An action based on the right of publicity is a state-law claim.... In Missouri, "the elements of a right of publicity action include: (1) That defendant used plaintiff's name as a symbol of his identity (2) without consent (3) and with the intent to obtain a commercial advantage." ... The parties all agree that CBC's continued use of the players' names and playing information after the expiration of the 2002 agreement was without consent. The district court concluded, however, that the evidence was insufficient to make out the other two elements of the claim, and we address each of these in turn.

With respect to the symbol-of-identity element, the Missouri Supreme Court has observed that "'the name used by the defendant must be understood by the audience as referring to the plaintiff.'" ...

Here, we entertain no doubt that the players' names that CBC used are understood by it and its fantasy baseball subscribers as referring to actual major league baseball players. CBC itself admits that: In responding to the appellants' argument that "this element is met by the mere confirmation that the name used, in fact, refers to the famous person asserting the violation," CBC stated in its brief that "if this is all the element requires, CBC agrees that it is met." We think that by reasoning that "identity," rather than "mere use of a name," "is a critical element of the right of publicity," the district court did not understand that when a name alone is sufficient to establish identity, the defendant's use of that name satisfies the plaintiff's burden to show that a name was used as a symbol of identity.

It is true that with respect to the "commercial advantage" element of a cause of action for violating publicity rights, CBC's use does not fit neatly into the more traditional categories of commercial advantage, namely, using individuals' names for advertising and merchandising purposes in a way that states or intimates that the individuals are endorsing a product.... But the Restatement, which the Missouri Supreme Court has recognized as authority in this kind of case, ... also says that a name is used for commercial advantage when it is used "in connection with services rendered by the user" and that the plaintiff need not show that "prospective purchasers are likely to believe" that he or she endorsed the product or service.... We note, moreover, that in Missouri, "the commercial advantage element of the right of publicity focuses on the defendant's intent or purpose to obtain a commercial benefit from use of the plaintiff's identity." ... Because we think that it is clear that CBC uses baseball players' identities in its fantasy baseball products for purposes of profit, we believe that their identities are being used for commercial advantage and that the players therefore offered sufficient evidence to make out a cause of action for violation of their rights of publicity under Missouri law.

B.

CBC argues that the first amendment nonetheless trumps the right-of-publicity action that Missouri law provides. Though this dispute is between private parties, the state action necessary for first amendment protections exists because the right-of-publicity claim exists only insofar as the courts enforce state-created obligations that were "never explicitly assumed" by CBC....

The Supreme Court has directed that state law rights of publicity must be balanced against first amendment considerations, ... and here we conclude that the former must give way to the latter. First, the information used in CBC's fantasy baseball games is all readily available in the public domain, and it would be strange law that a person would not have a first amendment right to use information that is available to everyone. It is true that CBC's use of the information is meant to provide entertainment, but "[s]peech that entertains, like speech that informs, is protected by the First Amendment because '[t]he line between the informing and the entertaining is too elusive for the protection of that basic right.'" ... We also find no merit in the argument that CBC's use of players' names and information in its fantasy baseball games is not speech at all. We have held that "the pictures, graphic design, concept art, sounds, music, stories, and narrative present in video games" is speech entitled to first amendment protection.... Similarly, here CBC uses the "names, nicknames, likenesses, signatures, pictures, playing records, and/or biographical data of each player" in an interactive form in connection with its fantasy baseball products....

Courts have also recognized the public value of information about the game of baseball and its players, referring to baseball as "the national pastime." ... A California court, in a case where Major League Baseball was itself defending its use of players' names, likenesses, and information against the players' asserted rights of publicity, observed, "Major league baseball is followed by millions of people across this country on a daily basis ... The public has an enduring fascination in the records set by former players and in memorable moments from previous games ... The records and statistics remain of interest to the public because they provide context that allows fans to better appreciate (or deprecate) today's performances." Gionfriddo v. Major League Baseball, 94 Cal. App. 4th 400, 411, 114 Cal. Rptr. 2d 307 (2001). The Court in Gionfriddo concluded that the "recitation and discussion of factual data concerning the athletic performance of [players on Major League Baseball's website] command a substantial public interest, and, therefore, is a form of expression due substantial constitutional protection." Id. We find these views persuasive.

In addition, the facts in this case barely, if at all, implicate the interests that states typically intend to vindicate by providing rights of publicity to individuals. Economic interests that states seek to promote include the right of an individual to reap the rewards of his or her endeavors and an individual's right to earn a living. Other motives for creating a publicity right are the desire to provide incentives to encourage a person's productive activities and to protect consumers from misleading advertising.... But major league baseball players are rewarded, and handsomely, too, for their participation in games and can earn additional large sums from endorsements and sponsorship arrangements. Nor is there any danger here that consumers will be misled, because the fantasy baseball games depend on the inclusion of all players and thus cannot create a false impression that some particular player with "star power" is endorsing CBC's products.

Then there are so-called non-monetary interests that publicity rights are sometimes thought to advance. These include protecting natural rights, rewarding celebrity labors, and avoiding emotional harm.... We do not see that any of these interests are especially relevant here, where baseball players are rewarded separately for their labors, and where any emotional harm would most likely be caused by a player's actual performance, in which case media coverage would cause the same harm. We also note that some courts have indicated that the right of publicity is intended to promote only economic interests and that noneconomic interests are more directly served by so-called rights of privacy....

Because we hold that CBC's first amendment rights in offering its fantasy baseball products supersede the players' rights of publicity, we need not reach CBC's alternative argument that federal copyright law preempts the players' state law rights of publicity.

III.

[The court also ruled against the players on their claim that CBC had contractually restricted itself by virtue of a provision relinquishing the right to challenge the assertion of ownership by the players, and a provision whereby CBC agreed to make no use of the players' information after the license agreement with the players had expired. These contract and estoppels claims by the players against CBC failed because the contract terms involved were not enforceable. The Players Association had warranted that it owned the state law publicity rights of the players relating to their statistics; this was not true, and because of this breach of a material obligation in the contract, the "no-challenge" and "no-use" provisions were not enforceable.]

IV.

For the foregoing reasons, the district court's grant of summary judgment to CBC is affirmed.

Notes

1. Although the Court of Appeals in *C.B.C.* affirmed the lower court's grant of summary judgment on the plaintiffs' claims, the reasoning of the two courts was quite different. Unlike the court of appeals, the district court rejected both the claim that the players had a right of publicity in their names and statistics, and the assertion that defendant had appropriated them to their commercial advantage. Moreover, whatever publicity rights the players might have had were outweighed by the First Amendment rights of the defendant to use the players' names and statistics, information which the court considered to be simply "bits of baseball's history." The district court decision can be found at 443 F. Supp. 2d 1077 (E.D. Mo. 2006).

2. The right of publicity is a state common law right. The *C.B.C.* decision is based on Missouri law. Is the decision simply the initial foray of a court into this issue? Might one expect that other courts will view these rights of publicity differently?

3. The court's decision talked about baseball's special position in American culture as "America's pastime," and the fact that baseball players were already rewarded "handsomely"

for their professional efforts. Are these relevant considerations for the court to consider? Are popular sports like football and basketball to be treated differently because they lack the historical and cultural roots of baseball? Is the fact that a player is well-paid for his efforts a reason to diminish his publicity rights?

4. One effect of *C.B.C.* is that other organizations sponsoring fantasy games are seeking to renegotiate their licensing agreements with the players' organizations. *See* Maureen C. Weston, *The Fantasy of Athlete Publicity Rights: Public Fascination and Fantasy Sports' Assertion of Free Use Place Athlete Publicity Rights On an Uncertain Playing Field*, 11 Chap. L. Rev. 581, 598 (2008) (noting that fantasy sports providers such as ESPN are seeking renegotiation of licensing deals in the wake of *C.B.C.*).

5. How relevant are the traditional cases in the publicity area to the issue of fantasy sports in the 21st century? *C.B.C.* makes no reference to the fact that fantasy sports are internet based. Is there a difference between using a player's name and statistics in a board game, and using it as a basis of a fantasy competition? Should the court's opinion at least have acknowledged that digital media are more difficult to restrict than traditional and tangible media like board games and magazines?

6. After the United States Supreme Court denied certiorari in the *C.B.C.* case, CBSSports.com offered a fantasy college football game using the names and statistics of actual college athletes. Previously, they had offered a fantasy game identifying players only as "Syracuse RB" or "Michigan WR." Fantasy sports based on college basketball is also being considered. *See* Nando Di Fino, *College Football Fantasy Game to Name Names*, Wall St. J., July 31, 2008, *available at* http://online.wsj.com/article/SB121733679819593215. html?mod=googlenews_wsj. The NCAA objected to the CBS action, and complained that NCAA bylaws were being violated because player likenesses were being used. This could jeopardize the player's amateur status under NCAA rules. However, the NCAA has taken no formal action against CBS to halt the games. *See also* Jack Carey, *NCAA Unlikely to Wage War on Fantasy Site*, USA Today, Oct. 28, 2008, *available at* http://www.usatoday.com/ sports/college/2008-10-27-knight-commission_N.htm.

7. The *C.B.C.* case has generated significant commentary. *See, e.g.*, Gustavo A. Otalvora, *Alfonso Soriano is Getting Robbed: Why the Eighth Circuit Court of Appeals Made a Bad Call in* C.B.C. Distribution and Marketing v. Major League Baseball, 2008 U. Ill. J.L. Tech. & Pol'y 383 (Fall 2008); Matthew J. Mitten, *A Triple Play for the Public Domain: Delaware Lottery to Motorola to C.B.C.*, 11 Chapman L. Rev. 569 (2008); Richard T. Karcher, *The Use of Players' Identities in Fantasy Sports Leagues: Developing Workable Standards for Right of Publicity Claims*, 111 Penn St. L. Rev. 557 (2007); Stacey B. Evans, *Whose Stats Are They Anyway? Analyzing the Battle Between Major League Baseball and Fantasy Game Sites*, 9 Tex. Rev. Ent & Sports L. 335 (2008); Matthew G. Massari, *Lessons from the Fantasy Sports Dispute*, 25 Ent. & Sports Law. 9 (Winter 2008); E. Jason Burke, *"Quasi-Property" Rights: Fantasy or Reality? An Examination of* C.B.C. Distribution & Marketing Inc. v. Major League Baseball Advanced Media, L.P. *and Fantasy Sports Providers' Use of Professional Athlete Statistics*, 27 Wash. U. J.L. & Pol'y 161 (2008).

4. Proscribed Sports Betting

As noted in the Introduction to this Chapter, the amount of money wagered on sports through legal channels is dwarfed by the amount bet illegally. Sporting events are a popular part of American culture. The opportunities to bet legally are limited. It is thus not surprising that ardent and even casual fans of the games look for outlets to bet on sporting events. Despite the widespread nature of such sports betting, the fact remains there are federal and state laws that make this activity illegal in one way or another. The materials that follow show the imperfect statutory tools that federal and state authorities have to curtail this betting.

A. Federal Law

United States v. Scavo
593 F.2d 837 (8th Cir. 1979)

HENLEY, Circuit Judge.

Frank Scavo appeals from his conviction of being engaged in the business of betting or wagering and knowingly using wire communication facilities for the transmission in interstate commerce of information assisting in the placing of bets or wagers, in violation of 18 U.S.C. § 1084(a) [Wire Act]. We affirm.

On December 20, 1976 Chief Judge Devitt of the District of Minnesota signed an order authorizing interception of communications conducted on telephones which were suspected of being used in connection with an illegal gambling business being conducted in violation of 18 U.S.C. s 1955 [Illegal Gambling Business Act]. The investigation centered on one Dwight Mezo, who operated a substantial bookmaking business in the Minneapolis area. As a result of this investigation, appellant, along with nine others, was indicted by a grand jury and charged with conducting an illegal gambling business in violation of 18 U.S.C. § 1955. Eight of appellant's co-defendants, including Mezo, pleaded guilty and charges against a ninth codefendant were dropped.

On March 8, 1978 appellant was charged by information with use of a communications facility to transmit wagering information in violation of 18 U.S.C. § 1084(a)....

At trial the government's evidence consisted principally of playing recordings of telephone conversations obtained from the court-authorized wiretaps on the telephones of Dwight Mezo. In addition, F.B.I. Special Agent William Holmes was qualified as an expert in gambling and testified about the nature of gambling operations, gambling terminology, and his opinion as to appellant's role in Mezo's bookmaking operation. He testified that appellant, then a resident of Las Vegas, provided Mezo with much-needed "line" information i.e., the odds or point spread established to equalize or induce betting on sporting events.

Appellant offered two exhibits for the purpose of showing the ready availability of line information from other sources, but introduced no other evidence. The jury returned a verdict of guilty and the district court sentenced appellant to one year on probation. This timely appeal ensued.

Appellant challenges his conviction on six grounds: (1) the evidence was insufficient to show a violation of 18 U.S.C. § 1084(a); (2) the court erred in its instructions to the jury; ...

A. Sufficiency of the Evidence.

Appellant first contends that the evidence was insufficient to support a conviction under 18 U.S.C. § 1084(a). The statute provides:

> (a) Whoever being engaged in the business of betting or wagering knowingly uses a wire communication facility for the transmission in interstate or foreign

commerce of bets or wagers or information assisting in the placing of bets or wagers on any sporting event or contest, or for the transmission of a wire communication which entitles the recipient to receive money or credit as a result of bets or wagers, or for information assisting in the placing of bets or wagers, shall be fined not more than $10,000 or imprisoned not more than two years, or both.

Appellant concedes that he used a wire communication facility (the telephone) to transmit information assisting in the placing of bets or wagers. Appellant argues, however, that a person who merely provides line information is not "engaged in the business of betting or wagering."

Appellant relies on a series of cases interpreting 18 U.S.C. § 1955. This statute provides in relevant part:

(a) Whoever conducts, finances, manages, supervises, directs, or owns all or part of an illegal gambling business shall be fined not more than $20,000 or imprisoned not more than five years, or both.

(b) As used in this section

(1) "illegal gambling business" means a gambling business which

(i) is a violation of the law of a State or political subdivision in which it is conducted;

(ii) involves five or more persons who conduct, finance, manage, supervise, direct, or own all or part of such business; and

(iii) has been or remains in substantially continuous operation for a period in excess of thirty days or has a gross revenue of $2,000 in any single day.

A number of cases decided under this statute have held that the mere occasional exchange of line information between two individuals is insufficient to show that they are so interdependent as to be part of a single "illegal gambling business." For example, in United States v. Guzek, 527 F.2d 552, 557–58 (8th Cir. 1975), we said:

(T)he mere placing of bets by one bookmaker with another or the mere furnishing of line information in and of itself may not be sufficient to establish the interdependence of the bookmakers so as to fuse them into one single business for the purpose of counting each of these participants toward the five persons necessary to establish a violation of s 1955....

Appellant contends that the phrase "conduct(ing) ... an illegal gambling business" used in § 1955 is synonymous with the phrase "being engaged in the business of a betting or wagering" used in § 1084(a) and thus the cases decided under § 1955 should also apply to alleged violations of § 1084(a).

We find appellant's argument unpersuasive. The issue in the cases decided under § 1955 is whether the person providing line information has such a close, ongoing, and substantial relationship to the person receiving the information as to make them both participants in a single gambling business. In enacting § 1955, Congress did not intend to make all gambling businesses subject to federal prosecution; rather the statute was "intended to reach only those persons who prey systematically upon our citizens and whose syndicated operations are so continuous and so substantial as to be of national concern...." H.R.Rep.No.1549, 91st Cong. 2d Sess. (1970), Reprinted in (1970) U.S. Code Cong. & Admin. News, pp. 4007, 4029. See also United States v. Box, 530 F.2d 1258, 1264–65 (5th Cir. 1976). The cases relied upon by appellant merely reflect a judicial sensitivity to the limited purpose of Congress in enacting § 1955.

In regard to § 1084(a), however, there is nothing to indicate that Congress intended only to punish large-scale gambling businesses. The basis of federal jurisdiction underlying § 1084(a) is the use of interstate communications facilities, which is wholly distinct from the connection between large-scale gambling businesses and the flow of commerce, which provides the jurisdictional basis for § 1955. See United States v. Sacco, 491 F.2d 995, 999 (9th Cir. 1974). Thus, the necessary showing of interdependence between individuals involved in an illegal gambling business under § 1955 is not required under § 1084(a). Moreover, § 1084(a) is not limited to persons who are exclusively engaged in the business of betting or wagering and the statute does not distinguish between persons engaged in such business on their own behalf and those engaged in the business on behalf of others. See Truchinski v. United States, 393 F.2d 627, 630 (8th Cir.), cert. denied, 393 U.S. 831 (1968).

Although we reject appellant's blanket assertion that suppliers of line information are outside the scope of § 1084(a), we must nevertheless determine whether the government introduced evidence sufficient to show that appellant was "engaged in the business of betting and wagering." At trial, the government proceeded on the theory that appellant was part of Mezo's bookmaking business and on this aspect of the case the authorities relied upon by appellant are relevant to a prosecution under § 1084(a). They are not controlling, however, because the evidence adduced showed more than a mere occasional exchange of line information between appellant and Mezo.

Viewed in the light most favorable to the government, the evidence showed that appellant furnished line information to Mezo on a regular basis; that Mezo relied on this information; that some sort of financial arrangement existed between appellant and Mezo; that appellant was fully aware of Mezo's bookmaking operation; and that accurate and up-to-date line information is of critical importance to any bookmaking operation.

Given this evidence, we conclude that the government has shown that appellant was an important part of the Mezo bookmaking operation and that appellant was indeed "engaged in the business of betting or wagering" within the meaning of § 1084(a).

B. The Court's Instructions.

Appellant contends that the court made two errors in instructing the jury. First, he claims that the court erred in refusing to give the following instruction in relation to the elements of the offense under § 1084(a):

> That defendant must have been aware of the statute in question; that he must have known that he was violating the law in providing the line information before he can be found guilty of the offense charged.

Appellant contends that such a specific intent instruction is mandated by Cohen v. United States, 378 F.2d 751 (9th Cir.), cert. denied, 389 U.S. 897 (1967). In Cohen, the court held that Congress intended knowledge of the statutory prohibition to be an element of the offense under § 1084(a), but also held that there is a rebuttable presumption that the accused in fact had knowledge of the law. 378 F.2d at 757.

The parties have not cited, nor has our independent research disclosed, any other case which has accepted the Cohen rationale. Indeed, in a subsequent case, the Ninth Circuit, in a brief per curiam opinion, upheld a conviction under § 1084(a) against a challenge that the defendant had no intent to commit a violation of federal law. See United States v. Swank, 441 F.2d 264, 265 (9th Cir. 1971).

Given the facts of this case, we have no occasion to decide whether Cohen correctly states the law. In Cohen, the court approved the following instruction:

Unless and until outweighed by evidence in the case to the contrary, the presumption is that every person knows what the law forbids and what the law requires to be done.

378 F.2d at 756 n.5. In the instant case, the record is devoid of any evidence from which it could be inferred that appellant acted because of ignorance of the law. Thus, there was nothing to rebut the presumption approved in *Cohen*, and failure to give a specific intent instruction, if error at all, was harmless.

Appellant's second contention relates to the instruction defining the phrase "engaged in the business of betting or wagering." Appellant offered, and the court rejected, an instruction limiting application of this phrase to "bookmakers" i.e., persons who accept, exchange, or lay off bets. Instead, the court instructed the jury as follows:

The first of these essential elements that the government must prove is that the defendant engaged in the business of betting or wagering if and when he used the wire communications facility. The term "business" is to be applied according to its usual and ordinary meaning.

An individual engages in the business of betting or wagering if he regularly performs a function which is an integral part of such business. The individual need not be exclusively engaged in the business nor must he share in the profits or losses of the business. He may be an agent or employee for another person's business, but the function he performs must provide a regular and essential contribution to that business. If an individual performs only an occasional or nonessential service or is a mere bettor or customer, he cannot properly be said to engage in the business.

A business enterprise usually involves a continuing course of conduct by persons associated together for a common purpose.

We find no error in the court's instruction, which is in accord with the law in this circuit. See Truchinski v. United States, supra, 393 F.2d at 630.

United States v. Schullo

363 F. Supp. 246 (D. Minn. 1973)

NEVILLE, District Judge.

Defendants were tried before a jury and found guilty of violating 18 U.S.C. § 1955, the Federal anti-gambling statute. The court instructed the jury that, under that law, before any defendant could be found guilty the government must establish beyond a reasonable doubt:

1) that a gambling business was conducted in the State of Minnesota;

2) that the business violated the laws of the State of Minnesota;

3) that the business had a gross revenue of at least $2,000 in any single day;

4) that there were five or more persons who did "conduct, finance, manage, supervise, direct or own all or a part of a gambling business ..."

The evidence was very clear that three co-defendants, not presently on trial i.e., William Wolk, Jack Capra and Myron Fishman, conducted a gambling business in the State of Minnesota in violation of state law. Wolk, Capra and Fishman pled guilty to another offense and at least two of them were in jail at the time of this trial. These three ran and operated a bookmaking business between at least the dates of February 21, 1971 and approximately June 22, 1971. There is no question but what their activities violated the laws of the State of Minnesota and in final argument counsel for Schullo and Petrangello (though not counsel for Thomas) conceded that the evidence had established the first two statutory requirements and that Schullo and Petrangello had been engaged in a gambling business in violation of Minnesota State law. Though not so admitted by Thomas' counsel, the uncontroverted evidence as to him and the others was so strong as to leave no doubt of fulfillment of requirements 1 and 2 and the court so commented to the jury.

Counsel for all defendants made challenges to elements 3 and 4 as to not being sustained in the evidence and affected by alleged error in the manner in which the court instructed the jury. As to element 3, a required showing of gross revenue of at least $2,000 in any single day, the government introduced transcripts of telephonic conversations with the "book" showing that on February 20th bets totaling in excess of $25,000 were placed and again on March 3rd bets in excess of $7,000 were placed. The statute provides that a gambling business must receive *gross revenue* in excess of $2,000 in any single day. Defendants' contention is that the court erred in instructing the jury in regard to total bets placed as a measure of gross revenue. It is their view, as nearly as the court has understood it, that gross revenue is an accounting concept and in effect should be analogized to the cost of goods sold in a financial statement for a normal business, i.e., total revenue less the cost of purchasing and manufacturing the products sold, arriving at gross profit before any deductions for overhead, depreciation, taxes or miscellaneous expenses. The court rejected this and instructed the jury that gross revenue as used in the statute means all wagers or bets accepted, i.e., the total of all bets and wagers placed including credit as well as cash transactions. Counsel contend that in operating a "book" some bets are won and collected but that some bets are lost and must be paid off. Therefore, according to defendants, the proper way to determine gross revenue is to deduct the pay offs from the total receipts, thereby arriving at the bookmaker's net figure. The court is unequivocally convinced that if Congress had intended that definition it would have phrased the statute in different terms. Gross revenue must mean total amount of bets handled, dealt with or received as distinguished from any net figure or amount from which deductions have been taken. This court patterned its instruction after the definition in United States v. Ceraso, 467 F.2d 653, 657 (3d Cir. 1972), where the appellate court stated:

> The legislative history indicates that Congress contemplated that the $2000 figure would refer simply to the amount wagered in any one day. Throughout the discussion of the legislation, many Congressmen relied heavily on the Report of the President's Commission on Law Enforcement and Administration of Justice, The Challenge of Crime in a Free Society. The report used the term 'gross revenue' to indicate the amount that it believed was wagered during any one period in the United States. It carefully distinguished that figure from the profit it believed organized crime made on such activity.... During the debate, Congressmen picked up this terminology, and used the term 'gross revenue' to mean the total amount bet. Most significantly, Senator Hruska, who added the provision relating to syndicated gambling to the Organized Crime Statute, stated:
>
> > 'The suggested standard for determining that such an operation is of sufficient size to warrant Federal intervention is entirely reasonable and practicable. *Any bookmaking or numbers operation which does* more than $2000 in business in one day ... must have a substantial adverse effect on the flow of moneys and goods in interstate commerce (emphasis in original) 115 Cong. Rec. 10736 (1969).'

The concern of Congress was the amount of daily business transacted by gamblers, not the sum of their profits.

It is a severe task for the Government to obtain sufficient evidence to sustain any convictions under any definition of gross revenue. It would complicate their task enormously if they had to attempt to show the net profits from such an operation in any one day. Gambling records are obviously not public documents. The amount of profits could generally be proven only by seizure of carefully secreted files. The interpretation suggested by appellants would render the enforcement of this statute a mockery. We, therefore, conclude that there was sufficient evidence to sustain the conviction and that the verdict was not against the weight of the evidence. This court adopted the rationale and language of *Ceraso* and believes there was no error here.

In regard to the question of the fourth requirement i.e., "conduct, finance, manage, supervise, direct or own all or a part of a gambling business", the court instructed the jury as follows:

> The words 'conduct, finance, manage, supervise, direct or own all or part of' are to be given their normal, customary meaning. If it is proven beyond a reasonable doubt that a defendant here on trial is a bookmaker himself and exchanges line or other information or places or accepts layoff bets with another bookmaker, you may consider that defendant is conducting, financing, managing, directing or owning all or part of the gambling business of the other bookmaker.

> On the other hand, if a person is merely a customer placing a bet with a bookmaker he does not fit within the definition of those words.

> So if a person is merely a customer placing a bet or bets with a bookmaker, without being a bookmaker himself, or without being an employee or agent or runner of a bookmaker, then the defendant is not a person who conducted, financed, managed, supervised, directed or owned all or part of an illegal gambling business.

The court obtained this definition from the *Ceraso* case above cited, and from a synthesis of the language found in United States v. Becker, 461 F.2d 230, 232 (2d Cir. 1972), and United States v. Harris, 460 F.2d 1041, 1049 (5th Cir. 1972). These cases trace the legislative history of the 1970 Organized Crime Control Act. *Becker* portrays Section 1955 as having been enacted *in pari materia* with Section 18 U.S.C. § 1511 which uses the same language and has explicit legislative history to support the conclusions of this court. Thus Congress' intent was to include all those who participate in the operation of a gambling business, regardless of how minor their roles, and whether they be labeled agents, runners, independent contractors or the like. Only customers of the business were to be excluded. Perhaps this court's instruction did not go even that far for no reference therein was made to the term "operation".

The court recognizes that the controversy here centers mostly around the word "conduct", and perhaps the word "finance", as there was no claim by the government that the three movant-defendants now before the court were owners or that they directly managed, supervised or directed the Wold-Capra-Fishman "book."

From the evidence before the jury however reasonable minds could find beyond a reasonable doubt that the operation of a successful "bookmaking" business requires an opportunity to "lay off" bets, i.e., to obtain sort of a re-insurance. If too many people bet only one side of an athletic contest a bookmaker assumes too great a risk of loss and endeavors to find another bookmaker where he can "lay off" his excess so as to keep his bets on each side of a game or event as equal in amount as possible. Lay off betting then is a necessity for successful bookmaking operation.

The jury further could find under the evidence that it is necessary or at least very desirable that a bookmaker be continuously informed on other bookmakers' "lines" i.e., apprised of "line" information comprising point spreads and odds being used by other bookmakers. Such is necessary to prevent undue betting on another book because the odds are better. In addition, clever betters and gamblers will attempt to "middle" two bookmakers if possible. That is, they will bet both sides of the same game with different bookmakers who are using different "line" information in hopes of winning against both bookmakers if the final score is in the middle.

There is no question but what the jury could find beyond a reasonable doubt that all three defendants took lay-off bets from the Wolk-Capra-Fishman "book", although they, as separate bookmakers, did not directly operate that book. The jury could find that these movant-defendants did furnish and exchange "line" information up to several times on some days. Premised on the theory that these exchanges are necessary to the successful operation of book, the jury could and apparently did find that these three men were conducting and/or financing the Wolk-Capra-Fishman bookmaking business and thus comprised part of the five persons who must be involved in a gambling business to violate the statute.

The court recognizes that the Congressional language used is perhaps inept to some extent but the court's function is to attempt to instruct the jury so as to permit it to act upon the Congressional intent and the Congressional history set out in the three cases above. Although the Eighth Circuit has not passed upon the matter, this court reaches the conclusion from the above three circuit court cases and from studying the statute that the words "conduct" and "finance" should receive a broad definition to accomplish the purpose of the Organized Crime Act. This court is satisfied with the construction used by the three circuits in the above cases. *See* United States v. Harris, *supra,* in support of the definition that the word "conduct" means that "this section applies generally to persons who participate in the ... conducting of an illegal gambling business." Defense counsel's argument that the strict dictionary definition of the words "conduct" and "finance" should be adopted is not well taken. Attention of the court is called to an excerpt from 13 Criminal Law Reporter 3015, quoting a proposed amendment to 18 U.S.C. § 1955, said to be recommended by the present Executive. This would insert that one is guilty of violating § 1955 if he "Receives lay off wagers or otherwise provides re-insurance in relation to persons engaged in gambling." From this springs the familiar argument that such is not presently the law; else why would such an amendment be proposed. The court rejects this. At least two of the three circuit court cases above cited have in effect included the above as encompassed in the term "conduct" or "finance" and while the proposed amendment would of course make the issue more clear, it does not follow that such is required nor that the law is to the contrary unless amended....

Other assignments of error are without merit. [Defendants' motions denied.]

Notes

1. The federal laws considered in these cases were the Wire Act, 18 U.S.C. § 1084, and the Illegal Gambling Business Act (sometimes referred to as the Federal Antigambling Statute), 18 U.S.C. § 1955. Prosecutions for illegal gaming activity occur most commonly under these provisions. *See, e.g.,* Cohen v. United States, 378 F.2d 751 (9th Cir. 1967)

(defendant must have knowledge of interstate nature of telephone calls for Wire Act to be violated); United States v. Kelley, 395 F.2d 727 (2d Cir. 1968) (case also involved violation of federal gambling tax statutes); United States v. Fuller, 441 F.2d 755 (4th Cir. 1971) (unsuccessful challenge to wiretap warrants establishing Wire Act violations); United States v. Vigi, 363 F. Supp. 314 (E.D. Mich. 1973) (violation of IGBA).

While these are the most likely tools federal prosecutors will employ against bookmakers, there are several other federal laws that may be implicated, either alone or in addition to these statutes. This includes the Travel Act, 18 U.S.C. § 1952, the Paraphernalia Act, 18 U.S.C. § 1953, and a law prohibiting sports bribery, 18 U.S.C. § 224. As the main cases above suggest, prosecution for violations of multiple federal statutes is not unusual. *See also* United States v. Kaczowski, 114 F. Supp. 2d 143 (W.D.N.Y. 2000) (prosecution under Wire Act, Travel Act, and IGBA).

2. In *Scavo* and *Schullo*, the courts noted that the federal statutes applied to those in the business of betting, and did not apply to those placing the bets. If the federal government really believes that interstate sports gambling is pernicious, why not attack the "demand" side of the equation as well, that is, the bettor himself? Would such prosecutions, similar to prosecutions of those using the services of prostitutes and those using illegal drugs, cut down even further on such illegal gambling? Why might the federal government not be inclined to amend federal law to do this?

B. State Law

i. Gambling

Many states have separate prohibitions for placing a bet, "gambling," and accepting the bet, "bookmaking." Where a state statute prohibits gambling, sports betting is often included in the statutory language. For example, Texas' statute provides:

§ 47.02. Gambling

(a) A person commits an offense if he:

(1) makes a bet on the partial or final result of a game or contest or on the performance of a participant in a game or contest;

(2) makes a bet on the result of any political nomination, appointment, or election or on the degree of success of any nominee, appointee, or candidate; or

(3) plays and bets for money or other thing of value at any game played with cards, dice, balls, or any other gambling device.

See also ALA. CODE § 13A-12-20 (2005); COLO. REV. STAT. § 18-10-102 (2009); HAW. REV. STAT. § 712-1220 (1993).

ii. Bookmaking

Santoro v. State
959 So. 2d 1235 (Fla. App. 2007)

LaROSE, Judge.

Joseph Salvatore Santoro appeals his convictions and sentences for eighteen counts of felony bookmaking. We affirm. Mr. Santoro argues that the State failed to prove that he committed the crimes in Florida. We write to address his claim that United States v. Truesdale, 152 F.3d 443 (5th Cir.1998), a case dealing with offshore bookmaking, compels reversal. As we explain below, *Truesdale* is unavailing. Mr. Santoro also argues that the State failed to prove his intent to commit multiple offenses and that the State relied on improper identification evidence to convict him. Mr. Santoro failed to preserve these alleged errors in the trial court; he has not demonstrated fundamental error. Thus, we reject these arguments without further discussion.

Between late 2001 and early 2002, the Collier County Sheriff's Office investigated Mr. Santoro's bookmaking operations. Mr. Santoro contacted an undercover officer and asked if he wanted to place bets. Mr. Santoro confirmed the events on which the officer would like to place bets, informed the officer of his dollar limits, and provided toll-free service numbers and an identification number for placing bets. Mr. Santoro also gave the officer his personal phone number. Thereafter, the undercover officer placed numerous bets by phone with unknown individuals using the service numbers provided by Mr. Santoro.

On one occasion, Mr. Santoro met the officer in Naples and paid him $1500 for bets made during the undercover operation. A week later, the officer and Mr. Santoro spoke by phone to arrange a $1150 payment by the officer. Mr. Santoro instructed the officer to send the money to Mr. Santoro's Fort Lauderdale address. The sheriff's office sent the money to that address. The betting continued after Mr. Santoro arranged for an increase in the undercover officer's betting limits. A final meeting occurred at an exit off Interstate 75 in mid-February, where the officer paid a $1200 betting debt to Mr. Santoro.

The State filed an information charging Mr. Santoro, as a principal, with bookmaking.

The term "bookmaking" means the act of taking or receiving, while engaged in the business or profession of gambling, any bet or wager upon the result of any trial or contest of skill, speed, power, or endurance of [man] ... or upon the result of any chance, casualty, unknown, or contingent event whatsoever.

See § 849.25(1)(a), Fla. Stat. (2001). The bookmaking statute lists factors to be considered in determining whether a person has engaged in the offense of bookmaking:

1. Taking advantage of betting odds created to produce a profit for the bookmaker or charging a percentage on accepted wagers.

2. Placing all or part of accepted wagers with other bookmakers to reduce the chance of financial loss.

3. Taking or receiving more than five wagers in any single day.

4. Taking or receiving wagers totaling more than $500 in any single day, or more than $1500 in any single week.

5. Engaging in a common scheme with two or more persons to take or receive wagers.

6. Taking or receiving wagers on both sides on a contest at the identical point spread.

7. Any other factor relevant to establishing that the operating procedures of such person are commercial in nature.

See § 849.25(1)(b).

The trial court instructed the jury that in order to convict Mr. Santoro, the State had to prove (1) that he engaged in the business or profession of gambling; (2) that while so engaged, he took or received a bet or wager; and (3) that the bet or wager was upon the result of a trial or contest of skill, speed, power, or endurance of man. *See* § 849.25(1)(a); Fla. Std. Jury Instr. (Crim.) 22.14. The trial court also instructed the jury to consider the section 849.25(1)(b) factors in making its deliberations. *See* Fla. Std. Jury Instr. 22.14.

Finally, the trial court gave the jury the standard principal instruction:

"If the defendant helped another person or persons commit or attempt to commit a crime, the defendant is a principal and must be treated as if he had done all the things the other person or persons did, if the defendant had a conscious intent that the criminal act be done and the defendant did some act or said some word which was intended to, and which did incite, cause, encourage, assist or advise the other person or persons to actually commit or attempt to commit the crime.

To be a principal, the defendant does not have to be present when the crime is committed or attempted."

Fla. Std. Jury Instr. 3.5(a); *see also* § 777.011, Fla. Stat. (2001). The jury found Mr. Santoro guilty of all charges.

Mr. Santoro claims that the bets were made offshore, most likely in Costa Rica. Therefore, he argues, the State failed to prove that gambling occurred in Florida. Mr. Santoro bases his argument on United States v. Truesdale, 152 F.3d 443. His reliance is misplaced. *Truesdale* involved a bookmaking prosecution under 18 U.S.C. § 1955. The federal statute prohibits conducting, financing, managing, supervising, directing, or owning "'all or part of an illegal gambling business,'" specifically a gambling business that "'violates state or local law.'" *Id.* at 446 (quoting § 1955). The *Truesdale* jury received instructions covering only the Texas bookmaking statute. *Id.* at 447. On appeal, the appellants argued a lack of evidence showing that they conducted illegal bookmaking in Texas. No bets were received, recorded, or forwarded in Texas; the bets were placed in Jamaica and in the Dominican Republic. *Id.*

The Fifth Circuit Court of Appeals reversed, concluding that the prosecution presented insufficient evidence to show beyond a reasonable doubt that the appellants conducted bookmaking in Texas. Significantly, although acting as a custodian of money used to place offshore bets violates the Texas statute, the federal indictment did not allege and the jury was not instructed that Mr. Truesdale violated that statutory provision. *Id.* at 448–49. But for these omissions, the convictions might have been sustained. *See* United States v. Atiyeh, 402 F.3d 354, 371 (3d Cir. 2005).

In Mr. Santoro's case, the jury heard evidence that he supplied the undercover officer in Florida with toll-free phone numbers and an identification number to call to place bets. Mr. Santoro also gave the officer his Broward County phone number in case any problems arose, so that Mr. Santoro could resolve any problems from Florida. The officer placed bets mostly on football games. Mr. Santoro told the officer in Florida that he could bet up to $500 per game and up to $1500 per week. The officer met with Mr. Santoro on multiple occasions in Florida to exchange gambling money, and Mr. Santoro, from Florida, arranged an increase in the officer's betting limit. The information specifically alleged violations of section 849.25(1)(a). The trial court properly instructed the jury on the statutory elements of the charged offenses and on the principal theory.

The circumstances surrounding Mr. Santoro's offenses render *Truesdale* inapposite. Accordingly, his convictions and sentences are affirmed.

Notes

1. Numerous state statutes criminalize what is variously called "bookmaking," "commercial gambling," or "keeping a gambling house." *See, e.g.*, Iowa Code Ann. § 725.7, 725.13 (2009); Ala. Code 1975 § 13A-12-20, 12-22 (2005); 18 Pa. Cons. Stat. Ann. § 5514 (2000); S.C. Code § 16-19-130 (2003). Minnesota law makes it a felony to engage in "sports bookmaking," defined as "the activity of intentionally receiving, recording, or forwarding within any 30-day period more than five bets, or offers to bet, that total more than $2,500 on any one or more sporting events." Minn. Stat. § 609.75 (7) (2009). In one case, a Minnesota appeals court ruled that it was no defense to a violation of the statute that one was a "beard"—a person who only relayed bets for others and risked no money himself. State v. Greenfield, 622 N.W.2d 403 (Minn. App. 2001). For other applications of bookmaking statutes involving sports betting, *see* State v. Cartwright, 510 P.2d 405 (Ariz. Ct. App. 1973) (under Arizona bookmaking statute, language "in the business of bookmaking" was intended to distinguish bookmakers from purely social bettors, not to define it as one ongoing offense; thus each separate recording and registering of a bet constitutes a separate offense under the statute); State v. Owens, 703 P.2d 898 (N.M. Ct. App. 1984) (discussing difference between social gambling and "commercial gambling" and affirming defendant's conviction for commercial gambling); State v. Benevento, 350 A.2d 485 (N.J. Super. App. Div. 1975) (acting as an intermediary between bettors and bookie does not protect a defendant from criminal liability).

2. Not all sports betting outside the "PASPA-exempt" states is conducted between bettor and bookmaker. The classic illustration of what might be called "social gambling" occurs every March when people, many of whom have only passing knowledge of the sport, fill in brackets for the NCAA Men's Basketball Tournament. Is this legal? Several states have exceptions to their gambling statutes for this type of activity. The language of the exceptions differs from state to state, but there are basically two ways the exception is written into state law: (1) by declaring that bets are exempt if they are non-banked and in a private place; or (2) by exempting bets, which, in the language of the statutes, are "incidental to a bona fide social relationship." *Compare* Iowa Code § 99B.12 ("exempting bets "incidental to a bona fide social relationship") *with* Tex. Penal Code § 47.02 (providing a defense to prosecution for bets that are made "in a private place," with no one receiving "any economic benefit other than personal winnings," and where, except for skill or luck, "the risks of losing and the chances of winning were the same for all participants."). In a similar vein is the Colorado statute, which provides:

> "Gambling" means risking any money, credit, deposit, or other thing of value for gain contingent in whole or in part upon lot, chance, the operation of a gambling device, or the happening or outcome of an event, including a sporting event, over which the person taking a risk has no control, but does not include ...
>
> d) Any game, wager, or transaction which is incidental to a bona fide social relationship, is participated in by natural persons only, and in which no person is participating, directly or indirectly, in professional gambling. Colo. Rev. Stat. Ann. § 18-10-102(2)(d).

Other statutes with social gambling exceptions include Va Code Ann. § 18.2-334 (2006); Me. Rev. Gaming L. Stat. Ann. tit. 17A, § 952 (2006); Conn. Gen. Stat. Ann. § 53-278b (West 2007); Colo. Rev. Stat. Ann. § 18-10-102(2)(d) (2009); Or. Rev. Stat. Ann. § 167.117(7) (West 2003). *See also* H. Wayne Clark Jr., *Who's In? The Bona Fide Future of Office Pools*, 8 GAMING L. REV. 202 (2004) (discussing legality of NCAA pools under PASPA and various state laws).

5. League and Amateur Organization Restrictions on Sports Betting

It is obviously in the interests of those operating sporting events to discourage and, more likely, prohibit betting by the participants on the events involved. The betting can be direct, placed by the participant himself, or indirect, where others compensate the participant in exchange for some action on the part of the participant. In sports betting, there have been several scandals involving "point shaving." One well-known example of "point shaving" involved the 1978–79 Boston College basketball team. In a criminal case against defendants convicted of violating several federal statutes, the court's statement of the facts provides a picture of how point shaving operates.

United States v. Burke

700 F.2d 70 (2d Cir. 1983)

. . . .

Background

The appellants' convictions arise from their participation in the Boston College (B.C.) basketball "point shaving scandal."[1] The evidence presented at trial, although somewhat sketchy, revealed that the point shaving scheme was born in Pittsburgh during the summer months of 1978 and was the brainchild of Rocco Perla and his brother Anthony (Tony). The Perla brothers were small-time gamblers with big-time ideas who viewed the 1978–79 B.C. basketball season as a perfect opportunity to implement these ideas. Their optimism was fueled by the prospect that they might recruit Richard Kuhn to join the scheme. Kuhn, a high school friend of Rocco Perla, was entering his senior year at B.C. and was expected to be a key member of the 1978–79 B.C. basketball team.

The Perlas proposed a simple scheme. They would select, in concert with Kuhn, certain basketball games where the projected point spread separating B.C. from its opponent was expected to be significant. Kuhn would be responsible for ensuring, by his play on the court, that B.C. fell short of the point spread. Thus, for example, if participating bookmakers determined B.C. to be an eight-point favorite in a particular game, Kuhn would be paid his bonus, usually $2,500, if B.C. won by less than eight points. Kuhn agreed to participate in this scheme.

Rocco and his brother Tony then mobilized a betting syndicate to maximize their potential gain from this illegal operation. They contacted a local friend, Paul Mazzei, who was known to have influence within major New York gambling circles. Mazzei in turn contacted Henry Hill, a reputed underworld figure from New York who had befriended Mazzei while both men were serving sentences in a federal penitentiary. Mazzei and the Perlas were particularly hopeful that Hill would enlist the support of his reputed underworld "Boss," defendant James Burke, to ensure protection for their enterprise in the event that the bookmakers discovered they were being swindled. Hill and Burke were brought into the scheme.

---

1. This scandal reached national prominence when *Sports Illustrated* (*SI*), in its February 16, 1981 issue, published an article by Henry Hill, in collaboration with Douglas Looney, entitled *How I Put The Fix In*. This article purported to be Henry Hill's first-hand account of the point shaving scheme and implicated the appellants in this scandal.

On November 16, 1978, Burke instructed Hill, Mazzei and Tony Perla to meet in Boston with Kuhn and any other member of the B.C. team interested in participating in their scheme. Hill, Mazzei and Tony Perla flew to Logan Airport in Boston and, after discussing their strategy with Kuhn, the defendants agreed that the upcoming Providence game would be an appropriate test for their scheme. Hill then paid Kuhn several hundred dollars good-faith money and Mazzei furnished him with some cocaine to seal the conspiracy.

The Providence game was played on December 6, 1978 and Boston College was favored to win by six to seven points. Kuhn was thus expected to keep the score below the six to seven point margin. The test run for the scheme proved unsuccessful, however, when B.C. established an early lead and ultimately won the game by nineteen points. Apparently enraged by their gambling loss, the appellants decided to recruit additional B.C. players to enhance their control over the outcome of the games. They approached Ernie Cobb, the leading scorer on the team, and Joseph Beaulieu, who shared the center position with Kuhn. Cobb agreed to cooperate, while Beaulieu rejected this offer.

The December 16 Harvard game was chosen as the second test for the scheme. B.C. was favored by twelve points, but won the game by only a three-point margin, 86 to 83. The bettors were very happy with this result and Kuhn was paid $2,500 for his efforts. The scheme continued to work successfully in the December 23 U.C.L.A. game, where U.C.L.A., a fifteen to eighteen point favorite, won the game by twenty-two points.

Suspecting that some bookmakers might be getting wise to the scheme, the defendants temporarily revised their strategy after the U.C.L.A. game. To allay any suspicions of foul play, the defendants decided to bet on B.C. to win by *more* than the point spread in a game that they were confident B.C. would win handily. The conspirators chose the January 17 University of Connecticut (UCONN) game to implement this plan. Their strategy was effective; B.C., a two to three point favorite, beat UCONN by a margin greater than the point spread.[4]

In early February, B.C. was scheduled to play two New York teams, Fordham and St. John's. The defendants decided that these games presented especially good opportunities because New York bookmakers generally accepted large bets for New York teams. They reintroduced the original strategy and it proved successful for the February 3 Fordham game when B.C., a thirteen point favorite, won by seven points. The February 6 St. John's game was a "push:" the bettors neither won nor lost when St. John's prevailed by the exact betting margin established by participating bookmakers.

Confident from their recent success, the defendants viewed the February 10 Holy Cross game as an opportunity to reap the full benefits of their scheme. They were aware that bookmakers generally accepted large bets on this game because B.C. and Holy Cross were traditional rivals and also because the game was being televised nationwide. Holy Cross was favored to win and, consistent with the scheme, the defendants bet on Holy Cross to win by a margin greater than the point spread. Holy Cross ultimately won by only two points, however, and the defendants lost a substantial amount of money. The scheme thus concluded on an unsuccessful note.

---

4. The trial testimony relating to the UCONN game highlights the inconsistencies between Henry Hill's testimony at trial and his representations in the SI article. Hill maintained at trial that the game was played on January 17, that B.C. was favored by two or three points and that B.C. ultimately won by a margin greater than the point spread. The SI article indicates that the game was played on January 27, that B.C. was a five to six point favorite and that B.C. won the game by one point, 78–77. We are, however, bound by the evidence presented at trial and our discussion of the facts reflects this limitation.

The criminal conspiracy unraveled when Henry Hill was indicted by state authorities on drug conspiracy charges and subsequently was implicated in the Lufthansa robbery at Kennedy Airport in New York.[5] While being questioned on these charges, Hill revealed that he had recently participated in a point shaving scheme involving the B.C. basketball team and various underworld figures. Hill offered to relate the full story of the swindle if federal officials would guarantee him full immunity and would agree to intercede on his behalf to convince state officials to drop the drug charges pending in state court. The grand jury indicted Burke, Mazzei, Kuhn, Rocco Perla and Tony Perla on the basis of testimony given by Hill. Hill was indicted as a co-conspirator, but was not named as a defendant.

At trial, the government's case consisted principally of the testimony of Henry Hill and three other witnesses, James Sweeney and Joseph Beaulieu, both B.C. players, and Barbara Reed, a 23-year-old nurse who lived with Kuhn during the 1978–79 B.C. season. The government also introduced two confessions, one made by Kuhn and the other by Tony Perla. Finally, the government presented telephone records showing evidence of extensive communications between the conspirators during the 1978–79 season, and records provided by Western Union and various hotels which further corroborated government testimony.

[There was a four week trial after which the jury convicted defendants Burke, Kuhn, Mazzei and Tony and Rocco Perla of the charges of RICO conspiracy, conspiracy to commit sports bribery, and interstate travel with the intent to commit bribery. After considering a number of claims by the defendants on appeal, the court affirmed the convictions of all the defendants.]

Notes

1. The problem of athletes conspiring to affect the outcomes of games is ongoing, and is not confined to basketball. Several athletes from the University of Toledo have been implicated in efforts to fix both basketball and football games between 2003 and 2006. In one instance, an offensive lineman was told he would receive $1000 for committing penalties. *See* A.J. Perez & Kevin Johnson, *Indictments Unsealed in Toledo Sports-Fixing Schemes*, USA TODAY, May 7, 2009, *available at* http://www.usatoday.com/sports/college/2009-05-06-toledo-points-shaving-indictment_N.htm; Mike Fish, *Alleged Toledo Fixers Played Both Sides*, ESPN.com, May 9, 2009, *available at* http://sports.espn.go.com/ncaa/news/story? id=4154321.

2. Because of concerns about this sort of corruption, the NCAA has strict rules against betting and betting-related activity by athletes. NCAA Bylaw 10.3 is specific in its prohibition against sports betting. The bylaw applies to student-athletes, staff members of an institution's athletics department, non-athletics department staff members who have athletic department connections or responsibilities (for example, the institution's faculty athletics representative), and staff members in the institution's conference office. In addition to proscribing sports wagering, the bylaw forbids these people from "provi[ding] information to individuals involved in or associated with any type of sports wagering activities concerning intercollegiate, amateur or professional athletics competition." The penalties for violations of the Bylaw are directed at the student-athlete:

> (a) A student-athlete who engages in activities designed to influence the outcome of an intercollegiate contest or in an effort to affect win-loss margins ("point

---

5. On Friday, December 8, 1978, one of the largest armed robberies in United States history occurred at the Lufthansa cargo warehouse in Kennedy Airport. The criminals involved in that robbery absconded with $5 million in cash and $1 million in jewelry. *See generally* United States v. Werner, 620 F.2d 922, 924–27 (2d Cir. 1980).

shaving") or who participates in any sports wagering activity involving the student-athlete's institution shall permanently lose all remaining regular-season and postseason eligibility in all sports.

(b) A student-athlete who participates in any sports wagering activity through the Internet, a bookmaker or a parlay card shall be ineligible for all regular-season and postseason competition for a minimum of a period of one year from the date of the institution's determination that a violation occurred and shall be charged with the loss of a minimum of one season of eligibility. If the student-athlete is determined to have been involved in a later violation of any portion of Bylaw 10.3, the student-athlete shall permanently lose all remaining regular-season and postseason eligibility in all sports.

Note that the penalty for point-shaving or participating in any sports wagering activity involving the student's school results in a permanent loss of all athletic eligibility. Other sports wagering activity results in a loss of one year of eligibility. The bylaws of the NCAA may be viewed online in their entirety at the following address: http://www.ncaapublications.com/productdownloads/D110.pdf.

3. Professional sports leagues also have a history of having to deal with participants who bet on the outcome of games in which they participate. In baseball, the "Black Sox" scandal of 1919 stands as an icon. Eight Chicago White Sox players were banned from baseball for life for working to fix the World Series. This included "Shoeless Joe Jackson." This episode in sports history has inspired considerable scholarly and popular attention. See FIELD OF DREAMS (Universal Studios 1989) (an Iowa farmer hears a heavenly voice tell him, "If you build it, he will come." He interprets this message as an instruction to build a baseball field on his farm, upon which appear the spirits of Shoeless Joe Jackson and the other seven Chicago White Sox players banned from the game for throwing the 1919 World Series); W.P. KINSELLA, SHOELESS JOE (Mariner Books 1999) (1982) (movie based on this book); DAVID L. FLEITZ, SHOELESS: THE LIFE AND TIMES OF JOE JACKSON (McFarland & Co. 2001) (a scholarly book examining arguments for and against his innocence. The book highlights the theory that Jackson was a wise businessman whose love of money was stronger than his love of the game.); DONALD GROPMAN & ALAN M. DERSHOWITZ, SAY IT AIN'T SO JOE: THE TRUE STORY OF SHOELESS JOE JACKSON, (Citadel 2d ed. 1999) (lays out evidence supporting Jackson's innocence); KENNETH RATAJCZAK, THE WRONG MAN OUT (AuthorHouse 2008) (a compilation of historical facts. The last chapter includes a mock trial in which the reader is encouraged to be a juror. The author encourages readers who think Shoeless Joe is innocent to e-mail Major League Baseball and urge his reinstatement.); ELIOT ASINOF, EIGHT MEN OUT (Holt Paperbacks 2000) (historical examination of the motives, backgrounds, and conditions of the players that made fixing the 1919 World Series possible); Daniel A. Nathan, *Arnold Rothstein Rigged the 1919 World Series. Or Did He?*, 2004 LEGAL AFFAIRS 52, (March/April, 2004) (discussion of the scandal and who might have been the mastermind behind it); James R. Devine, *Baseball's Labor Wars in Historical Context: The 1919 Chicago White Sox as a Case-Study in Owner-Player Relations*, 5 MARQ. SPORTS L.J. 1 (1994) (analysis of why the players might have thrown the game from a labor perspective, i.e. it was the only avenue they had to air their grievances regarding shared ownership and operation of the game with the owners).

4. Modern baseball has its own icon of sports betting: Pete Rose. In early 1989 Major League Baseball received reports that Pete Rose, then manager of the Cincinnati Reds, had bet on baseball games, including games involving his own team. The Commissioner Bart Giamatti hired John M. Dowd to investigate. Dowd had developed a reputation as a tenacious and skilled lawyer, and is often credited with building the case against organized crime kingpin Meyer Lansky. On May 9, 1989, less than three months after he was hired,

Dowd submitted his 225 page report to the Commissioner's Office. The report detailed what Dowd called "overwhelming" proof that Rose had bet on baseball games, including games involving his team. The report did not conclude that Rose had bet *against* his team, however. The Commissioner then scheduled a hearing to address these allegations. Rose was able to forestall this hearing by seeking and obtaining a temporary restraining order in state court against Giamatti. After the Commissioner removed the case to federal court, Giamatti and Rose entered into an agreement whereby Rose agreed to a lifetime ban from baseball. While Rose did not admit to betting on baseball, he "acknowledge[d] that the Commissioner ha[d] a factual basis" for imposing the penalty of lifetime banishment. Rose was permitted to petition for reinstatement at some future date.

In light of what he calls "much renewed interest in the Dowd Report and in Pete Rose's lifetime banishment from baseball," Dowd created a web site that contains the Dowd Report, the supporting documentary proof, and the agreement Rose reached with the Commissioner. *See* http://www.dowdreport.com. Rose continues to make his case that he should be readmitted to the good graces of baseball. PETE ROSE & RICK HILL, MY LIFE WITHOUT BARS (Rodale Books 2004). Some have voiced agreement with this. Paul Weiler, *Renovating Our Recreational Crimes*, 40 NEW ENG. L. REV. 809 (2006) (article about changing sports betting and marijuana laws. He advocates that now that Pete Rose has admitted betting on baseball he should be allowed into the Hall of Fame.). There has also been considerable scholarship devoted to the Rose affair. Ronald J. Rychlak, *Pete Rose, Bart Giamatti, and the Dowd Report*, 68 MISS. L.J. 889 (1999) (brief recap of the scandal, the investigation, the report, the fallout from Pete Rose's book, and his tax and criminal problems as part of an effort by the Mississippi Law Journal to be part of the process to bring to light never before released facts for public inspection); Matthew B. Pachman, *Limits on the Discretionary Powers of Professional Sports Commissioners: A Historical and Legal Analysis of Issues Raised by the Pete Rose Controversy*, 76 VA. L. REV. 1409 (1990) (analysis of the powers of the Commissioner of Baseball and issues raised by the Pete Rose controversy). Parallels and comparisons between the Black Sox and Rose also have been explored. Thomas J. Ostertag, *From Shoeless Joe to Charley Hustle: Major League Baseball's Continuing Crusade Against Sports Gambling*, 2 SETON HALL J. SPORT L. 19 (1992) (examining the debate between proposed federal sports gambling statute and state desire for revenue against the background of MLB's historical anti-gambling stance); Michael W. Klein, Comment, *Rose is in Red, Black Sox are Blue: A Comparison of* Rose v. Giamatti *and the 1921 Black Sox Trial*, 13 HASTINGS COMM. & ENT. L.J. 551 (1991) (comparison of the two scandals, the laws of both eras, and the power of the Commissioner to impose sanctions).

5. It is unfair to single out baseball. All the other major sports have experienced problems with athletes violating league sports wagering prohibitions. For example, in addition to getting arrested and jailed for running an illegal dog-fighting ring, Michael Vick also got in trouble with the NFL for the gambling associated with the activity. George Vecsey, *Vick Gambled with Career, and Lost*, N.Y. TIMES, Aug. 21, 2007, *available at* http://select.nytimes.com/2007/08/21/sports/football/21vecsey.html?scp=1&sq=vick%20gambled%20with%20career&st=cse. Hockey player Jaromir Jagr gambled on sports owing as much as $500,000 to an internet gambling company. See Michael Farber & Don Yaeger, *Capital Losses*, SPORTS ILLUSTRATED, Mar. 17 2003, *available at* http://vault.sportsillustrated.cnn. com/vault/article/magazine/MAG1028225/index.htm. There was suspicion that tennis star Nikolay Davydenko fixed a tennis in which he played in August 2003. Greg Garber, *Suspicions Follow Davydenko Heading to U.S. Open*, ESPN.COM, Aug. 23, 2007, *available at* http://sports.espn.go.com/sports/tennis/news/story?id=2984805.

6. Not surprisingly, professional leagues also prohibit those who officiate contests from engaging in sports wagering. In 2007, NBA referee Tim Donaghy admitted that he bet

on N.B.A. games, including some that he officiated. He also admitted that he advised professional gamblers about which teams to pick and provided the gamblers with information about referee assignments, relationships between referees and players, and the health of players. In 2008, Donaghy was sentenced to fifteen months in prison for his role in the gambling scandal. The Commissioner of the NBA, David Stern, hired Lawrence Pedowitz to conduct an investigation into whether there was evidence of gambling by other NBA referees. Following fourteen months of investigation and more than two hundred interviews with referees and team and league personnel, the 133-page Pedowitz report concluded that there was no evidence of similar activity by other officials. The report is *available at* http://hosted.ap.org/specials/interactives/_documents/100208nba_pedowitz.pdf. *See also* Howard Beck & Michael S. Schmidt, *Former N.B.A. Referee Pleads Guilty*, N.Y. Times, Aug. 16, 2007 *available at* 2007 WLNR 15844349 (article describing facts of case); Robert I. Lockwood, Note, *The Best Interests of the League: Referee Betting Scandal Brings Commissioner Authority and Collective Bargaining Back to the Frontcourt in the NBA*, 15 Sports. L.J. 137 (Spring 2008) (an analysis of the different powers of the major sports commissioners focusing on the NBA and how Commissioner Stern's authority has become a subject for debate again after the Donaghy and other referee scandals).

7. For other analysis of the problems of participant sports wagering issues, *see* Richard H. McLaren, *Corruption: Its Impact on Fair Play*, 19 Marq. Sports L. Rev. 15 (2008) (in-depth analysis of the corrupting influence of match-fixing and gambling on sports, including tennis, the Olympic games (referees and coaches involved), professional soccer, and international boxing and wrestling); Symposium: *Regulating Coaches' and Athletes' Behavior Off the Field*, 8 DePaul J. Sports L. & Contemp. Probs. 141 (2007) (discussing how gambling has affected sports at the professional and collegiate level); Jeffrey Standen, *The Beauty of Bets: Wagers As Compensation For Professional Athletes*, 42 Williamette L. Rev. 639 (2006) (author argues allowing professional athletes to bet on their own games is not necessarily bad); John Grady & Annie Clement, *Gambling and Collegiate Sport*, 15 J. Legal Aspects of Sport 95 (2005) (discussion of pre- and post-PASPA betting scandals involving college athletes, the NCAA and legislative responses, the weaknesses of those responses, and suggested improvements); John Warren Kindt & Thomas Asmar, *College and Amateur Sports Gambling: Gambling Away Our Youth?*, 8 Vill. Sports & Ent. L.J. 221 (2002) (discussion of gambling incidents involving student athletes, citing surveys/studies on that topic, and discussing the freedom of Olympic athletes to bet on their own events).

6. Poker: America's Game

The ascendance of poker in the United States since 2000 has been meteoric. According to the American Gaming Association, more than 37 million Americans played poker in 2005. Others say the number is even higher, with participation rates exceeding golf. The Poker Players Alliance estimates that 55 million Americans play poker. In the 2008 World Series of Poker, 7319 players competed for a prize pool of nearly $69,000,000.

Much of the popularity of poker can be traced to the rapid growth of internet gaming. It is likely that a substantial number of poker players in the United States rarely, if ever, set foot in a poker room. One source maintains that nearly 2 million people play poker on the internet *each day*. Aaron Levy, Note, *A Risky Bet: The Future of Pay-to-Play Fan-*

tasy Sports, 39 Conn. L. Rev. 325, 343 (2006). The legal issues of internet gaming, including the Unlawful Internet Gaming Enforcement Act, are explored in detail in chapter 12.

There are many different card games that fall under the category of poker. The legal treatment of the game is not limited to any one game, and can extend to card games that technically aren't poker.

A. Social Poker — The "Home Game"

Fondren v. State

179 S.W. 1170 (Tex. Crim. 1915)

HARPER, J

Appellant was convicted of gaming, and his punishment assessed at a fine of $12.50.

"I live at Warren, Tex. I am deputy sheriff of Tyler county, and was on January 16, 1914. I remember the occurrence on the night of January 16, 1914, where two parties and myself found Pink Fondren and Albert Pennington and Joe Williford. This occurred in an old store building and warehouse used one time by George Wooley; the back used as warehouse. It is composed of two rooms, the front room used at one time as a cold drink stand. We found the door on north side of back room barred and paper in the keyhole. We came around to the window and couldn't get in on that side. Got a stick, then got out my knife and cut a hole in an old comfort that was used as a blind over the window. It was a cheap comfort, with the cotton scattered in it, and you could see through it; cost about 75 cents or $1. They had two boards placed edge on edge at the bottom of the quilt as a dead fall. I could see motions of cards through the comfort, and after I cut it I could see them good. They were playing cards. I know they were playing cards. I watched them about 15 minutes, until I got tired." ...

By the above testimony, it is seen that the state's witnesses testified that appellant, Albert Pennington, and Joe Williford were playing together. When the defendant called Joe Williford as a witness, the state objected and proved by him that he was under indictment for the same offense. The objection to the witness testifying should have been sustained. Article 791, C. C. P., specifically declares that Williford was not a competent witness for defendant. Article 792 provides that evidence may be introduced to prove him an incompetent witness. Consequently, there was no error in permitting the state to introduce evidence that Williford was indicted, charged with the same offense. The only error committed was in permitting the witness to testify after the state had made this proof. As the defendant called Williford as a witness, he will not be heard to complain that the state offered proof showing that he was an incompetent witness And especially has he no ground of complaint, since the court erroneously overruled the objection and permitted the witness to testify at his instance.

As to Albert Pennington, it was permissible for the state to seek also to disqualify him as he was also indicted for the same offense. However, there was no error in permitting him to testify for the defendant, as he testified he had paid his fine. When he was convicted and paid his fine, this removed the bar of incompetency as a witness. The fact the court said he would permit the state to make the inquiry to affect the credit of the witnesses does not render the inquiry improper; it was only giving a wrong reason. The testimony was not admissible to affect their credit, but was admissible on the issue of whether or not they were competent to testify as witnesses for appellant. As before stated, the court erred in permitting Williford to testify for defendant after the proof had been made, but there was no error in permitting Pennington to testify as he showed he had paid the penalty. As the defendant got the benefit of both the competent and incompetent witness, it is a matter of which he cannot be heard to complain.

Appellant contends that, if he did play at a game of cards (which he denies), it was in his room in Poland's boarding house. W. I. Poland testified:

> "I lived in Warren. Tex., on the night of January 16, 1914. Was then, and my family are now, running the boarding house at Warren. I have two houses, about 100 yards apart. One we live in, and the other I use for my boarders to room in, and the house in question where Joe Williford and Dick Barclay slept at that time was then used by me as a sleeping apartment for my boarders, and Joe Williford occupied the middle room, slept there and had all his clothes, a grip, etc., in that room, also at that time a man named Geo, Crone had his household goods in that room of Joe Williford. He asked me to let him store them in there for a few days, and I let him do so. They were moved in about two weeks, just so soon as he could get him a house. Joe Williford used that room just as any boarder uses a room to live and sleep in; it was his private room. He had been working and boarding with me about two or three months using the room in that manner."

Counsel cite a great many old authorities holding that it is no offense to play in one's room at a boarding house, but he apparently does not recall that this is no longer the law in this state. The statute now provides, and has provided for several years, that card playing in any place, other than a private residence occupied by a family, is an offense. See Pen. Code, art. 518, as amended in 1901. Since the amendment of that article of the Code, it has always been held to be an offense to play cards in the private room of a boarder at a hotel or boarding house. In this case it was not contended that appellant was a married man, and his family resided in the room. All of the record demonstrates that no family occupied the room. The evidence of the absent witness was therefore material to no issue in the case, and the facts it was alleged could be proven by him were not contested, and were proven by Mr. Poland and other witnesses, and if true would be no defense.

The judgment is affirmed.

Notes

1. *Fondren* is an early recognition that even when states generally proscribe gambling at poker and other card games, there are often exceptions for the "home game." In Texas, the relevant statute makes it a misdemeanor for a person to "bet ... at any game played with cards." However, "(1) it is a defense to prosecution that: the actor engaged in gambling in a private place; (2) no person received any economic benefit other than personal winnings; and (3) except for the advantage of skill or luck, the risks of losing and the chances of winning were the same for all participants." Texas Penal Code § 47.02.

2. Many other states have laws which exempt "social gaming." Some of these laws are referred to above in the material on sports betting. Some make specific reference to card games. *See, e.g.,* Ala. Code 1975 § 13A-12:21 (a defense to charge of simple gambling that person was engaged in a social game in a private place); Va. Code Ann. § 18.2-334 (West 2006) (not illegal to engage in game of chance conducted in a private residence); Maine Stat. Ann. Tit. 17A, § 952; Conn. Gen. Stat. Ann. § 53-278(b); Colo. Rev. Stat. Ann. § 18-10-102(2)(d); Ore. Rev. Stat. Ann. § 167.117(7); N.D. Cent. Code

§ 12.1-28-02 (2009) (allowing social poker up to a limit of $25 per hand played); Iowa Code Ann. § 99B.12 (allowing social poker provided that no person can lose more than $50 in a 24 hour period). Many cases, some of considerable age, have addressed the legalities of the "home game." *See* People v. Dubinsky, 31 N.Y.S.2d 234 (1941) (when host/owner of premises accepts some take of the pool or other consideration for providing the venue, game is not exempted as "social game"); State v. Hansen, 816 P.2d 706 (Or. Ct. App. 1991) (percentage of poker dealers' tips paid to defendants who managed operation of poker tables constituted house income directly resulting from games, thus making games "unlawful gambling" and not social games); State v. Schlein, 854 P.2d 296 (Kan. 1993) (defendant argued that state had to prove that duplex where a poker tournament had taken place had previously been used for gambling in order to be a "gambling place" under Kansas law. The court affirmed the conviction, holding that statute contained no requirement that premises had previously been used as a gambling place).

B. Poker Rooms

Due in part to the popularity of poker, several states have laws that permit "poker rooms" that are licensed by the state. For example, Montana code provisions regulate poker rooms under the Montana Card Games Act of 1974. Operators must obtain a license to operate a card room. Although the prize for winning any one card game cannot exceed $300, that limit does not apply to authorized tournaments, which require a separate permit. Mont. Code Ann. §§ 23-5-301–321 (2009).

Similar detail is found in Delaware's statute. Passed in 2005, it authorized certain nonprofit organizations to hold Texas Hold 'em tournaments for the purpose of raising funds for the promotion of charitable or civic purposes. The Delaware Code Chapter is entitled "No Limit Texas Hold'Em Poker," and has literally codified the rules of Texas Hold 'em, from the ranks of the hands, to antes, and to the procedure for placing and calling bets. *See* Del. Code Ann. tit. 28, §§ 1801–1835 (2009).

California, on the other hand, takes a different approach. Participants in certain listed games commit the crime of gaming. The games listed are banked or "percentage" games, such as roulette and twenty-one (blackjack). It also includes lesser known games as "faro, monte, ..., lansquenet, rouge et noire, rondo, tan, fan-tan, seven-and-a-half, ... [and] hokey-poke." Poker was removed from this list in 1991, thus opening the door to card rooms in the state. The California State Assembly enacted legislation in 2003 to allow local governments to regulate and tax cardrooms. *See* Cal. Bus. & Prof. Code. § 19960, and Gambling Control Act & Regulations, Cal. Bus. & Prof. Code § 19800 et seq. Arts 1–17, *available at* http://ag.ca.gov/gambling/pdfs/gca2009.pdf.

C. State Court Prosecutions

State v. Duci
727 P.2d 316 (Ariz. 1986)

FELDMAN, Justice.

Appellees, defendants below, allegedly organized at least 45 poker games in Arizona between October 1983 and July 1984. Defendants were indicted criminally under A.R.S.

§ 13-3307 for engaging in the business of accepting bets or wagers or setting up gambling pools on the "result of any game of skill or chance." A.R.S. § 13-3307(A)....

FACTS

The state alleges that Edward Duci, Robert Lewis ("Fat Louie") Amuso, Carol Ann Aanenson, Robert Clarence Graham, Charles Edward Keenan, Helen Elaine Ryan, Vincent Paul ("Mooney") Snyder, and Michael Aaron Zemel (defendants) conducted casino poker games at several locations from October 1983 to July 1984. Some of the games were conducted by a single defendant while others were conducted by two or more defendants. Defendants solicited players for their games, provided cards and regulation poker tables, and acted as dealers and bankers. Defendants also provided free drinks and cigarettes to all participants. Most of the games were held in apartments rented by defendants and apparently used only as locations for defendants' games. The games were moved to new locations every two or three months. In return for their services, defendants took ten percent of each pot up to a maximum of $3. Only those defendants actually running a given game shared in the profits from that game. Based on a ledger seized from one of the defendants, the state estimates that the games generated approximately $150,000 in profits for the operators. There is no record of the profits, if any, realized by the participants.

DISCUSSION

1. *Issues*

Like State v. American Holiday Ass'n, 727 P.2d 807 (Ariz. 1986), this case requires us to consider the scope of A.R.S. § 13-3307(A). In pertinent part, A.R.S. § 13-3307(A) provides that

> no person may engage for a fee ... in the business of accepting ... any bet [or] wager or engage for a fee in the business of selling wagering pools ... with respect to the result ... of any ... game of skill or chance....

The statute contains four elements relevant to this case. The state must prove that defendants (1) for a fee (2) engaged in the business (3) of accepting bets or wagers or selling wagering pools (4) on the results of games of skill or chance. Defendants concede, as they must, that elements 1, 2, and 4 are satisfied. The only question is whether taking a percentage of each pot in exchange for dealing and setting up the games satisfies the element of accepting bets or selling wagering pools.

Defendants do not seriously dispute that the participants in their poker games were *placing* bets. As we stated in *American Holiday,* "a bet is a situation in which the money or prize belongs to the persons posting it, each of whom has a chance to win it." 727 P.2d 810. Defendants concede this point but argue that they were not "accepting" the bets for two reasons: first, A.R.S. § 13-3307 is a bookmaking statute and casino poker games are not, defendants assert, bookmaking operations; and second, A.R.S. § 13-3301 specifically covers defendants' conduct. The court of appeals based its decision on a third argument— that defendants were not "accepting" bets because they did not personally participate in the poker games. We address each of these arguments in turn.

2. *The Scope of A.R.S. § 13-3307*

In *American Holiday, supra,* we read A.R.S. § 13-3307's legislative history as suggesting that professional bookmaking operations were the legislature's primary target in enacting A.R.S. § 13-440, the predecessor to A.R.S. § 13-3307. *American Holiday,* 727 P.2d at 811–812. We held that the absence of any stated broad legislative objective supported narrowing the interpretation of the statutory terms "bet or wager" to exclude "entrance fees charged by the sponsor of a contest to participants competing for prizes." *Id.* at 810–811.

The absence of broad legislative objectives underlying A.R.S. § 13-3307 may justify narrow interpretations of the statute in other situations unlike that under review in *American Holiday*. However, we need not define the precise reach of A.R.S. § 13-3307 in this case because we believe that defendants' conduct is covered even under a restrictive view of the statute.

First, defendants' poker games closely resemble classic bookmaking operations. A bookie takes bets on the results of some contest. He makes his money by taking bets and adjusting the odds or laying off side bets, so that he makes a percentage of the money bet no matter who wins the event on which the bets are placed. Similarly, defendants accepted bets on each hand of poker and, by taking a percentage of each pot, assured themselves a profit regardless who won the hand.

Defendants recognize that their conduct is similar to classic bookmaking when they admit in their briefs that they would be guilty of violating A.R.S. § 13-3307 if they had taken a percentage of a pot consisting of bets on the outcome of the World Championship of Poker held in Reno every year. The difference, defendants argue, is that in the games from which this case arose the bettors were also participants. This factor does distinguish defendants' games. However, it seems absurd to read A.R.S. § 13-3307's meager legislative history as establishing that the statute covers only bookmaking operations that accept bets *on contests involving third parties* and as legitimizing bookmaking operations in which the bet is made by a participant in the game.

Defendants' argument is similar to that advanced in *People v. Dugan*, 485 N.E.2d 315 (Ill. 1985). In that case the defendants were convicted under a bookmaking statute of conducting casino poker games similar to those run by defendants in the instant case. The statute in *Dugan* applied to persons accepting "'bets or wagers upon the results of any ... contests ... or upon any lot, chance, casualty, unknown or contingent event whatsoever....'" *Id.* at 317 (quoting Ill. Rev. Stat. ch. 38, para. 28-1.1(d) (1981)). Like defendants here, the defendants in *Dugan* argued that "bookmaking occurs when a wager is made on an event such as a horse race or sports contest in which neither the bettor nor the bookmaker is a participant." *Id.* The Illinois Supreme Court rejected defendants' argument, holding that the plain language of the statute encompassed the defendants' conduct. *Id.* We reach a similar conclusion in the case before us.

The plain language of A.R.S. § 13-3307(A) is broad enough to cover defendants' conduct. Like classic bookmakers, defendants accepted bets on the result of games of skill or chance. The statute does not require that those placing the bets be nonparticipants; it is not for us to add an element to the plain language of the statute. People v. Dugan, 466 N.E.2d 687, 692 (Ill. App. Ct.1984) ("the plain language of the bookmaking statute does not ... limit its application to situations where the bookie and bettor are nonparticipants in the event wagered upon"), *aff'd in relevant part, rev'd in part on other grounds*, 485 N.E.2d 315 (Ill. 1985).

Defendant's conduct also falls within the statute's proscription on selling wagering pools for a fee. "Pool selling" is generally defined as "the receiving from several persons of wagers on the same event, the total sum of which is to be given the winners, subject ordinarily to a deduction of a commission by the seller of the pool." State v. Rafanello, 199 A.2d 13, 15 (Conn. 1964). This definition is easily broad enough to include defendants' conduct. We recognize that betting pools are usually arranged with respect to horse races or some other contest in which the bettors are not participating. *Id.* As noted, however,

A.R.S. § 13-3307(A) does not impose a nonparticipation requirement. *Cf.* State ex rel. Corbin v. Pickrell, 667 P.2d 1304, 1307 (Ariz. 1983) ("where the statutory language is unambiguous, that language must be ordinarily regarded as conclusive, absent a clearly expressed legislative intent to the contrary"). Furthermore, no rationale justifying a nonparticipation requirement comes easily to mind. Indeed, reading a nonparticipation requirement into the statute would allow even classic bookmakers to escape the statute simply by participating in their own betting pools.

3. A.R.S. § 13-3307 or § 13-3301

Defendants' second argument is that their conduct falls within A.R.S. § 13-3301 rather than § 13-3307. Section 13-3301 prohibits gaming with cards and specifically proscribes conducting poker games; violation of the statute is a misdemeanor, rather than a class 6 felony as under A.R.S. § 13-3307.

This argument has some intuitive appeal, but it too seems incorrect. First, as the court of appeals recognized in State v. Cartwright, 510 P.2d 405 (Ariz. App.1973), the key element of A.R.S. § 13-3307(A) is the requirement that defendants be engaged in *the business* of accepting bets or wagers. That element is absent from A.R.S. § 13-3301 and provides a persuasive justification for classifying violations of A.R.S. § 13-3307(A) as class 6 felonies. *Cf.* People v. Dugan, 466 N.E.2d 687, 692 (Ill.App.Ct.1984) (gambling statutes covering identical conduct distinguished by one statute's focus on those engaging in the business of gambling). Defendants systematically organized and conducted casino poker games generating approximately $150,000 in profits. We believe these activities are sufficient to establish that defendants were engaged in the *business* of accepting bets or wagers or selling wagering pools for a fee. A.R.S. § 13-3307(A).

Second, our research discloses no Arizona cases authorizing this court to construe penal statutes to avoid the possibility that illegal conduct can be charged under more than one statute. On the contrary, A.R.S. § 13-104 abrogates the common law rule that penal statutes are to be strictly construed. Instead, we are instructed to construe penal statutes "according to the fair meaning of their terms to promote justice and effect the objects of the law...." *Id.* The objective of § 13-3307 is apparently to classify those engaged in the *business* of accepting bets or selling wagering pools as felons.

4. The Court of Appeals' Decision

The court of appeals did not expressly adopt either argument advanced by defendants. Instead, it held that defendants' conduct was not covered by the statute because defendants were not actually "accepting" bets or wagers. The court reasoned that taking a percentage of the pot is not "accepting" a bet or wager because defendants were not actually participating in the games and therefore did not stand to win or lose something depending on the outcome. State v. Duci, No. 1 CA-CR 8786, memorandum op. at 6–7 (Ariz. Ct. App. Dec. 26, 1985) (memorandum decision).

We disagree with the court of appeals' construction of the statute for several reasons. First, by adding a participation requirement not present in the statute itself, the court of appeals' decision excludes even classic bookmakers from the reach of A.R.S. § 13-3307. Like defendants' profits, a classic bookie's profits are dependent on the amount of betting and the break in the odds; profits are not contingent on the outcome of a given contest. Similarly, like defendants, bookies usually do not participate in or bet on the contests on which they are "accepting" bets. *E.g., Cartwright,* 510 P.2d at 406 (bookie accepting bets on football games but not participating in the betting could violate A.R.S. § 13-440). All one need do to avoid prosecution under a participation standard is avoid participating in or betting on the contest for which one is "accepting" bets or wagers. Professional gamblers would fall within the statute while those running professional gambling operations would not. Given the statute's emphasis on those in the business of accepting bets or wagers, the court of appeals' construction of the statute is unpersuasive.

CONCLUSION

A.R.S. § 13-3307 is a broad statute. In *American Holiday* we noted several reasons for adopting a narrow definition of the statutory terms "bets" and "wagers." Another possible factor limiting the statute's scope is the "engaging in the business" requirement. *See Cartwright, supra.* In this case, however, neither limitation is relevant. Defendants were engaged in the business of conducting casino poker games. If taking a percentage of each pot in a series of poker games does not involve the business of "accepting" bets or wagers, or pool selling, it is difficult to imagine any conduct prohibited by the statute.

We hold that under the facts before us A.R.S. § 13-3307(A) applies to persons in the business of operating casino poker games for profit. It is irrelevant that those placing the bets are participants and that those running the games are nonparticipants. The court of appeals' decisions are vacated. The judgments of dismissal entered by the trial courts are reversed. The cases are remanded for proceedings consistent with this opinion.

HOLOHAN, C.J., GORDON, V.C.J., and HAYS and CAMERON, JJ., concur.

D. Is Playing Poker Gambling?

Joker Club, L.L.C. v. Hardin
643 S.E.2d 626 (N.C. App. 2007)

CALABRIA, Judge.

Joker Club, L.L.C., ("plaintiff") appeals from an order of the trial court, denying its request for injunctive relief against former District Attorney James E. Hardin ("defendant") and concluding that poker is a game of chance that is illegal in North Carolina. We dismiss in part and affirm the order of the trial court.

On 11 August 2004, plaintiff's attorney wrote to defendant, stating his client's intent to open a poker club within the territorial limits of Durham County and seeking defendant's opinion as to the legality of the establishment. On 24 September 2004, defendant responded to plaintiff's inquiry and stated plaintiff's proposed activity was illegal under North Carolina law and local law enforcement would enforce the applicable statutes. Subsequently, on 12 November 2004, plaintiff executed a lease with a third party, which contained a specific provision requiring the plaintiff to obtain written approval from defendant stating poker was a legal activity. In the absence of such approval, the third party would cancel plaintiff's lease and retain the security deposit.

Plaintiff then filed this action and sought a declaratory judgment that poker was a game of skill, as opposed to a game of chance, and thus not in violation of N.C. Gen. Stat. § 14-292 (2005). Plaintiff also sought a temporary restraining order to prevent defendant from enforcing N.C. Gen. Stat. § 14-292. The Durham County Superior Court heard this matter on 23 May 2005 and ruled in favor of defendant, concluding that poker was a game of chance under N.C. Gen. Stat. § 14-292. Accordingly, the trial court denied plaintiff's request for a temporary restraining order. From the trial court's order, plaintiff appeals.

We initially consider whether plaintiff has complied with the mandatory Rules of Appellate Procedure so as to properly preserve its arguments for appellate review. We conclude that plaintiff has committed numerous rule violations, subjecting this appeal to partial dismissal....

However, we conclude that plaintiff's second assignment of error sufficiently complies with the rules and we will thus consider it on appeal. That assignment of error requires us to determine whether the trial court erred in concluding that poker is a game of chance and thus illegal under N.C. Gen. Stat. § 14-292 (2005). That statute provides as follows:

> Except as provided in Chapter 18C of the General Statutes or in Part 2 of this Article, any person or organization that operates any game of chance or any person who plays at or bets on any game of chance at which any money, property or other thing of value is bet, whether the same be in stake or not, shall be guilty of a Class 2 misdemeanor. This section shall not apply to a person who plays at or bets on any lottery game being lawfully conducted in any state.

Id.

We first note that plaintiff has not challenged the trial court's findings of fact, and those findings are thus binding on appeal. *State v. Fleming,* 106 N.C. App. 165, 168, 415 S.E.2d 782, 784 (1992). We must then determine whether the conclusions of law are supported by the findings. However, the findings set forth in Superior Court Judge Orlando Hudson's order amount to a summary of the evidence presented, with no additional facts being found from the presentation of evidence.

Here, four witnesses testified for the plaintiff and one for the State. Roy Cooke ("Cooke"), a professional poker player from Las Vegas, Nevada, testified that he had spent most of his adult life studying poker. Cooke testified that there are certain strategies to poker that allow a player to improve his mathematical odds over the course of a game. He indicated that while in a single hand of poker, chance may defeat a skilled and experienced player, the skilled player is likely to prevail when multiple hands are played.

Frank Martin ("Martin"), a Florida-based consultant who runs poker tournaments, also testified that skill will prevail over luck over a long period of time in the course of a poker tournament. He further stated that there are certain skills that players can develop to consistently win at poker, including patience, memory, and the ability to analyze odds.

Anthony Lee ("Lee"), a casino manager in the Bahamas, testified that there are numerous skills needed for a player to succeed in poker, and that he has failed to develop them himself. Lee testified that patience, knowledge of the odds, the ability to read people, and self-control are all necessary skills.

Chris Simmons ("Simmons"), who plays poker in North Carolina, testified that his poker skills have improved greatly since he began studying poker and reading books on winning poker strategies. Simmons stated that in his experience, poker is a game where skill prevails over chance.

Richard Thornell ("Thornell"), a North Carolina Alcohol Law Enforcement officer, was the only witness to testify for the State. Thornell, who stated that he has played poker for more than 39 years, testified that while there was skill involved in poker, luck ultimately prevailed. He testified that he had seen a television poker tournament in which a hand with a 91% chance to win lost to a hand with only a 9% chance to win.

The evidence, as presented by these witnesses, establishes that poker is both a game of skill and chance. All witnesses appeared to agree that in a single hand, chance may predominate over skill, but that over a long game, the most skilled players would likely amass the most chips. From the evidence, Judge Hudson was unable to determine whether skill or chance predominated in poker, but concluded that poker is a game of chance. After a careful examination of the case law interpreting North Carolina's prohibition against wagering on games of chance, we agree.

We have held that an inquiry regarding whether a game is a game of chance or skill turns on whether chance or skill predominates. State v. Eisen, 192 S.E.2d 613, 615–16 (N.C. App. 1972). In State v. Stroupe, the North Carolina Supreme Court considered whether a certain type of pool was a game of skill or chance. 76 S.E.2d 313, 317 (1953). The *Stroupe* Court stated the applicable test as such:

> [T]he test of the character of any kind of a game of pool as to whether it is a game of chance or a game of skill is not whether it contains an element of chance or an element of skill, but which of these is the dominating element that determines the result of the game, to be found from the facts of each particular kind of game. Or to speak alternatively, whether or not the element of chance is present in such a manner as to thwart the exercise of skill or judgment.

Id. at 317.

The *Stroupe* Court, in articulating its test, relied on Chief Justice Ruffin's classic summary of the law with respect to games of chance. In State v. Gupton, Chief Justice Ruffin wrote:

> [W]e believe, that, in the popular mind, the universal acceptation of "a game of chance" is such a game, as is determined entirely or in part by lot or mere luck, and in which judgment, practice, skill, or adroitness have honestly no office at all, or are [thwarted] by chance. As intelligible examples, the games with dice which are determined by throwing only, and those, in which the throw of the dice regulates the play, or the hand at cards depends upon a dealing with the face down, exhibit the two classes of games of chance. A game of skill, on the other hand, is one, in which nothing is left to chance; but superior knowledge and attention, or superior strength, agility, and practice, gain the victory. Of this kind of games chess, draughts or chequers, billiards, fives, bowles, and quoits may be cited as examples. It is true, that in these latter instances superiority of skill is not always successful—the race is not necessarily to the swift. Sometimes an oversight, to which the most [skillful] is subject, gives an adversary the advantage; or an unexpected puff of wind, or an unseen gravel in the way, may turn aside a quoit or a ball and make it come short of the aim. But if those incidents were sufficient to make the games, in which they may occur, games of chance, there would be none other but games of that character. But that is not the meaning of the statute; for, as before remarked, by the very use of those terms, the existence of other kinds of games, not of chance, is [recognized]. The incidents mentioned, whereby the more [skillful] may yet be the loser, are not inherent in the nature of the games. Inattention is the party's fault, and not his luck; and the other obstacles, though not perceived nor anticipated, are occurrences in the course of nature and not chances.

State v. Gupton, 30 N.C. 271, 273–74 (1848).

Chief Justice Ruffin's analysis clarifies the logic underpinning North Carolina's interpretation of the predominate-factor test. It makes clear that while all games have elements of chance, games which can be determined by superior skill are not games of chance. For example, bowling, chess, and billiards are games of skill because skill determines the outcome. The game itself is static and the only factor separating the players is their relative skill levels. In short, the instrumentality for victory is in each player's hands and his fortunes will be determined by how skillfully he uses that instrumentality.

Poker, however, presents players with different hands, making the players unequal in the same game and subject to defeat at the turn of a card. Although skills such as knowledge of human psychology, bluffing, and the ability to calculate and analyze odds make it more likely for skilled players to defeat novices, novices may yet prevail with a simple run of luck. No amount of skill can change a deuce into an ace. Thus, the instrumentality for victory is not entirely in the player's hand. In State v. Taylor, our Supreme Court noted this distinction. 16 S.E. 168 (N.C. 1892).

> It is a matter of universal knowledge that no game played with the ordinary playing cards is unattended with risk, whatever may be the skill, experience or intelligence of the gamesters engaged in it. From the very nature of such games, where cards must be drawn by and dealt out to players, who cannot anticipate what ones may be received by each, the order in which they will be placed or the effect of a given play or mode of playing, there must be unavoidable uncertainty as to the results. *Id.* at 169.

This is not so with bowling, where the player's skill determines whether he picks up the spare; or with billiards, where the shot will find the pocket or not according to its author's skill. During oral arguments, counsel for plaintiff analogized poker to golf, arguing that while a weekend golfer might, by luck, beat a professional golfer such as Tiger Woods on one hole, over the span of 18 holes, Woods' superior skill would prevail. The same would be true for a poker game, plaintiff contended, making poker, like golf, a game of skill. This analogy, while creative, is false. In golf, as in bowling or billiards, the players are presented with an equal challenge, with each determining his fortune by his own skill. Although chance inevitably intervenes, it is not inherent in the game and does not overcome skill, and the player maintains the opportunity to defeat chance with superior skill. Whereas in poker, a skilled player may give himself a statistical advantage but is always subject to defeat at the turn of a card, an instrumentality beyond his control. We think that is the critical difference.

For the reasons stated above, we determine that chance predominates over skill in the game of poker, making that game a game of chance under N.C. Gen. Stat. § 14-292 (2005). Accordingly, the decision of the trial court should remain undisturbed.

Affirmed.

Notes

1. Chapter 1 discusses the basics of gambling: prize, chance, and consideration. As noted, many states apply what is sometimes called the "predominance" test. This analysis considers an activity gambling if a person risks something of value on an activity predominately determined by chance for the opportunity to win a prize. In Pennsylvania v. Dent, Case No: 733 of 2008 (Pa. C.P. 26th Dist. Columbia County January 14, 2009), a trial court judge took a different view of this issue than did the court in *Duci*:

> Using the predominance test, in conjunction with analyzing skill versus chance using the four prong dominant factor test, it is apparent that skill predominates over chance in Texas Hold'em poker. First, each player has a distinct possibility of exercising skill and has sufficient data available to make an informed judgment. Second, each player has the opportunity to exercise the skill, and they do possess the skill (albeit in varying degrees). Third, each

player's skill and efforts sufficiently govern the results. Fourth, the standard skill is known by the players and governs the results. Skill comes with varying degrees of competence, but that is the case with any competition involving skill.

The academic studies and the experts generally agree that a player must be skillful to be successful at poker. At the outset, chance is equally distributed among the players. But the outcome is eventually determined by skill. Successful players must possess intellectual and psychological skills. They must know the rules and the mathematical odds. They must know how to read their opponents "tells" and styles. They must know when to hold and fold and raise. They must know how to manage their money. This court finds that Texas Hold'em poker is a game where skill predominates over chance. Thus, it is not "unlawful gambling" under the Pennsylvania Crimes Code.

2. The question of whether poker constitutes gambling has captured the imaginations of many people, and even some courts. For case considerations, *see* Town of Mt. Pleasant v. Chimento, case No. 98045DB (S.C. Mun. Ct. Feb. 19, 2009) *available at* http://www.scribd.com/doc/12654899/SC-Judges-Decision-on-MtPleasant-Poker-Case-021909 ("This court finds ... that Texas Hold-em is a game of skill. The evidence and studies are overwhelming that this is so."); Bell Gardens Bicycle Club v. Dept. of Justice, 42 Cal. Rptr. 2d 730, 748 (Cal. Ct. App. 1995) ("[T]he testimony unequivocally showed that winning the jackpot, unlike winning the poker pot, *is based predominately on chance not skill*."); Charnes v. Cent. City Opera House Ass'n., 773 P.2d 546, 551 (Colo. 1989) (holding that poker is an illegal game of chance); Indoor Recreation Enters., Inc. v. Douglas, 235 N.W.2d 398, 401 (Neb. 1975) (holding poker is a game of chance). It has also been a fertile source of legal and mathematical commentary. *See* Anthony N. Cabot, Glenn J. Light & Karl F. Rutledge, *Alex Rodriguez, A Monkey, and the Game of Scrabble: The Hazard of Using Illogic to Define the Legality of Games of Mixed Skill and Chance*, 57 DRAKE L. REV. 383, 401–402 (2009) ("Poker has been described both as a game of chance and as a game of skill. Differences, however, can be attributed to the determination of skill and chance as being a question of fact as opposed to a question of law. Therefore, the skill or chance decision can be influenced by the quality of evidence presented, the experience and qualifications of counsel, and the experience, qualifications, and biases of the triers of fact."); Ingo C. Fiedler & Jan-Philipp Rock, *Quantifying Skill In Games: Theory and Empirical Evidence for Poker*, 13 GAMING. L. REV. 50 (2009) (discussing the mathematical and statistical aspects of poker); Michael A. DeDonno & Douglas K. Detterman, *Poker is a Skill*, 12 GAMING L. REV. 31 (2008) (description of a series of studies using university students, some of whom were taught poker using instructive software. They were pitted against those who were not trained to see if poker was a skill you could learn); Anthony Cabot & Robert Hannum, *Poker: Public Policy, Law, Mathematics, and the Future of an American Tradition*, 22 T.M. COOLEY L. REV. 443 (2005) (comprehensive recap of poker case law, statutes, poker statistics, and expert opinions to effect that poker is a game of skill); JOHN VON NEUMANN & OSKAR MORGENSTERN, THE THEORY OF GAMES AND ECONOMIC BEHAVIOR (1994) (book on game theory with an entire chapter devoted to poker).

3. Some have argued that whether the debate over poker is gambling or not overlooks the educational value of poker. A group of students at Harvard law School and a professor created an organization called the Global Poker Strategic Thinking Society. This group is dedicated to the idea that poker "which is probability-based and requires risk assessment, situational analysis and a gift for reading people, can be an effective teaching tool, whether for middle school math or in business and law classes." *See* Gary Rivlin, *High Stakes Poker*

as a Learning Tool, N.Y. Times, Dec. 12, 2007, http://www.nytimes.com/2007/12/12/ny region/12poker.html?scp=5&sq=high+stakes+poker+&st=nyt.

E. Federal Law and Poker

There are three federal laws that have potential application to poker, though to a somewhat limited extent. Because these laws are primarily aimed at bookmaking—believed to be a source of funding for organized crime—and because there is the requirement of interstate activity, they are not widely applied to poker.

The language of the Wire Act, 18 U.S.C. § 1084, seems to have little application to poker, as it prohibits using the means of interstate communication for betting on "a sporting event or related contest."

The Travel Act, 18 U.S.C. § 1952 makes it a crime to "travel in interstate commerce or use the mail or any facility in interstate of foreign commerce" with intent to distribute the proceeds of an unlawful activity. The statute includes "any business enterprise involving [illegal] gambling as "unlawful activity."

The Illegal Gambling Business Act requires the government to prove that there is a gambling operation, (1) that is in violation of state or local law where conducted; (2) involves five or more persons that conduct, finance, manage, supervise, direct or own all or part of the business; and (3) remains in substantially continuous operation for more than thirty days or has a gross revenue of $2,000 in any given day.

The latter two statutes have occasionally played a role in federal poker prosecutions. In United States v. Pack, No. 92-3872, 1994 WL 19945 (6th Cir. Jan. 25, 1994), defendant Pack, a police officer, was convicted under the Illegal Gambling Business Act for conducting an illegal gambling business with four other co-defendants. The business involved bookmaking, lotteries, poker machines, and casino style poker games in Liverpool, Ohio. The portion of the case most involved with poker was the defendant's argument that the evidence was not sufficient, because "the weekly poker game that took place at one of the co-defendants' houses was simply not the type of activity contemplated by [the ILGBA]", and he was "merely a player in this social poker game." The court affirmed his conviction, finding that a reasonable jury could find that the group who played in these weekly poker games, and were involved in other gambling activities together, were conducting an illegal gambling business. Further, the court found that Pack was not merely a player, but, based on the record, was a regular dealer, who took five percent from every pot for the house, coordinated the games, and was seen giving the rake money to a co-conspirator. The court concluded that anyone—including a dealer—who causes a business to function, "conducts" the business under the Act, and is criminally liable.

In United States v. Rieger, 942 F.2d 230 (3rd Cir. 1991), defendant was convicted under the Illegal Gambling Business Act. An undercover police officer had infiltrated an illegal poker game held by the defendant on the second floor of a restaurant located in Erie, Pennsylvania. During these games, the officer witnessed defendant Rieger, or one of his employees, cut the rake on each hand of poker. Rieger later admitted that he had been operating the game for two years. Rieger appealed his conviction, arguing that the government failed to establish that five or more persons were involved in the operation of a gambling business at all times during a period of more than thirty days, and that those who were involved in its operation had a financial interest in the gambling business. The appellate court affirmed the conviction, holding that, (1) there was sufficient evidence that more than five persons were involved (including doormen, cutmen, and the defendant) and that the poker game was conducted for more than thirty days; (2) the persons involved in operating the game need not have had a financial stake in the game, but had to be more than mere bettors; and (3) the five person requirement and the thirty day requirement were separate and, thus, the same five people did not need to be operating the game for the entire period.

The Travel Act was applied in United States v. Jones, 642 F. 2d 909 (5th Cir. 1981). Defendant Jones was convicted of conspiracy and violating the Travel Act for conduct relating to his playing in, and attempting to cash checks representing his winnings, in an illegal poker game. Jones received two checks as part of his winnings in an illegal poker game conducted at the Black Garter Club in Tom Bean, Texas. The following day, he drove to a bank in Cartwright, Oklahoma where he cashed one of the checks and had the other returned "non-sufficient funds." Jones appealed his Travel Act conviction, arguing that the government must establish that the activity conducted in the destination state subsequent to the interstate travel was unlawful, and because his acts of presenting checks in Oklahoma were lawful, he did not violate the Travel Act. Further, Jones argues that in order to be found guilty under the Travel Act, the travel must be necessary to facilitating the illegal gambling. With respect to Jones' first argument, the court held, "As long as the interstate travel or use of the interstate facilities and the subsequent facilitating act make the unlawful activity easier, the jurisdictional requisites under [the Travel Act] are complete." Further, with respect to Jones's argument that the travel must facilitate the illegal gambling, the court held that the act of traveling to collect the proceeds of an illegal poker game satisfied the "facilitation requirement," reasoning that, "attempts to gather the wagered funds which involve the use of interstate facilities can be an essential part of the gambling enterprise."

See also United States v. Payne, No. 92-2430, 1993 WL 218770 (4th Cir. June 21, 1993) (forfeiture of truck and cash under Illegal Gambling Business Act upheld when officers found room set up for poker games, and there were poker machines and other gambling paraphernalia in Defendant's apartment); United States v. Zemek, 634 F.2d 1159 (9th Cir. 1980) (upholding convictions under Illegal Gambling Business Act and federal racketeering laws for running poker games). In addition, several Illegal Gambling Business Act prosecution cases exist that deal with maintenance of "poker machines." *See* United States v. Massino, 546 F.3d 123 (2d Cir. 2008); United States v. Gotti, 459 F.3d 296 (2d Cir. 2006); United States v. Lynn, 178 F.3d 1297 (6th Cir. 1999); United States v. Conley, 92 F.3d 157 (3d Cir. 1996).

Chapter 15

Pari-Mutuel Gaming

1. Introduction

In the United States, pari-mutuel betting is principally used for various types of horse racing, greyhound racing, and jai alai. Pari-mutuel gambling has characteristics that distinguish it from other types of gambling. The name "pari-mutuel" roughly translates from the French as "to wager among ourselves." All bets of a particular type are grouped together in a pool and then a specified percentage is deducted for taxes and the house take. The payoffs are then determined by the number of winning bets and the remaining pool is shared among the winners. This system of betting is sometimes called "pool sharing." Because the pool remains open even after one places a bet, the payouts are not determined until the pool is closed, for example, when a horse race begins. This differs from the "fixed odds" bet where the potential payout is known at the time the bet is made. The invention that made pari-mutuel betting more fluid and popular was the "totalisator." Initially conceived in the 19th century in Europe, a totalisator is a specialized, mechanical calculating machine that can calculate the odds and approximate payouts for certain types of bets to bettors as the betting pool grows. The innovation was brought to the United States in the late 1920s.

2. The Licensing Process

Bedford Downs Management Corp. v. State Harness Racing Commission
926 A.2d 908 (Pa. 2007)

In this appeal by allowance we review whether the Pennsylvania State Harness Racing Commission ("Commission") abused its discretion in denying two license applications to conduct harness race meetings at which pari-mutuel wagering is permitted. In light of the significant deference that the Commission enjoys in making decisions regarding the granting or denying of harness racing license applications, and for the reasons set forth in greater detail below, we affirm in part and reverse in part the order of the Commonwealth Court, and in doing so, uphold the Commission's denial of both harness racing license applications. We render our decision, however, without prejudice to the applicants to reapply for a harness racing license and for reconsideration by the Commission, consistent with our opinion today.

The relevant facts and procedural history are as follows. On December 27, 2002, Valley View Downs, LP ("Valley View") filed with the Commission an "Application for a Li-

599

cense to Conduct a Harness Horse Race Meeting with Pari-Mutuel Wagering" pursuant to the Race Horse Industry Reform Act, 4 P.S. § 325.101 *et seq.* ("Racing Act"). Valley View's harness racing facility was to be located approximately 35 miles northwest of Pittsburgh in South Beaver Township, Beaver County Pennsylvania.

On April 3, 2003, the Commission announced a new Statement of Policy ("Statement of Policy"), effective May 3, 2003, which applied to pending and new license applications. 7 Pa. Code §§ 133.1–133.7. The Statement of Policy declared, *inter alia,* that the Commission would treat applicants as a comparative group and that the Commission would not be obligated to issue any license despite the fact that a license was available. On May 24, 2003, a notice was published in the Pennsylvania Bulletin establishing a 60-day license application period from May 24, 2003 through July 22, 2003.

Thereafter, on June 9, 2003, Bedford Downs Management Corporation ("Bedford") filed an "Application for a License to Conduct a Harness Horse Race Meeting with Pari-Mutuel Wagering" with the Commission. Bedford's proposed racetrack was to be located approximately three miles east of the Ohio/Pennsylvania border in Mahoning Township, Lawrence County, Pennsylvania.

Approximately one year later, on July 5, 2004, the Governor of Pennsylvania, Edward G. Rendell, signed into law the Pennsylvania Race Horse Development and Gaming Act ("Gaming Act" or "Act 71"). 4 Pa. C.S. §§ 1101–1904. The Gaming Act authorized limited gaming by the installation and operation of slot machines with the intention of, *inter alia,* protecting the public through the regulation and policing of activities involving gaming; enhancing live horse racing, breeding programs, entertainment and employment; and providing a new source of revenue to the Commonwealth. 4 Pa. C.S. § 1102(1), (2), and (3). Importantly, for purposes of this appeal, under the Gaming Act, a person who has been approved by the Commission to conduct harness horse race meetings could apply to the Pennsylvania Gaming Control Board ("Gaming Control Board") for a license to operate slot machines at a licensed racetrack facility. 4 Pa. C.S. § 1302(a)(3).

The Commission held public comment hearings on the applications. Furthermore, a pre-hearing conference was held on October 12, 2004 and evidentiary hearings were conducted from October 25–27, 2004, and on November 9–12, 2004, November 30, 2004, and February 21, 2005.

After the hearings, Bedford and Valley View filed proposed findings of fact and conclusions of law with supporting briefs. In a supplemental brief to the Commission, Valley View raised allegations regarding Bedford's principals' alleged links to "organized crime." The Commission through its investigative staff conducted further background investigations of individuals and transactions relating to both applicants. On June 24, 2005, the Commission, *sua sponte,* reopened the evidentiary record. While the Commission's investigative staff sought a hearing to present its findings regarding Bedford and Valley View, in lieu of a hearing, the parties entered into certain stipulations and a protective order in light of the sensitive nature of the personal background information presented to the Commission. On September 21, 2005, the Commission approved the stipulations and the official docket and evidentiary record were formally closed.

On November 3, 2005, the Commission issued a unanimous final order denying both applications. Six days later, on November 9, 2005, the Commission issued an Adjudication in support of its earlier order. The Adjudication included 238 Findings of Fact and 21 Conclusions of Law.

Specifically, the Commission denied Valley View's application because: (1) its plan to have patrons and horsemen share one main entrance would not be safe; (2) the tight track radius and increased banking was not safe for horses; (3) its plan for a paddock on the backside of the track would be inconvenient for owners and would prevent the public from being able to see and have access to the horses; and (4) the topography of the land would prevent having a separate gate or entrance on the backside of the track.

The Commission denied Bedford's application because: (1) the deceased grandfather of Bedford's principal owners had conducted business with reputed organized crime figures through the companies that he owned; (2) the deceased grandfather acquired most of the land upon which Bedford planned to build its facility while his companies were dealing with reputed organized crime figures; and (3) although Bedford presented to the Commission a "highly confident" letter from Merrill Lynch, which appeared to evidence adequate financing for the project, the letter did not identify the borrower, the letter required more conditions than Valley View's highly confident letter, and the letter was issued, in substantial part, based on the original involvement of Isle of Capri Casinos, Inc. ("Isle of Capri") and CIBC World Markets ("CIBC"), rather than Merrill Lynch's own review of the Bedford project or of the individuals involved in the project.

On December 1, 2005, Bedford filed a petition for reconsideration with the Commission. On December 8, 2005, Valley View filed a petition for hearing and reconsideration. As the applicants thereafter filed appeals in the Commonwealth Court, the Commission found that it no longer had jurisdiction over the petitions for reconsideration.

On December 9, 2005, Bedford and Valley View filed petitions for review with the Commonwealth Court (footnote omitted). A divided *en banc* Commonwealth Court affirmed the denial of the Valley View license application; however, it vacated the denial of the Bedford license application and remanded that application to the Commission for reconsideration in light of its opinion. *Bedford Downs v. State Harness Racing Commission*, 901 A.2d 1063 (Pa. Cmwlth. 2006).

Concerning the Valley View license application, the Commonwealth Court majority, in an opinion authored by Judge Rochelle Friedman, found, *inter alia*, that one main entrance for patrons and horsemen was not in the best interests of racing and this finding was supported by the substantial evidence of record; that the proposed tight track radius and increased banking was not in the best interests of racing and this determination was supported by the substantial evidence of record; that Valley View's proposed backside paddock was not in the best interests of racing and that this finding was supported by the substantial evidence of record; and finally, that the Commission's conclusion that the topography, which prevented Valley View from having a separate backside entrance which was not in the best interests of racing was supported by the substantial evidence of record. *Id.* at 1071–72.

With respect to the Bedford license application, the Commonwealth Court majority concluded that the Commission improperly focused upon the deceased grandfather of the Bedford principals and allegations that he did business with reputed organized crime figures through family-owned companies that still exist. According to the Commonwealth Court majority, the Commission may under the Racing Act refuse to grant a license if the experience, character, or fitness of any officer, director or stockholder is such that his or her participation in horse racing or related activities would be inconsistent with the public interest or with the best interests of racing, 4 P.S. § 325.209(e), but the deceased grandfather was not an officer, director, or stockholder of Bedford; thus, it was error to deny Bedford's application on this ground. Additionally, the Commonwealth Court found that the Commission erred in concluding that the appearance of a connection between organized crime and the ground upon which Bedford proposed to construct the facility was inconsistent with the best interests of racing, reasoning that the law is concerned with the adverse influence of people, not the ground. *Id.* at 1072–73.

Finally, the Commonwealth Court majority addressed three aspects of Bedford's proposed financing. First, it determined that the failure of Merrill Lynch's "highly confident" letter to identify the precise borrower had no effect on Bedford's ability to obtain financing. Second, the majority concluded that the fact that Merrill Lynch's highly confident letter contained more conditions than Valley View's financing letter was inconsequential as there was no finding that Bedford would be unable to meet any of the conditions. Finally, the Commonwealth Court addressed and rejected the Commission's concern that Merrill Lynch based its letter, in substantial part, on the high level of confidence that Merrill Lynch had with Isle of Capri and CIBC, not on its own review of the project or the individuals involved in the project. More specifically, the Commonwealth Court reasoned that the departure of Isle of Capri and CIBC from the project was not due to financial concerns, but rather, was a result of a disagreement over management philosophy. Moreover, the Commonwealth Court found that there was no reason to believe, or substantial evidence to support the proposition, that if Merrill Lynch had reviewed the project and the individuals involved, that it would not have issued its letter. Accordingly, the majority of the Commonwealth Court vacated the Commission's order to the extent that it denied the Bedford application and remanded the case to the Commission for reconsideration in light of its decision. *Id.* at 1073–75....

On January 19, 2007, our Court granted the Commission's petition for allowance of appeal, 458 MAL 2006, and Valley View's petition for allowance of appeal, 540 MAL 2006, regarding the Commonwealth Court's order reversing the Commission's denial of Bedford's license application. We also granted Valley View's petition for allowance of appeal regarding the Commonwealth Court's order affirming the denial of Valley View's license application. 541 MAL 2006 (footnote omitted). Our grant of allocatur with respect to Valley View's petition was limited to two issues:

> Whether the State Harness Racing Commission exceeded its statutory powers, acted in an arbitrary and capricious fashion, and violated a harness racing applicant's due process rights by changing the manner in which the application would be evaluated, based on a Statement of Policy and undisclosed preferences in circumstances where the new procedure treated similarly-situated, simultaneously pending applications differently?

> and

> Whether the Commission's failure to afford an applicant an opportunity to cure purported deficiencies and/or to address previously undisclosed agency preferences rendered the agency's conduct arbitrary and capricious?

In addressing the issues raised by the parties, we will first discuss the substantive standards to be used in the consideration of harness racing with pari-mutuel wagering licensure and then we will set forth the proper standard and scope of review which governs this appeal. Thereafter, we will turn to the issues relating to the Bedford license application, and finally address the questions raised concerning the Valley View license application.

Pursuant to the Racing Act, passed in 1981, the General Assembly permits and regulates harness racing in the Commonwealth. This includes the issuance of licenses to engage in harness racing with pari-mutuel wagering. The Commission, a departmental administrative commission of the Department of Agriculture, has general jurisdiction over all pari-mutuel harness racing activities in the Commonwealth. The Commission is specifically entrusted with the responsibility to determine the grant or denial of licenses to conduct pari-mutuel harness racing activities. The Racing Act provides that no more than five corporations may be licensed by the Commission to conduct harness racing meetings with pari-mutuel wagering. 4 P.S. § 325.205(b). At the time relevant to this appeal, only one remaining harness racing license was available.

Section 209 of the Racing Act authorized the Commission to issue a harness racing license if "the public interest, convenience or necessity will be served and a proper case for the issuance of a license is shown...." 4 P.S. § 325.209(a). Additionally, no party disputes that the applicant must show that its application is consistent with the "best interests of racing." *See* Man O'War Racing Association v. State Horse Racing Commission, 250 A.2d 172 (Pa. 1969).

Moreover, the Commission may refuse to grant a license for a number of reasons set forth in the statute, including *inter alia:* if the officer, director, member or stockholder of the corporation applying for a license has been convicted of a crime involving moral turpitude; engaged in bookmaking; has been found guilty of fraud or misrepresentation in connection with racing or breeding; or has violated any law of a racing jurisdiction or violated any rule of the Commission. Also, a license may be denied if the experience, character, or fitness of any officer, director or stockholder of any such corporation is such that the participation of the person in horse racing or related activities would be inconsistent with the public interest, convenience or necessity or with the best interests of racing. 4 P.S. § 325.209(e) (footnote omitted) ....

Consistent with the substantive standards applicable to the review of a license application and the significant discretion that the Commission enjoys with respect to license approval, the standard of review of the Commission's decision to grant or deny a harness racing license is one of great deference.... In *Man O'War,* we explained that judicial review was "severely limited" and that a decision by the State Horse Racing Commission would only be overturned on appellate review when there was "a clear abuse of discretion." 250 A.2d at 181. The reasoning for this deferential standard of review is equally applicable to the review of harness racing license applications. First, the General Assembly delegated to the Commission exclusively this "important and sensitive" task. *Id.* at 180. Second, decisions regarding the grant or denial of a harness racing license include "balancing many competing interests." *Id.* Thus, the number of "technical and precise factors" that the Commission must evaluate and analyze point to an exercise of discretion with which an appellate court should not unnecessarily interfere. *Id.* Related thereto, the Commission has special "expertise and judgment" in making licensing decisions. *Id.* at 181.

Especially in light of the multifaceted-decision making that is part and parcel with the review of racing licenses, it is important to emphasize that an abuse of discretion may not be found simply because an appellate court may have reached a different conclusion and chosen different applicants. That is not the judicial function here. An abuse of discretion is not simply an error of judgment. It requires much more....

With this significantly deferential standard of review in mind, we turn to the challenges regarding the Bedford license application.

The Commission first contends that with respect to the Bedford license application, the Commonwealth Court erred by interfering with the authority and responsibility of the Commission to interpret and apply the "best interests of racing" standard in conjunction with the suitability standards set forth in the Gaming Act. Specifically, the Commonwealth Court rejected consideration of the criteria under the Gaming Act in addressing a harness racing application:

> To the extent that the Commission relied on Act 71 in considering the deceased grandfather's business dealings, the Commission erred. The Commission has no authority to act under Act 71. Bedford applied to the Commission for a license to conduct harness racing with pari-mutuel wagering, not a license to offer slot machine gaming at its proposed facility. The licenses, the statutes and the governing agencies are separate and distinct.

Bedford Downs, 901 A.2d at 1073 n.11.

The Commission maintains that it did not act under the authority of the Gaming Act as suggested by the Commonwealth Court. At all times, according to the Commission, it focused solely on the application for a harness racing license and acted solely under the Racing Act. At no time did it consider whether Bedford should receive a gaming license in the event that it were to ultimately apply for one and it did not in any fashion usurp the power or jurisdiction of the Gaming Control Board to determine whether Bedford should receive a license for slot machine gaming at its proposed facility. Rather, the Commission offers that it was only concerned with the best interests of racing. The Commission found it necessary to consider Bedford's likely suitability for licensure under the Gaming Act because that statute inextricably linked harness racing and gaming. The Commission supports its position by pointing to both the purpose of the Gaming Act, including to enhance live horse racing, breeding programs, entertainment, and employment in the Commonwealth, 4 Pa. C.S. § 1102, but also to the connection between the two statutes as evidenced by Section 1302 of the Gaming Act which makes the approval of a horse or harness pari-mutuel license a condition precedent to eligibility for a Category 1 slot license. 4 Pa. C.S. § 1302(a)(1). While the Commission candidly acknowledges that if it were to rely solely upon the suitability standards set forth in the Gaming Act, that would constitute legal error, the Commission goes on to offer that the provisions of the Gaming Act provided guidance to the Commission and nothing more. Valley View adds that it was incumbent upon the Commission to consider suitability under the Gaming Act as Bedford's project was predicated upon gaming revenues to service debt and fund operations of Bedford's harness racing and gaming operations.

Bedford counters that the Commonwealth Court properly held that each agency is only empowered to act under its own jurisdiction and the Commission may only exercise its decision making authority under the Racing Act. Indeed, according to Bedford, there is no authority for the Commission to expand its jurisdiction to consider suitability or any other factor under the Gaming Act. Therefore, to the extent the Commission decided Bedford's application under the Gaming Act, it committed error (footnote omitted).

We agree with the Commonwealth Court's admonition and Bedford's general argument that the Commission has no jurisdiction to determine whether an applicant will be a successful applicant for a gaming slots license under the Gaming Act. Simply stated, the Commission does not have the authority to decide issues within the province of the Gaming Control Board. While as noted above, obtaining a harness racing license under the Racing Act could certainly impact the ability of an applicant to obtain a slots license under the Gaming Act, and thus, the two statutes have some clear relationship—the two are not *necessarily inextricably* linked. Thus, to this extent, we find that the Commission has no jurisdiction to act under the Gaming Act. To the extent that the Commission's adjudication can be interpreted to give it such jurisdiction or to decide issues under the Gaming Act, it is hereby rejected.

This limitation on the Commission's authority and power to grant or deny a license under the Racing Act, however, does not end our analysis—the question with respect to Bedford is more nuanced than a simple determination of whether the Commission has jurisdiction to decide issues under the Gaming Act. As acknowledged by Bedford, it introduced to the Commission a proposal of not only a harness racing facility, but a "racino" that is, a combined racing and gaming facility. Thus, Bedford would require licensure by two separate Commonwealth agencies. Yet, even the requirement of obtaining two licenses to operate such a facility would not in and of itself give the Commission the ability to act under the Gaming Act. In this situation, Bedford does not refute that it made the financing and financial projections for its harness racing facility dependent upon revenue to be generated from the gaming operations at its facility. Thus, the viability of the proposed harness racing facility was linked to its gaming operations.

As the showing of financial viability for the proposed harness racing facility was dependent upon the acquisition of a gaming license, rather than usurp the authority of the Gaming Control Board's jurisdiction under the Gaming Act, we find that the Commission was merely ensuring the financial integrity of Bedford's harness racing proposal and the mere consideration by the Commission of Bedford's general suitability or potentiality as a likely candidate for a license under the Gaming Act in the circumstances of this license application was legitimate and not in error (footnote omitted).

The second issue raised by the Commission was whether the Commonwealth Court erroneously substituted its judgment for that of the Commission with respect to the Commission's expertise, judgment, and discretion in matters of credibility and suitability regarding the denial of the Bedford application which the Commission contends is in conflict with the significant discretion enjoyed by the Commission pursuant to our Court's decision in *Man O'War*.

The Commission urges that the General Assembly has vested significant discretion in the Commission because of its expertise and judgment in making decisions regarding the issuance of harness racing licenses. Related thereto, the Commission is the ultimate fact finder and is free to accept or reject the testimony of any witness—in whole or in part. Finally, the Commission offers that it is the applicant that must demonstrate that its request for a license is in the best interests of racing generally. The Commission stresses that based upon these standards, the Commonwealth Court nevertheless disregarded the Commission's expertise and judgment when the Commission concluded that the mere appearance of a connection and involvement of Bedford principals with family-owned companies with reputed ties to organized crime is inconsistent with the best interests of racing. Furthermore, in the Commission's view, the Commonwealth Court substituted its judgment for that of the Commission regarding the ownership of the land upon which the Bedford track was to be built. Finally, the Commission takes issue with the Commonwealth Court's disregard of its concerns pertaining to Bedford's financing. We will address each of these contentions *seriatim*.

The Commission was concerned that Carmen Ambrosia, the deceased grandfather of Bedford's principals, Carmen Shick, Kenneth Shick, and Kendra Tabak, had financial dealings in the 1980s with organized crime. These dealings were purportedly conducted through family-owned businesses, including Ambrosia Coal and Construction Company and New Castle Lime and Stone Company. These family-owned businesses exist today; the Bedford principals are involved with these entities; and Bedford would potentially look to these businesses for financing. Bedford asserts that the denial of its application on the basis of decades old actions of a deceased patriarch, with which none of the Bedford principals had any involvement was a clear abuse of discretion, and that the Commonwealth Court's decision repudiating such concerns was proper.

We initially determine that to the extent that the Commission's adjudication can be read as denying the Bedford application solely on the basis of the deceased grandfather's ties to organized crime figures, it is hereby rejected. We agree with Bedford that Carmen Ambrosia's alleged ties to organized crime in and of themselves should not be a basis to deny the Bedford license application. Plainly stated, guilt by ancestry, without more, is impermissible under our current system of law. *See* NAACP v. Claiborne Hardware Co., 459 U.S. 898, 932, (1982) ("[g]uilt by association is a philosophy alien to the traditions of a free society....").

We find, however, that the situation before us is more complicated than the neat scenario of a grandchild being tainted by the purported sins of the grandfather. The parties do not dispute that an applicant for a harness racing license must demonstrate that its application is consistent with the "best interests of racing." *Man O'War*, 250 A.2d at 180. Furthermore, we agree with the Commonwealth Court when it concluded over twenty years ago that one of the purposes of the Racing Act is to "foster an image of horse racing that would make the image of that 'industry' an irreproachable one, even in the eyes of the skeptical public." Helad Farms v. State Harness Racing Commission, 470 A.2d 181, 184 (Pa. Comm. 1984). Therefore, we do not quibble with the proposition that the Commission is well within its discretion to consider an applicant's ties to organized crime in determining whether an applicant should be awarded a harness racing license. The difficulty comes, however, in applying these admirable concepts to a particular applicant.

Specifically, the Commission found that Carmen Ambrosia along with his wife acquired most of the property upon which the proposed Bedford facility was to be located. As the Commission found:

> What is most troubling and ultimately why this Commission cannot award the pari-mutuel license is that Carmen Ambrosia (now deceased) along with his wife acquired most, if not all of the land upon which Bedford intended to build the proposed facility. As the Commission specifically found, at least two of Ambrosia's companies, Ambrosia Coal and Construction Company and New Castle Lime and Stone Co. were earning money or attempting to earn money by virtue of dealing with organized crime figures. These companies exist today. These are the very same companies whose assets Mr. Shick would tap into for financial assistance in developing the Bedford project. He asserted that his companies have millions of tons of coal and limestone reserves and thousands of acres of real estate. At worst, the accumulation of those reserves or those companies, have direct ties or dealings with members of organized crime. At best, there is a cloud of doubt as to the suitability of the land and the assets for this project. The assets of these companies as well as the land acquired by Carmen Ambrosia are clearly part of Bedford's project.

Commission Adjudication at 81.

The Commission concluded that, "[t]he mere appearance of connection and involvement of Ambrosia Coal and Construction Co. (and other family-owned companies) with organized crime and the ownership of the ground upon which Bedford intends to construct the project reflects negatively upon the racing industry and is therefore inconsistent with the best interests of racing." Commission Adjudication Conclusion of Law No. 16.

There appears to be, however, a certain tension in the findings and conclusions of the Commission. On one hand, as noted above, the Commission was troubled by the connections between Mr. Ambrosia and his family businesses' ties to organized crime. The businesses are the same as are currently in operation and the entities to which Mr. Shick indicated that he was now involved and to which he could turn for financial assistance in developing the Bedford facility. Yet, the Commission recognized that Mr. Ambrosia was deceased and it made clear that it was not "asserting or implying that Carmen Shick or any of the other principals of Bedford had any direct dealing or ties to members of organized crime." Commission Adjudication at 80. Related thereto, the Commission found that the experience, character and fitness of Bedford's officers, directors, and shareholders was consistent with the public interests, convenience or necessity and would be in the best interests of racing generally. Commission Adjudication, Conclusion of Law 15.

Moreover, it is unclear to what extent the Commission denied the Bedford application on the basis that the actual property on which Bedford was to site the facility was originally acquired by Carmen Ambrosia. Commission Adjudication at 81. The Commonwealth Court opined that the Commission abused its discretion to the extent that it relied upon a connection between organized crime and "the ground upon which Bedford intends to construct the facility...." *Bedford Downs*, 901 A.2d at 1073. Indeed, the Commonwealth Court admonished the Commission that, "[i]t is absurd to believe that the *ground* upon which the racing facility is built will induce Bedford to violate the racing laws." *Id.* (emphasis original). The Commission refutes that it was basing its determination on the fact that illicit funds were used to purchase the property itself. According to the Commission, Bedford's proposal linked the property to the assets of the family-owned businesses and it properly denied the Bedford application on this basis.

The import of the interplay between a historical connection to organized crime, current connections of an applicant to organized crime, and the effect of past connections on a pending application may not always be clear. We caution that while the Commission may certainly consider ties to organized crime in denying a harness racing license, such ties must be of such a nature as to be directly relevant to a pending application.

We need not, however, definitively resolve whether the Commission erred in its consideration of Carmen Ambrosia's alleged past ties to organized crime and its implications with respect to the current Bedford application. As more fully discussed below, we find that independent of any alleged ties to organized crime, Bedford's financing raised sufficient concerns to uphold the Commission's denial of the racing application on this basis alone.

Specifically, the Commission contends that the Commonwealth Court substituted its judgment for the Commission's regarding concerns pertaining to Bedford's financing. In its adjudication, the Commission determined that it was concerned that Merrill Lynch's "highly confident" letter contained a far greater number of conditions than the highly confident letter issued by Bear Stearns to Valley View. Furthermore, Merrill Lynch's letter indicated that the actual borrower of the funds was not identified. Moreover, the Commission found that Merrill Lynch's highly confident letter was based substantially on the high level of confidence that Merrill Lynch had with Isle of Capri and CIBC and not on extensive review of the Bedford project itself and the individuals involved in that project.

The Commonwealth Court rejected the Commission's concerns with Bedford's financing. First, the Commonwealth Court reasoned that in its view, the fact that the borrower was not identified "has no effect on Bedford's ability to obtain financing." *Bedford Downs*, 901 A.2d at 1074. Specifically, the Commonwealth Court explained that the individual who drafted the letter explained that the structure of a deal varies by project; sometimes a company will create subsidiary corporations to divide casino operations from horse track operations; and the desire was to have a letter which would encompass the various options.

With respect to the greater number of conditions contained in Merrill Lynch's highly confident letter, the Commonwealth Court opined that the Commission did not make any findings of fact with respect to the conditions that Merrill Lynch imposed upon Bedford and whether Bedford would be unable to meet the conditions. According to the Commonwealth Court, absent some finding that Bedford could not meet the conditions imposed by Merrill Lynch, "there can be no reason for concern about Bedford's ability to finance the project based upon those conditions." *Id.*

Finally, the Commonwealth Court rejected the Commission's concern that Merrill Lynch based its highly confident letter on the high level of confidence Merrill Lynch had with Isle of Capri and CIBC. Specifically, the Commonwealth Court offered that Isle of Capri and CIBC ended their relationship with Bedford due to a failure to reach an agreement over the management of the racino and not due to financing. When negotiations with Isle of Capri failed, Bedford pursued a previous offer of a highly confident letter from Innovation Capital Holding, a gaming transaction consulting business with a relationship with Merrill Lynch. Citing to testimony of record not mentioned by the Commission, the Commonwealth Court asserted that Merrill Lynch did not simply rely on the previous involvement of Isle of Capri and CIBC, but that Merrill Lynch reviewed the project and the individuals involved in the project prior to issuing its highly confident letter. Therefore, the Commonwealth Court found that the Commission abused its discretion in "questioning, without any valid reason, the 'highly confident' letter issued by Merrill Lynch." *Id.* at 1075.

We agree with the Commission that based upon the broad discretion vested in the Commission coupled with an appellate court's deferential standard of review, the Commonwealth Court erred in rejecting the Commission's concerns regarding Bedford's financing. Specifically, we find that the Commonwealth Court's dismissal of the Commission's reasoning failed to give the Commission's concerns regarding Bedford's financing appropriate effect and failed to recognize the credibility determinations made by the Commission.

Initially, we note that the Commission's reasoning regarding financing cannot be viewed in a vacuum. Indeed, the Commission discussed the context of how Bedford's final financing proposal came into being. Specifically, Bedford filed its application on June 9, 2003 and through the course of the proceedings intended to finance its project in conjunction with an equity investment by Isle of Capri. Isle of Capri possessed a highly confident letter from CIBC. On January 11, 2005, however, Bedford advised the Commission that negotiations with Isle of Capri had ceased but that it was securing another highly confident letter for the financing of the project. On January 17, 2005, Merrill Lynch issued its "highly confident" letter regarding the financing of the Bedford project. In its adjudication, the Commission focused upon certain testimony of Mr. Avid Laurence of Merrill Lynch, who signed the "highly confident" letter. Mr. Laurence indicated that because Isle of Capri had been willing to engage in the deal, and not due to Bedford, it gave them a great deal of confidence and comfort. The Commission also noted that before issuing the highly confident letter, Merrill Lynch did not conduct background checks on the principals of Bedford and was not aware of litigation involving the Shick family.

It is in this context that the Commission properly voiced its concerns regarding the number of conditions in the Merrill Lynch highly confident letter, the lack of the identity of the borrower of the funds, and the Merrill Lynch letter being based, to a substantial part, on confidence with Isle of Capri and CIBC, rather than an extensive review of the Bedford project itself and the individuals involved in that project. Each of these determinations was based to one degree or another on credibility determinations. Incomplete and questionable independent due diligence regarding financing are certainly legitimate reasons to deny an application. This is especially true when financial suitability is a fundamental consideration in awarding a racing license. These determinations were for the Commission to make and not the Commonwealth Court.

Related thereto, the Commonwealth Court failed to understand that the license application process was a comparative review process. Thus, the ultimate question was not solely that considered by the Commonwealth Court, viz., whether Bedford could obtain, and meet financing; rather, the issue centered on the integrity and sufficiency of Bedford's financial resources and in part on how Bedford's financing compared to the other license applicant. While the Commonwealth Court majority may have come to a different conclusion regarding the integrity of Bedford's financing than that reached by the Commission, that is not the appropriate role of appellate review of these matters. In the end, we find that the Commission was well within its discretion to be concerned about the terms and conditions of Bedford's financing and the events surrounding the obtaining of such financing; the Commonwealth Court erred in substituting its own judgment in rejecting the Commission's determination.

Therefore, we conclude, for all of the reasons stated above, that the Commission properly denied the Bedford license application.

We now turn to consider Valley View's challenges to the denial of its license application.

Valley View first argues that the Commission's Statement of Policy, and its decision to apply a comparative review process to harness racing applications thereunder, violated Valley View's due process rights. Specifically, Valley View offers two distinct grounds by which it challenges the Statement of Policy. First, Valley View maintains that the Commission's Statement of Policy was not properly promulgated as a regulation or a rule, and thus, is not entitled to the force and effect of law and that the procedures imposed pursuant to the Statement of Policy were in conflict with existing law and regulations. Second, according to Valley View, the Statement of Policy led to unfair and inequitable treatment of similarly situated applicants and placed Valley View on unequal footing with another prior applicant, Chester Downs. In this regard, Valley View asserts that Chester Downs was awarded a license without having to compete against other applicants and that the Chester Downs facility proposed a 5/8 mile track which was acceptable to the Commission, whereas Valley View's application was denied, in part, due to a 5/8 mile track.

In response, the Commission and Bedford first offer that Valley View failed to properly and timely file a challenge to the Commission's Statement of Policy and the comparative review process, including assertions regarding the Chester Downs application. Specifically, the Commission submits, *inter alia,* that Valley View did not make its challenge until it filed a petition for reconsideration. According to the Commission, this was the first time Valley View asserted its due process challenges, and thus, they are waived....

We conclude that Valley View's various challenges to the Commission's Statement of Policy, the comparative process, and the due process challenges based upon the Statement of Policy are waived. The Commission adopted the Statement of Policy on April 3, 2003, which became effective May 3, 2003. Approximately one and one-half years after the adoption of the Statement of Policy, on October 12, 2004, the Commission held the first pre-hearing conference in these matters. Valley View failed to raise any challenge to the Statement of Policy during this pre-hearing conference, at subsequent pre-hearing conferences, in pre-hearing memoranda, during public comment hearings, or during any of the evidentiary hearings regarding Valley View or Bedford. *See* 58 Pa. Code § 185.83(o).

Valley View attempts to salvage its challenge to the Statement of Policy by pointing to letters it sent to the Commission on April 7, 2003, May 7, 2003, and May 27, 2003, as well as its petition for reconsideration. The letters, which are attached to Valley View's Brief as Appendix C, merely make a "recommendation" that the policy only apply to new applications, Letter Dated April 7, 2003 Appendix C, Valley View Brief; seek "clarification" regarding the applicability of the Statement of Policy (and suggesting that a comparative assessment should not be conducted with respect to Valley View and that the policy should have been proposed as a formal regulation), Letter Dated May 7, 2003 Appendix C, Valley View Brief; and while purportedly agreeing to proceed under the Statement of Policy, "reserve the right to raise additional arguments about the new 'group consideration' standard included in the Statement of Policy and Procedures for License Application Review." Letter Dated May 27, 2003 Appendix C, Valley View Brief.

We find Valley View's position to be unpersuasive. First, even though the letters were apparently written a year and one-half prior to the commencement of the Valley View hearings on November 4, 2004, they were never introduced into the evidentiary record or into the certified record before the Commission. It must be remembered that the proceedings concerning both Valley View and Bedford were ones in which hearings were held before a Hearing Examiner, both sides were permitted to participate, object, cross-examine, and to make argument. Proposed findings of fact and conclusions of law were presented by the parties, yet no objection to the Statement of Policy was lodged in any of these proceedings, even though Valley View had the opportunity to make such a challenge. Even assuming, *arguendo* that the letters which are attached to Valley View's brief are properly before us, we find that the mere forwarding of letters to agencies outside of the formal administrative proceedings in which parties are active participants is simply insufficient to preserve an issue on appeal. Thus, we conclude that Valley View's failure to make any formal objection during the proceedings to the framework under which the Commission was clearly operating constitutes waiver of Valley View's various challenges to the Statement of Policy and the comparative review process....

Valley View's second challenge is that the Commission failed to afford it an opportunity to cure the defects cited by the Commission as the basis for the denial of its license application. According to Valley View, Bedford was permitted four opportunities to correct defects in its application while it was refused this ability. Finally, Valley View suggests that the Commission should have provided preliminary decision-making before a final decision was rendered, akin to that in the land use arena, and that it should have had the ability to cure any deficiencies in its plan prior to a final adjudication.

The Commonwealth Court determined that the Commission properly considered the plan before it and had no obligation to permit revisions after a final adjudication was rendered. We agree. In the matter *sub judice,* Valley View requests the ability to modify its plan, not during the ongoing pre-adjudication process but after a final adjudication was made. In essence, Valley View wants the Commission to re-open the record to allow it to address and purportedly correct its deficiencies. Valley View offers no authority requiring the Commission to take such a post-final adjudication approach to its decision making. Moreover, Valley View was permitted the opportunity to revise its proposal numerous times over the course of the proceedings prior to the Commission's final adjudication. All proceedings must have a point at which at final decision must be made. Therefore, we reject Valley View's demand for a post-final adjudication opportunity to cure its application.[9]

---

9. Furthermore, with respect to Valley View's assertion that Bedford was permitted to correct a defect while it was not, Valley View fails to recognize that Bedford's request to re-open the record took place *prior* to the Commission's final order and adjudication. Valley View's request in this matter came thirty days *after* the Commission's final adjudication. While Valley View claims that given the oppor-

In conclusion, for the reasons set forth above, the order of the Commonwealth Court is reversed with respect to the Bedford license application and affirmed with respect to the Valley View application. In sum, we uphold the Commission's broad discretion and its denial of both harness racing license applications. Finally, our decision today is rendered without prejudice for Bedford and Valley View to reapply for a harness racing license and for reconsideration of those applications by the Commission consistent with our opinion today.

Notes

1. *Bedford Downs* reflects one characteristic of pari-mutuel racing: the central role played by a state licensing body that has been given statutory authority to handle many areas of the racing industry. This entity typically is empowered with the authority to grant (or deny) licenses to operate racing venues, and the licensing of individuals who are part of the activity. The powers granted to this administrative agency are usually quite comprehensive. *See, e.g.,* Ky. Rev. Stat. Ann. § 230.225 (West 2009), "The Kentucky Horse Racing Authority is created as an independent agency of state government to regulate the conduct of horse racing and pari-mutuel wagering on horse racing, and related activities within the Commonwealth of Kentucky." *See also* Ky. Rev. Stat. Ann. § 230.260 (West 2009) (setting out fourteen enumerated powers held by the Horse Racing Authority).

As an administrative body, these agencies typically promulgate regulations that help to give effect to the statutory language. In a state with a well-established racing industry, the regulations will be extensive. Also illustrated in *Bedford Downs* is the fact that courts defer to the reasonable judgments of these administrative bodies when applying the regulations.

2. Perhaps the most fundamental power of the state agency is the power to license. An entity wanting to conduct pari-mutuel racing must be licensed to do so. The costs of pursuing such a license are substantial and there may be competition among those seeking licenses, as *Bedford Downs* illustrates. *See also* Livingston Downs Racing Ass'n, Inc. v. Jefferson Downs Corp., 192 F. Supp. 2d 519 (M.D. La. 2001) (determined effort by one licensee to prevent another entity seeking a license from gaining one. The defendant had attempted to halt a referendum by local citizens to support the license, filed court challenges to efforts by the plaintiff to gain the license, and attempted to influence state legislators and regulators. The litigation focused on antitrust and RICO claims.).

3. Even after an entity has obtained a license to operate a pari-mutuel facility, it may be in competition with other licensees for the most desirable dates to conduct racing. The power to set these dates is held by the state agency which is typically bound by statutory and/or administrative rules. In Balmoral Racing Club, Inc. v. Illinois Racing Board, 603 N.E.2d 489 (Ill. 1992), the plaintiff challenged the Illinois Racing Board's application of five statutory requirements for granting licensees and allocating racing dates. The statutory factors were:

> (1) the character, reputation, experience and financial integrity of the applicants and of any other or separate person that either:
>
> > (i) controls, directly or indirectly, such applicant, or

---

tunity to cure its deficiencies, it would have met all of the "now-disclosed" requirements, as noted above, Valley View may take the opportunity to reapply to the Commission, without prejudice, for reconsideration of its application.

(ii) is controlled, directly or indirectly, by such applicant or by a person which controls, directly or indirectly, such applicant;

(2) their facilities and accommodations for the conduct of horse race meetings;

(3) the location of the tracks of the applicants in relation to the principal centers of population of the State;

(4) the highest prospective total revenue to be derived by the State from the conduct of such meets;

(5) the good faith affirmative action plan of each applicant to recruit, train and upgrade minorities in all classifications within the association. Ill. Rev. Stat. 1991, ch. 8, par. 37-21(c).

The plaintiff complained that the Board had only considered factor 4, the maximization of state revenue. The court agreed and remanded the case to the Board for consideration of all five statutory elements.

Under some state regulatory regimes, pari-mutuel facilities must not be located within a certain distance of another facility. But is this an appropriate consideration? Should market forces be allowed to operate, with facilities offering the most attractive package of races naturally gaining market share? Or would such a free-for-all undermine the objective of maximizing state tax revenues? Some states have effectively "de-regulated" the process of assigning racing dates. The Florida Pari-Mutuel Commission was vested with non-delegable discretionary power to allocate racing dates among permit holders under FLA. STAT. §§ 550.011 (related to fixing dates for racing) and 20.16. *See, e.g.,* Gulfstream Park Racing Ass'n, Inc. v. Dep't Bus. Regulation, 441 So. 2d 627, 629 (Fla. 1983). However, those statutes were repealed by Laws 1992, c. 92-348, §67, effective Dec. 16, 1992 and Laws 1993, c. 93-220, § 12, effective July 1, 1993 respectively. *See also* Joseph Durso, *On Horse Racing; Racetracks in Florida Are Jockeying for Dates,* N.Y. TIMES, June 16, 1992, *available at* http://www.nytimes.com/1992/06/16/sports/on-horse-racing-racetracks-in-florida-are-jockeying-for-dates.html; *Florida Jai Alai Deregulation Rejected,* L.A. TIMES, May 19, 1989 *available at* http://articles.latimes.com/1989-05-19/sports/sp-436_1_alai-jai-house-committee.

4. An entity which obtains a license may have it revoked if it does not follow the terms of the license grant. In Hialeah Racing Ass'n, LLC v. Department of Business and Professional Regulation, Div. of Parimutuel Wagering, 907 So. 2d 1235 (Fla. Dist. Ct. App. 2005), plaintiff Hialeah sought review of an order of the Department of Business and Professional Regulation revoking the association's pari-mutuel wagering thoroughbred racing permit and denying its annual thoroughbred racing license application, after the association decided not to run scheduled races. The District Court of Appeal held that the association's financial hardship, which caused an inability to field enough horses to compete against other racetracks, did not constitute just cause for failure to operate races on the date and times specified. Rehearing was denied, August 19, 2005. *See also* Paul Moran, *Can Hialeah Park Rise Again?,* ESPN.com, Aug. 12, 2008, http://sports.espn.go.com/sports/horse/columns/story?columnist=moran_paul&id=3531315.

5. In addition to the licensing of racetrack facilities, state racing boards also require individuals involved in racing to apply for and be granted a license. This may apply even if the individual is only remotely connected with racing. The provisions for licensing can be quite detailed. *See, e.g.,* 810 Ky. Admin. Regs. 1:025 (2009) (listing grounds for an applicant to be determined unsuitable); Ariz. Rev. Stat. § 5-107.01(B) ("No trainer, driver, jockey, apprentice jockey, horse owner, dog owner, greyhound racing kennel owner or operator, breeder of racing greyhounds, exercise boy, agent, jockey's agent, stable fore-

man, groom, valet, veterinarian, horseshoer, steward, stable watchman, starter, timer, judge, food and beverage concessionaire, manager or other person acting as a participant or official at any racing meeting including all employees of the pari-mutuel department and any other person or official the department deems proper shall participate in racing meetings without having first obtained and having in full force and effect a license or credentials that are issued by the department, pursuant to such rules as the commission shall make. The department shall not revoke a license except for cause and after a hearing. For the purposes of this subsection, participate in a dog racing meeting includes breeding, raising and training a dog and certifying as an Arizona bred dog."); Ariz. Rev. Stat. § 5-107.01(E) ("All applicants for a permit or license shall Submit to the department a full set of fingerprints, background information and the fees that are required pursuant to § 41-1750. The department of racing shall submit the fingerprints to the department of public safety for the purpose of obtaining a state and federal criminal records check pursuant to § 41-1750 and public law 92-544. The department of public safety may exchange this fingerprint data with the federal bureau of investigation. The applicant shall pay the fingerprint fee and costs of the background investigation in an amount that is determined by the department. For such purpose the department of racing and the department of public safety may enter into an intergovernmental agreement pursuant to title 11, chapter 7, article 3. The fees shall be credited pursuant to § 35-148.").

In addition, the license process may also accomplish other important objectives. In Nevada, for example, a person can be denied a license if he is subject to a court order to pay child support and has not complied. Nev. Rev. Stat. § 466.172 (1997). When challenges are made to denials of licenses, courts typically show deference to the decision of the administrative body. *See, e.g.,* Cohen v. Dep't of Bus. Regulation, Div. of Parimutuel Wagering, 584 So. 2d 1083 (Fla. Dist. Ct. App. 1991) (applicant for greyhound license appealed his denial. Court held that applicant was sufficiently put on notice that his application was denied because he was deemed to not possess "good moral character," and the consideration of the applicant's lengthy record of arrests and convictions did not constitute reversible error).

6. In addition to having the authority to grant licenses to individuals, state racing boards have the authority to revoke them. The following section on Animal Welfare will consider how this relates to trainers. As for other licensees, a similar range of discretion is granted to the state board to take steps to protect the integrity of the pari-mutuel activity. *See, e.g.,* Reed v. Kansas Racing Comm'n, 860 P.2d 684 (Kan. 1993) (in an appeal by a racetrack general manager from the revocation of his license, the court held there was sufficient evidence to find that he had perjured himself related to an incident involving the receipt of gambling information, and therefore sufficient evidence to conclude he was unqualified to perform his duties as general racetrack manager); Rice v. New York State Racing and Wagering Bd., 653 N.Y.S.2d 601 (N.Y. App. Div. 1997) (court upheld appeal jockey's thirty day suspension for driving horse with lack of effort); Cordero v. Corbisiero, 565 N.Y.S.2d 109 (N.Y. App. Div. 1991) (upholding jockey's ten day suspension for "riding foul" in a race as not arbitrary and capricious). These actions by the state racing board have to be supported by an adequate record.

3. Where Can Pari-Mutuel Betting Take Place?

It may seem odd to ask the question this section poses. The most obvious site for a bettor to engage in pari-mutuel betting is at the facility where the racing is taking place. But as the following notes describe in detail, the number of patrons actually attending live racing has plummeted. In response to this fact, a variety of different ways of placing pari-mutuel bets have developed. This has created considerable controversy.

State Ex Rel. Stenberg v. Omaha Exposition and Racing, Inc.
644 N.W.2d 563 (2002)

NATURE OF CASE

In this original action, the Attorney General (relator) asks the court to declare (1) that the conduct of "telephonic wagering" pursuant to Neb. Rev. Stat. §§ 2-1230 to 2-1242 (Reissue 1997) violates Neb. Const. art. III, § 24, and (2) that licenses to conduct telephonic wagering are void due to the unconstitutionality of the statutes under which they were issued. The relator also seeks to permanently enjoin the respondents from acting pursuant to licenses granted by the Nebraska State Racing Commission (Commission).

SCOPE OF REVIEW

The burden of establishing the unconstitutionality of a statute is on the one attacking its validity....

Statutes are afforded a presumption of constitutionality, and the unconstitutionality of a statute must be clearly established before it will be declared void....

FACTS

The respondents are entities licensed by the Commission to conduct parimutuel wagering on live horseracing and on horseracing events conducted both within and outside the state, including simulcast wagering. Named as respondents are Omaha Exposition and Racing, Inc., which operates Horsemen's Park Racetrack in Omaha; the Nebraska State Board of Agriculture, which operates State Fair Park Racetrack in Lincoln; the Hall County Livestock Improvement Association, which operates Fonner Park Racetrack in Grand Island; the Platte County Agricultural Society, which operates Columbus Agricultural Park Racetrack in Columbus; and South Sioux City Exposition and Racing, Inc., which operates Atokad Downs Racetrack in South Sioux City. In May 2001, the Commission, acting pursuant to §§ 2-1232 and 2-1241, approved licenses for the respondents which allow them to conduct telephonic wagering at the respective racetracks. Omaha Exposition and Racing, Inc., began operating telephonic wagering pursuant to its license on October 24.

The relator asserts that a portion of 1992 Neb. Laws, L.B. 718, now codified at §§ 2-1230 to 2-1242, violates article III, § 24, which states in pertinent part:

Nothing in this section shall be construed to prohibit (a) the enactment of laws providing for the licensing and regulation of wagering on the results of horseraces, wherever run, either within or outside of the state, by the parimutuel method, when such wagering is conducted by licensees within a licensed racetrack enclosure....

Sections 2-1230 to 2-1242 purport to authorize telephonic wagering which does not occur within the confines of a licensed racetrack enclosure in the state.

In Nebraska, betting on the outcome of horseraces is authorized when conducted by the parimutuel method. Bettors attempt to predict the outcome of one or more races. All wagers on any of the horses to win in a specific race constitute a pool. After deductions for taxes, for promotion of agriculture and breeder's awards, and for payment to the entity conducting the races, the amount remaining in the pool is paid out to the bettors in proportion to their bets, e.g., the winner who has wagered $20 receives 10 times as much as the winner who wagered $2....

A computer known as a totalizator is used to manage the wagers. The computer continuously computes and recomputes the amount of each pool, the amount bet upon each prediction for each horse, and the amount that would theoretically be paid out for each $2 bet on each horse if the race is finished and that horse wins, places, or shows.

According to the parties, when telephonic wagering is not available, an individual who wishes to place a bet on a horserace is required to go to a licensed racetrack; select the race, the horse, and the order of finish; and then place the bet at a terminal station, which is either operated by the bettor or a parimutuel clerk at a parimutuel window. When the bet is entered into the totalizator, a ticket showing the transaction is issued and given to the bettor. If the bettor is successful, the ticket is presented to the racetrack for payment.

As a result of the Commission's issuance of licenses for telephonic wagering, a person outside the confines of a licensed racetrack enclosure may place a telephone call to a racetrack and give instructions to an employee of the racetrack concerning the wager of money that the individual has on deposit at a telephone deposit center in his or her own deposit account. After the racetrack employee at the telephone deposit center has received a call and determined that the individual has sufficient funds in the deposit account, the employee places the wager on behalf of the caller. The wager is entered into the totalizator, which records the transaction and places the money in the applicable parimutuel pool. Any winnings are credited to the individual's deposit account, and any losses are deducted from the account. The employee is allowed to enter a wager only if the individual has sufficient funds available in the deposit account at the time the wager is placed by the employee.

ISSUES BEFORE COURT

The court is asked to determine (1) whether the authorization of telephonic wagering on horseraces pursuant to §§ 2-1230 to 2-1242 violates article III, § 24, which authorizes parimutuel wagering on the results of horseraces within or outside the state only "when such wagering is conducted by licensees within a licensed racetrack enclosure"; (2) whether licenses issued by the Commission authorizing the respondents to conduct telephonic wagering are void due to the unconstitutionality of the statutes under which they were issued; and (3) whether the respondents should be permanently enjoined from acting pursuant to the telephonic wagering licenses issued by the Commission.

ANALYSIS
L.B. 718

The statutes in question were passed by the Legislature as 1992 Neb. Laws, L.B. 718. The Legislature stated that "horseracing, horse breeding, and parimutuel wagering industries are important sectors of the agricultural economy of the state, provide substantial revenue for state and local governments, and employ many residents of the state." § 2-1230(1)(a). Teleracing facilities provide a potential for strengthening the horseracing industry and its economic contributions to the state. § 2-1230(1)(b). The Legislature found that "it is in the best interests of the state to encourage experimentation with parimutuel wagering through licensed teleracing facilities" and telephonic wagering. § 2-1230(1)(b) and (c). The experimentation would determine whether teleracing and telephonic wagering would promote growth of the horseracing industry and provide additional revenue to the state. § 2-1230(1)(d). The Legislature also found that teleracing and telephonic wagering should be authorized and regulated so that it would not jeopardize horseracing or employment opportunities. § 2-1230(1)(e).

Telephonic wagering is defined as "the placing of parimutuel wagers by telephone to a telephone deposit center at a licensed racetrack as authorized by the commission." § 2-1231(5). A teleracing facility is "a detached, licensed area occupied solely by a licensee for the purpose of conducting telewagering and containing one or more betting terminals, which facility is either owned or under the exclusive control of the licensee during the period for which it is licensed." § 2-1231(6). Telewagering is "the placing of a wager through betting terminals electronically linked to a licensed racetrack, which … instantaneously transmits the wagering information to the parimutuel pool for acceptance and issues tickets as evidence of such wager." § 2-1231(7).

At the present time, the Commission issues licenses to racetracks for the operation of telephonic wagering facilities. § 2-1232. A licensee may deduct up to 5 percent from the winnings of any winning ticket purchased through telephonic wagering. § 2-1236. A licensed racetrack that conducts live races may establish a telephonic wagering system if the racetrack establishes and maintains a telephone deposit center. All wagers must be entered into the parimutuel pool and are subject to all laws and conditions applicable to any other wagers. § 2-1239.

Under the law, only the holder of the deposit account may place a telephonic wager. § 2-1240. Any violation of that rule constitutes a Class II misdemeanor. *Id.* Telephonic wagering is allowed at licensed racetracks which conduct either intrastate simulcasting or interstate simulcasting as approved by the Commission. § 2-1241. The racetracks must pay one-half of 1 percent of the amount wagered through telephonic wagering to the Department of Revenue for credit to the Commission's cash fund. § 2-1242.

CONSTITUTIONALITY of L.B. 718

This court has previously been asked to consider the constitutionality of portions of L.B. 718. In 1994, upon an original action filed by the relator, we held that the provisions of L.B. 718 which authorized teleracing facilities to conduct telewagering were unconstitutional in violation of article III, § 24. *See* State ex rel. Stenberg v. Douglas Racing Corp., 524 N.W.2d 61 (Neb. 1994).

Douglas Racing Corp. was licensed to operate a teleracing facility in Bennington, Nebraska, at which terminals were electronically linked to its totalizator located in Omaha. The bets were entered by either the bettor or the parimutuel clerk and then sent to the totalizator at the racetrack. The bettors received tickets as evidence of their wagers. We held that the relator had met the burden to establish that certain statutes were unconstitutional to the extent they authorized telewagering.

In *Douglas Racing Corp.,* the relator argued that telewagering at a teleracing facility was unconstitutional because parimutuel wagering on horseraces must be conducted within a licensed racetrack enclosure and that telewagering was equivalent to offtrack betting, which was not constitutionally authorized. The respondent unsuccessfully asserted that because the licensee conducted his end of the wagering within the confines of the licensed racetrack, telewagering was constitutional.

We concluded that article III, § 24, was unambiguous and required no construction. State ex rel. Stenberg v. Douglas Racing Corp., *supra,* citing State ex rel. Spire v. Conway, 472 N.W.2d 403 (Neb. 1991). The Constitution's provision that parimutuel wagering is authorized only when conducted within a licensed racetrack enclosure "plainly requires that (1) the wagering must be conducted by an entity licensed to do so and (2) the wagering must be conducted by licensees at a racetrack enclosure which is licensed to operate horseraces." *Douglas Racing Corp.*, 524 N.W.2d at 64. Wagering which takes place outside a licensed racetrack enclosure or a detached facility "cannot logically occur within a licensed racetrack enclosure as required by our Constitution." *Id.* We determined that telewagering at teleracing facilities was the functional equivalent of offtrack betting, which was not conducted within a licensed racetrack enclosure and which violated the state Constitution. *Id.*

We held that Douglas Racing Corp.'s license for the operation of the Bennington facility was void because it was licensed pursuant to an unconstitutional statute. We enjoined the respondent from acting pursuant to the license issued by the Commission. While we held that Neb. Rev. Stat. §§ 2-1203, 2-1203.01, 2-1207, 2-1208, 2-1216, 2-1221, 2-1222, and 2-1230 through 2-1242 (Cum.Supp.1994) were all unconstitutional to the extent they authorized telewagering at teleracing facilities, we did not address any other portions of L.B. 718.

Here, we are asked to consider the remainder of L.B. 718 as it purports to authorize telephonic wagering. We first address whether the remainder of L.B. 718 is severable from the provisions previously held to be unconstitutional....

There is no dispute between the parties concerning the severability of L.B. 718.... [W]e conclude that it is possible to sever the telewagering provisions from the telephonic wagering provisions.

We next examine whether telephonic wagering is unconstitutional. The burden of establishing the unconstitutionality of a statute is on the one attacking its validity. Bergan Mercy Health Sys. v. Haven, 620 N.W.2d 339 (Neb. 2000). Statutes are afforded a presumption of constitutionality, and the unconstitutionality of a statute must be clearly established before it will be declared void. *Id.* Constitutional provisions, like statutes, are not open to construction as a matter of course; construction of a constitutional provision is appropriate only when it has been demonstrated that the meaning of the provision is not clear and that construction is necessary. State ex rel. Stenberg v. Douglas Racing Corp., *supra.*

As noted earlier, article III, § 24, does not prohibit wagering on horseracing by the parimutuel method "when such wagering is conducted by licensees *within a licensed racetrack enclosure*" (emphasis supplied). The key issue here is whether telephonic wagering occurs within a licensed racetrack enclosure.

Section 2-1231(5) defines telephonic wagering as "the placing of parimutuel wagers by telephone to a telephone deposit center at a licensed racetrack" as authorized by the Commission. For purposes of this opinion, the person placing the wager is not at the racetrack, but is calling from a telephone away from the facility. The parties stipulated that "a person located outside the confines of a racetrack will be allowed to place a call to a licensed racetrack enclosure to give instructions to an employee of the racetrack concerning the wager of money that the individual has on deposit at a telephone deposit center."

In attempting to allow different forms of parimutuel wagering, the Legislature stated that "[w]agers placed ... by approved telephonic wagering as authorized by sections 2-1230 to 2-1242 shall be deemed to be wagers placed and accepted within the enclosure of any racetrack." See § 2-1207 (Reissue 1997). However, as the relator notes, the Legislature may not circumvent or nullify the constitution by defining terms in statutes. In MAPCO Ammonia Pipeline v. State Bd. of Equal., 471 N.W.2d 734, 739 (Neb. 1991), *cert. denied* 508 U.S. 960 (1993), we held that the Legislature's "power to define [terms] is limited, since (1) the Legislature cannot abrogate or contradict an express constitutional provision and (2) the legislative definition must be reasonable, and cannot be arbitrary or unfounded."

Pursuant to stipulation, under telephonic wagering, the person making the wager calls the licensed racetrack directly to instruct an employee on the placing of a wager. Thus, it is undisputed that the person placing the call is outside the licensed racetrack enclosure.

Nebraska's Constitution is not a grant, but, rather, is a restriction on legislative power, and the Legislature is free to act on any subject not inhibited by the constitution. State ex rel. Stenberg v. Douglas Racing Corp., 524 N.W.2d 61 (Neb. 1994). The question is whether the wager is placed within the licensed racetrack enclosure when the telephone call is initiated outside the racetrack enclosure. Simply stated, does the constitution require that the person making the call to the licensee also be located within the licensed racetrack enclosure?

The respondents argue that the constitution requires only that the licensee's activity in conducting wagering on horseraces occur within a licensed racetrack enclosure. This is distinguished from wagers made at a teleracing facility, where at least a part of the licensee's activity occurs outside the racetrack enclosure. They assert that the wager occurs within the confines of the racetrack enclosure because the wager is placed by a racetrack employee pursuant to instructions from a person outside the enclosure. They conclude that it is only the actions of the licensee's employee that constitute the placing of the wager.

The respondents argue that telephonic wagering is substantially different from telewagering. They assert that the only action taken by a person who is outside the racetrack enclosure is to give instructions to an employee of the licensed racetrack, who then places the wager from within the enclosure. In their brief, they claim that telephonic wagering is conducted every day by persons who go to the racetrack with a cellular telephone and place wagers for friends who are located outside the racetrack enclosure. They argue that the wager occurs only when the person inside the racetrack enclosure places the wager with the licensee.

The relator argues that both telephonic wagering and telewagering involve the same conduct-placing wagers on horseraces from an offtrack location. The relator claims that it is the caller who directs the racetrack employee to follow his instructions and that, therefore, it is the offtrack caller who is engaged in wagering on the horserace.

Minnesota has faced a similar challenge to its constitution, which was amended in 1982 to provide that "'[t]he legislature may authorize on-track parimutuel betting on horseracing in a manner prescribed by law.'" Rice v. Connolly, 488 N.W.2d 241, 244 (Minn. 1992). In 1985, the Minnesota Racing Commission adopted rules implementing a telephone account wagering system, in which account holders maintained a minimum balance against which wagers were debited and winnings were credited. The account holder telephoned a licensed employee at a racetrack to place and record wagers on behalf of the account holder. "[T]he wagerer need not be present at the racetrack or a teleracing facility—all that is required is access to a telephone." Id. at 246.

When asked whether the constitution "contemplate[d] other than on-track, i.e., on the racetrack premises, parimutuel betting," the Minnesota Supreme Court found that it did not. See id. The court found that "[i]n its literal sense, the word 'on' as a part of the phrase 'on-track' is more precisely defined as 'at' to denote a location for the placement of a parimutuel bet." Id. at 247. The state's voters had specifically approved "'on-track parimutuel betting on horseracing,'" and the court found, as a practical matter, that "bets not physically placed at the racetrack cannot be, by definition, 'on-track,' no matter how they are transmitted to the track, electronically recorded or accepted into the pool of funds." Id.

The Minnesota court noted, as the respondents had pointed out, that advances in technology facilitated remote wagering. However, the court found that its own mandate required it to "refrain from expansive interpretation by looking beyond the clear, unambiguous and ordinary meaning of the language of the constitutional provision." *Id.* at 248. It held: "Wagering at facilities remote from the racetrack or by telephonic means are beyond the scope of the activities authorized by the voters and are therefore impermissible." *Id.*

Following the rationale of the Minnesota Supreme Court, resolution of the case at bar is relatively simple. In the context of telephonic wagering, wagers are not placed by a licensee until the licensee has been instructed to do so by a caller, and the instructions do not originate from within a licensed racetrack enclosure. We conclude the constitution requires that the instructions to place the wager must originate from within the licensed racetrack enclosure.

Nebraska voters have previously rejected an attempt by the Legislature to change the constitutional provisions concerning parimutuel betting. In 1995, the Legislature adopted L.R. 24CA, which placed before the voters a constitutional amendment proposing the elimination of the location requirement in article III, § 24. The amendment provided that parimutuel wagering on racehorses could be conducted by licensees "at such locations and by such means as are authorized by the Legislature." The introducer's statement of intent noted this court's decision in State ex rel. Stenberg v. Douglas Racing Corp., 524 N.W.2d 61 (Neb. 1994), and stated that L.R. 24CA would delete the location provision and provide the Legislature with the authority to determine the location and means of wagering on horseraces. See Statement of Intent, L.R. 24CA, General Affairs Committee, 93d Leg., 2d Sess. (Jan. 23, 1995). At the general election in November 1996, the constitutional amendment was defeated by a vote of 388,462 against and 236,600 in favor.

Nebraska's Constitution permits wagers on horseracing when the "wagering is conducted by licensees within a licensed racetrack enclosure." See Neb. Const. art. III, § 24. As this court held in *Douglas Racing Corp.*, the constitutional language allows wagering only by those who are within a racetrack enclosure. Telephonic wagering differs from telewagering only as to the form used to transmit the wager. It is a distinction without a difference. Telephonic wagering violates the constitution because it does not occur within a licensed racetrack enclosure. The relator has met the burden of establishing that the telephonic wagering statutes are unconstitutional.

CONCLUSION

We have held that "[a]n unconstitutional statute is a nullity, is void from its enactment, and is incapable of creating any rights or obligations." *Douglas Racing Corp.*, 524 N.W.2d at 65. The statutes purporting to authorize telephonic wagering, §§ 2-1230 to 2-1242, are unconstitutional. The licenses issued to the respondents to conduct telephonic wagering are void because they were issued pursuant to these statutes. The respondents are permanently enjoined from acting pursuant to the licenses issued by the Commission, and judgment is entered for the relator.

JUDGMENT FOR RELATOR.

Notes

1. The number of thoroughbred races run in North America declined 2.2% in 2008 from 2007. Gross purses in North America in 2008 slipped 1.3% from the record level achieved in 2007, as a decline of more than $1 billion in pari-mutuel handle in 2008 reduced the

contribution to purses. A "handle" is the total amount of money wagered on a given event. Current figures indicate that this decline continues, as thoroughbred declined another 2.5% in 2009. But a better indication of the problems facing the industry is the decline in track attendance from approximately 75 million in the mid-1980s to approximately 42 million in 1997. *See* Joan S. Howland, *Let's Not "Spit the Bit" In Defense of "The Law of the Horse:" The Historical and Legal Development of American Thoroughbred Racing,* 14 MARQ. SPORTS L. REV. 473 (2004) (comprehensive historical analysis of the history of thoroughbred racing from ancient times, colonial America, and the present); Thomas H. Meeker, *Thoroughbred Racing—Getting Back on Track,* 78 KY. L.J. 435 (1989–1990) (analysis of the decline of American racing by the President and CEO of Churchill Downs with suggestions on how the industry can turn around). The role of horseracing in American post-Depression history and culture is thrillingly described in the Laura Hillenbrand book, *Seabiscuit: An American Legend,* published in 2001. The book was the basis of the movie, *Seabiscuit,* released in 2003. Interest in horseracing spikes from time-to-time, usually due to a race like the Kentucky Derby, held on the first Saturday in May. Particular horses may also capture the public's interest. Examples include: Ruffian, a filly considered one of the greatest thoroughbreds of all time, who was euthanized in 1975 when she broke down in a match race against Foolish Pleasure, that year's Kentucky Derby winner; Barbaro, the winner of the 2006 Kentucky Derby who broke down in the Preakness Stakes two weeks later, shattering bones in a rear leg; the owners tried to rehabilitate Barbaro through extensive surgical treatment but he had to be euthanized in January 2007, eight months after his injury; Rachel Alexandra, a filly who defeated male horses in stakes races, broke several track records, was undefeated in 2009, and then was retired by her owners in 2010; and Zenyatta, a mare who won all nineteen of her races until she lost the 2010 Breeders Cup Classic by a short head. Still, the interest in these, and other, horses has not stanched diminished interest in the sport.

2. If horseracing is struggling for an audience, the other prominent form of pari-mutuel activity, greyhound racing, is in even more dire condition. In 2010, greyhound racetracks were operating in seven states: Alabama, Arizona, Arkansas, Florida, Iowa, Texas, and West Virginia. Oregon, Connecticut, Kansas, Colorado, and Wisconsin still permit Greyhound racing, but no tracks are currently offering races. Greyhound racing is also legal in South Dakota, but the state has no operating racetracks. In addition, seven states specifically banned live greyhound racing: Idaho, Maine, North Carolina, Nevada, Vermont, Virginia, and Washington. Florida has thirteen greyhound racetracks, by far the most of any state. From 1994 to 2003, the greyhound racing handle in Florida dropped from $850 million to $533 million. *See* Library Index, *Sports Gambling—Pari-Mutuel Gambling,* http://www.libraryindex.com/pages/1611/Sports-Gambling-PARI-MUTUEL-GAMBLING.html.

3. Jai alai is a sport with a tradition of pari-mutuel betting. Jai alai peaked in popularity during the early 1980s, when more than $600 million was wagered on the sport. By 1996 the total handle was down to around $240 million.

In 2004 pari-mutuel gambling on jai alai was conducted in only two states: Florida at five frontons and Rhode Island at one fronton. The sport used to be conducted in Connecticut, but the last jai alai fronton in that state closed in 2002. As of 2010, Florida was the sole surviving venue for jai alai. In fiscal year 2008, bets on jai alai in Florida fell nearly sixteen percent from the previous year, from $81.4 million to $68.7 million, according to the Florida Department of Business and Professional Regulation. A law was passed in 2004 permitting frontons to offer high stakes poker tables which would generate additional revenue. Fronton owners have been pushing for statutory authority to add slot machines as well. *See* Bill Andrews, *Jai Alai, a Bettors' Sport, Struggles to Stay Relevant,* N.Y.

TIMES STUDENT JOURNALISM INST., Jan. 9, 2009, *available at* http://www.nytimes-institute.com/miami09/2009/01/09/jai-alai-a-bettors'-sport-struggles-to-stay-relevant/.

4. The background of the *Stenberg* case is instructive. There has been horseracing in Nebraska for many years, and racing in Omaha was particularly successful. The track there—Ak-Sar-Ben (Nebraska spelled backwards)—was one of the nation's leading tracks. In the mid-1980s, Ak-Sar-Ben was tenth in the nation in racetrack attendance, and weekend racing handles sometimes reached $2 million. But in 1986, a greyhound facility opened just across the border in Council Bluffs, Iowa. Racing was year round and interest in Ak-Sar-Ben's racing began to decline. As other forms of gambling developed, the leaders of Ak-Sar-Ben failed to respond to and anticipate how much damage could be done to their enterprise. By 1995 Ak-Sar-Ben was closed. Efforts to save what was left of the racing industry in the state led to the efforts described in Stenberg. *See* Omaha Track Enduring Hard Times, Wash. Post, Aug. 21, 1991 (abstract), http://www.highbeam.com/ doc/1P2-1080974.html (last visited June 9, 2010); Ak-Sar-Ben Seeks Simulcast Deal, Wash. Post, Feb. 8, 1994. (abstract), http://www.highbeam.com/doc/1P2-875046.html (last visited June 8, 2010) ("Ak-Sar- Ben will not offer live horse racing this spring unless new simulcasting agreements are reached ..."); Ak-Sar-Ben Racetrack is on the Selling Block, Wichita Eagle, Nov. 21, 1990, at 3B (abstract), *available at* http://nl.newsbank.com/nl-search/we/Archives?p_product=WE&s_site=kansas&p_multi=WE&p_theme=realcities&p_action=search&p_max-docs=200&p_topdoc=1&p_text_direct-0=0EADB4155CAC050B&p_ field_direct-0=document_id&p_perpage=10&p_sort=YMD_date:D&s_trackval=GooglePM (last visited June 8, 2010).

5. One of the first responses to the decline of live track betting was off-track betting (OTB). In 1971, several years after a city-wide referendum, New York city opened the nation's first legal off-track pari-mutuel betting facility in the United States. Bettors could wager on races at the OTB facilities. By 1983, the telecasts of live racing could be watched by patrons. This is what is called simulcasting. In New York, large teletheaters were opened offering betting as well as dining. In 1997, the NYCOTB responded to the increased interest in wagering from home by broadcasting races on television. But nothing, ultimately, could save the New York OTB industry. In December of 2010, after the New York State Senate refused to approve a rescue plan, off-track betting sites in New York closed.

Numerous other states have statutory provisions for simulcasting of some sort. *See, e.g.,* 4 Pa. Stat. Ann. § 325.216 (West 2009) (Interstate Simulcasting of Horse Races); Ky. Rev. Stat. Ann. § 230.377 (West 2009) (Award of Simulcasting and Intertrack Wagering Dates); Idaho Admin. Code r. 11.04.02.000 (Rules Governing Simulcasting). One commentator has noted that, "Eighty percent of the money wagered on horseracing is placed on simulcast races broadcast from another state." M. Shannon Bishop, *And They're Off: The Legality of Interstate Pari-Mutuel Wagering and Its Impact on the Thoroughbred Horse Industry*, 89 KY. L.J. 711, 712 n.6 (2001). The eighty percent figure can only have grown in the ensuing years.

The problem in *Stenberg* was that the Nebraska Constitution allowed for pari-mutuel wagering only "when such wagering is conducted by licensees within a licensed racetrack enclosure." The state legislature was unsuccessful in its effort to allow for wagering at venues other than the racetracks themselves. Clearly, relevant statutory and state constitutional language must be addressed when considering this.

6. Another way to provide support for pari-mutuel horseracing or greyhound racing is to link the activity with one that is a proven winner: the slot machine, or sometimes a video lottery terminal. In 1989, the state of Iowa created the first "racino." A horsetrack

in suburban Des Moines, Prairie Meadows, had gone into bankruptcy soon after it began operating. As a racino, the horseracing operation became subsidized by slot machines, and eventually table games. Now Prairie Meadows is a thriving operation with high-level stakes races. At least twelve states have embraced the racino model to support horseracing and greyhound racing, including New York, Pennsylvania, and Florida. The addition of video gaming devices has saved, at least temporarily, some racetracks. The Dover Downs racetrack in Delaware increased its revenue from $14 million to $141 million following the addition of slot machines in 1994. The number of slot machines at racetracks is expected to triple during the first decade of the twenty-first century. *See* Library Index, *Sports Gambling — Pari Mutuel Gambling*, http://www.libraryindex.com/pages/1611/Sports-Gambling-PARI-MUTUEL-GAMBLING.html.

There is some question whether the pari-mutuel industry can be saved by the racino model. *See* John Cheves, *Are Racinos Saving the Horse Industry in Other States?* Lexington Herald-Leader, June 15, 2009 (providing case studies on the problems, benefits, and effects of racinos in Indiana, West Virginia, and Pennsylvania). *See also* Alan B. Koslow & David S. Romanik, *Gaming at Florida Pari-Mutuels: Racinos Are a Sure Bet for the Sunshine State*, 10 Gaming L. Rev. 107 (2006) (discussing implementation of racinos in Florida); Edward W. McClenathan, *Land Use Implications of Casinos and Racinos on Local Governments in New York State*, 39 Urb. Law. 111 (2007) (discussing the loss of local land-use control that often occurs with the introduction of racinos).

Another question raised by the racino is whether it is proper to divert gaming revenues to an industry that cannot "pay its own way." Even if the racino model can save the racing industry, are there other more beneficial uses states could put these funds to?

7. In response to concerns that interstate wagering would financially injure racetracks, Congress enacted the Interstate Horseracing Act of 1978 (IHA), 15 U.S.C. §§ 3001–3007. The Act was passed to "regulate interstate commerce with respect to wagering on horseracing, in order to further the horseracing and legal off-track betting industries in the United States." The Act generally prohibited the acceptance of "interstate off-track wager[s]," but provided a number of exceptions whereby simulcast wagering would be legal with local consent.

In 2000, Congress amended the Act to allow wagers placed "by an individual in one State via telephone or other electronic media and accepted by an off-track betting system in the same or another State." The use of the terms "electronic media" suggests that the Act now allows online betting over the Internet on horseracing. This view was supported in 2006 when Congress exempted "any activity that is allowed under the Interstate Horseracing Act of 1978" when it passed the Unlawful Internet Gaming Enforcement Act (UIGEA). 31 U.S.C.A. § 5362(10)(D)(i) (2006). IHA did not preempt state law, and therefore states are free to prohibit interstate pari-mutuel wagering. *See* Gulfstream Park Racing Ass'n, Inc. v. Tampa Bay Downs, Inc., 294 F. Supp. 2d 1291, 1302 (M.D. Fla. 2003) (holding Interstate Horseracing Act did not preempt Florida from regulating intertrack wagering).

Under the IHA, states can authorize a form of wagering that allows individuals to set up accounts, usually with a credit card, either at in-state or out-of-state racetracks or with corporations that act as agents for racetracks. Individuals with accounts can then wager via telephone or Internet while watching the races from home or other locations. The amount of their wagers is deducted from their accounts and the money is sent to combined pools at sponsoring tracks. However, some states only allow individuals to place bets while actually "present in a licensed racetrack enclosure ..." *See, e.g.,* Iowa Code

ANN. § 99D.11(3) (West 2009). Individuals in these states would be unable to set up these types of accounts because they are required to physically be at the racetrack to place a valid bet. For an analysis of whether the service offered by one such enterprise, TVG Corp., complies with state racing regulations, *see* Op. Att'y Gen., 04-005, 2004 WL 3095821 (Ky. 2004). For a more detailed discussion of the Interstate Horseracing Act of 1978, see Chapter 11.

4. Patron Disputes

Ryan v. New Jersey Racing Commission
764 A.2d 486 (2001)

ALLEY, J.A.D.

Defendant, the New Jersey Racing Commission, appeals from a judgment for $3,995.20 and court costs in favor of plaintiff, Martin Ryan, entered after a trial in Special Civil Part on plaintiff's claim for payment on an allegedly stolen winning superfecta parimutuel racing ticket he purchased at the Meadowlands Racetrack. We reverse.

Plaintiff contended that on March 4, 1998, he purchased several winning tickets for a horse race at the Meadowlands Racetrack, among which was the "stolen" ticket that is the subject of his claim. He alleges that he bought this ticket at the same time as his other tickets. He testified that after the race was completed, unaware that the ticket in question was a winning superfecta ticket, he handed the ticket to a stranger, who walked away with it without any protest by plaintiff. The trial judge accepted plaintiff's testimony and entered judgment accordingly.

The Racing Commission asserts on appeal that the trial court's judgment is contrary to the applicable regulations, which it contends preclude payment on racing bets except on presentation of the ticket. It contends further that the ticket was never cashed, that it expired six months after it was issued, and that the expired ticket could not be paid even if it had remained in plaintiff's possession and he had attempted to surrender it in exchange for payment. It also contends that the trial court lacked jurisdiction because plaintiff's recourse was to appeal from the Racing Commission to the Appellate Division, rather than to begin an action in the Law Division, Special Civil Part.

We reverse because the trial judge erred in determining first that physical surrender of a racing ticket is not a prerequisite to obtaining payment of the ticket, and second that a ticket can be paid after its six month expiration date.

To protect the public from the dangers inherent in all forms of gambling, the Legislature vested the Racing Commission with powers necessary to enable it to carry out the Racing Act of 1940, *N.J.S.A.* 5:5-22. Horsemen's Benev. and Protective Ass'n, New Jersey Div. v. Atlantic City Racing Ass'n, 487 A.2d 707 (N.J. 1985) (regulation of horse racing is within the authority of the Legislature to protect the health, safety, and general welfare of the people). The Racing Commission's powers include the authority to prescribe rules, regulations and conditions under which horse racing is to be conducted in this State. N.J.S.A. 5:5-30. Pursuant to this broad authority, the Racing Commission promulgated N.J.A.C. 13:70-29.13, which reads in material part:

N.J.A.C. 13:70-29.13 Ticket claims ...

(b) No claim shall be considered thereafter and no claim shall be considered for tickets thrown away, lost, changed, destroyed or mutilated beyond identification.

(c) Payment of wagers will be made only on presentation of appropriate pari-mutuel tickets.

The parties have not cited, nor has our own research disclosed, any case in this jurisdiction that deals directly with a denial of payment to a race track patron who cannot produce the winning ticket. At least one court, however, has upheld such a denial as to another form of legalized gambling.

In Karafa v. New Jersey State Lottery, 324 A.2d 97 (Ch.Div.1974), the Lottery Commission refused to pay a claim to a person who alleged that he had purchased a winning lottery ticket. There, six or seven people observed plaintiff with the winning ticket, which was worth $50,000. The plaintiff gave the ticket to his mother for safekeeping. The plaintiff's mother inadvertently discarded the winning ticket with a batch of old, worthless tickets. The director of New Jersey's lottery rejected plaintiff's claim because he could not produce the ticket. In upholding the Lottery Commission's refusal to pay on the ticket, the court relied upon N.J.S.A. 5:9-7(a)(5), a statute containing language nearly identical to N.J.A.C. 13:70-29.13(c). The statute authorized the Lottery Commission to promulgate regulations dictating the conditions for the payment of prizes "to the holders of winning tickets[.]" The court found that this statutory language indicated a legislative intent to restrict payment to persons who physically possessed the ticket and that the Lottery Commission's promulgation of a regulation mandating possession was consistent with this intent. Karafa, supra, 324 A.2d 97. The court explained that

> [T]he clear legislative purpose was to keep the administrative machinery geared for the payment of winnings as simple and as efficient as possible. That machinery was not to become bogged down in the resolution of claims, conflicting or otherwise, in the event of misplaced, lost or destroyed tickets. The procedure simply calls for the production of the winning ticket. Unless that is done, payment cannot be made. Ibid. at 504, 324 A.2d 97.

In this appeal, plaintiff argues that the Racing Commission's intent in promulgating N.J.A.C. 13:70-29.13(b) was to enable a person whose ticket was stolen to be able to claim the proceeds if he could prove he purchased it. We disagree. The legal and policy issues examined in Karafa are fundamentally indistinguishable from those involved here.

Horse racing is a highly regulated industry, as are other forms of legalized gambling. This is due in large part to "the danger of clandestine and dishonest activity inherent in horse racing, as in all forms of gambling...." De Vitis v. New Jersey Racing Commission, 495 A.2d 457 (N.J. App. Div.), certif. denied, 508 A.2d 213 (N.J. 1985). See also Jersey Downs, Inc. v. Division of New Jersey Racing Commission, 246 A.2d 146 (N.J. App.Div.1968). The policy rationale respecting lottery regulation addressed in Karafa applies with equal force to the regulations promulgated by the Racing Commission, namely N.J.A.C. 13:70-29.13.

Plaintiff's contention that he need not surrender his ticket to obtain payment is not supported by his interpretation of N.J.A.C. 13:70-29.13(b).Other jurisdictions that have dealt with this issue have uniformly denied recovery where the wagerer could not physically produce a valid ticket. See, e.g., Carr v. State of New York, 15 A.D.2d 709, 223 N.Y.S.2d 229 (App. Div.1962), appl. dism. 371 U.S. 14 (1962) (stating that by restricting payment of prizes to "holder[s] of winning tickets[,]" the legislature intended to exclude one who was a holder of a winning ticket or one who is entitled to be but is not presently a holder of a winning ticket); State v. Nebraska State Bd. of Agric., 350 N.W.2d 535 (Neb. 1984)

("A pari-mutuel ticket is an instrument payable on demand when the demand is accompanied by presentation of the ticket."); Register v. Oaklawn Jockey Club, Inc., 811 S.W.2d 315 (Ark. 1991); Oregon Racing Comm'n v. Multnomah Kennel Club, 411 P.2d 63 (Or. 1966); Hochhalter v. Dakota Race Management, 524 N.W.2d 582 (N.D. 1994).

The trial court found plaintiff's testimony credible and entered judgment in his favor based largely on the court's construction of N.J.A.C. 13:70-29.13(b). In so ruling the court attempted to make it appear that the holding applied only to this case, but it would not be so limited. Instead, the decision would substitute the court's own perceptions for those set forth in duly adopted administrative regulations, N.J.A.C. 13:70-29.13(c). It would also contravene the sound principles articulated in *Karafa*. We are thus persuaded that the trial court's ruling in this respect must be reversed.

We also conclude that N.J.A.C. 13:70-29.60 barred payment of the ticket more than six months after its purchase. That regulation reads in pertinent part, "[a]ll mutuel tickets and vouchers shall expire six months and one day from the date of issue[.]" This regulation implements N.J.S.A. 5:5-68.1, which deals with "amounts resulting from parimutuel tickets remaining unclaimed after six months which are paid to the Racing Commission for deposit in the general fund…," and N.J.S.A. 5:5-64, which directs that "[a]ll sums held by any permitholder for payment of outstanding parimutuel tickets not claimed by the person or persons entitled thereto within six months from the time such tickets are issued shall be paid upon the expiration of such six-month holding period as [specified by the statute]…."

Defendant contends that the trial court disregarded the clear language of the regulation by holding that plaintiff "made every attempt within the time frame of the six months to retrieve his winnings" and "was led to delay his pursuit of his claim so that the Racing Commission could determine in its investigation whether the missing ticket would be cashed by some other third party or presumable culprit." We conclude that this was an error of law and presents an independent basis for vacating the trial court's judgment. Equitable estoppel is only "rarely" employed against a governmental agency, O'Malley v. Dept. of Energy, 537 A.2d 647 (N.J. 1987). There is no basis in this record for doing so here. In any event, the alleged representations on which plaintiff claims to have relied were not made by representatives of the Racing Commission but of the Meadowlands, and are not attributable to the Commission.

We do not take issue with the trial court's findings as to plaintiff's credibility, but unfortunately for plaintiff, even if we accept his version of the evidence, this does not translate into a legal basis for approving the errors of law embraced in the trial court's judgment. In light of our foregoing determinations, which fully dispose of the appeal, we need not rule upon the jurisdictional issue or the other errors said to have been committed by the trial court.

The judgment appealed from is reversed.

Bourgeois v. Fairground Corp.

480 So.2d 408 (La. App. 1985)

Lynn Bourgeois appeals a summary judgment which denied his right to collect a racehorse bet due to a faulty tote machine. No other case has presented this question.

Bourgeois attempted to buy a $20 exacta ticket and the tote machine jammed. The clerk told him to go to another window, but the race started before he could place a bet. The numbers he selected finished in the proper order and paid $13,840.80. Bourgeois sued the Fair Grounds and American Totalisator in contract and tort.

The pari-mutuel clerk, John Cronin, said Bourgeois put his money on the counter and the bet was entered into the tote machine. The ticket came out partially printed with a proper bar code. The machine jammed and a "call tote man" signal lit up. Cronin called for a technician and William Dietz tried to repair the malfunction. The machine could not be fixed so Dietz cancelled the ticket. Bourgeois' money was never accepted.

Cronin stated that despite regular maintenance the tote machines jam about seven to nine times a day. Sometimes no ticket comes out, it is not printed, or only the bar code prints. In every instance the routine practice is to cancel the attempted bet because there is no ticket to evidence a winner.

Bourgeois claims when his bet was punched into the machine there was a contract and the Fair Grounds cannot unilaterally cancel the agreement. He also argues there was negligence due to the equipment failure and the cancellation of the ticket by an unauthorized employee.

Racehorse bets go into a pari-mutuel pool and the track merely acts as a statutorily created agency for taking, holding and distributing the pool. Holberg v. Westchester Racing Commission, 184 Misc. 581, 53 N.Y.S.2d 490 (Sup. Ct. App. Term 1st Dept.1945).

The track's only obligation is to distribute the pool to the winning ticket holders. Shapiro v. Queens County Jockey Club, 184 Misc. 295, 53 N.Y.S.2d 135 (Mun.Ct.1945). The right of a bettor to a winning share results not from buying a ticket but solely from having a ticket which evidences the winning bet. Hochberg v. New York City Off-Track Betting Corporation, 74 Misc. 2d 471, 343 N.Y.S.2d 651 (Sup. Ct. 1973), aff'd 43 A.D.2d 910, 352 N.Y.S.2d 423 (A.D. 1st Dept.1974); Oregon Racing Commission v. Multnomah Kennel Club, 242 Or. 572, 411 P.2d 63 (1966); Carr v. State, 15 A.D.2d 709, 223 N.Y.S.2d 229 (A.D. 3rd Dept.1962), appeal denied 11 N.Y.S.2d 645, 229 N.Y.S.2d 1025, 183 N.E.2d 329 (1962), appeal dismissed, 371 U.S. 14, 83 S. Ct. 44, 9 L.Ed.2d 49 (1962); Mattson v. Hollywood Turf Club, 101 Cal.App. 2d 215, 225 P.2d 276 (1950).

The Fair Grounds acts as a stakeholder for all wagers and has no interest in the outcome of a race. The track receives a percentage of the bets, hence, its objective is to collect as many as possible. Unfortunately for Bourgeois and the track, the bet was not consummated. Bourgeois' argument as to a contract has no merit.

Without a winning ticket Bourgeois has no right to demand payment. Valois v. Gulfstream Park Racing Association, 412 So. 2d 959 (Fla. Ct. App. 1982). American Totalisator, owner of the machine, owed no duty to Bourgeois and there is no showing that it was negligent.

The facts are basically undisputed and there is no genuine issue as to a material fact. La. C.C.P. Art. 966; Thompson v. South Central Bell Telephone Company, 411 So.2d 26 (La. 1982). Defendants are entitled to summary judgment as a matter of law.

The judgment is affirmed.

Hochhalter v. Dakota Race Management
524 N.W.2d 582 (N.D. 1994)

SANDSTROM, Justice.

Dakota Race Management (DRM) has appealed a district court judgment in favor of Clinton Hochhalter for DRM's allocated share of the amount of money Hochhalter would have won if he had been issued the ticket he requested when betting on a parimutuel horse race. We reverse.

I

DRM provides electronic simulcast racing services to James River Aerie # 2337 (Jamestown Eagles) and other operators conducting off-track parimutuel betting on horse races viewed on television at the simulcast site. DRM provides the computer terminals for taking bets at the simulcast site and trains the tellers who operate the equipment. A patron places a bet through a teller who uses a computer keyboard to record the bet and produce a ticket for the patron. The ticket shows the amount of the bet, the horse selection, and the nature of the bet.

On October 3, 1992, Hochhalter placed a $2.00 bet on a twin trifecta, which involves selecting the first, second, and third place horses in two races. Hochhalter correctly selected the first three horses in the first trifecta, which entitled him to participate in the second race of the twin trifecta. He took his winning ticket from the first race to the teller to make his selections for the second race. The teller had trouble entering the bet and telephoned DRM for assistance. The teller entered Hochhalter's selections and a ticket was issued. Almost immediately, betting was shut down by the track steward and the totalisator was locked.

Neither the teller nor Hochhalter examined the ticket, except to ascertain it reflected Hochhalter's selection of horses. The ticket issued to Hochhalter for the second race was for a straight trifecta, rather than for a twin trifecta. Hochhalter correctly selected the first three horses in the second race included in the twin trifecta. Hochhalter was not included in the twin trifecta parimutuel pool, and he refused payment of the smaller amount he was entitled to collect on the straight trifecta.

Hochhalter sued DRM and the Jamestown Eagles for breach of contract and negligence and sought to recover the amount he would have won ($6,257.60) if he had been issued the correct ticket for the second race of the twin trifecta. The trial court found Hochhalter not negligent, Jamestown Eagles 30 percent negligent, and DRM 70 percent negligent. Judgment was entered in favor of Hochhalter against Jamestown Eagles for $1,877.28 plus 30 percent of his costs and disbursements, and against DRM for $4,380.32, plus 70 percent of his costs and disbursements. DRM appealed.

The trial court had jurisdiction under Art. VI, §§ 1 and 8, N.D. Const., and N.D.C.C. § 27-05-06. This court has jurisdiction under Art. VI, §§ 1 and 2, N.D. Const., and N.D.C.C. § 28-27-01. The appeal was timely under Rule 4(a), N.D.R. App. P.

II

DRM contends recovery is precluded by N.D.A.C. § 69.5-01-08-11, which provides, in part:

> 1. No parimutuel tickets may be sold except by the association conducting the races on which such wagers are made, and the same must be sold only at regular 'seller' windows properly designated by signs showing the type and denomination of tickets to be sold at such windows if there are restrictions of any kind. No parimutuel tickets may be sold after the totalisator has been locked and *no association is responsible for ticket sales entered into but not completed by issuance of a ticket before the totalisator has been locked.*
>
> 2. Any claim by a person that the person has been issued a ticket other than that which the person requested must be made before such person leaves the seller window and before the totalisator is locked (emphasis added).

DRM argues the underscored part of subsection 1 "is clear and unambiguous in absolving any association from responsibility for ticket sales which are entered into but not completed before the totalisator has been locked" and contends "the transaction requested by Hochhalter was not completed before the totalisator was locked because the teller failed to issue the appropriate ticket." The record establishes, however, Hochhalter was issued a ticket and left the window. A ticket sale was "entered into" and "completed by issuance of a ticket," even though the ticket issued was not the one requested.

Hochhalter admits he did not make a claim that he had "been issued a ticket other than that which [he] requested" before he left the seller window and before the totalisator was locked. Hochhalter's claim is, therefore, barred by N.D.A.C. §69.5-01-08-11(2). "One who gambles must do so in accordance with the rules of the game." Mattson v. Hollywood Turf Club, 225 P.2d 276, 279 (Cal. App. 1950).

As DRM argues, other "courts have uniformly and consistently held that a bettor's right to collect winnings is absolutely conditioned upon presentation of a winning ticket."....

The court in Mattson v. Hollywood Turf Club, 225 P.2d at 279, explained the parimutuel system of betting:

> A licensed track sells tickets and acts as custodian of the funds, which are accumulated in pools for win, place and show; the track takes the share of its partner, the State, and its own share, from the top, and divides what is left in the several pools among the holders of winning tickets. The tickets in a given pool in a given race are identical as to form. A holder who has lost his ticket has no means of identifying it. Possession is his only evidence of ownership. It is also the only evidence upon which the track makes distribution.... Such are the terms offered to the betting public, and they constitute the essential features of the implied contract between the track and its bettors.

"[T]he nature of the pari-mutuel system of betting necessarily requires a ticket to evidence the bettor's participation in the pool and ... payment could not practicably be made without presentation of such ticket." Aliano v. Westchester Racing Ass'n, 265 App. Div. 225, 38 N.Y.S.2d 741, 745 (1942). Without "the purchase and presentation of a winning ticket," a complaint alleging breach of contract and negligence of the issuance of the wrong tickets does not state a cause of action. Bastone v. Yonkers Racing Corp., 360 N.Y.S.2d at 150. "The right of a bettor to a winning share results not from buying a ticket but solely from having a ticket which evidences the winning bet." Bourgeois v. Fairground Corp., 480 So.2d at 409. Without a winning ticket, Hochhalter's complaint is insufficient as a matter of law. Seder v. Arlington Park Race Track Corp. Because he did not have a winning ticket and did not claim an error before leaving the window, Hochhalter did not join the pool of participants entitled to share in the winnings of the twin trifecta. "Since plaintiff does not possess a winning ticket, he cannot recover payment of a winning share." Hochberg v. New York City Off-Track Betting Corp., 343 N.Y.S.2d at 655.

DRM, as the owner of the machine involved, owed no duty to Hochhalter. Bourgeois. DRM's contract with the Jamestown Eagles to provide electronic simulcast racing services specifically excludes any duty to others. Gambling differs from other business transactions and ordinary remedies are not usually available to enforce gambling debts. Carr. "Where there is a statute applicable to a gambling contract, recovery is enforceable only in accordance with its provisions." Carr, 221 N.Y.S.2d at 638. Recovery is enforceable only in accordance with N.D.A.C. §69.5-01-08-11(2). Because he did not make a claim that he was issued a ticket other than what he requested before he left the seller window, Hochhalter is barred from recovery.

III

The judgment is reversed.

VANDE WALLE, C.J., and NEUMANN, LEVINE and MESCHKE, JJ., concur.

Szadolci v. Hollywood Park Operating Co.

17 Cal. Rptr. 2d 356 (Cal. App. 1993)

BACKGROUND

James Farenbaugh went to Hollywood Park on June 14, 1989, and put down $4,860 on a "Pick-9" ticket. A Pick-9 requires the bettor to pick the winners of the nine races run that day. Picking all nine winners results in a large return.

But Farenbaugh had something else in mind. He cancelled the ticket and bribed the parimutuel clerk to let him keep the worthless ticket. Farenbaugh then set out to sell shares in the ticket to other patrons at the track. The record does not reveal whether this was an ongoing scam by Farenbaugh. In any event, since the chance of hitting a big winner is remote, any shares sold would result in clear profit to Farenbaugh, who, having cancelled the ticket, had none of his own money at risk.

Plaintiffs Jim Szadolci and Daniel Teich bought into the ticket before the first race started. Each paid approximately $240 for a 5 percent share. Teich left the track shortly thereafter. Plaintiff Mardy Loewy apparently bought in for 5 percent after the day's racing program had commenced. The record is not clear at what point Loewy invested (he said probably after the second or third race) or how much he paid for his share (possibly around $300).

But, lo and behold, Farenbaugh (much to his dismay, we assume) picked all nine winners. A valid ticket would have paid $1,380,000. Farenbaugh's cancelled ticket was worth zero.

Szadolci and Loewy (jubilant, we presume, at the prospect of realizing $69,000 each) accompanied Farenbaugh (feigning aplomb, no doubt) to the pay window, only to learn of the ticket cancellation. Unfortunately, the record does not reveal what happened at that moment.

The three plaintiffs sued Hollywood Park, the parimutuel clerk, another track employee, and Farenbaugh for negligence, conspiracy, and negligent hiring. Defendants secured summary judgment and plaintiffs appeal....

DISCUSSION

The trial court's ruling was based on the conclusion that the transactions between plaintiffs and Farenbaugh were illegal bets. Since plaintiffs' complaint relied on a theory which put them *in pari delicto*, the trial court held, they were barred from recovery. "'The general rule is that the courts will not recognize such an illegal contract [betting] and will not aid the parties thereto, but will leave them where it finds them. This rule has been rigidly enforced in this state to deny any relief in the courts to parties seeking to recover either their stakes or their winnings under a wagering contract which is in violation of law, …'" Bradley v. Doherty, 30 Cal. App. 3d 991, 994, 106 Cal. Rptr. 725 (1973).

Plaintiffs seek to distinguish themselves from the above rule by arguing that the transactions here did not constitute illegal bets. They argue that the trial court found these to be illegal "lay off bets" by erroneously relying on People v. Oreck, 168 P.2d 186 (Cal. App. 1946) which held that a "lay off man" was engaged in illegal bookmaking. What is a lay off bet/man? "If a customer of a bookie bets $5.00 on horse X to win a certain race, and the track odds are 5–1, if that horse wins the bookie must pay the customer $25, while if it loses the bookie wins $5.00. Now, if before the race, the bookie lays off that $5.00 bet with a lay off man, what is the result? If the horse wins, the bookie must pay the customer $25, but he is reimbursed to the extent of $25 by his bet with the lay off man. In a very real sense the bookie has won that bet with the lay off man, and the lay off man has lost. But if the horse loses, the bookie wins $5.00 from his customer, but he must pay the lay off man $2.50. In a very real sense the bookie has lost and the lay off man has won on that transaction...." (*Id.* at pp. 220–221, 168 P.2d 186.)

But here, argue plaintiffs, unlike in *Oreck,* Farenbaugh's bet with the track was legal, so their investments did not constitute lay off bets. Farenbaugh possessed, they claim, a chose in action ("a right to recover money or other personal property by a judicial proceeding" (Civ. Code, § 953)), interest in which could be transferred. See Mattson v. Hollywood Turf Club, 225 P.2d 276 (Cal. App. 1950), which holds there is at least an implied contract between the track and its bettors. *Mattson* also aptly points out that whether betting on horses "is a game of skill, as some believe, or of chance, as many have learned, it provides a legal method for getting rid of one's money." *Id.* at p. 219, 225 P.2d 276.

We agree that the transactions between Farenbaugh and plaintiffs did not constitute lay off bets, but for a different reason than proffered by plaintiffs. There was no underlying bet between Farenbaugh and any person or entity. Farenbaugh had withdrawn his legitimate bet and had no stake with the track in the outcome of the race, so he was laying nothing off when he fleeced plaintiffs. Farenbaugh had no chose in action. Plaintiffs bought a share of a worthless ticket, which entitled Farenbaugh and them to recover nothing from the track. If there was any kind of implied contract, it was between plaintiffs and Farenbaugh, who impliedly had offered plaintiffs a return if the selected horses won. A lay off bet provides a bookie with a backup. Farenbaugh, who could have used the help, had no backup.

Business and Professions Code section 19595 provides in part: "Any form of wagering or betting on the result of a horse race other than that permitted by this chapter is illegal." The basic approved betting format is for a bettor to give his money to the track, where it is then placed in the parimutuel pool, out of which winning bettors are paid. See Bus. And Prof. Code, § 19594 — "Any person within the enclosure where a horse racing meeting is authorized may wager on the result of a horse race held at that meeting by contributing his money to the parimutuel pool operated by the licensee under this chapter...." One of the advantages of this system is that it should eliminate the type of problem that occurred here.

Any way we look at it, plaintiffs laid direct wagers with Farenbaugh, who took their money and impliedly agreed to a 5 percent winner's share for each plaintiff. None of the money involved ended up in the parimutuel pool. So, while these were not lay off bets, they were unauthorized direct bets with Farenbaugh, and illegal.

Plaintiffs argue that these were not bets because Farenbaugh received no compensation, had no interest in the outcome of the races, and was on the same side as plaintiffs. But Farenbaugh had a very real stake in the outcome. For his scam to work, the ticket had to be a loser, because he could then offer his condolences to plaintiffs and walk away with their money. Only when the ticket "won" did Farenbaugh's problems arise. So, Farenbaugh was directly betting against plaintiffs. If their horses won, his scam was revealed and he acquired a measure of grief. If they lost, he kept several hundred dollars of plaintiffs' money without having risked one dime.

Plaintiffs offer the example of friends going to the track and pooling their money, with one of them purchasing the ticket. If the purchaser actually takes his friends' money and hands it to the parimutuel clerk, the bet is legal, plaintiffs argue, because the friends' money has been placed in the parimutuel pool. If he spends his own money and is then reimbursed by his friends, the bet is an illegal lay off bet according to defendants' analysis. This, plaintiffs argue, is illogical. But, since we have a different situation here, we need not analyze whether either of the above situations constitutes legal or illegal betting. Here, no one's money was in the parimutuel pool. There was no lay off bet. The transactions were direct and face-to-face between Farenbaugh and plaintiffs. Plaintiffs laid bets with Farenbaugh. The bets were not as authorized by the Business and Professions Code. They were illegal bets. Plaintiffs have no remedy. Whether the trial court relied on the wrong theory or not, its result was correct....

DISPOSITION

The judgment is affirmed.

Notes

1. The first three cases in this section deal with situations, respectively, where the bettor gave away a winning ticket, was victimized by a faulty machine, and was given the wrong ticket by the clerk. In all three instances the courts emphasized the requirement of the presentation of a winning ticket. This rule has been applied in many other cases. *See, e.g.,* Register v. Oaklawn Jockey Club, Inc., 821 S.W.2d 475 (Ark. 1991) (clerk mistakenly told bettor that a particular horse had been scratched from a race, and bettor lost out on $28,000 winning pool; none of the claims, whether tort or contract based, changed requirement of the presentation of a winning ticket); Seder v. Arlington Park Race Track Corp., 481 N.E.2d 9 (Ill. App. 1985) (bettor claimed he presented his selections for the "sweep six" wager at one of the track's windows, but that defendants refused to place and register his bet, that he correctly selected the winning horses in races two through seven, and that had defendants accepted his wager he would have won the wager pool of $154,000; in action of first impression, court noted that plaintiff failed to even allege that he held a winning pari-mutuel ticket for the sweep six wagering pool on the date in question, so that presentment requirement barred claim); Valois v. Gulfstream Park Racing Ass'n, 412 So. 2d 959, 960 (Fla. App. 1982) (plaintiff alleged she attempted to place certain bets at the defendant's race track, but due to a malfunction in the pari-mutuel machine she was unable to complete the wagers that would have given her a winning pari-mutuel ticket; claims for breach of contract, negligence, negligent misrepresentation and violation of a statutory duty, dismissal affirmed, "[T]here can be no valid pari-mutuel wager without a pari-mutuel ticket which is absolutely essential to the bettor's right to collect winnings from the pari-mutuel pool.").

There are cases where courts hold the track accountable for mistakes made by its employees. *See, e.g.,* Palmisciano v. Burrillville Racing Ass'n, 603 A.2d 317 (R.I. 1992) (machine malfunctioned and agent was unable to issue "Twin Trifecta" ticket requested by bettor that would have paid him over $39,000; summary judgment ruling amounted to a holding that presentation of winning ticket was not essential and that defendant had duty to use reasonable care to effect bettor's wager); DePasquale v. Ogden Suffolk Downs, Inc., 564 N.E.2d 584 (Mass. App. 1991) (Twin Trifecta bettor was not issued alleged winning ticket because of machine malfunction; absent presentation of a winning ticket, elaborate state statutory scheme regulating racing provides that bettor is not entitled to payment; however, bettor also claimed defendant engaged in unfair and deceptive trade practices in not returning his cancelled ticket promptly, and these claims were neither within, nor foreclosed by, the racing regulations).

2. Occasionally, the results of races are changed due to disqualifications. While this affects the payment of purses to the horse owners, if the results have been declared final and payment has been made accordingly, no later change in results can cause a redistribution of the mutuel payout. *See* 810 Ky. Admin. Regs. 1:016(17); 810 Ky. Admin. Regs. 1:017 §7 ("Revised Order of Finish after Race Declared Official for Pari-mutuel Payoff. If a horse is disqualified after a race has been declared official for pari-mutuel payoff and thereby causes revision of the order of finish in the race: (1) The pari-mutuel payoff shall in no way be affected.")

See also White v. Turfway Park Racing Ass'n, 909 F.2d 941 (6th Cir. 1990) (Bettor learned days after a race that prerace "workout time" for the official winner of one race may not have been announced, as required by rules of racing. He claimed that he would have won "Pick-Six" wager if that winning horse had been disqualified, and second place horse declared winner of race. Court held that Kentucky rule of finality applied when racetrack stewards posted "official" sign on horse race result board. Therefore district court was barred from reordering finish and redistributing parimutuel payoff.).

3. Winning tickets are not always presented for payment. When this happens, state racing regulations provide for the money to go to the state after a prescribed period of time. *See, e.g.*, Ark. Code Ann. §23-110-406 (b) (West 2009) ("However, all winning pari-mutuel tickets not presented to the franchise holder for redemption on or before the one hundred eightieth day next following the last racing day of each racing meet hereafter held shall be void."); Mahurin v. Oaklawn Jockey Club, 771 S.W.2d 19 (1989) (plaintiff argued that he was not given notice that his winning racing ticket would be declared void if not cashed within 180 days of the last race; court held there was no taking of his property in violation of due process).

4. As some of the cases set out above illustrate, a bettor seeking payment of a disputed wager may have to exhaust administrative remedies before filing a civil action. *See, e.g.*, R.I. Gen. Laws §41-2-7 ("Notwithstanding the provisions of §42-20-13, or other provisions of laws, the procedures established by §§41-2-3, 41-2-4, and 41-2-6 shall constitute the exclusive remedies for persons aggrieved by any order or decision of the division of racing and athletics or of the racing and athletics hearing board."); Ambeault v. Burrillvill Racing Ass'n, No. 74-3361, 1975 WL 169983 (R.I. Super. Ct. Jul. 8, 1975) (bettor who alleged harm because the defendant racetrack followed the rules of the racing commission, was required to exhaust all administrative remedies before superior court would assume jurisdiction).

5. Trainer Regulation and Animal Welfare

A. Trainer's Responsibility

Hudson v. Texas Racing Commission
455 F.3d 597 (5th Cir. 2006)

REAVLEY, Circuit Judge:

This appeal involves an issue of first impression, whether the Texas absolute insurer rule, 16 Tex. Admin. Code §311.104(b), which provides, *inter alia,* that "[a] trainer shall ensure that a horse ... that runs a race while in the care and custody of the trainer ... is free from all prohibited drugs, chemicals, or other substance," violates the due process clause. We hold that it does not and therefore affirm the judgment of the district court.

I.

James Hudson is licensed by the Texas Racing Commission (the "Commission") as an owner and trainer of race horses.[1] On June 8, 2002, the horse named St. Martin's Cloak, which was owned and trained by Hudson and in his custody and care, finished first in the sixth race at Lone Star Park, thereby earning a share of the purse money. A post-race urine sample obtained from St. Martin's Cloak tested positive for Torsemide, a prohibited drug. A split sample analyzed by Louisiana State University also tested positive for Torsemide.

Hudson received notice that the Board of Stewards (the "Stewards") at Lone Star Park would conduct a hearing. Hudson participated in the hearing along with his counsel. Following the hearing, the Stewards suspended Hudson for sixty days, declared St. Martin's Cloak unplaced in the race, and ordered that the purse money won by St. Martin's Cloak be redistributed. Hudson timely appealed the Stewards' ruling to the Commission.

A hearing was conducted before an administrative law judge ("ALJ"). The ALJ determined that a prima facie case was made that St. Martin's Cloak participated in a race with a prohibited drug in its body, in violation of Commission rules. The ALJ determined that it was irrelevant that there was no evidence of Hudson's intent or overt act in administering the Torsemide. The ALJ further determined that the facts supported a finding that the absolute insurer rule had been violated. The ALJ recommended that the ruling of the Stewards should be upheld.

The Commission adopted the ALJ's findings and upheld the Stewards' ruling. Hudson then filed a petition in a Texas state district court seeking judicial review of the Commission's decision. He claimed that, *inter alia,* that the absolute insurer rule violated the due process clause.

The Commission timely removed the action to federal district court. The district court, proceeding sua sponte, granted summary judgment in favor of the Commission on Hudson's federal constitutional claims. The district court determined, *inter alia,* that the absolute insurer rule did not violate due process. This appeal followed.

II.

The sole issue on appeal is whether the Texas absolute insurer rule, 16 Tex. Admin. Code § 311.104(b), both facially and as applied, violates the due process clause. Hudson

---

1. Horse racing came to Texas with the passage of the Texas Racing Act ("the Act") in 1986. *See* Acts 1986, 69th Leg., 2nd C.S., ch. 19, § 1. The express purpose of the Act is "to provide for the strict regulation of horse racing and greyhound racing and the control of pari-mutuel wagering in connection with that racing." Tex. Rev. Civ. Stat. Ann. art. 179e, § 1.02 (Vernon Supp. 2005). A Commission was created and the Act mandated that

> [t]he commission shall regulate and supervise every race meeting in this state involving wagering on the result of greyhound or horse racing. All persons and things relating to the operation of those meetings are subject to regulation and supervision by the commission. The commission shall adopt rules for conducting greyhound or horse racing in this state involving wagering and shall adopt other rules to administer this Act that are consistent with this Act. The commission shall also make rules, issue licenses, and take any other necessary action relating exclusively to horse racing or to greyhound racing.

Id. § 3.02(a). The Act permits the commission or a section of the commission to appoint a committee of experts, members of the public, or other interested parties to advise the commission or a section of the commission about a proposed rule. *Id.* § 3.02(f). The Act further mandates that the commission, in adopting rules and in the supervision and conduct of racing, shall consider the statewide effect of a proposed commission action on the state's agricultural, horse breeding, and horse training industries. *Id.* § 3.02(g).

argues that the district court erred in granting summary judgment in favor of the Commission on his claim that the absolute insurer rule violates due process.

Section 311.104(b) of the Texas Administrative Code, entitled "Absolute Insurer," provides:

(1) A trainer shall ensure the health and safety of each horse or greyhound that is in the care and custody of the trainer.

(2) A trainer shall ensure that a horse or greyhound that runs a race while in the care and custody of the trainer or kennel owner is free from all prohibited drugs, chemicals, or other substances.

(3) A trainer who allows a horse or greyhound to be brought to the paddock or lockout kennel warrants that the horse or greyhound:

(A) is qualified for the race;

(B) is ready to run;

(C) is in a physical condition to exert its best efforts; and

(D) is entered with the intent to win.[2]

Hudson claims that the absolute insurer rule, facially and as applied to him, violates due process. He argues that the rule "creates a conclusive, mandatory, and irrebuttable" presumption that a trainer has committed a violation when a horse tests positive for a prohibited substance, irrespective of who actually administered the drug to the horse or the intent of the trainer. Hudson contends that the rule deprives a trainer of the right to negate his responsibility regarding administration of a prohibited drug.

To establish a due process violation under 42 U.S.C. § 1983, Hudson must first show that he was denied a constitutionally-protected property right.[3] This court has held that such property rights must be established by state law.[4]

The Supreme Court has determined that a horse trainer licensed in New York had a property interest in his racing license.[5] Examining New York law, the Court noted that a racing license "may not be revoked or suspended at the discretion of the racing authorities."[6] The Court determined that "state law has engendered a clear expectation of continued enjoyment of a license absent proof of culpable conduct by the trainer."[7] This gave the trainer a "legitimate claim of entitlement ... that he may invoke at a hearing."[8]

This court has not addressed whether a horse trainer licensed by the Commission has a constitutionally-protected property right. Certain provisions of Texas law, however, lead us to conclude that such a right exists. The Texas Administrative Code provides that

---

2. 16 Tex. Admin. Code § 311.104(b). All references to Texas law are to provisions in force in 2002, when Hudson's violation and the related hearing took place.

3. *See* Bryan v. City of Madison, 213 F.3d 267, 274–75 (5th Cir. 2000).

4. *Id.* at 275. The Commission questions whether Hudson has a property right in his racing license sufficient to merit the protections of due process. They note, that under state law, participation in racing is a privilege rather than a right. The distinction between rights and privileges, however, does not control the issue. *See* Bd. of Regents of State Colleges v. Roth, 408 U.S. 564, 571 (1972) (stating that the Supreme Court "has fully and finally rejected the wooden distinction between 'rights' and 'privileges' that once seemed to govern the applicability of procedural due process rights.").

5. *See* Barry v. Barchi, 443 U.S. 55, 64 & n. 11 (1979).

6. *Id.* at 64 n. 11.

7. *Id.*

8. *Id.* (internal quotation marks and citation omitted).

a license issued by the Commission may be denied, suspended, or revoked after notice and a hearing.[9] Section 311.6(b) enumerates several grounds for the denial, revocation, and suspension of racing licenses, including, among others, violations of racing rules, a felony conviction, a conviction of a crime of moral turpitude that is reasonably related to the licensee's fitness to hold a license, and providing false information in a license application. Based on the above provisions, we conclude that Hudson has a protected property interest in his racing license. *See Barry,* 443 U.S. at 64 & n. 11, 99 S. Ct. at 2649 & n. 11.

We turn to Hudson's two substantive due process arguments. Hudson first argues that § 311.104(b) violates substantive due process because it creates an irrebuttable presumption of fault. He contends that whenever a prohibited substance is found in a horse's system, the absolute insurer rule creates an irrebuttable presumption that the trainer of the horse administered the substance. We disagree. The absolute insurer rule, as it name implies, makes a trainer of a horse that is entered in a race the absolute insurer that the horse is free from all prohibited substances. No presumption of trainer fault is created when the presence of a prohibited substance is found. The absolute insurer rule does not assign fault, but instead, requires the trainer to bear the responsibility of the horse's condition, as a contingency to being licensed as a trainer by the state.

Hudson also argues that the absolute insurer rule violates substantive due process because it subjects a trainer to disciplinary action without a showing of wrongdoing. In essence, Hudson contends that the state lacks the power to impose absolute liability. This argument is also without merit. It has long been held that due process does not require proof of guilty knowledge before punishment may be imposed.[10] In areas of activity requiring strong police regulation to protect public interests, strict liability may be imposed upon individuals "otherwise innocent but standing in responsible relation to a public danger."[11] Horse racing requires strong police regulation to protect the public interests.[12]

Because horse raising for money can be prohibited all together in Texas, the legislature may condition a license to engage in legalized racing upon compliance with any regulation that is reasonably appropriate to the accomplishment of the Act. To ensure the health of the horse, to protect the integrity of the sport, and to protect the betting public, the state has a valid objective in seeking to prevent the doping of horses. The absolute insurer rule for horse trainers is a reasonable and valid exercise of the state's police power to achieve that objective.[13]

---

9. 16 Tex. Admin. Code § 311.6(a).

10. *See, e.g.,* United States v. Balint, 258 U.S. 250, 252–53 (1922); United States v. Ayo-Gonzalez, 536 F.2d 652, 657 (5th Cir.1976) (stating that due process is not violated merely because mens rea is not a required element of a prescribed crime).

11. United States v. Dotterweich, 320 U.S. 277, 281 (1943).

12. Western Turf Ass'n v. Greenberg, 204 U.S. 359, 363–64 (1907).

13. A Michigan appellate court upheld an absolute insurer provision based on a due process challenge on the following grounds: "Horse racing is accompanied by legalized gambling, making the activity especially susceptible to fraud and corruption. Strong regulation protects not only the wagering public but also advances the state's economic interests in the racing business by preserving public confidence in the activity." Berry v. Mich. Racing Comm'r, 321 N.W.2d 880, 884 (Mich. App. 1982). Addressing due process concerns, the Michigan court continued:

> Due process would not forbid a complete ban on horse racing as a legalized form of gambling. The imposition of strict liability is reasonable because the trainer is the person best able to prevent illegal drugging. The insurer rule provides maximum protection against illegal drugging; arguably it is the only practical means of reducing such corrupt practices. If, as plaintiff proposes, we were to conclude that due process necessitates a finding of guilty knowledge or intent prior to the imposition of sanctions, enforcement of the prohibition on horse drugging would be virtually impossible, and the interests of the public and state

The majority of jurisdictions have upheld the same or similar absolute insurer rule.[14] Illinois and Maryland are the only jurisdictions that have held the absolute insurer rule to be unconstitutional.[15] We agree with the majority of jurisdictions that the absolute insurer rule does not violate due process. While the absolute insurer rule may be harsh, it is constitutional.

III.

We affirm the judgment of the district court because (1) Hudson has not shown that the Texas absolute insurer rule establishes an irrebuttable presumption of guilt, and (2) the absolute insurer rule is a reasonable regulation that does not violate due process either facially or in its application to Hudson.

AFFIRMED.

Notes

1. *Hudson* provides a good overview of the trainer's responsibility for the condition of the horse. Under the absolute insurer rule, the trainer bears the responsibility when his or her horse tests positive for a prohibited medication. This is the case even when the drug may have been administered by someone else, either inadvertently or maliciously. The rule is a venerable one. One of the leading cases upholding the constitutionality of the absolute insurer rule is Sandstrom v. California Horse Racing Board, 189 P.2d 17 (Cal. 1948). In that case, the court emphasized that the rule did not amount to an assessment of fault on the trainer's part in administering an injection or failing to monitor the horse. Rather, it was a form of strict liability designed to assure the public of the integrity of the racing. The rule has also been applied to greyhound trainers. *See* D'Avignon v. Ark. Racing Comm'n, 651 S.W.2d 87 (Ark. 1983).

2. The absolute insurer rule emanates from administrative and regulatory sources, not statutory ones. *See, e.g.,* N.J. Admin. Code 13:70-14A.6 ("(a) A trainer shall be the absolute insurer of and is responsible for the condition of a horse within his care and custody."); Md. Code Regs. 09.10.03.04 ("F. Trainer Responsibility. A trainer is the absolute insurer of, and responsible for, the condition of each horse the trainer enters in a race, regardless of the acts of third parties.").

3. Even with the absolute insurer rule, a trainer may challenge the fairness of the evidence against him. *See* LaBorde v. La. State Racing Comm'n, 506 So. 2d 634 (La. App. 1987) (while horse trainer is absolute insurer of horse's condition, state racing commission could not unfairly limit evidence in disciplinary proceedings against trainers whose horses tested positive for prohibited drug). *See also* Monaci v. State Horse Racing Comm'n, 717 A.2d 612 (Pa. Commw. Ct. 1998).

---

would go unprotected. The insurer rule is a reasonable alternative to either leaving those interests unprotected or forbidding legalized racing.
Id. (internal citation omitted).

14. *See* Div. of Pari-Mutuel Wagering v. Caple, 362 So.2d 1350, 1354–55 (Fla. 1978); O'Daniel v. Ohio State Racing Comm'n, 307 N.E.2d 529 (Ohio 1974); Jamison v. State Racing Comm'n, 507 P.2d 426 (N.M. 1973); State v. W. Va. Racing Comm'n, 55 S.E.2d 263 (W. Va. 1949); Sandstrom v. Cal. Horse Racing Bd., 31 Cal.2d 401, 189 P.2d 17 (1948); DeGroot v. Ariz. Racing Comm'n, 686 P.2d 1301 (Ariz. 1984); Briley v. La. State Racing Comm'n, 410 So.2d 802 (La. Ct. App. 1982); Dare v. State, 388 A.2d 984 (N.J. App. Div. 1978); Fioravanti v. State Racing Comm'n, 375 N.E.2d 722 (Mass. App. 1978).

15. *See* Brennan v. Ill. Racing Bd., 247 N.E.2d 881 (Ill. 1969); Mahoney v. Byers, 48 A.2d 600 (Md. 1946). We note that *Mahoney* was distinguished by Goldman v. Maryland Racing Commission, 584 A.2d 709 (Md. App. 1991).

4. As noted in Hudson, some decisions have struck down the absolute insurer rule as unconstitutional. *See also* Schvaneveldt v. Idaho State Horse Racing Comm'n, 578 P.2d 673 (1978) (without ruling on the constitutionality of a properly worded absolute insurer rule, the court held that the Idaho provision was vague and could not be applied against the trainer. Although the rule declared that the trainer was the absolute insurer, it did not say: "(1) what condition the trainer insures; or (2) the consequences to the trainer if the unstated condition is or is not present." *Id.* at 675).

5. Some states employ a rebuttable presumption rule for banned substances in a horse's system. For example, Kentucky regulations provide that the findings of banned substances in a horse after a race constitute "prima facie evidence" that the horse was drugged and that, "the licensed trainer of a horse found to have been administered a medication, drug, or substance in violation of Section 1 or 2 of this administrative regulation shall bear the burden of proof showing freedom from negligence in the exercise of a high degree of care in safeguarding such horse from tampering; and, failing to prove such freedom from negligence (or reliance on the professional ability of a licensed veterinarian) shall be subject to disciplinary action." 810 Ky. Admin. Regs. 1:018.2(5); 811 Ky. Admin. Regs. 2:096.3(2). In New York, the regulations state that, "The trainer shall be held responsible for any positive test unless he can show by substantial evidence that neither he nor any employee nor agent was responsible for the administration of the drug or other restricted substance. Every trainer must guard each horse trained by him in such manner and for such period of time prior to racing the horse so as to prevent any person, whether or not employed by or connected with the owner or trainer, from administering any drug or other restricted substance to such horse...." N.Y. Comp. Codes R. & Regs. tit. 9, § 4043.4. Such provisions have withstood constitutional scrutiny in the states employing that standard. *See, e.g.,* Harbour v. Col. State Racing Comm'n, 505 P.2d 22 (1973) (although even the rebuttable presumption rule could be harsh, "the difficulty in controlling the business of horse racing and the importance of doing so in the interest of the public necessitates such rules and renders them reasonable"); Seely v. Okla. Horse Racing Comm'n, 743 P.2d 685, 690 (Okla. Civ. App. 1987) ("The rule in question, Rule 902, does not impose strict liability on the trainer for the condition of his horses, but establishes that positive drug tests constitute "prima facie" evidence that a foreign substance was administered by, or with the knowledge of the trainer. This type of rule, which allows a trainer to introduce evidence to rebut the prima facie case, is not violative of the due process clause."); Commonwealth v. Webb, 274 A.2d 261(Pa. Commw. Ct. 1971).

6. In light of the paucity of cases where trainers successfully challenge action against them under the rebuttable presumption standard, one may question whether there is any real difference in application between the absolute insurer and rebuttable presumption standards. One such successful challenge involved a trainer claiming that the horse's owner administered a prohibited type of cough syrup to the horse without the trainer's knowledge. Although the Racing Board did not believe the presumption had been overcome, on appeal the court held that the trainer had proven, "by substantial evidence that the owner (not he, the trainer, nor any employee nor agent) was responsible for the administration of the cough syrup containing the restricted substance." Wetzel v. N.Y. State Racing & Wagering Bd., 487 N.Y.S.2d 218, 220 (N.Y. App. Div. 1985).

7. Despite its presence in many regulations and success in the courts, the absolute insurer rule has been widely criticized. *See, e.g.,* Bennett Liebman, *The Trainer Responsibility Rule in Horse Racing*, 7 Va. Sports & Ent. L.J. 1 (2007); Luke P. Iovine, III & John E. Keefe, Jr., *Horse Drugging: The New Jersey Trainer Absolute Insurer Rule: Burning Down the House to Roast the Pig*, 1 Seton Hall J. of Sport Law 61 (1991).

B. Animal Welfare

Notes

1. There is reason to question the commitment of racing officials to the safety and welfare of the animals. In the 2009 Breeder's Cup, a number of trainers who had serious drug violations related to horses they trained, saddled horses for the Breeder's Cup races. Some critics say the trainers' conduct reflects a desire to win by any means necessary. Likewise, trainers found to have violated these rules should be seriously punished and not allowed to train the horses. For an alarming description of this issue, *see* Joe Drape, *Barred for Drugs, Horse Trainers Return to Track*, N.Y. Times, Nov. 5, 2009.

The article raises troubling issues about the treatment of racing horses. While the absolute insurer rule seems to be directed primarily at making sure there is fair competition, it apparently offers little protection for the animals. If trainers who are caught using prohibited medications on their horses can escape with minimal punishment, the disincentives for such conduct are diluted. Part of the problem is the absence of uniformity in the states regarding the legality of administering drugs to the animals. Some have suggested a model statute that all racing states would adopt. Is this an area where Congress would have the power to legislate national standards? Would that be appropriate?

For a thorough treatment of many of these medication issues, *see* Kimberli Gasparon, *The Dark Horse of Drug Abuse: Legal Issues of Administering Performance-Enhancing Drugs to Racehorses*, 16 Vill. Sports & Ent. L.J. 199 (2009). *See also* Joe Drape, *Derby Nears, but Safety Rules Don't*, N.Y. Times, March 24, 2009, *available at* http://www.nytimes.com/2009/03/24/sports/othersports/24derby.html.

2. Another controversial safety issue involves the composition of the track on which the horses race. Historically, in the United States, races have been run on dirt, or less often, turf. Alarmed by the number of fatal breakdowns suffered by horses on dirt tracks, some tracks switched to a synthetic track surface. The synthetic surface is often made of a composite of sand, synthetic fibers and recycled rubber that is chemically treated to allow for good drainage. It is hotly disputed whether a synthetic surface is safer for the horse. According to one study, the number of fatal breakdowns declined by 40% in California after the state switched to synthetic surfaces. At one California track the fatality rate fell from 3.09 per 1000 starts to 1.70. At another California track, the fatality number dropped from 2.89 per 100 starts to 1.59. Opponents to the synthetic tracks argue that the tracks cause more soft tissue injuries in the horses.

See Joe Drape, *Although Critics Remain, Synthetic Tracks Show Progress*, N.Y. Times, November 6, 2009; Jim Squires, *Hollow Safety Promises at Hallowed Starting Gates*, N.Y. Times, May 3, 2009.

3. Claims of animal abuse are even more common for greyhound racing. *See, e.g.*, Erin N. Jackson, *Dead Dog Running: The Cruelty of Greyhound Racing and the Bases for Its Abolition in Massachusetts*, 7 Animal L. 175 (2001). For an industry rejoinder to the attacks of animal rights proponents, see The Greyhound Racing Association of America, *As Nature Designed them — Greyhound Racing*, http://www.gra-america.org/the_sport/articles/a_nature.html.

Chapter 16

Lotteries

1. History and Background of Lotteries

Lotteries are one of the most venerable forms of gambling in the United States. They have alternately been hailed as an effective means of governmental fund-raising as a "voluntary" tax, and reviled as governmental exploitation of the poor. Lotteries have ridden waves of popularity and suffered periodic banishment.

Colonial America was replete with lotteries, both public and private. In the mid-18th century, colonial legislatures authorized over 100 lotteries. The lotteries helped to fund churches, schools, public buildings, and even institutions that have become some of the most prestigious universities in the United States. Columbia, Princeton, and Yale all were assisted by proceeds from lotteries. As relations between the colonies and Britain deteriorated and led to revolution, lotteries helped to pay for the military expenses of the colonists as they built their defenses for the war. By the mid-1800s, however, lotteries had fallen on hard times in the United States. This resulted from the convergence of two seemingly disparate sets of concerns. On the one hand, there were those who viewed lotteries as a pernicious activity that exploited the poor. But after a slave won a lottery prize, purchased his freedom, and plotted an insurrection, lotteries were criticized for fomenting "social upheaval":

> The poor and the powerless might, through a stroke of luck, gain a fortune. Such tumult flew in the face of the emerging Protestant capitalist ethic, which prescribed hard work and self-sacrifice as the only path to success. Working hard felt a little less satisfying when one's neighbor, or even employee, might become wealthier simply by holding a lucky ticket. Those who felt apprehensive about the lottery's leveling effects soon joined forces with others who felt that the poor who bought lottery tickets should be 'protected' from scheming lottery agents.

DAVID G. SCHWARTZ, ROLL THE BONES: THE HISTORY OF GAMBLING 150 (Gotham Books 2006). Hostility toward the lottery was exhibited not only by existing states outlawing it, but by newly admitted states that forbade lotteries in their constitutions. This aversion to the lottery in the mid-1800s had one notable exception: the Louisiana Lottery. Known by the name of the "Octopus" or the "Serpent," it was originally chartered in 1868. Until its demise in 1907, it had a nationwide reach. Profits were in the millions of dollars, year after year. But soon, stories of corruption contributed to efforts to kill the Serpent. Because the Louisiana Lottery used mail services for much of its distribution, the United States government moved to close it down. The United States was joined by states whose citizens were purchasing tickets and thereby taking money out of the state. Such was the sordid history of the Louisiana Lottery that it would be many decades before a state would again hazard the creation of a state lottery.

It was in 1964 that New Hampshire, a state far removed from Louisiana, geographically and presumably otherwise, reinstituted and began operating a lottery. Since that time, lotteries have swept the nation. As of 2009, forty-three states and the District of Columbia have lotteries of some form. According to La Fleur's, a magazine that follows the lottery industry, lottery sales in the United States for fiscal year 2008 were $52.7 billion. Its detailed World Lottery Almanac refers to lotteries as a "$227 billion worldwide ... industry." However, the prevalence of lotteries in the United States has not reduced the controversy generated by having the state as a partner to this form of gambling. Many social issues and legal problems are implicated by lotteries.

Not surprisingly, states are vigilant in the protection of their lotteries from private lotteries or sweepstakes contests. In Chapter 1, there is discussion of the characteristics of activities that might be considered gambling. The basic formula is to look for the existence of the three elements of prize, chance, and consideration. See Chapter 1 for further discussion of this topic.

Notes

1. Much has been written about the history of lotteries. *See, e.g.*, John Samuel Ezell, Fortune's Merry Wheel: The Lottery in America (Harv. U. Press, 1960) (classic study of the prevalence of gaming and lotteries in America, especially during colonial times); Anisha S. Dasgupta, *Public Finance and the Fortunes of the Early American Lottery*, 24 Quinnipiac L. Rev. 227 (2006) (comprehensive examination of early lotteries; analyzing many lotteries of the 18th century and their failure to achieve their promise as a funding device for government; and arguing that the "dynamics of adoption and disappointment in the public finance context" determine a lottery's success. *Id.* at 230.); Ronald J. Rychlack, *Lotteries, Revenues and Social Costs: A Historical Examination of State-Sponsored Gambling*, 34 B.C. L. Rev. 11 (1992) (thorough study of the many issues lotteries have implicated in their long history).

2. Since early in their appearance in the United States, lotteries have been criticized on many grounds. One persistent criticism is that lotteries exploit the most economically vulnerable members of society, i.e., the poor. These complaints focus in part on the claim that the poor play the lottery more often, a claim that is often disputed by the lottery industry. The industry tends to portray most lottery players as middle-class with some college education. They also like to emphasize that the racial composition of players is closely tied to the racial makeup of state populations. *See e.g.*, North American Association of State and Provincial Lotteries, *Demographics Study Highlights*, http://www.naspl.org/index.cfm?fuseaction=content&PageID=33 (last visited June 5, 2010); Texas Lottery Commission, *2008 Demographic Survey of Texas Lottery Player*, *available at* http://www.uh.edu/cpp/txlottery2008.pdf (last visited June 5, 2010). The Oregon Lottery declares that, "The typical Oregon Lottery player is the typical Oregonian. Income, education, and age levels match the populations in each category and sub-set. The average Oregon Lottery player has some college education, a household income of $45,000 per year, is about 41 years old, and is equally likely to be male or female." *See* Oregon Lottery, http://www.oregonlottery.org/general/games_revenue.php#demograph. Some argue that in addition to playing the lottery more often, the poor are the target audience for lottery advertising, and do not receive the same level of benefits from lottery proceeds. *See* Kana A. Ellis, *Finding the Winning Numbers: State Lotteries for Education and Their Impact on the Poor*, 14 Geo. J. on Poverty L. & Pol'y 317 (2007); Pamela Mobilia, *A Little Bit More Evidence of Lottery Regressivity: The Kansas State Lottery*, 8 J. Gambling Stud. 361 (1992) (analyzes charge of regressiv-

ity of lottery using the mean of bets expressed as a percentage of income. The results showed that populations of lower income counties bet more as a percentage of income.); Todd A. Wyett, *State Lotteries: Regressive Taxes in Disguise*, 44 TAX LAW. 867, 877, 883 (1991) ("Lotteries are regressive taxes whose incidence of taxation falls most heavily on low-income families.... Thus, there is in effect a redistribution of wealth from poor families to families in all income classes.").

Not everyone agrees that it is a fool's errand to play the lottery. One author argues that playing the lottery is neither irrational nor uninformed. The author discusses the role of mathematics in influencing a person's decisions of when to buy a lottery ticket. Also, between the time the ticket is purchased and the numbers are actually drawn, a player has a "sense of open-ended possibility" that is not inconsequential. Lloyd R. Cohen, *The Lure of the Lottery*, 36 WAKE FOREST L. REV. 705 (2001). Could the concern about the lottery having a disparate impact on the poor be addressed by forbidding marketing of the lottery? Could a lottery be successful by being responsive only to unsolicited demand? Is there a parallel between the lottery and the way in which states regulate the sale of liquor? Excessive "participation" in either of these activities creates social costs. With liquor, these costs are addressed by advertising limitations or by a government monopoly in the sale of liquor. Liquor sales are aimed more at servicing the demand for alcohol than as a revenue source. But the lottery has become much more the latter than the former.

3. Lotteries typically offer several types of "products." One product is a scratch-off ticket, where the purchaser can determine immediately whether he has a winner. Formerly, scratch-off tickets were in small denominations such as $1, $2, or $5. In the past few years, however, some states, such as Texas, have introduced scratch-off games with $50 tickets. Those who treat gambling addicts estimate that one-third of the calls to addiction hot lines are from lottery players, the majority of whom play the scratch-off games. They argue that these high stakes lottery tickets take particular advantage of vulnerable members of society who view the lottery as a way of "hitting it big." One critic has said that, "Scratch-off tickets are to the lottery what crack is to cocaine." Lottery officials say the future of the lottery business depends on instant games with bigger winning prizes, and that the games are not aimed at compulsive gamblers or intended to be addictive. For an interesting description of the debate, and the appeal of these games to many players, *see* Nelson D. Schwartz, *The $50 Ticket: A Lottery Boon Raises Concern*, N.Y. TIMES, Dec. 27, 2007. The article also addresses the demographics of lottery customers. Because lotteries involve state governments, and there are questions about the effect of lotteries on poorer people, shouldn't a state have a duty to develop detailed demographic information on who plays the lottery, and to what extent?

4. Another basic type of lottery product involves the drawing of numbers on a daily, weekly or bi-weekly basis. These games often go by the name of Lotto or Powerball. Some of these games involve the pooling of money from several states. These "numbers" games follow a long tradition of games that developed in the United States when lotteries were not legal. Sometimes these games flourished even when there was a lottery. In some ways, the existence of the state-sanctioned lottery removed the taint, if not the fact, of illegality of the numbers game. For a fascinating description of the numbers game known as "policy," *see* MATTHEW SWEENEY, THE LOTTERY WARS: LONG ODDS, FAST MONEY, AND THE BATTLE OVER AN AMERICAN INSTITUTION 65–67 (Bloomsbury 2009).

Other lottery products include raffles, keno, and video lottery terminals. For a detailed description of the various lottery products and the revenues they generate, *see* Charles T. Clotfelter & Philip J. Cook, *The Importance of a Good Cause: Ends and Means in State Lotteries*, in GAMBLING: MAPPING THE MORAL LANDSCAPE 19–23 (Alan Wolfe & Erik C. Owens, eds., Baylor U. Press 2009).

5. As noted above, lotteries have long served as a means of financing government operations. They are especially attractive to states since they are viewed as a type of "self-taxing" device, producing additional government revenues without an explicit tax. One might question whether government should fund its operations this way. Often, lotteries have been promoted as a benefit for public education within a state. But it is far from certain that lotteries have been a substantial bonanza for public education. *See, e.g.,* Kana A. Ellis, *Finding the Winning Numbers: State Lotteries for Education and Their Impact on the Poor,* 14 Geo. J. on Poverty L. & Pol'y 317, 325 (2007) (author claims that states often reduce direct funding for education when they start lotteries and that this often creates a net loss to education funds when the lottery fails to make up the previous balance); Donald E. Miller & Patrick A. Pierce, *Lotteries for Education: Windfall or Hoax?* 29 St. & Loc Gov't Rev. 34, 40 (1997) (statistical analysis of the effect of lotteries on education spending suggests that education spending does not increase markedly as a result of lottery revenues); Ron Stodghill & Ron Nixon, *For Schools, Lottery Payoffs Fall Short of Promises,* N.Y. Times, Oct. 7, 2007 (comprehensive study of states that tie lottery revenues to funding of education; authors find that as lotteries have increased the amount of the prizes for players, the percentage of each dollar going to education has shrunk; further, in many instances lottery dollars are not supplemental, they simply replace public funds directed to education).

2. State Constitutions and Lotteries

As discussed above, lotteries fell into disfavor in the 19th century and many of the newly admitted states contained provisions in their constitutions forbidding lotteries from operating in the state. Beginning in the 1960s, when states once again warmed to the idea of a lottery, state constitutions were construed, or more often, amended, to allow lotteries. This has led to considerable litigation.

State ex rel. Six v. Kansas Lottery
186 P.3d 183 (Kan. 2008)

This case comes before the court on a direct appeal pursuant to K.S.A. 2007 Supp. 60-2102(b)(2). The appellant seeks review of an order of the district court upholding the constitutionality of the Kansas Expanded Lottery Act (KELA), K.S.A. 2007 Supp. 74-8733 *et seq.*

This appeal asks us to resolve tension among the historical ban on lotteries contained in the Kansas Constitution, later amendments to the constitution that permit lotteries under certain circumstances, and recent legislative action seeking to increase state revenues by establishing supervised gambling venues. The issue before this court is narrow: Does the legislative scheme provide for a lottery that is owned and operated by the State of Kansas? An integrated study of the history of lotteries in Kansas, the language of the Kansas Constitution, the interpretation of similar laws in other states, and the legislative provisions contained in KELA leads us to conclude that KELA complies with the constitutional prohibitions and mandates.

Background

Since the admission of Kansas into the Union in 1861, art. 15, § 3, of the Kansas Constitution has provided: "Lotteries and the sale of lottery tickets are forever prohibited." A series of cases proceeded to define what constitutes a lottery....

In the 1974 general election, the state adopted a constitutional amendment permitting games of bingo to be conducted by certain nonprofit organizations. This amendment was later amended to allow instant bingo games. Kan. Const. art. 15, §3a. On November 1, 1986, the citizens of Kansas voted to amend the Kansas Constitution to permit pari-mutuel wagering in horse and dog racing and to authorize a "state-owned and operated lottery." Sixty-four percent of Kansas voters approved the lottery amendment. [Kan. Const. art. 15, §3c]

Following approval of the 1986 amendments, Kansas enacted legislation allowing horse and dog racing (K.S.A. 74-8801 *et seq.*) and enabling a state-owned and operated lottery (K.S.A. 74-8701 *et seq.*).... In 1990, the Kansas Legislature extended the life of the state-owned lottery. L.1990, ch. 370. The lottery is now scheduled to expire on July 1, 2022. K.S.A.2007 Supp. 74-8723(a).

Two earlier cases before this court have addressed the interplay between the constitutional ban on lotteries and the subsequent amendments permitting limited lotteries: State ex rel. Stephan v. Finney, 867 P.2d 1034 (Kan. 1994) (definition of lottery includes gambling enterprises in general); and State ex rel. Stephan v. Parrish, 887 P.2d 127 (Kan. 1994) ("instant bingo" exceeds constitutional boundaries for legal bingo games). No constitutional challenges under the constitutional lottery provisions have come to this court since *Parrish* was decided in 1994, and this court has never been asked to address the constitutionality of the 1987 Kansas Lottery Act.

During the 2007 legislative session, the Kansas Legislature passed, and the Governor signed, SB 66, "An act concerning lotteries; enacting the Kansas expanded lottery act, authorizing operation of certain gaming facilities, electronic gaming machines and other lottery games at certain locations...." KELA became effective April 19, 2007. L.2007, ch. 110. It is codified at K.S.A.2007 Supp. 74-8733 *et seq.* It generally provides for gaming in casinos and pari-mutuel racetracks in four gaming zones....

On August 23, 2007, the attorney general filed an original action in quo warranto and mandamus.... The [Shawnee County] district court filed a 41-page memorandum decision and order on February 1, 2008, holding that the statute passed constitutional muster. The State of Kansas, through the attorney general, filed a timely notice of appeal and amended notice of appeal.

The constitutionality of a statute is a question of law, and this court applies a de novo standard of review to the judgment of the district court....

It is not the duty of this court to criticize the legislature or to substitute its view on economic or social policy; it is the duty of this court to safeguard the constitution....

Before striking down a statute, the court must find that the statute clearly violates the constitution. This court will not strike down a legislative enactment on the mere ground that it fails to conform with a strictly legalistic definition or a technically correct interpretation of constitutional provisions. Instead, the test is whether the legislation conforms with the "'common understanding of the masses'" at the time they adopted the constitutional provisions, and the presumption favors the natural and popular meaning in which the words were understood by the adopters....

The legislative record contains little evidence of what the Kansas legislators and voters thought or intended when approving art. 15, §3c. *Finney*, 254 Kan. at 650, 867 P.2d 1034. It appears, however, that the voters intended "to allow closely regulated gambling and to raise money for the state." 254 Kan. at 650, 867 P.2d 1034 (quoting Att'y Gen. Op. No. 87-16, citing Minutes of the House Federal and State Affairs Committee, January 21, 1986, testimony of Secretary of Revenue Harley Duncan).

The intention underlying both § 3 and § 3c of article 15 involves promoting the economic welfare and growth of this state. This unity of intention compels us to read § 3c to favor the constitutionality of legislation purporting to create a state-owned lottery, as we have read § 3 to foreclose gambling schemes in the past....

The intended purpose of KELA conforms with the intended purpose of § 3c of article 15, and we will therefore read the statute with a presumption that it meets the constitutional requirements.

Ownership and Operation

What does the phrase "state-owned and operated lottery" mean in the context of our state constitution? The petitioner advocates a narrow meaning: the state must own the facility where the lottery is played or where game tickets are dispensed, must own the gaming equipment, must hire workers at the facilities and issue their paychecks, and must make both large and small management decisions. In other words, the state must hold the title to the principle (sic) tangible property associated with the lottery, and the principle (sic) decision-makers must be state employees. The respondent, on the other hand, argues for an expansive meaning: It suffices that the state have an ownership interest in the enterprise and that it actively supervise the management of the enterprise. Further, for constitutional purposes, the state may own an intangible interest and may direct the control of the activities of nonstate employees.

Neither § 3c nor the explanatory notes presented to the electorate contained definitions of "owning," "operating," or "lotteries." "From all the testimony for and against the proposed amendment to allow a state-owned lottery ... [t]here is no indication that during the hearings and debate the legislature intended to define what constituted a 'state-owned lottery' or attempted to limit what types of gambling the State could constitutionally own and operate." *Finney*, 254 Kan. at 651–52, 867 P.2d 1034. Because the constitutional provision is not self-defining, the courts must function as the definers of the words of the constitution. *Finney*, 254 Kan. at 652–53, 867 P.2d 1034; see also *Parrish*, 256 Kan. at 755, 887 P.2d 127 (court has authority and duty to define constitutional provisions).

The parties disagree on exactly what the state must own and operate. This court has previously defined the subject matter as follows:

> "A state-owned lottery, as that term is used in art. 15, § 3c of the Kansas Constitution, means any state-owned and operated *game, scheme, gift, enterprise, or similar contrivance* wherein a person agrees to give valuable consideration for the chance to win a prize or prizes" (emphasis added). *Finney*, 254 Kan. at 656, 867 P.2d 1034.

It is unnecessary that the state own the physical plant associated with the lottery. It suffices that the state own the game, or the scheme, or the enterprise. Such a definition is consistent with a standard of review favoring the constitutionality of KELA.

The words "own" and "ownership" are not technical terms or terms of art but common terms, the precise legal meaning of which depends upon the context in which they appear....

Ownership is "[t]he bundle of rights allowing one to use, manage, and enjoy property, including the right to convey it to others." Black's Law Dictionary 1138 (8th ed.2004)....

Although ownership may exist without operation and operation may exist without ownership, the two concepts are closely intertwined. Wide-ranging operational discretion implies ownership, and ownership implies discretion in making operating decisions....

Ownership does not necessarily mean absolute dominion over the subject property. Marsh v. Alabama, 326 U.S. 501, 506 (1946). Operation likewise does not imply absolute control, especially in the business context. Control of a corporation need not mean control of business minutiae; the owner can be "'enmeshed in the direction and control of the business without being involved in the actual management.'" Trudgeon v. Fantasy Springs Casino, 71 Cal. App. 4th 632, 641, 84 Cal.Rptr.2d 65 (1999) (quoting Gavle v. Little Six, Inc., 555 N.W.2d 284, 295 (Minn. 1996))....

The essence of [earlier Kansas cases] is that a public entity may retain both ownership and operation of an enterprise—in those cases, a public park and a racing facility—while allowing private entities to profit from the ownership of businesses that promoted the social benefit of the public enterprise. These cases demonstrate that ownership of a business enterprise does not require legal title or exclusivity of ownership interests. They also demonstrate that operation is a fluid concept that may be manifested through supervision, subcontracting, or leasing.

Analysis Of The Issue In Other Jurisdictions

The parties urge this court to consider the outcomes in other jurisdictions to constitutional challenges to gaming operations. Those cases have limited application to the issue before us, because the language of the Kansas Constitution and the intention of its adopters require unique construction. See *Nelson,* 210 Kan. at 444, 502 P.2d 841. We nevertheless find it instructive to review cases from several other jurisdictions.

In State v. West Virginia Economic Dev. Auth., 588 S.E.2d 655 (W. Va. 2003), the West Virginia Supreme Court of Appeals considered a video lottery act in light of a constitutional provision that allows the legislature to "'authorize *lotteries which are regulated, controlled, owned and operated* by the State of West Virginia in the manner provided by general law, either separately by this State or jointly or in cooperation with one or more states[.]'" (emphasis added). The purpose of the act "was to establish a single state owned and regulated video lottery thus allowing the State to collect revenue there from, control the operations of the machines, and stem the proliferation of gambling in the State [citation omitted]." 214 W.Va. at 289, 588 S.E.2d 655. The act allowed video lottery games to be placed in licensed private establishments. 588 S.E.2d 655.

Opponents of the act argued that the video lottery was not sufficiently regulated, controlled, owned, and operated by the state. They contended that "the video lottery machines are operated, controlled and owned by their private manufacturers, operators, and retailers." 214 W.Va. at 291, 588 S.E.2d 655. In finding the statute constitutional, the court pointed to numerous indicia of state regulation, control, ownership, and operation. These included mandatory approval of the lottery terminals at licensed racetracks by the Lottery Commission, a central monitoring system that could immediately disable the games, mandatory licensing qualifications, and ownership by the Lottery Commission of the main logic boards and all erasable programmable read-only memory chips. 588 S.E.2d 655.

In Dalton v. Pataki, 835 N.E.2d 1180 (2005), the New York Court of Appeals considered a constitutional provision generally prohibiting lotteries but making an exception for lotteries "operated by the state." The court found that participation in a multi-state lottery did not violate the state constitution, because New York retained sufficient control over the sale of lottery tickets so as to operate the lottery within the state. New York retained the authority to specify where and in what manner the lottery tickets might be sold, the power to license ticket agents and determine their compensation, and the freedom to withdraw from the multi-state agreement. 835 N.E.2d 1180. Although the state regularly contracted with outside vendors and other entities for equipment and services, operation remained under the control of the state. "While the State may not have exclusive control over every aspect of the Mega Millions lottery, it operates the multistate lottery within New York as required by the Constitution [citation omitted]." 835 N.E.2d 1180.

A similar question was presented in South Dakota, where the central issue involved discrimination against out-of-state business interests. Article III, § 25 of the South Dakota Constitution provides:

> "The legislature shall not authorize any game of ... lottery.... However, it shall be lawful for the legislature to authorize by law, a state lottery or video games of chance, or both, which are regulated by the state of South Dakota, either separately by the state or jointly with one or more states, and which are *owned and operated* by the state of South Dakota, either separately by the state or jointly with one or more state or persons" (emphasis added).

South Dakota participates in a video lottery business called the South Dakota Lottery. South Dakota does not own the video machines on which the games of chance are played or the modems attached to the machines, but the state owns the dominant software programs that operate the machines. The state bills the owners/operators of the machines for its portion of the revenue. Chance Management, Inc. v. State of S.D., 97 F.3d 1107, 1109 (8th Cir. 1996). The Eighth Circuit concluded that this arrangement constituted a "state business" within the gaming market and that South Dakota "owns and operates" the gaming enterprise. 97 F.3d at 1109, 1111 ...

These cases from our sister jurisdictions demonstrate that sufficient indicia of state ownership and operation may lie in diverse areas such as ownership of gaming software, centralized monitoring and control of electronic games, retention of the authority to approve or veto individual games, control of how and where lottery games are played, and the flow of gaming revenues directly to and from the state.

KELA and the Indicia of Ownership and Operation

Our analysis of the concepts of ownership and operation, in concert with the approaches that our sister states have taken to lottery ownership and operation, leads us to the conclusion that the constitution does not mandate physical ownership of the gaming plant or immediate control of all aspects of gaming operations. We instead will look at the statute to determine whether it establishes sufficient indicia of ownership and operation to comply with the constitutional requirements.

KELA explicitly places "full, complete and ultimate ownership and operational control of the gaming operation of the lottery gaming facility with the Kansas lottery." K.S.A. 2007 Supp. 74-8734(h)(17). It also provides that the lottery "shall retain full control over all decisions concerning lottery gaming facility games." K.S.A. 2007 Supp. 74-8734(h)(17). In addition, the statute provides the Kansas lottery with the authority to overrule without prior notice any action by a lottery gaming facility manager. K.S.A. 2007 Supp. 74-8734(h)(17).

The statutory scheme, when read in its entirety, shows that these direct statements of ownership and operational control are not mere verbal camouflage. KELA mandates that the Kansas lottery shall be the licensee and owner of all the software programs used at the lottery gaming facilities for all lottery games. K.S.A. 2007 Supp. 74-8734(n)(1). The games themselves are to be leased or purchased for the Kansas lottery. K.S.A. 2007 Supp. 74-8734(n)(2). Electronic gaming machines will be directly linked to a central lottery communications system to provide monitoring, auditing, and other available program information to the Kansas lottery and will be online and in constant communication with a central computer. K.S.A. 2007 Supp. 74-8749(a)(2), (3). These machines will be subject to deactivation at any time by order of the executive director. K.S.A. 2007 Supp. 74-

8749(a)(4). These provisions place ownership and control of key lottery elements squarely in the hands of the Kansas lottery.

The games themselves will all be purchased or leased for the Kansas lottery, and the games will be subject to the ultimate control of the Kansas lottery. K.S.A. 2007 Supp. 74-8734(n)(2) ...

The flow of the monetary proceeds into and out of the gaming facilities—another key indicium of ownership and operation—also resides directly with the Kansas lottery. All lottery gaming-facility revenues from lottery gaming facilities and all net electronic gaming machine income from racetrack gaming facilities will be paid daily and electronically to the executive director of the racing and gaming commission....

Although KELA allows the Kansas lottery to contract for the management of gaming facilities, any management contract must include provisions for the Kansas Racing and Gaming Commission to oversee all lottery gaming facility operations, including internal controls; security facilities; performance of background investigations; determination of qualifications and credentials of employees, contractors, and agents of the managers; auditing of facility revenues; enforcement of all state laws; and maintaining the integrity of gaming operations. K.S.A. 2007 Supp. 74-8734(h). The state may enter into these contracts to manage or to construct and manage gaming facilities on behalf of the state and subject to the operational control of the state. K.S.A. 2007 Supp. 74-8734(d).

While the state is not the exclusive owner and operator of all aspects of the lottery enterprise under KELA, the state owns and operates the enterprise itself and owns and operates key elements of the lottery. The payment of gaming revenues directly to the state, the ownership by the state of software licenses, the central monitoring of electronic games, and the authority to enter into management contracts and to supervise the managers constitute substantial indicia of ownership by the state and concomitant operation.

[The court also found that there was not an improper delegation of power by the legislature to the operators of the casinos.]

Conclusion

Ownership and operation are flexible concepts. This court will read a constitutional provision so as to carry out the intention of the citizens when they enacted the provision, and the court will read a statute with a presumption of constitutionality. The legislature and citizens amended the constitution in order to provide a mechanism for raising revenues for the state and for promoting economic growth, goals that KELA is structured to accomplish. KELA, while not providing for total and unambiguous ownership and operation by the state, contains sufficient indices of ownership and control for it to comply with the constitutional mandate.

The decision of the district court is affirmed.

Notes

1. There have been a number of other decisions where state supreme courts grapple with issues concerning state constitutions and re-institution or modification of a lottery. One problem area involves the constitutional authority for a state to participate in a multi-state lottery. In State ex rel Ohio Roundtable v. Taft, No.02 AP-911, 2003 WL 21470307 (Ohio Ct. App. June 26, 2003), the challenge was to the state's participation in a multi-state lottery. The Ohio state constitution permitted the General Assembly to "authorize an agency of the state to conduct lotteries." Lottery opponents claimed that a state law

authorizing the Lottery Commission to participate in a multi-state lottery "if the governor so directed" violated that constitutional provision. Moreover, when the Lottery Commission delegated certain functions to other states as part of the multi-state lottery, it ran afoul of the constitutional requirement that an agency of the state "conduct" the lottery. The court rejected all these claims, holding that the statutes implementing the constitutional provision did not improperly cede authority. A similar constitutional attack was likewise unsuccessful in Tichenor v. Missouri State Lottery Commission, 742 S.W.2d 170, 174 (Mo. 1988) ("We conclude that the phrase [in the Missouri state constitution] 'Missouri State Lottery' should not be read as a limitation on the authority of the State Lottery Commission to enter into a multi-state lottery venture otherwise complying with the details of the Missouri statute.").

2. Many cases have dealt with other alleged constitutional infirmities with a lottery proposal. Some challenges can be on quite technical grounds. *See* Heatherly v. State of North Carolina, 658 S.E.2d 11, 13 (N.C. Ct. App. 2008) (suit seeking declaratory judgment that lottery was unconstitutional because it did not receive three readings as required for revenue bills in the state; court ruled that lottery act was not a revenue bill because it "was not enacted to raise money on the credit of the state, or to pledge the faith of the state directly or indirectly for the payment of debt, or to impose any tax upon the people of the state" (internal citations omitted)). *See also* Ecumenical Ministries of Oregon v. Oregon State Lottery Commission, 871 P.2d 106, 108 (1994) (detailed analysis of Oregon constitution's evolution from its 1857 prohibition of lotteries to recent amendments authorizing a lottery, with the funds being "used for the purpose of creating jobs and furthering economic development in Oregon.").

3. Constitutional questions have also arisen when the uses of lottery proceeds apparently depart from that which was constitutionally approved. *See, e.g.,* In re Great Outdoors Colorado Trust Fund, 913 P.2d 533 (Colo. 1996). The case discusses Colorado's experience when a 1980 amendment to the Colorado constitution, which originally provided that net proceeds from the lottery would be allocated to the conservation trust fund for park, recreation, and open space purposes, unless otherwise provided by statute. The "unless otherwise provided by statute" provision resulted in the General Assembly directing money away from environmental projects and to capital and construction projects. Eventually, the amount used for the originally approved environmental purposes shrank to a very low percentage of lottery proceeds. Colorado voters then approved an amendment in 1992 requiring that most lottery proceeds go to environmental causes. However, certain lottery proceeds had already been dedicated to capital construction projects. The 1992 Amendment provided that those commitments should be honored. This case focused on questions regarding funding of the "transitional" projects.

4. One of the reasons historically given for lotteries periodically being banned is a concern about fraud. Lottery fraud can take many forms. One concern is that insiders or the sellers of lottery products will defraud the purchasers. In Iowa, the State Ombudsman conducted a two-and-a-half year investigation that uncovered at least three retailers who pocketed some lottery winnings by not giving the full amount to the holders of winning tickets. The Ombudsman report recommended more than sixty changes to lottery operations to curtail the risk of fraud. The Iowa Lottery's own investigation turned up no improper prize payments to or by the lottery retailers. *See* Clark Kauffman, *Investigation Looks at Lottery Security*, Des Moines Register, Jan. 24, 2008. *See also Lottery Officials Report No Problems With Security*, Globe Gazette, Aug. 7, 2009, *available at* http://www.globegazette.com/articles/2009/08/07/news/state/doc4a7baf 2160556929184503.txt#vmix_media_id=6762568 (last visited June 5, 2010); Chase Davis,

Report: Iowa Lottery Passive About Fraud, Des Moines Register, Apr. 22, 2009 *available at* http://m.dmregister.com/news.jsp?key=449234 (last visited June 5, 2010).

One notable case of fraud involved collusion between a television announcer and a lottery official that would alter the way that ping pong balls were drawn up into the machine that displayed the winning numbers. This led to the successful prosecution of the conspirators. *See* Commonwealth v. Katsafanas, 464 A.2d 1270 (Pa. Super. Ct. 1983). *See also* State v. Kimiinski, 474 N.W.2d 385 (Minn. App. 1991) (charging defendant with two counts of state lottery fraud for knowingly redeeming stolen lottery tickets; lottery fraud statute made it crime to claim lottery prize by means of fraud, deceit, or misrepresentation, and was held to be applicable to knowing redemption of stolen lottery tickets); United States v. Valavanis, 689 F.2d 626 (6th Cir. 1982) (convictions of the Ohio State Lottery's Drawing Coordinator and an accomplice for mail fraud while engaged in scheme to defraud the lottery upheld).

5. Other claims of lottery fraud are more subtle than the outright criminal activity suggested above. Some claim that lotteries misrepresent aspects of their "product." A university professor sued the Virginia Lottery contending that purchasers of an estimated 26.5 million tickets over the past five years had no chance of winning the top prize because it had already been won; yet, the lottery continued to sell tickets. The professor's effort to convert the case into a class action failed. *See Class-Action Appeal Denied in Lottery Case*, Richmond Times-Dispatch, Apr. 23, 2009, *available at* http://www2.times dispatch.com/rtd/news/state_regional/article/LOTT23_20090422-222213/263026/ (last visited June 5, 2010). In *Robinson v. Colorado State Lottery Division*, 179 P.3d 998 (Colo. 2008), the court held that an action against the lottery for continuing to sell tickets after all advertised prizes had been awarded was based on a tort misrepresentation theory, and was thus barred by the state's Governmental Immunity Act. *See also* Darren A. Prum, *Lottery Tickets Sold after the Featured Prize is Claimed: Will the Courts Force the Practice to be Stopped?*, 13 Gaming L. Rev. & Econ. 286 (2009).

Another claim of misrepresentation relates to the way the lottery advertises the amount that can be won. Lotteries commonly market a jackpot according to the gross amount that can be won. What isn't mentioned is that if a player takes the winnings in a lump sum, the amount actually paid will be far less than the amount advertised. For example, if the lottery jackpot is $10 million, a single winner would receive $10 million reduced to present value over a twenty or thirty year amortization period. Thus, the single winner would, with a twenty year amortization receive a lump sum of far less than $10 million even before the reduction for taxes. Only if the winner took the winnings over the twenty year period would he receive $10 million. Of course, because of inflation and the time value of money his true winnings are far less than $10 million in "real" dollars. *See* La Bo J P'-ship v. Louisiana Lottery Corp., 6 So. 3d 191 (La. Ct. App. 2009) *writ denied* 5 So. 3d 168 (2009) (plaintiffs claimed lottery misrepresented that winner could elect lump sum payment when in fact winnings were payable only over twenty years. Court held that the only representation made by the lottery was to award a specified jackpot in accordance with the rules as stated on the ticket. It was plaintiffs' responsibility to verify any alleged ambiguities.); *see also* Zapata v. Quinn, 707 F.2d 691 (2d Cir. 1983) (lottery winner who claimed a deprivation of property without due process of law because her winnings were to be paid partly by a ten year annuity instead of a lump sum failed to state a claim upon which relief could be granted); Rice v. Ohio Lottery Commission, 708 N.E.2d 796 (Ohio Ct. Cl. 1999) (lottery player held to have either actual or constructive notice that when he elected the lump-sum payment over the annuity payments, the "present cash value" prize would be less than the "present value" that would be paid out under the annuity option; no breach of contract claim against the lottery commission would lie).

When lottery winners elect to take the payout over a term of years, they often have the option of assigning their winnings to a third party which pays them a discounted lump sum for the remaining money. For an engaging description of the lump sum industry and its dealings with lottery winners, *see* EDWARD UGEL, MONEY FOR NOTHING: ONE MAN's JOURNEY THROUGH THE DARK SIDE OF LOTTERY MILLIONS (2007).

3. Lottery Players Suing the Lottery

Smith v. State Lottery Comm'n of Indiana
812 N.E.2d 1066 (Ind. Ct. App. 2004)
OPINION

BAILEY, Judge.

Case Summary

Appellants-Plaintiffs Tom Smith ("Smith") and George Frankl ("Frankl"), individually and as Class representatives of all others similarly situated, (collectively, "the Class"), appeal the trial court's grant of summary judgment in favor of Appellee-Defendant the State Lottery Commission ("the Lottery") on the Class's breach of contract claim.[1] We affirm in part, reverse in part, and remand for further proceedings.

Issue

The Class presents a single issue for review, which we restate as follows: whether the trial court erroneously granted summary judgment to the Lottery because the Lottery closed instant games and refused payment of prizes absent compliance with a contractual obligation to announce game end dates.

Facts and Procedural History

On direct appeal from the trial court's previous dismissal of Smith's claim, this Court recited the pertinent facts as follows:

The Lottery began selling instant win scratch-off tickets through its retailers on October 13, 1989, and has since offered hundreds of such games, some running simultaneously. Tickets for some of the games sell for a few months, others for over a year. When Smith purchased his ticket, on September 15, 1996, the back of the card contained the following statement: "All prizes must be claimed within 60 days of announced end of game."[2]

Having discovered that he had a winning ticket, Smith filled out the back of the ticket as required and presented it to the retailer on January 20, 1997, demanding his five dollar prize. Unbeknownst to Smith, the game had ended September 30, 1996, and the last day to claim prizes was on November 29, 1996. The retailer informed Smith that it was

---

1. In light of the Lottery's decision to publish game end dates at Lottery retailers' establishments, in the Indiana Register, on its website, and on individual tickets, the Class has abandoned its claim for injunctive relief.

2. Some time after Smith purchased his ticket, the Lottery changed the language on the back of the instant win scratch-off tickets, deleting "announced" before "end of game" and adding advice about where players could learn the game end date. The message now reads: "All prizes must be claimed within 60 days after the end of the game. Ask the game ending dates at any Hoosier Lottery Retailer or call 1-800-955-6886 for customer service." R. at 323.

too late to redeem his ticket. On January 22, 1997, Smith went to the principal office of the Hoosier Lottery in Indianapolis in an attempt to claim his prize. There he was told that the game was over and that nothing could be done to obtain his prize. There were no signs posted at the retailer's site announcing a closing date for the game,[3] nor was Smith advised by the retailer or the Lottery of an administrative appeal process or given a claim form.

On April 25, 1997, Smith filed a complaint in the trial court against the Lottery for breach of contract seeking damages for himself and for a Class of all persons whose winning scratch-off lottery tickets were rejected by the Lottery as having been untimely presented. Smith also sought equitable relief on behalf of a subclass of future lottery game players in the form of an order requiring the Lottery to either cease denying players their winnings or take reasonable steps to announce the end of instant scratch-off games in the future.

On June 24, 1997, the Lottery filed a motion to dismiss, or in the alternative, for summary judgment. The Lottery claimed that Smith's complaint must be dismissed for lack of subject matter jurisdiction, or alternatively that it was entitled to summary judgment because Smith failed to claim his prize in a timely manner. Smith responded to the dismissal and summary judgment motions, and filed a cross motion for summary judgment, claiming that he was entitled to judgment as a matter of law because the Lottery had never publicly announced the end of the games and could not, under either its contractual obligations to ticket holders or its own regulations, deny ticket holders their winnings. Smith also filed a motion for Class certification which was still pending when the case was dismissed. Following a hearing on October 14, 1997, the trial court granted the Lottery's motion to dismiss. In relevant part, the order of dismissal provided that the court lacked subject matter jurisdiction because Smith had not exhausted his administrative remedies; that an administrative process existed under the Indiana Administrative Orders and Procedures Act, IND. CODE § 4-21.5 et seq.; and that Smith had failed to demonstrate that he was not required to exhaust administrative remedies.

Smith v. State Lottery Comm'n of Ind., 701 N.E.2d 926, 928 (Ind. Ct. App.1998), *trans. denied.* This Court determined that Smith's claim came under the Administrative Orders and Procedures Act ("the AOPA") but that he was entitled to judicial review because he had exhausted all available remedies. *Id.* at 933. The case was remanded for judicial review under the criteria of Indiana Code Section 4-21.5-5-14, with the recommendation that the trial court consider certification of a class action. *Id.*

On February 7, 2002, the trial court granted Smith's motion to certify the case as a class action and divided the Class into two subclasses: (A) purchasers of scratch-off lottery tickets between 1989 and 1997 who actually presented a winning ticket to the Lottery or a retailer and were refused or denied payment ("Class A"); and (B) all other purchasers of winning scratch-off tickets between 1989 and 1997 who have not received payment for the winning tickets ("Class B"). The trial court found that Smith was an adequate representative for Class A, but not for Class B. On February 15, 2002, Frankl pe-

---

3. During the period in question, the Lottery did not instruct retailers to publicly post the game end dates, nor did it publish game end dates in the Indiana Administrative Code, where it publishes other, detailed information about the Instant Winner games. *See* 65 IAC 4. This section consists of 317 pages of rules regarding these games. Subsequent to Smith bringing this action, the Lottery, apparently for the first time, began announcing to the public, through postings at retailers' places of business, the last date for winning players to claim their prizes. R. at 220–222, 226.

titioned to intervene and represent Class B.[4] The trial court granted Frankl's petition on July 2, 2002.

Initially, in addition to compensation for breach of contract, the Class sought injunctive relief in the form of a court order requiring public announcement of game end dates. However, the Lottery issued formal repeals of each game involved in the class action, and adopted various methods for publishing game end dates prospectively, obviating the necessity of a court order.[5]

On March 11, 2003, the Class filed its motion for summary judgment. On May 27, 2003, the Lottery filed a cross-motion for summary judgment. On July 30, 2003, the trial court heard oral argument on the respective motions. On October 16, 2003, the trial court granted summary judgment to the Lottery. The summary judgment order provides in pertinent part as follows:

1. Plaintiff alleges in his Complaint that the class members are improperly denied the proceeds of winning instant game tickets by Defendant because it requires that all prizes must be claimed within 60 days of the announced end of game and Defendant never announces the end of instant games.

2. Plaintiff argues that Defendant failed to announce and publish the end of its instant games and that public announcement, and a publication of game ending dates in the Indiana Administrative Code are required.

3. Plaintiff contends that the parties' dispute centers on the meaning of the term "announced end of game."

4. The Defendant Lottery Commission is required to adopt rules under IND. CODE § 4-22-2 for verification of tickets claimed to win prizes and to make payment of prizes. IND. CODE § 4-30-11-1.

5. 65 I.A.C. 4 contains the rules which have been promulgated regarding the Defendant's instant games.

6. 65 I.A.C. 4-2-2 provides:

"Any person who purchases an instant ticket agrees thereby to comply with and abide by IC 4-30 ... and all procedures and instructions established by and final decisions of the director in connection with the conduct of the instant game for which the instant ticket is purchased."

7. 65 I.A.C. 4-2-3(a) provides:

"An instant game will end when all instant tickets for that instant game have been sold or on a date announced in advance by the director. The director may suspend or terminate an instant game without advance notice...."

8. Plaintiff contends that the claim of the class is supported by 65 I.A.C. 4-3-2(e) which provides:

---

4. Frankl purchased an instant win scratch-off lottery ticket during 1996. The ticket indicated that Frankl won a prize of one dollar. However, Frankl did not tender his ticket in order to claim his prize, but retained possession of it.

5. Effective September 12, 1996, the Lottery repealed 103 instant games. Effective June 15, 1998, the Lottery repealed 132 instant games. Effective July 7, 1999, the Lottery repealed 34 instant games. Effective June 30, 2000, the Lottery repealed 39 instant games. The repeal decisions were published in the Indiana Administrative Code. The parties agree that the Lottery has now repealed all games for which the tickets herein at issue were sold.

"An instant prize must be claimed within sixty (60) days of the announced end of the instant game in which the prize was won or it will be forfeited...."

9. IND. CODE § 4-30-11-7 provides that in the case of an instant game " ... the right to claim prizes exists for sixty (60) days *after the end of the lottery game*. If a valid claim is not made for [a] prize within the applicable period, the prize is considered an unclaimed prize...." (emphasis added).

10. 65 I.A.C. 4-3-4 also provides:

"All liability of the state, its officials, officers, and employees, and of the commission, the director, and employees of the commission for any instant prize terminates upon payment of an instant prize *or upon the expiration of sixty (60) days after the end of the instant game in which the instant prize was won....*" (emphasis added).

11. IND. CODE § 4-30-11-9 provides "All unclaimed prize money shall be added to the pool from which future prizes are to [be] awarded or used for special prize promotions."

12. 65 I.A.C. 4-3-2(e) also provides in part:

"All unclaimed prize money or other prizes required to be paid or delivered by the commission shall be added to the pool from which prizes are to be awarded or used for special prize promotions."

13. Any regulation that conflicts with statutory law is invalid, *Lee Alan Bryant Health Care Facilities, Inc. v. Hamilton*, 788 N.E.2d 495, 500 (Ind.Ct.App.2003), and rules and regulations may not be inconsistent with the statute that the commission is administering. *Leslie v. State*, 755 N.E.2d 1147, 1149 (Ind.Ct.App.2001).

14. 65 I.A.C. 4-3-2(e), upon which Plaintiffs rely, conflicts not only with other rules promulgated for the instant games, but also with applicable statutory provisions which Defendant is administering.

15. Plaintiffs are not entitled for [sic] judgment as a matter of law.

16. By reason of the foregoing, Defendant is entitled to judgment as a matter of law.

(App. 15-17.) The Class appeals.

....

A lottery is contractual in nature, historically having elements of a chance, a consideration and a prize. *Thao v. Control Data Corp.*, 790 P.2d 1239, 1241 (Wash. App. 1990). "'[The lottery] is designed to induce many contracts. The entire scheme is presented to the public as a general offer. The scheme prescribes the conditions of acceptance. These conditions require the acceptors to pay something or do something, or both.'" *Seattle Times Co. v. Tielsch*, 495 P.2d 1366, 1369 (Wash. 1972) (citing F. Williams, *Flexible Participation Lotteries* § 278, at 275 (1938)). A purchaser agrees to the established rules for determining prizes. *Id.; see also* 65 IAC 4-2-2.

The elements of a breach of contract action include: (1) the existence of a contract; (2) the defendant's breach of that agreement; and (3) damages. *Wilson v. Lincoln Federal Sav. Bank*, 790 N.E.2d 1042, 1048 (Ind. Ct. App. 2003).

The parties herein stipulated to the existence of a contract. Moreover, it is undisputed that a term of the lottery contract at issue is the statement printed on the back of the scratch-off tickets, as follows: "All prizes must be claimed within 60 days of announced end of game."[6] The breach of contract dispute centers upon whether the Lottery breached a material obligation to "announce" a game's end date to facilitate prize claims.

Generally, contract language will be given its plain and ordinary meaning. Colonial Penn Ins. Co. v. Guzorek, 690 N.E.2d 664, 669 (Ind. 1997). In pertinent part, "announce" is defined as "to give public notice of; make known officially or publicly; deliver news of" in Webster's Third New International Dictionary (2002).

The trial court concluded that, assuming that the Lottery promised to "announce" a game end, it had no legal obligation to do so because of a conflict between its regulation and statutory law. In essence, the trial court declared the contractual provision providing for game end announcement (mirroring the language of I.A.C. 4-3-2(e)) to be illegal because of irreconcilable conflict with Indiana Code Section 4-30-11-7. We disagree with the trial court's conclusion that an irreconcilable conflict exists.

Indiana Code Section 4-30-11-7 prescribes payment within sixty days of the end of an instant game. It does not relieve the Lottery of its assumed duty to announce when that game ends. The contractual term providing for "announcement" of game endings is presumptively valid. "As a general rule, the law allows competent adults the utmost liberty in entering into contracts which, when entered into freely and voluntarily, will be enforced by the courts." Peoples Bank & Trust Co. v. Price, 714 N.E.2d 712, 716 (Ind. Ct. App.1999), *trans. denied.* Thus, our focus turns to whether the Lottery established, as a matter of law, that it did not breach a material term of the contract by failing to "announce" the ending of the games at issue.

The Class contends that the Lottery did not "announce" game endings because the dates were not disseminated in a manner calculated to reach the public. In the view of the Class, the Lottery materially breached the contract and effectively decreased the likelihood that prizes would be awarded. In response, the Lottery maintains that it fulfilled its obligation of announcement by posting a copy of an "Instant Game Information Sheet" having game end dates in each of its regional office lobbies. The Lottery also provided the information sheets to lottery retailers, with no obligation to publicly post the sheets. Some retailers chose to display the information sheets, either in employee areas or public areas of the businesses. Too, the Lottery employed telephone customer service representatives whose duties included answering inquiries about game end dates. The Lottery argues that it thereby met the reasonable expectations of the purchasers.

Whether a party is in material breach of contract is a question of fact contingent on the following factors:

> (a) The extent to which the injured party will obtain the substantial benefit which he could have reasonably anticipated;
>
> (b) The extent to which the injured party may be adequately compensated in damages for lack of complete performance;
>
> (c) The extent to which the party failing to perform has already partly performed or made preparations for performance;
>
> (d) The greater or less hardship on the party failing to perform in terminating the contract;

---

6. At some point, the Lottery also began printing on the tickets the Lottery's toll-free customer service telephone number.

(e) The willful, negligent or innocent behavior of the party failing to perform; and

(f) The greater or less uncertainty that the party failing to perform will perform the remainder of the contract.

Wilson, 790 N.E.2d at 1048–49 (citing Tomahawk Village Apts. v. Farren, 571 N.E.2d 1286, 1293 (Ind. Ct. App. 1991)). Material questions of fact are not appropriate for resolution by summary judgment. T.R. 56(C). It is for the fact-finder to decide whether the conduct of the Lottery precluded purchasers who tendered their prize-winning tickets from obtaining a substantial benefit of the contract. We therefore reverse the summary judgment order in favor of the Lottery and against the members of Class A.

However, summary judgment was properly granted to the Lottery with respect to the claims of the members of Class B because the Lottery's designated materials negated the damages element of their breach of contract claim. The members of Class B elected not to timely tender any lottery ticket for a prize—after either the end date or official repeal of the games—and thus suffered no damages attributable to the conduct of the Lottery.

Affirmed in part, reversed in part, and remanded.

BAKER, J., and DARDEN, J., concur.

Reifschneider v. State

17 P.3d 907 (Kan. 2001)

LARSON, J.:

This is the second appeal of an attempt by Harold Reifschneider to claim the entire amount of the November 26, 1994, cash lotto jackpot for which he held one of two winning lottery tickets.

The factual scenario and proceedings in the previous appeal, Reifschneider v. Kansas State Lottery, 969 P.2d 875 (Kan. 1998) (*Reifschneider I*), were set forth as follows:

"On November 26, 1994, appellant Joyce Reifschneider, at the time known as Joyce Eldridge, purchased a Cash Lotto ticket with a winning combination of numbers. Another winning ticket with the same combination of numbers was sold in Wichita for the same game. Appellant Harold Reifschneider presented the ticket purchased by Joyce, along with a claim form, on November 28, 1994. Because another winning ticket had been sold, the Reifschneiders were paid $177,442, which represented one-half of the total jackpot. On November 22, 1995, the remaining winning ticket had still not been presented and the Reifschneiders, through counsel, sent a letter and a claim form seeking the unclaimed prize share. On April 17, 1996, the Executive Director of the Kansas Lottery through its attorney informed the Reifschneiders' counsel by letter that the Lottery was denying their claim.

"On November 26, 1996, the Reifschneiders filed a petition in the district court of Shawnee County for breach of contract. They alleged that the Lottery had breached its obligation to pay the full amount of the jackpot. The Lottery filed a motion to dismiss, claiming among other things that the KJRA [Kansas Act for Judicial Review and Civil Enforcement of Agency Actions Act] was the sole avenue of relief available to the Reifschneiders and that even if their petition could be construed as a petition for judicial review, it was untimely as it was filed in excess of the 30 days following the agency decision. The Lottery also argued that pursuant to applicable statutes and regulations, the Reifschneiders were only entitled to one-half of the jackpot, notwithstanding the fact that the other half went unclaimed.

"The district court noted that the Reifschneiders' action was for breach of contract but determined that their sole avenue of relief was under the KJRA. The district court also determined that even if the Reifschneiders' petition could be construed as a petition for judicial review under the KJRA, it was untimely. Accordingly, the district court granted the Lottery's motion to dismiss.

"In their appeal, the Reifschneiders contend that (1) an appealable order was not issued by the Kansas Lottery and (2) the letter denial by the Kansas Lottery of their claim denied them due process of law. As a part of this contention, they claim that the Kansas Administrative Procedure Act (KAPA), K.S.A. 77-501 *et seq.*, applies or, at the very least, minimal requirements of notice and an opportunity for hearing are required before a valid order may be entered denying their interest in the claimed property." 266 Kan. at 339–40, 969 P.2d 875.

We held in *Reifschneider I* that (1) the sole action for a person aggrieved by a decision of the Executive Director of the Kansas Lottery (Lottery) is an action under the Kansas Act for Judicial Review and Civil Enforcement of Agency Actions (KJRA), K.S.A. 77-601 *et seq.*, but (2) the letter sent to Reifschneider's counsel did not strictly comply with the notice provisions of K.S.A. 77-613(e) because it was not also sent to Reifschneider. The letter also failed to state the agency officer who was to receive service of a petition for judicial review on behalf of the agency. Consequently, the 30-day period within which a petition for review was required to be filed would begin only after proper service of the final order of the agency. 266 Kan. at 341–43, 969 P.2d 875.

Eleven days after our opinion in *Reifschneider I* was filed, the former Executive Director of the Lottery notified Reifschneider and his counsel by letter of his final order denying Reifschneider's claim in the following manner:

"You presented a claim for the $354,884 jackpot for the Cash Lotto drawing on November 26, 1994, and were advised that yours was one of two tickets bearing the winning combination of numbers. In accordance with rules and regulations adopted by the Kansas Lottery Commission, the Kansas Lottery paid your claim in the sum of $177,442, representing one-half of the jackpot prize. No claim was ever presented for the other ticket bearing the same winning combination of numbers, which was sold by the Quik Trip store, 2838 West Central, Wichita, Kansas. Your claim for the other half of the winning jackpot, since the other ticket containing the winning combination of numbers was never claimed, was presented to me for review and consideration. Based upon the limitations imposed by the *Kansas Lottery Act* and by administrative rules and regulations, I directed Assistant Attorney General Carl M. Anderson to deny your claim for the unclaimed prize, representing the other one-half of the Cash Lotto jackpot. This was done in the form of a letter to your attorney, Thomas Berscheidt, on April 17, 1996. Your claim was denied in that letter, and at this time, for the following reasons:

"Subsection (d) of K.A.R. 111-7-5 of the Cash Lotto game rules provides that 'the prize money allocated to the jackpot prize category for matching six (6) of six (6) shall be divided equally by the number of game boards winning a jackpot prize.' In this case, there were two game boards bearing winning combinations of numbers, the one submitted by you and the one issued at 11:49 a.m. on November 26, 1994, by the QuikTrip store in Wichita.

"An on-line generic rule applicable to all on-lines games, including Cash Lotto, provides at subsection (e) of K.A.R. 111-6-5 addressing the payment of prizes that, 'all prizes must be claimed within 365 days including the first day of the game or the drawing on which the prize was won.... Any prizes not claimed within the specific period shall be added to the prize pools of subsection Kansas lottery games.'

"The *Kansas Lottery Act*, at subsection (f) of K.S.A. 74-8720 provides that 'Unclaimed prize money not payable directly by lottery retailers shall be retained for the period established by rules and regulations, and if no claim is made within such period, then such unclaimed prize money shall be added to the prize pools of subsequent lottery games.' Since the rules require that the Cash Lotto jackpot prize be divided equally by the number of game boards winning a jackpot prize,' and only one valid claim was presented, the balance would be considered an unclaimed prize and treated as required by statute and the administrative rules and regulations adopted by the Kansas Lottery.

"The denial of your claim for the unclaimed $177,442 represents final agency action by the Kansas Lottery. You may seek judicial review of this action by the Kansas Lottery by filing a petition for judicial review within 30 days after service of this letter which represents a final order with reference to your claim. In the event you wish to seek judicial review on the subject matter addressed here, you should serve such a petition for judicial review upon me as Executive Director for the Kansas Lottery."

Reifschneider timely filed a petition for review of this order under the KJRA. The Lottery's answer denied Reifschneider's claim to the prize because he did not produce a winning ticket for the second portion of the prize. The Lottery also contended he had been paid in full, that the State was discharged from liability upon payment of the prize pursuant to K.A.R. 111-6-14 (7 Kan. Reg. 216 [1988]), release, accord and satisfaction, and a general denial.

In Reifschneider's initial memorandum brief, among other arguments, he contended that the Lottery had no evidence, "substantial or otherwise," to even establish that another winning ticket was in fact sold.

The Lottery, in obvious response to this allegation, in its reply brief, argued that we had held in *Reifschneider I* that the Kansas Administrative Procedure Act (KAPA), K.S.A. 77-501 *et seq.*, does not apply to the Kansas Lottery. The Lottery now argues K.S.A. 77-619 allows receipt of additional evidence by a court during the course of an appeal from an administrative decision. The lottery proffered evidence of the existence of a second winning lottery ticket for the November 26, 1994, drawing through the affidavit of its Executive Director with attached business records in the form of computer documentation.

The records showed the time, date, and location of the winning tickets as well as the numbers selected on the winning game boards (05, 06, 16, 23, 26, and 32). The records showed that at 11:49:06 a.m. an unknown person purchased winning lottery ticket number 16421313 at terminal 228 at a QuikTrip convenience store in Wichita, Kansas. It further showed that at 1:17:35 p.m. Reifschneider purchased a winning lottery ticket number 11370729 from terminal 659 at the Schaffer Standard in LaCrosse, Kansas.

The Lottery further argued in its brief that Reifschneider, by accepting payment of $177,442, had discharged the Lottery from further liability, that the decision of the Executive Director of the Lottery was entitled to great deference, that unclaimed prize money is required to be placed in subsequent prize pools by K.S.A. 74-8720(f), and that substantial competent evidence showed the sale of two winning lottery tickets with one being unclaimed.

Reifschneider specifically objected to the Lottery's proffer and contended he was being denied the opportunity of challenging all or part of the proffered exhibits. He failed, however, in any manner to counter the evidence submitted or show how it was in error. He argued that by insisting it is not governed by the KAPA, the Lottery chose for there to be no agency record under K.S.A. 77-619(a). He claimed no additional evidence was necessary to determine the basic issue in the appeal, which he framed as follows:

"The only issue to be considered herein is whether a second winning ticket, allegedly sold but not presented for the available prize permits the Respondent to conclude that the remaining portion of the total prize should be returned to the prize pool. If for the sake of argument it is conceded that ten tickets were sold with the same winning combination of numbers and the Petitioner was the only one to present the 'actual ticket' within 365 days of the drawing, the same issue would remain. Petitioner is the only person who possesses a validated 'winning ticket'. A 'winning ticket' properly submitted is the only way to claim a prize, according to the Respondent's own regulations [K.A.R. 111-7-5(g)]."

With this record and based upon these arguments, the trial court made findings of fact that two tickets with a winning combination of numbers had been sold. Reifschneider's ticket was presented. The second ticket was never presented. Reifschneider had been paid one-half of the jackpot amount and later presented a claim to the Lottery seeking the unclaimed prize share allotted to the other winning ticket, which was denied by a final order issued by the Executive Director of the Lottery.

The trial court's conclusions of law stated the Lottery's actions were subject to the KJRA, specifically K.S.A. 77-621(a)(1), which states that "the burden of proving the invalidity of agency action is on the party asserting invalidity," and placing the burden on Reifschneider to prove the Lottery erred in its interpretation of the law and factual conclusions, contrary to K.S.A. 77-621(c)(4) and (7).

A statement in the concurring opinion of *Reifschneider I* was relied on by the trial court for a holding that the Lottery is not subject to the KAPA. But, the trial court relied on K.S.A. 77-620 to hold an agency record consists of documents reflecting the agency action, which was shown by the Executive Director's letter to Reifschneider dated December 22, 1998.

The trial court further held that this agency record could be supplemented by additional evidence in the form of computer records submitted pursuant to K.S.A. 77-619(a) showing the sale of the two winning lottery tickets. The court found "the Kansas Lottery's determination that there was a second winning ticket, number 16421313, is a finding of fact supported by substantial evidence in the form of computer documentation of the second prize winning ticket."

The trial court then held that a specialized agency's interpretation of a statute it has the duty to implement should be entitled to great deference if the agency's interpretation is supported by a rational basis, citing State Dept. of Administration v. Public Employees Relations Bd., 894 P.2d 777 (Kan. 1995).

The issue of law that the trial court stated it was required to resolve is whether the holder of one of two winning lottery tickets, who has been paid one-half of the prize, has a right to the other half if it is not claimed within the prescribed time period. This issue requires construction of the statutes and agency regulations.

K.A.R. 111-7-5(d) (7 Kan. Reg. 1192-93 [1988]) states: "The prize money allocated to the jackpot prize category for matching six (6) of six (6) shall be divided equally by the number of game boards winning a jackpot prize." A game board is defined in K.A.R. 111-7-2(d) (7 Kan. Reg. 1192 [1988]) as "that area of the play slip which contains thirty-three (33) squares, numbered one (01) through thirty-three (33)."

The trial court looked to the provision of the Kansas Lottery Act at K.S.A. 74-8720(f) that states: "Unclaimed prize money not payable directly by lottery retailers shall be retained for the period established by rules and regulations and if no claim is made within such period, then such unclaimed prize money shall be added to the prize pools of subsequent lottery games." K.A.R. 111-6-5(e) (7 Kan. Reg. 214-15 [1988]) provides prizes must be claimed within 365 days and restates the requirement of adding unclaimed prizes to the prize pools of subsequent Kansas lottery games.

This led the trial court to the question: "Is a winner's entitlement determined by the number of tickets sold or the number of tickets presented to the lottery?" Reifschneider contends the lottery would need ticket number 16421313 to prove the existence of the other winning ticket. The trial court quoted K.A.R. 111-7-5(g): "A validated ticket shall be the only proof of a game play or plays, and the submission of a winning ticket to and receipt of the ticket by the Lottery or its authorized retailer shall be the *sole method of claiming a prize.*" This regulation relates only to the process of claiming a lottery prize and applies to the players, not to the Lottery.

The trial court held K.A.R. 111-7-5(g) does not mean the Lottery has to be in possession of the actual winning lottery tickets in order to establish their existence, which is shown by the Lottery's computer records that show the time, date, and location where winning tickets are sold and the number selected. In this case the computer records show the existence of two winning lottery tickets sold on November 26, 1994.

The trial court found the Executive Director acted within the provisions of K.A.R. 111-7-5(d) and K.S.A. 74-8720(c) in paying Reifschneider one-half of the jackpot prize and that the default of the owner of the other winning ticket does not entitle him to the entire jackpot. The court specifically held: "The amount of the prize is determined by the number of tickets sold and not by the number of tickets presented." The trial court concluded:

"This Court finds that the Petitioner has not met his burden of proving the invalidity of the Kansas Lottery's action. The Kansas Lottery has not erroneously interpreted or applied the law. Further, the Lottery's action is supported by substantial evidence and is not unreasonable, arbitrary, or capricious."

The decision of the Lottery was affirmed.

Reifschneider appeals.

He contends the final order issued by the Lottery is a clear denial of due process, that the trial court's decision is contrary to law and the rules and regulations applicable to the Lottery, and finally that he is entitled to interest on the unpaid portion of the cash lottery prize.

The scope of review of an administrative agency under the KJRA is defined in K.S.A. 77-621, which provides in applicable part:

"(a)....

(1) The burden of proving the invalidity of agency action is on the party asserting invalidity; and

....

"(c) The court shall grant relief only if it determines any one or more of the following:

...

(4) the agency has erroneously interpreted or applied the law;

....

(7) the agency action is based on a determination of fact, made or implied by the agency, that is not supported by evidence that is substantial when viewed in light of the record as a whole, which includes the agency record for judicial review, supplemented by any additional evidence received by the court under this act."

We have further held:

"The interpretation of a statute by an administrative agency charged with the responsibility of enforcing a statute is entitled to judicial deference and is called the doctrine of operative construction. Deference to an agency's interpretation is particularly appropriate when the agency is one of special competence and experience. Although an appellate court gives deference to the agency's interpretation of a statute, the final construction of a statute lies with the appellate court, and the agency's interpretation, while persuasive, is not binding on the court. Interpretation of a statute is a question of law over which an appellate court's review is unlimited." In re Appeal of United Teleservices, Inc., 983 P.2d 250 (Kan. 1999)....

In first considering Reifschneider's contention that he has been denied due process, we point out that while it was not so held in the majority opinion in *Reifschneider I,* we agree with that portion of the concurring opinion therein that states:

"The Reifschneiders contend that their due process rights are guaranteed under the Kansas Administrative Procedure Act (KAPA), K.S.A. 77-501 *et seq.* However, the KAPA applies 'only to the extent that other statutes expressly provide that the provisions of this act govern proceedings under those statutes.' K.S.A. 77-503. Nothing in the Kansas Lottery Act, K.S.A. 74-8701 *et seq.,* expressly provides that the KAPA governs proceedings regarding the Lottery. Therefore, by its own terms, the KAPA does not apply." 969 P.2d 875 (Davis, J., concurring).

With the various hearing requirements of the KAPA not implemented, we next consider if the trial court's actions in considering the Lottery's business records under a K.S.A. 77-619(a) submission require reversal herein and a full and complete hearing before the Lottery's Executive Director. We hold that under the limited and restrictive facts of this particular case, it does not.

While Reifschneider now appears to claim that only one winning ticket has been sold, that was not the argument he presented to the Lottery when he filed his claim for the additional unclaimed portion of the November 26, 1994, jackpot. He did not contend that his ticket was the only one sold with the winning number combination, but rather he argued that under the laws and regulations governing the Lottery, he was legally entitled to the money irrespective of whether a second ticket existed as long as the second ticket was never claimed.

We generally hold that a party cannot raise an issue to the district court which has not been raised at the administrative level, U.S.D. No. 500 v. Womack, 890 P.2d 1233 (Kan. App. 1995), and it is also clear that none of the exceptions to that rule found in K.S.A. 77-617(a), (b), (c), or (d) apply to this case. In addition, Reifschneider presented no valid reason in his objection to the Lottery's proffer to require a hearing and offered no evidence that would question the Lottery's records or show they were unreliable or erroneous.

It has been clear throughout these proceedings that Reifschneider's sole claim before the Lottery is a legal issue rather than a claim that his ticket was the only winning ticket sold. In his objection to the Lottery's brief, which is previously in this opinion set forth in full, he candidly states: "The only issue to be considered herein is whether a second winning ticket, allegedly sold but not presented for the available prize permits the Respondent to conclude that the remaining portion of the total prize should be returned to the prize pool." This is the sole issue that is raised, and as such it does not matter whether the trial court properly admitted the additional documents. We need not address the issue further and turn to the legal issue which is determinative of this case.

Reifschneider argues the district court erred in upholding the Lottery's decision. He contends that under the statutes and regulations governing the Lottery with regard to unclaimed prize money, he should be awarded the unclaimed half of the disputed jackpot.

We have previously set forth the standard of review and the deference which we give to agency interpretations, although such interpretations while persuasive, are not binding upon us.

K.S.A. 74-8720 is the only applicable statute concerning lottery prizes. It states, in pertinent part:

"(b) The prize to be paid or awarded for each winning ticket or share shall be paid to one natural person who is adjudged by the executive director, the director's designee or the retailer paying the prize, to be the holder of such winning ticket or share, or the person designated in writing by the holder of the winning ticket or share on a form satisfactory to the executive director, except that the prize of a deceased winner shall be paid to the duly appointed representative of the estate of such winner or to such other person or persons appearing to be legally entitled thereto.

"(c) The executive director shall award the designated prize to the holder of the ticket or share upon the validation of a claim or confirmation of a winning share. The executive director shall have the authority to make payment for prizes by any means deemed appropriate upon the validation of winning tickets or shares."

K.S.A. 74-8720(f) provides that unclaimed prize money "shall be retained for the period established by rules and regulations and if no claim is made within such period, then such unclaimed prize money shall be added to the prize pools of subsequent lottery games."

In enacting K.S.A. 74-8720, the legislature gave the Executive Director of the Lottery or his or her designee the sole authority to determine who is a holder of a winning ticket. Fowles v. Kansas State Lottery, 867 P.2d 357 (Kan. 1994). Of course, this authority is limited by the Kansas statutes and by the administrative regulations promulgated by the Lottery. See Director of Taxation v. Kansas Krude Oil Reclaiming Co., 236 Kan. 450, Syl. ¶2, 691 P.2d 1303 (1984) (stating that an administrative agency may not substitute its judgment for that of the legislature); Tew v. Topeka Police & Fire Civ. Serv. Comm'n, 237 Kan. 96, 100, 697 P.2d 1279 (1985) (stating that generally an agency may not disregard its own rules and regulations).

K.S.A. 74-8720 does not speak directly to the controversy at issue here. Therefore, it is necessary to examine the administrative regulations promulgated by the Lottery. K.S.A. 74-8710 authorizes the Kansas Lottery Commission to adopt rules and regulations governing the operation of the lottery, including the manner of selecting the winning tickets or shares and the manner of payment of prizes to the holders of winning tickets or shares. See K.S.A.1999 Supp. 74-8710(a)(2) and (3).

K.A.R. 111-7-5 (9 Kan. Reg. 986 [1990]), is one of the regulations governing Cash Lotto games such as the one in which Reifschneider participated. It provides: "The prize money allocated to the jackpot prize category for matching six (6) of six (6) shall be divided equally by the number of game boards winning a jackpot prize." K.A.R. 111-7-5(d). While this regulation provides that the prize money be divided among winning game boards, it does not answer the question of whether the tickets, in order to be classified as "winning game boards," must be claimed or merely must be sold.

Reifschneider argues that in order to qualify, the tickets must be claimed, pointing to K.A.R. 111-7-3(c) (11 Kan. Reg. 1796 [1992]), which states: "A validated ticket shall be the only proof of a game play or plays, and the submission of a winning ticket to and receipt of the ticket by the Lottery or its authorized retailer shall be the sole method of claiming a prize or prizes." The fallacy of this argument is that this regulation is directed towards the steps necessary to claim a prize rather than addressing the question of whether the prize should be divided. See *Fowles*, 254 Kan. at 560–61, 867 P.2d 357.

The Lottery argues that it was precluded from paying the remainder of the jackpot to Reifschneider because he did not meet the validation requirements set forth in K.A.R. 111-6-7 (11 Kan. Reg. 1477 [1992]). As part of the requirements for a valid ticket, K.A.R. 111-6-7(a)(7) requires that the ticket not have been previously paid. The Lottery contends that because it previously paid Reifschneider one-half of the jackpot, the ticket had been previously paid. This is disingenuous, however, as it is clear that this regulation addresses situations where a ticket is presented twice in hopes of obtaining a double recovery rather than the situation at issue here. The same may be said of the Lottery's assertion that it cannot pay Reifschneider the remaining part of the jackpot because he no longer has a winning ticket.

Nothing in the administrative regulations promulgated by the Kansas Lottery exactly addresses this situation. The Lottery's decision denying Reifschneider's claim was based on its interpretation of K.S.A. 74-8720(f), K.A.R. 111-7-5 (9 Kan. Reg. 986 [1990]), and K.A.R. 111-6-5 (7 Kan. Reg. 214 [1988]), which is a valid interpretation of the language. Under our standard of review, the Lottery's interpretation of its regulations was neither clearly erroneous nor inconsistent with the regulations. *See* Murphy v. Nelson, 921 P.2d 1225. We agree with the ruling of the Lottery and with the analysis of the district court which is previously set forth herein.

We defer to the Lottery's interpretation and hold that where two or more tickets bearing the same winning number combination are sold, the jackpot is to be split between those tickets, even in cases where one or more of the tickets go unclaimed. The trial court was correct in upholding the Lottery's determination that Reifschneider is not entitled to the remaining $177,442 in the jackpot. In accordance with K.S.A. 74-8720(f), the unclaimed prize money held by the Lottery is to be added to the prize pools of subsequent lottery games.

Affirmed.

(dissenting opinion omitted).

Notes

1. For a case similar to *Reifschneider*, *see* Fullerton v. Dep't of Rev. Servs., 714 A.2d 1203 (Conn. 1998) (when one of two winning jackpots went unclaimed, plaintiff sought to recover the unclaimed proceeds to add to his winnings. The court held that the term "winner" does not require that a winning ticket be submitted for payment. Rather, a winner is determined after the results of the drawing are known, regardless of whether the ticket is presented for payment. Lottery regulations provided for reversions of unclaimed prizes.). One characteristic of many of the cases where players sue the lottery is the court's insistence that plaintiff exhaust the administrative remedies provided by the lottery statute and regulations.

2. The complaints of lottery players take many forms; the player may claim a procedural irregularity; that he was given the wrong ticket by the lottery agent; mistakenly discarded a winning ticket; or submitted a winning ticket after the deadline. *See, e.g.,* Granton v. Wash. State Lottery Comm'n, 177 P.3d 745 (Wash. 2008) (player claimed that a "draw

break" (a ticket-buying cut off) occurred earlier than scheduled and this prevented him from buying a winning lottery ticket. Court held that it suspected case was frivolous and that because there was no ticket purchased plaintiff would not be eligible for prize.); Palese v. Del. State Lottery Office, No. CA 1546-N, 2006 WL 1875915 (Del. Ch. June 29, 2006) (buyer of lottery ticket sought to collect on a "play slip," even though the actual ticket had been allegedly destroyed in the laundry. Court concluded that an individual had to actually hold the ticket to collect and that the actions of the commission did not result in unjust enrichment, nor did commission break any promise it might have made to investigate plaintiff's claim.); Haynes v. Dep't of Lottery, 630 So. 2d 1177 (Fla. Dist. Ct. App. 1994), reh'g denied, 642 So. 2d 746 (Fla. 1994) (player claimed that either through computer malfunction or clerk error, tickets with the eventual winning numbers requested by player were not dispensed. Player had play slips with winning numbers as evidence. Court held lottery laws were clear that play slips were not valid receipts or the equivalent of tickets, and that player should have checked tickets at time purchase); Stern v. State, 512 N.Y.S.2d 580 (App. Div.), appeal dismissed, 514 N.E.2d 390 (N.Y. 1987) (player destroyed ticket after liquor store posted wrong winning numbers. The court held that player's claim was untimely and that, in any event, New York Lottery regulations exempt the Lottery from liability for tickets thrown away by mistake.); Madara v. Commonwealth, 323 A.2d 401 (Pa. Commw. Ct. 1974) (state was under no obligation to pay player for a winning ticket after the player presented the ticket two days after the submission deadline had expired.).

3. Some cases brought against lottery officials claim the lottery game was misleading, that there was a misprinted ticket, or some other mistake made by the lottery was to the player's disadvantage. See, e.g., Maffett v. Ohio Lottery Comm'n, No. 2004-09967-AD, 2005 WL 1190713 (Ohio Ct. Cl. Apr. 20, 2005) (plaintiff claimed that the rules/instructions on the ticket read "match two like prize amounts and win that prize." In fact, the game actually required the matching of 3 like prizes or two like prizes and a bell symbol. Plaintiff's ticket had neither of those combinations. The court held that the lottery commissioner properly exercised his power to void misprinted tickets.); Triano v. Div. of State Lottery, 703 A.2d 333 (N.J. Super. Ct. App. Div. 1997) (player claimed that lottery brochure induced her to buy ticket, that symbol on ticket entitled her to prize, and that lottery acted fraudulently in denying her claim; court ruled that questions relating to meaning of instructions on ticket had to be submitted first to administrative processes); Keefe v. Ohio Lottery Comm'n, No. 06AP-14, 2006 WL 1990814 (Ohio Ct. App. July 18, 2006) (lottery winner alleged breach of contract because commission awarded him $5 million instead of $6 million. The jackpot had been advertised for $5 million but the commission's website said the jackpot was for $6 million and the lottery secretary wrote $6 million on the claim form. Court held the claim form was not a contract and plaintiff's estate was only entitled to the $5 million.).

4. One source of litigation is the prohibition that exists in many states against allowing a player to assign his winnings to another. As one court declared, the justification for the prohibition is "to protect the Lottery from administrative hassles.... The regulations make clear that, once a winner has been determined, and the Lottery has begun payments pursuant to the regulations, it has no further responsibility to answer for what a lottery winner later does with his prize. Otherwise the Lottery could not rely on the determination of the winner to discharge its obligations. There could be endless administrative expense and risk of potential liability if the Lottery were required to reexamine the status of the prize winners on a regular basis." Midland States Life Ins. Co. v. Cardillo, 797 N.E.2d 11, 16 (Mass. App. Ct. 2003). Courts across the country interpreting similar anti-assignment provisions have reached the same conclusion. See, e.g., In re Koonce, 262 B.R. 850 (Bankr. D. Nev. 2001); Petition of Singer Asset Fin. Co.,

L.L.C., 714 A.2d 322 (N.J. Super. 1998) (court order sanctioning an assignment of lottery winnings is limited to circumstances of necessity); In re Meyers, 139 B.R. 858 (Bankr. N.D. Ohio 1992) (assignment of lottery prize void under Ohio law prohibiting assignment absent court order); McCabe v. Director of New Jersey Lottery Commission, 363 A.2d 387 (N.J. Super. Ct. Ch. Div. 1976) (allowing lottery winner to obtain a lump sum of money by assignment would contravene intent of state anti-assignment law); Converse v. Lottery Commission, 783 P.2d 1116 (Wash. Ct. App. 1989); Lotto Jackpot Prize of December 3, 1982 Won by Marianov, 625 A.2d 637 (Pa. 1993); In re Louisiana Lottery Corp. Grand Prize Drawing of March 21, 1992, 643 So. 2d 843 (La. Ct. App. 1994); Singer Asset Fin. Co., L.L.C. v. Bachus, 741 N.Y.S.2d 618 (N.Y. App. Div. 2002). Typical statutory language is, "Except as otherwise provided in Section 13.1, no prize, nor any portion of a prize, nor any right of any person to a prize awarded shall be assignable. Any prize, or portion thereof remaining unpaid at the death of a prize winner, may be paid to the estate of such deceased prize winner, or to the trustee under a revocable living trust established by the deceased prize winner as settlor...." 20 Ill. Comp. Stat. 1605/13 (2004).

4. Contractors and Third Parties Suing the Lottery

Hawkeye Commodity Promotions, Inc. v. Vilsack
486 F.3d 430 (8th Cir. 2007)

BENTON, Circuit Judge.

In March 2006, Iowa enacted legislation ending the TouchPlay lottery game. Hawkeye Commodity Promotions, Inc., a licensed TouchPlay retailer, tried to enjoin the law before it took effect. Hawkeye argued that the law violates the Contracts, Takings, Equal Protection, and Due Process clauses of the federal constitution. The district court ... rejected those claims. Hawkeye appeals, reiterating those claims and asserting that the district court should have admitted the deposition testimony of the president of the Iowa Lottery Authority (the Lottery). This court affirms.

I.

Following revenue shortfalls in 2000 and 2001, the Iowa General Assembly authorized the Lottery to "establish a plan to implement the deployment of pull-tab vending machines with video monitors." The Lottery then added the TouchPlay game. A TouchPlay machine is "a vending machine that dispenses or prints and dispenses lottery tickets that have been determined to be winning or losing tickets by a predetermined pool drawing machine prior to the dispensing of the tickets." Iowa Admin. Code r. 531-14.3. With flashing lights and captivating sounds, TouchPlay machines resemble slot machines. Unlike slot machines, which are random, TouchPlay is not random. Tickets are loaded into the machine electronically, and like pull-tab tickets, the outcome of each game is predetermined.

The Lottery never owned any TouchPlay machines. They were manufactured and distributed to retailers, who purchased or leased them. The Lottery contracted for the manufacture of TouchPlay machines; licensed the retailers to put them in businesses; set the number of winning tickets and the amount paid out on each machine; collected data from the machines; and split the revenue with manufacturers and retailers. TouchPlay began with 30 machines in May 2003, expanding rapidly: By April 2006, more than 6,400 machines operated at 3,800 businesses across Iowa.

Hawkeye was incorporated and capitalized solely as an Iowa TouchPlay retailer. On January 3, 2005, Hawkeye applied for an MVM (monitor vending machines) retailer license, which was issued on January 10. Accompanying the license were: a letter including a five-year revenue-sharing formula; door decals for Hawkeye's machines; and, a memo entitled "Licensing Terms and Conditions (January 2005)," summarizing the applicable laws and regulations. Hawkeye owns 724 TouchPlay machines, 581 of which operated at 187 Iowa businesses in April 2006. Hawkeye invested about $6.8 million in this venture—$4.7 million to buy the machines, and $2.1 million in start-up and operational costs.

Responding to concerns about the "proliferation of gambling," in January 2006 Governor Thomas J. Vilsack ordered a 60-day moratorium on new TouchPlay licenses while a task force studied it. In March the task force recommended restrictions to protect gambling addicts and minors. Governor Vilsack extended the moratorium "to give the Iowa Legislature time to act on the matter if it so chooses." The General Assembly passed legislation banning TouchPlay, which the Governor signed March 20 (to be codified at Iowa Code § 99G.30A(4)). The ban took effect May 4.

On April 5, Hawkeye sued for declaratory and injunctive relief, invoking the Contracts, Takings, Equal Protection, and Due Process clauses of the United States Constitution. An expedited trial occurred April 12, with testimony by affidavit. Hawkeye later moved to re-open the record to add the deposition of Dr. Edward J. Stanek, president of the Lottery. On April 26, the district court denied the motion and issued a decision. This court reviews the district court's factual findings for clear error, and its legal and constitutional conclusions de novo. Daggitt v. United Food & Commercial Workers Int'l Union, Local 304A, 245 F.3d 981, 986 (8th Cir. 2001).

II.

No state shall pass any law "impairing the Obligation of Contracts." U.S. Const. art. I, § 10, cl. 1. Hawkeye's main argument is that SF 2330 (the bill number of the TouchPlay law) "completely destroyed" Hawkeye's contracts with the Lottery, and with over 200 Iowa businesses.

Much of Hawkeye's discussion addresses its license. Hawkeye emphasizes at length that its license could not be terminated without good cause, 60 days' notice, and a hearing. Iowa Admin. Code r. 531-14.1 to -14.20. But Hawkeye's license has not been terminated; Hawkeye still has its license. The Licensing Terms and Conditions, which Hawkeye agreed to in its application, state: "If a provision in this document conflicts with an applicable statutory or regulatory provision, the statutory or regulatory provision preempts the conflicting provision in this document." The abolition of TouchPlay did not trigger the administrative rules governing Hawkeye's license.

A.

A three-part test determines whether a statute violates the Contracts Clause. "The first question is whether the state law has, in fact, operated as a substantial impairment on pre-existing contractual relationships." Equip. Mfrs. Inst. v. Janklow, 300 F.3d 842, 850 (8th Cir. 2002). This question "has three components: whether there is a contractual relationship, whether a change in law impairs that contractual relationship, and whether the impairment is substantial." Gen. Motors Corp. v. Romein, 503 U.S. 181, 186 (1992).

i.

The parties appear to assume that the existence of a contract is governed by state law. Indeed, the district court looks only to Iowa law, finding an implied-in-fact unilateral contract of indefinite duration, which either party could cancel at any time. See *Hawkeye*, 432 F. Supp.2d at 843–46. But "whether a contract was made is a federal question for purposes of Contract Clause analysis." *Romein*, 503 U.S. at 187, (citing Irving Trust Co. v. Day, 314 U.S. 556, 561 (1942)).

In Stone v. Mississippi, 101 U.S. 814 (1879), the Supreme Court rejected a private company's Contracts Clause challenge to the state's cancellation of its lottery charter. Any one, therefore, who accepts a lottery charter does so with the implied understanding that the people, in their sovereign capacity, and through their properly constituted agencies, may resume it at any time when the public good shall require, whether it be paid for or not. All that one can get by such a charter is a suspension of certain governmental rights in his favor, subject to withdrawal at will. He has in legal effect nothing more than a license to enjoy the privilege on the terms named for the specified time, unless it be sooner abrogated by the sovereign power of the State. It is a permit, good as against existing laws, but subject to further legislative and constitutional control or withdrawal.... In Douglas v. Kentucky, 168 U.S. 488, 502 (1897), the Supreme Court said flatly, "a lottery grant is not, in any sense, a contract within the meaning of the Constitution of the United States, but is simply a gratuity and license, which the State, under its police powers, and for the protection of the public morals, may at any time revoke, and forbid the further conduct of the lottery." ...

Stone and *Douglas* are clear: A lottery "grant" or "charter" is not protected by the Contracts Clause. Hawkeye responds that *Stone* and *Douglas*, while "certainly good law," involve "an entirely different circumstance." On the contrary, *Stone* and *Douglas* are not distinguishable: in both cases, the legislature allowed a private party to operate a lottery, which was later nullified (in *Stone*, by the state's Reconstruction constitution; in *Douglas*, by act of the legislature and then by amendment to the state constitution). That fairly describes the history of TouchPlay in Iowa. Whatever agreement existed between Hawkeye and the Lottery is not protected by the Contracts Clause of the federal constitution.

ii.

As to the location contracts, it is undisputed on appeal—and this court decides—that they are contracts within the Contracts Clause, and are impaired by SF 2330. This court therefore asks whether the impairment of Hawkeye's contracts—with its locations and with the Lottery (assuming the district court is correct that they are protected by the Contracts Clause)—is substantial.

iii.

Substantial impairment depends on "the extent to which the [parties'] reasonable contract expectations have been disrupted. Reasonable expectations are affected by the regulated nature of an industry in which a party is contracting." In re Workers' Comp. Refund, 46 F.3d 813, 819 (8th Cir. 1995) (citations omitted). "In determining the extent of the impairment, we are to determine whether the industry the complaining party has entered has been regulated in the past." Energy Reserves Group v. Kan. Power & Light Co., 459 U.S. 400, 411 (1983).

Like Hawkeye, the public utility in Energy Reserves was "operating in a heavily regulated industry. State authority to regulate natural gas prices is well established." *Id.* at 414 (citations omitted). State authority to regulate gambling is similarly well-established: "No one would question that [the State] has the power to regulate gambling in the interest of the public health, safety, and general welfare." Neb. Messenger Servs. Ass'n v. Thone, 611 F.2d 250, 251–52 (8th Cir. 1979) (quoting the district court to uphold a Nebraska statute prohibiting service fees on pari-mutual betting against federal constitutional challenges).

In this case, the contracts themselves demonstrate Hawkeye's diminished contract expectations. The location contracts provide:

> In consideration of the sum of $10.00, Proprietor hereby grants unto HCP [Hawkeye] the exclusive right for five (5) years to install and maintain all Monitor Vending Machines, Lottery TouchPlay, and lottery vending machines *as may be allowed by law or promulgated regulation....*

(emphasis added)

In regard to any agreement with the Lottery, the Licensing Terms and Conditions memorandum that Hawkeye agreed to in January 2005 state at the top of the first page:

> The provisions of Iowa Code chapter 99G, 531 Iowa Administrative Code, and any other applicable statutory or regulatory provisions are herein incorporated by reference. If a provision in this document conflicts with an applicable statutory or regulatory provision, the statutory or regulatory provisions preempts the conflicting provision in this document.

Likewise, the contracts in Energy Reserves "expressly recognize the existence of extensive regulation by providing that any contractual terms are subject to relevant present and future state and federal law." *Id.* at 416. This court holds that, like the plaintiff in *Energy Reserves*, Hawkeye's "reasonable expectations have not been impaired." *Id.* SF 2330 does not substantially impair any Lottery or location contracts. Hawkeye's Contracts Clause argument fails on the first prong of *Janklow*.

B.

Alternatively, assuming a substantial impairment, the second and third prongs of the Contracts Clause analysis come into play. The second prong of the three-part test is whether the state has a "significant and legitimate public purpose behind the regulation." *Janklow*, 300 F.3d at 850. If, as Hawkeye claims, "the State offers no significant and legitimate public purpose for abolishing TouchPlay while continuing all other lottery games," then SF 2330 is unconstitutional under the Contract Clause. The state has the burden to show this purpose. *Id.* at 859–60.

The state identifies the need "to curb the expansion of gambling" as the purpose of SF 2330. Gambling is illegal in Iowa. Iowa Code § 725.7. Gambling in Iowa is permissible only if authorized by a specific statutory exception. *See, e.g.,* Iowa Code §§ 725.14, .15 (ban on gambling does not apply to pari-mutual betting regulated by the state racing and gaming commission, or to state lottery games regulated by the Iowa Lottery Authority). Existing at the sufferance of the Legislature, gambling is a heavily regulated industry in Iowa. See Iowa Code §§ 99G.1–.42; Iowa Admin. Code r. 531-1.1 to -20.23. The regulation of gambling—including its expansion and contraction—is a significant and legitimate public purpose for SF 2330.

The third prong is "whether the adjustment of the 'rights and responsibilities of contracting parties [is based] upon reasonable conditions and [is] of a character appropriate to the public purpose justifying [the legislation's] adoption.'" *Janklow*, 300 F.3d at 850 (alteration in original). This court finds that it is. TouchPlay began with 30 machines in bars and fraternal clubs in May 2003. Within three years, more than 6,400 machines functioned in nearly 3,000 Iowa business of all sorts, including grocery stores, restaurants, gas stations, truck stops, convenience stores, bowling alleys, and laundromats. As Touch-Play expanded, the public became concerned about protecting minors and compulsive gamblers. A state's police power encompasses controlling gambling, even to the point of abolishing a particular lottery game. *See, e.g., Stone*, 101 U.S. at 818, 11 Otto 814 (the police power "extends to all matters affecting the public health or the public morals. Neither can it be denied that lotteries are proper subjects for the exercise of this power.") (citations omitted); *Douglas*, 168 U.S. at 502; *Neb. Messenger*, 611 F.2d at 251–52.

Iowa's abolition of TouchPlay does not violate the Contracts Clause.

III.

Private property shall not "be taken for public use, without just compensation." U.S. Const. amend. V. Hawkeye considers SF 2330 a legislative taking of its property (i.e., the TouchPlay machines, its overall "business," the Lottery contract, and the location contracts).

A.

First, Hawkeye must show property interests protected by the Takings Clause.... The Constitution "protects rather than creates property interests." ... This court therefore looks to Iowa law to evaluate Hawkeye's property interests. *See* Bd. of Regents of State Colls. v. Roth, 408 U.S. 564, 577 (1972) ("the existence of a property interest is determined by reference to 'existing rules or understandings that stem from an independent source such as state law.'").

No doubt the machines are property under the Takings Clause. Hawkeye also claims a property interest in its TouchPlay business, and continued operation of its enterprise. The district court finds (and the state does not dispute) that Hawkeye "has some property interest" in the business itself. *Hawkeye*, 432 F. Supp.2d at 852 (citing Kimball Laundry Co. v. United States, 338 U.S. 1, 5 (1949) (Takings Clause protects "intangible" business assets like trade routes, goodwill, and earning power)).

As to the continued operation of the business, Hawkeye's participation in TouchPlay required an MVM license. "The possession of an MVM license ... is a privilege personal to that person or entity and is not a legal right." Iowa Admin. Code r. 531-14.12. As the district court explains, because Hawkeye's MVM license cannot be sold, assigned, or transferred, it "lacks the indicia of a property interest." See Iowa Admin Code r. 531-14.6 ("MVM licenses may not be transferred to any other person or entity...."). See generally Cent. States Theatre Corp. v. Sar, 66 N.W.2d 450, 455 (Iowa 1954) ("when a business is inherently illegal [e.g., liquor, tobacco] a permit to operate may be granted or refused at the will of the licensing body, is a privilege rather than a property right") (bracketed text added); Smith v. Iowa Liquor Control Comm'n, 169 N.W.2d 803, 807 (Iowa 1969) (upholding the revocation of a liquor license because "a license to sell beer, is a privilege granted by the state and is in no sense a property right."); ... Hawkeye does not have a property right in the continuation of its TouchPlay business for Takings Clause purposes.

As to Hawkeye's property-in-contracts argument, the district court holds that because the location contracts "allow for termination of the contract due to a change in law or regulation," they "do not constitute a property interest for the purposes of the takings clause." Hawkeye, 432 F.Supp.2d at 854. The January 2005 Licensing Terms and Conditions say, "If a provision in this document conflicts with an applicable statutory or regulatory provision, the statutory or regulatory provisions preempts the conflicting provision in this document." Contract rights are "a form of private property" in Iowa, but to qualify as a "protectable property interest" under the Takings Clause, "a contract must establish rights more substantial in nature than a mere unilateral expectation of continued rights or benefits." Crippen v. City of Cedar Rapids, 618 N.W.2d 562, 572 (Iowa 2000). Hawkeye's expectation that its contracts would not be modified or nullified by the state is undermined by: (1) its participation in a heavily regulated industry (gambling); (2) the "as may be allowed by law or promulgated regulation" language in the location contracts; (3) the analogous language in the Licensing Terms and Conditions; and, (4) the experience of its owners with South Carolina's video-poker ban. *See* Armstrong v. Collins, 621 S.E.2d 368 (S.C. 2005). Hawkeye's contracts are not a cognizable property interest under Iowa law for Takings Clause purposes.

B.

Having identified Hawkeye's property interests (the machines and the TouchPlay business itself), the issue becomes whether Hawkeye suffered a taking without just compensation. Two kinds of takings are: (1) per se, involving the "direct government appropriation of or physical invasion of private property"; and (2) regulatory, where a regulation affecting private property "goes too far." Lingle v. Chevron U.S.A., Inc., 544 U.S. 528, 537–38 (2005) (quoting Pa. Coal Co. v. Mahon, 260 U.S. 393, 415 (1922)).

This case is not a per se taking. Hawkeye did not suffer a "permanent physical invasion." ... Nor does the statute constitute a total regulatory taking in which Hawkeye has "been called upon to sacrifice all economically beneficial uses in the name of the common good." Lucas v. S.C. Coastal Council, 505 U.S. 1003, 1019 (1992) (emphasis in original). The parties dispute whether *Lucas* applies to non-real property. The district court holds that it does not. *Hawkeye*, 432 F. Supp.2d at 855. *Lucas* involved land, not personal property. And the Court in *Lucas* recognized that landowners have different expectations than owners of personal property about the potential impact of government regulation:

> "And in the case of personal property, by virtue of the state's traditionally high degree of control over commercial dealings, he ought to be aware of the possibility that new regulation might even render his property economically worthless (at least if the property's only economically productive use is sale or manufacture for sale)."

Id. at 1027–28.... Thus, it appears that Lucas protects real property only.

Even if Lucas applies to non-real property, Hawkeye still owns working TouchPlay machines. Even without TouchPlay, Hawkeye may take them to another state (or nation) that allows monitor-vending-machine gambling. Hawkeye's President states in an affidavit that the machines "have virtually no market value outside Iowa." But the district court finds that Hawkeye "could sell TouchPlay machines (e.g. salvage value) or reconfigure the TouchPlay machines for a different use." *Hawkeye*, 432 F. Supp.2d at 856 [footnote omitted]. SF 2330 did not deprive Hawkeye of "all economically beneficial uses" of its property.

Hawkeye next proposes that SF 2330 is a regulatory taking without just compensation under Penn Central Transportation Co. v. New York City, 438 U.S. 104 (1978). *Penn Central* provides "no set formula" to determine when the Fifth Amendment requires compensation. "Whether a particular restriction amounts to a taking depends on the circumstances of each case." Outdoor Graphics, Inc. v. City of Burlington, 103 F.3d 690, 694 (8th Cir. 1996). Factors to consider in this "ad hoc, factual inquiry" include: "(1) the economic impact of the regulation on the claimant; (2) the extent to which the regulation has interfered with distinct, investment-backed expectations; and (3) the character of the government regulation." Id. The first two factors are "primary"; the third "may be relevant in determining whether a taking has occurred." *Lingle*, 544 U.S. at 538–39. Weighing the *Penn Central* factors, the district court concludes that "the cost of banning Touch-Play machines must not be borne by the public." *Hawkeye*, 432 F. Supp.2d at 858. This court agrees. As to the first prong, SF 2330 had a "devastating economic impact" on its multi-million-dollar TouchPlay investment. But in terms of the second prong, Hawkeye's expectations in its TouchPlay business are discounted by: (1) the heavily regulated nature of gambling in Iowa; (2) the "as may be allowed by law or promulgated regulation" language in the location contracts; (3) the statement in the Licensing Terms and Conditions that, "If a provision in this document conflicts with an applicable statutory or regulatory provision, the statutory or regulatory provisions preempts the conflicting provision in this document"; and, (4) the owners' experience with South Carolina's video-poker ban. No doubt Hawkeye hoped that the Legislature would not stringently regulate or abolish TouchPlay before calendar year 2009 when it would have recouped its investment. However, a "'reasonable investment-backed expectation' must be more than a 'unilateral expectation or an abstract need.'" *Ruckelshaus*, 467 U.S. at 1005.

As to the third prong, the district court is correct that SF 2330 "will only prevent a specific use of TouchPlay Machines," and that usage is "a single stick in the bundle of property rights." *Hawkeye*, 432 F.Supp.2d at 857. SF 2330 may deprive Hawkeye's Touch-Play machines of their most immediately profitable use, but Hawkeye still "has the right to possess, lease and sell" the machines. *Id.* As to Hawkeye's business, Hawkeye can still use its trade routes and goodwill in any legal business other than TouchPlay. Under *Penn Central*, SF 2330 is not a regulatory taking of Hawkeye's property.

IV.

States shall not deprive any person of "life, liberty, or property, without due process of law", or of "the equal protection of the laws." U.S. Const. amend. XIV, § 1. Hawkeye argues that SF 2330 violates both provisions.

A.

"When an equal protection claim is neither based on a 'suspect class' or grounded in a fundamental right, it is subject to a rational basis review." Gilmore v. County of Douglas, 406 F.3d 935, 937 (8th Cir. 2005). SF 2330 implicates neither. For social and economic legislation like SF 2330, "the Equal Protection Clause allows the States wide latitude, and the Constitution presumes that even improvident decisions will eventually be rectified by the democratic process." City of Cleburne v. Cleburne Living Ctr., 473 U.S. 432, 440 (1985). As to SF 2330, therefore, the Constitution requires merely that "there is a plausible public policy reason for the classification, the legislative facts on which the classification is apparently based may have been considered to be true by the governmental decisionmaker, and the relationship of the classification to its goal is not so attenuated as to render the distinction arbitrary or irrational." Nordlinger v. Hahn, 505 U.S. 1, 11 (1992).

First, Hawkeye must show that it is "similarly situated to another group for purposes of the challenged government action." Carter v. Arkansas, 392 F.3d 965, 969 (8th Cir. 2004). Hawkeye contends that TouchPlay is similar to all other lottery games, and even to non-lottery amusement devices that dispense tickets redeemable for prizes instead of cash. The district court concludes otherwise. *Hawkeye*, 432 F. Supp.2d at 860. But the district court allows that "even if" TouchPlay is sufficiently similar to other forms of gambling that SF 2330 does not affect, Hawkeye still must negate "'every conceivable basis which might support' the classification." *Id.* (quoting *Gilmore*, 406 F.3d at 939).

Hawkeye claims that "Appellees have been unable to offer" a reason for banning Touch-Play. To the contrary, the Governor imposed a moratorium on new TouchPlay licenses because of concerns about the "proliferation of gambling," and appointed a task force to study ways to protect minors and compulsive gamblers. Regulating gambling is a legitimate public purpose. The Legislature chose to ban TouchPlay entirely. The district court is correct that this "incremental reform of the gaming industry" is not "so attenuated to its asserted purpose that the distinction it draws is wholly arbitrary and irrational." *Id.*; *Nordlinger*, 505 U.S. at 11.

Hawkeye also attacks the district court's speculation that "perhaps" the purpose of SF 2330 "might have been" "in part" TouchPlay's "inadequate safeguards." *Id.* The Equal Protection Clause "does not demand for the purpose of rational-basis review that a legislature or governing decision maker actually articulate at any time the purpose or rationale supporting its classification." *Nordlinger*, 505 U.S. at 15. Hawkeye cites statistics that most compulsive gambling happens in casinos, and that there are only two confirmed cases of minors using TouchPlay machines. But "a legislative choice is not subject to courtroom fact-finding and may be based on rational speculation unsupported by evidence or empirical data." FCC v. Beach Communications, Inc., 508 U.S. 307, 315 (1993). The district court properly rejects Hawkeye's equal protection claim.

B.

Hawkeye asserts that SF 2330 also "cannot satisfy rational basis review" under the Due Process Clause. The burden is on Hawkeye "to establish that the legislature has acted in an arbitrary or irrational way." Koster v. City of Davenport, 183 F.3d 762, 768 (8th Cir. 1999). As discussed, SF 2330 is neither arbitrary nor irrational, and serves a legitimate public purpose. Hawkeye's due process argument fails....

VI.

The judgment of the district court is affirmed.

Notes

1. Despite the success of the state in the federal court litigation in the TouchPlay case, state court litigation threatened the state with the potential for paying significant damages. After a state trial court judge refused to grant summary judgment for the state and a number of the TouchPlay cases were headed for trial, a series of settlements were reached between the state and various vendors and MVM interests. The state ended up paying over $15.5 million to settle the cases. *See* Jeff Eckhoff, State Moves Toward Settlement With 32 Touchplay Operators, Des Moines Register, July 18, 2008, *available at* http://m.dm-register.com/news.jsp?key=288152 (last visited June 7, 2010); William Petroski, Touchplay Suits Are Winding Down, Des Moines Register, Aug. 8, 2008, *available at* http://m.dm-register.com/news.jsp?key=297981 (last visited June 7, 2010).

For a description of the events relating to the creation of the TouchPlay game and its elimination, *see* Keith C. Miller, *The Iowa Lottery's TouchPlay Debacle*, 11 GAMING L. REV. 88 (2007).

2. A common element of many of these disputes is the deference courts give to the relevant state legislature to make changes to gambling laws solely because of political considerations. Is this deference wise, given that private investors would be justifiably reluctant to partner with the state if the state could change course without consequence? If the state is not viewed as a reliable partner, might these decisions have the long-term effect of chilling private investment in the lottery when it is needed?

5. Lottery Player v. Lottery Player

Sokaitis v. Bakaysa

975 A.2d 51 (Conn. 2009)

ZARELLA, J.

The dispositive issue in this appeal is whether General Statutes § 52-553[2] applies to, and makes void, a contract entered into by the plaintiff, Theresa Sokaitis, and the defendant, Rose Bakaysa, to share equally the proceeds of their legal gambling activities. On appeal, the defendant challenges the Appellate Court's determination that the contract between the parties was not covered by § 52-553. We affirm the judgment of the Appellate Court.

The following undisputed factual and procedural history, as set forth in the Appellate Court's opinion, are relevant to our disposition of this appeal. "On April 12, 1995, the plaintiff and the defendant, who are sisters, created and signed a written agreement. The agreement stated: 'This is a letter of agreement between [the defendant] and [the plaintiff]. This letter is dated on 4/12/95. This letter states that we are partners in any winning we shall receive, to be shared [equally]. (Such as slot machines, cards, at Foxwoods Casino, and [lottery] tickets, etc.).'" On June 20, 2005, a winning Powerball lottery ticket, worth $500,000, from the June 18, 2005 drawing was presented to the Connecticut lottery officials for payout. The winning ticket was presented by Joseph F. Troy, Sr., the brother of the parties, who indicated that he held the ticket jointly with the defendant. Lottery officials paid Troy and the defendant each $249,999, less federal tax withholding. The defendant did not provide the plaintiff with any portion of the lottery winnings.

"As a result, on August 19, 2005, the plaintiff brought an action against the defendant for breach of contract. The plaintiff sought money damages equal to [one-half] of the defendant's Powerball winnings plus interest. On August 17, 2006, the defendant filed a motion for summary judgment, alleging that there was no genuine issue of material fact and that the agreement on which the plaintiff was suing was unenforceable under § 52-553, thereby entitling the defendant to judgment as a matter of law. On September 14, 2006, the court granted the defendant's motion for summary judgment and rendered judgment in the defendant's favor." Sokaitis v. Bakaysa, 938 A.2d 1278 (Conn. App. 2008).

The plaintiff appealed to the Appellate Court, which reversed the trial court's judgment, concluding that § 52-553 is not applicable to the parties' agreement because the agreement was not a wagering contract within the terms of the statute. Id., at 666, 938 A.2d 1278. The Appellate Court reached this conclusion by examining the contract and determining that "the plaintiff and the defendant promised to share equally in any winnings they received from various forms of legalized gambling, including the lottery. They did not make promises that were induced by the consideration of 'money ... won ... at any game [pursuant to § 52-553]....' Therefore, the consideration for the agreement was not

---

2. General Statutes § 52-553 provides: "All wagers, and all contracts and securities of which the whole or any part of the consideration is money or other valuable thing won, laid or bet, at any game, horse race, sport or pastime, and all contracts to repay any money knowingly lent at the time and place of such game, race, sport or pastime, to any person so gaming, betting or wagering, or to repay any money lent to any person who, at such time and place, so pays, bets or wagers, shall be void, provided nothing in this section shall (1) affect the validity of any negotiable instrument held by any person who acquired the same for value and in good faith without notice of illegality in the consideration, or (2) apply to the sale of a raffle ticket pursuant to section 7-172."

the money that they won but rather their mutual promises to one another to share in any winnings they received." *Id.,* at 667, 938 A.2d 1278. This certified appeal followed.

On appeal to this court, the defendant claims that the Appellate Court improperly determined that the parties' contract was not within the proscriptive reach of § 52-553. She asserts that the Appellate Court mischaracterized the consideration supporting the contract which, she claims, was indeed "money … won … at any game.…" General Statutes § 52-553. The plaintiff, on the other hand, urges this court to uphold the judgment of the Appellate Court, arguing that the Appellate Court's determination that the parties' contract was not a wagering contract as defined by § 52-553 was correct.

The plaintiff also offers two closely related alternative grounds for affirmance should this court conclude that the parties' contract was indeed a wagering contract. First, the plaintiff argues that § 52-553 simply is not applicable to wagering contracts involving legal forms of gambling because such activities do not run afoul of this state's public policy against gambling. Second, the plaintiff argues that the statute is inapplicable to the contract at issue because § 52-553 has been implicitly repealed by subsequent legislation legalizing various forms of gambling to the extent that it may not be applied to void agreements to share winnings from legal forms of gambling. The plaintiff asserts that any other interpretation of § 52-553 would make it irreconcilable with the legislature's decision to alter public policy and to enact statutes legalizing certain forms of gambling. We agree with the plaintiff that the parties' agreement is not governed by § 52-553 and affirm the judgment of the Appellate Court, albeit on different grounds.… (footnote omitted).

The principle of legislative consistency is vital to our consideration of the subject statute's "relationship to existing legislation … governing the same subject matter.…" *Id.,* at 182, 914 A.2d 533. "[T]he legislature is always presumed to have created a harmonious and consistent body of law.… [T]his tenet of statutory construction … requires [this court] to read statutes together when they relate to the same subject matter.… Accordingly, [i]n determining the meaning of a statute … we look not only at the provision at issue, but also to the broader statutory scheme to ensure the coherency of our construction.… [T]he General Assembly is always presumed to know all the existing statutes and the effect that its action or [nonaction] will have upon any one of them" (internal quotation marks omitted). Stone-Krete Construction, Inc. v. Eder, 280 Conn. 672, 678, 911 A.2d 300 (2006). Thus, in considering whether § 52-553 is applicable to the parties' contract in the present case, we are bound to consider the existence of other statutes and regulations concerning gambling in order to ensure that our construction of the statute makes sense within the overall legislative scheme.

With these principles in mind, we turn to an examination of the statute at issue. In accordance with the mandate of § 1-2z that we consider the relationship of § 52-553 to other statutes in discerning its meaning, we note that a literal reading of the statute results in several conflicts with other, more recent, statutes related to legal wagering. The statute first declares that "[a]ll wagers … shall be void.…" General Statutes § 52-553. Clearly, this cannot be the absolute law of a state that has authorized the operation of a lottery; see General Statutes §§ 12-800 through 12-818; the establishment of off-track betting facilities; see General Statutes § 12-571a; pari-mutuel betting at licensed events; see General Statutes § 12-575; and the operation of jai alai frontons; see General Statutes § 12-573a. *See generally* Hilton International Co. v. Arace, 35 Conn. Supp. 522, 527–28, 394 A.2d 739 (1977) (Appellate Session of Superior Court explaining that authorization of various forms of legalized gambling has "attenuated" and "ero[ded]" public policy against gambling). Moreover, the legislature has entered into tribal-state compacts with the Mashantucket Pequot Tribal Nation and the Mohegan Tribe of Indians of Connecticut to administer the operation of casinos on tribal lands at which many forms of gambling occur. See General

Statutes §§ 12-586f and 12-586g. It is beyond peradventure that the laws of the state of Connecticut permit many forms of wagering. Thus, it cannot be that § 52-553 truly prohibits or makes unenforceable "[a]ll wagers," as such a reading of the statute is irreconcilable with this state's various forms of legalized wagering.[4] Thus, at least with respect to the act of wagering, § 52-553 can only be read sensibly to include the implicit caveat "except as otherwise provided by law."[5]

The second provision of the statute proves to be equally inconsistent with the legalized wagering provisions, without the implicit caveat "except as otherwise provided by law." In addition to prohibiting "[a]ll wagers," § 52-553 also makes void "all contracts ... of which the whole or any part of the consideration is money ... won, laid or bet, at any game, horse race, sport or pastime...." Read literally, this portion of the statute would prevent many forms of legal wagering, which involve an express or implied contract under which the consideration is "money ... bet," such as pari-mutuel wagering, casino gaming and even the lottery. Although perhaps not often stated explicitly, every legal wager is, in essence, a gambling contract. For example, the purchase of a lottery ticket represents a contract between the purchaser and the state lottery corporation, pursuant to which the purchaser wagers the purchase price of the ticket in exchange for a promise that, should a particular set of numbers be chosen, he will win a specified prize. See Talley v. Mathis, 453 S.E.2d 704 (Ga. 1995) (lottery is gambling contract between state and player). The parties to the gambling contract have agreed to "engage in a gamble"; Black's Law Dictionary (9th Ed.2009); the consideration for which, on the bettor's side, is "money ... bet...." General Statutes § 52-553; ....

---

4. In a 2003 amendment to § 52-553, the legislature found it necessary to exempt explicitly "the sale of a raffle ticket pursuant to § 7-172" from the operation of § 52-553. Public Acts 2003, No. 03-60, § 2. The legislative history clearly indicates that the purpose of this exemption was to allow the purchase of raffle tickets with a credit card, a form of wagering on credit. The remarks of Senator David J. Cappiello in support of the amendment make this clear: "As many of you already know, Connecticut is one of the only states that does not allow the use of a credit card to purchase raffle tickets.... [T]hey can go to the casinos and gamble with their credit cards, but for some reason, they cannot use them because of an antiquated 1940s law to purchase raffle tickets.... I urge you to please pass this law." Conn. Joint Standing Committee Hearings, Public Safety, Pt. 1, 2003 Sess., pp. 10–11. Senator Ernest E. Newton's remarks on the floor of the Senate are similarly illuminating: "Basically what this bill does, it allows organizations, nonprofits, an opportunity to use credit cards to [sell] raffle tickets and the nonprofit organizations really need this tool to help them in their fundraising efforts." 46 S. Proc., Pt. 6, 2003 Sess., p. 1886. Representative Stephen D. Dargan expressed the same understanding in the House of Representatives: "[B]asically what this bill will do, it will permit nonprofits to [sell] raffle tickets with a debit or credit card...." 46 H.R. Proc., Pt. 10, 2003 Sess., p. 3148. This legislative commentary bolsters our interpretation of § 52-553 as allowing wagering contracts, even those made on credit under certain circumstances, when the underlying gambling activity itself is legal. We surmise that the legislature has not substantively overhauled § 52-553 because, despite its erosion in recent years, the public policy and positive laws of this state remain opposed to all forms of unregulated gambling; see, e.g., General Statutes § 53-278b (criminalizing gambling generally); and making contracts facilitating illegal gambling unenforceable is both consistent with and supportive of this policy.

5. In reality, this is merely another way of saying that the more specific and recent statutes authorizing certain forms of wagering represent a partial, implicit repeal of the inconsistent aspects of § 52-553. "So far as pre-existing [statutory] provisions, by their repugnancy or inconsistency, stand in the way of the full and effective operation of the final expressed will of the legislature, they stand, in law, as pro tanto repealed. Not only is this true of those provisions which are on their face inconsistent with the [more recent statutes], but of any others which upon examination and analysis are found to hamper or interfere with its workability." Connelly v. Bridgeport, 104 Conn. 238, 253, 132 A. 690 (1926). Thus, to the extent that § 52-553 is inconsistent or interferes with the various statutes authorizing gambling, we conclude that it implicitly has been repealed.

If such a contract were to be deemed unenforceable under the broad language of § 52-553, we presume that the Connecticut Lottery Corporation would quickly find itself bereft of clientele. We must infer, therefore, in the course of construing this statute within the broader context of those statutes authorizing various forms of legalized gambling, that the legislature intended to exempt from the operation of § 52-553 those contracts supported by consideration in the form of money won or bet in the course of *legal* gambling.[7]

Indeed, an examination of General Statutes §§ 53-278a and 53-278b, the statutes defining and criminalizing "'[g]ambling,'" respectively, strongly supports our understanding of § 52-553. Section 53-278a (2) defines "'[g]ambling,'" in relevant part, as "risking any ... thing of value for gain contingent in whole or in part upon lot, chance or the operation of a gambling device, including the playing of a casino gambling game such as blackjack, poker, craps, roulette or a slot machine, but *does not include ... other acts or transactions expressly authorized by law* on or after October 1, 1973...." (emphasis added). Section 53-278b makes engaging in gambling a class B misdemeanor. When reading § 53-278b together with § 52-553, it is clear that, in combination, these statutes are intended both to criminalize gambling not otherwise authorized by law, and to deter illicit gambling by rendering all contracts facilitating such activities void and unenforceable. It stands to reason, therefore, that the legislature intended § 52-553 to be construed consistently with §§ 53-278a and 53-278b and to be applied only to contracts related to *illegal* gambling. Reading these related statutes in this manner is not only consistent with the mandate of § 1-2z but also serves to explain the continued existence and usefulness of § 52-553 in an age of pervasive legalized gambling.

Finally, § 52-553 provides in relevant part: "[A]ll contracts to repay any money knowingly lent at the time and place of such game, race, sport or pastime, to any person so gaming, betting or wagering, or to repay any money lent to any person who, at such time and place, so pays, bets or wagers, shall be void...." This provision prohibits the enforcement of contracts facilitating any type of gambling on credit, and largely has remained untouched by the legislature's "substantial inroads into the public policy against gambling"; Casanova Club v. Bisharat, 458 A.2d 1 (Conn. 1983); represented by its sanctioning of certain forms of legalized gambling. Indeed, this court has recognized that "[n]one of these statutes ... permits gambling on credit, and that is the vice at which the underlying statutes forbidding wagering contracts; General Statutes §§ 52-553 and 52-554; are particularly directed." *Id.* Even this core provision is not absolutely sacrosanct, however, as the legislature specifically has authorized a form of gambling on credit by permitting the use of credit cards to purchase raffle tickets under § 52-553. See footnote 4 of this opinion. Thus, even this part of the statute must be read to include an implicit caveat in order to remain consistent with the other legalized gambling statutes.

It is noteworthy that both the Connecticut Lottery Corporation and the state tax laws explicitly recognize that lottery winnings may be shared by agreement, and provide guidelines and forms regulating and taxing such shared winnings.[9] Indeed, the defendant and

---

7. We note, as the Appellate Court did, that there exists serious doubt as to whether the parties' agreement in this case constitutes a gambling contract within the common definition of that term. See footnote 6 of this opinion. We need not reach this issue, however, because we conclude that § 52-553 does not apply to the agreement in question in any case.

9. Section 12-705(b)-2 (e)(2) of the Regulations of Connecticut State Agencies provides: "If more than one individual is entitled to a share of the gambling winnings, one federal Form 5754 (Statement by a Person(s) Receiving Gambling Winnings) shall be completed, identifying each of the persons entitled to a share. Form 5754 is also used when the recipient is an individual not entitled to a share. This Form lists the name, address, and taxpayer identification number of all individuals enti-

her brother completed federal Form 5754 in the present case, indicating that they were entitled to equal shares of the lottery winnings. It certainly would be extraordinary for the legislature to permit the existence of regulations that facilitate the sharing of lottery winnings if private agreements to divide such winnings were barred by §52-553. We are persuaded that the legislature intended no such conflict, and we are bound to interpret §52-553 so as to avoid it if reasonably possible. *See* Stone-Krete Construction, Inc. v. Eder, *supra*, 280 Conn. at 678, 911 A.2d 300.

Construing the statute in light of the foregoing, we conclude that the parties' agreement in the present case, even if it is a wagering contract, is not governed by §52-553. The defendant has not offered an alternative interpretation of §52-553 that would make it consistent with the legislature's policy of permitting some forms of regulated gambling. Nevertheless, the defendant asserts that this court's decision in Ciampittiello v. Campitello, 134 Conn. 51, 54 A.2d 669 (1947), supports her position that the purported contract with the plaintiff is "void in Connecticut as pernicious and contravening Connecticut's deep-rooted public policy opposing gambling contracts." We believe *Ciampittiello* is distinguishable and that the defendant's reliance on the case, therefore, is misplaced.

The contract at issue in *Ciampittiello* was an agreement between two brothers to share equally in any proceeds or losses incurred as a result of pari-mutuel betting conducted by the parties on horse races over the course of several days. *Id.*, at 53, 54 A.2d 669. The agreement was made, and the wagering conducted, in Rhode Island, where wagering on horse races was legal. *Id.*, at 53–54, 54 A.2d 669. The reasoning this court employed in determining that the contract was valid in Rhode Island is instructive: "The agreement to share the proceeds of the gaming was a legal contract where it was made. Pari-mutuel betting on horse races is lawful in Rhode Island...." *Id.*, at 54, 54 A.2d 669. This statement suggests that the brothers' agreement to share their winnings was valid, at least in part, because the underlying wagering was legal. This surmise is further supported by the court's subsequent statement: "The defendant does not claim that such wagering is lawful in Connecticut but contends that our public policy does not prevent the enforcement of the claim by our courts." *Id.* Again, this statement suggests, at least implicitly, that the court's conflict of laws analysis hinged primarily on the legality of the underlying gambling activity, giving the distinct impression that, had the wagering been legal in Connecticut, the court would have been inclined to enforce the foreign contract.

Our reading of *Ciampittiello* also is buttressed by the fact that, when the decision was released in 1947, there was no legalized gambling in this state. Furthermore, not only had "[r]epeated efforts to legalize pari-mutuel betting in [Connecticut] ... failed"; *id.*, at 55, 54 A.2d 669; but betting on horse racing was actually a crime under General Statutes (1930 Rev.) §6316. *Id.* This court went so far as to declare that "[s]ince the establishment of our government wagering has been held to be, if not absolutely immoral, yet so injurious in its results as to require suppression by penal legislation" (internal quotation marks omitted). *Id.*, at 56, 54 A.2d 669. Thus, in *Ciampittiello*, we relied on this state's "ancient and deep-rooted public policy" against all forms of gambling; *id.*, at 57, 54 A.2d 669; and held that the parties' agreement to share their winnings was unenforceable in Connecticut because enforcing it "would violate some fundamental principle of justice, some preva-

---

tled to any share of the winnings. In the event the identity or residence of any individual entitled to share in the winnings cannot be satisfactorily established by the individual receiving the winnings, the share of the winnings to which such individual is entitled shall be considered to have been won by a resident of Connecticut and the income tax shall be withheld. The Form shall be signed, under penalties of perjury, by the individual(s) receiving the winnings."

lent conception of good morals, some deep-rooted tradition of commonweal" (internal quotation marks omitted). *Id.*

Manifestly, the public policy of this state with respect to gambling, as reflected in subsequent revisions of the General Statutes, has evolved considerably since *Ciampittiello* was decided. Our legislature has deemed it appropriate to legalize wagering in multiple forms and forums, to the extent that the "ancient and deep-rooted" public policy against gambling; *id.;* while still cognizable in some respects, is but a dusty relic of its former self. *See* Hilton International Co. v. Arace, supra, 35 Conn. Supp. at 527–28, 394 A.2d 739. We believe that, if *Ciampittiello* were to be decided today, the court would find the contract enforceable because it would, in fact, be legal in this state and there would be no conflict with the laws of the jurisdiction where the contract was made. By the same reasoning, we conclude that the parties' contract in the present case is not unenforceable under § 52-553. It would be, in our view, contrary to the statutory scheme as a whole to conclude that an agreement to share the spoils of legal wagering is illegal and unenforceable.[11]

The judgment of the Appellate Court is affirmed.

Meyer v. Hawkinson
626 N.W.2d 262 (N.D. 2001)

KAPSNER, Justice.

Clyde and Dorothy Meyer appeal from the district court's grant of summary judgment for Donald M. and Marilyn F. Hawkinson, dismissing Meyers' claim for enforcement of an alleged contract to share proceeds of the Western Canadian Lottery. The district court found there was a genuine issue as to the existence of a contract between the parties, but granted summary judgment because the alleged contract had an unlawful object and would be unenforceable as contrary to North Dakota's public policy against gambling. We hold the public policy of the state of North Dakota would not allow our courts to enforce an alleged contract to share proceeds of a winning lottery ticket. We affirm.

I

On August 16, 1997, Clyde Meyer drove his wife, Dorothy Meyer, and their friends, Donald and Marilyn Hawkinson, from Fargo, North Dakota to Winnipeg, Canada to attend the horse races. They planned to split the cost of gas for the trip, as was their custom. After checking into the hotel, Donald Hawkinson purchased a lottery ticket with three quick pick numbers at the hotel gift shop, and then he returned to the lounge to tell Marilyn Hawkinson and the Meyers about his purchase. Clyde Meyer claims Donald Hawkinson said to Clyde, "Go buy three lottery tickets and we'll split." According to Dorothy Meyer, Donald Hawkinson said, "I just bought three tickets for the lottery, and you go in and buy three, and if we win, we'll split." Hawkinson claims he said he felt "pretty lucky" and suggested to Meyer, "Why don't you go buy some," not mentioning any split.

Dorothy Meyer claims Clyde Meyer said, "Okay," and left the lounge. Clyde Meyer testified he directly turned around, walked to the gift stand, and bought three lottery tickets. Donald Hawkinson testified that when Clyde Meyer returned to the lounge, Meyer

---

11. We express no opinion, however, as to the enforceability of the parties' agreement pursuant to the principles of the law of contracts. That is a determination left to the trial court after the facts of the case have been fully developed.

may have said he got some lottery tickets. However, according to both of the Meyers and Marilyn Hawkinson, Clyde Meyer said nothing about the lottery or tickets when he returned to the table. It is undisputed that when Meyer returned, he said nothing about the number of tickets he had purchased, and he did not show anyone any lottery tickets.

The following day Donald Hawkinson discovered that one of his lottery ticket numbers was a winner of $1.6 million Canadian ($1.2 million U.S.). Clyde claims he went to meet his wife in the restaurant and thought he told her, "We won the lottery, Don's ticket."

The parties had been friends for over forty years, often gambling together. Donald frequently bought lottery tickets, but the parties never pooled their funds to purchase lottery tickets. During their stay in Winnipeg, the parties did not pool their money to bet on horses or to gamble in the casinos. They did have a custom of pooling their money before buying pull tabs, and they would open their pull tabs together and split any proceeds immediately. They also had a custom of splitting the cost of drinks. On this occasion, after Donald won the lottery, he paid for all the Meyers' drinks and meals.

The Hawkinsons called their children with the news and invited them to come to Winnipeg to celebrate. Clyde Meyer never telephoned anyone to tell them he had won the lottery. Dorothy Meyer testified she talked on the telephone to one of the Hawkinsons' children and may have said Donald Hawkinson won the lottery and was now a millionaire. Dorothy called her own son and thought she said, "Don had won the lottery." She also called her friend and thought she told her, "Don won the lottery."

The Hawkinsons and their children arranged for safekeeping the ticket in the hotel safe and later in a safety deposit box. The Meyers did not take part in these arrangements. Later the parties rode together back to Fargo, but there was no mention of splitting the lottery. Two to three weeks later, Donald told Clyde there would be no equal sharing of the winnings, and Clyde said he understood there would be no equal split, but he thought Donald would share the winnings. On about September 17, 1997, Donald sent each of the Meyers $2,500 as a gesture of friendship. Dorothy Meyer stated Clyde expected Donald to buy him a motor home, and so their friendship ended.

Clyde and Dorothy Meyer filed a civil action against Donald and Marilyn Hawkinson to enforce a contract to share equally in the lottery winnings. The Hawkinsons moved for summary judgment, arguing no reasonable mind could find from the evidence the existence of an enforceable contract, and even if a contract existed, it would be unenforceable as illegal and against public policy. The district court found there was a genuine issue as to whether a contract existed between the parties, making summary judgment inappropriate on that issue. Nevertheless, the district court granted summary judgment for the Hawkinsons, reasoning even if the alleged contract existed, such an agreement would be contrary to North Dakota's public policy against gambling. The district court concluded the alleged contract would be unenforceable because its object, although lawful in Canada, is unlawful in North Dakota as it violates state anti-gambling statutes. The Meyers appealed....

III

The Meyers argue the district court erred in granting Hawkinsons' motion for summary judgment by finding as a matter of law the alleged contract between the parties is unenforceable because it is contrary to the public policy of North Dakota. We disagree.

Gambling differs from other business transactions, and ordinary remedies usually are not available to enforce gambling debts. Hochhalter v. Dakota Race Mgmt., 524 N.W.2d 582, 584 (N.D. 1994). It is essential to the existence of a contract to have a lawful object.

N.D.C.C. §9-01-02. A contract is void if the consideration given for the contract is unlawful. N.D.C.C. §9-05-04. A contract is unlawful if it is (1) contrary to an express provision of law; (2) contrary to the policy of express law, although not expressly prohibited; or (3) otherwise contrary to good morals. N.D.C.C. §9-08-01.

A

The Meyers argue the alleged contract is not contrary to an express provision of law because it was entered into in Canada where the lottery is legal and because the alleged contract does not violate the laws of North Dakota. However, whether the alleged contract is contrary to express provision of law in North Dakota is essential to determining whether the contract is enforceable. The question is whether such a contract is enforceable in the courts of North Dakota or whether our courts will not be used to enforce such contracts because they are contrary to the public policy of this state.

The Constitution of North Dakota, Article XI, §25, provides:

> The legislative assembly shall not authorize any game of chance, lottery, or gift enterprises, under any pretense, or for any purpose whatever. However, the legislative assembly may authorize by law bona fide nonprofit veterans', charitable, educational, religious, or fraternal organizations, civic and service clubs, or such other public-spirited organizations as it may recognize, to conduct games of chance when the entire net proceeds of such games of chance are to be devoted to educational, charitable, patriotic, fraternal, religious, or other public-spirited uses.

In 1976, a constitutional amendment gave the legislature limited authority to authorize some forms of gambling. *See* N.D. Op. Att'y Gen. L-178, L-179 (1993). Under that limited constitutional authorization, the legislature enacted N.D.C.C. ch. 53-06.1 describing which games of chance are authorized in North Dakota, the persons and organizations authorized to hold such games of chance, and a regulatory licensing structure to ensure fairness and to ensure proceeds are devoted to purposes required by the constitution. *Id.* at L-179-80. Under N.D.C.C. §53-06.1-11.1(2), a licensed organization shall disburse gambling proceeds only for a specified list of educational, charitable, patriotic, fraternal, religious, or public-spirited uses.

Under North Dakota law, gambling is defined as risking any money or other thing of value for gain, contingent on a lot, chance, or the happening or outcome of an event over which the person taking the risk has no control. N.D.C.C. §12.1-28-01(1). In addition, N.D.C.C. §12.1-28-02(2) makes it a class A misdemeanor to:

a. Sell, purchase, receive, or transfer a chance to participate in a lottery, whether the lottery is drawn in state or out of state, and whether the lottery is lawful in the other state or country;

b. Disseminate information about a lottery with intent to encourage participation in it, except that a legal lottery may be advertised in North Dakota; or

c. Engage in gambling on private premises where the total amount wagered by an individual player exceeds five hundred dollars per individual hand, game, or event.

Clearly, an alleged contract to share proceeds of a $1.2 million lottery would be illegal if entered into in North Dakota. (Footnote omitted that discussed whether the contract would also have been illegal under Canadian law.)

Our state constitution expressly forbids lotteries and games of chance unless the entire net proceeds are devoted to public-spirited uses statutorily specified as educational, charitable, patriotic, fraternal, and religious. N.D. Const. art. XI, § 25; *see also* N.D.C.C. § 53-06.1-11.1(2). In addition, N.D.C.C. § 12.1-28-02(2), which criminalizes sales, purchases, receipt, or transfer of lottery chances, comprehensively forbids such activities whether the lottery is in state or out of state. By express terms, the statute prohibits these activities even if the lottery is legal in the other state or country. The statute also criminalizes dissemination of information about a lottery with intent to encourage participation in the lottery. Although § 12.1-28-02(2) refers to lottery chances, not proceeds, a chance to share proceeds is really a chance to participate in a lottery.

The alleged contract between the Meyers and Hawkinsons to share lottery winnings is a wager, or "risking any money . . . or other thing of value for gain, contingent [on a] lot, chance, . . . or the happening or outcome of an event . . . over which the person taking the risk has no control," and constitutes gambling under the statutory definition of gambling. *See* N.D.C.C. § 12.1-28-01(1). This Court will not enforce contracts which have an unlawful purpose or unlawful consideration. *See* N.D.C.C. §§ 9-01-02, 9-05-04; *see also* Erickson v. North Dakota State Fair Ass'n of Fargo, 211 N.W. 597, 599 (N.D.1926) (refusing to enforce an alleged contract to run an illegal horse race for prize money because courts will not aid parties engaged in illegal transactions, but rather will leave the parties where it finds them); Drinkall v. Movius State Bank, 88 N.W. 724, 727 (N.D. 1901) (holding neither party to an illegal contract may be aided by the courts, either to set it aside or enforce it).

We conclude the alleged contract if entered into in North Dakota would violate the express law against gambling. However, the contract was not created in North Dakota, so that does not end our inquiry. The contract may still be unlawful if contrary to the public policy underpinning express law, although not expressly prohibited. N.D.C.C. § 9-08-01; *see also* Cont'l Cas. Co. v. Kinsey, 499 N.W.2d 574, 580 (N.D. 1993) (noting the importance of enforcing contracts unless they clearly contravene public policy or express law).

B

The Meyers argue the alleged contract to share lottery proceeds is not void as against public policy. We are not persuaded.

Public policy is a principle of law whereby contracts will not be enforced if they have a tendency to be injurious to the public or against the public good. Johnson v. Peterbilt of Fargo, Inc., 438 N.W.2d 162, 163 (N.D. 1989). Whether the contract is against public policy is generally provided for by the state constitution or statute. *Id.; see, e.g.,* N.D.C.C. § 9-08-02 (providing that all contracts which have for their object exemption of persons from responsibility for their own fraud or willful injury to the person or property of another, or wilful or negligent violation of law, are against the policy of the law). However, when a contract is inconsistent with fair and honorable dealing, contrary to sound policy, and offensive to good morals, the courts have the authority to declare the contract void as against public policy. *Johnson,* at 164; *see also* N.D.C.C. § 9-08-01 (deeming contracts unlawful if contrary to express law; contrary to policy of express law, although not expressly prohibited; or contrary to good morals).

Despite the constitutional amendment authorizing some limited forms of gambling, the legislature's anti-gambling message remains especially strong regarding lotteries. Section 12.1-28-02(2), N.D.C.C., prohibits the sale, purchase, receipt, or transfer of a chance to participate in a lottery, *whether the lottery is drawn in state or out of state, and whether the lottery is lawful in the other state or country* (emphasis added). We regard the underlined language as clear indication of the public policy against lotteries. The use of our courts in the manner requested by the Meyers would frustrate that policy. In addition to the legislature, the voters have demonstrated opposition to lotteries. In 1986, a constitutional amendment proposed authorizing a state-operated lottery for the purpose of providing tax relief for the citizens of North Dakota. *See* 86-31 N.D. Op. Att'y Gen. Op. 152, 152–53 (1986); *see also* N.D. Const. art. XI, § 25. This proposed amendment met strong resistance. *See* 86-31 N.D. Att'y Gen. Op., at 152. Ultimately, the proposed amendment to establish a North Dakota lottery was defeated in the November 1986 general election. *See id.*

Other attempts to authorize lotteries in North Dakota have also failed. For example, when the City of Grand Forks inquired whether cities could allow lotteries or other non-licensed games of chance to be conducted within city limits, the Attorney General indicated cities lack that authority. *See* 85-15 N.D. Att'y Gen. Op. 46, 46 (1985). The Attorney General also indicated a private club, which was licensed to conduct games of chance, was prohibited from holding a drawing. *See* 82-7 N.D. Att'y Gen. Op. 17, 17 (1982). The Attorney General determined that a drawing in which members sign their names when entering the club, contribute money, and then the name of one member is drawn who wins the entire pot would constitute a prohibited lottery. *Id.* at 18.

Accordingly, the public policy in North Dakota runs consistently against lotteries. On the basis of public policy, our courts will not enforce contracts deemed injurious to the public or against the public good. *Johnson*, 438 N.W.2d at 163–64 (indicating that whether a contract is against public policy is generally provided by the state constitution or by statute)....

The Meyers argue that by refusing them an opportunity to enforce this contract, the courts would only reward those who convert the property of others. They cite cases from other jurisdictions which have enforced alleged contracts to split the proceeds of lotteries, although the lotteries were not legal in the state where the contract was formed. *See, e.g.*, Pearsall v. Alexander, 572 A.2d 113, 115–16 (App. D.C. 1990) (enforcing an agreement to share the winnings of a jointly purchased lottery ticket as not against public policy, because the parties did not wager against one another on the lottery's outcome, so the agreement was not a prohibited gaming contract); Talley v. Mathis, 453 S.E.2d 704, 705–06 (Ga. 1995) (enforcing an agreement to jointly purchase a lottery ticket and to share the proceeds, as not violative of either Georgia's statute prohibiting gambling contracts or public policy, because the lottery was legal in Kentucky where the ticket was purchased); Kaszuba v. Zientara, 506 N.E.2d 1, 1–3 (Ind. 1987) (enforcing a contract entered into in Indiana, whereby Kaszuba would travel to Illinois with Zientara's money to purchase an Illinois lottery ticket for Zientara, because despite the long-standing Indiana public policy against lotteries, prohibiting this contract would not shelter Indiana citizens from legal lotteries in sister states); Miller v. Radikopf, 228 N.W.2d 386, 386–87 (Mich. 1975) (enforcing an agreement, to jointly buy and divide winnings of an Irish sweepstakes ticket as not against public policy, because state statutes did not prohibit accepting proceeds of winning lottery tickets, but only prohibited selling the tickets); Castilleja v. Camero, 414 S.W.2d 424, 425–28 (Tex.1967) (enforcing as not against public policy an agreement made in Texas to jointly purchase a Mexican lottery ticket and split the proceeds, because this contract did not violate the laws of Mexico and, since the parties both had lawful ownership rights to the proceeds, refusal to enforce the contract would violate Texas' strong public policy against conversion of property).

Other jurisdictions have refused to enforce contracts to split lottery proceeds because if the winning ticket is not jointly owned, then the parties are wagering against each other on the outcome of the lottery, which violates state statutes against wagering on the outcome of uncertain events over which no party has control. In Dickerson v. Deno, 770 So.2d 63, 64 (Ala. 2000), the court voided an agreement to share winnings between Alabama holders of individually owned Florida lottery tickets. Because the tickets were owned by each individual party, they could only receive the proceeds from the winning lottery ticket as a result of their side agreement to share, not as a result of an ownership interest in the winning ticket. *Id.* at 66. Thus, the court reasoned the contract was founded on gambling consideration as it was a wager, hedging their bets in an attempt to increase each party's odds of winning the Florida lottery, an uncertain event none of the parties controlled. *Id.* at 66–67.

One jurisdiction even refused to enforce an agreement to split lottery proceeds between joint owners of the winning ticket, reasoning their joint venture was formed for the purpose of wagering on the outcome of a contingent event. *See* Cole v. Hughes, 442 S.E.2d 86, 88–89 (N.C. App. 1994) (voiding a joint venture agreement entered into in North Carolina to purchase Virginia lottery tickets and equally share winnings because North Carolina statute prohibits wagers depending on any chance event and voids contracts for the purpose of such wagering). When the parties then tried to enforce their joint venture agreement in Virginia, where the winning lottery ticket was purchased legally, that jurisdiction also refused to enforce the contract because the agreement was based on gambling consideration. *See* Hughes v. Cole, 465 S.E.2d 820, 827 (Va. 1996) (voiding the joint venture agreement entered into in North Carolina to purchase Virginia lottery tickets and share winnings, because a Virginia statute prohibited gaming contracts, even though the lottery was legal in Virginia).

In this case, the Meyers and Hawkinsons did not pool their money to jointly purchase the winning lottery ticket, and therefore Hawkinsons are not converting Meyers' property. Rather, Clyde Meyer and Donald Hawkinson were allegedly exchanging promises to share winnings from their individually owned lottery tickets on the happening of the uncertain event that the numbers drawn in the Canadian lottery matched one of their ticket numbers. Consequently, the alleged contract between Hawkinson and Meyer was a wager or side bet, that is, an attempt to hedge their bets and increase their odds of winning the Canadian lottery.

We have recognized that courts must be mindful of the right of individuals to enter contracts, when the court is faced with deciding whether a contract is against public policy. Martin v. Allianz Life Ins. Co. of North America, 1998 ND 8, ¶ 20, 573 N.W.2d 823. We have also acknowledged that the legislature is much better suited than the courts for setting the public policy of the state. *Id.* The statutory language, as well as the legislative and electoral history, comprehensively and clearly convey the policy underlying North Dakota's repeated rejection of a state-operated lottery and high-stakes gambling. *See* Trinity Med. Ctr., Inc. v. Holum, 544 N.W.2d 148, 152 (N.D. 1996) (providing the "cardinal rule" of statutory construction is that our interpretation must be consistent with legislative intent and done in a manner which will accomplish the policy goals and objectives of the statute). Therefore, we affirm the trial court's grant of summary judgment by finding as a matter of law the alleged contract between Clyde Meyer and Donald Hawkinson is contrary to public policy of the state of North Dakota and unenforceable in our courts.

IV

The Meyers further argue that summary judgment was inappropriate because, taking the evidence in the light most favorable to the Meyers, who opposed the summary judgment, there is a genuine issue as to the existence of an enforceable agreement between the parties. Because we affirm the trial court's decision the contract, if it existed, is unenforceable in the courts of North Dakota, consideration of this issue is unnecessary. *See*

Thompson v. First Nat'l Bank in Grand Forks, 269 N.W.2d 763, 765 (N.D. 1978) (determining it was unnecessary to decide whether the parties were precluded from enforcing the contract on other grounds when we disposed of the case on the ground of public policy considerations).

V

The judgment of dismissal is affirmed.

GERALD W. VANDE WALLE, C.J., and MARY MUEHLEN MARING, J., concur.

(concurring opinion omitted)

SANDSTROM, Justice, dissenting.

Because the majority misapprehends the history of gambling in North Dakota and the working of our gambling laws, and misstates the public policy of our state, I respectfully dissent.

I

Although a quarter of a century ago, a credible argument might have been made that the public policy of North Dakota opposed the enforcement of a contract relating to gambling, no such argument can prevail today.

The early years of our statehood were shaped by the corruption of the Louisiana Lottery, the last of the so-called "great national lotteries." So corrupt that it was kicked out of Louisiana, the lottery company, seeking to establish the state as its new base of operations, came to "buy" the North Dakota legislature during its first session. Elwyn B. Robinson, *History of North Dakota* 219–20 (1969); *see also* Report of Investigating Committee, Senate Journal 1019–94, 1st N.D. Legis. Sess. (1889–1890) (detailing the Senate's investigation of the corruption). The report of the Pinkerton detectives would establish there was good reason to believe the legislature was for sale. *Report of the Pinkerton Detective Agency Made to Governor John Miller on the Effort Made to Legalize the Louisiana Lottery During the Session of the First Legislative Assembly in North Dakota* (1890). Governor John Miller, and others of great integrity, had secretly hired the Pinkerton Detectives to document the buying of votes at $500 per vote. Senate Bill 167 was introduced to permit lotteries. *See* Senate Journal 842–46, 1st N.D. Legis. Sess. (1889–1890) (detailing the bill). While the bill passed the Senate, Senate Journal 448–49, 1st N.D. Legis. Sess. (1889–1890), when the investigation of the Pinkerton Detectives was revealed, the reaction was so strong that the bill was indefinitely postponed in the House. House Journal 688, 1st N.D. Legis. Sess. (1889–1890); *see also* Senate Journal 486, 1st N.D. Legis. Sess. (1889–1890) (reporting indefinite postponement). The people sent virtually a whole new legislature to Bismarck for the Second Legislative Assembly and proceeded as rapidly as the cumbersome procedures of the day would permit to adopt the First Amendment to the North Dakota Constitution, prohibiting all "lottery, or gift enterprises." ...

Over the next 85 years, North Dakota had a rather mixed history on gambling, ranging from Attorney General Nels Johnson, 1945–48, driving the slot machines out of the state, to Elmo Christiansen, in 1954, being convicted of conspiracy to bring illegal gambling into the state. Attorney General of North Dakota, *Gambling in North Dakota: A Historical and Legal Perspective* (1976). In 1964 and 1968, constitutional amendments to permit parimutuel betting on horse and dog races were defeated. *Id.* at 6; *see also* 1965 N.D. Sess. Laws ch. 478; 1969 N.D. Sess. Laws ch. 587. In 1972, the text of the First Amendment to the North Dakota Constitution was submitted separately to the voters considering a new state constitution. The gambling provision failed to get the majority vote needed for inclusion in the new constitution and therefore would have been omitted had the new constitution been adopted. *Id.*

The 1973 legislature, in adopting the New Criminal Code to be effective July 1, 1975, greatly increased the penalties for gambling — from misdemeanors to mostly felonies. 1973 N.D. Sess. Laws ch. 116, §27; *see also* N.D.C.C. §12.1-28-02 (1973) (identifying the offense classification scheme).

The 1975 legislature, at the urging of then-Attorney General Allen I. Olson, proposed a constitutional amendment to legalize gambling for charitable purposes. 1975 N.D. Sess. Laws ch. 616. The aftermath of Watergate and the resignation of President Richard Nixon emphasized the importance of obeying the law and changing, rather than violating, laws with which the people did not agree. Olson cracked down on widespread illegal gambling and urged the people to speak with their ballots. Allen I. Olson, Guest Editorial, *Gambling a Controversial Issue,* Grand Forks Herald, March 14, 1976, at 4.

After the 1976 approval of the constitutional amendment, the 1977 legislature legalized charitable gambling, requiring the entire net proceeds go to "[n]onprofit veterans, charitable, educational, religious, and fraternal organizations, civic and service clubs, and public-spirited organizations." 1977 N.D. Sess. Laws ch. 473, §2.

The 1981 legislature made North Dakota only the third state in the nation — following Nevada and New Jersey — to legalize "Blackjack" or "Twenty-one." 1981 N.D. Sess. Laws ch. 514, §7 (identifying twenty-one as a permissible game of chance); *see also Gambling at a Crossroads,* Grand Forks Herald, November 3, 1991 (identifying North Dakota as the third state to legalize blackjack). North Dakota became the third state with casinos — this before state lotteries became widespread, before modern riverboat gambling, and before the rise of Indian gambling. *See First Interim Report of the Commission on the Review of the National Policy Toward Gambling* (1975); Melinda Beck & Sylvester Monroe, *Reno on the Red River,* Newsweek, May 17, 1982, at 56.

In 1993, after the rise of modern state lotteries, the North Dakota legislature repealed the ban on lottery advertising — as long as the lottery was legal where it was conducted. 1993 N.D. Sess. Laws ch. 124; N.D.C.C. §12.1-28-02(2)(b). North Dakota's legalization of advertising of out-of-state lotteries cannot be reconciled with the majority's claimed public policy against them.

II

The majority misperceives the meaning of "lotteries and gift enterprises" as used in the First Amendment to North Dakota's Constitution and now in the current N.D. Const. art. XI, §25. The term is very broad....

The meaning of lottery as intended in the First Amendment to the North Dakota Constitution is consistent with the general definition. The definition was established in the Territorial Code of 1877 and incorporated into North Dakota law at statehood.

Lottery defined. A lottery is any scheme for the disposal or distribution of property by chance among persons who have paid, or promised or agreed to pay, any valuable consideration for the chance of obtaining such property, or a portion of it, or for any share of or interest in such property, upon any agreement, understanding, or expectation that it is to be distributed or disposed of by lot or chance, whether called a lottery, a raffle, or a gift enterprise, or by whatever name the same may be known.

Revised Codes of the Territory of Dakota, Penal Code, §373 (1877). With the exception of slight changes in punctuation, the 1877 definition remained the same when incorporated into North Dakota law. *See* N.D.R.C. Ch. 36, §7217 (1895).

The majority's analysis is seriously flawed by its misunderstanding of the meaning of "lottery, or gift enterprises" as used in our constitution.

The majority's analysis is further flawed by its misperception of recent state lottery proposals. The campaigns in opposition to state lotteries in 1986, 1988, and 1996 focused not on the evils of lotteries as opposed to "other forms of gambling," but on the evils of all forms of gambling and on the State entering into gambling competition with private charities. *See, e.g., King: Lotteries Won't Hurt Charitable Gaming,* Grand Forks Herald, May 26, 1988 (identifying Gorman King Sr. as a "lottery backer," and attributing statements to him that a lottery would not reduce profits of existing charitable gaming); *Lottery Could Wipe Out Many Charities,* Grand Forks Herald, June 9, 1988 (suggesting charities would be devastated by a lottery).

III

The majority ... holds "the public policy of the state of North Dakota would not allow our courts to enforce an alleged contract to share proceeds of a winning lottery ticket." The majority misstates the public policy of this State....

A

North Dakota public policy does not forbid gambling, but North Dakota does have a public policy against the undue influence and illicit activity that may accompany it. The North Dakota criminal code, substantially revised and effective July 1, 1975, increased the severity of punishment for gambling offenses. Although once wholly prohibited, after the adoption of a constitutional amendment in 1976, limited gambling became lawful in North Dakota. With the addition of gaming on Indian reservations in North Dakota, games of chance are now commonplace in this State. Although lawful, gambling remains highly regulated. *See* N.D.C.C. ch. 53-06.1 (the regulatory system for gambling in North Dakota). The majority is correct that lotteries remain unlawful in North Dakota. N.D.C.C. § 12.1-28-02(2). North Dakota's public policy permits gambling, and North Dakota's law establishes a regulatory system.

Whether a contract or one of its provisions "is against public policy is generally provided for by statute or by the State Constitution." Johnson v. Peterbilt of Fargo, Inc., 438 N.W.2d 162, 163 (N.D. 1989) (footnote omitted). "It is primarily the prerogative of the legislature to declare what agreements and acts are contrary to public policy, and to forbid them." 17A Am. Jur. 2d *Contracts* § 262 (1991) (footnote omitted). As reflected by legislation authorizing the advertisement in this state of out-of-state lotteries, an agreement to gamble or to share gambling proceeds in Canada is not contrary to our public policy.

Our public policy applies neither extraterritorially, nor, as in this case, internationally. For example, this Court recently held that although common-law marriages cannot be lawfully entered in this State, we may still recognize a common-law marriage validly entered in Canada. Pearson v. Pearson, 2000, ... 606 N.W.2d 128. We did not exalt our public policy against common-law marriages in *Pearson.* Without support, ... the majority states, "whether the alleged contract is contrary to express provision of law in North Dakota is essential to determining whether the contract is enforceable." In *Pearson,* an opinion authored by Justice Kapsner, the Court stated that although our own statutes and public policy prohibit common-law marriages, a common-law marriage validly entered into in Canada may be entitled to recognition in North Dakota. *Pearson,* at ¶ 8. Also in *Pearson,* the majority declined to terminate spousal support because of an alleged violation of North Dakota public policy against cohabitation, concluding the practice was acceptable in Canada.

Id. at ¶ 23. In this case, Canada has clearly authorized lotteries. A contract entered in Canada—that is permissible in Canada—is entitled to recognition here.

The majority, ... citing N.D.C.C. § 12.1-28-02(2), places great emphasis on the fact that it is a class A misdemeanor to "Sell, purchase, receive, or transfer a chance to participate in a lottery, whether the lottery is drawn in state or out of state, and whether the lottery is lawful in the other state or country." The majority, however, omits the crucial introductory clause, "Except as permitted by law."

[T]he majority cites N.D.C.C. § 9-01-02, stating a lawful object is necessary for a valid contract. In fact, N.D.C.C. § 9-01-02 states, "there *should* be ... [a] lawful object" (emphasis added).

The majority also cites § 9-05-04..., stating a contract is void "if the consideration given for the contract is unlawful." Illegal consideration is "any act or forbearance, or a promise to act or forbear, which is contrary to law or public policy." 17A Am. Jur. 2d *Contracts* § 240 (1991). The parties do not dispute that the money, consideration, or promises exchanged by the parties in this case were wholly legal in Canada. The statutes cited by the majority apply to contracts and conduct in North Dakota, but not to the alleged agreement between the Meyers and the Hawkinsons. As demonstrated by the persuasive analysis of other courts interpreting this issue, all of these facts are immaterial. The important fact is the parties do not dispute that the alleged agreement was wholly lawful in Canada, where it was entered. Canada's criminal code, Part VII—entitled Disorderly Houses, Gaming and Betting—at §§ 202–206 allows lotteries and private bets between individuals who are not in the business of betting.

The majority and concurring opinions seek to raise the specious argument of whether the alleged contract was valid in Canada. Whether the alleged agreement violated the law of Canada would likely involve questions of fact and law and therefore would not be suitable for summary judgment. More importantly, however, the plaintiffs argued the agreement was legal in Canada, and the defendants did not dispute the legality in Canada, but merely argued that the agreement violated North Dakota law. We have repeatedly held that issues not raised in the trial court cannot be raised for the first time on appeal. *See, e.g.,* Cermak v. Cermak, 1997 ND 187, ¶ 15, 569 N.W.2d 280. The issue was raised neither in the trial court nor on appeal. It is raised for the first time in the majority and concurring opinions here.

Although North Dakota's public policy may be demonstrated to a certain extent through the statutes cited by the majority, the clear intent of our public policy is to allow regulated gaming. Seeking to enforce a contract made in Canada to share proceeds of the Canadian lottery does not offend the public policy of this State.

B

Courts, including this Court, increasingly decline to render contracts invalid on the basis of public policy....

The concept of not enforcing a contract on public policy grounds is based on the notion that enforcing such a contract would have "a tendency to be injurious to the public or against the public good." *Johnson,* 438 N.W.2d at 163 (citing Ness v. City of Fargo, 251 N.W. 843 (N.D. 1933))....

If the contract at issue here had been made in North Dakota, North Dakota's public policy would apply. Because enforcement of this contract does not implicate our public policy or our laws, however, there is no "tendency" of enforcement of the contract "to be injurious to the public or against the public good." *Johnson,* 438 N.W.2d at 163 (citation omitted)....

The efficacy of our laws and the regulation of gambling in North Dakota would remain unaffected by enforcement of this agreement. It is infirm to refuse enforcement of this alleged contract, based on a purported North Dakota public policy that would not be implicated by enforcement of the agreement.

IV

The majority, ... cites a few cases in which this Court declined to enforce contract provisions on the basis of public policy. In each of those cases, enforcement of the respective contracts would have offended the public policy of this State by contravening our own statutes. Any agreement between Meyer and Hawkinson was lawful in Canada. There is no support for the proposition that our contract law is to have extraterritorial or international application. The majority cites no law or case that would allow this Court to apply our laws or purported public policy extraterritorially.

A

The two cases cited by the majority as support for the proposition that this alleged agreement cannot be enforced by our courts deserve little weight.

Unlike the states in cases relied on by the majority, North Dakota does not specifically prohibit the enforcement of a gaming contract....

B

The majority cites, but does not analyze, numerous cases in which courts have allowed enforcement of contracts similar to the alleged contract in this case. Perhaps most on point is Castilleja v. Camero, 414 S.W.2d 424 (Tex. 1967). In *Castilleja,* two Texas families agreed "to jointly purchase a lottery ticket in the Mexican National Lottery." *Id.* at 425. When one ticket won, the purchaser denied the existence of any proceed-sharing agreement. *Id.* The Texas Supreme Court stated:

> The agreement ... to jointly purchase a ticket in the National Lottery of Mexico and to divide the proceeds, if any, was not an illegal contract. It neither violated nor aided in the violation of any gaming statute of Texas. The only other jurisdiction involved was Mexico. In Mexico, the purpose of the contract had the express approval of the Mexican government in that the Mexican government has a revenue interest in the lottery. Thus the agreement was to do a lawful thing—participate in the National Lottery of Mexico, in a lawful manner—by going to Mexico.

Id. at 426. The court held, "A contract which is made in one jurisdiction but which relates to and is performed in another jurisdiction is governed by the law of the place of performance." *Id.* (citations omitted). Although the majority ignores the choice-of-law question, under our choice-of-law analysis, Canadian law would apply to this alleged contract. *See* Daley v. American States Preferred Ins. Co., 1998 ND 225, ¶¶ 13–17, 587 N.W.2d 159 (North Dakota's choice-of-law test for contracts is one of significant contacts followed by choice-influencing considerations). Like the *Castilleja* agreement that "did not relate to or involve Texas law," the alleged contract here does not involve North Dakota law. *Castilleja,* 414 S.W.2d at 427.

The *Castilleja* court concluded Texas policies and interests were not "sufficiently involved to deny recognition of the right [to enforce the contract] by Texas courts." *Id.* The court stated:

> To justify a court in refusing to enforce a right of action which accrued under the laws of another state, because against the policy of our laws, it must appear

that it is against good morals or natural justice, or that for some other reason the enforcement of it would be prejudicial to the general interests of our own citizens.

Id. The court concluded that although Texas public policy prohibited lotteries, conversion was more offensive and was the paramount act "contrary to natural justice." *Id.* at 427–28....

C

There exists no case to support the majority's belief that North Dakota's purported public policy against lotteries can be used to deny enforcement of an obligation that was wholly legal where made. The majority's lack of cited authority on point is telling. The majority ignores the persuasive analysis of the numerous courts that have considered this concept and have concluded the paramount public policy is enforcement of lawful obligations. I decline to join the majority's effort to be the first to establish such a tenuous legal position.

V

Because the majority misperceives our history, misunderstands our law, and misstates our public policy, I cannot concur. Because the majority ignores its duty to enforce lawful contracts, I respectfully dissent.

Domingo v. Mitchell

257 S.W.3d 34 (Tex. App. 2008)

PATRICK A. PIRTLE, Justice.

Presenting two issues, Appellant, Betty Domingo, challenges the trial court's order granting summary judgment in favor of Appellee, Brenda Mitchell. Specifically, by her first issue, she maintains the trial court erred in granting Mitchell's no-evidence summary judgment because she presented more than a scintilla of competent evidence in support of every element of her breach of contract claim. By issue two, she contends the trial court erred in granting Mitchell's traditional motion for summary judgment because genuine issues of material fact exist. We reverse and remand.

Background Facts

According to the summary judgment evidence, beginning in 2004, Domingo and Mitchell, who were co-workers and friends, played the Texas Lottery on numerous occasions. Their arrangement included an agreement to pool their money to purchase tickets and split all winnings equally. At times, Mitchell would purchase the tickets without requiring advance payment from Domingo and Domingo would promptly reimburse Mitchell, win or lose.

On March 9, 2006, Cindy Skidmore sent an e-mail to Mitchell asking if she was interested in joining a lottery group. After enlisting a select group of friends and co-workers, including Mitchell, Skidmore formed LGroup, a Texas Limited Partnership, for the purpose of pooling money to play the lottery. On March 23rd, she sent a follow-up e-mail to members of the group notifying them of a meeting on March 30th at a local restaurant to pay and select numbers for the April 2006 drawings. The e-mail also provided, "[i]f there is someone else you want to invite (& you feel pretty sure they won't drop out) let me know." Mitchell did not ask Skidmore if Domingo could participate in the April 2006 drawings.

Domingo alleges that sometime after the March 23rd e-mail, Mitchell invited her and Cindy Ruff, another co-worker, to participate in the lottery group for April 2006, specifically, Lotto Texas and Mega Millions. Ruff declined the offer due to insufficient funds. When Domingo inquired about how much her contribution would be, Mitchell offered to cover for her and be reimbursed at a later time.

On March 30th, Mitchell and other members of the group met at a restaurant to pay their share for the April 2006 tickets and contribute their numbers. Domingo was not present at this meeting. It was determined that each member of the group owed $17. Mitchell paid her contribution, but did not contribute for Domingo's share. According to Mitchell's deposition testimony, she did not have enough money with her to pay for her share and also advance $17 for Domingo to participate.[1]

On April 29, 2006, one of the tickets purchased by the group won. After choosing the cash value option, the winnings totaled $20,925,315.23. Domingo's exclusion from a share of the winnings eventually prompted her to consult an attorney because Mitchell had told her she would cover her share of the tickets. She filed suit against Mitchell and the LGroup for breach of contract and also alleged violations of the Texas Revised Partnership Act. Mitchell filed a combination no-evidence and traditional motion for summary judgment and without specifying a ground, the trial court granted summary judgment in favor of Mitchell.

By her no-evidence motion, Mitchell alleged there was no evidence of a valid contract because:

(1) she never made a valid offer to Domingo;

(2) Domingo never tendered a valid acceptance;

(3) she and Domingo never reached a "meeting of the minds" regarding the essential terms of the contract; and

(4) Domingo never tendered sufficient consideration.

Domingo responded to the no-evidence motion by asserting there was sufficient evidence of an offer, acceptance, meeting of the minds, and consideration to defeat the motion.

By her traditional motion, Mitchell alleged she was entitled to summary judgment as a matter of law on the breach of contract claim because Domingo did not present evidence of a valid, enforceable contract. Specifically, she contended the summary judgment evidence disproved:

(1) she made a valid offer to Domingo;

(2) Domingo tendered a valid acceptance; and

(3) they reached a "meeting of the minds."

Mitchell also alleged that any oral agreement violated the Statute of Frauds because Domingo was seeking to enforce a promise to answer for the debt of another. Domingo responded that Mitchell did not conclusively establish the absence of a genuine issue of material fact regarding the elements of a contract. She also asserted that the agreement was not a promise to answer for the debt of another and thus, did not violate the Statute of Frauds.

By two issues, Domingo challenges the no-evidence and traditional summary judgment motions that resulted in summary judgment being rendered against her....

---

1. Several witnesses testified that Mitchell did not have enough to pay for Domingo's share and also pay for her dinner also. However, Mitchell testified that she paid for her dinner with a food card.

I. Analysis of Elements of a Contract

Domingo sued Mitchell for breach of contract. The basis for Mitchell's no-evidence motion was that there was no evidence of the elements of a valid contract between herself and Domingo. The burden then shifted to Domingo to present more than a scintilla of evidence to raise a fact issue on whether the parties formed a contract. The grounds for Mitchell's traditional motion was that there was no disputed material fact issue regarding the elements of offer, acceptance, and meeting of the minds, and there was no writing to indicate the existence of an agreement, in violation of the Statute of Frauds.

A. Contract

The threshold question is whether Mitchell and Domingo entered into a contract. For a contract to exist, there must be an offer, acceptance, and consideration. *See* Harco Energy, Inc. v. Re-Entry People, Inc., 23 S.W.3d 389, 392 (Tex. App.-Amarillo 2000, no pet.). The existence of an oral contract may be proved by circumstantial evidence as well as direct evidence. Harris v. Balderas, 27 S.W.3d 71, 77 (Tex. App.-San Antonio 2000, pet. denied). In determining the existence of an oral contract, courts look at the communications between the parties and the acts and circumstances surrounding those communications. Palestine Water Well Services, Inc. v. Vance Sand and Rock, Inc., 188 S.W.3d 321, 325 (Tex. App.-Tyler 2006, no pet.). To determine whether there was an offer and acceptance, and therefore a "meeting of the minds," courts use an objective standard, considering what the parties did and said, not their subjective states of mind. *See* Komet v. Graves, 40 S.W.3d 596, 601 (Tex. App.-San Antonio 2001, no pet.).

B. Breach of Contract

The elements of a breach of contract claim are (1) the existence of a valid contract; (2) performance or tendered performance by the plaintiff; (3) breach by the defendant; and (4) damages sustained by the plaintiff as a result of that breach. Southwell v. University of Incarnate Word, 974 S.W.2d 351, 354–55 (Tex. App.-San Antonio 1998, pet. denied).

C. Offer

To prove that an offer was made, a party must show (1) the offeror intended to make an offer, (2) the terms of the offer were clear and definite, and (3) the offeror communicated the essential terms of the offer to the offeree. KW Const. v. Stephens & Sons Concrete Contractors, Inc., 165 S.W.3d 874, 883 (Tex. App.-Texarkana 2005, pet. denied).

D. Acceptance

An acceptance must be identical to the offer; otherwise, there is no binding contract. Long Trusts v. Griffin, 144 S.W.3d 99, 111–12 (Tex. App.-Texarkana 2004, pet. denied).

E. Meeting of the Minds

A "meeting of the minds" is not an independent element of a valid contract. It is merely a mutuality subpart of the offer and acceptance elements. A "meeting of the minds" is a mutual understanding and assent to the expression of the parties' agreement. *See* Weynand v. Weynand, 990 S.W.2d 843, 846 (Tex. App.-Dallas 1999, pet. denied). If evidence of the parties' mutual agreement consists of their conduct and course of dealing with one another, their mutual agreement may be inferred from the circumstances, in which case the contract is "implied" as opposed to "express." Double Diamond, Inc. v. Hilco Elec. Co-op., Inc., 127 S.W.3d 260, 267 (Tex. App.-Waco 2003, no pet.). An implied contract involves an inference from circumstantial evidence and is a question of fact. *Id.*

F. Consideration

A contract must be based on valid consideration. *See* Texas Gas Utilities Co. v. Barrett, 460 S.W.2d 409, 412 (Tex. 1970). Consideration is a bargained for exchange of promises that consists of benefits and detriments to the contracting parties. Roark v. Stallworth Oil & Gas, Inc., 813 S.W.2d 492, 496 (Tex. 1991). "It is quite elementary that the promise of one party is a valid consideration for the promise of the other party." *See* Texas Farm Bureau Cotton Ass'n v. Stovall, 253 S.W. 1101, 1105 (Tex. 1923). A contract that lacks consideration lacks mutuality of obligation and is unenforceable. Fed. Sign v. Tex. So. Univ., 951 S.W.2d 401, 409 (Tex. 1997); Belew v. Rector, 202 S.W.3d 849, 854 n.4 (Tex. App.-Eastland 2006, no pet.). Mutual promissory obligations by the parties to the agreement furnishes sufficient consideration to constitute a binding contract. Iacono v. Lyons, 16 S.W.3d 92, 94 (Tex. App.-Houston [1st Dist.] 2000, no pet.).

II. Analysis of Elements of the Contract as Between Mitchell and Domingo

Mitchell alleges she did not make an offer to Domingo, but if she did, some of the material terms of the offer were lacking, making the contract invalid. She argues that price had not been agreed to and that Domingo failed to submit numbers for the drawings, which was an essential element of the agreement. In response, Domingo asserts that a reasonable price can be implied. She also asserts that submitting numbers was not an essential term of the agreement. We agree with Domingo.

When all other elements of a contract have been met, a court may imply a reasonable price. *See* Buxani v. Nussbaum, 940 S.W.2d 350, 353 (Tex. App.-San Antonio 1997, no writ), citing Bendalin v. Delgado, 406 S.W.2d 897, 900 (Tex. 1966). According to Domingo's affidavit, she was an experienced lottery player and estimated that playing Lotto Texas and Mega Millions for the month of April 2006 would have cost approximately $20 to $25. According to the evidence, Mega Millions was played every Tuesday and Friday and Lotto Texas was played every Wednesday and Saturday. Looking at a calendar for April 2006 at $1 per ticket, there were eight drawings for Mega Millions and nine drawings for Lotto Texas, for a total cost of $17 per participant. Thus, a reasonable price could have been implied.

Whether a term forms an essential element of a contract depends primarily upon the intent of the parties. Potcinske v. McDonald Property Investments, Ltd., 245 S.W.3d 526, 531 (Tex. App.-Houston [1st Dist.] 2007, no pet.), citing Neeley v. Bankers Trust Co. of Texas, 757 F.2d 621, 628 (5th Cir. 1985). The question is whether the parties regarded the term as a vitally important ingredient of their bargain. *Id.*

Mitchell contends that submitting numbers was an essential term of the agreement and that without Domingo complying, there was no valid contract. However, the evidence suggests that submitting numbers for the April drawings was not an essential element of the contract. Copies of e-mails established that different numbers were selected on the day after the LGroup met for dinner to decide on a price and submit numbers. Members of the LGroup were also notified by e-mail and given a deadline of noon on April 1st in which to pick different numbers. Thus, any numbers submitted at the meeting on March 30th were an uncertainty as they were subject to being changed and thus, could not have been regarded by the parties as an essential element of the contract.

According to Domingo, she and Mitchell frequently participated in lottery pools with co-workers. They occasionally covered for each other and when Mitchell would advance Domingo's share, Domingo would promptly reimburse her. Shondra Stewart and Ellen Clemons, co-workers of Domingo and Mitchell, both gave deposition testimony that

Cindy Ruff, another co-worker, claimed she was present when Mitchell agreed to cover for Domingo's share of the April 2006 lottery tickets.

Mitchell testified that while she and Ruff were involved in a conversation about the lottery pool on the day after the LGroup met to discuss the April drawings, Domingo entered and asked Mitchell "why didn't you pay my—did you pay my money?" Mitchell responded, "no, I didn't have enough money last night." Although she did not tell Domingo she was excluded because she had not been invited to play with the LGroup, she did testify that she did not cover for Domingo because she had not been invited to play for the April drawings. Ruff testified that she recalled Domingo asking Mitchell why she did not cover her for the April drawings.

Domingo testified that she asked Mitchell "when do we need to pay our money for the April drawing?" Mitchell then informed her that she did not put in for her because she did not have enough money to pay for both of them. Mitchell added that the group was already set for April and instead invited Domingo to play for the May 2006 drawings.

This summary judgment evidence, coupled with Mitchell and Domingo's conduct and course of prior dealings with one another, is sufficient to raise a genuine issue of material fact concerning the offer and acceptance elements of the alleged contract between Mitchell and Domingo.

Regarding the element of consideration, the evidence shows that Mitchell agreed to advance Domingo's share of the lottery tickets and Domingo agreed to reimburse Mitchell. This exchange of promises is sufficient consideration to create a binding contract. *See Iacono*, 16 S.W.3d at 94. *See also* Walker v. Lorehn, 355 S.W.2d 71, 73–74 (Tex. Civ. App.-Houston 1962, writ ref'd n.r.e.).

III. Statute of Frauds

By her traditional motion for summary judgment, Mitchell contended that the alleged oral agreement was unenforceable because it was a promise to answer for the debt of another which the Statute of Frauds requires to be in writing. *See* Tex. Bus. & Com. Code Ann. § 26.01(b)(2) (Vernon Supp.2007). According to Mitchell, the oral agreement to cover Domingo's share of the lottery tickets was a debt that Domingo owed the LGroup. Mitchell's argument presupposes that she informed the LGroup that Domingo had been invited to play for the April 2006 drawings. The evidence however, showed that she did not inform the members of the LGroup that in March 2006 she had invited Domingo to participate in the April 2006 drawings. Hence, there could be no debt owed by Domingo to the LGroup. *See Walker*, 355 S.W.2d at 73–74. Because Domingo's financial obligation was her contractual obligation to reimburse Mitchell and not a promise to answer for the debt of another, the agreement did not violate the Statute of Frauds.

IV. Conclusion

Viewing the evidence in the light most favorable to Domingo, we conclude she presented more than a scintilla of evidence to raise a genuine issue of material fact on whether the parties entered into a valid oral contract and whether Mitchell breached the contract, thereby defeating Mitchell's no-evidence summary judgment. Simultaneously, accepting as true the evidence favorable to Domingo and indulging every reasonable inference in her favor, we conclude the summary judgment evidence raised a genuine issue of material fact defeating Mitchell's entitlement to summary judgment as a matter of law. We hold that the summary judgment in favor of Mitchell based on Domingo's breach of contract claim was improvidently granted. Resultantly, we sustain issues one and two.

Accordingly, the trial court's judgment is reversed and the cause is remanded to the trial court for further proceedings.

Notes

1. As *Domingo* illustrates, if the "public policy" issue is removed from consideration, these cases become fairly standard contracts disputes. As such, the relevant issues relate to whether there was an agreement to share winnings, what the terms of the agreement were, and whether there was consideration given. *See, e.g.,* Pearsall v. Alexander, 572 A.2d 113 (D.C. 1990) (court found sufficient "meeting of the minds" for an oral agreement between two friends through the exchange of bargained-for promises to share winnings); Johnson v. Johnson, 594 N.Y.S.2d 259 (N.Y. App. Div. 1993) (signed and witnessed agreement between the parties established their intent to share the winnings); Stepp v. Freeman, 694 N.E.2d 510 (Ohio Ct. App. 1997) (court found that a group of coworkers had entered into an implied-in-fact contract to purchase lottery tickets and that the contract was breached when one of the group's members was involuntarily dropped from the group and was not told about the purchase of a winning ticket).

2. On the other hand, when courts view the case through the public policy lens, the case becomes more complicated, as the *Sokaitis* and *Meyer* cases reflect. In these cases, courts will examine the state's statutory provisions to determine whether there are good reasons not to enforce any agreement that has been found to exist. The dissenting opinion in *Meyer* offers a particularly vivid historical account of one state's contradictory impulses with gambling legalization and regulation. *See also* Cole v. Hughes, 442 S.E.2d 86 (N.C. Ct. App. 1994) (court held a joint venture agreement under which parties pooled money to purchase lottery tickets was illegal and against public policy); Talley v. Mathis, 453 S.E.2d 704 (Ga. 1995) (agreement made in Georgia to purchase tickets in Kentucky for the Kentucky Lottery and share proceeds if they won was not an unenforceable "gambling contract" under Georgia law, and the agreement was not contrary to Georgia public policy).

3. There is a considerable literature that has developed on the many aspects of player vs. player litigation. *See, e.g.,* Steven F. Thompson, *Contracts to Split Lottery Prizes: What Happens When the Ticket is a Winner?*, 18 Am. J. Trial Advoc. 201 (1994); Matthew J. Gries, *Judicial Enforcement of Agreements to Share Winning Lottery Tickets*, 44 Duke L.J. 1000 (1995); Robert Birmingham, *Proving Miracle and The First Amendment*, 5 Geo. Mason L. Rev. 45 (1996) (interesting article examining a case where fourteen year old was given money to purchase lottery tickets with the understanding the child would pray to a saint for guidance. When the prayers apparently were answered, the ticket holder did not want to divide the proceeds according to an earlier agreement between the parties. The article examines the case of Pando v. Daysi, 499 N.Y.S.2d 950 (N.Y. App. Div. 1986) through the lens of the first amendment and religious freedom. *See also* Katie Foster, *Dividing Lottery Winnings During Dissolution of Marriage*, 18 J. Am. Acad. Matrimony L. 535 (2003) (discusses the factors and the differences between division of lottery winnings during divorce in community property and marital property states, as well as the factors courts consider when determining an equitable distribution of assets); Jennifer L. Reas, *His, Hers, and Ours: Determining How Courts Will Characterize Lottery Winnings Won Prior to Marriage*, 37 Brandeis L.J. 843 (1999).

4. The lawyer whose client wins a substantial lottery prize has a number of issues to consider. There are tax issues, estate planning problems, and ownership issues, to name but a few. For a discussion of some of these issues, *see* Dan W. Holbrook, *So Your Client Just*

Won the Lottery..., 40 Tenn. B.J. 32 (Apr. 2004) (discusses issues involved with winning the lottery such as who should own the ticket, can/should they take a lump sum payment; what will be the income tax burden; and how can client reduce gift and estate taxes); Linda Suzzanne Griffin, *The Lottery: A Practical Discussion on Advising the Lottery Winner*, 72 Fla. B.J. 84 (Apr. 1998); David L. MacGregor & Chris K. Gawart, *Advising Lottery Winners*, 67 Wis. Law. 17 (July 1994). For a completely tax-oriented analysis of lottery jackpot issues, *see* Thomas G. Sinclair, *Limiting the Substitute-For-Ordinary-Income Doctrine: An Analysis Through It's Most Recent Application Involving the Sale of Future Lottery Rights*, 56 S.C. L. Rev. 387 (2004); Kyla C.E. Grogan, *Lucky for Life: A More Realistic and Reasonable Estate Tax Valuation for Nontransferable Lottery Winnings*, 79 Wash. L. Rev. 1153 (2004); Matthew S. Levine, *Lottery Winnings as Capital Gains*, 114 Yale L.J. 195 (2004).

5. There is an urban legend about a "lottery curse." This is based on stories of bad fortune that are visited upon lottery winners. One notorious case involved Jack Whittaker, a winner of $314.9 million lottery prize in 2002. Subsequently his home and car were repeatedly burglarized. At a strip club, thieves broke into his Lincoln Navigator and stole a briefcase stuffed with $245,000 in $100 bills, and three $100,000 cashier's checks. He has been repeatedly sued, was divorced, lost a granddaughter to a drug overdose, and said he wishes he could give it all back. *See Powerball Curse? Record Jackpot Winner Reflects*, MSNBC.com, Sept. 13, 2007, *at* http://www.msnbc.msn.com/id/20763630/ns/us_news-life// (last visited June 7, 2010); Curse of the Lottery Winners, ABC News, Mar. 11, 2007 *at* http://i.abcnews.com/GMA/story?id=2941589 (last visited June 7, 2010) (chronicling the hardships of lottery winners. In one case, a $20 million winner was kidnapped and murdered by his sister-in-law).